THE
AMERICAN
FILM
INSTITUTE
DESK REFERENCE

THE
AMERICAN
FILM
INSTITUTE
DESK REFERENCE

INTRODUCTION BY CLINT EASTWOOD
PREFACE BY JEAN PICKER FIRSTENBERG

MELINDA COREY ★ GEORGE OCHOA

A STONESONG PRESS PRODUCTION

DK

LONDON, NEW YORK, DELHI, MUNICH AND MELBOURNE

Senior Art Editor: Mandy Earey
Editorial Director: Chuck Wills
Creative Director: Tina Vaughan
Production Manager: Chris Avgherinos
DTP: Russell Shaw and Milos Orlovic
Publisher: Sean Moore

Produced by: The Stonesong Press, Inc.
President: Paul Fargis
Vice President, Development: Alison Fargis
Vice President, Editorial: Ellen Scordato
Assistant Editor: Sarah Parvis

Art Direction and Production: Oxygen Design
Design: Sherry Williams, Tilman Reitzle

Senior Photo Researcher: Michele Camardella
Photo Researchers: Tilman Reitzle, Sherry Williams

For photo credits, see page 606

First American edition, 2002

2 4 6 8 10 9 7 5 3 1

Published in the United States by Dorling Kindersley Publishing, Inc.
375 Hudson Street, New York, New York 10014

A catalog record for this book is available from the
Library of Congress

US ISBN 0-7894-8934-1
UK ISBN 0751349895

021569

Color reproduction by Colourscan, Singapore
Printed and bound by Graphicom, Italy

see our complete product line at
www.dk.com

THE AMERICAN FILM INSTITUTE DESK REFERENCE

EDITORS-IN-CHIEF
Melinda Corey
George Ochoa

SENIOR WRITERS
Gene Brown
Michele Camardella
Jennifer Gauthier
Marshall Robinson
Christopher Smets
Burt Solomon

AMERICAN FILM INSTITUTE CONTRIBUTORS
Trevor Daley
Pat Hanson
Patti Johnson
Rochelle Levy Lazar
Liz McDermott
Nancy Ostertag
Caroline Sisneros
Ken Wlaschin
Jennifer Wolfe
Tony Wyatt

CONTENTS

MOVIE HISTORY

Traces the evolution of the cinema, from the first experiments in the 1800s to the high-tech global movie industry of the 21st century.

Jimmy Stewart and Donna Reed in It's a Wonderful Life *(1946).*

MOVIE BASICS

Outlines the fundamentals of film—the who, what, when, and where of how movies get made, from "pitch" to projection room.

Audrey Tautou in Amélie *(2001).*

MOVIE CRAFTS

Explores the "hands-on" aspects of the movie business—the myriad skills and talents needed to turn a simple idea into cinematic reality.

PEOPLE IN FILM

Profiles of the most accomplished historical and contemporary film-industry insiders, from producers to players.

Terry Gilliam's Time Bandits *(1981).*

Solveig Dommartin in Wings of Desire *(1987).*

FILMS

Lists the most significant movies ever made, as ranked by several eminent institutions according to a variety of criteria.

SOURCES

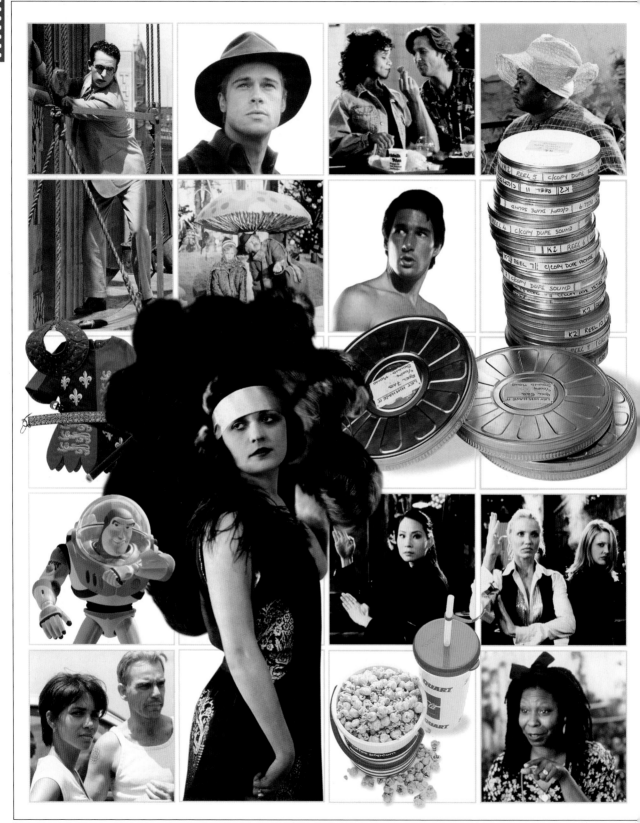

PREFACE

THE AMERICAN FILM INSTITUTE (AFI) is the preeminent national organization dedicated to advancing and preserving film, television, and other forms of the moving image. AFI's programs promote innovation and excellence through teaching, presenting, preserving, and redefining this art form. In 1965, President Lyndon Baines Johnson called for the establishment of AFI in order to "bring together leading artists of the film industry, outstanding educators and young men and women who wish to pursue this 20th century art form as their life's work."

Nearly four decades after its establishment, AFI is a nation-wide, independent, nonprofit organization. It trains many of the world's most prominent filmmakers at its prestigious Conservatory and helps coordinate the preservation of America's great film heritage through archives, databases, and the *American Film Institute Catalog of Feature Films*, which currently consists of 15 volumes. In 1997, AFI discovered and preserved the oldest surviving American feature film—the 1912 silent version of William Shakespeare's *Richard III*. And, AFI presents the best new movies and moviemakers at the annual AFI Los Angeles International Film Festival in Hollywood.

AFI also serves as the intersection between the creative community and Silicon Valley, exploring new technologies at its state-of-the-art media labs and working in collaboration with some of the world's most successful technology companies. The AFI National Theater at the Kennedy Center in Washington, D.C., offers film programs to the public, and the AFI Showcase at Disney-MGM Studios in Orlando, Florida, draws millions of visitors each year.

AFI is perhaps most recognizable to the public through its annual, nationally-televised Life Achievement Award, which for 30 years has been the highest honor bestowed for a career in film, given to cinema luminaries such as Orson Welles, James Stewart, and Martin Scorsese. Since 1998, AFI's 100 Years…series has been celebrating the centennial of American cinema, effectively raising interest in film history. And the annual AFI Awards have begun to recognize, preserve and honor excellence in the moving image during the 21st century, by honoring numerous categories in both film and television, including those in front of and behind the camera.

The art of the moving image is a unique collaboration amongst highly skilled artisans. The ability to enlighten, inform, and emotionally reach an audience is what makes film so accessible to all people, all ethnicities and all nationalities. The purpose of *The American Film Institute Desk Reference* is to function as a home and library reference, as well as an online resource that extends beyond the walls of AFI's Campus. *The American Film Institute Desk Reference* provides a new venue to effectively advance AFI's mission for education, preservation and recognition of film.

—Jean Picker Firstenberg
AMERICAN FILM INSTITUTE, CEO

INTRODUCTION

By Clint Eastwood

MOVIES TOUCH ALL OF OUR LIVES. We quote lines from our favorite films, refer to scenes we've loved and mimic our favorite characters. Filmmaking is an art form that's universally revered. And movies can take us on journeys we could have only dreamed; whether it's comedy, adventure, drama or science fiction, they are our greatest escape.

It's amazing there has never been a source to turn to for all the basic information about the movies: something handy to tell you when things happened in movie history, who was important and why, where to look for an agent or even whom to write or call for information about renting a movie for public showing. This book will help you out whether you are simply a fan who wants to know what a "gaffer" is, a film buff who wants the lowdown on an unfamiliar screenwriter, a student who quickly needs to find out the difference between lens aperture and camera aperture, or a professional who's looking for a phone number.

I don't know off the top of my head which film won the Oscar for best picture in 1957 (although I can tell who won in 1992 with no effort at all). I haven't memorized the IATSE phone number, and if you're like most moviegoers, you may not know which organization I just referred to. That's okay; you can find that and all the other important abbreviations in here. You're likely to find just about any basic film fact you need between these two covers, backed up by the authority of one of the entertainment community's most respected organizations, the AFI. *The American Film Institute Desk Reference* will make your day.

Clint Eastwood directed and starred in the powerful western Unforgiven *(1992). The film won four Academy Awards, including best director and best picture.*

ABOUT THIS BOOK

THE AMERICAN FILM INSTITUTE DESK REFERENCE provides a treasure trove of information about movies and the people behind them— from brief biographies and in-depth chronologies to award-winning films and important sources of information. **PART ONE: MOVIE HISTORY** provides a comprehensive timeline of cinema history from 1830 to present day. Each year's notable films are highlighted throughout, births and deaths of important film personalities are included, and decade descriptions help the reader grasp the scope of over one hundred years of movie-making. **PART TWO: MOVIE BASICS** outlines the lifecycle of a film. Everything from salaries to screenplays are explained.

The ABC's of film can be found in **PART THREE: MOVIE CRAFTS.** Glossaries defining the filmmaking process are organized by profession, including writing, editing, cinematography, and acting. **PART FOUR: PEOPLE IN FILM** provides biographies of the major players in the film industry. You can trace the depiction of historical and fictional characters portrayed on screen over the years, and discover where some of your favorite stars got their start. **PART FIVE: FILMS** celebrates Academy Award-winning films, cinema genres, and great movie quotes. **PART SIX: SOURCES** is your own film industry Rolodex. Address, phone numbers, web sites, and recommended reading for every facet of the film world can be found in this section.

MOVIE HISTORY SPREAD

Detailed cinema history is arranged year by year.

Blue tinted boxes in the side columns list birth and death dates of important film personalities.

MOVIE BASICS SPREAD

Yellow tinted boxes list important film releases worldwide that year.

Articles give practical information about everything from who's who in a film to what actors get paid.

MOVIE CRAFTS SPREAD

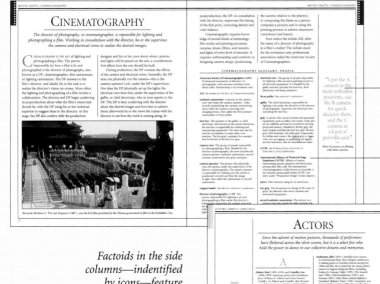

CINEMATOGRAPHY

The director of photography, or cinematographer, is responsible for lighting and photographing a film. Working in consultation with the director, he or she supervises the camera and electrical crews to realize the desired images.

Quotes from film personalities appear in the side columns throughout the book.

Extensive glossaries provide easy reference for film-related terms.

PEOPLE IN FILM SPREAD

ACTORS

Since the advent of motion pictures, thousands of performers have flickered across the silver screen, but it is a select few who hold the power to dance in our collective dreams and memories.

Factoids in the side columns—indentified by icons—feature fascinating anecdotes, gossip, and trivia about the films and people that have shaped film.

"Can't act. Slightly bald. Can dance a little."

FILMS SPREAD

FACTS ABOUT AFI'S 100 FUNNIEST AMERICAN MOVIES OF ALL TIME

Annotated lists of films are grouped using various criteria, such as genre, international films and award-winners, and many more. Includes AFI's celebrated lists of 100 Top American Movies of the last 100 years, and the 100 Funniest American Movies.

MOVIE HISTORY

Legendary slapstick comedian Charlie Chaplin debuted his trademark character "The Tramp" in Kid Auto Races at Venice *in 1914.*

1830–1899

First there was the optical illusion of the persistence of vision. Then new technologies and the shrewd inventiveness of Thomas Edison and the Lumière brothers gave birth to the movies.

THE ART AND INDUSTRY of motion pictures is built on an optical illusion. When a series of still pictures, each slightly different from the last, is projected on a screen in rapid succession, the human brain interprets the succession as continuous motion. In the 1830s, this phenomenon, called *persistence of vision,* was investigated as a scientific novelty by such inventors as Joseph Plateau and William George Horner. There the story of motion pictures might have ended, if not for the conjunction of several new technologies and a few canny business-men who, by century's end, had invented the movies.

One innovation essential to the birth of cinema was photography, which became commercially viable in 1839, when Louis Daguerre developed the daguerreotype, a method of making photographs on metal plates. Photography provided a means for capturing successive stills of people or things in motion, while devices like Eadweard Muybridge's zoöpraxiscope, a lantern that projected images in rapid succession onto a screen from photos printed on rotating glass, produced the illusion of moving pictures. Another important technology was electric power, first harnessed with the discovery of electromagnetic induction by British physicist Michael Faraday and American physicist Joseph Henry in 1831. Celluloid, the first commercially successful plastic, was invented by John Wesley Hyatt in 1869, and later became the base of motion picture film stock. In the 1870s, incandescent light bulbs were invented, later to be incorporated in projectors. Even with all these elements in place, the invention of the movies was not a foregone conclusion. It took creative leaps by inventors on both sides of the Atlantic to make the new art form possible. American inventor and entrepreneur Thomas Alva Edison was one of the first to realize that motion pictures could attract a paying audience. He designed a viewing device called the Kinetoscope, a coin-operated machine inside a wooden box: viewers could peep inside the box and watch amusing short films. Edison's first films – called Kinetoscope records – premiered on April 14, 1894, in a Kinetoscope parlor at 1155 Broadway in New York City. The first one to be copyrighted, on January 7, 1894, was *Edison Kinetoscopic Record of a Sneeze,* which showed his employee Fred Ott sneezing.

ACROSS THE ATLANTIC, French inventors Louis and Auguste Lumière learned about the Kinetoscope and decided they could do Edison one better. In 1895, they demonstrated a machine called the Cinématographe that could project movies on a screen, allowing an audience to watch the same film together rather than peeping at it individually. On December 28, 1895, a date many people consider the birthday of cinema, the Lumière brothers projected their films for the first time to a paying audience at the Grand Café on the Boulevard des Capucines in Paris. The program of short films included their first production, *La Sortie des Usines Lumière,* which showed workers leaving their factory; a train hurtling toward the audience; and *L'Arroseur Arrosé,* a very short farce that was the world's first fiction film.

Not to be outdone, Edison quickly acquired his own system for projecting films on a screen, the Vitascope, and began using it to show films in 1896. By the end of the decade, other movie companies,

AT LEFT: *Parisian audiences were startled by the train racing towards them in Louis and Auguste Lumière's 1895 film* Arrivée d'un Train en Gare de la Ciotat.

including Biograph and Vitagraph, were competing with him, churning out films. Patent-infringement lawsuits proliferated, but the mostly working-class audiences at the "flickers," as these early movies were called, knew nothing about those. They were too busy going to the movies.

The term *shooting a film* may have originated with the photographic gun invented by Etienne-Jules Marey in 1882.

--- C H R O N O L O G Y ---

1831

British physicist Michael Faraday and American physicist Joseph Henry discover the principle of electromagnetic induction, which will, by century's end, make electric power available for many machines, including motion picture equipment.

1832

Belgian inventor Joseph Plateau invents the Phenakistiscope (also called the Phenakistiscope or Fantascope), which produces an apparently moving picture by placing a rotating disk with drawings in front of a mirror.

1834

British inventor William George Horner demonstrates the Daedalum (also known as the Zoetrope or Zoötrope), a revolving drum with mounted drawings that creates an apparently moving picture.

1839

French inventor Louis-Jacques-Mandé Daguerre, building on the work of French chemist Joseph Nicéphore Niepce, develops the daguerreotype, the first commercially viable process for producing still photographs – in this case, positives on copper plates.

1841

British inventor William Henry Fox Talbot patents the calotype, a process for printing negative photographs on paper.

1869

American inventor John Wesley Hyatt invents celluloid, the first commercially successful plastic. It will later be used as a base for motion picture film stock.

1872

British-born American photographer Eadweard Muybridge begins his series of photographic studies of animal locomotion. His successive images of a horse in motion, later projected with a device called a zoöpraxiscope, influence the invention of motion pictures.

1876

French inventor Emile Reynaud develops the Praxinoscope, a device for viewing an apparently moving sequence of pictures. The device improves on Horner's Zoetrope (*see* 1834).

The Praxinoscope, invented in 1876, used picture strips and a mirrored drum to give the appearance that pictures were moving.

1879

American inventor Thomas Alva Edison patents his carbon-filament incandescent lightbulb. British inventor Joseph Swan invented a similar device the year before but is not as quick to capitalize on it. When film projectors are invented, lightbulbs will be an essential component.

1882

French inventor Etienne-Jules Marey invents a photographic gun with a multichamber revolving disk capable of taking 12 pictures per second. Later modifications will achieve up to 700 pictures per second.

1889

American inventor George Eastman invents perforated celluloid film, used by Thomas Alva Edison in his motion picture devices (*see* Kinetophonograph, below, and Kinetoscope, 1891).

PRE-1900: BIRTHS

1875
D.W. GRIFFITH, JAN. 22

1878
LIONEL BARRYMORE, APR. 28

1879
W.C. FIELDS, FEB. 10
WILL ROGERS, NOV. 4

1880
TOM MIX, JAN. 6
MACK SENNETT, JAN. 17

1881
CECIL B. DE MILLE, AUG. 12

1882
JOHN BARRYMORE, FEB. 15
BELA LUGOSI, OCT. 20
THOMAS INCE, NOV. 6

1883
FRANCIS X. BUSHMAN, JAN. 10
LON CHANEY, APR. 1
DOUGLAS FAIRBANKS, MAY 23

1885
WALLACE BEERY, APR. 1

American inventors Thomas Alva Edison and W.K.L. Dickson develop the Kinetophonograph (or Kinetophone), a precursor of the Kinetoscope (*see* 1891), which synchronizes film projection with a phonograph record.

1891

American inventor Thomas Alva Edison invents the first motion picture system, the Kinetograph camera and the Kinetoscope, a peep-show style viewer.

1893

Thomas Edison builds the world's first film studio, a tar-paper-covered structure called the "Black Maria," near his laboratories in West Orange, New Jersey.

The world's first public exhibition of a motion picture takes place in Brooklyn when Edison demonstrates his Kinetoscope. The film exhibited shows three people pretending to be blacksmiths.

The International Alliance of Theatrical Stage Employees (IATSE), which will become the principal labor group in the film industry, is founded.

1894

Edison's Kinetoscope begins commercial operation in an amusement arcade in New York City.

1895

French inventors Louis and Auguste Lumière demonstrate the camera-projector system called the Cinématographe. Unlike Edison's peep-show-like Kinetoscope, the Cinématographe can project a movie on a screen for group viewing.

American inventor Major Woodville Latham invents the Latham Loop, an essential component of later film projectors.

American inventors Thomas Armat and Charles Francis Jenkins develop the Phantascope, an improved device with an intermittent-motion mechanism, for projecting movies on a screen.

1896

Thomas Edison's Edison Company acquires rights to the Phantascope (*see* 1895) and renames it the Vitascope. Commercial showings of movies projected on a screen begin in New York City.

The American Mutoscope and Biograph Company demonstrates its Biograph (or American Biograph) projector in New York City. The company becomes known as the Biograph Company.

British-born Americans J. Stuart Blackton and Albert E. Smith form Vitagraph, a movie production company.

1897

The Biograph Company starts making films on a rooftop in New York City.

Vitagraph releases its first fictional film, *The Burglar on the Roof.*

Mutoscope

French inventor Raoul Gromoin-Sanson patents the Cineorama, the world's first multiscreen projection system. Presenting a circular panoramic view by using ten synchronized projectors, it will debut publicly at the 1900 World's Exposition in Paris.

1898

Edison files a patent-infringement suit against Biograph. Patent suits will proliferate in the years that follow.

Until early in the next decade, films are sold, not rented, to exhibitors. The film companies also sell the necessary projection machinery.

Immigrant and working-class audiences dominate early moviegoing audiences.

Nickelodeons, protomovie houses usually located in urban centers, are common viewing sites. Often converted stores, nickelodeons are so called because they typically charge a nickel for admittance.

In Britain, what may be the first film textbook is published: *Animated Photography or the ABC of the Cinematography* by filmmaker Cecil Hepworth.

1899

Kinetoscope parlors will be eclipsed by movie halls during the early twentieth century.

In Britain, Cecil Hepworth produces his first films.

Japan records its first films.

1900–1909

*Starting as immigrant fare at nickelodeons and vaudeville houses, movies
began to develop middle-class respectability with story-driven films like
The Great Train Robbery (1903) and D.W. Griffith's first directorial effort,
The Adventures of Dollie (1908).*

THE TWENTIETH CENTURY'S MAJOR NEW ART form began the century as cheap one- or two-reel entertainments for the working classes. In the US, early exhibition sites were often sandwiched into vaudeville theaters and lodge halls. A 1900 strike by US vaudevillians led theater owners to fill in for the missing acts with "flickers." Also springing up were nickelodeons, storefront screening rooms where the admission was five cents for a program of single-reel shorts. Most of these film sites were located in urban areas and frequented by immigrant laborers.

Within a decade, movies would begin to appeal to the middle and upper classes. Some credit for the changing perception of movies goes to the breakthrough films of US director Edwin S. Porter, notably two 1903 movies: the pioneering narrative *The Life of an American Fireman*, and the epic *The Great Train Robbery*. The latter film, which ran an unprecedented 12 minutes and suggested the possibilities for story-driven movies, lured audiences accustomed to sustained dramatic narratives. In Europe, the French company Film d'Art, founded in 1908, improved the quality of film with productions (and coproductions) based on great literary works and starring eminent stage actors. Their features influenced filmmakers worldwide, in the 1910s leading to the increased production of lengthy spectacles offered at premium prices, including *La Reine Elisabeth/ Queen Elizabeth* (1912) and

The Birth of a Nation (1915). D.W. Griffith, the director of *The Birth of a Nation*, got his start in 1908 with *The Adventures of Dollie.*

France and New York City were filmmaking centers; France's Gaumont was the world's largest studio. Reflecting the growing international appeal of films, Gaumont made and sold films in Europe, Russia, and the US. By the end of the decade, another French studio, Pathé, had become the world's largest film factory.

Notable US companies included Edison, Biograph, and Vitagraph, which initially made money by selling films by the foot and projection equipment to exhibitors. However, as production increased and exhibitors wished to rent rather than buy films, companies formed regional rental exchanges, beginning in 1902.

SIMILARLY, MAJOR FILM COMPANIES ended an ongoing (since 1897) war over patents for exhibition equipment and increased profit potential by forming the Motion Picture Patents Company (known as the Edison Trust) in 1908. The Edison Trust controlled distribution, production, and exhibition, requiring filmmakers to purchase Trust-approved stock and exhibitors to rent only Trust films and projectors. Through the end of the decade, independent companies were unable to exhibit films in prime locations. As movie houses appeared, so did far-reaching improvements in film technology. First was the refining of the projection process through the development of the loop and the Maltese cross, the former by US inventor Woodville Latham and British inventor R.W. Paul (in 1897), the latter by

AT LEFT: *The three-reel French film* La Reine Elisabeth *starred stage legend Sarah Bernhardt as Queen Elizabeth and in 1912 was the longest film ever released.*

Paul alone (in about 1905). Together, the loop and Maltese cross fed and routed 35mm film frame-by-frame through the projector with less wear and tear to the film. This projection process is largely unchanged today.

By 1908, the US had nearly 10,000 nickelodeons showing movies seen by millions of viewers every day. The nickelodeon was nearing its peak in popularity, but its days were numbered, as the movie star and Hollywood studios were being born.

— CHRONOLOGY —

1900

Real-life nonfiction films dominate output for most of the decade.

Film showings increase at vaudeville houses after vaudeville performers mount a strike, and theater owners fill in for the missing live acts with screenings.

Moviegoing begins to spread into small town America, with projection sites in dance halls and penny arcades.

Major studios of the decade are Biograph, the Edison Company, and Vitagraph.

Already the Lumière brothers have created more than 2,000 films, recording international sites, everyday activities, and action stories.

1901

France's Pathé is the dominant international studio.

Major British filmmakers of the day include Cecil Hepworth, A.G. Smith, US-born Charles Urban, and James Williamson, among others.

Finland opens its first movie house.

1902

The first film distribution office or exchange is established in San Francisco.

The first theater for movie exhibitions opens in Los Angeles.

Georges Méliès experiments with animation in *The Man With the Rubber Head* and with special effects in *A Trip to the Moon*.

A US Court of Appeals ruling determines that Thomas Edison is not the sole inventor of the movie camera.

George Méliès's 1902 film A Trip to the Moon *ran for an extraordinary 13 minutes, used 30 different sets, and dazzled audiences with its special effects.*

1903

In his film *Life of an American Fireman*, Edwin S. Porter builds dramatic tension with such pioneering editing techniques as interior-to-exterior shots that move from inside a building to outside. It also offers early examples of intercutting and close-ups.

Edwin S. Porter's hit film *The Great Train Robbery* is the first western and is highly influential in establishing storytelling conventions.

Hollywood is voted to become an incorporated village.

Harry, Albert, Sam, and Jack Warner open their first theater in New Castle, Pennsylvania. The Warner brothers will open the Duquesne Amusement Supply Company, a precursor to Warner Bros. Pictures, in 1907.

Japan's first theater opens in Tokyo.

Known as "America's Sweethearts" in the 1930s, Nelson Eddy and Jeanette MacDonald were born in the same month of the same year – June 1901. Jeanette (June 18) was 11 days older than Nelson (June 29). Their popularity reached its height with such operatic musicals as *Rose Marie* (1936) and *Maytime* (1937).

Made by the Edison Manufacturing Company in 1903, Edwin S. Porter's The Great Train Robbery *set new standards for storytelling and was film's first true "western."*

1905

Pioneered by the Lumière brothers, the 35mm-film width, with 1.33 x 1 image, and a film speed of 16 frames per second, is by now accepted as an industry standard.

What may be the first chase scene played for laughs appears in the Biograph film *Personal.*

The first nickel-odeon opens in Pittsburgh, offering a mix of films and vaudeville acts.

1904: BIRTHS

SIR CECIL BEATON, JAN. 14
CARY GRANT (ARCHIBALD ALEXANDER LEACH), JAN. 18
JOAN CRAWFORD (LUCILLE FAY LE SUEUR), MAR. 23
SIR JOHN GIELGUD, APR. 14
BING CROSBY (HARRY LILLIS CROSBY), MAY 2
EDGAR G. ULMER, SEPT. 17
DICK POWELL, NOV. 14
GEORGE STEVENS, DEC. 18

1905: BIRTHS

HENRY FONDA, MAY 16
PAULETTE GODDARD, JUNE 3
LILLIAN HELLMAN, JUNE 20
CLARA BOW, JULY 29
MYRNA LOY, AUG. 2
HENRY WILCOXON, SEPT. 8
CLAUDETTE COLBERT, SEPT. 13
GRETA GARBO, SEPT. 18
MICHAEL POWELL, SEPT. 30
EMLYN WILLIAMS, NOV. 26
OTTO PREMINGER, DEC. 5
HOWARD HUGHES, DEC. 24

1904

For most of the decade, the standard one-reel feature runs about ten minutes and does not identify actors by name.

France's Pathé opens a studio in New York.

Denmark opens its first movie theater in Copenhagen.

Variety, a trade newspaper for the entertainment community, begins publication.

For the next decade, France's Gaumont Film Company dominates the film industry in terms of quantity and international reputation.

Japanese film production increases with the onset of the Russo-Japanese War.

NOTABLE FILMS 1900–1905

1900:	1901:	1902:	1903:	1904:	1905:
United States	***United States***	***United States***	***United States***	***United States***	***United States***
FAUST AND MARGUERITE	A DAY AT THE CIRCUS	CHARLESTON CHAIN GANG	A GENTLEMAN OF FRANCE	COHEN'S ADVERTISING SCHEME	PERSONAL
THE MYSTIC SWING	TERRIBLE TEDDY THE GRIZZLY KING	UNCLE JOSH AT THE MOVING PICTURE SHOW	THE GREAT TRAIN ROBBERY	THE EX-CONVICT	RAFFLES, THE AMATEUR CRACKSMAN
WHY MRS. JONES GOT A DIVORCE			LIFE OF AN AMERICAN FIREMAN		
	France	***France***		***France***	***France***
France	BARBE-BLEU (BLUEBEARD)	THE MAN WITH THE RUBBER HEAD	***France***	AU CLAIR DE LA LUNE (PIERROT MALHEUREUX)	LE PALAIS DES MILLE ET UNE NUITS (A THOUSAND AND ONE NIGHTS)
JEANNE D'ARC (JOAN OF ARC)	LE PETIT CHAPERON ROUGE (LITTLE RED RIDING HOOD)	LE SACRE D'EDOUARD VII	LE CAKE-WALK INFERNAL (THE CAKE-WALK INFERNAL)	DAMNATION DÛ DOCTEUR FAUST	A PRESIDENT-ELECT ROOSEVELT
LE RÊVE DE NOËL (THE CHRISTMAS DREAM)		LE VOYAGE DANS LA LUNE (A TRIP TO THE MOON)	COMMENT MONSIEUR PREND SON BAIN		
	United Kingdom		LES MOUSQUETAIRES DE LA REINE		***United Kingdom***
United Kingdom	THE BIG SWALLOW	***Germany***			RESCUED BY ROVER
GRANDMA'S READING GLASS	FIRE!	SALOME	***United Kingdom***		
			ALICE IN WONDERLAND		
			THE UNCLEAN WORLD		

1906

Nickelodeons open in large numbers across the US, largely in urban areas.

Vitagraph opens a studio in Brooklyn, New York.

One of the first animated cartoons is made: *Humorous Phases of a Funny Face*, by Vitagraph cofounder James Stuart Blackton.

The first movie theater in Iceland opens.

The world's first feature film longer than one hour is the Australian film *The Story of the Kelly Gang*.

1907

Comedies will comprise about two-thirds of film production for the rest of the decade.

Nickelodeon attendance surpasses two million, reports the *Saturday Evening Post*. Movies are denounced by churches and the press for inciting criminal behavior.

Chicago establishes censorship regulations.

In France, Pathé's Boireau comedies starring André Deed demonstrate the popularity of comedy and make Deed a star.

So far, British films have enjoyed international acclaim and popularity. In coming years, artistic stasis and the growth of the US film industry will reduce the importance of the UK film industry.

Major British studios during this decade and the next include Hepworth and the British and Colonia Kinematograph Company. Serials are among their strongest genres.

Finland produces its first film, *Salavinanpolttajat (Bootleggers)*.

1908

The Motion Picture Patents Company (a.k.a. the Edison Trust) is established to regulate and control film production and distribution. It hopes to broaden audiences to include middle-class viewers, increasing the medium's prestige.

The Motion Picture Machine Operators is founded, the first filmmaking craft union.

D.W. Griffith refines "crosscutting," the technique of editing two different narratives together so that, as the story jumps between the two, tension results.

Biograph Studios contracts with D.W. Griffith, a struggling playwright and actor, to direct his first film, *The Adventures of Dollie*.

1906: BIRTHS
LOU COSTELLO, MAR. 6
MARY ASTOR, MAY 3
ROBERTO ROSSELLINI, MAY 8
BILLY WILDER, JUNE 22
ANTHONY MANN, JUNE 30
JOHN HUSTON, AUG. 5
JANET GAYNOR, OCT. 6
SIR CAROL REED, DEC. 30

1907: BIRTHS
FRED ZINNEMANN, APR. 29
SIR LAURENCE OLIVIER, MAY 22
JOHN WAYNE, MAY 26
JESSICA TANDY, JUNE 7
MICHAEL "MIKE" TODD, JUNE 22
BARBARA STANWYCK, JULY 16
GENE AUTRY, SEPT. 29
EDITH HEAD, OCT. 28
KATHARINE HEPBURN, NOV. 8

1908: BIRTHS
REX HARRISON, MAR. 5
BETTE DAVIS, APR. 5
JAMES STEWART, MAY 20
FRED MACMURRAY, AUG. 17
CAROLE LOMBARD, OCT. 6

1909: BIRTHS
JOSEPH L. MANKIEWICZ, FEB. 11
DAVID NIVEN, MAR. 1
JAMES MASON, MAY 15
ERROL FLYNN, JUNE 20
MARCEL CARNÉ, AUG. 18
ELIA KAZAN, SEPT. 7

Director D.W. Griffith (with megaphone) on the set. Griffith influenced virtually every aspect of filmmaking, from storytelling to camera angles to set design.

NOTABLE FILMS 1906–1909

1906:

United States
THE HAUNTED HOTEL
(ANIMATED)

HUMOROUS PHASES
OF A FUNNY FACE
(ANIMATED)

SEVEN AGES

Australia
THE STORY OF THE
KELLY GANG

Germany
APACHETANZ

United Kingdom
THE BLACKSMITH'S
DAUGHTER

1907:

United States
BEN-HUR

AN EXCITING
HONEYMOON

KATHLEEN
MAVOURNEEN

THE LIFE OF A COWBOY

THE MAGIC
FOUNTAIN PEN
(ANIMATED)

THE MIDNIGHT
RIDE OF PAUL REVERE

Finland
SALAVINANPOLTTAJAT
(BOOTLEGGERS)

France
HAMLET

LE TUNNEL SOUS
LA MANCHE
(TUNNELING THE
ENGLISH CHANNEL)

1908:

United States
THE ADVENTURES
OF DOLLIE

THE FATAL HOUR

FOR LOVE OF GOLD

STENKA RAZIN

THE TAVERN-
KEEPER'S DAUGHTER

France
NICK CARTER,
ROI DES DÉTECTIVES
(NICK CARTER,
KING OF THE DETECTIVES)
(SERIAL)

LE RAID PARIS–NEW
YORK EN AUTOMOBILE

Norway
FISKERLIVETS FARER:
ET DRAMA PØ HAVET
(THE PERILS OF FISHING:
A DRAMA OF THE SEA)

1909:

United States
A FOOL'S REVENGE

HER FIRST BISCUITS

IN OLD KENTUCKY

THE LIFE OF MOSES

THE LONELY VILLA

RANCH LIFE IN THE
GREAT SOUTHWEST

THE SEVENTH DAY

France
LA GIGUE
MERVEILLEUSE

Germany
WILDSCHÜTZENRACHE
(A POACHER'S REVENGE)

Italy
DANTE'S INFERNO

FALL OF TROY

Film was already an inexpensive form of entertainment. Turn-of-the-century vaudeville houses charged 25 cents for a movie and live entertainment. A Broadway show ticket at the time was about $2.

In pre-war German cinema, most films concentrate on domestic matters and do little to prefigure postwar expressionism.

Norway produces its first nondocumentary film, *Fiskerlivets Farer: Et Drama pø Havet (The Perils of Fishing: A Drama of the Sea).*

In Britain, newly built movie houses gain popularity.

Japan's first film studio opens in Tokyo.

Russia creates its first film, *Stenka Razin,* directed by Vladimir Romashkov.

1909

Carl Laemmle establishes the renegade studio Independent Motion Picture Company of America (IMP), unaffiliated with the Motion Picture Patents Company (MPPC).

Other independent filmmakers skirt the MPPC rules on using only approved raw stock and projectors by filming in California, far from MPPC headquarters. The practice helps establish California as a filmmaking center.

Tom Mix, a wrangler for a wild west show hired as a crew member appears in a scene of *Ranch Life in the Great Southwest* and launches his acting career.

D.W. Griffith pioneers the practice of actor rehearsal, necessitated by the growing complexity of his scenarios and his own aesthetic of a naturalistic acting style.

Mary Pickford debuts in *Her First Biscuits;* Ben Turpin is the first actor cited in a film publication, *Moving Picture World.*

Nearly 10,000 US movie houses are in operation.

New York establishes a State Board of Censorship.

In France, Pathé comedies starring Max Linder become popular.

In Paris, the Société du Film d'Art is established to produce films linked to the fine arts, in an attempt to raise the perceived caliber of the film medium.

The British govern-ment passes the Cinematograph Films Act to regulate film exchanges and other industry matters.

Initially hired as a crew member for the 1909 film Ranch Life in the Great Southwest, *Tom Mix's career was launched after he appeared in a scene of the film.*

1910–1919

Early movie stars like Mary Pickford and Charlie Chaplin drew wider audiences to increasingly complex films at larger theaters. The decade's most popular and controversial movie was the 1915 Civil War saga The Birth of a Nation.

IN 1910, INDEPENDENT MOVIE PRODUCER Carl Laemmle shocked the industry by making actress Florence Lawrence a star. Not only did he lure the popular player to his Independent Motion Pictures (IMP) from Biograph (where she was simply known as "the Biograph Girl"), he popularized her name through a high-profile publicity campaign. Biograph favorite Mary "the Girl with the Golden Hair" Pickford joined IMP later that year. In addition to Pickford and Lawrence, other actors received strong press coverage and became household names of the time, including Charlie Chaplin, William S. Hart, Pearl White, and Roscoe "Fatty" Arbuckle. Vampish Theda Bara became the first studio-created film personality.

Imported from Europe, multireel spectacular literary adaptations like *La Dame aux Camélias* (1911) and *Les Misérables* (1912, both French) and *Henry VIII* (1911) and *Hamlet* (1913, both British) enticed middle-class viewers, although they offered no technical breakthroughs. US director D.W. Griffith blended spectacle, editing, and cinematographic innovation with *Judith of Bethulia* (1914), and most notably with *The Birth of a Nation* (1915), which was easily the decade's most influential movie. Later noted for his spectacles, US director Cecil B. De Mille was successful during the late 1910s with sex comedies, which reflected post-Victorian mores, including *Old Wives for New* (1918) and *Don't Change Your Husband* (1919). Aside from Griffith, other notable US filmmakers included producer/director Thomas Ince and the comedy genius Mack Sennett, who introduced the

AT LEFT: *Cecil B. De Mille's gift for knowing what the public wanted made him one of Hollywood's enduring legends.*

wildly popular Keystone Kops around 1912. The rise of independent studios, as well as a two-year federal antitrust suit instigated by William Fox and his Greater New York Film Rental Company (1913–15), ended the stranglehold on distribution and exhibition by the Motion Picture Patents Company. Also contributing to MPPC's end was the concurrent decline in nickelodeons and their set one-reel programming. Audiences were ready for multireel films, or features.

INTERNATIONALLY, THE US AND FRANCE dominated the film market, with Pathé continuing to reign as the major French studio. In the US, newly prominent studios included Laemmle's IMP and Jesse Lasky's Famous Players–Lasky Corporation, which would merge by decade's end with Paramount, the distribution arm led by Adolph Zukor. Sweden entered a highly fruitful period of film production, largely through the works of directors Victor Sjöström (*Ingeborg Holm*, 1913, *A Girl from the Marsh Croft*, 1919) and Mauritz Stiller (*Love and Journalism*, 1916). Mexico (*The Gray Automobile*, 1919) and other countries yielded their first major film productions as well.

World War I curtailed production throughout Europe, making it possible for US imports to gain a large percentage of screens. (Sweden, remaining neutral, was one of the few exceptions, and its production rate remained stable.) The UK, for example, lost part of its 15 percent portion of the film market it held in the mid-1910s. As World War I ended, the movie business was greatly changed. Low-rent nickelodeons were nearly extinct, replaced by middle-class movie palaces. Now public figures,

In 1910 the average feature film had three reels and ran about 30 minutes. By 1920, an average feature film would run 80 to 90 minutes.

film actors, and directors were making demands. In 1919, D.W. Griffith, Charlie Chaplin, Douglas Fairbanks, and Mary Pickford rebelled against corporate control by creating their own distribution company: United Artists. But the big story was the rise of the US film industry and the growth of Hollywood, which would dominate the movie business in the 1920s and capitalize on the 1927 invention one Hollywood mogul called a fad: talkies.

CHRONOLOGY

1910

Title cards begin to be used in films.

Loew's Consolidated Enterprises is formed in February as a multiple-entertainment company including 400 theaters. Adolph Zukor is treasurer.

The Motion Picture Patents Company (the Edison Trust) tries to control film distribution through its General Film Company but meets with opposition from independent producers, including Carl Laemmle and William Fox. Their efforts over the next years lay the groundwork for the Hollywood film industry.

The Edison Trust attempts to limit foreign film exhibition in the US by restricting the import of foreign films.

Heavyset British-born John Bunny becomes the first film comic with the premiere of his first feature for Vitagraph, *Jack Fat and Jim Slim at Coney Island.*

Canadian-born Florence Lawrence becomes the first American movie star to be known to the public by name. She was formerly known only as "The Biograph Girl."

"Little Mary" Pickford is hired from D.W. Griffith's Biograph Studios by Carl Laemmle's International Motion Picture Company of America (IMP). Advertisements read, "Little Mary is an Imp now." Similarly, Florence Lawrence is hired from Biograph by IMP; she will be known as "the Imp Girl."

Alice Guy-Blaché, the first woman filmmaker and possibly the first director of a fiction film, forms her own production company, Solax, in New York.

Actress Florence Lawrence was one of film's first "stars." Tagged "The Biograph Girl," by 1910, she was one of few actresses known to the public by name.

NOTABLE FILMS 1910

United States	
A PLAIN SONG	RAMONA
THE BROKEN OATH	SUNSHINE SUE
IN OLD CALIFORNIA	THE THREAD OF DESTINY
IRONY OF FATE	TWELFTH NIGHT
JACK FAT AND JIM SLIM AT CONEY ISLAND	*France*
	BÉBÉ
JANE EYRE	MAX ET SON BELLE MÈRE
THE KID	(MAX AND HIS MOTHER-IN-LAW)
THE LAD FROM OLD IRELAND	*Germany*
THE MARTYRDOM OF THOMAS À BECKET	AFGRUNDEN (THE ABYSS)
IN NEIGHBORING KINGDOMS	DETECTED BY HER DOG
THE NEW MAGDALENE	

In one of the first film rights sales, the rights to Helen Jackson's *Ramona*, an 1884 historical romance about a mixed-race marriage, are sold to D.W. Griffith. The practice of buying book rights will continue through the century.

The Kinetoscope is reintroduced by inventor Thomas Edison as public entertainment but fails to attract a following.

Mary Pickford sets a fashion trend with her blonde corkscrew curls. She is known as "The Girl with the Golden Hair."

The Pathé Gazette, a French newsreel, debuts in Britain and the US Created by brother cinematographers Charles and Emile Pathé, it will eventually offer international news coverage.

Denmark, France, and Italy are the main film exporters to the US during the decade.

In Germany, movie houses begin to appear.

From now until 1913, the Danish company, Nordisk Film (a.k.a. Great Northern Co.) produces movies that gain international repute.

1911

D.W. Griffith's two-reelers are released in two parts, *His Trust* and *His Trust Fulfilled*, and *Enoch Arden, Parts I and II*. Audiences complain, leading Biograph to release the entire work at once.

The technique of crosscutting, introduced in the last decade, is being greatly refined by D.W. Griffith, as demonstrated in this year's *The Lonedale Operator*.

Florence Lawrence is interviewed in *Motion Picture Story*, perhaps the first movie star interview.

Mary Pickford is released from her IMP contract because she was a minor at signing. Later this year, she joins Majestic Studios.

Comedies cease to dominate film production; instead, various types of drama, including westerns and costume dramas, proliferate.

The Nestor Company becomes the first studio to open in California.

The Motion Picture Exhibitors' League is founded, the first professional organization for exhibitors.

Pathé's Weekly is the first newsreel screened in the US.

In Europe, films are frequently longer than the standard 15 minutes, with film stories becoming increasingly complex.

The British film industry declines in importance internationally, losing ground to French and US works.

Pennsylvania establishes a censorship board for films.

In Europe before World War I, genteel documentaries supporting the government are popular.

Vilnius-born (then Poland, now Lithuania) filmmaker Wladyslaw Starewicz (Ladislas Starewitch) makes his first animated film for entertainment purposes, *Prekvasnya Lukanida (The Fair Lucanida)*. He will continue making films in the 1920s using the puppet animation techniques employed in this film.

1912

Two new studios open: Adolph Zukor founds Famous Players, and Carl Laemmle starts Universal Film Manufacturing Company, which will become Universal Studios.

Mack Sennett's Keystone Comedy Studio releases its first comedies and "Kops" films. Over the decade, Keystone will become the dominant US silent comedy studio, boasting such stars as Ben Turpin, Charlie Chaplin, Chester Conklin, and Roscoe "Fatty" Arbuckle.

NOTABLE FILMS 1911

United States	Italy
ALKALI IKE'S AUTO	LA CADUTA DI TROIA (THE FALL OF TROY)
THE COURTING OF MARY	LE GERUSALEMME LIBERATA (THE CRUSADERS)
ENOCH ARDEN	**Poland**
FIGHTING BLOOD	PREKVASNYA LUKANIDA (THE FAIR LUCANIDA) (ANIMATED)
HIS TRUST	
HIS TRUST FULFILLED	**Russia**
THE LONEDALE OPERATOR	THE KREUTZER SONATA
ROMEO AND JULIET	MIEST KINOOPERATORA (THE CAMERAMAN'S REVENGE) (ANIMATED)
A TALE OF TWO CITIES	
THEIR FIRST MISUNDERSTANDING	**United Kingdom** HENRY VIII
VANITY FAIR	RACHEL'S SIN

Film hero Francis X. Bushman and Beverly Bayne become the first romantic screen couple when they are teamed in *The House of Pride*.

What Happened to Mary? paves the way for the US adventure serial; this sequence of 12 Edison films makes actress Mary Fuller a star.

Keystone Comedy Studio, the preeminent silent comedy studio founded by Mack Sennett, released the first film featuring the inept antics of the Keystone Kops in 1912.

NOTABLE FILMS 1912

United States
CARDINAL WOLSEY
COHEN COLLECTS
  A DEBT
THE COUNT OF
  MONTE CRISTO
THE CRY OF THE
  CHILDREN
HOFFMYER'S
  LEGACY
THE HOUSE
  OF PRIDE
MAN'S GENESIS
MAY'S HAT
THE MUSKETEERS OF
  PIG ALLEY
THE NEW YORK HAT

OLIVER TWIST
RICHARD III
AN UNSEEN ENEMY
WAR ON
  THE PLAINS
THE WATER NYMPH
WHAT HAPPENED
  TO MARY?
France
LES MISÉRABLES
LA REINE ELISABETH
  (QUEEN ELIZABETH)
Russia
ROZHDYESTVO
OBITATELI LYESA
  (THE INSECTS'
  CHRISTMAS)
  (ANIMATED)

Richard III, the oldest surviving American feature film, is released.

Queen Elizabeth, starring Sarah Bernhardt, runs four reels, prefiguring the standard multireel feature. The long historical work continues to broaden the appeal of movies among middle class audiences.

Sisters Dorothy and Lillian Gish appear in their first film, *An Unseen Enemy.*

Pioneering the role of independent producer, actress Helen Gardner founds the Helen Gardner Picture Corporation.

The power of the Edison Trust to control film length and distribution erodes with the growth of independent filmmakers.

The Edison Trust is sued by the US government for trade restrictions; distributor William Fox of the Greater New York Film Rental Company sues the Patent Company on antitrust violations.

Major French studios include Pathé, Gaumont, Eclair, and Film d'Art.

An independent British Board of Film Censors proposes a two-tier film ratings system.

In Japan, several studios (Yoshizawa, Yokoya, Pathé, and Fukujodo) attempt to control the market by merging into Nippon Katsudoshashin Co.

Stage actor William S. Hart is hired by filmmaker Thomas Ince.

Mary Pickford joins Famous Players Film Company; Charlie Chaplin signs with Keystone Comedy Studio.

D.W. Griffith moves from Biograph and joins Mutual. He leaves a legacy of 500 Biograph films.

Offscreen romances begin with the love affair between Dustin Farnham and Winifred Kingston on the set of *The Squaw Man.*

Lon Chaney plays a hunchback in *The Sea Urchin*, beginning a string of grotesque and pathetic roles that depend on cosmetic transformation. He will become known as "the Man of a Thousand Faces."

Jesse Lasky founds the Jesse L. Lasky Feature Play Company.

Cecil B. De Mille rents a barn in Hollywood for location shooting of *The Squaw Man;* it becomes the site of Paramount Studio.

US screen magazine *Photoplay* appears, the first popular fan magazine.

1913: BIRTHS

LORETTA YOUNG, JAN. 6
DANNY KAYE, JAN. 18
JOHN GARFIELD, MAR. 4
TYRONE POWER, JR., MAY 5
STEWART GRANGER, MAY 6
PETER CUSHING, MAY 26
ALAN LADD, SEPT. 3
STANLEY KRAMER,
  SEPT. 23
(SOME SOURCES SAY SEPT. 29)
BURT LANCASTER, NOV. 2
GIG YOUNG, NOV. 4
VIVIEN LEIGH, NOV. 5
HEDY LAMARR, NOV. 9

1913

New York City passes an ordinance establishing building code regulations for exhibition halls, requiring wider aisles and better ventilation. One result is the movie palace, the first of which opens in 1914.

Italy's eight-reel biblical epic *Quo Vadis* popularizes the genre internationally and plays for months in New York City at a record $1.50 admission.

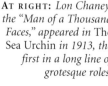

AT RIGHT: *Lon Chaney, the "Man of a Thousand Faces," appeared in* The Sea Urchin *in 1913, the first in a long line of grotesque roles.*

The talking picture is demonstrated in New York City by the Edison Company, but the synchronized phonograph-and-film apparatus does not work properly.

Germany competes with France's high-class *film d'art* with its *Autorenfilm* (author's film), hiring noted writers of the day, including Arthur Schnitzler.

Yiddish film flourishes with the founding of Kosmofilm in Warsaw. It produces Yiddish films until 1915.

NOTABLE FILMS 1913

United States	
THE ADVENTURES OF KATHLYN (SERIAL)	INSEL DER SELIGEN (ISLAND OF THE BLESSED)
THE GANGSTERS	*Italy*
A NOISE FROM THE DEEP	QUO VADIS
THE PICKWICK PAPERS	*Russia*
THE SEA URCHIN	TWILIGHT OF A WOMAN'S SOUL
TRAFFIC IN SOULS	*Sweden*
THE WAITER'S PICNIC	INGEBORG HOLM
Germany	TRÄDGÅRDSMÄSTEREN (THE GARDENER)
DER ANDERE (THE OTHER ONE)	*United Kingdom*
DIE FILMPRIMADONNA (THE FILM STAR)	DAVID COPPERFIELD
	HAMLET

1914

Cecil B. De Mille's *The Squaw Man*, an early US feature film, is among the first works filmed in Hollywood. It is a huge hit.

Italy's three-hour Roman-era epic, *Cabiria*, opens in New York and becomes a popular success.

Charlie Chaplin debuts as "The Tramp" character in the comedy *Kid Auto Races at Venice*.

Charlie Chaplin begins directing his own films.

Tillie's Punctured Romance is the first US multireel comedy feature.

Forty-nine-year-old William S. Hart begins appearing in films produced by friend Thomas H. Ince. Rarely smiling, Hart is soon a star, the "Good-Bad Man" of realistic westerns. His first feature-length film is *The Bargain*.

Winsor McKay's cartoon *Gertie the Dinosaur* opens, and the title character becomes one of the first animated film stars.

Felix the Cat makes his first appearance in Paramount cartoons, animated by Pat Sullivan.

Pearl White stars in the US adventure serial *The Perils of Pauline*, beginning a multiyear run of spunky girl–driven serials starring White, Grace Cunard, and others.

Winsor McKay's 1914 cartoon made the title character Gertie the Dinosaur *one of animation's early heroines.*

Tillie's Punctured Romance *starring Charlie Chaplin and Marie Dressler, was the first feature-length comedy film and was released by Keystone Comedy Studio in 1914.*

NOTABLE FILMS 1914

United States
THE BARGAIN

DOUGH AND DYNAMITE

IN THE SAGE
BRUSH COUNTRY

JUDITH OF BETHULIA

KID AUTO RACES
AT VENICE

THE LIFE OF
GENERAL VILLA

LUCILLE LOVE,
GIRL OF MYSTERY
(SERIAL)

MAKING A LIVING

MILLION DOLLAR
MYSTERY
(SERIAL)

NEPTUNE'S DAUGHTER

THE PERILS OF
PAULINE
(SERIAL)

THE PRISONER
OF ZENDA

THE SPOILERS

THE SQUAW MAN

TESS OF THE STORM
COUNTRY

TILLIE'S PUNCTURED
ROMANCE

THE TRAIL OF THE
LONESOME PINE

TYPHOON

THE VIRGINIAN

Italy
CABIRIA

SPERDUTI
NEL BUIO
(LOST IN THE DARK)

Russia
A CHILD OF THE
BIG CITY
(THE GIRL FROM
THE STREETS)

United Kingdom
GERTIE
(ANIMATED)

LIEUTENANT PIMPLE
AND THE STOLEN
INVENTION

A STUDY IN
SCARLET

1915: BIRTHS
VICTOR MATURE, JAN. 29

ANN SHERIDAN, FEB. 21

ANTHONY QUINN, APR. 21

ORSON WELLES, MAY 6

LEO GORCEY, JUNE 3

YUL BRYNNER, JULY 12

EDMOND O'BRIEN, SEPT. 10

INGRID BERGMAN, SEPT. 29

CORNEL WILDE, OCT. 13

ELI WALLACH, DEC. 7

FRANK SINATRA, DEC. 12

1915: DEATHS
JOHN BUNNY

The National Association for the Advancement of Colored People (NAACP) launched a formal protest campaign against *The Birth of a Nation* for its racist depiction of African-Americans. The film was banned in five states and 19 cities.

The first movie palace opens, the 3,000-seat Strand in Times Square. It is operated by Samuel "Roxy" Rothapfel.

The first movie column appears, by Louella Parsons in the *Chicago Record-Herald*.

Britain's first animated films are shown.

During World War I, German-occupied countries, including Belgium, significantly reduce film production. Neutral countries such as Sweden capitalize on war-related financial incentives and increase production.

1915

D.W. Griffith's Civil War epic *The Birth of a Nation* opens in Los Angeles and later in New York. A film event, it has an admission price of $2, the same as a theatrical production. It is the first US film with its own score, and the title song, "The Perfect Song," becomes a popular hit.

Protests against the racism depicted in *The Birth of a Nation* erupt in US cities, leading President Woodrow Wilson to express disapproval of the film.

The Motion Picture Patents Company is charged with trade infringement by a federal court. Already the company has lost control of the industry to largely Hollywood-based independent producers like Adolph Zukor and Carl Laemmle.

Unknown Theda Bara (Theodosia Goodman) becomes a sex star as "the Vamp" in *A Fool There Was*.

Stage star Ethel Barrymore signs with Metro Pictures.

The first Rin Tin Tin is born in Germany.

Douglas Fairbanks makes his film debut in *The Lamb*.

W.C. Fields debuts in *Pool Sharks*.

The film corporation, Triangle, is founded by Harry Aitken with Adam Kessel and Charles Baumann. D.W. Griffith, Mack Sennett, and Thomas Ince are the studio's three key directors.

D.W. Griffith's depiction of the Civil War and the Ku Klux Klan in 1915's The Birth of a Nation *incited riots and controversy.*

NOTABLE FILMS 1915

United States
THE BATTLE CRY
OF PEACE

THE BIRTH OF
A NATION

THE CHAMPION

THE CHEAT

A FOOL THERE WAS

JUST NUTS

THE LAMB

A NIGHT AT
THE SHOW

POLICE

POOL SHARKS

THE SCOURGE
OF THE DESERT

THE TRAMP

A WOMAN

France
LES MYSTÈRES DE
NEW YORK
(THE MYSTERIES
OF NEW YORK)
(SERIAL)

LES VAMPIRES

Poland
THE REPUDIATED
DAUGHTER

United Kingdome
JANE SHORE

ULTUS THE MAN
FROM THE DEAD

Stage actor William S. Hart made the transition to film in 1914 at age 49. He was both the star and the director of 1916's The Gun Fighter.

1916

Two company beginnings: Famous Players–Lasky Corporation and the Goldwyn Company are founded. Famous Players–Lasky is formed from the merger of the Famous Players Film Company and the Jesse L. Lasky Feature Play Company. Samuel Goldfish leaves to form the Goldwyn Company with Edgar Selwyn. Goldfish changes his last name to Goldwyn.

Paramount Pictures stock is acquired by Adolph Zukor and Famous Players–Lasky Corporation.

The New York State Board of Censorship becomes the National Board of Review.

The Lincoln Motion Picture Company is founded, the first African-American-owned film company.

Charlie Chaplin joins Mutual; Mary Pickford signs a two-year, million-dollar contract with Adolph Zukor's Famous Players Film Company that includes a percentage of the profits.

Comic star Mabel Normand sets up the Mabel Normand Feature Film Company with director Mack Sennett and others. Their first release, *Mickey* (1918), is a big hit.

The Fox Studio in Hollywood is destroyed by fire.

The first star autobiography is published, Pearl White's *Just Me.*

The first feature with a nude scene appears in *A Daughter of the Gods,* starring world-class swimmer Annette Kellerman.

Russia suspends film production in Norway during World War I.

NOTABLE FILMS 1916

United States
BEHIND THE SCREEN
CIVILIZATION
THE COSSACK WHIP
A DAUGHTER OF THE GODS
THE GUN FIGHTER
HELL'S HINGES
HIS PICTURE IN THE PAPERS
HOODOO ANN
INTOLERANCE
JOAN OF ARC
LASS OF THE LUMBERLANDS (SERIAL)
MANHATTAN MADNESS
NUGGET JIM'S PARTNER

ONE A.M.
THE PAWNSHOP
THE PURPLE MASK (SERIAL)
THE REALIZATION OF A NEGRO'S AMBITION
THE RETURN OF DRAW EGAN
TO HAVE AND TO HOLD
THE VALLEY OF DECISION
WHERE ARE MY CHILDREN
United Kingdom
ARSENE LUPIN
SHE
SWEET LAVENDER

1917

Film production is now done consistently in Hollywood.

Tom Mix appears in feature-length westerns at Fox, where his colorful performances make him the major cowboy star of the 1920s. Other cowboy stars of the 1920s include Harry Carey and Hoot Gibson.

Comedy film star Harold Lloyd begins wearing his trademark black glasses.

Mabel Normand signs with Goldwyn.

The First National Exhibitors Circuit is formed to protect exhibitors from the harsh practices of film distributors.

1916: BIRTHS

JACKIE GLEASON, FEB. 26
STERLING HAYDEN, MAR. 26
GREGORY PECK, APR. 5
GLENN FORD, MAY 1
OLIVIA DE HAVILLAND, JULY 1
KEENAN WYNN, JULY 27
VAN JOHNSON, AUG. 25
PETER FINCH, SEPT. 28
TREVOR HOWARD, SEPT. 29
KIRK DOUGLAS, DEC. 9
BETTY GRABLE, DEC. 18

1917: BIRTHS

HOWARD KEEL, APR. 13
DEAN MARTIN, JUNE 7
LENA HORNE, JUNE 30
ROBERT MITCHUM, AUG. 6
MEL FERRER, AUG. 25
JUNE ALLYSON, OCT. 7
JOAN FONTAINE, OCT. 22

1917: DEATHS

ERIC CAMPBELL
PAULINE "BABY SUNSHINE" FLOOD

NOTABLE FILMS 1917

United States BETWEEN		Japan

United States
BETWEEN
BIRTH CONTROL
A.K.A. THE NEW WORLD
THE BUTCHER BOY
THE CURE
EASY STREET
THE GULF
THE HEART OF
TEXAS RYAN

THE IMMIGRANT
JOAN THE WOMAN
MAX IN A TAXI
THE NARROW TRAIL
OVER THE FENCE
PEGGY
POLLY OF THE CIRCUS
POOR LITTLE RICH GIRL
PRIDE OF THE CLAN

STRAIGHT SHOOTING
A TALE OF TWO CITIES
THAIS
WILD AND WOOLLY
Argentina
EL APÓSTOL
(ANIMATED)
France
JUDEX
(SERIAL)

Japan
TAII NO MUSUME
(THE DAUGHTER OF
THE LIEUTENANT)
Sweden
TERJE VIGEN
(A MAN THERE WAS)
United Kingdom
MASKS AND FACES

Mary Pickford and Douglas Fairbanks are lovers, and later become the most beloved movie star couple of the 1920s.

The National Board of Review bans nudity in film.

Triangle troubles: Douglas Fairbanks and Mack Sennett cease or change distribution agreements with Triangle.

Studio changes: Select Pictures is created after Adolph Zukor buys half of Lewis J. Selznick Productions; Mack Sennett is bought out by Triangle. Sennett begins working with Paramount.

World War I affects films: Newsreels are censored by the US government during the war, and the Committee on Public Information forms a film division to monitor the rendering of US interests in films.

In Germany, industrialist General Erich Ludendorff and the government acquire smaller studios to form film producer/distributor UFA (Universum Film Aktien Gesellschaft). It becomes the dominant national studio.

Japanese films begin to incorporate Western filmmaking influences, including flashbacks and close-ups. Increasingly, women break tradition by playing female roles, eclipsing the traditional practice of *oyama* in which men portray women.

1918

Following years of lawsuits, the MPPC is defunct.

After some critically praised but not highly popular films, Cecil B. De Mille attracts large audiences with his sex comedy, *Old Wives for New.*

Warner Bros. releases its first film, *Four Years in Germany;* Ebony Film Corporation releases its first feature with an all-black cast, *Black Sherlock Holmes.*

Francis X. Bushman is divorced from wife Josephine Flaudume on infidelity charges and marries frequent co-star Beverly Bayne later in the year. The scandal tarnishes his career and leads theaters to refuse to show his films.

Tarzan of the Apes, starring Elmo Lincoln, is the first Tarzan movie.

Studio swaps: Mary Pickford joins First National with a production deal; Gloria Swanson signs with Famous Players–Lasky Corporation.

War notes: Stars make propaganda films and sell war bonds; filmmaking is considered an essential incentive for the selective service draft.

Swashbuckling actor Douglas Fairbanks, Sr. and "America's Sweetheart" Mary Pickford, began their relationship in 1917 and married in 1920. Here, the two attend a Hollywood premiere.

The **influenza epidemic** closes movie houses and prompts studios to suspend production for a month.

Sid Grauman opens his first movie theater, Sid Grauman's Million Dollar Theater, in Los Angeles.

NOTABLE FILMS 1918

United States	THE PRODIGAL WIFE
BLACK SHERLOCK HOLMES	SALOME
THE BLUEBIRD	SELFISH YATES
BLUE BLAZES RAWDEN	SHOULDER ARMS
THE BOND	THE SILENT MAN
A DOG'S LIFE	THE SINKING OF THE LUSITANIA (ANIMATED)
HEARTS OF THE WORLD	STELLA MARIS
LAUGHING BILL HYDE	TARZAN OF THE APES
MICKEY	THE WHISPERING CHORUS
MY FOUR YEARS IN GERMANY	*Germany and Poland* DER GELBE SCHEIN (THE YELLOW TICKET)
OLD WIVES FOR NEW	

1919

US studio United Artists is formed by Charlie Chaplin, Mary Pickford, Douglas Fairbanks, and D.W. Griffith to release and distribute its founders' films. It gains prestige and profits from the release of films by its founders and other famous directors and stars, including Keaton, Valentino, and Swanson.

Loew's Inc. is established by exhibitor Marcus Loew.

Studios buy into theater chains: Famous Players–Lasky Corporation gains Stanley theaters and part of Sid Grauman's theaters.

Self-censorship: Filmmaker members agree to submit their films to review by the National Association of the Motion Picture Industry.

Mary Miles Mintner signs with Famous Players–Lasky Corporation.

Harold Lloyd loses two fingers when a publicity-related bomb explodes.

Gloria Swanson gains stardom with the release of *Don't Change Your Husband.*

Oscar Micheaux, the first African-American director, makes his first film, *The Homesteader,* which is based on his own novel from 1917.

Fox News Newsreel debuts.

Distribution company Associated Producers is formed by directors Thomas Ince, Mack Sennett, and others.

The US dominates the European film market by the end of World War I. US films are seen as representing positive internationalism.

European comedies lose their pre-war hold on continental audiences.

Soviet cinema is nationalized by Vladimir Lenin after the revolution. Some directors will emigrate to Europe and the US, notably Wladyslaw Starewicz (Ladislas Starewitch) and Ryszard Boleslawski (Richard Boleslawsky).

The release of 1919's Don't Change Your Husband brought fame to Gloria Swanson, who became the highest paid actress in Hollywood by the mid-1920s.

1919: BIRTHS

CAROLE LANDIS, JAN. 1
JACK PALANCE, FEB. 18
JENNIFER JONES, MAR. 2
CELESTE HOLM, APR. 29
VERONICA LAKE, NOV. 19

NOTABLE FILMS 1919

United States	HIS MAJESTY, THE AMERICAN	*Denmark* PRESIDENTEN (THE PRESIDENT)
BACK STAGE		
BLIND HUSBANDS	MALE AND FEMALE	*France* J'ACCUSE (I ACCUSE)
BROKEN BLOSSOMS	THE MIRACLE MAN	
DADDY LONG LEGS	THE NEW MOON	*Germany* MADAME DUBARRY
DON'T CHANGE YOUR HUSBAND	SQUARE DEAL SANDERSON	
	SUNNYSIDE	DIE SPINNEN (THE SPIDERS) (SERIAL)
ELMO, THE MIGHTY (SERIAL)	THE UNWRITTEN CODE	
THE GRIM GAME	THE WILDERNESS TRAIL	

1920–1929

Post–World War I movies came of age with the flapper sensibilities of Clara Bow, the smart comedies of Buster Keaton, the smoldering sensuality of Rudolph Valentino, and the speaking voice of Al Jolson that introduced the sound era.

POSTWAR CYNICISM AND WORLDLINESS resulted in the wide variety and licentiousness of movies during the 1920s. In the US, sexy melodramas from Cecil B. De Mille like *The Affairs of Anatol* (1921) continued to appear, as did spectacles like Rex Ingram's *The Four Horsemen of the Apocalypse* (1921) and westerns like James Cruze's *The Covered Wagon* (1923). Comedies featured a staggering array of talent, including Charlie Chaplin (*The Gold Rush,* 1925), Buster Keaton (*Sherlock Jr.,* 1924), and Harold Lloyd (*The Freshman,* 1925). Feature documentaries debuted, with Robert Flaherty's *Nanook of the North* (1922), as did gangster movies, with Josef von Sternberg's *Underworld* (1927).

To fit their screen roles, movie stars had exotic personas. Rudolph Valentino became a smoldering lover with *The Sheik* (1921), and his death in 1926 was the cause of international mourning. Colleen Moore and Clara Bow (the "It" Girl) portrayed carefree flappers, and even long-tressed Mary Pickford bobbed her hair. Rin Tin Tin approximated human emotions and saved scores of humans in extremes of weather (*Frozen River,* 1929) and climate (*Rinty of the Desert,* 1928).

Sensational scandals were soon associated with Hollywood life. Despite being acquitted of manslaughter in the death of starlet Virginia Rappe, comedian Fatty Arbuckle was forced into retirement. In 1918, exhibitors refused to air films of matinee idol Francis X. Bushman, once an extramarital affair was revealed, but public knowledge of an affair between Pola Negri and Rudolph Valentino in the mid-1920s made the exotic actress more popular.

AT LEFT: *Dubbed the "It" Girl, Clara Bow epitomized the flapper in the films she made throughout the 1920s.*

Another clean-cut matinee idol, Wallace Reid, died from complications of drug addiction in 1923. In France, postwar cinema was marked by the commercial successes of Abel Gance (*Napoléon,* 1927, three connecting images side-by-side on the screen) and Jacques Feyder (*Crainquebille,* 1923), and the avant-garde experiments of Man Ray (*Le Retour à la Raison,* 1923) and Luis Buñuel (*Un Chien Andalou,* 1928). In Germany, dark, exaggerated, expressionist films dominated the first half of a decade called Germany's golden film era. Among major expressionist films were Robert Wiene's *The Cabinet of Dr. Caligari* (1919) and F. W. Murnau's *Nosferatu* (1922). After years of propagandistic films following the Russian Revolution, Soviet cinema became a creative center (officially sanctioned) with works by Lev Kuleshov, Alexander Dovzhenko, and most notably, Sergei Eisenstein (*Strike, Potemkin,* 1925). India enjoyed an active film industry during the silent era, producing up to 100 titles per year during the late 1920s.

To reward excellence in the film medium and to mark its growing importance, the Academy of Motion Picture Arts and Sciences began presenting Academy Awards in 1927.

INVENTORS THOMAS EDISON and Lee DeForest experimented with sound-film technology for decades (the Kinetophone and the Phonofilm process, respectively). But it was the upstart Vitaphone Company, formed by Warner Bros. and Western Electric, that made the first successful sound shorts in August 1926 and the first sound feature in October 1927: Alan Crosland's *The Jazz Singer,* starring Al Jolson.

Sound films were an immediate success with audiences, a challenge for the studios, and the death knell for the careers of many silent film stars. Among those felled by their voices were the heavily accented Pola Negri and John Gilbert, whose reedy voice during his sound premiere provoked audience laughter. Other actors, such as Mary Pickford, could not escape their silent screen personas and were unable to make a successful transition to sound films. After losing her audience with her more sophisticated sound-film image, Pickford retired in 1933.

By the end of the 1920s, over 40 percent of US movie theaters were wired for sound. Talking pictures would transform the film industry in the 1930s, further enlarging and refining the studio system. As would an event unrelated to movies – the collapse of the US stock market in October 1929 and the resulting worldwide economic depression.

CHRONOLOGY

1920

In an early union of Hollywood royalty, swashbuckling star Douglas Fairbanks marries "America's Sweetheart" Mary Pickford on March 2. For years, they will be filmdom's favorite couple. As a wedding gift, Pickford receives the mansion known as Pickfair.

The Americanization Committee is formed by Hollywood film executives and politicians to encourage patriotism through films. Among its members are Adolph Zukor and Secretary of the Interior Franklin K. Lane.

More than 20,000 movie houses are operating in the US.

US independent film producers attempt to control distribution by purchasing newly built movie palaces.

With Hollywood already known as the world's film production center, its Chamber of Commerce discourages would-be actors from coming to California with advertisements warning, "Please Don't Try to Break into the Movies."

With the 1919 release of *The Cabinet of Dr. Caligari*, Germany pioneers expressionist drama. Practitioners will include Robert Wiene, F.W. Murnau, and Fritz Lang.

Teenage vaudevillian Archie Leach arrives in America from England. He will later make films as Cary Grant.

In Brazil, films are shown for the first time with records, providing "synchronized" sound.

Italian film critic Ricciotto Canudo, who has coined the phrase "the seventh art" to define film as an art form, founds the Club des Amis du 7e Art (Club of Friends of the Seventh Art) in Paris.

The first Polish film studio is built in Warsaw.

Films related to the revolution dominate nationalized Soviet filmmaking.

Director Ernst Lubitsch's *Madame Dubarry/Passion* in 1919 and this year's *Anna Boleyn/Deception* popularize elaborate costume dramas.

In Germany, the theatrical productions of Max Reinhardt influence film genres, lighting, and directorial styles for the decade. Reinhardt-influenced directors include Ernst Lubitsch, Otto Preminger, and F. W. Murnau.

An often-imitated masterpiece of German expressionism, The Cabinet of Dr. Caligari (1919) used canvas and distorted perspectives to create its eerie sets.

NOTABLE FILMS 1920

United States
THE DEVIL'S PASS KEY

DR. JEKYLL AND
MR. HYDE

HUMORESQUE

KATHLEEN
MAVOUREEN

THE LAST OF THE
MOHICANS

MADAME X

THE MARK OF ZORRO

THE MOLLYCODDLE

ONE WEEK

THE PENALTY

POLLYANNA

THE RETURN OF TARZAN

THE ROUND UP

THE TOLL GATE

WAY DOWN EAST

WHY CHANGE YOUR
WIFE?

France
L'ILLUSTRE ATTRICE
CICALA FORMICA
(THE FAMOUS ACTRESS
CICADA ANT)

Germany
ANNA BOLEYN
(DECEPTION)

THE GOLEM

SUMURUN
(ONE ARABIAN NIGHT)

Norway
PRÄNKÄSTAN
(THE PARSON'S WIDOW)

Sweden
KLOSTRET I SENDOMIR
(THE MONASTERY OF
SENDOMIR)

USSR
DOMESTIC AGITATOR

MOTHER

ON THE RED FRONT

United Kingdom
ALF'S BUTTON

NOTHING ELSE
MATTERS

1921

Comedian Roscoe "Fatty" Arbuckle is arrested on September 11 in San Francisco for the murder of actress Virginia Rappe. Charges are reduced to manslaughter, and a December trial results in a hung jury.

German state film studio UFA signs agreement with Famous Players–Lasky Corporation to bring German films to the US.

Sweden suffers a talent drain over the coming decade, as actors and directors such as Greta Garbo, Mauritz Stiller, and Victor Sjöström leave for Hollywood.

The US release of *The Cabinet of Dr. Caligari* sparks a May 7 anti–film importation riot at a Hollywood theater.

1922

Former US Postmaster General Will Hays is appointed head of the Motion Picture Producers and Distributors of America, Inc. (MPPDA), a self-monitoring organization for the depiction of morals in the movies.

Toll of the Sea, the first two-color Technicolor feature, is made.

Writer, director, and explorer Robert Flaherty pioneers documentary filmmaking with the 1922 release of *Nanook of the North*, which details the daily life of an Inuit and his family.

Within Our Gates, written and directed by Oscar Micheaux in 1920, is the oldest surviving film made by an African-American. The only surviving copy was found by the American Film Institute in Spain and restored by the Library of Congress.

NOTABLE FILMS 1921

United States
A SAILOR-MADE MAN

THE AFFAIRS OF
ANATOL

DREAM STREET

THE FOUR HORSEMEN
OF THE APOCALYPSE

THE KID

LITTLE LORD
FAUNTLEROY

ORPHANS OF
THE STORM

THE SHEIK

THE THREE
MUSKETEERS

TOL'ABLE DAVID

China
SEA OATH

France
L'ATLANTIDE

Germany
DANTON
(ALL FOR A WOMAN)

DER MÜDE TOD
(DESTINY)

Sweden
THE PHANTOM
CARRIAGE
(THY SOUL SHALL
BEAR WITNESS)

United Kingdom
KIPPS

SQUIBS

USSR
HUNGER-HUNGER-
HUNGER

The daily life of a northern Canadian Eskimo family was brought to the screen in Nanook of the North – *film's first documentary – in 1922.*

NOTABLE FILMS 1922

United States	THE PRISONER OF ZENDA	**China**	NOSFERATU
ARABIAN LOVE	ROBIN HOOD	BEAUTIES AND SKELETONS	PHANTOM
BLOOD AND SAND	SKY HIGH	**France**	**Norway**
THE CHAMPION	TESS OF THE STORM COUNTRY	CRAINQUEBILLE	PAN
THE CRADLE	THE POWER OF LOVE (IN 3-D STEREOSCOPIC PROCESS)	**Germany**	**USSR**
FOOLISH WIVES		DAS WEIB DES PHARAO (THE LOVES OF PHARAOH)	INFINITE SORROW
GRANDMA'S BOY			
NANOOK OF THE NORTH	TOLL OF THE SEA	DR. MABUSE, DER SPIELER (DR. MABUSE, THE GAMBLER)	
ONE TERRIBLE DAY (FIRST "OUR GANG" COMEDY)	WHEN KNIGHTHOOD WAS IN FLOWER	LUKREZIA BORGIA	

The average big-budget film in the 1920s costs about $250,000.

In February, the second trial of Roscoe "Fatty" Arbuckle for manslaughter in the death of Virginia Rappe ends in a hung jury. In the third trial, in April, he is acquitted. The trials prompt Will Hays to suspend Arbuckle temporarily from filmmaking.

Foreign competition, particularly from the US and Germany, reduces Italy's film production and representation on local movie screens.

In China, the pioneering wholly owned film company Ming Hsing is created.

In Japan, the practice of using an *oyama,* or female impersonator for female roles, is ending, a change instigated in large part by the writings of critic and filmmaker Norimasa Kaeriyama.

1923

Matinee idol Wallace Reid dies at age 32 from an overuse of drugs and alcohol. His early death prompts further public scrutiny of the film community in Hollywood.

With the release of James Cruze's *The Covered Wagon,* westerns become popular with audiences.

Cowboy star William S. Hart retires following divorce proceedings charging him with fathering an illegitimate child. Later this year, purported mother Elizabeth MacCauley reveals that she lied about Hart's involvement, and Hart returns to filmmaking.

In *Binderup v. Pathé Exchange,* the US Supreme Court rules that the shipment of film within a state constitutes an extension of interstate commerce and therefore can be regulated by the federal government.

Despite the misgivings of Paramount studio chief Adolph Zukor, Cecil B. De Mille's $1 million epic *The Ten Commandments* is a huge success.

Sixteen-millimeter film is introduced by Eastman Kodak Company for use by amateur filmmakers. It gains popularity in industrial and educational markets.

A major earthquake in September destroys many of Japan's studios and movie houses, largely in Tokyo and Yokohama. During rebuilding, foreign films reshape areas of public film interest and promote experimentation by Japanese filmmakers.

A large wooden sign advertising HOLLYWOODLAND is erected by a real estate developer. Later shortened to HOLLYWOOD, the sign will remain for decades and become a symbol of the movie business.

1923's 2½ hour epic The Ten Commandments, *from flamboyant director Cecil B. De Mille, cost over $1 million, far exceeding his original budget.*

NOTABLE FILMS 1923

United States	
THE CHRISTIAN	THE TEN COMMANDMENTS
FLAMING YOUTH	WHERE THE NORTH BEGINS
THE GREEN GODDESS	WHY WORRY?
THE HUNCHBACK OF NOTRE DAME	WILD BILL HICKOK
LITTLE OLD NEW YORK	A WOMAN OF PARIS
NORTH OF HUDSON BAY	**France** LE GAMIN DE PARIS
OUR HOSPITALITY	**Japan** IN THE RUINS
PLUNDER (SERIAL)	**United Kingdom** WOMAN TO WOMAN
ROSITA	**USSR** LOCKSMITH AND CHANCELLOR
RUGGLES OF RED GAP	
SAFETY LAST	
SOULS FOR SALE	
THE SPOILERS	

From this year through 1932, Japan has the most prolific filmmaking industry in the world.

The Soviet government establishes the creative unit Proletino to create politically oriented films.

1924

Throughout the decade in American films, the sexually liberated flapper and the honorable cowboy dominate popular movies. The flapper is epitomized by Colleen Moore and Clara Bow; the cowboy by William S. Hart, Tom Mix, and Harry Carey.

Double features are offered in some US cities.

In Britain, producer Michael Balcon founds Gainsborough Studios, where Alfred Hitchcock will direct his first films, beginning with *The Pleasure Garden* (1925).

In Britain, once-dominant film innovator Cecil Hepworth is forced into bankruptcy and closes his studios. His decline reflects, in part, the increasing international popularity of American films.

"Poverty Row," a maze of shabby offices around Sunset Boulevard in Hollywood, is the site of Harry and Jack Cohn's new business, C.B.C. Films Sales Company, which becomes major studio Columbia Pictures.

Metro-Goldwyn Pictures is formed from the merger of Metro Pictures, Goldwyn Pictures, and Louis B. Mayer Productions. Mayer heads production.

US film producer and director Thomas Ince dies under mysterious circumstances aboard William Randolph Hearst's yacht, possibly shot by his host Hearst.

Film production company Famous Players–Lasky is eclipsed in importance by its distributor Paramount and is forced to share credit in all films. For the past five years, Paramount has been gaining strength through its acquisition of dozens of US motion picture houses.

Charlie Chaplin marries his 16-year-old *Gold Rush* co-star Lita Grey (Lolita McMurray).

NOTABLE FILMS 1924

United States	France
BEAU BRUMMEL	NANA
THE DRAMATIC LIFE OF ABRAHAM LINCOLN	**Germany** DER LETZTE MANN (THE LAST MAN)
ENTR'ACTE	KRIEMHILDS RACHE (KRIEMHILD'S REVENGE)
GIRL SHY	
GREED	DAS WACHSFIGUREN-KABINETT (WAXWORKS)
HE WHO GETS SLAPPED	**Germany and United Kingdom** DECAMERON NIGHTS
THE IRON HORSE	
THE MARRIAGE CIRCLE	**Japan** JOGASHIMA
MONSIEUR BEAUCAIRE	SEISAKU'S WIFE
THE NAVIGATOR	**Sweden** GÖSTA BERLINGS SAGA (THE ATONEMENT OF GÖSTA BERLING)
PETER PAN	
ROMOLA	
THE SEA HAWK	**USSR** THE EXTRAORDINARY ADVENTURES OF MR. WEST IN THE LAND OF THE BOLSHEVIKS
SEVEN CHANCES	
SHERLOCK JR.	
THE THIEF OF BAGDAD	KINO-GLAS
Denmark MIKAEL (MICHAEL CHAINED; A.K.A. HEART'S DESIRE AND THE INVERT)	

1925

With *Tumbleweeds,* cowboy star William S. Hart hangs up his spurs. Partly self-financed, the film is later re-released with a sound farewell speech in which Hart calls filmmaking "the breath of life to me."

Cowboy actor Tom Mix becomes Hollywood's highest-paid movie star, signing a contract with Fox for $20,000 per week. The flamboyant Mix heralds a new generation of western stars.

1924: BIRTHS

LEE MARVIN, FEB. 19
FREDDIE BARTHOLOMEW, MAR. 15
SABU, MAR. 15
MARLON BRANDO, APR. 3
DORIS DAY, APR. 3
SIDNEY LUMET, JUNE 20
AUDIE MURPHY, JUNE 20
EVA MARIE SAINT, JULY 4
ARLENE DAHL, AUG. 11
LAUREN BACALL, SEPT. 16
GERALDINE PAGE, NOV. 24

1924: DEATHS

THOMAS INCE

1925: BIRTHS

PAUL NEWMAN, JAN. 26
JACK LEMMON, FEB. 8
ROD STEIGER, APR. 14
JEANNE CRAIN, MAY 25
TONY CURTIS, JUNE 2
DONALD O'CONNOR, AUG. 30
PETER SELLERS, SEPT. 8
CLIFF ROBERTSON, SEPT. 9
RICHARD BURTON, OCT. 16
ANGELA LANSBURY, OCT. 16
ROCK HUDSON, NOV. 23
GLORIA GRAHAME, NOV. 28
SAMMY DAVIS, JR., DEC. 8

1925: DEATHS

MAX LINDER (GABRIEL-MAXIMILIEN LEUVIELLE)

For the 1924 film *Tess of the D'Urbervilles,* MGM head Louis B. Mayer ordered director Marshall Neilan to add a happy ending. Author Thomas Hardy could not veto the change – he had sold the rights to his novel to MGM.

1926: BIRTHS

PATRICIA NEAL, JAN. 20
JERRY LEWIS, MAR. 16
ROGER CORWIN, APR. 5
MARILYN MONROE, JUNE 1
JEAN PETERS, OCT. 12

1926: DEATHS

BARBARA LA MARR
RUDOLPH VALENTINO

The Lost World introduces dinosaurs to the science fiction/fantasy film genre. Special effects are created by Willis O'Brien, whose later films will include *King Kong* (1933).

After a contest sponsored by *Movie Weekly*, MGM renames Broadway actress Lucille Le Sueur "Joan Crawford."

Louise Brooks debuts in *Street of Forgotten Men.*

Journalist Louella Parsons begins to report on Hollywood for the Hearst newspaper chain.

Newspaper tycoon William Randolph Hearst moves into his Pacific estate, San Simeon. As Xanadu, it appears in the 1940 Orson Welles film *Citizen Kane.*

Paramount expands its theater ownership by merging its theater chain with that of Balaban & Katz.

In a program of expansion, Warner Bros. launches a radio station, KFWB, acquires the Vitagraph Company, and joins with Western Electric to develop sound apparatus for new talking films.

In *Potemkin,* Russian filmmaker Sergei Eisenstein introduces the technique of montage, or the dynamic juxtaposition of disparate shots to create a new meaning.

Light in Asia, a dramatic biography of the Buddha, marks India's emergence as a filmmaking center.

A Politburo decision in the Soviet Union sanctions some experimentation in national filmmaking; the works of Alexander Dovzhenko, Vsevolod Pudovkin, and Sergei Eisenstein will distinguish the next few years of Soviet filmmaking.

Czech filmmaking experiences a resurgence, with increased production and critical acclaim that continues through the silent era.

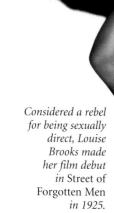

Considered a rebel for being sexually direct, Louise Brooks made her film debut in Street of Forgotten Men *in 1925.*

NOTABLE FILMS 1925

United States
THE BIG PARADE
THE EAGLE
THE FRESHMAN
GO WEST
THE GOLD RUSH
LADY WINDERMERE'S FAN
LIGHTNIN'
THE LOST WORLD
MADAME SANS-GÊNE
THE MERRY WIDOW
THE PHANTOM OF THE OPERA
THE PONY EXPRESS
RIDERS OF THE PURPLE SAGE
SALLY OF THE SAWDUST
THE SALVATION HUNTERS
SEVEN CHANCES
STELLA DALLAS
TUMBLEWEEDS
THE UNHOLY THREE

Japan
STREET SKETCHES

Sweden
DIE FREUDLOSE GASSE (JOYLESS STREET)

United Kingdom
THE PLEASURE GARDEN

USSR
THE BATTLESHIP POTEMKIN (POTEMKIN)
STACHKA (THE STRIKE)

1926

Screen idol Rudolph Valentino dies on August 23 at age 31, following an operation for a perforated ulcer. Intense public reaction prompts a near-riot at his funeral. Hollywood studios shut down for the ceremony.

Swedish beauty Greta Garbo electrifies US audiences with three films this year: *The Torrent, The Temptress,* and *Flesh and the Devil.*

Detective Charlie Chan is introduced in the US serial *House Without a Key.*

In a review of Robert Flaherty's film *Moana,* the term *documentary* is coined for a nonfiction film.

Vitaphone, a sound-synchronizing process for film developed by Warner Bros. and Western Electric, is introduced. Patents for the sound-recording process that will soon be known as Movietone are bought by William Fox.

Flesh and the Devil co-stars Greta Garbo and John Gilbert plan to marry in September, but Garbo leaves him at the altar.

The first film with Vitaphone sound effects and a musical score, *Don Juan,* opens in New York City. Starring John Barrymore, it has no spoken dialogue on the sound track.

Broadway producer David Belasco renames stage actress Ruby Stevens "Barbara Stanwyck."

Al Jolson's famous phrase, "You ain't heard nothing yet!" came to epitomize the pioneering period of sound movies. He spoke these words, and a few others, in *The Jazz Singer*, an essentially silent film with a few cued-for-sound sentences of dialogue and exuberant musical numbers by Jolson in blackface. When *The Jazz Singer* was released in 1927, only 400 US theaters were wired for sound. It broke box-office records at all of them.

Hollywood royalty Mary Pickford and Douglas Fairbanks travel to Moscow, where they are received by adoring crowds.

Animated filmmakers Max and Dave Fleischer move to Paramount after their five-year-old Red Seal Studio collapses.

Don Juan *starring John Barrymore and Mary Astor was released in 1926 with Vitaphone sound effects and a musical score, but no spoken dialogue.*

1927

Al Jolson accepts the lead in *The Jazz Singer* (in May), after George Jessel and Warner Bros. fail to reach an agreement on payment for the sound portion of the film and Eddie Cantor declines the offer to star.

Alan Crosland's *The Jazz Singer,* starring Al Jolson, debuts from Warner Bros. on October 6 as the first feature-length "talking" film, with sound dialogue provided through Vitaphone disk transfer. Public reaction is enthusiastically positive.

Actress Clara Bow becomes the "It" Girl after the February release of *It.* "It" is sex appeal and, with her cupid's-bow mouth and bobbed hair, Bow epitomizes the liberated flapper.

The Academy of Motion Picture Arts and Sciences, a nonprofit organization, is established to "improve the artistic quality of the film medium."

With the success of *Seventh Heaven,* stars Janet Gaynor and Charles Farrell become known as "America's Lovebirds" and go on to make 11 additional films together.

The first Academy Awards for film excellence will consider films made from August 1, 1927, through July 31, 1928.

NOTABLE FILMS 1926

United States	
BEAU GESTE	TRAMP, TRAMP, TRAMP
BEN-HUR	WHAT PRICE GLORY?
THE BLACK PIRATE	THE WINNING OF BARBARA WORTH
LA BOHÈME	*Czechoslovakia*
DON JUAN	THE GOOD SOLDIER SCHWEIK
FAUST	THE KREUTZER SONATA
FLESH AND THE DEVIL	
THE GRAND DUCHESS AND THE WAITER	*Denmark*
THE GREAT K&A TRAIN ROBBERY	KLOVNEN (CLOWNS)
HANDS UP!	*France*
METROPOLIS	NAPOLÉON
MOANA	*Spain*
OLD IRONSIDES	LA MALCASADA
THE SCARLET LETTER	*United Kingdom*
SO THIS IS PARIS	THE LODGER
THE SON OF THE SHEIK	THE PLEASURE GARDEN
SPARROWS	*USSR*
THE STRONG MAN	MOTHER (MOTHER 1905)
THE TEMPTRESS	SHETAYA CHAST SVETA (ONE SIXTH OF THE WORLD)
VARIETY	

1927: BIRTHS

HARRY BELAFONTE, MAR. 1
JANET LEIGH, JULY 6
CARL "ALFALFA" SWITZER, AUG. 8 (SOME SOURCES REPORT 1926)
ROBERT SHAW, AUG. 9
PETER FALK, SEPT. 5
GEORGE C. SCOTT, OCT. 15

1927: DEATHS

MARCUS LOEW
SAM WARNER
EARLE WILLIAMS

In 1927, Fritz Lang's chilling and visionary science fiction work Metropolis *impressed critics, but left German film studio UFA in serious financial trouble.*

Hollywood studios issue the "Don't and Be Carefuls," an attempt at self-censorship that prohibits the showing of white slavery, interracial romance, and drug use on screen.

The film actor–employer agreement is reached through the Academy of Motion Picture Arts and Sciences in December.

Animators Walt Disney and Ub Iwerks create *Oswald the Lucky Rabbit,* a cartoon series.

The Photophone sound system is demonstrated by RCA.

Famous Players–Lasky Corporation becomes Paramount studios.

Egypt produces its first major full-length feature, *Laila,* a drama.

In the UK, the Cinematograph Films Act of 1927, which mandates increases in domestic film bookings, results in a marked increase in financial and creative output from British studios.

Norwegian cinema moves into the limelight with *Troll-elgen (The Magic Leap),* directed by Walter Fürst.

Former World War I flying ace William Wellman directed the thrilling air fights in 1927's *Wings,* recipient of Hollywood's very first best picture award. Starring Charles "Buddy" Rogers, Richard Arlen, and Clara Bow, *Wings* was a silent film but featured a musical sound track and the synchronized sound effects of propellers and whirring motors as planes took off and landed.

Stan Laurel and Oliver Hardy appear in their first film, *Duck Soup,* a comedy produced by the Hal Roach Studio.

MGM production supervisor Irving Thalberg marries MGM star, Norma Shearer, who will become known as "the First Lady of the Screen."

After being fired by Hal Roach, Frank Capra is employed as a director by Columbia Pictures. He will play an instrumental part in that studio's success in the 1930s.

David O. Selznick moves from MGM to Paramount to head its story and writing departments.

Fox Movietone News is inaugurated and its first scoop is the filmed coverage of the transatlantic flight made by Charles Lindbergh.

Grauman's Chinese Theater opens with the May Hollywood premiere of Cecil B. De Mille's *The King of Kings.* Douglas Fairbanks, Mary Pickford, and Norma and Constance Talmadge are the first movie stars to leave their handprints and footprints in the forecourt of the theater, a privilege granted Hollywood "royalty."

The Roxy Theater in New York City opens as the largest movie house in the world, with seating for 6,214.

NOTABLE FILMS 1927

United States	WINGS
CAMILLE	
THE CAT AND THE CANARY	***Egypt***
	LAILA
CHILDREN OF DIVORCE	***France***
COLLEGE	CASANOVA
EXIT SMILING	NAPOLÉON
THE GENERAL	UN CHAPEAU DE PAILLE D'ITALIE (THE ITALIAN STRAW HAT)
IT	
THE KID BROTHER	***Germany***
KING OF KINGS	MANON LESCAUT
LONG PANTS	METROPOLIS
LOVE (ANNA KARENINA)	SPIONE (SPIES)
THE LOVE OF SUNJA	***Norway***
MY BEST GIRL	TROLL-ELGEN (THE MAGICLEAP)
SEVENTH HEAVEN	***United Kingdom***
THE STUDENT PRINCE	THE RING
SUNRISE: A SONG OF TWO HUMANS	***USSR***
THE MAN WHO LAUGHS	THE END OF ST. PETERSBURG
UNDERWORLD	

1928

Lights of New York, the first all-talking feature, debuts from Warner Bros. The film is directed by Brian Foy. All ten of the year's all-talking films are made by Warner Bros.

Using an improvised sound system, Walt Disney and Ub Iwerks produce the animated sound cartoon *Steamboat Willie,* starring Mickey Mouse. Disney himself provides the voice of Mickey.

With the August release of *Loves,* silent star Pola Negri becomes an early casualty of sound films. Her heavy Polish accent renders her unintelligible to most audiences.

Mary Pickford bobs her hair, flapper-style. Her career never recovers.

Clara Bow becomes the highest-paid movie star, receiving $35,000 per week.

Paramount announces it will make only talking films as of 1928.

Al Jolson has the first film-related hit record: "Sonny Boy," from *The Singing Fool,* which sells two million copies this year.

An all-talking trailer advertising coming attractions is used for the first time to advertise the movie *Tenderloin.*

Darryl Zanuck becomes head of Warner Bros. production.

Louis B. Mayer appears as a delegate at the Republican National Convention.

RKO (Radio-Keith-Orpheum) Pictures is established. Controlling the new studio's exhibition sites is Joseph P. Kennedy.

B. P. Schulberg becomes the head of Hollywood production at Paramount.

The surrealistic film *Un Chien Andalou (An Andalusian Dog)* written and directed by Luis Buñuel and Salvador Dali premieres in Paris. Despite its disturbing and bizarre scenes, the film receives an enthusiastic response.

1928: BIRTHS

JAMES GARNER, APR. 3
SHIRLEY TEMPLE, APR. 23
JAMES IVORY, JUNE 7
STANLEY KUBRICK, JULY 26
ANN BLYTH, AUG. 16
JAMES COBURN, AUG. 31
RODDY McDOWALL, SEPT. 17
LAURENCE HARVEY, OCT. 1
GEORGE PEPPARD, OCT. 1
GEORGE "SPANKY" McFARLAND, OCT. 2
ROGER MOORE, OCT. 14
ANTHONY FRANCIOSA, OCT. 28
GRACE KELLY, NOV. 12

1928: DEATHS

THEODORE ROBERTS
LARRY SEMON
MAURITZ STILLER
FRED THOMSON

1928's classic surrealistic short film Un Chien Andalou (An Andalusian Dog), *which featured striking and disturbing images, was both written and directed by Luis Buñuel and Salvador Dali.*

As it has for the past few years, India produces approximately 100 films in 1928.

The statuette given to Academy Award winners was designed by art director Cedric Gibbons. The gold-plated metal trophy is 13½ inches tall and shows a man holding a sword and standing on a reel of film.

NOTABLE FILMS 1928

United States		**France**	**Germany**
ALIAS JIMMY VALENTINE	THE PATSY	ETOILE DE MER	ASPHALT
THE BIG CITY	QUEEN KELLY	(STAR OF THE SEA)	PANDORA'S BOX
THE CAMERAMAN	SADIE THOMPSON	LA CHUTE DE	**Japan**
THE CIRCUS	SHOW PEOPLE	LA MAISON USHER	DREAMS OF YOUTH
THE CROWD	THE SINGING FOOL	LES DEUX TIMIDES	JUJIRO
THE GAUCHO	STEAMBOAT BILL, JR.	LA PASSION DE	(CROSSROADS)
GLORIOUS BETSY	SPEEDY	JEANNE D'ARC	**United Kingdom**
KIT CARSON	STREET ANGEL	(THE PASSION OF	DAWN
THE LAST COMMAND	TENDERLOIN	JOAN OF ARC)	SHOOTING STARS
LIGHTS OF NEW YORK	THE WEDDING	LES NOUVEAUX	UNDERGROUND
THE LOVE PARADE	MARCH	MESSIEURS	**USSR**
OUR DANCING	WEDDING NIGHT	(THE NEW GENTLEMEN)	OKTYABR
DAUGHTERS	THE WIND	THÉRÈSE RAQUIN	(OCTOBER OR
OUR DANCING	A WOMAN	TIRE AU FLANC	TEN DAYS THAT
MOTHERS	OF AFFAIRS	(LAZE ABOUT)	SHOOK THE WORLD)
		UN CHIEN ANDALOU	ZVENIGORA
		(AN ANDALUSIAN DOG)	

Soviet directors Eisenstein, Alexandrov, and Pudovkin present a theoretical statement on sound cinema, "The Future of the Sound Film."

The Soviet government criticizes Sergei Eisenstein's film *October* for its suspicious "formalism," and the government-sponsored All-Union Party Conference concludes that Soviet films must be made in such a way as to be "understood by the millions."

1929

The first Academy Award winners are announced in February by the Academy of Motion Picture Arts and Sciences. The awards are presented at a banquet in May.

John Gilbert's voice is the subject of audience ridicule at screenings of the silent star's first talking film, *His Glorious Night.*

Cartoon breakthroughs include Walt Disney's first "Silly Symphony" cartoon, *The Skeleton Dance,* in May and the pioneering synchronized talking cartoon, *Bosco the Talking Kid,* from Hugh Harman and Rudolph Ising.

"Our Gang" all-talking films begin with the opening of *Small Talk.*

The Marx Brothers star in their first film, *The Cocoanuts,* in May, as does Maurice Chevalier, in *Innocents of Paris* in April.

Mary Pickford speaks in *Coquette,* her first all-talking film.

King Vidor's *Hallelujah!* is the first major sound feature with an all-black cast.

Paramount acquires 50 percent of CBS.

Warner Bros. purchases several music publishing houses to gain control of music rights for use in films.

On With the Show from Warner Bros., released in May, is the first all-color sound musical.

The US Justice Department charges Fox and Warner Bros. with violation of antitrust laws.

Groucho, Chico, and Harpo Marx starred in films from 1929 until 1949. Brother Zeppo appeared with his brothers for the first five years of their career.

Douglas Fairbanks and Mary Pickford make their first co-starring appearance together in *The Taming of the Shrew.*

To reduce charges of favoritism, the Motion Picture Academy of Arts and Sciences announces that starting next year, Academy Award winners will be chosen by all Academy members, not by the elite Central Board of Judges.

Joseph Stalin announces that USSR film production must devote 30 percent of its efforts to works supporting the Five Year Plan.

By the end of the 1920s, several European countries including Austria, Britain, France, and Hungary, as well as Australia, impose quotas on the importation of foreign films.

Italy passes a law requiring all films to be exhibited in Italian.

The number of French cinemas nearly triples over the decade, from 1,444 after World War I to 4,200 in 1929.

Alfred Hitchcock's *Blackmail* is the UK's first talking picture.

Director Alfred Hitchcock's 1929 film Blackmail *was the first talking picture released in the UK. Hitchcock, seen here as a subway patron, made cameo appearances in his films.*

NOTABLE FILMS 1929

United States			United Kingdom
APPLAUSE	HALLELUJAH!	THE TAMING OF THE SHREW	BLACKMAIL
THE BRIDGE OF SAN LUIS REY	IN OLD ARIZONA	THE VIRGINIAN	PICCADILLY
BROADWAY MELODY OF 1929	INNOCENTS OF PARIS	*Czechoslovakia*	*USSR*
BULLDOG DRUMMOND	THE IRON MASK	THE ORGANIST OF ST. VITUS	THE GENERAL LINE (OLD AND NEW)
THE COCOANUTS	LUCKY STAR	SUCH IS LIFE	THE MAN WITH A MOVIE CAMERA
COQUETTE	ON WITH THE SHOW	*Egypt*	
DISRAELI	THE PAGAN	DAUGHTER OF THE NILE	STORM OVER ASIA (THE HEIR TO GENGHIS KHAN)
THE DIVINE LADY	RED HOT RHYTHM	*Japan*	
GOLD DIGGERS OF BROADWAY	RIO RITA	TOKYO MARCH	
	THE RIVER	*Spain*	
	SMALL TALK	LA ALDEA MALDITA (THE ACCURSED VILLAGE)	
	SPITE MARRIAGE		

1929: BIRTHS
JEAN SIMMONS, JAN. 23
JANE POWELL, APR. 1
CAROLYN JONES, APR. 28
AUDREY HEPBURN, MAY 4
JOHN CASSAVETES, DEC. 9

1929: DEATHS
JEANNE EAGELS
DUSTIN FARNUM
WILLIAM RUSSELL

1930–1939

With gangster movies, lavish musicals, and romantic comedies, the sound era and the US studio system reached full flower in the 1930s, culminating in the golden film year 1939 and its most honored representative, Gone with the Wind.

THE INDEPENDENT COMPANIES that had rebelled against the controls of the Motion Picture Patents Company in the early 1920s were now the filmmaking power centers themselves. MGM, Warner Bros., Paramount, RKO, Universal, Columbia, Disney, and Fox controlled most US screens, with up to 778 features annually. By mid-decade, each studio would have an individual identity: high-toned MGM offered big stars and high-quality production; "Poverty Row" Columbia traded on Harry Langdon–trained Frank Capra's comedies; Warner Bros. made gritty social dramas and gangster films. Although some critics called silents a purer form of cinema, audiences preferred sound, and by 1930, more than 60 percent of US theaters were equipped for it. The silent era had effectively ended, and what would be known as the golden era of movies had begun.

Sound transformed the film business. It required actors with trained voices, and the leading studios mined the Broadway and London stages for naturally emotive actors like Katharine Hepburn, Henry Fonda, and James Stewart. Sound required streamlined recording devices, with Edison's sound-on-disk process replaced by optical sound recording. It put title-card writers out of work and forced screenwriters to define characters through words.

Sound also made possible a new genre: the musical. Popular novelties in the 1920s, musicals emerged in great variety and defined studios and stars of the 1930s. Paramount in the early 1930s produced musicals starring Maurice Chevalier; MGM prospered with Jeanette MacDonald–Nelson Eddy vehicles.

AT LEFT: *Clark Gable and Vivien Leigh in* Gone with the Wind, *the first color film to win an Academy Award for best picture.*

Warner Bros. had annual Gold Diggers musicals; and RKO made stars of Fred Astaire and Ginger Rogers. Other popular genres of the 1930s included the gangster film, notably those produced by Warner Bros., which released such classics as *Public Enemy* (1931) starring James Cagney, *Little Caesar* (1931) starring Edward G. Robinson, *Scarface* (1932) starring Paul Muni, and *The Roaring Twenties* (1939) starring Cagney and Humphrey Bogart. Literary adaptations (*David Copperfield*, 1935), romantic comedies (*It Happened One Night*, 1934), and westerns (*Stagecoach*, 1939) also dominated US cinema.

FRENCH DIRECTORS, LED BY JEAN RENOIR, were instead celebrated for an often dark vision of the human condition that presaged the impending world war. Among Renoir's films are *La Grande Illusion (Grand Illusion)* (1937) and *La Règle du Jeu (The Rules of the Game)* (1939). Other notable French filmmakers of the 1930s include René Clair (*A Nous la Liberté*, 1931), Jean Vigo (*Zéro de Conduit [Zero for Conduct]* 1933), and Marcel Carné (*Le Jour se lève [Daybreak]* 1939). Pre-war Germany produced up to 200 films per year, marked by the works of Fritz Lang (*M*, 1931) and G. B. Pabst (*Westfront 1918*, 1930). After Hitler's rise to power in 1933, the industry was controlled by minister of propaganda Joseph Goebbels, which resulted in such nationalistic homages to fascism as Leni Riefenstahl's *Triumph des Willens (Triumph of the Will)* (1935). Spanish cinema came under the control of the production company Compañia Industrial del Film Español, S.A., in 1931. But by the end of the 1930s and with the rise of dictator Francisco Franco, films were subject to government control. In the Soviet Union, sound-film production began in 1930 with *The Earth Thirsts*. Dramas, literary adaptations, and works based on Russian history were the fundamentals of early Soviet film, notably Sergei Eisenstein's *Alexander Nevsky* (1938). It came after his first project, *Bezhin Meadow*, about collectivization, was terminated by the government following a change in farm policy.

COLOR FILM TECHNOLOGY, in development since the 1890s, reached a milestone in 1932 with the development of the three-color separation process. First used for the Walt Disney cartoon *Flowers and Trees* (1933) and the 1935 feature *Becky Sharp*, it is best known for the 1939 Civil War epic *Gone with the Wind*.

Winning a record eight Academy Awards, *Gone with the Wind* was the biggest movie sensation since the 1915 Civil War epic *The Birth of a Nation*. Yet it was but one of many enduring movies made in what many have called the finest year in US film. Other outstanding projects that year included *Stagecoach, Goodbye, Mr. Chips, Ninotchka, Wuthering Heights, Mr. Smith Goes to Washington, Only Angels Have Wings, Dark Victory, Young Mr. Lincoln, The Women, Gunga Din*, and *The Wizard of Oz*.

CHRONOLOGY

1930

Greta Garbo appears in her first talkie, *Anna Christie*, advertised with the slogan "Garbo Talks!"

Joan Crawford and Clark Gable team up in *Dance, Fools, Dance*, the first of eight features together.

John Wayne stars in the western, Raoul Walsh's *The Big Trail*, but the film fails at the box office. Wayne will not become a star until the release of *Stagecoach* in 1939.

Prison melodramas debut as a genre with *The Big House*, directed by George Hill.

Notable film music includes "Falling in Love Again" (*The Blue Angel*) and "Hooray for Captain Spaulding" (*Animal Crackers*).

With her husky voice, Swedish-born Greta Garbo survived the transition to sound with her 1930 film Anna Christie, *for which the advertisements proclaimed, "Garbo Talks!"*

Hungarian-accented silent star Vilma Banky is dropped by Samuel Goldwyn, another casualty of sound film. Likewise, silent star Norma Talmadge is forced out, her exit prompted by her unsatisfactory performance as a sound actress in *DuBarry, Woman of Passion*.

Fox Studio head William Fox is forced to sell the studio to bankers for $18 million after losing his fortune in the 1929 stock market crash. He faces a federal antitrust investigation.

NOTABLE FILMS 1930	
United States	THE SEA WOLF
ABRAHAM LINCOLN	THE VIRTUOUS SIN
ALL QUIET ON THE WESTERN FRONT	WHOOPEE!
ANIMAL CRACKERS	**France**
ANNA CHRISTIE	SOUS LES TOITS DE PARIS (UNDER THE ROOFS OF PARIS)
BILLY THE KID	
THE BLUE ANGEL	
THE BIG HOUSE	**Germany**
THE BIG TRAIL	DIE DREIGROSCHENOPER (THE 3 PENNY OPERA)
CITY GIRL	
DANCE, FOOLS, DANCE	**Spain**
DRACULA	ZALACAIN EL AVENTUERERO (ZALACAIN, THE ADVENTURER)
HELL'S ANGELS	
MIN AND BILL	
MONTE CARLO	**United Kingdom**
MOROCCO	A COTTAGE ON DARTMOOR (ESCAPE FROM DARTMOOR)
OUTWARD BOUND	
ROMANCE	MURDER

Italy releases its first talking film, *La Canzone dell'Amore*, directed by Gennaro Righelli.

Germany bans *All Quiet on the Western Front* for its pacifist message.

Paramount, Warner Bros., and Fox are the biggest owners of movie theaters in the industry.

More than one-third of the 23,000 US movie theaters are wired for sound.

The Hollywood Reporter debuts, the first film industry daily newspaper.

The Production Code is adopted in March by the industry to codify practices when filming scenes that involve sex, violence, religion, and other sensitive subjects.

1931

The Great Depression leads to a sharp decrease in movie theater attendance. Average weekly attendance drops to 70 million this year (from 90 million in 1930) and will drop to 60 million in 1932 and 1933. The studios suffer financial difficulties, and theaters resort to such giveaway gimmicks as dish nights and double features to attract audiences.

RKO acquires the French Pathé Company.

The Hollywood studios, enmeshed in disputes about raiding each other's stars by persuading them to switch from one studio to another, agree to submit such matters to arbitration and to limit the practice in the future.

Universal releases *Dracula* and *Frankenstein*. The films make stars of Bela Lugosi (Dracula) and Boris Karloff (Frankenstein's monster) and begins Universal's classic cycle of horror films.

Warner Bros. invents the gangster genre with *Little Caesar,* starring Edward G. Robinson, and *Public Enemy,* starring James Cagney.

Clark Gable has his first nonextra role, as the villain in the western *The Painted Desert*. Signed by MGM, he appears in 12 movies this year (notably *A Free Soul*) and quickly becomes a major star.

Bette Davis signs her first contract with Warner Bros. The association will last until 1949.

Warner Oland, the screen's best-known Charlie Chan, plays the role for the first time in *Charlie Chan Carries On.*

Helen Hayes makes her film debut in *The Sin of Madelon Claudet.*

Clara Bow elopes with western star Rex Bell and settles with him on his ranch in Nevada. The move speeds the end of her career; she will retire from films two years later, in 1933.

French director Jean Renoir makes the first of his great movies of the decade, *La Chienne,* a critical success but a box-office disappointment.

The first gangster films, such as Little Caesar *starring Edward G. Robinson (pictured) and* Public Enemy, *were made by Warner Bros. in 1931.*

India releases its first talkie, *Alam Ara.*

Japan releases its first full-length talkie, *The Neighbor's Wife and Mine.*

The film *M*, directed by Fritz Lang, is released in Germany.

RKO won its only best picture Oscar with the now rarely seen western *Cimarron* (1931).

NOTABLE FILMS 1931

United States	Canada
AN AMERICAN TRAGEDY	THE VIKING
CIMARRON	*France*
CITY LIGHTS	LA CHIENNE
DRACULA	LE MILLION
FRANKENSTEIN	A NOUS LA LIBERTÉ
A FREE SOUL	*Germany*
THE FRONT PAGE	KAMERADSCHAFT
HISTORY IS MADE AT NIGHT	DER KONGRESS TANZT
LITTLE CAESAR	M
MONKEY BUSINESS	*India*
PLATINUM BLONDE	ALAM ARA
PUBLIC ENEMY	*Japan*
THE SIN OF MADELON CLAUDET	THE NEIGHBOR'S WIFE AND MINE
	United Kingdom
	DANCE PRETTY LADY
	THE W PLAN

1931: BIRTHS

ROBERT DUVALL, JAN. 5
JAMES EARL JONES, JAN. 17
GENE HACKMAN, JAN. 30
JAMES DEAN, FEB. 8
WILLIAM SHATNER, MAR. 22
LEONARD NIMOY, MAR. 26
ANNE BANCROFT, SEPT. 17
ANGIE DICKINSON, SEPT. 30
MIKE NICHOLS, NOV. 6

1931: DEATHS

THOMAS ALVA EDISON
F.W. MURNAU

Olympic swimming champion Johnny Weissmuller made his debut as Tarzan in 1932's Tarzan, the Ape Man *and portrayed the vine swinger until 1948.*

1932: BIRTHS

PIPER LAURIE, JAN. 22
FRANÇOIS TRUFFAUT, FEB. 6
ELIZABETH TAYLOR, FEB. 27
DEBBIE REYNOLDS, APR. 1
ANTHONY PERKINS, APR. 4
OMAR SHARIF, APR. 10
PETER O'TOOLE, AUG. 2
LOUIS MALLE, OCT. 30

1932: DEATHS

RIN TIN TIN (ORIGINAL DOG)

NOTABLE FILMS 1932

United States		
AMERICAN MADNESS	IF I HAD A MILLION	SHANGHAI EXPRESS
A BILL OF DIVORCEMENT	THE KID FROM SPAIN	RED DUST
BLONDE VENUS	LETTY LYNTON	**France**
DR. JEKYLL AND MR. HYDE	THE MASK OF FU MANCHU	BOUDU SAVED FROM DROWNING
A FAREWELL TO ARMS	NO MAN OF HER OWN	**Germany**
FREAKS	ONE HOUR WITH YOU	THE REBEL
GRAND HOTEL	RAIN	**United Kingdom**
HORSE FEATHERS	TARZAN, THE APE MAN	ROME EXPRESS
I AM A FUGITIVE FROM A CHAIN GANG	TROUBLE IN PARADISE	**USSR**
	SCARFACE	A SIMPLE CASE (LIFE IS BEAUTIFUL)

1932

Harry Cohn becomes president of Columbia Pictures.

Jesse Lasky resigns from Paramount.

Paramount ends its ownership of the Astoria Studios in Queens, New York. The studios become an independent production center.

MGM executive Irving Thalberg has a heart attack. Following his convalescence in Europe, he will return to MGM with greatly reduced authority.

Fearing competition from radio, film exhibitors ask the studios to stop permitting their stars to appear in that medium. Some studios briefly ban radio appearances by stars.

Walt Disney releases his first color cartoon, *Flowers and Trees,* which is also the first film in three-color Technicolor.

Katharine Hepburn makes her screen debut in *A Bill of Divorcement.*

MGM signs "Blonde Bombshell" Jean Harlow, who will become a major star. MGM's screenwriting department hires future Nobel Prize winner William Faulkner.

Jean Harlow marries MGM producer Paul Berg, who commits suicide two months later.

Tarzan, the Ape Man, the first in a series of Tarzan films starring Olympic swimming champion Johnny Weissmuller, is released.

At age three, Shirley Temple is signed to appear in a series of one-reel films called *Baby Burlesks,* which will mark her film debut.

Kodak introduces 8mm film for amateur filmmakers.

In Britain, Alexander Korda founds London Films.

In Mexico, Soviet director Sergei Eisenstein's ambitious film project *Que Viva Mexico!* is halted when its sponsor, the author Upton Sinclair, withdraws funding.

L'Armata Azzurra, a tribute to Mussolini's air force, is Fascist Italy's first heavily propagandistic film.

Egypt releases its first talkie, *The Song of the Heart.*

German psychologist Rudolf Arnheim publishes *Film as Art,* a seminal work of formalist film theory. It details how the constraints of the film medium affect its defining characteristics.

1933

The US government enacts the Code of Fair Competition for the Motion Picture Industry, which permits the major studios to act as vertically integrated monopolies, each controlling the production, distribution, and exhibition of its films.

Paramount Publix, the parent company of Paramount Pictures, is forced into bankruptcy, as is RKO, the parent company of RKO Pictures. Both companies are placed in receivership.

The Screenwriters Guild and the Screen Actors Guild are formed.

A one-day strike by carpenters and electricians protesting temporary wage cuts shuts down the major Hollywood studios on March 13.

In July and August, members of the International Alliance of Theatrical Stage Employees (IATSE) go on strike against the studios.

Daily Variety begins publication.

MGM signs Nelson Eddy.

Paramount releases *Popeye the Sailor,* a Betty Boop cartoon that features the first appearance by Popeye.

The Disney short *Three Little Pigs* introduces the song "Who's Afraid of the Big Bad Wolf?"

Fred Astaire and Ginger Rogers debut as a dancing team in *Flying Down to Rio.*

The first drive-in movie opens near Camden, New Jersey.

In Germany, the Nazis seize power and take control of the country's film industry, forcing Jews from their jobs. Hollywood studios accede to Nazi demands that they bar Jews from their German offices.

Alexander Korda's *The Private Life of Henry VIII,* starring Charles Laughton, catapults British cinema to a new level of international prestige.

Hedy Lamarr (then Hedy Kiesler) gains international notoriety for appearing nude in the Czech film *Ecstasy.*

NOTABLE FILMS 1933

United States
THE BITTER TEA OF GENERAL YEN
BLONDE BOMBSHELL
CAVALCADE
DANCING LADY
DUCK SOUP
FLYING DOWN TO RIO
42ND STREET
I'M NO ANGEL
THE INVISIBLE MAN
ISLAND OF LOST SOULS
KING KONG
LITTLE WOMEN
THE MUMMY
QUEEN CHRISTINA
ROMAN SCANDALS
SHE DONE HIM WRONG
STATE FAIR

Brazil
GANGA BRUTA

China
WILD TORRENT

Czechoslovakia
ECSTASY

France
QUATORZE JUILLET
ZÉRO DE CONDUITE
(ZERO FOR CONDUCT)

Germany
THE TESTAMENT OF DR. MABUSE

Japan
TWO STONE LANTERNS

United Kingdom
THE PRIVATE LIFE OF HENRY VIII

USSR
THE GREAT CONSOLER

1933: BIRTHS

KIM NOVAK, FEB. 13
MICHAEL CAINE, MAR. 14
JAYNE MANSFIELD, APR. 19
JOAN COLLINS, MAY 23
ROMAN POLANSKI, AUG. 18

1933: DEATHS

ROSCOE "FATTY" ARBUCKLE

Charles Laughton starred as the British monarch Henry VIII in the lavish UK production The Private Life of Henry VIII *(1933).*

1934

The Production Code, a self-censorship code devised by the Hollywood studios in 1930, begins to be strictly enforced, as it will be until the mid-1960s.

MGM chief Louis B. Mayer uses studio newsreels to malign author Upton Sinclair, the socialist Democratic candidate for governor in California. Sinclair loses the election.

Frank Capra's *It Happened One Night* is released. The film does much to establish the new genre of screwball comedy and will be the first movie to win all four major Academy Awards: best picture, best actor, best actress, and best director.

Zeppo Marx leaves the Marx Brothers and becomes a talent agent.

Columbia's first Three Stooges comedy, *Woman Haters,* is released. The Stooges' series of 190 films will run through 1959, the longest-running series of two-reel comedies in sound-film history.

Bette Davis becomes a star with her role as the waitress Mildred in *Of Human Bondage.*

Donald Duck makes his first appearance, in Walt Disney's *The Wise Little Hen.*

The popular Thin Man series, based on the Dashiell Hammett novels, premieres with *The Thin Man,* starring William Powell and Myrna Loy as Nick and Nora Charles.

1934: BIRTHS

GEORGE SEGAL, FEB. 13
ALAN BATES, FEB. 17
ALAN ARKIN, MAR. 26
SHIRLEY MACLAINE, APR. 24
GENA ROWLANDS, JUNE 19
DONALD SUTHERLAND, JULY 17
SOPHIA LOREN, SEPT. 20
MAGGIE SMITH, DEC. 28
RUSS TAMBLYN, DEC. 30

1934: DEATHS

MARIE DRESSLER
JEAN VIGO

NOTABLE FILMS 1934

United States	OF HUMAN BONDAGE
BABES IN TOYLAND	THE SCARLET EMPRESS
THE BLACK CAT	THE THIN MAN
CLEOPATRA	TREASURE ISLAND
DEATH TAKES A HOLIDAY	TWENTIETH CENTURY
THE GAY DIVORCEE	VIVA VILLA
THE HOUSE OF ROTHSCHILD	WOMAN HATERS
IMITATION OF LIFE	**France** L'ATALANTE
IT HAPPENED ONE NIGHT	**India** SEETA
LITTLE MISS MARKER	**Italy** 1860
THE LOST PATROL	**USSR** PETERSBURG NIGHTS
MADAME BOVARY	THREE SONGS ABOUT LENIN
THE MERRY WIDOW	

Gangster John Dillinger dies in a hail of police bullets when he leaves Chicago's Biograph Theater, where he has just seen Clark Gable in *Manhattan Melodrama.*

Promising French director Jean Vigo dies of leukemia at age 29, the same year that his masterpiece, *L'Atalante,* is released.

Warner Bros. closes its distribution office in Berlin in reaction to the anti-Semitic policies of the Nazi government.

Myrna Loy and William Powell portrayed amateur detectives Nick and Nora Charles in the Thin Man series, which debuted in 1934.

1935

Hollywood studios
begin financial recovery following lean years during the early part of the Great Depression.

20th Century–Fox is formed from the merger of Twentieth Century Pictures and the Fox Film Corp.

Republic Pictures is founded. Among its first year's releases is Gene Autry's first western feature, *Tumbling Tumbleweeds.*

Errol Flynn becomes a star in *Captain Blood.*

Mary Pickford and Douglas Fairbanks divorce.

David O. Selznick leaves MGM to become an independent producer. His company, Selznick International, will produce *Gone with the Wind* (1939), one of the top-grossing films of all time. Though that film will be released by MGM, most Selznick productions will be released by United Artists until 1947.

The Sixth Nazi Party Congress, held in Nuremberg, Germany, in 1934, was documented by Leni Riefenstahl in the Nazi propaganda film Triumph of the Will *released in 1935.*

In New York City, the Museum of Modern Art film library is established.

The first three-color Technicolor feature, *Becky Sharp,* is released.

In Rome, Western Europe's first film school, Centro Sperimentale di Cinematografia, is established.

In Germany, Leni Riefenstahl directs the propaganda classic *Triumph of the Will,* a documentary about the Nazi Nuremberg rally of 1934.

In Britain, J. Arthur Rank begins building his film empire, systematically gaining dominance in every aspect of the film industry, from production to exhibition.

1935: BIRTHS

ELVIS PRESLEY, JAN. 8
RICHARD CHAMBERLAIN, MAR. 11
CHARLES GRODIN, APR. 21
ROY SCHEIDER, NOV. 10
WOODY ALLEN, DEC. 1
LEE REMICK, DEC. 14

1935: DEATHS

W. K. L. DICKSON
WILL ROGERS
THELMA TODD

NOTABLE FILMS 1935

United States			France
ALICE ADAMS	THE INFORMER	MUTINY ON THE BOUNTY	TONI
BECKY SHARP	LIVES OF A BENGAL LANCER	NAUGHTY MARIETTA	**Germany**
BLACK FURY	MAGNIFICENT OBSESSION	ONE MORE SPRING	TRIUMPH OF THE WILL
BRIDE OF FRANKENSTEIN	THE MAN WHO KNEW TOO MUCH	RUGGLES OF RED GAP	**United Kingdom**
CAPTAIN BLOOD	A MIDSUMMER NIGHT'S DREAM	A TALE OF TWO CITIES	SANDERS OF THE RIVER
CHINA SEAS	LES MISÉRABLES	TOP HAT	THE SCARLET PIMPERNEL
THE DEVIL IS A WOMAN		TUMBLING TUMBLEWEEDS	THE 39 STEPS
G-MEN		WEREWOLF OF LONDON	

Charlie Chaplin's 1936 film Modern Times *dealt with the perils of modern technology and machinery using his trademark slapstick comedy.*

1936

The Screen Directors Guild is incorporated.

Walt Disney switches distributors, dropping United Artists in favor of RKO.

Carl Laemmle sells Universal Films, the studio he founded, to a group of investors for a little over $5 million.

Supported by Pathé, a new studio, Grand National, is launched in Hollywood. James Cagney signs on as a star-producer but will return to Warner Bros. in 1938.

Pioneer Pictures merges with Selznick International.

The accounting firm Price-Waterhouse begins its long run as tabulator of votes for the Academy Awards.

1936: BIRTHS

TROY DONAHUE, JAN. 27
ALAN ALDA, JAN. 28
BURT REYNOLDS, FEB. 11
JIM BROWN, FEB. 17
DEAN STOCKWELL, MAR. 5
URSULA ANDRESS, MAR. 19
DENNIS HOPPER, MAY 17
LOUIS GOSSETT, JR., MAY 27
BRUCE DERN, JUNE 4
STELLA STEVENS, OCT. 1

1936: DEATHS

JOHN GILBERT
O.P. HEGGIE
IRVING THALBERG

David O. Selznick buys the rights to Margaret Mitchell's best selling novel *Gone with the Wind;* the movie version will be released and cofinanced by MGM (*see* 1939).

In an encyclical, a letter to all the bishops of the Catholic Church, Pope Pius XI denounces indecent films.

The Lux Radio Theater begins broadcasting radio versions of movies and plays.

Lana Turner, now 16, is discovered at Schwab's Drugstore in Hollywood by an editor of *The Hollywood Reporter,* who recommends her to director Mervyn LeRoy.

Olympic skating star Sonja Henie signs with 20th Century–Fox. She debuts in *One in a Million* (1937).

Fifteen-year-old singer Deanna Durbin's feature debut in *Three Smart Girls* is a commercial success, saving Universal from bankruptcy.

Mary Astor's career is threatened, but not ended, by a scandal involving an affair with playwright George S. Kaufman.

Bette Davis is temporarily fired from Warner Bros. over a contract dispute; she is back at work at the studio by year's end.

Bugs Bunny is created by a group of Warner Bros. cartoon animators.

Chasen's, a now-famous Hollywood eatery, begins life as Dave Chasen's Southern Pit Barbecue.

In Paris, the Cinémathèque Française, a film archive, is founded.

NOTABLE FILMS 1936

United States	
ANTHONY ADVERSE	THE PETRIFIED FOREST
FLASH GORDON (SERIAL)	THE PRISONER OF SHARK ISLAND
FOLLOW THE FLEET	ROMEO AND JULIET
FURY	SAN FRANCISCO
THE GARDEN OF ALLAH	SHOW BOAT
THE GREAT ZIEGFELD	THE STORY OF LOUIS PASTEUR
THE GREEN PASTURES	SYLVIA SCARLETT
LITTLE LORD FAUNTLEROY	SWING TIME
LLOYDS OF LONDON	SYLVIA SCARLETT
MR. DEEDS GOES TO TOWN	THINGS TO COME
MODERN TIMES	TRAIL OF THE LONESOME PINE
MY MAN GODFREY	*United Kingdom*
ONE IN A MILLION	THE SECRET AGENT

1937

The Supreme Court upholds the Wagner Act, which guarantees workers the right to form a union and bargain collectively, prompting film industry unions to put pressure on the Hollywood studios to permit closed shops and collective bargaining.

20th Century–Fox is the first studio to focus on radio advertising to promote its movies.

The Academy of Motion Picture Arts and Sciences presents the first Irving G. Thalberg Memorial Award, to producer Darryl Zanuck.

Snow White and the Seven Dwarfs, made by Disney, is the first feature-length animated film.

Though Cary Grant has worked in films since 1932, his witty, debonair star persona only begins to take shape in this year's *Topper* and *The Awful Truth.*

Ronald Reagan signs with Warner Bros. and appears in his first film, *Love Is on the Air.*

Director, screenwriter, and actor John Huston signs with Warner Bros.

In response to a poll, Clark Gable and Myrna Loy are crowned King and Queen of Hollywood at the El Capitan Theater.

The Japanese invasion of Shanghai, China, forces the substantial film community in that city to disperse; many go to Hong Kong or Taiwan. The Japanese use the captured film studios to make propaganda films.

Saint Tukaram is the first Indian film to win an international award, at this year's Venice Film Festival.

NOTABLE FILMS 1937	
United States	A STAR IS BORN
THE AWFUL TRUTH	STELLA DALLAS
CAMILLE	THEY WON'T FORGET
CAPTAINS COURAGEOUS	THREE SMART GIRLS
A DAY AT THE RACES	WINGS OF THE
DEAD END	MORNING
THE GOOD EARTH	***France***
THE HURRICANE	GRAND ILLUSION
LOST HORIZON	PÉPÉ LE MOKO
LOVE IS ON THE AIR	***Germany***
THE LIFE OF EMILE	THE RULER
ZOLA	***India***
NOTHING SACRED	SAINT TUKARAM
THE PLAINSMAN	***Italy***
THE PLOUGH AND	SCIPIONE L'AFRICANO
THE STARS	***Japan***
THE PRISONER OF	HUMANITY AND PAPER
ZENDA	BALLOONS
SAN QUENTIN	***Poland***
SNOW WHITE AND	PEOPLE OF THE VISTULA
THE SEVEN DWARFS	***USSR***
STAGE DOOR	PETER THE FIRST
	(1937–39)

1937: BIRTHS

MARGARET O'BRIEN, JAN. 15
VANESSA REDGRAVE, JAN. 30
TOM COURTENAY, FEB. 25
WARREN BEATTY, MAR. 30
BILLY DEE WILLIAMS, APR. 6
JACK NICHOLSON, APR. 22
MORGAN FREEMAN, JUNE 1
DUSTIN HOFFMAN, AUG. 8
ROBERT REDFORD, AUG. 18
CLAUDE LELOUCH, OCT. 30
JANE FONDA, DEC. 21
ANTHONY HOPKINS, DEC. 31

1937: DEATHS

COLIN CLIVE
GEORGE GERSHWIN
JEAN HARLOW
RALPH INCE
MARIE PREVOST

AT LEFT: *1937's* The Awful Truth, *starring Cary Grant and Irene Dunne, helped mold Grant's suave persona and propel him to stardom after years of minor roles.*

1938

The Justice Department files *United States v. Paramount Pictures Inc., et al.* The antitrust litigation will eventually bring about the end of the studio system (*see* 1948, 1949).

The International Alliance of Theatrical Stage Employees (IATSE) leader William Bioff resigns under accusations of corruption.

A late-Depression financial slump rocks the Hollywood film industry in 1938–39.

In 1938, actress turned gossip queen Hedda Hopper embarked on a career as a newspaper gossip columnist that would last 28 years.

Hedda Hopper publishes her first Hollywood gossip column in the *Los Angeles Times.*

British director Alfred Hitchcock agrees to make his first US film, with producer David O. Selznick.

Howard Hawks's film *Bringing Up Baby* is a box-office failure, prompting the releasing studio, RKO, to buy out the director's contract.

Five of the top six stars on the exhibitors' annual list are MGM performers. 20th Century–Fox's Shirley Temple leads at No. 1, but Nos. 2 to 7, respectively, are MGM's Clark Gable, Mickey Rooney, Spencer Tracy, Robert Taylor, and Myrna Loy.

Soviet director Mark Donskoy releases *The Childhood of Maxim Gorky,* the first of three biographical films about the Russian author known collectively as the "The Maxim Gorky Trilogy" (1938–40).

In Britain, the Cinematograph Films Act increases the quota ceiling, the percentage of films shown on British screens that must be made in Britain, and encourages American investment in coproductions with British studios.

NOTABLE FILMS 1938

United States
THE ADVENTURES OF ROBIN HOOD
ALEXANDER'S RAGTIME BAND
ALGIERS
ANGELS WITH DIRTY FACES
THE BIG BROADCAST OF 1938
BLOCKADE
BLONDIE
BOYS TOWN
BRINGING UP BABY
FOUR DAUGHTERS
HOLIDAY
IN OLD CHICAGO

JEZEBEL
THE LONE RANGER (SERIAL)
LOVE FINDS ANDY HARDY
MARIE ANTOINETTE
THE SAINT IN NEW YORK
SUEZ
THREE COMRADES
UNDER WESTERN SKIES
A YANK AT OXFORD
YOU CAN'T TAKE IT WITH YOU
YOUNG DR. KILDARE

France
THE HUMAN BEAST

LA MARSEILLAISE
PORT OF SHADOWS

Germany
OLYMPIA

United Kingdom
BANK HOLIDAY (THREE ON A WEEKEND)
THE LADY VANISHES
PYGMALION

USSR
ALEXANDER NEVSKY
THE CHILDHOOD OF MAXIM GORKY
THE GREAT CITIZEN (TWO PARTS, 1938–39)
VOLGA-VOLGA

1939

The studio system achieves what will be considered its peak year of artistic success, as Hollywood releases a record number of critically acclaimed films.

Arthur Freed becomes a producer at MGM, where he will shape many of the great musicals of the 1940s and 50s.

Grand National files for bankruptcy.

Gone with the Wind is released. It will long be the industry's biggest money-maker, and is still considered one of the greatest American films ever made.

Hattie McDaniel wins the Oscar for best supporting actress for her role as Mammy in *Gone with the Wind*. She is the first African-American to win an Academy Award.

Stagecoach and *Dodge City* are among several films marking the return of the big-budget western after a period in which the genre was mainly represented by B-films.

Stagecoach makes former B-actor John Wayne a star.

Frank Capra's *Mr. Smith Goes to Washington* solidifies Jimmy Stewart's appeal and continues the string of highly successful films directed by Capra for Columbia.

William Holden gains stardom in *Golden Boy*.

Sweater-clad Ann Sheridan, a Warner Bros. actress, is promoted as "the Oomph Girl."

Judy Garland, Jack Haley, and Ray Bolger are off to see the wizard in the beloved 1939 classic The Wizard of Oz.

The Wizard of Oz, MGM's most expensive film production in the studio's history, premieres at Grauman's Chinese Theater.

In September, movie theaters temporarily close in Britain in response to the outbreak of World War II.

The National Film Board of Canada is established.

French director Jean Renoir's masterpiece, *The Rules of the Game,* is a flop upon first release. It is now considered a classic.

Three of Hollywood's leading directors of the 1970s — Peter Bogdanovich, Francis Ford Coppola, and William Friedkin — were born in Hollywood's greatest year, 1939.

1939: BIRTHS

YVETTE MIMIEUX, JAN. 10
SAL MINEO, JAN. 10
PETER FONDA, FEB. 23
JAMES CAAN, MAR. 26
FRANCIS FORD COPPOLA, APR. 7
HARVEY KEITEL, MAY 13
PETER BOGDANOVICH, JULY 30
GEORGE HAMILTON, AUG. 12
WILLIAM FRIEDKIN, AUG. 29
LILY TOMLIN, SEPT. 1
FRANKIE AVALON, SEPT. 18
F. MURRAY ABRAHAM, OCT. 24
JOHN CLEESE, OCT. 27
JANE ALEXANDER, OCT. 28

1939: DEATHS

DOUGLAS FAIRBANKS, SR.
CARL LAEMMLE, SR.
BERYL MERCER

NOTABLE FILMS 1939

United States			Czechoslovakia
BABES IN ARMS	GUNGA DIN	THE ROARING TWENTIES	HUMORESQUE
BEAU GESTE	HOLLYWOOD CAVALCADE	STAGECOACH	**France**
CONFESSIONS OF A NAZI SPY	THE HOUND OF THE BASKERVILLES	THE STORY OF ALEXANDER GRAHAM BELL	DAYBREAK
DARK VICTORY	THE HUNCHBACK OF NOTRE DAME	THEY MADE ME A CRIMINAL	THE RULES OF THE GAME
DESTRY RIDES AGAIN	INTERMEZZO	UNION PACIFIC	**United Kingdom**
DODGE CITY	JESSE JAMES	WINGS OF THE NAVY	THE FIRST DAYS
EACH DAWN I DIE	JUAREZ	THE WIZARD OF OZ	THE FOUR FEATHERS
FLYING DEUCES	MR. SMITH GOES TO WASHINGTON	THE WOMEN	THE STARS LOOK DOWN
GOLDEN BOY	NINOTCHKA	WUTHERING HEIGHTS	**USSR**
GONE WITH THE WIND	THE OLD MAID	YOUNG MR. LINCOLN	SCHORS
GOODBYE, MR. CHIPS	ONLY ANGELS HAVE WINGS		TRACTOR DRIVERS
THE GREAT MAN VOTES			

1940–1949

World War II curtailed European film production but fostered many patriotic US films such as Casablanca *(1942). The postwar years brought a dark realism and declining movie attendance fostered by the growing popularity of television.*

ALTHOUGH THE WAR HAD ALREADY SLOWED European film production by 1940, the year was choice for US films. There was the social conscience drama in *The Grapes of Wrath*, stylish suspense in *Rebecca*, witty comedy in *The Philadelphia Story* and *His Girl Friday*, and Nazi satire in *The Great Dictator*. A year later, the US entered World War II and Hollywood followed. Enlisting or called to duty were Jimmy Stewart, Clark Gable, Frank Capra, William Wyler, and scores of others. One of those who remained in Hollywood was World War I veteran Humphrey Bogart, who starred in the most enduring propaganda film of the war, Warner Bros.' *Casablanca* (1942). Other major wartime films included *The Lady Eve* (1941), *Mrs. Miniver* (1942), *The More the Merrier* (1943), *Since You Went Away* (1944), *This Is the Army* (1943), and *Thirty Seconds Over Tokyo* (1944).

Nearly kept from release in 1941 was a film about a newspaperman: *Citizen Kane*, written by, directed by, and starring 25-year-old Orson Welles. Its thinly veiled subject, press mogul William Randolph Hearst, tried to quash the film and managed to limit release and publicity. The film lost money on its first release.

IN EUROPE, the war had profound effects on the film industry. Following the USSR's entry into the war in 1941, the country's film output centered on propagandistic documentaries, entertainments, and dramas, including Sergei Eisenstein's masterwork *Ivan the Terrible Part 1* (1945). Some countries saw

AT LEFT: *In 1940's* The Philadelphia Story, *Katharine Hepburn portrays haughty socialite Tracy Lord, whose proper wedding plans are upended by a reporter (Jimmy Stewart) and an ex-husband (Cary Grant).*

film output all but cease: Czechoslovakia, for example, made only 12 films a year during World War II. Germany's film industry remained active, with over 1,000 films produced during Hitler's dictatorship. Most were anti-Semitic (*Jud Süss*, 1940) or elaborate histories (*Münchhausen*, 1943). After the war, the 1949 division of Germany led to separate, diametrically opposed republics with different artistic visions. In France, those directors who did not flee to Hollywood concentrated on historical and allegorical works. Notable directors of the decade include Marcel Carné (*Les Enfants du Paradis*) (*Children of Paradise*) (1945) and Robert Bresson (*Les Dames du Bois de Boulogne*) (*Ladies of the Park*) (1945). Postwar, in 1946, the French film industry formed the Centre National du Cinéma Française to fight US and other countries' encroachment and encourage national cinema. Similar protective measures were enacted by other European countries.

THE US FILM INDUSTRY began the postwar era with its most profitable year ever in 1946. But studio labor clashes and inflation raised production costs, while European import restrictions, the responsibilities of young baby-boom families, and television reduced movie attendance. In 1949, average weekly attendance was 87.5 million, declining slightly from 1948's 90 million. Ten years later, in 1959, weekly attendance had dropped to less than 50 million.

The Hollywood studios' power was more seriously diminished by the US federal government's antitrust ruling against Paramount and four other studios. In May 1948, the studios were ordered to divest themselves of their theaters, their pipeline to income. This year also saw the beginning of the House Committee on Un-American Activities (HUAC), which began investigating so-called political subversives in the film industry.

In 1946, the Academy Award winner for best picture was William Wyler's drama of returning veterans, *The Best Years of Our Lives.* In light of the three-decade decline that would follow, the title was prophetic.

CHRONOLOGY

1940

The five largest Hollywood studios sign consent decrees that outlaw blind selling, the practice of forcing exhibitors to rent films they have not seen, and reduce block booking, the practice of requiring an exhibitor to book several films at once (including less desirable ones) to groups of five movies. The consent decrees limit the studios' ability to tie the sale of B-features to A-features by giving exhibitors more freedom to refuse the B-features. The major studios adapt by phasing out their B-movie units and concentrating on production of A-movies.

The demand for B-pictures is taken up by the so-called major minors, Universal and Columbia, and minor studios like Monogram and Republic, which step up production of low-budget films.

RKO, reorganized, leaves the state of receivership in which it was placed in 1933.

"Soundies" begin to be produced. These short musical films, played on machines resembling jukeboxes, will be produced through 1946.

Broadway director Vincente Minnelli is lured to MGM by Alan Freed as an advisor on its musicals. He will soon direct such classics as *Meet Me in St. Louis, An American in Paris,* and *Gigi.*

Romanoff's, a restaurant that will become a nexus of Hollywood society, opens.

Alfred Hitchcock's first American film, *Rebecca,* is a critical and box-office success.

Bing Crosby, Bob Hope, and Dorothy Lamour begin their series of Paramount "road" comedies with *Road to Singapore.*

Alfred Hitchcock's first American film, Rebecca (1940), featuring Joan Fontaine and Judith Anderson, was his only film to win the Oscar for best picture.

In one of the film industry's more tempestuous unions, Laurence Olivier and Vivien Leigh marry, after divorcing their respective spouses. The couple will divorce in 1960.

Sterling Hayden signs with Paramount. He will make his screen debut in next year's *Virginia.*

Betty Grable signs with 20th Century–Fox, where she will become a major star of musicals and the number one pinup girl of the World War II years.

Following the Nazi takeover of France, filmmaker Jean Renoir leaves France for Lisbon. He will live in the US from 1941 until after the war.

Brazil's film industry, which had produced an average of 15 feature films a year in the 1920s, produces only one this year, the result of a steady Depression-era decline.

NOTABLE FILMS 1940

United States	
BOOM TOWN	PINOCCHIO
DOWN ARGENTINE WAY	PRIDE AND PREJUDICE
THE FIGHTING 69TH	REBECCA
FANTASIA	ROAD TO SINGAPORE
FOREIGN CORRESPONDENT	SANTA FE TRAIL
THE GRAPES OF WRATH	THE SEA HAWK
THE GREAT DICTATOR	THE SHOP AROUND THE CORNER
THE GREAT McGINTY	WATERLOO BRIDGE
HIS GIRL FRIDAY	THE WESTERNER
KNUTE ROCKNE ALL–AMERICAN	**Germany**
THE LETTER	JUD SÜSS
THE MORTAL STORM	**Italy and France**
MY FAVORITE WIFE	LA TOSCA
NORTHWEST PASSAGE	**Japan**
ONE NIGHT IN THE TROPICS	NISHIZUMI
OUR TOWN	**USSR**
THE PHILADELPHIA STORY	LIBERATION
	United Kingdom
	LONDON CAN TAKE IT
	THE THIEF OF BAGDAD

Orson Welles produced, wrote, directed, and starred in Citizen Kane, *a hallmark in American cinema released in 1941 and based on the life of William Randolph Hearst.*

1941

The movies *High Sierra* (with a screenplay cowritten by John Huston) and *The Maltese Falcon* (directed by John Huston) establish Humphrey Bogart as a star.

As Universal's top moneymaker Deanna Durbin's screen career fades, the studio's fortunes are revived by Bud Abbott and Lou Costello; their film *Buck Privates* is a major success this year. The comedy duo will make a series of hits for the studio.

As the US draws closer to entry into World War II, war movies become popular, including *Sergeant York, Dive Bomber,* and *A Yank in the RAF.*

Soon after the US entry into World War II in December, about 40,000 of the film industry's 240,000 employees will join the armed forces.

Producer Samuel Goldwyn breaks his ties to United Artists and begins to distribute his films through RKO.

Joseph Schenck, chairman of 20th Century–Fox, is convicted of income-tax fraud. He will serve four months in prison.

Citizen Kane, the first film by director Orson Welles (who also stars in, cowrote, and produced it), is hailed by critics for its cinematic innovation and dramatic achievement. Publishing magnate William Randolph Hearst, the model for the hero Charles Foster Kane, is unsuccessful in his efforts to suppress the film.

Ava Gardner debuts in *H. M. Pulham Esq.,* though stardom will not come for several years *(see 1946).*

A *Life* **magazine photograph** of Rita Hayworth (starring in this year's *Blood and Sand*) in a negligee becomes a popular GI pinup.

NOTABLE FILMS 1941

United States
BLOOD AND SAND
BUCK PRIVATES
CITIZEN KANE
DIVE BOMBER
DR. JEKYLL AND MR. HYDE
DUMBO
HERE COMES MR. JORDAN
HIGH SIERRA
HOW GREEN WAS MY VALLEY
I WANTED WINGS
JOHNNY EAGER
KITTY FOYLE
THE LADY EVE
THE LITTLE FOXES
THE MALTESE FALCON
THE SEA WOLF
SERGEANT YORK
SULLIVAN'S TRAVELS

SUSPICION
THEY DIED WITH THEIR BOOTS ON
THE WOLF MAN
A YANK IN THE RAF

France
REMORQUES (STORMY WATERS)

Italy
UN COLPO DI PISTOLA

Mexico
PASSION ISLAND

United Kingdom
49TH PARALLEL (THE INVADERS)
KIPPS
MAJOR BARBARA

USSR
SWINEHERD AND SHEPHERD (THEY MET IN MOSCOW)

Due to the shortage of metals during World War II, Academy Award statuettes are made of plaster during the war years. Oscar winners will later have their plaster statuettes replaced with gold-plated versions.

1942: BIRTHS

SUSANNAH YORK, JAN. 9
SHELLEY FABARES, JAN. 19
SCOTT GLENN, JAN. 26
KATHARINE ROSS, JAN. 29
CAROL LYNLEY, FEB. 13
MICHAEL YORK, MAR. 27
MARSHA MASON, APR. 3
SANDRA DEE, APR. 23
BARBRA STREISAND, APR. 24
ROGER EBERT, JUNE 18
MICHELE LEE, JUNE 24
KAREN BLACK, JULY 1
GENEVIEVE BUJOLD, JULY 1
HARRISON FORD, JULY 3
GIANCARLO GIANNINI, AUG. 1
MADELINE KAHN, SEPT. 29
BRITT EKLAND, OCT. 6
PETER COYOTE, OCT. 10
BOB HOSKINS, OCT. 26
MARTIN SCORSESE, NOV. 17
JOHN AMOS, DEC. 27

1942: DEATHS

JOHN BARRYMORE
GEORGE M. COHAN
LAURA HOPE CREWS
CAROLE LOMBARD
EDNA MAY OLIVER
MAY ROBSON
HELEN WESTLEY

NOTABLE FILMS 1942

United States	ROAD TO MOROCCO
ACROSS THE PACIFIC	SABOTEUR
BAMBI	TALES OF MANHATTAN
THE BLACK SWAN	THE TALK OF THE TOWN
CASABLANCA	
CAT PEOPLE	THIS GUN FOR HIRE
FLYING TIGERS	TO BE OR NOT TO BE
FOR ME AND MY GAL	WAKE ISLAND
GENTLEMAN JIM	WOMAN OF THE YEAR
THE GLASS KEY	YANKEE DOODLE DANDY
HOLIDAY INN	
I MARRIED A WITCH	YOU WERE NEVER LOVELIER
JOURNEY INTO FEAR	MRS. MINIVER
JUNGLE BOOK	NOW, VOYAGER
KINGS ROW	*France*
THE MAGNIFICENT AMBERSONS	LETTRES D'AMOUR (LOVE LETTERS)
THE MAJOR AND THE MINOR	*Italy*
	OSSESSIONE
THE MAN WHO CAME TO DINNER	*Mexico*
ORCHESTRA WIVES	MARIA CANDELARIA
THE PALM BEACH STORY	*United Kingdom*
	IN WHICH WE SERVE
THE PRIDE OF THE YANKEES	ONE OF OUR AIRCRAFT IS MISSING
RANDOM HARVEST	*USSR*
REAP THE WILD WIND	LENINGRAD IN COMBAT

1942

Casablanca, released in a limited run in November, will become one of the most popular films of all time. Starring Humphrey Bogart and Ingrid Bergman, it will enter general release in 1943 and win three 1943 Oscars, for best picture, best director, and best screenplay.

The US government forms the Office of War Information to coordinate wartime propaganda and maintain relations with the Hollywood film industry. It employs various forms of de facto film censorship.

US filmmakers experience wartime restrictions on set construction, location shooting, and bright lights at Hollywood premieres.

George Murphy and Judy Garland starred in For Me and My Gal *with Gene Kelly. The 1942 musical marked Kelly's screen debut.*

As many male stars enlist, Hollywood experiences a shortage of leading men.

Bob Hope begins a tradition of entertaining the US troops abroad with a ten-week tour of about 100 army camps.

The Hollywood Canteen, cofounded by Bette Davis, John Garfield, and others, provides entertainment and hospitality for visiting servicemen. The institution will spawn a musical, *Hollywood Canteen* (1944), and will close its doors in 1945.

The year's biggest hit, *Mrs. Miniver,* starring Greer Garson, inspires sympathy from audiences for its portrayal of a brave English family during the Blitz.

Paramount takes over the Fleischer animation studio.

Gene Kelly debuts and Judy Garland appears for the first time with her name above the title in the hit musical *For Me and My Gal.*

In Germany, the Nazi government nationalizes the film industry.

Censors objected to the focus on Jane Russell's breasts in her motion picture debut, the Howard Hughes film The Outlaw.

1943

The Hollywood Foreign Correspondents Association is founded. Later known as the Hollywood Foreign Press Association, it will begin presenting the Golden Globe Awards in 1944.

After several scuffles with the law, actress Frances Farmer is placed under psychiatric observation.

War films, such as *This Is the Army* and *Stage Door Canteen,* dominate the box office.

Frank Capra releases *Prelude to War,* the first in his series of Why We Fight documentaries.

Jane Russell debuts in *The Outlaw,* produced and directed by Howard Hughes. The film's focus on her 38-inch bust draws the ire of the Hays Office, the studios' self-censorship authority, which keeps the film out of widespread circulation until later in the 1940s.

1943: BIRTHS

FABIAN, FEB. 6
JOE PESCI, FEB. 9
LYNN REDGRAVE, MAR. 8
ERIC IDLE, MAR. 29
CHRISTOPHER
WALKEN, MAR. 31
MICHAEL PALIN, MAY 5
MALCOLM
MCDOWELL, JUNE 13
EDWARD HERRMANN, JULY 21
ROBERT DE NIRO, AUG. 17
TUESDAY WELD, AUG. 27
VALERIE PERRINE, SEPT. 3
CHEVY CHASE, OCT. 8
PENNY MARSHALL, OCT. 15
CATHERINE DENEUVE, OCT. 22
SAM SHEPARD, NOV. 5
BEN KINGSLEY, DEC. 31

1943: DEATHS

HOBART BOSWORTH
WADE BOTELER
SPENCER CHARTERS
DWIGHT FRYE
LESLIE HOWARD
MONTAGU LOVE
MAX REINHARDT
W.S. "WOODY" VAN DYKE
CONRAD VEIDT
GUSTAV VON SEYFFERTITZ

NOTABLE FILMS 1943

United States			
ACTION IN THE NORTH ATLANTIC	GUADALCANAL DIARY	THE MORE THE MERRIER	WATCH ON THE RHINE
AIR FORCE	A GUY NAMED JOE	THE NORTH STAR	SAHARA
CABIN IN THE SKY	HEAVEN CAN WAIT	THE OX-BOW INCIDENT	**Denmark** DAY OF WRATH
DESTINATION TOKYO	HITLER'S CHILDREN	PHANTOM OF THE OPERA	**France** THE RAVEN
FIVE GRAVES TO CAIRO	I WALKED WITH A ZOMBIE	SHADOW OF A DOUBT	**Germany** MÜNCHHAUSEN
FOR WHOM THE BELL TOLLS	LASSIE COME HOME	SO PROUDLY WE HAIL!	**United Kingdom** THE LIFE AND DEATH OF COLONEL BLIMP
FRANKENSTEIN MEETS THE WOLF MAN	MADAME CURIE	THE SONG OF BERNADETTE	
	MISSION TO MOSCOW	STORMY WEATHER	
	MR. LUCKY		

1944

Bing Crosby's portrayal of an affable priest in *Going My Way* makes this film the year's biggest hit.

Lauren Bacall makes her screen debut in *To Have and Have Not.* She and co-star Humphrey Bogart fall in love on the set and will marry the following year.

The Academy Awards, previously a private ceremony, are presented as part of a variety show at Grauman's Chinese Theater. The event is broadcast over the radio – another first.

Producer Hal Wallis, formerly with Warner Bros., signs with Paramount.

In Britain, the distributor Eagle-Lion Films is founded.

Barry Fitzgerald and Bing Crosby appeared as priests whose methods clash in the 1944 Oscar-winning musical comedy Going My Way.

Olivia de Havilland wins in Los Angeles Superior Court in a contract dispute with Warner Bros. The studio is deemed to have no claims on her following the expiration of her contract, despite the time she spent on suspension.

The first television advertisement for a film is aired: in a 30-minute promotion for *The Miracle of Morgan's Creek.*

Alexander Korda sells his London Film operations to United Artists.

In Spain from 1944 to 1973, film production comes under the control of Franco's minister of culture, Luis Carrero Blanco.

NOTABLE FILMS 1944

United States			
ARSENIC AND OLD LACE	HAIL THE CONQUERING HERO	NATIONAL VELVET	THE UNINVITED
BRAZIL	HOUSE OF FRANKENSTEIN	PASSAGE TO MARSEILLE	THE WOMAN IN THE WINDOW
A CANTERBURY TALE	JANE EYRE	PHANTOM LADY	*Germany*
THE CANTERVILLE GHOST	LAURA	THE SEVENTH CROSS	DIE FEUERZANGENBOWLE
COVER GIRL	LIFEBOAT	SINCE YOU WENT AWAY	*Spain*
THE CURSE OF THE CAT PEOPLE	THE MASK OF DIMITRIOS	THE SULLIVANS (THE FIGHTING SULLIVANS)	THE TOWER OF THE SEVEN HUNCHBACKS
DOUBLE INDEMNITY	MEET ME IN ST. LOUIS	TALL IN THE SADDLE	*Sweden*
THE FIGHTING SEABEES	THE MIRACLE OF MORGAN'S CREEK	THIRTY SECONDS OVER TOKYO	HETS (TORMENT)
GASLIGHT	MR. SKEFFINGTON	TO HAVE AND HAVE NOT	*United Kingdom*
GOING MY WAY	MURDER, MY SWEET		HENRY V

1945

During the period of national mourning following the death of President Franklin Delano Roosevelt on April 12, movie theaters close and the Hollywood studios shut down in his memory.

On August 15, the studios stop production to celebrate the end of World War II.

In late August, the US government ends the allocation of raw film stock.

After the war ends, the Hollywood Victory Committee announces that 4,012 film personalities made 53,056 war-related appearances to entertain and raise funds.

The name of the Motion Picture Producers and Distributors of America is changed to the Motion Picture Association of America (MPAA).

After an eight-month strike by set designers and decorators, the Conference of Studio Unions wins the right to represent set dressers in labor negotiations with the studios.

Recording star Frank Sinatra enjoys his first major screen appearance in *Anchors Aweigh.*

***Mildred Pierce* revitalizes** the career of its star, Joan Crawford, and will net her the first Academy Award for best actress she has won in 20 years of movie stardom.

Musical-comedy star Dick Powell changes his screen persona as he portrays detective Philip Marlowe in *Murder, My Sweet.*

Comedy team Abbott and Costello perform their stage routine "Who's on First?" in the film *The Naughty Nineties.*

Casper the Friendly Ghost debuts in the Paramount cartoon The Friendly Ghost.

NOTABLE FILMS 1945

United States
ANCHORS AWEIGH

AND THEN THERE WERE NONE

BACK TO BATAAN

THE BELLS OF ST. MARY'S

BLOOD ON THE SUN

THE BODY SNATCHER

CHRISTMAS IN CONNECTICUT

DEAD OF NIGHT

DETOUR

THE ENCHANTED COTTAGE

THE HOUSE ON 92ND STREET

I ACCUSE MY PARENTS

LEAVE HER TO HEAVEN

THE LOST WEEKEND

LOVE LETTERS

MILDRED PIERCE

MINISTRY OF FEAR

MURDER, HE SAYS

THE NAUGHTY NINETIES

OBJECTIVE, BURMA!

THE PICTURE OF DORIAN GRAY

PRIDE OF THE MARINES

SCARLET STREET

SPELLBOUND

STATE FAIR

THEY WERE EXPENDABLE

THE THIN MAN GOES HOME

THE THREE CABALLEROS

A TREE GROWS IN BROOKLYN

A WALK IN THE SUN

WONDER MAN

France
LES ENFANTS DU PARADIS (CHILDREN OF PARADISE)

Italy
ROMA, CITTÁ APERTA (OPEN CITY)

Sweden
CRISIS

United Kingdom
HENRY V

I KNOW WHERE I'M GOING!

USSR
IVAN GROZNYJ I (IVAN THE TERRIBLE, PART 1)

1945: BIRTHS

TOM SELLECK, JAN. 29
MIA FARROW, FEB. 9
BRENDA FRICKER, FEB. 17
BARRY BOSTWICK, FEB. 24
ROB REINER, MAR. 6
JOHN HEARD, MAR. 7
LINDA HUNT, APR. 2
STEVE MARTIN, APR. 14
JOHN LITHGOW, OCT. 19
GOLDIE HAWN, NOV. 21
BETTE MIDLER, DEC. 1
TERI GARR, DEC. 11

1945: DEATHS

HENRY ARMETTA
ROBERT BENCHLEY
FRANK CRAVEN
CHARLES EVANS
JEROME KERN
ALLA NAZIMOVA
GEORGE SIDNEY

Crooner Frank Sinatra made his first major film appearance in Anchors Aweigh *in 1945, which also featured Gene Kelly dancing with an animated mouse.*

1946

Hollywood enjoys its most profitable year ever, with theater attendance at an all-time high.

A labor dispute results in a 25 percent raise for studio employees.

Universal merges with International Pictures, becoming Universal-International.

The Best Years of Our Lives, directed by William Wyler, captures the mood of returning veterans attempting to adjust to civilian life after World War II.

The NAACP objects to Disney's *Song of the South* for giving "an impression of an idyllic master/slave relationship which is a distortion of the fact."

Ava Gardner (in films since 1941) and Burt Lancaster (in his screen debut) are catapulted to stardom with their roles in *The Killers.*

In Japan, the recovering postwar film industry begins to boom, as theater attendance reaches 733 million – nearly twice the pre-war annual average of 400 million.

France institutes the Centre National du Cinéma Française to regulate the film industry.

The first Cannes Film Festival is held on the French Riviera.

1946: BIRTHS

DIANE KEATON, JAN. 5
DOLLY PARTON, JAN. 19
DAVID LYNCH, JAN. 20
GENE SISKEL, JAN. 26
GREGORY HINES, FEB. 14
ALAN RICKMAN, FEB. 21
LIZA MINNELLI, MAR. 12
JOHN WATERS, APR. 22
TALIA SHIRE, APR. 25
JOHN WOO, MAY 1
CHER, MAY 20
HELEN MIRREN, JULY 2
SYLVESTER STALLONE, JULY 6
CHEECH MARIN, JULY 13
TOMMY LEE JONES, SEPT. 15
TWIGGY, SEPT. 19
MARY BETH HURT, SEPT. 26
SUSAN SARANDON, OCT. 4
IVAN REITMAN, OCT. 27
SALLY FIELD, NOV. 6

1946: DEATHS

GEORGE ARLISS
LIONEL ATWILL
NOAH BEERY, SR.
MAE BUSCH
CHARLES BUTTERWORTH
W.C. FIELDS
WILLIAM S. HART
RONDO HATTON
SYDNEY HOWARD
MILES MANDER
ETTA MCDANIEL
DONALD MEEK
PAUL PORCASI
SLIM SUMMERVILLE
FLORENCE TURNER
CHARLES D. WALDRON

Bombshell Ava Gardner became a star with The Killers, *based on an Ernest Hemingway story. The 1946 film also featured co-star Burt Lancaster's screen debut.*

NOTABLE FILMS 1946

United States			Germany
ANNA AND THE KING OF SIAM	GILDA	ROAD TO UTOPIA	THE MURDERERS ARE AMONG US
THE BEAST WITH FIVE FINGERS	GREEN FOR DANGER	SONG OF THE SOUTH	SOMEWHERE IN BERLIN
BEDLAM	THE HARVEY GIRLS	THE SPIRAL STAIRCASE	*Italy*
THE BEST YEARS OF OUR LIVES	IT'S A WONDERFUL LIFE	THE STRANGE LOVE OF MARTHA IVERS	PAISAN
THE BIG SLEEP	THE JOLSON STORY	THE STRANGER	*United Kingdom*
BLITHE SPIRIT	THE KILLERS	THE TIME OF THEIR LIVES	CAESAR AND CLEOPATRA
THE BLUE DAHLIA	MY DARLING CLEMENTINE	TO EACH HIS OWN	GREAT EXPECTATIONS
BRIEF ENCOUNTER	NIGHT AND DAY	THE YEARLING	A MATTER OF LIFE AND DEATH (STAIRWAY TO HEAVEN)
CLUNY BROWN	A NIGHT IN CASABLANCA	ZIEGFELD FOLLIES	
DUEL IN THE SUN	NOTORIOUS	*France*	
	THE POSTMAN ALWAYS RINGS TWICE	BEAUTY AND THE BEAST	
	THE RAZOR'S EDGE	GATES OF THE NIGHT	

1947

The House Committee on Un-American Activities (HUAC) begins hearings investigating alleged communist infiltration of the Hollywood film industry.

David O. Selznick ends his association with United Artists; he will in the future distribute his films himself.

Dore Schary becomes head of RKO Studios.

Actor Ronald Reagan becomes president of the Screen Actors Guild.

Deborah Kerr, already a star of British films, has her first Hollywood success in *The Hucksters.*

The steamy drama *Forever Amber* sets a new opening record at New York City's Roxy theater, despite having received a "condemned" rating from the Legion of Decency. It stars Linda Darnell as 17th-century climber Amber St. Clair.

Richard Widmark has his screen debut in *Kiss of Death,* as a psychopathic killer with a terrifying laugh. He receives an Oscar nomination for best supporting actor.

NOTABLE FILMS 1947

United States	
ANGEL AND THE BADMAN	MONSIEUR VERDOUX
THE BACHELOR AND THE BOBBY-SOXER	MY FAVORITE BRUNETTE
THE BISHOP'S WIFE	NIGHTMARE ALLEY
BODY AND SOUL	ODD MAN OUT
BRUTE FORCE	OUT OF THE PAST
CAPTAIN FROM CASTILE	THE PARADINE CASE
DARK PASSAGE	THE SECRET LIFE OF WALTER MITTY
DEAD RECKONING	SONG OF THE THIN MAN
A DOUBLE LIFE	UNCONQUERED
THE EGG AND I	*China*
THE FARMER'S DAUGHTER	SPRING RIVER FLOWS EAST (TEARS OF THE YANGTSE)
FOREVER AMBER	*Czechoslovakia*
GENTLEMAN'S AGREEMENT	THE STRIKE
THE GHOST AND MRS. MUIR	*Germany*
THE HUCKSTERS	MARRIAGE IN THE SHADOWS
KISS OF DEATH	*Italy*
LADY IN THE LAKE	OUTCRY
LIFE WITH FATHER	*United Kingdom*
MIRACLE ON 34TH STREET	BLACK NARCISSUS

Gangster and Hollywood hanger-on Bugsy Siegel is murdered in Beverly Hills.

In New York City, the Actors Studio, a rehearsal group for professional actors, is founded by Elia Kazan and others. Under the artistic direction of Lee Strasberg, it will become the center for "the Method," an acting technique inspired by Stanislavski's teachings, and train such actors as Marlon Brando, James Dean, and Paul Newman.

The UK institutes a 75 percent import duty on all US films. US film producers retaliate with an embargo on exports of their products to Britain. The tax will be repealed in 1948.

The postwar years bring a surge in production of the dark, fatalistic, morally ambiguous movies known as "film noir."

1948

The Supreme Court declares the Big Five major movie studios guilty of monopolistic practices in restraint of trade. Block booking, fixing of admission prices, and discriminatory pricing and exhibition arrangements are prohibited. The major studios are ordered to divest themselves of their theater holdings. The divestitures will take place gradually and be completed in the 1950s.

The Hollywood Ten (*see* box) are convicted of contempt of Congress for refusing to cooperate with the House Committee on Un-American Activities. They are each sentenced to a year in jail and a fine of $1,000, and are blacklisted by the film industry.

1947: BIRTHS

FARRAH FAWCETT, FEB. 2
TYNE DALY, FEB. 21
EDWARD JAMES OLMOS, FEB. 24
BILLY CRYSTAL, MAR. 14
GLENN CLOSE, MAR. 19
PETER RIEGERT, APR. 11
JAMES WOODS, APR. 18
SONDRA LOCKE, MAY 28
JONATHAN PRYCE, JUNE 1
BRYAN BROWN, JUNE 23
DANNY GLOVER, JULY 22
ROBERT HAYS, JULY 24
ARNOLD SCHWARZENEGGER, JULY 30
ANNE ARCHER, AUG. 25
CINDY WILLIAMS, AUG. 27
SAM NEILL, SEPT. 14
KEVIN KLINE, OCT. 24
RICHARD DREYFUSS, OCT. 29
JOE MANTEGNA, NOV. 13
BEN CROSS, DEC. 16
STEVEN SPIELBERG, DEC. 18
TED DANSON, DEC. 29

1947: DEATHS

OLIVE BORDEN
HARRY CAREY
DUDLEY DIGGES
BRANDON HURST
LESLIE KING
ERNST LUBITSCH
GRACE MOORE
SIDNEY TOLER

THE HOLLYWOOD TEN

IN 1948, THE FOLLOWING PEOPLE, known as the Hollywood Ten, were convicted of contempt of Congress for refusing to co-operate with the House Committee on Un-American Activities.

Alvah Bessie
screenwriter

Herbert Biberman
director-producer

Lester Cole
screenwriter

Edward Dmytryk
director

Ring Lardner, Jr.
screenwriter

John Howard Lawson
screenwriter

Albert Maltz
screenwriter

Samuel Ornitz
screenwriter

Adrian Scott
producer-writer

Dalton Trumbo
screenwriter

Edward Dmytryk

1948: BIRTHS

CARL WEATHERS, JAN. 14
CHRISTOPHER GUEST, FEB. 5
BARBARA HERSHEY, FEB. 5
BERNADETTE PETERS, FEB. 28
MERCEDES RUEHL, FEB. 28
BONNIE BEDELIA, MAR. 25
DIANNE WIEST, MAR. 28
LINDSAY CROUSE, MAY 12
ROBERT ENGLUND, JUNE 6
JOHN CARPENTER, JUNE 16
KATHY BATES, JUNE 28
JEREMY IRONS, SEPT. 19
MARGOT KIDDER, OCT. 17
SAMUEL L. JACKSON, DEC. 21
(SOME SOURCES SAY 1949)
GÉRARD DEPARDIEU, DEC. 27

1948: DEATHS

JOHN AGAR
MARY EATON
SERGEI EISENSTEIN
VERA GORDON
D.W. GRIFFITH
SAMUEL S. HINDS
EDGAR KENNEDY
ELISSA LANDI
CAROLE LANDIS
GREGG TOLAND
DAME MAY WHITTY
WARREN WILLIAM

A consent decree in an antitrust case requires the Eastman Kodak Company to open its color-film processing patents for general use.

Italian director Vittorio De Sica releases the neorealist classic *The Bicycle Thief.*

Lamberto Maggiorani and Enzo Staiola played father and son in Vittorio De Sica's simple yet masterful 1948 tale The Bicycle Thief.

Red River, directed by Howard Hawks and starring John Wayne, is a box-office success; it will be acclaimed as one of the greatest westerns of all time.

The Boy with Green Hair is the first feature film by American director Joseph Losey. He will move to Europe in the 1950s, after he is blacklisted as a former communist.

Dore Schary quarrels with RKO's new boss, Howard Hughes, and returns to MGM as head of production.

Britain imposes limits on how much money American companies can take out of the country annually; other European countries will follow suit. The restrictions encourage American studios to use the frozen funds to make a growing percentage of their movies in these countries.

NOTABLE FILMS 1948

United States	I REMEMBER MAMA	PORTRAIT OF JENNIE	UNFAITHFULLY YOURS
ABBOTT AND COSTELLO MEET FRANKENSTEIN	JOAN OF ARC	RED RIVER	*France*
ADVENTURES OF DON JUAN	JOHNNY BELINDA	ROPE	DEDEE
APARTMENT FOR PEGGY	KEY LARGO	THE SEARCH	JOUR DE FÊTE (BIG DAY)
THE BABE RUTH STORY	THE LADY FROM SHANGHAI	SITTING PRETTY	THE STORM WITHIN
THE BIG CLOCK	LETTER FROM AN UNKNOWN WOMAN	THE SNAKE PIT	*Germany*
THE BOY WITH GREEN HAIR	MACBETH	A SONG IS BORN	THE TRIAL
CALL NORTHSIDE 777	MR. BLANDINGS BUILDS HIS DREAM HOUSE	SORRY, WRONG NUMBER	*Italy*
EASTER PARADE	THE NAKED CITY	STATE OF THE UNION	LADRI DI BICICLETTE (THE BICYCLE THIEF)
FORCE OF EVIL	OLIVER TWIST	SUPERMAN (SERIAL)	WITHOUT PITY
A FOREIGN AFFAIR	THE PALEFACE	3 GODFATHERS	*United Kingdom*
FORT APACHE	THE PIRATE	THE THREE MUSKETEERS	HAMLET
		THE TREASURE OF THE SIERRA MADRE	THE RED SHOES

1949

Anticommunism becomes an increasingly powerful force in Hollywood. The Motion Picture Industry Council is founded to combat communist influence in the film business. The California State Senate committee on Un-American Activities links several film personalities to communism.

A federal statutory court order requires 20th Century-Fox, Warner Bros., and Loew's (MGM) to divest themselves of their theater holdings. It is one of several antitrust actions taken this year by the government against the major motion picture studios.

The affair between actress Ingrid Bergman and director Roberto Rossellini, both married to other people, becomes publicly known. The scandal will hurt their careers.

Marilyn Monroe poses nude for a calendar. This year, she will appear with the Marx Brothers in their last film as a team, *Love Happy*. (Groucho, Harpo, and Chico Marx will all appear in *The Story of Mankind*, in 1957, but in separate scenes.)

Rita Hayworth marries Prince Aly Khan in France.

Bette Davis quits Warner Bros. after an eighteen-year affiliation.

Elia Kazan's *Pinky* premieres, a racial drama about a black woman (Jeanne Crain) passing for white. It is one of several race-related films this year. Others include *Intruder in the Dust, Lost Boundaries,* and *Home of the Brave*.

Fred Astaire and Ginger Rogers appear in their tenth and final film together, *The Barkleys of Broadway*.

My Friend Irma is released, the first film starring the comedy team of Dean Martin and Jerry Lewis.

The musical On the Town, filmed on location in New York City, speeds the industry's movement toward location filming.

Kirk Douglas's star turn as a boxer in *Champion* makes him a leading man, after years of supporting roles.

In an effort to encourage domestic film production, Britain's government establishes the National Film Finance Corporation to make loans to the film industry.

Britain's Ealing Studios begins to be known for its sophisticated "Ealing comedies," including this year's *Kind Hearts and Coronets,* in which actor Alec Guinness plays eight parts, including a woman.

Germany is officially divided into the Federal Republic of Germany (West Germany) and the German Democratic Republic (East Germany), leading to the development of two separate film industries.

Brazilian filmmaker Alberto Cavalcanti returns to Brazil after many years working abroad to head the production house Vera Cruz Films.

Kirk Douglas gained distinction for his role as Midge Kelly, an ambitious boxer in the 1949 film Champion, *also featuring Lola Albright.*

NOTABLE FILMS 1949

United States
ADAM'S RIB
ALL THE KING'S MEN
BATTLEGROUND
CHAMPION
A CONNECTICUT YANKEE IN KING ARTHUR'S COURT
THE HEIRESS
I WAS A MALE WAR BRIDE
JOAN OF ARC
JOLSON SINGS AGAIN
A LETTER TO THREE WIVES
MIGHTY JOE YOUNG
SAMSON AND DELILAH
THE SANDS OF IWO JIMA
SHE WORE A YELLOW RIBBON
THE SNAKE PIT
THEY LIVE BY NIGHT
TWELVE O'CLOCK HIGH
WHITE HEAT

France
JOUR DE FÊTE
LES ENFANTS TERRIBLES
LE SILENCE DE LA MER

Germany
THE LAST ILLUSION

Italy
STROMBOLI

Japan
STRAY DOG

United Kingdom
THE BLUE LAGOON
CHRISTOPHER COLUMBUS
CONSPIRATOR
THE HASTY HEART
THE HISTORY OF MR. POLLY
KIND HEARTS AND CORONETS
PASSPORT TO PIMLICO
THE THIRD MAN

1949: BIRTHS

JOHN BELUSHI, JAN. 24
CYBILL SHEPHERD, FEB. 18
JESSICA LANGE, APR. 20
BRUNO KIRBY, APR. 28
MERYL STREEP, JUNE 22
SHELLEY DUVALL, JULY 7
KEITH CARRADINE, AUG. 8
SHELLEY LONG, AUG. 23
RICHARD GERE, AUG. 31
ARMAND ASSANTE, OCT. 4
SIGOURNEY WEAVER, OCT. 8
WHOOPI GOLDBERG, NOV. 13
JEFF BRIDGES, DEC. 4
TOM WAITS, DEC. 7
SISSY SPACEK, DEC. 25

1949: DEATHS

WALLACE BEERY
VICTOR FLEMING
CHARLES MIDDLETON
FRANK MORGAN
SIDNEY OLCOTT
MARIA OUSPENSKAYA
BILL "BOJANGLES" ROBINSON
SAM WOOD

1950–1959

American studios offered color spectacles like The Robe *and technical advances like CinemaScope to entice viewers back to theaters. European filmmaking was invigorated by iconoclastic new talents such as François Truffaut and Ingmar Bergman.*

WHILE SCREENS IN THE EARLY 1950s were filled with realistic dramas like *On the Waterfront* (1954) and *The Men* (1950), the film community encountered an uglier real-life drama with the House Committee on Un-American Activities (HUAC) investigations.

In 1948, Congress issued a citation of contempt to the filmmakers and screenwriters known as the "Hollywood Ten" for refusing to divulge their political affiliations; the HUAC resumed its investigations in 1951. Acting on information provided by Hollywood Ten informant Edward Dmytryk and others, including Elia Kazan, the HUAC blacklisted dozens of filmmakers and actors, including Jules Dassin, Zero Mostel, Robert Rossen, and Lionel Stander. The HUAC investigation ended in the mid-1950s, but blacklisted film professionals would not become eligible for Oscar consideration until 1959.

Meanwhile, some US studios (such as MGM and 20th Century–Fox in 1952) by order of the Supreme Court divested themselves of their theaters and tried to recoup declining profits in various ways. By 1958, the major studios (including Paramount, the last holdout) had sold their rights to pre-1948 films to television. Others, like Disney, began television production.

The studios also invested in technical advances they hoped would attract audiences back to the theaters. Cinerama, Paramount's wide-screen process, debuted to huge success in 1952, with *This Is Cinerama.* The process would be discontinued in 1962, but 20th Century–Fox's wide-screen process,

AT LEFT: *Like many performers, Marilyn Monroe did her part for the war effort, including traveling to Korea to entertain the troops in 1954.*

CinemaScope, became a lasting contribution to filmmaking debuting with 1953's *The Robe,* and was eventually adopted by all the major studios. VistaVision was Paramount's wide-screen contribution. Stereoscopic viewing, or 3-D, premiered to much hoopla in 1952 with *Bwana Devil.* But the special 3-D glasses needed for viewing turned the innovation into a novelty, and by decade's end, regular production of 3-D movies had ceased.

WHEN ALL ELSE FAILED, Hollywood turned to bigger movies. Top-grossing color spectacles included *The Ten Commandments* (1956), *The Greatest Show on Earth* (1952), and *Around the World in 80 Days* (1956). Lavish musicals, largely under the (Arthur) Freed unit at MGM, reinvigorated the genre. Notable titles included *Singin' in the Rain* (1952), *The Band Wagon* (1953), and *An American in Paris* (1951). Westerns also began to reflect darker postwar sensibilities. Notable titles included *High Noon* (1952), *Shane* (1953), *The Naked Spur* (1953), and *The Searchers* (1956).

In France, established directors made some of their finest films, among them Max Ophüls's *Lola Montès* (1955) and Robert Bresson's *Le Journal d'un Curée de Campagne (Diary of a Country Priest)* (1951). Offering a new, freer filmmaking approach were the critics of *Cahiers du Cinéma,* many of whom became the filmmakers of the *Nouvelle Vague* (New Wave). Its debut film, Roger Vadim's *Et Dieu Créa la Femme (And God Created Woman),* appeared in 1956 to national success, but it was François Truffaut's *Les Quatre Cents Coups (The 400 Blows)* (1959) that fully launched the movement. Other notable films included Alain Resnais's *Hiroshima, Mon Amour* (1959).

The voice of Universal's Francis the Talking Mule was provided by character actor Chill Wills.

In Sweden, director Ingmar Bergman refined his psychological dramas with three films that established his international reputation: *Smiles of a Summer Night* (1955), *The Seventh Seal* (1957), and *Wild Strawberries* (1957). Similarly, Italian cinema was reinvented through the works of Michelangelo Antonioni, Bernardo Bertolucci, and particularly Federico Fellini (*The Nights of Cabiria,* 1956, and *La Strada,* 1954).

In 1959, 42 million Americans went to movies weekly – less than half the attendance numbers during World War II. One reason was television. Director Alfred Hitchcock was one filmmaker who found success in both media. From 1955, he hosted the television series *Alfred Hitchcock Presents.* Then, borrowing television's black-and-white graininess and capitalizing on the growing, thrill-seeking youth market, he made a low-budget movie in 1960 that prefigured a new kind of raw, subversive moviemaking: *Psycho.*

CHRONOLOGY

1950

Warner Bros., Loews, and 20th Century-Fox are ordered to sell off their theaters in a federal antitrust ruling.

RKO divests itself of its theaters to comply with federal antitrust rulings.

United Artists is taken over by an investment group headed by Paul McNutt.

Judy Garland attempts suicide and agrees with MGM to end her nearly 15-year association with the studio.

Ingrid Bergman gives birth to an out-of-wedlock child with director Roberto Rossellini in February, prompting public disapproval in the US, including Senate condemnation by Colorado Senator Edwin Johnson.

Frank Sinatra is banished from his house by wife Nancy for his affair with Ava Gardner and departs MGM after starring in unsatisfying features.

Lucille Ball and husband Desi Arnaz found Desilu Productions.

Treasure Island is the Disney studio's first all-live-action feature.

Producer Arthur Freed continues to drive the MGM musical to lavish heights in the 1950s, notably with directors Vincente Minnelli and Stanley Donen.

The western enters its most majestic era in the 1950s, with landmark films by John Ford, Howard Hawks, Anthony Mann, Budd Boetticher, and others.

1950: BIRTHS

WILLIAM HURT, MAR. 20
CHRISTINE LAHTI, APR. 4
TOM BERENGER, MAY 31
JOHN SAYLES, AUG. 31
BILL MURRAY, SEPT. 21
RANDY QUAID, OCT. 1
JOHN CANDY, OCT. 31
ED HARRIS, NOV. 28

1950: DEATHS

SARA ALLGOOD
HOBART CAVANAUGH
ALAN HALE, SR.
WALTER HUSTON
REX INGRAM (HITCHCOCK)
EMIL JANNINGS
AL JOLSON
LOU LEHR
FLORENCE NASH
JOHN M. STAHL

NOTABLE FILMS 1950

United States
ALL ABOUT EVE
ANNIE GET YOUR GUN
THE ASPHALT JUNGLE
BORN YESTERDAY
BROKEN ARROW
CHEAPER BY THE DOZEN
CINDERELLA
CYRANO DE BERGERAC
DESTINATION MOON
FATHER OF THE BRIDE
THE FLAME AND THE ARROW
FRANCIS
THE GUNFIGHTER
HARVEY
IN A LONELY PLACE
KING SOLOMON'S MINES
THE MEN
PANIC IN THE STREETS
RIO GRANDE
THE RIVER
SCANDAL
STAGE FRIGHT
SUMMER STOCK
SUNSET BOULEVARD
THE THIRD MAN
TREASURE ISLAND
WINCHESTER '73

China and USSR
VICTORY OF THE CHINESE PEOPLE

France
LA RONDE
ORPHÉE (ORPHEUS)

India
BABUL
JOGAN
MANTHIRI KUMARI

Italy
MIRACOLO A MILANO (MIRACLE IN MILAN)

Japan
RASHOMON

Mexico
LOS OLVIDADOS

Sweden
ILLICIT INTERLUDE (SUMMER INTERLUDE)
MISS JULIE
THE NAKED NIGHT (STARDUST AND TINSEL)

United Kingdom
THE ELUSIVE PIMPERNEL
FAMILY PORTRAIT
GONE TO EARTH
SEVEN DAYS TO NOON

USSR
PADENIYE BERLINA (THE FALL OF BERLIN)

1951

Television attracts two stars: Cowboy star Gene Autry signs for a series, and Groucho Marx transfers to the small screen with *You Bet Your Life.*

Screen Directors Guild president Joseph Mankiewicz refuses to sign a mandatory US loyalty oath, prompting mass member resignations, including Cecil B. De Mille's.

Oscar nominees Judy Holliday and José Ferrer are among those investigated by the US government for alleged communist leanings. Ferrer is subpoenaed by HUAC.

The French film industry is distinguished in the 1950s by works of established directors like Robert Bresson and Marcel Carné.

French film output during the 1950s will average 100 to 120 films annually.

The first Sino-Soviet feature from the two nation-alized industries is *Victory of the Chinese People.*

West German films during the 1950s will be restricted in scope and creativity, limited by funds and national film policies.

The Japanese film industry gains two new production companies, Shin-Toho and Toei.

Independence melodramas are popular staples of postindependence India during the 1950s.

During the early 1950s, up to 150 features are made annually in Mexico.

The British government establishes the British Film Production Fund to encourage film production, with limited success.

Anti-Western films dominate the Russian film industry in the early 1950s, until Joseph Stalin's death in 1953.

Despite a high entertainment tax that curtails film production, Sweden distinguishes itself with the 1950s domestic dramas of Ingmar Bergman and others.

Betty Grable is named the top female box office star, according to a poll of exhibitors by Quigley Publications. John Wayne is named the top male star.

The US House Committee on Un-American Activities continues its investigation of writers and directors who are suspected communists. Among those investigated are Larry Parks, Budd Schulberg, and Sterling Hayden, all of whom admit to former Party membership.

1950 Oscar-winner José Ferrer and John Garfield testify before the HUAC that they were never members of the Communist Party.

Actor Sterling Hayden and director Edward Dmytryk provide HUAC with the names of possible political subversives.

Unstable cellulose nitrate–based film stock is no longer used in the industry. Its use will cause the destruction of half of all previously made American films.

The Production Code amends its rules to forbid narcotics and abortion as film subjects.

Louis B. Mayer resigns as head of MGM; producer, Dore Schary replaces him.

20th Century–Fox agrees to divest itself of its theaters.

Marilyn Monroe signs a long-term contract with 20th Century–Fox.

Mary Astor unsuccessfully attempts suicide.

AT LEFT: Betty Grable, who traveled to the front lines in an effort to boost morale among the troops, was the most popular pinup of World War II and the top female star of 1950.

NOTABLE FILMS 1951

United States	Sun	India
ACE IN THE HOLE	QUO VADIS?	DEEDAR
THE AFRICAN QUEEN	THE RED BADGE OF COURAGE	*Italy*
ALICE IN WONDERLAND	ROYAL WEDDING	BELLISSIMA
AN AMERICAN IN PARIS	SAILOR BEWARE	*Japan*
BEDTIME FOR BONZO	SHOW BOAT	BAKUSHU (EARLY SUMMER)
DAVID AND BATHSHEBA	STRANGERS ON A TRAIN	THE IDIOT
THE DAY THE EARTH STOOD STILL	A STREETCAR NAMED DESIRE	*Spain*
THE DESERT FOX	THE THING FROM ANOTHER WORLD	ESA PAREJA FELIZ (THE HAPPY FAMILY)
DETECTIVE STORY	*France*	*United Kingdom*
GERALD MCBOING BOING (ANIMATED)	LE JOURNAL D'UN CURÉ DE CAMPAGNE (DIARY OF A COUNTRY PRIEST)	CAPTAIN HORATIO HORNBLOWER
THE GREAT CARUSO	LE PLAISIR	THE LAVENDER HILL MOB
I WAS A COMMUNIST FOR THE FBI		THE MAN IN THE WHITE SUIT
A PLACE IN THE		THE TALES OF HOFFMANN

The first 3-D movie was Bwana Devil, released in 1952. 3-D films and the required 3-D glasses soon became a novelty and never reached their expected potential.

Musical star Dan Dailey returns to Hollywood after five months of mental rehabilitation at Menninger Clinic in Kansas.

Judy Garland opens a hugely successful concert run at New York City's Palace Theater.

Maurice Chevalier is prohibited from entering the US due to suspected support of communist-affiliated groups.

A version of pay television is tested in Chicago, offering new movies for a fee.

Columbia establishes Screen Gems, a subsidiary devoted to making television programs.

In France, journalists and critics André Bazin and Jacques Doniol-Valcroze found the influential film journal *Cahiers du Cinéma*.

The Japanese film industry is reinvigorated when *Rashomon* (1950) wins the top prize at the 1951 Venice Film Festival.

Spanish filmmakers gain inspiration after viewing previously unavailable neorealist films at an Italian-sponsored film festival.

1952

US movie attendance drops to 51 million, from a 1948 high of 90 million.

Studios combat the threat of television with such screen gimmicks as 3-D and Cinerama.

This Is Cinerama, the first feature made with the wide-angle process, grosses more than $32 million in limited release. *Bwana Devil* is the first 3-D release and requires 3-D glasses for viewing.

The first contract granting payment for television residuals is negotiated by the Screen Actors Guild.

20th Century–Fox divests itself of its theaters.

RKO's Jerry Wald becomes production head at Columbia.

Warner Bros. and 20th Century–Fox announce that they will cease making B-movies.

At HUAC hearings, director Elia Kazan reveals that he and playwright Clifford Odets were communists. Odets later confirms to the committee his former Party membership.

NOTABLE FILMS 1952

United States
THE AFRICAN QUEEN
THE BAD AND THE BEAUTIFUL
BWANA DEVIL
COME BACK, LITTLE SHEBA
THE GREATEST SHOW ON EARTH
HANS CHRISTIAN ANDERSEN
HIGH NOON
IVANHOE
THE MEMBER OF THE WEDDING
MOULIN ROUGE
MY COUSIN RACHEL
PAT AND MIKE
THE QUIET MAN
RANCHO NOTORIOUS
SINGIN' IN THE RAIN
THE SNOWS OF KILIMANJARO
SON OF PALEFACE
THIS IS CINERAMA
VIVA ZAPATA!

WITH A SONG IN MY HEART

France
LES BELLES DE NUIT (BEAUTIES OF THE NIGHT)
CASQUE D'OR
FANFAN LA TULIPE (FANFAN THE TULIP)

Italy
EUROPA '51
OTHELLO
UMBERTO D

Mexico
EL

Poland
YOUNG CHOPIN

Spain
BIENVENIDO, MR. MARSHALL (WELCOME, MR. MARSHALL)

United Kingdom
THE CARD (THE PROMOTER)

USSR
REVIZOR (THE INSPECTOR GENERAL)
VASILI'S RETURN (THE RETURN OF VASILI)

Playwright Lillian Hellman declines to answer HUAC questions. The committee rejects her offer to answer only questions about herself but none about her acquaintances.

Frank Sinatra's recording contract with Columbia is not extended.

Mario Lanza is sued by MGM for not appearing on the set of *The Student Prince*.

Sales of a Marilyn Monroe nude calendar massively increase her popularity in the US, as does her appearance on the cover of *Life*.

Mickey Rooney and MGM agree to end their association.

Producer Walter Wanger is sentenced to four months in jail for the 1951 shooting of agent Jennings Lang.

James Stewart is among the first to share in a film's profits, with the film *Bend in the River*.

In Canada, noteworthy films are made throughout the 1950s in Quebec, but relatively few are made in other provinces.

From the early 1950s, many noteworthy East German films are concerned with personal problems and contemporary life.

Egypt's film industry turns toward social realism with the 1952 national revolution.

Government pressures hinder Polish film production during the 1950s and demand works of socialist realism.

1953

The wide-screen CinemaScope process is introduced with the biblical epic *The Robe.* At New York City's Roxy Theater, where it premieres, it is proclaimed the "Modern Entertainment Miracle You See Without the Use of Glasses."

Director Robert Rossen is a cooperative witness for HUAC investigators, naming names and admitting his own former tie to communism.

HUAC testimony by actors Lucille Ball and Lee J. Cobb is made public.

Monogram Studios is renamed Allied Artists.

Otto Preminger's *The Moon Is Blue* uses the word *virgin* and is denied the MPAA Production Code Seal of Approval.

Frank Sinatra resuscitates his career with his performance as Maggio in *From Here to Eternity.*

The Academy Awards ceremony is televised for the first time.

Living in Switzerland, Charlie Chaplin relinquishes his reentry papers to the US. He faces morals and political investigations if he returns.

Marilyn Monroe appears on the cover and as the centerfold of December's *Playboy* magazine.

Marlene Dietrich has a successful three-week cabaret stint, beginning a new phase in her career.

The Screenwriters Guild allows the names of writers suspected of communist affiliations to be removed from film credits.

International coproductions among the US and European countries will be popular throughout the 1950s.

Italian cinema rebounds from the decline of neorealism this decade with the works of directors like Michelangelo Antonioni and Federico Fellini.

German actress Marlene Dietrich performed in a successful three-week Las Vegas cabaret show in 1953, revitalizing her career.

NOTABLE FILMS 1953

United States
THE BAND WAGON
THE BEAST FROM 20,000 FATHOMS
THE BIG HEAT
CALAMITY JANE
CALL ME MADAM
FROM HERE TO ETERNITY
GENTLEMEN PREFER BLONDES
HOUSE OF WAX
HOW TO MARRY A MILLIONAIRE
IT CAME FROM OUTER SPACE
JULIUS CAESAR

MISS SADIE THOMPSON (IN 3-D)
MOGAMBO
THE MOON IS BLUE
NIAGARA
PETER PAN
THE ROBE
ROMAN HOLIDAY
SHANE
STALAG 17
THE SUN SHINES BRIGHT
THE WAR OF THE WORLDS
THE WILD ONE

Brazil
O CANGACERIO

France
THÉRÈSE RAQUIN (THE ADULTERESS)
LES VACANCES DE MONSIEUR HULOT (MR. HULOT'S HOLIDAY)

France and Italy
LA CAROZZA D'ORO (THE GOLDEN COACH)
FRENCH CANCAN
LILI
MADAME DE... (THE EARRINGS OF MADAME DE)
LE SALAIRE DE LA PEUR (THE WAGES OF FEAR)

Italy
I VITELLONI

Japan
GATE OF HELL
HIROSHIMA
TOKYO MONOGATARI (TOKYO STORY)
WILD GEESE (THE MISTRESS)

Poland
FIVE FROM BARSKA STREET

Spain
CÓMICOS (COMICS)

United Kingdom
THE BEGGAR'S OPERA
THE CRUEL SEA

1953: BIRTHS

AMY IRVING, SEPT. 10
TOM HULCE, DEC. 6
KIM BASINGER, DEC. 8
JOHN MALKOVICH, DEC. 9

1953: DEATHS

NIGEL BRUCE
WILLIAM FARNUM
FRANCIS FORD
PORTER HALL
HERMAN J. MANKIEWICZ
CHRIS-PIN MARTIN
HERBERT RAWLINSON
RICHARD ROSSON
LEWIS STONE
HANK WILLIAMS, SR.
DOOLEY WILSON

1954

Blacklist-related hiring prohibitions are upheld by the Los Angeles Supreme Court.

Howard Hughes acquires all stock in RKO, becoming the first sole owner of a studio.

Walt Disney announces it will start distributing films through its new company, Buena Vista Film Distributing Company.

Joseph Breen, Production Code administrator for two decades, retires.

Paramount's wide-screen VistaVision process is introduced with the Irving Berlin musical *White Christmas,* directed by Michael Curtiz, which becomes the year's top-grossing US film.

Marilyn Monroe marries New York Yankee Joe DiMaggio in January and divorces him in October.

RKO sells its film library to television. In coming years, other studios will follow suit with deals that do not include residuals.

Shirley MacLaine replaces an injured Carol Haney in Broadway's *The Pajama Game* and signs a film contract later in the year.

Debbie Reynolds and singer Eddie Fisher are engaged.

Clark Gable leaves MGM after 23 years and signs with 20th Century–Fox in a multifilm profit-sharing deal.

Errol Flynn leaves Warner Bros.

In the early 1950s, British features from the Ealing, Korda, and Rank studios are the first movies made available to US television.

Veteran actor Charles Buchinsky changes his name to Charles Bronson.

Danny Kaye becomes UNICEF's ambassador-at-large. His public service and philanthropic endeavors will continue for the rest of his life.

In *Cahiers du Cinéma,* French critic François Truffaut introduces the term *politique des auteurs* to shake up approaches to film criticism. His ideas will be central to what in the 1960s US critic Andrew Sarris calls the auteur theory of director-centered filmmaking.

Polish cinema is revitalized with the debut of the first film in Andrzej Wajda's trilogy, *A Generation.*

The Soviet film industry creates more humanistic films following the 1953 death of Joseph Stalin.

With the release of *Godzilla,* Japan begins a 15-year run of international success with science fiction/action films.

Brazil's inventive Vera Cruz film company goes bankrupt.

NOTABLE FILMS 1954

United States	THEM!
THE BAREFOOT CONTESSA	20,000 LEAGUES UNDER THE SEA
BEAT THE DEVIL	ULYSSES
THE CAINE MUTINY	VERA CRUZ
CARMEN JONES	WHITE CHRISTMAS
THE COUNTRY GIRL	**Italy**
THE CREATURE FROM THE BLACK LAGOON (IN 3-D)	LA STRADA
	SENSO
DIAL M FOR MURDER	VIAGGIO IN ITALIA (JOURNEY TO ITALY)
THE EGYPTIAN	**Japan**
EXECUTIVE SUITE	GODZILLA
THE GLENN MILLER STORY	SANSHO THE BAILIFF
THE HIGH AND THE MIGHTY	SEVEN SAMURAI (THE MAGNIFICENT SEVEN)
JOHNNY GUITAR	**Poland**
MAGNIFICENT OBSESSION	A GENERATION
	Sweden
ON THE WATERFRONT	SALKA VALKA
REAR WINDOW	**United Kingdom**
RIOT IN CELL BLOCK 11	ANIMAL FARM
SABRINA	DOCTOR IN THE HOUSE
SEVEN BRIDES FOR SEVEN BROTHERS	FATHER BROWN (THE DETECTIVE)
A STAR IS BORN	**USSR**
	A BIG FAMILY

1955

James Dean dies in an automobile accident in September. He had just finished filming *Giant,* the third feature in which he starred.

Todd-AO is the latest wide-screen process, introduced in *Oklahoma!* and *Around the World in 80 Days.*

Warner Bros. expands into the television market by producing small-screen shows, including *Maverick* and *77 Sunset Strip.*

The Man With the Golden Arm and *I Am a Camera* are denied Production Code seals by the Motion Picture Association of America; the former for its topic of drug addiction, the latter for its discussion of abortion.

Columbia leases its pre-1948 films to television without residuals.

Charlie Chaplin sells his portion of United Artists to the studio; Mary Pickford unsuccessfully attempts to buy his share but is outbid by Samuel Goldwyn.

Bud Abbott and Lou Costello end their relationship with Universal after dozens of successful comedies.

Grace Kelly meets Prince Rainier of Monaco.

Alfred Hitchcock and Judy Garland have television successes: Hitchcock in the series *Alfred Hitchcock Presents* and Garland in a special.

Britain's Ealing Studios closes.

Satyajit Ray distinguishes the Bengali film industry with the debut of *Pather Panchali,* the first of the Apu trilogy.

James Dean starred in just three films, including Giant, *before his death in 1955 at the age of 24. He was nominated posthumously for a best actor Academy Award in 1956 for* East of Eden *and in 1957 for* Giant.

1955: BIRTHS

KEVIN COSTNER, JAN. 18
BRUCE WILLIS, MAR. 19
ELLEN BARKIN, APR. 16
DEBRA WINGER, MAY 17
WILLEM DAFOE, JULY 22

1955: DEATHS

JAMES AGEE
LLOYD BACON
THEDA BARA
CHIEF THUNDERCLOUD
CONSTANCE COLLIER
JAMES DEAN
WILLIAM C. DE MILLE
PAUL HARVEY
JOHN HODIAK
SHEMP HOWARD
ALICE JOYCE
CARMEN MIRANDA
ROBERT RISKIN
S.Z. "CUDDLES" SAKALL

NOTABLE FILMS 1955

United States
ALL THAT HEAVEN ALLOWS
BAD DAY AT BLACK ROCK
BATTLE CRY
THE BIG KNIFE
THE BLACKBOARD JUNGLE
THE BRIDGES AT TOKO-RI
CINERAMA HOLIDAY
THE DESPERATE HOURS
EAST OF EDEN
GUYS AND DOLLS
HOUSE OF BAMBOO
I'LL CRY TOMORROW
IT'S ALWAYS FAIR WEATHER

KILLER'S KISS
LADY AND THE TRAMP (ANIMATED)
LOVE IS A MANY SPLENDORED THING
LOVE ME OR LEAVE ME
THE MAN WITH THE GOLDEN ARM
MARTY
MR. ARKADIN
MISTER ROBERTS
THE NIGHT OF THE HUNTER
NOT AS A STRANGER
OKLAHOMA!
OTHELLO
REBEL WITHOUT A CAUSE

THE ROSE TATTOO
THE SEVEN-YEAR ITCH
SUMMERTIME
TO CATCH A THIEF
TO HELL AND BACK
THE TROUBLE WITH HARRY
France
BOB LE FLAMBEUR (BOB THE GAMBLER)
DU RIFIFI CHEZ LES HOMMES/RIFIFI
NANA
France and Germany
LOLA MONTÈS
Italy
LE AMICHE (THE GIRL FRIENDS)

IL BIDONE (THE SWINDLE)
Japan
YANG KWEI-FEI
Mexico
ENSAYO DE UN CRIMEN (THE CRIMINAL LIFE OF ARCHIBALDO DE LA CRUZ)
Spain
MUERTE DE UN CICLISTA (DEATH OF A CYCLIST)
Sweden
SMILES OF A SUMMER NIGHT
USSR
RESTLESS YOUTH

The first feature film to be broadcast on US television in its entirety during prime time was *The Wizard of Oz* on November 3, 1956. It was seen on over 13 million of 40 million television sets.

1956: BIRTHS

MEL GIBSON, JAN. 3
ROBBY BENSON (ROBERT SEGAL), JAN. 21
SPIKE LEE (SHELTON LEE), MAR. 20
ANDY GARCIA (ANDRES ARTURO GARCIA MENDEZ), APR. 12
ERIC ROBERTS, APR. 18
TOM HANKS, JULY 9
CARRIE FISHER, OCT. 21
BO DEREK (CATHLEEN COLLINS), NOV. 20

1956: DEATHS

FRED ALLEN
EDWARD ARNOLD
GEORGE BANCROFT
LOUIS CALHERN
TOMMY DORSEY
CHARLEY GRAPEWIN
JEAN HERSHOLT
PAUL KELLY
GUY KIBBEE
SIR ALEXANDER KORDA
CHARLES LEMOYNE
BELA LUGOSI
RALPH MORGAN
JED PROUTY
MARGARET WYCHERLY

1956

A five-day workweek is adopted by the movie industry.

Darryl Zanuck leaves 20th Century–Fox to become an independent producer.

Grace Kelly marries Prince Rainier of Monaco, becoming Her Serene Highness, Princess Grace of Monaco. She abandons her film career.

Marilyn Monroe marries playwright Arthur Miller, author of *Death of a Salesman*.

The Production Code restrictions on abortion and other sensitive issues are eased for filmmakers.

American sex symbol Marilyn Monroe married playwright Arthur Miller in 1956.

Warner Bros. sells rights to its pre-1950 movies to an investment group.

Dore Schary is fired as production head at MGM.

Friendly Persuasion's best screenplay nominee, Michael Wilson, is prohibited from being listed as a nominee because he is blacklisted. When questioned by the HUAC in 1952, he pleaded the Fifth Amendment.

Elvis Presley is signed to a film deal; so is Jayne Mansfield.

Dean Martin and Jerry Lewis dissolve their comedy partnership.

"Que Sera, Sera" (from *The Man Who Knew Too Much*) and "True Love" (from *High Society*) are popular song hits.

A suggestive 135-foot billboard of Carroll Baker in *Baby Doll* is condemned by the Catholic Church.

The Warner-Pathé newsreel is discontinued, a victim of television.

In Britain, the anti-establishment Free Cinema movement is led by young filmmakers, including Lindsay Anderson and Tony Richardson.

NOTABLE FILMS 1956

United States	
ANASTASIA	PICNIC
AROUND THE WORLD IN 80 DAYS	RICHARD III
BABY DOLL	THE SEARCHERS
THE BAD SEED	SEVEN MEN FROM NOW
THE BRAVE ONE	THE SOLID GOLD CADILLAC
BUS STOP	SOMEBODY UP THERE LIKES ME
CAROUSEL	TEA AND SYMPATHY
FORBIDDEN PLANET	TEAHOUSE OF THE AUGUST MOON
FRIENDLY PERSUASION	THE TEN COMMANDMENTS
GIANT	TRAPEZE
THE HARDER THEY FALL	WAR AND PEACE
HIGH SOCIETY	WORLD WITHOUT END
INVASION OF THE BODY SNATCHERS	THE WRONG MAN
THE KILLERS	*Spain*
THE KING AND I	CALLE MAYOR (MAIN STREET)
LOVE ME TENDER	LOS JUEVES, MILAGRO (A MIRACLE EVERY THURSDAY)
LUST FOR LIFE	*USSR*
THE MAN WHO KNEW TOO MUCH	MOTHER (1905)
MOBY DICK	OTHELLO
PATTERNS	

1957

Legends end: Humphrey Bogart dies from lung cancer in January; MGM mogul Louis B. Mayer dies in October.

RKO ceases making feature films; Republic Films also stops making feature films but plans television productions.

Universal Films leases its films to television.

Paramount discontinues its newsreel, the *Paramount News.*

Frank Sinatra and Ava Gardner finalize their divorce in July.

Elizabeth Taylor divorces Michael Wilding in January and marries Mike Todd in February.

Ingrid Bergman returns to the US and to Hollywood filmmaking.

The first international film festival in the US is held — the San Francisco Film Festival.

The Jean Hersholt Humanitarian Award is established by the Motion Picture Academy of Arts and Sciences. Y. Frank Freeman is the first recipient.

United Artists rebounds in the 1950s under its syndicate ownership by pursuing independent filmmakers such as Stanley Kramer and Otto Preminger.

A three-month libel trial against the gossip magazine *Confidential* results in a hung jury; the magazine decides to discontinue publishing tell-all articles.

In France, *Cahiers du Cinéma* co-editor and founder André Bazin supports the auteur theory (that the director is the "author" of the film) through his writings during this decade.

In Czechoslovakia, films such as Vojtech Jasny's *September Nights,* begin to criticize the Stalinist era.

Australian company Ealing Films and director Joris Ivens elevate the national cinema with films, including *Three in One,* released this year.

1958

Paramount sells the rights to its films that do not require residuals (pre-1948) to MCA. It is the last of the major studios to sell these rights.

Paramount makes its studios available to independent producers.

Columbia Pictures's new head is Sam Briskin; MGM's new production chief is Sol C. Siegel.

Charlie Chaplin pays $425,000 in back taxes, canceling his debt to the US government.

Lana Turner's teen daughter, Cheryl Crane, fatally stabs Turner's boyfriend, Johnny Stompanato, after he threatens the actress. The death is ruled "justifiable homicide."

Mike Todd dies in a crash in his plane *Lucky Liz,* named for wife Elizabeth Taylor. Taylor was ill and had been unable to accompany him.

Elizabeth Taylor and Eddie Fisher become romantically involved. Fisher leaves his spouse Debbie Reynolds.

Paul Newman and Joanne Woodward are married.

Kim Novak dates Dominican dictator's son General Rafael Trujillo, Jr. He is married.

Horror movie impresario William Castle publicizes his film *Macabre* by taking out a $1,000 insurance policy for death by fright.

1957: BIRTHS

GEENA DAVIS (VIRGINIA DAVIS), JAN. 21
JOHN TURTURRO, FEB. 28
MICHELLE PFEIFFER, APR. 29
KELLY MCGILLIS, JULY 9
MELANIE GRIFFITH, AUG. 9

1957: DEATHS

WILLIAM "BILLY" BEVAN
HUMPHREY BOGART
JACK BUCHANAN
JIMMY DORSEY
FRANK FENTON
HARRISON FORD (SILENT ACTOR)
OLIVER HARDY
JOSEPHINE HULL
ERICH WOLFGANG KORNGOLD
GENE LOCKHART
LOUIS B. MAYER
GRANT MITCHELL
EZIO PINZA
NED SPARKS
NORMA TALMADGE
ARTURO TOSCANINI
ERICH VON STROHEIM
JAMES WHALE
CORA WITHERSPOON

NOTABLE FILMS 1957

United States			*Italy*
AN AFFAIR TO REMEMBER	HEAVEN KNOWS, MR. ALLISON	SILK STOCKINGS	LE NOTTI BIANCHE (WHITE NIGHTS)
BACHELOR PARTY	I WAS A TEENAGE WEREWOLF	THE SPIRIT OF ST. LOUIS	LE NOTTI DI CABIRIA (THE NIGHTS OF CABIRIA)
THE BRIDGE ON THE RIVER KWAI	THE INCREDIBLE SHRINKING MAN	THE SUN ALSO RISES	*Japan*
THE CURSE OF FRANKENSTEIN	THE LEFT HANDED GUN	SWEET SMELL OF SUCCESS	THE LOWER DEPTHS
THE DELICATE DELINQUENT	LOVE IN THE AFTERNOON	TAMMY AND THE BACHELOR	THE MYSTERIANS
DESK SET	MAN OF A THOUSAND FACES	THE THREE FACES OF EVE	RODAN
A FACE IN THE CROWD	PAL JOEY	TWELVE ANGRY MEN	THRONE OF BLOOD
FEAR STRIKES OUT	PATHS OF GLORY	*Argentina*	*Poland*
FUNNY FACE	PEYTON PLACE	LA CASA DEL ANGEL	KANAL
LES GIRLS	THE PRINCE AND THE SHOWGIRL	*Australia*	*Sweden*
THE GREAT MAN	RAINTREE COUNTY	THREE IN ONE	THE SEVENTH SEAL
GUNFIGHT AT THE OK CORRAL	SAYONARA	*Czechoslovakia*	WILD STRAWBERRIES
A HATFUL OF RAIN	SEVEN WONDERS OF THE WORLD	SEPTEMBER NIGHTS	*United Kingdom*
		France	A KING IN NEW YORK
		AND GOD CREATED WOMAN	*USSR*
			AND QUIET FLOWS THE DAWN

In France, newly elected president Charles De Gaulle institutes a government progam to support film production, particularly for mainstream films.

In Britain, Hammer Films enjoys successes in the late 1950s with horror films.

Many Canadian directors, including Norman Jewison and Arthur Hiller, have relocated to the US for richer career opportunities.

1959

Nouvelle Vague films, including *The 400 Blows* and *Hiroshima, Mon Amour*, reignite French cinema and gain worldwide attention.

Blacklisted film professionals may be nominated for Oscars, according to a ruling by the Academy of Motion Picture Arts and Sciences.

Debbie Reynolds divorces Eddie Fisher in February; Elizabeth Taylor marries Fisher in May.

Soviet president Nikita Khrushchev visits Hollywood and disapprovingly watches the filming of *Can-Can*.

The Screenwriters Guild of America strikes against independent studios over residuals.

Cary Grant reveals his experiments with LSD and his visits to a psychiatrist in *Look* and the *New York Herald Tribune*.

Elvis Presley was inducted into the US Army in 1958 and began his tour of duty in March of that year.

Elvis Presley is one of many entertainers to enlist in the military.

The screenwriter of *The Defiant Ones* is revealed to be blacklisted writer Nedrick Young.

Writers linked to the film journal *Cahiers du Cinéma* and others form an anti-establishment filmmaking movement known as *la Nouvelle Vague* (New Wave). Among its practioners are Claude Chabrol and François Truffaut.

1958: BIRTHS

HOLLY HUNTER, MAR. 20
GARY OLDMAN, MAR. 21
ALEC BALDWIN, APR. 3
DANIEL DAY-LEWIS, APR. 29
KEVIN BACON, JULY 8
MADONNA CICCONE, AUG. 26
TIM ROBBINS, OCT. 16
MARY ELIZABETH MASTRANTONIO, NOV. 17
JAMIE LEE CURTIS, NOV. 22

1958: DEATHS

HERBERT BRENON
HARRY COHN
RONALD COLMAN
ROBERT DONAT
ROBERT GREIG
JESSE L. LASKY
FRANKLIN PANGBORN
PARKYAKARKUS
TYRONE POWER
EDNA PURVIANCE
MIKE TODD
HELEN TWELVETREES
H. B. WARNER
HARRY M. WARNER
SAMUEL ZIMBALIST

NOTABLE FILMS 1958

United States		France	Japan
AUNTIE MAME	THE LONG HOT SUMMER	LES AMANTS (THE LOVERS)	THE HIDDEN FORTRESS
THE BIG COUNTRY	MACABRE		Mexico
THE BLOB	MARJORIE MORNINGSTAR	ASCENSEUR POUR L'ESCHAFAUD (FRANTIC)	NAZARÍN
THE BRAVADOS	NO TIME FOR SERGEANTS		Poland
THE BROTHERS KARAMAZOV	THE OLD MAN AND THE SEA	LE BEAU SERGE	ASHES AND DIAMONDS
	RUN SILENT, RUN DEEP	MON ONCLE (MY UNCLE)	Sweden
CAT ON A HOT TIN ROOF	SEPARATE TABLES		THE MAGICIAN
DAMN YANKEES	SOME CAME RUNNING	Germany	United Kingdom
THE DEFIANT ONES	THE TARNISHED ANGELS	DAS LIED DER MATROSEN (SAILOR'S SONG)	CARRY ON, SERGEANT
THE FLY	TOUCH OF EVIL		A NIGHT TO REMEMBER
GIGI	VERTIGO	Italy	
I WANT TO LIVE!	THE VIKINGS	I SOLITI IGNOTI (BIG DEAL ON MADONNA STREET)	USSR
INDISCREET	THE YOUNG LIONS		IVAN THE TERRIBLE PART II
			POEM OF THE SEA

Cary Grant found himself dangling from Mount Rushmore and dodging crop dusters in North by Northwest *(1959) when a group of spies mistook him for someone else.*

Elizabeth Taylor's films are banned in Egypt following her fund-raising for Israel.

John Wayne is accused by Panama's government of interfering with national politics after the actor pays half a million dollars to activist Roberto Arias.

The theme from *A Summer Place* becomes a pop hit.

Janus Films becomes a successful foreign film distributor in the US, in part by handling the films of Ingmar Bergman.

Hercules, an Italian film dubbed in English, becomes the first of several Italian import hits.

The average US movie ticket price declines through the 1950s (from $.53 in 1950 to $.51 in 1959), in an effort to compete with television.

1959: BIRTHS

LINDA BLAIR, JAN. 22
AIDAN QUINN, MAR. 8
MATTHEW MODINE, MAR. 22
EMMA THOMPSON, APR. 15
BRONSON PINCHOT, MAY 20
ROSANNA ARQUETTE, AUG. 10
SEAN YOUNG, NOV. 20
VAL KILMER, DEC. 31

1959: DEATHS

GILBERT ADRIAN
JOSS AMBLER
MAX BAER
ETHEL BARRYMORE
ERIC BLORE
HELEN BRODERICK
CHARLES CONKLIN
LOU COSTELLO
IRVING CUMMINGS, SR.
CECIL B. DE MILLE
PAUL DOUGLAS
ROSETTA "TOPSY" DUNCAN
ERROL FLYNN
JAMES GLEASON
EDMUND GOULDING
EDMUND GWENN
HAROLD HUBER
KAY KENDALL
WANDA LANDOWSKA
LUPINO LANE
MARIO LANZA
LASSIE (ORIGINAL)
LUCIEN LITTLEFIELD
VICTOR MCLAGLEN
UNA O'CONNOR
HELEN PARRISH
GEORGE "SUPERMAN" REEVES
LEE SHUMWAY
RUSSEL SIMPSON
PRESTON STURGES
CARL "ALFALFA" SWITZER
CHARLES VIDOR
GRANT WITHERS

NOTABLE FILMS 1959

United States		Some Like It Hot	Italy
ANATOMY OF A MURDER	IMITATION OF LIFE	SUDDENLY, LAST SUMMER	HERCULES
BEN-HUR	NORTH BY NORTHWEST	A SUMMER PLACE	Japan
COMPULSION	THE NUN'S STORY	THE TINGLER	FLOATING WEEDS
THE DIARY OF ANNE FRANK	ON THE BEACH	France	OHAYO (GOOD MORNING)
THE HANGING TREE	OPERATION PETTICOAT	THE COUSINS	United Kingdom
HAPPY ANNIVERSARY	PILLOW TALK	LES QUATRE CENTS COUPS (THE 400 BLOWS)	LOOK BACK IN ANGER
HAVE ROCKET, WILL TRAVEL	PORGY AND BESS	HIROSHIMA, MON AMOUR	ROOM AT THE TOP
THE HOUSE ON HAUNTED HILL	RIO BRAVO	France and Brazil	TIGER BAY
	SHAKE HANDS WITH THE DEVIL	BLACK ORPHEUS	USSR
	SLEEPING BEAUTY (ANIMATED)		BALLAD OF A SOLDIER

1960–1969

Transition marked the decade, as the Production Code ended and US studios moved from traditional movies like The Sound of Music *(1965) to adult dramas like* Midnight Cowboy *(1969).*

EUROPEAN DIRECTORS LIKE Jean-Luc Godard and Federico Fellini redefined international cinema. The youth market that *Psycho* so successfully targeted in 1960 had many film choices in the early 1960s. Nine Elvis Presley vehicles were released before 1964; the American International Pictures (AIP) Poe horror series and beach party series had been launched; and *Tammy* and *Gidget* movies were popular. But there were as yet no young filmmakers.

The big Hollywood films were the early-1960s well-made, if familiar, spectacles such as *West Side Story* (1961), *El Cid* (1961), *How the West Was Won* (1962), *Cleopatra* (1963), and *It's a Mad, Mad, Mad, Mad World* (1963). There were swan songs, too: Frank Capra's last movie (*Pocketful of Miracles,* 1961) and John Ford's last western (*The Man Who Shot Liberty Valance,* 1962). De Mille could no longer update or reinvent the spectacle: he had died in 1959.

In 1965, the enormously successful *The Sound of Music* looked as if it might reinvigorate the musical. Although some musicals, like *Funny Girl* (1968), were box-office successes, many musicals of the late 60s showed the form's age, such as *Paint Your Wagon* (1969) and *Star!* (1968).

WORLD CINEMA CONTINUED to present an array of refined experimentation often lacking in American films. In France, New Wave directors commanded world cinema through definitive works from Jean-Luc Godard (*Breathless,* 1960), Alain Resnais (*Last Year at Marienbad,* 1961), and Claude Chabrol (*The Girlfriends,* 1968). Other notable French films

included Claude Lelouch's *A Man and a Woman* (1966) and Luis Buñuel's *Belle de Jour* (1967). Italian cinema was dominated by Federico Fellini, with works including *La Dolce Vita* (1960), *8½* (1963), and *Juliet of the Spirits* (1965), and by Michelangelo Antonioni with *L'Avventura* (1960) and *Red Desert* (1964). Luchino Visconti directed the dramas *Rocco and His Brothers* (1960) and *The Leopard* (1963). During the early 1960's, Polish cinema thrived as younger compatriots of director Andrzej Wajda made their directorial marks: Roman Polanski with *Knife in the Water* (1961) and Jerzy Skolimowski with *Wallover* (1965). In India, producer Ismail Merchant and US director James Ivory completed their first of many films dealing with the clash of culture between East and West, *Shakespeare Wallah* (1965).

IN 1967, TWO MOVIES reenergized the US film community: Arthur Penn's *Bonnie and Clyde* and Mike Nichols's *The Graduate.* Each subverted its putative genre (gangster movie, coming-of-age, love story), and both were popular successes. More dark, antiheroic films followed, including *The Wild Bunch* (1969), *Easy Rider* (1969), and *Midnight Cowboy* (1969), the first X-rated movie to win an Academy Award for best picture.

On November 1, 1968, the decades-old Production Code was replaced by a multipart ratings system, administered by a division of the Motion Picture Association of America. The four original ratings were G (general audiences); M (later GP, and still later PG/parental guidance suggested); R (restricted, no one under 17 admitted without parent or guardian); and X (no one under 17 admitted). A print advertisement for 1967's *The Graduate* showed

AT LEFT: *The shower scene in Alfred Hitchcock's 1960 suspense thriller* Psycho, *starring Janet Leigh and Anthony Perkins, became one of the most famous moments in film history.*

Filmed in 1960, *Splendor in the Grass* (1961) was not only Warren Beatty's first film but also the first screenplay by playwright William Inge. He wrote the film's male lead role specifically for Beatty, who had drawn favorable notices in Inge's play *A Loss of Roses* (1959). The movie also provided Sandy Dennis with her first film role.

a confused Dustin Hoffman, a woman's leg in the foreground, and the caption: "This is Benjamin. He's a little worried about his future." The same was true for the major studios of the 1960s. Given the range of top-grossing movies for 1969 – *Butch Cassidy and the Sundance Kid, The Love Bug, Midnight Cowboy, Easy Rider* and *Hello, Dolly!* – the change was already happening, but the way wasn't clear.

CHRONOLOGY

1960

The Roxy, New York City's fabled movie palace, closes.

The Screenwriter's Guild and the Screen Actors Guild each go on strike over residual payments for films sold to television.

American International Pictures' *The House of Usher* is the first of the studio's cycle of eight films directed by Roger Corman and based on the works of Edgar Allan Poe.

Universal and Columbia defeat the government's suit charging them with price-fixing films sold to television.

Dalton Trumbo, author of the screenplays for *Exodus* and *Spartacus,* is the first blacklisted writer to receive screen credit.

Sidney Poitier charges that racism in Hollywood has made it difficult for him to secure living quarters while filming *A Raisin in the Sun.*

Sidney Poitier not only starred in A Raisin in the Sun *in 1960 but also vocalized the discrimination he encountered while trying to find a place to live during filming.*

NOTABLE FILMS 1960

United States		France	HERCULES UNCHAINED
THE ALAMO	PLEASE DON'T EAT THE DAISIES	LES BONNES FEMMES (THE GIRLS)	ROCCO E I SUOI FRATELLI (ROCCO AND HIS BROTHERS)
THE APARTMENT	POLLYANNA	A BOUT DE SOUFFLE (BREATHLESS)	*Sweden*
BELLS ARE RINGING	PSYCHO	TESTAMENT D'ORPHÉE (THE TESTAMENT OF ORPHEUS)	JUNGFRUKALLAN (THE VIRGIN SPRING)
BUTTERFIELD 8	SERGEANT RUTLEDGE		*United Kingdom*
THE DARK AT THE TOP OF THE STAIRS	SHADOWS	TIREZ SUR LE PIANISTE (SHOOT THE PIANO PLAYER)	CONSPIRACY OF HEARTS
ELMER GANTRY	SONS AND LOVERS	*France and Italy*	THE ENTERTAINER
EXODUS	SPARTACUS	PLEINE SOLEIL (PURPLE NOON)	THE LEAGUE OF GENTLEMEN
FROM THE TERRACE	THE SUNDOWNERS	*Greece*	OUR MAN IN HAVANA
HOUSE OF USHER	SUNRISE AT CAMPOBELLO	POTE TIN KYRIAKI (NEVER ON SUNDAY)	PEEPING TOM
INHERIT THE WIND	SWISS FAMILY ROBINSON	*Italy*	SATURDAY NIGHT AND SUNDAY MORNING
JAZZ ON A SUMMER'S DAY	TALL STORY	L'AVVENTURA	SINK THE BISMARCK!
LET'S MAKE LOVE	THE TIME MACHINE	LA DOLCE VITA (THE SWEET LIFE)	TUNES OF GLORY
THE MAGNIFICENT SEVEN	THE UNFORGIVEN		VILLAGE OF THE DAMNED
MIDNIGHT LACE	WILD RIVER		
NORTH TO ALASKA	WHERE THE BOYS ARE		

The Hollywood Walk of Fame is inaugurated. The sidewalk is studded with bronze stars celebrating actors, directors, and other entertainment personalities.

Jane Fonda makes her screen debut in *Tall Story*.

Elizabeth Taylor's series of illnesses create havoc on the set of *Cleopatra*.

The box office is taking a beating in Britain, with films on television identified as one of the culprits.

Peeping Tom, Michael Powell's violent study of a man who literally kills women with his camera, has some critics in Britain calling the film obscenely perverse.

Marlene Dietrich, on a concert tour, returns to Germany for the first time since 1930. Well known to be one of the more prominent Hollywood figures who supported the Allied war effort in the 1940s, she receives a mixed reception.

Federico Fellini's *La Dolce Vita (The Sweet Life),* the unanimous choice for the Golden Palm at Cannes, is nevertheless booed by some at its showing. Michelangelo Antonioni's seemingly plotless *L'Avventura* draws public censure at the festival and elicits a letter defending it, signed by prominent filmmakers.

1961

Central Casting begins to give African-American actors equal access to available assignments.

The Supreme Court rules that local and state governments can censor films.

Hollywood stars turn out for the inauguration of the new American president, John F. Kennedy.

Joseph L. Mankiewicz takes over from Rouben Mamoulian as director of *Cleopatra,* and Lewis Milestone replaces Carol Reed at the helm of the remake of *Mutiny on the Bounty.*

TWA pioneers regular in-flight movies in first class.

A revised Production Code permits the portrayal of homosexuality on the screen.

Marilyn Monroe divorces Arthur Miller, spends time in a mental hospital, and is introduced to President Kennedy.

NBC premieres Saturday Night at the Movies, beginning the regular showing of recent Hollywood films on television. The first film is *How to Marry a Millionaire.*

After a widely publicized search for an actor to play the character of James Bond in a series of films based on novels by Ian Fleming, the producers choose Scottish actor Sean Connery. The result will be next year's *Dr. No.*

Director Jean-Luc Godard marries actress Anna Karina.

Fascists disrupt the Rome premiere of Pier Paolo Pasolini's *Accatone,* a realistic melodrama about a pimp killed by the police.

Luis Buñuel's *Viridiana,* winner of the Golden Palm at Cannes, is attacked by the Vatican and by the government of the director's native Spain for being "sacrilegious." The film is a witty, surreal tale of a novice nun corrupted by her wicked uncle.

NOTABLE FILMS 1961

United States
THE ABSENT-MINDED PROFESSOR
BLUE HAWAII
BREAKFAST AT TIFFANY'S
THE CHILDREN'S HOUR
EL CID
THE COMANCHEROS
THE ERRAND BOY
FANNY
FLOWER DRUM SONG
THE GUNS OF NAVARONE
THE HOODLUM PRIEST
THE HUSTLER
JUDGMENT AT NUREMBERG
KING OF KINGS
LOVER COME BACK
THE MISFITS
ONE-EYED JACKS
101 DALMATIANS
ONE, TWO, THREE
THE PARENT TRAP
THE PIT AND THE PENDULUM
POCKETFUL OF MIRACLES
A RAISIN IN THE SUN
SPLENDOR IN THE GRASS
SUMMER AND SMOKE
TWO RODE TOGETHER
WEST SIDE STORY

France
UNE FEMME EST UNE FEMME (A WOMAN IS A WOMAN)
JULES ET JIM (JULES AND JIM)

France and Italy
L'ANNÉE DERNIÈRE À MARIENBAD (LAST YEAR AT MARIENBAD)
LA NOTTE (THE NIGHT)

Italy
ACCATONE
LA CIOCIARA (TWO WOMEN)
DIVORZIO ALL'ITALIANA (DIVORCE ITALIAN STYLE)

Japan
NINGEN NO JOKEN (A SOLDIER'S PRAYER)
YOJIMBO (THE BODYGUARD)

Spain
VIRIDIANA

Sweden
SÅSOM I EN SPEGEL (THROUGH A GLASS DARKLY)

United Kingdom
THE INNOCENTS
A TASTE OF HONEY
VICTIM
WHISTLE DOWN THE WIND

1961: BIRTHS
EVAN HANDLER, JAN. 10
EDDIE MURPHY, APR. 3
GEORGE CLOONEY, MAY 6
VING RHAMES, MAY 12
TIM ROTH, MAY 14
MICHAEL J. FOX, JUNE 9
LOLITA DAVIDOVICH, JULY 15
FOREST WHITAKER, JULY 15
ELIZABETH MCGOVERN, JULY 18
WOODY HARRELSON, JULY 23
LAURENCE FISHBURNE, JULY 30
REBECCA DE MORNAY, AUG. 29
JENNIFER TILLY, SEPT. 16
LUC PICARD, SEPT. 24
ERIC STOLTZ, SEPT. 30
RALPH MACCHIO, NOV. 4
TILDA SWINTON, NOV. 5
D.B. SWEENEY, NOV. 14
MEG RYAN, NOV. 19
MARIEL HEMINGWAY, NOV. 22
JULIANNE MOORE, DEC. 3
SAM ROBARDS, DEC. 16

1961: DEATHS
LEO CARRILLO
JEFF CHANDLER
RUTH CHATTERTON
CHARLES COBURN
GARY COOPER
MARION DAVIES
JOAN DAVIS
BARRY FITZGERALD
GEORGE FORMBY
ZOLTÁN KORDA
BELINDA LEE
CHICO MARX
NITA NALDI
HENRY O'NEILL
GAIL RUSSELL
JOSEPH M. SCHENCK
ANITA STEWART
MAURICE TOURNIER
ANNA MAY WONG

1962

MCA absorbs Universal-International.

West German judge Hermann Markl is forced to resign after *Judgment at Nuremberg* publicizes his Nazi past.

Film production in Hollywood has dropped off precipitously, although box-office receipts remain healthy.

Darryl Zanuck takes over as president of 20th Century–Fox. Mounting budget overruns on the studio's *Cleopatra* threaten its solvency.

Fearing an increase in filming abroad, the Screen Actors Guild shelves demands for higher wages.

Plot elements involving pedophilia in *Lolita* and homosexuality in *Advise and Consent* signal the end of old filmmaking taboos.

Bette Davis advertises for acting roles with a "Situation Wanted" ad in *The Hollywood Reporter.*

The drug overdose death of Marilyn Monroe shocks and saddens movie fans around the world.

Elizabeth Taylor's romance with *Cleopatra* co-star Richard Burton dominates entertainment head-lines to such an extent that it elicits a negative response from the Vatican.

Robert Duvall makes his screen debut in *To Kill a Mockingbird.*

Citizen Kane (1941) takes the top spot as the best movie ever made in an international poll of film critics conducted by the British film magazine, *Sight and Sound.* The second-best picture, according to the poll, is Michaelangelo Antonioni's *L'Avventura* (1960).

The release of *Dr. No* in Great Britain initiates the spectacularly successful series of films based on Ian Fleming's character James Bond. Its star, Sean Connery, will play agent 007 in seven films.

The French film periodical *Cahiers du Cinéma* devotes a special issue to the French New Wave, featuring an interview with director Jean-Luc Godard.

NOTABLE FILMS 1962

United States
ADVISE AND CONSENT
BIRDMAN OF ALCATRAZ
BOYS NIGHT OUT
CARNIVAL OF SOULS
CAPE FEAR
DAVID AND LISA
DAYS OF WINE AND ROSES
FREUD
GAY PURR-EE
GIGOT
GYPSY
HATARI!
HELL IS FOR HEROES
HOW THE WEST WAS WON
THE INTERNS
LOLITA
THE LONELINESS OF THE LONG DISTANCE RUNNER
LONELY ARE THE BRAVE
LONG DAY'S JOURNEY INTO NIGHT
THE LONGEST DAY
THE MAN WHO SHOT LIBERTY VALENCE

THE MANCHURIAN CANDIDATE
THE MIRACLE WORKER
THE MUSIC MAN
MUTINY ON THE BOUNTY
REQUIEM FOR A HEAVYWEIGHT
RIDE THE HIGH COUNTRY
THE ROAD TO HONG KONG
SWEET BIRD OF YOUTH
THAT TOUCH OF MINK
TO KILL A MOCKINGBIRD
TWO FOR THE SEESAW
WHAT EVER HAPPENED TO BABY JANE?

US and UK
BILLY BUDD

France
LE CAPORAL ÉPINGLÉ (THE ELUSIVE CORPORAL)
CLÉO DE 5 À 7 (CLEO FROM 5 TO 7)
LES DIMANCHES DE VILLE D'AVRAY (SUNDAYS AND CYBÈLE)

VIVRE SA VIE (MY LIFE TO LIVE)

France and Italy
CARTOUCHE

Italy
BOCCACCIO '70
L'ECLISSE (ECLIPSE)

Japan
CUSHINGURA (THE LOYAL 47 RONIN)
SANJURO
SANMA NO AJI (AN AUTUMN AFTERNOON)

Mexico
EL ANGEL EXTERMINADOR (THE EXTERMINATING ANGEL)

Poland
NOZ W WODZIE (KNIFE IN THE WATER)

United Kingdom
DR. NO
A KIND OF LOVING
LAWRENCE OF ARABIA

USSR
MY NAME IS IVAN

1962: BIRTHS

SUZY AMIS, JAN. 5
JIM CARREY, JAN. 17
JENNIFER JASON LEIGH, FEB. 5
LOU DIAMOND PHILLIPS, FEB. 17
RAE DAWN CHONG, FEB. 28
EMILIO ESTEVEZ, MAY 12
ALLY SHEEDY, JUNE 13
TOM CRUISE, JULY 3
MATTHEW BRODERICK, AUG. 21
KRISTY MCNICHOL, SEPT. 11
JOAN CUSACK, OCT. 11
VINCENT SPANO, OCT. 18
CARY ELWES, OCT. 26
LORI SINGER, NOV. 6
DEMI MOORE, NOV. 11
JODIE FOSTER, NOV. 14
ANDREW MCCARTHY, NOV. 29
FELICITY HUFFMAN, DEC. 9
RALPH FIENNES, DEC. 22

1962: DEATHS

LOUISE BEAVERS
REX BELL
WILLIE BEST
CLARA BLANDICK
TODD BROWNING
FRANK BORZAGE
MICHAEL CURTIZ
LOUISE FAZENDA
HOOT GIBSON
ERNIE KOVACS
LEW LANDERS
CHARLES LAUGHTON
FRANK LOVEJOY
THOMAS MITCHELL
MARILYN MONROE
VICTOR MOORE
JERRY WALD
BILLY WILKERSON
GUINN "BIG BOY" WILLIAMS

1963

The NAACP pressures the movie industry to abolish African-American stereotyping in films and provide more employment opportunities for blacks in the movie business.

Hollywood executives and labor leaders ask for government help to curb "runaway productions," those productions filmed abroad to save money.

United Artists' Santa Monica Boulevard lot and the Hal Roach Studio are slated to become shopping centers.

James Caan makes his screen debut in a small role in *Irma la Douce.*

Beach Party, starring Frankie Avalon and Annette Funicello, is the first of a cycle of "beach films."

The opening of *Cleopatra* is an anticlimax. The romance between Elizabeth Taylor and Richard Burton, stars of 20th Century–Fox's budget-busting, nearly studio-breaking film, has dominated headlines for months.

Although both were married, Elizabeth Taylor and Richard Burton – who later married, divorced, and married again – began their relationship while filming Cleopatra, *released in 1963.*

The New York Film Festival debuts with a showing of Luis Buñuel's *El Angel Exterminador (The Exterminating Angel)* (Mexico, 1962).

It's a Mad, Mad, Mad, Mad World features a bevy of comedians from silent days to the present.

The auteur theory of cinema, already prominent in the French film journal *Cahiers du Cinéma,* makes an impact in America. The theory holds that the director is the "author" of a film.

The Paris Cinémathèque's new theater, Palais de Chaillot, opens with a series of Charlie Chaplin films.

An Italian court convicts director Pier Paolo Pasolini of blasphemy for a scene in which he parodied biblical epics in *La Ricotta,* his contribution to an anthology film.

India bans *Nine Hours to Rama,* which is about the assassination of Mahatma Gandhi.

NOTABLE FILMS 1963

United States		Brazil	Spain
AMERICA, AMERICA	IRMA LA DOUCE	VIDAS SECAS	LOS TARANTOS
BEACH PARTY	IT'S A MAD, MAD, MAD, MAD WORLD	(BARREN LIVES)	**Sweden**
THE BIRDS	LILIES OF THE FIELD	**France and Italy**	TYSTNADEN
BYE BYE BIRDIE	THE LIST OF ADRIAN MESSENGER	IL GATTOPARDO (THE LEOPARD)	(THE SILENCE)
CAPTAIN NEWMAN, M.D.	LOVE WITH THE PROPER STRANGER	LE MEPRIS (CONTEMPT)	**United Kingdom** BILLY LIAR
THE CARDINAL	McLINTOCK!	**France, Italy, and West Germany**	FROM RUSSIA WITH LOVE
CHARADE	MOVE OVER DARLING	THE TRIAL	JASON AND THE ARGONAUTS
CLEOPATRA	THE NUTTY PROFESSOR	**Italy**	THE L-SHAPED ROOM
COME BLOW YOUR HORN	THE RAVEN	MONDO CANE (A DOG'S LIFE)	LORD OF THE FLIES
THE DAY OF THE TRIFFIDS	SHOCK CORRIDOR	OTTO E MEZZO (8½)	THE SERVANT
DONOVAN'S REEF	SOLDIER IN THE RAIN	**Italy and France**	THIS SPORTING LIFE
55 DAYS AT PEKING	THE STRIPPER	IL BOOM, IERI OGGI DOMANI	TOM JONES
THE GREAT ESCAPE	SUNDAY IN NEW YORK	(YESTERDAY, TODAY, AND TOMORROW)	THE V.I.P.s
THE HAUNTING	THE SWORD IN THE STONE		
HUD	THE THRILL OF IT ALL		

Although Luchino Visconti's 1963 film *Il Gattopardo (The Leopard)* (France and Italy) won the Golden Palm at Cannes, Visconti disowned it when its worldwide distributor, 20th Century–Fox, edited the release print from 205 to 161 minutes.

1964: BIRTHS

NICOLAS CAGE, JAN. 7
BRIDGET FONDA, JAN. 27
LAURA LINNEY, FEB. 5
CHRIS FARLEY, FEB. 15
MATT DILLON, FEB. 18
JULIETTE BINOCHE, MAR. 9
ROB LOWE, MAR. 17
ANNABELLA SCIORRA, MAR. 24
CRISPIN GLOVER, APR. 20
HANK AZARIA, APR. 25
COURTENEY COX, JUNE 15
JOHN LEGUIZAMO, JULY 22
SANDRA BULLOCK, JULY 26
MARY-LOUISE PARKER, AUG. 2
JOANNE WHALLEY, AUG. 25
KEANU REEVES, SEPT. 2
ROSIE PEREZ, SEPT. 6
JANEANE GAROFALO, SEPT. 28
BEATRICE DALLE, DEC. 19
MARISA TOMEI, DEC. 4

1964: DEATHS

GRACIE ALLEN
WILLIAM BENDIX
NACIO HERB BROWN
EDDIE CANTOR
SIR CEDRIC HARDWICKE
BEN HECHT
PERCY KILBRIDE
ALAN LADD
PETER LORRE
HARPO MARX
RUDOLPH MATÉ
COLE PORTER
JOSEPH SCHILDKRAUT
DIANA WYNYARD

1964

Made-for-television movies become a regularly scheduled staple for the networks.

Universal Studios begins its wildly popular studio tours.

Although public opinion is pressing for the end of Hollywood film censorship, avant-garde filmmakers are still fair game for police action. Kenneth Anger's sexually explicit *Scorpio Rising* is seized at a New York City showing.

In New York City, the Paramount Theater, one of the great movie palaces of the 1920s, shows its last regularly scheduled film; in Los Angeles, a real estate developer announces that the RKO Hill Street, another grand theater, will become a garage.

Three major Hollywood films, *Dr. Strangelove, Seven Days in May,* and *Fail-Safe,* vilify the American military establishment.

Peter Sellers stars in *The Pink Panther,* the first film in that series, and plays three roles in Stanley Kubrick's *Dr. Strangelove.*

In California, former film star George Murphy is elected to the US Senate.

Clint Eastwood, star of television's *Rawhide,* becomes an Italian film sensation in *Per un Pugno di Dollari (A Fistful of Dollars),* the first of several "spaghetti westerns" that will invigorate his US film career.

Sidney Poitier is the first African-American actor to win the Oscar for best actor, for *Lilies of the Field* (1963).

Traffic comes to a halt in central London as throngs of Beatles fans mob the theater where *A Hard Day's Night* is premiering.

Pier Paolo Pasolini, who has incurred the Vatican's wrath in recent years for his iconoclasm, is back in the church's good graces after the premiere of his *Il Vangelo Secondo Mateo (The Gospel According to St. Matthew).*

1965

A landmark nude scene in *The Pawnbroker* signals a major liberalization in the enforcement of Hollywood's Production Code. The Supreme Court furthers this progressive trend by striking down two state film-censorship laws.

The Motion Picture Association of America reaches an out-of-court settlement with 12 people excluded from film work in the 1950s because of the blacklist but will not admit that there ever was a blacklist.

There is an upsurge in production on Hollywood lots. Also rapidly increasing is the amount of money producers are paying for rights to the novels on which they base films.

Hollywood begins to organize entertainment units to perform for US troops in Vietnam.

The Legion of Decency changes its name to the National Catholic Office of Motion Pictures.

Julie Christie vaults to international stardom with lead roles in *Darling* and *Dr. Zhivago.*

NOTABLE FILMS 1964

United States			La Peau Douce (The Soft Skin)	*Japan*
The Americanization of Emily	Marnie	Viva Las Vegas		Kwaidan
	Mary Poppins	What a Way to Go!	*France and Italy*	Woman in the Dunes
Becket	The Masque of the Red Death	The World of Henry Orient	Le Journal d'une Femme de Chambre (Diary of a Chambermaid)	*United Kingdom*
The Best Man				Goldfinger
The Carpetbaggers	My Fair Lady	Zorba the Greek	*Italy and France*	A Hard Day's Night
Cheyenne Autumn	Night of the Iguana	*Brazil*	Matrimonio all'Italiana (Marriage Italian Style)	King and Country
Dr. Strangelove	The Pink Panther	Deus e o Diabo na Terra do Sol (Black God, White Devil)		Séance on a Wet Afternoon
Fail-Safe	Scorpio Rising		Il Vangelo Secondo Mateo (The Gospel According to St. Matthew)	The Yellow Rolls-Royce
The Fall of the Roman Empire	Seven Days in May			Zulu
	Seven Faces of Dr. Lao	*France*	*Italy, Spain, and West Germany*	*UK and Yugoslavia*
Father Goose	A Shot in the Dark	L'Homme de Rio (That Man from Rio)		The Long Ships
Good Neighbor Sam	Topkapi	Les Parapluies de Cherbourg (The Umbrellas of Cherbourg)	Per un Pugno di Dollari (A Fistful of Dollars)	*USSR*
The Incredible Mr. Limpet	The Unsinkable Molly Brown			Shadows of Our Forgotten Ancestors
Lilith				

In 1965, Omar Sharif and Julie Christie starred in the poignant love story, Doctor Zhivago, *based on the Nobel Prize-winning novel by Boris Pasternak.*

Audrey Hepburn is not nominated for a best actress Oscar for playing the role of Eliza Doolittle in the film version of *My Fair Lady*. Ironically, Julie Andrews, who played Eliza on Broadway and was passed over for the movie role, is not only nominated but wins the best actress statuette for *Mary Poppins*.

Walt Disney announces that his company will construct a major theme park in Orlando, Florida.

Directors George Stevens and Otto Preminger each bring their studios to court over the issue of licensing their films to television and allowing them to be interrupted by commercials.

Producer Samuel Bronston declares bankruptcy, his studio toppled by *The Fall of the Roman Empire*, the multimillion-dollar disaster released last year.

Cahiers du Cinéma deemphasizes its coverage of American films.

Glauber Rocha, the intensely political Brazilian director whose *Deus e o Diabo na Terra do So* (*Black God, White Devil*) (1964) typifies his work, delivers a manifesto on "The Aesthetics of Hunger" to a conference in Genoa.

NOTABLE FILMS 1965

United States
THE AGONY AND THE ECSTASY
BATTLE OF THE BULGE
CAT BALLOU
THE CINCINNATI KID
THE COLLECTOR
DOCTOR ZHIVAGO
THE GREAT RACE
THE GREATEST STORY EVER TOLD
HARLOW
THE HILL
HUSH...HUSH, SWEET CHARLOTTE
KING RAT
LORD JIM
THE LOVED ONE
MAJOR DUNDEE
OPERATION CROSSBOW
A PATCH OF BLUE
THE PAWNBROKER
THE SANDPIPER
SHENANDOAH
SHIP OF FOOLS
THE SONS OF KATIE ELDER
THE SOUND OF MUSIC
THE SPY WHO CAME IN FROM THE COLD
THAT DARN CAT!
THOSE MAGNIFICENT MEN IN THEIR FLYING MACHINES
A THOUSAND CLOWNS
THE TRAIN
VON RYAN'S EXPRESS
WHAT'S NEW, PUSSYCAT?

Czechoslovakia
LOVES OF A BLONDE
OBCHOD NA KORZE (THE SHOP ON MAIN STREET)

France
LE BONHEUR (HAPPINESS)
LA VIEILLE DAME INDIGNE (THE SHAMELESS OLD LADY)

France and Italy
PIERROT LE FOU (PIERROT GOES WILD)
VIVA MARIA!

Italy
GIULIETTA DEGLI SPIRITI (JULIETTE OF THE SPIRITS)

Italy, Spain, and West Germany
PER QUALCHE DOLLARO IN PIÙ (FOR A FEW DOLLARS MORE)

United Kingdom
DARLING
HELP!
THE IPCRESS FILE
THE KNACK, AND HOW TO GET IT
REPULSION
THUNDERBALL

1965: BIRTHS

DIANE LANE, JAN. 22
SARAH JESSICA PARKER, MAR. 25
ROBERT DOWNEY, JR., APR. 5
MARTIN LAWRENCE, APR. 16
BROOKE SHIELDS, MAY 31
ELIZABETH HURLEY, JUNE 10
EMMANUELLE BÉART, AUG. 14
KYRA SEDGWICK, AUG. 19
MARLEE MATLIN, AUG. 24
KEVIN DILLON, AUG. 19
CHARLIE SHEEN, SEPT. 3
BEN STILLER, NOV. 30
GONG LI, DEC. 31

1965: DEATHS

IRVING BACON
CONSTANCE BENNETT
MARY BOLAND
CLARA BOW
NANCY CARROLL
RAY COLLINS
DOROTHY DANDRIDGE
LINDA DARNELL
MARGARET DUMONT
JUDY HOLLIDAY
STAN LAUREL
JEANETTE MACDONALD
MAE MURRAY
ZACHARY SCOTT
DAVID O. SELZNICK
EVERETT SLOANE

1966

Who's Afraid of Virginia Woolf?, despite foul language, and *Alfie*, which mentions an "abortion" on the sound track, receive Production Code approval, further indicating the decline of film censorship. The Production Code itself is soon revised to reflect the new permissiveness.

Jack Valenti, the new head of the Motion Picture Association of America, pushes for a film industry rating system so as to avoid government censorship.

Former film star and Screen Actors Guild president Ronald Reagan is elected governor of California.

Gulf & Western Industries buys Paramount Pictures. Robert Evans becomes head of production at the studio.

George Hamilton, who is dating President Johnson's daughter Lynda Bird, is criticized for his draft deferment, which was granted because he is his mother's and brother's sole support.

Michael Caine, who has been appearing in films for a decade, becomes a star with his role in *Alfie.*

The Sound of Music is the new all-time box-office leader, surpassing *Gone with the Wind.*

The sexual explicitness of *Nattlek (Night Games),* a Swedish entry at the San Francisco Film Festival, precipitates Shirley Temple Black's resignation as a director of the festival.

Georgy Girl, a British import, is the first film labeled "Suggested for Mature Audiences Only."

French intellectuals and film critics protest the delayed release of New Wave director Jacques Rivette's *Suzanne, la Religieuse de Diderot (The Nun).* French censors deplore its portrayal of a lesbian Mother Superior.

François Truffaut's book *Le Cinéma elon Hitchcock (Hitchcock/Truffaut)* is published.

The theme from *Un Homme et Une Femme,* written by Frances Lai, becomes a popular hit.

Tunisia, bidding to become a center of Third World film, holds its first film festival.

1967

Bank America absorbs United Artists through its Transamerica subsidiary.

The American Film Institute begins operations. The Motion Picture Association of America, the National Endowment for the Arts, and the Ford Foundation are major funders.

The last newsreel distributor, Universal Newsreel, folds its operations.

Jack Warner sells a controlling interest in Warner Bros. to Seven Arts. Warner founded the studio with his brothers in the 1920s.

The Graduate makes Dustin Hoffman a star, opening the way for a generation of unconventional film actors.

Bonnie and Clyde influences American fashions and reflects a new sensibility that incorporates sex, violence, and humor into the movies.

Shirley Temple Black loses her bid for election to Congress from California.

Sultry Jayne Mansfield is decapitated in an auto accident.

Critics attack the re-release of *Gone with the Wind* in a wide-screen format, claiming it distorts the pictorial values of the original.

The death of Spencer Tracy shortly after the

NOTABLE FILMS 1966

United States		France	United Kingdom
ANY WEDNESDAY	LT. ROBIN CRUSOE, USN	AU HASARD BALTHAZAR (BALTHAZAR)	ALFIE
ARABESQUE	OUR MAN FLINT	UN HOMME ET UNE FEMME (A MAN AND A WOMAN)	BORN FREE
BATMAN	THE PROFESSIONALS		CUL-DE-SAC
THE BLUE MAX	THE RUSSIANS ARE COMING, THE RUSSIANS ARE COMING		FAHRENHEIT 451
THE CHASE	THE SAND PEBBLES	*France and US*	THE FAMILY WAY
CHELSEA GIRLS	SECONDS	IS PARIS BURNING?	GEORGY GIRL
THE ENDLESS SUMMER	THE SILENCERS	*France and Sweden*	KHARTOUM
FANTASTIC VOYAGE	TORN CURTAIN	MASCULINE-FÉMININE (MASCULINE-FEMININE)	A MAN FOR ALL SEASONS
THE FORTUNE COOKIE	WILD ANGELS	*France and UK*	MARAT (SADE)
A FUNNY THING HAPPENED ON THE WAY TO THE FORUM	WHO'S AFRAID OF VIRGINIA WOOLF?	LE ROI DE COEUR (KING OF HEARTS)	MODESTY BLAISE
GRAND PRIX	THE WRONG BOX	*Italy*	MORGAN!
THE GROUP	*Algeria and Italy*	IL BUONO IL BRUTTO IL CATTIVO (THE GOOD, THE BAD, AND THE UGLY)	ONE MILLION YEARS B.C.
HARPER	LA BATTAGLIA DI ALGERI (THE BATTLE OF ALGIERS)	*Sweden*	*UK and Italy*
HOW TO STEAL A MILLION	*Czechoslovakia*	PERSONA	BLOW-UP
	OSTRE SLEDOVANÉ VLAKY (CLOSELY WATCHED TRAINS)		*USSR*
			ANDREI RUBLEV

One of the all-time great Hollywood romances, between Katharine Hepburn and Spencer Tracy, ended with Tracy's death following the filming of Guess Who's Coming to Dinner *in 1967.*

1967: BIRTHS

EMILY WATSON, JAN. 14
SHERYL LEE, APR. 22
SANDRINE BONNAIREM, MAY 31
MIA SARA, JUNE 19
NICOLE KIDMAN, JUNE 20
HARRY CONNICK, JR., SEPT. 11
MIRA SORVINO, SEPT. 28
JULIA ROBERTS, OCT. 28
LISA BONET, NOV. 16

1967: DEATHS

MISCHA AUER
CHARLES BICKFORD
SMILEY BURNETTE
MARTINE CAROL
ANDY CLYDE
JANE DARWELL
REGINALD DENNY
NELSON EDDY
BERT LAHR
VIVIEN LEIGH
ANTHONY MANN
JAYNE MANSFIELD
ANTONIO MORENO
PAUL MUNI
NAT PENDLETON
CLAUDE RAINS
BASIL RATHBONE
SIG RUMAN
ANN SHERIDAN
TOTÒ
SPENCER TRACY
ANTON WALBROOK
FRANZ WAXMAN

filming of *Guess Who's Coming to Dinner* ends a great Hollywood career and his fabled film and personal partnership with Katharine Hepburn.

John Boorman's *Point Blank,* starring Lee Marvin, is released to little fanfare but later will be praised as a landmark film noir in color.

The widespread popularity of the Swedish film *Elvira Madigan* makes a "hit" of Mozart's Piano Concerto No. 21, prominent on its sound track.

Charlie Chaplin reacts bitterly to the London critics who have disparaged what will prove to be his final film, *A Countess from Hong Kong.*

Claude Lelouch's *Un Homme et une Femme (A Man and a Woman)* (1966) is a box-office success in the US, where it has become Allied Artists's most profitable release.

Right-wing teenagers vandalize a theater in Paris showing the antiwar film *Far from Vietnam.*

NOTABLE FILMS 1967

United States
BAREFOOT IN THE PARK
BONNIE AND CLYDE
CAMELOT
COOL HAND LUKE
THE DIRTY DOZEN
DOCTOR DOLITTLE
DON'T LOOK BACK
EL DORADO
FAR FROM THE MADDING CROWD
FIVE MILLION YEARS TO EARTH
THE FLIM-FLAM MAN
THE GRADUATE
GUESS WHO'S COMING TO DINNER
A GUIDE FOR THE MARRIED MAN

HALF A SIXPENCE
HOMBRE
HOW TO SUCCEED IN BUSINESS WITHOUT REALLY TRYING
IN COLD BLOOD
IN THE HEAT OF THE NIGHT
THE JUNGLE BOOK
POINT BLANK
THE PRESIDENT'S ANALYST
REFLECTIONS IN A GOLDEN EYE
THOROUGHLY MODERN MILLIE
TO SIR, WITH LOVE
THE TRIP
VALLEY OF THE DOLLS
WAIT UNTIL DARK

THE WAR WAGON

US and Italy
THE TAMING OF THE SHREW

Czechoslovakia
HOŘÍ, MÁ PANENKO (THE FIREMEN'S BALL)

France
LES DEMOISELLES DE ROCHEFORT (THE YOUNG GIRLS OF ROCHEFORT)
DEUX OU TROIS CHOSES QUE JE SAIS D'ELLE (TWO OR THREE THINGS I KNOW ABOUT HER)
LE VIEIL HOMME ET L'ENFANT (THE TWO OF US)
LE VOLEUR (THE THIEF OF PARIS)

France and Italy
WEEKEND
BELLE DE JOUR

Spain and Switzerland
CHIMES AT MIDNIGHT

Sweden
ELVIRA MADIGAN

United Kingdom
BEDAZZLED
CASINO ROYALE
A COUNTESS FROM HONG KONG
THE FEARLESS VAMPIRE KILLERS
TWO FOR THE ROAD
YOU ONLY LIVE TWICE

1968: BIRTHS

CUBA GOODING, JR., JAN. 2
JOSH BROLIN, FEB. 12
MOLLY RINGWALD, FEB. 14
PATSY KENSIT, MAR. 4
MOIRA KELLY, MAR. 6
PATRICIA ARQUETTE, APR. 8
ASHLEY JUDD, APR. 19
BILLY CRUDUP, JULY 8
WILL SMITH, SEPT. 25
PARKER POSEY, NOV. 8
BRENDAN FRASER, DEC. 3

1968: DEATHS

NICK ADAMS
ANTHONY ASQUITH
FAY BAINTER
TALLULAH BANKHEAD
BJÖRN BERGLUND
WENDELL COREY
FINLAY CURRIE
ALBERT DEKKER
CARL DREYER
BOBBY DRISCOLL
DAN DURYEA
KAY FRANCIS
DOROTHY GISH
MAE MARSH
TOMMY NOONAN
RAMON NOVARRO
HUNT STROMBERG
BASIL SYDNEY
FRANCHOT TONE
LEE TRACY
WALTER WANGER
BERT WHEELER

Death of a Gunfighter, released this year, was notable for its directorial credit: "Allen Smithee," a pseudonym chosen by the Directors Guild of America after Don Siegel and Robert Totten, who directed the film, disowned it. "Allen Smithee" would be credited with other films over the coming years.

1968

The Motion Picture Association of America institutes a rating system, running from G for general audiences to X, restricted to those over 16 or older (later 17 or older).

Avco buys Joseph E. Levine's Embassy Films.

FBI head J. Edgar Hoover decries the "sex, sadism, degeneracy and violence" in American films.

Film stars such as Barbra Streisand, Paul Newman, Shirley MacLaine, and Robert Ryan speak out against the war in Vietnam. Jane Fonda campaigns for Native American rights.

Valerie Solanis shoots artist/filmmaker Andy Warhol.

The Academy Awards ceremonies are delayed for two days because of the assassination of Martin Luther King, Jr.

Underground filmmaker Jack Smith's *Flaming Creatures* (1963), which features an orgy scene, is embroiled in a courtroom struggle over censorship.

Recognizing that the vast majority of films are now in color, the Motion Picture Academy drops the dual Oscars for black-and-white and color cinematography.

George Romero's *Night of the Living Dead,* a horror movie filmed in Pittsburgh for $114,000, brings in $12 million in rentals worldwide.

The groundbreaking special effects in *2001: A Space Odyssey* set a new standard for science fiction films and will be widely copied.

Woody Allen directs his first film, *Take the Money and Run.* Peter Bogdanovich's first picture as a director, *Targets,* is also actor Boris Karloff's last.

The Cannes Film Festival closes early when directors withdraw their films and jury members resign in response to director Jean-Luc Godard's plea that the festival support students and workers demonstrating and striking throughout France.

The Wild One (1954), starring Marlon Brando, is finally released in Britain. Censors had feared that the movie would provoke British teenagers to violence.

In the face of stiff resistance from the film community, the French government ends its attempt to control the Cinémathèque Française, the world's most famous film archive, and will allow André Langlois to continue to run it.

Soviet director Sergei Bondarchuk's seven-hour *War and Peace* is shown in two sections on successive days in its US engagement.

NOTABLE FILMS 1968

United States	
THE BOSTON STRANGLER	THE SWIMMER
BULLITT	TARGETS
CHARLIE BUBBLES	THE THOMAS CROWN AFFAIR
CHARLY	WILL PENNY
CHITTY CHITTY BANG BANG	*France*
COLOSSUS: THE FORBIN PROJECT	BAISERS VOLÉS (STOLEN KISSES)
COOGAN'S BLUFF	LA MARIÉE ÉTAIT EN NOIR (THE BRIDE WORE BLACK)
THE DETECTIVE	*France and Italy*
FACES	BARBARELLA
FINIAN'S RAINBOW	*Italy*
FLESH	TEOREMA (THEOREM)
THE FOX	*Italy and US*
FUNNY GIRL	C'ERA UNA VOLTA IL WEST (ONCE UPON A TIME IN THE WEST)
THE GREEN BERETS	
HEAD	*Sweden*
THE HEART IS A LONELY HUNTER	SKAMMEN (SHAME)
HELL IN THE PACIFIC	*United Kingdom*
ICE STATION ZEBRA	THE CHARGE OF THE LIGHT BRIGADE
MADIGAN	IF…
NIGHT OF THE LIVING DEAD	THE LION IN WINTER
THE ODD COUPLE	OLIVER!
THE PARTY	SHALAKO
PETULIA	2001: A SPACE ODYSSEY
PLANET OF THE APES	YELLOW SUBMARINE
PRETTY POISON	*UK and Italy*
THE PRODUCERS	ROMEO AND JULIET
ROSEMARY'S BABY	*USSR*
STAR!	WAR AND PEACE

1969

The Equal Employment Opportunities Commission puts Hollywood on notice: take positive steps to end racial job discrimination or the government will sue the film industry to end the practice. (The Nixon administration does not enforce this threat.)

MGM goes through three presidents in less than a year. The third, hotel executive Kirk Kerkorian, will de-emphasize film production, making MGM more of an entertainment conglomerate.

Barry Diller, 27, newly appointed head of ABC's film division, is a media star on the rise.

Producer Hal Wallis ends his 25-year association with Paramount and moves to Universal.

Midnight Cowboy, *released in 1969, was the first X-rated film to receive an Academy Award for best picture. Both Jon Voight and Dustin Hoffman were nominated for their performances.*

The Killing of Sister George, which has a lesbian theme, is banned in Boston.

The Carthay Circle theater, which has hosted many film premieres, including the Hollywood opening of *Gone with the Wind* in 1939, closes to make way for an office building.

Judy Garland dies from an overdose of sleeping pills. Her viewing and funeral in New York City draw 20,000 fans.

The murder of actress Sharon Tate, wife of director Roman Polanski, and four others by the Charles Manson "family" shocks the nation.

Midnight Cowboy is the first major production to draw an X rating and will be the only one to win an Oscar for best picture.

Graphic violence and liberalized sexual mores in Hollywood films, epitomized this year by *The Wild Bunch* and *Bob & Carol & Ted & Alice,* continue to be controversial.

Jag är nyfiken-en film i gult (I Am Curious-Yellow) (Sweden, 1967) has difficulty passing US Customs and creates a sensation with its explicit depictions of sex.

Although the French film industry remains vigorous artistically, the number of movie theaters continues to decline.

Algeria nationalizes all film organizations.

Director Miloš Forman remains in the West as the "Prague Spring" in his native Czechoslovakia gives way to stricter controls by the Communist Party.

1969: BIRTHS

JENNIFER ANISTON, FEB. 11
ROBERT SEAN LEONARD, FEB. 28
RENÉE ZELLWEGER APR. 25
CATE BLANCHETT, MAY 14
ANNE HECHE, MAY 25
ICE CUBE, JUNE 15
LOREN DEAN, JULY 31
EDWARD NORTON, AUG. 18
CHRISTIAN SLATER, AUG. 18
MATTHEW PERRY, AUG. 19
CATHERINE ZETA-JONES, SEPT. 25
MATTHEW MCCONAUGHEY, NOV. 4

1969: DEATHS

JOHN BOLES
CHARLES BRACKETT
JUDY GARLAND
LEO GORCEY
GABBY HAYES
SONJA HENIE
JEFFREY HUNTER
BORIS KARLOFF
ROD LA ROCQUE
LEO MCCAREY
BARTON MACLANE
ERIC PORTMAN
THELMA RITTER
JOSEF VON STERNBERG
ROBERT TAYLOR
RHYS WILLIAMS

NOTABLE FILMS 1969

United States
ALICE'S RESTAURANT
BOB & CAROL & TED & ALICE
A BOY NAMED CHARLIE BROWN
BUTCH CASSIDY AND THE SUNDANCE KID
CACTUS FLOWER
EASY RIDER
GOODBYE COLUMBUS
HELLO, DOLLY!
LAST SUMMER
THE LOVE BUG
MEDIUM COOL
MIDNIGHT COWBOY
MORE
PAINT YOUR WAGON
PUTNEY SWOPE
THE STERILE CUCKOO
SWEET CHARITY
TAKE THE MONEY AND RUN
THEY SHOOT HORSES, DON'T THEY?
TOPAZ
TRUE GRIT
THE WILD BUNCH

Algeria and France
Z

France
UNE FEMME DOUCE
MA NUIT CHEZ MAUD (MY NIGHT AT MAUD'S)

France and Brazil
ANTONIO DAS MORTES

France and Italy
LA SIRÈNE DU MISSISSIPPI (MISSISSIPPI MERMAID)

Italy and France
FELLINI SATYRICON (SATYRICON)

Italy and West Germany
GOTTERDAMMERUNG (THE DAMNED)

Switzerland
CHARLES—MORT OU VIF (CHARLES—DEAD OR ALIVE)

United Kingdom
ANNE OF THE THOUSAND DAYS
KES
OH! WHAT A LOVELY WAR
ON HER MAJESTY'S SECRET SERVICE
THE PRIME OF MISS JEAN BRODIE
WHERE EAGLES DARE
WOMEN IN LOVE

1970–1979

The decade that began bleakly with MGM's auction of Judy Garland's ruby slippers saw the art of film revitalized through iconoclastic young directors. Their hits included The Godfather *(1972) and* Star Wars *(1977).*

IN THE EARLY 1970s, Hollywood hit bottom. The years 1969-71 marked a depression for the American film industry, with 1971 the nadir of the 25-year economic decline begun after the peak year 1946. In 1970 MGM, once Hollywood's grandest studio, had sunk so low as to auction off its costumes and props – everything from the ruby slippers worn by Judy Garland in *The Wizard of Oz* to Ben-Hur's chariot. Hollywood, it seemed, had forgotten how to attract audiences to theaters and had no idea how to deal with the youth culture and social and racial polarization.

Hollywood's salvation came from a new generation of filmmakers: Francis Ford Coppola, Martin Scorsese, Steven Spielberg, George Lucas, William Friedkin, and Brian De Palma. Having grown up on Hollywood movies and lived through a time of social transformation, these directors proceeded to reinvent whole genres. They were given relatively free rein by studios that didn't know what else to do. Coppola's *The Godfather* (1972) and *The Godfather Part II* (1974) recast the gangster film as dark historical epic. Friedkin brought a new kind of urban realism to the crime film with *The French Connection* (1971) and a new level of shock to the horror film with *The Exorcist* (1973).

All these films were big moneymakers, but none compared to Spielberg's *Jaws* (1975) and Lucas's *Star Wars* (1977), the first films to earn more than $100 million in rentals. These two movies, one a man-versus-shark thriller, the other a science fiction swashbuckler, permanently changed Hollywood economics. From here on, the studios focused on

the annual production of a few huge blockbusters, usually youth-oriented, genre-based, action-packed, and laden with special effects. Before that trend solidified in the 1980s, commercial filmmakers enjoyed an unusual degree of latitude to innovate and experiment. Robert Altman's *M*A*S*H* (1970) and *Nashville* (1975), Scorsese's *Taxi Driver* (1976), Stanley Kubrick's *A Clockwork Orange* (1971), Michael Cimino's *The Deer Hunter* (1978), Mel Brooks's *Blazing Saddles* (1974), and Woody Allen's *Annie Hall* (1977) could not have been made in an earlier time and would perhaps be difficult to make today. Hollywood found profit in more traditional venues as well, such as the disaster-film cycle that began with *Airport* (1970) and *The Poseidon Adventure* (1972), and the comeback of the musical, represented by *Saturday Night Fever* (1977) and *Grease* (1978).

AIDING IN HOLLYWOOD'S ECONOMIC resurrection was the introduction of multiplexes – theaters with many screens that could show more films profitably; new cable outlets, such as Home Box Office; and the discovery, with *Jaws*, that saturation advertising on television coupled with wide release could translate into big box-office profits.

In many other countries, the 70s were bleaker. In Britain, domestic film production declined precipitously, although the country's top-notch studio facilities attracted many American filmmakers. The once-thriving film industries of Italy and Japan suffered through economic crises. Other countries experienced great creative ferment and won new audiences abroad. In Germany, youthful directors like Rainer Werner Fassbinder (*The Marriage of Maria Braun*, 1978) and Wim

AT LEFT: *Carrie Fisher and Mark Hamill starred in* Star Wars, *released in 1977. This timeless tale of good versus evil is one of the biggest box-office hits of all time.*

1970: BIRTHS

PAUL THOMAS ANDERSON, JAN. 1
SKEET ULRICH, JAN. 20
HEATHER GRAHAM, JAN. 29
MINNIE DRIVER, JAN. 31
LARA FLYNN BOYLE, MAR. 24
UMA THURMAN, APR. 29
SAMANTHA MATHIS, MAY 12
JOSEPH FIENNES, MAY 27
CHRIS O'DONNELL, JUNE 26
JENNIFER LOPEZ, JULY 24
RIVER PHOENIX, AUG. 23
EMILY LLOYD, SEPT. 29
MATT DAMON, OCT. 8
ETHAN HAWKE, NOV. 6
JENNIFER CONNELLY, DEC. 12

1970: DEATHS

ED BEGLEY
BILLIE BURKE
FRANCES FARMER
PRESTON FOSTER
EDWARD EVERETT HORTON
ROSCOE KARNS
ANITA LOUISE
CONRAD NAGEL
ALFRED NEWMAN
CATHY O'DONNELL
MARJORIE RAMBEAU
CHARLES RUGGLES
INGER STEVENS
SYLVIE
PERC WESTMORE

Marlon Brando came close to not playing the title role in *The Godfather*. Director Francis Ford Coppola favored the English actor Laurence Olivier for the part of Don Corleone, and Paramount was not anxious to work with the ever-difficult Marlon Brando. But Mario Puzo, who wrote the novel *The Godfather* and also cowrote the screenplay, insisted on Marlon Brando. When the offer came, Brando could not refuse it.

Wenders led the Young German Cinema, notable for its leftist critique of bourgeois life, to international recognition. Australian filmmakers like Peter Weir (*Picnic at Hanging Rock,* 1975), Bruce Beresford, and Gillian Armstrong put their country in the world cinema spotlight for the first time. Similarly, Poland's Andrzej Wajda and Krzysztof Kieslowski and Brazil's Bruno Barreto brought worldwide attention to their countries' film industries.

--- CHRONOLOGY ---

1970

Pressured by the Justice Department to end discrimination, the American film industry institutes a job pool for minorities.

PG replaces GP (which had previously replaced M) in the rating system, and the minimum age for admission to R and X designated films is raised to 17.

Richard D. Zanuck is forced out at 20th Century–Fox, where big losses from recent films put the studio's future in jeopardy. The other major studios are also coping with steady losses.

Paramount's new president, 30-year-old Stanley Jaffe, is the youngest studio head in Hollywood history.

The first of a chain of Jerry Lewis Cinemas opens.

MGM relocates its executive offices from New York to Hollywood and auctions off its costumes and props, including Tarzan's loincloth.

Vice President Spiro Agnew attacks rock films that "brainwash" youth into finding the drug culture appealing.

The US Army and Air Force ban the showing of *M*A*S*H* – a Grand Prix winner at Cannes – on their bases because of the film's cynical attitude toward the military.

At the singer/actor's request, President Nixon appoints Elvis Presley an honorary special agent in the antidrug task force.

John Wayne's portrayal of Rooster Cogburn in last year's *True Grit* gains him his first Oscar, for best actor.

Exploitation filmmaker Russ Meyer's *Beyond the Valley of the Dolls* has a screenplay by movie critic Roger Ebert.

As the year begins, the British film industry has only four major productions under way.

A drive-in opens near Paris, the first in the metropolitan area.

In Italy, *Investigation of a Citizen Above Suspicion* creates an uproar with its cynical portrayal of police corruption.

Akira Kurosawa's *Dodes'ka-den* is his first film in five years.

NOTABLE FILMS 1970

United States	
AIRPORT	WOODSTOCK
THE ARISTOCATS	ZABRISKIE POINT
THE BALLAD OF CABLE HOGUE	**US and Japan** TORA! TORA! TORA!
BENEATH THE PLANET OF THE APES	**US and Yugoslavia** KELLY'S HEROES
BEYOND THE VALLEY OF THE DOLLS	**France** BORSALINO
THE BOYS IN THE BAND	DOMICILE CONJUGAL (BED AND BOARD)
BREWSTER MCCLOUD	L'ENFANT SAUVAGE (THE WILD CHILD)
CATCH-22	LE GENOU DE CLAIRE (CLAIRE'S KNEE)
COTTON COMES TO HARLEM	**France and Italy** LE BOUCHER (THE BUTCHER)
DARLING LILI	
FIVE EASY PIECES	**France, Italy, and Spain** TRISTANA
THE GREAT WHITE HOPE	**Italy** INDAGINE SU UN
HUSBANDS	CITTADINO AL DI SOPRA
JOE	DI OGNI SOSPETTO
LITTLE BIG MAN	(INVESTIGATION OF A CITIZEN ABOVE
LOVE STORY	SUSPICION)
A MAN CALLED HORSE	**Italy, France, and West Germany**
M*A*S*H	IL CONFORMISTA
MYRA BRECKENRIDGE	(THE CONFORMIST)
ON A CLEAR DAY YOU CAN SEE FOREVER	**Japan** DODES'KA-DEN
THE OWL AND THE PUSSYCAT	**United Kingdom** PERFORMANCE
PATTON	THE PRIVATE LIFE OF SHERLOCK HOLMES
RIO LOBO	
START THE REVOLUTION WITHOUT ME	RYAN'S DAUGHTER
TOO LATE THE HERO	SCROOGE
THE TWELVE CHAIRS	10 RILLINGTON PLACE
WHERE'S POPPA?	

1971

The average ticket price in American theaters is $1.65, but many second-run houses find success by dropping their admission to $1.

Hollywood executives get the investment tax credit they and California governor Ronald Reagan have requested from the federal government to aid an ailing domestic film industry.

Italian-Americans have successfully pressured Francis Ford Coppola not to use the word *Mafia* in his film of Mario Puzo's *The Godfather*.

Barbra Streisand and Gregory Peck are among the film figures on President Nixon's "Enemies List."

Samuel Goldwyn is awarded the Presidential Medal of Freedom.

Stanley Kubrick's *A Clockwork Orange* is one of the few major films to draw an X rating.

The actor making the biggest news at this year's Oscar ceremonies isn't there. George C. Scott has said he would refuse the best actor award for *Patton* (1970) but wins it nevertheless.

Georgia bans Mike Nichols's *Carnal Knowledge* for obscenity, a ruling that the Supreme Court will overturn.

The government-run French television network declines to show Marcel Ophüls's *Le Chagrin et la Pitié (The Sorrow and the Pity)*, a documentary about French collaboration with the Germans in World War II.

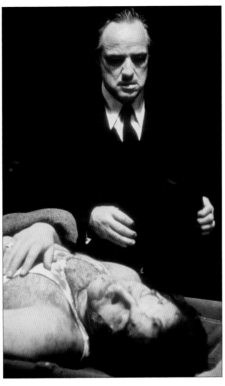

Director Pier Paolo Pasolini is again in trouble with Italian censors, this time over *The Decameron*.

Five years after Andrei Tarkovsky's *Andrei Rublev* (1966) was celebrated at Cannes, Soviet authorities have authorized its release in the USSR.

In 1971, Marlon Brando starred as Don Vito Corleone in The Godfather, *the first of a trilogy that has become an American cultural institution.*

1971: BIRTHS

SEAN ASTIN, FEB. 25
ANNABETH GISH, MAR. 13
EWAN MCGREGOR, MAR. 31
MARK WAHLBERG, JUNE 5
TUPAC SHAKUR, JUNE 16
COREY FELDMAN, JULY 16
DAVID ARQUETTE, SEPT. 8
WINONA RYDER, OCT. 29
CHRISTINA APPLEGATE, NOV. 25
COREY HAIM, DEC. 23
JUDE LAW, DEC. 29

1971: DEATHS

BRONCO BILLY ANDERSON
PIER ANGELI
SPRING BYINGTON
TULLIO CARMINATI
CHESTER CONKLIN
BEBE DANIELS
GLENDA FARRELL
FERNANDEL
JAY C. FLIPPEN
BILLY GILBERT
THOMAS GOMEZ
RAYMOND HATTON
VAN HEFLIN
HAROLD LLOYD
EDMUND LOWE
PAUL LUKAS
AUDIE MURPHY
CHIPS RAFFERTY
MICHAEL RENNIE
DOUGLAS SHEARER
MAX STEINER
PAUL TERRY

NOTABLE FILMS 1971

United States
THE ABOMINABLE DR. PHIBES
THE ANDERSON TAPES
THE ANDROMEDA STRAIN
BANANAS
BEDKNOBS AND BROOMSTICKS
BILLY JACK
BLESS THE BEASTS AND CHILDREN
A CLOCKWORK ORANGE
DIRTY HARRY
$ (DOLLARS)
FIDDLER ON THE ROOF
THE FRENCH CONNECTION
HAROLD AND MAUDE

THE HOSPITAL
KLUTE
THE LAST PICTURE SHOW
A NEW LEAF
MCCABE AND MRS. MILLER
THE OMEGA MAN
THE PANIC IN NEEDLE PARK
PLAY MISTY FOR ME
SHAFT
SILENT RUNNING
SUPPORT YOUR LOCAL GUNFIGHTER
SUMMER OF '42
SWEET SWEETBACK'S BADASSSSS SONG

TAKING OFF
EL TOPO
TWO-LANE BLACKTOP
WILLY WONKA AND THE CHOCOLATE FACTORY
WILLARD

Australia
WALKABOUT

France
LE SOUFFLE AU COEUR (MURMUR OF THE HEART)

France, Switzerland, and Germany
LE CHAGRIN ET LA PITIÉ (THE SORROW AND THE PITY)

Italy
MORTE A VENEZIA (DEATH IN VENICE)

Italy and Germany
IL GIARDINO DEI FINZI-CONTINI (THE GARDEN OF THE FINZI-CONTINIS)

United Kingdom
AND NOW FOR SOMETHING COMPLETELY DIFFERENT
THE BOY FRIEND
THE DEVILS
DIAMONDS ARE FOREVER
THE GO-BETWEEN
MACBETH
STRAW DOGS
SUNDAY, BLOODY SUNDAY

1972

The inauguration of Home Box Office movie broadcasts on a limited scale is the beginning of a new venue for recent feature films: premium cable channels and, ultimately, pay-per-view service.

CBS drops out of the feature-film production business.

The refusal of many theaters to show X-rated films and of newspapers to accept ads for them forces Stanley Kubrick to re-edit *A Clockwork Orange* to earn an R rating.

The pornographic film *Deep Throat* is the subject of legal action in many localities.

After almost four decades, *Life* magazine, which has helped sustain the popularity of Hollywood's films and movie stars, ends weekly publication.

Francis Ford Coppola's crime drama *The Godfather* opens to record box-office and considerable controversy over its violence and portrayal of Italian-Americans.

The Poseidon Adventure is the first of a cycle of popular disaster films.

Superfly and *Blacula* are two of a string of blaxploitation films starring African-American actors.

The publication of the shooting script of *Citizen Kane* (1941) provokes a controversy over the relative contributions of Orson Welles and Herman J. Mankiewicz.

Jane Fonda's visit to Hanoi enrages many Americans.

Charlie Chaplin visits the US for the first time in two decades, accepting an award from the Film Society of Lincoln Center and an honorary Academy Award.

Anti-Castro youth disrupt the first Cuban Film Festival in New York City.

Die-hard partisans and opponents of the former French occupation of Algeria exchange punches at a Bordeaux theater showing *La Battaglia di Algeri (The Battle of Algiers)* (1965).

In Paris, the Gaumont Palace cinema, built in 1911 to seat 6,000, closes to make way for a shopping center and hotel.

The Johannesburg Film Society abandons its best picture award because censorship by the South African government will not permit the screening of the best films.

1972: Births

CATHERINE McCORMACK, JAN. 1
JENNIFER ESPOSITO, APR. 19
ALISON EASTWOOD, MAY 22
ROBIN TUNNEY, JUNE 19
SELMA BLAIR, JUNE 23
CLAIRE FORLANI, JULY 1
BEN AFFLECK, AUG. 15
CAMERON DIAZ, AUG. 30

1972: Deaths

WILLIAM BOYD
BRUCE CABOT
LEO G. CARROLL
MAURICE CHEVALIER
BRANDON DE WILDE
WILLIAM DIETERLE
BRIAN DONLEVY
MIRIAM HOPKINS
ISABEL JEWELL
MARILYN MAXWELL
LOUELLA PARSONS
J. ARTHUR RANK
MARGARET RUTHERFORD
GEORGE SANDERS
GIA SCALA
AKIM TAMIROFF
FRANK TASHLIN
EDGAR G. ULMER
MARIE WILSON

NOTABLE FILMS 1972

United States
AVANTI!
BLACULA
CABARET
THE CANDIDATE
DELIVERANCE
EVERYTHING YOU ALWAYS WANTED TO KNOW ABOUT SEX (BUT WERE AFRAID TO ASK)
FAT CITY
FRITZ THE CAT
THE GETAWAY
THE GODFATHER
THE HOT ROCK
JEREMIAH JOHNSON
THE KING OF MARVIN GARDENS
LADY SINGS THE BLUES
THE LIFE AND TIMES OF JUDGE ROY BEAN
THE NEW CENTURIONS
PINK FLAMINGOS
PLAY IT AGAIN SAM
THE POSEIDON ADVENTURE
1776
SLAUGHTERHOUSE-FIVE
SOUNDER
SUPERFLY
WHAT'S UP, DOC?

France
LE GRAND BLOND AVEC UNE CHAUSSURE NOIRE (THE TALL BLOND MAN WITH ONE BLACK SHOE)

France and Italy
ULTIMO TANGO A PARIGI (LAST TANGO IN PARIS)

France, Italy, and Spain
LE CHARME DISCRET DE LA BOURGEOISIE (THE DISCREET CHARM OF THE BOURGEOISIE)

France, Italy, and UK
L'ASSASSINIO DI TROTSKY (THE ASSASSINATION OF TROTSKY)

Germany
AGUIRRE, DER ZORN GOTTES (AGUIRRE, THE WRATH OF GOD)

Italy
IL CASO MATTEI (THE MATTEI AFFAIR)
FELLINI'S ROMA
MIMI METALLURGIO FERITO NELL'ONORE (THE SEDUCTION OF MIMI)

Sweden
VISKNINGAR OCH ROP (CRIES AND WHISPERS)

United Kingdom
FRENZY
THE RULING CLASS
SLEUTH

1973

The Supreme Court revises the criteria state and local governments may use for censorship, making the appeal to "prurient interest" and offense to "community standards" key tests.

MGM announces it will release its films through United Artists.

Jerry Lewis withdraws from participation in the chain of movie theaters that bears his name.

The First American Film Institute Life Achievement Award is presented to director John Ford.

Major film openings are moved from midweek to Fridays.

Columbia Pictures moves its executive offices from New York City to Los Angeles.

The soon-to-be scandal-plagued David Begelman becomes president of Columbia Pictures.

The American Film Theater releases its first picture, *The Iceman Cometh,* based on the play by Eugene O'Neill.

Marlon Brando, supporting rights for Native Americans, sends a woman who identifies herself as Sacheen Littlefeather, an Apache, to the Oscars in his place to decline his best actor award for *The Godfather* (1972). She is later revealed to be an actress named Maria Cruz.

Inspired by a true story, the 1973 film The Exorcist, *with Kitty Winn and Jason Miller, featured Linda Blair as a child possessed by a demon.*

Deep Throat (1972) faces legal challenges for pornography throughout the US

The Exorcist is the first of a string of popular films focusing on the occult.

Bruce Lee's mysterious death comes just as his martial arts films are bringing big popularity to that genre.

Charlie Chaplin finally permits the release of *A King in New York* (1957) in the US.

British actor Roger Moore is the new James Bond.

An Italian court finds director Bernardo Bertolucci not guilty of obscenity for his film *Ultimo Tango a Parigi (Last Tango in Paris)* (1972).

Director Marco Ferreri's *La Grande Bouffe (Blow-Out)* about people eating themselves to death, causes an uproar at Cannes, where audiences find it in poor taste.

The first International Festival of Horror and Fantasy Films, held in Avoriaz, France, awards first prize to *Duel,* the first feature film (1971, made-for-television) directed by Steven Spielberg.

1973: BIRTHS

OMAR EPPS, MAY 16
JULIETTE LEWIS, JUNE 21
STEPHEN DORFF, JULY 29
PAUL WALKER, SEPT. 12
GWYNETH PALTROW, SEPT. 28
NEVE CAMPBELL, OCT. 3
GRETCHEN MOL, NOV. 8

1973: DEATHS

ROBERT ARMSTRONG
SIDNEY BLACKMER
JOE E. BROWN
LON CHANEY, JR.
MERIAN C. COOPER
NOËL COWARD
BOBBY DARIN
JOHN FORD
ARTHUR FREED
BETTY GRABLE
LAURENCE HARVEY
JACK HAWKINS
SESSUE HAYAKAWA
VERONICA LAKE
ROCKY LANE
BRUCE LEE
LILA LEE
ANNA MAGNANI
KEN MAYNARD
J. CARROL NAISH
KATINA PAXINOU
EDWARD G. ROBINSON
ROBERT RYAN
ROBERT SIODMAK
CONSTANCE TALMADGE
BUD WESTMORE
WALLY WESTMORE

NOTABLE FILMS 1973

United States
AMERICAN GRAFFITI
BADLANDS
BANG THE DRUM SLOWLY
CHARLEY VARRICK
CHARLOTTE'S WEB
CINDERELLA LIBERTY
ELECTRA GLIDE IN BLUE
EMPEROR OF THE NORTH
ENTER THE DRAGON
THE EXORCIST
HIGH PLAINS DRIFTER
THE ICEMAN COMETH
JESUS CHRIST SUPERSTAR
THE LAST DETAIL
THE LAST OF SHEILA
THE LONG GOODBYE
MAGNUM FORCE
MEAN STREETS
THE PAPER CHASE
PAPER MOON
PAPILLON
PAT GARRETT & BILLY THE KID
SAVE THE TIGER
SERPICO
SISTERS
SLEEPER
SOYLENT GREEN
STEELYARD BLUES
THE STING
WALKING TALL
THE WAY WE WERE
WESTWORLD

France
LA NUIT AMÉRICAINE (DAY FOR NIGHT)
LACOMBE LUCIEN
LA PLANÈTE SAUVAGE (FANTASTIC PLANET)

Italy
LA GRANDE BOUFFE (BLOW-OUT)

Italy and UK
FRATELLO SOLE SORELLA LUNA (BROTHER SUN SISTER MOON)

Jamaica
THE HARDER THEY COME

Spain
THE SPIRIT OF THE BEEHIVE

United Kingdom
THE LEGEND OF HELL HOUSE
LIVE AND LET DIE
O LUCKY MAN!
THEATRE OF BLOOD
A TOUCH OF CLASS
THE WICKER MAN

UK and France
THE DAY OF THE JACKAL

UK, France, and Italy
DON'T LOOK NOW

1974

Members of the Screen Actors Guild no longer have to take the loyalty oath instituted during the blacklist period.

Richard Heffner heads the office that enforces the Motion Picture Association rating system.

A fire sweeps through the Samuel Goldwyn Studios causing $3 million worth of damage.

MGM's profits increase but from the studio's Las Vegas hotel-casino, not its films.

The inauguration of the Telluride Film Festival is marred by protests against an award to Leni Riefenstahl, whom critics charge with making films for Hitler.

People **magazine** begins publication, assuming *Life* magazine's role of publicizing the movies and their stars. Mia Farrow is on the first cover.

Walt Rostow, who helped plan the war in Vietnam, tries unsuccessfully to block the opening of Peter Davis's *Hearts and Minds,* a documentary about the conflict.

A streaker runs on camera as David Niven speaks at the Academy Awards ceremony.

The first woman producer to share a best picture Oscar is Julia Phillips, who receives the honor for *The Sting.*

Warner Bros. and 20th Century–Fox, in a unique feature-film venture, jointly produce *The Towering Inferno.*

Indicative of the new strain of violence in film culture, *The Texas Chainsaw Massacre* becomes a cult classic.

The production of feature films in France hits a new high of 234 this year.

Soviet director Sergo Paradjanov (*Shadows of Our Forgotten Ancestors,* 1964) is imprisoned in the USSR for homosexuality and other charges.

Mexico opens a cinémathèque patterned after the one in France.

A nude scene in *Siddhartha* creates a controversy at the India Film Festival.

Egyptian censors bow to protests and permit the release of director Youssef Chahine's *The Sparrow,*(1973) about the 1967 Six-Day War with Israel.

1975

The Screen Actors Guild elects its first female president, Kathleen Nolan.

SONY demonstrates a $2,000 home videotape machine for the upscale market, called a Betamax.

Michael Ovitz and several colleagues from the William Morris Agency establish the Creative Artists Agency.

The American Film Institute unveils the first issue of its monthly film magazine, *American Film.* The cover features *All the President's Men* stars Dustin Hoffman and Robert Redford.

1974: BIRTHS

CHRISTIAN BALE, JAN. 30
PENÉLOPE CRUZ, APR. 28
HILARY SWANK, JULY 20
NATASHA HENSTRIDGE, AUG. 15
RYAN PHILLIPPE, SEPT. 10
JEREMY SISTO, OCT. 6
JOAQUIN PHOENIX, OCT. 28
LEONARDO DI CAPRIO, NOV. 11
CHLOÉ SEVIGNY, NOV. 18

1974: DEATHS

BUD ABBOTT
JACK BENNY
WALTER BRENNAN
CLIVE BROOK
JOHNNY MACK BROWN
BETTY COMPSON
DONALD CRISP
VITTORIO DE SICA
LARRY FINE
SAMUEL GOLDWYN
OTTO KRUGER
ANATOLE LITVAK
AGNES MOOREHEAD
MARCEL PAGNOL
TEX RITTER

NOTABLE FILMS 1974

United States		A WOMAN UNDER THE INFLUENCE	Italy
ALICE DOESN'T LIVE HERE ANYMORE	HARRY AND TONTO	YOUNG FRANKENSTEIN	AMARCORD
BENJI	LENNY	**Canada**	C'ERAVAMO TANTO AMATI (WE ALL LOVED EACH OTHER SO MUCH)
BLAZING SADDLES	THE LONGEST YARD	THE APPRENTICESHIP OF DUDDY KRAVITZ	**Sweden**
CALIFORNIA SPLIT	THE LORDS OF FLATBUSH	**France**	TROLLFLÖJTEN (THE MAGIC FLUTE)
CHINATOWN	THE MAGIC FLUTE	LE FANTÔME DE LA LIBERTÉ (THE PHANTOM OF LIBERTY)	**United Kingdom**
THE CONVERSATION	THE PARALLAX VIEW		THE GOLDEN VOYAGE OF SINBAD
DARK STAR	PHANTOM OF THE PARADISE	L'HORLOGER DE SAINT-PAUL (THE CLOCKMAKER)	JUGGERNAUT
DEATH WISH	THE SUGARLAND EXPRESS	LES VALSEUSES (GOING PLACES)	THE MAN WITH THE GOLDEN GUN
DIRTY MARY CRAZY LARRY	THE TAKING OF PELHAM ONE TWO THREE	**Germany**	MURDER ON THE ORIENT EXPRESS
EARTHQUAKE	THE TEXAS CHAIN SAW MASSACRE	ANGST ESSEN SEELE AUF (ALI FEAR EATS THE SOUL)	THE ODESSA FILE
THE FRONT PAGE	THAT'S ENTERTAINMENT		THE THREE MUSKETEERS
THE GODFATHER, PART II	THUNDERBOLT AND LIGHTFOOT		
THE GREAT GATSBY	THE TOWERING INFERNO		

The Walt Disney Company sues to force the producers of the pornographic film *The Happy Hooker* to delete the *Mickey Mouse Club* theme song from an orgy scene.

At the Academy Awards ceremony, a coproducer of the winning documentary, *Hearts and Minds,* reads a telegram from the Viet Cong recognizing the support of sympathetic Americans. Under pressure from his cohost Bob Hope, Frank Sinatra responds by reading a statement that disassociates the Academy from the telegram.

Twenty years after he won an Oscar for his screenplay *The Brave One,* blacklisted writer Dalton Trumbo actually receives the statuette.

Steven Spielberg's 1975 blockbuster adaptation of Peter Benchley's novel Jaws *left the public terrified of the water and inordinately fearful of 25-foot killer sharks.*

FBI and CIA harassment and surveillance of Hollywood activist Jane Fonda comes to light.

Steven Spielberg's *Jaws* innovates massive television advertising of films opening in wide release.

George Burns, whose last film appearance was in 1939, begins a new stage of his career with *The Sunshine Boys.*

The US issues a stamp honoring D.W. Griffith.

France announces its own version of the Oscar: the César.

The French government withdraws subsidies from all X-rated films.

Controversial Italian director Pier Paolo Pasolini is murdered in Bologna, Italy.

NOTABLE FILMS 1975

United States
A BOY AND HIS DOG
THE DAY OF THE LOCUST
DEATH RACE 2000
DOG DAY AFTERNOON
ESCAPE TO WITCH MOUNTAIN
THE FRENCH CONNECTION II
FUNNY LADY
THE GREAT WALDO PEPPER
HARD TIMES
HEARTS OF THE WEST
THE HINDENBURG
JAWS
LOVE AND DEATH
NASHVILLE
NIGHT MOVES
ONE FLEW OVER THE CUCKOO'S NEST
ROLLERBALL
ROOSTER COGBURN
SHAMPOO
THE STEPFORD WIVES
THE SUNSHINE BOYS
THREE DAYS OF THE CONDOR
THE WIND AND THE LION
THE YAKUZA

Australia
PICNIC AT HANGING ROCK

France
COUSIN COUSINE
L'HISTOIRE D'ADÈLE H. (THE STORY OF ADELE H.)

Germany
JEDER FÜR SICH UND GOTT GEGEN ALLE (EVERY MAN FOR HIMSELF AND GOD AGAINST ALL)
DIE VERLORENE EHRE DER KATHARINA BLUM (THE LOST HONOR OF KATHARINA BLUM)

Italy
TRAVOLTI DA UN INSOLITO DESTINO NELL'AZZURRO MARE D'AGOSTO (SWEPT AWAY)

United Kingdom
BARRY LYNDON
FAREWELL, MY LOVELY
THE MAN WHO WOULD BE KING
MONTY PYTHON AND THE HOLY GRAIL
RETURN OF THE PINK PANTHER
THE ROCKY HORROR PICTURE SHOW
TOMMY

USSR and Japan
DERSU UZALA

Mark Frechette once had the world at his feet. An unknown actor, he landed the male lead in Michelangelo Antonioni's first English-language film, *Zabriskie Point* (1970). But the reviews weren't good, and his career languished. In 1973 he was arrested in Boston for robbing a bank. He died in prison in 1975 under mysterious circumstances.

1976

The number of drive-in screens in the US, which peaked at slightly more than 4,700 in the late 1950s, has declined to 3,600.

Hollywood Boulevard, long a tourist mecca in the nation's film capital, has become run-down and infested with adult bookstores.

Paramount announces that it will release films from its library in Sony's Betamax video format.

Columbia president David Begelman forges actor Cliff Robertson's signature on a check, touching off a major scandal.

Alan Ladd, Jr., heads film production at 20th Century–Fox, while Michael Eisner, a television executive, heads film production and is CEO at Paramount.

The filming of *Rocky* sees the first major use of the handheld Steadicam.

Francis Ford Coppola films *Apocalypse Now* in the Philippines. This year and next, the production is delayed by a typhoon, Martin Sheen's heart attack, and the late arrival of Marlon Brando.

About 34 million people, the most ever to see a feature film on television, watch the first broadcast of *Gone with the Wind* (1939) on two successive nights.

Elizabeth Taylor divorces Richard Burton for the second and last time.

John Wayne ends six decades in films with his lead performance in the elegiac western *The Shootist*.

Britain imposes a tax of 75 percent on the worldwide film earnings of foreign producers who live in Great Britain.

Director Jean Renoir is inducted as an officer in the French Legion of Honor.

An Italian court declares *Ultimo Tango a Parigi (Last Tango in Paris)* (1972) obscene and declares anyone connected with the film, including star Marlon Brando, liable to arrest.

Swedish director Ingmar Bergman says that his arrest in Sweden for tax evasion – which resulted in a nervous breakdown – will force him to live and work abroad.

Both Japanese and US censors ban Nagisa Oshima's *Ai No Corrida (In the Realm of the Senses)*, a film about obsessive sex.

1976: Births

FREDDIE PRINZE, JR., MAR. 8
REESE WITHERSPOON, MAR. 22
LUKAS HAAS, APR. 16
ALICIA SILVERSTONE, OCT. 4

1976: Deaths

RICHARD ARLEN
STANLEY BAKER
BUSBY BERKELEY
LEE J. COBB
RAY CORRIGAN
FRANKIE DARRO
JEAN GABIN
JAMES WONG HOWE
HOWARD HUGHES
FUZZY KNIGHT
FRITZ LANG
MARGARET LEIGHTON
ROGER LIVESEY
SAL MINEO
CAROL REED
PAUL ROBESON
ROSALIND RUSSELL
ALASTAIR SIM
SYBIL THORNDIKE
DALTON TRUMBO
LUCHINO VISCONTI
ADOLPH ZUKOR

Apocalypse Now, *filmed in the Philippines in 1976–77, was plagued with problems, including a typhoon that destroyed sets, Martin Sheen's heart attack, and the outbreak of civil war.*

NOTABLE FILMS 1976

United States	
ALL THE PRESIDENT'S MEN	THE SHOOTIST
ASSAULT ON PRECINCT 13	SILENT MOVIE
THE BAD NEWS BEARS	SILVER STREAK
THE BINGO LONG TRAVELING ALL-STARS & MOTOR KINGS	A STAR IS BORN
	TAXI DRIVER
BOUND FOR GLORY	**Canada**
BREAKHEART PASS	THE LITTLE GIRL WHO LIVES DOWN THE LANE
CAR WASH	**France**
CARRIE	L'ARGENT DE POCHE
THE ENFORCER	**France and US**
FAMILY PLOT	LE LOCATAIRE (THE TENANT)
THE FRONT	**Germany**
KING KONG	IM LAUF DER ZEIT (KINGS OF THE ROAD)
THE LAST TYCOON	**Italy**
LOGAN'S RUN	ALLEGRO NON TROPPO
MARATHON MAN	PASQUALINO SETTEBELLEZZE (SEVEN BEAUTIES)
THE MISSOURI BREAKS	**Italy, France, and Germany**
MURDER BY DEATH	NOVECENTO (1900)
NETWORK	**Switzerland**
NEXT STOP, GREENWICH VILLAGE	JONAS QUI AURA 25 ANS EN L'AN 2000 (JONAH WHO WILL BE 25 IN THE YEAR 2000)
THE OMEN	
THE OUTLAW JOSEY WALES	**United Kingdom**
THE PINK PANTHER STRIKES AGAIN	BUGSY MALONE
	THE EAGLE HAS LANDED
ROCKY	THE MAN WHO FELL TO EARTH
THE SEVEN-PER-CENT SOLUTION	ROBIN AND MARIAN

1977

Entering wide release in May, *Star Wars* brings in $127 million in rental earnings this year and ultimately sells $2.5 billion in movie-related merchandise.

Star Wars ensures the success of Dolby stereo sound tracks.

20th Century–Fox begins to release its films on videotape.

The American Film Institute's poll of its 350,000 members declares *Gone with the Wind* America's greatest film.

Columbia reveals that its president, David Begelman, has embezzled $60,000. His reinstatement after a suspension raises the issue of possible widespread corruption in the industry.

The showing of *Mohammed, Messenger of God* is temporarily suspended in major markets when Black Muslims protest the film by taking hostages in Washington, D.C.

Italian director Lina Wertmuller enjoys enormous popularity in America. *New York* magazine calls her "the most important film director since Bergman."

Piper Laurie makes her first film apprearance in 15 years, as Sissy Spacek's mother in *Carrie*.

Director Roman Polanski is arrested for statutory rape.

Bette Davis is the first woman to receive the American Film Institute Life Achievement Award.

Director Francis Ford Coppola is forced to mortgage his home as collateral on a loan to finish the beleaguered *Apocalypse Now*.

The man-tailored attire of Diane Keaton in *Annie Hall* starts a new fashion trend.

Left-wing film director Claude Autant-Lara publicly blames France's New Wave directors and their films for the decline in French film attendance.

With Francisco Franco's death, Spain abolishes censorship, finally permitting the release of Luis Buñuel's *Viridiana* (1961).

NOTABLE FILMS 1977

United States		
ANNIE HALL	PUMPING IRON	L'UNE CHANTE L'AUTRE PAS (ONE SINGS, THE OTHER DOESN'T)
BETWEEN THE LINES	SATURDAY NIGHT FEVER	
BLACK SUNDAY	SLAP SHOT	
A BRIDGE TOO FAR	SMOKEY AND THE BANDIT	**France and Ivory Coast**
CLOSE ENCOUNTERS OF THE THIRD KIND	SORCERER	NOIRS ET BLANCS EN COULEURS (BLACK AND WHITE IN COLOR)
EQUUS	THE SPY WHO LOVED ME	
FUN WITH DICK AND JANE	STAR WARS	**Germany**
THE GAUNTLET	TELEFON	DER AMERIKANISCHE FREUND (THE AMERICAN FRIEND)
THE GOODBYE GIRL	THREE WOMEN	
HIGH ANXIETY	THE TURNING POINT	**Italy**
THE ISLAND OF DR. MOREAU	**US and Germany**	SUSPIRIA
.JULIA	TWILIGHT'S LAST GLEAMING	**Poland**
THE KENTUCKY FRIED MOVIE	**Australia**	MAN OF MARBLE
THE LATE SHOW	THE LAST WAVE	**Spain and France**
LOOKING FOR MR. GOODBAR	**France**	CET OBSCUR OBJET DU DÉSIR (THAT OBSCURE OBJECT OF DESIRE)
NEW YORK, NEW YORK	L'HOMME QUI AIMAIT LES FEMMES (THE MAN WHO LOVED WOMEN)	
OH, GOD!	MR. KLEIN	**United Kingdom**
		THE DUELLISTS

1978

The decline in the production of Hollywood films is evident in this year's 354 releases, down from last year's 560.

Hollywood studio executives are uneasy about the inroads that feature films on home video (this year on laser disks as well as tape) may make in theater attendance.

Most films will be protected for 75 years under the new US copyright law.

A substantial collection of old newsreels is lost in a fire at the National Archives.

Five United Artists executives resign and form Orion Pictures.

Vanessa Redgrave sparks protests at the Oscar ceremony when she makes a pro-Palestinian speech upon accepting her award for best supporting actress.

In June, three months after the uproar over Vanessa Redgrave at the Oscar awards ceremony, a bomb goes off during the night at a Los Angeles theater screening Redgrave's documentary, *The Palestinian*.

The day before facing sentencing for corrupting a minor, Roman Polanski flees the US for France.

1978: BIRTHS
Katie Holmes, Dec. 18

1978: DEATHS
Ford Beebe
Charles Boyer
John Cazale
Dan Dailey
Claude Dauphin
Louis de Rochemont
Lee Garmes
Leo Genn
Oscar Homolka
Tim McCoy
Jack Oakie
Robert Shaw
Jack Warner
Gig Young

Marlon Brando's compensation for his brief appearance in *Superman* was $2,225,000, almost half the production cost of an average Hollywood film. Jamie Lee Curtis received a mere $8,000 for her debut starring role, in *Halloween*.

A scene involving Russian roulette in Michael Cimino's *The Deer Hunter* provokes concern that impressionable people may imitate it.

Robert De Niro was nominated for an Academy Award for The Deer Hunter, *which won the 1978 Oscar for best picture and best director (Michael Cimino).*

NOTABLE FILMS 1978

United States
Blue Collar
The Boys from Brazil
The Boys in Company C
The Buddy Holly Story
California Suite
Capricorn One
The Cheap Detective
Coma
Coming Home
Days of Heaven
The Deer Hunter
The End
Eraserhead
Eyes of Laura Mars
Foul Play
The Fury
Girlfriends
Grease
Halloween
Heaven Can Wait
Hooper
Interiors
Invasion of the Body Snatchers
The Last Waltz
Midnight Express
National Lampoon's Animal House
Pretty Baby
Same Time, Next Year
Straight Time
Superman
An Unmarried Woman
Up in Smoke
The Wiz
Who Is Killing the Great Chefs of Europe?
Who'll Stop the Rain?

Australia
The Chant of Jimmie Blacksmith

Brazil
Doña Flor e Seus Dois Moridos (Doña Flor and Her Two Husbands)

France
Diabolo Menthe (Peppermint Soda)

France and Belgium
Préparez vos Mouchoirs (Get Out Your Handkerchiefs)

France and Italy
La Cage aux Folles

Germany
Die Ehe der Maria Braun (The Marriage of Maria Braun)

Sweden
Herbstsonate (Autumn Sonata)

United Kingdom
Death on the Nile
Watership Down

Bowing to protests, the Hollywood Chamber of Commerce rescinds its previous refusal to grant the leftist singer-actor Paul Robeson a star in the Hollywood Walk of Fame.

Gene Siskel and Roger Ebert begin to review films on public television.

Canada bans Louis Malle's first English-language feature, *Pretty Baby*, in which teenage Brooke Shields plays a 12-year-old prostitute.

Ingrid Bergman's appearance in Ingmar Bergman's *Herbstsonate (Autumn Sonata)* is her first film in her native Sweden in four decades.

Ingmar Bergman returns to Sweden.

Celebrated throughout the world as a major figure in film, director Satyajit Ray is having trouble in his native India finding a distributor for his latest picture, *The Chess Players*.

Under more liberal censorship guidelines in India, kissing is now acceptable in films.

With the end of the Cultural Revolution, China's Beijing Film Academy reopens.

1979

Shootings and stabbings occur in California theaters showing *The Warriors* and *Boulevard Nights,* both gang films.

The FBI acknowledges harassing Jane Fonda and Jean Seberg over their leftist political activities.

Gays protest William Friedkin's filming of *Cruising,* a film about homosexual sadomasochism.

The China Syndrome, a film starring Jane Fonda, about a mishap at a nuclear power plant, opens less than a month before the crisis at the Three Mile Island plant in Pennsylvania.

Bela Lugosi's heirs lose a suit in California contending that they, rather than Universal, should control rights to his image.

The image of Bo Derek is everywhere, thanks to an enormous publicity campaign for her appearance in Blake Edwards's *10.*

Alan Ladd, Jr., resigns from 20th Century–Fox to become an independent producer. His clash with the "management by objectives" style of former investment banker and Fox chairman Dennis Stanfill symbolizes the clash between the new and old Hollywood.

David Begelman now heads film production at MGM.

John Wayne, in the final stages of terminal cancer, is a presenter at the Academy Awards.

Radio City Music Hall ends its regular showing of motion pictures.

An 18-theater cineplex, the world's largest, opens in Toronto.

Communist countries exit the West Berlin Film Festival over the showing of *The Deer Hunter* (1978), a Vietnam War film that portrays the North Vietnamese as sadistic and brutal.

Producer Carlo Ponti, husband of Sophia Loren, faces charges of smuggling currency and art out of Italy.

Bo Derek became a sex symbol in 1979 after playing the dream girl in the Blake Edwards film 10, *starring Dudley Moore and Julie Andrews.*

1979: BIRTHS

JENNIFER LOVE HEWITT, FEB. 21

CLAIRE DANES, APR. 12

RACHAEL LEIGH COOK, OCT. 4

1979: DEATHS

DOROTHY ARZNER

JOAN BLONDELL

GEORGE BRENT

EDGAR BUCHANAN

DOLORES COSTELLO

JOHN CROMWELL

ANN DVORAK

GRACIE FIELDS

DICK FORAN

CORINNE GRIFFITH

JACK HALEY

JON HALL

DARLA HOOD

MERLE OBERON

MARY PICKFORD

NICHOLAS RAY

JEAN RENOIR

JEAN SEBERG

DIMITRI TIOMKIN

JOHN WAYNE

DARRYL F. ZANUCK

NOTABLE FILMS 1979

United States	A LITTLE ROMANCE	STARTING OVER	*France and UK*
ALIEN	LOVE AT FIRST BITE	10	TESS
ALL THAT JAZZ	MANHATTAN	THE WARRIORS	*Germany*
APOCALYPSE NOW	MOONRAKER	WISE BLOOD	DIE BLECHTROMMEL (THE TIN DRUM)
BEING THERE	THE MUPPET MOVIE	*US and Netherlands*	NOSFERATU: PHANTOM DER NACHT (NOSFERATU: THE VAMPYRE)
BEST BOY	1941	ZULU DAWN	
THE BLACK STALLION	NORMA RAE	*Australia*	
BREAKING AWAY	NORTH DALLAS FORTY	"BREAKER" MORANT	*Netherlands*
THE CHINA SYNDROME	THE ONION FIELD	MY BRILLIANT CAREER	SOLDIER OF ORANGE
ESCAPE FROM ALCATRAZ	OVER THE EDGE	MAD MAX	*United Kingdom*
THE EUROPEANS	ROCKY II	*Brazil*	LIFE OF BRIAN
GOING IN STYLE	THE ROSE	BYE BYE BRASIL (BYE BYE BRAZIL)	QUADROPHENIA
THE GREAT SANTINI	THE SEDUCTION OF JOE TYNAN	*Canada and UK*	TIME AFTER TIME
THE JERK	STAR TREK—THE MOTION PICTURE	MURDER BY DECREE	*USSR*
KRAMER VS. KRAMER			MOSCOW DOES NOT BELIEVE IN TEARS

1980–1989

It was a time of blockbusters, from E.T. *(1982) to* Die Hard *(1988), but also of a burgeoning independent film movement, from the founding of the Sundance Institute to* sex, lies, and videotape *(1989).*

HOLLYWOOD IN THE 80S was dominated by blockbusters and sequels. *Jaws* (1975) and *Star Wars* (1977) had proven that thrill-packed genre spectacles would attract hordes of youthful moviegoers; *The Empire Strikes Back* (1980) and *Return of the Jedi* (1983) proved they would come back for more. Moviemaking became a competition to see who could produce the most astonishing special effects, generate the most sequels, and sell the most tie-in merchandise. Escapist fare like *Raiders of the Lost Ark* (1981), *E.T.* (1982), *Ghostbusters* (1984), *Rambo* (1985), *Lethal Weapon* (1987), *Die Hard* (1988), and *Batman* (1989) ruled the box office. Release schedules were organized around summer and Christmas, when kids were out of school. Films about real life aimed at adults (such as *Driving Miss Daisy,* 1989) became scarce.

Huge sums of money were needed to produce and advertise these spectacles, and Hollywood protected its investments by courting stars, directors, and producers who had proven their worth in previous outings. The fees of a few select stars, aided by powerful agencies such as Creative Artists Agency (CAA), climbed astronomically. Even so, the big box-office hits kept the American film industry in economic health, assisted by the spread of the home videocassette recorder (VCR) and cable television access, which offered new outlets for its products. The increasing American dominance of foreign markets also helped Hollywood prosper.

With the major studios reluctant to take chances on offbeat material, the demand for quality and

AT LEFT: *The old Saturday-morning-serial style was revived in 1981 with* Raiders of the Lost Ark, *starring Harrison Ford as an adventure-seeking archaeology professor.*

experimentation in films began to be filled by independent film companies such as New Line Cinema and Miramax, a trend that would grow even stronger in the 90s. Robert Redford's Sundance Institute, founded in 1980 to encourage young filmmakers, gradually began to attract attention to independent films, particularly those showcased at the annual Sundance Film Festival. By hook or by crook, filmmakers in the 80s managed to release a number of innovative and unusual films, including Martin Scorsese's *Raging Bull* (1980), John Waters's *Polyester* (1981), Barry Levinson's *Diner* (1982), David Lynch's *Blue Velvet* (1986), Jim Jarmusch's *Down By Law* (1986), John Sayles's *Matewan* (1987), Steven Soderbergh's *sex, lies, and videotape* (1989), and Spike Lee's *Do the Right Thing* (1989).

IN THE SOVIET UNION, the 80s were a time of great creativity, aided by the ascension to power of the liberalizing leader Mikhail Gorbachev in 1985. The Fifth Congress of Soviet Filmmakers in 1986 inaugurated a new era of openness and independence in Soviet filmmaking. Andrei Tarkovsky (*The Sacrifice,* 1986), Nikita Mikhalkov (*A Private Conversation,* 1983), Elem Klimov, Gleb Panfilov, and Tengiz Abuladze all produced impressive works. China, also undergoing cultural reform, experienced a similar cinematic renaissance, as the Beijing Film Academy graduated its first class since its closing during the Cultural Revolution of the 60s. Zhang Yimou (*Red Sorghum,* 1988), Chen Kaige (*Yellow Earth,* 1983), and Huang Jianxin, among others, became internationally known as the "fifth generation" of Chinese filmmakers. Other countries also took heart in the quality of their filmmakers of the 80s, even as Hollywood imports claimed greater shares of their audiences. In France, notable filmmakers included Diane Kurys (*Entre Nous*, 1983) and Bertrand Tavernier; in Canada, Denys Arcand (*Jesus of Montreal*, 1989) and David Cronenberg; in Britain, Stephen Frears (*My Beautiful Laundrette*, 1985) and Neil Jordan; in Spain, Pedro Almodóvar (*Women on the Verge of a Nervous Breakdown*, 1988), and in Japan, Juzo Itami (*Tampopo*, 1986).

--- CHRONOLOGY ---

1980

Former Screen Actors Guild president and movie star Ronald Reagan is elected president of the United States.

Sherry Lansing, the new president of 20th Century–Fox, is the first woman to hold such a position in Hollywood. She will resign in 1982.

Dawn Steel becomes vice-president for production at Paramount.

The Screen Actors Guild strikes for ten weeks over money issues. The strike, which closed production, is said to have cost the industry $400 million.

Martin Scorsese takes a leading role in the campaign for film preservation.

W. C. Fields is honored on a US commemorative stamp. He became a cult figure after his 1946 death.

Melvyn Douglas, at 79 the oldest person to win an Oscar for best supporting actor, beats out nine-year-old Justin Henry, the youngest ever nominated for one.

Francis Ford Coppola sets up his Zoetrope Studios.

John Huston's *Let There Be Light,* a 1945 documentary about mentally ill US soldiers, suppressed by the military since it was filmed, is shown publicly for the first time.

Director Michael Cimino's three-hour-plus western, *Heaven's Gate,* becomes the new touchstone for budget bloat. The reviews are almost universally negative.

Britain's Rank Organization ceases film production to concentrate on distribution and exhibition.

Lew Grade is forced out as head of the major British studio ITC after its *Raise the Titanic* is a $22 million box-office failure.

The film archives of the Cinémathèque Française, founded in 1936, suffers a disastrous fire.

India creates a National Film Development Corporation for the promotion of Indian movies.

1980: BIRTHS

CHRISTINA RICCI, FEB. 12
BRENDAN SEXTON III, FEB. 21
DOMINIQUE SWAIN, AUG. 12
MACAULAY CULKIN, AUG. 26
MICHELLE WILLIAMS, SEPT. 9

1980: DEATHS

TEX AVERY
DON "RED" BARRY
JIMMY DURANTE
HUGH GRIFFITH
ALFRED HITCHCOCK
CHARLES MCGRAW
STEVE MCQUEEN
STROTHER MARTIN
LEWIS MILESTONE
GEORGE PAL
GEORGE RAFT
RACHEL ROBERTS
DORE SCHARY
PETER SELLERS
RAOUL WALSH
MAE WEST

NOTABLE FILMS 1980

United States	
AIRPLANE!	9 TO 5
ALTERED STATES	ORDINARY PEOPLE
AMERICAN GIGOLO	POPEYE
THE BIG RED ONE	PRIVATE BENJAMIN
THE BLUES BROTHERS	PROM NIGHT
BRONCO BILLY	RAGING BULL
BRUBAKER	RETURN OF THE SECAUCUS SEVEN
CADDYSHACK	SEEMS LIKE OLD TIMES
COAL MINER'S DAUGHTER	THE SHINING
DRESSED TO KILL	STARDUST MEMORIES
THE ELEPHANT MAN	STIR CRAZY
THE EMPIRE STRIKES BACK	URBAN COWBOY
FAME	USED CARS
FLASH GORDON	WILLIE AND PHIL
THE FOG	**Canada and France**
FRIDAY THE 13TH	ATLANTIC CITY
GLORIA	**France**
HEAVEN'S GATE	LE DERNIER MÉTRO (THE LAST METRO)
HIDE IN PLAIN SIGHT	**Japan**
HOPSCOTCH	KAGEMUSHA
THE LONG RIDERS	**United Kingdom**
MELVIN AND HOWARD	BAD TIMING: A SENSUAL OBSESSION
	THE DOGS OF WAR

1981

MGM buys United Artists.

The Disney Company expands into cable television with the creation of the Disney Channel.

Marvin Davis, who made his fortune in oil, takes control of 20th Century–Fox.

The Screenwriters Guild of America goes on a three-month strike over monetary compensation.

The new president of the Screen Actors Guild is Ed Asner.

A congressional committee holds hearings into the use of drugs by people in the entertainment business.

Yale student Jodie Foster, who played the young prostitute in *Taxi Driver* (1976), is stalked by John Hinckley, whose obsession becomes public when he attempts to assassinate President Reagan.

One of America's most respected actresses, Meryl Streep starred in The French Lieutenant's Woman *in 1981. She is known for her uncanny ability to mimic accents.*

The new *Life* magazine proclaims Meryl Streep "America's Best Actress."

Ragtime is James Cagney's first film in 20 years.

Young actors Tom Cruise and Sean Penn gain notice in the film *Taps.*

Even with a quarter of its length trimmed, *Heaven's Gate,* last year's monumental failure, fails again in re-release.

Radio City Music Hall shows French director Abel Gance's *Napoléon* (1927) on three connecting screens.

The premiere of *On Golden Pond* is a poignant event, with co-star Henry Fonda hospitalized for a cardiac problem.

Actress Melina Mercouri becomes Greece's minister of culture.

Kurdish screenwriter and director Yilmaz Guney, who had been serving a 19-year sentence in a Turkish prison for murder on trumped-up charges, manages to escape from Turkey while free on a pass.

1981: BIRTHS

ELIJAH WOOD, JAN. 28
NATALIE PORTMAN, JUNE 9

1981: DEATHS

BEULAH BONDI
RICHARD BOONE
PADDY CHAYEFSKY
RENÉ CLAIR
MELVYN DOUGLAS
ABEL GANCE
GLORIA GRAHAME
C. Y. "YIP" HARBURG
ANN HARDING
EDITH HEAD
WILLIAM HOLDEN
BERNARD LEE
ROBERT MONTGOMERY
ARTHUR O'CONNELL
NORMAN TAUROG
NATALIE WOOD
WILLIAM WYLER

NOTABLE FILMS 1981

United States
ABSENCE OF MALICE
AN AMERICAN WEREWOLF IN LONDON
ARTHUR
BLOW OUT
BODY HEAT
THE CHOSEN
ESCAPE FROM NEW YORK
EYE OF THE NEEDLE
EYEWITNESS
FORT APACHE, THE BRONX
THE FOUR SEASONS
THE HOWLING
MOMMIE DEAREST
MY DINNER WITH ANDRE
ON GOLDEN POND
PENNIES FROM HEAVEN
POLYESTER
THE POSTMAN ALWAYS RINGS TWICE
PRINCE OF THE CITY

RAGTIME
RAIDERS OF THE LOST ARK
REDS
STRIPES
SUPERMAN 2
TAPS
WHOSE LIFE IS IT ANYWAY?
WOLFEN

Australia
GALLIPOLI
MAD MAX 2 (THE ROAD WARRIOR)

Botswana
THE GODS MUST BE CRAZY

Brazil
PIXOTE: A LEI DO MAIS FRACO (PIXOTE)

Canada
HEAVY METAL
PORKY'S
SCANNERS

France
COUP DE TORCHON (CLEAN SLATE)

France and Canada
LA GUERRE DU FEU (QUEST FOR FIRE)

Germany
DAS BOOT (THE BOAT)

Hungary
MEPHISTO

Poland
CZIOWIEK Z ZELAZA (MAN OF IRON)

Scotland
GREGORY'S GIRL

United Kingdom
CLASH OF THE TITANS
CHARIOTS OF FIRE
EXCALIBUR
FOR YOUR EYES ONLY
THE FRENCH LIEUTENANT'S WOMAN
THE GREAT MUPPET CAPER
THE LONG GOOD FRIDAY
TIME BANDITS

Barry Levinson's first film, *Diner,* which earned him a place among cinema's up-and-coming directors, almost never opened. Some executives at MGM/UA argued for canceling its release when previews in St. Louis and Phoenix flopped. But praise from the critics present at the preview and a crucial boost from Pauline Kael in *The New Yorker* helped jump-start an important career.

1982

Steven Spielberg's *E.T.* is released. It will surpass *Star Wars* (1977) as the film with the highest total of domestic rentals. The films that had previously held this record were *Gone with the Wind* (1939), *The Sound of Music* (1965), *The Godfather* (1972), and *Jaws* (1974).

Coca-Cola buys Columbia Pictures.

Filming abroad by the major American studios is up 75 percent over last year.

The Canadian theater chain Cineplex expands to the US.

Nova, a new production company that will eventually become Tri-Star, is formed by Columbia Pictures, CBS, and HBO.

Although the proportion of American homes with VCRs will not hit the ten percent mark until next year, film revenue from the sale of videos has already reached eight percent and is becoming a factor in financing film production.

Sherry Lansing, the first female studio president, leaves 20th Century–Fox to become an independent producer.

The passing of the Golden Age of Hollywood is underlined by this year's Motion Picture Academy Players Directory. Only 26 of the 1,800 names that were in the 1937 edition are still listed.

Jane Fonda is one movie star who profits directly from the medium of videotape. Her workout tape, released this year, will become a best-seller.

Francis Ford Coppola's attempt to use videotape and computers in film production spells financial disaster for his film *One from the Heart.*

Eddie Murphy, a comedian who has been appearing on NBC's *Saturday Night Live,* becomes a movie star with his first film, *48 HRS.*

A helicopter accident during the filming of *Twilight Zone–The Movie* (1983) kills actor Vic Morrow and two children, and leads to the indictment of director John Landis for involuntary manslaughter.

Britain's Channel 4, which goes on the air this year, will eventually help revive the nation's film industry by commissioning films it will show after their theatrical run.

The Polish government, threatened by the Solidarity movement, steps up its political persecution of such artists as director Andrzej Wajda, and dissolves the pro-Solidarity actors union.

NOTABLE FILMS 1982

United States
ANNIE
THE ATOMIC CAFE
BLADE RUNNER
CANNERY ROW
COME BACK TO THE FIVE AND DIME, JIMMY DEAN, JIMMY DEAN
CONAN THE BARBARIAN
DEAD MEN DON'T WEAR PLAID
DINER
EATING RAOUL
E.T.: THE EXTRA-TERRESTRIAL
FAST TIMES AT RIDGEMONT HIGH
48 HRS.
FRANCES
A MIDSUMMER NIGHT'S SEX COMEDY
MISSING
THE SECRET OF NIMH
SHOOT THE MOON
SOPHIE'S CHOICE
STAR TREK 2: THE WRATH OF KHAN
SWAMP THING
TOOTSIE

TRON
THE VERDICT
VICTOR/VICTORIA
THE WORLD ACCORDING TO GARP

Australia
THE MAN FROM SNOWY RIVER

Canada
THE GREY FOX

France
DIVA
LE RETOUR DE MARTIN GUERRE (THE RETURN OF MARTIN GUERRE)

Germany
FITZCARRALDO
VERONIKA VOSS

Turkey and Switzerland
YOL

United Kingdom
THE DARK CRYSTAL
THE DRAUGHTSMAN'S CONTRACT
MOONLIGHTING

UK and India
GANDHI

1983

The average ticket price in American theaters rises above $3.

Frank Mancuso is named head of Paramount's film division.

20th Century-Fox is the first major studio to openly solicit deals for the display of brand names in its films.

With the opening of *The Return of the Jedi,* the THX sound system (a quality sound system for movies and theaters developed by George Lucas) begins to make a positive impact on film sound technology.

The special effects used in Woody Allen's *Zelig,* in which Allen appears to be standing next to historical figures in live-action sequences, paves the way for Robert Zemeckis's use of similar effects in *Forrest Gump* (1994).

A fire destroys or damages several sets on the Paramount lot, including its layout of New York City streets.

Richard Pryor's five-year deal with Columbia and Eddie Murphy's five-year deal with Paramount signal the return of the long-term contract for at least a few of the more bankable Hollywood names.

The Big Chill is widely discussed as a landmark film heralding the aging of the baby-boomer generation in the US.

Jack Lang, French minister of culture, is credited for helping to revive the French film industry, most notably by making it easier to finance production. Theater attendance in France this year drops more than five percent from 1982.

Swedish director Ingmar Bergman announces his retirement after the release of his film *Fanny och Alexander* (*Fanny and Alexander*). He returns to filmmaking (for television) the next year.

Gandhi (1982) is the most popular foreign film ever released in India.

Ben Kingsley played the title role in Gandhi *(1982) which won eight Academy Awards in 1983 including best picture, best director, and best actor.*

NOTABLE FILMS 1983

United States	TO BE OR NOT TO BE
BABY IT'S YOU	TRADING PLACES
THE BIG CHILL	TWILIGHT ZONE—
A CHRISTMAS STORY	THE MOVIE
THE DEAD ZONE	UNDER FIRE
FLASHDANCE	VALLEY GIRL
GORKY PARK	WAR GAMES
KOYAANISQATSI	YENTL
THE KING OF COMEDY	ZELIG
LIANNA	**Australia**
THE LORDS OF	THE YEAR OF LIVING
DISCIPLINE	DANGEROUSLY
MR. MOM	**France**
NATIONAL LAMPOON'S	ENTRE NOUS
VACATION	(AT FIRST SIGHT)
NEVER SAY	**Poland and France**
NEVER AGAIN	DANTON
EL NORTE/	**Sweden, W. Germany,**
THE NORTH	**and France**
THE OUTSIDERS	FANNY OCH ALEXANDER
RETURN OF THE JEDI	(FANNY AND
THE RIGHT STUFF	ALEXANDER)
RISKY BUSINESS	**United Kingdom**
RUMBLE FISH	THE DRESSER
SCARFACE	EDUCATING RITA
SILKWOOD	LOCAL HERO
THE STAR CHAMBER	MONTY PYTHON'S
SUDDEN IMPACT	THE MEANING OF LIFE
TENDER MERCIES	OCTOPUSSY
TERMS OF ENDEARMENT	THE PLOUGHMAN'S
TESTAMENT	LUNCH
	UK and Japan
	MERRY CHRISTMAS,
	MR. LAWRENCE

1984

Complaints of excessive violence in recent films spark the adoption of a new rating classification, PG-13, strongly cautioning that some material may be inappropriate for children under 13.

The Supreme Court declares that home-videotaping for personal use does not violate copyright laws.

AMC, the American Movie Classics cable television channel, begins operations.

The Walt Disney Company sets up Touchstone Pictures to make films that appeal to an adult audience. Its first production, *Splash,* is a big hit.

Barry Diller becomes head of 20th Century–Fox.

Conservative Charlton Heston and liberal Screen Actors Guild president Ed Asner clash over what direction the union movement in the entertainment world should take.

1983: DEATHS

ROBERT ALDRICH
LUIS BUÑUEL
BUSTER CRABBE
GEORGE CUKOR
MARCEL DALIO
LOUIS DE FUNÈS
DOLORES DEL RIO
WILLIAM DEMAREST
IRA GERSHWIN
CAROLYN JONES
RAYMOND MASSEY
DAVID NIVEN
PAT O'BRIEN
RALPH RICHARDSON
NORMA SHEARER
WALTER SLEZAK
GLORIA SWANSON
TENNESSEE WILLIAMS

Muscular action heroes like John Rambo, played by Sylvester Stallone, hit the big screen in the 1980s, attracting audiences to films full of stunts and explosions.

NOTABLE FILMS 1984

United States
ALL OF ME

AMADEUS

BEVERLY HILLS COP

BIRDY

BLOOD SIMPLE

BODY DOUBLE

BROADWAY DANNY ROSE

THE BROTHER FROM ANOTHER PLANET

THE COTTON CLUB

COUNTRY

DUNE

THE FLAMINGO KID

GHOSTBUSTERS

GREMLINS

GREYSTOKE, THE LEGEND OF TARZAN, LORD OF THE APES

ICEMAN

INDIANA JONES AND THE TEMPLE OF DOOM

THE KARATE KID

MOSCOW ON THE HUDSON

THE MUPPETS TAKE MANHATTAN

THE NATURAL

A NIGHTMARE ON ELM STREET

ONCE UPON A TIME IN AMERICA

PARIS, TEXAS

PLACES IN THE HEART

POLICE ACADEMY

THE POPE OF GREENWICH VILLAGE

PURPLE RAIN

RED DAWN

REPO MAN

REVENGE OF THE NERDS

THE RIVER

ROMANCING THE STONE

A SOLDIER'S STORY

SPLASH

STOP MAKING SENSE

STAR TREK 3: THE SEARCH FOR SPOCK

STARMAN

STRANGER THAN PARADISE

SWING SHIFT

THE TERMINATOR

THIS IS SPINAL TAP

THE TIMES OF HARVEY MILK

THE WOMAN IN RED

France
UN DIMA A LA CAMPAGNE (A SUNDAY IN THE COUNTRY)

Germany
MARLENE

DIE UNENDLICHE GESCHICHTE (NEVER ENDING STORY)

United Kingdom
THE KILLING FIELDS

A PASSAGE TO INDIA

1984: DEATHS

RICHARD BASEHART

RICHARD BURTON

JACKIE COOGAN

CARL FOREMAN

PEGGY ANN GARNER

JANET GAYNOR

YILMAZ GUNEY

NEIL HAMILTON

BYRON HASKIN

SAM JAFFE

WILLIAM KEIGHLEY

ERNEST LASZLO

PETER LAWFORD

JOSEPH LOSEY

MAY MCAVOY

JAMES MASON

MARY MILES MINTER

SAM PECKINPAH

WALTER PIDGEON

WILLIAM POWELL

FLORA ROBSON

FRANÇOIS TRUFFAUT

JOHNNY WEISSMULLER

OSKAR WERNER

Michael Eisner takes over the helm at the Walt Disney Company as chairman and chief executive officer.

Metropolis (1926), the Fritz Lang silent classic, is re-released with a digital stereo sound track.

James Cagney is awarded the US Medal of Freedom.

The Canadian theater chain Cineplex buys the Odeon group of theaters.

The French government honors Jerry Lewis as a "genius of film comedy."

France and the Disney Company announce that Disney will build a theme park near Paris.

Italian studios produce 30 films this year, compared to the 294 they released in 1968.

1985

More than 25 percent of American households now own VCRs.

Alan Ladd, Jr., takes on the leadership of MGM/United Artists.

Australian media magnate Rupert Murdoch now controls 20th Century–Fox.

Dawn Steel heads production at Paramount.

Colorized films are shown on television for the first time.

The success of Susan Seidelman's *Desperately Seeking Susan* reaffirms the growing significance of independent films.

The revelation that Rock Hudson, a classic Hollywood leading man, is gay and has AIDS shocks movie fans.

The Brown Derby restaurant, an integral part of old Hollywood's celebrity culture, closes.

Sylvester Stallone's Rambo character becomes a controversial political symbol associated with right-wing militarism.

The **British film** industry stages a promotion called "The British Film Year." In its Films Act of this year, the Thatcher government has largely withdrawn state subsidies from its national cinema.

The **British film** company Goldcrest reaches too far when it casts a big American star, Al Pacino, in *Revolution,* a film about the American Revolution. When the film is a failure, it bankrupts Goldcrest.

The **soft-core** pornographic film *Emmanuelle* (1974) ends a more than ten-year run at the Triomphe theater in Paris.

Jean-Luc Godard is hit in the face with a pie at Cannes.

The first Tokyo International Film Festival is beset by controversy over the censorship of a film about right-wing author Yukio Mishima.

The end of military rule in Brazil allows social and political themes to be reintroduced into Brazilian films.

NOTABLE FILMS 1985

United States	
AFTER HOURS	THE PURPLE ROSE OF CAIRO
AGNES OF GOD	RAMBO: FIRST BLOOD, PART 2
BACK TO THE FUTURE	RUNAWAY TRAIN
BRAZIL	ST. ELMO'S FIRE
THE BREAKFAST CLUB	SILVERADO
CLUE	SPIES LIKE US
COCOON	THE SURE THING
THE COLOR PURPLE	THE TRIP TO BOUNTIFUL
DESPERATELY SEEKING SUSAN	WITNESS
THE EMERALD FOREST	YOUNG SHERLOCK HOLMES
ENEMY MINE	*US and Brazil*
THE FALCON AND THE SNOWMAN	KISS OF THE SPIDER WOMAN
FLETCH	*Argentina*
FRIGHT NIGHT	LA HISTORIA OFICIAL (THE OFFICIAL STORY)
THE GOONIES	*France*
JAGGED EDGE	SHOAH
LADYHAWKE	*Japan and France*
LOST IN AMERICA	RAN
MAD MAX BEYOND THUNDERDOME	*Sweden*
MASK	MITT LIV SOM HUND (MY LIFE AS A DOG)
OUT OF AFRICA	*United Kingdom*
PALE RIDER	LETTER TO BREZHNEV
PEE-WEE'S BIG ADVENTURE	MY BEAUTIFUL LAUNDRETTE
PRIZZI'S HONOR	A VIEW TO A KILL

1986

The video release of Disney's *Sleeping Beauty* (1959) sells more than a million copies.

Swearing and narcotics use on film bring an automatic rating of PG (parental guidance).

Ted Turner acquires the vast MGM/United Artists film library.

British producer David Puttnam is the new chief at Columbia Pictures. The first British film figure to head a major US studio, he will leave after a year of contentious relationships with his colleagues.

Tri-Star Pictures buys Loew's Theaters.

The Supreme Court permits local governments to prevent the showing of films with nude scenes at drive-ins if passing motorists can see them.

Colorization of films on television is becoming an artistic issue. Director John Huston protests its application to his *Maltese Falcon* (1941).

The new mayor of Carmel-by-the-Sea, California, is Clint Eastwood.

Martin Sheen serves jail time for leading a protest against nuclear weapons.

Spike Lee makes his directing debut (*She's Gotta Have It*), and Oliver Stone directs his first major film (*Platoon*).

Sigourney Weaver's strong, assertive Ripley character in *Aliens* draws enthusiastic support from many feminists.

Brat Pack actor Molly Ringwald stars in *Pretty in Pink,* the third film of the informally named "Molly Trilogy," which also includes *Sixteen Candles* (1984) and *The Breakfast Club* (1985).

The gender gap in movie star earnings continues, with Sylvester Stallone currently topping the men at up to $12 million a film and Barbra Streisand commanding about $5 million per picture.

Sigourney Weaver's portrayal of the tough, determined Ripley in the 1986 sci-fi film Aliens *established an assertive role model for women.*

1986: DEATHS

BRIAN AHERNE
ELISABETH BERGNER
GUNNAR BJÖRNSTRAND
JAMES CAGNEY
YAKIMA CANUTT
BRODERICK CRAWFORD
CARY GRANT
STERLING HAYDEN
ELSA LANCHESTER
BESSIE LOVE
GORDON MACRAE
UNA MERKEL
RAY MILLAND
VINCENTE MINNELLI
ANNA NEAGLE
LILLI PALMER
OTTO PREMINGER
DONNA REED
BLANCHE SWEET
ANDREI TARKOVSKY
FORREST TUCKER
RUDY VALLEE
HAL WALLIS
KEENAN WYNN

"Crocodile" Dundee, 1986's surprise hit from Down Under, was the first foreign film to deliver the biggest annual box-office gross in the US. It was a sleeper success, to which Paramount obtained distribution rights only because two other companies had turned it down. Paul Hogan, its star, was no stranger to the screen – the television screen that is, where he had been doing commercials for Australian tourism.

NOTABLE FILMS 1986

United States		Peggy Sue Got	Australia
ABOUT LAST NIGHT …	THE FLY	MARRIED	"CROCODILE" DUNDEE
ALIENS	F/X	PLATOON	*France*
BACK TO SCHOOL	HANNAH AND	PRETTY IN PINK	JEAN DE FLORETTE
BIG TROUBLE IN	HER SISTERS	A ROOM WITH	MANON DES SOURCE
LITTLE CHINA	HEARTBREAK	A VIEW	(MANON OF
BLACK WIDOW	RIDGE	RUTHLESS PEOPLE	THE SPRING)
BLUE VELVET	HEARTBURN	SALVADOR	*Italy, France, and*
BRIGHTON	HIGHLANDER	SHE'S GOTTA	*West Germany*
BEACH MEMOIRS	HOOSIERS	HAVE IT	THE NAME OF
CHILDREN OF A	LABYRINTH	SID AND NANCY	THE ROSE
LESSER GOD	LEGAL EAGLES	STAR TREK 4:	*Japan*
THE COLOR	LITTLE SHOP OF	THE VOYAGE HOME	TAMPOPO
OF MONEY	HORRORS	STAND BY ME	*Netherlands*
DOWN AND OUT IN	LUCAS	TOP GUN	THE ASSAULT
BEVERLY HILLS	MANHUNTER	*U.S. and France*	*United Kingdom*
FERRIS BUELLER'S	THE MOSQUITO COAST	AU DE MINUIT	THE MISSION
DAY OFF	9½ WEEKS	(ROUND MIDNIGHT)	MONA LISA

Thorn-EMI, successor to Associated British, is forced by economic constraints to sell its film operations, including the famed Elstree Studios, to the Cannon Group, headed by Menahem Golan and Yoram Globus.

The Australian film *"Crocodile" Dundee* becomes the most profitable foreign film released in the US to date.

Attendance at French cinemas is just over 1.6 million

1987

Congress holds hearings on the legalities of colorizing old black-and-white films.

Dawn Steel becomes president of Columbia Pictures.

An earthquake centered near Los Angeles causes some damage and holds up production at Hollywood studios.

Michael Douglas's one-night stand with Glenn Close in 1987's Fatal Attraction *provoked controversy and drew attention to the consequences of marital infidelity.*

Premiere **magazine** begins publication in the US.

Elizabeth Taylor, whose friend Rock Hudson died of AIDS, is active in raising funds for AIDS research.

Director John Landis is cleared of criminal responsibility for the death of three people on the set of *Twilight Zone–The Movie* (1983).

Alex Forrest, the obsessive, murderous woman played by Glenn Close in *Fatal Attraction,* prompts serious discussions about gender relations in America.

Full Metal Jacket is Stanley Kubrick's first film in seven years; *The Dead* is John Huston's last film.

The career of Dennis Hopper, which had been derailed by personal problems, is revived by his role in David Lynch's offbeat *Blue Velvet.*

NOTABLE FILMS 1987

United States	SOMEONE TO
BEVERLY HILLS COP 2	WATCH OVER ME
THE BIG EASY	SUSPECT
BROADCAST NEWS	SWIMMING TO
CRY FREEDOM	CAMBODIA
THE DEAD	THREE MEN
DIRTY DANCING	AND A BABY
84 CHARING	THROW MOMMA
CROSS ROAD	FROM THE TRAIN
EMPIRE OF	TIN MEN
THE SUN	THE UNTOUCHABLES
FATAL ATTRACTION	WALL STREET
FULL METAL	THE WITCHES OF
JACKET	EASTWICK
GOOD MORNING,	WISH YOU
VIETNAM	WERE HERE
HELLRAISER	*Canada*
HOPE AND GLORY	THE DECLINE OF THE
HOUSE OF GAMES	AMERICAN EMPIRE
ISHTAR	*Denmark*
LA BAMBA	BABETTE'S GÆSTEBUD
LETHAL WEAPON	(BABETTE'S FEAST)
THE LIVING	*Denmark and Sweden*
DAYLIGHTS	PELLE EROBREREN
MATEWAN	(PELLE THE
MOONSTRUCK	CONQUERER)
MAURICE	*France*
NO WAY OUT	AU REVOIR,
PLANES, TRAINS &	LES ENFANTS
AUTOMOBILES	(GOODBYE, CHILDREN)
PREDATOR	*Italy, UK, and China*
RADIO DAYS	THE LAST EMPEROR
RAISING ARIZONA	*Mali*
ROBOCOP	YEELEN
ROXANNE	(BRIGHTNESS)
	West Germany
	DER HIMMEL
	ÜBER BERLIN
	(WINGS OF DESIRE)

Timothy Dalton replaces Roger Moore in the role of James Bond in *The Living Daylights.*

Pinewood Studios, where films were made by the Rank Organization, becomes merely a facility for rent.

Almost 350 cinemas have closed in France in the past year, and Denmark is losing movie theaters at the rate of about two a month.

Brigitte Bardot, retired from films, auctions off some of her personal property in Paris to raise money for the care of animals, a cause with which she is becoming closely identified.

1988

Under the new Film Preservation Act, the US government will designate 25 films annually that must carry disclaimers if colorized, stating that the artists who created them did not consent to the use of the process.

Where once there were more than 6,000 American drive-ins, now there are slightly more than 1,500.

The number of Hollywood horror films has doubled in the past three years.

The Screenwriters Guild goes on strike for six months over the issue of compensation. The strike costs the industry an estimated $150 million.

Martin Scorsese's *The Last Temptation of Christ* upsets many religious fundamentalists, who regard it as blasphemous.

Sales of the video of *E.T.* have surpassed 15 million.

Willem Dafoe (center) played Jesus Christ in Martin Scorsese's highly controversial 1988 film The Last Temptation of Christ.

1987: DEATHS

FRED ASTAIRE
MARY ASTOR
RAY BOLGER
CLARENCE BROWN
MADELEINE CARROLL
BOB FOSSE
JACKIE GLEASON
RITA HAYWORTH
JOHN HUSTON
DANNY KAYE
MERVYN LEROY
JOSEPH E. LEVINE
ROUBEN MAMOULIAN
LEE MARVIN
DAVID MAYSLES
POLA NEGRI
ROBERT PRESTON
GERALDINE PAGE
RANDOLPH SCOTT
DOUGLAS SIRK
ALICE TERRY
ANDY WARHOL

Chinese director Zhang Yimou was awarded the Golden Bear at the Berlin Film Festival for his 1988 debut film Red Sorghum.

NOTABLE FILMS 1988

United States	MARRIED TO THE MOB	*China*
ABOVE THE LAW	MIDNIGHT RUN	RED SORGHUM
THE ACCIDENTAL TOURIST	THE MILAGRO BEANFIELD WAR	*France*
THE ACCUSED	MISSISSIPPI BURNING	LA LECTRICE (THE READER)
ALIEN NATION	THE NAKED GUN	*France and Netherlands*
ANOTHER WOMAN	RAIN MAN	THE VANISHING
BAGDAD CAFE	RUNNING ON EMPTY	*India and UK*
BEACHES	STAND AND DELIVER	SALAAM BOMBAY!
BEETLEJUICE	TALK RADIO	*Italy and France*
BIG	THE THIN BLUE LINE	NUOVA CINEMA PARADISO (CINEMA PARADISO)
BILOXI BLUES	TUCKER: THE MAN AND HIS DREAM	*Spain*
BIRD	TWINS	MUJERES AL BORDE DE UN ATAQUE DE NERVIOS (WOMEN ON THE VERGE OF A NERVOUS BREAKDOWN)
BULL DURHAM	THE UNBEARABLE LIGHTNESS OF BEING	
COLORS	WHO FRAMED ROGER RABBIT	*United Kingdom*
COMING TO AMERICA	WORKING GIRL	THE LAIR OF THE WHITE WORM
CROSSING DELANCEY	YOUNG GUNS	STORMY MONDAY
DANGEROUS LIAISONS	*Canada*	*USSR*
THE LAST TEMPTATION OF CHRIST	DEAD RINGERS	LITTLE VERA

Jane Fonda reaches out to Vietnam veterans antagonized by her antiwar views.

The Museum of the Moving Image opens in London.

The famed Elstree Studios in Britain, only recently earmarked for demolition, are saved at the last minute.

In an interview in *Le Monde,* New Wave director Jean-Luc Godard declares, "The cinema is dead."

The awarding of the Berlin Film Festival's Golden Bear to Chinese first-time director Zhang Yimou's *Red Sorghum* is emblematic both of his talents and of the revival of Chinese film.

The portrait of alienated youth in the new Soviet film *Little Vera* is indicative of the change brought about in the USSR's cultural climate by Mikhail Gorbachev. The film is an international success.

1989

Warner Communications merges with Time Inc. to form Time-Warner Inc.

Columbia merges with Tri-Star Pictures.

Sony buys Columbia and Tri-Star from Coca-Cola for $3.4 billion and then merges with Guber-Peters Entertainment Company. Jon Peters and Peter Guber head Sony's new film division.

The Motion Picture Export Association complains that film piracy and import and distribution quotas abroad cost the American film industry as much as $1 billion a year.

The Disney Company negotiates for months to buy the company that controls Jim Henson's Muppets, but the deal falls through.

Joe Roth is the new head of 20th Century–Fox films.

Former President Ronald Reagan apologizes for the remark he made while in Japan that Japanese participation in Hollywood production might mean "cleaner" films.

Bill & Ted's Excellent Adventure is the first of a cycle of movies featuring "stupid humor."

The $8 million gross pulled in by *Roger & Me* is the highest ever earned by a nonmusical documentary. Writer/director Michael Moore uses his attempts to meet with General Motors (GM) chairman Roger Smith as a backdrop for examining the effects of a GM plant closing in Flint, Michigan.

Last year's heralded documentary, Errol Morris's *The Thin Blue Line,* which aimed to show that a man was wrongfully convicted of murder in Texas, leads to the over-turning of his conviction.

Computer animation is given a boost when the Oscar for best animated short film is awarded to Pixar's *Tin Toy.*

The ailing French film industry tries to revive the languishing market for its product in the US by holding the first Festival of French Films in New York City.

South Korean directors protesting US domination of the local film market release snakes in several movie theaters.

The 1989 documentary Roger & Me – *which focused on the repercussions of the closing of the General Motors auto plant in Flint, Michigan – grossed $8 million.*

1989: DEATHS

LUCILLE BALL
IRVING BERLIN
MEL BLANC
BERNARD BLIER
JOHN CASSAVETES
GEORGE COULOURIS
BETTE DAVIS
SERGIO LEONE
SILVANA MANGANO
LIONEL NEWMAN
LAURENCE OLIVIER
JOHN PAYNE
ANTHONY QUAYLE
FRANKLIN J. SCHAFFNER
LEE VAN CLEEF
CORNEL WILDE

The success of Steven Soderbergh's *sex, lies, and videotape,* an independent, low-budget film, would be a mixed blessing for the Sundance Film Festival. The festival had been known for its laid-back atmosphere, but once distributors could see the potential profit from independent productions, it would lose much of its distinction and become more of a mainstream marketplace.

NOTABLE FILMS 1989

United States	DEAD POETS SOCIETY	LETHAL WEAPON 2	*US and UK*
THE ABYSS	DO THE RIGHT THING	THE LITTLE MERMAID	SHIRLEY VALENTINE
THE ADVENTURES OF BARON MUNCHAUSEN	DRIVING MISS DAISY	LOOK WHO'S TALKING	*Australia*
ALWAYS	DRUGSTORE COWBOY	NATIONAL LAMPOON'S CHRISTMAS VACATION	DEAD CALM
BATMAN	EARTH GIRLS ARE EASY	NEW YORK STORIES	*Canada*
BILL & TED'S EXCELLENT ADVENTURE	ENEMIES, A LOVE STORY	PARENTHOOD	JÉSUS DE MONTRÉAL (JESUS OF MONTREAL)
BLACK RAIN	THE FABULOUS BAKER BOYS	ROGER & ME	*China and Japan*
BORN ON THE FOURTH OF JULY	FIELD OF DREAMS	SAY ANYTHING	JU DOU
CHANCES ARE	GLORY	SCANDAL	*France and UK*
THE COOK, THE THIEF, HIS WIFE AND HER LOVER	HEATHERS	SEA OF LOVE	VALMONT
CRIMES AND MISDEMEANORS	HONEY, I SHRUNK THE KIDS	SEX, LIES, AND VIDEOTAPE	*Hong Kong*
	INDIANA JONES AND THE LAST CRUSADE	STEEL MAGNOLIAS	THE KILLER
	LEAN ON ME	THE WAR OF THE ROSES	*Ireland*
		WHEN HARRY MET SALLY…	MY LEFT FOOT
			United Kingdom
			HENRY V

1990–1999

The Hollywood studios, including newcomer DreamWorks SKG, dueled for critical and popular attention with the independent makers of such films as Shakespeare in Love *(1998) and* The Blair Witch Project *(1999).*

IN THE 1990s, the costs of making a Hollywood film continued to spiral. Fees for top stars climbed to $20 million; budgets for the most expensive films broke the $100 million mark and approached $200 million. With the stakes so high, studio executives faced enormous pressure to deliver hits, even though many films were doomed to lose money. Yet just when it seemed the system should be scrapped, another spectacle would rack up staggering earnings. *Terminator 2: Judgment Day* (1991), *Jurassic Park* (1993), *Forrest Gump* (1994), *Independence Day* (1996), and *Titanic* (1997) were all phenomenal box-office successes.

Even while Hollywood films became bigger and to many critics, blander, an assortment of independent films, made at much lower cost, began to win critical and popular acclaim. They included Quentin Tarantino's *Pulp Fiction* (1994), Kevin Smith's *Clerks* (1994), Edward Burns's *The Brothers McMullen* (1995), Todd Solondz's *Welcome to the Dollhouse* (1996), and the Coen brothers's *Fargo* (1996). The independent film movement, which had been growing since the creation of the Sundance Institute in the 80s, was now forcing Hollywood to take notice. Independent distributors were proliferating, ready to feed the insatiable hunger of video stores, cable stations, megaplexes, and the Internet for new products.

THE ULTIMATE EMBARRASSMENT for Hollywood may have come at the Oscars in the late 1990s, when indie upstart Miramax (an autonomous subsidiary of Disney since 1993) twice won best picture, for *The*

AT LEFT: *Teenager Mena Suvari occupies Kevin Spacey's dreams in* American Beauty, *which won five Oscars in 1999, including best picture, best actor, and best director.*

English Patient (1996) and *Shakespeare in Love* (1998). As sobering as that news was, Hollywood was even more astonished by the box-office success of the shoestring independent production *The Blair Witch Project* (1999): grossing more than $140 million, it did better than many costly studio blockbusters.

Despite its reputation for glossy insubstantiality, Hollywood managed to produce some critically praised films in the 90s, including Jonathan Demme's *The Silence of the Lambs* (1991), Clint Eastwood's *Unforgiven* (1992), Steven Spielberg's *Schindler's List* (1993) and *Saving Private Ryan* (1998), and Sam Mendes's *American Beauty* (1999).

BEHIND THE CAMERAS, several studios changed corporate owners. Disney became a powerhouse in the 90s, riding a new wave of animated hits such as *The Lion King* (1994). Orion, founded in 1978, declared bankruptcy in 1991. One new studio was formed, DreamWorks SKG, named for its founding partners, Steven Spielberg, Jeffrey Katzenberg, and David Geffen. As the new millennium approached, Hollywood faced substantial changes, including the ongoing digital revolution. For a growing number of filmmakers, digital video was becoming preferable to film, and progress was made toward digital distribution.

British films of the peroid included James Ivory's *Howards End* (1992), Neil Jordan's *The Crying Game* (1992), Sally Potter's *Orlando* (1993), and Mike Leigh's *Secrets and Lies* (1996). Denmark's Dogma 95 movement produced several works of note, including *The Celebration* (1998). Jane Campion (*The Piano*, 1993) brought attention to New Zealand's film industry, while Ousmane

Sembène (*Guelwaar,* 1992) did the same for Senegal's. Hong Kong gained greater attention from the West in the 90s, as stars such as Jackie Chan and Chow Yun-Fat and directors such as John Woo crossed over to Hollywood. Cinema in general was becoming increasingly globalized. Two Italian-language films, *Il Postino (The Postman)* (1994) and *La Vita é Bella (Life is Beautiful)* (1997), received an honor that had rarely before been bestowed on foreign-language films when they were nominated for best picture Academy Awards.

── CHRONOLOGY ──

1990

AT RIGHT: *In 1990, Macaulay Culkin skyrocketed to stardom as a little boy inadvertently left by himself who must defend his house from burglars in* Home Alone.

Giancarlo Paretti, shortly to be convicted of fraud in an Italian court, takes control of MGM/United Artists.

Matsushita Industrial Inc., a Japanese corporation, buys MCA/Universal.

Time Warner gets the video rights to United Artists' films.

Dawn Steel leaves Columbia Pictures to produce indepen-dently; Mike Medavoy leaves Orion for Tri-Star.

A fire damages movie sets at Universal.

Billy Crystal serves for the first time as host of the Oscar ceremonies, a role he will reprise often.

Action star Arnold Schwarzenegger becomes chairman of President George Bush's Council on Physical Fitness and Sport.

Hollywood has a new child star: Macaulay Culkin, featured in *Home Alone.*

The X rating is replaced by NC-17 – No Children Under 17 Admitted.

Arnold Schwarzenegger's reported $13 million fee for *Total Recall* sparks controversy over the issue of ballooning salaries for movie stars.

The number of drive-ins in the US has dropped below 1,000.

Martin Scorsese and other film luminaries create the Film Foundation to promote film preservation.

British actress Maggie Smith becomes a Dame of the British Empire.

Jane Campion's *An Angel at My Table* almost doesn't make it to theaters. She directed it for New Zealand television, and only its success at several film festivals convinces her to arrange a general release.

1990: DEATHS

EVE ARDEN
MADGE BELLAMY
JOAN BENNETT
CAPUCINE
SAMMY DAVIS, JR.
JACQUES DEMY
HOWARD DUFF
IRENE DUNNE
CHARLES FARRELL
GRETA GARBO
AVA GARDNER
PAULETTE GODDARD
REX HARRISON
JIM HENSON
JILL IRELAND
ARTHUR KENNEDY
MARGARET LOCKWOOD
JOEL MCCREA
GARY MERRILL
SERGEI PARADJANOV
MICHAEL POWELL
MARTIN RITT
DELPHINE SEYRIG
BARBARA STANWYCK
TERRY-THOMAS
UGO TOGNAZZI

NOTABLE FILMS 1990

United States			France and Italy
ARACHNOPHOBIA	HENRY AND JUNE	POSTCARDS FROM THE EDGE	LA FEMME NIKITA
AVALON	HENRY: PORTRAIT OF A SERIAL KILLER	PRESUMED INNOCENT	**Germany**
AWAKENINGS	HOME ALONE	PRETTY WOMAN	THE NASTY GIRL
THE BONFIRE OF THE VANITIES	THE HUNT FOR RED OCTOBER	Q & A	**Japan**
DANCES WITH WOLVES	INTERNAL AFFAIRS	QUICK CHANGE	AKIRA KUROSAWA'S DREAMS
DICK TRACY	JACOB'S LADDER	REVERSAL OF FORTUNE	**New Zealand**
DIE HARD 2	MERMAIDS	THE SHELTERING SKY	AN ANGEL AT MY TABLE
EDWARD SCISSORHANDS	METROPOLITAN	TEENAGE MUTANT NINJA TURTLES	**Spain**
THE FRESHMAN	MISERY	TOTAL RECALL	ATAME! (TIE ME UP! TIE ME DOWN!)
GHOST	MOUNTAINS OF THE MOON	WHITE HUNTER, BLACK HEART	**Switzerland**
THE GODFATHER, PART III	MR. AND MRS. BRIDGE	WILD AT HEART	JOURNEY OF HOPE
GOODFELLAS	PACIFIC HEIGHTS	**France**	**United Kingdom**
THE GRIFTERS	PARIS IS BURNING	CYRANO DE BERGERAC	THE KRAYS
HAMLET			LIFE IS SWEET
			THE WITCHES

NOTABLE FILMS 1991

United States
THE ADDAMS
FAMILY
BACKDRAFT
BARTON FINK
BEAUTY AND
THE BEAST
BOYZ N THE HOOD
BUGSY
CAPE FEAR
CITY SLICKERS
DEAD AGAIN
DEFENDING YOUR LIFE
THE DOORS
THE FISHER KING
FRANKIE AND JOHNNY
FRIED GREEN
TOMATOES
GRAND
CANYON

HOOK
HOT SHOTS!
JFK
JUNGLE FEVER
LITTLE MAN
TATE
MADONNA,
TRUTH OR DARE
MY OWN
PRIVATE IDAHO
NEW JACK CITY
NIGHT ON
EARTH
PRINCE OF TIDES
RAMBLING ROSE
ROBIN HOOD,
PRINCE OF THIEVES
THE SILENCE OF
THE LAMBS
SLACKER

SLEEPING WITH
THE ENEMY
STAR TREK 6: THE
UNDISCOVERED COUNTRY
TERMINATOR 2:
JUDGMENT DAY
THELMA & LOUISE
WHAT ABOUT BOB?

Australia
PROOF

**Belgium, France,
and Germany**
TOTO THE HERO

Burkina Faso
TILAÏ

Canada and UK
NAKED LUNCH

**China, Taiwan,
and Hong Kong**
RAISE THE
RED LANTERN

France
DELICATESSEN
TOUS LES MATINS
DU MONDE
(EVERY MORNING
OF THE WORLD)

France and Germany
EUROPA, EUROPA

Italy
MEDITERRANEO

United Kingdom
THE COMMITMENTS
LET HIM
HAVE IT
35 UP
TRULY, MADLY,
DEEPLY

UK and Netherlands
PROSPERO'S
BOOKS

1991: DEATHS

IRWIN ALLEN
JEAN ARTHUR
VILMA BANKY
RALPH BELLAMY
FRANK CAPRA
JAMES FRANCISCUS
WILFRED HYDE-WHITE
DEAN JAGGER
KLAUS KINSKI
DAVID LEAN
KEYE LUKE
FRED MACMURRAY
YVES MONTAND
ALEX NORTH
JOE PASTERNAK
ALDO RAY
LEE REMICK
TONY RICHARDSON
DON SIEGEL
RICHARD THORPE
GENE TIERNEY
REGIS TOOMEY

1991

Despite the success of *The Silence of the Lambs,* Orion is deeply in debt. Lacking promotion and distribution money, it postpones the release of several films and finally goes bankrupt. Woody Allen moves from Orion to Tri-Star.

Credit Lyonnais forces Giancarlo Paretti to give up control of what is now MGM-Pathé, but MGM continues to flounder at the box office under new chief Alan Ladd, Jr.

Brandon Tartikoff is the new chairman of Paramount.

Ghetto dramas *Boyz N the Hood* and *New Jack City* provoke violence in theaters.

Vanessa Redgrave is criticized for what some say are pro-Iraqi statements made during the Persian Gulf crisis.

The "production cost spiral" becomes a Hollywood obsession.

Producer Julia Phillips's Hollywood exposé book, *You'll Never Eat Lunch in This Town Again,* is the talk of the town.

Movie patrons are treated to the phenomenon of computerized "morphing" in *Terminator 2: Judgment Day.*

Joel and Ethan Coen's *Barton Fink* is the first film to sweep three major awards at Cannes: the Golden Palm, the director's prize, and best actor.

The Planet Hollywood theme restaurant opens a New York City branch.

Cyrano de Bergerac (1990) wins a record ten César Awards, the French equivalent of the Oscar.

Tilaï, which takes the special jury prize at Cannes and the top prize at the Pan-African Film Festival, places director Idrissa Ouedraogo of Burkina Faso firmly in the forefront of African filmmakers.

American films now account for 86 percent of the Egyptian market.

The French actor Yves Montand died this year, a man at peace with himself. He had become a father for the first time, at age 67, only three years earlier. He was also touted as a possible presidential candidate. Still, his passing was eerie: shortly before he died of a heart attack, he filmed a scene in a movie in which his character dies of a heart attack.

The Silence of the Lambs, *a 1991 film, swept the 1992 Academy Awards, winning best picture, best actor (Anthony Hopkins), best actress (Jodie Foster), and best director (Jonathan Demme).*

This year there was a bittersweet feel to the César Awards, given to France's best. Director Cyril Collard's autobiographical film about AIDS and sex, *Les Nuits Fauves (Savage Nights)* (1992), became the first picture to win for both best film and best French film. Three days earlier he had died from the disease.

1992

Americans now spend more than twice as much on renting or buying videotapes as on movie theater tickets.

Brandon Tartikoff leaves Paramount, where Sherry Lansing becomes head of production.

Barry Diller and Joe Roth leave 20th Century–Fox.

MGM leaves its long-time headquarters in Culver City, California. Sony moves into the vacated space.

Spike Lee's filming of *Malcolm X* is partly financed by African-American entertainers. Some African-American intellectuals have questioned whether Lee is capable of depicting the charismatic leader on the big screen.

Hollywood movie studios, fearing violence, close early the day a verdict in the Rodney King case involving police brutality is announced.

Presidential candidate Bill Clinton draws strong support from many Hollywood stars.

Motion Picture Association head Jack Valenti, a former member of the Kennedy administration, attacks the veracity of Oliver Stone's *JFK* (1991).

Pop star Madonna and director James Cameron sign long-term, multimillion-dollar deals with major studios.

Basic Instinct, which makes Sharon Stone a star, is notorious for its steamy sex scenes.

Spike Lee's 1992 film Malcolm X, *a biography of the 1960s activist starring Denzel Washington in the title role, sparked controversy within the African-American community.*

The ongoing custody battle between Woody Allen and Mia Farrow dominates newspaper headlines.

In Britain, the BBC comes under fire from the House of Lords for broadcasting Martin Scorsese's *The Last Temptation of Christ.*

A Disney theme park opens near Paris.

The South Korean government permits the release of director Chung Ji-Yoing's *White Badge,* the first antiwar film to get past the South Korean censors.

The Tokyo Film Festival refuses to show the Belgian film *Man Bites Dog,* a satire on film violence, although it has already been honored at Cannes.

NOTABLE FILMS 1992

United States			China
ALADDIN	HONEYMOON IN VEGAS	RED ROCK WEST	THE STORY OF QUI JU
BAD LIEUTENANT	HUSBANDS AND WIVES	RESERVOIR DOGS	*France*
BASIC INSTINCT	THE LAST OF THE MOHICANS	A RIVER RUNS THROUGH IT	UN COEUR EN HIVER (A HEART IN WINTER)
BATMAN RETURNS	A LEAGUE OF THEIR OWN	SCENT OF A WOMAN	LES NUITS FAUVES (SAVAGE NIGHTS)
BOB ROBERTS	LEAP OF FAITH	SISTER ACT	*Mexico*
THE BODYGUARD	LETHAL WEAPON 3	SINGLE WHITE FEMALE	COMO AGUA PARA CHOCOLATE (LIKE WATER FOR CHOCOLATE)
BRAM STOKER'S DRACULA	LORENZO'S OIL	SINGLES	
BUFFY THE VAMPIRE SLAYER	MALCOLM X	THUNDERHEART	*Spain*
CANDYMAN	EL MARIACHI	UNFORGIVEN	BELLE EPOQUE (THE AGE OF BEAUTY)
CHAPLIN	OF MICE AND MEN	WAYNE'S WORLD	*United Kingdom*
A FEW GOOD MEN	A MIDNIGHT CLEAR	WHITE MEN CAN'T JUMP	THE CRYING GAME
FOREVER YOUNG	MISSISSIPPI MASALA	*Australia*	HOWARDS END
GLENGARRY GLEN ROSS	MY COUSIN VINNY	STRICTLY BALLROOM	ORLANDO
HERO	PATRIOT GAMES	*Belgium*	PETER'S FRIENDS
HOFFA	THE PLAYER	MAN BITES DOG	

1993

The Disney Company buys Miramax.

Creative Artists Agency's consulting contract with Credit Lyonnais, the bank that controls MGM, causes controversy when it is revealed that the agency also represents clients who deal with MGM.

Frank G. Mancuso replaces Alan Ladd, Jr., as the head of MGM.

More than three-quarters of all American households that have television sets now also own VCRs.

Vivien Leigh's *Gone with the Wind* Oscar sells for $500,000 at auction.

A US postage stamp honors Elvis Presley. After a national vote, a young Elvis is pictured.

Jane Alexander becomes chairperson of the National Endowment for the Arts.

Martial-arts star Bruce Lee's son Brandon is killed on the set of *The Crow* (1994) in a gunshot accident.

Kim Basinger files for bankruptcy after losing a suit brought against her by Main Line Pictures for her withdrawal from *Boxing Helena.*

The arrest of Heidi Fleiss, a madam who catered to many in the movie industry, creates a scandal.

The death of River Phoenix in Los Angeles from a lethal mix of alcohol and drugs shocks the movie community.

France successfully fends off US efforts to diminish the French tax on film imports in the current negotiations on international tariffs.

Germinal, starring Gérard Depardieu and directed by Claude Berri, comes in at a final cost of 175 million francs, a European record for expenditure.

1994

The January earthquake in Los Angeles damages some production facilities.

Viacom absorbs Paramount.

Sony takes a multibillion-dollar write-off on its movie investments, and Peter Guber resigns as head of its film division.

Disney Company president Frank Wells dies in a helicopter crash.

Steven Spielberg, Jeffrey Katzenberg, and David Geffen, create a new studio, DreamWorks SKG.

Many members of the Motion Picture Academy, who vote in the Oscar competition, now view films on videotapes received from the studios rather than in a theater.

The failure of the acclaimed basketball documentary *Hoop Dreams* to receive an Oscar nomination (although it wins the Golden Globe Award for best documentary) forces the Academy to reconsider how it judges documentaries.

1993: DEATHS

DON AMECHE
RAYMOND BURR
CANTINFLAS
EDDIE CONSTANTINE
CYRIL CUSACK
FEDERICO FELLINI
LILLIAN GISH
STEWART GRANGER
AUDREY HEPBURN
RUBY KEELER
MYRNA LOY
HELEN HAYES
JOSEPH L. MANKIEWICZ
SPANKY MCFARLAND
JEAN NEGULESCO
RIVER PHOENIX
VINCENT PRICE
IRENE SHARAFF
ALEXIS SMITH
ANN TODD

NOTABLE FILMS 1993

United States			US and Taiwan
ADDAMS FAMILY VALUES	IN THE LINE OF FIRE	RISING SUN	THE WEDDING BANQUET
THE AGE OF INNOCENCE	THE JOY LUCK CLUB	SCHINDLER'S LIST	**Australia and France**
BENNY & JOON	JURASSIC PARK	SEARCHING FOR BOBBY FISCHER	THE PIANO
A BRONX TALE	KALIFORNIA	SHADOWLANDS	**China**
CARLITO'S WAY	MANHATTAN MURDER MYSTERY	SHORT CUTS	FAREWELL MY CONCUBINE
DAVE	MENACE II SOCIETY	SIX DEGREES OF SEPARATION	**France**
DAZED AND CONFUSED	MRS. DOUBTFIRE	SLEEPLESS IN SEATTLE	GERMINAL
FALLING DOWN	THE NIGHTMARE BEFORE CHRISTMAS	THIS BOY'S LIFE	TROIS COULEURS: BLEU (BLUE)
FEARLESS	THE PELICAN BRIEF	TOMBSTONE	**France and Vietnam**
THE FIRM	A PERFECT WORLD	WHAT'S EATING GILBERT GRAPE?	THE SCENT OF GREEN PAPAYA
FREE WILLY	PHILADELPHIA	WHAT'S LOVE GOT TO DO WITH IT?	**United Kingdom**
THE FUGITIVE	THE REMAINS OF THE DAY	**US and Ireland**	MUCH ADO ABOUT NOTHING
GETTYSBURG		IN THE NAME OF THE FATHER	NAKED
GROUNDHOG DAY			

The 1994 British film Four Weddings and a Funeral, *starring Hugh Grant and Andie MacDowell, was a surprise number one hit in America.*

Documents obtained from the Brown and Williamson Tobacco Company show that it paid $1 million from 1979 to 1983 to have its cigarettes displayed prominently in 22 films.

The Bravo cable network launches the Independent Film Channel.

Filmmaker Quentin Tarantino triumphs with *Pulp Fiction*, winner of the Golden Palm at Cannes.

With *Ace Ventura, Pet Detective; The Mask;* and *Dumb and Dumber* following in quick succession, Jim Carrey is suddenly the new clown prince of US cinema.

A prominent role in *Forrest Gump* brings stage actor Gary Sinise to the fore as a film star.

Two million copies of Walt Disney's *The Lion King* sound track are in the stores three weeks before the animated film opens.

Britain places tighter restrictions on the screening of violent films that attract young people.

The British production *Four Weddings and a Funeral* is a surprise hit in the US market.

Ireland bans the US film *Natural Born Killers*.

Several Arab nations ban *Schindler's List*, ostensibly on the basis of sex and violence.

NOTABLE FILMS 1994

United States			Italy
BULLETS OVER BROADWAY	THE LAST SEDUCTION	SWIMMING WITH SHARKS	IL POSTINO (THE POSTMAN)
CLEAR AND PRESENT DANGER	THE LION KING	TRUE LIES	*Macedonia, UK, and France*
CLERKS	LITTLE WOMEN	WOLF	BEFORE THE RAIN
THE CLIENT	LIVING IN OBLIVION	*Australia*	*New Zealand*
DEATH AND THE MAIDEN	NATURAL BORN KILLERS	ADVENTURES OF PRISCILLA, QUEEN OF THE DESERT	HEAVENLY CREATURES
DISCLOSURE	NOBODY'S FOOL	MURIEL'S WEDDING	ONCE WERE WARRIORS
DON JUAN DEMARCO	THE PAPER	*France*	*Russia and France*
DUMB AND DUMBER	PULP FICTION	LÉON (THE PROFESSIONAL)	BURNT BY THE SUN
ED WOOD	QUIZ SHOW	*France and Poland*	*Taiwan*
FORREST GUMP	SERIAL MOM	TROIS COULEURS: BLANC (THREE COLORS: WHITE)	EAT DRINK MAN WOMAN
HOOP DREAMS	THE SHAWSHANK REDEMPTION	TROIS COULEURS: ROUGE (THREE COLORS: RED)	*United Kingdom*
THE HUDSUCKER PROXY	SPEED		FOUR WEDDINGS AND A FUNERAL
INTERVIEW WITH THE VAMPIRE	STAR TREK: GENERATIONS		THE MADNESS OF KING GEORGE

1995

Seagram buys MCA/Universal from Matsushita Industrial Company. Ron Meyers leaves Creative Artists Agency to head MCA.

Michael Ovitz, formerly head of Creative Artists Agency, is the new chief at the Disney Company.

The cost of making a Hollywood feature film is double what it was five years ago.

The cable television network Showtime, in partnership with Robert Redford, creates the Sundance Channel, an outlet for independent films.

Winston Groom, author of the book on which *Forrest Gump* (1994) was based, challenges Paramount's claim that the film has lost $62 million. Studio accounting practices, in general, are coming under close scrutiny.

Sales of *The Lion King* (1994) video have reached 20 million copies.

The showing of *The Last Seduction* on HBO before its release in theaters is an example of the growing convergence between television and other media – an issue that will present problems in determining Oscar eligibility.

The O.J. Simpson trial competes with the Oscar ceremonies for media attention.

Pocahontas **has the** biggest premiere of any film ever – a free showing in New York City's Central Park, viewed by nearly 100,000 people.

Toy Story **is the** first completely computer-animated feature-length film.

The Net **is one** of several recent films in which malevolent activities are perpetrated through computers.

Coverage of the Cannes Film Festival on several sites on the World Wide Web, and Warner Bros.'s heavy Web promotion of *Batman Forever,* indicate of the rise of a new medium for film publicity and news.

Theater attendance in China is estimated at about five billion, approximately four times that in the US Hollywood executives express an interest in penetrating the Chinese market.

China refuses director Zhang Yimou permission to attend the New York Film Festival for a showing of his films because the festival is also screening *The Gate of Heavenly Peace,* a documentary about the 1989 crackdown in Beijing's Tiananmen Square.

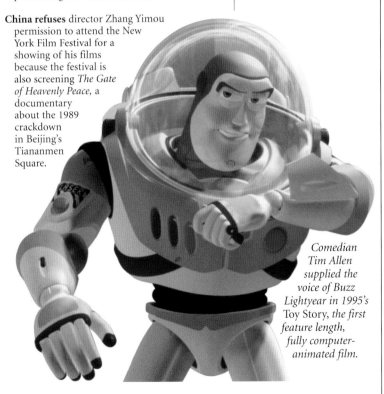

Comedian Tim Allen supplied the voice of Buzz Lightyear in 1995's Toy Story, *the first feature length, fully computer-animated film.*

NOTABLE FILMS 1995

United States
THE AMERICAN PRESIDENT
APOLLO 13
BABE
BATMAN FOREVER
THE BRADY BUNCH MOVIE
BRAVEHEART
THE BRIDGES OF MADISON COUNTY
CASINO
CLUELESS
COPYCAT
CRIMSON TIDE
DEAD MAN WALKING
DESPERADO
DIE HARD: WITH A VENGEANCE
GET SHORTY
GOLDENEYE
HEAT
JUMANJI
KIDS
LEAVING LAS VEGAS
MIGHTY APHRODITE
MR. HOLLAND'S OPUS
MURDER IN THE FIRST
THE NET
NIXON
OUTBREAK
POCAHONTAS
ROB ROY

SABRINA
SEVEN
SMOKE
STRANGE DAYS
THINGS TO DO IN DENVER WHEN YOU'RE DEAD
TO DIE FOR
TOY STORY
TWELVE MONKEYS
THE USUAL SUSPECTS
WELCOME TO THE DOLLHOUSE
WHILE YOU WERE SLEEPING

China
THE CHUNGKING EXPRESS

China and France
SHANGHAI TRIAD

France
LA CITÉ DES ENFANTS PERDUS (CITY OF LOST CHILDREN)
LA HAINE (HATE)

France, Germany, and Hungary
UNDERGROUND

Netherlands
ANTONIA'S LINE

United Kingdom
RICHARD III
SENSE AND SENSIBILITY

1996

The blockbuster hit Independence Day *featured stunning special effects and enjoyed the biggest opening-day gross in film history when it opened in 1996.*

The Golden Globe Awards, which have garnered increased attention in recent years, are televised for the first time.

Former Disney studio head Jeffrey Katzenberg sues the company for profits to which he says he is entitled.

Michael Ovitz resigns his position at the Disney Company over clashes with Michael Eisner.

Independence Day grosses $100 million in its first six days – the biggest opening ever.

Marlon Brando apologizes for saying that Jews "own" Hollywood (on the *Larry King Live* show on CNN).

Steven Spielberg buys the Oscar statuette won by Clark Gable for *It Happened One Night* (1934) at auction and returns it to the Motion Picture Academy.

The presentation of pornographer Larry Flynt as a First Amendment hero in Miloš Forman's *The People vs. Larry Flynt* creates controversy.

Director David Cronenberg's *Crash*, with its eroticizing of automobile crashes, creates controversy and leaves many people appalled.

1996: DEATHS

ANNABELLA
KYOSHI ATSUMI
LEW AYRES
MARTIN BALSAM
SAUL BASS
PANDRO S. BERMAN
ALBERT R. BROCCOLI
GEORGE BURNS
MARCEL CARNÉ
RENÉ CLÉMENT
CLAUDETTE COLBERT
JOANNE DRU
MAX FACTOR
GREER GARSON
BEN JOHNSON
GENE KELLY
KRZYSZTOF KIESLOWSKI
DOROTHY LAMOUR
LAURA LA PLANTE
MARCELLO MASTROIANNI
DON SIMPSON
LYLE TALBOT

NOTABLE FILMS 1996

United States	THE HUNCHBACK OF NOTRE DAME	ROMEO & JULIET	*Australia*
BEAUTIFUL GIRLS	INDEPENDENCE DAY	SCREAM	SHINE
BIG NIGHT	JERRY MAGUIRE	SLEEPERS	*Canada*
THE BIRDCAGE	LONE STAR	SLING BLADE	CRASH
BOUND	LOOKING FOR RICHARD	STAR TREK: FIRST CONTACT	*Denmark*
COURAGE UNDER FIRE	MARVIN'S ROOM		BREAKING THE WAVES
THE CRUCIBLE	MISSION: IMPOSSIBLE	THAT THING YOU DO!	*France, Italy, and UK*
EMMA	THE NUTTY PROFESSOR	A TIME TO KILL	STEALING BEAUTY
THE ENGLISH PATIENT	ONE FINE DAY	TREES LOUNGE	*Japan*
ERASER	101 DALMATIANS	TWISTER	SHALL WE DANCE?
EVERYONE SAYS I LOVE YOU	THE PEOPLE VS. LARRY FLYNT	2 DAYS IN THE VALLEY	*United Kingdom*
EVITA	PRIMAL FEAR	UP CLOSE AND PERSONAL	BEAUTIFUL THING
EXECUTIVE DECISION	RANSOM	WHEN WE WERE KINGS	HAMLET
FARGO	THE ROCK	*US and Iceland*	SECRETS AND LIES
		MICHAEL COLLINS	TRAINSPOTTING
			UK and US
			BRASSED OFF

Shine, a film about the recovery from mental illness of pianist David Helfgott, boosts sales of his recordings. Most of the reviews for his concert tour, however, are negative.

The success of foreign-language films in the US has diminished to the point where very few can hope to earn more than $1 million, the point below which their distribution is not profitable.

Italy's *Il Postino* (*The Postman*) is the first foreign-language film since Ingmar Bergman's *Cries and Whispers* (1973) to be nominated for a best picture Oscar.

China pressures the Disney Company not to coproduce *Kundun* (1997), a film about the Dalai Lama. Beijing threatens to limit Disney's access to the lucrative Chinese market if the studio parti-cipates in the production. (It does participate.)

The US pushes China to crack down on the video piracy of Hollywood films.

1997

The total cost of making and distributing a feature film has risen 150 percent over the past decade.

A *New York Times*/**CBS** poll shows that 64 percent of Americans prefer to watch movies at home.

Ticket sales to Hispanic-Americans are up 22 percent over last year and now outnumber the total number of theater tickets bought by African-Americans.

With the exception of *Jerry Maguire*, independent films dominate the Oscar nominations.

Movie soundtrack albums capture four of the top ten spots on *Billboard's* best-sellers chart.

Loews' Theaters, owned by Sony, merges with Cineplex Odeon.

Columbia and MGM/UA fight over the rights to the James Bond character.

Old movie posters shoot up in price – part of the hot market for all movie memorabilia.

Anne Heche acknowledges her lesbian relationship with television actress Ellen DeGeneres, raising discussion of whether audiences will accept Heche as a heterosexual romantic lead.

First Lady Hillary Rodham Clinton attacks films that glamorize cigarettes, singling out Julia Roberts's smoking in *My Best Friend's Wedding*.

Titanic defies expectations that the most expensive production ever will not recover its cost. It grosses more than $600 million in the US alone.

The National Lottery pours $150 million into the British film industry. Funds from the lottery and tax breaks increase production to 124 films this year, up from 48 in 1992.

The Cannes Film Festival celebrates its fiftieth anniversary.

The film industries in the former countries of the Soviet Bloc have reached their nadir, with Hollywood movies dominating and many artists emigrating to work abroad.

Movie audiences in China are largely rejecting the domestic product in favor of Hollywood films, which are shown weekday evenings and on weekends.

The Cairo Film Festival is hit with celebrity cancellations because of the recent massacre by Islamic militants of 58 foreign tourists at Luxor.

NOTABLE FILMS 1997

United States	
ABSOLUTE POWER	JACKIE BROWN
AFFLICTION	KUNDUN
AIR FORCE ONE	L.A. CONFIDENTIAL
AMISTAD	LIAR LIAR
THE APOSTLE	MEN IN BLACK
AS GOOD AS IT GETS	MY BEST FRIEND'S WEDDING
AUSTIN POWERS: INTERNATIONAL MAN OF MYSTERY	THE PEACEMAKER
	PRIVATE PARTS
BOOGIE NIGHTS	THE RAINMAKER
BREAKDOWN	SCREAM 2
CHASING AMY	SEVEN YEARS IN TIBET
CONSPIRACY THEORY	STARSHIP TROOPERS
CONTACT	TITANIC
DECONSTRUCTING HARRY	TOMORROW NEVER DIES
THE DEVIL'S ADVOCATE	ULEE'S GOLD
THE DEVIL'S OWN	WAG THE DOG
DONNIE BRASCO	**Canada**
EVE'S BAYOU	THE SWEET HEREAFTER
FACE/OFF	**France**
GATTACA	THE FIFTH ELEMENT
GOOD WILL HUNTING	**Italy**
GROSSE POINTE BLANK	LA VITA È BELLA (LIFE IS BEAUTIFUL)
I KNOW WHAT YOU DID LAST SUMMER	**United Kingdom** THE FULL MONTY
THE ICE STORM	**UK and France**
IN & OUT	LOLITA
IN THE COMPANY OF MEN	**UK, US, and Ireland** MRS. BROWN

With all the fuss made over the expensive special effects in *Titanic*, it can be easy to forget that the sinking of the great ocean liner had been effectively depicted before on the screen at a considerably lower cost. The 1953 film with the same title, starring Clifton Webb, used a model of the ship that was only 20 feet long. And the truly memorable *A Night to Remember* (1959) was made on a budget of less than $2 million.

1998

The Disney Company is hit hard by the sluggish box office of Oprah Winfrey's *Beloved,* which cost $80 million. Another Disney film, *Armageddon,* is the top-grossing new film of this year, but its success is dampened by its high production cost: at $200 million, it is Disney's most expensive film ever.

Warner Bros. and Disney cut back on production to reduce costs.

Titanic's **11 Oscars** tie it with *Ben-Hur* (1959).

The restored Egyptian Theater reopens in Hollywood.

The diminished success of Woody Allen's films at the box office forces him to disband the production staff he's worked with for two decades.

Terrence Malick's *The Thin Red Line* is the first film he has directed in 20 years.

Michael Ovitz launches the Artists Management Group.

Citizen Kane (1941) heads the American Film Institute's list of the 100 greatest American films.

Gone with the Wind (1939) is re-released in its original aspect ratio (that is, in its original height and width) and with its color digitally restored.

Adrian Lyne's *Lolita* (1997) premieres on the Showtime cable channel when it cannot find a major US distributor.

Barry Levinson's *Wag the Dog* benefits from analogies people make between its plot and the President Clinton/Monica Lewinsky scandal.

Responding to the protests of Greek-Americans, Antonio Banderas cancels plans to star in a film about Mustafa Kemal Ataturk, the founder of modern Turkish nationalism.

The French Ministry of Culture announces the establishment of a $41 million Maison du Cinéma, a cultural center dedicated to film study and preservation.

In Italy, where 75 percent of films exhibited are imports, a strike by film dubbers severely impedes the movie business.

The Japanese share of its domestic film market has reached a new low of 30 percent.

Titanic **is the first** English-language film to do well in India before being dubbed into Hindi.

1998: Deaths

Gene Autry
Binnie Barnes
Lloyd Bridges
Dane Clark
Richard Denning
John Derek
Marius Goring
Akira Kurosawa
Jean Marais
E.G. Marshall
Roddy McDowall
Maureen O'Sullivan
Mae Questel
Roy Rogers
Frank Sinatra
J.T. Walsh
Robert Young

NOTABLE FILMS 1998

United States	
AMERICAN HISTORY X	RONIN
ANTZ	RUSH HOUR
ARMAGEDDON	RUSHMORE
BELOVED	SAVING PRIVATE RYAN
THE BIG LEBOWSKI	SHAKESPEARE IN LOVE
A BUG'S LIFE	THE SIEGE
BULWORTH	A SIMPLE PLAN
CIVIL ACTION	THE SPANISH PRISONER
DARK CITY	STAR TREK: INSURRECTION
DEEP IMPACT	THERE'S SOMETHING ABOUT MARY
ENEMY OF THE STATE	THE THIN RED LINE
EVER AFTER	THE TRUMAN SHOW
GODS AND MONSTERS	THE WEDDING SINGER
GODZILLA	WHAT DREAMS MAY COME
HAPPINESS	WILD THINGS
HENRY FOOL	THE X-FILES
THE HORSE WHISPERER	YOU'VE GOT MAIL
THE LAST DAYS OF DISCO	**Brazil and France** CENTRAL DO BRASIL (CENTRAL STATION)
THE MASK OF ZORRO	**Denmark**
MULAN	DOGME 1 (THE CELEBRATION)
THE NEGOTIATOR	**Japan**
THE OBJECT OF MY AFFECTION	HANA-BI (FIREWORKS)
THE OPPOSITE OF SEX	**United Kingdom**
OUT OF SIGHT	ELIZABETH
A PERFECT MURDER	HILARY AND JACKIE
PLEASANTVILLE	**UK and US**
PRIMARY COLORS	LITTLE VOICE
THE PRINCE OF EGYPT	

1999

In its opening weekend, *American Beauty* earns $861,531. Showing in only 16 theaters, that averages out to $53, 846 per screen. DreamWorks cancels its original slow roll-out plan and instead adds 500 screens for the following week and 1000 more for the next.

Average production costs decline 2.3 percent, the second annual decline in a row, suggesting that producers are finally exerting control over the famed cost spiral.

In the past decade, the US share of the European film market has risen from 50 percent to at least 70 percent. US filmmakers now expect to take, on average, about half of their grosses from foreign markets.

There are now five million DVD players in use.

An honorary Oscar presented to Elia Kazan draws protests over the director's cooperation with the House Committee on Un-American Activities (HUAC) in the 1950s.

Giancarlo Paretti, who less than a decade ago controlled MGM, is indicted for fraud in the US and is the subject of criminal investigations in other countries.

Jim Wiatt, co-chair of International Creative Management, quits to head the William Morris Agency.

DreamWorks SKG drops plans for a multimillion-dollar Hollywood studio facility after facing financial difficulties.

MGM promotes the now decades-old James Bond character among young people with 100 hours of programming about 007 on MTV.

The popularity of the MPEG, a digital file format for compressing and playing video and audio on home computers, now used mostly for music, worries the film industry, which fears that it will also be used to pirate films.

To secure an R rating for Stanley Kubrick's *Eyes Wide Shut,* an orgy scene is digitally altered with computer-generated figures.

The power of the World Wide Web as a marketing tool is confirmed by the runaway success of *The Blair Witch Project.* Within weeks, the $30,000 film grosses over $100 million, thanks in large part to the film's clever Web site.

A line begins to form at Mann's Chinese Theater in Hollywood three weeks before the opening of *Star Wars: Episode I—The Phantom Menace.*

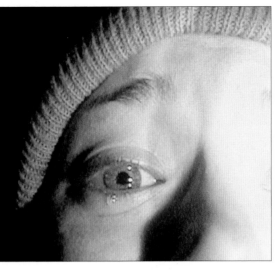

The Blair Witch Project, (1999) shot on 16mm black and white and color digital video, was commended for its documentary style, blurring the lines between reality and fiction.

A spate of teenage shootings is partly blamed on film violence. Theater owners respond by requiring photo ID for admission to R-rated films.

French-made films have lost ten percent of their market share in France since 1990, the biggest decline in domestic market share suffered by any European film industry in the decade. In the past year, the domestic share of French films slipped below 30 percent.

Chinese director Zhang Yimou cancels a showing of two of his films at Cannes, arguing that the Cannes organizers have a biased view of Chinese films. Previously at odds with Chinese censors, Zhang is believed to have gained the censors' approval for these films, *Not One Less* and *My Mother and Father.*

Kurdish filmmaker Yilmaz Guney's *Yol* (1982) is shown for the first time in Turkey.

1999: DEATHS

REX ALLEN
IAN BANNEN
DIRK BOGARDE
HILLARY BROOKE
RORY CALHOUN
EDWARD DMYTRYK
HUNTZ HALL
MADELINE KAHN
GARSON KANIN
STANLEY KUBRICK
VICTOR MATURE
CLAYTON MOORE
ABRAHAM POLONSKY
OLIVER REED
RUTH ROMAN
GEORGE C. SCOTT
GENE SISKEL

NOTABLE FILMS 1999

United States				*Canada and UK*	*Germany, US, France, and Cuba*
AMERICAN BEAUTY	BOYS DON'T CRY	GO	SOUTH PARK	THE WORLD IS NOT ENOUGH	BUENA VISTA SOCIAL CLUB
ANALYZE THIS	BRINGING OUT THE DEAD	THE GREEN MILE	SUMMER OF SAM	*Canada and UK*	*Italy and UK*
ANY GIVEN SUNDAY	THE CIDER HOUSE RULES	THE HURRICANE	THE TALENTED MR. RIPLEY	EXISTENZ	A MIDSUMMER NIGHT'S DREAM
ARLINGTON ROAD	COOKIE'S FORTUNE	THE INSIDER	TARZAN	FELICIA'S JOURNEY	*Spain and France*
AUSTIN POWERS: THE SPY WHO SHAGGED ME	DOGMA	THE IRON GIANT	THREE KINGS	*China*	TODO SOBRE MI MADRE
BEING JOHN MALKOVICH	ED TV	THE LIMEY	STAR WARS: EPISODE I—THE PHANTOM MENACE	MY MOTHER AND FATHER	(ALL ABOUT MY MOTHER)
THE BLAIR WITCH PROJECT	ENTRAPMENT	MAGNOLIA	TRUE CRIME	NOT ONE LESS	*United Kingdom*
BOWFINGER	FIGHT CLUB	MAN ON THE MOON	*US and UK*	*China, France, and Japan*	NOTTING HILL
	THE GENERAL'S DAUGHTER	THE MATRIX	EYES WIDE SHUT	THE ASSASSIN	TOPSY-TURVY
	GIRL, INTERRUPTED	MUSIC OF THE HEART	AN IDEAL HUSBAND	*France and US*	
		OCTOBER SKY		THE STRAIGHT STORY	
		THE SIXTH SENSE			
		SLEEPY HOLLOW			

2000–2002

The digital revolution put the tools of cinema into the hands of the masses, even while violence and cartoon mayhem continued to saturate the box office. But when terrorists attacked America on the morning of September 11th, 2001, Hollywood was forced to confront a scenario that no filmmaker could have imagined.

As THE NEW MILLENNIUM BEGAN, Hollywood faced substantial changes. The cost of making movies was higher than ever. The threat of simultaneous writer and actor strikes panicked the industry, inspiring a yearlong frenzy of production before both were narrowly averted in 2001. Studios, always looking for ways to save money, began to explore the possibilities of digital exhibition and distribution. And in an election year, Tinseltown came under heavy fire from politicians on the campaign trail, forcing studio heads to rethink practices in the marketing of its violent films to minors.

Meanwhile, for a growing number of filmmakers, digital video was becoming preferable to film. Taking their cues from Denmark's Dogma 95 approach, established directors such as Spike Lee, Mike Figgis, Barbet Schroeder, Richard Linklater, and Steven Soderbergh all made low budget, improvisational films shot with hand-held digital cameras. Other directors, such as George Lucas and Robert Rodriguez, used higher quality digital cameras that reproduced the look and feel of film at a fraction of the cost.

By 2001, computer animated films like *Shrek* (2001) and *Monsters, Inc.* (2001) were outgrossing not only more traditional offerings like Disney's *Atlantis: The Lost Empire* (2001), but most live action films as well. For young independent filmmakers, the development of new software suddenly made it easy to create high-quality movies using a home computer. And the increasing popularity of DVD technology, with its emphasis on high-quality presentation, director commentaries, and behind-the-scenes material, provided a greater understanding of the filmmaking process.

The terrorist attacks of September 11th, 2001, brought a different kind of change, forcing reconsideration of current projects and uncertainty about the future. Among the delays was *Collateral Damage* (2002), a terrorism-themed Arnold Schwarzenegger vehicle, as well as such disparate offerings as *Sidewalks of New York* (2002) (a lightweight romance set in Manhattan), *Big Trouble* (2002) (a broad comedy that featured a bomb on a plane), and the WWII action picture, *Windtalkers* (2002).

With America on high alert, many pundits predicted a greater return of the kind of frothy, escapist entertainment popular during the Second World War, and analysts watched the box office for signs of shifting public taste. Two big budget fantasies, *Harry Potter and the Sorcerer's Stone* (2001) and *The Lord of the Rings: The Fellowship of the Ring* (New Zealand and US, 2001), seemed to provide relief, dominating audience attention throughout the holiday season. But by early 2002, when Ridley Scott's *Black Hawk Down*, a blistering recreation of a failed US military operation in Somalia, opened at number one, it became apparent that the tragedy's true effect on the industry – if any – would not be known for many years to come.

AT LEFT: *Daniel Radcliffe played a fledgling wizard in* Harry Potter and the Sorcerer's Stone *(2001), based on the J.K. Rowling's bestselling novel of the same name.*

2000

Summer box office returns are disappointing compared to the previous year, when *Star Wars: Episode I — The Phantom Menace* led a huge audience turnout. But 2000 nevertheless registers record revenues of about $7.7 billion, driven by a late-year rally with films such as *Dr. Seuss' How the Grinch Stole Christmas*. It is the ninth straight year of increasing revenues.

In a sign of the increasing globalization of cinema, the martial arts fantasy *Crouching Tiger, Hidden Dragon* (China/ Hong Kong/Taiwan/US) is nominated for an Academy Award for best picture and wins four other Academy Awards, including best foreign language film. The film grosses about $100 million at the US box office.

Digital filmmaking becomes more widely practiced by such well-known directors as Mike Figgis, Eric Rohmer, and Arturo Ripstein, who shoot all or part of their new features on digital video.

Sony Pictures Entertainment invests in Ifilm.com, an Internet resource involved in distributing short and feature-length films over the Internet.

The animated science-fiction film *Titan A.E.* is the first Hollywood feature to be projected digitally over the Internet from a studio, 20th-Century Fox, to a theatrical audience. However,

Ziyi Zhang starred in the highly acclaimed Ang Lee film Crouching Tiger, Hidden Dragon *(2000).*

the technology is still cumbersome, and the notion of Internet distribution of major features remains elusive.

Producers of short films benefit from increasing demand for their product on the Web.

After many delays and some cuts to avoid an NC-17 rating, Mary Harron's adaptation *American Psycho*, an adaptation of Bret Easton Ellis's 1991 novel about a yuppie serial killer, reaches the screen.

The marriage of Meg Ryan and Dennis Quaid breaks up following Ryan's high-profile affair with Russell Crowe, her co-star in *Proof of Life* (2000).

NOTABLE FILMS 2000

United States
ALMOST FAMOUS
BEFORE NIGHT FALLS
CAST AWAY
CHARLIE'S ANGELS
CHICKEN RUN
THE CONTENDER
DINOSAUR
DR. SEUSS' HOW THE GRINCH STOLE CHRISTMAS
DR. T & THE WOMEN
ERIN BROCKOVICH
GIRLFIGHT
GLADIATOR
ME, MYSELF & IRENE

MEET THE PARENTS
MISSION: IMPOSSIBLE II
NURSE BETTY
THE PATRIOT
THE PERFECT STORM
POLLOCK
O BROTHER, WHERE ART THOU?
QUILLS
REQUIEM FOR A DREAM
SCARY MOVIE,
SPACE COWBOYS
TRAFFIC
U-571

UNBREAKABLE
WHAT LIES BENEATH
WONDER BOYS
X-MEN
YOU CAN COUNT ON ME

Belgium, France, and Netherlands
IEDEREEN BEROEMD! (EVERYBODY'S FAMOUS!)

China and Germany
SUZHOU HE (SUZHOU RIVER)

China, Hong Kong, Taiwan, And Us
WO HU CANG LONG (CROUCHING TIGER, HIDDEN DRAGON)

Czech Republic
MUSÍME SI POMÁHAT (DIVIDED WE FALL)

Denmark, Sweden, and France
DANCER IN THE DARK

France
BAISE-MOI (RAPE ME)

France and UK
VATEL

France, UK, Germany, and Spain
INTIMITÉ (INTIMACY)

Italy Aand US
MALÈNA

Mexico
AMORES PERROS (LOVE'S A BITCH)

Mexico, France, and Spain
ASÍ ES LA VIDA (SUCH IS LIFE)

UK and France
BILLY ELLIOT

UK and Spain
SEXY BEAST

UK and US
CHOCOLAT
SHADOW OF THE VAMPIRE

Dogma 95, a Danish filmmaking movement calling for a fresh, simple aesthetic, seems to come to an end as co-founder Thomas Vinterberg declares, "I'm pretty much done with Dogma."

International interest in Latin American film is renewed with acclaimed new features by Mexican filmmakers Alejandro González Iñárritu (*Amores Perros*) and Arturo Ripstein (*Así es la vida*).

Many critics consulted by Film Comment deem Iranian director Abbas Kiarostami the most important film person of the 1990s.

The Hong Kong government promises to help boost the territory's struggling film industry. In recent years, the entire Asian film industry has been hurt by the Asian financial crisis and rampant piracy.

NOTABLE FILMS 2001

United States		*Bosnia, Belgium, France, Italy, Slovenia, And UK*	*Italy, UK, US and Germany*
A BEAUTIFUL MIND	MONSTERS, INC.	NO MAN'S LAND	GOSFORD PARK
A.I. ARTIFICIAL INTELLIGENCE	MULHOLLAND DRIVE	*Chile*	*Spain*
ALI	THE OTHERS	TAXI PARA TRES (A CAB FOR THREE)	JUANA LA LOCA (MADNESS IN LOVE)
BLACK HAWK DOWN	PEARL HARBOR	*France and Germany*	*Taiwan and France*
DONNIE DARKO	PLANET OF THE APES	LE FABULEUX DESTIN D'AMÉLIE POULAIN (AMÉLIE)	NI NEIBIAN JIDIAN (WHAT TIME IS IT THERE?)
THE FAST AND THE FURIOUS	THE ROYAL TENENBAUMS	*India*	QIANXI MANBO (MILLENNIUM MAMBO)
FROM HELL	SERENDIPITY	ASOKA	*US, UK, and France*
GHOST WORLD	SHREK	*Italy and France*	BRIDGET JONES'S DIARY
HANNIBAL	SPY KIDS	LA STANZA DEL FIGLIO (THE SON'S ROOM)	
IN THE BEDROOM	TRAINING DAY		
THE MAN WHO WASN'T THERE	WAKING LIFE		
MEMENTO	*Austria and France* LA PIANISTE (THE PIANO TEACHER)		

2001

The September 11 terrorist attacks on the World Trade Center and the Pentagon prompt reconsideration of Hollywood films depicting terrorism, violence, or scenes of the World Trade Center. The Arnold Schwarzenegger action film *Collateral Damage,* about to be released, is shelved; other films are reedited or have their release dates postponed. Security is tightened at movie studios.

Most of the year's summer films exhibit a marked box-office dropoff after the first weekend, reflecting aggressive advance marketing campaigns and an abundance of screens. Exceptions include the long-running hit *The Others.*

Steven Soderbergh has the distinction of having each of two directorial efforts, *Traffic* and *Erin Brockovich,* receive Academy Award nominations for best picture and best director. He wins for best director for *Traffic.*

Actors' and screenwriters' strikes are narrowly averted by negotiated agreements. Left unsettled are writers' opposition to the possessory "film by" credit for directors, and actors' concerns about "runaway production," the trend of studios filming abroad to save money.

George Clooney criticizes a Screen Actors Guild (SAG) decision to expel three strikebreakers during the previous year's commercials strike. Clooney argues that a double standard exists, instituting harsher penalties for unknowns than for celebrities.

An estimated 28 million DVD players are sold worldwide this year, compared to about 50 million VCRs.

Sony Pictures Entertainment suspends two advertising executives for creating a fictitious film critic, David Manning of the *Connecticut Ridgefield Press,* who provided phony review blurbs for films.

After more than a decade in film, Julia Roberts finally wins her first Oscar, a best actress Academy Award for *Erin Brockovich.*

Tom Cruise and Nicole Kidman divorce.

The British Board of Film Classification (BBFC) relaxes film censorship restrictions, passing the 1972 US sex film *Deep Throat* uncut for the first time.

The French film industry dominates its own box office for the first time, enjoying 54% of the domestic box office share in the first five months of 2001. In recent years, French films have claimed only about 30% of the market.

India's film industry, known as *Bollywood,* sees the overseas market for Hindi films slacken after the September 11 attacks.

2001: DEATHS

SAMUEL Z. ARKOFF
LEWIS ARQUETTE
JEAN-PIERRE AUMONT
JOHN CHAMBERS
TROY DONAHUE
DALE EVANS
JANE GREER
JACK GROSSBERG
GEORGE HARRISON
NIGEL HAWTHORNE
PAULINE KAEL
HOWARD W. KOCH
STANLEY KRAMER
JACK LEMMON
DOROTHY MCGUIRE
TED MANN
JASON MILLER
ANTHONY QUINN
MICHAEL RITCHIE
HERBERT ROSS
ANN SOTHERN
KIM STANLEY
BEATRICE STRAIGHT
DEBORAH WALLEY
RAY WALSTON

AT LEFT: *Renée Zellweger starred as a British single, thirtysomething in* Bridget Jones's Diary, *(2001) based on Helen Fielding's bestselling novel of the same name.*

Director Martin Scorsese examined gang warfare in mid-1800s New York City in Gangs of New York *(2002), starring Leonardo DiCaprio, Daniel Day-Lewis, Henry Thomas, and David Schofield.*

2002: DEATHS

TED DEMME
EILEEN HECKART
CHUCK JONES
HILDEGARD KNEF
PEGGY LEE
DUDLEY MOORE
PAULINE MOORE
JULIA PHILLIPS
HAROLD RUSSELL
RICHARD SYLBERT
BILLY WILDER

2002

The American Film Institute holds the inaugural AFI Awards ceremony on January 5th. *The Lord of the Rings: The Fellowship of the Ring* receives the award for best film.

Filmmaker David Lynch promotes *davidlynch.com*, a years-in-development website that allows paid subscribers to access exclusive photos and short films by the director, thus bypassing the studio system to create a direct conduit between creator and audience.

Digitally-shot dramatic features make a splash at the 2002 Sundance Film Festival. Rebecca Miller's *Personal Velocity* snagging both the Grand Jury Prize and the award for best cinematography, while Gary Winick's *Tadpole* wins for best direction and is purchased by Miramax for $5 million.

Stolen Summer, writer-director Pete Jones' first feature, is released in theatres. The film's entire production had been documented for HBO's *Project Greenlight,* a reality series produced by Ben Affleck and Matt Damon that gave the novice filmmaker $1 million dollars to make a movie based on his script.

Black Hawk Down, Ridley Scott's depiction of a failed 1993 US military operation in Somalia, gets its unofficial premiere in Mogadishu when a bootlegged videotape of the film is shown. Audiences cheer whenever American helicopters are brought down and US soldiers are killed.

The 74th Annual Academy Awards are staged at the new Kodak Theater. It marks the first time in 42 years that the Oscars are held in Hollywood.

Halle Berry wins an Academy Award for best actress for her role in *Monster's Ball*—the first time ever for an African-American actress in a lead role. Denzel Washington wins the best actor Oscar for *Training Day.* It's his second career Academy Award and he is the first black actor to win for a leading role since 1963.

New Line Cinema is forced by MGM, the studio behind the James Bond franchise, to pull advertising of its third Austin Powers film, *Goldmember,* due to similarities to 1964's *Goldfinger.* The conflict is resolved only months before the picture's release, when New Line is allowed to keep the original title.

Collateral Damage, the terrorist-themed Arnold Schwarzenegger film postponed in the wake of September 11th, opens at number one.

Star Wars: Episode II – Attack of the Clones becomes the first major Hollywood film to be shot entirely without film. Instead, *Clones* is photographed using a new 24 frame-per-second digital process that allows for all of the quality of motion picture stock while eliminating the unavoidable wear-and-tear associated with traditional film negatives and theatrical prints. However, Lucas's dream of digitally projecting the film in 2,000 theatres goes unrealized when less that 200 theatres in the nation are properly equipped to do so, forcing the filmmaker to release most *Clones* prints on old-fashioned celluloid.

The film adaptation of the first part of J.R.R. Tolkien's epic trilogy brought hobbits, elves, wizards, and other characters to life in The Lord of the Rings: The Fellowship of the Ring *(2001). The film was named "Movie of the Year" at the first annual AFI Awards, held on January 5, 2002.*

NOTABLE FILMS 2002

United States		
ABOUT SCHMIDT	INSOMNIA	STAR WARS: EPISODE 2 –
ADAPTATION	THE KID STAYS IN	ATTACK OF THE CLONES
CHICAGO: THE MUSICAL	THE PICTURE	TADPOLE
CONFESSIONS OF A	MINORITY REPORT	THE TRUTH ABOUT
DANGEROUS MIND	MEN IN BLACK 2	CHARLIE
FULL FRONTAL	PANIC ROOM	WE WERE SOLDIERS
HARRY POTTER AND THE	PERSONAL VELOCITY	**Germany, Italy and US**
CHAMBER OF SECRETS	REIGN OF FIRE	GANGS OF NEW YORK
THE HOURS	ROAD TO PERDITION	**New Zealand and US**
ICE AGE	SIGNS	THE LORD OF THE RINGS:
	SPIDER-MAN	THE TWO TOWERS

MOVIE
BASICS

Kevin Spacey plays a detective who grapples with corruption in the 1997 film L.A. Confidential, *set against the backdrop of 1950s Hollywood.*

STUDIOS

Movies all have a similar life cycle. Each begins as a concept developed on paper, then is filmed, edited, and exhibited. But a movie will never make it from paper to film without financing, and for the most part, financing means studios.

ENTITIES THAT FINANCE FILM PRODUCTION CAN consist of anything from a millionaire investor to a bank to a student filmmaker's family to a church. But most American commercial movies are funded by studios, for-profit companies that specialize in financing and distributing movies. The largest studios are called the "majors," and there are currently eight: Disney, DreamWorks SKG, MGM, Paramount, Sony (Columbia/TriStar), 20th Century–Fox, Universal, and Warner Bros.

The studios, for the most part, no longer produce or exhibit movies themselves. They did in the "studio era," from the 1920s to the 1950s, when films were made on the studios' own premises with salaried employees as cast and crew and were exhibited in theaters owned by the studios. Since antitrust legislation and changing economics ended that system, studios have adopted a

Founded in 1914, Paramount Pictures remained one of the major Hollywood studios throughout the 20th century and into the 21st century.

different role. They consider proposals ("pitches") by independent producers, help to develop them, and, if they think a project is worthy, agree to finance the making of the movie. The producers make the movie, using locations and facilities that they decide are suitable. Studio executives stay in touch to ensure that the project is progressing. Once the movie is finished, the studios distribute or sell the film to exhibitors or theater owners, who are generally unconnected to the studios. (Some studios do own theaters, but the theaters will book anyone's films, not just those of the studio.) Thus, the functions of *production, distribution,* and *exhibition* are separated from one another.

The majors are not the only game in town. Recent decades have seen the rise of a number of small film financing, production, and distribution entities called independent companies, or *independents.* Some have grown large and influential enough to qualify as "mini-majors": these include Miramax, New Line Cinema, and Polygram. To make things more confusing, some "independents" are now owned by the majors: Miramax, for example, has been an autonomous subsidiary of Disney since 1993. Other countries have their own film studios, but with two differences. First, in many nations outside the US, it is common for filmmaking to be heavily subsidized by the government. In Canada, for example, the Canadian Film Development Corporation invests public money in feature film production; in France, the Centre National de la Cinématographie (CNC) assists filmmakers at every stage; in African countries such as Senegal and Burkina Faso, government support has made emerging film industries possible. Second, many foreign film companies rely on coproductions with companies in other countries to defray the huge costs of feature filmmaking. It is rare in the U.S. to see two studios collaborating on a film, but this is fairly common overseas.

STAGES IN FILMMAKING:

The life cycle of a Hollywood feature film can be divided into the following general stages:

Development. The phase that begins when a studio acquires or options a literary property (such as a screenplay; a treatment, which is a synopsis of a film story; a novel; or a play). It involves packaging the key talent (director, producer, screenwriter, and principal cast), continues through one or more screenplay drafts until a satisfactory screenplay and budget are attained, and ends with a green light from the studio – a go-ahead to begin preproduction.

Preproduction. This phase begins with the green light and ends before shooting begins. It includes signing cast and crew, finalizing the script and shooting schedule, designing the sets, and finding locations.

Production. This includes all aspects of filming, from the physical preparations for the shoot, such as building sets and rehearsing, to shooting the principal cast (called principal photography) and setting and background action (called second-unit photography).

Postproduction. This phase begins after shooting is complete when the film is edited, visual effects are added, and sound tracks are mixed. The result is the release print, the final film ready for distribution.

Release. This is when prints of the film are distributed to theater owners or exhibitors and shown to paying audiences. Frequently, the film's investors also benefit from sales to television, cable, and video/DVD markets, and ancillary sales such as toys, T-shirts, and sound track albums.

A STUDIO STAFF LIST:

These are some of the key people employed by Hollywood studios to acquire and develop properties and oversee production. Actual titles may vary.

Studio chief: the chief executive officer (CEO) or chairperson

President of worldwide production: oversees the selection, development, production, and distribution of movies

Vice president of creative affairs: looks for and develops projects and oversees productions; may be called vice president of production

Vice president of development: works with writers to develop scripts

Creative executive: works on developing scripts, but at a lower level than the VP of development; sometimes called a development executive or production executive

Production executive: visits sets and monitors progress on projects currently being produced; may also be called a creative executive

Business affairs executive: negotiates contracts with talent; often the person holding this job is a lawyer

Story editor: head of the story department, which reviews the scripts, books, plays, treatments, etc., that agents and producers have submitted to the studio for consideration as possible projects; supervises story analysts

Story analyst: an entry-level person who supplies coverage, that is, who reads submissions and writes synopses, with comments about whether the property is recommended; also called a reader

Development assistant: entry-level assistant to a development executive or story department; reads scripts and does clerical work

In the world of motion pictures, the creative people, or talent, are the artists and technical craft workers who actually make a film – everyone from the star to the director to the assistant editor to the grips, or stagehands. The business-people are those who finance and distribute the film, or who work for companies that do so, and include the agents, business managers, and lawyers who represent the creative people in their dealings with the financing entities.

CREATIVE PEOPLE

Movie stars get the fame, but they are only part of the artistic team that brings a movie to life. Among the other creative people: producers, screenwriters, directors, directors of photography, production designers, composers, and editors.

THE CREATIVE PEOPLE ARE routinely divided into those *above the line* and those *below the line*. The "line" is the one printed in a film budget that divides up costs. Above the line are the costs of acquiring the literary material (the screenplay and rights to any source material, such as a novel or play), and signing the key creative talent: the producer, director, writer, and principal actors. (Principal actors are those with dialogue, as opposed to extras, who have no dialogue.) Below the line are all other production costs, including the technical crew, such as the director of photography and the editor, the people who assist them, and the extras.

The reason for this distinction is that above-the-line costs vary wildly, while below-the-line costs are fairly predictable. One can know in advance how much a professional camera crew and editing department will cost per week. But the same actress who accepted $50,000 for the leading role that launched her career may not accept less than $20 million 12 years later – a price differential of 40,000 percent. (These figures are, respectively, what Julia Roberts was paid for *Mystic Pizza* in 1988 and *Erin Brockovich* in 2000.) Hence in many cases a movie's budget is determined by who the above-the-line people are, and how much they are in demand.

In March of 2000, Forbes *named Julia Roberts the most powerful celebrity in the world. She has grossed over $1.6 billion worldwide in the span of her career.*

Above-the-line people generally have higher status and make more money than below-the-line people. They are regarded as the genuine authors of a film, those most responsible for its success, while below-the-line people may be regarded as merely technical, even blue-collar. However, movies are an inherently collaborative process, and some cinematographers, production designers, and editors gain such renown in the industry and among movie fans that they can rival the reputations of the above-the-line talent. Furthermore, many a film career has started below the line – as an editor, production assistant, or extra – before proceeding above the line, to director or producer.

ABOVE THE LINE PEOPLE:
Producer. The person most broadly responsible for getting the movie made. As the liaison between the people financing the movie and the people filming it, he or she is concerned with getting it done on time and keeping it within budget, with a level of quality appropriate to its budget. The producer delegates many day-to-day duties to the production manager or line producer.
Screenwriter. The person who writes the screenplay, the text that is the basis for filming the movie. Several screenwriters may work on a screenplay, which normally goes through multiple revisions before it is ready for filming.

Director. The person hired by the producer to be in charge of creating the movie. During production, he or she gives day-to-day direction to the cast (the actors) and crew (the behind-the-scenes craft workers, such as the director of photography). During postproduction, he or she directs the efforts of editors, sound mixers, composers, and others who put the final film together.

Actors. The people who play the characters in the filmed story. These include stars – actors so famous and popular that their very presence in a film helps attract audiences – along with many lesser-known performers. The casting director is responsible for selecting the nonstarring actors, in consultation with the producer and director.

Many different below-the-line personnel are involved in the making of a film. The most important are as follows:

BELOW THE LINE PEOPLE:

Director of photography. The person responsible for how the film is lit and photographed. Heading the camera crew (which includes the camera operator, the person who actually runs the camera), he or she makes sure that the images envisioned by the director are realized on film.

Production designer. The person responsible for the look of the physical world that is put on film, from sets to props.

Costume designer. The person who creates the actors' wardrobe, in consultation with the production designer. Makeup artists and hairstylists also contribute to the look of the actors.

Visual effects supervisor/Special effects supervisor. The person who creates effects too dangerous, expensive, or fantastic to achieve by normal means: everything from flying reptiles to vanished cities to battle wounds.

Sound editor/Sound effects editor. The person responsible for the quality of the dialogue and sound effects tracks, and for creating many of the sound effects.

Composer. The person who creates the film's musical score.

Mixer. The person who blends all the recorded sound tracks, including dialogue, sound effects, and music, into a master sound track, which becomes part of the finished version, or release print.

Editor. The person who, in consultation with the director, selects and assembles pieces of footage into a finished film.

> "The producer is an authoritarian figure who risks nothing, presumes to know public taste, and always wants to change the end of the film."
>
> —
>
> *Frederico Fellini*

The director of photography is responsible for the film's lighting and how it is photographed. Above, the camera crew films A Passage to India *(1984) on location in India as Sir David Lean (seated, center) directs.*

BUSINESSPEOPLE

Somebody has to watch the bottom line. In film, that job falls to the businesspeople, including executives protecting the interests of the studios; and agents and managers protecting those of the talent.

BUSINESSPEOPLE CAN BE DIVIDED into those who work for studios and other financing companies, and those who represent talent, the creative people, the ones who receive the financing. The former control the purse strings; the latter try to get for their clients more of what is in the purse.

At the top of the studio personnel list is the CEO or chairperson, the *studio chief.* He or she has final power to green light a movie: to authorize production to begin. Proposed projects percolate up to him or her from the creative department, which is staffed by creative executives looking for story ideas, making deals, and developing projects. *Production executives* monitor progress on the set, while *business affairs executives* negotiate contracts with talent. The studio chief oversees many other departments, including financial, legal, marketing, advertising and publicity, distribution, and merchandising.

Talent may be represented by one or more of these kinds of business people:

Agent. A person who procures work for clients and negotiates contracts for them in return for a commission, usually ten percent. Powerful agents may offer packages, in which, for example, the studio will obtain the services of a star and director, both represented by the agent.

Manager. A person who guides the career of a client, usually in return for 10 to 20 percent of all paychecks.

Business manager. A person who manages a client's financial affairs in return for a percentage.

Lawyer. An attorney who negotiates for a client and may act as a broker, putting together deals.

After working at Warner Bros., Darryl Zanuck founded 20th Century Pictures in 1933, which later merged with Fox Film Corporation, establishing 20th Century–Fox.

THE BOTTOM LINE

Once the movie is made, the studio or other financing entity is the one that most stands to gain or lose. It therefore invests large sums in promoting the film and distributing it to exhibitors, who pay rental fees to the studio for the right to show the film to ticket-buying audiences. Market research, advertising, and publicity are used to attract audiences. Even though the creative people have already been paid, they also have an incentive to see the film succeed. For one thing, the top talent may enjoy profit participation, a cut of the take. But there is more involved than profits. There is also power. If a film is a hit, everyone associated with the project, from studio executives to stars and producers, will rise in power and status. In an uncertain industry, where, as William Goldman famously put it, "Nobody knows anything," people linked to a hit are regarded as geniuses. Something called the "halo effect" shines upon them, however small their contribution. If they are involved in enough hits, they will become "players," people with the clout to demand huge compensation for their efforts and win studio approval for the projects of their choice.

But if a film is a bomb, a black mark is placed in the ledger of those associated with it. Make enough bombs, and heads will roll at the studio. Directors' careers will go into decline. Stars will be downgraded from A-list to B-list (the informal ranking that divides top talent from lower talent), or drop off the scale entirely. Power will dissipate.

Hence, there is the fascination in Hollywood – and increasingly among movie fans – with box-office grosses, the overall amount of money a film earns for its studio. On the one hand, movies are works of both art and entertainment, made by artists and entertainers, judged by critics, embraced or rejected by audiences. On the other hand, they are usually commercial products, intended to turn a profit.

A film's aesthetic merit is often hard to determine. It is a matter of opinion that is sometimes not settled for years. Some films die in their first weeks of exhibition, justly fading into cinematic oblivion. Some are hits on their first release but later disappear from view, unwanted even by local television stations. (How many people still want to see *The Trial of Billy Jack,* a smash hit in 1974) Others, although initially unpopular, may become critical or cult classics, honored as immortal works, beloved by future generations. The test of time takes time. But no one can argue with box-office receipts, and that answer comes right away.

For independent filmmakers, the bottom line may be different. For a filmmaker who has raised money independently to produce a super-low-budget film, the primary goal may not be commercial success but artistic quality, as measured by the appreciation of filmmaking peers. Of course, having it be a commercial hit would be nice, too – the fortunate situation of such recent films as *Clerks* (made for $27,000) and *The Blair Witch Project* (made for $30,000). Even if commercial success doesn't come, success may be measured by awards and recognition at such gatherings as the Sundance Film Festival and the Independent Feature Film Market.

Finding a good distributor for an independently made film is a big reward in itself; so is the seductive attention Hollywood often gives to independent filmmakers who prove they can make commercially viable films without big budgets. Many a director has started by making little art films and ended by controlling huge Hollywood blockbusters. Whether that should be considered success or failure depends upon the filmmaker.

Whatever its artistic merits, every film that makes money does one good thing for the cinematic art: it plows profits back into the studios and production companies, where they can be used to finance new movies, some of which may be tomorrow's classics. Further, every film that is released has a chance of offering ideas to other filmmakers, who may bend and shape them in original ways. In these senses, a movie reaches the true climax of its life cycle when it gives birth to other movies.

Independent films have far smaller budgets than films produced by major studios. Director Kevin Smith made 1994's Clerks *for a mere $27,000.*

> "Nobody knows anything."
>
> —
>
> *William Goldman, screenwriter, in* Adventures in the Screen Trade, *on the ability of those in the industry to predict which movies will succeed*

The Changing Fundamentals

An Interview with William Goldman, 2000

SCREENWRITER AND NOVELIST William Goldman has been in the movie business for over 35 years. He has won two Academy Awards, for *Butch Cassidy and the Sundance Kid* (1969, best original screenplay) and *All the President's Men* (1976, best adapted screenplay). Other screenplays include *Harper* (1966), *Marathon Man* (1976, from his novel), *The Princess Bride* (1987, from his novel), *Maverick* (1994), and *The General's Daughter* (1999). His nonfiction books include *Adventures in the Screen Trade* (1983) and *Which Lie Did I Tell?* (2000).

Q *How has the movie business changed since you first entered it?*

The crucial thing is that the money that movies cost now has led to a necessary change in what studios will make. I first heard about it in the 70s when there was a prize-winning director who had an inexpensive movie with two young stars. It was what we would call now an independent film. He went to a studio, and the studio head said, "I can only make a million dollars out of this movie and I'm not in business to make a million dollars." And I thought, "What are you smoking? There's nothing wrong with a million dollars."

What happened was, as we all know, sadly, *Jaws*. A brilliant movie on its own, but it made so much money so quickly that special effects movies became the vogue and still are. Special effects are expensive, so what's happened is, costs have risen ferociously. Example: thirty years ago, *Butch Cassidy and the Sundance Kid* cost, essentially, $4.8 million to make.

That's including a big director, George Roy Hill, and one of the two biggest stars on earth at the time, Paul Newman (the other was John Wayne). Today that would be inconceivable. It's not just inflation. Movies were not that expensive then.

Q *What made the cost go up? Just special effects?*

Well, stars have gone insanely out of control. Studios want to be protected with stars, and they'll pay anything to have them. But as movies get more expensive, stars, are within certain parameters, worthless. Julia Roberts had three huge hits in the last year and a half. Four years ago she was doing *Mary Reilly.* The star has to do something that audiences want to see.

Paul Newman said something to me once, years ago. We were shooting *Harper*. And he said, essentially, "I'm not worth anything in a rotten movie. I'm not worth anything in a movie where I'm miscast. But if I'm cast properly, in a quality movie, I believe I'm worth more than somebody else would have been in that part." And I think that's true.

The studios try to protect themselves now. They have all these idiots who sit in on meetings and then give you their notes. The first time this ever happened to me was *Maverick*. I'm meeting with [director] Dick Donner and Mel Gibson, and these three studio executives, Happy, Smiley, and Dopey, were sitting there taking notes. And I got a note once saying, "We feel *Maverick* would be better if it were funnier and more exciting." And I thought, "Who are you people? Get down in the trenches with me, tell me how to do that. I think it would be better too if it were funnier and more exciting." But that happens on every movie now. Because their costs are so high, they tend to make lowest-common-denominator movies. A great quote from [Disney chairman] Michael

Eisner: "I am not in business to make art films. I'm in business to return a profit to my investors." A hundred percent right. His job at Disney is to make sure Disney survives. They make all these people rich; they should have a say in it. I'm not saying it's wrong what they're doing. I'm saying it is a change.

Q *Have movies gotten worse?*

I think the 90s are by far the worst decade in history. I can't come up with the ten best movies of the 90s. I think each decade's been worse since the 30s. It's not just the studio thing. We don't know why, but talent tends to cluster. I believe right now is a time of low talent not just in the movies but in all the arts. I don't think you walk around saying, "God, isn't it great reading novels today? I can't wait for the next Hemingway." He's not here. Who are the great painters, who are the great tenors, who are the great anything? In three years we could be booming. What we need is a bunch of new talent. And it could happen at any time. And then all of a sudden, you say, "God, aren't movies wonderful?" I hope that happens.

Q *You've written [in* Adventures in the Screen Trade*] that movies are a group endeavor, and that the success of any movie depends on several elements, including actor, cameraman, director, editor, producer, production designer, and writer. But are screenwriters still regarded as less important than other people who work on films?*

I'm sure that's true. I was once asked by a bunch of European writers on the entertainment business how I could say what I said in my books and articles and still work in Hollywood. I said, "Because I'm a screenwriter. They don't care what I say. It's the usual whine. If a director said it, or a star, that's a whole different thing."

Q *What's the most important moment in making a film? When is it most likely to go wrong or right?*

[Director of photography] Gordon Willis once told me, in an interview for *Adventures in the Screen Trade*, that his greatest skill was not lighting, but that he remembered where the filmmakers were going when they started the movie. He said, "One thing I'm proud of about myself is that I generally don't get confused because I set my sights on something before we start. Then maybe in the middle I'll say, 'This wasn't the idea before, it's not the idea now, we're going the wrong way, we're making another movie.'"

In the case of an adaptation, a producer will come to the writer and say, "I've optioned this book or play; would you like to make a screenplay out of it?" and the screenwriter says yes or no. There was a story kernel that moved the producer. If that same story kernel moves the screenwriter, they can go forward and try to tell the story on film. If the studio gives you money, you hire a director. More people get involved with the story. If we all see the same story, we have a chance. When the story starts to get shredded, that's when you're heading into murky waters. Very often people are not making the same story.

I give directors full credit for the brutal work they do. It's physically exhausting. They're getting eaten alive by the studios. They've only got this room for today. It's supposed to be raining out and it's sunny. The star's supposed to go hype a movie in Paris, and he has to leave at four. There's awful stuff directors have to deal with. And it's very hard to say, "We started to make a movie about two kids and a canoe." Because maybe the rowboat starts shooting better, and somebody says, "Wait a minute. We'll make a movie about two kids and a canoe and a rowboat." Suddenly you're shifting the story.

A story's a very fragile thing. Where movies get in trouble is they begin to put blemishes and alterations on the original piece of narrative.

Q *What advice would you give to someone who wants to write screenplays or otherwise enter the movie business?*

Well, I say the same thing over and over: You'd better give a damn. You'd better care about the story you're telling. There were several movies last year I loved, but the one I could not have come close to doing was *The Matrix*. I'm not interested in special effects. I don't know how to write them. I have very severe limitations. I cannot write farce. I don't have that particular plotting skill. So don't do *The Matrix* unless you love it. Because it will show.

FEATURES AND OTHER FILMS

Feature films are usually about two hours long, fictional, and first released in theaters. All these factors set the feature apart from other types of films, including shorts, documentaries, and made-for-TV films.

FEATURE FILMS ARE DEFINED primarily by their duration: usually 90 minutes to two hours long, although they may be as short as an hour or longer than three hours. They usually tell a fictional story with live actors, are first released in movie theaters, and are notable for their high professional and technical quality. These characteristics of feature films set them apart from various other types of film.

Shorts, for example, are usually less than 30 minutes long. In the silent and early sound era, shorts were viewed widely: until the 1910s, most films were shorts. Afterward, and into the 1940s, they were added attractions, accompanying the main feature and making for a full evening of entertainment. Nowadays, shorts (also called short films or short subjects) function mainly as a medium for art filmmakers and as showcases for beginning filmmakers' talents. Production costs are relatively low and audiences small, perhaps just the cognoscenti at film festivals or Hollywood executives considering whether to hire a young filmmaker.

One of the greatest makers of shorts was American director-producer Mack Sennett (1880–1960). From 1912 to 1917, his Keystone Film Company turned out hundreds of silent comedy shorts, each full of frenzied sight gags and slapstick humor. The company's pace was dizzying: a splitreel every week, that is, a reel of film containing two short subjects, each running less than five minutes. Director-star Charlie Chaplin got his start in Sennett films, which also showcased such performers as Mabel Normand, Fred Mace, Ford Sterling, Roscoe "Fatty" Arbuckle, and the clumsy policemen called the Keystone Kops. Sennett went on cranking out shorts into the 1930s, but his trade was hurt by the growing popularity of features, while the advent of sound in the late 1920s made his emphasis on physical comedy seem old-fashioned.

Sennett's shorts were fiction films, using actors to dramatize a story, however thin. Most feature films are also fiction films, whether their material is wholly invented or based on real events. In contrast, *documentary films,* whether feature length or short, use real people to tell a nonfiction story. Documentary filmmakers may shoot their film without a script, on a relatively low budget, with no performers except the real people who are interviewed or filmed going about their business. Other documentaries rely mostly on archival material, sometimes with text read aloud by actors. Some documentaries reach a fairly wide theatrical audience: *Roger & Me* (1989) and *The War Room* (1993) are examples. But many are never seen except on television or at film festivals, such as the Double Take Documentary Film Festival.

The earliest films were, in a sense, short documentaries, because they depicted real events: examples include the Lumiére Brothers' *La Sortie des Usines Lumiére* (1895), which showed workers leaving their factory, and the newsreels that flourished in the years that followed, depicting events such as presidential inaugurations. Yet a true documentary is not just a photographed record of events, but a narrative with a point of view. One of the great early documen-tary filmmakers was American director Robert J. Flaherty (1884–1951), whose *Nanook of the North* (1922) told the factually accurate, dramatically crafted story of the struggle of an Eskimo named Nanook to survive in his harsh environment.

ANIMATED FILMS, WHETHER feature-length or short, do away entirely with on-screen humans, depending instead on animated figures. The figures may be hand drawn, computer generated, or consist of three-dimensional puppets animated by a process called stop motion. In traditional hand-drawn animation films (commonly called cartoons), animated figures are painted on transparent plastic sheets called cels. Each cel is placed atop a background of static scenery and photographed individually. Since the figures in each cel are drawn at a different stage of motion, the figures appear to move once the film is projected. In stop-motion animation, the position of the solid figures is changed slightly from frame to frame, with the camera filming each position in succession: the projected result again is lifelike motion. In computer animation, digital technology creates the illusion of motion. In all three cases, a sound track consisting of music, sound effects, and dialogue recorded by actors may be added in the studio to complete the film.

Short animated films became popular by the end of the first decade of the 20th century, but the American whose name is most identified with animation, Walt Disney (1901–1966), did not found his Walt Disney Company until 1923. His work was famed for its excellence, innovation, and endearing characters, whether these appeared in silents, as Mickey Mouse did in his first cartoons in 1928, or in Disney features, the first of which was *Snow White and the Seven Dwarfs* (1937). Disney and other studios have continued to make popular animated features, most of them aimed primarily at children.

The last thing that sets feature films apart from other kinds of films is where they are shown: in movie theaters. Unlike movies that premiere on broadcast television or cable channels, or that are released straight to video/DVD, feature films are designed to lure audiences into paying ticket prices and viewing the film away from home.

To accomplish this feat, most features have a high level of professional and technical quality. They are typically filmed on 35mm or even 65mm film, either of which yields a richer, more detailed image than video or 16mm – the two formats commonly used for shorts and documentaries. (However, digital video is beginning to make inroads even in making features.) Features are cast with attractive stars, loaded with elaborate sets, and brought to life by skilled crews. All of this is expensive and risky, undertaken by companies that need deep pockets and experience to succeed. The companies that dominate American moviemaking, as well as the global film marketplace, are collectively known as the Hollywood studios, or simply Hollywood for short.

"Making a movie is a bit like having babies. It lasts nine months, and you go through morning sickness."
—
Guy Hamilton, director of James Bond films

Released in 1937, Disney's Snow White and the Seven Dwarfs *was the first full-length animated feature film.*

FILM, CAMERA, PROJECTOR

Painters work with oils, sculptors with bronze, and filmmakers with emulsions coated on celluloid. At its most elemental, that is film: chemicals exposed in a camera, processed in a laboratory, and run through a projector.

ALL THE WONDERFUL STORIES Hollywood tells and the breathtaking moments experienced in a movie theater depend on the reactions of chemicals on plastic. That is the material basis of the movies: the stuff movies are made of.

Digital equipment may eventually revolutionize how films are made, but for the present the basic technology of most major motion pictures remains unchanged. A thin strip of transparent plastic called celluloid, the film's base or support, is coated with an emulsion, a grainy mixture of chemical compounds called silver halides, which are sensitive to light. Upon exposure to light, the tiny grains of silver halide become unstable and turn to metallic silver. The more light, the more metallic silver is formed, producing what is called a latent image. Upon development (immersion in a chemical bath), the areas that received more light show up as dark areas; the ones that received less light show up as light areas. The result is the negative: a portrait in reverse of whatever people or objects had been reflecting light toward the film.

16mm film was introduced in 1923.

COLOR FILM IS more complicated. The emulsion has three separate layers, each containing both silver halides and chemical dyes called sensitizers or couplers. Each layer is sensitive to one color – cyan, magenta, or yellow. When this type of film, known as tripack, is processed, the result is a negative image with colors complementary to the colors of the objects or people being filmed.

To control how much light reaches the film, the film is placed in a camera – a dark box with a small hole, or aperture, through which light can momen-tarily be admitted by opening a shutter. A movie camera has two apertures: a diaphragm or iris, which is an adjustable aperture that controls how much light reaches the film; and a fixed aperture, whose shape controls the size and shape of the frame. The latter is located in the aperture plate. Movie frames are rectangular because the opening in the aperture plate is rectangular. In front of the aperture is a lens, a piece of glass ground as to gather light from the field of view – the area in front of the camera – and focus it on the film. In professional movie production, the field of view is generally part of a set, a constructed stage for action where variables are tightly controlled. Light sources are precisely placed to achieve an aesthetically pleasing image.

Inside a motion picture camera, film is stored in a magazine, which is a container with two reels – a feed reel and a take-up reel. The feed reel houses the film that will be exposed; the take-up reel collects film that has been exposed. Film is fed into the camera body by means of a motorized mechanism containing a sprocket wheel, which is a wheel with precisely positioned teeth. As the wheel turns and the teeth engage the sprocket holes (perforations along the film's edges), the film advances. A particular frame of film is held steady behind the shutter, which momentarily opens to admit light; then the shutter closes and the next frame is pulled into place. Because each frame of film stops for a moment, the process is called intermittent movement.

Made in France, the compact and lightweight Debrie Parvo camera was a favorite of many filmmakers from its creation in 1908 throughout the first half of the 20th century.

After the film is processed in the laboratory and a negative is prepared, prints, or positives, have to be made. A machine called a printer performs this task: it uses projected light to transfer the image of the negative onto raw film stock, creating a positive image in which objects that had been light on the set appear light and colors run true.

FOR EXHIBITION, the print is run through a projector, which has a shutter, aperture, lens, and intermittent mechanism similar to the camera, but which projects light from a lamp inside. The light is projected through the film onto a screen one frame at a time, with darkness between frames. Because of the phenomenon of persistence of vision, the rapid succession of frames (24 frames per second in professional filmmaking) creates an illusion of motion. If one frame shows actors in a certain position, and the next shows them in a slightly different position, the human eye interprets the changing positions as continuous motion.

Sound adds a further complication. On a film set, sound is recorded on a magnetic tape recorder synchronized to the film image; but many additional sound tracks are usually mixed with the initial track in postproduction before a final sound track is complete. In the end, that sound track is transferred directly onto the film in the form of a set of lines (an optical sound track) read by the projector.

Sound and color greatly changed the moviegoing experience. Currently, digital technology, with which filmmakers can record, manipulate, and play back images and sound in the form of binary data, is further expanding the possibilities of the medium. Filmmakers have begun to experiment with digital distribution and exhibition of film, though at present the technical and practical hurdles remain high. For the moment, the original technology of film, camera, and projector remains the foundation of the movies.

"To me the camera represents the eyes of a person through those whose mind is one watching the events on screen. It must whirl and peep and move from place to place as swiftly as thought itself..."

—

F.W. Murnau, 1928

HOW TO BREAK INTO THE MOVIES

How can you get started on a film career? Go to film school, get training from craft unions and guilds, read, network, and find a way to make a film – even a small one.

PROBABLY THE MOST frequently asked question about the film industry is: "How do I break in?" Unlike law, medicine, teaching, and many other professions, there are no clear-cut routes that open the doors to employment.

Instead, there are a number of career paths, myriad theories, and advice as varied as the careers of those offering it.

Arthur Hiller, former president of the Academy of Motion Picture Arts and Sciences, is a highly successful and respected director with such film credits as the box-office smash *Love Story, The Americanization of Emily, The Out-of-Towners,* and *The In-Laws.* Mr. Hiller began his career in Canadian radio and then worked in television during the golden era of live drama before launching his film career. "When young people say they want to direct," Hiller explains, "I ask them if they have ever made a film. If the answer is 'no,' there is not enough there."

He believes that those who want to break in and really care will find a way to make a film – "an 8-millimeter, a 16-millimeter or video, a five-minute film with a friend."

"Make a film," he advises. "It doesn't have to be two hours; make a little film to start learning."

"Prepare yourself," he adds. "Keep on trying to find your way. Go to school and study; go to workshops and work."

Arthur Hiller was the President of the Directors Guild of America from 1989 to 1993, and president of the Academy of Motion Picture Arts and Sciences from 1996 to 1998.

Preparing oneself may mean attending such schools as New York University, the University of California at Los Angeles, AFI Conservatory, the University of Southern California, or any number of other universities and colleges with first-rate film programs and drama departments. Respected acting schools such as the American Academy of Dramatic Arts are another way for would-be actors and actresses to get professional training.

Many of the unions and guilds representing the various crafts of the film industry maintain Web sites. Of particular interest to aspiring directors is the Directors Guild of America (DGA) site (www.dga.org). The DGA notes that once a year, it awards "$2,500 each to an African-American, a woman, and a Latino student filmmaker." It also "occasionally" offers clerical scholarships at its Los Angeles office to "full-time matriculated students eligible for internship credit from a fully accredited college or university."

For information on film schools, the DGA cites *The Complete Guide to American Film Schools and Cinema and Television Courses,* by director Ernest Pintoff, and the Cinemedia directory of film schools.

Hiller notes, "You need a lot of luck. It is not easy. Many talented people want to break in. You must keep your faith and your belief in yourself."

"Basic Information for Those Considering a Professional Acting Career" can be found on the Web site of the Screen Actors Guild (SAG). Under "Getting Started in Hollywood, New York, or Any City," SAG recommends that an aspiring actor, "…have enough savings to live without any income" while attempting to break into the acting business. It continues, "Success in this business is an unpredictable combination of talent, training, residence, 'look,' energy, attitude, and the completely uncontrollable factor—luck!"

THE SAG WEB SITE (www.sag.com) features a resource list that includes a section titled "So You Wanna Be an Actor." It also recommends a number of books: its own publication, *Young Performers Handbook: How to Be a Working Actor,* by Mari Lyn Henry and Lynne Rogers; *Directory of Professional Theatre Training Programs and Summer Theatre Directory* (no author listed); *Summer Theatre Guide,* by John Allen; *Professional Actor Training in New York City,* by Jim Monos; *The Camera Smart Actor,* by Richard Brestoff, and *Your Film Acting Career,* by M.K. Lewis and Rosemary Lewis.

SAG also offers valuable insights into such essentials as finding a talent agent and/or a personal manager and obtaining professional photographs. On the Web site of the Screen Producers Guild (www.producersguild.com), hopefuls have the opportunity to e-mail questions that will be answered by members of the guild. The site also includes valuable definitions of the roles of the producer, executive producer, and associate producer, along with a list of 26 producer functions. Another Web site of interest is www.employmentnow.com, supported by the Film, TV & Commercial Employment Network. The site includes a wide range of information on jobs and a section in which actors and actresses can post photographs and credits.

Some of the craft unions and guilds offer apprentice training programs; others do not and expect would-be practitioners to obtain their training at schools before attempting to find work.

Networking is key to success in finding a job in the industry, according to Robert G. Rehme, current president of the Academy of Motion Picture Arts and Sciences and producer of such films as *Patriot Games, Clear and Present Danger, Beverly Hills Cop III,* and *Gettysburg.*

"Get any kind of job," Rehme advises. "Then network with as many producers, directors, and writers as you can. If you are interested in a craft, work as a production assistant first."

GEOGRAPHY ALSO COUNTS. Rehme states, "It is important to be in Hollywood or New York City. I hear from people living in Tucson and Phoenix and Denver. They want to break into films, but they don't plan to move. That makes it very difficult."

"Persevere," he adds. "You must never stop. Knock on every door. Take advantage of every opportunity. Never take no for an answer and you can succeed."

Nicholas Meyer is a director, screenwriter, and best-selling novelist. He wrote the Academy Award–nominated screenplay from his own novel, *The Seven-Percent Solution,*

Before finding fame with his 1995 film, *The Brothers McMullen,* writer, director, and actor Edward Burns got his start as a production assistant on the television show *Entertainment Tonight.*

"In Hollywood, anything can happen. Anything at all."

—
Raymond Chandler, writer of The Long Goodbye *(1953)*

made his directorial debut with the 1979 film *Time After Time,* and directed such motion pictures as *Star Trek II: The Wrath of Khan* and *Star Trek IV: The Undiscovered Country.* After graduation from the University of Iowa, Meyer took the first step on his way to Hollywood when he joined the publicity department of Paramount Pictures in New York. He then worked as a unit publicist on Arthur Hiller's *Love Story.*

Regarded as an erudite filmmaker and writer, Meyer laces his work with references to literary classics, including the works of Arthur Conan Doyle. On the topic of a career in movies, Meyer begins by noting, "Any anecdotal autobiographical detail I could provide would be completely irrelevant. It would be like telling someone how I fall asleep." He notes that breaking into the industry is "completely idiosyncratic," that filmmakers and performers can come from almost anywhere, including "film schools, advertising agencies, and MTV." But, he notes, "Whatever you do, be prepared to put in ten years. That's how long it will take. After ten years, if there is no sign of progress, sit down and ask yourself some serious questions." Meyer goes on, "How you enter depends on who you are and, metaphorically, where you are coming from. Coming from a film school in Los Angeles is different than coming from Wichita or even New York City. It also depends on what you want to do. There are an infinite number of variables based on what you want to do."

Meyer's bottom line: "Persistence is the name of the game." And, he adds, "A simple answer would be simplistic."

WOULD-BE NICHOLAS MEYERS will find an Online Mentor Service on the Web site of the Writers Guild of America (WGA) (www.wga.org). Provided free of charge, the service is described as "a unique effort in the field of entertainment connecting professional Hollywood film and television writers with those who aspire to be," but notes that the guild "does not instruct writers on how or what to write." WGA members will, however, answer questions about "crafting a story, developing characters or dialogue...." The mentor section also includes Frequently Asked Questions and a recommended reading list consisting of *Adventures in the Screen Trade,* by William Goldman ("The bible for aspiring screenwriters wanting to know what it's really like"); Aristotle's *Poetics; The Art of Dramatic Writing,* by Lajos Egri; *Becoming a Writer,* by Dorothea Brande; *Bird by Bird,* by Anne Lamott; *The Comic Toolbox,* by John Vorhaus; *How to Sell Your Screenplay: The Real Rules of Film and Television,* by Carl Sautter; *Lew Hunter's Screenwriting 434,* by Lew Hunter (the author's screenwriting class at UCLA Graduate Film School in book form); *Making a Good Script Great* (2d ed.), by Linda Seger; *Monster: Living Off the Big Screen,* by John Gregory Dunne; *The Screenwriter Looks at the Screenwriter* and *Screenwriting Tricks of the Trade,* both by William Froug; *Structures of Fantasy,* by Richard Michaels; and *The Writer's Journey: Mythic Structure for Storytellers and Screenwriters,* by Christopher Vogler.

A more emotional approach comes from veteran screen publicist

Kimberly Peirce's first feature film was *Boys Don't Cry,* based on the true story of Teena Brandon, a transgendered teenager who chose to lead her life as man. Inspired by a 1994 article in *The Village Voice,* Peirce chose the topic for her Columbia Film School thesis and spent nearly five years researching the story and writing the script.

Stuart Fink, who numbers among his many credits the 1999 Academy Award nominated film *The Insider* as well as *Clueless* and *A League of Their Own.*

FINK BELIEVES THAT PASSION is the key to breaking into the film industry and becoming a success. "You have to be sure that your passion about this kind of work is stronger than anything you've ever felt over a period of time. No one can talk you out of it if you really want it."

He warns, "The amount of rejection and humiliation which seem to be part of the experience of working in the film industry needs to be balanced by this passion." If you have tested your passion and found "you are willing to walk on hot coals, then do it," Fink says. "Do it in every ethical way you can imagine."

He continues, "Start in mailrooms. Take a job as an intern even if it pays no money. Work as a production assistant on a film and run for coffee. Take any entry-level job – even part-time work – you can get in the area that interests you."

"And remember," he adds, "communication is the essence. Schools of journalism for publicists, English-lit courses for writers, MBA degrees for the business end, film institutes or schools for actors and directors – anything that will give you a leg up, plus *communication skills.*"

BUFFY SHUTT, A UNIVERSAL PICTURES producer, got her start in the film industry through serendipity. Her first job after college was with *Harper's Bazaar* magazine. Her boss heard of a publicity staff opening at Paramount Pictures and recommended Shutt. She rose rapidly in the corporate ranks, eventually becoming Universal's president of marketing, and was one of the few high-ranking women executives at the time. "Now people study for film careers," she states. But in addition to film studies, she recommends, "Read a lot, acquire wide knowledge, rather than specific film knowledge. And develop your memory."

The final word is Arthur Hiller's: "Keep knocking and one day a door will open. And when it does, you'd better be good!"

"If one wanted to emulate a career it would be Spike's. He did exactly what he always wanted to do, first in the independent arena and then with the studios."

—

Director Kevin Smith on Spike Lee

Spike Lee, seen here filming Crooklyn *(1994), started his career by financing his first film,* She's Gotta Have It *(1988), with his own credit cards.*

Buzzwords: A Compendium of Hollywood Slang

Whether they're talking about hyphenates, legs, or turnaround, Hollywood moviemakers have a language all their own. Some Hollywood slang terms, such as "buzz," are often used outside the filmmaking community; others, such as "going indie prod," are mainly for insiders only.

"Ann Sheridan walked in, and they said, 'That's the "Oomph" Girl.' I said, 'Excuse me' and went up to my room to look in my dictionary to see what 'oomph' meant."

—

Ingrid Bergman, 1972

A-list The short roster of stars, directors, and other talent presumed to have the power to attract audiences to the box office. Stars on the decline may fall to the B-list or C-list.

A-picture A first-class film production with big stars, a big budget, and high production values, as opposed to a low-budget B-picture or a super-low-budget Grade-Z picture.

ankle To leave a job, either by quitting or being fired.

back end The movie profits in which talent may share, in the form of percentage points. A star's back end may be gross points (a share of gross profits) or the less desirable net points (a share of the profits after expenses are recouped; creative studio accounting may ensure that these "profits" never materialize).

bankable Adjective for a star whose mere presence in a film will attract audiences, as in "the movie became a hit despite the lack of bankable stars."

bankroll To finance a film.

B.O. Box office or box-office receipts.

boffo or boff, boffola Outstandingly good, usually with reference to box-office receipts, as in "His new movie's doing boffo B.O." "Socko" has a similar meaning; "whammo" means it's even more successful.

bomb A movie that is a failure, particularly at the box office.

business, the *See* INDUSTRY, THE

buzz Word of mouth about a project, particularly among industry cognoscenti before a film's release, as in "Her new movie has good buzz."

click a hit to connect with audiences, as in "The picture never clicked."

development hell A particularly long and tortured case of development, the process between optioning a property and the studio's green light. Incessant script revision and chaotic hiring and firing of talent are hallmarks of development hell.

D-girl Derogatory term for a fairly low-level female working in development, acquiring, and refining literary properties. D-boy and D-person are variants of the term.

distrib A distributor.

element A high-level creative person attached to a film production, such as a star, director, writer, or producer. Several elements make a package.

first look A deal in which a certain studio has a first option on a filmmaker's projects.

flavor of the month A previously unknown creative person who is currently in high demand and presumed to have great talent, but whose moment of fame may soon vanish. Young independent directors are often discovered by Hollywood and become flavors of the month.

flop A movie that fails at the box office.

go indie prod Become an independent producer. Since many studio and production company executives do this upon being fired, the term can be synonymous with "get fired" or "become unemployed."

go picture A movie project that has been green-lighted.

green light A studio's go-ahead for a film to be made; or to give such a go-ahead.

heat Good buzz about a creative talent, such as a star or director, reflected in high demand and the general sense that he or she can do no wrong. A player with this quality is hot.

helm To direct a film. A director is a helmer.

history The existing relationship between two Hollywood players, particularly if it is negative, for example, if they have quarreled, are former lovers, or have sued each other. If they have history, they may not be able to work together.

housekeeping deal An arrangement in which a studio gives a producer free space on its premises and possibly other amenities (fees, staff salaries, etc.) in return for first look at the producer's properties.

hyphenate A person who does more than one job in film, such as an actor-producer or director-producer-writer.

in the can A completed film; from the round metal container in which a film is stored.

indie An independent movie, director, producer, or distributor, as in "Indies have swept the Oscar nominations this year."

indie prod *See* GO INDIE PROD

industry, the The entertainment industry, especially the movie and television industry. Also called the business, show business, showbiz, or simply the biz.

legs What a movie has if it enjoys good box office over a prolonged period. If ticket sales peter out after the opening weekend, the movie doesn't have legs.

lens or lense To film or be filmed, as in "Her new movie is currently lensing."

major One of the eight major film studios: Disney, DreamWorks SKG, MGM, Paramount, Sony (Columbia/TriStar), 20th Century–Fox, Universal, and Warner Bros.

mini-major Film production/distribution companies that are smaller than the majors but big enough to compete with them. Leading mini-majors include Miramax, New Line Cinema, and Polygram.

open To attract a big audience in the first few days of release, as in "The advance buzz was good, but the movie didn't open."

package A proposed movie project that includes several promising elements, such as an A-list star and director and a hot script.

pay or play A deal obligating a studio or production company to pay a creative person, such as a star or director, even if the project ends up not being green-lighted or the person's talents are never used.

sell-through The practice of pricing a movie videocassette low enough so that consumers will buy it rather than rent it; or a videocassette priced this way.

shoe size A measurement of an executive's or star's power, as in "His shoe size has gone down."

short list The select group of people being considered for a given creative role on a film production, as in "He's on the short list to play the lead."

show business *See* INDUSTRY, THE

socko *See* BOFFO

suit A film industry person who has to wear a suit to work, such as a studio executive or lawyer, as opposed to one who does not, such as a director, actor, or other creative type.

topper The chief executive of a studio or other company.

town, the Hollywood, or the entertainment industry as a whole.

turnaround When a project has been dropped by one studio and is searching for another, with or without eventual success, as in "The project is in turnaround."

whammo *See* BOFFO

word of mouth What audience members tell each other about a movie they have just seen; more generally, what people say about a project. An expensive ad campaign cannot save a movie from bad word of mouth.

wrap The end of principal photography of a film.

With more than 100 films to his credit, sound designer Mark Berger has won an Academy Award every time he has been nominated. The four-time Oscar winner has won in the best sound category for *Apocalypse Now* in 1979, *The Right Stuff* in 1983, *Amadeus* in 1984 and *The English Patient* in 1996.

Woody Allen and Diane Keaton, seen here in Annie Hall *(1977), have "history." They enjoyed an on-screen and offscreen relationship that spanned multiple years and films.*

HOW MUCH ARE THEY PAID?

Movie pay scales vary wildly. An actor may make $108 for a day as an extra, or $20 million for starring in a blockbuster. For an original screenplay, a writer may make $40,000 or $4 million.

THE STARS OF AMERICAN society – film actors, best-selling authors, athletes, and computer entrepreneurs – command attention for what they do and for how much they earn. Most readers of *Entertainment Weekly* or *People,* and viewers of *Access Hollywood* and *Entertainment Tonight,* are familiar with the Hollywood stars and directors who are earning seven-figure salaries – and more – per picture, and with the writers who are in the six-figure class.

But what is the reality of movie industry salaries? Who earns what?*

PERFORMERS

As much as the scandalous rumors and their on- and offscreen romances, it is the salaries of actors and actresses that make motion pictures the glamour industry of American society.

At the top of the profession are stars who reportedly earn $20 million to $25 million per film. They frequently earn even more by negotiating "points," or participation in the film's profits. Earners in this category presently include Tom Hanks, Tom Cruise, Mel Gibson, Harrison Ford, Julia Roberts, Bruce Willis, Adam Sandler, Mike Myers, Jim Carrey, Will Smith, Eddie Murphy, and Nicolas Cage.

At present, most top female stars make less than their male counterparts. Actresses in the $10 million to $15 million range include Meg Ryan, Michelle Pfeiffer, Jodie Foster, Jennifer Lopez, and Sigourney Weaver. Male performers in this range include Denzel Washington and George Clooney.

Tom Hanks – who began his career as a sitcom star on TV's Bosom Buddies *– reportedly commands a salary of $20 million per movie for films like* Saving Private Ryan *in 1998.*

*(Note: By the time you read this, the salary information may well be out of date.)

For recent films, Ben Affleck, Matt Damon, Samuel L. Jackson, Catherine Zeta-Jones, and Ashley Judd have all received in the $5 million to $10 million range.

Some actors earn still more by wearing more than one hat – for example, by directing, writing, or co-producing their films. Occasionally, an actor will go in the other direction – working below his or her standard fee if particularly interested in a project. A recent example was Nick Nolte, who accepted $1 million for his role in Terrence Malick's critically acclaimed *The Thin Red Line*.

By comparison, it is interesting to note that in the 1930s, Greta Garbo was the screen's highest-paid performer at $250,000 per film, and screen immortal Clark Gable, at his peak, was compensated at somewhere between $50,000 and $75,000 for each appearance.

For those actors who have not attained star status, the difference in salary levels is vast. Screen Actors Guild minimums for actors or actresses working in Hollywood is $636 a day for principal performers and $105 a day for background players (also known as extras).

PRODUCERS

The salaries of producers are perhaps the most elusive number in the industry. Most other industry professionals belong to unions or guilds that set minimum salary levels. This is not a function of the Screen Producers Guild. Instead, each filmmaker's compensation is the result of individual contract negotiations between the filmmaker and the studio and/or investors. However, according to one source in the mid-1990s, producer compensation for specific assignments might fall within the following categories:

Finder's fees: These are typically between $10,000 and $25,000 for bringing a project – in which the producer is not later involved – to a studio. Often this is the role of the first-time producer. An experienced producer is more likely to remain involved with such a project and earn more money.

Development money: In many ways, this is a consultant's fee and may total between $15,000 and $50,000. It is paid while a studio develops a project and works with writers.

Green-lighted project fees: Once a producer gets the go-ahead on a project, fees may grow to between $100,000 and $350,000. If the filmmaker is powerful enough, the deal may include participation in the profits, known as points.

Line-producing fees: This is the producer's compensation for actually getting the film made, and often ranges from $150,000 to $300,000.

DIRECTORS

As is the case with most of the creatives, headline directors can command special deals and large salaries – sometimes into six-figures plus – and perks, including points. However, minimum salaries under the Directors Guild of America are substantial but not stratospheric. A director working on a feature film budgeted up to $500,000 (low budget) earns a minimum of $7,608 per week with a guarantee of two weeks of preparation time and eight weeks of shooting. Compensation for time worked beyond the guarantee is $1,420

Jack Nicholson, at his own request, received neither credit nor salary for his role as an anchorman in James Brooks's 1987 film *Broadcast News*.

Legendary director Orson Welles at work. More recently, directors command salaries ranging from more than $7,000 to more than $11,000 per week.

"I've got America's best writer for $300 a week."

—

Jack L. Warner on signing William Faulkner in the 1930s

per day. On medium-budget films – between $500,000 and $1.5 million – directors earn $8,647 a week with the guaranteed shooting period expanded to ten weeks. Compensation for each additional day is $1,729. On high-budget films – those over $1.5 million – the weekly salary grows to $12,106, shooting time stays at ten weeks, and compensation for additional work is $2,421 a day. Directors of shorts and/or documentaries are paid at the same rate as those working on medium-budget films. The salary minimums apply to both the East and West Coasts.

WRITERS

Joe Eszterhas sold his original script for *Basic Instinct* for $3 million and reportedly has earned between $3 million and $4 million for subsequent scripts (including *Showgirls* for $3.7 million and $2.5 million for a synopsis of *Jade*). Eszterhas has become the gold standard for screenwriters, but under the contractual terms of the Writers Guild of America, the

minimum salary, although a handsome one, falls far short of his level.

For an original screenplay, including treatment, the guild minimum ranges from a low of $48,738 to a high of $91,495. For a nonoriginal screenplay, again with a treatment, compensation starts at $42,647 with a high of $79,308. Minimums are the same on both coasts.

CAMERA

Cinematography translates the scenes created by directors and writers into moving images on film. Specifically, the cinematographer, also known as the director of photography, is in charge of lighting the set and photographing the scene. Such Academy Award–winning cinematographers as Conrad Hall and Haskell Wexler can negotiate fees in excess of the West Coast minimum of $589.57 for an eight-hour day plus time and a half, and the East Coast base of $614.26 for an eight hour day. Camera operators earn $2,830.62 per week in California and $2,620.42 on the East Coast.

EDITORS

The names of five film editors are in the spotlight each year at Academy Awards time; otherwise, editors tend to labor in anonymity outside of the industry. Working in Hollywood, an editor earns a minimum of $2,233.98 per 56-hour week, "on call wait."

MAKEUP ARTISTS AND HAIRSTYLISTS

Another relatively unsung craft is that practiced by makeup artists and hairdressers. In Hollywood, makeup artists earn a minimum of $2,004.93 for a 54-hour week and hairstylists have a base salary of $1,602.12 for a 48.6-hour week cumulative hours, five consecutive days, time and half afterward.

WARDROBE SUPERVISORS

West Coast wardrobe supervisors are paid a minimum of $1,666.19 for a 54-hour week. West Coast set costumers are paid a minimun of $1,444.54 for a 54-hour week.

COSTUME DESIGNERS

A few costume designers – such as the legendary Edith Head, Orry-Kelly, and Theoni V. Aldredge – have found fame and won Academy Awards. Most West Coast costume designers earn a starting salary of $1,782 for a four-day week. Assistant designers have a base pay of $1,455.

SCENIC ARTISTS

Hollywood scenic artists have an hourly base pay of $37.01 per hour. Lead scenic artists, with a crew, begin at $40.96 per hour.

UNIT PUBLICIST

Unit publicists are responsible for creating written materials and generating publicity during the production of a film. Those in the senior publicist category have a starting salary of $1,586.38 per week and, when working on location, are also reimbursed for expenses. This rate prevails on both coasts.

EXECUTIVES

The public is often aware of the most extreme examples of executive salaries. Michael Eisner, chairman and chief executive officer of the Walt Disney Company, made business-news headlines in 1998 when his base annual salary was frozen at $754,000 until the year 2006 and he received "only" a $5 million bonus. By contrast, senior publicists working at a studio earn $1,586.38 a week – the same as their unit publicist counterparts working outside the studio. The middle and lower ranks of studio personnel are likely to reflect the economics of the rest of corporate America, with the highest paychecks going to top-level executives and average or below-average salaries earmarked for the rest of the staff. For example, it is not unusual for senior executives in charge of marketing to earn $500,000 a year. Film companies have been known to offer some employees a glamorous atmosphere and perks in lieu of high salaries.

Many of the unions and guilds maintain Web sites that include information, on the minimum salaries they negotiate. In addition, many unions and guilds negotiate residuals, payments due to an actor or other talent when a film is shown on televison.

In 1994, syndicated writer Jack Mathews commented that film stars are "worth whatever somebody is willing to pay them. The process is called free enterprise market economics, and in this screwy society…there are greater outrages to ponder than the $15 million being paid to Eddie Murphy for *Beverly Hills Cop III*." Mathews's assessment applies equally to the rest of the industry.

The 1963 film *Cleopatra*, starring Elizabeth Taylor and Richard Burton, cost approximately $40 million dollars to make. This was an unprecedented budget for that time and would equal roughly a quarter of a billion dollars today.

Designers have been creating costumes for Count Dracula since the silent era, this one was created for Drakula, made in 1921.

MOVIE
CRAFTS

Werner Herzog directs the action on the set during the filming of Fitzcarraldo (1982), which was shot in Brazil and Peru.

PRODUCING

The producer gets a movie made. The many jobs of a producer may include obtaining financing, making script suggestions, bringing together the creative team, and devising a shooting schedule and budget.

WHAT IS A PRODUCER? What is the difference between an executive producer and an associate producer? William Goldman's answer to questions like these in *Adventures in the Screen Trade* is, "I haven't the foggiest." The term *producer* itself is vague: writers write, actors act, but what does it mean to say "I produce"? Adding to the lack of clarity is the absence of a guild that effectively governs producers. There is no one to insist that only properly qualified people are awarded the title. (There is a Producers Guild of America, but its powers are limited.) If a bankable star wants his wife to be credited as a producer, she gets credited.

DESPITE THE MURKINESS of the terminology, some things can be said about producing. In essence, a producer is the person responsible for getting a movie made. In contemporary Hollywood, a producer often puts together a package and acquires or develops a story, bringing the creative elements (writer, director, actor, etc.) together and obtaining the necessary financing. This kind of producer typically heads a production company that may or may not have a long-term partnership arrangement with a studio, and is compensated by producer fees and sometimes by profit participation.

The chores described above are sometimes called *creative producing,* to distinguish them from *line producing* or *hands-on producing.* A line producer ensures that the film stays within budget, crises are

Ambitious Samuel Goldwyn served as an independent producer for more than 80 films, including such classics as The Pride of the Yankees *(1942),* The Best Years of Our Lives *(1946), and* Guys and Dolls *(1955).*

resolved, and whatever is needed is supplied on time. The working styles of line producers vary: some micromanage; some leave most decisions to the director, although they will keep track of daily progress and troubleshoot when needed. The line producer may continue to shepherd the project through the exploitation phase, when it is exhibited and sold to ancillary markets. Sometimes the creative and line producers are the same person: a single individual who is the first one on the project and the last one off. Sometimes the two jobs are separated, as when a creative producer who heads a production company hires a different line producer for each of several concurrent projects. In that case, the line producer may be billed as a production manager, unit production manager, or associate producer.

The function of the producer has changed greatly since the studio era. In those days, most producers were essentially line producers: salaried studio employees assigned to supervise projects within tight constraints determined by the studio. There were also a few independent producers (such as Samuel Goldwyn) who financed their own films and thus exercised total control.

Most producers today are independent in the sense that they are not studio employees. But only a fraction are independent in the sense that they do not rely on the studios for financing. These truly independent producers are either rich enough to finance their films themselves or they are capable of

PRODUCER'S TASKS: A PARTIAL LIST

NOT EVERY PERSON BILLED as a producer does all the tasks listed below on each film. But these are the kinds of things a producer might do:

- Conceive the idea
- Assemble the package (for example, story, stars, director, writer)
- Sell the package to a studio or other financial backer
- Read drafts of the script and make suggestions
- Select locations
- Devise a breakdown (a scene-by-scene itemization of what will be needed)
- Devise a shooting schedule and budget
- Hire the crew, including the director of photography, production designer, costume designer, editor, and composer, and oversee their efforts
- Manage the production of the film
- Gather input from the production manager, first assistant director, and the production accountant about problems in production, such as falling behind schedule or going over budget
- Consult with the director about how to address problems
- Supply the financial backers with progress reports and rushes or selected takes
- Oversee editing
- Oversee previews and make decisions about how to respond
- Make plans for distributing and marketing the film

raising money from private investors, whether banks, churches, relatives, or wealthy investors. Often a producing credit can be won without much actual involvement in producing. Someone who does nothing but arrange financing or persuade the star to come aboard may be credited as a producer or, more commonly, as an executive producer. If the director or star has enough clout, he or she may demand and get credit as producer – while doing nothing more than directing or acting.

PRODUCING STYLES

Directors are often treated as if they were auteurs, sole authors of their films, each with a recognizable style or recurrent set of themes. Yet a few producers have made an equally recognizable mark on their films.

In the studio era, these included the independent producers Samuel Goldwyn and David O. Selznick, who once said, "Great films, successful films, are made in their every detail according to the vision of one man." A few studio employees, like RKO's

horror master Val Lewton and MGM's musical producer Arthur Freed, also enjoyed a considerable degree of independence and left their signature on all the films they produced.

Since the decline of the studio era, few producers are well-known to the public, unless they also happen to be directors (such as Steven Spielberg). Yet some have been just as distinctive in their filmmaking as Selznick or Goldwyn. The team of Don Simpson and Jerry Bruckheimer, for example, created a fast-paced, testosterone-laced action-movie style that marked films from *Beverly Hills Cop* to *Crimson Tide* and has been continued by Bruckheimer since Simpson's death in 1996.

Even so, some of the best producers have been precisely those who were least visible. Director Don Siegel described Walter Wanger, his producer on *Riot in Cell Block 11* (1954), in this way: "Walter is a producer who produces; he doesn't direct. He wouldn't direct traffic." A producer, Siegel added, "should encourage the director to give the film the director's signature."

The job of producer may be vague, but it ranks high. Traditionally, "Produced by" is the last opening credit to roll before "Directed by." Should the film win a best picture Oscar, it is the producer who runs up on stage to accept it.

PRODUCING GLOSSARY: PEOPLE

> "[Line producers] are the working class among the elite in town. This is probably because they actually work."
>
> —
>
> *Gail Resnik and Scott Trost,*
> All You Need to Know About the Movie and TV Business

assistant producer An assistant to the producer who may do some supervising in the producer's absence.

associate producer Traditionally, the producer's second-in-command, who helps with such tasks as on-set problem solving and coordinating location shoots. But the credit may also be awarded to someone only tangentially involved with line producing, such as a writer or studio executive. Or it may be the only title given to the person who does all the actual work of line producing, while the producer credit goes to someone less involved but more powerful.

crew The group of people involved in making a film, or in some aspect of making the film, such as the camera crew.

executive producer A person in some way responsible for a film who rarely participates in the nitty-gritty of filmmaking to the degree that creative or line producers do. The title itself gives no clue as to what the person does. The executive producer may raise money to get the film made; may be very involved in business aspects; or may do nothing more than place a phone call to help close the deal. She may be the head of the production company, the star's business manager, or the star herself.

location department The group of people who find locations, arrange to make them available, and manage the transportation of equipment and personnel to the location.

location manager The person who arranges contracts for the use of locations. Sometimes this person is also a location scout, finding locations appropriate to the film; in other cases, the location scout works under the location manager.

location scout A person who searches for locations to use in a film.

producer The person in charge of getting a movie made, including securing the financing, acquiring or developing a story, and bringing the creative elements together. See also "Producing: Introduction."

Producers Guild of America The national organization for film and television producers, based in Beverly Hills.

producer's representative or **producer's rep** An individual or organization that helps a producer find a distributor and acts as liaison between them.

production accountant or **production auditor** The person who pays the bills, maintains records of expenditures, and reports to the studio or other financing body on how money is being spent.

production assistant Despite the name, this person generally works not under the producer but under the director, running errands of various kinds. (*See* "Directing" in this chapter.)

production company A firm that develops and makes movies, but does not usually finance or distribute its own products.

production coordinator or **production office coordinator** The person in charge of the production office. Acts as liaison among the different personnel who are shooting the film and between them and the production company's main office. Sometimes this person is the same as the production secretary; sometimes the production secretary works for this person.

production department The group of people responsible for calculating the costs of shooting and preparing for shooting the film.

production manager The person in charge of the everyday details of filmmaking. This person may also be the line producer or may work under the line producer. Tasks of the production manager include hiring and negotiating deals with the crew, signing up vendors, making the breakdown for each day's shoot, and maintaining budget and schedule. He or she may also be called the unit manager or unit production manager. Note: despite their title, production managers are members of the director's guild.

shooting company The crew of a particular movie.

technical adviser A person from outside the film industry hired to advise the makers of a film about a particular area of expertise, such as a doctor about medical procedures or a soldier about war.

unit or **production unit** The crew making a film.

unit manager (or **unit production manager**) This may be a synonym for production manager, or may be someone who works under the production manager, taking care of such details as preparing each day's shoot and obtaining transportation and housing on location.

utility man A low-ranking worker on a film production who runs errands and performs manual labor.

PRODUCING GLOSSARY: THINGS

above the line In a film budget, the costs of signing key creative talent such as producer, director, screenwriter, author of source material (if any), and principal actors. Above-the-line costs are distinguished from below-the-line costs.

backup schedule Shooting schedule to be followed if the regular schedule cannot proceed, for instance, because of bad weather.

below the line In a film budget, all expenses that are not above the line (and related to key creative talent); includes crew salaries, extras, equipment, location-shooting expenses, etc.

breakdown A scene-by-scene, day-by-day itemization of what will be needed (actors, props, extras, etc.) to shoot a movie. Scenes are usually grouped out of sequence to minimize expenses (for example, all shots in one location may be filmed at the same time, even if they will appear in separate parts of the movie). The breakdown is usually prepared by the production manager and is the basis for preparing a breakdown board and shooting schedule. Also called breakdown sheets, breakdown script, or script breakdown.

breakdown board A large wood panel (typically five feet or longer) that displays the breakdown for shooting a film. The board is used to juggle information from the breakdown sheets until an optimum shooting sequence is determined. Cardboard breakdown strips show the type of scene (interior or exterior, day or night), the location, and who or what is needed (actors, special equipment, vehicles). Also called a production board, production breakdown board, or production strip board.

budget (1) The total sum of money to be spent making a movie. (2) The document that outlines how the money will be spent. The budget is prepared in preproduction, usually by the production manager.

call The shooting schedule for a particular day, distributed or posted the previous day. It lists which members of cast and crew are expected and includes times for makeup and costuming. Also called the call sheet or shooting call.

crew call The call sheet for a film production crew that tells the members when and where to come for shooting.

cross-plot An abridged, one-page breakdown sheet.

location A place other than a studio where shooting is performed. When a film is shot "on location," it sometimes means that it is filmed at or near the actual places where the story is set, but most location filming takes place far from the film's setting: Vancouver, British Columbia, for example, has doubled for many American cities. While offering greater realism (natural sunlight and scenery; real buildings), location shooting presents logistical problems: having to house and feed the cast and crew; supplying power; controlling lighting and sound. Hence many films combine some location filming and some studio filming. The location department is in charge of finding locations and making them available for filming.

log sheet A record of activities by a film technician. Log sheets are made for camera work (a camera report), sound work (the sound report), and often editing. The continuity clerk records continuity sheets (*See also* "Directing Glossary: People" in this chapter).

production breakdown *See* BREAKDOWN

production number (1) A number the studio assigns to a movie for reference in bookkeeping and other kinds of records. (2) A big musical performance in a film musical.

production office The command center for getting a movie made.

production report A report giving detailed infor-mation about a day's shoot, including number of shots and takes, amount of film used, people employed, etc. Also called the daily production report.

production schedule The schedule for each day's shoot.

shooting or **shoot** The process of putting action on film.

shooting schedule An advance plan for filming on a particular day or series of days, including scenes and shots to be filmed, time and location of shooting, and people and things needed.

Director Leo McCarey surveyed the action during the production of 1944's Going My Way.

DIRECTING

The director brings artistic order out of the potential chaos of a film set. He or she directs the actors and leads the crew to make sure the story envisioned is the story put on screen.

THE DIRECTOR IS in charge of the creative aspects of a film production. The director orchestrates what is filmed by guiding the actors and working with the technical crew to make each scene as effective as possible in all respects – lighting, camera placement, sound, etc. The actors and the technical crew answer to the director, while the director answers to the producer, who answers to the studio or other financial backers.

Throughout the filmmaking process, the director is usually the person with the most complete understanding of how all the pieces of a film-in-progress will fit into an artistic whole. In pre-production, directors often help shape the script, plan the shooting schedule, consult on casting, and work with the director of photography and the production designer on the film's overall look. During production, the director may order script rewrites and will begin consulting with the editor on how the film should be assembled. In postproduction, the director continues to be involved with editing, scoring, sound, and visual effects. His involvement typically will not end until the final print is in the can.

ALTHOUGH IN THE EARLIEST DAYS of silent filmmaking directors such as D.W. Griffith had a great deal of artistic control, the rise of the studio system reduced most American directors to a workmanlike role. As studio employees, Hollywood directors of the 1930s and 40s were largely not free to develop their own projects but were assigned scripts, casts, schedules, and budgets. Their on-set decisions were closely monitored and controlled by studio producers.

Director Martin Scorsese on the set of The Age of Innocence *(1993), with Winona Ryder and Daniel Day-Lewis.*

Within this system, a few directors, such as John Ford, Howard Hawks, and Alfred Hitchcock, successfully maintained a fair degree of independence, while others, such as Orson Welles, bore the career scars of lost battles with the studios. With the demise of the studio system and the rise of independently packaged films, directors once more had a chance to shine. The auteur theory, coming out of France in the 1950s, praised directors who impressed a personal stamp on their movies and made every detail serve a coherent vision. This approach influenced future generations of filmmakers, notably the "movie brats" of the 1970s, who included Steven Spielberg, George Lucas, Francis Ford Coppola, and Martin Scorsese.

A director stands a better chance of truly controlling a film's artistic content if he or she is a hyphenate – someone who writes (or cowrites) and produces (or coproduces) films. This is common among independent filmmakers working with small-to medium-size budgets, but rare among Hollywood directors responsible for turning vast sums of studio money into commercial hits. In such cases, it takes an enormous degree of box-office success to give a director the clout to continue making films exactly as he or she wants.

For a director, ultimate control is the right to approve the final cut – as opposed to leaving the final editing choices in the hands of the producer or studio. Many directors can now have it both ways by issuing a "director's cut" on video – one edited differently from the studio cut shown in theaters.

DIRECTING GLOSSARY: PEOPLE

assistant director (A.D.) The director's second-in-command, who acts something like a foreman on the set. The A.D. is responsible for giving the call (the summons to actors and crew for a given day's shoot), organizing crowd scenes, arranging logistics, maintaining order, and helping with other tasks as requested by the director. There may be more than one A.D.; the first will then be called the "first assistant director," with a "second" and possibly a "third" working under him or her. It is the A.D. who yells "Quiet on the set!" and "Roll!," sometimes through a megaphone.

auteur French word for "author," applied in auteur theory to directors who express a consistent personal vision in their works.

continuity clerk The person stationed beside the camera who is responsible for maintaining a film's continuity. Often a woman, she takes detailed notes about each shot, recording such particulars as number and duration of takes, exact position of actors, costumes, direction of movement, dialogue spoken (including any changes from the script), etc. Her notes are the basis for daily continuity sheets, and they help ensure that shots filmed out of sequence match when placed in correct order. Also called a continuity girl, script girl, script clerk, or script supervisor.

dialogue director A person who rehearses performers and coaches them in learning and saying their lines. The position is not as common now as it was in the early sound days, when many film directors and actors lacked experience with dialogue.

director The person in charge of the creative aspects of a film production. (*See* "Directing: Introduction.")

Directors Guild of America Union of film and television directors and assistant directors.

filmmaker A person who makes films, particularly one who uses them to express a distinctive vision or style. In commercial cinema, this term is usually reserved for the director, though it can also mean a producer. More precisely, "filmmakers" are independent, often avant-garde directors who take charge of several aspects of production, possibly including writing, producing, photographing, or editing.

metteur-en-scène Older French term for "director," used pejoratively by auteur theorists for a director who, unlike an "auteur," puts together a film mechanically and does not use it to express a personal vision. The more neutral contemporary French term for director is *réalisateur.*

production assistant (P.A.) An assistant to the director or production manager who runs errands, distributes papers, and generally acts as a gopher (as in "go for coffee"). An entry-level position for many an aspiring filmmaker.

script clerk, script girl, or **script supervisor** *See* CONTINUITY CLERK

second unit A group of personnel, headed by the second-unit director, that films separately from the main unit, handling crowd scenes, action and stunt sequences, and location background shots. Neither the stars nor the director need be present, though the director supervises the planning of second-unit shooting.

second-unit director The person in charge of the second unit. Usually someone skilled in handling action and crowd scenes.

Smithee, Allen (Alan) Pseudonym appointed by the Directors Guild of America as a screen credit for a director who insists on removing his name from a film. A director might do so, for example, if the producers have crafted a final cut that strongly deviates from his wishes. Allen (or Alan) Smithee films are usually mediocre to horrible, from the first one, *Death of a Gunfighter* (1967; released 1969), to more recent examples like *Sub Down* (1997).

> "What is directing? It's trying to use a lot of people and some very, very heavy apparatus and give it the lightness of a pen while you are writing."
>
> —
>
> *David Lean*

Japanese director Akira Kurosawa brought feudal Japan to the big screen. He directed more than thirty films prior to his death in 1998, including Ran *(1985), pictured here.*

OPPOSITE:

Born in London, England, Alfred Hitchcock directed his first films in the 1920s and continued to direct into the 1970s. Audiences reveled in his signature cameo appearances.

blocking Planning a scene by rehearsing actors' positions and movements, along with the positions of cameras and lights.

continuity The logical progression of a film from shot to shot and scene to scene. Since movies are typically photographed out of sequence, care must be taken to maintain the illusion of continuity by having action flow smoothly and by matching all appropriate details. For example, if an actor has a bruised cheek in one shot, in a second shot does not, and in a third shot does again, the illusion that the bruise is real will disappear. The job of safeguarding continuity falls especially to the continuity clerk, who keeps continuity sheets for that purpose. *Continuity* is also a term for a highly detailed shooting script.

continuity sheets The log of each take maintained by a continuity clerk to ensure continuity from shot to shot. It records such details as number and duration, position of actors, direction of movement, dialogue spoken, etc. Also called continuity notes and take sheets.

dailies Rough prints of a day's shooting, usually made overnight for viewing the next day by key personnel, particularly the director and the producer. The viewing ensures that the shots are acceptable and permits prompt retakes if they are not; it also serves as the basis for decisions about light and color corrections in future prints. Also called rushes.

director's cut The rough cut, or rough initial version of a movie, adhering strictly to the director's wishes. Working in tandem with the editor, the director has complete freedom to develop it, but the final cut may be quite different, embodying changes required by the producer or initiated by the director.

director's viewfinder Small device that allows a director or director of photography to see an image through various lenses, aiding in the selection of the best lens for the shot. A viewfinder can often be found hanging on a chain from the director's neck. Also called a director's finder.

dry run A rehearsal with actors before shooting or with the crew, but without the cameras running. Also called a run-through.

running lines Rehearsing dialogue.

run-through *See* DRY RUN

rushes *See* DAILIES

storyboard A series of sketches or still photographs outlining a proposed film. Generally used in planning animated films, the storyboard is also used by some feature-film directors who like to plan their films shot by shot.

tempo The pace at which a movie seems to advance. The pace is the result of numerous factors, including the pace of the screenplay, movement of the actors, movement of the camera, and rhythm of the editing. On the set, the director controls tempo by controlling the timing with which the actors play their scenes.

WHO SAYS WHAT ON A FILM SET

BEFORE THE TAKE, IN THIS SEQUENCE:

ORDER	GIVEN BY	MEANING
"Quiet on the set!"	assistant director	everyone be quiet, shooting is about to start
"Roll 'em!"	assistant director	camera operator, start the camera; variants include *"Roll"* and *"Roll it"*
"Speed!"	recordist	the camera and sound recorder are in sync and running at the correct operational speed
"Action!"	director	actors, start acting

AT THE END OF THE TAKE, IN THIS SEQUENCE:

"Cut!"	director	the shot is over, stop shooting and acting; a variant, *"Cut and hold,"* means stop shooting and acting but maintain places in case shot has to resume
"Print it!"	director	this take is good, send it to the laboratory and have it printed; variants include *"Print," "Save it,"* and *"Take it"*

WRITING

The screenwriter is not just a supplier of snappy dialogue. Telling the story on paper before it reaches film, the screenwriter designs a film's narrative structure and conceives its characters and scenes.

BEFORE A MOVIE CAN BE MADE, a screenwriter has to imagine it. He or she has to frame the story, conceive in detail what the audience will see and hear, and decide what the characters will say and do. All of this must be set down clearly in the printed text, called the screenplay or script, which becomes the blueprint for making the movie. Without a screenplay, no contemporary feature film could exist.

Historically, despite the obvious importance of their work, screenwriters have held a lowly position in the Hollywood hierarchy, somewhere below stars, directors, producers, and studio executives. In the 1950s and 60s, auteur theory claimed that directors were the real authors of movies, further downgrading the position of screenwriters. Their status has improved somewhat in recent decades, with news of multimillion-dollar screenplay sales and a plethora of books celebrating the art of screenwriting. Even so, Nobel and Pulitzer prizes have yet to be awarded on the basis of a writer's screenwork. And screenwriters have become inured to having their work revised and remolded by other screenwriters, not to mention directors, producers, executives, and stars.

SCREENPLAYS BEGIN LIFE either as an original concept or as a piece of source material, such as a novel, play, short story, article, or another movie. If the latter, the makers of the movie have to obtain rights to the source material. Would-be screenwriters, working unpaid and on their own, usually have to develop their concept into a completed "spec screenplay" (on

The screenplay for Harold Pinter's The Servant, *released in 1963.*

spec, or on speculation) before they can hope to sell it to a producer or get it represented by an agent. Established screenwriters, however, can often sell a concept as a pitch, an oral recounting of the story to production or studio executives. (This often takes place at the Hollywood institution called a pitch meeting.) The project may also be sold on the basis of a written outline or treatment, a detailed synopsis of the film. If a pitch is successful, the next step is a development deal or step deal, the process by which a concept becomes a screenplay. The studio contracts the writer for a series of development steps, often two drafts and a polish (light rewrite), paying her or him something at each step. During development, other voices chime in with rewrite suggestions—studio executives, producer, director, stars. The studio may decide to drop the project along the way, or to keep the project but drop the writer (often softening the blow with the euphemism "We're going in a different direction," which means "You're fired"). New writers may be called in to write completely new drafts, or a script doctor (a seasoned screenwriter specializing in fixing troubled scripts) may tinker with the most problematic parts.

A long and tortured development process is called "development hell." If the process is successful, the studio will green-light the picture, or authorize production. If it fails, the project is either shelved, which means the studio is not making it but no one else can either, or goes into turnaround, which means another studio is free to pick it up. Even after production begins, the script may be altered: the director may decide to make changes once he or she sees the actors playing the scenes before the camera, or an audience's negative reaction to a preview may compel the studio to rewrite and reshoot parts of the film. But major script changes after production begins are horribly expensive, much more so than working out problems on the page before production begins. Hence the "development hell" process to write and rewrite until the script is as trouble-free as possible.

Screenwriters who have written hits are in great demand and may command exorbitant fees. But even the most famous scribes do not have much control over what becomes of their scripts, unless they also happen to be producers or directors. Hence some screenwriters take on just those roles on a few projects, thereby gaining more claim to the title auteur.

SCREENPLAY STRUCTURE

Some writers plot their films by using scene cards. In this method, each scene is described on an index card (or a digital equivalent), then the cards are arranged and rearranged until the optimum structure is worked out. Others use a step outline, a method in which major scenes are described and numbered in the order in which they occur. Still others plot their stories in a narrative treatment.

Whatever writing method is used, a script will have certain elements, including description, dialogue, and structure. Of these three, structure is the most abstract and the most important. William Goldman goes so far as to say, "Screenplays are structure."

The structure of the script – the broad shape of its action, from opening fade-in to final fade-out – is what will make the script a coherent, exciting story—a leaden exercise, or an incoherent mess.

Structure is composed of scenes and sequences. Scenes are units of action, usually occurring in a single time and place. Scenes are grouped into sequences, or a connected series of scenes, like the wedding sequence in *The Godfather*. Sequences, in turn, are grouped into acts. The Hollywood film traditionally has three acts: (I) setup; (II) complication or confrontation; (III) resolution. In a two-hour movie, Act I usually lasts about 30 minutes, Act II 60 minutes, and Act III 30 minutes. In screenplay terms, where a minute of screen time translates roughly into a page of script, this means Act I is 30 pages, Act II 60 pages, and Act III 30 pages. The three-act structure has been described this way: "In the first act you get your hero in a tree; in the second act you throw rocks at him; in the third act you get him down from the tree."

Most contemporary Hollywood films have two major plot points or turning points, which are decisive moments in the action: one near the end of Act I and the other near the end of Act II. Both of these plot points (sometimes called Plot Points I and II) turn the action in a new and surprising direction.

It should be noted that not all screenwriters strive to adhere to this structure, and not all moviegoers can easily locate Plot Points I and II. Says Alex Epstein, "three-act structure is overrated. In comedy, if you keep them laughing, they'll forgive you anything.

"A film director can take a great script and make a great film. Or he can take a great script and make a terrible film. But he can't take a terrible script and make a great film. No way."

—

Syd Field, screenwriter and screenwriting teacher, in Screenplay: The Foundations of Screenwriting

In adventure stories and thrillers, tell a good yarn, and you can chuck the turning points out the window."

The opening (first 10–15 minutes) and ending (last 10–15 minutes) are widely considered to be the most important parts of the film, and of the screenplay. By the end of the first ten minutes, most audience members will have already decided whether or not they like the film. They also will have formed some definite expectations about what kind of film it is – its genre, tone, etc. Yet even if they like and understand it, a bad ending will leave them unsatisfied and complaining, while a good ending will send them out of the theater sated and singing the movie's praises. From such reactions flow good and bad word of mouth, movies with "legs," and movies that disappear after opening day.

> "Q: Why shouldn't an outline or treatment be longer than 30 pages? A: The producer's lips get tired."
>
> —
>
> *Why an outline or treatment should be short, according to an old Hollywood joke.*

SCREENPLAY TERMINOLOGY: A GLOSSARY

angle on What the camera is aimed at; what the audience sees; also written as FAVORING

another angle Change the way the camera points at a subject; also written as NEW ANGLE

back to scene Return from a distinctive shot (POV, CLOSE SHOT, INSERT, etc.) to a more neutral camera setup

beat A pause for dramatic emphasis; or a plot point, a moment that significantly advances the action

close shot A shot in which the character's face occupies all or most of the frame; *see also* INSERT

cut to Shift to a new scene

ext. Exterior scene, intended to take place outdoors (though it may be filmed on a studio set simulating the outdoors)

fade in Gradually make the transition from blackness to a complete image. Fade-ins and fade-outs are typically used to mark a significant change in time or location. Since fade-ins often begin a movie, FADE IN is traditionally the opening direction in a screenplay.

fade out Gradually make the transition from image to blackness. Since fade-outs often end a movie, FADE OUT is traditionally the last direction in a screenplay. Also written as GO TO BLACK. *See* FADE IN.

favoring *See* ANGLE ON

go to black *See* FADE OUT

insert A CLOSE SHOT of an object, such as a watch face, photograph, or headline

int. Interior scene, intended to take place indoors

montage *See* SERIES OF SHOTS

moving shot A shot in which the camera moves along with a moving character or vehicle, for example, a shot inside a moving car; also written as "moving."

new angle *See* ANOTHER ANGLE

o.s. Off scene; refers to a sound whose source cannot be seen on screen. A voice heard off scene is often described as a voice-over, or V.O. More precisely, a voice is O.S. when the speaker is understood to be speaking in the scene but is not present in the shot (as when a character listens to someone speaking on the other side of the room). A voice is a V.O. when the speaker is understood not to be speaking in the scene, such as a narrator or a voice from the character's past.

over the shoulder shot A shot in which the character's head is in the foreground of the frame and what the character sees is in the background; often used in POV and REVERSE ANGLE shots

pov A character's point of view; how the scene looks to him or her

reverse angle A 180-degree change in perspective; instead of Character A looking west at Character B, we now have Character B looking east at Character A

series of shots A succession of short shots, often used to show the passage of a longer period of time, also written as MONTAGE

v.o. Voice-over; a voice whose source is not visible in the shot; *See also* O.S.

wider angle Include more of the scene than in the previous shot

SCREENPLAY FORMAT

- Type or word-process using the Courier 12-point font. Do not boldface, right-justify, or vary fonts. It should look like it came out of a typewriter. Underlining is preferable to italics.
- Single-space, except for the title page; there the script title, byline, and writer's name are double spaced.
- Left margin is 1.5 inches, right margin 1.00 inch. The wider left margin leaves room for the three-hole punch. The top and bottom margins should each be 1.00 inch.
- Bind the screenplay between plain cardstock covers with two or three brass brads. There should be no writing on the covers. Fancy covers are the mark of an amateur.
- The optimum length for a script is 120 pages (at about a page per minute of screen time, this should translate into a two-hour movie). Avoid writing much longer or shorter than that, but especially longer: a 180-page first screenplay is the mark of someone who doesn't know how to edit his or her own work.
- Descriptive text is 60 characters wide.
- Dialogue is 30 characters wide.
- Title page: Nothing on top. In the middle, center the title (in all caps) and screenwriter's name, like this:

THE GREATEST MOVIE EVER
by
John Smith

The bottom left or right of the title page should give the screenwriter's name, address, and phone number. Something like this:

```
John Smith
222 Maple St.
Anytown, NY 10000
(555)555-1212
```

- First page begins with FADE IN. Do not repeat name of screenplay or writer. Beginning with the second page, the page number appears in the upper right.
- When starting a new scene or changing location, insert a slugline, like this:

INT. WITCH'S CASTLE —
HALLWAY — NIGHT

- Sluglines must always say whether the scene is interior (INT.) or exterior (EXT.) and whether it is DAY or NIGHT.
- Do not number sluglines. That is done in the shooting script, long after the project has already been sold.
- When a character is first introduced, his or her name is CAPITALIZED. Afterward, it is set upper- and lowercase in descriptive text, but remains ALL CAPS when heading dialogue.
- Dialogue: Indent the character name in ALL CAPS at 3.7 to 4.2 inches. Under that, indent the dialogue spoken by that character at 3.0 inches:

DOROTHY
Toto, I've a feeling we're
not in Kansas anymore.

- Avoid giving explicit camera directions like "Camera pans left to follow the intruder" or "JUMP CUT, followed by DISSOLVE." This is called "directing on the page" and is damaging for several reasons, not least because it breaks the spell of your story by drawing attention to the camera. (It also usurps the job of the director, who will most likely ignore your instructions anyway.) Instead, simply describe what the viewer will see: "The intruder walks left."
- Prose style should be clear, vivid, and enjoyable. Only describe things the viewer could see or hear, but remember that a reader will have to get through your script first. Be kind to that reader.
- Capitalize sounds other than dialogue. For example: "the car SCREECHES to a halt, HORN going wild."
- When completely changing place and time, you may insert "CUT TO:" at the right margin, with a space before and a space after. However, some writers dispense with this, preferring not to clutter the page. There is no need to use it when you are merely shifting locations within a continuous scene.

WRITING GLOSSARY: PEOPLE

dialogue writer A person who specializes in writing dialogue for a film.

gagman A screenwriter whose specialty is writing jokes, either visual or verbal. Gagmen were especially prominent in the writing of silent-film comedy.

screenwriter A person who writes or revises a screenplay, the text from which a movie is filmed.

scribe Slang for a screenwriter.

script consultant *See* SCRIPT DOCTOR

script doctor A person hired to consult on or rewrite a script, often a troubled one in need of fixing. Also called a script consultant.

Writers Guild of America (WGA) Union representing writers who write for film, television, and radio.

> "They were treated much like butlers, socially."
>
> —
>
> *Ben Hecht on the status of screenwriters in studio-era Hollywood*

WRITING GLOSSARY: THINGS

adaptation A movie based on, or adapted from, a work in another medium, such as a play, novel, history, or an article.

backstory The background to the story seen on screen, sometimes seen in flashback or alluded to in dialogue or exposition. The backstory to *Casablanca* includes Rick Blaine's service in the Spanish Civil War and his days with Ilsa in Paris.

caption A printed line shown on screen to describe time or place or translate a foreign phrase. *See also* SUBTITLE

continuity title *See* INTERTITLE

crawl title, creeping title *See* ROLLING TITLE

credits Titles listing the people who made the movie and naming their contributions.

crosscutting Shifting back and forth between two events happening at once. Also called intercutting.

dialogue Lines spoken by actors.

episode A self-contained part of an anthology film or serial.

flashback A scene depicting events that happened prior to the time of the main narrative.

flashforward A scene depicting events that will happen or are imagined as happening after the time of the main narrative. Also called flash-ahead.

high concept Term for a film that heavily depends on an intriguing and unusual premise, such as "mermaid visits Manhattan and falls in love with a man," the premise of the high-concept film *Splash*.

insert title See INTERTITLE

intertitle A full screen of printed text inserted between segments of photographed action, rather than at the film's beginning or end. In silent films, intertitles were used extensively to display dialogue. In sound films, they have been used sparingly, usually to describe a time or place change or offer exposition. Also called insert titles or CONTINUITY TITLES.

John Turturro plays a writer who encounters strange characters at his hotel in the movie Barton Fink *(1991).*

MacGuffin or **McGuffin** Term coined by Alfred Hitchcock for an object or goal about which the characters care a great deal but about which the audience does not care; its narrative purpose is only to drive the action. Hitchcock's favorite example was the vague "government secrets" that drove the action in his film *North by Northwest.*

main title Printed text that gives the name of the film, usually at the beginning.

option Agreement in which rights to a screenplay or story material are "rented" for a specified period, during which no one else can buy the film; the optioned material may be made into a movie, or the project may be dropped without being made when the option expires.

outline A synopsis of a proposed film story. If accepted, the screenwriter will be asked to prepare either a full screenplay or a more detailed treatment.

overlap dialogue Different dialogue spoken by two or more characters simultaneously, so that it is difficult to make out specific words.

parallel action Action taking place simultaneously in two or more settings, with the camera cutting back and forth from one to the other.

parenthetical A brief instruction on how a line should be delivered, placed between parentheses and inserted between the character's name and his or her line of dialogue in a script. Also called a "wryly," for the overuse of the parenthetical "wryly," as in:

```
            JANE
          (wryly)
        Nice tie.
```

pat-the-dog scene A scene in which the screen hero does something nice (for example, patting a dog), thereby gaining audience sympathy. Sometimes inserted artificially to satisfy studio demands for a more likable hero.

photoplay Archaic term, common in the silent era, for a screenplay or movie.

plot point A moment that significantly advances the action.

production script A script of the completed film, including all dialogue and action as filmed.

rolling title Text that rolls up from the bottom of the screen and vanishes at the top. Typically used for closing credits, though occasionally for other purposes, such as the opening exposition in *Star Wars.* Also called a title crawl, crawl title, creeping title, or running title.

scenario A completed screenplay, or an outline or treatment for a screenplay.

scene (1) A unit of action, normally taking place in a single location at a single time. A series of connected shots makes up a scene; a series of connected scenes makes up a sequence. (2) The setting or location of a unit of action.

screenplay The written text from which a movie is made. It includes dialogue, descriptions of action and setting, and some camera and sound directions. Also called script, scenario, or photoplay.

script *See* SCREENPLAY

selling script An unsold screenplay that is being marketed to industry people, rather than a shooting script formatted for use as a blueprint for filming.

sequence A series of scenes connected by a single idea. Examples include the wedding in *The Godfather* and crossing the Nefud Desert in *Lawrence of Arabia.* Each sequence has a beginning, a middle, and an end.

shooting script The final, approved screenplay used by the director in making a film. It includes not only dialogue and action but detailed camera instructions, with individual shots numbered consecutively.

shot A single continuous action that is filmed or appears to be filmed in one take, from one camera setup. The shot is the basic unit of film grammar; several shots make up a scene.

slugline In a screenplay, the line of text that gives a scene's location and states whether it is an interior or exterior, day or night, e.g.,

```
    "INT.—WITCH'S CASTLE—
       HALLWAY—NIGHT."
```

spec script A screenplay written on spec, or on speculation, that is, with no commitment from a studio or other buyer.

spine The essence of a story; that which holds the story together.

subtitle A caption printed across the bottom of the screen, particularly a translation of a foreign-language phrase.

synopsis A brief summary of a film or potential film. Often precedes a more detailed outline or treatment, as a means of interesting buyers.

title Text that appears on screen to convey information to the audience. Includes credits, main title, and subtitles.

treatment A detailed summary of a film story. Often used to sell a project before the script is written.

The footage for the 1960s flashback scenes of Terence Stamp in Steven Soderbergh's 1999 film *The Limey,* was taken directly from the 1967 film *Poor Cow.*

"Ben [Hecht] was always good at pressure jobs. He worked on *Gone with the Wind* for David Selznick – never read that either. Claimed reading the book would only confuse him."

—

Leland Hayward, 1971

ACTING

Actors perform a film story. They include stars whose names and faces are widely known, and lesser-known players without whom a movie could not create its illusion of multitudes.

ACTORS ARE THE PEOPLE who play the characters in a film. They are cast, or selected for their parts, in two ways, depending on whether they are stars or lesser-known players. Stars are courted by studios and producers, and usually do not need to audition for a role. These actors are presumed to be qualified to play the principal characters to best advantage, and famous and popular enough to attract audiences to the film. Often they are the main thing people mention in talking about the movie ("Did you see the new Bruce Willis movie?" or "I don't remember the title, but Julia Roberts was in it"). Sometimes the star is part of the package that sells the movie to the studio. They are paid a great deal: some stars currently command up to $20 million per movie, often with a cut of the gross.

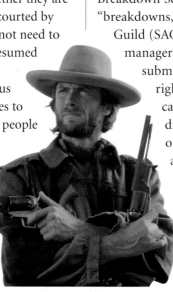

Clint Eastwood first met with film success starring in spaghetti westerns. Later he became synonymous with the vigilante cop Dirty Harry, a character he played in multiple films.

OTHER ACTORS ARE RECRUITED by the casting director, a freelance professional hired to do this job, often in consultation with the producer and director. Their names are largely unknown to the general public, yet movies could not be made without them. Some earn a decent living, appearing regularly in character parts; others spend most of their careers scrounging for work, temping or waiting tables to make ends meet, but are able to point to a few moments where they shone on-screen.

Casting directors have tremendous power over the careers of these journeymen actors. The casting director usually begins by breaking down a script

to see what roles have to be cast. To search for talent, he or she may employ the private company Breakdown Services, which distributes daily lists, or "breakdowns," of available roles to Screen Actors Guild (SAG) franchised agents and personal managers. The agents and managers then submit names of clients who might be right for the part. Auditions before the casting director follow; the casting director then either makes the choice or selects a small pool of candidates to audition before the director and producer. The casting director also negotiates contracts. Payment varies according to performer and role, but for many jobs it is no more than scale, the minimum salary for work by a member of SAG. (Often, it is scale plus ten – scale plus the ten percent the agent receives, if the actor has an agent.)

Occasionally, a lead role in a Hollywood movie will go to a little-known actor – a strategy that can lend a freshness to a film, although it risks burdening the film with a central figure lacking in star quality. When this strategy is used, the unknown actor is paid less than usual star rates and is often paired with better-known talent, as a sort of insurance policy. Thus Kevin Costner, unknown when he starred in *The Untouchables*, was paired with screen veteran Sean Connery; that film's success propelled Costner into movie star ranks. Sofia Coppola's performance in *The Godfather Part III*, however, failed to establish her as a screen phenomenon. Powerful stars are often involved in the script development process. Screenwriters are sometimes infuriated by their suggested revisions if these feed the stars' egos at the expense of the script. Often, however, a star knows best what kind of dialogue or touches of characterization work best with his or her established screen persona.

ACTORS PREPARE for their roles in different ways. Some, influenced by the naturalistic "Method" style of the Actors Studio (a New York City group founded in 1947), attempt a deep understanding of their characters' background and motivation: they may extensively research their characters and inhabit the role even between takes. Marlon Brando, Dustin Hoffman, and Robert De Niro are all exemplars of this approach. Others prepare less exhaustively or use other acting techniques.

Some actors, such as Hoffman and De Niro, pride themselves on playing a variety of parts, and may be all but unrecognizable in different roles. Most Hollywood stars, however, develop a definite persona, a screen personality that viewers enjoy seeing over and over, with variations: Audrey Hepburn, the childlike romantic heroine; Tom Hanks, the decent everyman. Wise stars manage their careers by choosing roles consistent with their screen personas, not antagonistic to them. Clint Eastwood has played many variations on the tough, laconic, masculine hero, but has yet to venture a *Dumb and Dumber*–type Jim Carrey role. On the set, film actors face certain challenges their stage brethren do not. They must portray credible emotion even when their scenes are filmed out of sequence and repeated several times to accommodate different camera setups.

They may get little, if any, time to rehearse, and have no audience beyond the director and crew. On the other hand, if they flub a line or the scene falls flat, they can do a retake. They can express emotion through small and subtle gestures, easily visible on the big screen but invisible if performed in a large theater. And they have the benefit of cinematography, music, and editing to enhance and underscore their performances.

WHO DOES THE STUNTS?

Their faces are unknown to audiences, but their bodies are highly visible – crashing through windows, grappling in fights, burning in explosions. They are Hollywood's stuntmen and -women, the performers who substitute for the principal actors in scenes that require dangerous physical activity. Most are members of the Stuntmen's Association of Motion Pictures as well as the Screen Actors Guild. They are highly trained in the business of doing risky things safely.

Stunt people are invisible. In publicity interviews, stars talk about how they "do their own stunts," without mentioning that real danger has usually been kept far away from them, if only to avoid an injury that might bring production to a halt. Instead, the stuntmen and -women, dressed in identical costumes and with similar physical appearances, double (substitute) for them. In some shots, digital imagery and matte photography

In an effort to be taken more seriously as an actress, Marilyn Monroe studied under Lee Strasberg at the esteemed Actors Studio in New York City.

Barbara Stanwyck starred in nine films with the word *lady* or *ladies* in the title – *Ladies of Leisure* (1930), *Ladies They Talk About* (1933), *Gambling Lady* (1934), *A Lost Lady* (1934), *The Lady Eve* (1941), *The Great Man's Lady* (1942), *Lady of Burlesque* (1943), *The Lady Gambles* (1949), and *To Please a Lady* (1950).

are used to make the star's actions seem more risky than they are (for example, superimposing a precipitous ten-story drop when the actor's feet are actually only inches from the ground).

Shirley Temple made her first feature film in 1932 at age four and danced, sang, smiled, and pouted through more than 40 movies before age 15. She later became the U.S. Ambassador to Czechoslovakia.

IT WAS NOT ALWAYS SO. In the silent era, some stars were famous for risking life and limb in hazardous stunts. One, comedian Harold Lloyd, lost his right thumb and forefinger when a prop bomb exploded in his hand during the filming of *Haunted Spooks* (1920). Undeterred, he went on to perform many other thrilling acts, most notably hanging from the hand of a clock atop a tall building in *Safety Last* (1923). Nowadays, one of the few action stars to carry on in Lloyd's daring tradition is Jackie Chan, whose broken bones testify to his insistence on performing his own stunts.

Perhaps the most famous of all stuntmen was Yakima Canutt (1895–1986). In addition to performing some amazing stunts for the likes of John Wayne and Gene Autry, he was also a minor actor in westerns and a top second-unit director, directing action sequences in such classics as *Stagecoach* (1939) and *Ben-Hur* (1959). In 1966, he received a special Oscar "for creating the profession of stuntman as it exists today and for the development of many safety devices used by stuntmen everywhere."

German shepherd Rin Tin Tin was discovered during World War I in a German trench by Captain Lee Duncan, who brought him to Hollywood and made him a star. Many of his movies were written by future 20th Century–Fox head Darryl F. Zanuck.

CHILDREN AND ANIMALS

Actors traditionally warn each other against doing scenes with children and animals. Audience interest inevitably goes to kids and beasts, leaving the hapless grown-up performer upstaged. Even so, Hollywood long ago learned that children and animals make good box office: they had only to look at the profits brought in by Jackie Coogan and Shirley Temple, Rin Tin Tin and Lassie. Even more than the stage, film is a natural showcase for child and animal actors. Directors can shoot many takes until a recalcitrant toddler or a lazy collie does exactly what the scene calls for, then print only that take, making the performer appear a born thespian.

VARIOUS UNSEEN TRICKS enhance these performances. To comply with federal and state labor laws limiting the hours young children can work, identical twins often play a single part: with the children dressed identically, the audience never notices the switch from scene to scene. As for animals, look-alikes are often used to play a single role, with each trained to perform one required behavior while trainers stand offscreen, dangling a food treat as a reward. Films like *Babe* (1995) and the 1998 remake of *Doctor Dolittle* combine such old-fashioned animal-filming tricks with newfangled techniques: animatronic animals to replace the real animals in key scenes; digital compositing to place the animal where the director wants it to be. With all these aids, it is no wonder that animals and children often shine so much brighter than adult actors, who must rely on nothing more than talent and experience.

ACTING GLOSSARY: PEOPLE

action hero An actor who specializes in playing the lead in action-adventure films, which often involve fighting and mayhem.

actor or **actress** Respectively, a man or woman who plays roles in films or plays. Also called a player or performer. Actor is sometimes used gender-neutrally, referring to either a man or a woman.

antagonist The main adversary of the protagonist, or lead character, in a film. If particularly evil, sometimes called the villain or HEAVY.

bit player An actor performing a bit, a small speaking part. A silent bit is a part with no lines (such as a doorman or cab driver) but visible enough to make the player more than an extra.

body double See DOUBLE

cameo A brief, sometimes unbilled screen appearance by a famous person, such as a star or director. Alfred Hitchcock was known for doing cameos in his films.

cast The set of performers in a film. To cast a film is to find performers for every part.

casting director The person who selects, or advises in the selection of most performers in a film. The casting director also negotiates contracts with these performers.

character actor An actor who specializes in character roles, supporting roles that represent a distinct type of personality. Walter Brennan, for example, made a living playing feisty, cackling sidekicks to gunslingers and other leading men.

comedian or **comedienne** Respectively, a man or woman specializing in comedic roles, ones that make people laugh. Sometimes called a comic.

contract player A performer under contract with a studio or producer.

double A person who takes the place of an actor in a shot, usually when the action in the shot is too dangerous, requires some special expertise, or is distasteful to the star. A double resembles the actor in build and general appearance and is usually filmed in long shot, so that the audience will not notice the switch. A stunt double fills in for dangerous stunts (see STUNT PERFORMER); a body double fills in for close-ups of the exposed body.

extra A performer who speaks no lines and is used as background or as part of a crowd. Unlike bit players, extras usually receive no screen credit.

featured player or **feature player** A performer in a featured part, an important supporting role but not a starring one.

guest star A well-known star who plays a brief supporting role in a film, usually to enhance its marquee value.

heavy The villain or bad guy in a film, or an actor specializing in such parts. *See also* ANTAGONIST

hero and **heroine** Respectively, the leading male and female parts in a film. See also PROTAGONIST

ingenue The role of innocent, attractive young woman, or an actress playing such parts.

juvenile The role of a young man, usually age 16 to 20, or an actor playing such parts.

lead The main role in a film, or a performer who plays such roles. Many films have both a male and a female lead.

performer An actor or other artist (singer, dancer, stuntman, trapeze artist, etc.) who appears in a role on-screen.

player See ACTOR

Actor Christopher Walken has built a career playing the role of the "heavy" in films such as 1990's King of New York.

"I get sent lots and lots of heroines and nice-girl parts. You know, there's some man who moves the plot, and his sidekick is a girl who has one nude scene and is vulnerable and kind of funny at times…the kind of thing you just never want to see again. I want to do something gritty, something real funny, a real smelly part."
—
Meryl Streep, 1980

protagonist The main character in a film, the focus of audience sympathy. Sometimes called the hero or heroine. His or her adversary, if any, is the antagonist, sometimes called the villain or heavy.

Screen Actors Guild (SAG) A union for motion picture performers established in 1933.

silent bit *See* BIT PLAYER

stand-in A person who substitutes for a star during the lengthy process of setting up camera and lighting equipment. A stand-in is usually similar to the star in build, coloring, and general appearance. A stand-in sometimes appears in long shots on screen, but is then better known as a double.

star A lead character in a film, or the performer who plays the part. More generally, a star is an actor or actress who is well known, attracts audiences, delivers memorable screen performances, and is regularly cast in lead roles.

starlet A young, attractive woman who has achieved some notice, usually in small roles, and is said to have potential for becoming a star. In the studio era, starlets were regularly promoted as future stars by studio publicity machines, but their careers often died quickly with their alleged promise unrealized.

straight man A performer who acts as a foil for a comedian, drawing laughs by his or her serious reactions to the comic's antics.

straight part A normal dramatic role that is not excessively comedic, villainous, action-oriented, or otherwise exaggerated or stereotypical.

stunt coordinator The person who plans and supervises the stunts, or dangerous physical actions, in a film.

stuntman or **stuntwoman** A performer who substitutes for an actor or actress in scenes that call for dangerous physical activity, such as driving fast, fighting on the roofs of trains, or falling off buildings. Filmed in long shot, the stunt player must have a superficial resemblance to the actor for whom he or she substitutes.

supporting player An actor who plays a supporting role in a film, a part that is important but secondary. A person specializing in such roles is usually called a CHARACTER ACTOR.

vamp The role of a seductive, scheming woman, or an actress specializing in such roles. Theda Bara was the first actress to be called a vamp, for playing such a role in *A Fool There Was* (1914), which was based on Rudyard Kipling's *The Vampire*.

villain *See* HEAVY

voice-over A voice whose source is not visible in the shot. An actor's role is a "voice-over" when it does not entail appearing visually on screen, for example, in the case of a narrator, the voice of an animated character, or an English-speaking voice dubbed over a foreign-language speaker's performance.

walk-on A small nonspeaking part, usually smaller than a bit but bigger than an extra role, or the actor playing such a part.

ACTING GLOSSARY: THINGS

billing The placement of an actor's name in the credits, usually according to presumed box-office power. A top-billed actor is placed first; an actor with second billing comes second.

cue A signal to an actor to begin performing.

cue card Large panel printed with lines of dialogue and held next to the camera for the benefit of an actor who can't remember his lines. The TelePrompTer, an electronic version of the cue card, can perform the same service. Also called, disparagingly, idiot card or idiot sheet.

persona The on-screen image or personality associated with a star.

photogenic Having the quality of looking good on film. A crucial trait for movie stars, one that is searched for in screen tests.

screen test A filmed audition to determine whether an actor is right for a particular movie role.

star quality What actors have if they have sufficient appeal to draw people to their movies. Being photogenic is only part of it; being able to dominate a scene, inspire audience sympathy, and project an appealing persona are other elements.

star system The set of practices by which a few performers are regularly cast in lead roles by virtue of their presumed ability to attract audiences. Stars are highly sought after when their films make money, but a series of flops can make them former stars.

typecasting Assigning an actor the sort of role for which he or she is already well known. Casting against type is assigning a role to an actor that does not fit his or her established screen persona.

Headshot An 8″ x 10″ photo of an actor listing his or her acting credits; usually given out at auditions for the casting directors to keep.

CINEMATOGRAPHY

The director of photography, or cinematographer, is reponsible for lighting and photographing a film. Working in consultation with the director, he or she supervises the camera and electrical crews to realize the desired images.

CINEMATOGRAPHY IS THE ART of lighting and photographing a film. The person responsible for how a film is lit and photographed is the director of photography, also known as a DP, cinematographer, first cameraman, or lighting cameraman. The DP answers to the film's director, and ideally his or her task is to realize the director's vision on-screen. More often, the lighting and photographing of a film involve a collaboration. The director and DP begin conferring in preproduction about what the film's visual style should be, with the DP using his or her technical expertise to suggest ideas to the director. At this stage, the DP also confers with the production designer and his or her crew about where cameras and lights will be placed on the sets, a consideration that affects how the sets should be built.

During production, the DP oversees the efforts of the camera and electrical crews. Generally, the DP does not physically run the camera—this is the camera operator's job, under the DP's supervision. Nor does the DP physically set up the lights: the electrical crew does that, under the supervision of the gaffer, or chief electrician, who in turn reports to the DP. The DP is busy conferring with the director about the desired images and how best to achieve them; afterwords he or she views the rushes with the director to see how the work is coming along. In

Bernardo Bertolucci's The Last Emperor (1987), *was the first film permitted by the Chinese government to film in the Forbidden City.*

postproduction, the DP, in consultation with the director, supervises the timing of the first print, correcting density and color balance.

Cinematography requires knowledge of several kinds of technology: film stocks and printing processes; cameras, lenses, filters, and mounts; and lights of every level of intensity. It requires craftsmanship and creativity in designing camera setups (positioning the camera relative to the players); in composing the frame as a painter composes a picture; and in using the printing process to achieve maximum consistency and beauty.

Ever notice the initials ASC after the name of a director of photography in a film's credits? The initials stand for the invitation-only professional association called the American Society of Cinematographers.

CINEMATOGRAPHY GLOSSARY: PEOPLE

American Society of Cinematographers (ASC) Professional association of directors of photography, with associate members from allied crafts. Membership is by invitation only.

ASC See AMERICAN SOCIETY OF CINEMATOGRAPHERS

assistant cameraman A person in the camera crew who helps the camera operator. Tasks include maintaining the camera; maintaining focus while the camera is moving; and changing lenses. Also called the first assistant cameraman or focus puller.

best boy The assistant to the gaffer, or chief electrician. Also known as the second electrician, the best boy is responsible for ordering and maintaining equipment. The term may also be used for an assistant to some other crew member. The key grip's assistant, for example, may be known as the best boy grip.

camera crew The group of people responsible for photographing a film. Headed by the director of photography, the crew includes the camera operator, assistant cameraman, second assistant cameraman, key grip, and grips.

camera operator The person who physically runs the camera, under the supervision of the director of photography. The camera operator is responsible for making sure the camera is positioned correctly and that the image is right. Also called the cameraman or second cameraman.

clapper loader See SECOND ASSISTANT CAMERAMAN

director of photography or **DP** The person responsible for lighting a set and photographing a film under the director's supervision; supervises the camera crew and the gaffer, who heads the electrical crew. Also called a cinematographer, first cameraman, or lighting cameraman.

electrical crew The group of people responsible for lighting a film set and supplying current to all electrical equipment. It is headed by the gaffer and also includes the best boy, third electrician, and lamp operators.

focus puller See ASSISTANT CAMERAMAN

gaffer The chief electrician, responsible for lighting a set under the direction of the director of photography. Supervises the electrical crew, including the best boy.

grip A person who moves cameras and associated equipment, such as dollies and cranes. Grips also set up scaffolds and may be involved in moving props and scenery. Headed by the key grip, the team of grips includes the best boy grip (the key grip's first assistant), the dolly grip (responsible for dollies and cranes), the rigging grip or rigger (who sets up rigging, or scaffolding, for lights), and the hammers, who do miscellaneous tasks.

IATSE See INTERNATIONAL ALLIANCE OF THEATRICAL STAGE EMPLOYEES

International Alliance of Theatrical Stage Employees (IATSE) Alliance of unions representing camera operators and electricians, among other film craft. The International Cinematographers Guild, known as Local 600, is the national camera guild within IATSE. (See entry under "Production Design" in this chapter.)

juicer Film industry slang for an electrician.

key grip The foreperson in charge of the team of grips, the laborers who move cameras and associated equipment.

second assistant cameraman The person on a camera crew who marks the slate, operates the clapboard, and changes film magazines. Also called the camera loader, clapper loader, clapper boy, slateman, or slate boy.

> "I put the A camera in the most orthodox positions, use the B camera for quick, decisive shots, and the C camera as a kind of guerrilla unit."
>
> —
>
> *Akira Kurosawa on filming with three cameras*

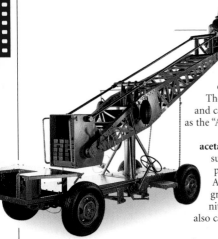

CINEMATOGRAPHY GLOSSARY: THINGS

Academy standards Standard requirements for film technology set by the Academy of Motion Picture Arts and Sciences. They govern such aspects as film leaders and camera and projector apertures (known as the "Academy aperture").

acetate base or **triacetate base** A film support to which a light-sensitive photographic emulsion is attached. Acetate came into use in the late 1940s, gradually replacing the more flammable nitrate base. Film with an acetate base is also called safety film.

The extendable arm of the crane that supports the camera is called the "boom," hence the term "boom camera." There are also microphone booms and lighting booms.

acutance A measure of the sharpness of a filmed image, taken with a densitometer, which measures density change across the image.

anaglyphic process See PROCESS

angle, camera The relative height or direction from which a subject is photographed. Placement of the camera determines the angle. An eye-level angle, for example, results when the camera is placed at about the performer's eye level; a high-angle shot when the camera is placed above the performer, looking down. Each kind of angle yields a different aesthetic effect. A high-angle shot, for example, tends to make the character look smaller and weaker; a low-angle shot, filmed from below the character, tends to make him or her look larger and more formidable. *See also* the box on "Camera Angles."

aperture (1) The opening in a lens that controls how much light reaches the film (also called a lens aperture, diaphragm, or iris). (2) The opening in a camera that determines the area of each frame exposed, that is, the camera aperture. (3) The opening in a projector that determines the area of each frame projected, that is, the projector aperture. (4) The opening in a printer that determines how much light exposes a film during the printing process, that is, the printer aperture.

artificial light Light created specifically for filming purposes as opposed to available light, the light that would normally be found in the setting of a given scene (for example, sunlight for outdoor shots; table lamps or fireplaces for interior shots).

ASA speed rating A number that indicates a film's emulsion speed, that is, the emulsion's sensitivity to light. Originally named for the American Standards Association, later renamed the American National Standards Institute. Also called ASA standard, ANSI standard, or ANSI speed rating.

aspect ratio The ratio of width to height of a film image. From the silent era to the 1950s, the standard aspect ratio was 4:3, or 1.33:1. The wide-screen cinema of the 50s introduced a variety of new aspect ratios, from 1.65:1 to 2.7:1. *See* WIDE-SCREEN PROCESSES.

available light *See* ARTIFICIAL LIGHT

background lighting *See* LIGHTING

base The transparent component of film, usually celluloid, onto which a light-sensitive emulsion is coated; examples of bases have included nitrate base and acetate base.

bath Any of the chemical solutions used in processing film, or the container that holds the solutions.

blow up To enlarge a photographic image, or to enlarge an entire film from a smaller to larger gauge, such as from 16mm to 35mm. An optical printer is used in blowing up an image; the result is called a blow-up.

boom In a crane, the extendable arm that supports a camera; also called a camera boom, to distinguish it from a microphone boom, which supports a microphone, and a light boom, which supports a light.

camera The basic machine of filmmaking. It contains an intermittent mechanism to advance film so that each frame is exposed, one at a time, by light admitted through an aperture. A lens focuses light from the field of view onto the film. Film is stored in a magazine, a lightproof container attached to the top of the camera: it advances from a feed roll in the magazine through the camera body and back into the magazine, where it is taken up by the take-up roll. A viewfinder enables the camera operator to view the field of action that will be captured on film. Cameras range in size and weight from heavy studio cameras to portable cameras and still lighter handheld cameras. (*See also* the essay "Film, Camera, Projector".)

camera report A daily sheet sent with the film to the processing laboratory. It contains information about the day's shoot, including details about the film's emulsion, and a breakdown of footage shot. The first or second assistant cameraman usually prepares the report.

CAMERA ANGLES

SOME OF THE MOST COMMON kinds of camera angles:

- EYE-LEVEL ANGLE: filmed at the performer's eye level; considered a normal or neutral angle

- HIGH ANGLE: filmed from above the performer

- LOW ANGLE: filmed from below the performer

- OBLIQUE ANGLE: filmed by tilting the camera so that the characters seem to lean to one side

- DUTCH ANGLE: filmed at a pronounced diagonal tilt, to convey a sense of disorder or uneasiness

- SUBJECTIVE ANGLE: filmed from the point of view of a specific character, such as a panning shot to indicate a character examining a scene

can A round metal container used to store film. If a film is "in the can," it has been completed.

candela Unit of measurement for the intensity of a light source. Abbreviated "cd."

celluloid Any of several transparent cellulose derivatives used as a base, the part of film stock on which emulsion is coated.

clapboard A slate with a pair of hinged boards. The slate is filmed at the start of each take, to give infor-mation about the take and to synchronize sound and picture. Information, such as the date, name of the film, and numbers of scene and take, is written on the slate and read aloud. Then the boards are clapped together, providing a distinct reference point for later sound synchronization by the editor. Electronic synchronization is often used today in place of the old-fashioned clap. The second assistant cameraman (sometimes called the slateman or slate boy) usually operates the clapboard. Also called a clapper board, clapstick board, number board, slate board, slate, production board, and take board.

The slamming sound that clapboards make is used to synchronize the sound of the film with the images of the film.

clapsticks The two hinged boards attached to a slate in a clapboard.

composition The arrangement of elements in a frame and, more generally, in a scene. The elements include shapes, lines, light and dark, and movement. Part of the DP's task, in consultation with the director, is to produce pleasing and meaningful compositions.

crane A camera mount consisting of a trolley with an attached extendable arm, or boom, that ends in a platform capable of holding the camera and up to three seated people (the camera operator, assistant cameraman, and director). Operated by hydraulic, electrical, or manual means, the crane can move the camera in any direction. A continuous shot that quietly shifts levels and angles is called a crane shot or boom shot.

deep focus A style of cinematography in which all objects in the frame are sharply defined, including those in the foreground, middle ground, and background. It contrasts with the more usual style of shallow focus, where only the plane of action is sharply focused, with everything else appearing blurred. Deep focus requires special lenses and lighting techniques. The premier example is Gregg Toland's cinematography in *Citizen Kane* (1941).

definition The sharpness and level of detail in a filmed image. It is a function of both the lens and the film stock. Also called resolution.

density The degree of opacity in a cinematic image; the degree to which it stops light from passing through. It is measured with a densitometer.

develop To make visible the latent image in exposed film, using chemical agents called developers. The person at the laboratory who runs the developing machine is also called a developer. It is one stage in film processing, which also includes fixing, washing, and drying, although the term developing is sometimes used synonymously with processing.

diaphragm An adjustable camera opening, usually composed of overlapping thin metal blades, that controls the amount of light passing through a lens and reaching the film. Also called an iris or lens aperture.

diffuser Translucent material placed in front of a light source or lens to diffuse or soften light.

digital camera A camera that records images in the form of binary information stored on a silicon chip. Also called a digital video camera, it is increasingly being used as a cheaper, more flexible alternative to traditional film cameras. At the low end, such as the handheld mini-DV, the quality of digital cameras can be unsatisfying, but professional-caliber high-definition (HD) cameras, such as the 24p, can achieve effects comparable to traditional film equipment.

dolly A wheeled platform on which a camera is mounted. Moving noiselessly, often on tracks, it permits the camera to make moving shots. It is driven or pushed by the dolly grip.

emulsion The light-sensitive substance coated on one side of a film base. It consists mainly of gelatin and silver halides.

Estar A polyester film support, tougher and longer lasting than an acetate base, used for many films, particularly internegatives for making release prints.

exposure The subjection of raw film stock to light so that a latent image is formed.

field of view The area covered by a camera lens and recorded on film. Also called field of action.

"I think films of the future will use more and more of these 'camera angles,' or, as I prefer to call them, these 'dramatic angles.' They help photograph thought."

—

F.W. Murnau, 1928

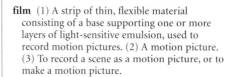

In an attempt to create a new and more honest form of cinema, a collective of four well-known Danish filmmakers, christened "Dogma 95," set forth a manifesto in 1995 calling for a Vow of Chastity in modern-day moviemaking. Of their ten rules, one stated, "The film must be in colour. Special lighting is not acceptable. (If there is too little light for exposure the scene must be cut or a single lamp be attached to the camera)."

The metal panels, or "barn doors," help to shape the beam that is projected from the light.

film (1) A strip of thin, flexible material consisting of a base supporting one or more layers of light-sensitive emulsion, used to record motion pictures. (2) A motion picture. (3) To record a scene as a motion picture, or to make a motion picture.

filter A sheet of glass or gelatin that selectively absorbs part of the light spectrum and is placed in front of a lens or light source to modify a film image's tone or color balance.

focal length The distance between the center of the lens and the point on the film when a remote object, measured at infinity, comes into sharp focus. Infinity, in photography, means that all light rays coming from that distance are virtually parallel to the lens, so that all objects within the field of view are in focus. Focal length is usually given in millimeters.

focus (1) The point behind the lens where light rays converge to form an image. Also called focal point. (2) The degree of sharpness of an image. (3) To adjust the lens so that light rays converge to form a maximally sharp image. This is done by turning the focus ring to change the focal length, the distance between the lens and the film.

footage A particular length of film measured in feet.

frame One of the successive, individual photographs that compose a motion picture, or the bounded space occupied by one or more of these photographs.

f-stop A camera setting that indicates the relative width of the aperture at different diaphragm openings, and therefore the amount of light being admitted. Smaller f-stops represent larger apertures, or more light; larger f-stops represent less light.

gauge The width of film, in millimeters (mm). Standard gauge for professional filmmakers is 35mm; narrow gauge, used by amateurs and some professionals, is 16mm. Other gauges include 70, 65, and 8mm.

grain A particle of silver halide in a film's emulsion that turns to metallic silver upon exposure to light, forming the latent image. When these particles are visible on-screen, because of defects in processing or use of a small gauge of film, the result is a grainy image.

high-key lighting Bright, low-contrast illumination that results from putting the key light, or principal light, high and using fill lights to minimize shadows. Frequently found in comedies, where it affords a cheerful tone.

image The picture that results from the photographic process.

integral tripack Color film with three layers of emulsion, each sensitive to a different primary color.

intensity The power of a light source, measured in candelas, or the degree of illumination in an image.

iris *See* DIAPHRAGM

key light The main source of light for a scene or subject, usually in front, higher than, and to the side of the subject. It is supplemented by other sources of illumination, such as fill lights and back light.

leader (1) A blank strip of film at the beginning of a reel of a release print. It facilitates threading, protects the film from damage, and gives information to the projectionist, such as the name of the film and the number of the reel. Specifications for this kind of leader are set either by the Academy of Motion Picture Arts and Sciences (for "Academy leaders") or by the Society of Motion Picture and Television Engineers (for "universal leaders" or "SMPTE universal leaders"). (2) A blank strip of film at the end of a reel. (3) A blank strip of film used to fill in space during editing of a work print.

lens A transparent optical device, usually made of glass, shaped to gather light and form a sharp image at a particular distance behind the lens. When film is placed at that distance, which is known as focal length, it captures the image. The camera lens is mounted in a lens barrel, a cylindrical case with a focus ring that can be used to focus the picture. Lenses can be normal, covering a medium field of view; wide angle, covering a broader field of view but reducing the proportional size of the elements; or telephoto (long focus), covering a small field of view but magnifying the elements. Zoom lenses, which have a variable focal length, combine qualities of all three; one can "zoom in" from a wide-angle shot to a tight telephoto close-up, or "zoom out" in the reverse direction. The most extreme wide-angle lens is called a fisheye lens: it takes in a field of view of nearly 180 degrees but distorts the image. Wide-angle lenses have short focal lengths; telephoto lenses have long focal lengths; and normal lenses have medium focal lengths (usually 50mm for a 35mm camera). Swing/shift lenses allow depth-of-field extremes, dramatically focusing on one part of the frame while blurring other parts.

lighting The illumination of a scene. Lighting is a major component of the cinematographer's art, since the arrangement of light and dark affects the aesthetic beauty of a scene and its emotional impact. Low-key (dark, high-contrast) lighting communicates sadness or menace; high-key (bright, even) lighting communicates glamour and good cheer. Stars are made more gorgeous or imposing by artful lighting, with small spotlights called obies to minimize lines in their faces; kicker or eye lights to highlight their eyes; and rim or edge lights to highlight their outlines. There are three basic light sources on a film set: (1) the key light, or principal light, to the front and side of the subject; (2) fill or filler lights, which fill in shadows and minimize contrast; (3) and back lights, which add depth to the subject by highlighting edges. Rim lighting, in which the performer's outlines are brightly illuminated but the front relatively dim, is an example of back light. Unless a scene is filmed with available light (from the sun or ordinary, scene-appropriate sources such as a fireplace), it relies on artificial light from luminaires. These are complete movie lighting units, including lamp, stand, and housing. Luminaires come in many varieties (*see* the box "A Menagerie of Lights") but can be broadly classified as floodlights, which offer a large, diffuse area of illumination, or spotlights, which sharply illuminate a specific area. Many luminaires are arc lamps, high-intensity lights that rely on electric current flowing between rods; those with carbon rods, long used by Hollywood, are called carbon-arc lamps. Incandescent lights, especially tungsten-halogen lamps, are also used. Movie lights are often softened by translucent materials called diffusers, placed in front of the lens or the light source. The scrim, a translucent screen usually made of wire gauze, is an example of a diffuser.

line up To choose the distance and angle for a shot and set up the camera accordingly.

low-key lighting A lighting arrangement in which areas of darkness predominate, contrasting sharply with the key light and other sources of illumination. Frequently found in dramas, mysteries, and other movies with a somber or fearful tone.

luminaire A lighting fixture, including housing, lamp, and stand.

monochrome Exhibiting a single color. The term is most often applied to black-and-white film.

negative A film image in which dark and light areas are reversed and colors are complementary.

nitrate base A film support made of cellulose nitrate, which is highly flammable; a fire hazard, it was gradually phased out in favor of the less-combustible acetate base beginning in the late 1940s.

A MENAGERIE OF LIGHTS

MOVIE LIGHTS HAVE RECEIVED some of the more colorful appellations in the Hollywood lexicon. Here are some of the members of the luminaire menagerie:

ASHCAN: a 1,000-watt floodlight
BABY SPOT: a 1,000-watt spotlight
BANK: a row of lights
BASHER: a small lamp of 250–500 watts
BROAD: a floodlight for a large area
BRUTE: a high-intensity arc spotlight
CONE: a cone-shaped lamp
DEUCE: a 2,000-watt spotlight
DINKY or DINKY INKY: a small 100-watt spotlight
KLIEG LIGHT: a strong searchlight
MIDGET: a 200-watt spotlight
OBIE: a small spotlight
RIFLE SPOT: a long, narrow spotlight
SKY PAN: a luminaire of 5,000–10,000 watts
SUN GUN: a small portable high-intensity light

---

notch A mark made on the edge of a piece of film to indicate a correction in printing density.

pan Horizontal movement of the camera around a fixed axis from one part of the scene to another.

positive A film in which lighting values and colors correspond directly to those of the photographed subject rather than corresponding in reverse, as in a negative. The films projected in a theater are positives. Also called prints.

print A positive copy of a film made from a negative.

printer A machine that makes prints, or positive copies, of a film from a negative. There are two basic types, contact and optical. (1) In a contact printer, the emulsion of the processed negative comes into direct contact with the emulsion of raw film stock, as both pass in front of an aperture. Light transfers the image onto the raw film stock, forming a positive print. There are two kinds of contact printers: continuous, where the film runs past the aperture without stop; and step or intermittent, where each frame stops briefly before the light. Continuous contact printing is fast and cheap, so it is often used to make multiple release prints for distribution to theaters. Step printing is used when perfect registration is needed, as in the traveling matte process. (*See* "Special Effects" in this chapter). (2) An optical printer consists of a synchronized projector and

---

"I didn't create a 'Garbo face.' I just did portraits of her [as] I would have done for any star. My lighting of her was determined by the requirements of a scene. I didn't, as some say I did, keep one side of the face light and the other dark. But I did always try to make the camera peer into the eyes, to see what was there."

—

*Cinematographer
William Daniels, 1970*

Charlton Heston starred in Cecil B. DeMille's $13 million extravaganza of 1956,
The Ten Commandments, *which exemplified the vividness and brilliance of Technicolor films.*

> "If it is a tense scene…then, despite all rules of technique to the contrary, I claim that the scene demands a 'close-up' of the actor's face cut quickly into the main scene."
>
> —
> *William S. Hart, silent screen actor, 1917*

camera. The projector projects the negative image onto raw film stock in the camera. Optical printing is ideal for traveling mattes. Most optical printers are of the step variety, though continuous optical printers also exist; these are used to reduce film from one gauge to another.

process To develop the latent image in a film, and to treat the film so that it is washed free of chemicals and dried, with the image fixed. Processing may refer just to the stage that ends with a negative, or it may also include the printing stage, in which a positive print is produced.

projector A machine that throws motion picture images onto a screen. It contains a lamp, shutter, aperture, lens, and intermittent mechanism to bring the film before the lamp and project it on a screen, one frame at a time. The rapid succession of frames creates the illusion of motion.

ramping The use of in-camera speed shifts within a single shot, so that the action suddenly slows down or speeds up.

reel A metal or plastic spool, on which film is wound. The term is also used as a unit of measurement, denoting about ten minutes worth of running time, or about a thousand feet of 35mm film.

resolution See DEFINITION

running speed The rate at which film runs through a camera or projector, 24 frames per second for 35mm sound film.

running time The duration of a film.

safety film See ACETATE BASE

saturation The degree of purity or vividness in a color. Old Technicolor films had highly saturated colors, as opposed to the more diluted, grayer colors of today's films.

setup The positioning of the camera, lights, sound equipment, and actors before the filming of a shot begins. More specifically, it refers to the positioning of the camera.

shoot To photograph a scene or story with a motion picture camera.

shot A single continuous action that is filmed or appears to be filmed in one take, from one camera setup. The shot is considered the basic unit of film grammar. Shots can be categorized in several ways: by camera angle used (*see* ANGLE); by distance from the subject (e.g., close-ups versus long shots); by narrative or continuity function (for example, an establishing shot is a long shot or full shot used to establish the location or mood of a scene); by whether and how the camera is moving; or by other considerations, such as style of lighting. Many shots filmed are never seen by the audience: a single scene may be photographed from several different angles, with the director and editor selecting the ones that work best. In the master-scene or master-shot technique, a traditional Hollywood procedure, the actors first play a scene as a long shot in one continuous take, then replay parts of the scene for medium shots and close-ups. When this technique works, it gives the director and editor adequate "coverage," that is, a sufficient selection of shots to choose from. *See* the box on "Shots."

slate The part of a clapboard on which take information is marked, including production number, date, and numbers of scene and take. Also used as a synonym for clapboard, or as a director's order ("Slate!") to tell the second assistant cameraman to operate the clapboard and announce the numbers of scene and take.

tone (1) The mood or atmosphere of a scene. (2) The specific shade of a color. (3) The range of contrast or brightness in a film image.

tracks Rails attached to the floor of a set upon which a dolly can move easily.

tripack *See* INTEGRAL TRIPACK

tripod A three-legged camera support.

wide-screen processes Projection systems in which the aspect ratio, the image's ratio of width to height, is larger than the standard 4:3, or 1.33:1. In the 1950s, many wide-screen processes were introduced. CinemaScope and others were anamorphic systems, which use an anamorphic camera lens to squeeze a wide image to one-half its width on 35mm film, then use an anamorphic projector lens to unsqueeze it on the screen. VistaVision, a nonanamorphic system, relied on passing 35mm film through the camera horizontally instead of vertically, permitting a wider frame. Todd-AO and Super Panavision relied on wider-gauge, 65mm film to create a wide-screen image.

SHOTS

A SELECTION OF THE MANY different kinds of shots used by cinematographers:

BOOM SHOT: a shot filmed from a moving boom, incorporating different camera levels and angles

CAMEO SHOT: a shot in which the subject is filmed against a black or neutral background

CHOKER: a tight close-up, typically showing only the actor's face

CLOSE SHOT (CS): a shot in which the subject is filmed from top of head to waist; closer than a medium shot but not as tight as a close-up

CLOSE-UP (CU): a shot of a detailed part of a person or object, such as the subject's head

CUTAWAY: a shot that is related to the main action but briefly leaves it, for example, an audience member's reaction to a show

DOLLY SHOT: a moving shot accomplished by moving the camera on a dolly; also called a tracking, trucking, moving, or traveling shot

ESTABLISHING SHOT: a long shot that establishes a scene or mood

EXTREME CLOSE-UP (ECU, XCU): a magnified shot of a small detail, such as the actor's eyes

EXTREME LONG SHOT (ELS, XLS): a wide-angle shot from a great distance, such as an aerial shot of a location

FLASH: a very brief shot, often for shock effect

FOLLOW SHOT: a shot in which the camera moves to follow a subject

FREEZE FRAME: a shot that results from repeatedly printing a single frame, so the subject seems frozen

FULL SHOT (FS): a long shot that captures the subject's entire body, from feet to head

HEAD-ON SHOT: a shot where the action seems to come directly at the camera

HIGH-ANGLE SHOT: a shot filmed from above the subject, as opposed to a low-angle shot, filmed from below, or the more normal eye-level shot, filmed at eye level

LONG SHOT (LS): a shot in which the subject is at a distance, often including both people and their surroundings

MEDIUM-LONG SHOT (MLS): a shot wider than a medium shot but narrower than a long shot

MEDIUM SHOT (MS): a shot in which the subject is filmed from about the knees up, and several actors may be shown; intermediate between a close shot and a long shot

PAN SHOT: a shot in which the camera moves horizontally around a fixed axis from one part of a scene to another

POINT-OF-VIEW SHOT: a shot from the point of view of a character in the scene

REACTION SHOT: a close shot of a character reacting to something off scene or in an earlier shot

REVERSE-ANGLE SHOT: a shot in which the angle is opposite to that in the preceding shot; used in alternating between the points of view of two characters speaking, in a pattern called shot/reverse-shot

TIGHT SHOT: a shot in which the subject fills almost the whole frame, as opposed to a loose shot, in which there is space on both sides of the subject

TILT SHOT: a shot in which the camera moves up or down along a vertical axis, as when it surveys a building from bottom to top

TWO-SHOT: a medium or close shot just wide enough for two people; often used to film conversation

PRODUCTION DESIGN

Part architect, part decorator, part dreamer, the production designer envisions the physical world that is photographed in a movie. Everything from house exteriors to handheld props falls under his or her purview.

THE PRODUCTION DESIGNER IS THE PERSON who creates the look of the world within a film. Among his or her duties are designing and overseeing construction of sets and scenery; designing props and overseeing their procurement (some may be constructed, some bought or rented); and working with the costume designer to make sure that the wardrobe of the actors fits the film's overall look. The job typically requires knowledge of architecture, engineering, painting and drawing, and theater and film arts. Depending on the movie's subject matter, the production designer must be able to research and re-create historical periods; grasp the material particulars of various contemporary subcultures, from Mafia social clubs to corporate boardrooms; and imagine worlds that have never existed.

WORKING WITH THE DIRECTOR and producer, the production designer comes up with sketches of proposed sets, then revises them to better fit the director's vision. Budgetary and technical constraints are always considerations. A number of people may work under the production designer's supervision, including the art director, set designer, set decorator, scenic artist, production buyer, property master, construction coordinator, and greensman. These are sometimes collectively called the art department.

The production designer for 1930's Just Imagine *created sets meant to depict what was then considered a futuristic vision of New York City in 1980.*

PRODUCTION DESIGN GLOSSARY: PEOPLE

art department The group of people working under the production designer's supervision. In addition to those named below, the group may include illustrators, storyboard artists (who create storyboards depicting the action), matte painters (*see* "Special Effects" in this chapter), set painters, title designers (who design the film's titles), ornamental plasterers, and mold makers.

art director Former term for the production designer; nowadays, the term is most often used for the set designer or for an assistant to the production designer.

buyer *See* PRODUCTION BUYER

construction coordinator The person who oversees construction of sets, prepares a construction budget, and hires a construction crew. The latter includes the construction foreperson, labor foreperson, paint foreperson, carpenters, and standby painters.

greensman A person who dresses sets with real and artificial plants, including trees, shrubs, and flowers, and tends the live fauna.

grip A person who moves props and scenery, lays dolly tracks and pushes dollies, and performs other manual jobs. Also called a stagehand.

IATSE *See* INTERNATIONAL ALLIANCE OF THEATRICAL STAGE EMPLOYEES

International Alliance of Theatrical Stage Employees (IATSE) Alliance of unions, affiliated with the AFL-CIO, that represents many film technical crafts, including those in the art department, such as art directors, set designers, set painters, and grips. Other film crafts represented by IATSE include camera operators, electricians, editors, script supervisors, sound technicians, laboratory technicians, and distribution and exhibition employees.

lead person *See* SET DECORATOR

production buyer A person who buys or rents props and obtains materials for making sets or costumes. Also called a buyer or property buyer.

production designer The person who creates and is responsible for the look of the world in which a film is set. He or she supervises all

those involved in production design, such as the set designer and scenic artist. Formerly known as the art director, a term now usually reserved for an assistant to the production designer.

prop man *See* PROPERTY MASTER

property master The person in charge of obtaining or constructing props; and ensuring they are available when needed. Also called the prop man.

scenic artist A person who paints scenery or sets.

set decorator A person who dresses a set with props, furnishings, and decorative trimmings, working under the set designer's supervision. Also called a set dresser, he or she supervises the set dressing crew, which consists of a lead person at the head of a swing gang; these are the people who physically move and place the set dressings.

set designer A person who drafts architectural plans and provides specifications for set construction, based on the sketches of the production designer or art director. Sometimes called an art director.

set dresser *See* SET DECORATOR

set estimator A person who prepares cost estimates for constructing sets.

stagehand *See* GRIP

swing gang *See* SET DECORATOR

The minature set of The Empire Strikes Back *(1980) was dressed with fake snow and featured a painted backdrop. Above, special effects artist's arrange a snow walker.*

Mistakes are bound to happen in any film, and searching for goofs is an obsession for some moviegoers. Sometimes a viewer can spot a piece of out-of-place equipment, like a boom mike hanging over an actor's head, crew members reflected in a window, or an anachronistic object in the movie, like a wristwatch on a Roman slave.

OPPOSITE:

The intricacy of set design is seen in this outdoor set that was built at MGM studios for the filming of National Velvet *in 1944.*

"...a director gets whatever he asks for without argument, no matter how crazy or impossible the request."

—

Jesse Lasky

apple box Box kept out of camera view and used to elevate objects and people, such as short actors, to the desired height. Also called a riser.

back lot An open-air section on film studio grounds used for filming exteriors. It may contain outdoor sets, such as city streets, that are maintained for use in future productions. Also called the lot.

backdrop *See* BACKING

backing A large painting or photographic blowup used as background for a scene, often glimpsed through a window. May be made of cloth or from wooden boards called flats. Also called a backdrop or drop.

cyclorama A large, curved backdrop, often representing the sky and lit by a bank of lights called a cyclorama strip or cyc strip.

downstage The part of the set closest to the camera.

dress To prepare a set for filming by placing and arranging props, decorations, and furniture.

flat A piece of scenery consisting of a flat piece of plywood or some other lightweight material. Scenery is painted on flats, which fit together to form the backing for a scene.

floor The part of the studio where shooting is taking place.

forced perspective In set design, a technique that gives an illusion of greater depth and distance. It consists of making foreground objects full size but background objects appropriately smaller in scale.

limbo A set with a neutral or black background, sometimes used for close-ups.

location A place other than a studio where shooting is performed. (*See also* "Producing Glossary: Things" in this chapter.)

lot The entire area of a film studio, inside and outside; or simply the back lot, which is outside.

production values The general quality of a film production, considered independently from the quality of the script, acting, or directing. It includes such characteristics as production design, sets, props, costumes, music, cinematography, and sound.

prop or **property** A movable object seen on film that is not a structural part of the set or a component of an actor's costume. Props range from furniture to tableware to computers to weapons.

prop plot A layout for a set showing where all the props go.

revamp To change an existing set by altering some of its contents, such as props or backing. Revamping may be done to prepare the set for another scene in the same film or for a different film.

riser *See* APPLE BOX

scenery The part of a set that represents the outdoors, such as a backing, seen through a window and showing mountains or skyscrapers.

set A constructed location where filmed action takes place. Sets can be built indoors or outdoors; indoor sets can represent both interior and exterior locales. Sets are usually made of lightweight, movable materials and need possess only as much reality as will be captured by the camera: a house exterior, for example, may be nothing but a facade supported by beams. Interior sets often have only three walls and no ceilings, allowing for easier camera movement and lighting and microphone placement.

stage The part of a studio where sets are built for filming. Often called a soundstage because it is usually soundproof and acoustically engineered for recording sound.

strike To take apart a set once filming is complete, or to remove a prop or a part of the set.

upstage The rear part of a set, the part furthest from the camera. An actor is metaphorically "upstaged" if another actor steals a scene from him or her by doing something that attracts the audience's attention.

The set of Things to Come *(1936) gives the illusion of greater depth and distance by making foreground objects full size and background objects smaller in scale.*

COSTUMES, MAKEUP, HAIR

What the production designer does for the world of a film, the costume designer, makeup artist, and hairstylist do for its stars. They design the actors' physical appearance: clothes, skin tones, and hairstyles.

COSTUMES

The costume designer researches and creates or oversees the procurement of clothing and accessories used in a film. Part of the film staff since the 1920s, he or she works closely with the director, cinematographer, and production designer. As head of the costume department, he or she may supervise other members of the department, including the costume supervisor, costumer/stylist, dresser, key costumer, set costumer, tailor/seamstress, and wardrobe attendant.

To determine wardrobe needs, the costume designer studies the script for the number of costumes needed; researches the historical period depicted in the film; sketches costumes with the correct style, color, and fabric for the set design and actors' body types; and oversees sewing, maintenance, and liaison activities between other departments.

Wardrobe items that can be purchased or acquired off the rack are handled by the stylist, among others.

Most Los Angeles–based designers belong to the Costume Designers Guild, a once–independent union now (since 1976) a local of IATSE. New York–based designers may belong to IATSE Local 829. An organization known as Motion Picture Costumers is also an IATSE local.

Patrick Bergin wore this costume for the 1991 film Robin Hood.

MAKEUP

The makeup artist is the person who prepares the actor's face, neck, forearms, and hands to reflect the character's physicality. These artists compose the makeup department, which has been responsible for cosmetic appearances since the later years of the silent era, after actors ceased applying their own makeup. Although the makeup artist discusses strategies with the director and cinematographer, he or she works intimately with the actors, artist to artist. All actors, from principal to extra, are the makeup artist's responsibility.

The makeup artist sets up the makeup schedule, manages staff, and is the liaison to the hairstylists.

Supervised by the makeup artist is the assistant, who is responsible for applying facial makeup. Makeup applied below the neck is the responsibility of the body makeup artist. Special effects makeup is created by the special effects department (see "Special Effects" in this chapter).

From 1982, makeup has constituted a regular Academy Award category. Unionized makeup artists belong to the Makeup Artists & Hair Stylists local of the IATSE. Film makeup is specially designed to be photographed, to look right under the given conditions of lighting, resolution, and color rendition. It is also designed to look clean, as if the the actor is not wearing any makeup but appears beautiful just the same (unless the character is supposed to look ugly or overly made-up).

HAIR

The hairstylist is the person who styles and colors the actor's hair, wig, mustache, beard, and eyebrows to create the character's look. While the stylist works under the production designer and with director, costume designer, and actor, he or she is most closely aligned with the makeup artist. The two collaborate to achieve a look consistent with the era and emotional makeup of the character. The hairstylist is also responsible for maintaining hair between takes. Hair and makeup people are the first staff members whom actors encounter every day, usually very early in the morning.

A wig dresser or hairpiece stylist specializes in preparing wigs and hairpieces, attaching them to the head, and combing and setting them. She may cut wigs and hairpieces to specified length and style, and wash and dry them after use. Unionized hairstylists belong to the Makeup Artists & Hair Stylists local of the IATSE.

A dresser puts the finishing touches on Elizabeth Taylor, who was outfitted in elaborate costumes, hairdos, and makeup for the 1963 version of Cleopatra.

COSTUMES AND MAKEUP GLOSSARY

body makeup artist Person responsible for creating and applying makeup below the collarbone and on the rest of the body except (in most cases) forearms and hands.

costume or wardrobe designer A person who researches, designs, and creates or procures clothing for a film.

costume supervisor A person who writes the costume budget and oversees other departmental duties, including hiring personnel, inventory control, fittings, and costume maintenance.

costumer/stylist A person who acquires wardrobe and accessories for the film.

dresser A person who gets actors into costume.

hairstylist A person who styles and colors the actors' hair and hairpieces to fit their characters.

key costumer A person who assists the costume designer and fits the actors.

makeup artist A person who prepares the actors' face, neck, forearms, and hands to produce the desired effects on-screen.

makeup call The time at which actors report to the makeup department to be prepared for shooting.

set costumer A person who remains on the set to ensure costume continuity from scene to scene, costume availability for upcoming scenes, and the actor's appearance in the costume.

tailor/seamstress A person who sews the wardrobe, following the costume designer's plan.

wardrobe attendant A person who maintains and alters wardrobe items.

SPECIAL EFFECTS

Need a live dinosaur? A space battle? A sinking ship? Special effects artists are in charge of manufacturing these and any other illusions a film may demand.

SPECIAL EFFECTS ARE ILLUSIONS USED TO CREATE scenes that would otherwise be impossible or difficult to film. The parting of the Red Sea and E.T. flying on a bicycle are famous examples, but many special effects are less obtrusive and are meant to reduce costs or simplify shoots. The last shot of *Raiders of the Lost Ark* shows a workman delivering the ark into a vast warehouse filled with crates. The warehouse is actually a matte painting, integrated into the frame through special effects. It would not have been impossible to build a real warehouse on that scale, just needlessly expensive.

There are two kinds of special effects (abbreviated as FX, SFX, SPFX, or EFX): visual or photographic effects, achieved by manipulating the film image; and mechanical or physical effects, achieved through the use of mechanical devices on the set. The term *special effects* is sometimes used exclusively for mechanical effects as distinct from visual effects, though sometimes (as in this book) the term is used for both types. Visual effect techniques include computer-generated imagery, matte paintings, traveling mattes, rotoscopes, rear projection, front projection, stop-motion animation, and miniatures. Mechanical effects include explosions, wires attached to actors, full-scale mock-ups, animatronic puppets, rain and snow machines, and squibs used to simulate bullet hits. A complicated FX sequence may include a variety of visual and mechanical effects.

A MOVIE'S VISUAL EFFECTS TEAM is usually headed by a visual effects supervisor; its mechanical effects team is headed by a special effects supervisor. Visual and mechanical effects are often farmed out to special effects companies, of which the most famous is Industrial Light & Magic (ILM), the company founded by George Lucas to provide the effects for *Star Wars* (1977). Other FX companies include Digital Domain, Pacific Data Images, and Stan Winston Studio. On an FX-laden film, such as a science fiction blockbuster, several companies may collaborate on the project.

Matte shots combine elements filmed separately, to create special effects such as Harrison Ford hanging precariously from a building ledge in 1982's Blade Runner.

SPECIAL EFFECTS GLOSSARY: PEOPLE

digital effects supervisor A person responsible for a movie's digital effects.

explosives specialist A person who creates explosions on the set. Also called a pyrotechnician.

matte painter A person who paints backgrounds for matte shots, either with brushes or on a computer.

model maker A person who builds models for use in special effects photography.

pyrotechnician *See* EXPLOSIVES SPECIALIST

special effects makeup artist A makeup artist who specializes in monstrous makeup, sometimes with mechanical components such as functioning tentacles or a third eye.

special effects supervisor The person in charge of a film's special effects, particularly its mechanical effects.

visual effects supervisor The person in charge of a film's visual effects.

Industrial Light & Magic's senior visual effects supervisor, Dennis Muren, has more Academy Awards than anyone else alive today. The eight-time winner in the best visual effects category received Oscars for *Jurassic Park* in 1993, *Terminator 2: Judgment Day* in 1991, *The Abyss* in 1989, *Innerspace* in 1987, *Indiana Jones and the Temple of Doom* in 1984, *Return of the Jedi* in 1983, *E.T. The Extra-Terrestrial*, in 1982, and *The Empire Strikes Back* in 1980.

SPECIAL EFFECTS GLOSSARY: THINGS

animatronics Internal electronic mechanisms used to animate puppets, allowing their movements to be precisely controlled.

blue-screen process Technique used to create traveling mattes, in which actors or models are filmed against a blue screen, and their photographed figures subsequently matted into some other sequence through the use of an optical printer.

composite To combine images that have been created separately into one shot, either digitally, in camera, using traveling mattes, or by some other means. The resulting image is a composite shot or composite.

computer animation Animation technique in which an image stored on a computer is made to move by digital manipulation. The animator may specify the position of the moving object in each frame, or may specify only key points, with the computer filling in the intervening movements according to its programming.

computer-generated imagery (CGI) Images created on a computer, often animated and combined digitally with live action. It may include creatures or more mundane elements, such as snow or scenery.

creature effects Mechanical effects used to realize monstrous creatures, such as dinosaurs and alien beings. The term is usually reserved for puppets of various kinds, rather than computer-generated creatures.

digital effects Visual effects created by manipulating images that are stored as binary data on a computer. Digital effects shots may include live-action elements filmed on a set and scanned into the computer, then warped or altered, as through the addition of shadows, removal of supporting wires, or morphing of one person into another. They may also include computer-generated images, often digitally composited with live actors into one shot.

front projection Compositing technique in which a photographed image, such as background scenery, is projected from the front of the set to a screen behind the live action. The effect is to combine the live action with the photographed image.

frozen moment Technique in which the camera appears to circle figures frozen in mid-action, even in mid-air. Also called virtual dolly.

glass shot A shot created through the use of a glass plate on which an element of a scene has been painted. The glass plate is placed between the camera and the actors, combining the painted element with the live action.

in-camera effect or **in-the-camera effect** A visual effect that is achieved within the camera prior to developing the film. It usually relies on blocking part of the lens with a matte, filming a shot, then rewinding the film, blocking the previously unblocked part, and filming a different element. When developed, the two elements will be combined in one shot.

matte A mask that covers part of a camera lens, keeping that part of the film unexposed, so that a different element can be added to the masked area. Stationary mattes are physically attached to the camera, often in a box called a matte box or effects box. Traveling mattes use one filmed image, such as an actor in motion, to mask another. A shot using a matte is called a matte shot. *See* TRAVELING MATTE.

Front projection combines live action with a photographed image that serves as the background.

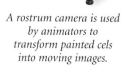

Scale or full-size models, like those used in the 1997 blockbuster Titanic *are often created and combined with a computer-generated background to create the look and effect desired by the director.*

A rostrum camera is used by animators to transform painted cels into moving images.

matte painting A painting photographed and composited with other elements in a matte shot. For example, a painting of a distant castle may be used to fill the unexposed area left when live actors were filmed by a camera partially covered by a matte.

mechanical effects Effects achieved through the use of mechanical devices on the set where the actors are filmed. Also called physical or practical effects. The term *special effects* is sometimes reserved for mechanical effects as opposed to visual effects.

miniature A small-scale model that, on film, appears to be the size of the real thing. Miniatures of ships, planes, buildings, spaceships, dinosaurs, and other massive objects, artfully combined with miniature backgrounds and live-action footage, are staples of special effects.

mock-up A full-scale model of part of a massive object, used on film to simulate the real thing. For example, in a pirate movie, a mock-up of part of the ship might be built for medium and close shots, while a miniature of the ship would be used for long shots.

model A scale replica of an object or part of an object, whether a miniature, a full-scale mock-up, or a larger-than-life model (such as giant prop tableware in movies about shrunken people).

morph To transform one digital image into another through computer animation. Used to make people change into werewolves, aliens shift their shapes, etc.

motion control A computerized system that allows precise control of camera and model movements. Used for such purposes as filming miniatures in action and matting them into composite shots.

optical composite A composite shot made with an optical printer. Also called an optical.

optical printer A machine that converts negatives to prints through the use of a synchronized projector and camera. The projector projects the negative image onto raw film stock in the camera. The optical printer is essential to the traveling matte technique. For example, the figure of an actor walking will be projected, frame by frame, onto an unexposed, actor-shaped hole in a piece of film showing the surface of an alien planet; the resulting composite shows the actor walking on the planet surface.

photographic effects *See* VISUAL EFFECTS

process camera Camera designed for visual effects work. Such cameras offer highly accurate registration, or steady placement of each frame before the aperture in precisely the intended position, an important feature in producing composite shots.

process photography *See* REAR PROJECTION

puppet A three-dimensional figure with movable parts, used in creature effects and other illusions. Some are animated by old-fashioned puppeteering techniques, such as rods and strings; some by performers wearing a costume with puppet extensions; some by stop-motion photography; some by animatronics, hydraulic systems, or other mechanisms.

rear projection Technique for creating backgrounds, in which a photographed image of background scenery is projected through a translucent screen behind the actors. The actors then appear to be present in that setting. Commonly used in the past to simulate driving scenes, with actors sitting in a mock-up car on the soundstage as rear-projected scenery rushed past their windows. The effect is often unconvincing, because of the difference in sharpness between the background and foreground images, and so is used less frequently today than other compositing methods, such as front projection and the blue-screen process. Also called back projection, rear-screen projection, and process photography.

rotoscope Animation technique in which individual frames are blown up, with elements of each frame traced one by one onto animation cels. Those elements can then be redrawn or repainted to look slightly different, then optically combined with the original footage. For example, an actor can be enhanced with a rotoscoped ghostly aura.

slow motion Effect caused by running the camera at faster-than-standard speed, then projecting at standard speed. In special effects, slow motion is used in filming miniatures and miniature explosions, giving them the appearance of greater mass and size.

special effects Visual and mechanical effects used to create illusions on film, or, more precisely, mechanical effects only as opposed to visual effects.

split screen Effect produced by matting, or masking, half of the lens, filming action in the uncovered area, then matting the other half and filming action in the previously covered area. The result is a composite of the two pieces of footage. Used for such effects as having an actor talk to what appears to be an identical twin.

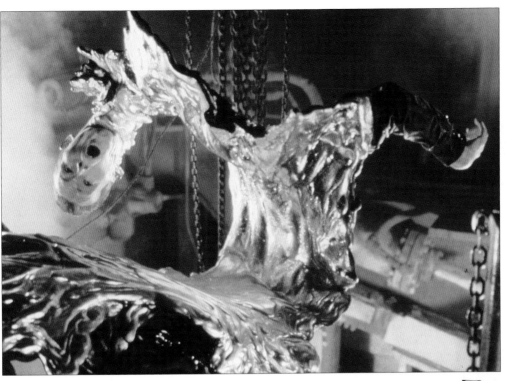

Terminator 2: Judgement Day, *released in 1991, was widely regarded for its use of morphing, or the transformation of a digital image into another image via computer animation.*

squib A small explosive charge fired electrically and used to simulate bullet hits. A squib attached to an actor's clothing will tear clothes and release fake blood on detonation, making it appear the actor has been shot.

stop motion Technique used to animate puppets. The position of the puppet is changed slightly from frame to frame, with the camera filming each position in succession. The projected result is that the puppet appears to move by itself. Stop-motion puppets are often miniatures of monsters or dinosaurs, optically or digitally combined with live action. The technique has lost ground in recent years to other creature techniques, such as animatronics and computer-generated imagery.

storyboard A series of sketches showing a proposed sequence of shots. Used in planning animation films and some live-action features, the storyboard is especially important for planning complicated effects shots.

traveling matte Technique for producing an optical composite, in which a moving element is filmed against a special background such as a blue screen, with that footage used to produce a moving, or traveling, matte. The system depends on rephotographing the film with a system of filters so that the moving element, for example an actor, is transformed into a moving black silhouette. That silhouette is optically combined with film of some other element, such as a mountainous background, so that each successive frame of the background contains a successively moving silhouette. When the image of the actor and of the background are combined in an optical printer, the actor appears to be moving against the background. *See also* BLUE-SCREEN PROCESS and OPTICAL PRINTER.

trick photography Somewhat derisive term for visual effects.

visual effects Special effects achieved by manipulating the film image. Also called photographic effects or trick photography.

weather effects Simulation of weather by various means, mechanical and visual. Mechanical devices may include a rainmaking sprinkler system mounted over the actors; a wind machine consisting of a large offscreen fan; a hopper that drops plastic flakes simulating snow; and chemical devices that emit smoke, fog, or haze. Weather effects, such as falling rain or condensing breath, can also be added optically or digitally.

A wind machine is just one of the many devices used to create weather effects in films.

SOUND AND MUSIC

Though film is often called a visual medium, most movies rely heavily on sound, including dialogue, sound effects, and music. The mixer, sound editor, and composer all contribute to what you hear at the movies.

THERE ARE THREE TYPES OF SOUND used in the movies: dialogue, sound effects, and music. Although experienced by the audience as one stream of sound, these three are, in fact, recorded and edited as separate tracks. The process of creating a movie's sound occurs in two distinct phases:

PRODUCTION

Most dialogue and some sound effects are recorded on the set. The sound crew, headed by the sound mixer or floor mixer, is in charge of making sure these sounds are recorded clearly and in the proper balance. The emphasis is on recording the actors' words

Silent films relied on live piano accompaniment to provide a sound track.

rather than background noises. If shooting is done on location, where sound quality is hard to control, both dialogue and sound effects may be dubbed later. In such cases, a guide track may be recorded, that is, an on-location sound track used as a guide for dubbing.

POSTPRODUCTION

Once photography is complete, there are four distinct tasks to accomplish before the movie's sound is complete:

(1) The sound editor, or sound effects editor, is responsible for working with the director and editor to create the dialogue and sound effects tracks. The sound editor identifies and fixes problems in the recorded sound, and supplies needed sounds. If necessary, looping sessions are held, in which actors in a studio record dialogue that was not properly recorded on set, or was only written after the fact to fill a dramatic hole. A Foley artist in a studio creates

sound effects (footsteps, punches, a creaking door, a briefcase being placed on a table) that were not recorded during shooting. Libraries of prerecorded sound effects may be used, along with computerized sound effects consoles, which enable the sound effects editor to manipulate sounds electronically.

(2) The composer is responsible for writing an original score for a movie; the music editor or music mixer for editing the music to fit into the complete sound mix. Once a film has been cut, the director and the editor meet with the composer and the music editor in spotting sessions, in which they view the film and discuss in detail what kind of music should go where. The composer uses this information as a guide. The result is recorded in scoring sessions, often with a full orchestra playing along. Some music may be obtained from outside sources (popular songs, classical melodies, etc.), in which case rights must be acquired.

(3) The final sound mix is the responsibility of the mixer, also called the dubbing, recording, or rerecording mixer. Working with the director and the editor, he or she may blend together more than 15 separate tracks, including dialogue, sound effects, and music, making sure that each sound gets just the emphasis it deserves and no more. Since most movies are in stereo, decisions must also be made about which sounds should be heard in which channels – left, middle, right, or surround.

(4) Once the mix is finished, it must be transferred onto the original negative. Film sound is recorded and edited on magnetic tape or with a

digital system, separate from the images. When the mix is complete, the magnetic sound track is reproduced in the finished film as an optical sound track, a set of squiggly lines running along the edge of the film.

This optical track is "read" by the projector during exhibition and transmitted through loudspeakers, so that the audience hears the sound in perfect synchronization with the picture. Nowadays, the final mix may be recorded not on an optical but on a digital sound track, which stores sound in the form of binary digital data, either directly on the film or on compact disks played in sync with the projector.

SOUND AND MUSIC GLOSSARY: PEOPLE

ADR technician The person who records in-studio line readings, in the process called automatic dialogue replacement, or ADR.

cableman or **cable puller** A person who handles cables and attachments for recording sound. Also called a location sound assistant, this person puts microphones on actors, sets up equipment, etc. The term *cable puller* may also refer to a person who handles camera cables.

composer The person who writes original music, or adapts preexisting music, for a film. This person may collaborate with a lyricist, who writes words for songs.

Foley artist The person who, in postproduction, creates sound effects, particularly the kind made by people rather than things. Examples include footsteps, punches, and kisses.

mixer The person who, in postproduction, blends several sound tracks into a single master sound track for a film. Also called the dubbing, recording, rerecording, or sound rerecording mixer. Sometimes called the sound mixer, although that term may be reserved for the floor mixer, the head of the sound crew.

music department The group of people who obtain, perform, or record music for a film. They may include the composer, lyricist, arranger-orchestrator, copyist, conductor, musicians, music supervisor (the studio official in charge of clearing rights for all music), music mixer, music librarian, and engineers.

music mixer The person who works with the composer to edit a film's music to fit into the total sound mix. Also called the music editor.

recordist *See* SOUND MIXER

sound crew The people responsible for recording sound during a shoot. The sound crew is headed by the sound mixer (also called the production sound mixer, floor mixer, or recordist), who has ultimate responsibility for making sure that sound recording is clear, balanced, and accurate. Skilled in recording dialogue and knowledgable about sound equipment and acoustics, he or she works closely with the film's director, and can object to a take if the sound is flawed. Under the sound mixer's supervision are the following individuals: the sound recorder, who assists in operating the sound recording equipment; the boom man or boom operator, who handles the microphone boom and keeps it out of camera view; one or more cablemen or cable pullers, who handle cables and attachments; and sometimes one or more playback operators or, simply, operators who perform various tasks, such as loading tape spools and monitoring playback machines.

sound cutter The person in charge of track laying, or the proper fitting of sound tracks to a film during editing.

sound editor or **sound effects editor** In postproduction, the person responsible for creating the dialogue and sound effects tracks for a film, though not the music track (which is the music mixer's job). The sound editor works with the director and editor to make optimum use of sound recorded on the set, to repair flaws in the recorded sound (such as differences in the level of dialogue), and to supply whatever other sounds are needed, whether it is sound effects or dialogue recorded in looping sessions. Under the sound editor is an assistant sound editor. On some films, several sound editors work under a supervising sound editor.

sound engineer A technician who works with sound tracks and assists in producing the final mix.

sound mixer The person who, as head of the sound crew, is responsible for recording sound on the set. Also called the floor mixer, recordist, or recording supervisor. The term is also sometimes used for the dubbing mixer or, simply, mixer, who in postproduction blends all the sound tracks into one master sound track. *See also* SOUND CREW.

The Academy Award for best sound goes to the mixer, or sound rerecording mixer, who blends all the sound tracks into a master sound track. The Academy Award for best sound effects editing goes to the sound effects editor, or supervising sound editor, who is responsible for creating the dialogue and sound effects tracks.

SOUND AND MUSIC GLOSSARY: THINGS

ADR *See* AUTOMATED DIALOGUE REPLACEMENT

aquarium Informal term for the booth where sound mixing is done.

asynchronous sound Sound not directly synchronized with the picture. It may be intentional, as when we hear someone's voice speaking offscreen, with the camera catching the reaction of the listener. Or it may be unintentional, as when a mixing flaw results in an actor's words preceding his lip movements.

audio Having to do with the sound of a film.

Technicians use a console or mixing board to create the film's final sound track.

automated dialogue replacement (ADR) A kind of looping session involving repetition of the previously recorded dialogue, with the corresponding image, as an assist to the actor rerecording the dialogue.

background music Music that the audience hears but that does not come from an on-screen source. It usually serves as a guide or catalyst for the audience's emotional response: for example, shrieking violins to make a scene scarier or romantic music to make the atmosphere more passionate.

background noise Noise such as car horns, crowd murmurs, and crashing waves, heard behind the dialogue and used to make a scene more realistic or atmospheric.

baffle (1) A portable, sound-absorbing wall used to prevent reverberations in studio recording. (2) A microphone attachment that accentuates high frequencies. (3) A sound-absorbing, fidelity-improving screen in a loudspeaker.

balance The arrangement of sound sources and microphones so that each sound has the right level relative to the others.

bloop The clicking noise produced by a splice in an optical sound track when it passes through a projector. The term may also refer to the blooping ink or blooping tape used to cover the splice and eliminate the noise.

boom A long telescopic arm that supports a microphone and is held over the head of the person speaking, outside of camera view.

bridge music Background music that accompanies a visual transition.

buzz track A sound track that records room tone, a low, unintelligible background noise that is used to avoid a jarring silence.

console A panel for mixing and controlling sound recording. Also called a mixing board.

cue breakdown or **cue sheet** A list of notes, or cues, to the composer, telling the latter at which moment in the film each bit of music is to begin or end.

dialing Controlling sound during filming. A given sound is either "dialed in" or "dialed out."

dialogue Spoken lines.

dialogue track A sound track that includes only dialogue. More than one dialogue track may be recorded for a particular film. If recorded during shooting, it may also be called the production track.

digital sound track A sound track in which sound is recorded in digital form, as a series of binary numbers stored in a computer.

directional microphone A microphone that picks up sound waves largely from a single direction. Used in recording dialogue. Also called a unidirectional microphone or cardioid.

Dolby Trademarked term for a noise-reduction system and stereo sound system (Dolby Stereo), both introduced in the 1970s and now widely used. The stereo system makes use of decoding technology to generate four-channel sound from an optical sound track.

double system The standard professional system for recording sound, in which sound and picture are recorded separately but in synchronization, the former on magnetic tape, the latter on film. This system offers better sound quality and more flexibility in editing than the alternative, the single system, in which image and sound are simultaneously recorded on the same film. The single system is still used for documentary and amateur filmmaking.

dubbing (1) The recording of dialogue or sound in postproduction, as when faulty dialogue is replaced in a looping session, or when a foreign film has its original dialogue replaced by a translation to a different language. (2) The mixing of all sound tracks into a single track.

echo chamber Enclosed space or electronic device that creates reverberations for an echo effect.

effects track Sound track containing sound effects only, not dialogue or music.

equalization Adjusting frequencies with the aid of an equalizer, or tone control system. The process improves signal-to-noise ratio, alters relative emphasis among frequencies, and modifies bass and treble. Also called filtering.

fidelity Accuracy in reproducing sound.

fishpole A lightweight pole to which a microphone is attached. Less cumbersome than a boom.

guide track A sound track made during location shooting but intended only as a guide for dubbing in postproduction.

i.p.s. Inches per second. A unit of measurement giving the speed at which a recording is taped.

lavalier or **lavaliere** A small microphone worn around the speaker's neck and usually hidden under his clothes.

level A measure of sound volume; or the volume at which a sound can be recorded with maximum fidelity.

lip-sync Synchronization of recorded speech with lip movement in the film image.

live sound Sound recorded on set, at the time of shooting.

looping The process by which actors rerecord dialogue in a studio in postproduction. A loop of film of a particular scene is played repeatedly to give the actor multiple opportunities to achieve synchronization of speech to the filmed lip movements.

M and E track A sound track containing music and effects but not dialogue. Used for dubbing a film in another language for release in a foreign country.

magnetic film Film coated with iron oxide for magnetic recording of sound. The magnetic film and the camera film run at the same speed, permitting perfect synchronization.

magnetic recording The process of capturing sound in the form of magnetic variations on film or tape, or the product of that process.

magnetic tape A ¼-inch tape that is coated with iron oxide for recording of sound. Also called audiotape.

mickey mousing A pejorative term for a style of scoring in which background music is so closely coordinated with on-screen action that every little emotional twist gets trumpeted on the music track. The effect may be to provoke laughter or annoyance.

microphone A device that converts sound waves into electric signals to be recorded on magnetic tape or film, ultimately to be converted back into sound waves by a speaker.

microphone boom See BOOM

mix The process by which several sound tracks are blended into one track; or the composite track that results. The process is also called dubbing or rerecording.

music track A sound track that contains only music, not dialogue or sound effects.

noise Unwanted sound audible in a recording.

off-mike or **off-microphone** Characteristic of sound directed away from a microphone, and therefore faint or unclear.

omnidirectional microphone A microphone that picks up sound from any direction, not just from one. Also called a nondirectional microphone.

optical sound track A sound track on photographic film, created by photographing a beam of light that varies in accordance with recorded sound variations. The sound track is converted back into audible sound by a projector.

out of sync The condition that results when recorded sound and filmed source do not match perfectly.

playback The conversion of recorded sound into audible sound, either for monitoring purposes or as a guide to performers on the set (as when recorded music is played back to guide singers and dancers during the shooting of a musical number; their movements, as a result, are synchronized to the recorded music).

postsynchronization or **postsync** The process of recording sound in postproduction to synchronize with filmed images. Looping is an example of postsynchronization. Also called dubbing or postrecording.

premix To combine several tracks into a single track, known as a premix, which in turn will be combined with one or more tracks in the final mix. For example, several different dialogue tracks may be premixed into one dialogue track. Also called predub.

prerecord To create a sound track prior to filming. This is often done with animated films.

Dissatisfied with his vocal performance, actor Mike Myers convinced DreamWorks Animation head Jeffrey Katzenberg to allow him not only to rework his interpretation of the character, but re-record every line of his dialogue for his role as the title ogre in the computer-animated *Shrek* (2001). Though the costly decision added millions of dollars to the budget of the partially-animated film, the grateful Myers waived his usual fee for re-recording, and the film went on to become one of the year's biggest grossing hits.

prescore To prepare and record a musical composition before a scene is shot. This is often done with musical numbers; performers then lip-sync and dance in time to the prerecorded music.

production track Sound recorded during shooting of a scene. It usually contains mainly dialogue and is also called the dialogue track.

rerecord To copy a recording or to mix sound tracks. Copying a recording is also called transferring the sound.

rifle mike A long directional microphone that can be aimed at a specific sound source.

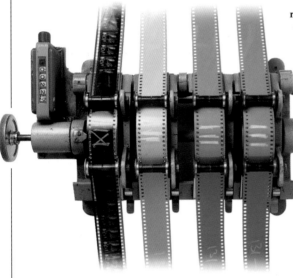

room tone The specific sound quality of a room, determined by the composition and dimensions of the room and its contents, or the room's ambient noise, and caused by such things as lamps and airconditioning systems.

score To write the background music for a film, or the music that results.

A synchronizer is used during editing to ensure that the sound track and film run together in harmony.

scoring stage A studio where a score is performed and recorded while the film is screened. The conductor watches the film on screen, using it to time his or her conducting; the musicians sit with their backs to the screen, watching the conductor.

SFX Abbreviation for sound effects.

single-system *See* DOUBLE-SYSTEM

sound effects (SFX) All sound in a film other than dialogue and music.

sound speed The rate (24 frames per second) at which film passes through a camera in the making of a sound movie. Sound recorders and projectors must run at the same speed for film and sound to be in synchronization; when they do, they are said to be at synchronous speed.

soundstage A studio for shooting a sound film. The stage is soundproof and acoustically engineered for recording sound.

sound track The set of sounds, including dialogue, sound effects, and music, that accompany the pictures in a film, or the physical medium in which those sounds are stored. In optical sound tracks, a narrow band on the left side of the film.

spotting The process of deciding when and where in a film a piece of background music should begin and end. The decision is made in spotting sessions that involve the composer, director, music editor, and editor.

stereophonic sound Sound that is recorded by two or more microphones on separate tracks, then played back through two or more loudspeakers, resulting in greater depth, fidelity, and range.

stripe To apply a band of magnetic iron oxide to a roll of film for sound recording, or the band that results.

synchronization or **sync** The process of getting a picture and sound track to run at matching speeds in correspondence with one another, so that the sound seems to come from the picture, or the condition of correspondence that results. A film that achieves this condition is said to be "in sync" or to have synchronous sound; one that fails to achieve it is said to be "out of sync" or to have asynchronous sound.

synchronization license The copyright permission needed to use recorded music in film.

synchronous speed *See* SOUND SPEED

track laying The process of fitting sound tracks to a film.

transfer *See* RERECORD

variable-area sound track An optical sound track in which the sound modulations take the form of a pattern of oscillations of light against dark. In making color films, this method is preferred over the alternative, the variable-density sound track.

variable-density sound track An optical sound track in which the sound modulations take the form of a series of horizontal striations that vary in density from black to light gray.

walla A sound effect consisting of an unintelligible crowd murmur (something like "walla walla walla...").

wild sound Sound that is recorded without the simultaneous and synchronous photographing of an image. For example, natural sounds at a location shoot may be recorded as wild sounds and later incorporated into the sound track. Also called nonsynchronous or nonsync sound. A sound track consisting of wild sounds is called a wild track.

EDITING

The editor takes the jumbled pieces of film that come out of production and, in consultation with the director and producer, transforms them into a coherent and well-paced story.

EDITING IS THE ART OF ASSEMBLING a film into finished form. Most movies are shot out of sequence, often with multiple takes covering each scene from different angles and recording different nuances in performance. Shots are often allowed to run longer than needed, so as to be sure to capture the key emotional moment. The result is a jumbled mass of film that must be winnowed down and cut and pasted into a coherent, continuous, well-paced story. This is the job the editor does, working in an editing or cutting room in consultation with the director and producer. So important is this task that Soviet theorist and director V.I. Pudovkin argued that it was the most vital and creative aspect of filmmaking.

SOME DIRECTORS WORK closely with the editor in selecting each shot and determining how to snip it. Other directors leave many of these decisions to the editor. Some directors "cut in the camera" – filming very little footage in roughly the intended sequence, so that only minimal editing will be needed. (This is one way of maintaining directorial control, although it increases the risk that expensive reshoots will be needed.) A good editor must be able to work with all kinds of directors, adapting his or her style to theirs. Occasionally, a director edits his or her own films: David Lean, for example, was a gifted director-editor. *Cutting* and *cutter* are sometimes used as synonyms for *editing* and *editor*, but because *cutting* implies a routine, mechanical activity rather than an artistic and intellectual one, *editing* is the preferred term. Properly speaking, a cutter is a person who cuts and splices film under an editor's supervision.

The splicer allows two pieces of film to be joined together.

STEPS IN THE EDITING PROCESS

PREPRODUCTION
• Sometimes the director and editor will do advance planning about the editing.

DURING FILMING
• The editor confers with the director about the rushes (the film shot the previous day) and begins assembling parts of the film, in what is known as a work print. Film may be transferred to videotape or digital format for greater ease in selecting and arranging shots. The version of the film that results from this assembly phase is called the assembly.

POSTPRODUCTION
• Working with the director, the editor refines the assembly into a rough cut, the first completely edited work print. Shots are arranged in what seems the best order, and sound tracks are put in sync with the images, but individual shots are not refined. Because the director's vision dominates this phase, this version of the film is often called the director's cut.
• After conferring with the director, the editor refines the rough cut; this may be done several times.
• The editor produces the fine cut, a seemingly final arrangement of shots, each cut precisely to the correct length. Optical effects, such as transitional and visual effects, are included.

German-born Leni Riefenstahl participated in every aspect of filmmaking during her career: editing, directing, producing, acting, and screenwriting.

• The editor works with the mixer to supervise final integration of all sound tracks (including dialogue, sound effects, and music) into a master track. The master track is integrated with the images in the fine cut.
• The original negative is cut, using the fine cut as a blueprint.
• The original negative and the final sound mix are printed together on the answer print, also called the trial composite. During this step, final timing, the process of adjusting density and color quality, is done.
• Following audience previews and further discussions between director and editor, additional changes may be made to the fine cut.
• Master prints are made from the original negative; from these, duplicate negatives are made for the production of release prints.

CHANGING TECHNOLOGY

In the old days, editing depended completely on marking up, cutting, and cementing together strips of film. Today, video and digital technology makes it possible for some phases of editing to be done with push-button ease. Films are transferred to videotape or digital format and computer coded, enabling editors to shave frames off a shot and try out different editing sequences on a screen, without the labor of physically cutting film. Eventually, when the original negative is produced, real film must be cut and spliced, but that process is now usually guided by the electronic editing that has taken place beforehand.

> "The cutting room is the last place where any problems of story or acting or directing that have accumulated along the way can be fixed. The buck stops in the cutting room."
>
> —
>
> *Dede Allen, editor*

EDITING GLOSSARY: PEOPLE

apprentice editor An editor in training, who learns the craft by assisting the assistant editor and/or the editor.

assistant editor Aide to a film editor. Among his or her tasks are maintaining records of pieces of film, cutting and splicing film, labeling cans, working with video and digital technology, and keeping order in the cutting room. If the assistant editor works with videotape, he or she may be called a videotape operator.

cutter A person, such as an assistant editor, who cuts and splices film under the supervision of the editor. The editor is also sometimes called a cutter.

doctor An editor who specializes in creating a passable film from a particularly bad collection of shots. Doctors sometimes suggest additional scenes that will solve whatever problems exist, and may even direct the second unit to obtain the needed scenes.

editor A person who selects and assembles pieces of film into a finished whole.

off-line and **on-line editors** *See* VIDEOTAPE EDITOR

production editor A person who assembles rushes (the product of a day's shooting, viewed the following day) and synchronizes them with recorded sound.

videotape editor An editor who works with videotape. An off-line videotape editor is one who works with the director during the production to create an edit list, a selection of shots that should go in the final film. An on-line videotape editor works in postproduction, creating final edits based on the edit list.

videotape operator A person who prepares videotape for editing, puts together rough cuts, and assists with final edits. May also be called an assistant editor.

EDITING GLOSSARY: THINGS

A and B editing A method of editing in which two matching rolls of film are used to produce a master print. The method is used to create transitional effects such as dissolves and fades, and, in 16mm filmmaking, to eliminate visible splices. Pictures on one roll correspond to blank leader on the other roll, until the moment when a dissolve is to begin; at that point, the other roll begins to carry the pictures while the first roll goes blank until the succeeding dissolve. The shots from both rolls are printed in order on a single film (a process called A and B printing). A and B editing is also called checkerboard cutting.

accelerated montage Rapid cutting, with very brief shots, to increase the pace of action and raise the level of excitement and suspense.

answer print The first edited print of a film that contains both sound and picture. Sent to the producer for approval, it may require changes before a final release print is approved. Also called the approval print, trial print, or trial composite.

assembly The initial process, in preparation for making a rough cut, of selecting takes, putting together shots, and trimming scenes. The product assembled as a result of this process is also called the assembly, although it may be called the editor's cut, to distinguish it from the rough cut or director's cut.

bin A receptacle for storing unwound film, used in editing rooms. Also called a trim bin, it has a rack from which pieces of film are hung.

china pencil Grease pencil used for marking up a work print, e.g., with instructions for transitional effects. Also called a china marker or chinagraph pencil.

code numbers Corresponding numbers printed at one-foot intervals along the edges of both picture and sound work prints, to provide a guide to synchronization.

composite print A print containing both picture and sound in synchronization. Also called a married print.

content curve The length of time an audience needs to register the significant information in a shot. A shot should be cut at the peak of the curve. Cut too early and the sequence is choppy or incoherent; too late and it is plodding.

continuity cutting Editing unobtrusively to keep the film advancing in a clear, smooth, linear way. Among the techniques employed are cutting on action. Also called invisible cutting, it contrasts with dynamic cutting.

crosscutting The technique of cutting back and forth between two parallel, separately filmed actions to show their relationship. May be used to build suspense or to have one action comment on the other. Also called parallel cutting or parallel editing. *See also* INTERCUTTING.

cue mark A scratched or penciled mark on a work print, to signal a particular point in editing or synchronization.

cut A sudden transition from one shot to another, achieved by juxtaposing the last frame of one shot with the first frame of another. Also called a straight cut or direct cut.

cutaway A momentary shift away from the main action, as when a cut is made from a dance scene to the audience watching, then quickly back to the dance scene.

cutting Editing, or the art of assembling pieces of film into a finished whole. More precisely, the mechanical process of cutting and splicing pieces of film, or their video or digital equivalents, as part of the business of editing.

cutting negative *See* NEGATIVE CUTTING

cutting on action Cutting unobtrusively from one shot to another while the subject of the shot is moving. The cut is unobtrusive because the audience's attention is focused on the moving actor or vehicle.

cutting room The room where film is edited. It is typically furnished with such equipment as a workbench, flatbed editing machine, bin, and storage shelves. Also called the editing room.

diagonal splicing The oblique joining together of sound film or magnetic tape to minimize noise.

digital editing Editing film by transferring it to digital format and cutting and assembling it on the computer. Digital editing equipment includes the Avid, Lightworks, and D-Vision systems.

direct cut *See* CUT

dynamic cutting Juxtaposition of discontinuous shots of various subjects to form a significant whole. Often used to create ambiguity or tension. Opposed to continuity cutting.

edge numbers A series of numbers, with key letters, printed at one-foot intervals on the edge of raw negative film and duplicated on positive prints. During negative cutting, edge numbers facilitate matching of an edited work print with the negative. Also called key numbers, footage numbers, and negative numbers.

The first Academy Award for best film editing was given in 1934 to Conrad Nervig for Eskimo.

edit list A list of shots designated to be included in a film.

editing The art of assembling a film into finished form.

editing bench or **editing table** A work table holding editing equipment.

editing room *See* CUTTING ROOM

Editola Trade name for an editing machine similar to a Moviola.

editorial sync The state that results from the exact matching of picture and sound by the synchronizer. Also called editorial synchronization, editing sync, edit sync, and dead sync.

editor's cut *See* ASSEMBLY

Once filming is complete, the editor uses an editing table to synchronize the sound track and the accompanying images, linking sequences of film to put the images in order.

final cut The last version of a film, the one released to exhibitors.

fine cut A version of a film that is considerably more refined than the rough cut and close to the final version. The final version, or final cut, is also sometimes called the fine cut.

flange A metal or plastic disk used in conjunction with a core to facilitate rewinding.

flatbed editing machine A table that incorporates editing equipment. Reels containing pictures and sound run horizontally, on the table surface, instead of upright, as in the Moviola. Some tables allow for transfer of film to video. Also called flatbed editor, table editing machine, editing table, or horizontal editor.

horse A device, employing a rod through cores, for holding reels of film.

intercutting Cutting back and forth between two or more locations to make one coherent scene. May be used as a synonym for crosscutting, though intercutting is sometimes used more precisely for two closely related actions that make up one scene (say, two people talking to each other on the telephone), while crosscutting is reserved for two independent actions shown concurrently so that the two comment on one another (for example, the baptism and the multiple murders near the end of *The Godfather*). *See also* CROSSCUTTING.

invisible cutting *See* CONTINUITY CUTTING

jump cut A cut that seems abrupt because the subject appears to jump suddenly from one point to another. In traditional filmmaking, it is considered undesirable, a sign of poor shooting or editing. But some directors favor it as a way of unsettling the audience or emphasizing a point.

match cut A cut from one shot to another in which a certain subject or action is carried over, or matched. Cutting on action is an example of a match cut.

matching The stage in which the original negative is cut to match the editing of the work print.

montage (1) A sequence composed of a succession of brief shots depicting the passage of time or a series of memories; also called compilation cuts. (2) A style of editing that emphasizes the often jarring juxtaposition of disparate images, rather than the continuity cutting (or invisible cutting) traditional in Hollywood films. (3) The editing process as envisioned by Russian film theorists Pudovkin and Eisenstein, who saw editing as the central way in which films communicate meaning. (4) Any juxtaposition of images through editing.

Moviola Trade name for an upright, motor-driven editing machine. Sometimes used generically for any machine of this type. Once a staple of cutting rooms, it has been replaced in many cases by flatbed editing machines and video and digital systems.

negative cutting The process of cutting a negative to match the final work print. It involves matching the negative frame by frame with the work print, employing edge numbers as a guide. Also called conforming. The person who cuts the negative is called the negative cutter or conformer.

numbering machine A device for printing edge numbers on a piece of film.

outtake A take or shot not used in the finished film. *See also* TRIM.

overlap (1) The filming of identical actions at the end of one shot and the beginning of another. This is often done to allow the editor to join the shots unobtrusively by cutting on action. In some cases, audiences may be permitted to see the identical action repeated from different angles, for the sake of dramatic emphasis. (2) The continuation of sound from one shot to another. (3) The extension of one end of film over another for splicing. (4) The extension of a shot to allow for a transitional effect such as a dissolve or fade.

rack A frame for hanging pieces of film over a bin.

rough cut The first completely edited version of a film, in which shots are selected and arranged in the correct order but without fine cutting. Because the editor produces this version in accordance with the director's wishes, without interference from the studio, the rough cut is sometimes called the director's cut.

scraper An instrument, either separate from or part of a splicer, that scrapes emulsion from the end of a piece of film in preparation for splicing.

shooting ratio The ratio of footage shot to footage used in the final cut. 5:1 or 10:1 are common ratios, though more apparently wasteful ratios of 15:1 or even 30:1 sometimes occur.

slug A piece of blank leader spliced into a work print for temporary replacement of a missing piece of footage. Also called buildup or spacing.

splice (1) To join together two pieces of film. (2) A point in the film where two pieces are joined. The traditional method of splicing is to scrape the emulsion from the end of one strip of film, apply cement to the scraped surface, and attach the surface to the overlapping end of another strip of film. This is called an overlap cement, lap, or cement splice. If the cement is dried rapidly by being electrically heated, it is called a hot splice. Another method is the butt or dry splice, in which two film ends are cut and joined with transparent tape to create a nonoverlapping butt joint. It may also be called a Mylar splice, for the Mylar that composes the tape. The butt splice is weaker and blurrier than the lap splice but also easier to do, and so it is used for work prints, while final cuts employ lap splices. In 16mm filmmaking, where lap splices are more easily visible than on studio-quality 35mm film, a method called A and B editing, or checkerboard cutting, may be used. This requires the use of two rolls of film to prepare a master print with no visible splices.

splicer A device for splicing, or joining together, pieces of film. Splicers include hand splicers (operated by hand), machine splicers (operated by both hands and feet), and hot splicers (which use heat for rapid drying of cement). Cement splicers make use of cement, tape splicers tape.

split reel A film reel with a removable side, permitting the editor to insert or remove film without winding or rewinding.

straight cut *See* CUT

synchronizer Machine with linked sprocket wheels attached to a revolving shaft, used to keep a film and sound tracks in synchronization.

transitional effect Any effect other than a straight cut for marking a change of scene (e.g., dissolve, fade, wipe). Once produced exclusively in camera, most are now added optically in the laboratory. (*See also* the box on "Transitional Effects".)

trial composite *See* ANSWER PRINT

trim To shorten a shot or scene by cutting out a portion. Trims are pieces of film cut from shots or scenes. The trims (also called clips or cuts) are registered and stored in case they are needed later. The term trim may be used interchangeably with outtake or out, though an outtake is more precisely an entire take, shot, or scene not used in the final film.

trim bin *See* BIN

video editing system A machine that transfers film images to videotape and transmits them to monitors, enabling the editor to inspect and rearrange them electronically.

viewer A machine for fast viewing of film, equipped with a lamp to illuminate frames and a motorized or manual crank for advancing and rewinding film.

work print The print with which the editor works in putting together a film. It evolves from an assembly to a rough cut to a fine cut to a final cut. In its finished form, it serves as the model for cutting the original negative. Also called workprint or cutting copy.

When a scene is filmed but omitted from a movie, it is said to be "left on the cutting room floor," as if it will later be swept up as trash. In fact, pieces left out of a film are usually registered and stored, in case of a decision to reinstate them.

TRANSITIONAL EFFECTS

DISSOLVE: one scene fades out while another fades in, with the two scenes briefly overlapping on screen; also called a lap dissolve

FADE: the scene gradually emerges out of blackness (a fade-in) or gradually darkens into blackness (a fade-out); many films begin with a fade-in and end with a fade-out

IRIS-IN/IRIS-OUT: the scene begins as a pinpoint circle of light surrounded by black; the circle expands to fill the entire frame (iris-in). The scene ends by reversing the procedure: the image becomes a circle that shrinks until it becomes a pinpoint and disappears (iris-out). Also called circle-in or circle-out.

SWISH PAN: a rapid pan from one point to another, blurring the scene and serving as a transition to the next scene

TRANSITION FOCUS: the scene goes out of focus; a new scene comes into focus

WIPE: one scene gradually erases and replaces another, as if the new scene were a cloth wiping the other off the screen. Wipes may have straight, sharp edges or soft or jagged ones. There are several distinct subgenres of wipes, including the burst or explosion wipe, in which the new scene seems to burst onto the screen, and the flipover (or flip) wipe, in which a scene seems to rotate or flip over, with the new scene apparently printed on its back.

DISTRIBUTION AND EXHIBITION

Once a movie is in the can, a new phase begins: distribution and exhibition.
The distributor gets the completed movie to theater owners, or exhibitors.
The exhibitors show the movie to audiences.

THE PRECEDING SECTION, "THE FINE DETAILS," focused on how a movie is produced. But production is only one phase of a movie's life. Distribution and exhibition are needed for the film to reach an audience. The distributor is the middleman between the producer, the one who makes the movie, and the exhibitor, the one who shows the movie to paying audiences.

These three functions – production, distribution, and exhibition – are, for the most part, separated in today's film industry. Independent production companies, run by independent producers, make movies, usually financed by a

Modern-day movie theaters that show multiple films are called multiplexes.

film studio that helps to develop a given project. A particular production company may have a long-term contract or multipicture deal with a studio, giving the studio exclusive rights to projects the production company generates for a given period. But the production company is still legally independent and may set up shop elsewhere when the contract expires.

SOME STUDIOS ARE CONNECTED to theaters either directly or through a corporate parent. But today's studio-owned theaters do not operate as mere showcases for the studio's films; rather, they operate independently of the studio, booking films the exhibitor thinks will bring in the biggest audiences, and aiming for deals that benefit the

exhibitor, not the distributor. With production and exhibition kept separate, today's studios operate largely as distributors – albeit distributors with deep pockets. During development, they operate as quasiproducers, using their financing money to influence what films will be made and how. Once the film is completed, the studio acts as a distributor: booking, advertising, promoting, and tracking its product with zeal and savvy.

Studios generally distribute the movies they develop and finance. Warner Bros. Distributing Corp. distributes the product of its sister company Warner Bros. Pictures; Buena Vista (the distribution arm of Disney) distributes Disney films. But they may also distribute independently financed films.

This is called a negative pickup – a "picking up" by the studio of a completed, or nearly completed, negative. The studio pays the producer for the privilege of distributing the film to theaters.

If an independent filmmaker fails to interest any of the majors in his or her film, there are many other distributors who might offer it a home. Independent film distributors – some of them autonomous units of studios, as Miramax is of Disney – shop at the film festivals, looking for quirky, promising, and relatively cheap product from young filmmakers.

Whether a film's distributor is a major or an indie, the same set of tasks is involved. In practice, the distributor may have as little as four months to prepare to launch the film.

PLANNING A RELEASE STRATEGY

The release date for the film must be thought through. Christmas and summer are traditional peak times for moviegoing, but release schedules are crowded then, so a distributor may opt to release at a time when there is less competition. The release pattern must be decided upon. Films anticipated to have wide appeal, such as sequels to blockbusters, usually get a wide release (also called a broad, general, or saturation release), opening simultaneously in 800 or more theaters nationwide. Films of less certain appeal might get a limited release, opening in only a few hundred theaters. Risky, arty films might get a platform or slow release, opening first in just two or three cities, perhaps in New York and L.A., then gradually spreading to a few hundred theaters, after word of mouth and good reviews (if they come) have had a chance to generate interest in it.

BOOKING THE FILM INTO THEATERS

Distributors do not sell new releases to theaters or theater chains. Rather, they license them or book them, granting the right to show a rented print of the movie on a specified series of dates at a specified location, in return for a fee called a rental. Film rental agreements are fiendishly complicated (*see* below), but the rentals collected more or less reflect how many people are seeing the film and are crucial to how studios make money. A film's box-office gross, strictly speaking, is the sum of all ticket prices paid by audiences, the money handed over to the clerk in the theater's ticket booth, or box office. But the term *box-office gross* is often used interchangeably with film rentals, fees paid by exhibitors to distributors, even though these sums are more properly described as distributor's gross. In strict terminology, film rentals are always a percentage of box-office gross.

OBTAINING AND DISTRIBUTING PRINTS

Someday, digital film distribution may make exhibition as simple as downloading a file from the Internet. For now, however, distributors have to provide physical copies of the film. They have to order sufficient prints for the theaters that have booked them, control the prints' quality, and transport them to the theaters. If the print isn't there on the day promised, moviegoers fume and the theater owner loses money.

ADVERTISING AND PUBLICIZING THE FILM

This includes market research; development of television, radio, newspaper, and other ads; creation of trailers or previews, those brief "coming attractions" spots shown in theaters that highlight the best parts of upcoming films; creation of posters (called one-sheets), lobby cards, stills, and other marketing materials; distribution of press kits and press releases to the media; arranging for stars and other talent to be interviewed; and anything else that might let people know the film exists and persuade them to see it.

"For a national release, movies have become a three-day business; if the opening grosses are not strong, the picture will not survive for an extended run."

—

Robert G. Friedman, film executive

Tracking the Film's Performance

Films have only a short time in which to make money in theaters: after a few weeks or months, the public will usually lose interest. Therefore distributors have to analyze grosses quickly and carefully. If the film is doing better than expected, perhaps the number of screens showing it should be expanded. If it's doing worse than expected, perhaps the ad campaign should be pulled and replaced with a backup. Distributors don't rely only on domestic theatrical release to make money. A film's earning potential is extended by release in foreign theaters; by home-video/DVD sales; and by licensing of a variety of television rights: pay-per-view, premium cable channels, basic cable channels, and broadcast television. The distributor can also license merchandising rights to makers of everything from toys, mugs, and T-shirts to records and computer games. Nowadays, a film that performs poorly at the domestic box office may still turn a profit in these ancillary markets.

A film's production costs are only the beginning. P&A, the exorbitant cost agreement of prints and advertising, is another hurdle feature films have to clear in order to recoup the studio's investment.

The Arcane World of Film Rentals

When a studio books a major new release in a theater, it doesn't do so for a flat fee, nor for a fixed percentage. Instead, it relies on an arcane system that has evolved gradually to balance competing interests: a sliding scale of percentages, with a number of variables, including the theater's operating costs, known as the "nut" or "house nut."

An arrangement called 90/10 is common. Here the distributor demands 90 percent of the gross box-office take (ticket sales) minus the nut, the house allowance. Like almost everything else in the movie business, the nut is a negotiated figure and may include a

---

THE MOTION PICTURE RATING SYSTEM

BEFORE BEING RELEASED THEATRICALLY IN THE US, MOST films seek a rating from the Ratings Board of the Motion Picture Association of America (MPAA). Since 1968, the MPAA has administered this rating system, which tries to advise the public about a film's suitability for younger audiences. No filmmaker is legally required to obtain an MPAA rating, but in practice most commercial producers and distributors do, since most theaters will not show films that lack a rating. The criteria used to assign a rating include violence, sensuality, nudity, language, and drug abuse. Other countries have their own distinct ratings systems.

These are the MPAA ratings, what they mean officially, and what might cause a film to earn that rating.

G   GENERAL AUDIENCES. ALL AGES ADMITTED.
Nothing deemed improper for young children. Minimal violence, no nudity, no words naughtier than preschool bathroom euphemisms. Nowadays, the G rating is associated with children's movies and otherwise avoided by filmmakers.

PG   PARENTAL GUIDANCE SUGGESTED. SOME MATERIAL MAY NOT BE SUITABLE FOR CHILDREN.
May include some profanity, violence, or brief, nonsexually oriented nudity.

PG-13   PARENTS STRONGLY CAUTIONED. SOME MATERIAL MAY BE INAPPROPRIATE FOR CHILDREN UNDER 13.
A step naughtier than PG, with the addition of drug-abuse content, scarier violence, or one (but not more than one) sexually derived profanity.

R   RESTRICTED. UNDER 17 REQUIRES ACCOMPANYING PARENT OR ADULT GUARDIAN.
May include persistent raw language, rough or persistent violence, nudity in sexual contexts, or drug abuse.

NC-17   NO CHILDREN UNDER 17 ADMITTED.
May include abundant sex, nudity, violence, profanity, drug abuse, or some combination thereof.

little built-in profit for the exhibitor. If the two sides agree to set the nut at $20,000, and the first week's gross box-office take is $50,000, the distributor's rental fee that week would be 90 percent of $30,000, or $27,000, which amounts to 54 percent of the gross box-office take.

But this arrangement is usually complicated by the addition of a floor, a minimum percentage of the gross that is guaranteed to the distributor. Each week, the distributor gets either the 90/10 deal or the floor, whichever is higher. Often the floor is set at 70 percent for the first few weeks, so that, in the case above, the distributor would be guaranteed at least 70 percent of $50,000, or $35,000. In successive weeks, the percentage goes down: floors might be at 70 percent for three weeks, then at 60 percent for two weeks, all the way down to 35 percent in the last weeks. This arrangement is called "90/10 over an approved house allowance with minimums."

Further complicating the picture is the fact that the most hotly anticipated releases are frequently auctioned off to the exhibitor who offers the sweetest terms for the distributor. On the other hand, distributors have an interest in booking their films into well-located or well-equipped theaters, even if the bids from those theaters are lower. Often, an exhibitor will pay upfront money to the distributor, either in the form of a nonrefundable guarantee or a refundable advance (that is, refundable if the picture doesn't meet expectations).

Sometimes a distributor suspects that the exhibitor is not accurately calculating the percentage owed under

TYPES OF THEATERS

ART HOUSE A theater specializing in art, foreign, or independent films considered to be of high quality but low mass appeal.

CINEMA Term for a movie theater, more commonly used in Europe than in the US.

DRIVE-IN Outdoor theater where the audience watches a movie from their automobiles. Also called an ozoner or passion pit.

DUMP Pejorative term for a low-priced movie theater showing films late in their run.

FIRST-RUN THEATER A theater that specializes in new releases at premium prices, typically in comfortable and well-equipped surroundings. Contrasts with

a second-run house, which shows movies later in their release at discount prices, sometimes in a more spartan environment.

MEGAPLEX A movie theater with 16 or more screens. *See* MULTIPLEX.

MULTIPLEX A movie theater with more than one screening room, able to show several films at one time. If it has 16 or more screens, it is called a megaplex.

NEIGHBORHOOD THEATER A theater away from a major city center, serving a neighborhood or region. Also called a nabe or regional theater.

the 90/10 arrangement. Often exhibitors feel distributors are taking advantage of them. The result may be quarrels, overdue film rentals, and negotiated settlements. But the two sides need each other. Without exhibitors, distributors have no place to show films; without distributors, exhibitors have nothing to show.

NOT JUST POPCORN ANYMORE
Popcorn, soda, and candy used to be the sole staples of movie theater concession stands. Now in many theaters a veritable smorgasbord is available, from espresso and chocolate truffles to hot dogs and grilled chicken. The reason: theaters profit more from concession sales than ticket prices. The bulk of box-office grosses goes to distributors, whereas concession sales go entirely to the exhibitors.

The average American eats 68 quarts of popcorn a year, which adds up to 17.3 billion quarts of popcorn consumed each year!

The Voluntary Movie Rating System

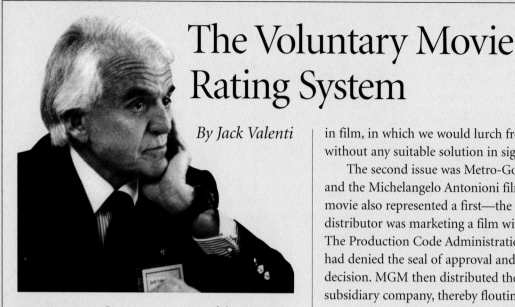

By Jack Valenti

W HEN I BECAME PRESIDENT of the Motion Picture Association of America (MPAA) in May 1966, the slippage of Hollywood studio authority over content of films collided with an avalanching revision of American mores and customs. By summer of 1966, the national scene was marked by insurrection on the campus, riots in the street, rise in women's liberation, doubts about the institution of marriage, and the crumbling of social traditions. It would have been foolish to believe that movies, that most creative of art forms, could have remained unaffected by the change and torment in our society.

THE RESULT OF ALL THIS was the emergence of a "new kind" of American movie—frank and open, and made by filmmakers subject to very few self-imposed restraints.

Almost within weeks in my new duties, I was confronted with controversy, neither amiable nor fixable. The first issue was the film *Who's Afraid of Virginia Woolf?* in which, for the first time on screen, the word "screw" and the phrase "hump the hostess" were heard. The MPAA's general counsel and I met with Jack Warner and his top aide, Ben Kalmenson. The result was the deletion of "screw" and retention of "hump the hostess," but I was uneasy over the meeting. I was uncomfortable with the thought that this was just the beginning of an unsettling new era

in film, in which we would lurch from crisis to crisis, without any suitable solution in sight.

The second issue was Metro-Goldwyn-Mayer and the Michelangelo Antonioni film *Blow Up.* This movie also represented a first—the first time a major distributor was marketing a film with nudity in it. The Production Code Administration in California had denied the seal of approval and I backed the decision. MGM then distributed the film through a subsidiary company, thereby flouting the voluntary agreement of MPAA member companies that no one would distribute a film without a Code seal.

Finally, in April 1968, the U.S. Supreme Court upheld the constitutional power of states and cities to prevent the exposure of children to books and films that could not be denied to adults.

It was plain that the old system of self-regulation, begun with the formation of the MPAA in 1922, had broken down. What few threads there were holding together the structure created by Will Hays, one of my two predecessors, had now snapped. From the very first day of my own succession to the MPAA President's Office, I had sniffed the Production Code constructed by the Hays Office. There was about this stern, forbidding catalogue of "Dos and Don'ts" the odious smell of censorship. I determined to junk it at the first opportune moment.

I knew that the mix of new social currents, the irresistible force of creators determined to make "their" films, and the possible intrusion of government into the movie arena demanded my immediate action. Within weeks, discussion of my plan for a movie rating system began with the president of the National Association of Theatre Owners (NATO) and with the governing committee of the International Film Importers & Distributors of America (IFIDA), an assembly of independent producers and distributors.

By early fall, my colleagues in the National Association of Theatre Owners joined with me in affirming our objective of creating a new and, at the time, revolutionary approach to how we would fulfill our obligation to the parents of America.

My first move was to abolish the old Hays Production Code. Then on November 1, 1968, we announced the birth of the new, voluntary film rating system of the motion picture industry, with three organizations, NATO, MPAA and IFIDA, as its monitoring and guiding groups. The initial design called for four rating categories:

- G FOR GENERAL AUDIENCES—all ages admitted.
- M FOR MATURE AUDIENCES—parental guidance suggested, but all ages admitted.
- R FOR RESTRICTED—children under 16 would not be admitted without an accompanying parent or adult guardian.
- X FOR NO ONE UNDER 17 ADMITTED.

The rating system trademarked all category symbols, except X. Under the plan, anyone not submitting his or her film for rating could self-apply the X or any other symbol or description, except those trademarked by the rating program.

So, the emergence of the industry rating system filled the vacuum provided by my dismantling of the Hays Production Code. The movie industry would no longer "approve or disapprove" the content of a film, but we would now see our primary task as giving advance cautionary warnings to parents so that parents could make the decision about the movie going of their young children.

CHANGES IN THE RATING SYSTEM

We found early on that the M category (M meaning "Mature") was regarded by most parents as a sterner rating than the R category. To remedy this misconception, we changed the name from M to GP (meaning General audiences, Parental guidance suggested). A year later we revised the name to the current label, "PG: Parental Guidance Suggested."

On July 1, 1984 we made another adjustment. We split the PG category into two groupings, PG and PG-13. PG-13 meant a higher level of intensity than was found in a film rated PG. Over the past years, parents have approved of this amplifying revision in the rating system.

On September 27, 1990, we announced two more revisions. First, we introduced brief explanations of why a particular film received its R rating. Since, in the opinion of the Rating Board, R rated films contain adult material, we believed it would be useful to parents to know a little more about the film's content before they allowed their children to accompany them. Sometime later, we began applying the explanations in the PG, PG-13 and NC-17 categories as well. These explanations are available to parents at the theater (by telephone or at the box office), in certain media reviews and listings, and are also made available on the MPAA's Internet home page—http://www.mpaa.org.

Second, we changed the name of the X category to NC-17: NO ONE UNDER 17 ADMITTED. The X rating over the years appeared to have taken on a surly meaning in the minds of many people, a meaning that was never intended when we created the system. Therefore, we chose to reaffirm the original intent of the design we installed on November 1, 1968, in which this "adults only" category explicitly describes a movie that most parents would want to have barred to viewing by their children. That was and is our goal, nothing more, nothing less.

THE PURPOSE OF THE RATING SYSTEM

The basic mission of the rating system is a simple one: to offer to parents some advance information about movies so that parents can decide what movies they want their children to see or not to see. The entire rostrum of the rating program rests in the assumption of responsibility by parents. If parents don't care, or if they are languid in guiding their children's' movie going, the ratings system becomes useless. Indeed, if you are 18 or older, or if you have no children, the rating system has no meaning for you. Ratings are meant for parents, no one else.

CRITIQUING FILM

From ordinary moviegoers to film reviewers and film scholars, everyone likes to form and express views about cinema. The practice of film criticism ranges from simple praise and pans to highly theoretical analysis.

THE FINAL PHASE FOR MOVIES is their reception by audiences, including professional critics. Everyone in the audience is at least an amateur critic, in that they form opinions about the film ("It was great"; "It stunk"; "It had a terrific twist ending"). These opinions get transmitted to friends in the form of word of mouth, a force that can make sleeper hits out of little movies and sink megabudget spectacles. Some people, however, make their living by judging the aesthetic merits of film: these are professional reviewers, who work for print, broadcast, and on-line media. Their praise or condemnation may not guarantee the film's outcome but it can be influential. Distributors spend a lot of money organizing advance screenings for critics, excerpting the most laudatory reviews as blurbs in ads. Understandably, when a distributor has a strong reason to think a film will be critically reviled, advance screenings may be withheld. In that case, blurbs may be solicited from obscure media outlets known to be easy with praise.

Yet the task of reviewing is only one aspect of film criticism. Scholarly critics seek to analyze, interpret, and judge films, or "film texts," in a more systematic way, often with reference to other films and to one or more film theories, interpretive frameworks for understanding film as a distinct artistic medium. Such film criticism is carried out in journals and universities, and is one part of the larger field of film studies. Film studies is an eclectic field, in which such disciplines as history, economics,

In the award-winning 1989 film Cinéma Paradiso, *an audience in a small village in Italy enjoys a film.*

philosophy, cultural studies, gender studies, psychoanalysis, semiotics, and literary criticism may all be brought to bear in understanding film.

WAS THAT A MOVIE OR A FILM?

Movie, film, motion picture, and *cinema* all seem to refer to the same thing, but there are subtle differences. *Movie* is the entertaining thing you see on the weekend to relax. *Film* is the work of art you study, perhaps in film studies courses or film research centers (no one talks about "movie studies" or "movie research centers"). *Motion picture* is a more formal way of saying "movie," sometimes used in technical or business descrip-tions, sometimes in publicity materials seeking to inflate a movie's importance: "A Major Motion Picture," not "A Major Movie."

Cinema is the grandest of all the terms: it refers to film in general, not to any one particular film, and connotes serious consideration of the aesthetic qualities of the medium. In Britain, *cinema* means movie theater, so one can talk about "going to the cinema," but most Americans don't go to the cinema or to films; for a good time, they go to the movies.

In practice all these terms can be used to refer to the same work. *The Godfather* is a movie because it's entertaining. It's also a film by Francis Ford Coppola, his masterpiece. It's a motion picture, a major Paramount release. And it's an example of cinema, exhibiting all sorts of distinctively cinematic qualities. What you call it depends on how you're discussing it and with whom.

HOW TO WATCH A MOVIE

In a famous scene in *Annie Hall*, Woody Allen stands in a movie line and overhears so much mindless chatter about film and the writings of communications theorist Marshall McLuhan that he conjures up McLuhan to tell the chatterer, "You know nothing of my work." If you want to avoid a similarly embarrassing encounter, here are ten tips on how to watch a movie and talk about it in an interesting way.

AIM AT SAYING SOMETHING MORE THAN "IT WAS GREAT." "It was great" or "It was boring" are conversation stoppers, unless you add some explanation of why the film was great or why it was boring. You want to be able to say something like "The screenplay fell apart in the last act, but there was a great supporting performance by so-and-so," or "The cinematography was gorgeous, but the characterizations were weak." To do that, you have to be able to tease apart the various elements that go into the film experience.

CONSIDER EACH FILM CRAFT INDIVIDUALLY. To tease the film production crafts apart, look over the movie crafts described in this chapter. Notice how many different kinds of talent go into the making of a film: producing, directing, writing, acting, cinematography, production design, costume design, makeup, hair, special effects, sound, music, editing. A great film results from the collaboration of all these people doing great work. Rare is the film that bombs in every department; most do well in some departments but not all. Look at the way the stars communicate emotion (acting) and how the film makes use of your expectations about the actors based on previous films (casting); examine the balance of lights and darks (cinematography); consider the expressiveness of the sets (production design); listen to how the score punctuates action (music); see how the film flows from shot to shot (editing). All these aspects affect a film's quality.

DON'T ASSUME THE SCREENPLAY IS JUST DIALOGUE. Even film buffs have a tendency to talk as if the director thought up the action, or the actors created their characters, while the screenwriter just scripted lines for the actors to say. In fact, the screenplay supplies the action of the film, its narrative structure, and its characters, as well as the dialogue. When you think of it that way, you'll notice more about how the movie is constructed and how character is established. The decisive plot points that often appear about 25 minutes and 85 minutes into a two-hour movie; the small actions that make you like the hero or distrust the hero's friend.

FOCUS ON THE DIRECTOR. Controversy still rages over whether any one person deserves to be called the author of a film: director, writer, and producer can all have a strong authorial impact on the end result. Yet it is the director who is theoretically in charge of creative decisions, so there is some reason to accept the auteurist convention of talking about "Orson Welles's *Citizen Kane*" and "John Ford's *The Searchers*." In general, it is wise to think about a film in the context of the director's entire oeuvre. Does it seem to present a variation on themes he or she often

"The words 'Kiss Kiss Bang Bang,' which I saw on an Italian movie poster, are perhaps the briefest statement imaginable of the basic appeal of the movies."

—

Pauline Kael, 1968

revisits? Does it exhibit a distinctive style, a way of placing the camera, pacing the film, directing the actors? Note, however, that this can get ridiculous when talking about a film like Peter Bonerz's *Police Academy 6*.

THINK ABOUT WHAT THE MOVIE MEANS. Even a movie that is clearly intended as entertainment – say, *Night of the Living Dead* – can be analyzed for its thematic content and symbolic suggestiveness. What do the zombies mean? Why is a black man the hero? Why does it end as it does? Is it significant that the film came out in 1968, at the height of

The cult classic Night of the Living Dead (1968), *director George Romero's first film, influenced the works of later directors such as Wes Craven and Sam Raimi.*

youth protest against what was considered a corrupt society? This need not be an imposition on the film: every narrative that keeps an audience enthralled, whether a fairy tale or an epic, does so by making use of the audience's hopes, fears, anxieties, tensions, and expectations. Don't worry about whether the writer or director thought consciously of the meaning;

you don't know, and it may not matter. What matters is that somehow you have thought consciously of it, and it is worth thinking about what elements of the film may have contributed to the meaning you have found there.

CONSIDER HOW THE MOVIE FITS INTO ITS GENRE. To do this, think about all the movies that came before it in its category and those that came after. *Night of the Living Dead* is a far different experience than the old Universal horror movies – *Frankenstein, Dracula,* etc. – and seems to have inspired many subsequent slasher pics, from *Halloween* to *Scream*. How? Why? The same kinds of questions can come up with regard to any genre – musicals, westerns, detective films, science fiction films, soap operas. Was the film original or clichéd? Did it elaborate on clichés in new ways? Is it so original as to create a new genre, or does it fall into an existing genre?

THINK ABOUT HOW THE MOVIE USES FILM GRAMMAR. The shot is the basic unit of any film: a single continuous take, before the camera cuts to something else. To analyze a shot, you think about how characters move within the frame, how light and dark are balanced in the frame, how the camera is positioned relative to the characters: above them, making them look small, or close up, emphasizing one character's reaction? Shots build into scenes: by analyzing how one shot follows another, you understand the scene better. Scenes build into sequences: by analyzing how one scene follows another in a connected way, you understand the sequence better.

DON'T ASSUME THE ONLY GOOD MOVIES ARE ONES WITH "IMPORTANT" TOPICS. In the short run, people have a tendency to judge films by their subject matter, paying more attention if a film deals with current social or political issues, or if it is based on a serious literary work or an artist's life. Yet the movies that are most revered in the long run often seem like mere entertainment when first released. *The Wizard of Oz, Casablanca, Singin' in the Rain* – everyone nowadays considers them fit objects for serious discussion. But *Singin' in the Rain* won no Oscars in its year (1952), while *Moulin Rouge,* a respected but now little-seen life of Toulouse-Lautrec, won two. Similarly, as good as 1998's best picture *Shakespeare in Love* was, are you sure it was a better film than that year's gross-out comedy hit *There's Something About Mary*? Maybe it was, but don't assume it was just because of their respective subject matter.

WATCH A LOT OF MOVIES. Sample all genres and all time periods. Make the video store your second home. Don't just go for new releases: study the beat-up racks of older titles, the ones hardly anyone takes out. Start with actors, directors, and genres you like, but don't just stay with them: try everything. Study lists of classic films (like those in Chapter Four) and try to see as many of those as you can. See what's available at your local library. Go to art theaters as well as multiplexes – but don't make the mistake of thinking the movies are better just because they're foreign or independent; maybe they are, maybe they aren't. The more movies you've seen, the richer your appreciation of any given movie will be.

STAY THROUGH THE END OF THE CREDITS. You'll get to hear the full score, you'll see how many different kinds of professionals worked on the movie, and you'll have time to let the film sink in before returning to the wider world.

Although Moulin Rouge *won two Oscars in 1953, films like* Casablanca *and* Singin' in the Rain *are remembered more today.*

A GLOSSARY OF CRITICAL TERMS

absolute film Nonnarrative experimental film that relies on images to suggest an alternative reality. An absolute film emphasizes the visual aspects of the medium, using such techniques as action, movement, and rhythm to call attention to the filmic space and time.

abstract film A type of nonnarrative film that is organized around visual elements such as color, shape, rhythm, and size. Shots are related to each other by repetition and variation rather than causal links.

action The movement that takes place in front of the camera or the series of events that occurs in the film's narrative.

apparatus Refers to the mechanical technology of filmmaking and exhibition. Theorist Jean-Louis Baudry (1970) was one of the first to propose that film technology has a specific effect on the spectator. Although it presents the cinematic image as real, the technology actually hides the process of construction that goes into making a film, masking as natural what is actually a construction. The spectator looking at the image on screen becomes an all-knowing subject and identifies with the apparatus. In this process the cinematic apparatus constructs its own viewing subject.

atmosphere The overall mood of a film evoked by such elements as lighting, sets, costumes, music, and camera work. Films by Orson Welles, Jean Renoir, Federico Fellini, and Fritz Lang rely heavily on atmosphere to create an emotional tone.

auteur theory A theory of film that positions the director as the film's "author." This approach identifies common themes and stylistic traits that characterize films by the same director. The idea arose in the 1920s with the theoretical writings of certain French critics and directors. In the 1950s André Bazin and other *Cahiers du Cinéma* contributors linked auteur theory to *mise-en-scène*. It was then used in the 1960s by American film critic Andrew Sarris as an evaluative method to distinguish good (auteur) films from bad ones, and as a strategy for elevating American film directors to a respected status. Despite many dissenting voices, the theory remains influential.

avant-garde A film movement that seeks to break with tradition and often makes a political statement. This term was first used in the 1920s by a group of French filmmakers who experimented with new stylistic techniques, narrative formats, and genres. Avant-garde filmmakers hope to call attention to the dominant codes of cinema by challenging them. Some examples of this kind of filmmaking are Dadaism, surrealism, expressionism, and other noncommercial film movements.

balance The harmonious arrangement of visual elements in a shot. Generally speaking, film, like other visual arts, strives to create a total image that is pleasing to the eye.

Cahiers du Cinéma A film review journal launched in 1951 and headed by French film critic André Bazin. Its authors expanded the auteur theory to include attention to elements of *mise-en-scène* and promoted a new appreciation of Hollywood films. Filmmakers François Truffaut and Jean-Luc Godard wrote for *Cahiers* before turning to production work.

caligarisme A cinematic style that refers to a 1919 film by Robert Wiene, *The Cabinet of Dr. Caligari*. This German expressionist film is characterized by an exaggerated and stylized *mise-en-scène*: distorted angles, heavy makeup, and geometric shadows. Caligarisme was used by avant-garde filmmakers as an experiment in abstract cinema. They thought of film as "painting-in-motion," rather than as a realistic depiction of natural events and settings.

caméra-stylo Term that translates literally as "camera pen." It was coined in 1948 by French director Alexandre Astruc to suggest that film is an independent art with its own language and style. It also refers to the film director as an artist who writes his or her own scripts and exercises creative control over the production. This idea formed the basis for auteur theory.

cinéaste A film enthusiast, or someone involved in filmmaking.

cinéma verité Refers to unstaged, documentary-style filmmaking. This French phrase means "cinema truth." The style was made popular in the 1950s with the French New Wave movement and uses portable cameras and synchronized sound recording equipment to capture live events.

cinematic Having the qualities of a film.

counterpoint Term imported from music theory to describe the juxtaposition of image and sound in a film. Although the visual image and the sound track may suggest different meanings, they work together to represent the same object or idea.

cultural studies A interdisciplinary field of scholarship that considers the social, economic, and historical context of a film in addition to its formal and narrative properties. It began in the late 1950s and 60s in Birmingham, England, when such figures as Stuart Hall and Raymond Williams began to examine the impact of popular culture on individuals and societies. A cultural studies approach to film takes note of the circuit of production, distribution, and reception in which all films participate. Often

Many of the principal members of the French New Wave movement, including François Truffaut, Eric Rohmer, Jean-Luc Godard, and Claude Chabrol, began their career in cinema as contributors to the influential film magazine, *Cahiers du Cinéma*.

leftist in political orientation, it borrows concepts from philosophy, linguistics, sociology, and literary criticism.

diagonal action Refers to action that occurs from the lower left corner to the upper right corner of the image. Diagonal action is used to create a heightened sense of excitement in the viewer.

diegesis The fictional world of the film's story. *Diegesis* is Greek for "recounted story." Elements of the film that are not directly related to the story are called extradiegetic.

expressionism A style of filmmaking in which the appearance of the visible world is based on subjective emotional states. The color, texture, and shape of the filmed image draws upon human sensations for inspiration. This style was used primarily by German artists and filmmakers in the 1920s and 30s.

feminism An approach to film criticism that specifically considers the effect of gender on the production and reception of a film. Feminist film scholars like Molly Haskell, Laura Mulvey, Kaja Silverman, and Teresa de Lauretis examine the relationship between the female spectator and the cinematic image. In her well-known essay "Visual Pleasure and Narrative Cinema" (1975), Mulvey uses psychoanalysis to argue that it is difficult for the female spectator to identify with the active male protagonist of a film, so she must adopt a passive position.

film aesthetics Study of the formal, artistic qualities of a film. This approach considers film as a unique art form and examines the viewer's emotional and psychological responses to the medium.

film criticism A body of work that analyzes the narrative and stylistic features of film. This approach may also place the film within a historical context or compare it with other films by the same director, judging its relative merits.

film history A body of research that traces the technological and stylistic developments of the film medium, as well as economic changes in the industry and the impact of social history on each of these elements. It also highlights the contributions of directors, producers, and stars as they occur chronologically.

film theory A body of knowledge that uses a variety of analytical approaches to investigate and explain film as an art form distinct from all others. Film theory considers the distinctive techniques of the industry, the components of the cinematic image, the relationship between film and society, the psychological responses of the viewer, and the spatial and temporal constraints of the film. Film theory borrows ideas from such movements as feminism, cultural studies, Marxism, structuralism, semiotics, poststructuralism, and psychoanalysis. Some of the earliest film theorists were Lev Kuleshov, Sergei Eisenstein, and André Bazin, who focused on the question of cinema's ability to represent life.

filmic time The flow of time within a film narrative, as opposed to the film's running time. While running time is usually only about two hours, filmic time can be sped up so that many years pass in a second of running time (as when *2001: A Space Odyssey* cuts from a bone thrown in the air in humanity's prehistoric past to a spacecraft in orbit), or slowed down so that a single instant is examined from many angles. Filmic time can also flash backward or flash forward before returning to the narrative present.

filmology An approach to film that focuses on the psychological foundations of the artistic qualities of the medium. It examines how these elements impact the viewer socially, emotionally, and morally. Filmology originated in 1947 at the French Institute of Filmology with its journal, *The International Review of Filmology.*

formalism A filmmaking style that calls attention to the formal qualities of a film. As practiced by Soviet director Sergei Eisenstein, it was characterized by the use of fast editing and montage. In early film theory, this style was contrasted to the style of realism celebrated by André Bazin.

gaze Refers to the exchange of looks that occurs in the cinema both between the spectator and the film and between the characters in the film. Beginning in the 1970s, French and American film theorists used ideas from psychoanalysis to explain the relationship between the viewer and the image on the screen. The viewer unconsciously identifies with the image, but also feels control over it, because of the conventions of perspective. Feminist film theorists utilize the concept to suggest that in classic cinema women are often the passive objects of a powerful male gaze.

genre studies An approach to the study of film that organizes films by type according to common features of narrative or style. Examples of genres include westerns, horror films, musicals, and documentaries.

FILMIC TIME: AN EXAMPLE

A WOMAN BEGINS TO WALK down a long street; the camera cuts to a man watching the woman; in the next shot, the woman reaches the man, as if she had traversed the street instantly. How did she get there so fast? Answer: filmic time. By a visual convention, audiences tacitly understand that during the time a camera cuts away from the action, the filmic time that passes may be indefinitely greater or less than the running time that passes.

"Several tons of dynamite are set off in this picture – none of it under the right people."

—

James Agee on the 1947 film Tycoon

impressionism A film style that uses a series of brief shots linked together in a sequence to create a subjective impression rather than a faithful representation of reality. The term refers to late-nineteenth-century painting in France, when artists such as Monet, Renoir, and Degas rebelled against the romantic tradition and painted their impressions of the world. French filmmakers such as Germaine Dulac, Louis Delluc, and Abel Gance are known for their impressionist works.

Marxism Emphasizes consideration of the economic conditions of film production. It may also suggest an analysis based on a close examination of the class issues represented in the film's narrative. Marxism suggests that control of the means of production is in the hands of a small group of people.

minimal cinema A type of filmmaking that strips both the narrative and the style down to a bare minimum. These films create a feeling of intense realism by minimizing the use of equipment and camera work or utilizing found objects. An example of minimal cinema is Robert Bresson's *Diary of a Country Priest* (1951).

mise-en-scène The composition and contents of the cinematic image, as opposed to the editing, or montage, that links one image to the next. It refers to such features as lighting, costumes, sets, acting style, and other visual properties in a scene. The term, taken from the French for "put into the scene," was imported into film criticism from its use in the theater. The study of a film's *mise-en-scène* is often used in auteur theory to document features common to specific directors. Some critics, such as André Bazin, have made a point of contrasting directors who emphasize *mise-en-scène* with those who emphasize montage.

modernism An idea based upon a twentieth-century cultural movement characterized by the self-conscious questioning of moral and social values and the obvious manipulation of the artistic medium. Modernist films are recognized by their abstract themes and their attempt to expose the illusions created by the apparatus. Avant-garde styles such as surrealism and Dadaism are examples of a modernist impulse.

montage Editing together different cinematic images. According to Soviet filmmaker Sergei Eisenstein, montage is characterized by collision and conflict between the individual shots. The linking of two different images through montage creates new meaning. Some of the most vivid examples of montage can be seen in Eisenstein's films *Strike* (1924) and *Battleship Potemkin* (1925).

mythic criticism A form of criticism that focuses on the use of archetypal stories and characters in a film's narrative. Myths seek to explain features of the world around us and take a general form that is often repeated. Although films strive to create unique worlds and characters, many film narratives employ traditional mythic patterns such as the struggle between good and evil and the search for identity. Westerns, in particular, often rely on mythic elements.

neorealism An Italian film movement of the 1940s and 50s that was concerned with capturing real-life events, in particular, the struggle of common people against social forces beyond their control. Neorealist directors such as Roberto Rossellini, Vittorio De Sica, and Luchino Visconti often used nonactors and shot on location to reveal the hardships of everyday life. Critics credit Visconti's *Ossessione* (*Obsession*, 1942) with ushering in the movement. Other well-known examples are Rossellini's *Roma, Città Aperta* (*Rome, Open City*, 1945), and De Sica's *Ladri di Bicicletti* (*The Bicycle Thief*, 1948).

Nouvelle Vague The term translates to "New Wave" and refers to a style of French filmmaking in the late 1950s and 60s characterized by a break with previous cinematic traditions. Nouvelle Vague films feature no stars, a cinéma-verité style combined with fast editing and jump cuts, and an interest in everyday life. Some of the most important French New Wave directors were also critics for the *Cahiers du Cinéma*: Jean-Luc Godard, François Truffaut, and Claude Chabrol.

open and closed worlds Refers to the world of the film and how self-sufficient or self-contained it is. A closed world (or form) makes few references to anything outside of the frame, suggesting a highly constructed and tightly constrained *mise-en-scène*. An open world is more spontaneous and informal, creating a more natural environment.

parallelism Describes a relationship between the visual and aural properties of a film that is the opposite of counterpoint. Parallelism occurs when the image and the sound are parallel or mutually reinforcing.

phenomenology An approach to cinema that focuses on the viewer's perceptions and experiences. Phenomenology is a philosophical inquiry that deals with worldly phenomena as the product of human observations and perceptions. Developed by German philosopher Edmund Husserl, it has influenced American film scholars such as Vivian Sobchack and Allan Casabier.

postmodernism A term used to describe an aesthetic position that challenges the constraints of modernism. In the cinema, its features include repetition and simulation, self-conscious reference to previous films, the assembling of different styles or genres, and the subversion of traditional cinematic codes.

Gene Siskel and Roger Ebert, cohosts of the syndicated television show, *Siskel & Ebert*, turned their "thumbs up/thumbs down" movie rating technique into a universally recognized review system.

psychoanalysis Sigmund Freud's theory of identity formation has been imported into film theory to explain the interaction between the viewer, the apparatus, and the filmed image. French theorists Christian Metz and Jean-Louis Baudry use psychoanalysis to argue that the spectator comes to identify with the camera's gaze. Psychoanalysis may also be used to interpret a film's narrative. Classic narrative cinema is said to follow a formula similar to Freud's Oedipal complex as the main character resolves a crisis and attains a measure of stability in life.

realism Style of filmmaking that seeks to represent reality directly and truthfully. The term comes from an artistic and literary movement of the nineteenth century that challenged idealism. Realism can describe a film's narrative or its formal style. This approach to filmmaking was praised by French critic André Bazin in the 1940s.

semiology or **semiotics** Refers to the study of signs within society. Semiology originated with the work of Swiss linguist Ferdinand de Saussure in the early twentieth century, and the term semiotics was coined by C.S. Peirce, an American philosopher. Roland Barthes popularized the term in the 1950s. Semiology calls for an analysis of the meaning of images and objects in relation to the system in which they are found.

shot analysis Method of film analysis that focuses on each shot as an individual unit. The shot analysis considers such things as photographic properties of the image (tone, speed, perspective), framing, action, and *mise-en-scène*.

socialist realism Refers to the depiction of social and economic conditions within society. The style began with documentary films of the 1930s and is best exemplified by Italian neorealist films.

structuralism Philosophical tradition dating from the early twentieth century that examines language as an organized system of meaning construction. The impact of structuralism on film theory was such that film analysis became a rigid, scientific process. Structuralism is closely related to semiology and was brought to popular attention by French philosopher Roland Barthes. Its ideas were later taken up by Christian Metz.

surrealism Film style that depicts the irrational inner workings of the unconscious. The term dates back to a literary and artistic movement of the 1920s made famous by such figures as Salvador Dali and Man Ray. Surrealist films draw upon fantasy and are often composed of a series of seemingly unrelated images. The most well-known example is the Dali—Luis Buñuel film, *Un Chien Andalou* (1929).

theme The overriding idea that guides a film.

"Just another manhunt story wrapped up in pseudo-psychoanalysis."

—

Director Alfred Hitchcock on his 1945 film Spellbound

Some of the most vivid examples of montage can be seen in Sergei Eisenstein's films Strike *(1924) and* Battleship Potemkin *(1925), shown here.*

PEOPLE
IN FILM

Classically trained English actor Ralph Fiennes portrayed Almasy in the tragic love story The English Patient *(1996). Fiennes's other films include* Schindler's List *(1993),* Quiz Show *(1994), and* Oscar and Lucinda *(1997).*

ACTORS

Since the advent of motion pictures, thousands of performers have flickered across the silver screen, but it is a select few who hold the power to dance in our collective dreams and memories.

A

Woody Allen was doing stand-up comedy in New York's Greenwich Village when he was approached by Warren Beatty and producer Charles Feldman and offered $30,000 to write *What's New, Pussycat?* as a vehicle for Beatty. Allen agreed, but only if he could write a part for himself as well. Beatty eventually bowed out, and Peter O'Toole later filled the role.

Abbott, Bud (1895–1974) and **Costello, Lou** (1906–1959) American actors and comedians. Born William A. Abbott and Louis Francis Cristillo. As Abbott and Costello, they formed one of the major comedic duos of the 1940s and 50s. The pair mixed wordplay (e.g., their "Who's on First" routine) and physical comedy in performances on radio, stage, and television and in highly popular films. They made their screen name with their second feature, *Buck Privates* (1941), which led to a string of box-office hits, including *Hold That Ghost* (1941) and *Abbott and Costello Meet Frankenstein* (1948). They disbanded in 1957.

Affleck, Ben (1972–) American actor and screenwriter. Since 1992, the lanky actor has performed in leading and supporting roles in such films as *Good Will Hunting* (1997); for which he (and Matt Damon) won an Academy Award for best screenplay; *Shakespeare in Love* (1998); *Armageddon* (1998); and *Pearl Harbor* (2001).

Allen, Woody (1935–) American actor, director, and screenwriter. Born Allen Konigsberg. The essential postwar nebbish and one of film's greatest comedic talents was a comedy writer and club entertainer before he began to write and appear in offbeat films such as *What's New Pussycat?* (1965). In the 1970s, he was the director-writer-star of such comedies as *Take the Money and Run* (1969) and *Sleeper* (1973), then went in a more serious direction with *Annie Hall* (1977), which won Academy Awards for best picture, director, and original screenplay (Allen and Marshall Brickman). In the 1980s, he combined comedy and drama in films including *Manhattan* (1979), *Zelig* (1983), *Hannah and Her Sisters* (1986; Academy Award winner for best original screenplay), and *Crimes and Misdemeanors* (1989). Although he acted in all of these, he has also made films in which he did not act (e.g., *Bullets over Broadway*, 1994) and has acted in other people's films. He returned to light comedy with *Small Time Crooks* (2000) and *The Curse of the Jade Scorpion* (2001).

Andersson, Bibi (1935–) Swedish-born actress in international films. Born Birgitta Andersson. A leading player in Swedish cinema during the 1950s and 60s, she is noted for her many performances in Ingmar Bergman films, including *Smiles of a Summer Night* (1955), *The Seventh Seal* (1956), *Wild Strawberries* (1957), and *Persona* (1967). Other films include *Babette's Gæstebud (Babette's Feast)* (1987, Denmark) and *Drømspel (Dreamplay)* (1994, Norway/Sweden).

Andrews, Dana (1909–1992) American actor. Born Carver Dana Andrews. A reliable dramatic star from the 1940s into the 80s, he was alternately hard-boiled and vulnerable in his best-known roles, in *Laura* (1944) and *The Best Years of Our Lives* (1946). Other films include *The Ox-Bow Incident* (1943) and *Boomerang* (1947). He was the brother of actor Steve Forrest.

Andrews, Julie (1935–) British-born American actress. Born Julia Elizabeth Wells. On the stage since childhood, she became a theatrical star in the 1950s, when she was the first to play Eliza Doolittle in the musical *My Fair Lady*. Moving to film, she became an upright, clear-voiced musical star in *Mary Poppins* (1964), for which she won an Academy Award for best actress. She is perhaps best remembered as the indefatigable governess Maria Von Trapp in *The Sound of Music* (1965). Other films include *Star!* (1968); *10* (1979) and *Victor/Victoria* (1982), both directed by her husband, Blake Edwards; and *The Princess Diaries* (2001).

Ann-Margret (1941–) Swedish-born American actress. Born Ann-Margaret Olsson. In her debut opposite Bette Davis in *Pocketful of Miracles* (1961) and her performance as a starstruck teen in the musical *Bye Bye Birdie* (1963), she displayed the playful womanliness and sexuality that became her trademark. The red-haired actress emerged as a sex symbol among the early rock and roll set, playing opposite Elvis Presley in *Viva Las Vegas* (1964). She was nominated for best supporting actress Academy Awards for *Carnal Knowledge* (1971) and *Tommy* (1975). Her later films, including *Grumpy Old Men* (1993), capitalize on her comedic abilities.

Arbuckle, Roscoe "Fatty" (1887–1933) American comedian, director, and screenwriter. A portly former plumber's assistant, he became a top silent comedian in Keystone Kops comedies and other films during the 1910s. From 1916, he frequently wrote and directed the films in which he acted. Acting credits include *Mother's Boy* (1913), *Bathing Beauty* (1914), and *His Wedding Night* (1917; also dir.). His acting career came to an end when starlet Virginia Rappe was found dead at his home in 1921 and he was charged with manslaughter. After two mistrials, Arbuckle was acquitted in the third trial. He later directed films under the pseudonym William B. Goodrich, including *Keep Laughing* (1932). He was married to Minta Dufree.

Arliss, George (1868–1946) British-born American actor. Born George Augustus Andrews. Trained on the stage, he became a lead player in silent and sound films, known for his portrayals of historical figures, including the title role in *Disraeli* (1929), for which he won an Academy Award for best actor. Other films include *Alexander Hamilton* (1931) and *Cardinal Richelieu* (1935).

Arquette, Patricia (1968–) American actress. In films from the 1980s, she gained notice for dramatic and comedic abilities in *Ed Wood* (1994), *Flirting with Disaster* (1996), and *Bringing Out the Dead* (1999). She is the sister of actors Alexis, David, and Rosanna Arquette and the granddaughter of comedian Cliff "Charley Weaver" Arquette.

Arthur, Jean (1905–1991) American actress. Born Gladys Georgianna Greene. After steady but unspectacular work in silent films, she became a prominent light comedian from the 1930s to the 50s, distinguished by her cockeyed outlook and throaty voice. She particularly shone in Frank Capra's comedies *Mr. Deeds Goes to Town* (1936), *You Can't Take It with You* (1938), and *Mr. Smith Goes to Washington* (1939) and was nominated for a best actress Academy Award for John Ford's *The Whole Town's Talking* (1935). Dramatic appearances include roles in *Only Angels Have Wings* (1939), *History Is Made at Night* (1937), and *Shane* (1953), her final film.

Astaire, Fred (1899–1987) American dancer, actor, singer, and choreographer. Born Frederick Austerlitz. In the ten musicals in which he danced with Ginger Rogers, he became the icon of perfect elegance. He was known for his relaxed song styling, pleasant screen persona, and inventive staging of dance numbers. Before coming to Hollywood, he had danced on stage with his sister and partner Adele. The Astaire-Rogers collaboration began with *Flying Down to Rio* (1933) and included *The Gay Divorcee* (1934), *Top Hat* (1935), *Swing Time* (1936), and *Shall We Dance* (1937). Later musicals, in which he was paired with such actresses as Judy Garland and Cyd Charisse, include *Easter Parade* (1948), *The Band Wagon* (1953), and *Funny Face* (1957). Dramatic appearances include a role in *On the Beach* (1959). He received a special Academy Award in 1949 and AFI's Life Achievement Award in 1981.

Astor, Mary (1906–1987) American actress. Born Lucille Vasconcellos Langhanke. A star of silent and early sound films, she was known for her portrayals of worldly, sophisticated women. Her apex came as Brigid O'Shaughnessy opposite Humphrey Bogart's Sam Spade in *The Maltese Falcon* (1941). Other films include *Beau Brummel* (1924), *Red Dust* (1932), *Dodsworth* (1936), *The Hurricane* (1937), *The Palm Beach Story* (1942), and *Hush…Hush, Sweet Charlotte* (1965).

Autry, Gene (1907–1998) American actor, singer, and songwriter. A singing cowboy on radio from the 1920s after he was discovered by Will Rogers, he went on to star (with his horse Champion) in popular western features during the 1930s and early 40s. Films include *Tumblin' Tumbleweeds* (1935) and *The Singing Cowboy* (1937). He also wrote more than 200 popular songs.

"Can't act. Slightly bald. Can dance a little."

—

Verdict of a studio executive after Fred Astaire's first screen test, 1930s

A veteran of the vaudeville circuit since the age of seven, song-and-dance man Fred Astaire helped shape the movie musicals of the 1930s, 1940s, and 1950s.

B

In 1994, Albright College fraternity brothers Craig Fass, Brian Turtle, and Mike Ginelli created a movie trivia game called Six Degrees of Kevin Bacon. Its premise states that every actor, living or dead, can be linked to Bacon through his extensive filmography. An online database known as *The Oracle of Bacon* has since connected Bacon to 240,000 other performers, including Buster Keaton, Elvis Presley, and E.T.

Bacall, Lauren (1924–) American actress. Born Betty Joan Perske. A confidently glamorous star of sound films, best known as the insolent partner to Humphrey Bogart in *To Have and Have Not* (1944), her debut feature. After meeting on the set, she and Bogart were married (from 1945 to his death in 1957) and paired on the screen again in *The Big Sleep* (1946), *Dark Passage* (1948), and *Key Largo* (1949). Films without Bogart include *How to Marry a Millionaire* (1953), *Designing Woman* (1957), *The Shootist* (1976), and *Misery* (1990).

Bacon, Kevin (1958–) American actor. An all-American player who first appeared in popular youth films such as *National Lampoon's Animal House* (1978) and *Friday the 13th* (1980), he established himself as a strong ensemble performer in *Diner* (1982) and romantic lead in *Footloose* (1984). He has continued in lead and character roles in Hollywood films including *JFK* (1991), *Apollo 13* (1995), and *Hollow Man* (2000). He is married to actress Kyra Sedgwick.

Baldwin, Alec (1958–) American actor. Active on stage and television before entering film, the steely-eyed actor has played lead and support in comedies (*Notting Hill,* 1999), dramas (*Glengarry Glen Ross,* 1992), and thrillers (*The Hunt for Red October,* 1990). He has been married to actress Kim Basinger and is the brother of actors Daniel, Stephen, and William Baldwin. Other films include *Pearl Harbor* (2001).

Bancroft, Anne (1931–) American actress. Born Anna Maria Louise Italiano. Also active in theater and on television, she is best known on screen for her portrayal of the seductress Mrs. Robinson in *The Graduate* (1967). She won a best actress Academy Award for her performance in *The Miracle Worker* (1962). Other notable films include *The Turning Point* (1977) and *Up at the Villa* (2000, UK/US). She is married to director Mel Brooks.

Banderas, Antonio (1960–) Spanish-born actor in Spanish and American films. Handsome and dashing, he was an established leading man in Spain when he gained international notice with *Mujeres al Borde de un Ataque de Nérvios (Women on the Verge of a Nervous Breakdown)* (1988) and *Atame! (Tie Me Up! Tie Me Down!)* (1990). US films include *Philadelphia* (1993), *The Mask of Zorro* (1998), and *Spy Kids* (2001). He is married to actress Melanie Griffith.

Bankhead, Tallulah (1903–1968) American actress. An accomplished stage actress from the 1920s, known for her smart, freethinking performances, she appeared only sporadically in American and British silent and sound films, most memorably in Alfred Hitchcock's *Lifeboat* (1944). Other films include *Stage Door Canteen* (1943) and *A Royal Scandal* (1945).

Bara, Theda (1890–1955) American actress. Born Theodosia Goodman. She became known as "the Vamp" following her performance in *A Fool There Was* (1915), which was based on the Kipling poem "The Vampire." Following this success, the Broadway-trained actress starred in dozens of films through the end of World War I, among them *The Eternal Sappho* (1916), *Madame Du Barry* (1918), and *Salome* (1918). Her popularity declined in the 1920s, and she left the screen in 1926.

Barrymore, Drew (1975–) American actress. The granddaughter of actor John Barrymore, she became known as a child actress in *E.T.: The Extra-Terrestrial* (1982) and later became an adult lead and supporting player in such films as *Scream* (1996), *The Wedding Singer* (1998), *Charlie's Angels* (2000), and *Riding in Cars with Boys* (2001). In her adult roles, she projects an alternately fun-loving and world-weary outlook.

Barrymore, Ethel (1879–1959) American actress. Born Ethel Blythe. Sister of actors John and Lionel Barrymore, she was a leading stage actress when she came to silent film in 1914. After appearing in *The Divorcee* (1919), she went back to the stage, returning to film for only one appearance—with her brothers, in *Rasputin and the Empress* (1933)—until the 1940s. She continued in cinema through the 1950s, appearing in such dramas as *The Spiral Staircase* (1946), *The Farmer's Daughter* (1947), *Pinky* (1949), and *None but the Lonely Heart* (1944), for which she won an Academy Award for best supporting actress.

Barrymore, John (1882–1942) American actor. Born John Sidney Blythe. Son of stage actor Maurice Barrymore (Herbert Blythe), and youngest member of the Barrymore generation of actors that also included his brother Lionel and sister Ethel, and he was a famed stage performer before becoming a silent and sound film idol. Darkly handsome, he was known as the Great Profile in silent romances, including *Beau Brummel* (1924) and *Don Juan* (1926), and excelled in character roles, such as those in *The Sea Beast* (1926) and *Dr. Jekyll and Mr. Hyde* (1926). While his sound career was distinguished by acclaimed performances in *Grand Hotel* (1932), *A Bill of Divorcement* (1932), *Dinner at Eight* (1934), and *Twentieth Century* (1934), it was diminished by age and alcohol abuse. His son John Barrymore, Jr. (a.k.a. John Drew Barrymore) has also been a film actor, as is John Jr.'s daughter Drew Barrymore.

Barrymore, Lionel (1878–1954) American actor. Born Lionel Blythe. Brother of actors Ethel and

John Barrymore, he was a Broadway star before becoming a featured silent film player, notably in such D.W. Griffith films as *The New York Hat* (1912) and *Judith of Bethulia* (1914). In sound films, he was a seasoned character actor, even after partial paralysis in 1938 put him in a wheelchair. Credits include *A Free Soul* (1931; best actor Academy Award), *Grand Hotel* (1932), *Dinner at Eight* (1933), *Young Dr. Kildare* (1940), and *Key Largo* (1948). He also played the villainous banker Potter in *It's a Wonderful Life* (1946). His memoir is *We Barrymores* (1951). He was also a painter, novelist, and composer.

Barthelmess, Richard (1895–1963) American actor. Manly and fine-featured, he was a leading performer in silent films, notably in D.W. Griffith features such as *Broken Blossoms* (1919) and *Way Down East* (1920). Other silent films include *Tol'able David* (1921) and *The Noose* (1928; Academy Award nomination for best actor). He moved into character parts in the 1930s, in such sound films as *The Dawn Patrol* (1932) and *Only Angels Have Wings* (1939).

Basinger, Kim (1953–) American actress. A former model, she became known for on-screen radiance and vulnerability in leading and supporting roles in such films as *Batman* (1989) and *L.A. Confidential* (1997), for which she won an Academy Award for best supporting actress. Other features include the notorious erotic film *9 ½ Weeks* (1986). She has been married to actor Alec Baldwin.

Bates, Kathy (1948–) American actress. Born Kathleen Bates. A Tony Award–winning Broadway actress, she became known for deft, often intense screen characterizations in such films as *Misery* (1990), for which she won a best actress Academy Award, *Fried Green Tomatoes* (1991), *Dolores Clairborne* (1995), and *Titanic* (1997).

Baxter, Anne (1923–1985) American actress. A child performer on Broadway, she became a leading film player in the 1940s and 50s, most notably as the shamelessly aspiring actress Eve Harrington in *All About Eve* (1950), for which she received an Academy Award nomination for best actress. She won the Oscar for her supporting performance in *The Razor's Edge* (1946). Other notable films include *The Magnificent Ambersons* (1942) and *The Ten Commandments* (1956). She was married to actor John Hodiak.

Baxter, Warner (1891–1951) American actor. The slender, handsome, fast-talking leading actor of the 1930s first became known in silent films such as *The Great Gatsby* (1926). He gained greater fame in the early sound era, winning an Academy Award for best actor as the Cisco Kid in *In Old Arizona* (1929). In the 1930s, he appeared in a variety of genres, including musicals such as *42nd Street* (1934) and comedies such as *Broadway Bill* (1934).

Beatty, Warren (1937–) American actor, director, screenwriter, and producer. Born Henry Warren Beaty. The tall, handsome younger brother of actress Shirley MacLaine established himself as a romantic powerhouse with *Splendor in the Grass* (1962). Later in the decade, after several films and much gossip about his love life, he became part of a cult phenomenon as the male lead in *Bonnie and Clyde* (1967). Through the early 1980s, he appeared in several notable films, including *McCabe and Mrs. Miller* (1971); *Shampoo* (1975), which he produced and coscripted; and *Reds* (1981), which he produced, coscripted, and directed, and for which he won a best director Academy Award. In the 1990s, he directed, produced, and starred in *Dick Tracy* (1990) and *Bulworth* (1998) and wrote the screenplay for the latter. On the set of *Bugsy* (1991), he met wife Annette Bening. In 2000, he received the Jean Hersholt Humanitarian Award. Other films include *Town & Country* (2001).

Beery, Wallace (1885–1949) American actor. Hefty and sandpaper-voiced, he appeared widely in silent films, such as *So Big* (1925) and *Fireman Save My Child* (1927), before becoming a major sound star in the 1930s. He won a best actor Academy Award for *The Champ* (1931). Other films include *Min and Bill* (1930), *Tugboat Annie* (1933), and *Dinner at Eight* (1933). He was married (1916–18) to actress Gloria Swanson.

Bellamy, Ralph (1904–1991) American actor. A stage-trained player largely remembered by moviegoers as the character who loses the leading lady to Cary Grant in two comedies, *The Awful Truth* (1937) and *His Girl Friday* (1940). As a dramatic leading man, he portrayed Franklin Delano Roosevelt in *Sunrise*

Dolores Claiborne (1995), written by well-known horror novelist Stephen King, featured Jennifer Jason Leigh (right) as the estranged daughter of an accused murderer played by Kathy Bates (left).

at Campobello (1960), a role he originated on stage. He received an honorary Academy Award in 1986.

Belmondo, Jean-Paul (1933–) French-born actor. Active in films from the 1950s, he became internationally famous as the rebellious yet likable lead in Jean-Luc Godard's *À Bout de Souffle (Breathless)* (1960). He embodied that persona in other films, including *L'Homme de Rio (That Man from Rio)* (1964) and *Borsalino* (1970).

Belushi, John (1949–1982) American actor. Part of the original cast of the television series *Saturday Night Live* during the 1970s, he transferred his outsize talent to the screen in the highly successful comedies *National Lampoon's Animal House* (1978) and *The Blues Brothers* (1980), the latter a reprise of the television duo he and Dan Aykroyd created. Belushi died of a drug overdose.

Benigni, Roberto (1952–) Italian-born actor, director, screenwriter, and producer. A leading comic, he has appeared widely in US and Italian films, such as *Down by Law* (1986) but gained international recognition for his Holocaust comedy-drama *La Vita e Bella (Life Is Beautiful)* (1997). The film won an Academy Award for best foreign film, and Benigni was named best actor.

Bening, Annette (1958–) American actress. Known for her worldly, quick-thinking characters. After receiving acclaim on Broadway, she turned to film, gaining notice in *Valmont* (1989) and *The Grifters* (1990). She was nominated for a best actress Academy Award for *American Beauty* (1999). She is married to actor Warren Beatty, whom she met when she starred with him in *Bugsy* (1991). Other films include *What Planet Are You From?* (2001).

Bennett, Constance (1904–1965) American actress. Daughter of silent film star Richard Bennett and sister of actress Joan Bennett, she appeared in silent films (e.g., *Reckless Youth,* 1922) but is best known for smart performances in sound comedies, including *Topper* (1937) and *It Should Happen to You* (1954). Among her husbands was actor Gilbert Roland.

Benny, Jack (1894–1974) American comedian and actor. Born Benjamin Kubelsky. The eternal skinflint of vaudeville, radio, and television, he appeared in comic roles in several films, including *Broadway Melody of 1936* (1935), *To Be or Not to Be* (1942), and *The Horn Blows at Midnight* (1945).

Bergman, Ingrid (1915–1982) Swedish-born American actress. Radiant beauty and top Hollywood star, most memorable as Ilsa, the haunted former lover of Rick (played by Humphrey Bogart) in *Casablanca* (1942). After

Before finally settling on Ingrid Bergman, producer Hal Wallis considered both Ann Sheridan and Hedy Lamarr to play opposite Humphrey Bogart in *Casablanca* (1942).

first gaining notice in the Swedish film *Intermezzo* (1936), she came to the United States and appeared in major dramas of the 1940s, including *For Whom the Bell Tolls* (1943), *Gaslight* (1944; best actress Academy Award), *Spellbound* (1945), *The Bells of St. Mary's* (1945), and *Notorious* (1946). Shunned by Hollywood from 1950 for deserting her husband to marry director Roberto Rossellini, she returned to the US screen in 1956 with *Anastasia,* winning a second Oscar for best actress. She won a best supporting actress Academy Award for her performance in *Murder on the Orient Express* (1974) and was nominated for a best actress Academy Award for *Autumn Sonata* (1978).

Blondell, Joan (1909–1979) American actress. Daughter of comedian Eddie Blondell, she appeared on stage in the 1920s and became a Hollywood fixture from the 1930s, epitomizing the softhearted, smart-mouthed dame in such films as *Public Enemy* (1931), *The Crowd Roars* (1932), *Gold Diggers of 1933* (1933), *A Tree Grows in Brooklyn* (1945), and *Desk Set* (1957). Among her husbands were Dick Powell (1932–36) and producer Mike Todd (1947–50).

Bogarde, Dirk (1921–1999) British-born actor. Born Derek Jules Gaspard Ulric Niven van den Bogaerde. Internationally known character actor famed for his subtle portrayals of troubled souls in films including *The Servant* (1963), *Darling* (1965), *Morte a Venezia (Death in Venice)* (1971), and *Le Serpent (The Serpent)* (1973). Among his memoirs is *A Postillion Struck by Lightning.*

Bogart, Humphrey (1899–1957) American actor. Born Humphrey DeForest Bogart. The most enduring male star of sound films entered film in 1930 and appeared in his first gangster role in *The Petrified Forest* (1936). He continued with other defining tough-guy roles in *The Roaring Twenties* (1939) and *High Sierra* (1941). He emerged as a major star with *The Maltese Falcon* (1941), in which he played hard-edged but heroic private eye Sam Spade, and *Casablanca* (1942), in which he embodied the haunted idealism of nightclub owner Rick Blaine. With these films, he established the darkly noble Bogart persona, which continued to develop in *To Have and Have Not* (1944), on the set of which he met wife Lauren Bacall; *The Big Sleep* (1946); and *The African Queen* (1951). He played complicated leads in *The Treasure of the Sierra Madre* (1948) and *The Caine Mutiny* (1954) and offered a self-deprecatory light turn in the comedy *Sabrina* (1954).

Bond, Ward (1903–1960) American actor. Gruff, often amiable character actor who appeared in over 200 films, often as part of the John Ford repertory. Notable films directed by Ford include *The Grapes of Wrath* (1940), *My Darling Clementine* (1946), *Three Godfathers* (1948),

Kenneth Branagh wrote the screenplay, directed, and starred in a 1989 adaptation of Shakespeare's Henry V.

Boyer, Charles (1897–1978) French actor. A suave, silky-voiced romantic lead who worked in French films from the 1920s and American films from the 1930s, including *L'Homme du Large* (1920, France), *Liliom* (1934, France), *History Is Made at Night* (1937), *Algiers* (1938), *Love Affair* (1939), *Back Street* (1941), and *Gaslight* (1944). Later films, such as *Madame de... (The Earrings of Madame De...)* (1953, France/ Italy), highlighted his on-screen world-weariness. Among the many actresses he played against were Ingrid Bergman, Jean Arthur, and Irene Dunne.

Branagh, Kenneth (1960–) Irish-born British actor and director. Trained on the London stage, he became famous for starring in, directing, and adapting *Henry V* (1989), a vigorous reenvisioning of Shakespeare's play that earned him Academy Award nominations for best actor and best director. As an actor-director, his later Shakespearean films include *Much Ado About Nothing* (1993), *Hamlet* (1996), and his contemporary films include *Peter's Friends* (1992). He has also appeared in films by other directors, such as *Celebrity* (1998), and *Harry Potter and the Chamber of Secrets* (2002).

"He looked to me like a kid who delivers groceries."
—
Playwright Clifford Odets, on first seeing Marlon Brando in Stella Adler's acting class, 1940s.

Wagonmaster (1950), and *The Searchers* (1956). Other memorable films include *The Maltese Falcon* (1941) and *It's a Wonderful Life* (1946).

Bow, Clara (1905–1965) American actress. This flapper star of the 1920s was a beauty-contest winner and minor silent actress until studio publicity and the film *It* (1927) transformed her into the "It" girl. She represented the era's liberated young woman in such films as *Wings* (1927) and *Get Your Man* (1927). Her distinctive look included dark bobbed hair, short skirts, and painted bow lips. Her career ground to a halt soon after the advent of sound; she retired in 1933.

Boyd, William (1895–1972) American actor and producer. A popular silent star during the 1920s (*Two Arabian Nights, 1927*), the good-looking lead became a movie fixture during the 1930s and 40s in the role of upright western hero Hopalong Cassidy. Beginning with *Hop-A-Long Cassidy* in 1935, he appeared in more than 60 series episodes before 1950. The films were later shown on TV, to great popularity. He is not to be confused with actors William "Stage" Boyd (1890–1935) or Bill Boyd (1910–1977), "the Cowboy Rambler."

Brando, Marlon (1924–) American actor. Born Marlon Brando, Jr. The masculine Broadway lead revolutionized postwar cinema when he brought his brutal stage performance as Stanley Kowalski in *A Streetcar Named Desire* to the screen in 1951. Beginning with that role, he was nominated for a best actor Academy Award four years running; the other nominations were for *Viva Zapata!* (1952), *Julius Caesar* (1953), and *On the Waterfront* (1954), for which he at last won the prize. Twenty years later, he offered another iconic performance as Don Vito Corleone in *The Godfather* (1972), for which he won a second best actor Academy Award, which he refused in the name of Native American rights. Later films include *Apocalypse Now* (1979), *Don Juan DeMarco* (1995), and *The Score* (2001).

Brennan, Walter (1894–1974) American actor. One of the cinema's most versatile supporting players, he appeared in movies from the 1920s into the 70s and was the first actor to win three Academy Awards. In the supporting actor category, he won for *Come and Get It* (1936), *Kentucky* (1938), and *The Westerner* (1940). Other notable films include *Tearin' into Trouble* (1927), *Sergeant York* (1941), *Meet John Doe*

(1941), *Red River* (1949), *Rio Bravo* (1959), and *Smoke in the Wind* (1975).

Bridges, Jeff (1949–) American actor. Son of actor Lloyd Bridges (1913–1998) and brother of actor Beau Bridges (1941–), he was an effective ensemble player in the elegaic film *The Last Picture Show* (1972), which earned him the first of several Academy Award nominations. He followed with a wide range of strong character-driven films of varying box-office success, including *Stay Hungry* (1976), *Tucker: The Man and His Dream* (1988), *The Fabulous Baker Boys* (1989), *The Fisher King* (1991), *The Contender* (2000), and *K-Pax* (2001).

Bronson, Charles (1921–) American actor. Born Charles Bunchinsky (changed variously to Buchinski and Buchinsky). In films from the 1950s, notably *The Dirty Dozen* (1967), the tough but beleaguered character actor became a top box-office star in the 1970s with *Death Wish* (1974). The violent vigilante fantasy led to several sequels and other action films, including *Hard Times* (1975) and *Kinjite: Forbidden Subjects* (1989). He has also been a major lead in European films, including *Città Violenta (The Family)* (1970, Italy/France) and *Soleil Rouge* (1971, France/Italy/Spain). He was married to actress Jill Ireland from 1968 until her death from cancer in 1990.

Brooks, Louise (1906–1985) American actress. A bobbed-hair brunette, she distinguished herself in US features, including *A Girl in Every Port* (1928) and *The Canary Murder Case* (1929), but became an enduring international sensation in G.W. Pabst's German film *Die Büchse der Pandora (Pandora's Box)* (1929), in which she played the tempestuous flower girl Lulu. She followed it with Pabst's *Das Tagebuch einer Verlorenen (Diary of a Lost Girl)* (1929). Her career ebbed in the 1930s, but she returned to the spotlight late in life with her memoiristic essay collection, *Lulu in Hollywood.*

Brosnan, Pierce (1951–) Irish-born actor. Trained on the London stage and television, he appeared in films from the 1980s but did not became a romantic and action lead until he assumed the James Bond mantle with *Goldeneye* (1995), *Tomorrow Never Dies* (1997), and *The World Is Not Enough* (1999). He applied aplomb and amusement to the role of Bond, as he did to the role of the larcenous title character in *The Thomas Crown Affair* (1999).

Brynner, Yul (1915–1985) American actor born on Sakhalin, an island southeast of the Russian mainland. After serving as a member of various acting troupes, he gained fame on Broadway in 1951 as the commanding King of Siam in *The King and I* and became a screen star with the film version in 1956. For a few years following, he was a top box-office draw in films such as

The Ten Commandments (1956), *The Buccaneer* (1958), and *The Magnificent Seven* (1960). Later films include *Westworld* (1973).

Bullock, Sandra (1966–) American actress. Experienced in made-for-television films and supporting roles in features, she established her carefree, wisecracking persona opposite Keanu Reeves in *Speed* (1994). Several star turns followed, including *While You Were Sleeping* (1995), *Practical Magic* (1998), *28 Days* (2000), and *Miss Congeniality* (2000).

Burns, George (1896–1996) and **Allen, Gracie** (1902–1964) American comedians and actors. The married vaudeville and radio stars appeared in more than a dozen film comedies that showcased their practiced wordplay. Among the best known are *The Big Broadcast* (1932), *International House* (1933), *We're Not Dressing* (1934), *The Big Broadcast of 1936* (1935), *The Big Broadcast of 1937* (1936), and *A Damsel in Distress* (1937). Allen's solo films include *The Gracie Allen Murder Case* (1939) and *Mr. and Mrs. North* (1942). The pair were television stars as well. Following his wife's death, Burns became known as a solo performer in such films as *The Sunshine Boys* (1975; best supporting actor Academy Award) and *Oh, God!* (1977), in which he played the title role.

Burton, Richard (1925–1984) Welsh-born star of international films. Born Richard Walter Jenkins, Jr. A major British stage actor from the 1940s, he became a dramatic lead in Hollywood big-budget films, including *The Robe* (1953), *The Longest Day* (1962), and *Cleopatra* (1963), on the set of which he met actress Elizabeth Taylor. Amid a tumult of publicity in the ensuing 13 years, the two married and divorced twice and appeared together in such films as *Who's Afraid of Virginia Woolf?* (1966) and *The Comedians* (1967, US/France). Other films include *Becket* (1964, UK/US), *The Night of the Iguana* (1964), and *Anne of the Thousand Days* (1969, UK).

Busch, Mae (1897–1946) Australian-born American actress. As a silent film lead, she is best known for dramas, such as *The Devil's Pass Key* (1920), *Foolish Wives* (1922), and *Souls for Sale* (1923). In the 1930s, she was a frequent presence in Laurel and Hardy films, including *Sons of the Desert* (1933).

Bushman, Francis X. (1883–1966) American actor. Born Francis Xavier Bushman. One of the most handsome and popular stars of the silent screen, he was a romantic lead in such films as *Romeo and Juliet* (1916) and *Daring Hearts* (1919). Straight dramatic performances include Messala in *Ben-Hur* (1926). In later films, such as *Sabrina* (1954), he offered supporting performances.

Jeff Bridges has played characters named Jack or Jackson in several of his most notable films, ranging from *The Last Picture Show* (1971) and *King Kong* (1976), to *Jagged Edge* (1985), *The Fabulous Baker Boys* (1989), *The Fisher King* (1991), and *The Contender* (2000).

C

Caan, James (1939–) American actor. Active in films from the 1960s, including *El Dorado* (1967), he made his mark in the 70s as a dramatic actor, notably in the TV movie *Brian's Song* (1970) and as gangster Sonny Corleone in *The Godfather* (1972). He has since appeared regularly as a character lead or supporting player in such films as *Misery* (1990) and *Mickey Blue Eyes* (1999).

Cage, Nicolas (1964–) American actor. Born Nicholas Coppola. The nephew of director Francis Ford Coppola, he is known for incendiary performances in such dramas as *Leaving Las Vegas* (1995; best actor Academy Award), *Wild at Heart* (1990), *Captain Corelli's Mandolin* (2001, UK/France/US), and such action films as *Face/Off* (1997). His comedy performances, in such films as *Raising Arizona* (1987) and *Peggy Sue Got Married* (1986), exhibit similar intensity.

Cagney, James (1899–1986) American actor. Born James Francis Cagney, Jr. Trained on Broadway and in vaudeville, he started in film in 1930 and developed into one of the archetypal film gangsters in the 1930s and 40s, defining the urban tough guy in such features as *The Public Enemy* (1931), *Angels with Dirty Faces* (1938), *The Roaring Twenties* (1939), and *White Heat* (1949). Throughout his long career, he starred in westerns (*The Oklahoma Kid,* 1939), war films (*Mister Roberts,* 1955), comedies (*The Strawberry Blonde,* 1941), dramas (*City for Conquest,* 1940), and musicals (*Yankee Doodle Dandy,* 1942), for which he received a best actor Academy Award for his portrayal of George M. Cohan. Cagney received AFI's Life Achievement Award in 1974. His final film was *Ragtime* (1981).

Caine, Michael (1933–) British-born actor in British and American films. Born Maurice Joseph Micklewhite. The alternately rough and roguish dramatic lead and supporting player is best known for morally complex characters, such as those he played in *Hannah and Her Sisters* (1986) and *The Cider House Rules* (1999), both of which earned him Academy Awards for best supporting actor. A prolific actor he has appeared in many genres, including mystery (*Sleuth,* 1972), adventure (*The Man Who Would Be King,* 1975), drama (*Mona Lisa,* 1986), and comedy (*Dirty Rotten Scoundrels,* 1988). Other films include *Alfie* (1972), *Educating Rita* (1983), and *Quills* (2000).

Cantinflas (1911–1993) Mexican actor in international films. Born Mario Moreno Reyes. A major comic film star in Mexico from the 1930s to the 70s, he appeared in such films as *No te Engañes Corazón* (1936) and *El Ministro y Yo* (1976). He gained international notice with two US films, *Around the World in 80 Days* (1956) and *Pepe* (1960).

Cantor, Eddie (1892–1964) American comedian, singer, and actor. Born Edward Israel Iskowitz. One of the most popular entertainers of the 1920s and 30s, he starred in the Ziegfeld Follies, in Broadway shows, and on radio. The wide-eyed comic entered films with adaptations of his stage hits *Kid Boots* (1926) and *Whoopee!* (1930). Other films include *Roman Scandals* (1933) and *Strike Me Pink* (1936). He received a special Academy Award in 1956.

Carradine, John (1906–1988) American actor. Born Richmond Reed Carradine. One of the screen's foremost character actors, he provided Shakespearean intonation and ironic sensibility in dozens of films from the 1930s through the 80s. Notable films include *The Grapes of Wrath* (1940), *The Kentuckian* (1955), and *The Man Who Shot Liberty Valance* (1962). He was the father of actors David, Keith, and Robert Carradine.

Carrey, Jim (1962–) Canadian-born American actor and comedian. Born James Eugene Carrey. After honing his physical comedy skills on television, he gained cinematic fame for *Ace Ventura, Pet Detective* (1994) and followed with such broad comedies as *Dumb and Dumber* (1994) and *The Mask* (1994). In later roles, he has blended comedic and dramatic elements, notably in *The Truman Show* (1998) and *Man on the Moon* (1999). Other films include *Me, Myself & Irene* (2000) and *Dr. Seuss' How the Grinch Stole Christmas* (2000).

Chan, Jackie (1955–) Hong Kong–born actor, writer, director, and producer. Born Chan Kwong-Sang. After training in acrobatics and martial arts at the Peking Opera School, he moved from stuntman to international star with films that combine humor and death-defying stunts, such as *Half a Loaf of Kung-Fu* (1978) and *The Big Brawl* (1980). In recent

> "When I drove through that studio gate and the thrill was gone, I knew it was time to quit."
>
> —
>
> *James Cagney, 1960s*

Jackie Chan, pictured in Rumble in the Bronx *(1996), was instrumental in developing the genre of comedy kung fu.*

years, he has appeared in several US productions, including *Rush Hour* (1998) and *Shanghai Noon* (2000).

Chaney, Lon (1883–1930) American actor. Born Alonso Chaney. Known as "the Man of a Thousand Faces," he became a silent film star with his portrayals of horrific or troubled characters in films such as *The Hunchback of Notre Dame* (1923) and *The Phantom of the Opera* (1925). A makeup pioneer, he often created his own looks. He made one sound film, *The Unholy Three* (1930). He is the father of actor Lon Chaney, Jr.

Chaplin, Charlie (Sir Charles Spencer Chaplin) (1889–1977) British-born actor, director, producer, and screenwriter. After a penurious childhood and stage training, he entered silent films in 1913 and within two years was an international star. From 1914, he generally wrote and directed his films and sometimes produced them. His Tramp persona, established in such films as *The Tramp* (1915), was a mainstay in his films, including *The Kid* (1921) and *The Gold Rush* (1925), considered by some his finest work. In 1919, he became a cofounder of the United Artists Corporation. His sound films took on a darker tone, such as *The Great Dictator* (1940)—which marked the Tramp's last appearance—and his autumnal work *Limelight* (1952). His marriages to young women, including Paulette Goddard and Oona O'Neill (daughter of playwright Eugene O'Neill), made him a press magnet, and he was also scrutinized by the US government after World War II for his communist leanings. He was denied reentry to the country in 1952 following a European trip. He returned to accept an honorary Academy Award in 1972. Actress Geraldine Chaplin (1944–) is his daughter.

Chase, Chevy (1943–) American actor. Born Cornelius Crane Chase. An actor and writer on the television series *Saturday Night Live* in the 1970s, he entered film at that time and parlayed his bumbling yet self-mocking persona into a string of comedic successes, including *Caddyshack* (1980), *National Lampoon's Vacation* (1983), and *Fletch* (1985). Later films include *Memoirs of an Invisible Man* (1991).

Cher (1946–) American singer and actress. Born Cherilyn Sarkisian LaPierre. With husband Salvatore "Sonny" Bono, she had several hit records and a successful TV series, *The Sonny & Cher Comedy Hour*. When the marriage and show ended in the 1970s, she embarked on a solo recording, television, and film career. Film roles highlighted her soulful earthiness, particularly *Moonstruck* (1987), for which she won an Academy Award for best actress. Other films include *Silkwood* (1983), *Mask* (1985), *The Witches of Eastwick* (1987), and *Tea with Mussolini* (1999, Italy/UK).

Chevalier, Maurice (1888–1972) French-born entertainer and actor. The internationally known performer appeared in films from 1908 and became known on screen as an amiable rogue in sophisticated comedies including *The Love Parade* (1929), *One Hour with You* (1932), and *Love Me Tonight* (1932). Later films, such as *Gigi* (1958), played on his previously established rakish persona. He received a special Academy Award in 1958.

Christie, Julie (1941–) Indian-born British actress. Alluring dramatic lead best known for her morally ambiguous roles in films such as *Darling* (1965), for which she won an Academy Award for best actress, and *McCabe and Mrs. Miller* (1971). Other notable films include *Doctor Zhivago* (1965), *Don't Look Now* (1973), *Shampoo* (1975), and *Afterglow* (1997).

Clarke, Mae (1907–1992) American actress. A female lead of the 1930s, she appeared in *Frankenstein* (1931), *The Front Page* (1931), and *The Public Enemy* (1931), as James Cagney's grapefruit target. Postwar, she appeared sporadically in such films as *Magnificent Obsession* (1954).

Clift, Montgomery (1920–1966) American actor. Born Edward Montgomery Clift. Trained on Broadway, he established himself as an intense, intelligent screen loner from his earliest films, *The Search* (1948) and *Red River* (1948). He appeared in such star vehicles as *A Place in the Sun* (1951) and *From Here to Eternity* (1953). He moved into more introspective character leads after a disfiguring auto accident in 1957. Films from that period include *Judgment at Nuremberg* (1961) and *Freud* (1962).

Close, Glenn (1947–) American actress. A distinguished stage actress who appeared in such plays as *The Real Thing* and *Sunset Boulevard*, she is known in films for her sharply drawn characterizations. Screen credits include *The World According to Garp* (1982), *The Big Chill* (1983), *Fatal Attraction* (1987), *Dangerous Liaisons* (1988), and *Cookie's Fortune* (1999). She is also a naturalistic television performer, notably in the TV movie *Sarah, Plain and Tall*.

Coburn, James (1928–) American actor. Stage-trained, he first became known for his no-nonsense presence in action films such as *The Magnificent Seven* (1960) and *The Great Escape* (1963) but gained his greatest popularity as an insouciant spy in *Our Man Flint* (1966) and *In Like Flint* (1967). Other films include *The President's Analyst* (1967) and *Candy* (1968). His performance in *Affliction* (1998) earned an Academy Award for best supporting actor.

Colbert, Claudette (1905–1996) French-born American actress. Born Claudette Lily Chauchoin. Initially playing exotic types in

Glenn Close was only five years older than Robin Williams when she played his mother in *The World According to Garp* (1982).

Cecil B. De Mille's *The Sign of the Cross* (1932) and his *Cleopatra* (1934), she gained broader casting notice as a runaway bride in Frank Capra's comedy *It Happened One Night* (1934). It won her a best actress Academy Award and established her comedic touch and ability to play top leads. Projecting a knowing acceptance of life's absurdities, she sparkled in such films as *Imitation of Life* (1934), *Bluebeard's Eighth Wife* (1938), *Boom Town* (1940), *The Palm Beach Story* (1942), *Since You Went Away* (1944), and *The Egg and I* (1947).

Colman, Ronald (1891–1958) British-born American actor. A suave silent and sound leading man, he became known for starring in lush dramas in the 1920s, including *Stella Dallas* (1925) and *Beau Geste* (1926). In the sound era, his sonorous voice and regal bearing made him the standard choice for literary film adaptations and serious dramas. Films include *Condemned* (1929), *Bulldog Drummond* (1929), *Arrowsmith* (1931), *A Tale of Two Cities* (1935), *Lost Horizon* (1937), *The Prisoner of Zenda* (1937), *Random Harvest* (1942), and *The Talk of the Town* (1942). He won a best actor Academy Award for *A Double Life* (1948).

Connery, Sean (1930–) Scottish actor. Born Thomas Connery. In *Dr. No* (1962), the virile, unperturbable Connery created the role of the world's most famous postwar spy, James Bond. Several sequels followed, each cementing his superstar status, including *From Russia with Love* (1963), *Goldfinger* (1964), *Thunderball* (1965), and *Diamonds Are Forever* (1971). He later became known for adroit character performances, particularly as an aging Robin Hood in *Robin and Marian* (1976), Indiana Jones's father in *Indiana Jones and the Last Crusade* (1989), and a tough Chicago cop in *The Untouchables* (1987), for which he received an Academy Award for best supporting actor. He was married to actress Diane Cilento (1962–1973). Other films include *Finding Forrester* (2000).

Cooper, Gary (1901–1961) American actor. Born Frank James Cooper. In silent and sound films, often opposite Hollywood's leading femmes fatales, he was a laconic, easygoing lead who projected both moral rectitude and a mischievous streak. After silent successes, including *The Winning of Barbara Worth* (1926), he became a 1930s romantic comedy star in such films as *Trouble in Paradise* (1932) and *Mr. Deeds Goes to Town* (1936). In 1941, he won a best actor Academy Award for *Sergeant York* and was memorable as ballplayer Lou Gehrig in *The Pride of the Yankees* (1942). Later performances include *Friendly Persuasion* (1956) and the western *High Noon* (1952), for which he won another best actor Academy Award. He received a special Academy Award for lifetime achievement in 1961, shortly before his death.

Cortez, Ricardo (1899–1977) Viennese-born American actor. Born Jacob Krantz (or Kranze). Darkly handsome with smoldering eyes, he became known for portraying exotic lovers and other lead characters in silent and early sound films. Features include *Argentine Love* (1924), *The Torrent* (1926), and the original *Maltese Falcon* (1931), in which he plays the first on-screen Sam Spade.

Costner, Kevin (1955–) American actor and director. Theater-trained, he became known as a rangy, humanistic leading man in *The Untouchables* (1987) and an athletic sex symbol in *Bull Durham* (1988), *Field of Dreams* (1989), and *The Bodyguard* (1992). He won Academy Awards for best director and best picture for his revisionist western *Dances with Wolves* (1990). Subsequent, less successful big-budget spectaculars include *Waterworld* (1995). Other films include *Thirteen Days* (2000).

Cotten, Joseph (1905–1994) American actor. Broadway-trained, the serious-looking actor debuted on screen in Orson Welles's *Citizen Kane* (1941). Dramatic leads followed in the 1940s and 50s, including *The Magnificent Ambersons* (1942) and several films with top female stars, such as *Shadow of a Doubt* (1943, with Teresa Wright), *The Farmer's Daughter* (1947), *Portrait of Jennie* (1948), and *Niagara* (1953, with Marilyn Monroe).

Crain, Jeanne (1925–) American actress. A former beauty queen, she was a leading actress in domestic comedies during the 1940s, including *Apartment for Peggy* (1948), *Cheaper by the Dozen* (1950), and *A Letter to Three Wives* (1949). She was nominated for a best actress Academy Award for her performance in the racial drama *Pinky* (1949).

Crawford, Broderick (1911–1986) American actor. Born William Broderick Crawford. The hulking Broadway actor is best known for his performance in *All the King's Men* (1949), which earned him an Academy Award for best actor. Other films include *Born Yesterday* (1950) and *Il Bidone (The Swindle)* (1955, Italy). He starred in various TV series of the 1950s and 60s. He was the son of stage performers Lester (Robert) Crawford and Helen Broderick.

Scotsman Sean Connery first played suave secret agent James Bond in Dr. No *(1962) and reprised the role in six later films.*

Crawford, Joan (1904–1977) American actress. Born Lucille Fay Le Sueur. Broadway-trained, she acquired her professional name in a studio publicity contest and became known as a streetwise flapper in such films as *Our Dancing Daughters* (1928) and *Dance, Fools, Dance* (1931). In the 1930s, she continued as a major sex symbol in such movies as *Grand Hotel* (1932), *The Women* (1939), and *Strange Cargo* (1940). She is best remembered as the tough and tragic working woman in *Mildred Pierce* (1945), which won her a best actress Academy Award. Later films include *Possessed* (1947), *Sudden Fear* (1952), and *What Ever Happened to Baby Jane?* (1962). Among her four husbands was Douglas Fairbanks, Jr. (1928–33). Adopted daughter Christina publicly castigated Crawford's mothering in the tell-all book *Mommie Dearest* (1978).

Crosby, Bing (1903–1977) American singer and actor. Born Harry Lillis Crosby. He was the leading popular crooner during the 1930s and soon became one of Hollywood's leading box-office attractions in light musical comedies, including *Anything Goes* (1936) and *Rhythm on the Range* (1936). In the 1940s, he made his most memorable films, both dramatic and comedic. With Bob Hope and Dorothy Lamour, he began the series of zany road comedies, so called for their theme of travel to exotic places, including *Road to Singapore* (1940), *Road to Zanzibar* (1941), *Road to Morocco* (1942), and *Road to Hong Kong* (1962). As a dramatic actor, he was a convincing priest opposite Barry Fitzgerald in *Going My Way* (1944; best actor Academy Award) and its sequel *The Bells of St. Mary's* (1945). Still a strong presence in the 1950s, he appeared in such films as *High Society* (1956) and *The Country Girl* (1954).

> "He's a kid off a Wheaties box."
>
> —
>
> *Oliver Stone on Tom Cruise, 1989*

Crowe, Russell (1964–) New Zealander actor. A former child star, he became a commanding leading man of Australian cinema in the early 1990s in films such as *Crossing* (1990) and *Romper Stomper* (1992). In the US from the mid-90s, he showed subtlety and power in such films as *L.A. Confidential* (1997), *The Insider* (1999), and the epic *Gladiator* (2000), for which he won a best actor Academy Award.

Cruise, Tom (1962–) American actor. Born Thomas Cruise Mapother IV. The contemporary epitome of vulnerable brashness, he came to prominence in his role as a suburban teenager seeking sexual experience in *Risky Business* (1983). A string of box-office successes cemented his stardom, including *Top Gun* (1986), *The Color of Money* (1986), *Rain Man* (1988), and *Born on the Fourth of July* (1989). Later films include *Mission: Impossible* (1996), *Jerry Maguire* (1996), *Magnolia* (1999), and *Mission Impossible II* (2000). He was married to actress Nicole Kidman (1990-2001), with whom he co-starred in *Eyes Wide Shut* (1999).

Curtis, Jamie Lee (1958–) American actress. A television series regular while still in her teens, she established herself as a horror-movie queen with her debut in *Halloween* (1978) and subsequent horror films such as *The Fog* (1980). Through the 1980s and 90s, she has been a sassy lead in comedies including *A Fish Called Wanda* (1988, UK) and *True Lies* (1994). Her parents are actors Tony Curtis and Janet Leigh. She is married to actor-director Christopher Guest.

Curtis, Tony (1925–) American actor. Born Bernard Schwartz. A mix of urban toughness and sculpted beauty, he became a star during the 1950s and 60s in period pieces such as *Houdini* (1953) and contemporary dramas such as *The Sweet Smell of Success* (1957) and *The Defiant Ones* (1958). Yet he is best known as a saxophonist in drag in the comedy *Some Like It Hot* (1959). Subsequent comdeies include *Operation Petticoat* (1959) and *The Great Race* (1965). He was married to actress Janet Leigh (1951–62); their daughter is actress Jamie Lee Curtis.

Cusack, Joan (1962–) American actress. A former regular on television's *Saturday Night Live,* she distinguished herself on screen in several comedic character performances in films such as *Working Girl* (1988), *In and Out* (1997), and *Toy Story 2* (1999, voice). She has appeared in films with her brother John Cusack.

Cusack, John (1966–) American actor. Brother of actress Joan Cusack, he has been an appealing, cerebral lead in mostly offbeat films since the 80s, including *The Sure Thing* (1985), *The Grifters* (1990), *Being John Malkovich* (1999), and *Serendipity* (2001). Other films include *Grosse Pointe Blank* (1997) and *High Fidelity* (2000), both of which he cowrote and coproduced.

John Cusack played a thirtysomething music lover who visits his past girlfriends in order to examine the failure of his current relationship in High Fidelity *(2000).*

D

Damon, Matt (1970–) American actor and screenwriter. After leaving Harvard shortly before graduating, he collaborated with friend Ben Affleck on the screenplay for *Good Will Hunting* (1997). He played the title role of a troubled young genius, and he and Affleck won an Academy Award for best screenplay. Later films have capitalized on his clean-cut intensity, including *Saving Private Ryan* (1998), *The Talented Mr. Ripley* (1999), and *All the Pretty Horses* (2000).

Dandridge, Dorothy (1923–1965) American actress and entertainer. One of the first African-American leading ladies, she was nominated for a best actress Academy Award for *Carmen Jones* (1954). Other films include *A Day at the Races* (1937), *Since You Went Away* (1944), and *Porgy and Bess* (1959). Among her husbands was dancer Harold Nicholas of the Nicholas Brothers.

Davis, Bette (1908–1989) American actress. Born Ruth Elizabeth Davis. An unparalleled star of Hollywood's golden age, she became the cinematic archetype of the strong-willed woman, particularly in Warner Bros. films of the 1930s. Films of that decade include *Of Human Bondage* (1934), *Dangerous* (1935), *The Petrified Forest* (1936), and *Jezebel* (1938), for which she received a best actress Academy Award. In the late 1930s and 40s, she became known for melodramas, including *Dark Victory* (1939), *The Letter* (1940), and *Now, Voyager* (1942). She made a comeback as aging Margo Channing in *All About Eve* (1950) and continued making films into the late 1980s (*What Ever Happened to Baby Jane?*, 1962; *The Whales of August*, 1989). In 1977, she received the AFI Life Achievement Award. Her fourth and last husband was actor Gary Merrill (1950–60). Her autobiographies include *The Lonely Wife* (1962) and *This 'n That* (1987).

Davis, Geena (1957–) American actress. Born Virginia Davis. The lanky, red-haired beauty first gained screen notice in *Tootsie* (1982) and became known as an earthy, self-deprecating performer, particularly in *The Accidental Tourist* (1988), for which she won an Academy Award for best supporting actress, and *Thelma & Louise* (1991). Other films include *The Fly* (1988) and *A League of Their Own* (1992). She was married to actor Jeff Goldblum and later to director Renny Harlin.

Day, Doris (1924–) American actress and singer. Born Doris von Kappelhoff. A fresh-faced big-band vocalist in the 1940s (with the Bob Crosby and Les Brown bands), she entered film in 1948 and became a top box-office draw during the 1950s, usually as a light, warm presence in musicals and dramas, including *Calamity Jane* (1954), *Young at Heart* (1955), and *The Pajama Game* (1957). Shining performances in darker films include *Love Me or Leave Me* (1955) and *The Man Who Knew Too Much* (1956). She revealed comedic skills in sex farces with Rock Hudson, including *Lover Come Back* (1962) and *Pillow Talk* (1959), for which she was nominated for a best actress Academy Award.

Day-Lewis, Daniel (1957–) British actor. Son of poet C. Day-Lewis, he is one of the most respected romantic and dramatic leads of his generation. Stage-trained, he came to cinematic prominence in *My Beautiful Laundrette* (1985, UK) and *A Room with a View* (1985, UK) and won a best actor Academy Award for *My Left Foot* (1989, Ireland). Continuing to specialize in period literary dramas, he played the male lead in *The Last of the Mohicans* (1992), *The Age of Innocence* (1993), and *The Crucible* (1996).

Dean, James (1931–1955) American actor. Born James Byron Dean. He graduated from TV commercials, Broadway, and bit movie roles to stardom in three films over two years: *Rebel Without a Cause* (1955), *East of Eden* (1955), and *Giant* (1956). His premature death in a car accident only intensified his cult following, as fans proved perennially fascinated by his image of troubled, sensitive, doomed youth.

de Havilland, Olivia (1916–) Tokyo-born American actress. Older sister of Joan Fontaine, she appeared in films from the 1930s, notably as Errol Flynn's love interest in such screen pairings as *The Adventures of Robin Hood* (1938) and *Dodge City* (1939). Her performance as Melanie in *Gone with the Wind* (1939) defined her for generations afterward. Postwar, she won best actress Academy Awards for *To Each His Own* (1946) and *The Heiress* (1949). Other films include *Hold Back the Dawn* (1941) and *The Snake Pit* (1948).

Delon, Alain (1935–) French-born actor and producer. Good-looking tough-guy leading man, he has appeared in French and international films since the 1950s and been a producer since the 60s. Among his notable acting credits are *Rocco e i Suoi Fratelli* (*Rocco and His Brothers*) (1960), *Il Gattopardo* (*The Leopard*) (1963), *Paris Brûle-t-il?* (*Is Paris Burning?*) (1966), and *Notre Histoire* (1984).

Dench, Dame Judi (1934–) British-born actress in British and American films. The highly regarded stage actress in Britain has made an impression on film audiences with her witty and subtle characterization of Queen Victoria in *Mrs. Brown* (1997) and Queen Elizabeth in *Shakespeare in Love* (1998); the latter role

Dorothy Dandridge received an Oscar nomination for Carmen Jones *(1954).*

To prepare for his role in *The Crucible* (1996), Daniel Day-Lewis arrived weeks early to the film's New England location so he could personally construct his character's 17th-century-style home.

Johnny Depp portrayed one of the worst directors of all time in Ed Wood *(1994).*

player has been one of France's and later Hollywood's most respected and versatile leads, displaying command in dramas and period works. Films include *Stavisky* (1974, France), *1900* (1976, Italy), *The Return of Martin Guerre* (1981, France), *Danton* (1982, Poland/France), *Cyrano de Bergerac* (1990, France), and *Hamlet* (1996, US/UK), and *Vatel* (2001).

Depp, Johnny (1964–) American actor. TV-trained, he appeared in increasingly diverse character leads, notably in *Edward Scissorhands* (1990), *What's Eating Gilbert Grape?* (1993), *Ed Wood* (1994), *Donnie Brasco* (1997), and *From Hell* (2001). He usually portrays a complicated man worthy of sympathy and understanding.

Dern, Laura (1966–) American actress. Stage-trained daughter of actors Bruce Dern and Diane Ladd, she displays a broad range and a quiet sexuality, largely in serious dramas and dark comedies. Among her films are *Smooth Talk* (1985), *Blue Velvet* (1986), *Rambling Rose* (1991), *Citizen Ruth* (1996), and *Focus* (2001).

De Vito, Danny (1944–) American actor, director, and producer. From stage and television (the series *Taxi*), he became a respected, popular comic character player in films of the 1980s, often as an energetic con man. Films include *Romancing the Stone* (1984), *Tin Men* (1987), *Junior* (1994), and *Heist* (2001). With *Throw Momma from the Train* (1987), he began directing films, including *The War of the Roses* (1989). He has also been successful as a producer. He is married to actress Rhea Perlman.

Diaz, Cameron (1972–) American actress. This blond lead radiated warm beauty and comedic talent in *My Best Friend's Wedding* (1997) and *There's Something About Mary* (1998). Later films, include *Being John Malkovich* (1999), *Charlie's Angels* (2000), and *Shrek* (2001, voice only).

DiCaprio, Leonardo (1974–) American actor. Born Leonardo Wilhelm DiCaprio. Trained in television, he gained critical notice for his performances in serious features such as *This Boy's Life* (1993) and *What's Eating Gilbert Grape?* (1993) and became a full-fledged teen idol as the male lead in *Titanic* (1997). Subsequent credits include *The Man in the Iron Mask* (1998), *The Beach* (2000) and *Gangs of New York* (2002).

Dietrich, Marlene (1901–1992) German-born American actress. Born Maria Magdalene Dietrich. She received international attention as the sexually dangerous Lola Lola in *The Blue Angel* (1930). Later, in Hollywood, she starred in such films as *Morocco* (1930), *Destry Rides Again* (1939), *Rancho Notorious* (1952), *Witness for the Prosecution* (1958), and *Touch of Evil* (1958). Projecting androgynous allure, she helped make trousers an acceptable option for women.

earned her an Academy Award for best supporting actress. She has also portrayed the spymaster M in the James Bond films *Golden-eye* (1995), *Tomorrow Never Dies* (1997), and *The World Is Not Enough* (1999).

Deneuve, Catherine (1943–) French actress in international films. Born Catherine Dorléac. In *The Umbrellas of Cherbourg* (1964, France), *Repulsion* (1965, UK), *Belle de Jour* (1967, France/Italy), and *Tristana* (1970, France/Spain), she epitomized cool French beauty and became a worldwide star. Later films include *The Dernier Métro (The Last Metro)* (1980, France), *Indochine* (1992, France), and *Dancer in the Dark* (2000, Denmark/Sweden/France).

De Niro, Robert (1943–) American actor, director, and producer. A highly respected actor famous for his ability to play starkly different characters, he first gained notice in *Bang the Drum Slowly* (1973) and *Mean Streets* (1973), the latter establishing his long working relationship with director Martin Scorsese. Their subsequent films included *Taxi Driver* (1976), *Raging Bull* (1980; best actor Academy Award), *The King of Comedy* (1983), *GoodFellas* (1990), and *Casino* (1995). He received a best supporting actor Academy Award for his performance as young Vito Corleone in *The Godfather Part II* (1974). Other films include *The Deer Hunter* (1978), *The Untouchables* (1987), *Wag the Dog* (1997), *The Score* (2001), and *Meet the Parents* (2000). He directed, coproduced, and starred in *A Bronx Tale* (1993).

Depardieu, Gérard (1948–) French actor in international films. From the 1970s, the craggy-faced

Dillon, Matt (1964–) American actor. In films since the 1970s, he became known for unaffected performances in teen-oriented films, including *Rumble Fish* (1983) and *The Flamingo Kid* (1984). He gained acclaim for his dark humanism in *Drugstore Cowboy* (1989) and for his goofy rakishness in *There's Something About Mary* (1998). Actor Kevin Dillon is his brother.

Donat, Robert (1905–1958) British actor. Experienced on stage, this suave leading man became a respected actor in American and British films from the 1930s to the 50s. He won a best actor Academy Award for his sentimental performance as a teacher in *Goodbye, Mr. Chips* (1939). He was known for his roles in historical dramas, including *The Private Life of Henry VIII* (1933) and *The Count of Monte Cristo* (1934), but he is probably best remembered as the lead in Alfred Hitchcock's *The 39 Steps* (1935).

Douglas, Kirk (1916–) American actor and producer. Born Issur Danielovitch (changed to Isidore Demsky). Leading man who delivered forceful, energetic performances in lush dramas and biographies beginning in the 1940s, notably in *Champion* (1949), *The Bad and the Beautiful* (1953), and *Lust for Life* (1956). Other films include *Paths of Glory* (1958), *Spartacus* (1960), and *Seven Days in May* (1964). He produced films as head of Bryna Productions. Douglas received AFI's Life Achievement Award in 1991. He is the father of actor Michael Douglas.

Douglas, Michael (1944–) American actor and producer. The son of actor Kirk Douglas, he first became known as a television actor and film producer, especially for *One Flew over the Cuckoo's Nest* (1975), which won the Academy Award for best picture. During the 1980s, he developed into a film leading man, adept in roles depicting questionable morality, such as in *Fatal Attraction* (1987) and *Wall Street* (1987), for which he won a best actor Academy Award. Other films include *Romancing the Stone* (1984), *The American President* (1995), *Wonder Boys* (2000), *Traffic* (2000), and *Don't Say a Word* (2001). He is married to actress Catherine Zeta-Jones.

Downey, Robert, Jr. (1965–) American actor. On screen since age five, he appeared widely in films during early adulthood, including *Less Than Zero* (1987) and *Soapdish* (1991), and achieved acclaim for his portrayal of the title role in *Chaplin* (1992). Later films include *Two Girls and a Guy* (1998). His career has been interrupted by drug problems. Filmmaker Robert Downey is his father.

Dressler, Marie (1869–1964) Canadian-born actress. Born Leila Marie Koerber. A Broadway and vaudeville headliner, the large, plain-faced actress was a leading silent comedian in films such as *Tillie's Punctured Romance* (1914) and

The Callahans and the Murphys (1927). She was acclaimed for her performances in sound films that included *Min and Bill* (1930), for which she won a best actress Academy Award, and *Dinner at Eight* (1933), in which she delivers the notable last line. Her autobiography is *The Life Story of an Ugly Duckling*.

Dreyfuss, Richard (1947–) American actor. The wiry, intense player was a top character lead in the 1970s, beginning with his appearances in the sleeper *American Graffiti* (1973) and *The Apprenticeship of Duddy Kravitz* (1974). Memorable credits of the decade include such big-budget hits as *Jaws* (1975) and *Close Encounters of the Third Kind* (1977). He won a best actor Academy Award for *The Goodbye Girl* (1977). Later films include *Tin Men* (1987) and *Mr. Holland's Opus* (1995).

Dunaway, Faye (1941–) American actress. The stately blond created a sensation with her title role performance as Bonnie Parker in *Bonnie and Clyde* (1967), which earned an Academy Award nomination for best actress. She displayed her trademark coolness in lead roles in films such as *The Thomas Crown Affair* (1968) and *Chinatown* (1974). She won a best actress Academy Award for her performance as a hard-driving TV executive in *Network* (1976) and memorably impersonated Joan Crawford in *Mommie Dearest* (1981). Later films include *The Yards* (2000).

Dunne, Irene (1898–1990) American actress. Born Irene Marie Dunn. A warm, self-possessed, urbane presence in several genres during the studio era, including romantic comedies such as *The Awful Truth* (1937), melodramas such as *Penny Serenade* (1941), and period pieces such as *Life with Father* (1947) and *I Remember Mama* (1948). She received the Kennedy Center honors for lifetime achievement in 1985 and was nominated five times for a best actress Academy Award.

Durante, Jimmy (1893–1980) American comedian, actor, and entertainer. Born James Francis Durante. The self-deprecating Broadway star, nicknamed Schnozzola for his big nose, appeared in comic films from the 1930s to 60s, including *Sally, Irene and Mary* (1938), *It Happened in Brooklyn* (1947), and *Jumbo* (1962). His films were infused with his affability and talent for jokes.

Durbin, Deanna (1921–) Canadian-born American actress. Born Edna Mae Durbin. Bubbly child star of the 1930s and 40s on a par with Judy Garland in popularity. Films include *Three Smart Girls* (1936), *100 Men and a Girl* (1937), and *It's a Date* (1940). In 1938, she won a special Academy Award for juvenile performances. She retired from films in 1948.

Kirk Douglas originated the role of the iconoclastic R.P. McMurphy in the failed Broadway adaptation of Ken Kesey's *One Flew over the Cuckoo's Nest* in the early 1960s. He then spent 13 years trying to produce and star in a film version. A discouraged Douglas eventually passed along the rights to his son Michael, and the resulting film—starring Jack Nicholson as McMurphy—was a box-office smash that swept the 1975 Academy Awards in all major categories, the first movie to do so since *It Happened One Night* in 1934.

Jimmy Durante appeared in over 35 films in 33 years.

Duvall, Robert (1931–) American actor. Beginning with his first film, *To Kill a Mockingbird* (1962), in which he played the mysterious Boo Radley, the stage-trained actor has been a strong, chameleon-like character player. Notable films include *The Godfather* (1972), *The Godfather Part II* (1974), *Apocalypse Now* (1979), *The Great Santini* (1980), *Rambling Rose* (1991), and *Sling Blade* (1996), and *The 6th Day* (2000). He won a best actor Academy Award for *Tender Mercies* (1983). He wrote, directed, executive-produced, and starred in *The Apostle* (1997).

E–F

Eastwood, Clint (1930–) American actor, director, and producer. Born Clinton Eastwood, Jr. After starring in the TV series *Rawhide,* he established himself as an enigmatic film lead in the Sergio Leone Italian westerns *A Fistful of Dollars* (1964), *For a Few Dollars More* (1965), and *The Good, the Bad, and the Ugly* (1966). In the 1970s, he directed his first film, *Play Misty for Me* (1971), in which he also starred, and became known as "Dirty Harry" Callahan in *Dirty Harry* (1971) and sequels such as *Sudden Impact* (1983), which he also directed. His persona, then and now, is tough, laconic, and towering; over the years, he gained acclaim for his spareness in both acting and directing. Later acting credits include *Escape from Alcatraz* (1979); *Unforgiven* (1992), which he directed and produced and for which he won Academy Awards for best picture and director; *In the Line of Fire* (1993); and *A Perfect World* (1993), *The Bridges of Madison County* (1995) and *Space Cowboys* (2000), all of which he directed. Eastwood received AFI's Life Achievement Award in 1996.

Eddy, Nelson (1901–1967) American singer and actor. The opera singer and concert performer became a top box-office draw in the 1930s as partner to Jeanette MacDonald in several film operettas, including *Naughty Marietta* (1935) and *Rose Marie* (1936). Eddy and MacDonald, known as America's Sweethearts, were the most popular singing duo of pre–World War II cinema.

Fairbanks, Douglas (1883–1939) American actor. Born Douglas Elton Ulman. The handsome, rakish Broadway player was the premier swashbuckler of the silent screen and a major star of light comedy and drama. Films include *Manhattan Madness* (1916), *Till the Clouds Roll By* (1919), *The Mark of Zorro* (1920), *The Three Musketeers* (1921), *Robin Hood* (1922), and *The Thief of Baghdad* (1924). He helped define Hollywood royalty when he married actress Mary Pickford in 1920; they divorced in 1936. In 1919, he cofounded United Artists. His son was actor Douglas Fairbanks, Jr.

Farnum, William (1876–1953) American actor. One of the first major leading men of the silent era, he began his screen career with *The Spoilers* (1914) and went on to act in such films as *A Tale of Two Cities* (1917) and *Les Misérables* (1917). His career was hampered by a serious on-set accident in 1925; he turned to character roles during the sound era, in films such as *Hangmen Also Die* (1943) and *Samson and Delilah* (1949).

Faye, Alice (1912–1998) American actress and singer. Born Alice Jeanne Leppert. A major star in musicals of the 1930s and 40s, she helped to define the genre in its early years, appearing in such films as George White's *Scandals* (1934), *In Old Chicago* (1938), *Alexander's Ragtime Band* (1938), and *The Gang's All Here* (1943). Trained on Broadway, she was appreciated for her liveliness and light melodious voice. She retired from the screen in 1945, except for occasional appearances. Among her husbands were singer Tony Martin and bandleader Phil Harris.

Ferrer, José (1909–1992) Born José Vicente Ferrer de Otero y Cintron. An accomplished stage actor, he was a top film star during the 1950s and won a best actor Academy Award for his performance in *Cyrano de Bergerac* (1950). Other notable films include *Moulin Rouge* (1952), *The Caine Mutiny* (1953), *Lawrence of Arabia* (1962), and *Ship of Fools* (1965). Among his wives were actress Uta Hagen and singer Rosemary Clooney. He is the father of actor Miguel Ferrer.

Fetchit, Stepin (1892–1985) American actor. Born Lincoln Theodore Monroe Andrew Perry. By receiving featured billing and earning a small fortune from his film work, he was a pioneer for African-Americans in cinema, but the mincing, fearful characters he played have since come to epitomize negative racial caricature. Among his films, which span the silent and sound eras, are *In Old Kentucky* (1927), *Show Boat* (1929), *Judge Priest* (1934), and *Bend of the River* (1952).

Field, Sally (1946–) American actress. Originally a TV comedy actress, she became a working-class heroine for her title performance in the film *Norma Rae* (1979), for which she won a best actress Academy Award. This was followed by several plainspoken roles in such films as *Places in the Heart* (1984), for which she won a second Academy Award for best actress; *Steel Magnolias* (1989); and *Forrest Gump* (1994). She is the stepdaughter of actor Jock Mahoney.

Fields, Dame Gracie (1898–1979) British singer and actress. Born Grace Stansfield. The leading box-office draw in British films of the 1930s, she offered comic uplift in *Looking on the Bright Side* (1932), *Look Up and Laugh* (1935), and *Keep Smiling/Smiling Along* (1938, US/UK). American films include *Holy Matrimony* (1943) and *Stage Door Canteen* (1943). In 1979, she was named Dame Commander of the Order of the British Empire. One of her husbnds was actor-director Monty Banks.

Fields, W.C. (1879–1946) American actor and screenwriter. Born William Claude Dukenfield. An internationally known vaudevillian, he appeared in several silent films from 1915, including *Tillie's Punctured Romance* (1928), but did not become a major film star until the sound era. Before World War II, he was a top box-office draw and an icon of humorous misanthropy and surly braggadocio in films including *It's a Gift* (1934), *You Can't Cheat an Honest Man* (1939), *My Little Chickadee* (1940), *The Bank Dick* (1940), and *Never Give a Sucker an Even Break* (1941). Using his real name or pseudonyms, he was also screenwriter or co-screenwriter of several of his films.

Fiennes, Ralph (1962–) British actor. Born Ralph Nathaniel Fiennes. The brooding actor worked on the London stage before gaining acclaim for his performance as a conflicted Nazi officer in *Schindler's List* (1993). He became a dramatic and romantic lead in British and American films, including *Quiz Show* (1994), *The English Patient* (1996), and *The End of the Affair* (1999). Actor Joseph Fiennes is his brother.

Finney, Albert (1936–) British actor in British and American films. He came to prominence in British cinema for his dark performance in *Saturday Night and Sunday Morning* (1960) and his lively title take in *Tom Jones* (1962). His frequently antiheroic roles in later films were equally varied. Credits include the British films *Two for the Road* (1967), *Charlie Bubbles* (1967, which he also directed), *Murder on the Orient Express* (1974), and *The Dresser* (1983), along with the American films *Shoot the Moon* (1982), *Under the Volcano* (1984), and *Erin Brockovich* (2000).

Fishburne, Laurence (1961–) American actor. Born Laurence Fishburne III. Making an early appearance in *Apocalypse Now* (1979), he became known from the 1980s for performances that were both measured and explosive. Films include *What's Love Got to Do with It?* (1993), *Searching for Bobby Fischer* (1993), *Othello* (1995), and *The Matrix* (1999).

Fitzgerald, Barry (1888–1961) Irish-born actor. Trained at Ireland's Abbey Theatre and on Broadway, he played a variety of Irish characters in films including *The Plough and the Stars* (1937), *Bringing Up Baby* (1938), *How Green Was My Valley* (1941), and *Going My Way* (1944), for which he won an Academy Award for best supporting actor.

Flynn, Errol (1909–1959) Tasmanian-born American actor. Lean and dashing, he was the archetypal swashbuckler hero in the 1930s and 40s, with some forays into western roles. His frequent on-screen love interest was Olivia de Havilland. He rose to stardom in *Captain Blood* (1935) and continued in a string of glossy spectacles, including *The Adventures of Robin Hood* (1938), *The Dawn Patrol* (1938), *Dodge City* (1939), *The Private Lives of Elizabeth and Essex* (1939), *The Sea Hawk* (1940), *They Died with Their Boots On* (1942), and *Objective Burma!* (1946). In later years, he made films only occasionally, notably *The Sun Also Rises* (1957). He was married to actress Lili Damita (1935–42). His autobiography is *My Wicked, Wicked Ways* (1959).

Fonda, Bridget (1964–) American actress. The daughter of Peter Fonda and granddaughter of Henry Fonda, she appeared in films beginning in the late 1980s. After making an impression of intelligence and energy in *Scandal* (1989), she became a lead in comedies, dramas, and thrillers. Other films include *Single White Female* (1992), *Point of No Return* (1993), *It Could Happen to You* (1994), and *A Simple Plan* (1998).

Fonda, Henry (1905–1982) American actor. The image of plainspoken decency in sound films, he is best known as the dispossessed tenant farmer and ex-con Tom Joad in John Ford's *The Grapes of Wrath* (1940). Trained on Broadway, he entered film in 1934 and soon became a top box-office lead in dramas including *Jezebel* (1938), *Young Mr. Lincoln* (1939), and *The Ox-Bow Incident* (1943). He also excelled in comedies, making simplemindedness look easy in *The Lady Eve* (1941). His moral stature grew in the 1950s with *Twelve Angry Men* (1957) and *Mister Roberts* (1955), in which he re-created his title Broadway role. He received a special Academy Award in 1980, and in 1981 a best actor Academy Award for his performance in *On Golden Pond,* his only film with daughter Jane Fonda. Fonda received AFI's Life Achievement Award in 1978. He is also the father of actor Peter Fonda and grandfather of actress Bridget Fonda. He was married to actress Margaret Sullavan (1931–33).

Though he appeared in well over 100 films, Henry Fonda played a villain only once, in Sergio Leone's *Once Upon a Time in the West* (1968).

AT LEFT: *Following in the footsteps of Sir Laurence Olivier and Orson Welles, Laurence Fishburne played* Othello *in the 1995 adaptation of Shakespeare's tragedy.*

Fonda, Jane (1937–) American actress. Daughter of Henry Fonda, she was one of the most respected and controversial actresses of the late 1960s and 70s, known for her left-wing activism, particularly against the Vietnam War. Her fiery performances include two that won best actress Academy Awards, in *Klute* (1971) and in *Coming Home* (1978). Other films include *Julia* (1977), *The China Syndrome* (1979), *On Golden Pond* (1981, co-starring her father), and *The Morning After* (1986). During the early and mid-1960s, she appeared primarily in comedies, including *Cat Ballou* (1965), *Barefoot in the Park* (1967), and the cult favorite *Barbarella* (1965), directed by then husband Roger Vadim. She left acting in 1989.

Fonda, Peter (1939–) American actor. After appearing on Broadway in the early 1960s, he turned to films, establishing himself and making countercultural statements in *The Wild Angels* (1966) and *Easy Rider* (1969), which he also produced and wrote. Later films include *Ulee's Gold* (1997). He is the father of actress Bridget Fonda. Actor Henry Fonda is his father; actress Jane Fonda is his sister.

Jane Fonda won an Academy Award for best actress for her performance as an aspiring actress/prostitute in Klute *(1971).*

Fontaine, Joan (1917–) Tokyo-born British actress. Born Joan de Beauvoir de Havilland. Sister of Olivia de Havilland, she originally portrayed trusting leads in films including *Rebecca* (1940), *Suspicion* (1941; best actress Academy Award), and *Jane Eyre* (1944). Later she performed in more worldly roles, notably in *Letter from an Unknown Woman* (1948) and *September Affair* (1951).

Ford, Glenn (1916–) Canadian-born actor. Born Gwyllyn Samuel Newton Ford. A no-nonsense Broadway-trained dramatic and comedy actor, he is best remembered for *Gilda* (1946), *A Stolen Life* (1946), and *The Blackboard Jungle* (1955). He displayed humor in *The Courtship of Eddie's Father* (1963) and *Pocketful of Miracles* (1961). Among his wives was actress Eleanor Powell.

Ford, Harrison (1942–) American actor. Open-faced and disarming, he first gained notice as a cocky driver in George Lucas's *American Graffiti* (1973) but became a pop-culture hero as Han Solo in Lucas's next film, *Star Wars* (1977), a role he reprised in *The Empire Strikes Back* (1980) and *Return of the Jedi* (1983). He won even greater fame and turned out another piece of pop iconography as the adventurous archaeologist Indiana Jones in *Raiders of the Lost Ark* (1981), *Indiana Jones and the Temple of Doom* (1984), and *Indiana Jones and the Last Crusade* (1989). He matured into a top action star in such films as *The Fugitive* (1993), *Clear and Present Danger* (1994), and *Air Force One* (1997). Other films include *Working Girl* (1988) and *What Lies Beneath* (2000). He combined the characteristics of action and romantic hero in the police drama *Witness* (1985), for which he received an Academy Award nomination for best actor. In 2000, Ford received AFI's Life Achievement Award.

Foster, Jodie (1962–) American actress and director. Born Alicia Christian Foster. A child actress in TV and film, she made a strong impression at age 13 as a young prostitute in *Taxi Driver* (1976). After several other films, she established herself as a forceful adult player in *The Accused* (1988), for which she won a best actress Academy Award. She received her second best actress Academy Award for *The Silence of the Lambs* (1991). Later films include *Contact* (1997) and *Panic Room* (2002). From the 1990s, she has devoted part of her career to directing; directorial credits include *Little Man Tate* (1991) and *Home for the Holidays* (1995).

Freeman, Morgan (1937–) American actor. A respected supporting player and lead from the 1970s, he typically portrays wise, caring characters in such films as *Driving Miss Daisy* (1989) and *The Shawshank Redemption* (1994), both of which gained him Academy Award nominations for best actor. Other films include *Unforgiven* (1992) and *Along Came a Spider* (2001).

G

Gable, Clark (1901–1960) American actor. Born William Clark Gable. The essence of virile self-deprecation and toughness, he was so popular with male and female fans that he was dubbed "the King." Stage-trained, he worked sporadically in silent films before making his name in a number of 1930s melodramas, including *A Free Soul* (1931), *Red Dust* (1932), and *Dancing Lady* (1933), and comedies, particularly as a reporter in *It Happened One Night* (1934), a performance that earned him an Academy Award for best actor. He went on to star in many top films of the mid- to late 1930s, including *Mutiny on the Bounty* (1935) and *San Francisco* (1936), and most memorably as Rhett Butler in *Gone with the Wind* (1939). He remained a leading man to the end of his life, with highlights including

Boom Town (1940), *Mogambo* (1953), and *The Misfits* (1961), and played opposite the greatest leading ladies of his day, including Norma Shearer, Jean Harlow, Joan Crawford, Vivien Leigh, Greer Garson, and Marilyn Monroe. He was married to actress Carole Lombard when she died in a plane crash in 1942. He served in the air force in World War II.

Garbo, Greta (1905–1990) Swedish-born American actress. Born Greta Louise Gustafsson. Star of silent and sound films known on and off screen for her lovely elusiveness and androgyny. Introduced in Sweden in films such as *Gösta Berling's Saga (The Legend of Gösta Berling)* (1924), she began her Hollywood career with *The Temptress* (1926). Many star vehicles followed, including *Love* (1927), *Anna Christie* (1930), *Camille* (1937), and *Ninotchka* (1939). She retired from the screen in 1941, following *Two-Faced Woman* (1941), and afterward lived largely in seclusion.

Gardner, Ava (1922–1990) American actress. Famed for her sultry beauty, she rose to national attention in *The Killers* (1946). She was then showcased in several features, including *Show Boat* (1951), *Mogambo* (1953), and *The Barefoot Contessa* (1954). In the 1950s, she was the dark-haired alternative to blonds Grace Kelly and Marilyn Monroe. Her private life was of equal public interest, including her marriages to Mickey Rooney, musician Artie Shaw, and Frank Sinatra.

Garfield, John (1913–1952) American actor. Born Julius Garfinkle. Trained in New York theater, he brought a vulnerable toughness to the screen, gaining an Academy Award nomination for best supporting actor for his first film, *Four Daughters* (1938). In the 1940s, he appeared in several dark dramas, including *Destination Tokyo* (1944), *The Postman Always Rings Twice* (1946), *Gentleman's Agreement* (1947), and *Body and Soul* (1947), for which he received an Academy Award nomination for best actor. His career ended with his blacklisting by the House Un-American Activities Committee. He died of a heart attack shortly afterward.

Garland, Judy (1922–1969) American actress and singer. Born Frances Gumm. The biggest Hollywood musical star of the 1940s began as part of a vaudeville sister act before being signed by MGM at age 16. She had already appeared in her first Andy Hardy film, *Love Finds Andy Hardy* (1938), when she became a major star with her performance as Dorothy in *The Wizard of Oz* (1939), for which she won a special juvenile Academy Award. In the 1940s, her musicals included *Easter Parade* (1948) and *Meet Me in St. Louis* (1944), directed by her future husband Vincente Minnelli. Drug problems (beginning with an early studio introduction to diet pills), marital discord, nervous breakdowns, and suicide attempts limited her subsequent roles. She was nominated for a best actress Academy Award for her performance in the musical remake of *A Star Is Born* (1954), and also received an Academy Award nomination for best supporting actress for *Judgment at Nuremberg* (1961). Offscreen, she offered stupendously successful engagements at the Palladium and the Palace Theater in New York. One of the handful of Hollywood stars known by their first names, she was publicly mourned after her 1969 death from a drug overdose. Her daughters are singer-actresses Liza Minnelli and Lorna Luft.

Garr, Teri (1949–) American actress. Memorable as the ditzy assistant to the title character in *Young Frankenstein* (1974), the blond comedian has also brightened such films as *Close Encounters of the Third Kind* (1977), *Tootsie* (1982), and *Michael* (1996). Usually cast in supporting roles in films, she has worked in television in both lead and supporting roles.

Garson, Greer (1908–1996) Irish-born American actress. Stage-trained in Britain, she established a stately, humorous screen presence beginning with *Goodbye, Mr. Chips* (1939). Other films include *Mrs. Miniver* (1942), for which she won a best actress Academy Award; *The Valley of Decision* (1945); and *Sunrise at Campobello* (1960). She was married to Richard Ney (1943–47), the actor who played her son in *Mrs. Miniver*.

Gaynor, Janet (1906–1984) American actress. Born Laura Gainor. A respected lead actress of the early sound era, the wide-eyed actress was the first recipient of the best actress Academy Award, for performances in *Sunrise* (1927), *Seventh Heaven* (1927), and *Street Angel* (1928). Other notable films before her retirement in the late 1930s were *State Fair* (1933) and *A Star Is Born* (1937). Her frequent co-star was Charles Farrell. In 1978, she won a special award from the Academy of Motion Picture Arts and Sciences for her contribution to film. Among her husbands was fashion designer Gilbert Adrian.

Gere, Richard (1949–) American actor. The stage-trained actor became a screen sex symbol with *Days of Heaven* (1978), *American Gigolo* (1980), and *An Officer and a Gentleman* (1982). Later roles have played off his cocky yet removed persona, including those in *Primal Fear* (1996); *Pretty Woman* (1990) and *Runaway Bride* (1999), both opposite Julia Roberts; and *Dr. T & the Women* (2000).

Gibson, Mel (1956–) Australian-American actor. Born in the United States but raised partly in Australia, he emerged as one of the top screen stars of Australian film in the early 1980s, and of American film by the end of the decade. He

When sullen screen star Greta Garbo appeared opposite Melvyn Douglas in Ernst Lubitsch's 1939 romantic comedy *Ninotchka,* studio publicity made the most of the unlikely casting, boldly proclaiming "Garbo laughs!"

projects a persona of unpredictability and warm masculinity in dramas and action movies. Australian successes include *Mad Max* (1979), *Gallipoli* (1981), *Mad Max 2/The Road Warrior* (1981), and *The Year of Living Dangerously* (1983). American films include *Lethal Weapon* (1987) and its sequels, *Hamlet* (1990), *The Patriot* (2000), and *What Women Want* (2000). An occasional director, he won Academy Awards for best director and best picture for *Braveheart* (1995), in which he also starred.

Sir John Gielgud starred in The Human Factor *(1979).*

Gielgud, Sir John (1904-2000) British-born actor in British and American films. An eminent Shakespearean stage actor, he appeared in silent and sound films in a variety of roles, but it was one of his latest and lightest that earned him an Academy Award for best supporting actor: Hobson the butler to Dudley Moore's title character in *Arthur* (1981). Other films include three versions of *Hamlet* (1939, UK, documentary; 1964; 1996, US/UK); *Julius Caesar* (1953); *Becket* (1964, UK); *Murder on the Orient Express* (1974, UK); and *Gandhi* (1982, UK).

Gish, Dorothy (1898–1968) American actress. The sister of Lillian Gish, she was a leading star of silent films, with particular command of light drama and comedy. Films include *Hearts of the World* (1918), *Orphans of the Storm* (1922), *The Country Flapper* (1922), and *Our Hearts Were Young and Gay* (1944).

In 1970, Lillian Gish received a special Oscar for achievement in a career that then spanned close to 60 years. Nearly two decades later, she would make her final screen appearance, in *The Whales of August* (1987).

Gish, Lillian (1896–1993) American actress. Known as the First Lady of the Silent Screen, she radiated fragility and strength in dozens of silent films. Most were directed by her mentor D.W. Griffith, including *Judith of Bethulia* (1914), *The Birth of a Nation* (1915), *Broken Blossoms* (1919), *True Heart Susie* (1919), *Way Down East* (1920), and *Orphans of the Storm* (1922). She made relatively few sound features, her last being *The Whales of August* (1987). She received a special Oscar in 1970 and the AFI Life Achievement Award in 1984. Her sister was silent actress Dorothy Gish.

Glover, Danny (1947–) American actor. Theater-trained, this powerful character lead made his film debut in *Escape from Alcatraz* (1979) and

became better known following Steven Spielberg's *The Color Purple* (1985). He was half of the crime-fighting team (with Mel Gibson) in *Lethal Weapon* (1987) and its sequels. Other films include *Witness* (1985) *To Sleep with Anger* (1991), and *Beloved* (1998).

Goddard, Paulette (1905–1990) American actress. Born Pauline Marion Levee (or Levy). A lead and supporting actress during the 1930s and 40s, she was famed for her sultry beauty and (in some films) worldly wit. Films include *Modern Times* (1936), *The Women* (1939), and *So Proudly We Hail* (1943). She was married to actor and director Charlie Chaplin, later to actor Burgess Meredith, and finally to writer Erich Maria Remarque.

Goldberg, Whoopi (1949–) American actress. Born Caryn Johnson. Stage-trained, inimitable character actress who made a major impression in her first film, *The Color Purple* (1985). She won a best supporting actress Academy Award for her performance as a medium in *Ghost* (1990). Other films include *The Long Walk Home* (1990); *The Player* (1992); *Sister Act* (1992), in which she played a lounge singer disguised as a nun; and *Rat Race* (2001). She has also appeared on television, notably in *Star Trek: The Next Generation*.

Goldblum, Jeff (1952–) American actor. An offbeat supporting and lead player, he is best known for playing weirdly intellectual types in such diverse films as *The Big Chill* (1982), *Jurassic Park* (1993), and *Cats and Dogs* (2001). He offered a poignant, horrific performance as the title role in *The Fly* (1986). He was married to his co-star in that film, Geena Davis.

Gould, Elliott (1938–) American actor. A leading man of the 1970s, he is best known for iconoclastic performances in such films as *M*A*S*H* (1970), *Bob & Carol & Ted & Alice* (1969), *The Touch* (1971, Sweden/US), and *The Long Goodbye* (1973). He later moved on to character roles, as in *Bugsy* (1991) and *Kicking and Screaming* (1995). He was married for a time to Barbra Streisand.

Grable, Betty (1916–1973) American actress. Born Elizabeth Ruth Grable. During World War II, she dominated popular imagery as a Hollywood pinup girl, with legs insured by Lloyds of London for $1 million. As an actress, she was a musical and comedic talent in films including *Down Argentine Way* (1940), *Moon over Miami* (1941), *The Beautiful Blonde from Bashful Bend* (1949), and *How to Marry a Millionaire* (1953).

Grahame, Gloria (1924–1981) American actress. Born Gloria Grahame Hallward. Best known as the tainted yet vulnerable type, the blond, sloe-eyed actress won a best supporting actress Academy Award for *The Bad and the Beautiful*

(1952). Other films include *It's a Wonderful Life* (1946), *In a Lonely Place* (1950), *The Greatest Show on Earth* (1952), and *Oklahoma!* (1955). Husbands included director Nicholas Ray (1948–52).

Granger, Stewart (1913–1993) British-born American actor. Born James Stewart. A top box-office draw in British films of the 1940s (e.g., *Secret Mission*, 1942; *Captain Boycott*, 1947), he was a consistent leading man in US films of the 1950s. These include *King Solomon's Mines* (1950) and *The Prisoner of Zenda* (1952). Among his wives was actress Jean Simmons (1950–60).

Grant, Cary (1904–1986) British actor. Born Archibald Alexander Leach. The epitome of wit and sophistication began as an acrobat, then turned to Broadway before entering film. He gained notice opposite Mae West in *She Done Him Wrong* (1933), then became a Hollywood leading man in several classic romantic comedies, including *The Awful Truth* (1937), *Bringing Up Baby* (1938), *Holiday* (1938), *His Girl Friday* (1940), and *The Philadelphia Story* (1941). At the same time, he displayed an aloof romanticism in dramas, including *Only Angels Have Wings* (1939), *None but the Lonely Heart* (1944), and *Notorious* (1946), which was directed by Alfred Hitchcock. Other Hitchcock films include *To Catch a Thief* (1955) and *North by Northwest* (1959). He was paired on screen with many leading actresses of his day, including Ingrid Bergman, Irene Dunne, Katharine Hepburn, Grace Kelly, Eva Marie Saint, and Loretta Young. He remains the icon of cool suavity on screen. Though he never won an acting Oscar, he was awarded a special Academy Award in 1969.

Grant, Hugh (1960–) British-born actor. Oxford-educated and stage-trained, he became known in part for playing idealistic, off-kilter romantic leads in films including *Four Weddings and a Funeral* (1994), *Notting Hill* (1999), and *Bridget Jones's Diary* (2001).

Greenstreet, Sydney (1879–1954) British-born American actor. Broadway-trained, the rotund, gravel-voiced actor became a popular supporting player during the 1940s, usually as an oily, suave villain or otherwise shady character. Films include his debut, *The Maltese Falcon* (1941), *Casablanca* (1942), and *Across the Pacific* (1942).

Griffith, Melanie (1957–) American actress. The daughter of actress Tippi Hedren, she has been a bubbly lead in comedy-dramas since *Something Wild* (1986) and the Cinderella story *Working Girl* (1988). Later films include *Paradise* (1991), and *Crazy in Alabama* (1999). Twice married to actor Don Johnson, she is now married to actor Antonio Banderas.

Guinness, Sir Alec (1914–2000) British actor in British and American films. One of Britain's top postwar stage and film talents, he excelled in comedy and drama, memorably in David Lean films such as *The Bridge on the River Kwai* (1957), for which he won a best actor Academy Award. Light comedic performances include multiple roles in *The Lavender Hill Mob* (1952); supporting performances include Obi-Wan Kenobi in *Star Wars* (1977) and two sequels. Other films include *Great Expectations* (1946), *Kind Hearts and Coronets* (1949), *The Man in the White Suit* (1951), *Lawrence of Arabia* (1962), and *Doctor Zhivago* (1965). He received a special Academy Award in 1980.

H

Hackman, Gene (1931–) American actor. He moved from Broadway to film to become one of the most accomplished lead and supporting actors in postwar Hollywood. After receiving an Academy Award nomination for best supporting actor for *Bonnie and Clyde* (1967), he appeared in several major dramas of the 1960s and 70s, including *I Never Sang for My Father* (1970), *The Conversation* (1974), and *The French Connection* (1971). He won a best actor Academy Award for the latter, which sealed his image as a craggy everyman. His role in *Unforgiven* (1992) garnered another Academy Award for best supporting actor. Other films include *Superman* (1978), *Mississippi Burning* (1988) and *The Royal Tennenbaums* (2001).

Hanks, Tom (1956–) American actor. After starring in the TV comedy *Bosom Buddies,* he became a major comedic film lead with his touching performance in *Splash* (1984). He followed with a funny, poignant turn in *Big* (1988), for which he received his first Academy Award nomination for best actor. With *Sleepless in Seattle* (1993) and subsequent films, he emerged as a major star, embodying the kind of everyman decency that was once associated with James Stewart. For *Philadelphia* (1993) and *Forrest Gump* (1994), he won best actor Academy Awards twice in a row. He was the lead character voice in *Toy Story* (1995) and was nominated for a best actor Academy Award for *The Green Mile* (1999). Other films include *Saving Private Ryan* (1998) and *Castaway* (2000). He is married to actress Rita Wilson. In 2002, Hanks received the AFI Lifetime Achievement Award.

Harlow, Jean (1911–1937) American actress. Born Harlean Carpenter. A platinum-blond sex symbol with comic flair, she starred in features throughout much of the 1930s, including *Platinum Blonde* (1931), *Red Dust* (1931), *Bombshell* (1933), *Dinner at Eight*

"Until I decide how a character walks, nothing happens."

—

Sir Alec Guinness, 1985

(1934), and *Libeled Lady* (1936). She died from a cerebral edema while filming *Saratoga* (1937).

Harrelson, Woody (1961–) American actor. A television star as the obtuse bartender Woody in *Cheers,* he became a film lead with *White Men Can't Jump* (1992) and followed with a variety of features, usually in the role of an iconoclast. Films include *Indecent Proposal* (1993), *Natural Born Killers* (1994), and *The People vs. Larry Flynt* (1996).

Harrison, Sir Rex (1908–1990) British-born actor. Born Reginald Carey Harrison. An alternately rakish and aloof leading man of the British and American stage, he is best remembered for his incarnation of Henry Higgins in the stage and screen versions of *My Fair Lady* (film, 1964). He won a best actor Academy Award for the performance. Other notable films include *Anna and the King of Siam* (1946), *The Ghost and Mrs. Muir* (1947), and *Cleopatra* (1963). Among his wives were actresses Lilli Palmer, Kay Kendall, and Rachel Roberts.

Hart, William S. (1865–1946) American actor. Broadway-trained but raised partly in the West, he became the leading western star of the pre–World War I years with realistic performances that defined the cowboy type. Notable films include *His Hour of Manhood* (1915) and *The Square Deal Man* (1917), which he also directed. By the time of his final film, *Tumbleweeds* (1925), his unaffected cowboy persona had been overtaken by more action-oriented heroes such as those portrayed by Tom Mix.

Hawn, Goldie (1945–) American actress. An unconventional beauty and deft comedian, she trained in TV comedy before entering film and winning a best actress Academy Award for her first role, in *Cactus Flower* (1969). She was nominated a second time for *Private Benjamin* (1980). Other films include *Swing Shift* (1984), *The First Wives Club* (1996), and *Town & Country* (2001). She lives with actor Kurt Russell and is the mother of actress Kate Hudson.

Hayes, Helen (1900–1993) American actress. Born Helen Hayes Brown. Known by the 1920s as the First Lady of American Theater, she appeared sporadically in silent films and began acting in Hollywood films at the beginning of the sound era. She won a best actress Academy Award for her first sound film, *The Sin of Madelon Claudet* (1931). Her films of the 1930s include *Arrowsmith* (1931) and *A Farewell to Arms* (1932). Although she made only a handful of films in the following decades, she won a best supporting actress Academy Award for *Airport* (1970).

Hayward, Susan (1918–1975) American actress. Born Edythe Marrener. Playing a tough woman on her own in a string of emotional dramas, the red-haired beauty was a top box-office draw in the 1950s. She won a best actress Academy Award for *I Want to Live!* (1958). Other films include *Smash-Up: The Story of a Woman* (1947), *My Foolish Heart* (1950), *With a Song in My Heart* (1952), and *I'll Cry Tomorrow* (1956). She left the movie business in 1964, except for occasional roles.

Hayworth, Rita (1918–1987) American actress. Born Margarita Carmen Cansino. Trained as a dancer and appearing in films as the dark-haired Rita Cansino from the 1930s, she changed her name and hair color and emerged as a luscious, red-haired femme fatale by the 1940s, becoming one of Hollywood's most glamorous stars. Films include *Only Angels Have Wings* (1939), *You Were Never Lovelier* (1942), *Cover Girl* (1944), and, most famously, *Gilda* (1946). During World War II, she (along with Betty Grable) was one of the top two servicemen's pinups. Later roles traded on her ripened beauty, including those in *Pal Joey* (1957) and *Separate Tables* (1958).

Henried, Paul (1908–1992) Trieste-born American actor. Born Paul George Julius von Henried. An aristocratic film lead during the 1930s and 40s, he is best known as the resistance leader and husband of Ingrid Bergman in *Casablanca* (1943) and as the suave partner to Bette Davis in *Now, Voyager* (1942). Other notable films include *Goodbye, Mr. Chips* (1939) and *Rope of Sand* (1949).

Hepburn, Audrey (1929–1993) Belgian-born American actress. Born Audrey Hepburn-Ruston. The slender, stage-trained actress became an immediate icon of natural yet cosmopolitan femininity upon her debut opposite Gregory Peck in *Roman Holiday* (1953). Winning a best actress Academy Award for the role, she followed it with several dramas, musicals, and comedies with Hollywood's leading directors and stars, including William Holden, Humphrey Bogart, Fred Astaire, Gary Cooper, and Cary Grant. Films include *Sabrina* (1954), *Funny Face* (1957), *Love in the Afternoon* (1957), *Breakfast at Tiffany's* (1961), *Charade* (1963), and *My Fair Lady* (1964). As a symbol of uncomplicated style, her influence on fashion remains strong. In later years, she devoted herself to charitable causes, particularly UNICEF.

Hepburn, Katharine (1907–) American actress. Commanding and patrician, she is the most respected dramatic actress of sound films and a twentieth-century icon of female independence. Over the course of six decades, she won four best actress Academy Awards, for *Morning Glory* (1933), *Guess Who's Coming to Dinner* (1967), *The Lion in Winter* (1968), and *On Golden Pond* (1981). She was nominated for eight other films: *Alice Adams* (1935), *The Philadelphia Story*

"No actress should be expected to be Audrey Hepburn. That dress by Mr. Givenchy has already been filled."

—

Billy Wilder, 1990s

(1940), *Woman of the Year* (1942), *The African Queen* (1951), *Summertime* (1955), *The Rainmaker* (1956), *Suddenly, Last Summer* (1959), and *Long Day's Journey into Night* (1962). Especially enjoyable are her screwball comic pairings with Cary Grant: *Holiday* (1938), *Bringing Up Baby* (1938), and *The Philadelphia Story.* She often played a spinster finding love, or a free-spirited woman clashing with society's constraints. *Woman of the Year* was the first of several films pairing her with Spencer Tracy, with whom she would have a decades-long relationship that ended with his death in 1967. Other Tracy-Hepburn films include *Adam's Rib* (1949) and *Pat and Mike* (1952).

Heston, Charlton (1923–) American actor. Born Charles Carter. Tall and golden-haired, with a booming voice, he was an icon of strength in religious epics during the 1950s and 60s, most memorably as Moses in *The Ten Commandments* (1956) and as the title character in *Ben-Hur* (1959), for which he received a best actor Academy Award. He was equally strong in domestic dramas of the time, notably in *The Greatest Show on Earth* (1952) and *Touch of Evil* (1958). Often cast in costume dramas, he has played major historical figures, including Andrew Jackson in *The Buccaneer* (1958), Michelangelo in *The Agony and the Ecstasy* (1965), and General Gordon in *Khartoum* (1966). He is also remembered as Taylor, the man beset by simians in *Planet of the Apes* (1968) and *Beneath the Planet of the Apes* (1970). He received the Jean Hersholt Humanitarian Award in 1977 and became known in later years for his support of right-wing causes.

Hoffman, Dustin (1937–) American actor. A struggling Off-Broadway player, the plain-looking Hoffman became an overnight star for a new generation with his performance as Benjamin Braddock in *The Graduate* (1967). He reinforced his position with his transformation into Ratso Rizzo in John Schlesinger's *Midnight Cowboy* (1969). He continued to be a top draw in unconventional roles, including *Little Big Man* (1970), *Lenny* (1974), and the domestic drama *Kramer vs. Kramer* (1979), for which he won his first of two best actor Academy Awards, after having been nominated several times. He triumphed as a forthright female in the comedy *Tootsie* (1982) and won his second best actor Academy Award for his performance as an autistic savant in *Rain Man* (1988). In the 1990s, notable films include *Wag the Dog* (1997). Hoffman received AFI's Life Achievement Award in 1999.

Holden, William (1918–1981) American actor. Born William Franklin Beedle, Jr. A top symbol of masculinity in the 1950s. From his early success in *Golden Boy* (1939), he developed into an antiheroic, virile star in the 1950s, in films such as *Sunset Boulevard* (1950); *Stalag 17*

(1953), for which he received a best actor Academy Award; *Picnic* (1956); and *The Bridge on the River Kwai* (1957). He exhibited a light comedic touch in *Born Yesterday* (1950) and *Sabrina* (1954). Later films include *The Wild Bunch* (1969) and *Network* (1976).

Holliday, Judy (1922–1965) American actress. Born Judith Tuvim. A Broadway star in the late 1940s for her warm, daffy turn in the play *Born Yesterday,* she brought the same qualities to the screen version in 1950, receiving an Academy Award for best actress. Other films include *Adam's Rib* (1949) and *Bells Are Ringing* (1960). She died of cancer.

Hope, Bob (1903–) British-born American comedian and actor. Born Leslie Townes Hope. Sweetly egotistical, he was one of the major comedic leads and top box-office stars of the 1940s. He is best known for his road comedies, so called for their theme of travel to exotic places, in which he co-starred with Bing Crosby and Dorothy Lamour; the series began with *Road to Singapore* (1940) and included *Road to Zanzibar* (1941), *Road to Morocco* (1942), and

Audrey Hepburn played the endearing but eccentric Holly Golightly in Breakfast at Tiffany's *(1961).*

Charlton Heston has played Marc Antony three times on screen: in both the 1950 and 1970 productions of *Julius Caesar* and in 1973's *Antony and Cleopatra.*

Road to Bali (1952). Other notable comedic incarnations include performances in *Monsieur Beaucaire* (1946), *My Favorite Brunette* (1947), *The Paleface* (1948), and *The Seven Little Foys* (1955). Hope continued making films into the 1980s. A longtime host of the Academy Awards telecast, he was honored with five special Oscars (1940, 1944, 1952, 1959, and 1965). He is also known for his wartime troop shows in World War II and subsequent conflicts and his television specials. In his film debut, *The Big Broadcast* of 1938, he first performed what would become his theme song, "Thanks for the Memories."

Hopkins, Sir Anthony (1937–) Welsh-born actor in British and American films. Trained on the London stage and Broadway, the meticulous, nuanced performer was a respected actor in films from the 1960s, including *The Lion in Winter* (1968), *A Bridge Too Far* (1977), and *84 Charing Cross Road* (1987). He did not become a household name until his performance as captive killer Hannibal Lecter in *The Silence of the Lambs* (1991), for which he won a best actor Academy Award; he reprised the role in *Hannibal* (2001). Other films include *Howards End* (1992), *The Remains of the Day* (1993), *Shadowlands* (1993), and *Nixon* (1995).

Hopkins, Miriam (1902–1972) American actress. Born Ellen Miriam Hopkins. A leading star of the 1930s, she is best known for her sprightly performances in films of varied genres from comedies to period pieces, including *Trouble in Paradise* (1932), *Barbary Coast* (1935), and *Becky Sharp* (1935). She returned to films in the 1950s and 60s, with credits including *Carrie* (1952) and *The Children's Hour* (1962). Among her husbands was director Anatole Litvak.

Hopper, Dennis (1936–) American actor, director, and screenwriter. A supporting actor in the 1950s (e.g., in *Rebel Without a Cause,* 1955; *Giant,* 1956), he became a counterculture icon in the 60s with *Easy Rider* (1969), which he also directed and cowrote. Considered a strong, unpredictable character actor, he has played varied roles, including those in *True Grit* (1969), *Apocalypse Now* (1979), *Blue Velvet* (1986), *Hoosiers* (1986), and *Speed* (1994).

Anthony Hopkins was hired to provide the voice of Laurence Olivier for the bath scene in the 1991 restoration of *Spartacus* (1960).

AT RIGHT: *Exotic-looking actress and singer Lena Horne was the first African-American performer signed to a long-term studio contract in Hollywood.*

Horne, Lena (1917–) American singer and actress. Launching her career as a chorus girl at the Cotton Club, she developed into an accomplished nightclub singer and was recruited by MGM. She became the first African-American actress to be fully glamorized and promoted by a major film studio. Among her films are *Stormy Weather* (1943), *Cabin in the Sky* (1943), and *Ziegfeld Follies* (1946). She received a Lifetime Achievement Award at the Kennedy Center in 1984.

Hoskins, Bob (1942–) British-born actor in British and American films. Everyman lead and supporting player. Films include *The Long Good Friday* (1980), *Mona Lisa* (1986, UK), *The Lonely Passion of Judith Hearne* (1987, UK),*Who Framed Roger Rabbit?* (1988, US), and *Enemy at the Gates* (2001, Germany/UK/Ireland/US).

Howard, Leslie (1893–1943) British-born actor in British and American films. Born Leslie Howard Stainer. The stage-trained, blond, blue-eyed actor appeared in silent films in Britain but became a star in the US during the 1930s in roles in films including *Of Human Bondage* (1934), *The Petrified Forest* (1936), *Intermezzo—A Love Story* (1939), and, most famously, *Gone with the Wind* (1939), in which he played Ashley Wilkes. He also produced and directed films in the 1940s. After returning to Britain at the outbreak of World War II, he was killed when his plane was attacked by Nazi fighters in 1943.

Hudson, Rock (1925–1985) American actor. Born Roy Harold Scherer, Jr. He represented engaging manliness in dramas and romantic comedies of the 1950s and 60s. Star-making films include Douglas Sirk's melodramas *Magnificent Obsession* (1954), *All That Heaven Allows* (1956), *Written on the Wind* (1957), and *The Tarnished Angels* (1958). He was nominated for a best actor Academy Award for *Giant* (1956). With *Pillow Talk* (1959), he began a lively series of romantic farces with Doris Day that also included *Lover Come Back* (1962) and *Send Me No Flowers* (1964). His death of complications due to AIDS helped draw attention to the disease.

Hunt, Helen (1963–) American actress. A television star who won Emmys for the sitcom *Mad About You,* she made occasional appearances in films from the 1980s (such as *Peggy Sue Got Married,* 1986). She became a movie star with *Twister* (1996) and *As Good as It Gets* (1997), for which she won a best actress Academy Award. Other films include *What Women Want* (2000).

Hunter, Holly (1958–) American actress. Stage-trained, she has balanced comedy and drama in such films as *Raising Arizona* (1987) and *Broadcast News* (1987). Her nuanced dramatic performances include her work in *The Piano* (1993, New Zealand/France), for which she received a best actress Academy Award.

Hurt, William (1950–) American actor. A star from his debut in *Altered States* (1980), he originally played offbeat romantic leads in such films as *Eyewitness* (1981), *Body Heat* (1981), and *The Accidental Tourist* (1988). He has also excelled as a character lead and ensemble player in such films as *The Big Chill* (1983), *Kiss of the Spider Woman* (1985, best actor Academy Award), and *A.I. Artificial Intelligence* (2001).

Huston, Anjelica (1952–) American actress. The daughter of director John Huston, and granddaughter of actor Walter Huston. Debuting in her father's *A Walk with Love and Death* (1968), she did not gain national notice until the 1980s, when she created tough characters in *Prizzi's Honor* (1985), for which she received a best supporting actress Academy Award; *The Dead* (1987); and *Enemies, a Love Story* (1989). Later films include *The Grifters* (1990) and *The Golden Bowl* (2001, UK).

Huston, Walter (1884–1950) American actor. Born Walter Houghston. The father of director John Huston and grandfather of actress Anjelica Huston, he was a Broadway regular when he debuted in film in 1929. During the 1930s, he played dramatic leads in dramas such as *Abraham Lincoln* (1930), *The Criminal Code* (1931), and *Dodsworth* (1936), while also taking on comedy-dramas, including *American Madness* (1932). For his performance in *The Treasure of the Sierra Madre* (1948), he received an Academy Award for best supporting actor.

Hutton, Betty (1921–) American actress and singer. Peppy blond musical and nonmusical lead of the 1940s and 50s. Films include *The Miracle of Morgan's Creek* (1944), *Red Hot and Blue* (1949), *Annie Get Your Gun* (1950), and *The Greatest Show on Earth* (1952).

I–J

Ingram, Rex (1895–1969) American actor. Trained as a medical doctor, he established a presence in mainstream films of the studio era despite the obstacles faced by African-American actors. Films include *The Green Pastures* (1936), *The Adventures of Huckleberry Finn* (1939), *The Thief of Bagdad* (1940), and *Cabin in the Sky* (1943). He continued his screen career into the 1960s, in such films as *Hurry Sundown* (1967). Not to be confused with Irish-born American director Rex Ingram (1892–1950).

Irons, Jeremy (1948–) British-born American actor. Trained on the London and New York stages, he became a romantic lead during the 1980s, in films including *The French Lieutenant's Woman* (1981) and *Betrayal* (1983). He achieved even greater fame as a character lead, usually in morally ambiguous roles, notably in *Dead Ringers* (1988) and *Reversal of Fortune* (1990), for which he won a best actor Academy Award. Other films include *The Lion King* (1994, voice only) and *Lolita* (1997, UK/France).

Jackson, Samuel L. (1949–) American actor. Lead and supporting player known for creating difficult, incendiary characters in such films as *Pulp Fiction* (1994) and *Jungle Fever* (1991). Other films include *Die Hard with a Vengeance* (1995), *Trees Lounge* (1996), *The Negotiator* (1998), and *Shaft* (2000).

Jannings, Emil (1884–1950) Swiss-born actor in German and American films. Born Theodor Friedrich Emil Janenz. Highly regarded silent actor in Germany and later in the US, he gained international notice for *Der Letzte Mann (The Last Laugh)* (1924) and *Varieté (Variety)* (1925) but is now best remembered as the unhappy paramour in *Der Blaue Engel (The Blue Angel)* (1930). At the first Academy Awards ceremony (for 1927–28), he was honored as best actor for *The Way of All Flesh* (1927) and *The Last Command* (1928).

Johnson, Ben (1918–1996) American actor and stuntman. He began his career as a rodeo performer and stunt rider in westerns and served as a stunt double for John Wayne, Gary Cooper, and James Stewart. He went on to become a supporting player in westerns and an occasional lead in such films as *Mighty Joe Young* (1949) and *Wagon Master* (1950). Other films include *Rio Grande* (1950), *Shane* (1953), and *The Wild Bunch* (1969). He won an Academy Award for best supporting actor for *The Last Picture Show* (1971).

Jolie, Angelina (1975–) American actress. Born Angelina Jolie Voight. The daughter of actor Jon Voight, she entered film in the 1990s and won a best supporting actress Academy Award for *Girl, Interrupted* (1999). Other films include *The Bone Collector* (1999), *Gone in 60 Seconds* (2000), and *Lara Croft: Tomb Raider* (2001). She is married to actor Billy Bob Thornton.

Jolson, Al (1886–1950) American singer and actor. Born Asa Yoelson. The leading US vaudeville singer and entertainer during the early 20th century, he introduced the sound film era with *The Jazz Singer* (1927), the first feature-length

> "I guess we got too busy shooting and chasing people to have time to stop and have some gratuitous sex."
>
> —
>
> *Samuel L. Jackson, on his relatively chaste portrayal of detective John Shaft.*

talkie, in which he proclaimed, "You ain't heard nothin' yet." His popularity declined as the sound era matured but was revived with the film biography *The Jolson Story* (1946), for which he dubbed songs. Other films include *The Singing Fool* (1928), *Hallelujah, I'm a Bum* (1933), and *Rose of Washington Square* (1939).

Jones, James Earl (1931–) American actor. Broadway-trained, the imposing actor has balanced stage and film careers since his first film performance in *Dr. Strangelove* (1964). In 1970, he reprised his stage role in *The Great White Hope,* and in 1977 he was the uncredited voice of Darth Vader in *Star Wars.* He also provided voice-overs for Darth Vader in *The Empire Strikes Back* (1980) and *Return of the Jedi* (1983) and has worked often in television. Later films include *Field of Dreams* (1989) and *The Lion King* (1994, voice).

Jones, Jennifer (1919–) American actress. Born Phyllis Isley. After being discovered by (and later married to) David O. Selznick, the dark-haired beauty became a leading actress of the 1940s and 50s, starring in high-profile films that began with *The Song of Bernadette* (1943), for which she won a best actress Academy Award. Other notable films include some of the top moneymakers of the era, such as *Since You Went Away* (1944), *Duel in the Sun* (1946), and *Love Is a Many-Splendored Thing* (1955).

Jones, Tommy Lee (1946–) American actor. This rough-looking, Broadway-trained actor was a respected supporting player (*Coal Miner's Daughter,* 1980) before emerging as a character star in *The Fugitive* (1993), for which he won a best supporting actor Academy Award. Subsequent films have drawn on his ability to mix gruff humor and intelligence, notably *Men in Black* (1997) and *Double Jeopardy* (1999).

K

Kahn, Madeline (1942–1999) American actress. Active on stage and TV, she was best known in film for her ribald performances in Mel Brooks comedies, including *Blazing Saddles* (1974), for which she received an Academy Award nomination for best supporting actress, and *Young Frankenstein* (1974). Other films include *What's Up, Doc?* (1972) and *Paper Moon* (1973). She won a Tony in 1992 for her performance in the play *The Sisters Rosenzweig.*

Karloff, Boris (1887–1969) British-born American actor. Born William Henry Pratt. After appearing in many silent films, the gentlemanly actor became the definitive movie monster as Dr.

Frankenstein's creation in *Frankenstein* (1931). Though he lent character support in some later films (*The Criminal Code,* 1931; *Scarface,* 1932), he primarily appeared as a monster or villain in horror films. Credits include *The Old Dark House* (1932), *The Mummy* (1932), *The Black Cat* (1934), *The Bride of Frankenstein* (1935), and *Targets* (1968), in which he played a horror film star.

Kaye, Danny (1913–1987) American actor. Born David Daniel Kaminski. Already famous on Broadway for his verbal dexterity, he became a favorite musical and comedy film star in the 1940s and 50s. His blithe everyman quality was showcased in such films as *The Secret Life of Walter Mitty* (1947), *Hans Christian Andersen* (1952), *White Christmas* (1954), and *The Court Jester* (1956). In 1954, he received a special Academy Award and, in 1991, the Jean Hersholt Humanitarian Award. He was an active spokesperson for UNICEF.

Keaton, Buster (1895–1966) American actor, director, producer, and screenwriter. Born Joseph Francis Keaton. A defining slapstick comedian of the silent era, he was an acrobat and vaudevillian before establishing his unsmiling "Stone Face" comic persona in silent shorts and, from the 1920s, in features. Alone or in collaboration, he directed, produced, and wrote many of his films, which included *Sherlock Jr.* (1924), *Seven Chances* (1925), *The General* (1927), and *Steamboat Bill, Jr.* (1928). He appeared widely in sound films during the 1930s, but to less acclaim. In the 1950s, he was rediscovered and praised for his occasional appearances in films, including *Sunset Boulevard* (1950), *Limelight* (1952), and *It's a Mad, Mad, Mad, Mad World* (1963). He was married to actress Natalie Talmadge (1921–33).

Keaton, Diane (1946–) American actress and director. Born Diane Hall. Broadway-trained, she became known as a fresh-faced urban neurotic in several comedies with then lover Woody Allen, including *Play It Again, Sam* (1972); *Annie Hall* (1977), for which she received a best actress Academy Award; and *Manhattan* (1979). Dramatic credits include the role of Kay Corleone in *The Godfather* (1972) and its sequels and parts in *Looking for Mr. Goodbar* (1977) and *Marvin's Room* (1996). Director credits include *Unstrung Heroes* (1995).

Keaton, Michael (1951–) American actor. Born Michael Douglas. Trained in television, he became a major star with intense, offbeat performances in the title roles of two Tim Burton films, *Beetlejuice* (1988) and *Batman* (1989). He followed with *Batman Returns* (1992), *Multiplicity* (1994), and a variety of quirky, sometimes disappointing films.

Keeler, Ruby (1909–1993) Canadian-born actress. A Broadway musical headliner, she came to Hollywood to join husband Al Jolson

> "I know crazy better now than I did years ago."
>
> —
>
> *Angelina Jolie on her early acting roles, 2001*

and soon became one of the top musical stars of the 1930s. She was famed for her wholesome characters in musicals concerning backstage life such as *42nd Street* (1933), *Footlight Parade* (1933), and *Gold Diggers of 1933* (1933). She and Jolson divorced in 1940 and she retired in the early 1940s, returning to Broadway in 1970 to appear in the revival of *No, No Nanette*.

Keitel, Harvey (1941–) American actor. A former Marine, the supporting and lead player established his hot-tempered, street-smart persona in several Martin Scorsese films, including *Mean Streets* (1973), *Alice Doesn't Live Here Anymore* (1975), and *Taxi Driver* (1976). Subsequent films as varied as *Thelma & Louise* (1991), *Bad Lieutenant* (1992), *The Piano* (1993, Australia/France), and *Pulp Fiction* (1994) have played off this volatility.

Kelly, Gene (1912–1996) American actor, dancer, choreographer, and director. Born Eugene Curran Kelly. He was the symbol of creative athleticism and virility in the film musical. He went to Hollywood after successes on Broadway, including the title role in the stage musical *Pal Joey,* and made his screen debut in *For Me and My Gal* (1942). He starred in and choreographed musicals including *Cover Girl* (1944), *Anchors Aweigh* (1945), and *An American in Paris* (1951) and codirected and starred in groundbreaking works with Stanley Donen: *On the Town* (1949), *Singin' in the Rain* (1952), and *It's Always Fair Weather* (1955). Dramatic roles include *Inherit the Wind* (1960). He won a special Academy Award in 1951, the Kennedy Center Lifetime Achievement Award in 1982, and the AFI Life Achievement Award in 1985.

Kelly, Grace (1928–1982) American actress. She was the 1950s icon of cool composure and hidden passions, sometimes offered with knowing humor. Following TV and Broadway experience, she gained acclaim for her performance in the film *High Noon* (1952), opposite Gary Cooper. Pairings with other top leading men followed, including those in three Alfred Hitchcock films: *Dial M for Murder* (1954), *Rear Window* (1954), and *To Catch a Thief* (1955). While on location shooting the last of these, she met husband Prince Rainier III of Monaco, whom she married in 1956, becoming Princess Grace of Monaco and retiring from films. She died in an auto accident, the circumstances of which remain unclear. She won a best actress Academy Award for *The Country Girl* (1954).

Kerr, Deborah (1921–) Scottish-born American actress. Trained in ballet and drama, she became known in the 1950s for her poise and subtle undertone of longing in such films as *Black Narcissus* (1947, UK), *King Solomon's Mines* (1950), *From Here to Eternity* (1953), *The King and I* (1956), *Tea and Sympathy*

(1956), *An Affair to Remember* (1957), and *Separate Tables* (1958). She was nominated six times for a best actress Academy Award. She retired from films in 1969.

Kidman, Nicole (1964–) American actress. Born in Hawaii but raised in Australia, she first appeared in Australian films (such as *Flirting,* 1990) but became better known for her beauty and range in such American and British films as *To Die For* (1995), *The Portrait of a Lady* (1996, UK), *Moulin Rouge* (2001), and *The Others* (2001). She was married to actor Tom Cruise (1990-2001), with whom she starred in *Far and Away* (1993) and *Eyes Wide Shut* (1999).

Kline, Kevin (1947–) American actor. The Tony Award–winning stage actor entered films in 1982 with the drama *Sophie's Choice.* He has since acted as a lead and supporting player in a wide range of films, displaying particularly high energy in comedies and comedy-dramas, including *The Big Chill* (1983); *A Fish Called Wanda* (1988, UK), for which he won a best supporting actor Academy Award; *Dave* (1993); *In and Out* (1997); and *Life as a House* (2001).

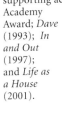

Classic beauty Grace Kelly made 11 movies in five years before retiring from films to marry Prince Rainier III of Monaco in 1956.

Michael Keaton portrayed cop Ray Nicolet in 1997's *Jackie Brown,* then played the same character again a year later—in a brief, uncredited turn—in *Out of Sight* (1998). Although the two films had different directors and were produced and released by opposing studios, both were based on crime novels by Elmore Leonard that featured Nicolet in a supporting role.

Becoming and Playing the Part

By Janet Leigh

Janet Leigh signed her first film contract with MGM Studios in 1947.

"CUT! PRINT! EXCELLENT!" Those are the words an actor longs to hear. They signify accomplishment, praise, and the much-needed boost in self-confidence.

Arriving at that point isn't always a smooth journey, however. Archaeologists search the innards of an excavation, hoping to find proof of a previous culture. Actors, when preparing for a role, go through a somewhat similar procedure. Only we dive into the abyss and create the clues that verify existence. In the construction process our own psyche inevitably melds with the invented person's. Thus, the actor reporting to work brings a predetermined complicated interpretation of the character to be portrayed.

Here come the dilemmas! As all the players gather with their director for the first rehearsal, each has their own personal agenda. But the director's canvas must show the whole design, not just individual segments, so the director has the unenviable task of channeling diverse goals into one common objective!

The actor is now faced with the challenge of clinging to his projected image while interacting with his likewise armed fellow thespians. Plus, he is expected to synchronize his concept with the director's vision. Not easy! But of course, that sense of adventure is why our profession is so inviting, why electricity tingles through our veins, why we give imagination full rein.

Every director has their own modus operandi, which the actor must adjust to. Mr. Hitchcock, for example, planned the camera setups for the entire production before shooting ever began. So rehearsals were never for positioning, they were for the crew to light and the performers to redo their thought processes to fit the camera's prearranged movements. If anyone required help to make the transition work for them, Mr. Hitchcock was ready and willing. But the camera remained absolute. I believe that this is a primary reason why Mr. Hitchcock's movies were always so taut and tight and suspenseful—there wasn't one superfluous frame of film in any of them.

Many actors ranted and raved, but the histrionics seldom were effective. If there was the rare exception where the star prevailed, I would wager that 1) Mr. Hitchcock managed to edit the scene very close to his original structuring, 2) the altered piece actually interfered with the desired pace of the finished project.

Orson Welles, on the other hand, could diagram setups prior to the time of shooting, as evidenced by his memorable three-minute-plus opening crane shot in *Touch of Evil*. But for the most part, I think he preferred the improvisational approach. A particular background could catch his eye, and he might say, "Let's do so-and-so sequence here!" Also, I believe he enjoyed giving his players a skeletal script and flushing out the characters in the rehearsals.

In these two instances, and naturally many more, the actor, after an exploratory discussion in which his views were aired, would be wise to follow the final decision of the person in command. Their track record speaks for itself, and like the old adage says, "If it ain't broke, don't fix it!"

Unfortunately we aren't always blessed with talented, qualified leaders. Very early in my career, I was laying the foundation for my next assignment with my mentor, Lillian Burns Sidney. She helped every contractee at Metro-Goldwyn-Mayer, from a neophyte like me to a pro à la Greer Garson. Miss Burns, incidentally, disliked the term "drama coach." She said no one can teach acting; one can only guide and show people the tools and how to use them.

I noticed she was more specific in this particular case. No explanation was offered but thankfully I was intuitive enough to not question but just pay special attention to the overall approach of my role and the intent of the picture in general that she presented. When I arrived on location and had the first encounter with the director, I realized the reason for her depth of information. The person was not able to lend any insight. He could, with the cinematographer, place the camera. But the execution of the scenes was up to the actors. Luckily, I had been briefed and the others were experienced so everything came out all right. At this point I suggest that if the actor finds himself in a cage with a mentally limited lion, protect yourself at all costs! But even then it must be done skillfully with great tact and diplomacy. Because we cannot ignore the fact that even this director is still the one who says, "Cut! Print!"

There are times when an actor can be self indulgent and stubborn, even when paired with a real professional. Alas, I was guilty of that—one time only!

The character was an alcoholic who had succumbed to her devils once again. It was quite an emotional sequence. After one take, the director, a very distinguished gentleman, quietly said, "That was absolutely wonderful. I need you to shorten it all a bit, otherwise I'll have to chop it up because of time, and I would like to have it without interruption, it's really that good!"

Charlton Heston and Janet Leigh starred in Touch of Evil *(1958).*

Miss Know-it-all heard him but didn't heed his words. I was too busy wallowing in the bottomless pit of this disease and emoting my little heart out. "If it's that effective," my overworking ego whispered, "they'll have to use it in total form!" Take two might have been even a mite longer!

He sighed. "Cut! Print one and two!" To his assistant, who was close by, he remarked, "We'll start with the first, cut to whoever is pounding at the door, and finish with the tail end of the second take."

I had committed the actor's cardinal sin. I had forgotten that not only is the director the one to say, "Cut! Print!", he also edits!

L

Ladd, Alan (1913–1964) American actor. Blank, cool dramatic actor particularly known for the title role in the western *Shane* (1953). After years of journeyman film roles, he emerged as a star in dark detective films, including *This Gun for Hire* (1942) and *The Glass Key* (1942).

Lamarr, Hedy (1913–2000) Austrian-born American actress. Born Hedwig Eva Maria Kiesler. The beautiful siren was active in European films—notably *Ecstasy* (1933, Czechoslovakia), in which she appeared nude—before coming to Hollywood in 1938. She appeared in dramas and melodramas, including *Boom Town* (1940), *White Cargo* (1942), and most memorably as Delilah in *Samson and Delilah* (1949), but never quite became a top-ranked star. Her autobiography is *Ecstasy and Me* (1966).

Lamour, Dorothy (1914–1996) American actress. Born Mary Leta Dorothy Slaton. Exotic and unflappable, she was a memorable foil to Bob Hope and Bing Crosby in the road comedies, so called for their theme of travel to distant places, including *Road to Zanzibar* (1941), *Road to Morocco* (1942), and *Road to Utopia* (1946). These and other roles, such as that of a South Seas islander in *The Hurricane* (1937), frequently required her to be garbed in a sarong. Other credits include *The Greatest Show on Earth* (1952) and *Donovan's Reef* (1963).

Lancaster, Burt (1913–1994) American actor and producer. Born Burton Stephen Lancaster. In his film leads, the one time circus performer was a vision of athletic, sometimes troubled, masculinity. He first gained fame for his lead role in *The Killers* (1946); subsequent films include *From Here to Eternity* (1953), *Elmer Gantry* (1960; best actor Academy Award), *Jim Thorpe—All American* (1951), *Come Back, Little Sheba* (1952), *The Rose Tattoo* (1955), *The Rainmaker* (1956), and *The Sweet Smell of Success* (1957). An early independent producer, he helped produce such films as *Marty* (1955). In the 1960s, he moved deeper into character roles in films including *Il Gattopardo (The Leopard)* (1963, Italy/France) and *The Swimmer* (1968). Later performances in films such as *Atlantic City* (1981) and *Field of Dreams* (1989) were elegaic and gentle.

Lange, Jessica (1949–) American actress. Trained in Paris theater, the lissome blond lead debuted as the giant ape's love interest in *King Kong* (1976) but soon became known as a serious, expressive actress in such dramas as *Frances* (1982), *Country* (1984), *Music Box* (1989), and *Titus* (1999). She won a best supporting actress

Academy Award for *Tootsie* (1982), which revealed her light comedic abilities, and a best actress Academy Award for *Blue Sky* (1994).

Lansbury, Angela (1925–) British-born American actress. From the 1940s, she was a respected character player, often cast as a jealous or cool schemer, as in *Samson and Delilah* (1949) and *The Manchurian Candidate* (1962). Other films include *Gaslight* (1944) and *The Picture of Dorian Gray* (1945). In later years, she became a warm, shrewd, maternal presence, as in her voice work for the animated *Beauty and the Beast* (1992) and her starring role in the TV series *Murder, She Wrote*. She was married to actor Richard Cromwell (1945–46).

LaRocque, Rod (1896–1969) American actor. Handsome silent-era screen idol who inspired great fan devotion. He appeared in many features of the 1910s and 20s, including *Ruggles of Red Gap* (1918), *The Ten Commandments* (1923), and *Our Modern Maidens* (1929). He continued working in sound film, ending his career with *Meet John Doe* (1941). He married silent-film vamp Vilma Banky in 1927.

Laughton, Charles (1899–1962) British-born American actor. Stage-trained, the portly actor became known for the range of characters he played and the joy he evoked in playing them. He worked mostly in American films from 1932. Notable performances include the title characters in *The Private Life of Henry VIII* (1933, UK), for which he won a best actor Academy Award, and *Ruggles of Red Gap* (1935); Javert in *Les Misérables* (1935); Captain Bligh in *Mutiny on the Bounty* (1935); Quasimodo in *The Hunchback of Notre Dame* (1939); and Sir Wilfrid in *Witness for the Prosecution* (1958). *The Night of the Hunter* (1955) was his only directorial effort. He was married to Elsa Lanchester.

Laurel, Stan (1890–1965) and **Hardy, Oliver** (1892–1957) American actors and comedians. Laurel was born Arthur Stanley Jefferson; Hardy was born Norvell Hardy. In over 100 silent and sound films, thin Laurel and rotund Hardy were one of film history's most popular and imitated comedy duos. Both acted separately in films from the 1910s, and by chance appeared together in *Lucky Dog* (1917), although not as a team. They emerged as the team Laurel and Hardy in 1927, when their joint films included *Duck Soup*, *Sailors Beware*, and *Putting Pants on Philip*. Dozens of other shorts and features followed, including the renowned *Sons of the Desert* (1933), *Babes in Toyland* (1934), and *The Flying Deuces* (1939). The team disbanded in 1945, but made one more film, *Atoll K/Utopia/ Robinson Crusoe-Land* (France/Italy), in 1950. Laurel was also a writer and producer and received a special Academy Award in 1960.

> "Why'd you use a midget? That man you used in the test, he's a midget."
>
> —
>
> *MGM studio executive on viewing the 5' 6" actor Alan Ladd's first screen test, circa 1940*

Lawrence, Florence (1886–1938) Canadian-born American actress. She is widely credited as the first American movie star to become known to the public by name, for the film *The Broken Oath* (1910), thus speeding the development of the star system. Her other films include *The Gypsy* (1911), *Elusive Isabel* (1916), and *The Johnstown Flood* (1926).

Lee, Bruce (1940–1973) American actor. Born Lee Yuen Kam. A child actor in Hong Kong and a young adult player on US television, as Kato in the series *The Green Hornet,* he emerged as an international cult cinema star with his string of Hong Kong martial-arts action films. Among them are *The Big Boss/Fists of Fury* (1971), *Enter the Dragon* (1973), and *Way of the Dragon/ Return of the Dragon* (1973). His son Brandon Lee (1965–1993) was also an action lead; like his father, Brandon suffered an untimely death.

Lee, Christopher (1922–) British actor. In numerous horror and action films, he has specialized in monsters and villains, particularly Count Dracula, but has also played some heroes, such as Sherlock Holmes. Many of his appearances were in modestly budgeted features produced by Britain's Hammer Films, often co-starring Peter Cushing. Among his films are *The Curse of Frankenstein* (1957), *Dracula/Horror of Dracula* (1958) and several sequels, *The Mummy* (1959), *The Hound of the Baskervilles* (1959), *The Three Musketeers* (1974), and *The Man with the Golden Gun* (1974).

Leigh, Janet (1927–) American actress. Born Jeanette Helen Morrison. A featured actress of films from the 1940s to 60s, she was noted for her on-screen combination of openness and knowing sexuality. She appeared in thrillers, including *Touch of Evil* (1958), *Psycho* (1960), and *The Manchurian Candidate* (1962), as well as light comedies and musicals, including *Bye Bye Birdie* (1963) and *Wives and Lovers* (1963). She was married to Tony Curtis (1951–62); actress Jamie Lee Curtis is their child.

Leigh, Vivien (1913–1967) Indian-born British actress in British and American films. Born Vivian Mary Hartley. In British films from 1934 (such as *Dark Journey,* 1937), she gained international celebrity as Scarlett O'Hara in the Hollywood blockbuster *Gone with the Wind* (1939), winning a best actress Academy Award. She further solidified her status as a serious actress playing Blanche Dubois in *A Streetcar Named Desire* (1951), for which she won a second Academy Award for best actress. Fragile health, including manic depression, limited her subsequent appearances, which included *Ship of Fools* (1965), her final film. From 1940 to 1960, she was married to Laurence Olivier, whom she met while filming *Fire over England* (1937, UK).

Lemmon, Jack (1925–2001) American actor. One of Hollywood's most respected character leads, he moved from the stage and TV in the 1940s and 50s to the screen. He refined his combination of earnestness and scheming in *Mister Roberts* (1955), for which he won a best supporting actor Academy Award. The next years brought his finest comedic performances, in *Some Like It Hot* (1959) and *The Apartment* (1960). Beginning with *The Days of Wine and Roses* (1962), he has been known for natural dramatic performances. He won a best actor Academy Award for *Save the Tiger* (1973). He often teamed with irascible Walter Matthau, notably in *The Fortune Cookie* (1966), *The Odd Couple* (1968), and *Grumpy Old Men* (1993). In 1988, Lemmon received the AFI Life Achievement Award.

Lewis, Jerry (1926–) and **Martin, Dean** (1917–1996) American actors and comedians. Lewis was born Joseph Levitch; Martin was born Dino Paul Crocetti. With Lewis as a zany comic and Martin as a singing straight man, the pair formed Martin & Lewis, the top film comedy duo of the 1950s. Beginning with *My Friend Irma* (1949), they appeared in more than 15 movies together, including *Sailor Beware* (1952), *Scared Stiff* (1953), and *The Caddy* (1953), generally with Lewis as a manic child-man and Martin as a suave straight man. After the pair disbanded in 1956, Lewis starred solo in a series of commercially successful movies, many of which he directed, produced, and/or wrote. Among these are *Cinderfella* (1960), *The Bellboy* (1960), and *The Nutty Professor* (1963). From the 1980s, Lewis has appeared sporadically in films, notably in *The King of Comedy* (1983). His charity work includes the *Muscular Dystrophy Telethon,* an annual television event he has hosted since the 1960s. Martin went on to solo acting and singing after the breakup of Martin & Lewis. His solo film credits include *Rio Bravo* (1959), *Toys in the Attic* (1963), *Robin and the 7 Hoods* (1964), and *The Silencers* (1966).

In addition to multiple turns as Sherlock Holmes and Fu Manchu, veteran actor Christopher Lee has portrayed Count Dracula in films including *The Horror of Dracula* (1958), *Dracula: Prince of Darkness* (1966), *Dracula Has Risen from the Grave* (1968), *Taste the Blood of Dracula* (1970), *Dracula A.D. 1972* (1972), *Satanic Rites of Dracula* (1974), and *Dracula and Son* (1977), for a grand total of 12 times. This figure, it should be noted, does not include the numerous times Lee has played vampires not named Dracula.

The legendary comedy team of straight man Dean Martin and goofball Jerry Lewis made more than 15 films between 1949 and 1956.

Lithgow, John (1946–) American actor. The Tony Award–winning actor (for *The Changing Room*, 1973) is known for intelligent supporting performances in such films as *The World According to Garp* (1982) and *Terms of Endearment* (1983), both of which garnered him Academy Award nominations for best supporting actor. He also offered a memorable turn in *Twilight Zone: The Movie* (1983) and has won a wide audience with the TV series *Third Rock from the Sun*.

Lloyd, Harold (1893–1971) American actor and comedian. The pioneering silent comedian combined an average-seeming countenance and then unparalleled stunts to become one of cinema's most popular comic talents. Among his dozens of silent shorts and features, some of the best known are *A Sailor-Made Man* (1921), *Never Weaken* (1921), *Safety Last* (1923), *Why Worry?* (1923), and *The Freshman* (1925). His sound films included *The Milky Way* (1936) and *Mad Wednesday/The Sins of Harold Diddlebock* (1947). He won a special Oscar for his comedic contributions in 1952.

Lloyd, Norman (1914–) American actor and producer. The stage actor was a member of the original company (1937–1938) of the Mercury Theatre before making his debut on screen as a villain in *Saboteur* (1942). His memorable portrayal led to other notable character roles in films including *Spellbound* (1945), *Limelight* (1952), and *The Age of Innocence* (1993). On television, he had a recurring role in the series *St. Elsewhere*.

Lombard, Carole (1908–1942) American actress. Born Jane Alice Peters. In silent and particularly in sound films, she displayed an easy glamour and a light comedic touch. Notable performances include those in *Twentieth Century* (1934), *My Man Godfrey* (1936), *Nothing Sacred* (1937), and her last film, *To Be or Not to Be* (1942). She was killed in a plane crash while on a trip to sell war bonds. Her first husband was actor William Powell; her second, actor Clark Gable.

Lopez, Jennifer (1970–) American actress and singer. Sultry actress who came to prominence playing the title role of the slain Tejano singer in *Selena* (1997). Other films include *My Family (Mi Familia)* (1995), *Out of Sight* (1998), and *The Wedding Planner* (2001). She is also a pop recording artist.

Loren, Sophia (1934–) Italian-born actress in international film. Born Sofia Scicolone. Rising from wartime poverty during the 1940s, the earthy, voluptuous young woman became one of the major postwar images of international beauty. Starring in both American and Continental productions, in both dramatic and common roles, she was memorable in *La Ciociara (Two Women)* (1961, Italy), for which she won a best actress Academy Award; *El Cid* (1961); *Ieri, oggi, domani (Yesterday, Today and Tomorrow)* (1963, Italy); and *Matrimonio all'Italiana (Marriage Italian Style)* (1964, Italy). She returned to Hollywood in the 1990s, for the comedy *Grumpier Old Men* (1995).

Lorre, Peter (1904–1964) Hungarian-born American actor. Born Laszlo Löwenstein. Character actor known for alternately melancholy and menacing performances in such German films as *M* (1931) and, from 1935, US films including *Mad Love* (1935), *Crime and Punishment* (1935), and particularly *The Maltese Falcon* (1941) and *Casablanca* (1942). Comedies include *Arsenic and Old Lace* (1946) and *My Favorite Brunette* (1947).

Loy, Myrna (1905–1993) American actress. Born Myrna Adele Williams. A leading player in silent and sound films, she is best known for her amused, sophisticated performances as Nora Charles opposite William Powell's Nick Charles in *The Thin Man* (1934) and its sequels. In silent films from the 1920s, including *Don Juan* (1926) and *So This Is Paris* (1926), she was often cast as the mysterious type, sometimes in Oriental roles. After World War II, she specialized in domestic comedies and dramas, including *The Best Years of Our Lives* (1946), *The Bachelor and the Bobby-Soxer* (1947), *Mr. Blandings Builds His Dream House* (1948), and *Cheaper by the Dozen* (1950). She continued in films until 1980. In 1998, she was honored by the Kennedy Center for the Performing Arts and, in 1991, she received a special Academy Award.

Lugosi, Bela (1882–1956) Hungarian-born American actor. Born Béla Blasko. From his definitive title performance in *Dracula* (1931), he was a leading screen icon of Gothic horror. He trained in Hungary and appeared on Broadway (as Dracula) before coming to Hollywood. Notable films made in Hungary include *Casanova* (1918) and *Lulu* (1918). Hollywood films include classics such as *Island of Lost Souls* (1932), *The Black Cat* (1934), *Ninotchka* (1939), and *The Wolf Man* (1941), plus low-quality features such as *Plan 9 from Outer Space* (1959).

Lupino, Ida (1918–1995) British-born American actress, director, and screenwriter. The daughter of song-and-dance man Stanley Lupino, she was known as a serious actress from the 1930s to 50s, usually portraying tough-born women. Notable film performances include those in *The Light That Failed* (1940), *They Drive by Night* (1940), *High Sierra* (1941), and *The Big Knife* (1955). As a director (a rarity for women

Jennifer Lopez became the highest-paid Latina actress in Hollywood history when she collected $1 million to star in *Selena* (1997).

Sophia Loren achieved success in both Italian and American cinema.

in midcentury Hollywood), she was known for social dramas, including *Never Fear* (1950), *The Hitch-Hiker* (1953), and *The Bigamist* (1953). Among her husbands was actor Howard Duff.

M

McCrea, Joel (1905–1990) American actor. The handsome, rugged actor was the epitome of reliability in silent and sound leads, particularly in westerns, such as *Ramrod* (1947), and comedies, such as *The Palm Beach Story* (1942). He was also memorable in Alfred Hitchcock's *Foreign Correspondent* (1940). Films include *Union Pacific* (1939), *The Primrose Path* (1940), *Sullivan's Travels* (1941), *The More the Merrier* (1943), and *Ride the High Country* (1962). He was married to actress Frances Dee.

McDaniel, Hattie (1895–1952) American actress and singer. A band vocalist, she became the first African-American actor to win an Academy Award, which she received for her supporting performance in *Gone with the Wind* (1939). Other films include *Imitation of Life* (1934), *Show Boat* (1936), *In This Our Life* (1942), and *Since You Went Away* (1944).

MacDonald, Jeanette (1901–1965) American actress and singer. In the 1930s, the red-haired soprano teamed with Nelson Eddy to become the most popular singing couple in history. Known as America's Sweethearts, they appeared in such films as *Naughty Marietta* (1935), *Rose Marie* (1936), *Maytime* (1937), *The Firefly* (1937), and *Sweethearts* (1938). Playing opposite Maurice Chevalier, she displayed lightness in lavish, sly musicals, including *The Love Parade* (1927) and *One Hour with You* (1932). She was married to silent film actor Gene Raymond.

McDormand, Frances (1958–) American actress. Stage-trained, she is known for practical, idiosyncratic characters. Films include *Mississippi Burning* (1988); *Fargo* (1996), for which she won a best actress Academy Award; *Almost Famous* (2000); and *The Man Who Wasn't There* (2001). She is married to director Joel Coen.

McLaglen, Victor (1886–1959) British-born American actor. Former boxer and Boer War soldier, he became a noted silent and sound character actor, winning a best actor Academy Award for his title role performance in John Ford's *The Informer* (1935). He appeared frequently in Ford films, including *She Wore a Yellow Ribbon* (1949) and *The Quiet Man* (1952). Other films include *Gunga Din* (1939) and *Klondike Annie* (1936).

MacLaine, Shirley (1934–) American actress, singer, and dancer. Born Shirley MacLean Beaty. The red-haired star of the 1950s, 60s, and onward got her big break when, as a Broadway understudy, she replaced an ailing actress (Carol Haney) in the stage musical *The Pajama Game* (1954). She was appealing in musicals, comedies, and dramas, including *Can-Can* (1957) and *Sweet Charity* (1969), and was nominated for a best actress Academy Award for *Some Came Running* (1959), *The Apartment* (1960), and *Irma La Douce* (1963). Later film roles have been character leads, such as in *Terms of Endearment* (1983), for which she won a best actress Academy Award. She is the sister of actor Warren Beatty. The first of her many memoirs and books, some on spiritual topics, is *Don't Fall off the Mountain* (1970).

McQueen, Butterfly (1911–1995) American actress. Born Thelma McQueen. In theater from childhood, she established her screen persona with her debut as a high-strung slave in *Gone with the Wind* (1939). Other films include *The Women* (1939), *Cabin in the Sky* (1943), and *Mildred Pierce* (1945). She appeared sporadically in film and television from the 1950s onward.

McQueen, Steve (1930–1980) American actor. Born Terrence Steve McQueen. The epitome of taciturn coolness and nonchalant sexuality, he was a major box-office star in the 1960s and 70s. Memorable films include *The Great Escape* (1963), *Bullitt* (1968), *The Thomas Crown Affair* (1968), and *Papillon* (1973). He was nominated for a best actor Academy Award for his performance in the war drama *The Sand Pebbles* (1966). Among his wives was actress Ali MacGraw.

Madonna (1958–) American singer and actress. Born Madonna Louise Veronica Ciccone. A pop star from the early 1980s, she has appeared sporadically in films that include *Desperately Seeking Susan* (1985), *Dick Tracy* (1990), *A League of Their Own* (1992), and *Evita* (1996), in which she played the title role.

Malden, Karl (1913–) American actor. Born Mladen Sekulovich. A major postwar character actor, he won an Academy Award for best supporting actor for reprising his Broadway performance as Mitch in *A Streetcar Named Desire* (1951). He followed with another Academy Award–nominated supporting performance in *On the Waterfront* (1954). Other notable films include *Baby Doll* (1956), *Birdman of Alcatraz* (1962), and *Patton* (1970). He was president of the Academy of Motion Picture Arts and Sciences (1989–93).

Steve McQueen's portrayal of a POW who attempts a daring escape in The Great Escape *(1963) cemented his star status.*

Malkovich, John (1953–) American actor. Trained in the theater in Chicago, where he was a cofounder of the Steppenwolf Ensemble, and in New York, he entered film in 1984 and became a lead and supporting actor, often playing seductive characters of ill-repute. Films include *Places in the Heart* (1984), *Dangerous Liaisons* (1988), *The Sheltering Sky* (1990), *In the Line of Fire* (1993), and *The Portrait of a Lady* (1996, UK). He turned in a self-mocking performance as himself in the arch comedy-fantasy *Being John Malkovich* (1999).

Lee Marvin commanded a group of World War II military prisoners in a mission against the Nazis in The Dirty Dozen *(1967).*

Mansfield, Jayne (1933–1967) American actress. Born Vera Jayne Palmer. The beauty-contest veteran and Broadway actress became a Marilyn Monroe–like sex symbol with dizzy performances in the comedies *The Girl Can't Help It* (1956) and *Will Success Spoil Rock Hunter?* (1957). In later years, she worked largely in European films. She died in a car accident.

March, Fredric (1897–1975) American actor. Born Ernest Frederick McIntyre Bickel. The Broadway-trained leading man was notable for his range and understated lead performances, including those in *Dr. Jekyll and Mr. Hyde* (1932) and *The Best Years of Our Lives* (1946), both of which earned him a best actor Academy Award. Other films include *A Star Is Born* (1937), *Nothing Sacred* (1937), *The Buccaneer* (1938), *Inherit the Wind* (1960), and *Seven Days in May* (1964).

Martin, Steve (1945–) American actor, comedian, screenwriter, and director. Trained in television from the 1960s, he became a box-office draw with *The Jerk* (1979). His next film was the dark Depression-era musical *Pennies from Heaven* (1981). A series of humane, off-the-wall comedies followed, many scripted or coscripted by him, including *The Lonely Guy* (1984), *All of Me* (1984), and *Roxanne* (1987). He continued as a major comedic lead in *Father of the Bride* (1991), *Housesitter* (1992), *Bowfinger* (1999), and other films. He is also a playwright, novelist, and essayist.

Marvin, Lee (1924–1987) American actor. Trained on the stage, he first became known in film dramas and westerns as a tough, tall heavy, notably in *Bad Day at Black Rock* (1955), *Seven Men from Now* (1956), and *The Man Who Shot Liberty Valance* (1962). He later distinguished himself in comedic and action roles, including those in *The Dirty Dozen* (1967) and *Cat Ballou* (1965), for which he won a best actor Academy Award.

Marx Brothers American comic actors. Chico Marx (born Leonard, 1886–1961); Harpo Marx (born Adolph, known as Arthur, 1888–1964); Groucho Marx (born Julius Henry, 1890–1977); Zeppo Marx (born Herbert, 1901–1979). A fifth brother, Gummo Marx (born Milton, 1893–1977), performed on stage with his brothers but left the act before 1920 and did not appear in their films. The most famous comedic family in film history headlined in vaudeville and on Broadway before appearing in a screen version of their stage hit *The Cocoanuts* (1929). The film established their screen characters: Groucho the mustached, wisecracking schemer; Chico the Italian-accented vagabond; Harpo the mute breeder of chaos; and Zeppo the straight man. They followed with a string of enduring acts of comic anarchy: *Animal Crackers* (1930), *Monkey Business* (1931), *Horse Feathers* (1932), and *Duck Soup* (1933), Zeppo's last film. The remaining brothers then changed studios from Paramount to MGM, where, after *A Night at the Opera* (1935) and *A Day at the Races* (1937), their films diminished in quality. Their final film together was *Love Happy* (1949), with a young Marilyn Monroe. Margaret Dumont (1889–1965) was Groucho's frequent comic foil. Films with Groucho alone include *Copacabana* (1947) and *Will Success Spoil Rock Hunter?* (1957). Films with Harpo alone include *Stage Door Canteen* (1943). Groucho went on to enjoy a successful solo career on television and in print.

Masina, Giulietta (1920–1994) Italian-born actress. Born Giulia Anna Masina. Considered by husband-director Federico Fellini a great influence on his work, she evoked a mixture of comedy and tragedy in many of his films, including *La Strada* (1954), *Le Notti di Cabiria (The Nights of Cabiria/Cabiria)* (1956), and *Giulietta degli Spiriti (Juliet of the Spirits)* (1965).

Mason, James (1901–1984) British actor in British and American films. In films from the 1930s, he was a suave villain and leading man in both US and UK productions. He is best known as the tortured actor Norman Maine in *A Star Is Born* (1954). Other films include *The Seventh Veil* (1945, UK), *Caught* (1949), *Julius Caesar* (1953), *North by Northwest* (1959), and *Lolita* (1962, UK/US), in which he played the nymphet-worshipping teacher Humbert Humbert.

Mastroianni, Marcello (1923–1996) Italian actor. Dark and worldly, he was a major postwar romantic lead in Italian cinema. Stage-trained under Luchino Visconti, he appeared in such Italian films as *Le Notte Bianche (White Nights)* (1957), *I Soliti Ignoti (The Big Deal in Madonna Street)* (1958), *Divorce—Italian Style* (1961), *Ieri, oggi, domani (Yesterday, Today, and Tomorrow)* (1963), and *Marriage Italian Style* (1964). He was frequently paired with Sophia Loren; in addition, he often appeared in Fellini films, including *La Dolce Vita* (1960), *Otto e Mezzo (8 ½)* (1963), *Ginger and Fred* (1985), and *City of Women* (1980).

Matthau, Walter (1920–2000) American actor. Born Walter Matuschanskayasky. This craggy-faced, gravel-voiced Broadway actor became a comedic lead in the 1960s. He was often paired with Jack Lemmon, as in *The Fortune Cookie* (1966), for which he won a best supporting actor Academy Award, and *The Odd Couple* (1968), in which he re-created his Broadway role. He continued in film comedies and dramas through the 1990s; credits include *Cactus Flower* (1969), *Kotch* (1971), *Plaza Suite* (1971), *The Sunshine Boys* (1975), and *Grumpy Old Men* (1993).

Mature, Victor (1915–1999) American actor. A beautifully sculpted dramatic actor of the 1940s and 50s, he was a national sensation as Samson in *Samson and Delilah* (1949). Other movies drew on his sword-and-sandals appeal, including *The Robe* (1953) and *Demetrius and the Gladiator* (1954), while others played on his mournfulness (*My Darling Clementine*, 1946) and noir abilities (*Kiss of Death*, 1947).

Midler, Bette (1945–) American singer and actress. Trained on Broadway and through performances in the New York City gay baths, she moved into film with the musical *The Rose* (1979) and went on to specialize in broad comedies such as *Down and Out in Beverly Hills* (1986), *Ruthless People* (1986), and *The First Wives Club* (1996). Other films include *Beaches* (1988) and *For the Boys* (1992).

Mifune, Toshiro (1920–1997) Chinese-born Japanese actor in Japanese and international films. Towering star of postwar Japanese films, most of them character-infused action dramas. Many of his films are classics of Japanese cinema, particularly those directed by Akira Kurosawa, such as *Rashomon* (1950), *The Seven Samurai* (1954), *Throne of Blood* (1957), *The Lower Depths* (1957), and *Yojimbo* (1961). He continued making films into the 1990s, with titles including the American films *Hell in the Pacific* (1975) and *1941* (1979).

Milland, Ray (1907–1986) Welsh-born American actor. Born Reginald Truscott-Jones. A suave dramatic leading man, he gained the highest accolades when he played somewhat against type, most memorably as an alcoholic writer in *The Lost Weekend* (1945), for which he won a best actor Academy Award. Other notable films include *Beau Geste* (1939), *Ministry of Fear* (1944), *The Big Clock* (1948), and *Dial M for Murder* (1954).

Minnelli, Liza (1946–) American singer and actress. The daughter of Judy Garland and director Vincente Minnelli, she is a successful stage and concert performer, best known on screen for a mix of showiness and sensitivity, notably displayed in her performance as Sally Bowles in *Cabaret* (1972), which earned an Academy Award for best actress. She was nominated for another best actress Academy Award for her performance as a troubled woman in *The Sterile Cuckoo* (1969) and proved a successful comedian in the comedy-drama *Arthur* (1981). She debuted in film as a young child in *In the Good Old Summertime* (1949).

Miranda, Carmen (1909–1955) Portuguese-born American actress. Born Maria do Carmo Miranda da Cunha; raised in Brazil. Often dressed in fruity headgear, the "Brazilian Bombshell" brought exotic looks, good humor, and stage-trained energy to Brazilian films of the 1930s, such as *A Voz do Carnaval* (1933), and US musicals of the 1940s. Among the latter were *Down Argentine Way* (1940), *The Gang's All Here* (1943), and *Copacabana* (1947). She died young, of a heart attack.

Mitchell, Thomas (1892–1962) American actor. An established stage actor, he became one of the screen's most recognizable character actors during the 1930s and beyond, appearing in dozens of films and winning an Academy Award for best supporting actor as the redeemed drunken doctor in *Stagecoach* (1939). Other memorable films include three others from 1939—*Gone with the Wind*, *Only Angels Have Wings*, and *Mr. Smith Goes to Washington*—as well as *Our Town* (1940), *It's a Wonderful Life* (1946), and *High Noon* (1952).

Mitchum, Robert (1917–1999) American actor. Cleft-chinned and heavy-lidded, he was the Hollywood epitome of insolence and disregard for authority in both heroic and villainous roles. His films include *Out of the Past* (1947), *River of No Return* (1954), *Night of the Hunter*

Liza Minnelli, daughter of actress Judy Garland and director Vincente Minelli, starred in Cabaret *(1972).*

"Don't worry, darling. This will be a very big hit, no matter what. And you can get a lot of maids in the morning."

—

Walter Matthau to his wife, Carol, on the eve of the opening-night performance of The Odd Couple *on Broadway, 1965*

(1955), and *Farewell, My Lovely* (1975). He was also adept at tender dramas and comedy-dramas, including *Rachel and the Stranger* (1948) and *Heaven Knows, Mr. Allison* (1957). He came to prominence in *The Story of G.I. Joe* (1944), for which he was nominated for a best supporting actor Academy Award, and continued making films into the 1990s.

Mix, Tom (1880–1940) American actor. Born Thomas Mix. The preeminent western silent star of the late 1910s and 20s, he replaced the somberness of cowboy star William S. Hart with an exuberance and showmanship that influenced later western actors. Among his films are *The Wilderness Trail* (1919), *Riders of the Purple Sage* (1925), and *Lone Star Ranger* (1923). His horse Tony had an avid following as well. Mix left film in 1934, appearing instead in the circus and on radio.

Monroe, Marilyn (1926–1962) American actress. Born Norma Jean Mortenson. Hollywood sexual icon who offered a much imitated blend of platinum sensuality and innocence. Her films include dramas, such as *All About Eve* (1950), *The Asphalt Jungle* (1950), and *River of No Return* (1954), and comedies and musicals, such as *Gentlemen Prefer Blondes* (1953), *The Seven Year Itch* (1955), and *Some Like It Hot* (1959). Her private life generated huge interest, given that her husbands included ballplayer Joe DiMaggio and playwright Arthur Miller. She died of an apparent drug overdose; her cult of fans has only grown since.

Montand, Yves (1921–1991) Italian-born actor and singer in French and international films. Born Ito Livi. One of the most beloved of French celebrities, he was an established music-hall singer when he made his name as an actor in *La Salaire de la Peur (The Wages of Fear)* (1953). He then played in a variety of international films, including *Let's Make Love* (1960), *Z* (1969), *Etat de Siège (State of Siege)* (1972), *Jean de Florette* (1986), and *Manon des Sources (Manon of the Spring)* (1986). He was married to actress Simone Signoret from 1951 until her death in 1985.

Montgomery, Robert (1904–1981) American actor and director. Born Henry Montgomery, Jr. Stage-trained, he became a leading light actor during the 1930s and 40s who also distinguished himself in more somber roles. Among his works are *The Big House* (1930), *Night Must Fall* (1937), and *Here Comes Mr. Jordan* (1941). A member of the US Naval Reserve, he participated in the D day invasion. After World War II, he concentrated on directing, television performances, and Republican politics.

Monty Python Collective name for six comic actors and writers who, in the 1960s and 70s, created and starred in the British television series *Monty Python's Flying Circus*, and made several feature films before disbanding in the early 1980s. Their absurdist, richly allusive humor still enjoys cult status. The group's members were Graham Chapman (1941–1989), John Cleese (1939–), Terry Gilliam (1940–, the only American-born member), Eric Idle (1943–), Terry Jones (1942–), and Michael Palin (1943–). The six went on to solo television and film

Monty Python and the Holy Grail *(1974), starring Graham Chapman, John Cleese, Eric Idle, Terry Jones, Terry Gilliam, and Michael Palin, spoofed the legend of King Arthur and the Knights of the Round Table.*

careers, either behind or in front of the lens. The group's features, all British, include *Monty Python and the Holy Grail* (1974, directed by Terry Gilliam), *Monty Python's Life of Brian* (1979, directed by Terry Jones), and *Monty Python's the Meaning of Life* (1983, directed by Terry Jones). Separately, Gilliam is the director-cowriter of such films as *Brazil* (1985) and *12 Monkeys* (1995); Cleese the actor-writer of such films as *A Fish Called Wanda* (1988, UK); Idle an actor in such films as *Nuns on the Run* (1990); Jones the director-writer-actor of such films as *Erik the Viking* (1989); Palin an actor in such films as *A Private Function* (1984); and Chapman, before his death, the actor-cowriter of *Yellowbeard* (1983).

Moore, Demi (1963–) American actress. Born Demetria Guynes. She gained prominence in movies that teamed her with other young leads of the 1980s, known collectively as the Brat Pack; these films included *St. Elmo's Fire* (1985) and *About Last Night* (1986). She was a soulful romantic lead in *Ghost* (1990). Subsequently her career has been marked by huge successes, such as *Indecent Proposal* (1993) and *A Few Good Men* (1992), and equally big flops, such as *Striptease* (1996) and *GI Jane* (1997). She was married to actor Bruce Willis (1987-2000).

Muni, Paul (1895–1967) American actor born in Lemberg, then part of Austria. Born Muni Weisenfreund. Stage-trained, he appeared in his first film, *Valiant*, in 1929. In the 1930s, he became a leading player in melodramas and historical films, such as *Scarface: The Shame of a Nation* (1932, title role); *I Am a Fugitive from a Chain Gang* (1932); *The Story of Louis Pasteur* (1936), for which he won a best actor Academy Award; *The Life of Emile Zola* (1937); and *The Good Earth* (1937).

Murphy, Eddie (1961–) American comedian and actor. Trained on TV's *Saturday Night Live*, he became a box-office sensation in the 1980s with his debut in *48HRS.* (1982). Even more successful was his performance as a wisecracking lawman in *Beverly Hills Cop* (1984), which generated two sequels (1987 and 1994). He gained praise for his humane performances in the title roles of *The Nutty Professor* (1996) and *Dr. Dolittle* (1998). Other films include *Shrek* (2001, voice only).

Murray, Bill (1950–) American actor and comedian. A veteran of TV's *Saturday Night Live*, he transferred his mix of cynicism and humanity to lead and supporting film roles beginning in the 1970s. Lead roles include those in *Ghostbusters* (1984) and the existential comedy-drama *Groundhog Day* (1993); supporting roles include those in *Tootsie* (1982), *Rushmore* (1998), and *Osmosis Jones* (2001). Other films include *Caddyshack* (1980) and *Stripes* (1981).

N

Neeson, Liam (1952–) Irish-born American actor. Theater-trained and in films since the 1980s, he became a major star with his performance as Oskar Schindler in *Schindler's List* (1993), for which he received a best actor Academy Award nomination. Other films span genres from historical drama (*Rob Roy*, 1995, US/Scotland; *Michael Collins*, 1996) to domestic drama (*The Good Mother*, 1988) to horror and action (*Darkman*, 1990) to science fiction (*Star Wars: Episode I—The Phantom Menace*, 1999). His wife is actress Natasha Richardson.

Negri, Pola (1894–1987) Polish-born American actress. Born Barbara Apolonia Chalupiec. An exotic leading lady of Polish and German silent cinema, working with directors Max Reinhardt and Ernst Lubitsch, she came to the US in 1923 and became an immediate star. Her mysteriousness and outlandish style were popular in such American films as *The Spanish Dancer* (1923), *Forbidden Paradise* (1924), and *East of Suez* (1925).

Neill, Sam (1947–) Irish-born international actor. Born Nigel Neill. He became a leading man in Australia with *My Brilliant Career* (1979) and soon became a lead and character actor in American films as well. Films include *Evil Angels/A Cry in the Dark* (1988, Australia), *The Hunt for Red October* (1990), *Jurassic Park* (1993), *The Piano* (1993, New Zealand/France), and *Jurassic Park III* (2001).

Newman, Paul (1925–) American actor, director, and producer. Tall and blue-eyed, he became a bona fide romantic superstar in the 1950s and 60s with knowing, naturalistic performances in *The Long, Hot Summer* (1958), *Cat on a Hot Tin Roof* (1958), *Exodus* (1960), *The Hustler* (1961), *Hud* (1963), and *Cool Hand Luke* (1967). He teamed with Robert Redford in two immensely popular adventures, *Butch Cassidy and the Sundance Kid* (1969) and *The Sting* (1973). In the 1980s, he turned to character leads, notably in *Absence of Malice* (1981), *The Verdict* (1982), and *The Color of Money* (1986), for which he won a best actor Academy Award. Films of the 1990s include *The Hudsucker Proxy* (1993) and *Nobody's Fool* (1994). As an occasional director and producer, his films include *Rachel, Rachel* (1968) and *Harry and Son* (1984). Since 1958, he has been married to Joanne Woodward, his frequent co-star. His many charitable endeavors are partly financed by his line of food products.

Nicholas Brothers American dancers and performers. Fayard Nicholas (1914–); Harold Nicholas (1921–2000). The self-trained pair were vaudeville and stage veterans when they

"The only thing I'm secure about is that I'm funny."
—
Eddie Murphy, 1982

brought their energetic and acrobatic choreography to film in the 1930s and 40s. Among their films are *The Big Broadcast of 1936* (1935), *Down Argentine Way* (1941), *Stormy Weather* (1943), and *The Pirate* (1948). Harold appeared in several films by himself, including *Uptown Saturday Night* (1974). He was married to actress Dorothy Dandridge.

Nicholson, Jack (1937–) American actor, producer, director, and screenwriter. The dominant antiestablishment character lead of the postwar era, he became a national sensation with his supporting performance in *Easy Rider* (1969). In the 1970s, he created memorable iconoclasts in such films as *Five Easy Pieces* (1970), *The Last Detail* (1973), *Chinatown* (1974), and *One Flew over the Cuckoo's Nest* (1975), for which he won a best actor Academy Award. His films of the 1980s include *Reds* (1981), *Prizzi's Honor* (1985), *Ironweed* (1987), *Batman* (1989, as the Joker), and *Terms of Endearment* (1983), which netted him an Academy Award for best supporting actor. In the 1990s, he won a third Oscar, his second best actor Academy Award, for his performance as an urban misanthrope in *As Good as It Gets* (1998). For a time, he was the romantic companion of actress Anjelica Huston. He has also written, produced, and directed films; directing credits include *The Two Jakes* (1990), a sequel to *Chinatown*. Other films include *The Pledge* (2001). He received the AFI Life Achievement Award in 1994.

Niven, David (1909–1983) Scottish-born American actor. Born James David Graham Niven. From the 1930s to the 80s, he was a debonair, witty presence in dozens of films across nearly all genres. Among his best-known works are *Wuthering Heights* (1939), *Raffles* (1940), *The Bishop's Wife* (1947), *The Moon Is Blue* (1953), *Around the World in 80 Days* (1956), and *Separate Tables* (1958), for which he won a best actor Academy Award. His autobiographies include *The Moon Is a Balloon* and *Bring on the Empty Horses*.

Nolte, Nick (1941–) American actor. A solid leading man, he moved from television to film in the 1970s and became a popular star in comedies and dramas, including *48HRS.* (1982) and *Down and Out in Beverly Hills* (1986). Later films include *Cape Fear* (1991), *The Prince of Tides* (1991), *Afterglow* (1997), *Affliction* (1997), and *The Golden Bowl* (2001, UK).

Norris, Chuck (1939–) American actor. Born Carlos Ray Norris. From the late 1970s, he used karate training and military experience in a series of straightforward action films, notably *Missing in Action* (1984) and *The Delta Force* (1986) and their sequels. Other films include *Firewalker* (1984); he has also starred in the television series *Walker: Texas Ranger*.

Novak, Kim (1933–) American actress. Born Marilyn Pauline Novak. Radiating a mixture of innocence and sexuality, she was a major box-office draw during the 1950s. She played opposite such stars as Frank Sinatra, in *The Man with the Golden Arm* (1955) and *Pal Joey* (1957); William Holden, in *Picnic* (1956); and James Stewart, in *Vertigo* (1958) and *Bell, Book, and Candle* (1958).

Novarro, Ramon (1899–1968) Mexican-born American actor. Born Ramon Samaniegos. An early example of the Latin lover style of leading man, he appeared widely in silent films, including *The Prisoner of Zenda* (1922), *The Arab* (1924), and *Ben-Hur* (1926) in the title role.

O–P

O'Hara, Maureen (1920–) Irish-born American actress. Born Maureen FitzSimmons. The red-haired leading lady of the 1940s and 50s became prominent with her performance as Angharad in John Ford's *How Green Was My Valley* (1941). She was equally stirring in another Ford film, *The Quiet Man* (1952), one of several films in which she played opposite John Wayne, including *Rio Grande* (1950) and *The Wings of Eagles* (1957). Other films include *Our Man in Havana* (1959, UK), *Mr. Hobbs Takes a Vacation* (1962), and *Only the Lonely* (1991).

Olivier, Lord Laurence (1907–1989) British-born actor, director, and producer of British and American films. Handsome, wily, and intense, he was one of the foremost stage actors of his day, excelling particularly in Shakespearean roles. He was also a Hollywood romantic lead through the 1940s and a major character lead and supporting player to the end of his life. His starring, directing, producing, and coscripting work on *Henry V* (1944) brought him a special Academy Award. For *Hamlet* (1948), which he also directed and produced, he won Academy Awards for best picture and best actor. He offered notable Shakespearean performances in *Richard III* (1955, also dir., prod.) and *Othello* (1965). Romantic leading roles of the 1930s and 40s included those in *Wuthering Heights* (1939), *Rebecca* (1940), and *Pride and Prejudice* (1940). Films from the 1950s onward include *The Entertainer* (1960), *Spartacus* (1960), and *Marathon Man* (1975), in which he played a memorable Nazi dentist. From 1940 to 1960, he was tumultuously married to actress Vivien Leigh; he later married actress Joan Plowright. His books include the autobiography *Confessions of an Actor* (1982).

O'Toole, Peter (1932–) Irish-born actor in British and American films. The golden-haired actor

> "Why don't you try *acting?* It's much easier."
>
> —
>
> *Classically trained Laurence Olivier to Method man Dustin Hoffman, on the set of* Marathon Man, *(1976)*

leapt to prominence and garnered an Academy Award nomination for best actor with his performance as T.E. Lawrence in *Lawrence of Arabia* (1962, UK). For the next two decades, he appeared in top-drawer productions, often historical dramas or spicy comedies. He received best actor Academy Award nominations for several films during that period: *Becket* (1964, UK/US), *The Lion in Winter* (1968, UK), *Goodbye, Mr. Chips* (1969, UK/US), and *The Ruling Class* (1972, UK). Appearances were more sporadic in the 1980s and 90s, yet he was nominated twice more for a best actor Academy Award, for *The Stunt Man* (1980) and *My Favorite Year* (1982). He was married to actress Sian Phillips.

Pacino, Al (1940–) American actor. Born Alfredo Pacino. He had already appeared to some acclaim in *The Panic in Needle Park* (1971) when he took on the memorable role of Michael Corleone, the son of Mob boss Don Corleone, in the blockbuster *The Godfather* (1972). He received Academy Award nominations for best supporting actor for that film and its sequel, *The Godfather Part II* (1974); he also starred in *The Godfather Part III* (1990). Since then, he has been a dramatic lead actor, usually playing driven urban types, with notable credits including *Serpico* (1973), *Dog Day Afternoon* (1975), *Sea of Love* (1989), *Glengarry Glen Ross* (1992), *Donnie Brasco* (1997), and *The Insider* (1999). After many nominations, he won a best actor Academy Award for his demonstrative performance in *Scent of a Woman* (1992).

Paltrow, Gwyneth (1972–) American actress. Trained in theater, she projects patrician grace and lightness, notably in period pieces such as *Emma* (1996) and *Shakespeare in Love* (1998), for which she won a best actress Academy Award. Contemporary films include *Sliding Doors* (1998, US/UK), *Bounce* (2000), and *Shallow Hal* (2001). Her mother is actress Blythe Danner; her father, TV producer Bruce Paltrow.

Peck, Gregory (1916–) American actor. Born Eldred Gregory Peck. Tall, lanky, and understated, he has represented moral integrity and quiet appeal, most famously as country lawyer Atticus Finch in *To Kill a Mockingbird* (1962), for which he won an Academy Award for best actor. Broadway-trained, he made an early impression in the 1940s with lead roles in major dramas, such as *Spellbound* (1945), *Gentleman's Agreement* (1947), and *Duel in the Sun* (1947). Active in all genres, he was a major

romantic lead in the 1950s, especially memorable opposite Audrey Hepburn in the fairy-tale romance *Roman Holiday* (1953). Other notable 50s films include *Twelve O'Clock High* (1950) and *The Man in the Gray Flannel Suit* (1956). Later films include *Cape Fear* (1962), *The Omen* (1976), and *The Boys from Brazil* (1977). He received the Academy's Jean Hersholt Humanitarian Award and, in 1989, the AFI Life Achievement Award.

Penn, Sean (1960–) American actor and director. Highly respected actor who became known for his comic performance as a spaced-out student in *Fast Times at Ridgemont High* (1982). Subsequent dramatic roles include those in *The Falcon and the Snowman* (1985), *Carlito's Way* (1989), *Dead Man Walking* (1995), and *Sweet and Lowdown* (1999). He has also directed films, including *She's So Lovely* (1997) and *The Pledge* (2001). He was married to Madonna (1984–89) and later married actress Robin Wright. His brother is actor Christopher Penn.

Perkins, Anthony (1932–1992) American actor. Known as a sensitive supporting player in such dramas as *Friendly Persuasion* (1956), he became associated with horror due to his standout performance as the troubled killer in *Psycho* (1960), a role he reprised in sequels. Other films include *Murder on the Orient Express* (1974, US/UK) and *Winter Kills* (1980). His father was actor Osgood Perkins.

Pesci, Joe (1943–) American actor. With his performance as boxer Jake LaMotta's brother in Martin Scorsese's *Raging Bull* (1980), he became a prominent character actor, largely in

Anthony Quinn and Peter O'Toole starred in Sir David Lean's masterful epic Lawrence of Arabia *(1962).*

> "You'll never know how lonely those years were for me when I was the only black star out there. Now I walk down the street and see Jim Brown's name big on the marquee and I feel good."
>
> —
>
> *Sidney Poitier, 1969*

volatile roles. His performance in another Scorsese film, *GoodFellas* (1980), earned him an Academy Award for best supporting actor. His best-known leading role was a comedic turn as a novice lawyer in *My Cousin Vinny* (1992).

Pfeiffer, Michelle (1957–) American actress. The willowy Hollywood lead gained notice in *Scarface* (1983) and dazzled audiences in *The Fabulous Baker Boys* (1989). She was recognized for her nuanced performances and inner sadness in films such as *Dangerous Liaisons* (1988), *Love Field* (1992), and *The Age of Innocence* (1993). She was a memorable Catwoman in *Batman Returns* (1992). Later films include *The Story of Us* (1999) and *What Lies Beneath* (2000). Her second husband is TV producer David Kelley.

Pickford, Mary (1893–1979) Canadian-born American actress. Born Gladys Smith. With her trademark golden curls and innocent mien, she was known as "Little Mary" and "America's Sweetheart," the greatest star of silent films. Made with many of the period's top directors, her films spanned the heyday of silent cinema. Among them were *In Old Kentucky* (1909), *Ramona* (1910), *The New York Hat* (1912), *The Poor Little Rich Girl* (1917), *Rebecca of Sunnybrook Farm* (1917), *Pollyanna* (1920), and *Tess of the Storm Country* (1922). An intelligent businesswoman, she moved among studios for higher salaries. In 1919, she cofounded United Artists with, among others, Douglas Fairbanks, who became her second husband. The two were an early example of Hollywood royalty. In 1928, she shocked fans by bobbing her hair. She won a best actress Academy Award for the sound film *Coquette* (1928), but audiences did not accept her more sophisticated image. She retired in the 1930s. Her third husband was actor Buddy Rogers.

Pitt, Brad (1963–) American actor. After a standout supporting performance in *Thelma & Louise* (1991), this edgy, smoldering performer stepped up to leads and top box-office appeal. Films include *A River Runs Through It* (1992), *Legends of the Fall* (1994), *Seven* (1995), *12 Monkeys* (1995), *Meet Joe Black* (1998), *Fight Club* (1999), and *The Mexican* (2001).

Poitier, Sidney (1924–) American actor. Popular and respected actor whose success made it acceptable for African-Americans to star in mainstream American films. He gained notice for his performance opposite Tony Curtis in *The Defiant Ones* (1958) and won a best actor Academy Award for *Lilies of the Field* (1963). Other films include *A Raisin in the Sun* (1961), *A Patch of Blue* (1965), *To Sir with Love* (1967), *In the Heat of the Night* (1967), and *Guess Who's Coming to Dinner* (1967). His later films include *Little Nikita* (1988) and *The Jackal* (1997). In 1992, he became the first African-American to

receive the AFI Life Achievement Award and received an honorary Oscar in 2002.

Porten, Henny (1888–1960) German actress. The first major star of German films, she appeared widely in silent films from 1906 through the 1920s. Films credits include *Lohengrin* (1907), *Eva* (1912), and *Die Blaue Laterne* (1918). The Nazi government curtailed her film appearances in the 1930s because of her second marriage, to a Jew.

Powell, Dick (1904–1963) American actor, singer, director, and producer. Born Richard E. Powell. In the 1930s, he was a singer and musical star, notably in films with Ruby Keeler depicting backstage life, such as *42nd Street* (1933), *Gold Diggers of 1933* (1933), and *Footlight Parade* (1933). In the 1940s, he became known for his roles in mysteries and film noir, such as *Murder, My Sweet* (1945). He was also a director-producer of films, including *The Enemy Below* (1957). He was married to actresses Joan Blondell (1936–45) and June Allyson (1945 until his death).

Powell, Eleanor (1910–1982) American actress and dancer. Broadway-trained, she is remembered on film for her athletic, stylish tap dancing in film musicals of the 1930s and 1940s. Partners included James Stewart and Fred Astaire, but she made her greatest impression dancing solo. Notable films include *Broadway Melody of 1936* (1935), *Born to Dance* (1936), *Broadway Melody of 1938* (1937), *Rosalie* (1937), and *Broadway Melody of 1940* (1940). Upon marrying Glenn Ford (1943–59), she mostly retired from films.

Powell, William (1892–1984) American actor. At first portraying villains in silent films, he became known as a sophisticated leading man and one of the top stars of sound films in the 1930s. He was most memorable as detective Nick Charles, opposite Myrna Loy's Nora Charles, in *The Thin Man* (1934) and many sequels. He played impresario Florenz Ziegfeld twice: in *The Great Ziegfeld* (1936) and in *Ziegfeld Follies* (1946). Other films include the screwball comedy *My Man Godfrey* (1936), the period saga *Life with Father* (1947), the war comedy-drama *Mister Roberts* (1955), and several Philo Vance mysteries, such as *The Canary Murder Case* (1929). He was married to Carole Lombard (1931–33).

Power, Tyrone (1914–1958) American actor. Born Tyrone Edmund Power, Jr. The son of silent film star Tyrone Power, he was a dashing lead in dramas, action movies, and lighter fare. Films include *In Old Chicago* (1938), *Alexander's Ragtime Band* (1938), *Jesse James* (1939), *Blood and Sand* (1941), and *The Mark of Zorro* (1940). Postwar films include *The Razor's Edge* (1946), *The Sun Also Rises* (1957), and *Witness for the Prosecution* (1958). He was married to actresses Annabella (1939–48) and Linda Christian (1949–55).

Presley, Elvis (1935–1977) American singer and actor. From 1956, the rock and roll phenomenon was an appealing presence in more than 30 star vehicles, some featuring notable actresses, including Ann-Margret, Barbara Stanwyck, and Mary Tyler Moore. Among his films are *Love Me Tender* (1956), *Jailhouse Rock* (1957), *Girls! Girls! Girls!* (1962), *Roustabout* (1964), and what some consider his best, *Viva Las Vegas* (1964).

Price, Vincent (1911–1993) American actor. The highly cultured actor worked in films from the 1930s, notably in *Laura* (1944) and *Leave Her to Heaven* (1945), but gained his greatest fame for projecting stylized evil and dread in such horror films as *House of Wax* (1953), *The Fly* (1958), *The Tingler* (1959), *The House of Usher* (1960), and *The Abominable Doctor Phibes* (1971, UK). He was married to actress Coral Browne from 1974 to her death in 1991.

Pryor, Richard (1940–) American actor, comedian, director, and screenwriter. An established television and stand-up comic known for exposing racial attitudes in his work, he entered films in the late 1960s as a performer (*The Busy Body,* 1968) and in the 1970s as a writer (*Blazing Saddles,* 1974, coscreenwriter). He gained further popularity in his films with Gene Wilder, which include *Silver Streak* (1976), *Stir Crazy* (1980), and *See No Evil, Hear No Evil* (1989).

Q–R

Quinn, Anthony (1915–2001) Mexican-born actor in American and international films. Born Anthony Rudolfo Oxaca Quinn. Highly masculine lead and supporting player in more than 100 films, he is best known for his lusty portrayal of the title character in *Zorba the Greek* (1964). His performances in *Viva Zapata!* (1952) and *Lust for Life* (1956), in which he portrayed Paul Gauguin, earned Academy Awards for best supporting actor. Other notable films include *La Strada* (1954), *The Guns of Navarone* (1961), *Lawrence of Arabia* (1962), *The Greek Tycoon* (1978), and *Jungle Fever* (1991).

Raft, George (1895–1980) American actor. Born George Ranft. In films from the 1920s, the professionally trained dancer made his name on screen with a single action: flipping a coin as a gangster in *Scarface* (1932). After that, he appeared widely in crime films, including *Each Dawn I Die* (1939), *They Drive by Night* (1940), and *Some Like It Hot* (1959).

Rainer, Luise (1910–) Austrian-born American actress. Trained on the European stage, she became an American film lead, winning two successive Academy Awards for best actress in *The Great Ziegfeld* (1936) and *The Good Earth* (1937). After her meteoric rise, she retired in the early 1940s. She was married to dramatist Clifford Odets (1937–40).

Rains, Claude (1889–1967) British-born American actor. Born William Claude Rains. An established stage actor, he moved to films in the mid-1930s and soon became known for his dapper, witty, yet often somber screen presence, usually in supporting roles. He offered dozens of memorable performances in films including *The Invisible Man* (1933), *Mr. Smith Goes to Washington* (1939), *Casablanca* (1943), *Mr. Skeffington* (1944), *Notorious* (1946), and *Lawrence of Arabia* (1962).

Reagan, Ronald (1911–) American actor and politician. A steady lead in films from the 1930s through the 1950s, best known for his performance as dying football player George Gipp, "the Gipper," in *Knute Rockne— All American* (1940) and as the co-star of a chimpanzee in *Bedtime for Bonzo* (1951). He hosted TV series in the 1950s and 60s before devoting himself to politics, becoming the governor of California and later the president of the United States (1981–89). Other films include *Santa Fe Trail* (1940), *Kings Row* (1942), and *Desperate Journey* (1942).

Redford, Robert (1937–) American actor, producer, and director. Born Charles Robert Redford, Jr. The Broadway-trained actor became a top star and sex symbol for his performance as the western outlaw the Sundance Kid in *Butch Cassidy and the Sundance Kid* (1969), in which he was teamed with Paul Newman. The two worked together again in *The Sting* (1973). Other films capitalizing on his unassuming, golden-haired masculinity include *The Way We Were* (1973), *All the President's Men* (1975), *Out of Africa* (1985), and *The Last Castle* (2001). Since founding the Sundance Institute for independent filmmakers in 1980, he has concentrated on producing and directing. Among his directorial credits are *Ordinary People* (1980), for which he won a best director Academy Award; *A River Runs Through It* (1992), *Quiz Show* (1994), and *The Legend of Bagger Vance* (2000).

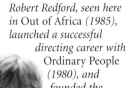

Robert Redford, seen here in Out of Africa *(1985), launched a successful directing career with* Ordinary People *(1980), and founded the Sundance Institute and its prestigious film festival.*

Redgrave, Lynn (1943–) British-born actress in British and American films. The daughter of Sir Michael Redgrave and the sister of Vanessa Redgrave, she gained early screen notice for her winsome lead performance in *Georgy Girl* (1966, UK). Over the next decades, she has appeared on television and stage as well as in film; notable films include *Shine* (1995) and *Gods and Monsters* (1998).

Redgrave, Sir Michael (1908–1985) British actor. The son of actor Roy Redgrave, he was active throughout his life on stage and was a leading man on screen from the 1930s, usually in high-quality productions, including *The Browning Version* (1951, US/UK), *The Importance of Being Earnest* (1952, UK), and *Oh! What a Lovely War* (1969, UK). He was knighted in 1959. He was the father of actresses Vanessa and Lynn Redgrave.

Redgrave, Vanessa (1937–) British-born actress in British and American films. The daughter of Sir Michael Redgrave, she became known for performances in historical films including *Julia* (1977), for which she won an Academy Award for best supporting actress. Other notable films include *Isadora* (1968) and *Mary, Queen of Scots* (1971). Since the 1980s, she has appeared in many character roles, including those in *Prick Up Your Ears* (1987) and *Cradle Will Rock* (2000). She is equally well known for her leftist political activism. She was married to director Tony Richardson, and is the mother of actresses Natasha and Joely Richardson. Her sister is actress Lynn Redgrave.

Reeve, Christopher (1952–) American actor. Handsome and stage-trained, he was a dramatic lead during the 1970s and 80s, best known for his incarnation of the title character in *Superman* (1978) and three sequels. Other films include *Noises Off* (1992) and *The Remains of the Day* (1993). A horseback riding accident in 1995 left him paralyzed from the neck down, but he has continued to act and direct, chiefly for television.

Reeves, Keanu (1965–) Lebanese-born American actor. Experienced on stage, this offbeat performer has been a screen lead since the 1980s, first in teen features such as *Bill and Ted's Excellent Adventure* (1989) and later in adult roles, often in action films, such as *Speed* (1994) and *The Matrix* (1999). Other films include *My Own Private Idaho* (1991) and *Sweet November* (2001).

Perhaps best known for his portrayal of Superman in four films, Christopher Reeve was paralyzed from the neck down after being thrown from his horse during a jumping competition in 1995.

Reid, Wallace (1891–1923) American actor, director, and screenwriter. Born William Wallace Reid. The child of a stage actor, he was one of silent film's early matinee idols, appearing in dozens of films, including *The Birth of a Nation* (1915), *Enoch Arden* (1915), *To Have and to Hold* (1916), and *Intolerance* (1916). He also directed and wrote several films from 1910 to 1915. While being treated for an on-set injury, he developed an addiction to morphine, which, with alcohol abuse, led to his early death.

Remick, Lee (1935–1991) American actress. A female lead of the 1950s and 60s, she became known for her steamy yet wily performances in *A Face in the Crowd* (1957), *The Long, Hot Summer* (1958), and *Anatomy of a Murder* (1959). Her performance as an alcoholic opposite Jack Lemmon in *Days of Wine and Roses* (1962) earned an Oscar nomination for best actress. From the 1970s, she appeared widely on TV, with occasional film work, including *The Omen* (1976) and *Emma's War* (1985, Australia).

Reynolds, Burt (1936–) American actor. The manly, self-deprecating lead was one of the top box-office draws and sex symbols of the 1970s after the success of *Deliverance* (1973) and *The Longest Yard* (1974). Especially popular were *Smokey and the Bandit* (1977) and its sequels and *The Cannonball Run* (1981). In *Starting Over* (1979) and *Semi-Tough* (1977), he revealed new levels of comedic skill. He later turned to television and to character roles in films, such as the porn director in *Boogie Nights* (1997).

Reynolds, Debbie (1932–) American actress. Born Mary Frances Reynolds. The pert blond actress became one of the top musical and comedy stars of the 1950s and 60s. Musicals include *Singin' in the Rain* (1952), *The Unsinkable Molly Brown* (1964), and *The Singing Nun* (1966); comedy-dramas include *The Tender Trap* (1955) and *Tammy and the Bachelor* (1957). Married to singer Eddie Fisher in the 1950s, she received much public sympathy when Fisher left her to wed actress Elizabeth Taylor in 1959. Her later film roles are edgier, notably the title role in *Mother* (1996).

Richardson, Sir Ralph (1902–1983) British actor. One of his generation's most accomplished stage actors, he appeared occasionally in films from 1933 to 1983, in a variety of character roles. Among his notable credits are *The Citadel* (1938), *Four Feathers* (1939), *The Heiress* (1949), *Anna Karenina* (1948), *The Fallen Idol* (1948), and *Greystoke: The Legend of Tarzan, Lord of the Apes* (1984). He was knighted in 1947.

Ringwald, Molly (1968–) American actress. A childhood singer and stage actress, she entered film in the 1980s, gaining notice for her representative characterizations of modern adolescence in *Sixteen Candles* (1984), *The Breakfast Club* (1985), and *Pretty in Pink* (1986). Later films include *Betsy's Wedding* (1990) and *Teaching Mrs. Tingle* (1999).

Rin Tin Tin (1916–1932) German-born American canine performer. The major animal star of the 1920s, the German shepherd appeared in top box-office adventure features and serials. He displayed exceptional intelligence and heroism in silent and sound films, including *The Man from Hell's River* (1922), *Rinty of the Desert* (1928), and *The Million Dollar Collar* (1929). He was followed in the 1930s by another dog, Rin Tin Tin, Jr. Rin Tin Tin's popularity paved the way for later canine movie series, such as the *Lassie* and *Benji* films.

Ritter, Thelma (1905–1969) American actress. The wisecracking supporting actress, who often played a domestic, cast her gimlet eye in more than two dozen films, including *All About Eve* (1950), *Rear Window* (1954), and *Pillow Talk* (1959). She received six Academy Award nominations.

Robards, Jason Jr. (1922–2000) American actor. An award-winning Broadway lead, he specialized in character roles on screen, winning best supporting actor Academy Awards for *All the President's Men* (1976) and *Julia* (1977). Other films include *Melvin and Howard* (1980) and *Quick Change* (1990). He was the son of actor Jason Robards. He was married to actress Lauren Bacall (1961–69).

Robbins, Tim (1958–) American actor and director. In films since the mid-1980s, the lanky actor was established as a lead after playing a callow baseball player tutored by Susan Sarandon in *Bull Durham* (1988). Other notable films include *The Player* (1992) and *The Shawshank Redemption* (1994). As a director, he is best known for the prison drama *Dead Man Walking* (1995), for which he was nominated for a best director Academy Award. He lives with Susan Sarandon.

Roberts, Julia (1967–) American actress. The radiant, dark-haired beauty gained notice in ensemble parts in *Mystic Pizza* (1988) and *Steel Magnolias* (1989) but reached stardom with her lead seriocomic performance in *Pretty Woman* (1990). Despite some later misses, she has sustained stardom with such films as *My Best Friend's Wedding* (1997), *Notting Hill* (1999), *Erin Brockovich* (2000), for which she won an Academy Award for best actress, and *America's Sweethearts* (2001).

Robertson, Cliff (1925–) American actor. Born Clifford Parker Robinson. Trained on stage and TV, he was a leading man in films of the 1960s and 70s, often serious dramas. He gave his best-known performances as John F.

Kennedy in *PT-109* (1963) and as a mentally retarded man who briefly becomes a genius in *Charly* (1969). He was married to actress Dina Merrill (1966–89).

Robeson, Paul (1898–1976) American actor and singer. The acclaimed concert performer and stage actor is best known to moviegoers for his towering performance as Joe in *Show Boat* (1936). Other silent and sound films include *Body and Soul* (1925), *The Emperor Jones* (1933), and *King Solomon's Mines* (1937, UK).

Robinson, Bill "Bojangles" (1878–1949) American dancer and actor. Born Luther Robinson. A pioneering African-American tap dancer, he appeared in film musicals during the 1930s and 40s, including *Stormy Weather* (1943), and opposite Shirley Temple in *The Little Colonel* (1935), *The Littlest Rebel* (1935), and *Rebecca of Sunnybrook Farm* (1938). He created and popularized stair dance routines.

Robinson, Edward G. (1893–1973) American actor. Born Emmanuel Goldenberg. One of the most masterful character actors and leads of the sound era, famous for helping to create the 1930s gangster in *Little Caesar* (1930) and for embodying biblical villainy as Dathan in *The Ten Commandments* (1956). Other films include *Dr. Ehrlich's Magic Bullet* (1940), *The Whole Town's Talking* (1935), and *Double Indemnity* (1944). During the 1950s, he was investigated for alleged communist associations and cleared of charges by the House Un-American Activities Committee. He posthumously received a special Academy Award.

Robson, Dame Flora (1902–1984) British actress in British and American films. A leading character player on the British stage, she appeared in many films, including several historical dramas. Among her films are *Catherine the Great* (1934, UK), *Fire over England* (1937, UK), *The Sea Hawk* (1940), and *Saratoga Trunk* (1946). In 1960, she was named Dame of the British Empire.

Rogers, Ginger (1911–1995) American actress. Born Virginia Katherine McMath. In ten films with Fred Astaire, she defined film musical fluidity and elegance. Trained in vaudeville and on Broadway, she was matched with Astaire at RKO in musicals beginning with *Flying down to Rio* (1933) and including *The Gay Divorcee* (1934), *Top Hat* (1935), and *Swing Time* (1936). Without Astaire, she demonstrated light comedic and dramatic skills in films from the 1930s to 50s, including *Stage Door* (1937); *Kitty Foyle* (1940), for which she won a best actress Academy Award; *Roxie Hart* (1943); and *Monkey Business* (1952).

Rogers, Roy (1911–1998) and **Evans, Dale** (1912–) American actors and singers. Born Leonard Franklin Slye and Frances Octavia

Since first acting together in *The Sure Thing* (1985), friends Tim Robbins and John Cusack jointly appeared in the films *Tapeheads* (1988), *The Player* (1992), *Bob Roberts* (1992), and *High Fidelity* (2000). In addition, Robbins directed Cusack in *Bob Roberts* (1992) and *Cradle Will Rock* (1999).

Ginger Rogers starred in musicals before transitioning to dramatic roles.

Smith, respectively. They were western stars in films in the 1940s and on TV in the 1950s, with Rogers known as the King of the Cowboys. The two appeared together in such westerns as *The Yellow Rose of Texas* (1944) and *Don't Fence Me In* (1945). They married in 1947. His horse was Trigger, hers Buttermilk.

Rogers, Will (1879–1935) American actor and humorist. Born William Penn Adair Rogers. The everyman wit of his day, Rogers was a top stage attraction by 1918, when he first appeared in silent films. With sound films he became a major draw, starring in features including *A Connecticut Yankee* (1931), *State Fair* (1933), *Judge Priest* (1934), and *Steamboat 'Round the Bend* (1935). He died in an airplane crash with flier Wiley Post.

Rooney, Mickey (1920–) American actor. Born Joe Yule, Jr. Energetic and funny, he was the embodiment of Depression-era youth and Hollywood's most popular star from 1939 to 1941. He is best remembered as Andy Hardy in the film series that began with *A Family Affair* (1937), and for his film musicals with Judy Garland, including *Babes in Arms* (1939) and *Strike Up the Band* (1940). He was also praised for serious films, including *A Midsummer Night's Dream* (1935), *Captains Courageous* (1937), and *Boys Town* (1938). In 1938, he received a special juvenile Academy Award. He has sustained one of Hollywood's longest careers, playing a variety of supporting characters in later years, as in *Breakfast at Tiffany's* (1961) and *The Black Stallion* (1979).

Roundtree, Richard (1937–) American actor. Trained in a stage ensemble troupe, he became famous as the pioneering African-American action hero *Shaft* (1971). He reprised the role in sequels—*Shaft's Big Score!* (1972) and *Shaft in Africa* (1973)—and played the role as a supporting character in the remake *Shaft* (2000). Other films include *Seven* (1995).

Rowlands, Gena (1934–) American actress. Born Virginia Rowlands. In films from the 1950s, the stage-trained actress is best known for lead performances in films directed by husband John Cassavetes, such as *A Woman Under the Influence* (1974) and *Gloria* (1980). She has appeared widely on television.

Russell, Jane (1921–) American actress. Born Ernestine Jane Geraldine Russell. Star of comedy and drama, she became notorious for the alluring way in which her body was presented in *The Outlaw* (1943). She projected a knowing persona in later films, including *The Paleface* (1948) and *Gentlemen Prefer Blondes* (1953).

Russell, Kurt (1951–) American actor. A popular young star in Disney films from the 1960s, such as *The Computer Wore Tennis Shoes* (1969), he developed into an action lead and character player who balanced stylized performances with naturalistic portrayals. Notable films include *Escape from New York* (1981), *Silkwood* (1983), *Swing Shift* (1984), *Tequila Sunrise* (1988), and *Executive Decision* (1996). He lives with actress Goldie Hawn.

Russell, Rosalind (1908–1976) American actress and singer. The stage-trained lead was one of the definitive sophisticated comedians during the late 1930s and 40s, notably in *The Women* (1939) and *His Girl Friday* (1940). She was nominated for best actress Academy Awards for two dramatic roles, in *Sister Kenny* (1946) and *Mourning Becomes Electra* (1947), as well as for her most flamboyant role, as the title character in the comedy-drama *Auntie Mame* (1958). Other dramatic turns included *Picnic* (1956). An accomplished musical-comedy star, she appeared in *My Sister Eileen* (1942; best actress Academy Award nomination) and as Mama Rose in *Gypsy* (1962).

Ryan, Meg (1961–) American actress. Born Margaret Hyra. The blond, TV-trained actress became one of Hollywood's top stars for her daffy lightness in romantic comedies and her emotional seriousness in dramas. Comedies include *When Harry Met Sally...* (1989) and *Sleepless in Seattle* (1994). Dramatic films include *Flesh and Bone* (1993), *Courage Under Fire* (1996), and *Proof of Life* (2000). She was married to actor Dennis Quaid.

Ryan, Robert (1909–1973) American actor. On screen from the 1940s, he portrayed both sympathetic and fearsome leads in such film noirs as *Caught* (1949), *Crossfire* (1947), and *Clash by Night* (1952) and westerns such as *The Naked Spur* (1953) and *The Wild Bunch* (1969).

Ryder, Winona (1971–) American actress. Born Winona Laura Horowitz. On screen by age 15, she established herself in roles reflecting delicacy and intensity, in both contemporary and period films. Among the features in which she has starred are *Heathers* (1989), *Edward Scissorhands* (1990), *The Age of Innocence* (1993), *Little Women* (1994), and *Girl, Interrupted* (1999).

S

Sanders, George (1906–1972) Russian-born British actor in American and international films. Prolific, urbane, sharp-witted actor who appeared in supporting and leading roles from the 1930s to the 70s. He is best known for his role as a critic in *All About Eve* (1950), for which he won an Academy Award for best supporting

Mickey Rooney was already a vaudeville veteran when he made his film debut at age six.

"The best part of the talkies is that when I say somethin', I say it and it sticks."

—

Will Rogers, 1929

actor. Other films include *Rebecca* (1940), *The Moon and Sixpence* (1942), *The Ghost and Mrs. Muir* (1947), and *Samson and Delilah* (1949). He starred in several Saint and Falcon movies of the 1940s, adventure films featuring heroes who went by those names. Wives included actresses Zsa Zsa Gabor and Magda Gabor.

Sarandon, Susan (1946–) American actress. Born Susan Abigail Tomalin. From early cult status for her performance in *The Rocky Horror Picture Show* (1975), she became a major dramatic lead in the 1980s and 90s, usually playing women driven by ideals. Perhaps the most memorable of these roles was the avenging waitress in *Thelma & Louise* (1991). Other films include *Atlantic City* (1980), *Lorenzo's Oil* (1992), *The Client* (1994), and *Joe Guold's Secret* (2000). She won a best actress Academy Award for her performance as Sister Helen Prejean in her partner Tim Robbins's film *Dead Man Walking* (1995) and was a believable Marmee in *Little Women* (1995).

Schwarzenegger, Arnold (1947–) Austrian-born American actor. Billed in some films of the 1970s as Arnold Strong, the muscular lead gained broader notice among film fans as a bodybuilder in the documentary *Pumping Iron* (1977). He went on to become an action hero, characterized by unstoppable strength and sly humor, in such films as *Conan the Barbarian* (1982), *The Terminator* (1984), *Total Recall* (1990), *Terminator 2: Judgment Day* (1991), and *The 6th Day* (2000). He has also proven an agreeable comic presence, particularly with Danny De Vito in *Twins* (1988) and *Junior* (1994). He is married to journalist Maria Shriver.

Scott, George C. (1926–1999) American actor. Born George Campbell Scott. Considered one of the finest actors of stage, television, and screen, he won a best supporting actor Academy Award for *The Hustler* (1961) and a best actor Academy Award for the title role in *Patton* (1970), although he refused the latter award. Other films include *Anatomy of a Murder* (1959) and *They Might Be Giants* (1971). He was married to actress Colleen Dewhurst (1960–65); their son is actor Campbell Scott. He later married actress Trish Van Devere.

Scott, Randolph (1898–1987) American actor. Born George Randolph Crane Scott. The tall, handsome World War I veteran began acting in films in the late 1920s, gaining a reputation for performances in westerns, notably the dark Budd Boetticher films of the 1950s, such as *The Tall T* (1957) and *Seven Men from Now* (1956). Earlier films include *Jesse James* (1939), *Western Union* (1941), and *Belle Starr* (1941).

Seagal, Steven (1952–) American actor and producer. Beginning in the 1980s, the massive actor starred in (and sometimes coproduced) action films that integrated his martial arts

training and amused sensibility, including *Hard to Kill* (1990), *Under Siege* (1992), *On Deadly Ground* (1994), which he also directed, and *Exit Wounds* (2001).

Sellers, Peter (1925–1980) British-born actor in British and American films. Born Richard Henry Sellers. In films from the 1950s, he was a dark and zany verbal and physical actor, best known for his multiple roles including the title role in *Dr. Strangelove* (1964), and for his Inspector Clouseau in *The Pink Panther* (1964) and many sequels. Other offbeat comedies include *The Mouse That Roared* (1959) and *Casino Royale* (1967). He offered a poignant performance in the comedy-drama *Being There* (1979). Among his wives was actress Britt Ekland (1964–68).

Shearer, Norma (1900–1983) American actress. Born Edith Norma Shearer. The poised and stately leading player was known in the 1930s as the First Lady of the Screen. Married to MGM mogul Irving Thalberg, her greatest success coincided with their marriage, from 1927 to his death in 1936. She won a best actress Academy Award for *The Divorcee* (1930). Defining roles include those in *Their Own Desire* (1929), *A Free Soul* (1931), *The Barretts of Wimpole Street* (1934), *Romeo and Juliet* (1936), and *The Women* (1939). She retired from film in 1942.

Sheen, Martin (1940–) American actor. Born Ramon Estevez. Stage-trained, the intense actor turned to films in the 1960s and won notice for his performance as a disaffected killer in *Badlands* (1973). He offered similarly striking performances in *Apocalypse Now* (1979) and *Wall Street* (1987). He has appeared widely on television and has been a cast member of the series *The West Wing*. Active in left-wing causes, he is the father of actors Emilio Estevez and Charlie Sheen.

Sheridan, Ann (1915–1967) American actress. Born Clara Lou Sheridan. Proclaimed by Warner Bros. as the Oomph Girl, she was featured in dramas, comedies, and musicals of the 1940s. Films include *Kings Row* (1942), *Angels with Dirty Faces* (1938), and *I Was a Male War Bride* (1949). Husbands included actors Edward Norris and George Brent.

Simmons, Jean (1929–) British-born American actress. A major dramatic lead of the 1950s and 60s, she was the picture of cultured grace and

Susan Sarandon and Geena Davis starred as best friends on the run in the female buddy film Thelma & Louise *(1991).*

beauty. Among her films are *Black Narcissus* (1947), *Hamlet* (1948), *The Robe* (1953), *Guys and Dolls* (1955), *Elmer Gantry* (1960), *Spartacus* (1960), and *The Happy Ending* (1969).

Sinatra, Frank (1915–1998) American singer and actor. Born Francis Albert Sinatra. The dominant male vocalist of the 20th century and a tough, sympathetic star of numerous films. Known as the Voice, he was the leading romantic singer of the 1940s and entered films with musicals such as *Anchors Aweigh* (1945), *It Happened in Brooklyn* (1947), and *On the Town* (1949). In 1945, he received a special Oscar for his appearance in the short patriotic film *The House I Live In.* After a professional decline in the early 1950s, he reestablished his popularity as an entertainer in part with his performance in *From Here to Eternity* (1953), for which he won an Academy Award for best supporting actor. Viewed afterward as a serious actor, he continued with performances in musical and nonmusical films, including *Suddenly* (1954), *The Man with the Golden Arm* (1955), *The Joker Is Wild* (1957), *Pal Joey* (1957), *Some Came Running* (1959), and *The Manchurian Candidate* (1962). With Rat Pack friends Sammy Davis, Jr., Peter Lawford, and others, he appeared in such frothy comedies as *Ocean's Eleven* (1960) and *Robin and the 7 Hoods* (1964, also prod.). In 1971, he received the Jean Hersholt Humanitarian Award and, in 1983, the Kennedy Center Honors. Involved with several famous women over the years, he was married to actresses Ava Gardner (1951–57) and Mia Farrow (1966–68).

Smith, Alexis (1921–1993) Canadian-born American actress. Born Gladys Smith. The cool, tall, stage-trained actress appeared widely in films of the 1940s and 1950s. Films include *Of Human Bondage* (1946), *The Two Mrs. Carrolls* (1947), *The Turning Point* (1952), and *The Young Philadelphians* (1959). In 1944, she married actor Craig Stevens.

Smith, Dame Maggie (1934–) British-born actress in British and American films. Acclaimed on stage in Britain and Broadway, she is best remembered on film as the eccentric title character in *The Prime of Miss Jean Brodie* (1969), for which she won a best actress Academy Award. She also won a best supporting actress Academy Award for *California Suite* (1978). Other notable films include *Travels with My Aunt* (1972) *The Lonely Passion of Judith Hearne* (1987), *Gosford Park* (2001) and *Harry Potter and the Sorcerer's Stone* (2001).

Smith, Will (1970–) American actor and singer. After starring in the TV series *Fresh Prince of Bel-Air* and enjoying success as a rap artist, he transferred his likable physicality to films, including *Independence Day* (1996), *Men in Black* (1997), *Enemy of the State* (1998), and *Ali* (2001).

Sissy Spacek chose to go unbilled in Steve Martin's 1983 mad scientist comedy, *The Man with Two Brains.* She provided the disembodied voice of Martin's cerebral love interest.

Sorvino, Mira (1968-) American actress. The daughter of actor Paul Sorvino, she combined dramatic subtlety and a light comedic touch in *Mighty Aphrodite* (1995), for which she won a best supporting actress Academy Award. Other films include *Quiz Show* (1994) and *Romy and Michele's High School Reunion* (1997).

Spacek, Sissy (1949–) American actress. Born Mary Elizabeth Spacek. A delicate, naturalistic southern actress, she is known for her early performance as half of a criminal couple in *Badlands* (1973). She won a best actress Academy Award for *Coal Miner's Daughter* (1980) and was nominated five other times, for *Carrie* (1976), *Missing* (1982), *The River* (1984), *Crimes of the Heart* (1986) and *In the Bedroom* (2001).

Spacey, Kevin (1959–) American actor. Trained on Broadway and in comedy clubs, he entered films in 1986 and has since specialized in portraying edgy, unpredictable characters in films including *Glengarry Glen Ross* (1992); *The Usual Suspects* (1995), for which he won a best supporting actor Academy Award; and *L.A. Confidential* (1997), and *K-Pax* (2001). He won a best actor Academy Award for his role in *American Beauty* (1999).

Stallone, Sylvester "Sly" (1946–) American actor, director, and screenwriter. Born Michael Sylvester Stallone. In the 1970s, the muscular figure rocketed to success with the boxing film *Rocky* (1976), which he wrote and starred in; the film won a best picture Academy Award and generated several sequels. In the 1980s, he continued his screen dominance with the Rambo action series, starting with *First Blood* (1982) and including *Rambo: First Blood Part II* (1985). His later career has been marred by box-office and critical disappointments; his more successful films of this period include *Cliffhanger* (1993) and *Cop Land* (1997). Films he has directed and written as well as starred in include *Paradise Alley* (1978).

Men in Black (1997) featured Will Smith and Tommy Lee Jones as secret government agents who investigate alien visits to Earth.

Stanwyck, Barbara (1907–1990) American actress. Born Ruby Stevens. Over several decades in film and television, she combined on-screen street smarts and vulnerability with offscreen professionalism. Definitive performances arose from her collaborations with director Frank Capra, including *The Bitter Tea of General Yen* (1933) and *Meet John Doe* (1941), and her work with director Billy Wilder in *Double Indemnity* (1944). Other starring roles include those in *Stella Dallas* (1937), *Ball of Fire* (1942), and *Sorry, Wrong Number* (1948). She received an honorary Academy Award in 1981. She appeared on television in the 1960s in two series, *The Barbara Stanwyck Show* and *The Big Valley*. In 1987, she received the AFI Life Achievement Award.

Steiger, Rod (1925–) American actor. Born Rodney Stephen Steiger. Major dramatic actor of the 1950s to 70s who moved from the teleplay *Marty* to pivotal character roles in the films *On the Waterfront* (1954) and *Oklahoma!* (1955), among others. He was nominated for a best actor Academy Award for his title performance in *The Pawnbroker* (1965) and won a best actor Academy Award for his performance opposite Sidney Poitier in *In the Heat of the Night* (1967). Other films include *Doctor Zhivago* (1965). A large actor with forceful demeanor, he has often portrayed larger-than-life historical figures, including Al Capone, W.C. Fields, Napoleon, and Mussolini.

Stewart, James (1908–1997) American actor. The tall, gangly icon of American idealism entered film in 1935 and soon gained acclaim for earnest, youthful performances in Frank Capra's Depression-era films *You Can't Take It with You* (1938) and *Mr. Smith Goes to Washington* (1939). He offered a more sophisticated turn in *The Philadelphia Story* (1940), winning a best actor Academy Award. After service in World War II, his screen persona took on a darker, more mature shading, beginning with *It's a Wonderful Life* (1946). In the 1950s, he revitalized the western genre with his morally troubled characters in *Winchester '73* (1951) and *The Naked Spur* (1953), among others. Working with director Alfred Hitchcock, he starred in several memorable suspense films, including *Rear Window* (1954) and *Vertigo* (1958); working with director John Ford, he starred in the westerns *The Man Who Shot Liberty Valance* (1962) and *Cheyenne Autumn* (1964). Among his most beloved characters are those of the clown-doctor in *The Greatest Show on Earth* (1952) and the pixilated Elwood P. Dowd in *Harvey* (1950). He continued making films into the 1990s; late roles include his voice work in the animated *An American Tail 2: Fievel Goes West* (1991). In 1980 he received the AFI Life Achievement Award, and in 1983, he was honored by the Kennedy Center. He received a special Oscar in 1985 for his contribution to cinema.

Stone, Sharon (1958–) American actress. A cool beauty trained in TV, she became a lead femme fatale with her sexually charged performances in *Total Recall* (1990) and *Basic Instinct* (1992). Since then, she has concentrated on serious dramas, notably *Casino* (1995) and *Gloria* (1999).

Stooges, the Three Trio of American comic actors. Moe Howard (1897–1975), Shemp [Samuel] Howard (1900–1955), and Larry Fine (1911–1974). Originally a vaudeville act formed in 1928, the trio began appearing in films in 1930. Shemp was soon replaced by brother Curly [Jerome] Howard (1906–1952) but returned in 1946 when Curly retired. The Three Stooges specialized in physical comedy shorts, of which they made about 200 from 1934 to 1958, all involving forms of minor mutual abuse. Features include *My Sister Eileen* (1942) and *Have Rocket Will Travel* (1959). Joe Besser replaced Shemp after he died in 1955; Joe De Rita replaced Besser in 1959.

Streep, Meryl (1951–) American actress. Since the 1970s, this dominant dramatic lead has been acclaimed for her ability to transform herself in difficult roles, in films such as *The French Lieutenant's Woman* (1981); *Sophie's Choice* (1982), for which she won a best actress Academy Award; *Silkwood* (1983), *Out of Africa* (1985), and *Music of the Heart* (1999). She gained recognition through her role in *The Deer Hunter* (1978), for which she was nominated for a best supporting actress Academy Award, and later won the award for the drama *Kramer vs. Kramer* (1979). She has played opposite many of the era's leading actors, but was particularly evocative opposite Clint Eastwood in the romantic drama *The Bridges of Madison County* (1995).

Streisand, Barbra (1942–) American singer, actress, and director. Born Barbara Joan Streisand. One of the great popular singers of the twentieth century, she became a leading actress during the 1960s and 70s and an often successful director during the 1980s. A Broadway star, she brought her stage performance as Fanny Brice to film in *Funny Girl* (1968), winning a best actress Academy Award for this, her first screen role. She had several hits in the 1970s, including *What's Up, Doc?* (1973) and *The Way We Were* (1973), in which she usually played a smart, assertive, but not always romantically lucky woman. Among her directing credits, the most memorable have been *Yentl* (1983) and *The Prince of Tides* (1991), in both of which she also acted. In 2001, Streisand received the AFI Life Achievement Award.

Sutherland, Donald (1934–) Canadian-born American actor. Although he appeared during the 1960s in Hollywood and foreign features, such as *The Dirty Dozen* (1967, US/UK), Sutherland gained popularity as an image of the

"Harry, forget Stanwyck. She's not an actress, she's a porcupine."

—

Frank Capra in the 1930s to studio head Harry Cohn on his first impression of Barbara Stanwyck, whom he would go on to direct in 1941's Meet John Doe

Art imitates life in 1950's *Sunset Boulevard*. For scenes in which Gloria Swanson's faded silent screen star Norma Desmond projects one of her old movies for screenwriter Joe Gillis (William Holden), director Billy Wilder used clips from Swanson's silent film *Queen Kelly* (1928). The director of *Queen Kelly*, Erich von Stroheim, co-stars as Swanson's faithful chauffeur, butler, and former director.

counterculture with lead performances in *M*A*S*H* (1970) and *Start the Revolution Without Me* (1970). In dramas from *Klute* (1971) to *Ordinary People* (1980) to *A Dry White Season* (1989) to *Space Cowboys* (2000), he has shown delicacy in playing average men in conflict. He is the father of actor Kiefer Sutherland.

Sutherland, Kiefer (1966–) American actor. The son of actor Donald Sutherland, he appeared in films beginning in the mid-1980s and gained notice for his role as a teen thug in *Stand By Me* (1986). He was teamed up with other young leads for ensemble films such as *The Lost Boys* (1987), *Young Guns* (1988), and *Flatliners* (1990). Other films include *A Few Good Men* (1992), *The Three Musketeers* (1993), and *A Time to Kill* (1996).

Swank, Hilary (1974–) American actress. From the early 1990s, the angular and intense actress worked in television (e.g., *Beverly Hills 90210*) and film—for example, *Buffy the Vampire Slayer* (1992). But she did not gain wide notice until she played a transgender youth in *Boys Don't Cry* (1999), for which she won a best actress Academy Award. She is married to actor Chad Lowe.

Swanson, Gloria (1893–1983) American actress. A high-living queen of the silent era, she appeared in a variety of melodramas and sex farces, including *Don't Change Your Husband* (1919), *Male and Female* (1919), *Sadie Thompson* (1928), and *Queen Kelly* (1928), before her retirement in 1934. Directors included Erich von Stroheim and Cecil B. De Mille; husbands included Wallace Beery. Financier Joseph Kennedy was a longtime lover and supporter. She made a lasting impression as a faded silent-film star in *Sunset Boulevard* (1950).

Swayze, Patrick (1954–) American actor. Trained as a dancer, the lithe, likable actor became a romantic lead with *Dirty Dancing* (1987) and *Ghost* (1990). Other films include *Point Break* (1991).

T

Talmadge, Norma (1893–1957) American actress. One of the first major silent stars, she appeared in both comedies and dramas, including *Love's Redemption* (1921), *Smilin' Through* (1922), and *Our Hospitality* (1923). In part, her career was managed by her husband Joseph Schenck. She was sister of silent film actresses Constance and Natalie Talmadge, the former also a silent film star (*Intolerance,* 1916; *A Virtuous Vamp,* 1919). After divorcing Schenck, she married entertainer and actor George Jessel.

Jessica Tandy played a stodgy southern matriarch in Driving Miss Daisy *(1989), also starring Morgan Freeman and Dan Aykroyd.*

Tandy, Jessica (1907–1994) British-born American actress. A great stage actress, she was an occasional but respected player in films from the 1930s, including *The Seventh Cross* (1944) and *The Valley of Decision* (1945). She won a best actress Academy Award for the title role in *Driving Miss Daisy* (1989). Other films include *Fried Green Tomatoes* (1991). She was married to actors Jack Hawkins (1932–40) and Hume Cronyn (1940–94).

Taylor, Elizabeth (1932–) British-born American actress. For decades, the violet-eyed film goddess has been one of the world's most beautiful women and the object of constant publicity. She emerged as a child star with *National Velvet* (1944), *Jane Eyre* (1944), and *A Date with Judy* (1948); she then graduated to young adult romantic leads, notably in *Father of the Bride* (1950) and *A Place in the Sun* (1951). Offscreen she moved from her first husband, hotelier Nicky Hilton, to her second, actor Michael Wilding. Through much of the 1950s and into the early 60s, she starred in vehicles drawing on her sultriness and vulnerability, notably *Giant* (1956), *Raintree County* (1957), *Cat on a Hot Tin Roof* (1958), *Suddenly, Last Summer* (1959), and *Butterfield 8* (1960), for which she won a best actress Academy Award. This period also saw her third and fourth marriages, to producer Mike Todd and singer Eddie Fisher. Taylor reached artistic maturity in the 1960s and 70s, a period dominated by her two marriages to (and divorces from) actor Richard Burton. They met during the making of *Cleopatra* (1963), their first film together. Other film pairings include *Who's Afraid of Virginia Woolf?* (1966), for which she won a second best actress Academy Award, and *The Comedians* (1967, US/France). In the 1980s and 90s, she married twice more (to politician John Warner and workingman Larry Fortensky) and appeared only sporadically in films. Taylor received AFI's Life Achievement Award in 1993. She remains a major celebrity and a hallowed Hollywood survivor.

Taylor, Robert (1911–1969) American actor. Born Spangler Arlington Brugh. Of classic profile, he was a major romantic lead during the 1930s, in films including *Magnificent Obsession* (1935), *The Gorgeous Hussy* (1936), and *Camille* (1937). In later, more varied films, he played both leads and character support. Notable among them were *Quo Vadis* (1951), *Westward the Women* (1952), and *Ivanhoe* (1952). He continued making movies until the end of his life. He was married to Barbara Stanwyck (1939–52).

Temple, Shirley (1928–) American actress. Hollywood's most famous child star, she dominated the box office in the 1930s, offering irrepressible pluck and cheer to Depression-era audiences. Her films were linked to a cornucopia of Shirley Temple merchandise. Titles include *Bright Eyes* (1934), *The Little Colonel* (1935), *Curly Top* (1935), and *Rebecca of Sunnybrook Farm* (1938). Her popularity petered out as she approached adulthood, with late films including *The Bachelor and the Bobby-Soxer* (1947) and *Fort Apache* (1948). Under the name Shirley Temple Black (from her 1950 marriage to TV executive Charles Black), she was appointed US ambassador to Ghana and later to Czechoslovakia.

Thompson, Emma (1959–) British-born actress in British and American films. After comedy improvisation at Cambridge University and on the London stage, she made an early cinematic impression with her intelligent performance as Katherine in *Henry V* (1989). Particularly praised for interpreting literary works, she won the best actress Academy Award for her performance in *Howards End* (1992) and was nominated for that award for *The Remains of the Day* (1993). Comedic turns have included *Junior* (1994) and *Primary Colors* (1998). She wrote the screen adaptation for *Sense and Sensibility* (1995), for which she won an Academy Award for best adapted screenplay. She was married for a time to actor-director Kenneth Branagh, in whose films, such as *Henry V,* she sometimes appeared.

Thornton, Billy Bob (1955–) American actor, director, and screenwriter. Plain and intense, he is best known for writing, directing, and starring in the morality play *Sling Blade* (1996), for which he won a best adapted screenplay Academy Award. He has also offered notable performances in *One False Move* (1991, for which he also wrote the screenplay) *A Simple Plan* (1998), and *Monster's Ball* (2001). He is married to Angelina Jolie.

Thurman, Uma (1970–) American actress. Tall, striking player who has distinguished herself in diverse leads and supporting roles, notably in *Dangerous Liaisons* (1988), *Henry & June* (1990), and *Pulp Fiction* (1994). Other films include the romantic comedy *The Truth About Cats and Dogs* (1996) and the drama *Tape* (2001).

Tierney, Gene (1920–1991) American actress. An elusive brunette beauty, she became famous in the title role of *Laura* (1944). She varied between romantic dramas such as *The Ghost and Mrs. Muir* (1947) and dark melodramas such as *Leave Her to Heaven* (1945), in which she played a scheming murderer. She made films into the 1960s.

Tracy, Spencer (1900–1967) American actor. Trained on Broadway, he was brought to films in 1930 and became a leading star for four decades, renowned for his authority and ease on screen. One of the top stars of the 1930s, he won best actor Academy Awards twice in a row for *Captains Courageous* (1937) and *Boys Town* (1938); other credits of the period include *San Francisco* (1936) and *Libeled Lady* (1936). In the 1940s, he played the title roles in *Edison the Man* (1940) and *Dr. Jekyll and Mr. Hyde* (1941) and began his on- and offscreen relationship with Katharine Hepburn. Their film pairings began with *Woman of the Year* (1942) and went on to include *State of the Union* (1948), *Adam's Rib* (1949), *Pat and Mike* (1952), *Desk Set* (1957), and *Guess Who's Coming to Dinner* (1967), his final film. Other notable films include *Father of the Bride* (1950), *Bad Day at Black Rock* (1955), and *Inherit the Wind* (1960).

Travolta, John (1954–) American actor. Broadway-trained, the blue-eyed actor became a top TV star in the 1970s and moved seamlessly into film prominence with leads in *Saturday Night Fever* (1977) and *Grease* (1978). After a career slump in the 1980s, he rebounded with *Pulp Fiction* (1994), again becoming a major star. Subsequent roles convey a mix of menace and soulfulness in films such as *Face/Off* (1997), *A Civil Action* (1998), *The General's Daughter* (1999), and *Domestic Disturbance* (2001).

Trevor, Claire (1909–2000) American actress. Born Claire Wemlinger. A dependable lead in dramas and westerns from the 1930s to the 50s, she often played a good-hearted woman with a past. She gained notice with *Dead End* (1937) and won a best supporting actress Academy Award for *Key Largo* (1948). She was particularly memorable playing opposite John Wayne in such films as *Stagecoach* (1939) and *The High and the Mighty* (1954).

"People used to ask Spencer Tracy, 'Don't you ever get tired of playing Spencer Tracy?' An' he'd say, 'Who the hell do you want me to play?'"

—

James Stewart, 1960s

Turner, Kathleen (1954–) American actress. The raspy-voiced actress gained early notice as a femme fatale in her debut film, *Body Heat* (1981), then went on to appear in black comedies such as *Prizzi's Honor* (1985) and thoughtful dramas such as *Peggy Sue Got Married* (1986). She has since appeared only occasionally in film, concentrating instead on stage performances.

Turner, Lana (1920–) American actress. Born Jean Mildred Frances Turner. From her legendary discovery in a drugstore, she rose to become a major blond femme fatale in the 1940s and a melodramatic lead in the 50s. Known as the "Sweater Girl," she is best remembered for her leads in *The Postman Always Rings Twice* (1946), *The Bad and the Beautiful* (1952), *Peyton Place* (1957, for which she was nominated for a best actress Academy Award), and *Imitation of Life* (1959). Among her husbands were bandleader Artie Shaw (1940–41) and actor Lex Barker (1953–57). She was at the center of publicity in 1957 when daughter Cheryl Crane killed Turner's boyfriend Johnny Stompanato in defense of her mother's safety.

Turpin, Ben (1874–1940) American comedian. Trained in burlesque, the cross-eyed comic appeared widely in silent films but did not become a major star until the late 1910s and 20s, when he worked for director and producer Mack Sennett in film parodies including *Uncle Tom without the Cabin* (1919), *The Shriek of Araby* (1923), and *The Reel Virginian* (1924).

> "His eyes look spooked, like a cat's, and you feel he'd be cold to the touch."
>
> —
>
> *Pauline Kael, reviewing Christopher Walken's performance in* The Dogs of War, *1981*

U–V

Ullmann, Liv (1939–) Tokyo-born Norwegian actress in international films. Trained on the Norwegian stage, she is known for deeply felt performances in major Swedish films directed by Ingmar Bergman, including *Shame* (1968), *The Passion of Anna/Passion* (1969), *Cries and Whispers* (1972), and *Scenes from a Marriage* (1973). The luminous actress has also appeared in American films, including *Gaby—A True Story* (1988). She had a multiyear relationship with Bergman in the 1970s and 80s.

Ustinov, Sir Peter (1921–) British-born actor, director, and screenwriter. Trained on the London stage, this versatile character actor began his life as a stage and screen renaissance man at the age of 17 in 1938. He sold his first screenplay in 1945, directed his first film in 1946 and earned an Academy Award nomination for his supporting role as Nero in *Quo Vadis?* in 1952. He won Academy Awards for his supporting roles in *Spartacus* (1960) and *Topkapi* (1964) and went on to play detective

Hercule Poirot in three Agatha Christie mysteries; *Death on the Nile* (1978, UK), *Evil Under the Sun* (1982, UK), and *Appointment with Death* (1988, UK).

Valentino, Rudolph (or Rodolph) (1895–1926) Italian-born American actor. Born Rodolfo Alfonzo Raffaele Pierre Philibert Guglielmi. The main icon of exotic male seductiveness during the 1920s and an early film star, he had a meteoric career cut short by death. In films from 1918, he gained public appeal with his lead in *Four Horsemen of the Apocalypse* (1921) and became a sensation the same year with *The Sheik*. Films such as *Blood and Sand* (1922) and *Monsieur Beaucaire* (1924) followed, but by the time he appeared in *The Son of the Sheik* (1926), his star was waning. A frenzy of fan mourning followed his death from peritonitis caused by a ruptured appendix.

Van Damme, Jean-Claude (1960–) Belgian-born American actor. Born Jean-Claude Van Varenberg. Nicknamed the "Muscles from Brussels", he is best known for over-the-top action films including *Double Impact* (1991), *Universal Soldier* (1992), and *Timecop* (1994).

Voight, Jon (1938–) American actor. As Buck in *Midnight Cowboy* (1969), for which he was nominated for a best actor Academy Award, the Broadway-trained actor became a dramatic movie lead in the 1970s. His film choices, even star turns, reflected his interest in character studies, notably *Deliverance* (1972) and the antiwar drama *Coming Home* (1978), for which he won a best actor Academy Award. Since the 1980s, he has focused on character roles, notably in *Mission: Impossible* (1996) and *Ali* (2001). He is the father of actress Angelina Jolie.

W–Y

Walken, Christopher (1943–) American actor. In films from the late 1960s, he won a best supporting actor Academy Award for his performance as a broken soldier in *The Deer Hunter* (1978) and has continued to play psychologically driven roles in films such as *The Dead Zone* (1983) and *King of New York* (1990). Early in his career, he played Diane Keaton's troubled brother in *Annie Hall* (1977).

Washington, Denzel (1954–) American actor. A respected film actor since the 1980s, he is known for projecting inner anger and moral strength in films including *Glory* (1989), for which he won a best supporting actor Academy Award, *Malcolm X* (1992), *The Hurricane* (1999), and *Remember the Titans* (2000). He has starred in big-budget features, including

Stagecoach *(1939),*
featuring George Bancroft,
John Wayne, and Louise
Platt, was a turning point
in Wayne's career.

Sigourney Weaver took
her stage name from
a minor character
in F. Scott Fitzgerald's
The Great Gatsby.

Crimson Tide (1995) *Courage Under Fire* (1996), and *Training Day* (2001), for which he won an academy award.

Waters, Ethel (1896–1977) American actress and singer. A pioneering African-American stage and screen actress, she is best known to film fans for *Cabin in the Sky* (1942), *Pinky* (1949), and *The Member of the Wedding* (1952). Before making films, she was a top nightclub singer and a Broadway musical star.

Wayne, John (1907–1979) American actor. Born Marion Michael Morrison; known as Duke. A symbol of America and the quintessential western star of sound films, he was the successor to earlier genre leads Harry Carey and Tom Mix. He was a B-movie western player until he starred in John Ford's *Stagecoach* (1939) as the Ringo Kid. In westerns directed by Ford and others over the next decades, Wayne dominated the genre, becoming a symbol of the heroic, if haunted, fight for justice. Westerns with Ford include *She Wore a Yellow Ribbon* (1949), *Fort Apache* (1948), *Rio Grande* (1950), *The Man Who Shot Liberty Valance* (1962), and *The Searchers* (1956), which features his most obsessed character, Ethan Edwards). He played a similarly dark character in Howard Hawks's *Red River* (1949). Wayne was a top box-office draw for four decades in war and action movies, including *Back to Bataan* (1945), *They Were Expendable* (1945), *Sands of Iwo Jima* (1951), and *The High and the Mighty* (1954). He also appeared in

other kinds of films, such as the comedy-drama *The Quiet Man* (1952). He won a best actor Academy Award for the western *True Grit* (1969). Wayne occasionally directed or codirected his own films, most notably *The Green Berets* (1968, codirector), which reflected his support for the Vietnam War. His final film was the elegaic western *The Shootist* (1976).

Weaver, Sigourney (1949–) American actress. Born Susan Alexandra Weaver. The stately, intense dramatic lead entered film as Ripley in the science fiction thriller *Alien* (1979), a role she reprised in three sequels (1986, 1992, and 1997). She is also known for romantic leads opposite major actors of the period, notably in *Eyewitness* (1981), with William Hurt; *The Year of Living Dangerously* (1983, Australia), with Mel Gibson; and *Ghostbusters* (1984), with Bill Murray. Later films include *Galaxy Quest* (1999) and *Heartbreakers* (2001).

Webb, Clifton (1891–1966) American actor. Born Webb Parmallee Hollenbeck. Trained in opera and on Broadway, he dabbled in silent film but made his mark in sound films as the acid-tongued columnist in *Laura* (1944). Other films drawing on his persnickety persona include *Sitting Pretty* (1948) and *Cheaper by the Dozen* (1950).

Weissmuller, Johnny (1904–1984) American actor. Born Peter John Weissmuller. A swimmer who won Olympic gold medals in 1924 and 1928, he turned his athletic prowess to the title role in *Tarzan the Ape Man* (1932) and 11 sequels. Among them are *Tarzan and His Mate* (1934) and *Tarzan Finds a Son* (1939). He later starred in film and TV in the *Jungle Jim* series. Among his wives was actress Lupe Velez.

Welch, Raquel (1940–) American actress. Born Raquel Tejada. The voluptuous star secured status as a 60s sex symbol with *Fantastic Voyage* (1966) and *One Million Years B.C.* (1966, UK). Later films include *The Three Musketeers* (1974, UK) and *Tortilla Soup* (2001).

Welles, Orson (1915–1985) American director, producer, screenwriter, and actor. Born George Orson Welles. With his first directorial feature, *Citizen Kane* (1941), which he also produced, coscripted, and starred in, the young filmmaker and actor established his name. The "Boy Wonder" made and appeared in other films but never achieved the same acclaim. He was a stylized, intense actor, adept at playing morally dubious characters. Other films in which he acted include *Jane Eyre* (1944), *The Lady from Shanghai* (1948, also directed and cowrote), *The Third Man* (1949, UK), *Touch of Evil* (1958, also directed and cowrote), *Compulsion* (1959), and *A Man for All Seasons* (1966, UK). He was married to Rita Hayworth (1943–48). He received the AFI Life Achievement Award in 1975.

West, Mae (1892–1980) American actress, screenwriter, and playwright. A self-parodying icon of sexuality, she established her risqué persona on Broadway by starring in, writing, directing, and producing the play *Sex* (1926) before becoming a Hollywood sensation in the 1930s. Her films, many of which she scripted or coscripted, include *She Done Him Wrong* (1933), *I'm No Angel* (1933), *Belle of the Nineties* (1934), *Klondike Annie* (1936), and *My Little Chickadee* (1940). She was one of the highest-paid actresses of her day. Her image as a freethinking, free-spirited woman continued throughout her life.

Widmark, Richard (1914–) American actor. Trained on Broadway and in radio, he became a dependable, hard-edged character actor in films from the 1940s to the 90s. He was believable as a villain, in films such as *Kiss of Death* (1947; best supporting actor Academy Award nomination), and a dark lead, in noir films such as *Panic in the Streets* (1950) and *Pickup on South Street* (1953) and in westerns such as *Two Rode Together* (1961) and *Cheyenne Autumn* (1964). Later films include *Against All Odds* (1983).

Wilder, Gene (1935–) American actor. Born Jerry Silberman. A Broadway-trained performer, he is best known for his comically neurotic performances in three Mel Brooks comedies: *The Producers* (1968), *Blazing Saddles* (1974), and *Young Frankenstein* (1974), and for his pairings with Richard Pryor in such comedies

as *Silver Streak* (1976) and *Stir Crazy* (1980). He was married to comedian Gilda Radner from 1984 until her death from cancer in 1989.

William, Warren (1895–1948) American actor. Born Warren Krech. Broadway-trained, he appeared in silent films in the 1920s but became a top name in the 30s, specializing in detectives and other smart leads. Among his notable films are *Gold Diggers of 1933* (1933), *The Dragon Murder Case* (1934, playing Philo Vance), *The Case of the Howling Dog* (1934, playing Perry Mason), *Madame X* (1937), and *The Man in the Iron Mask* (1939).

Williams, Esther (1923–) American actress. A prize-winning swimmer in her youth, she became known as Hollywood's Mermaid on screen, in swank swimfest musicals such as *Bathing Beauty* (1944), *Neptune's Daughter* (1949), and *Million Dollar Mermaid* (1952). Her husbands included the actor Fernando Lamas.

Williams, Robin (1952–) American actor and comedian. He first became known as the star of the TV situation comedy *Mork and Mindy*, then gained a reputation as a quirky dramatic actor in *Good Morning, Vietnam* (1987) and *Dead Poets Society* (1989), in both of which he blended pathos with free-flowing verbal wit. Later films ranged from the drama *The Fisher King* (1991) to the comedy *Mrs. Doubtfire* (1993) to the science-fiction film *Bicentennial Man* (1999). He won a best supporting actor Academy Award for his performance as a troubled doctor in *Good Will Hunting* (1997).

Willis, Bruce (1955–) German-born American actor. A top TV lead in the 1980s with the detective series *Moonlighting*, he became a fast-talking film action hero in *Die Hard* (1988) and its sequels (1990 and 1995). While continuing to appear in action movies, such as *Armageddon* (1998), he showed often underappreciated dramatic and comic abilities in other kinds of films, such as *Pulp Fiction* (1994), *12 Monkeys* (1995), *The Sixth Sense* (1999), *The Whole Nine Yards* (2000), and *Bandits* (2001). He was married to actress Demi Moore.

Winger, Debra (1955–) American actress. Female lead known for playing headstrong, wounded characters in films such as *Urban Cowboy* (1980), *An Officer and a Gentleman* (1982), *Terms of Endearment* (1983), and *Shadowlands* (1993).

Wood, Natalie (1938–1981) American actress. Born Natasha Gurdin. A child star remembered as the doubter of Kris Kringle in *Miracle on 34th Street* (1947), she became a leading Hollywood actress in the late 1950s and 60s, with starring roles in *West Side Story* (1961), *Splendor in the Grass* (1961), and *Gypsy* (1962). Noted for her dark-haired beauty and her vulnerable on-screen persona, she died in a boating accident. She was the sister of actress Lana Wood and mother of actress Natasha Wagner.

Woods, James (1947–) American actor. Following stage experience, he has been a steady player of morally challenged characters, notably in *Salvador* (1986), *Casino* (1995), *Ghosts of Mississippi* (1996), and *Riding in Cars with Boys* (2001).

Woodward, Joanne (1930–) American actress. From TV and Broadway, she emerged a major Hollywood star for her tour-de-force in the psychological drama *The Three Faces of Eve* (1957), for which she won a best actress Academy Award. Through the 1970s, she appeared in major studio productions, some literary-based melodramas, including *The Long, Hot Summer* (1958) and *From the Terrace* (1960), and some character dramas, including *Rachel, Rachel* (1968). Since 1958, she has been married to her frequent co-star and director Paul Newman.

Wright, Teresa (1918–) American actress. Born Muriel Teresa Wright. She projected feeling and moral stability in high-quality dramas of the 1940s and 50s, winning a best supporting actress Academy Award for *Mrs. Miniver* (1942). Other films include *The Pride of the Yankees* (1942), *The Little Foxes* (1941), *Shadow of a Doubt* (1943), and *The Best Years of Our Lives* (1946). She was married to screenwriter Niven Busch and writer Robert Anderson.

Wyman, Jane (1914–) American actress. Born Sarah Jane Fulks. In the 1940s and 50s, she starred as sensitive, well-grounded women in such dramas as *The Lost Weekend* (1945), *The Yearling* (1946), and *Johnny Belinda* (1948), for which she won a best actress Academy Award. In the 1950s, she teamed with Rock Hudson in the melodramas *Magnificent Obsession* (1954) and *All That Heaven Allows* (1956). In the 1980s, she starred on TV's *Falcon Crest*. Among her four husbands was Ronald Reagan.

Young, Gig (1913–1978) American actor. Born Byron Elsworth Barr. Originally billed as Byron Barr (not to be confused with another

Hollywood actor of the same name) and Bryant Fleming. A likable second lead and supporting player, he often appeared in domestic comedies and dramas. Among his films are *Come Fill the Cup* (1951), *Teacher's Pet* (1958), *Young at Heart* (1955), *Desk Set* (1957), and *They Shoot Horses, Don't They?* (1969, best supporting actor Academy Award). Among his wives was actress Elizabeth Montgomery (1956–63).

Young, Loretta (1913–2000) American actress. Born Gretchen Michela Young. A child actress in silent movies, as an adult she became known for her on-screen elegance and simplicity, particularly in *The Farmer's Daughter* (1947), for which she won a best actress Academy Award. Other notable performances include those in *Come to the Stable* (1949), *The Story of Alexander Graham Bell* (1939), and *The Bishop's Wife* (1947). She retired from films in 1953 and became the gown-wearing star of the TV drama anthology series *The Loretta Young Show*.

Young, Robert (1907–1998) American actor. From the 1930s to the 50s, he was a dependable lead and supporting actor who radiated warmth and understanding. Among his films are *Three Comrades* (1938), *The Mortal Storm* (1940), *Western Union* (1941), and *That Forsyte Woman* (1951). In the 1950s, he turned to TV, starring in *Marcus Welby, M.D.*

Based on the memoirs of Gypsy Rose Lee, Gypsy (1962) featured Natalie Wood as the famous striptease dancer.

Mann's Chinese Theatre Forecourt of the Stars: Foot- and Handprint Ceremonies (1927–2001)

PROBABLY THE WORLD'S MOST FAMOUS MOVIE THEATER, Mann's Chinese Theatre opened in Hollywood in 1927 as Grauman's Chinese Theatre, named for owner Sidney Patrick Grauman (1879–1950). Dazzling for its exotic Asian architecture and decor, it became even more famous for the handprints and footprints of film celebrities embedded in cement slabs in the forecourt. Movie stars also left their autographs; sometimes wrote messages, such as Humphrey Bogart's "Sid—May you never die till

Gary Cooper was immortalized in cement at Grauman's Chinese Theatre in Hollywood on August 13, 1943.

I kill you"; and occasionally left other kinds of marks in the wet cement: Jimmy Durante's nose, Betty Grable's legs, Groucho Marx's cigar. Exhibitor Ted Mann purchased the theater in 1973, after which it was renamed Mann's Chinese Theatre and became part of the Mann Theatres chain. Below is a list of the foot- and handprint ceremonies that made the theater's forecourt what it is today. To see the prints up close, visit Mann's Chinese Theatre, 6925 Hollywood Boulevard, Hollywood, CA.

CEREMONIES 1927–2001

1. **Mary Pickford** and **Douglas Fairbanks**, April 30, 1927
2. **Norma Talmadge**, May 18, 1927
3. **Norma Shearer**, August 1, 1927
4. **Harold Lloyd**, November 21, 1927
5. **William S. Hart**, November 28, 1927
6. **Tom Mix** and **Tony**, December 12, 1927
7. **Colleen Moore**, December 19, 1927
8. **Gloria Swanson**, circa 1927
9. **Constance Talmadge**, circa 1927
10. **Charles Chaplin**, circa January 1928
11. **Pola Negri**, April 2, 1928
12. **Bebe Daniels**, May 11, 1929
13. **Marion Davies**, May 13, 1929
14. **Janet Gaynor**, May 29, 1929
15. **Joan Crawford**, September 14, 1929
16. **Ann Harding**, August 30, 1930
17. **Raoul Walsh**, November 14, 1930
18. **Wallace Beery** and **Marie Dressler**, January 31, 1931
19. **Jackie Cooper**, December 12, 1931
20. **Eddie Cantor**, March 9, 1932
21. **Diana Wynyard**, January 26, 1933
22. **The Marx Brothers**, February 17, 1933
23. **Jean Harlow**, September 25, 1933
24. **Jean Harlow**, September 29, 1933
25. **Maurice Chevalier** and **Jeanette MacDonald**, December 4, 1934
26. **Shirley Temple**, March 14, 1935
27. **Joe E. Brown**, March 5, 1936
28. **Al Jolson**, March 12, 1936
29. **Freddie Bartholomew**, April 4, 1936
30. **Bing Crosby**, April 8, 1936
31. **Victor McLaglen**, May 25, 1936
32. **William Powell** and **Myrna Loy**, October 20, 1936
33. **Clark Gable** and **W.S. Van Dyke II**, January 20, 1937
34. **Dick Powell** and **Joan Blondell**, February 10, 1937
35. **Fredric March**, April 21, 1937
36. **May Robson**, April 22, 1937
37. **Tyrone Power** and **Loretta Young**, May 31, 1937
38. **Sonja Henie**, June 28, 1937
39. **The Ritz Brothers**, September 22, 1937
40. **Eleanor Powell**, December 23, 1937
41. **Don Ameche**, January 27, 1938
42. **Fred Astaire**, February 4, 1938
43. **Deanna Durbin**, February 7, 1938
44. **Alice Faye** and **Tony Martin**, March 20, 1938
45. **Edgar Bergen** and **Charlie McCarthy**, July 20, 1938
46. **The Dionne Quintuplets** and **Jean Hersholt**, October 11, 1938
47. **Mickey Rooney**, October 18, 1938
48. **Nelson Eddy**, December 28, 1938
49. **Ginger Rogers**, September 5, 1939
50. **Judy Garland**, October 10, 1939
51. **Jane Withers**, November 6, 1939
52. **Linda Darnell**, March 18, 1940
53. **Rosa Grauman** and **George Raft**, March 25, 1940
54. **John Barrymore**, September 5, 1940
55. **Jack Benny**, January 13, 1941
56. **Carmen Miranda**, March 24, 1941
57. **Barbara Stanwyck** and **Robert Taylor**, June 11, 1941
58. **Rudy Vallee**, July 21, 1941
59. **Cecil B. De Mille**, August 7, 1941
60. **The Judge James K. Hardy Family**, August 15, 1941
61. **Bud Abbott** and **Lou Costello**, December 8, 1941
62. **Edward Arnold**, January 6, 1942
63. **Joan Fontaine**, May 26, 1942
64. **Red Skelton**, June 18, 1942
65. **Mrs. Miniver** and **Greer Garson**, July 23, 1942
66. **Henry Fonda, Rita Hayworth, Charles Laughton, Edward G. Robinson,** and **Charles Boyer**, July 24, 1942
67. **Bob Hope** and **Dorothy Lamour**, February 5, 1943
68. **Betty Grable**, February 15, 1943
69. **Monty Woolley**, May 28, 1943
70. **Gary Cooper**, August 13, 1943
71. **Esther Williams** and **Private Joe Brain**, August 1, 1944

72. **Jack Oakie**, February 21, 1945
73. **Jimmy Durante**, October 31, 1945
74. **Sid Grauman** and **Gene Tierney**, January 24, 1946
75. **Irene Dunne** and **Rex Harrison**, July 8, 1946
76. **Margaret O'Brien**, August 15, 1946
77. **Humphrey Bogart**, August 21, 1946
78. **Louella O. Parsons**, September 30, 1946
79. **Ray Milland**, April 17, 1947
80. **Lauritz Melchior**, November 17, 1947
81. **James Stewart**, February 13, 1948
82. **Van Johnson**, March 25, 1948
83. **George Jessel**, March 1, 1949
84. **Roy Rogers** and **Trigger**, April 21, 1949
85. **Richard Widmark** and **Charles Nelson**, April 24, 1949
86. **Jeanne Crain**, October 17, 1949
87. **Jean Hersholt**, October 20, 1949
88. **Anne Baxter** and **Gregory Peck**, December 15, 1949
89. **Gene Autry** and **Champion**, December 1949
90. **John Wayne**, January 25, 1950
91. **Lana Turner**, May 24, 1950
92. **Bette Davis**, November 6, 1950
93. **William Lundigan**, December 29, 1950
94. **Cary Grant**, July 16, 1951
95. **Susan Hayward**, August 10, 1951
96. **Hildegarde Neff** and **Oskar Werner**, December 13, 1951
97. **Jane Wyman**, September 17, 1952
98. **Ava Gardner**, October 21, 1952
99. **Clifton Webb**, December 7, 1952
100. **Olivia de Havilland**, December 9, 1952
101. **Adolph Zukor**, January 5, 1953
102. **Ezio Pinza**, January 26, 1953
103. **Effie O'Connor** and **Donald O'Connor**, February 25, 1953
104. **Jane Russell** and **Marilyn Monroe**, June 26, 1953
105. **CinemaScope**, *The Robe* (1953), and **Jean Simmons**, September 24, 1953
106. **Danny Thomas**, January 26, 1954
107. **James Mason**, March 30, 1954
108. **Alan Ladd**, May 12, 1954
109. **Edmund Purdom**, August 30, 1954
110. **Van Heflin**, October 8, 1954
111. **George Murphy**, November 8, 1954
112. **Yul Brynner** and **Deborah Kerr**, March 22, 1956
113. **Elizabeth Taylor**, **Rock Hudson**, and **George Stevens**, September 26, 1956
114. **Elmer C. Rhoden**, September 16, 1958
115. **Rosalind Russell**, February 19, 1959
116. **Cantinflas**, December 28, 1960
117. **Doris Day**, January 19, 1961
118. **Natalie Wood**, December 5, 1961
119. **Charlton Heston**, January 18, 1962
120. **Sophia Loren**, July 26, 1962
121. **Kirk Douglas**, November 1, 1962
122. **Paul Newman** and **Joanne Woodward**, May 25, 1963
123. **Jack Lemmon** and **Shirley MacLaine**, June 29, 1963

John Barrymore added his imprints to those of other stars in front of Grauman's Chinese Theatre in Hollywood with a little help from Sid Grauman on September 5, 1940.

124. **Mervyn LeRoy**, October 15, 1963
125. **Hayley Mills**, February 22, 1964
126. **Dean Martin**, March 21, 1964
127. **Peter Sellers**, June 3, 1964
128. **Debbie Reynolds**, January 14, 1965
129. **Marcello Mastroianni**, February 8, 1965
130. **Frank Sinatra**, July 20, 1965
131. **Julie Andrews**, March 26, 1966
132. **Dick Van Dyke**, June 25, 1966
133. **Steve McQueen**, March 21, 1967
134. **Sidney Poitier**, June 23, 1967
135. **Anthony Quinn**, December 21, 1968
136. **Danny Kaye**, October 19, 1969
137. **Gene Kelly**, November 24, 1969
138. **Francis X. Bushman**, November 17, 1970
139. **Ali MacGraw**, December 14, 1972
140. **Jack Nicholson**, June 17, 1974
141. **Mayor Tom Bradley** and **Ted Mann**, May 18, 1977
142. **The Chinese Theatre's Fiftieth Anniversary**, May 24, 1977
143. *Star Wars* (1977) characters, **C-3PO, R2-D2, Lord Darth Vader**, and **Anthony Daniels**, August 3, 1977
144. **George Burns**, January 25, 1979
145. **John Travolta**, June 2, 1980
146. **Burt Reynolds**, September 24, 1981
147. **Rhonda Fleming**, September 28, 1981
148. **Sylvester Stallone**, June 29, 1983
149. **George Lucas** and **Steven Spielberg**, May 16, 1984
150. **Donald Duck** and **Clarence "Ducky" Nash**, May 21, 1984
151. **Clint Eastwood**, August 21, 1984
152. **Mickey Rooney**, February 18, 1986
153. **Eddie Murphy** and **Hollywood's 100th Anniversary**, May 14, 1987

154. *Star Trek*'s 25th anniversary, including its creator **Gene Roddenberry**, and featured players **William Shatner, Leonard Nimoy, DeForest Kelley, James Doohan, Walter Koenig, Nichelle Nichols**, and **George Takei**, December 5, 1991
155. **Harrison Ford**, June 4, 1992
156. **Michael Keaton**, June 15, 1992
157. **Tom Cruise**, June 15, 1992
158. **Mel Gibson**, August 23, 1993
159. **Arnold Schwarzenegger**, July 15, 1994
160. **Meryl Streep**, September 25, 1994
161. **Whoopi Goldberg**, February 2, 1995
162. **Bruce Willis**, May 18, 1995
163. **Steven Seagal**, July 10, 1995
164. **Jim Carrey**, November 1, 1995
165. **Johnny Grant**, May 13, 1997
166. **Robert Zemeckis**, July 8, 1997
167. **Michael Douglas**, September 10, 1997
168. **Al Pacino**, October 16, 1997
169. **Denzel Washington**, January 15, 1998
170. **Walter Matthau**, April 2, 1998
171. **Warren Beatty**, May 21, 1998
172. **Danny Glover**, July 7, 1998
173. **Tom Hanks**, July 23, 1998
174. **Robin Williams**, December 22, 1998
175. **Susan Sarandon**, January 11, 1999
176. **William F. "Bill" Hertz**, March 18, 1999
177. **Ron Howard**, March 23, 1999
178. **Sean Connery**, April 13, 1999
179. **Richard Gere**, July 26, 1999
180. **Terry Semel** and **Bob Daly**, September 30, 1999
181. **Sir Anthony Hopkins**, January 11, 2001
182. **Nicholas Cage**, August 14, 2001

Source: Mann Theatres official website, http://www.manntheatres.com/fore.html

HISTORICAL AND LEGENDARY FIGURES ON FILM: A SELECTION

Larger-than-life characters, whether honorable or evil, historical or legendary, make for memorable film appearances. On screen they can be even more of themselves than they were in legend or life.

TO IDENTIFY EVERY MEMORABLE CHARACTER from the movies would take a book in itself, not just a section of a chapter in a book. But movie characters are such an important part of the cinema experience that a chapter on film people hardly seems complete without paying homage to them. This section, then, honors film characters—not by providing an exhaustive compendium but simply by naming some of the greatest characters and listing the actors and films responsible for bringing them to life on screen. It includes four subsections: "Historical and Legendary," "Familiar Faces," "Minor Characters," and "Fictional."

This subsection lists more than 50 of the historical and legendary people most frequently portrayed on film. It includes those who actually lived, such as Julius Caesar; people who may have lived, such as Robin Hood; and

Richard Harris, Vanessa Redgrave, and Franco Nero starred as King Arthur, Guinevere, and Sir Lancelot in the musical Camelot *(1967).*

miscellaneous others dreamed up by the world's storytelling traditions, such as Sinbad. The principal criterion for selection: that the figure is widely known and has been portrayed in film many times.

For each figure, a brief identification is given, along with birth and death dates if the figure is historical. As with the fictional characters, identifications of these figures are kept short to put the focus on the films in which they were portrayed. Feature films in which the figures appeared are then listed, with the date of release and the actor who played the figure in that film. Many of these figures have been played so often, frequently in minor films, that space considerations make it impossible to include all these portrayals. Still, efforts have been made to include all or most of the major sound feature films that depict the historical figure, and at least a representative sampling of the silent films.

Aladdin Genie-mastering hero of Arabian tradition.
John Qualen, *Arabian Nights* (1942)
Cornel Wilde, *A Thousand and One Nights* (1945)
Johnny Sands, *Aladdin and His Lamp* (1952)
Robert Clary, *Thief of Damascus* (1952)
Dwayne Hickman, *1001 Arabian Nights* (1959)
Donald O'Connor, *Le Meraviglie di Aladino (The Wonders of Aladdin)* (1961, Italy)
Scott Weinger, *Aladdin* (1992; voice only)

Anastasia (1901–1918) Youngest daughter of Tsar Nicholas Romanov of Russia, assumed murdered with her family by the Bolsheviks but rumored to have survived.
Dawn O'Day, *Rasputin and the Empress* (1932)
Lilli Palmer, *Is Anna Anderson Anastasia?* (1956, Germany)
Ingrid Bergman, *Anastasia* (1956)
Fiona Fullerton, *Nicholas and Alexandra* (1971)
Meg Ryan, *Anastasia* (1997; voice only)

Antony, Marc (c. 82–30 B.C.E.) Roman soldier, avenger of Julius Caesar, and lover of Cleopatra.
Frank Benson, *Mark Antony* (1911, UK)
Henry Wilcoxon, *Cleopatra* (1934)
Charlton Heston, *Julius Caesar* (1950)
Marlon Brando, *Julius Caesar* (1953)
Raymond Burr, *Serpent of the Nile* (1953)
Bruno Tocci, *Caesar the Conqueror* (1962, Italy)
Richard Burton, *Cleopatra* (1963)
Sidney James, *Carry on Cleo* (1965, UK)
Charlton Heston, *Julius Caesar* (1970, UK)
Charlton Heston, *Antony and Cleopatra* (1972, UK/Switzerland/Spain)

Arthur Legendary medieval king of England and head of the Knights of the Round Table.
Billy Sullivan, *Over the Hill* (1917)
Charles Clary, *A Connecticut Yankee in King Arthur's Court* (1921)
William Farnum, *A Connecticut Yankee* (1931)
Cedric Hardwicke, *A Connecticut Yankee in King Arthur's Court* (1949)
Nelson Leigh, *The Adventures of Sir Galahad* (1949)
Mel Ferrer, *Knights of the Round Table* (1953, UK)
Brian Aherne, *Prince Valiant* (1954)
Anthony Bushell, *The Black Knight* (1954)
Brian Aherne, *Lancelot and Guinevere* (1963, UK)
Rickie Sorensen, *The Sword in the Stone* (1963; voice only)
Richard Harris, *Camelot* (1967)
Graham Chapman, *Monty Python and the Holy Grail* (1975, UK)
Nigel Terry, *Excalibur* (1981)
Trevor Howard, *Sword of the Valiant* (1982)
Sean Connery, *First Knight* (1995)
Joss Ackland, *A Kid in King Arthur's Court* (1995)
Sir John Gielgud, *Dragonheart* (1996)
Pierce Brosnan, *Quest for Camelot* (1998; voice only)

Beethoven, Ludwig van (1770–1827) German classical composer.
Harry Baur, *Un Grand Amour de Beethoven (The Life and Loves of Beethoven)* (1936, France)
Albert Bassermann, *New Wine* (1941)
Memo Benassi, *Rossini* (1941, Italy)
René Deltgen, *The Mozart Story* (1948)
Ewald Balser, *Eroica* (1949, Austria)
Erich von Stroheim, *Napoleon* (1954, France)
Ewald Balser, *Das Dreimäderlhaus (The House of the Three Girls)* (1958, Austria)
Gary Oldman, *Immortal Beloved* (1994)

Billy the Kid (1859–1881) Born William H. Bonney. Notorious outlaw of the Wild West.
Johnny Mack Brown, *Billy the Kid* (1930)
Roy Rogers, *Billy the Kid Returns* (1938)
Robert Taylor, *Billy the Kid* (1941)
Buster Crabbe, *Billy the Kid: Wanted* (1941; serial)
Jack Buetel, *The Outlaw* (1943)
Don Barry, *I Shot Billy the Kid* (1950)
Scott Brady, *The Law vs. Billy the Kid* (1954)
Paul Newman, *The Left-Handed Gun* (1958)
Chuck Courtenay, *Billy the Kid vs. Dracula* (1966)
Michael J. Pollard, *Dirty Little Billy* (1972)
Kris Kristofferson, *Pat Garrett & Billy the Kid* (1973)

Boleyn, Anne (1507–1536) Wife of King of England Henry VIII, mother of Queen Elizabeth I, executed for treason.
Laura Cowie, *Henry VIII* (1911, UK)
Merle Oberon, *The Private Life of Henry VIII* (1933, UK)
Elaine Stewart, *Young Bess* (1953)
Vanessa Redgrave, *A Man for All Seasons* (1966, UK)
Genevieve Bujold, *Anne of a Thousand Days* (1969, UK)
Charlotte Rampling, *Henry VIII and His Six Wives* (1973, UK)

Bonaparte, Napoléon (1769–1821) Emperor of France.
Albert Dieudonné, *Napoléon* (1927, restored 1981, France)
Rollo Lloyd, *Anthony Adverse* (1936)
Claude Rains, *Hearts Divided* (1936)
Charles Boyer, *Conquest* (1937)
Sergei Mezhinsky, *Kutuzov* (1944, USSR)
Marlon Brando, *Desirée* (1954)
Herbert Lom, *War and Peace* (1956, US/Italy)
Dennis Hopper, *The Story of Mankind* (1957)
Rod Steiger, *Waterloo* (1970, Italy/USSR)
Kenneth Haigh, *Eagle in a Cage* (1971, UK)

Buffalo Bill (1846–1917) Born William Frederick Cody. Wild West adventurer and entertainer.
William Fairbanks, *Wyoming* (1928)
Douglas Dumbrille, *The World Changes* (1933)
Moroni Olsen, *Annie Oakley* (1935)
Ted Adams, *Custer's Last Stand* (1936)
Roy Rogers, *Young Buffalo Bill* (1940)
Joel McCrea, *Buffalo Bill* (1944)
Richard Arlen, *Buffalo Bill Rides Again* (1947)
Louis Calhern, *Annie Get Your Gun* (1950)
Clayton Moore, *Buffalo Bill in Tomahawk Territory* (1952)
Charlton Heston, *Pony Express* (1953)
Malcolm Atterbury, *Badman's Country* (1958)
Gordon Scott, *Buffalo Bill* (1965, Italy/Germany/France)
Paul Newman, *Buffalo Bill & the Indians, or, Sitting Bull's History Lesson* (1976)
Ted Flicker, *The Legend of the Lone Ranger* (1981)
Keith Carradine, *Wild Bill* (1995)

Byron, Lord (George Gordon, 1788–1824) English poet and tempestuous freethinker.
George Beranger, *Beau Brummel* (1924)
Malcolm Graham, *The Last Rose of Summer* (1937, UK)
Dennis Price, *The Bad Lord Byron* (1949, UK)
Noel Willman, *Beau Brummel* (1954, UK)
Richard Chamberlain, *Lady Caroline Lamb* (1972, UK/Italy)
Hugh Grant, *Remando al Viento (Rowing in the Wind)* (1987, Spain)
Gabriel Byrne, *Gothic* (1987, UK)
Phillip Anglim, *Haunted Summer* (1988)
Jason Patric, *Frankenstein Unbound* (1990)

Caesar, Julius (101–44 B.C.E.) Roman dictator.
Charles Kent, *Julius Caesar* (1908)
Theo Frenkel, *Caesar's Prisoners* (1911, UK)
Guy Rathbone, *Julius Caesar* (1911, UK)
Warren William, *Cleopatra* (1934)
Claude Rains, *Caesar and Cleopatra* (1946, UK)
Louis Calhern, *Julius Caesar* (1953)
William Lundigan, *Serpent of the Nile* (1953)
John Gavin, *Spartacus* (1960)
Rex Harrison, *Cleopatra* (1963)
Kenneth Williams, *Carry on Cleo* (1965, UK)
John Gielgud, *Julius Caesar* (1970, UK)
Dom DeLuise, *History of the World Part One* (1981)

Capone, Al (1899–1947) Notorious American gangster and
  bootlegger.
Paul Muni, *Scarface* (1932; as Tony Camonte, based on Capone)
Rod Steiger, *Al Capone* (1959)
Neville Brand, *Spin of a Coin* (1962)
Jason Robards, *The St. Valentine's Day Massacre* (1967)
Ben Gazzara, *Capone* (1975)
Louis Giambalvo, *Gangster Wars* (1981)
Robert De Niro, *The Untouchables* (1987)
Titus Welliver, *Mobsters* (1991)
F. Murray Abraham, *Dillinger and Capone* (1995)

Casanova, Giovanni (1725–1798) Italian rogue and
  accomplished lover.
Michael Bohnene, *Casanova* (1928)
Georges Guétary, *Les Adventures de Casanova* (1946, France)
Arturo de Córdova, *The Adventures of Casanova* (1948)
Vincent Price, *Casanova's Big Night* (1954)
Marcello Mastroianni, *Casanova 70* (1965, Italy/France)
Donald Sutherland, *Fellini's Casanova* (1976)
Tony Curtis, *Casanova & Co.* (1977, Austria/France/Italy)
Marcello Mastroianni, *La Nuit de Varennes* (1982, France/Italy)
Alain Delon, *Le Retour de Casanova* (1992)

Cinderella European fairy-tale heroine who is
  transformed from reviled scullery maid to princess.
Florence La Badie, *Cinderella* (1911)
Mary Pickford, *Cinderella* (1914)
Ilene Woods, *Cinderella* (1950)
Leslie Caron, *The Glass Slipper* (1955)
Jerry Lewis, *Cinderfella* (1960; male version of
  Cinderella)
Pamela Baird, *The Wonderful World of the
  Brothers Grimm* (1962)
Gemma Craven, *The Slipper and the Rose*
  (1976, UK)
Drew Barrymore, *Ever After* (1998)

Cleopatra (68–30 B.C.E.)
  Egyptian queen, lover of
  Julius Caesar and Marc
  Antony.
Helen Gardner, *Cleopatra*
  (1912)
Theda Bara, *Cleopatra* (1917)
Claudette Colbert, *Cleopatra*
  (1934)
Vivien Leigh, *Caesar and
  Cleopatra* (1946, UK)
Pauline Letts, *Antony and
  Cleopatra* (1951, UK)

Rhonda Fleming, *Serpent of the Nile* (1953)
Sophia Loren, *Due Notti con Cleopatra* (1954, Italy)
Virginia Mayo, *The Story of Mankind* (1957)
Elizabeth Taylor, *Cleopatra* (1963)
Amanda Barrie, *Carry On Cleo* (1964, UK)
Lynn Redgrave, *Antony and Cleopatra* (1983, Italy/Germany/France)

Crockett, Davy (1786–1836) American frontiersman famous for
  his adventurous spirit, particularly at the Alamo.
Dustin Farnum, *Davy Crockett* (1916)
Cullen Landis, *Davy Crockett at the Fall of the Alamo* (1926)
Lane Chandler, *Heroes of the Alamo* (1937)
Robert Barrat, *Man of Conquest* (1939)
George Montgomery, *Davy Crockett, Indian Scout* (1949)
Trevor Bardette, *The Man from the Alamo* (1953)
Fess Parker, *Davy Crockett, King of the Wild Frontier* (1955)
Arthur Hunnicutt, *The Last Command* (1955)
John Wayne, *The Alamo* (1960)

Cromwell, Oliver (1599–1658) Puritan reformer and Lord
  Protector of England.
Booth Conway, *The Tavern Knight* (1920, UK)
Frederick Burton, *The Fighting Blade* (1923)
George Merritt, *The Vicar of Bray* (1937, UK)
John Le Mesurier, *The Moonraker* (1957, UK)
Patrick Wymark, *Matthew Hopkins: Witchfinder General* (1968, UK)
Richard Harris, *Cromwell* (1970, UK)

Cyrano de Bergerac, Savinien de (1619–1655) French poet and
  playwright famed for his literary talent, dueling skill, and nose.
  Immortalized in Edmond Rostand's play *Cyrano de Bergerac*
  (1897).
Pierre Magnier, *Cyrano de Bergerac* (1925, Italy/France)
Claude Dauphin, *Cyrano de Bergerac* (1945, France)
José Ferrer, *Cyrano de Bergerac* (1950)
José Ferrer, *Cyrano et d'Artagnan* (1963, France/Italy/Spain)
Steve Martin, *Roxanne* (1987; as modern update of Cyrano)
Gérard Depardieu, *Cyrano de Bergerac* (1990, France)

The Devil Fallen angel and prince of evil, also known as
Satan, Lucifer, or Beelzebub.
Edward Connelly, *The Devil* (1915)
Walter Huston, *All That Money Can Buy* (1941)
Alan Mowbray, *The Devil with Hitler* (1942)
Rex Ingram, *Cabin in the Sky* (1943)
Laird Cregar, *Heaven Can Wait* (1943)
Claude Rains, *Angel on My Shoulder* (1946)
Ray Milland, *Alias Nick Beal* (1949)
Stanley Holloway, *Meet Mr. Lucifer* (1953, UK)

*The tale of lovesick Cyrano de
Bergerac was revisited in the
1990 film of the same name
starring Gérard Depardieu.*

Yves Montand, *Marguerite de la Nuit (Marguerite of the Night)* (1956, France)
Vincent Price, *The Story of Mankind* (1957)
Stig Jarrel, *The Devil's Eye* (1960, Sweden)
Mickey Rooney, *The Private Lives of Adam and Eve* (1961)
Lon Chaney, Jr., *The Devil's Messenger* (1962, US/Sweden)
Donald Pleasance, *The Greatest Story Ever Told* (1965)
Peter Cook, *Bedazzled* (1967, UK)
Burgess Meredith, *Torture Garden* (1967, UK)
Clay Tanner, *Rosemary's Baby* (1968)
Ralph Richardson, *Tales from the Crypt* (1972, UK)
Ernest Borgnine, *The Devil's Rain* (1976)
John Ritter, *Wholly Moses* (1980)
Bill Cosby, *The Devil and Max Devlin* (1981)
George Burns, *Oh God! You Devil* (1984)
Terence Stamp, *The Company of Wolves* (1984)
Robert De Niro, *Angel Heart* (1987)
Jack Nicholson, *The Witches of Eastwick* (1989)
Bruce Payne, *Switch* (1991)
Al Pacino, *The Devil's Advocate* (1997)
David Moran, *Deconstructing Harry* (1997)
Elizabeth Hurley, *Bedazzled* (2000)
Harvey Keitel, *Little Nicky* (2000; as Satan)
Rodney Dangerfield, *Little Nicky* (2000; as Lucifer)

Dillinger, John (1903–1934) Notorious American gangster known as public enemy number one.
Lawrence Tierney, *Dillinger* (1945)
Leo Gordon, *Baby Face Nelson* (1957)
Nick Adams, *Young Dillinger* (1965)
Warren Oates, *Dillinger* (1973)
Robert Conrad, *The Lady in Red* (1979)
Martin Kove, *Baby Face Nelson* (1995)
Martin Sheen, *Dillinger and Capone* (1995)

Earp, Wyatt (1848–1929) Formidable lawman of the Wild West.
Walter Huston, *Law and Order* (1932)
Randolph Scott, *Frontier Marshal* (1939)
Richard Dix, *Tombstone, the Town Too Tough to Die* (1942)
Henry Fonda, *My Darling Clementine* (1946)
Will Geer, *Winchester '73* (1950)
Joel McCrea, *Wichita* (1955)
Burt Lancaster, *Gunfight at the O.K. Corral* (1957)
Buster Crabbe, *Badman's Country* (1958)
James Stewart, *Cheyenne Autumn* (1964)
Bill Canfield, *The Outlaws Is Coming* (1965)
James Garner, *Hour of the Gun* (1967)
Harris Yulin, *Doc* (1971)
James Garner, *Sunset* (1988)
Kurt Russell, *Tombstone* (1993)
Hugh O'Brian, *Wyatt Earp: Return to Tombstone* (1994)

Elizabeth I (1533–1603) Queen of England; powerful daughter of Queen Anne Boleyn and King Henry VIII.
Sarah Bernhardt, *Queen Elizabeth* (1912, France)
Miriam Nesbitt, *Mary Stuart* (1913)
Diana Manners, *The Virgin Queen* (1923, UK)
Athene Seyler, *Drake of England* (1935, UK)
Flora Robson, *Fire over England* (1937)
Bette Davis, *The Private Lives of Elizabeth and Essex* (1939)
Bette Davis, *The Virgin Queen* (1955)
Agnes Moorehead, *The Story of Mankind* (1957)
Glenda Jackson, *Mary, Queen of Scots* (1971, UK)
Jenny Runacre, *Jubilee* (1977)
Cate Blanchett, *Elizabeth* (1998)

God Supreme deity; creator of the universe.
George Grossmith, *God Is My Witness* (1931)
Charlton Heston, *The Ten Commandments* (1956; voice only)
Fernandel, *Le Diable et les Dix Commandements (The Devil and the Ten Commandments)* (1962, France)
George Burns, *Oh God!* (1977)
George Burns, *Oh God! Book II* (1980)
George Burns, *Oh God! You Devil* (1984)
Alanis Morissette, *Dogma* (1999)

Guinevere Legendary medieval Queen of England, wife of King Arthur and love to Sir Lancelot.
Marjorie Stapp, *The Adventures of Sir Galahad* (1949)
Jean Lodge, *The Black Knight* (1954)
Ava Gardner, *Knights of the Round Table* (1954, UK)
Jarma Lewis, *Prince Valiant* (1954)
Jean Wallace, *Lancelot and Guinevere* (1963)
Vanessa Redgrave, *Camelot* (1967)
Laura Duke Condominas, *Lancelot du Lac* (1974, Italy/France)
Carolyn Davies, *Lady of the Lake* (1986)
Lisa Flores, *A Young Connecticut Yankee in King Arthur's Court* (1995)
Julia Ormond, *First Knight* (1995)

Henry VIII (1491–1547) King of England and first head of the Anglican Church.
Arthur Bourchier, *Henry VIII* (1911, UK)
Charles Laughton, *The Private Life of Henry VIII* (1933, UK)
Montagu Love, *The Prince and the Pauper* (1937)
Lyn Harding, *Les Perles de las Couronne (The Pearls of the Crown)* (1937, France)
Charles Laughton, *Young Bess* (1953)
James Robertson Justice, *The Sword and the Rose* (1962, UK)
Robert Shaw, *A Man for All Seasons* (1966, UK)
Richard Burton, *Anne of a Thousand Days* (1969, UK)
Keith Mitchell, *Henry VIII and His Six Wives* (1972, UK)
Charlton Heston, *The Prince and the Pauper* (1977, UK)
Keith Barron, *God's Outlaw* (1986, UK)

Hercules Greek mythological hero famed for his superhuman strength.
Steve Reeves, *Le Fatiche di Ercole (Hercules)* (1959, Italy; reprised in sequels)
Samson Burke, *The Three Stooges Meet Hercules* (1962)
Nigel Green, *Jason and the Argonauts* (1963)
Arnold Schwarzenegger, *Hercules in New York* (1970)
Lou Ferrigno, *Hercules* (1983, Italy; reprised in sequel)
Tate Donovan, *Hercules* (1997; voice only)

Hitler, Adolf (1889–1945) Nazi dictator of Germany, instigator of World War II, and genocidal madman.
Charles Chaplin, *The Great Dictator* (1940; as Adenoid Hynkel, based on Hitler)
Carl Ekberg, *Man Hunt* (1941)
Bobby Watson, *The Devil with Hitler* (1942)
Ludwig Donath, *The Strange Death of Adolf Hitler* (1943)
V. Savelyov, *The Fall of Berlin* (1949, USSR)
Bobby Watson, *The Story of Mankind* (1957)
Richard Basehart, *Hitler* (1962)
Billy Frick, *Is Paris Burning?* (1966, US/France)
Sidney Miller, *Which Way to the Front?* (1970)
Alec Guinness, *Hitler: The Last Ten Days* (1973, UK/Italy)
Peter Sellers, *Soft Beds, Hard Battles* (1974, UK)
Kurt Raab, *Adolf and Marlene* (1977, Germany)
Gunther Bader, *Schtonk!* (1992, Germany)
Armin Mueller-Stahl, *Conversation with the Beast* (1996)

Holliday, Doc (1849–1885) Wild West dentist and gunfighter, friend of Wyatt Earp.
Harry Carey, *Law and Order* (1932)
Harvey Clark, *Law for Tombstone* (1937)
Cesar Romero, *Frontier Marshal* (1939)
Kent Taylor, *Tombstone, the Town Too Tough to Die* (1942)
Walter Huston, *The Outlaw* (1943)
Victor Mature, *My Darling Clementine* (1946)
Kirk Douglas, *Gunfight at the O.K. Corral* (1957)
Jason Robards, *Hour of the Gun* (1967)
Stacy Keach, *Doc* (1971)
Val Kilmer, *Tombstone* (1993)
Dennis Quaid, *Wyatt Earp* (1994)

Jack the Ripper Notorious serial killer of nineteenth century London, who was never caught.
Werner Krauss, *Das Wachsfigurenkabinett (Waxworks)* (1924, Germany)
Ivor Novello, *The Lodger* (1926, UK)
Laird Cregar, *The Lodger* (1944)
Jack Palance, *Man in the Attic* (1953)
Ewan Solon, *Jack the Ripper* (1959, UK)
John Fraser, *A Study in Terror* (1965, UK)
Don Herbert, *Terror in the Wax Museum* (1973)
David Warner, *Time After Time* (1979)
Ian Holm, *From Hell* (2001)

James, Jesse (1847–1882) Outlaw and gang leader of the Wild West.
Fred Thomson, *Jesse James* (1927)
Tyrone Power, *Jesse James* (1939)
Roy Rogers, *Days of Jesse James* (1939)
Roy Rogers, *Jesse James at Bay* (1941)
Alan Baxter, *Bad Men of Missouri* (1941)
Lawrence Tierney, *Badman's Territory* (1946)
Clayton Moore, *Jesse James Rides Again* (1947)
Reed Hadley, *I Shot Jesse James* (1949)
Willard Parker, *The Great Jesse James Raid* (1953)
Robert Wagner, *The True Story of Jesse James* (1956)
Henry Brandon, *Hell's Crossroads* (1957)
Wendell Corey, *Alias Jesse James* (1958)
John Lupton, *Jesse James Meets Frankenstein's Daughter* (1966)
Audie Murphy, *A Time for Dying* (1969)
Robert Duvall, *The Great Northfield Minnesota Raid* (1972)
James Keach, *The Long Riders* (1980)
Rob Lowe, *Frank and Jesse* (1994)

Jesus Christ (c. 6 B.C.E.–c. 30 C.E.) Judaean founder of Christianity, believed by Christians to be the son of God.
Robert Henderson-Bland, *From the Manger to the Cross* (1912)
Howard Gaye, *Intolerance* (1916)
H.B. Warner, *King of Kings* (1927)
Robert Le Vigan, *Golgotha* (1935, France)
Robert Wilson, *The Day of Triumph* (1954)
Claude Heater, *Ben-Hur* (1959)
Jeffrey Hunter, *King of Kings* (1961)
John Drew Barrymore, *Ponzio Pilato* (1961, Italy/France)
Enrique Irazoqui, *The Gospel According to St. Matthew* (1964, Italy/France)
Luis Alvarez, *The Redeemer* (1965, US/Spain)
Max von Sydow, *The Greatest Story Ever Told* (1965)
Bernard Verley, *The Milky Way* (1969, France/Italy)
John Bassberger, *The Thorn* (1971)
Robert Elfstrom, *The Gospel Road* (1973)
Ted Neeley, *Jesus Christ, Superstar* (1973)
Zalman King, *The Passover Plot* (1976, US/Israel)

Robert Powell, *Jesus of Nazareth* (1977, UK)
Brian Deacon, *Jesus* (1979)
Willem Dafoe, *The Last Temptation of Christ* (1988)

Joan of Arc (1412–1431) Impassioned French peasant girl burned as a heretic and celebrated as a Christian martyr.
Geraldine Farrar, *Joan the Woman* (1917)
Falconetti, *The Passion of Joan of Arc* (1928)
Simone Genevois, *La Merveilleuse Vie de Jeanne d'Arc (St. Joan—The Maid)* (1929, France)
Ingrid Bergman, *Joan of Arc* (1948)
Jean Seberg, *Saint Joan* (1957, UK)
Hedy Lamarr, *The Story of Mankind* (1957)
Milla Jovovich, *Messenger: The Story of Joan of Arc* (1999, France)

John (1167–1216) King of England and, as prince, the legendary enemy of Robin Hood.
George Courtnay, *Ivanhoe* (1913)
Sam de Grasse, *Robin Hood* (1922)
Ramsay Hill, *The Crusades* (1935)
Claude Rains, *The Adventures of Robin Hood* (1938)
George Macready, *Rogues of Sherwood Forest* (1950)
Guy Rolfe, *Ivanhoe* (1952, UK)
Nigel Terry, *The Lion in Winter* (1968, UK)
Peter Ustinov, *Robin Hood* (1973)
Richard Lewis, *Robin Hood: Men in Tights* (1993)

Lancelot Valiant English knight of medieval legend, subject of King Arthur and lover of Queen Guinevere.
Wilfred McDonald, *A Connecticut Yankee at King Arthur's Court* (1921)
Robert Taylor, *Knights of the Round Table* (1954, UK)
Don Megowan, *Prince Valiant* (1954)
Cornel Wilde, *Lancelot and Guinevere* (1963, UK)
Franco Nero, *Camelot* (1967)
Luc Simon, *Lancelot du Lac* (1974, France/Italy)
John Cleese, *Monty Python and the Holy Grail* (1975, UK)
Nicholas Clay, *Excalibur* (1981)
Ian Falconer, *A Young Connecticut Yankee in King Arthur's Court* (1995)
Richard Gere, *First Knight* (1995)
Marc Singer, *Lancelot: Guardian of Time* (1997)
Adrian Paul, *Merlin: The Return* (1999)

Lincoln, Abraham (1809–1865) Extraordinary US president who held office during the American Civil War.
Joseph Henabery, *The Birth of a Nation* (1915)
Benjamin Chapin, *The Lincoln Cycle* (1917)
Clarence Barr, *Madam Who* (1918)
Judge Charles Edward Bull, *The Iron Horse* (1924)
George Billings, *Abraham Lincoln* (1924)
Walter Huston, *Abraham Lincoln* (1930)
Frank McGlynn, *The Littlest Rebel* (1935)
John Carradine, *Of Human Hearts* (1938)
Henry Fonda, *Young Mr. Lincoln* (1939)
Raymond Massey, *Abe Lincoln in Illinois* (1940)
Austin Green, *The Story of Mankind* (1957)
Raymond Massey, *How the West Was Won* (1962)
John Anderson, *The Lincoln Conspiracy* (1977)

Liszt, Franz (1811–1886) Hungarian composer and pianist.
Daniel Lecourtois, *Un Amour de Frédéric Chopin* (1935, France)
Fritz Lieber, *The Phantom of the Opera* (1943)
Stephen Bekassy, *A Song to Remember* (1945)
Carlos Thompson, *Magic Fire* (1956)

Dirk Bogarde, *Song Without End* (1960)
Henry Gilbert, *Song of Norway* (1970)
Roger Daltrey, *Lisztomania* (1975, UK)
Julian Sands, *Impromptu* (1991, UK)
Geordie Johnson, *Liszt's Rhapsody* (1996, Canada)

Marian, Maid Paramour of legendary English bandit Robin Hood.
Barbara Tennant, *Robin Hood* (1912)
Enid Bennett, *Robin Hood* (1922)
Peggy Cartwright, *Robin Hood, Jr.* (1923)
Olivia de Havilland, *The Adventures of Robin Hood* (1938)
Patricia Morison, *Prince of Thieves* (1948)
Mary Hatcher, *Tales of Robin Hood* (1951)
Sarah Branch, *Sword of Sherwood Forest* (1960, UK)
Gay Hamilton, *A Challenge for Robin Hood* (1967, UK)
Ciaran Madden, *Wolfshead: The Legend of Robin Hood* (1973, UK)
Monica Evans, *Robin Hood* (1973)
Audrey Hepburn, *Robin and Marian* (1976)
Mary Elizabeth Mastrantonio, *Robin Hood: Prince of Thieves* (1991)

Merlin Sorcerer of English legend and adviser to King Arthur.
William V. Mong, *A Connecticut Yankee at King Arthur's Court* (1921)
Brandon Hurst, *A Connecticut Yankee* (1931)
Murvyn Vye, *A Connecticut Yankee in King Arthur's Court* (1949)
William Fawcett, *The Adventures of Sir Galahad* (1949)
Felix Aylmer, *Knights of the Round Table* (1953, UK)
Mark Dignam, *Lancelot and Guinevere* (1963, UK)
Karl Swenson, *The Sword in the Stone* (1963)
Laurence Naismith, *Camelot* (1967)
Nicol Williamson, *Excalibur* (1981)
Malcolm McDowell, *Kids of the Round Table* (1995)
Ron Moody, *A Kid in King Arthur's Court* (1995)
Michael York, *A Young Connecticut Yankee in King Arthur's Court* (1995)
John Gielgud, *Quest for Camelot* (1998)
Rik Mayall, *Merlin: The Return* (1999)

Moses Leader of the ancient Israelites who delivered God's Ten Commandments.
Patrick C. Hartican, *The Life of Moses* (1909)
Theodore Roberts, *The Ten Commandments* (1923)
Charlton Heston, *The Ten Commandments* (1956)
Francis X. Bushman, *The Story of Mankind* (1957)
Burt Lancaster, *Moses* (1975, UK/Italy)
Mel Brooks, *History of the World: Part I* (1981)
Val Kilmer, *The Prince of Egypt* (1998; voice only)

Mozart, Wolfgang Amadeus (1756–1791) Austrian composer and musical prodigy.
Stephen Haggard, *Whom the Gods Love* (1936, UK)
Hannes Stelzer, *Die Kleine Nachmusik* (1939, Germany)
Hans Holt, *Whom the Gods Love* (1942, Austria)
Hans Holt, *The Mozart Story* (1948, US/Austria)
Oscar Werner, *Mozart—Put Your Hand in Mine, Dear* (1955, Austria)
Diego Crovetti (young), *Mozart: A Childhood Chronicle* (1976, Germany)
Santiage Ziesmer (older), *Mozart: A Childhood Chronicle* (1976, Germany)
Tom Hulce, *Amadeus* (1984)

Oakley, Annie (1859–1926) Sharpshooter and entertainer with Buffalo Bill's Wild West show.
Barbara Stanwyck, *Annie Oakley* (1935)

Betty Hutton, *Annie Get Your Gun* (1950)
Gail Davis, *Alias Jesse James* (1959)
Nancy Kovack, *The Outlaws Is Coming* (1965)
Angela Douglas, *Carry On Cowboy* (1965, UK)
Geraldine Chaplin, *Buffalo Bill & the Indians, or, Sitting Bull's History Lesson* (1976)

Poe, Edgar Allan (1809–1849) American writer of mystery and horror.
Guy Oliver, *The Raven* (1912)
Henry B. Walthall, *The Raven* (1915)
John Sheppard, *The Loves of Edgar Allen [sic] Poe* (1942)
Joseph Cotten, *The Man with a Cloak* (1951)
Stanley Baker, *The Tell-Tale Heart* (1953)
Laurence Payne, *The Tell-Tale Heart* (1960, UK)
Robert Walker, Jr., *The Spectre of Edgar Allan Poe* (1974)

Presley, Elvis (1935–1977) American singer, the first rock and roll star.
John Gatti, *Let's Make Love* (1960)
Lele Dorazio, *Elvis! Elvis!* (1976)
Kurt Russell, *Elvis* (1979)
Don Johnson, *Elvis and the Beauty Queen* (1981)
David Keith, *Heartbreak Hotel* (1988)
Michael St. Gerard, *Great Balls of Fire!* (1989)
Harvey Keitel, *Finding Graceland* (1998)

Richard I (1157–1199) Also known as Richard Coeur de Lion or Richard Lion-Heart. King of England, crusader, and brother to John.
Walter Craven, *Ivanhoe* (1913)
Wallace Beery, *Richard the Lion-Hearted* (1923)
Henry Wilcoxon, *The Crusades* (1935)
Ian Hunter, *The Adventures of Robin Hood* (1938)
Patrick Barr, *The Story of Robin Hood and His Merrie Men* (1952, UK)
George Sanders, *King Richard and the Crusaders* (1954)
Patrick Holt, *Men of Sherwood Forest* (1954, UK)
Anthony Hopkins, *The Lion in Winter* (1968, UK)
Richard Harris, *Robin and Marian* (1976)
Aleksandr Baluyev, *Richard Lvinoye Serdtse (Richard the Lion-Hearted)* (1992, Russia)

Tom Hulce (right) played Wolfgang Amadeus Mozart in Amadeus *(1984), which focused on the rivalry between Mozart and composer Antonio Salieri.*

Richard III (1452–1485) The despotic, hunchbacked king of England.
Frank R. Benson, *Richard III* (1911, UK)
Frederick Warde, *Richard III* (1912)
Basil Rathbone, *Tower of London* (1939)
Laurence Olivier, *Richard III* (1954, UK)
Vincent Price, *Tower of London* (1962)
Ariel Garcia Valdès, *Richard III* (1986, France)
Ian McKellen, *Richard III* (1995, UK/US)
Al Pacino, *Looking for Richard* (1996)

Richelieu, Cardinal (1585–1642) Powerful advisor to French king Louis XIII, often cast as the chief enemy of the Three Musketeers.
Murdock MacQuarrie, *Richelieu* (1914)
Nigel De Brulier, *The Three Musketeers* (1921)
Edward Connelly, *Bardelys the Magnificent* (1926)
Nigel De Brulier, *The Iron Mask* (1929)
George Arliss, *Cardinal Richelieu* (1935)
Raymond Massey, *Under the Red Robe* (1937, UK)
Vincent Price, *The Three Musketeers* (1948)
Paul Cavanaugh, *The Sword of D'Artagnan* (1951)
Daniel Sorano, *The Three Musketeers* (1961, France)
Christopher Logue, *The Devils* (1971, UK)
Charlton Heston, *The Three Musketeers* (1973, Spain)
Charlton Heston, *The Four Musketeers* (1974, Spain)
Tim Curry, *The Three Musketeers* (1993)
Stephen Rea, *The Musketeer* (2001, Germany/US)

Robin Hood Folk hero of twelfth-century England who robbed from the rich and gave to the poor.
Robert Frazer, *Robin Hood* (1912)
William Russell, *Robin Hood* (1913)
Douglas Fairbanks, *Robin Hood* (1922)
Errol Flynn, *The Adventures of Robin Hood* (1938)
Russell Hicks, *The Bandit of Sherwood Forest* (1946)
Robert Clarke, *Tales of Robin Hood* (1951)
Richard Todd, *The Story of Robin Hood and His Merrie Men* (1952, UK)
Don Taylor, *Men of Sherwood Forest* (1954, UK)
Barrie Ingham, *A Challenge for Robin Hood* (1967, UK)
David Warbeck, *Wolfshead: The Legend of Robin Hood* (1973, UK)
Brian Bedford, *Robin Hood* (1973)
Sean Connery, *Robin and Marian* (1976)
John Cleese, *Time Bandits* (1981, UK)
Kevin Costner, *Robin Hood: Prince of Thieves* (1991)
Cary Elwes, *Robin Hood: Men in Tights* (1993)

Salome (first century C.E.) Judaean princess and daughter of Herodias, consort to Herod Antipas, the tetrarch of Galilee. As a reward for her dancing, Salome demanded the head of the prophet John the Baptist.
Florence Lawrence, *Salome* (1908)
Theda Bara, *Salome* (1918)
Diana Allen, *Salome* (1923)
Rita Hayworth, *Salome* (1953)
Brigid Bazlen, *King of Kings* (1961)
Paola Tedesco, *The Gospel According to St. Matthew* (1964, Italy/France)
Donyale Luna, *Salome* (1972, Italy)
Isabel Mestres, *Jesus of Nazareth* (1977, UK)
Jo Champa, *Salome* (1986, France/Italy)
Imogen Millais-Scott, *Salome's Last Dance* (1988, UK)

Santa Claus Bringer of yuletide spirit and Christmas gifts.
Ferdinand Munier, *Babes in Toyland* (1934)

Edmund Gwenn, *Miracle on 34th Street* (1947)
José Elías Moreno, *Santa Claus* (1959)
John Call, *Santa Claus Conquers the Martians* (1964)
John Bilyeu, *Santa's Christmas Circus* (1966)
David Huddleston, *Santa Claus* (1985)
John Malkovich, *Santabear's High Flying Adventure* (1987)
Richard Attenborough, *Miracle on 34th Street* (1994)
Tim Allen, *The Santa Clause* (1994; as Scott Calvin, the new Santa Claus)
John Goodman, *Rudolph the Red-Nosed Reindeer: The Movie* (1998; voice only)

Shakespeare, William (1564–1616) English playwright and poet, generally regarded as the greatest English-language writer.
Albert Ward, *The Life of Shakespeare* (1914, UK)
Basil Gill, *Immortal Gentleman* (1935, UK)
Anthony Kemble-Cooper, *Master Will Shakespeare* (1936)
Reginald Gardiner, *The Story of Mankind* (1957)
Joseph Fiennes, *Shakespeare in Love* (1998, US/UK)

Sheriff of Nottingham In medieval English legend, nemesis of bandit Robin Hood.
Alec B. Francis, *Robin Hood* (1912)
William Lowery, *Robin Hood* (1922)
Melville Cooper, *The Adventures of Robin Hood* (1938)
Lloyd Corrigan, *The Bandit of Sherwood Forest* (1946)
Tiny Stowe, *Tales of Robin Hood* (1951)
Peter Finch, *The Story of Robin Hood and His Merrie Men* (1952, UK)
Peter Cushing, *Sword of Sherwood Forest* (1960, UK)
John Arnatt, *A Challenge for Robin Hood* (1967, UK)
Pat Buttram, *Robin Hood* (1973)
Robert Shaw, *Robin and Marian* (1976)
Alan Rickman, *Robin Hood: Prince of Thieves* (1991)

Sinbad Sailor and monster slayer of Arabian legend.
Shemp Howard, *Arabian Nights* (1942)
Douglas Fairbanks, Jr., *Sinbad the Sailor* (1947)
Sebastian Cabot, *Babes in Baghdad* (1952)
Lon Chaney, Jr., *The Thief of Damascus* (1952)
Kerwin Matthews, *The Seventh Voyage of Sinbad* (1958)
Guy Williams, *Captain Sinbad* (1963)
Toshiro Mifune, *The Lost World of Sinbad* (1963, Japan)
John Phillip Law, *The Golden Voyage of Sinbad* (1974, UK)
Patrick Wayne, *Sinbad and the Eye of the Tiger* (1977, UK)
Lou Ferrigno, *Sinbad of the Seven Seas* (1989, US/Italy)
Vittorio Gassman, *Les 1001 Nuits* (1990, France/Italy)
Richard Grieco, *Sinbad: The Battle of the Dark Knights* (1998)

Victoria (1819–1901) Queen of Great Britain and Ireland and empress of India.
Mary Pickford, *Such a Little Queen* (1914)
Margaret Mann, *Disraeli* (1929)
Anna Neagle, *Victoria the Great* (1937, UK)
Fay Compton, *The Prime Minister* (1941, UK)
Irene Dunne, *The Mudlark* (1950, UK)
Muriel Aked, *The Story of Gilbert and Sullivan* (1953, UK)
Romy Schneider, *The Young Victoria* (1955, Germany)
Peter Sellers, *The Great McGonagall* (1974, UK)
Judi Dench, *Mrs. Brown* (1997, UK)

AT RIGHT: *In his semidocumentary* Looking for Richard *(1996), Al Pacino questioned how to interpret Shakespeare using an all-star cast that included Kevin Spacey.*

Great Character Actors and Actresses

By Angela Lansbury

W HEN I MADE MY FIRST motion pictures—*National Velvet* and *Gaslight*—in 1944, I learned something about filmmaking that has remained with me ever since. On those films I was privileged to work with some great stars and some great stars-to-be. But those who made the greatest impression on me were the supporting players, those who were and are described as "character actors."

Just what is a character actor? *The Film Encyclopedia* defines a character role as one "in a motion picture requiring a mature perform-ance on the part of an actor or actress in an attempt to represent a distinctive character type rather than a standard romantic lead, ingenue or juvenile part."

In *Gaslight* I met and worked with Dame May Whitty, a woman of extraordinary grace and talent, whose career in "talkies" began with the 1915 *Enoch Arden* and ended with three 1948 films. In between she appeared in such films as *Night Must Fall, Mrs. Miniver, The Lady Vanishes* (in which she played the title role), *Lassie Come Home,* and *Madame Curie*—and helped to make them classics.

And those wonderful character actors Donald Crisp and Anne Revere were on hand for *National Velvet*—providing the very young Elizabeth Taylor and the very young Angela Lansbury with daily living lessons on the art of acting. You may not know Donald Crisp's name, but if you saw such films as *Red Dust,* the 1935 *Mutiny on the Bounty, The Charge of the Light Brigade, Wuthering Heights, Jezebel, Lassie Come Home,* or *How Green Was My*

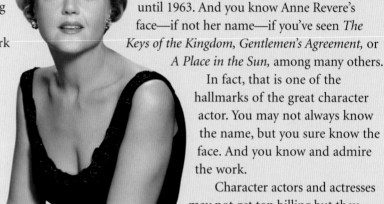

Angela Lansbury received an Academy Award nomination for best supporting actress for 1944's Gaslight.

Valley and many others—you probably admired this remarkable actor. Mr. Crisp's career began in silent films in 1907 and lasted until 1963. And you know Anne Revere's face—if not her name—if you've seen *The Keys of the Kingdom, Gentlemen's Agreement,* or *A Place in the Sun,* among many others.

In fact, that is one of the hallmarks of the great character actor. You may not always know the name, but you sure know the face. And you know and admire the work.

Character actors and actresses may not get top billing but they truly support the stars, elevating everyone's performances and making movies truly memorable. A classic example of a character actor was S.Z. Sakall, known as "Cuddles." This endearing Hungarian-born performer worked steadily in films of the 1940s and 1950s—mostly musicals. Film fans may have come to see Judy Garland and Van Johnson in *In the Good Old Summertime* or Betty Grable and June Haver in *The Dolly Sisters* or Doris Day in *Romance on the High Seas* or the great James Cagney in *Yankee Doodle Dandy,* but they often left the theater chuckling at and discussing Cuddles's accent and his exasperated airs.

TWO MORE OF MY PERSONAL FAVORITES were Agnes Moorehead, who held master's and doctorate degrees, and Beulah Bondi. Miss Moorehead was a recognized and honored actress—she won five Academy Award nominations. In the 1940s she actually starred in the radio production of *Sorry, Wrong Number,* a role that went to Barbara Stanwyck when the film was made. But Miss Moorehead was a familiar figure on the big screen. She made her debut in 1941 in Orson Welles's landmark *Citizen Kane,* playing the protagonist's mother. Incidentally, another outstanding but rarely recognized character actor appeared as Bernstein in *Citizen Kane;* that was Everett Sloane. Miss Moorehead appeared next in Welles's *The Magnificent Ambersons* and then in *Jane Eyre, Since You Went Away, Johnny Belinda,* the 1951 version of *Showboat, Pollyanna,* and *Hush…Hush, Sweet Charlotte.*

And Miss Bondi began with two 1931 films based respectively on an important stage play and a major novel—Elmer Rice's *Street Scene* and Sinclair Lewis's *Arrowsmith.* Actually, she began acting professionally on stage in 1899 when she was only seven. She worked through 1963, when at the age of 71 she appeared opposite Sandra Dee and Peter Fonda in *Tammy and the Doctor,* which featured two other strong character actors, MacDonald Carey and Reginald Owen. In between she graced the screen in dozens of films including *The Trail of the Lonesome Pine, Penny Serenade, Watch on the Rhine, The Snake Pit,* and two James Stewart classics—*Mr. Smith Goes to Washington* and *It's a Wonderful Life.*

Phillip Seymour Hoffman joined the ranks of well-known character actors with roles in films such as Flawless *(1999 - pictured),* Magnolia *(1999), and* Almost Famous *(2000).*

FORTUNATELY, GREAT CHARACTER ACTORS didn't vanish from the screen with the retirement of these wonder-fully talented performers. The tradition continues today. Take a look at films like *The Godfather* and *The Godfather II.* The brilliance of Al Pacino, Robert De Niro, Marlon Brando, Diane Keaton, and James Caan is dazzling. But think how much richer these films are for the work of Robert Duvall, Richard Castellano, Abe Vigoda, John Cazale, Morgana King, Bruno Kirby, Michael V. Gazzo, and the other character actors in this great ensemble. Happily, the art and magic of the character actor is alive and thriving today. Veteran stars and younger performers alike are

upholding and furthering the tradition. There is Joan Cusack. Although still a young actress, she has been working in films for 20 years and has been seen in *Sixteen Candles, Men Don't Leave,* and the more recent *Arlington Road* and *High Fidelity,* among others. Philip Seymour Hoffman has appeared in only a few films, but has already com-piled a record that many older actors would gladly accept. He caught the audience's collective eye in the provocative *Boogie Nights* and went on to such films as *Magnolia,* playing a male nurse; *Flawless,* as a drag queen; and a somewhat comic role in *The Talented Mr. Ripley.* Like the great Peter Lorre, Ving Rhames specializes in playing villains and rogues and has been seen in *Pulp Fiction, Con Air, Dave, Mission: Impossible, Entrapment,* and *Bringing Out the Dead.* Another in the long tradition of "the face is so familiar" actors is Hector Elizondo, whose work has been widely-praised since the 1970s and who numbers among his credits *American Gigolo, Runaway Bride,* and *Pretty Woman.* Arguably, the current King of the Character Actors is the estimable M. Emmet Walsh, who has appeared in more than 80 films beginning with an uncredited role in the 1969 *Midnight Cowboy* and whose résumé includes *Serpico, Silkwood, Raising Arizona, My Best Friend's Wedding, A Time to Kill,* and *The Iron Giant.* Although he often is cast as the heavy, Mr. Walsh was seen in a sympathetic role in the year 2000 in an installment of the widely acclaimed TV series, *NYPD Blue.*

The 1999 Academy Award nominations show-cased Michael Caine (who has switched between starring and character roles throughout his career) and young Haley Joel Osment. It is too soon to tell whether this talented young man will find a career as a leading man or a character actor, but if it is the latter, Haley Joel Osment will be following in great footsteps and a noble tradition.

FAMILIAR FACES

Character actors rarely or never star in films, but their excellent work in supporting roles is part of what makes movies memorable.

Edward Arnold (1890–1956)—unscrupulous mogul D.B. Norton in *Meet John Doe* (1941)

Eric Blore (1887–1959)—talky valet Bates in *Top Hat* (1935)

Beulah Bondi (1892–1981)—Andrew Jackson's wife Rachel in *The Gorgeous Hussy* (1936)

Spring Byington (1886–1971)—amiable eccentric Penny Sycamore in *You Can't Take It With You* (1938)

Charactor actor Porter Hall (standing at left, wearing glasses) played a reporter in His Girl Friday *(1940), featuring Rosalind Russell.*

Charles Coburn (1877–1961)—lecherous millionaire Sir Francis "Piggy" Beekman in *Gentlemen Prefer Blondes* (1953)

Elisha Cook, Jr. (c. 1903–1995)—two-bit gunsel Wilmer Cook in *The Maltese Falcon* (1941)

Jane Darwell (1879–1967)—steadfast matriarch Ma Joad in *The Grapes of Wrath* (1939)

William Demarest (1892–1983)—harried father Constable Kockenlocker in *The Miracle of Morgan's Creek* (1944)

Andy Devine (1905–1977)—shiftless sheriff Link Appleyard in *The Man Who Shot Liberty Valance* (1962)

Charley Grapewin (1869–1956)—likeable backwoodsman Jeeter Lester in *Tobacco Road* (1941)

Porter Hall (1888–1953)—busy reporter Murphy in *His Girl Friday* (1940)

Edward Everett Horton (1886–1970)—befuddled lawyer Egbert Fitzgerald in *The Gay Divorcee* (1934)

Sam Jaffe (1891–1984)—loyal water carrier Gunga Din in *Gunga Din* (1939)

Charles Lane (1905–)—disapproving foundation bookkeeper Larsen in *Ball of Fire* (1941)

Keye Luke (1904–1991)—"Number One Son" Lee Chan in *Charlie Chan in Paris* (1935)

Alan Mowbray (1893–1969)—title character's friend Tommy Gray in *My Man Godfrey* (1936)

Mildred Natwick (1908–1992)—widowed owner of Innisfree estate Sarah Tillane in *The Quiet Man* (1952)

Eugene Pallette (1889–1954)—exasperated father Mr. Pike in *The Lady Eve* (1941)

John Qualen (1899–1987)—stolid homesteader Lars Jorgensen in *The Searchers* (1956)

S.Z. "Cuddles" Sakall (1884–1955)—nightclub employee Carl in *Casablanca* (1942)

Woody Strode (1914–1994)—noble gladiator Draba in *Spartacus* (1960)

Akim Tamiroff (1899–1972)—The Boss in *The Great McGinty* (1940)

Ernest Thesiger (1879–1961)—mad scientist Dr. Septimus Pretorius in *The Bride of Frankenstein* (1935)

Henry Travers (1874–1965)—angel second class Clarence Odbody in *It's a Wonderful Life* (1946)

Mary Wickes (1910–1995)—wisecracking housekeeper Emma in *White Christmas* (1953)

MINOR CHARACTERS

Everyone has to start somewhere, here are some early roles of actors who later became movie stars.

Kevin Bacon Chip Diller, frat boy, *National Lampoon's Animal House* (1978)

Sandra Bullock Timid scientist, *Love Potion #9* (1992)

Michael Caine Gestapo agent, *The Two-Headed Spy* (1958)

Kevin Costner Frat Boy #1, *Night Shift* (1982)

Tom Cruise Billy, *Endless Love* (1981)

Robert De Niro Ma Barker's boy Lloyd, *Bloody Mama* (1970)

Danny De Vito Man in honeymoon suite, *Bananas* (1971)

Richard Dreyfuss Student in Berkeley rooming house, *The Graduate* (1967)

Clint Eastwood Lab technician, *Revenge of the Creature* (1955)

Laurence "Larry" Fishburne Mr. Clean, sailor, *Apocalypse Now* (1979)

Harrison Ford Bellhop, *Dead Heat on a Merry-Go-Round* (1966)

Danny Glover Inmate, *Escape from Alcatraz* (1979)

Jeff Goldblum "Freak #1," mugger, *Deathwish* (1974)

Tom Hanks Elliott, serial-killer victim, *He Knows You're Alone* (1981)

Dennis Hopper Goon, *Rebel Without a Cause* (1955)

James Earl Jones Lieutenant Lothar Zogg, *Dr. Strangelove* (1964)

Tommy Lee Jones Hank, *Love Story* (1970)

Diane Keaton Joan Vecchio, daughter of Bea Arthur's character, *Lovers and Other Strangers* (1970)

Jessica Lange Dwan, love interest, *King Kong* (1976)

Steve McQueen Steve Andrews, hero, *The Blob* (1955)

Steve Martin Dr. Maxwell Edison, *Sgt. Pepper's Lonely Hearts Club Band* (1978)

Walter Matthau Western heavy, *The Indian Fighter* (1955)

Demi Moore Heroine coping with monster parasites, *Parasite* (1982)

Liam Neeson Sir Gawain, *Excalibur* (1981)

Jack Nicholson Jimmy, juvenile delinquent, *The Cry-Baby Killer* (1958)

Gwyneth Paltrow Young Wendy, *Hook* (1991)

Michelle Pfeiffer Cordelia Farrington III, *Charlie Chan and the Curse of the Dragon Queen* (1981)

Meg Ryan Lisa, *Amityville 3-D* (1983)

Will Smith Homeless teen, *Where the Day Takes You* (1992)

Sylvester Stallone Stud in porn movie, *Party at Kitty and Studs/The Italian Stallion* (1970)

Sharon Stone Pretty girl on train, *Stardust Memories* (1980)

Donald Sutherland Old Hag and Policeman #1, *Castle of the Living Dead* (1964)

John Travolta Danny, Satanist, *The Devil's Rain* (1975)

Sigourney Weaver Date of Woody Allen's comedian character, Alvy Singer, *Annie Hall* (1977)

Bruce Willis Audience member during closing argument, *The Verdict* (1982)

> "The only way to be a success here is to be as obnoxious as the next guy."
>
> —
>
> *Sylvester Stallone on how to succeed in Hollywood*

Academy Award-winning actress Jessica Lange's first film role was in Dino DeLaurentis's 1976 remake of King Kong.

FICTIONAL CHARACTERS ON FILM: A SELECTION

Whether created for a film, novel, or a bestseller, fictional characters become part of one's imagination. These on-screen creations can touch us as deeply as their literary forebears.

THIS SECTION DESCRIBES MORE THAN 125 fictional characters who were either created specifically for film or who first came to life in literary works adapted for film. For the list compiled here, the net has been spread wide, to capture not only characters from great novels, such as Oliver Twist and Elizabeth Bennet, but pop-culture figures like James Bond and Indiana Jones. The characters include some who have been played by many actors, such as Charlie Chan, and some played just once but unforgettably, such as Thelma and Louise. Some are familiar from silent days, such as Jean Valjean, and some were created only in recent decades, such as the Terminator. The principal criterion for selection: that the character remains vivid in the memory of moviegoers.

Identifications of each character are kept short to put the focus on the films in which they appeared rather than on the literary source material. Where there is a literary source, the author and type of material—for example, a novel or play—are listed. Feature films in which the characters appeared are then listed, with dates of release and the actor who played the character in that film.

IF THE ACTOR PLAYED THE ROLE AGAIN in sequels, then a note says "reprised in sequels." But if a different actor played the role in a sequel or remake, then that actor is listed, along with the name and date of the new film. In cases where a role has been played since the silent era, the list of silent feature films may not be complete, due to the difficulty of isolating every silent film version. But in most cases, every major sound film portrayal has been listed.

Ahab, Captain   Monomaniacal sea captain hunting Moby Dick the White Whale, from the Herman Melville novel.
John Barrymore, *The Sea Beast* (1926)
John Barrymore, *Moby Dick* (1930)
Gregory Peck, *Moby Dick* (1956)

Alice   Girl who falls down a rabbit hole into a magical land, from the Lewis Carroll novels.
Ruth Gilbert, *Alice in Wonderland* (1931)
Charlotte Henry, *Alice in Wonderland* (1933)
Carol Marsh, *Alice in Wonderland* (1950, UK)
Kathryn Beaumont, *Alice in Wonderland* (1951; voice only)
Fiona Fullerton, *Alice's Adventures in Wonderland* (1972, UK)

Allnut, Charlie   Skipper of an African riverboat, from a C.S. Forester novel.
Humphrey Bogart, *The African Queen* (1951)

Bailey, George   Proprietor of a building-and-loan company and embodiment of small-town virtue, from a Philip Van Doren Stern story.
James Stewart, *It's a Wonderful Life* (1946)

Balboa, Rocky   Underdog boxer.
Sylvester Stallone, *Rocky* (1976; reprised in sequels)

Bambi   Amiable deer, from the Felix Salten novel.
Bobby Stewart, *Bambi* (1942; voice)

Bandello, Caesar Enrico "Rico"   Tough, doomed gangster known as Little Caesar, from a W.R. Burnett novel.
Edward G. Robinson, *Little Caesar* (1930)

Barbarella   Sexy space heroine, from the Jean-Claude Forest comic strip.
Jane Fonda, *Barbarella* (1968, France/Italy)

Bates, Norman   Insane proprietor of the Bates Motel, from a Robert Bloch novel.
Anthony Perkins, *Psycho* (1960; reprised in sequels)
Vince Vaughan, *Psycho* (1998)

Batman and Robin   Masked superheroes of Gotham City, from the Bob Kane comic book adventures. Secret identities: Bruce Wayne and Dick Grayson, respectively.
Adam West and Burt Ward, *Batman* (1966)

Michael Keaton, *Batman* (1989; Batman only)
Michael Keaton, *Batman Returns* (1992; Batman only)
Kevin Conroy, *Batman: Mask of the Phantasm* (1993; Batman only, voice only)
Val Kilmer and Chris O'Donnell, *Batman Forever* (1995)
George Clooney and Chris O'Donnell, *Batman & Robin* (1997)

Ben-Hur, Judah   Jewish prince turned galley slave and charioteer, from the Lew Wallace novel.
Ramon Novarro, *Ben-Hur* (1926)
Charlton Heston, *Ben-Hur* (1959)

Bennet, Elizabeth and **Darcy, Fitzwilliam**   Nineteenth-century romantic duo, from the Jane Austen novel.
Greer Garson and Laurence Olivier, *Pride and Prejudice* (1940)

Bickle, Travis   Deranged cabdriver.
Robert De Niro, *Taxi Driver* (1976)

Blaine, Rick   American expatriate and saloon keeper whose dormant idealism is awakened in World War II–era Casablanca, from a Murray Burnett play.
Humphrey Bogart, *Casablanca* (1942; with Ingrid Berman as old flame Ilsa Laszlo née Lund)

Block, Antonius   Medieval knight, a.k.a. the Knight, playing a metaphysically loaded game of chess against Death.
Max von Sydow, *Det Sjunde Inseglet (The Seventh Seal)* (1957, Sweden)

Martin Scorsese's Taxi Driver *(1976) featured Robert De Niro as a psychotic cabbie determined to save a child prostitute played by Jodie Foster.*

Blodgett, Esther and **Maine, Norman**   Rising star (born Blodgett but renamed Vicki Lester) married to fading star (Maine).
Janet Gaynor and Fredric March, *A Star Is Born* (1937)
Judy Garland and James Mason, *A Star Is Born* (1954)
Barbra Streisand and Kris Kristofferson (character names changed to Esther Hoffman and John Norman Howard), *A Star Is Born* (1976)

Blofeld, Ernst Stavros   Arch nemesis of James Bond and head of SPECTRE, from the Ian Fleming novels.
Donald Pleasence, *You Only Live Twice* (1967, UK)
Telly Savalas, *On Her Majesty's Secret Service* (1969, UK)
Charles Gray, *Diamonds Are Forever* (1971, UK)

Blondie   Housewife heroine, from the Chic Young comic strip.
Penny Singleton, *Blondie* (1938; reprised in many sequels, with Arthur Lake as hapless husband Dagwood Bumstead)

Bond, James   Suave British superspy, a.k.a. Agent 007, from the Ian Fleming novels.
Sean Connery, *Dr. No* (1962, UK; reprised in sequels)
David Niven, *Casino Royale* (1967, UK)
George Lazenby, *On Her Majesty's Secret Service* (1969, UK)
Roger Moore, *Live and Let Die* (1973, UK; reprised in sequels)
Timothy Dalton, *The Living Daylights* (1987, UK; reprised in *Licence to Kill*, 1989, UK)
Pierce Brosnan, *Goldeneye* (1995; reprised in sequels)

Braddock, Benjamin   Naive college graduate seduced by the worldly Mrs. Robinson, from a Charles Webb novel.
Dustin Hoffman, *The Graduate* (1967; Anne Bancroft as Mrs. Robinson)

Brown, Charlie   Long-suffering child star of Charles M. Schulz comic strip Peanuts.
Peter Robbins, *A Boy Named Charlie Brown* (1969; voice only; voice done by others in sequels)

Burns, Walter and **Johnson, Hildy**   Overbearing newspaper editor (Burns) trying to stop ace reporter (Johnson) from getting married, from a play by Ben Hecht and Charles MacArthur.
Adolphe Menjou and Pat O'Brien, *The Front Page* (1931)
Cary Grant and Rosalind Russell, *His Girl Friday* (1940)
Walter Matthau and Jack Lemmon, *The Front Page* (1974)
Burt Reynolds and Kathleen Turner, *Switching Channels* (1988; characters renamed John L. Sullivan IV and Christy Colleran)

Cabiria   Prostitute who remains ever hopeful despite a trail of misfortunes.
Giulietta Masina, *Le Notti di Cabiria (Nights of Cabiria)* (1957, Italy)
Shirley MacLaine, *Sweet Charity* (1969; as Charity Hope Valentine, based on Cabiria)

Caligari, Dr.   Villainous mountebank who hypnotically controls the somnambulist Cesare.
Werner Krauss, *The Cabinet of Dr. Caligari* (1919; with Conrad Veidt as Cesare)

Callahan, "Dirty" Harry
Tough San Francisco cop.
Clint Eastwood, *Dirty Harry* (1971; reprised in sequels)

Carton, Sydney (or Sidney)   Dissolute lawyer who sacrifices his life in the French Revolution, from a Charles Dickens novel.
Maurice Costello, *A Tale of Two Cities* (1911)
William Farnum, *A Tale of Two Cities* (1917)
John Martin Harvey, *The Only Way* (1925, UK)
Ronald Colman, *A Tale of Two Cities* (1935)
Dirk Bogarde, *A Tale of Two Cities* (1958, UK)

Chan, Charlie   Chinese-American detective, from the novels by Earl Derr Biggers.
E.L. Park, *Behind That Curtain* (1929)
Warner Oland, *Charlie Chan Carries On* (1931; reprised in sequels)
Sidney Toler, *Charlie Chan in Honolulu* (1938; reprised in sequels)
Roland Winters, *The Chinese Ring* (1947; reprised in sequels)
Peter Ustinov, *Charlie Chan and the Curse of the Dragon Queen* (1981)

Channing, Margo   Aging Broadway star, threatened by young newcomer Eve Harrington, from a Mary Orr story.
Bette Davis, *All About Eve* (1950; with Anne Baxter as Eve Harrington)

Charles, Nick and **Nora**   Rich married sleuths, from the Dashiell Hammett novel.
William Powell and Myrna Loy, *The Thin Man* (1934; reprised in sequels)

Clouseau, Inspector Jacques   Bumbling French policeman.
Peter Sellers, *The Pink Panther* (1964; reprised in sequels)
Alan Arkin, *Inspector Clouseau* (1968; UK)
Roberto Benigni, *Son of the Pink Panther* (1993; as Clouseau's son)

Corleone, Michael   Don of a crime family, son of Vito, from the Mario Puzo novel.
Al Pacino, *The Godfather* (1972; reprised in sequels)

Corleone, Vito   Founder and don of a crime family, from the Mario Puzo novel.
Marlon Brando, *The Godfather* (1972)
Robert De Niro, *The Godfather Part II* (1974)

Crown, Thomas   Wealthy adventurer who turns to theft.
Steve McQueen, *The Thomas Crown Affair* (1968)
Pierce Brosnan, *The Thomas Crown Affair* (1999)

Dallas, Stella   Self-sacrificing mother, from the Olive Higgins Prouty novel.
Belle Bennett, *Stella Dallas* (1925)
Barbara Stanwyck, *Stella Dallas* (1937)
Bette Midler, *Stella* (1990)

D'Artagnan   Swashbuckling companion of the Three Musketeers, from the novels by Alexandre Dumas.
Douglas Fairbanks, *The Three Musketeers* (1921)
Douglas Fairbanks, *The Iron Mask* (1928)
Walter Abel, *The Three Musketeers* (1935)
Don Ameche, *The Three Musketeers* (1939)
Warren William, *The Man in the Iron Mask* (1939)
Gene Kelly, *The Three Musketeers* (1948)
Michael York, *The Three Musketeers* (1974, UK; reprised in sequels)
Cornel Wilde, *The Fifth Musketeer* (1978)
Chris O'Donnell, *The Three Musketeers* (1993)
Gabriel Byrne, *The Man in the Iron Mask* (1998)
Justin Chambers, *The Musketeer* (2001, Germany/US)

Deeds, Longfellow   Small-town tuba player who inherits a fortune.
Gary Cooper, *Mr. Deeds Goes to Town* (1936)

Desmond, Norma   Faded silent-film star.
Gloria Swanson, *Sunset Boulevard* (1950)

Dietrichson, Phyllis   Seductive blond conspiring to murder her husband, from the James M. Cain novel.
Barbara Stanwyck, *Double Indemnity* (1944)

Doe, John   Decent jobless man, a.k.a. Long John Willoughby, snared to serve as a front for a corrupt bigwig.
Gary Cooper, *Meet John Doe* (1941)

Doinel, Antoine   Youth who survives a troubled childhood and grows up searching for love; alter ego of director-writer François Truffaut.
Jean-Pierre Léaud, *Les Quatre Cents Coups (The Four Hundred Blows)* (1959, France; reprised in sequels)

Dracula, Count   Preeminent vampire, from the Bram Stoker novel.
Max Schreck, *Nosferatu* (1922, Germany)
Bela Lugosi, *Dracula* (1931; later reprised)
Carlos Villarias, *Dracula* (1931, Mexico)
Lon Chaney, Jr., *Son of Dracula* (1943)
John Carradine, *House of Frankenstein* (1944; reprised in sequels)
Christopher Lee, *Dracula/Horror of Dracula* (1958, UK; reprised in sequels)
David Niven, *Old Dracula/Vampira* (1974, UK)
Klaus Kinski, *Nosferatu, the Vampyre* (1979, West Germany)
Frank Langella, *Dracula* (1979)
George Hamilton, *Love at First Bite* (1979)

Gary Oldman, *Bram Stoker's Dracula* (1992)
Leslie Nielsen, *Dracula: Dead and Loving It* (1995)
Gerard Butler *Dracula 2000* (2000)

Dubois, Blanche   Needy, aging Southern belle taunted by loutish brother-in-law Stanley Kowalski, from the Tennessee Williams play.
Vivien Leigh, *A Streetcar Named Desire* (1951; with Marlon Brando as Kowalski)

Dunson, Tom   Pioneering, tyrannical rancher, from a Borden Chase novel.
John Wayne, *Red River* (1948)

Edwards, Ethan   Relentless western hero searching for a girl taken captive by Indians, from an Alan LeMay novel.
John Wayne, *The Searchers* (1956)

Eyre, Jane   Governess in love with a man with a dark secret, from the Charlotte Brontë novel.
Ethel Grandin, *Jane Eyre* (1914)
Louise Vale, *Jane Eyre* (1915)
Mabel Ballin, *Jane Eyre* (1921)
Virginia Bruce, *Jane Eyre* (1934)
Joan Fontaine, *Jane Eyre* (1944)
Charlotte Gainsbourg, *Jane Eyre* (1996, France/Italy/US/UK)

Felson, Fast Eddie   Ace pool player, from the Walter Tevis novels.
Paul Newman, *The Hustler* (1961)
Paul Newman, *The Color of Money* (1986)

Finch, Atticus   Honorable country lawyer, from the Harper Lee novel.
Gregory Peck, *To Kill a Mockingbird* (1962)

Firefly, Rufus T.   Anarchic leader of mythical Freedonia.
Groucho Marx, *Duck Soup* (1933)

Fogg, Phileas   English gentleman who takes on a bet to go around the world in 80 days, from the Jules Verne novel.
David Niven, *Around the World in 80 Days* (1956)

Frankenstein's Monster   Creature brought to life by a scientist named Frankenstein; scientists include Colin Clive as Henry Frankenstein in *Frankenstein* (1931), Peter Cushing as Victor Frankenstein in *The Curse of Frankenstein* (1957, UK), and Gene Wilder as Frederick Frankenstein in *Young Frankenstein* (1974). From the Mary Shelley novel.
Charles Ogle, *Frankenstein* (1910)
Boris Karloff, *Frankenstein* (1931; reprised in sequels)
Lon Chaney, Jr., *The Ghost of Frankenstein* (1942)
Bela Lugosi, *Frankenstein Meets the Wolf Man* (1943)
Glenn Strange, *House of Frankenstein* (1944; reprised in sequels)
Christopher Lee, *The Curse of Frankenstein* (1957, UK)
Gary Conway, *I Was a Teenage Frankenstein* (1957)
Cal Bolder, *Jesses James Meets Frankenstein's Daughter* (1966)
Dave Prowse, *The Horror of Frankenstein* (1970, UK; reprised in sequel)
Peter Boyle, *Young Frankenstein* (1974)
Nick Brimble, *Frankenstein Unbound* (1990)
Robert De Niro, *Mary Shelley's Frankenstein* (1994)

Gale, Dorothy   Kansas girl whisked to the magical land of Oz, from the L. Frank Baum novel.
Dorothy Dwan, *The Wizard of Oz* (1925)
Judy Garland, *The Wizard of Oz* (1939)
Liza Minnelli, *Journey Back to Oz* (1974; voice only)

Diana Ross, *The Wiz* (1978)
Fairuza Balk, *Return to Oz* (1985)

Gatsby, Jay Wealthy man with a mysterious past, enamored of Daisy Buchanan, from the F. Scott Fitzgerald novel.
Warner Baxter, *The Great Gatsby* (1926)
Alan Ladd, *The Great Gatsby* (1949)
Robert Redford, *The Great Gatsby* (1974)

Geste, Beau Adventurer in the French Foreign Legion, a.k.a. Michael Geste, from the P.C. Wren novel.
Ronald Colman, *Beau Geste* (1926)
Gary Cooper, *Beau Geste* (1939)
Guy Stockwell, *Beau Geste* (1966)
Michael York, *The Last Remake of Beau Geste* (1977)

Golightly, Holly Urban free spirit, from the Truman Capote novella.
Audrey Hepburn, *Breakfast at Tiffany's* (1961)

Gunga Din Indian water-carrier, from the Rudyard Kipling poem.
Sam Jaffe, *Gunga Din* (1939)

HAL 9000 Troubled computer on board a spaceship to Jupiter.
Douglas Rain, *2001: A Space Odyssey* (1968, UK; voice only)
Douglas Rain, *2010* (1984; voice only)

Hall, Annie Dizzy beloved of Woody Allen's Alvy Singer.
Diane Keaton, *Annie Hall* (1977)

Hamlet Anguished prince of Denmark, from the Shakespeare play.
Charles Raymond, *Hamlet* (1912, UK)
Sir John Forbes-Robertson, *Hamlet* (1913, UK)
Sohrab Modi, *Hamlet* (1935, India)
Laurence Olivier, *Hamlet* (1948, UK)
Kishore Sahu, *Hamlet* (1954, India)
Maximilian Schell, *Hamlet* (1960, West Germany)
Innokenti Smoktunovski, *Hamlet* (1964, USSR)
Richard Burton, *Hamlet* (1964)
Nicol Williamson, *Hamlet* (1969, UK)
Mel Gibson, *Hamlet* (1990)
Kenneth Branagh, *Hamlet* (1996, US/UK)
Ethan Hawke, *Hamlet* (2000)

Hawkeye Frontier hero, a.k.a. Natty Bumppo, Leatherstocking, and the Deerslayer, from the James Fenimore Cooper novels. Also the nickname of Benjamin Franklin "Hawkeye" Pierce, Army surgeon played by Donald Sutherland in *M*A*S*H* (1970), from the Richard Hooker novel.
Randolph Scott, *The Last of the Mohicans* (1936)
Daniel Day-Lewis, *The Last of the Mohicans* (1992)

Heathcliff Smoldering lover of Catherine Earnshaw, from the Emily Brontë novel.
Laurence Olivier, *Wuthering Heights* (1939)
Jorge Mistral, *Wuthering Heights* (1953, Mexico)
Timothy Dalton, *Wuthering Heights* (1970, UK)
Ralph Fiennes, *Wuthering Heights* (1992, UK)

Higgins, Henry Insufferable elocution teacher of flower-seller Eliza Dolittle, from the George Bernard Shaw play.
Leslie Howard, *Pygmalion* (1938, UK; with Wendy Hiller as Eliza)
Rex Harrison, *My Fair Lady* (1964; with Audrey Hepburn as Eliza)

Holmes, Sherlock World's premier detective and paragon of logic, from the Arthur Conan Doyle stories and novels.

Alwin Neuss, *The Hound of the Baskervilles* (1915, Germany)
H.A. Sainsbury, *The Valley of Fear* (1916, UK)
John Barrymore, *Sherlock Holmes* (1922)
Clive Brook, *The Return of Sherlock Holmes* (1929; later reprised)
Arthur Wontner, *The Sleeping Cardinal* (1931, UK; reprised in sequels)
Raymond Massey, *The Speckled Band* (1931, UK)
Reginald Owen, *A Study in Scarlet* (1933)
Basil Rathbone, *The Hound of the Baskervilles* (1939; reprised in sequels)
Peter Cushing, *The Hound of the Baskervilles* (1959, UK)
Christopher Lee, *Sherlock Holmes and the Deadly Necklace* (1962, West Germany)
John Neville, *A Study in Terror* (1965, UK)
Robert Stephens, *The Private Life of Sherlock Holmes* (1970, UK)
Douglas Wilmer, *The Adventure of Sherlock Holmes' Smarter Brother* (1975)
Nicol Williamson, *The Seven-Per-Cent Solution* (1976)
Peter Cook, *The Hound of the Baskervilles* (1977, UK)
Christopher Plummer, *Murder by Decree* (1979)
Nicholas Rowe, *Young Sherlock Holmes* (1985)

Hunt, Laura Alluring woman at the center of a murder mystery, from the Vera Caspary novel.
Gene Tierney, *Laura* (1943)

Jekyll, Dr. Henry Scientist who transforms himself into the monstrous Mr. Edward Hyde, from the Robert Louis Stevenson novella.
John Barrymore, *Dr. Jekyll and Mr. Hyde* (1920)
Fredric March, *Dr. Jekyll and Mr. Hyde* (1932)
Spencer Tracy, *Dr. Jekyll and Mr. Hyde* (1941)
Boris Karloff, *Abbott and Costello Meet Dr. Jekyll and Mr. Hyde* (1953; transforms into Eddie Parker)
Ralph Bates, *Dr. Jekyll and Sister Hyde* (1970; transforms into Martine Beswick)
Tim Daly, *Dr. Jekyll and Ms. Hyde* (1995; descendant of Jekyll transforms into Sean Young)
John Malkovich, *Mary Reilly* (1996)

Jones, Indiana Adventurous archaeologist.
Harrison Ford, *Raiders of the Lost Ark* (1981; reprised in sequels)
River Phoenix, *Indiana Jones and the Last Crusade* (1989; as young Indiana)

Kane, Charles Foster Grasping newspaper magnate based on real-life publisher William Randolph Hearst.
Orson Welles, *Citizen Kane* (1941)

River Phoenix played a young Indiana Jones in Indiania Jones and the Last Crusade, *(1989).*

Kane, Will Marshal who stands alone against killers.
Gary Cooper, *High Noon* (1952)

Lecter, Hannibal Brilliant, imprisoned cannibal and serial killer, from the Thomas Harris novels.
Brian Cox, *Manhunter* (1986)
Anthony Hopkins, *The Silence of the Lambs* (1991; reprised in sequels)

Lolita Nymphet, a.k.a. Dolores Haze, who attracts the ardor of middle-aged scholar Humbert Humbert, from the Vladimir Nabokov novel.
Sue Lyon, *Lolita* (1962, UK; with James Mason as Humbert)
Dominique Swain, *Lolita* (1997, UK/France, with Jeremy Irons as Humbert)

Lord, Tracy Icy aristocrat who melts before her scheduled wedding, from the Philip Barry play.
Katharine Hepburn, *The Philadelphia Story* (1940)
Grace Kelly, *High Society* (1956)

McClane, John New York City supercop who regularly battles terrorists.
Bruce Willis, *Die Hard* (1988; reprised in sequels)

Mad Max Postapocalyptic action hero.
Mel Gibson, *Mad Max* (1979, Australia; reprised in sequels)

Maguire, Jerry Sports agent with a conscience.
Tom Cruise, *Jerry Maguire* (1996)

March, Jo Plucky young writer growing up with her sisters, from the Louisa May Alcott novels.
Katharine Hepburn, *Little Women* (1933)
Kay Francis, *Little Men* (1940)
June Allyson, *Little Women* (1949)
Winona Ryder, *Little Women* (1994)

Marlowe, Philip Hard-boiled private eye, from the Raymond Chandler novels.
Dick Powell, *Murder, My Sweet* (1944)
Humphrey Bogart, *The Big Sleep* (1946)
Robert Montgomery, *Lady in the Lake* (1946)
George Montgomery, *The Brasher Doubloon* (1947)
James Garner, *Marlowe* (1969)
Elliott Gould, *The Long Goodbye* (1973)
Robert Mitchum, *Farewell, My Lovely* (1975; reprised in sequel)

Maximus Gladiator who defies the Roman emperor Commodus.
Russell Crowe, *Gladiator* (2000)

Miniver, Mrs. Caroline Indomitable Englishwoman facing World War II, from the Jan Struther novel.
Greer Garson, *Mrs. Miniver* (1942)
Greer Garson, *The Miniver Story* (1950)

Ninotchka Female Soviet official who learns about love and capitalism in Paris.
Greta Garbo, *Ninotchka* (1939)
Cyd Charisse, *Silk Stockings* (1957)

O'Hara, Scarlett Fiery, tenacious Southern belle who survives the Civil War and Reconstruction and spars with Rhett Butler, from the Margaret Mitchell novel.
Vivien Leigh, *Gone with the Wind* (1939; with Clark Gable as Butler)

Pierce, Mildred Hardworking mother betrayed by ungrateful daughter, from the James M. Cain novel.
Joan Crawford, *Mildred Pierce* (1945)

Poppins, Mary Magical, "practically perfect" nanny, from the P.L. Travers novel.
Julie Andrews, *Mary Poppins* (1964)

Powers, Austin Time-traveling spy from swinging 60s London.
Mike Myers, *Austin Powers: International Man of Mystery* (1997; reprised in sequels)

Quasimodo Misshapen bell ringer of Notre Dame Cathedral, from the Victor Hugo novel.
Lon Chaney, *The Hunchback of Notre Dame* (1923)
Charles Laughton, *The Hunchback of Notre Dame* (1939)
Anthony Quinn, *The Hunchback of Notre Dame* (1957, France)
Tom Hulce, *The Hunchback of Notre Dame* (1996; voice only)

Quint Seasoned shark-hunter, from the Peter Benchley novel.
Robert Shaw, *Jaws* (1975)

Rambo, John Muscle-bound Vietnam vet and killing machine, from the David Morrell novel.
Sylvester Stallone, *First Blood* (1982; reprised in sequels)

Raskolnikov Cerebral student-murderer wracked with remorse, from the Feodor Dostoyevsky novel.
Grigori Khmara, *Crime and Punishment* (1923, Germany)
Peter Lorre, *Crime and Punishment* (1935)
Pierre Blanchar, *Crime and Punishment* (1935, France)
George Hamilton, *Crime and Punishment, USA* (1959; updated character named Robert)
Gueorgui Taratorkine, *Crime and Punishment* (1970, USSR)

Rizzo, Ratso Seedy companion of male prostitute Joe Buck, from the James Leo Herlihy novel.
Dustin Hoffman, *Midnight Cowboy* (1969; with Jon Voight as Joe Buck)

Sawyer, Tom and **Finn, Huckleberry** Pre–Civil War southern boys finding adventure on the Mississippi, from the Mark Twain novels.
Jack Pickford and Robert Gordon, respectively, *Huck and Tom* (1918)
Gordon Griffith and Lewis Sargent, respectively, *Huckleberry Finn* (1920)
Jackie Coogan and Junior Durkin, respectively, *Tom Sawyer* (1930)
Jackie Coogan and Junior Durkin, respectively, *Huckleberry Finn* (1931)
Billy Cook and Donald O'Connor, respectively, *Tom Sawyer, Detective* (1938)
Tommy Kelly and Jackie Moran, respectively, *The Adventures of Tom Sawyer* (1938)
Mickey Rooney (as Huckleberry only), *The Adventures of Huckleberry Finn* (1939)
Eddie Hodges (as Huckleberry only), *The Adventures of Huckeberry Finn* (1960)
Johnnie Whitaker and Jeff East, respectively, *Tom Sawyer* (1973)
Jonathan Taylor Thomas and Brad Renfro, respectively, *Tom and Huck* (1995)

Scrooge, Ebenezer Miser visited by ghosts on Christmas Eve, from the Charles Dickens story.
Seymour Hicks, *Scrooge* (1913, UK)
Rupert Julian, *The Right to Be Happy* (1916)
Seymour Hicks, *Scrooge* (1935, UK)

The 1994 remake of Little Women *featured Winona Ryder as Jo.*

Reginald Owen, *A Christmas Carol* (1938)
Alastair Sim, *Scrooge/A Christmas Carol* (1951, UK)
Albert Finney, *Scrooge* (1970, UK)
Bill Murray, *Scrooged* (1988, updated version)

Shaft, John Tough African-American private eye, from the Ernest Tidyman novels.
Richard Roundtree, *Shaft* (1971; reprised in sequels)
Samuel L. Jackson, *Shaft* (2000; as nephew of original John Shaft)

Shane Mysterious wandering gunman of the West, from the Jack Schaefer novel.
Alan Ladd, *Shane* (1953)

Skywalker, Luke Idealistic Jedi knight in training in galaxy far, far away. Son of Darth Vader.
Mark Hamill, *Star Wars* (1977; reprised in sequels)

Smith, Jefferson Idealistic senator who takes on Washington corruption.
James Stewart, *Mr. Smith Goes to Washington* (1939)

Spade, Sam Hard-boiled detective, from the Dashiell Hammett novel and stories.
Ricardo Cortez, *The Maltese Falcon* (1931)
Warren William, *Satan Met a Lady* (1936; with character renamed Ted Shayne)
Humphrey Bogart, *The Maltese Falcon* (1941)
George Segal, *The Black Bird* (1975; as Sam Spade, Jr.)

Superman Mighty, flying superhero from planet Krypton, from the Jerome Siegel and Joe Schuster comic book adventures.
George Reeves, *Superman and the Mole Men* (1951)
Christopher Reeve, *Superman* (1978; reprised in sequels)

Tarzan Jungle hero raised by apes, from the Edgar Rice Burroughs novels.
Elmo Lincoln, *Tarzan of the Apes* (1918; reprised in sequels)
Johnny Weissmuller, *Tarzan, the Ape Man* (1932; reprised in sequels, many with Maureen O'Sullivan as love interest Jane)
Buster Crabbe, *Tarzan the Fearless* (1933)
Herman Brix, *The New Adventures of Tarzan* (1935; reprised in sequel; actor's name later changed to Bruce Bennett)
Glenn Morris, *Tarzan's Revenge* (1938)
Lex Barker, *Tarzan's Magic Fountain* (1949; reprised in sequels)
Gordon Scott, *Tarzan's Hidden Jungle* (1955; reprised in sequels)
Dennis Miller, *Tarzan, the Ape Man* (1959)
Jock Mahoney, *Tarzan Goes to India* (1962, UK; reprised in sequel)
Mike Henry, *Tarzan and the Valley of Gold* (1966, US/Switzerland; reprised in sequels)
Ron Ely, *Tarzan's Jungle Rebellion* (1970; reprised in sequel)
Miles O'Keeffe, *Tarzan the Ape Man* (1981)
Christopher Lambert, *Greystoke: The Legend of Tarzan, Lord of the Apes* (1984)
Casper Van Dien, *Tarzan and the Lost City* (1998, Australia/US/Germany)
Tony Goldwyn, *Tarzan* (1999; voice only)

Terminator, The Unstoppable cyborg from the future, capable of fighting for evil or good.
Arnold Schwarzenegger, *The Terminator* (1984; reprised in sequel)

Thelma & Louise Women on the lam for the killing of an attempted rapist. Full names: Thelma Dickinson and Louise Sawyer.
Geena Davis and Susan Sarandon, respectively, *Thelma & Louise* (1991)

Thompson, Sadie Loose woman on South Sea island, from the W. Somerset Maugham story.
Gloria Swanson, *Sadie Thompson* (1928)
Joan Crawford, *Rain* (1932)
Rita Hayworth, *Miss Sadie Thompson* (1953)

Twist, Oliver Orphan boy struggling to survive in 19th-century London, from the Charles Dickens novel.
Vinnie Burns, *Oliver Twist* (1912)
Ivy Millais, *Oliver Twist* (1912, UK)
Marie Doro, *Oliver Twist* (1916)
Harold Goodwin, *Oliver Twist Jr.* (1921, updated version)
Jackie Coogan, *Oliver Twist* (1922)
Dickie Moore, *Oliver Twist* (1933)
John Howard Davies, *Oliver Twist* (1948, UK)
Mark Lester, *Oliver!* (1968, UK)
Joey Lawrence, *Oliver & Company* (1988; as voice of animated kitten Oliver)

Vader, Darth Villainous lord, a.k.a. Anakin Skywalker, representing the Dark Side of the Force. Father of Luke Skywalker.
David Prowse, body; James Earl Jones, voice, *Star Wars* (1977; reprised in sequels)
Sebastian Shaw, *Return of the Jedi* (1983, Darth Vader unmasked as Anakin Skywalker)
Jake Lloyd, *Star Wars Episode I: The Phantom Menace* (1999; the boy Anakin)

Valjean, Jean French fugitive pursued by implacable Inspector Javert, from the Victor Hugo novel.
Henry Krauss, *Les Misérables* (1913, France)
William Farnum, *Les Misérables* (1917)
Gabriel Gabrio, *Les Misérables* (1925, France)
Harry Baur, *Les Misérables* (1934, France)
Fredric March, *Les Misérables* (1935)
Domingo Soler, *Les Misérables* (1944, Mexico)
Gino Cervi, *Les Misérables* (1952, Italy)
Michael Rennie, *Les Misérables* (1952)
Jean Gabin, *Les Misérables* (1957, France/Germany)
Liam Neeson, *Les Misérables* (1998, Germany/UK/US)

Zelig, Leonard Chameleonlike celebrity of the 1920s.
Woody Allen, *Zelig* (1983)

Zhivago, Yuri Doctor and poet who lives through the Russian Revolution, from the Boris Pasternak novel.
Omar Sharif, *Doctor Zhivago* (1965)

Zorba, Alexis Passionate Greek peasant, from the Nikos Kazantzakis novel.
Anthony Quinn, *Zorba the Greek* (1964)

Zorro Masked, swashbuckling, Robin Hood–like hero of Spanish California, from the Johnston McCulley stories.
Douglas Fairbanks, *The Mark of Zorro* (1920; reprised in sequel)
Robert Livingston, *The Bold Caballero* (1937)
Tyrone Power, *The Mark of Zorro* (1940)
Frank Latimore, *Zorro* (1961, Spain)
Alain Delon, *Zorro* (1975, Italy/France, set in South America)
George Hamilton, *Zorro, the Gay Blade* (1981; as twin sons of Zorro)
Anthony Hopkins, *The Mask of Zorro* (1998; with Antonio Banderas as Zorro's successor)

• • •

1. Humphrey Bogart

2. Cary Grant

3. James Stewart

4. Marlon Brando

5. Fred Astaire

6. Henry Fonda

7. Clark Gable

8. James Cagney

9. Spencer Tracy

10. Charlie Chaplin

11. Gary Cooper

12. Gregory Peck

13. John Wayne

14. Laurence Olivier

15. Gene Kelly

16. Orson Welles

17. Kirk Douglas

18. James Dean

19. Burt Lancaster

20. The Marx Brothers

21. Buster Keaton

22. Sidney Poitier

23. Robert Mitchum

24. Edward G. Robinson

25. William Holden

AFI Screen Legends

THE AMERICAN FILM INSTITUTE DEFINES an American screen legend as an actor or a team of actors with a significant screen presence in American feature-length films whose screen debut occurred in or before 1950, or whose screen debut occurred after 1950 but whose death has marked a completed body of work. The list of actors in the side margins, released in 1999, was selected by leaders from the American film community, including artists, historians, critics, and other cultural leaders, who chose from a list of 250 nominees in each gender, as compiled by AFI historians.

FACTS ABOUT AFI'S 50 GREATEST AMERICAN SCREEN LEGENDS

Lillian Gish has the longest screen career of any AFI legend, male or female—75 years.

Laurence Olivier has the longest career span of any male legend—59 years.

There are five female living legends: Katharine Hepburn, Elizabeth Taylor, Shirley Temple, Lauren Bacall, and Sophia Loren.

There are four male living legends: Marlon Brando, Gregory Peck, Kirk Douglas, and Sidney Poitier.

Legends Marlon Brando, Sidney Poitier, and Sophia Loren all made their screen debuts in 1950, the year AFI designated as a cutoff point. Stars whose screen debuts occurred just after 1950, and therefore did not qualify as AFI legends, include Jack Lemmon, Paul Newman, Shirley MacLaine, and Clint Eastwood.

Eight of the screen legends comprised four legendary duos: Katharine Hepburn and Spencer Tracy, Humphrey Bogart and Lauren Bacall, Fred Astaire and Ginger Rogers, and Clark Gable and Carole Lombard. The Marx Brothers are the sole legendary team on the AFI legends list.

There are 12 legends who made the transition from silent pictures to "talkies": Joan Crawford, Barbara Stanwyck, Lillian Gish, Carole Lombard, Mary Pickford, Clark Gable, Charlie Chaplin, Gary Cooper, John Wayne, the Marx Brothers, Buster Keaton, and Edward G. Robinson.

Thirteen AFI screen legends were born outside the United States: Audrey Hepburn, Belgium; Elizabeth Taylor, England; Ingrid Bergman, Sweden; Greta Garbo, Sweden; Marlene Dietrich, Germany; Claudette Colbert, France; Vivian Leigh, India; Sophia Loren, Italy; Mary Pickford, Canada; Cary Grant, England; Charlie Chaplin, England; Laurence Olivier, England; and Edward G. Robinson, Romania.

Eight screen legends were born in New York City: Barbara Stanwyck, Mae West, Rita Hayworth, Lauren Bacall, Humphrey Bogart, James Cagney, Burt Lancaster, and the Marx Brothers.

Tales of Manhattan (1942) is the feature film that boasts the largest collection of screen legends: Henry Fonda, Ginger Rogers, Rita Hayworth, and Edward G. Robinson. A 20-minute short film to benefit a tuberculosis sanitarium titled *Slippery Pearls* (or *Stolen Jools*) from 1931 contains five AFI screen legends: Joan Crawford, Barbara Stanwyck, Gary Cooper, Buster Keaton, and Edward G. Robinson.

Joan Crawford visited Clark Gable on the set of Mutiny on the Bounty *(1935).*

AFI LIFE ACHIEVEMENT AWARD

EACH YEAR SINCE 1973, the AFI Life Achievement Award has honored an individual whose career in motion pictures or television has greatly contributed to the enrichment of American culture. The original criteria stated that "the recipient should be one whose talent has in a fundamental way advanced the film art; whose accomplishment has been acknowledged by scholars, critics, professional peers and the general public; and whose work has stood the test of time." In 1993, AFI trustees extended the criteria to encompass individuals with active careers and work of significance yet to be accomplished.

Bette Davis

1973: John Ford	1983: John Huston	1993: Elizabeth Taylor
1974: James Cagney	1984: Lillian Gish	1994: Jack Nicholson
1975: Orson Welles	1985: Gene Kelly	1995: Steven Spielberg
1976: William Wyler	1986: Billy Wilder	1996: Clint Eastwood
1977: Bette Davis	1987: Barbara Stanwyck	1997: Martin Scorsese
1978: Henry Fonda	1988: Jack Lemmon	1998: Robert Wise
1979: Alfred Hitchcock	1989: Gregory Peck	1999: Dustin Hoffman
1980: James Stewart	1990: Sir David Lean	2000: Harrison Ford
1981: Fred Astaire	1991: Kirk Douglas	2001: Barbra Streisand
1982: Frank Capra	1992: Sidney Poitier	2002: Tom Hanks

THE HOLLYWOOD WALK OF FAME

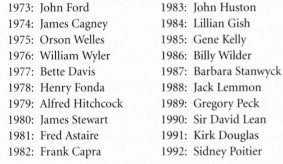

BILLED AS "THE WORLD'S MOST FAMOUS SIDEWALK," the Hollywood Walk of Fame is paved with some of entertainment's greatest names. Each name is engraved in a bronze star embedded in pink terrazzo, accompanied by an emblem identifying the honoree's primary area of achievement: Motion Pictures, Television, Radio, Recording, or Live Theatre. Since construction of the Walk of Fame began in 1960, more than 2,000 stars have been set in stone there, and more are still being added. The Motion Picture names are an ongoing Who's Who of film history, encompassing actors from Bud Abbott to Loretta Young and directors and producers from Samuel Z. Arkoff to Fred Zinnemann. They include screen legends such as Lauren Bacall, Humphrey Bogart, Clark Gable, Judy Garland, Katharine Hepburn, and Spencer Tracy; silent stars such as Roscoe "Fatty" Arbuckle; present-day stars such as Tom Cruise; animal stars such as Lassie; child stars such as Shirley Temple; and supporting players such as Beulah Bondi and Charles Ruggles.

The Walk of Fame, administered by the Hollywood Chamber of Commerce, lines both sides of Hollywood Boulevard from Gower to La Brea and both sides of Vine Street from Yucca to Sunset. For more information, including a complete directory of stars on the Walk of Fame, visit the Chamber's website at: http://www.hollywoodchamber.net.

1. Katharine Hepburn
2. Bette Davis
3. Audrey Hepburn
4. Ingrid Bergman
5. Greta Garbo
6. Marilyn Monroe
7. Elizabeth Taylor
8. Judy Garland
9. Marlene Dietrich
10. Joan Crawford
11. Barbara Stanwyck
12. Claudette Colbert
13. Grace Kelly
14. Ginger Rogers
15. Mae West
16. Vivien Leigh
17. Lillian Gish
18. Shirley Temple
19. Rita Hayworth
20. Lauren Bacall
21. Sophia Loren
22. Jean Harlow
23. Carole Lombard
24. Mary Pickford
25. Ava Gardner

DIRECTORS

They call "Action," and they decide when it's time to "Cut." When the men and women behind the camera speak, everyone listens.

A

Akerman, Chantal (1950–) Belgian director, screenwriter, and actress. Akerman employs an austere, minimalist style to explore the edges of feminine experience. An acclaimed example is *Jeanne Dielman, 23 Quai du Commerce, 1080 Bruxelles* (1975), which depicts 48 hours in the life of a prostitute. Other films include *Les Rendez-vous d'Anna* (1978, France/ Germany), about a filmmaker on a press tour, *Toute une Nuit (All Night Long)* (1982), *Histoires d'Amérique (American Stories)* (1988), and *La Captive (The Captive)* (2000, France/Belgium).

Aldrich, Robert (1918–1983) American director. His films often focus on violence, brutality, and action but also effectively use humor. A television writer and director, he made his feature debut with *The Big Leaguer* (1953). Films include *The Big Knife* (1955), *Attack!* (1956), *What Ever Happened to Baby Jane?* (1962), *The Flight of the Phoenix* (1966), the blockbuster *The Dirty Dozen* (1967), and *The Longest Yard* (1974). Aldrich was a president of the Directors Guild of America.

The films of director Robert Aldrich include Whatever Happened to Baby Jane? *(1962) and* The Longest Yard *(1974).*

Allégret, Marc (1900–1973) Swiss-born French director. His feature debut was *Les Amants de Minuit* (1931), which he codirected. His other credits include *Fanny* (1932), *Zou-Zou* (1934), *L'Amant de Lady Chatterley (Lady Chatterley's Lover)* (1955), *En Effeuillant La Marguerite (Please Mr. Balzac)* (1956), and *Les Parisiennes (Tales of Paris)* (1962, France/Italy). He advanced the careers of Simone Simon, Michèle Morgan, Jean-Pierre Aumont, Jeanne Moreau, and Brigitte Bardot. His brother was director Yves Allégret.

Allégret, Yves (1907–1987) French director. A practitioner of film noir who made his debut with *Tobie est un Ange* (1941), which was never released. Notable films include *Les Sept Péchés Capitaux (Seven Deadly Sins)* (1952), which he codirected, *Les Orgueilleux (The Proud and the Beautiful)* (1953), *L'Invasion* (1970), and *Mords pas—on t'aime* (1976). His brother was director Marc Allégret.

Allen, Woody (1935–) American director, writer, and actor. Brooklyn-born, he makes films that are usually New York–based and focus on the lives and loves of neurotics. His greatest success, critically and commercially, was *Annie Hall* (1977), winner of Academy Awards for best picture, best director, and best screenplay. Other films include *Broadway Danny Rose* (1983), *Hannah and Her Sisters* (1986), *Crimes and Misdemeanors* (1989), and *Bullets over Broadway* (1994), all of which earned him Academy Award nominations for direction. Other credits include *Bananas* (1971), *Manhattan* (1979), *Radio Days* (1987), *Sweet and Lowdown* (1999), and *The Curse of the Jade Scorpion* (2001).

Almodóvar, Pedro (1951–) Spanish director, screenwriter, actor, and composer. His films are generally irreverent comedies set in post-Franco Spain, often focusing on homosexuals or bisexuals. His first film, *Dos Putas* (1974), was filmed on an amateur basis, in Super-8mm. Subsequent features include *Atame! (Tie Me Up! Tie Me Down!)* (1990), *High Heels* (1991, Spain/France), and the award-winning *Mujeres al Borde de un Ataque de Nérvios (Women on the Verge of a Nervous Breakdown)* (1988). His most recent film, *Todo Sobre Mi Madre (All About My Mother)* (1999), won an Academy Award for best foreign film.

Altman, Robert (1925–) American director, screenwriter, and producer. He is best known for his idiosyncratic view of American society and an original cinematic approach that has inspired a number of disciples. He sometimes cowrites and coproduces his films. He made his directorial debut with an exploitation film, *The Delinquents* (1957). He gained international recognition with *M*A*S*H* (1970) and followed with such films as *McCabe and Mrs. Miller* (1971), *Nashville* (1975), *The Player* (1992), *Short Cuts* (1993), and *Gosford Park* (2001).

Anderson, Lindsay (1923–1994) Indian-born British director and writer. After working as a film critic, he directed the Academy Award–winning documentary *Thursday's Children* (1954), then made his feature debut with *This Sporting Life* (1963), followed by *If...* (1969), *O Lucky Man!* (1973), *In Celebration* (1975, UK/Canada), and *The Whales of August* (1987, US).

Antonioni, Michelangelo (1912–) Italian director and screenwriter. He began his directing career with documentary shorts during and after World War II, then moved into feature directing with *Cronaca di un Amore (Story of a Love Affair)* (1950). He became known for using innovative cinematic techniques to communicate modern alienation and malaise. He usually serves as story writer and coscreenwriter on his films. Credits include *Deserto Rosso (The Red Desert)* (1964), *L'Avventura* (1960), *Blow-Up* (1966, UK/Italy), *Zabriskie Point* (1970, US), *Professione: Reporter (The Passenger)* (1975), and *Identificazione di una Donna (Identification of a Woman)* (1982).

Apted, Michael (1941–) British director and producer of British and American films. A feature director, he is also well known for his documentary series on a small group of Britons, beginning with *7 Up* (1963) and tracking their lives with a new film every seven years, through *42 Up* (1998). Apted was a television researcher and soap-opera director before moving into film with *The Triple Echo* (1973). His other films include *Coal Miner's Daughter* (1980), *Gorky Park* (1983), *Gorillas in the Mist* (1988), *Thunderheart* (1992), and *The World Is Not Enough* (1999).

Armstrong, Gillian (1950–) Australian director of Australian and American films. After winning a scholarship to the Australian Film and Television School, Armstrong produced *Smokes and Lollies* (1975), the first in a decade-long coming-of-age trilogy. She came onto the international scene with *My Brilliant Career* in 1979, about the aspirations of a turn-of-the-century woman. Armstrong's other films include *Starstruck* (1982), *Mrs. Soffel* (1984), *High Tide* (1988), *The Last Days of Chez Nous* (1992), *Little Women* (1994), and *Oscar and Lucinda* (1997).

Arzner, Dorothy (1900–1979) American director and screenwriter. The first major female director, and the first female member of the Directors Guild of America. Arzner began as a script clerk at Famous Players, eventually working her way up to editor. She edited several movies, including *Old Ironsides* (1926), before she was assigned to direct *Fashions for Women* (1927) for Paramount. She directed *The Wild Party* (1929) with Clara Bow, *Merrily We Go to Hell* (1932), *Christopher Strong* (1933) with Katharine Hepburn, and *First Comes Courage* (1943). After World War II, she turned to television commercials and industrial films and taught at UCLA, counting director Francis Ford Coppola among her students.

Attenborough, Sir Richard (1923–) British director, actor, and producer of British and American films. He reached the zenith of his distinguished career with an Academy Award for his direction of *Gandhi* (1982, UK/India), which also was named best picture. After an exemplary career as a stage and screen actor, Attenborough turned to directing with *Oh! What a Lovely War* (1969). His subsequent works range from war films to musicals, including *Young Winston* (1972, UK), *A Bridge Too Far* (1977, UK), *A Chorus Line* (1985), *Shadowlands* (1993, UK/US), and *In Love and War* (1996, US/UK). Attenborough was knighted in 1976.

August, Bille (1948–) Danish director. A renowned cinematographer after graduating from the Danish Film School, August made his directorial debut with *Honning Måne (In My Life)* (1978). *Twist and Shout* (1985), which he also wrote, was a hit in his native Denmark, and he went on to international success with *Pelle Erobreren (Pelle the Conqueror)* (1987, Denmark/Sweden). He directed Ingmar Bergman's autobiographical script for *Den Godaviljan (The Best Intentions)* (1992, Sweden) before directing *The House of the Spirits* (1993), *Les Misérables* (1998, Germany/UK/US), and *En Sång för Martin (A Song for Martin)* (2001).

B

Beresford, Bruce (1940–) Australian-born American director. Beresford's *Driving Miss Daisy* (1989) won an Academy Award for best picture. He made his directorial debut with *The Adventures of Barry McKenzie* (1972, Australia), based on a comic strip. He subsequently directed such films as *Breaker Morant* (1980, Australia), *Tender Mercies* (1983), *Crimes of the Heart* (1986), and *Double Jeopardy* (1999, US/Canada/Germany).

The memorable image of the glowing briefcase that punctuates Robert Aldrich's classic detective thriller *Kiss Me Deadly* (1955) has been quoted in several films since, including *Heavy Metal* (1981), *Repo Man* (1984), and *Pulp Fiction* (1994).

The works of Swedish director and screenwriter Ingmar Bergman, pictured here with Liv Ullman, have been praised for their depiction of human relationships and philosophical issues.

Bergman, Ingmar (1918–) Swedish director and screenwriter. Experienced as a stage director, he was a script doctor and screenwriter (*Hets [Torment/Frenzy]*, 1944) before turning to film directing with *Kris (Crisis)* in 1945. His films *Kvinnodrö (Smiles of a Summer Night)* (1955) and *Det Sjunde Inseglet (The Seventh Seal)* (1957) won prizes at the Cannes Film Festival, bringing him international fame. He has been praised for his capacity to depict human relationships in intimate detail and for his exploration of philosophical issues and crises of faith. He writes his own screenplays. Other works include *Sommaren med Monika (Monika/Summer with Monika)* (1953), *Smultronstället (Wild Strawberries)* (1957), *Persona* (1966), *Viskningar och Rop (Cries and Whispers)* (1972), *The Magic Flute* (1974), *Das Schlangenei (The Serpent's Egg)* (1977, Germany/US), and *Fanny och Alexander (Fanny and Alexander)* (1983; best foreign language film Academy Award).

Bertolucci, Bernardo (1940–) Italian director. He helmed his first feature, *La Commare Secca (The Grim Reaper)* (1962), when he was 22 years old, and subsequently directed some of the most honored and controversial films of his time. His *Ultimo Tango a Parigi (Last Tango in Paris)* (1973, Italy/France) created worldwide controversy because of its graphic sexuality. *The Last Emperor* (1987, UK/China) received nine Academy Awards, including best director and best picture. His other films include *La Strategia del Ragno (The Spider's Strategem)* (1970), *Il Conformista (The Conformist)* (1971, Italy/France/West Germany), and *1900* (1977, Italy/France/Germany).

Besson, Luc (1959–) French director of French and American films. Director of stylized and visually dynamic films who became known to American audiences with the art-house hit *Subway* (1985). His subsequent films include *The Big Blue* (1988) and the inventive action film *La Femme Nikita* (1990), which spawned an American remake, *Point of No Return* (1993) as well as a television series. He also directed *The Professional* (1994), the imaginative *The Fifth Element* (1997), and *The Messenger: The Story of Joan of Arc* (1999).

Boetticher, Budd (1916–) American director. A onetime matador in Mexico, he began in films as a technical adviser on the bullfighting film *Blood and Sand* (1941). Two of his own films— *The Bullfighter and the Lady* (1951) and *The Magnificent Matador* (1965)—also reflect his early experience. Other credits include *The Cimarron Kid* (1951), *The Man from the Alamo* (1953), *Red Ball Express* (1952), and *The Rise and Fall of Legs Diamond* (1971).

Bresson, Robert (1907–) French director and screenwriter. His works are austere, introspective, and stylistically unified, often employing un-professional actors. His first film was *Les Affaires Publiques* (1934). After World War II, he directed such films as *Le Journal d'un Curé de Campagne (Diary of a Country Priest)* (1951), *Pickpocket* (1959), *Le Procès de Jeanne d'Arc (The Trial of Joan of Arc)* (1962), *Lancelot du Lac (Lancelot of the Lake)* (1974, France/ Italy), and *L'Argent (Money)* (1983, France/ Switzerland).

Brest, Martin (1951–) American director, screenwriter, producer, and actor. Trained at New York University film school and the American Film Institute, he became known for his spirited comedies and dramas. Directing credits include *Fast Times at Ridgemont High* (1982), *Midnight Run* (1984, also prod.), and *Scent of a Woman* (1992, also prod.).

Broca, Philippe de (1933–) French director. An assistant to French New Wave directors such as Truffaut, Broca became a director of documen-tary subjects as well as human comedies, the best known of which was the counterculture hit *Le Roi de Coeur (The King of Hearts)* (1966). Other films include *Le Diable par la Que (The Devil by the Tail)* (1969), *Tendre Pulet (Dear Inspector)* (1977), *L'Africain* (1983), *Les 1001 Nuits (Scheherazade)* (1990), and *Le Bossu (On Guard)* (1997).

Brooks, Albert (1947–) American director, actor, and screenwriter. Born Albert Einstein. Trained in television and as a stand-up comic, he entered films in the 1970s as an actor in *Taxi Driver* (1976) and as the actor-director-writer of *Real Life* (1979), which demonstrated his rueful comedic sensibilities. Later acting-directing-writing credits include *Modern*

Romance (1981), *Lost in America* (1985), *Mother* (1996), and *The Muse* (1999). His father was performer Harry "Parkyakarkus" Einstein.

Brooks, Mel (1926–) American director, screenwriter, producer, and actor. Born Melvin Kaminsky. A stand-up comic and TV comedy writer, he became a feature director-writer with *The Producers* (1968, best original screenplay Academy Award), which he adapted in 2001 into a smash Broadway musical. Since that film, he has made many genre spoofs and other comedies. His films as a director-writer, some of which he produced and acted in, include *Blazing Saddles* (1974), *Young Frankenstein* (1974), *High Anxiety* (1977), *History of the World Part One* (1981), and *Dracula: Dead and Loving It* (1995).

Buñuel, Luis (1900–1983) Spanish director. He is known for his outrageous, surrealist images and for his iconoclastic attacks on the Catholic church, the middle class, and other institutions. His style was established with his first film, the short *Un Chien Andalou (An Andalusian Dog)* (1928, France), which he codirected, coproduced, and cowrote with artist Salvador Dali. He cowrote most of his films, many of them made in Mexico or France. Works include *L'Age d'Or (The Golden Age)* (1930, France), *Los Olvidados (The Young and the Damned)* (1950, Mexico), *Viridiana* (1961, Spain/ Mexico), *El Angel Exterminador (The Extermin-ating Angel)* (1962, Mexico), *Belle de Jour* (1967, France/Italy), *Le Charme Discret de la Bourgeoisie (The Discreet Charm of the Bourgeoisie)* (1972, France; best foreign language film Academy Award), and *Cet Obscur Objet du Désir (That Obscure Object of Desire)* (1977, France).

Burton, Tim (1960–) American director and producer. Trained as an animator, he became known as a director for his use of dark, wildly horrific images filtered through a childlike sensibility. He sometimes coproduces his films. Directing credits include *Beetlejuice* (1988), *Batman* (1989), *Edward Scissorhands* (1990), *Ed Wood* (1994), *Sleepy Hollow* (1999), and *Planet of the Apes* (2001).

C

Cacoyannis, Michael (1922–) Greek director of international films. He enjoyed his greatest success with the Academy Award nominee *Zorba the Greek* (1974). He made his debut as a director with *Windfall in Athens/Sunday Awakening* (1953). His other directorial credits include *Stella* (1955), *The Day the Fish Came Out* (1967, UK/Greece), and *The Trojan Women* (1971, US/ Greece).

Cameron, James (1954–) Canadian-born American director, screenwriter, and producer. A director of blockbuster action films, he changed genres and achieved new levels of box-office success with the romantic epic *Titanic* (1997). He usually writes or cowrites his films and has produced some of them; he has also produced and written films of others. Other directorial efforts include *The Terminator* (1984), *Aliens* (1986), *Terminator 2: Judgment Day* (1991), and *True Lies* (1994).

Campion, Jane (1954–) New Zealand–born director of international films. Campion has vaulted into the top ranks of directors with only a handful of films. Her first feature, *Sweetie* (1989, Australia), was presented at Cannes. Her subsequent films are *An Angel at My Table* (1990, New Zealand), the widely acclaimed *The Piano* (1993, New Zealand/ France), *The Portrait of a Lady* (1996, UK/US), and *Holy Smoke* (1999, US/Australia).

Capra, Frank (1897–1991) Sicilian-born American director. Although best known for films pitting an idealistic individual against corrupt powers that be, such as *Mr. Deeds Goes to Town* (1936, best director Academy Award) and *Mr. Smith Goes to Washington* (1939), he made many kinds of films, including the pioneering screwball comedy *It Happened One Night* (1934), which won Academy Awards for best picture and best director. Other films include the Christmas favorite *It's a Wonderful Life* (1946) and *You Can't Take It with You* (1938; best director Academy Award). He received AFI's Life Achievement Award in 1982.

Carné, Marcel (1909–1996) French director. He began his career as an assistant to René Clair and other leading directors, making his own feature directorial debut with *Jenny* (1936), followed by such films as *Hotel du Nord* (1938), *Quai des Brumes (Port of Shadows)* (1938), and his greatest work, *Les Enfants du Paradis (Children of Paradise)* (1945).

Cassavetes, John (1929–1989) American director. Cassavetes was a highly regarded actor who turned to direction with equal success. He made his directorial debut with *Shadows* (1961) and followed with such films as *Faces* (1968), *A Woman Under the Influence* (1974), for which he earned a best director Academy Award nomination, and *Gloria* (1980). His wife, actress Gena Rowlands, appeared in a number of his films.

"Capra corn": Hollywood slang for the heartwarming, tear-inducing stories of ordinary decent people that were the specialty of American director Frank Capra.

Known for his quirkiness and innovation, Tim Burton directed Beetlejuice *(1988),* Batman *(1989),* Edward Scissorhands *(1990), and* Batman Returns *(1992, pictured).*

Director Martha Coolidge, seen here on the set of Out to Sea *(1997), achieved box office success with* Valley Girl *(1983).*

Joel Coen's first professional credit was as assistant film editor on Sam Raimi's low-budget 1983 splatterfest, *The Evil Dead.* The filmmakers would later collaborate (along with Joel's brother Ethan) on Raimi's *Crimewave* (1985) and Coen's *The Hudsucker Proxy* (1994).

Castle, William (1914–1977) American director and producer. He directed low-budget crime and adventure movies from the 1940s to mid-1950s (e.g., *The Whistler,* 1944; *Johnny Stool Pigeon,* 1949; *Drums of Tahiti,* 1954), then turned director-producer, specializing in horror films, often promoted with gimmicks and sometimes becoming cult classics. Films of this period include *House on Haunted Hill* (1959), *The Tingler* (1959, promoted with theater seats wired to give mild electric shocks), *The Spirit Is Willing* (1967), and *Rosemary's Baby* (1968, prod. only).

Chabrol, Claude (1930–) French director. After working as a publicist and a critic, Chabrol debuted as a director with *Le Beau Serge* (*Bitter Reunion*) (1959). He developed an international reputation with *Les Cousins* (*The Cousins*) (1959) and *Les Bonnes Femmes* (1960). Among his 50 features are such major films as *Landru* (*Bluebeard*) (1963, France/Italy), *Le Scandale* (*The Champagne Murders*) (1967), and *Les Innocents aux Main Sales* (*Dirty Hands*) (1975, France/Italy/West Germany).

Chaplin, Sir Charles (1889–1977) British-born American director, actor, producer, and screenwriter. Known as Charlie Chaplin, he was the silent screen's most honored comedian, who typically portrayed the Tramp character in films including *The Tramp* (1915) and *The Kid* (1921). From 1914, he wrote, directed, starred in, and sometimes produced and composed music for his films, which are characterized by pathos and satire as well as slapstick comedy. He was a cofounder of United Artists. Silent films include *The Gold Rush* (1925), *City Lights* (1931), and *Modern Times* (1936); sound films include *The Great Dictator* (1940), *Monsieur Verdoux* (1947), and *Limelight* (1952). Accused of communist ties, he was denied reentry to the US in 1952 and did not return for 20 years. He received special Academy Awards in 1927–28 and 1972. He was knighted in 1975.

Chen Kaige (1952–) Chinese director. One of the most important filmmakers to emerge since the Cultural Revolution of the 1960s, he makes films that combine high spectacle and emotional subtlety. Early films benefited from the cinematography of Zhang Yimou, later a director himself. Chen's directing credits include *Yellow Earth* (1984), *The Big Parade* (1985), *King of Children* (1987), and *Farewell My Concubine* (1993).

Cimino, Michael (1943–) American director, screenwriter, and producer. Known principally for directing and cowriting the acclaimed Vietnam War film, *The Deer Hunter* (1978, best director Academy Award), and following it by directing and writing one of Hollywood's most notorious flops, the western *Heaven's Gate* (1980). Later films include *Desperate Hours* (1990), which he also coproduced.

Clair, René (1898–1981) French director who also worked in the United Kingdom and the United States. He wrote his first film, *Paris qui Dort* (*The Crazy Ray*) (1924), in one night and completed filming in three weeks. He first drew international attention with the silent *Chapeau de Paille d'Italie* (*The Italian Straw Hat/The Horse Ate the Hat*) (1927). Other films include *Sour les Toits de Paris* (*Under the Roofs of Paris*) (1930), *Le Million* (1931), *A Nous la Liberté* (1931), and the classic mystery *And Then There Were None* (1945, US).

Coen, Joel (1954–) American director and screenwriter. He and brother Ethan (1957–), his cowriter and producer, create stylized, offbeat dramatic comedies. After finishing New York University film school, the Coen brothers made the striking *Blood Simple* (1984). Later films include *Raising Arizona* (1987), *Barton Fink* (1991), *Fargo* (1996), *The Big Lebowski* (1998), *O Brother, Where Art Thou?* (2000), and *The Man Who Wasn't There* (2001).

Coolidge, Martha (1946–) American director. A documentary director in the 1970s (*David Off and On,* 1972; *An Old-Fashioned Woman,* 1974), she turned to fiction films and gained acclaim for her lively youth comedy *Valley Girl* (1983). Later films include dramatic character studies such as *Rambling Rose* (1991) and *Angie* (1994).

Coppola, Francis Ford (1939–) American director, screenwriter, and producer. After getting his start with low-budget producer Roger Corman, for whom he directed and wrote the horror film *Dementia 13* (1963), he became renowned for *The Godfather* (1972) and *The Godfather Part II* (1974), winning a best director Academy Award for the latter. These Godfather films exhibited his talent for epic scale, intimate drama, and operatic staging. He often cowrites and coproduces his films and produces films by other directors. Other directorial efforts include *Apocalypse Now* (1979), *The Cotton Club* (1984), *Peggy Sue Got Married* (1986), *Tucker: The Man and His Dream* (1988), *The Godfather Part III* (1990), and *Bram Stoker's Dracula* (1992). He is the father of actress-director Sofia Coppola and the uncle of actor Nicolas Cage.

Corman, Roger (1926–) American director and producer. He is a prolific producer and director-producer of mainly low-budget films in many genres, most memorably horror and science fiction. He is notable not only for his films, many of which enjoy cult status, but for the start he gave to various filmmakers and actors now famous in their own right. As a director-producer, Corman's films include *It Conquered the World* (1956), *The Little Shop of Horrors* (1960), *Frankenstein Unbound* (1990, also co-sc.), and a series of films based on works by Edgar Allan Poe, including *The House of Usher* (1960), *The Raven* (1963), and *The Masque of the Red Death* (1964, UK/US). Films he produced or executive-produced but did not direct include *The Wild Ride* (1960; starring Jack Nicholson), *Dementia 13* (1963; dir. by Francis Ford Coppola), *Boxcar Bertha* (1972; dir. by Martin Scorsese), and *Battle Beyond the Stars* (1980; sc. by John Sayles).

Costa-Gavras, Constantin (1933–) Greek-born director and screenwriter of international films. Born Konstantinos Gavras; also known simply as Costa-Gavras. He is renowned for politically explosive films such as *Z* (1969, France/Algeria), winner of a best foreign film Academy Award; *L'Aveu (The Confession)* (1970, France); *Etat de Siège (State of Siege)* (1973, France); *Special Section* (1975, France/Italy/West Germany); and *Missing* (1982, US). He made his directorial debut with the suspense film *Compartment Tueurs (The Sleeping Car Murders)* (1965).

Cronenberg, David (1943–) Canadian director and screenwriter of Canadian and American films. He began his career with horror movies but has branched out into other kinds of stories. All, however, maintain his fascination with repulsive and frightening images and the dark recesses of the psyche. He usually writes or cowrites his films. Directing credits include *Shivers/They Came from Within* (1975), *Scanners* (1981), *The Fly* (1986), *Dead Ringers* (1988), *Naked Lunch* (1991), *Crash* (1996), and *eXistenZ* (1999).

Crowe, Cameron (1957–) American director and screenwriter. A writer and editor for *Rolling Stone* magazine, he entered film in 1982 with a screenplay adaptation of his book *Fast Times at Ridgemont High.* He later turned to directing and writing, focusing on the human foibles and yearnings of his generation in films such as *Singles* (1992), *Jerry Maguire* (1996), and *Almost Famous* (2000).

Curtiz, Michael (1888–1962) Hungarian-born American director. Curtiz made 145 films in his career—spanning drama, adventure, musical, romance, comedy, sports, and mystery—but is best known for one: the wartime adventure-romance *Casablanca* (1943), winner of Academy Awards for best picture and best director. He made his directorial debut with *Az Utolso Bohém (The Last Bohemian)* (1912, Hungary); his first American film was *The Third Degree* (1927). Among his better-known films are *The Sea Hawk* (1940), *Angels with Dirty Faces* (1938), *Yankee Doodle Dandy* (1942), *Mildred Pierce* (1945), and *White Christmas* (1954).

D

Dash, Julie (1952–) American director and producer. Beginning her directorial career in the 1970s, she became known for subtle explorations of women's lives, including *Four Women* (1975) and *Diary of an African Nun* (1977). In the 1980s, she became a producer as well as a director, for the films *Illusions* (1982) and *Daughters of the Dust* (1991, also sc.). Since then, she has directed several television dramas.

De Mille, Cecil B. (1881–1959) American director, producer, and screenwriter. A prolific director of the silent and sound eras, he often edited and wrote or cowrote his silent films. Recognized at first for spicy narratives of modern mores, he became known for religious and historical epics such as *The Ten Commandments* (1923 original, 1956 remake). He cofounded the Jesse L. Lasky Feature Play Company, later Paramount, and helped establish Hollywood as a film capital. Other films include *The Squaw Man* (in three versions: 1914, 1918, and 1931), *Forbidden Fruit* (1921), *The King of Kings* (1927), *The Sign of the Cross* (1932), *The Crusades* (1935), *The Plainsman* (1937), *Samson and Delilah* (1949), and *The Greatest Show on Earth* (1952).

Demme, Jonathan (1944–) American director. Demme made his directorial debut under producer Roger Corman with *Caged Heat* (1974) and followed with *Crazy Mama* (1975). He went on to make a series of offbeat and stylish films, including *Melvin and Howard* (1980), *Swing Shift* (1983), and *Something Wild* (1986). He achieved a new level of fame with the thriller *The Silence of the Lambs* (1991), which won Academy Awards for best picture and best director. This success was followed by the highly acclaimed drama *Philadelphia* (1993).

De Palma, Brian (1940–) American director. He first attracted attention with the low-budget film *Greetings* (1968) and its sequel *Hi Mom!* (1970), featuring a young Robert De Niro. De Palma's credits encompass suspense thrillers including *Dressed to Kill* (1980), violent crime dramas such as *Scarface* (1983) and *The Untouchables* (1987), and adventure films like *Mission: Impossible* (1996). His flair for generating suspense through adroit camera work is reminiscent of director Alfred Hitchcock.

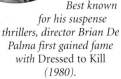

Best known for his suspense thrillers, director Brian De Palma first gained fame with Dressed to Kill *(1980).*

De Sica, Vittorio (1902–1974) Italian director, screenwriter, and actor. His *Sciuscia (Shoeshine)* (1946) and *Ladri di Biciclette (The Bicycle Thief)* (1948) were major works of Italian neorealism, both winning the best foreign language film Academy Award, as did his *Ieri, oggi, domani (Yesterday, Today, and Tomorrow)* (1963) and *Il Giardino dei Finzi-Contini (The Garden of the Finzi-Continis)* (1971). His films are notable for their humanity and tenderness. He coscripted many of his films and acted in both his own and others' films. Other directorial efforts include *Umberto D* (1952), and *I Sequestrati di Altoni (The Condemned of Altona)* (1962).

Dovzhenko, Alexander (1894–1956) Ukrainian director and screenwriter. Dovzhenko made his feature debut at the age of 32, codirecting *Vasya the Reformer* (1926) after a career as a diplomat and an artist. He directed two silent films accorded classic status—*Arsenal* (1929) and his masterpiece *Earth/ Soil* (1930). His other films include *Zvenigora* (1928) and two patriotic works—*Aerogard (Air City/Frontier)* (1935) and *Shchors/Shors* (1939).

Dreyer, Carl (1889–1968) Danish director and screenwriter. Dreyer made his debut with *The President* (1919); his later films include the acknowledged classics *The Passion of Joan of Arc* (1928, France) and *Day of Wrath* (1943). Among his films are *Leaves from Satan's Book* (1920), *Mikael/Chained/Heart's Desire/The Story of the Third Sex* (1924, Germany), *Vampyr/ Vampyr ou l'Etrange/Aventure de Allan Gray* (1932, France/ Germany), *Ordet (The Word)* (1955), and *Gertrud* (1964), his final film.

Duras, Marguerite (1914–1996) French director, screenwriter, and novelist. Born in French Indochina (now Vietnam) and educated in Paris at the Sorbonne, the prolific Duras wrote rich, meditative stories in many media, eschewing easy plotting for deep explorations into human relations. She coscripted the celebrated *Hiroshima, Mon Amour* (1959) before directing *La Musica* in 1966. Other notable films include *Jaune le Soleil* (1971), *India Song* (1975), *Le Camion (The Truck)* (1977), and *Les Enfants (The Children)* (1984). Her novel *The Lover* was adapted for the screen by Jean-Jacques Annaud in 1991.

Duvivier, Julien (1896–1967) French director and screenwriter. Noted for his "poetic realism," he was ranked with René Clair, Jacques Feyder, Jean Renoir, and Marcel Carné as one of the "Big Five" of French cinema. Duvivier made his directorial debut with *Haceldema (Le Prix du Sang)* (1919) and went on to make such films as *Le Golem (The Golem/Legend of Prague)* (1936, France/Czechoslovakia) and *Pépé le Moko* (1936). He is perhaps best remembered for two "light films": *Le Petit Monde de Don Camillo (The Little World of Don Camillo)* (1951) and its sequel, *Le Retour de Don Camillo (The Return of Don Camillo)* (1953, France/Italy).

"They do not realize that art has to be severe. It cannot be commercial. It cannot be for the producer, or even for the public. It has to be for oneself."

—
Vittorio De Sica, on the trouble with producers, 1972

E–F

Eastwood, Clint (1930–) American actor, director, and producer. Eastwood established himself as an actor in TV and Italian-made westerns. He went on to direct 22 films, beginning with *Play Misty for Me* (1971). Much of his output has been in the western genre, but he has demonstrated his versatility with such films as *Sudden Impact* (1983), *Bird* (1988), *The Bridges of Madison County* (1995), *Midnight in the Garden of Good and Evil* (1997), *True Crime* (1998), and *Space Cowboys* (2000). His western *Unforgiven* (1992) won Academy Awards for best picture and best director.

Edwards, Blake (1922–) American director, screenwriter, and producer. Edwards was one of the hottest American directors of the early 1960s with such films as *Breakfast at Tiffany's* (1961), *Days of Wine and Roses* (1962), and *The Pink Panther* (1964). Among his other major films are *10* (1979), *SOB* (1981), and *Victor/ Victoria* (1982). He has also directed six Pink Panther sequels. He is married to Julie Andrews.

Eisenstein, Sergei (1898–1948) Russian director, screenwriter, and film theoretician, born in Latvia (then part of Russia). His filmmaking and theorizing helped to formulate film language, establishing the importance of montage. He often wrote or cowrote his films. He had an uneasy relationship with the Soviet authorities, whose support for him varied. Works include *Potemkin (The Battleship Potemkin)* (1925), *October/Ten Days That Shook the World* (1928), *The General Line/Old and New* (1929), *Alexander Nevsky* (1938), and *Ivan the Terrible Part I* (1945; followed by *Part II,* unreleased until 1958, and an unfinished *Part III*). His books include *Film Sense* (1942) and *Film Form* (1949).

Emmerich, Roland (1955–) West German–born American director, screenwriter, and producer. Science fiction and action director who often collaborates in writing and producing his films, which include *Moon 44* (1990, West Germany), *Universal Soldier* (1992), *Stargate* (1994, France/ US), *Independence Day* (1996), *Godzilla* (1998), and *The Patriot* (2000).

Farrelly, Peter (1957–) and **Bobby** (1958–) American directors, screenwriters, and producers. This team of brothers, known as the Farrelly Brothers, collaborate in directing, writing, and producing outrageous comedies. Peter is credited as the sole director for *Dumb & Dumber* (1994); their joint directing credits include *Kingpin* (1996), *There's Something About Mary* (1998), *Me, Myself & Irene* (2000), and *Shallow Hal* (2001).

Fassbinder, Rainer Werner (1946–1982) German director, screenwriter, and actor. A premier representative of post–World War II German cinema, he made iconoclastic, engaging dramas about life in modern Germany. He made up to four films per year until his premature death from a drug overdose. He wrote and sometimes acted in his films. Works include *Götter der Pest (Gods of the Plague)* (1970), *Fontane Effi Briest (Effi Briest)* (1974), *Eine Reise ins Licht (Despair)* (1978), *Die Ehe der Maria Braun (The Marriage of Maria Braun)* (1979), *Lola* (1981), and *Die Sehnsucht de Veronika Voss (Veronika Voss)* (1982).

Fellini, Federico (1920–1993) Italian director and screenwriter. A screenwriter in the 1940s, he moved to directing in the 50s, cowriting his films. His humanistic, sharp-eyed works, rich in symbolism and sensuality, made him Italy's most renowned filmmaker. He won Academy Awards for best foreign language film for *La Strada* (1954), *Le Notti di Cabiria (The Nights of Cabiria/Cabiria)* (1957), *Otto e Mezzo (8 ½)* (1963), and *Amarcord* (1973). Other films include *I Vitelloni* (1953), *La Dolce Vita* (1960), *Giulietta degli Spiriti (Juliet of the Spirits)* (1965), *Fellini Satyricon* (1969), and *La Voce della Luna (Voices of the Moon)* (1990). He was awarded a Lifetime Achievement Award at the 1992 Academy Awards.

Feyder, Jacques (1885–1948) Belgian director. Feyder was a leader in the Poetic Realism movement in France. His first feature was *M. Pinson-Policier* (1916, France), which he codirected. His *L'Atlantide* (1921) was the most expensive French production of its time; he followed with such films as *Crainquebille* (1922), *Visages d'Enfants (Faces of Children)* (1925, Switzerland), and *Thérèse Raquin (Shadows of Fear)* (1928). After the government banned *Les Nouveaux Messieurs (The New Gentlemen)* (1928), he went to Hollywood and directed Greta Garbo in *The Kiss* (1929, US). After leaving Hollywood, he directed nine more films, including *La Kermesse Héroïque (Carnival in Flanders)* (1935).

Figgis, Mike (1949–) Kenyan-born British director. His first directorial work was *Stormy Monday* (1988), for which he also wrote the screenplay and composed the music. With fewer than a dozen credits, he carved out a reputation for engrossing and suspenseful films. His motion pictures include *Internal Affairs* (1990, US), *Leaving Las Vegas* (1995, US/France), *Miss Julie* (1999, US), and *Time Code* (2000, US).

Flaherty, Robert (1884–1951) American director. Flaherty has been called the father of the documentary. His *Nanook of the North* (1922), which he also produced, wrote, photographed, and edited, and *Man of Aran* (1934, UK) are still the gold standard for documentaries. In all, Flaherty directed 12 films—seven of them documentaries, including *The Twenty-Four Dollar Island* (1927), *Industrial Britain* (1933, UK), and *Louisiana Story* (1948). His feature films include *White Shadows of the South Seas* (1928), which he codirected with W.S. Van Dyke, and *Elephant Boy* (1937, UK), which he codirected with Zoltán Korda.

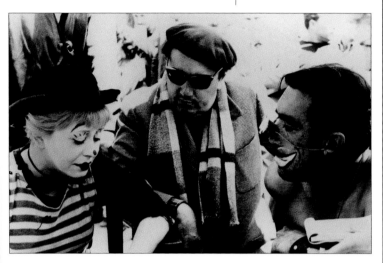

Italian director Federico Fellini (center) gained international acclaim with La Strada (1954), which starred his wife, Giulietta Masina and Anthony Quinn (right).

Ford, John (1895–1973) American director, producer, and screenwriter. Prolific director whose feature film career ran from the 1910s to the 60s. His characteristically American works were marked by strong narrative, engaging characters, and a visual style at once poetic and unobtrusive. He worked in many genres, but his greatest impact was on the western, which he elevated with meditations on the conflict between frontier and civilization. He won a best director Academy Award four times, for *The Informer* (1935), *The Grapes of Wrath* (1940), *How Green Was My Valley* (1941), and *The Quiet Man* (1952). Other films include *The Secret Man* (1917), *The Iron Horse* (1924), *The Lost Patrol* (1934), *Stagecoach* (1939), *Drums Along the Mohawk* (1939), *My Darling Clementine* (1946), *The Searchers* (1956), and *The Man Who Shot Liberty Valance* (1962). He produced, wrote, or cowrote some of his films. In 1973, Ford won AFI's Life Achievement Award.

Forman, Miloš (1932–) Czechoslovakian-born American director. Forman first won international acclaim with *Loves of a Blonde* (1966, Czechoslovakia) and *The Fireman's Ball* (1968, Czechoslovakia). After moving to the United States, he directed a number of films with uniquely American themes. He reached the pinnacle of his profession with *One Flew over the Cuckoo's Nest* (1975), which won Academy Awards in the top five categories, including best picture and best director. His subsequent films include *Hair* (1979), *Amadeus* (1984), winner of Academy Awards for best film and best director, and *Man on the Moon* (1999).

Franju, Georges (1912–1987) French director. Franju was a founder of the Cinémathèque Française, a film archive, and a successful director of shorts and documentaries, before turning to features with *La Tête Contre les Murs (The Keepers)* (1959). He followed this with such films as the horror classic *Les Yeux sans Visage (Eyes Without a Face/The Horror Chamber of Dr. Faustus)* (1960, France/Italy), *Thérèse Desqueyroux/ Therese* (1962), *Thomas l'Imposteur (Thomas the Imposter)* (1965), and *L'Homme sans Visage (Shadowman)* (1974).

Frankenheimer, John (1930–) American director. Frankenheimer was a veteran of 125 TV productions during the heyday of live drama, when he directed his first film, *The Young Stranger* (1957). He went on to direct films in a variety of genres, including *The Manchurian Candidate* (1962), *Seven Days in May* (1964), *The Fixer* (1968), *The Iceman Cometh* (1973), and *Reindeer Games* (2000).

Franklin, Carl (1949–) American director, screenwriter, and actor. While studying at the American Film Institute, he began working with director Roger Corman and offered his first directorial effort, *Nowhere to Run,* in 1989. Since then, he has gained acclaim for dramatically and structurally complex works, including *One False Move* (1991) and *Devil in a Blue Dress* (1995), for which he also wrote the screenplay.

Frears, Stephen (1941–) British director. After assisting other filmmakers, including Lindsay Anderson, and directing for British TV, Frears made his feature debut with *Gumshoe* (1972). He followed with such films as the widely acclaimed and award-winning *My Beautiful Laundrette* (1985), *Prick Up Your Ears* (1987), *The Grifters* (1990, US), and *High Fidelity* (2000, US).

Friedkin, William (1939–) American director. Trained in television, he became a top box-office director with *The French Connection* (1971; best director Academy Award) and *The Exorcist* (1973); later films have been less successful commercially. Noted for his cool visual style and tight editing, Friedkin's other films include *The Night They Raided Minsky's* (1968), *The Boys in the Band* (1970), *Sorcerer* (1977), *Cruising* (1980), and *Jade* (1995).

Fuller, Samuel (1911–1997) American director, writer, producer, and actor. A former crime reporter and pulp novelist who fought in Europe and North Africa during WWII, Fuller's bluntly poetic genre pictures were marked by a bold visual style, fierce morality, and near-tabloid narrative sense. His tough worldview and independent spirit penetrate such films as *Pickup on South Street* (1953), *The Steel Helmet* (1951), *Shock Corridor* (1963), *The Naked Kiss* (1964), and *The Big Red One* (1980).

Former actor Carl Franklin trained as a director at the American Film Institute.

Gance, Abel (1889–1981) French director. A pioneer of filmmaking techniques, Gance is best remembered for directing *Napoléon* (1927). A five-hour version of *Napoléon* was re-released in 1979 accompanied by live symphonic orchestras. Gance, whose name appeared on screen before his stars' names, died 18 days after the New York premiere. He made his feature debut with *La Digue* (1911) and followed with *Mater Dolorosa* (1917), *La Dixième Symphonie* (1918), *J'Accuse (I Accuse)* (1919), *La Roue* (1923), and *Cyrano et d'Artagnan* (1963, France/Italy/Spain).

Godard, Jean-Luc (1930–) French director and screenwriter. A film critic and maker of film shorts, he turned to feature directing and writing with *A Bout de Souffle (Breathless)* (1960). His visually experimental, improvisational films were pivotal examples of the French New Wave and have greatly influenced avant-garde film-making. Rich in political and philosophical content, his films include *Le Petit Soldat (The Little Soldier)* (1960; release delayed to 1963), *Alphaville* (1965), *Masculin/Féminin (Masculine Feminine)* (1966), *Weekend* (1968), *Prénom: Carmen (First Name: Carmen)* (1983), and *Nouvelle Vague (New Wave)* (1990).

Grierson, John (1898–1972) Scottish director. Grierson is considered to be the founder of the British documentary field. He was the first to use the term *documentary*, which he took from a French term for travelogues. He made his debut with *Drifters* (1929), a documentary about herring fisherman, and followed with his only other directorial credit, *The Fishing Banks of Skye* (1934). He spent the rest of his career as a producer.

Griffith, D.W. (1875–1948) American director, producer, and screenwriter. This landmark silent-film director helped to shape film grammar, pioneering essential techniques of cinematography, editing, and narrative. His most enduring work is *The Birth of a Nation* (1915), acclaimed for its epic form though controversial for its racist content. He produced, wrote, or cowrote many of his films. He was a cofounder of United Artists. Examples of his many films include *Judith of Bethulia* (1914), *Intolerance* (1916), *Broken Blossoms* (1919), *Orphans of the Storm* (1922), and *The Sorrows of Satan* (1926). His career ended soon after the coming of sound.

Haines, Randa (1945–) American director. She gained acclaim with her directorial debut about the life of a deaf woman, *Children of a Lesser God* (1986). Later films include *The Doctor* (1991) and *Wrestling Ernest Hemingway* (1993).

Hallström, Lasse (1946–) Swedish director and screenwriter of Swedish and American films. A professional filmmaker by the age of 16, Hallström was known in his native Sweden for his comedies, including *ABBA: The Movie* (1977) and *Jag är Med Barn (Father to Be)* (1979). He achieved international success with the bittersweet coming-of-age story, *Mitt Liv som Hund (My Life as a Dog)* in 1985. He began working for Hollywood with *Once Around* (1991), and continued specializing in poignant, gentle comedy with such films as *What's Eating Gilbert Grape?* (1993), *Something to Talk About* (1995), and *The Cider House Rules* (1999).

Hawks, Howard (1896–1977) American director, producer, and screenwriter. Over his long career, from the 1920s to 1970, he became famous for his spare, swift narrative style, often celebrating the ethos of men of action. Women in his films are typically brave and insolent, most memorably Lauren Bacall, whom he introduced in *To Have and Have Not* (1944). He often produced his films and sometimes cowrote them, working in many genres, from westerns to comedies to musicals. Films include *A Girl in Every Port* (1928), *Scarface* (1932), *Bringing Up Baby* (1938), *Only Angels Have Wings* (1939), *His Girl Friday,* (1940), *Red River* (1948), *Gentlemen Prefer Blondes* (1953), and *Rio Bravo* (1959). He received an honorary Academy Award in 1974.

Heckerling, Amy (1954–) American director. Trained at the New York University film school and the American Film Institute, Heckerling had a commercial and critical success with her first comic feature, *Fast Times at Ridgemont High* (1982). Since then, she has made a number of comedies of varying success, including *Johnny Dangerously* (1984), *National Lampoon's European Vacation* (1985), *Look Who's Talking* (1989), *Look Who's Talking Too* (1990), the hit *Clueless* (1995), and *Loser* (2000).

Hepworth, Cecil (1874–1953) British director. Hepworth was a pioneer of the film industry in his native land. His six-minute film *Rescued by Rover* (1906) was one of the first films to use sophisticated cutting. Four years later, Hepworth patented a system for providing sound for films with a phonograph. His first feature was *The Basilisk* (1915), and his subsequent credits include *Annie Laurie* (1916), *Sheba* (1919), *Wild Heather* (1921), and *Comin' Thro' the Rye* (1921).

Herzog, Werner (1942–) German director. Herzog has directed features—often focusing on themes of obsession, loneliness, and alienation—and documentaries. He made his feature debut with *Signs of Life* (1968) and moved to the forefront of German cinema with *Aguirre, the Wrath of God* (1972, West Germany/Mexico/Peru), starring Klaus Kinski. Among his subsequent credits are *Nosferatu: The Vampyre* (1979, West Germany/France/US) and the highly acclaimed *Fitzcarraldo* (1982). He also directed *Mein Liebster Feind (My Best Fiend)* (1999, Germany/ UK), a documentary about his relationship with Kinski.

Hiller, Arthur (1923–) Canadian-born American director. In 1957, he moved from radio and television work to become a feature film director, often of high-gloss entertainments. Films include *The Americanization of Emily* (1964), *Love Story* (1970), *The Hospital* (1971), *The In-Laws* (1979), and *The Babe* (1992).

Hitchcock, Alfred (1899–1980) British director and producer who worked in Britain until 1939, chiefly in the US afterward. Known as the Master of Suspense, he crafted entertaining thrillers that dealt with crime, espionage, and madness. Their innovative visual style and narrative techniques and profound psychological content have made them perennially fascinating to critics and to other filmmakers. He produced many of his films and also hosted TV mystery series. Films include *The Lodger* (1926), *The Man Who Knew Too Much* (1934 original, 1956 remake), *The 39 Steps* (1935), *The Lady Vanishes* (1938), *Spellbound* (1945), *Notorious* (1946), *Rear Window* (1954), *Vertigo* (1958), *North by Northwest* (1959), *Psycho* (1960), *The Birds* (1963), and *Frenzy* (1972). He received AFI's Life Achievement Award in 1979.

Howard, Ron (1953–) American director, actor, and producer. Howard's fame came first as a child actor, playing Opie on *The Andy Griffith Show,* then as a young man in George Lucas's *American Graffiti* (1973) and the television show *Happy Days.* Howard became a popular Hollywood director with films such as *Splash* (1984), *Cocoon* (1985), *Parenthood* (1989), *Backdraft* (1991), *Apollo 13* (1995), and *Ransom* (1996). His film *A Beautiful Mind* (2001) earned him an Oscar as best director and he and his partner in Imagine Entertainment, Brian Grazer, shared an Oscar for best picture.

Hughes, John (1950–) American director, producer, and screenwriter. A copywriter and writer for *National Lampoon* magazine, Hughes worked on the *National Lampoon* movie spoofs before his directing career began with *Sixteen Candles* (1984). The movie was a hit, and Hughes began a string of teen comedies including *Weird Science* (1985), *The Breakfast Club* (1985), and *Ferris Bueller's Day Off* (1986). He has directed, produced, or written such films as *Planes, Trains, and Automobiles* (1987), *Home Alone* (1990), *101 Dalmatians* (1996), and *Flubber* (1997).

The directorial career of Howard Hawks, seen here on the set of Today We Live *(1933) with Joan Crawford, spanned 40 years.*

"All I'm doing is telling a story."

—

Howard Hawks, circa 1970

John Huston holds the distinction of having directed both his father, Walter and his daughter, Anjelica, to Academy Award wins: he for best supporting actor in *The Treasure of the Sierra Madre* (1948), she for best supporting actress in *Prizzi's Honor* (1985).

Huston, John (1906–1987) American director, screenwriter, and actor. Huston was a master of virtually every film genre, often infusing high adventure with deep moral concerns. He made his directorial debut with the crackling mystery *The Maltese Falcon* (1941). His fourth feature, *The Treasure of the Sierra Madre* (1948), won Academy Awards for best picture and best direction; Huston's father, Walter, won for best supporting actor. Four of Huston's other films—*The Asphalt Jungle* (1950), *The African Queen* (1951), *Moulin Rouge* (1952), and *Prizzi's Honor* (1985)—were nominated for Academy Awards. Huston's 37 film credits include *The Red Badge of Courage* (1951), *The Misfits* (1961), and *The Dead* (1987). Huston received AFI's Life Achievement Award in 1983. He was the father of actress Anjelica Huston.

I–J

Ince, Ralph (1887–1937) American director and actor. The brother of filmmakers Thomas and John Ince, he worked as an actor before making his directorial bow with *The Godmother* (1912). By 1914, he reportedly had directed 150 silent films and acted in 500. After the advent of sound, he was employed mostly as an actor until 1934, when he directed in England. In 1937—the year of his death—he had five films in release. Credits include *His Wife's Money* (1920), *Hardboiled* (1929), and *The Perfect Crime* (1937, UK).

Director and screenwriter Jim Jarmusch has also acted in the films of other directors.

Ince, Thomas (1882–1924) American director, producer, and screenwriter. Born Thomas Harper Ince. A childhood stage actor, the film pioneer turned to film in 1910 out of economic necessity, joining Independent Motion Pictures (IMP) as an actor and director. In 1911, at New York Motion Pictures (NYMP), he established his production studio Inceville and became known for directing and/or producing high-quality films, notably westerns (e.g., *The Law of the West*, 1912). From 1915 onward, he worked at several studios, including Triangle Film Corporation, where he directed the epic *Civilization* (1916). Before his unexpected death, he oversaw thousands of movies at several studios and established lasting production standards for the medium. Among the actors or directors he nurtured were William S. Hart and Frank Borzage. Ince is a brother of director-actors John and Ralph Ince.

Ivory, James (1928–) American director. A director of lavish period films, often adaptations of classic novels, Ivory works with longtime collaborators, producer Ismail Merchant and screenwriter Ruth Prawer Jhabvala. Trained at the film school of the University of Southern California, Ivory began as a documentary film maker before directing a series of films with Indian themes: *Shakespeare Wallah* (1965), *The Guru* (1969), and *Bombay Talkie* (1970). Later, the creative team of Ivory, Merchant, and Jhabvala began to make rich, upscale films, such as *The Europeans* in 1979. *Heat and Dust* (1983) followed, as did *The Bostonians* (1984), the Academy Award–winning *A Room with a View* (1986), *Maurice* (1987), *Mr. and Mrs. Bridge* (1990), the popular Academy Award winner *Howards End* (1992), *Surviving Picasso* (1996), and *A Soldier's Daughter Never Cries* (1998), and *The Golden Bowl* (2001).

Jarmusch, Jim (1953–) American director, screenwriter, and actor. An independent voice in modern American film, Jarmusch creates comically haunting stories of alienation and miscommunication in an arresting, engaging style. Educated at Columbia University and the New York University film school, Jarmusch won critical praise for his first feature, the black-and-white art-house hit *Stranger Than Paradise* (1984). He continued with *Down by Law* (1986); *Mystery Train* (1989); *Night on Earth* (1991), a travelogue of taxi rides; *Dead Man* (1995); and *Ghost Dog: The Way of the Samurai* (1999).

Jewison, Norman (1926–) Canadian-born American director. A director of wide range, Jewison began his career at the BBC before honing his skills on Canadian television. He directed Doris Day in *The Thrill of It All* (1963) before making a splash with *The Cincinnati Kid* (1965). He continued to find success in a variety of genres across four decades. Films include *The Russians Are Coming, the Russians Are Coming* (1966), *In the Heat of the Night* (1967), *The Thomas Crown Affair* (1968), *Fiddler on the Roof* (1971), *Jesus Christ, Superstar* (1973), *Rollerball* (1975), *...And Justice for All* (1979), *A Soldier's Story* (1984), *Agnes of God* (1985), *Moonstruck* (1987), *Other People's Money* (1991), *Only You* (1994), and *The Hurricane* (1999).

Jordan, Neil (1950–) Irish-born director and screenwriter of Irish, British, and American films. His films, which he also writes, typically deal with darkness and redemption, and often involve encounters with a mysterious "other," from transvestites to vampires to God. Films include *The Company of Wolves* (1984), *Mona Lisa* (1986), *The Crying Game* (1992), *Interview with a Vampire* (1994), and *The End of the Affair* (1999).

K

Kapoor, Raj (1924–1988) Indian director and actor. A popular actor with a Chaplin-like screen persona, he was born into an acting family and made film appearances as a child. He directed his first film, *Aag (Fire)*, in 1948, and achieved international stardom with *Awara (The Vagabond)* (1951). Among his many films are *Shree 420 (Mr. 420)* (1955), *Sangam* (1964), *Mera Naam Joker (My Name Is Joker)* (1970), *Satyam, Shivam, Sundaram (Love Sublime)* (1978), and *Prem Rog* (1982). He is the brother of actor Shashi Kapoor.

Kasdan, Lawrence (1949–) American director, screenwriter, and producer. A Clio Award–winning copywriter, Kasdan received his big break as the screenwriter of *The Empire Strikes Back* (1980) and *Raiders of the Lost Ark* (1981). His successful directorial debut, *Body Heat* (1981), was a smoldering neo-noir thriller, which he followed up with the baby-boomer hit *The Big Chill* (1983). Kasdan also directed *The Accidental Tourist* (1988), *Grand Canyon* (1991), *Wyatt Earp* (1994), and *Mumford* (1999).

Kazan, Elia (1909–) Turkish-born American director. Born in Constantinople of Greek parentage, he was a stage director before turning to film. He made his debut as a feature director with the poignant *A Tree Grows in Brooklyn* (1941). Two films—*Gentlemen's Agreement* (1947) and *On the Waterfront* (1954)—won best picture Academy Awards, and Kazan was honored as best director for each. His other credits include *A Streetcar Named Desire* (1951), *Viva Zapata!* (1952), and *Splendor in the Grass* (1961). Both Marlon Brando and James Dean made career breakthroughs in Kazan films. Kazan's screen achievements have been overshadowed somewhat in recent years by political controversy focusing on his naming names before the House Un-American Activities Committee.

Kieslowski, Krzysztof (1941–1996) Polish director and screenwriter. He was a major player in Eastern European films during the 1970s and 80s. He made his directorial debut with *Picture* (1969) and followed with *Workers* (1972). He directed *Dekalog (The Ten Commandments)* (1988), a TV series comprised of ten films; two segments—*A Short Film About Killing* (1988) and *A Short Film About Love* (1988)—were released as features to high acclaim. Other films include *Blue* (1993). He often wrote or cowrote his films.

Konchalovsky, Andrei (1937–) Russian-born director and screenwriter of Russian and American films. A success in his native Russia,

Pictured with Marlon Brando while filming On the Waterfront *(1954), director Elia Kazan cofounded the Actors Studio and helped develop Method acting.*

Konchalovsky had several international critical hits before working in Hollywood to lesser effect. After his film-school thesis won a prize at the Venice Film Festival, he debuted with the feature *Pervyj Uchitel (The First Teacher)* (1965). He made other films, including *Dyadya Vanya (Uncle Vanya)* (1970), *Sibiriade* (1978), and *Istoria Asi Klyachinoi, Kotoraya Lyubila, da Nie Vshla Zamuszh (Asya's Happiness)* (1967), which was suppressed in the Soviet Union until 1988. His first American film was the thriller *Runaway Train* (1985), followed by *Shy People* (1987) and the Sylvester Stallone vehicle *Tango & Cash* (1989). Konchalovsky directed the television miniseries *The Odyssey* in 1997.

Korda, Sir Alexander (1893–1956) Hungarian-born British director, producer, and executive. After directing and producing films in Europe and the US, Korda founded London Films in the 1930s, emerging as a major force in British cinema. His first box-office success was *The Private Life of Henry VIII* (1933), which he followed with *The Private Life of Don Juan* (1934), *Rembrandt* (1936), and *That Hamilton Woman/Lady Hamilton* (1941). As a producer, he relied on the services of brothers Zoltán, a director, and Vincent, an art director. Korda was knighted in 1942.

Kramer, Stanley (1913–2001) American director and producer. An independent producer from the 1940s, he turned to directing as well as producing in the mid-50s. His films often explore serious social issues. His credits as a producer include only *The Men* (1950), *High Noon* (1952), and *The Caine Mutiny* (1954); as a producer-director, his films include *The Defiant Ones* (1958), *Inherit the Wind* (1960), *Judgment at Nuremberg* (1961), *It's a Mad, Mad, Mad, Mad World* (1963), and *Guess Who's Coming to Dinner* (1967). He received the Academy's Irving G. Thalberg Award in 1961.

Two of Norman Jewison's films have been remade by director John McTiernan: 1968's *The Thomas Crown Affair* in 1999, and 1975's *Rollerball* in 2002. The latter was produced by Jewison.

Kubrick, Stanley (1928–1999) American-born director, producer, writer, and cinematographer of American and British films. A still photographer, he became a creator of visually impressive, cerebral, sardonic films. Always a perfectionist, he became so meticulous that many years passed between films in his later career. He worked in the US until 1960, in Britain afterward. He produced and wrote or cowrote most of his films, sometimes providing cinematography and editing as well. Films include *The Killing* (1956), *Paths of Glory* (1957), *Spartacus* (1960), *Lolita* (1962), *Dr. Strangelove* (1964), *2001: A Space Odyssey* (1968), *A Clockwork Orange* (1971), *Full Metal Jacket* (1987), and *Eyes Wide Shut* (1999).

Sir David Lean directed such classics as The Bridge on the River Kwai *(1957),* Doctor Zhivago *(1965), and* A Passage to India *(1984).*

Kuleshov, Lev (Leo) (1899–1970) Russian director, screenwriter, and theorist. A central figure in early Russian cinema, Kuleshov developed the theories of montage that Sergei Eisenstein later used to great effect. Kuleshov filmed the Russian front during World War I and returned to help found the First National Film School, where he taught. In 1933, the Soviet government placed a moratorium on his filmmaking because of his Western influences, but he continued to write criticism and teach. Kuleshov's feature films include *Luch Smerti* (*The Death Ray*) (1925), *Po Zakonu* (*By the Law*) (1926), *Vesyolaya Kanareika* (*The Gay Canary*) (1929), *Gorizont* (*Horizon: The Wandering Jew*) (1933), *Sibiryaki* (*The Siberians*) (1940), *Sluchaj v Vulkane* (*Descent in a Volcano*) (1941), and *My s Urala* (*We Are from the Urals*) (1944).

Kurosawa, Akira (1910–1998) Japanese director, producer, and screenwriter. This humanistic filmmaker often worked on an epic scale, as in *The Seven Samurai* (1954). His works are steeped in Japanese culture, notably samurai history, but communicate universal themes and experiences. He produced and wrote or cowrote many of his films. *Rashomon* (1950) and *Dersu Uzala* (1975) won Academy Awards for best foreign language film. Other films include *One Wonderful Sunday* (1947), *Drunken Angel* (1948), *Hidden Fortress* (1958), *Yojimbo* (1961), *Throne of Blood* (1957), *Dodes' Kaden* (1970), and *Ran* (1985).

Kurys, Diane (1948–) French director, screenwriter, and actor. Member of a Parisian acting troupe and a performer in Fellini's *Casanova* (1976), Kurys won a grant to direct the semiautobiographical *Dibolo Menhe* (*Peppermint Soda*) (1978), an instant hit in France. She continued with *Cocktail Molotov* (1980) and *Coup de Foudre* (*Entre Nous*) (1983), which are also semiautobiographical. Other films include *Un Homme Amoureux* (*A Man in Love*) (1987), *A la Folie* (*Six Days, Six Nights*) (1994), and *Les Enfants du Siècle* (*The Children of the Century*) (1999).

L

Lang, Fritz (1890–1976) Austrian-born director, screenwriter, and producer of German and American films. He worked in Germany until 1933, in France in 1934 (making *Liliom*), and mostly in the US afterward. He created masterful images in narratives that often dealt with crime, fate, and corruption. His cinematic technique incorporated both expressionism and realism. Films include *Dr. Mabuse der Spieler* (*Dr. Mabuse the Gambler*) (1922), *Metropolis* (1927), *M* (1931), *Fury* (1936), *Hangmen Also Die* (1943), *Scarlet Street* (1945), *Rancho Notorious* (1952), and *The Big Heat* (1953). He often wrote or cowrote and sometimes produced his films.

Lean, Sir David (1908–1991) British director, screenwriter, producer, and editor. He created epics, literary adaptations, and small-scale dramas, all marked by breathtaking visual style, thoughtful narrative, and crisp characterizations. Having entered the film industry as an editor, he sometimes edited, cowrote, and produced his directorial efforts. Films include *Brief Encounter* (1945), *Great Expectations* (1946), *Oliver Twist* (1948), *The Bridge on the River Kwai* (1957; best director Academy Award), *Lawrence of Arabia* (1962; best director Academy Award), *Doctor Zhivago* (1965), and *A Passage to India* (1984). He was knighted in 1984. He received the AFI Life Achievement Award in 1990.

Leder, Mimi (1957–) American director. In the 1990s, she gained notice for her action-filled dramas *The Peacemaker* (1997) and *Deep Impact* (1998), and later, for her character work *Pay It Forward* (2000). She has also directed several works for television.

Lee, Ang (1954–) Taiwanese-born American director. Lee attended college in New York City and made his directorial debut with *Tui Shou* (*Pushing Hands*) (1991, Taiwan/US). His first English-language film was the award-winning *Sense and Sensibility* (1995, UK/US), based on the Jane Austen novel. He subsequently directed *The Ice Storm* (1996), *Ride with the Devil* (1998), and *Crouching Tiger, Hidden Dragon* (2000).

Lee, Spike (1957–) American director, producer, and screenwriter. Lee is noted for exploring provocative and often controversial racial themes. He made his professional directing debut with a comedy, *She's Gotta Have It* (1986), and followed up with *School Daze* (1988). His subsequent films include *Do the Right Thing* (1989), *Malcolm X* (1992), *Clockers* (1995), *Summer of Sam* (1999), and *Bamboozled* (2000). Lee has appeared as an actor in a number of his films.

Leigh, Mike (1943–) British director and screenwriter. Leigh made his screen debut with *Bleak Moments* (1971), an adaptation of his play. Finding no further assignments, he concentrated on the stage and TV until *High Hopes* (1988). He won international acclaim for *Secrets and Lies* (1996). His *Topsy-Turvy* (1999), a film about the creation of the operetta *The Mikado*, won the New York Film Critics Circle best picture and best director awards.

Leone, Sergio (1929–1990) Italian director. Leone popularized the spaghetti western, with three Man with No Name westerns starring Clint Eastwood—*Per un Pugno di Dollari* (*A Fistful of Dollars*) (1964, Italy/Spain/West Germany), *Per Qualche Dollaro in più* (*For a Few Dollars More*) (1965, Italy/Spain/West Germany), and *Il Bueno il Brutto il Cattivo* (*The Good, the Bad, and the Ugly*) (1966). He then directed *C'era una Volta il West* (*Once Upon a Time in the West*) (1969, Italy/US), and a nearly four-hour crime tale, *Once Upon a Time in America* (1984, US/Italy/Canada), featuring an American cast that included Robert De Niro.

Lester, Richard (1932–) American-born British director. Lester scored his greatest success in England and is best known for two madcap films featuring the Beatles—*It's a Hard Day's Night* (1964) and *Help!* (1965). Other credits include *A Funny Thing Happened on the Way to the Forum* (1966), *Robin and Marian* (1976), *Superman II* (1981, US/UK), and *Superman III* (1984, US).

Levinson, Barry (1942–) American director and screenwriter. Originally a writer for television star Carol Burnett and a screenwriter with director Mel Brooks, he demonstrated his keen feel for dialogue and setting with his debut film, *Diner* (1982). Set in his hometown of Baltimore during the late 1950s, it would be the first of four Baltimore-based films; the others are *Tin Men* (1987), *Avalon* (1990), and *Liberty Heights* (1999). Throughout his career, he has been able to move between intimate films and big-budget movies, and it is the latter that have brought the greatest popular success, notably *Rain Man* (1988), which won Academy Awards for best picture, best actor, best director, and best screenplay. Other notable films include *Good Morning, Vietnam* (1987) and *Bugsy* (1991), and *Bandits* (2001). Not to be confused with producer and writer Barry Levinson (1932–1987).

Losey, Joseph (1909–1984) American director. Losey, who studied film with the Russian master Sergei Eisenstein in Moscow, made his debut in Hollywood with a "message" film, *The Boy with Green Hair* (1948). After being blacklisted during the McCarthy era, he settled in England and worked abroad for the remainder of his career. Among his notable films are *The Servant* (1964, UK), *Accident* (1967, UK), and *The Go-Between* (1971, UK).

Lubitsch, Ernst (1892–1947) German-born American director, producer, screenwriter, and actor. He worked in Germany until 1922, in Hollywood afterward. He was known for witty, sophisticated, sexually laced comedies, musicals, and dramas. His unique style was known as the Lubitsch Touch. Films include *Carmen* (*Gypsy Blood*) (1918), *The Marriage Circle* (1924), *The Love Parade* (1929), *Monte Carlo* (1930), *Trouble in Paradise* (1932), *Design for Living* (1933), *Ninotchka* (1939), and *To Be or Not to Be* (1942). He received an honorary Academy Award in 1937. He sometimes acted in, produced, and wrote or cowrote his films.

Lucas, George (1944–) American director and producer. Lucas's name is permanently linked to his *Star Wars* movies, which revolutionized the science fiction genre. After debuting with *THX 1138* (1971), he directed the highly commercial *American Graffiti* (1973). With *Star Wars* (1977), Lucas joined his mentor Francis Ford Coppola and his associate Steven Spielberg in the vanguard of American filmmakers. He subsequently focused on producing and developing *The Empire Strikes Back* (1980) and *Return of the Jedi* (1983), which were directed by others. He produced three Indiana Jones films with Steven Spielberg directing and went behind the camera again to direct *Star Wars: Episode I—The Phantom Menace* (1999).

Lumet, Sidney (1924–) American director. A child of theatrical parents, Lumet began acting on stage at an early age. After duty in World War II, he returned to work on Broadway before joining CBS television as a director. His first film was the career-launching *Twelve Angry Men* (1957) with Henry Fonda. Lumet's other films, which are typically marked by intelligence and attention to detail, include *Fail Safe* (1964), *Serpico* (1973), *Dog Day Afternoon* (1975), *Network* (1976), and *The Verdict* (1982).

Lumière, Louis (1864–1948) and **Lumière, Auguste** (1862–1954) French brothers and pioneer filmmakers. With American inventor Thomas Edison, they are commonly credited as the inventors of cinema. The Lumière brothers invented the Cinématographe, a combination camera-projector on which they exhibited their first film, *La Sortie des Usines Lumière* in March 1895. On December 28, 1895, they showed their filmstrips—of everyday scenes—to a paying

It was déjà vu all over again when 20th Century–Fox re-released *Star Wars*—in a digitally restored special edition—in February 1997. Lines around the block and packed theaters re-created the mania experienced when George Lucas's space opera was originally unleashed in the summer of 1977. The 20-year-old film became the number one movie in the country for several weeks, raking in nearly $120 million for a combined total of over $460 million, and toppling Steven Spielberg's *E.T : The Extra-Terrestrial* (1982) to briefly become the all-time box-office champ. Briefly, that is, until the release of *Titanic* later that same year.

audience. The date is widely regarded as the birthday of cinema. Their farce *L'Arroseur Arrosé* was the first example of a fiction film. Louis Lumière directed 60 films and produced about 2,000 others before turning full-time to film exhibition after 1900.

Lynch, David (1946–) American director and screenwriter. Trained at the American Film Institute Center for Advanced Film Studies, he gained cult audiences with his outrageous film *Eraserhead* (1977), for which he also served as producer, art director, editor, lyricist, and special effects artist. Later, more mainstream, films encompass wider themes but remain true to his core unconventionality. He usually writes his own films, which include *Blue Velvet* (1986), *Wild at Heart* (1990), *The Straight Story* (1999), and *Mulholland Drive* (2001). He developed the curious television series *Twin Peaks* in the 1990s.

"Writing film and directing film are not, and should not be, separate and mutually exclusive functions."

—

Joseph L. Mankiewicz, 1972

M

McCarey, Leo (1898–1969) American director. McCarey was an accomplished director, particularly of comedy, but is probably best remembered for *Going My Way* (1944), a Bing Crosby heartwarmer that won him Academy Awards for best director and writer. McCarey also received a best director Academy Award for *The Awful Truth* (1937). He directed the Marx Brothers in *Duck Soup* (1933) and other major comic talents such as Eddie Cantor, W.C. Fields, Mae West, and Harold Lloyd. Among his other credits are *Ruggles of Red Gap* (1935), *The Bells of St. Mary's* (1945), and *An Affair to Remember* (1957).

McTiernan, John (1951–) American director. Director specializing in fast-paced, big-budget action films. Credits include *Predator* (1987), *Die Hard* (1988), *The Hunt for Red October* (1990), *Last Action Hero* (1993), *The Thomas Crown Affair* (1999), and *The 13th Warrior* (1999).

Malick, Terrence (1943–) American director, screenwriter, and producer. Malick, a Harvard graduate and Rhodes Scholar, taught philosophy at MIT before he began writing screenplays in the early 1970s. He then became a director, writing or cowriting and sometimes producing his films. Lush and hypnotic, his films are few and far between, yet notable for their haunting portrayals of life on the edge. His first film, *Badlands* (1973), starred Martin Sheen and Sissy Spacek as killers roaming the American plains. Five years later, Malick directed *Days of Heaven* (1978), a drama of migrant workers that starred Richard Gere. It was twenty years before he returned to directing with the World War II drama *The Thin Red Line* (1998).

Malle, Louis (1932–1995) French-born director and screenwriter of French and American films. A talented and diverse director whose films span undersea documentaries, light comedies, provocative dramas, and thrillers. Born into a wealthy family, Malle studied at the Sorbonne and the French film institute (IDHEC) before assisting Jacques Cousteau on *Le Mode de Silence* (*The Silent World*) (1956). Malle's first feature was the thriller *Ascenseur pour l'Echafaud* (*Frantic*) (1958). Malle filmed *Les Amants* (*The Lovers*) (1959), *Vie Privée* (*A Very Private Affair*) (1962), *Le Voleur* (*The Thief of Paris*) (1967), and *Le Souffle au Coeur* (*Murmur of the Heart*) (1971) before directing the controversial *Pretty Baby* (1978) in America. *Atlantic City* (1980) and *My Dinner with Andre* (1981) received much praise, as did *Au Revoir les Enfants* (*Goodbye Children*) (1987), a story of coming of age during World War II. Before his death, Malle filmed *Damage* (1993) and *Vanya on 42nd Street* (1994). He was married to actress Candice Bergen from 1980.

Mankiewicz, Joseph L. (1909–1993) American director, producer, and screenwriter. Mankiewicz made his directing debut with *Dragonwyck* (1946). His films were perhaps best known for their intellectual content and incisive dialogue. His *All About Eve* (1950), a classic about the theater, earned a best director Academy Award and was named best picture. Earlier, he received a directing Oscar for *A Letter to Three Wives* (1949). Among his other notable films are *Julius Caesar* (1953), *Suddenly, Last Summer* (1959), and *Cleopatra* (1963). His last film, *Sleuth* (1972, UK), earned him an Academy Award nomination for best director.

Mann, Anthony (1906–1967) American director. Mann was a Broadway director and actor before making his film debut with *Dr. Broadway* (1942), the first in a series of low-budget films. His first major film was *Winchester '73* (1950), starring James Stewart. Mann was regarded as a first-rate director of westerns, frequently working with Stewart. Among his credits are *Bend of the River* (1952), *The Glenn Miller Story* (1954), and *El Cid* (1961).

Marshall, Garry (1934–) American director, producer, and screenwriter. An established television writer, producer, and director (*The Dick Van Dyke Show, The Lucy Show*), he began writing screenplays in the 1960s (*How Sweet It Is*, 1968) and turned to directing films in the 80s. Among his crowd-pleasing comedies and comedy-dramas are *Beaches* (1989) and *Pretty Woman* (1990). He also acted in several films, including *A League of Their Own* (1992). He is the brother of director Penny Marshall.

Marshall, Penny (1942–) American director and actress. A popular television actress best known for her role as Shirley on the sitcom *Laverne & Shirley* (1976–83), Marshall has directed several commercial hits. After directing several episodes of *Laverne & Shirley,* she moved to film with *Jumpin' Jack Flash* (1986) and the popular *Big* (1988), starring Tom Hanks. Her other films include *Awakenings* (1990), *A League of Their Own* (1992), *The Preacher's Wife* (1996), and *Riding in Cars With Boys* (2001). Marshall is the sister of writer-director Garry Marshall.

Mazursky, Paul (1930–) American director, screenwriter, and actor. Trained at Lee Strasberg's Actors Studio in New York, and at the University of California, Los Angeles film school, Mazursky worked as a television comedy writer, screenwriter, and actor before his debut feature, *Bob & Carol & Ted & Alice* (1969). This send-up of middle-class sexual mores was followed by *Alex in Wonderland* (1970) and two well-received character comedies, *Blume in Love* (1973) and *Harry and Tonto* (1974). *An Unmarried Woman* (1978) followed, as did *Moscow on the Hudson* (1984), *Down and Out in Beverly Hills* (1986), and *Enemies: a Love Story* (1989). Mazursky's outings in the 1990s, such as *Scenes from a Mall* (1991), were less popular.

Méliès, Georges (1861–1938) French director and producer. Méliès was a professional magician who used magic-lantern effects in his stage productions. After seeing the historic exhibition of the Lumière brothers, he bought his own equipment and presented films as part of his presentations. He then created fantasy films, using trick photography. He directed more than 500 films but is best remembered for his 30-scene *Le Voyage dans la Lune* (*A Trip to the Moon*) (1902), which still fascinates students and film fans. He also directed a 20-scene *Jeanne d'Arc* (*Joan of Arc*) (1900).

Melville, Jean-Pierre (1917–1973) French director. Despite the fact that he made only 13 films—mostly on crime and war themes—he was a major influence on French New Wave. He debuted with *Le Silence de la Mer* (1949) and followed with *Les Enfants Terrible* (*The Strange Ones*) (1949), based on a Jean Cocteau novel. His subsequent credits include *Deux Hommes dans Manhattan* (1959) and *Un Flic* (*Dirty Money*) (1972).

Meyer, Nicholas (1945–) American director and screenwriter. After writing the screen adaptation of his Sherlock Holmes mystery, *The Seven-Per-Cent Solution* (1976), he ventured into writing-directing with the time-travel film *Time After Time* (1979). Subsequent directing credits include *Star Trek II: The Wrath of Khan* (1982) and *Company Business* (1991), for which he also wrote the script.

Mikhalkov, Nikita (1945–) Russian director, actor, and screenwriter. The brother of director Andrei Konchalovsky, Mikhalkov also studied at the Russian film institute. His body of work is varied in content and style but highly regarded. His films include *Svoj Sredi Chuzhikh, Chuzhoj Sredi Svoikh* (*At Home Among Strangers*) (1974), *Neokonchennaya Pyesa dlya Mekhanicheskogo Pianino* (*Unfinished Piece for Mechanical Piano*) (1977), *Rodnya* (*Family Relations*) (1981), *Dark Eyes* (1987, Italy/France), *Avtostop* (*Hitchhiking*) (1990), *Urga* (*Close to Eden*) (1991), *Anna* (1993), *Utomlyonnye Solntsem* (*Burnt by the Sun*) (1994), and *Sibirskij Tsiryulnik* (*The Barber of Siberia*) (1998).

Minnelli, Vincente (1910–1986) American director. The master of the movie musical, he debuted with *Cabin in the Sky* (1942). His films *An American in Paris* (1951) and *Gigi* (1958) both won the best picture Academy Award. His other notable film musicals include *Meet Me in St. Louis* (1944), *Ziegfeld Follies* (1946), *The Pirate* (1948), and *The Band Wagon* (1953). His nonmusical successes include *The Bad and the Beautiful* (1952), *Lust for Life* (1956), and *Tea and Sympathy* (1956). He was married to actress Judy Garland and is the father of actress Liza Minnelli.

Murnau, F.W. (1888–1931) German-born director of German and American films. He worked in German film until 1926, in the US afterward. His films were visually innovative and darkly psychological, influencing the development of the *mise-en-scène* tradition. Films include *Nosferatu—Eine Symphonie des Grauens* (*Nosferatu the Vampire*) (1922), *Der Letzte Mann* (*The Last Laugh*) (1924), *Sunrise* (1927), *Our Daily Bread* (1930), and *Tabu* (1931; codirected with Robert Flaherty).

Former television sitcom star Penny Marshall directed A League of Their Own *(1992), featuring Lori Petty and Geena Davis.*

N–O

Niblo, Fred (1874–1948) American director and producer. A former actor and vaudevillian, Niblo worked extensively in the theater before joining the Ince studio in 1917. He directed many silent comedies and dramas but was best known for his action-adventure films, including *The Mark of Zorro* (1920), *The Three Musketeers* (1921), and the spectacular *Ben-Hur* (1926). Among his other movies are *Blood and Sand* (1922), *Camille* (1927), and *Way Out West* (1930).

Nichols, Mike (1931–) German-born American director, screenwriter, and producer. Born Michael Igor Peschkowsky. With his family, Nichols fled Nazi Germany and grew up in Chicago. He studied acting at Lee Strasberg's Actors Studio, before forming a comedy troupe in Chicago. He toured with comedian Elaine May as Nichols and May before launching a career on Broadway. Soon after, he made his film debut, directing Elizabeth Taylor and Richard Burton in *Who's Afraid of Virginia Woolf?* (1966). His second feature, *The Graduate* (1967), was a smash and earned him an Academy Award for best director. Nichols went on with *Catch-22* (1970), *Carnal Knowledge* (1971), *Gilda Live* (1980), *Silkwood* (1983), *Heartburn* (1986), *Working Girl* (1988), *Postcards from the Edge* (1990), *Regarding Henry* (1991), *Wolf* (1994), *The Birdcage* (1996), and *Primary Colors* (1998), among others. He is married to television newswoman Diane Sawyer.

Ophüls, Max (1902–1957) German-born director and screenwriter of international films. He was noted for his fluid cinematography, his emphasis on *mise-en-scène*, and for the lush, baroque quality of his films. He cowrote some of his films. Credits include *Letter from an Unknown Woman* (1948, US), *La Ronde* (1950, US), *Madame de...* (*The Earrings of Madame De...*) (1953, France/Italy), and *Lola Montès* (*Lola Montez*) (1955, France/West Germany). His son is filmmaker Marcel Ophüls (1927–), director of the documentary *Le Chagrin et la Pitié* (*The Sorrow and the Pity*) (1971, France/Switzerland/West Germany).

Ouedraogo, Idrissa (1952–) Burkinabe director. Born in Burkina Faso, Ouedraogo studied film at the African Institute of Cinematography and in Kiev and Paris. He made his feature debut with *Yam Daabo* (*The Choice*) (1987), which was shown at the Cannes Film Festival. His subsequent credits include *Tilaï* (*The Law*) (1990), winner of the Special Jury Prize at Cannes, *The Three Friends* (1993), *La Cri du Coeur* (*Heart's Cry*) (1994), and *Afrique, Mon Afrique...* (1995).

> "Any film I enjoyed making I tend to like, whether it is any good or not."
>
> — *Yasujiro Ozu, 1974*

Ozu, Yasujiro (1903–1963) Japanese director. Known for simple, low-angled camera technique in exquisite dramas of Japanese middle-class life, he often wrote or cowrote his films. Credits include *Sword of Penitence* (1927), *Woman of Tokyo* (1933), *The Flavor of Green Tea over Rice* (1952), *Tokyo Story* (1953), *Early Spring* (1956), and *Late Autumn* (1961).

P

Pabst, G.W. (1885–1967) German director. Pabst was an exponent of "pessimistic realism" in German films. After his debut with *Der Schatz* (*The Treasure*) (1923), he directed *Die Freudlose Gasse* (*The Street of Sorrow/The Joyless Street*) (1925), starring Greta Garbo with Marlene Dietrich as an extra. After the advent of sound, he directed *Die Dreigroschenoper* (*The Threepenny Opera*) (1931) and made one Hollywood film—*A Modern Hero* (1934, US). He directed two films for the Nazis and, following the end of the war, reversed his stance, denouncing anti-Semitism in *Der Prozess/In Name der Menschlichkeit* (*The Trial*) (1948, Austria).

Pagnol, Marcel (1895–1974) French director and writer. Pagnol wrote plays and novels while teaching school and soon became known for his theatrical works. He moved eagerly from stage plays to screenplays and filmed his works in a static theatrical style. His scripts have been remade many times, and he himself filmed *Topaze* twice, in 1936 and 1951. With *Topaze*, his best-known contributions are the story "Fanny," *César* (1936), and *Manon des Sources* (*Manon of the Spring*) (1952), remade in 1986. Other major films include *Le Schpountz* (*Heartbeat*) (1938), *La Fille du Puisatier* (*The Well-Digger's Daughter*) (1940), and *Les Lettres de Mon Moulin* (*Letters from My Windmill*) (1954).

Parker, Alan (1944–) British-born American director and screenwriter. Before becoming a feature director, Parker was an award-winning star in British advertising circles, known for his striking atmospheric style and design. He teamed with producer David Puttnam to make *Bugsy Malone* in 1976. This musical gangster spoof, shot entirely with children, was followed by the dark, Academy Award–nominated *Midnight Express* (1978). Parker continued to develop his lush, sweeping visuals with such films as *Fame* (1980), *Shoot the Moon* (1982), and *Birdy* (1984). He fought to keep his controversial *Angel Heart* (1987) from receiving an X rating. After *Mississippi Burning* (1988) and *Come See the Paradise* (1990), he returned to musicals in the 1990s with *The Commitments* (1991) and *Evita* (1996).

Parks, Gordon (1912–) American director and producer. A noted photojournalist for *Life* magazine from 1948 to 1968, Parks became Hollywood's first African-American director-producer of a major film with his autobiographical story *The Learning Tree* (1969), for which he also wrote the script and music. In 1989, *The Learning Tree* was among the first films selected by the Library of Congress for its National Film Registry. Parks's next work was the phenomenally successful action film *Shaft* (1971). Other films include *Shaft's Big Score!* (1972), *The Super Cops* (1974), and the biographical *Leadbelly* (1976). Parks's son Gordon, Jr., also a director, filmed *Super Fly* (1972).

Pasolini, Pier Paolo (1922–1975) Italian director and screenwriter. Pasolini made his directorial bow with *Accatone!* (1961), based on his own novel. His films often reflected his Marxism and offbeat religious views, creating major controversies and leading, at one point, to his arrest. Among his best-known works are *Il Vangelo Secondo Matteo* (*The Gospel According to St. Matthew*) (1964), *Il Decamerone* (*The Decameron*) (1971, Italy/France/West Germany), *I Racconti di Canterbury* (*The Canterbury Tales*) (1972), and *Salò o le Centoventi Giorante di Sodoma* (*Salo: The Last 120 Days of Sodom*) (1975).

Peckinpah, Sam (1925–1984) American director. After working in TV, Peckinpah made his feature-film debut with *The Deadly Companions* (1961), the first of many westerns. His most notable film, *The Wild Bunch* (1969), is marked by what many consider to be gratuitous violence, as are many of his other works. Additional credits include *Ride the High Country* (1962), *Straw Dogs* (1971, UK), and *Bring Me the Head of Alfredo Garcia* (1974).

Penn, Arthur (1922–) American director. Penn was a successful director for the Broadway stage and live TV drama when he made his feature bow with *The Left-Handed Gun* (1958). After directing major stage hits, he returned to films with *The Miracle Worker* (1962), which earned him an Academy Award nomination for best director. He was also nominated for his direction of *Bonnie and Clyde* (1967) and *Alice's Restaurant* (1969). Penn, whose work is hard to categorize, has also directed such films as *Mickey One* (1965), *Little Big Man* (1970), and *Penn and Teller Get Killed/Dead Funny* (1989).

Petrie, Daniel (1920–) Canadian-born American director. A former Broadway actor and television director who turned to film in 1960, he has directed a wide range of character-rich dramas, including *A Raisin in the Sun* (1961), *Fort Apache, The Bronx* (1981), and *The Bay Boy* (1984, Canada/France). His son Daniel Petrie, Jr., is a screenwriter; son Donald Petrie is a director.

Polanski, Roman (1933–) French-born, Polish-educated director of international films. Polanski endured double tragedy in his life—the incarceration of his parents in a Nazi concentration camp (where his mother died), and later the murder of his wife, actress Sharon Tate. These traumas, reflected in the grim, depressing, and often macabre nature of his films, were followed by another bizarre episode, when a statutory rape charge drove him out of the US as a fugitive in the late 1970s. Polanski made his feature debut with *Knife in the Water* (1963, Poland), nominated for a best foreign film Academy Award. He subsequently directed such films as *Repulsion* (1965, UK) and *Rosemary's Baby* (1968, US). His direction on *Chinatown* (1974, US) and *Tess* (1980, France/UK) earned Academy Award nominations.

Pollack, Sydney (1934–) American director, actor, and producer. Trained as an actor under Sanford Meisner, Pollack began directing television shows in the early 1960s. After directing episodes of *Ben Casey*, *Alfred Hitchcock Presents*, and *The Fugitive*, Pollack filmed his first feature, *The Slender Thread* (1965). His first hit was *They Shoot Horses, Don't They?* (1969) after which he became known as an actor's director, for the performances he elicited from major stars. He directed Robert Redford and Barbra Streisand in *The Way We Were* (1972), and then Redford again in the thriller *Three Days of the Condor* (1975). He scored a huge hit in 1982 with the comedy *Tootsie* and won a best director Academy Award for *Out of Africa* (1983). Other films include *Havana* (1990), *The Firm* (1993), *Sabrina* (1995), and *Random Hearts* (1999). He frequently acts in his own films and others'.

Powell, Michael (1905–1990, born in Britain) and **Pressburger, Emeric** (1902–1988, born in Hungary) British filmmakers. Though they each worked on films separately, they are best known for their collaborations, which are visually impressive and literate. Their films together (as directors, producers, and writers) include *The Life and Death of Colonel Blimp* (1943), *I Know Where I'm Going* (1945), *Black Narcissus* (1947), and *The Red Shoes* (1948). Separately, Pressburger was mainly a screenwriter, working in Germany until 1933, in France and Britain afterward. Powell's directorial efforts without Pressburger include *The Man Behind the Mask* (1936) and *Peeping Tom* (1960).

Preminger, Otto (1905–1986) Viennese-born American director. Preminger directed one film in Europe, then worked on Broadway before

Pictured with Johnny Depp during the filming of The Ninth Gate *(1999), Roman Polanski directed and cowrote* Rosemary's Baby *(1968),* Tess *(1980), and* Frantic *(1988).*

"If I'm so bloody that I drive people out of the theater, then I've failed."

—

Sam Peckinpah, 1971

making his first American film, *Under Your Spell* (1936). He built a reputation for controversial themes and for his iron hand on the set, bringing his films in on time and on budget. His *The Moon Is Blue* (1953) and *The Man with the Golden Arm* (1955) caused censorship controversies. He earned Academy Award nominations for his direction of *Laura* (1944) and *The Cardinal* (1963). Among his other major films are *Anatomy of a Murder* (1959), *Exodus* (1960), and *Advise and Consent* (1962).

Pudovkin, Vsevolod I. (1893–1953) Russian director. Inspired by D.W. Griffith's *Intolerance*, Pudovkin worked as an actor and screenwriter before making his debut as a feature director with *Hunger-Hunger-Hunger* (1921) and *Chess Fever* (1925). These were followed by *Mother* (1926), considered to be his masterpiece. A master of the montage technique, he expounded his theories of filmmaking in a series of pamphlets. His most notable sound movies are *Deserter* (1933) and *Suvorov* (1941).

Q–R

Ray, Nicholas (1911–1979) American director. A stage actor and director, he made his debut as a film director with the highly regarded *The Twisted Road* (1948), released again in 1949 as *They Live by Night*. Ray, who achieved cult status, carved out a career marked by diversity. Among his major films are *Knock on Any Door* (1949), *Rebel Without a Cause* (1955), *King of Kings* (1961), and *55 Days at Peking* (1963).

Ray, Satyajit (1921–1992) Indian director, screenwriter, and composer. *Pather Panchali* (1955), the first entry in his Apu Trilogy about a young Bengali, brought Indian cinema to international attention. He wrote and often composed music for his films, which were renowned for their complex cinematic style and rich humanity. The other films in the Apu Trilogy are *Aparajito (The Unvanquished)* (1957) and *Apu Sansar (The World of Apu)* (1959). His credits include *Charulata (The Lonely Wife)* (1964), *Ashanti Sanket (Distant Thunder)* (1973), and *Ganashatru (An Enemy of the People)* (1989). He received an honorary Academy Award in 1992.

Reed, Sir Carol (1906–1976) British director. Reed made his debut as a director with *It Happened in Paris* (1935). During World War II, he directed two highly regarded documentaries, *The Way Ahead/The Immortal Battalion* (1944) and the Academy Award–winning *The True Glory* (1945). In the 1940s and 50s, Reed turned out such acclaimed films as *Odd Man Out*

(1947) and the internationally successful *The Third Man* (1949). His *Oliver!* (1968) won Academy Awards for best picture and director. Additional credits include *Our Man in Havana* (1959) and *The Agony and the Ecstasy* (1965).

Reiner, Rob (1945–) American director, actor, and producer. A comic actor and writer, and son of director Carl Reiner, Rob Reiner found fame as Mike "Meathead" Stivic in Norman Lear's popular and long-lived sitcom *All in the Family*. He debuted as a feature director with the mock-documentary *This Is Spinal Tap* (1984), a spoof on heavy-metal bands. He followed with *Stand by Me* (1996; based on a Stephen King novella), and *The Princess Bride* (1987; adapted from the novel by William Goldman). He found popular success with films such as *When Harry Met Sally...* (1989), *Misery* (1990), *A Few Good Men* (1992), and *The American President* (1995). Other films include *The Story of Us* (1999).

Reitman, Ivan (1946–) Czech-born Canadian-American director and producer. Reitman is best known for large-scale, high-concept comedies. A refugee child, he settled in Canada with his parents and became interested in film after college. He produced several low-budget films, including some of David Cronenberg's early works, before directing the feature *Foxy Lady* in 1971. His first popular success was *Meatballs* (1979), featuring his frequent star Bill Murray. *Stripes* (1981) followed, as did the hugely successful *Ghostbusters* (1984). Later films include *Legal Eagles* (1986), *Twins* (1988), *Dave* (1993), *Six Days, Seven Nights* (1998), and *Evolution* (2001).

Renoir, Jean (1894–1979) French director. He worked in France until 1939, in the US, India, and Italy until 1953, and back in France afterward. The son of Impressionist painter Auguste Renoir, he was acclaimed for his poetic, humanistic films, which emphasized *mise-en-scène*. *La Grande Illusion (Grand Illusion)* (1937) and *La Règle du Jeu (The Rules of the Game)* (1939) are among his best-known works. He often wrote or cowrote his films. Other films include *Boudu Sauvé des Eaux (Boudu Saved from Drowning)* (1932), *Toni* (1935), *Le Crime de M. Lange (The Crime of Monsieur Lange)* (1936), *The Woman on the Beach* (1947), and *French Cancan (Only the French Can)* (1955).

Resnais, Alain (1922–) French director, cinematographer, and actor. Resnais earned international attention for his short *Night and Fog* (1956), about Nazi concentration camps. His feature debut was an exploration of memory and reality, *Hiroshima, Mon Amour* (1959). His next film, the elusive *L'Année Dernié à Marienbad (Last Year at Marienbad)* (1961, France/Italy), won the grand prize at the Venice Film Festival. His subsequent films include *La Guerre est Finie (The War Is Over)* (1966, France/Sweden), *Stavisky* (1974), and *Providence* (1977, France/Switzerland).

The son of Impressionist painter Auguste Renoir, Jean Renoir directed films, such as Diary of a Chambermaid *(1946, pictured), for more than 45 years.*

Richardson, Tony (1928–1991) British director. Richardson rocketed to fame with a string of internationally acclaimed films beginning with his first, *Look Back in Anger* (1958). A leader of Britain's "Angry Young Men," he then directed such influential films as *The Entertainer* (1960), *A Taste of Honey* (1962), *The Loneliness of the Long Distance Runner* (1962), and *Tom Jones* (1989), which earned Academy Awards for best picture and best director. Richardson was married to actress Vanessa Redgrave and was the father of actresses Natasha and Joely Richardson.

Ritt, Martin (1914–1990) American director, producer, and actor. Sidestepping a law career, Ritt began acting in the theater and television. After achieving success in directing television, he was blacklisted in the 1950s and turned to teaching at the Actors Studio, counting among his students Paul Newman and Rod Steiger. Ritt made his film debut with *The Edge of the City* (1957). He directed adaptations of literary works as well as original screenplays, beginning with Faulkner's *The Long, Hot Summer* (1958). Other notable films include *Paris Blues* (1961), *Hud* (1963), *The Spy Who Came in from the Cold* (1965), *The Great White Hope* (1970), *The Front* (1976), *Norma Rae* (1979), *Murphy's Romance* (1985), and *Stanley & Iris* (1990).

Rivette, Jacques (1928–) French director and producer. Although he was a seminal figure in the French New Wave, Rivette's films have received less critical and popular acclaim than those of his colleagues Truffaut and Godard. A critic and editor at the film journal *Cahiers du Cinéma*, Rivette self-produced his first film, *Paris Nous Appartient* (*Paris Belongs to Us*) in 1960. *L'Amour Fou* (1968) and the unreleased *Out 1* (1971) were lengthy works of minimal narrative cohesion. One of his best-known films is *Céline et Julie vont en Bateau* (*Céline and Julie Go Boating*) (1974). Other films include *Duelle* (*Twilight*) (1976), *L'Amour par Terre* (*Love on the Ground*) (1984), *La Belle Noiseuse* (*The Beautiful Troublemaker*) (1991), *Haut Bas Fragile* (*Up, Down, Fragile*) (1995), *Lumière et Compagnie* (*Lumière and Company*) (1995), and *Va Savoir* (*Who Knows?*) (2000).

Robbe-Grillet, Alain (1922–) French director and screenwriter. Though best known as a novelist, he is also esteemed for his cinematic achievements. He wrote the screenplay for *Last Year at Marienbad,* directed by Alain Resnais, which was one of the most discussed films of 1961. He made his directorial debut with *L'Immortelle* (1963), following with such unconventional, sometimes disturbing films as *Trans-Europe Express* (1967), *L'Homme qui Ment* (*The Man Who Lies*) (1968, France/Czechoslovakia), *Glissements Progressifs du Plaisir* (*Progressive Slidings into Pleasure*) (1974), and *La Belle Captive* (*The Beautiful Prisoner*) (1983).

Rohmer, Eric (1920–) French director. Rohmer was editor of the New Wave publication *Cahiers du Cinéma* and a documentary filmmaker before directing *Le Signe du Lion/The Sign of Leo* (1959). He gained international recognition as an original, insightful director with his fifth film, *Ma Nuit chez Maud* (*My Night at Maud's*) (1969); he followed it with *Le Genou de Claire* (*Claire's Knee*) (1970) and *L'Amour l'après-midi* (*Chloe in the Afternoon*) (1972). His other credits include *The Marquise of O* (1976, France/West Germany), *Pauline à la Plage* (*Pauline at the Beach*) (1983), and *L'Anglaise et le Duc* (*The Lady and the Duke*) (2001).

Ross, Herbert (1927–2001) American director, choreographer, and producer. A stage and screen choreographer, Ross went on to direct a musical version of *Goodbye, Mr. Chips* (1969). He continued with a string of films, including *Play It Again, Sam* (1972), *Funny Lady* (1975), *The Sunshine Boys* (1975), *The Seven-Per-Cent Solution* (1976), *The Turning Point* (1977), *The Goodbye Girl* (1977), *Pennies from Heaven* (1981), *Footloose* (1984), and *Steel Magnolias* (1989).

Rossellini, Roberto (1906–1977) Italian director. A leading exponent of Italy's post–World War II neorealism, Rossellini made his feature debut with *La Nave Bianca* (*White Ship*) (1941). He gained international attention after the war with the powerful *Roma, Città Aperta* (*Open City*) (1945) and enhanced his reputation with *Paisà* (*Paisan*) (1946). He married Ingrid Bergman and cast her as the star of a number of films, including *Stromboli* (1949). Among his other credits are *Viaggio in Italia* (*Strangers*) (1953), also starring Bergman, and *Il Generale Della Rovere* (*General Della Rovere*) (1959, Italy/France), starring another Italian director, Vittorio De Sica.

Roy, Bimal (1909–1966) Indian director and producer. Roy worked his way up from being an assistant cameraman to director of photography before filming his first feature, *Udahir Pathey* (1944). He had an international success with *Do Bigha Zamin* (*Two Acres of Land*) (1953) and continued with such films as *Biraj Bahu* (1954), *Amanat* (1955), *Gautama the Buddha* (1955), *Sujata* (*Untouchable Girl*) (1959), *Bandini* (1963), and *Do Dooni Chaar* (1966).

Rudolph, Alan (1943–) American director and screenwriter. The cinematic heir to his mentor Robert Altman, Rudolph captures meditations on American life and alienation. After Rudolph released two low-budget movies, *Premonition* (1972) and *Nightmare Circus* (1973), Altman

Acclaimed Italian director Roberto Rossellini was chastised when he began a relationship with actress Ingrid Bergman while both were married to others.

produced Rudolph's dark *Welcome to L.A.* (1977). Rudolph went on to make such films as *Remember My Name* (1978), *Roadie* (1980), the popular *Choose Me* (1984), *Trouble in Mind* (1985), *Mrs. Parker and the Vicious Circle* (1994), and *Afterglow* (1997).

Russell, Ken (1927–) British director, screenwriter, and producer. This flamboyant, frequently outrageous filmmaker served in the Royal Air Force before becoming an actor and dancer and, eventually, a photographer. He produced a series of semifactual biographies of famous composers and artists for the BBC, then moved to directing features with *French Dressing* (1963) and later the commercial success *Women in Love* (1969). As a feature director who frequently produced and wrote or cowrote his films, he continued making fantasy biographies of musicians, including *The Music Lovers* (1971), *Mahler* (1974), and *Lisztomania* (1975). His other films include *The Devils* (1971), the Who's rock opera *Tommy* (1975), *Altered States* (1980), *Gothic* (1986), *Salome's Last Dance* (1988), and *Mindbender* (1995).

S

Saura, Carlos (1932–) Spanish director and screenwriter. Saura was a still photographer and a documentary director who vaulted into the vanguard of Spanish directors with *La Caza (The Hunt)* (1966) and then directed a group of films that were honored at prestigious film festivals: *Peppermint Frappé* (1968), *La Prima Angélica (Cousin Angelica)* (1974), *Cría Cuervos (Raise Ravens)* (1976), and *Deprisa, Deprisa (Hurry, Hurry)* (1981). He also directed three acclaimed musical films: *Bodas de Sangre (Blood Wedding)* (1981), *Carmen* (1983), and *El Amor Brujo (Love the Magician)* (1986).

Sautet, Claude (1924–2000) French director. Sautet, whose films focus on middle-class life, was a social worker and music critic. He produced and wrote for TV before becoming a screenwriter and then a director. After directing mysteries, he made his mark with *Les Choses de la Vie (The Things of Life)* (1969) and followed with *César et Rosalie (Cesar and Rosalie)* (1972, France/Italy/West Germany), *Vincent François Paul…et les Autres (Vincent, François, Paul and the Others)* (1974, France/Italy), *Une Histoire Simple (A Simple Story)* (1980), and *Un Coeur en Hiver (A Heart in Winter)* (1992).

Sayles, John (1950–) American director, screenwriter, actor, and novelist. He makes intensely personal, socially conscious, politically informed films, written by him and sometimes including him as an actor. He has also acted in

and written other people's films and is a novelist. Directorial efforts include *Return of the Secaucus Seven* (1980), *The Brother from Another Planet* (1984), *Matewan* (1987), *Eight Men Out* (1988), and *Lone Star* (1996).

Schlesinger, John (1926–) British director. Schlesinger scored with his first feature, *A Kind of Loving* (1962). A filmmaker equally at home in intimate dramas and big-budget thrillers, Schlesinger directed such films as *Billy Liar* (1963); *Darling* (1965), which earned him the New York Film Critics Circle best director award; and *Far from the Madding Crowd* (1967). Working in Hollywood for the first time, he directed the searing *Midnight Cowboy* (1969, US), which won Academy Awards for best picture and direction. Other credits include *Sunday, Bloody Sunday* (1970), *Marathon Man* (1976, US), and *The Next Best Thing* (2000, US).

Scorsese, Martin (1942–) American director, screenwriter, and producer. His films are marked by an energetic visual style and authentic evocations of urban and criminal life, with violence and redemption as frequent themes. He sometimes cowrites his films; he also produces other people's films and is active in film preservation. Many of his films have been set in New York City, including *Mean Streets* (1973), *Taxi Driver* (1976), *New York, New York* (1977), *The King of Comedy* (1983), *Raging Bull* (1980), and *GoodFellas* (1990). Other films include *The Color of Money* (1986), *The Last Temptation of Christ* (1988), *The Age of Innocence* (1993), and *Gangs of New York* (2002). Scorsese received AFI's Life Achievement Award in 1997.

Scott, Ridley (1937–) British-born director and producer of British and American films. He moved from creating TV commercials to feature directing with *The Duellists* (1977). His films are noted for visual style and trendsetting production design. Directing credits include *Alien* (1979), *Blade Runner* (1982), *Thelma & Louise* (1991), *Gladiator* (2000) and *Black Hawk Down* (2001). His brother is director Tony Scott (1944–), whose films include *Top Gun* (1986).

Seidelman, Susan (1952–) American director and producer. Seidelman had several commercial hits in the 1980s before moving primarily to television production in the 90s. She received acclaim for her debut, *Smithereens* (1982), and followed with her biggest hit, *Desperately Seeking Susan* (1985). Seidelman also directed *Making Mr. Right* (1987), *Cookie* (1989), *She-Devil* (1989), and *The Dutch Master* (1995).

Sembène, Ousmane (1923–) Senegalese director. His first feature, *La Noire de... (Black Girl)* (1966), is widely considered the first major achievement of sub-Saharan African cinema. A novelist before becoming a filmmaker, he

> "In most of my films I try to do the physically difficult bits first, because it breaks down any preconceived notion the actor may have about his or her solipsist self-importance."
>
> — *Ken Russell, 1973*

writes his own scripts, many of which focus on tensions between African and Western cultures. Other films include *Mandabi (The Money Order)* (1968), *Ceddo (The People)* (1977), and *Camp de Thiaroye* (1988).

Sidney, George (1916–) American director. A child star, he became one of MGM's (and later, other studios') leading directors of musical films during the 1940s through the 60s. He often handled stage adaptations, as in *Annie Get Your Gun* (1950), *Show Boat* (1951), *Pal Joey* (1957), and *Bye Bye Birdie* (1963), and worked with major stars, including Judy Garland (*The Harvey Girls*, 1946) and Elvis Presley (*Viva Las Vegas*, 1964).

Siegel, Don (1912–1991) American director. Siegel began his career directing a string of B movies. His *Riot in Cell Block 11* (1956) was a standout among his early works, and *Invasion of the Body Snatchers* (1956) is regarded as a science fiction classic. Siegel became a favorite of the young French filmmakers of the 1950s, but probably will be best remembered for the films he made starring Clint Eastwood, including *Coogan's Bluff* (1968), *The Beguiled* (1971), and *Dirty Harry* (1972). He directed John Wayne's final film, *The Shootist* (1976).

Singleton, John (1968–) American director, screenwriter, and producer. After attending the University of Southern California film school, Singleton made his directing and screenwriting debut with *Boyz N the Hood* (1991), a film that earned him (at age 24) the honor of being the youngest person to ever receive an Academy Award nomination for best director. His follow-up was *Poetic Justice* (1993), starring pop singer Janet Jackson. Other films include *Higher Learning* (1995), *Rosewood* (1997), and *Shaft* (2000).

Sirk, Douglas (1900–1987) Danish-born American director. Born Claus Detlev Sirk. Already an accomplished director in Europe when he emigrated to the US at the beginning of World War II, he brought his visual originality to several stylized melodramas, including *Magnificent Obsession* (1954), *All That Heaven Allows* (1955), *Written on the Wind* (1956), and *Imitation of Life* (1959). He was also adept at dark dramas and noirs, such as *Sleep My Love* (1948) and *Shockproof* (1949).

Smith, Kevin (1970–) American director, screenwriter, and actor. A comic book writer, he entered film in the 1990s as a director-writer-actor with the earthy, idiosyncratic comedy *Clerks* (1994). Later movies include *Chasing Amy* (1997), *Dogma* (1999), and *Jay and Silent Bob Strike Back* (2001). He was also a co–executive producer of *Good Will Hunting* (1997).

Soderbergh, Steven (1963–) American director and screenwriter. He won acclaim for his first feature, the independent film *sex, lies and videotape* (1989), and has since become a major Hollywood director. His directorial efforts, some of which he writes, are marked by full-bodied characterizations and cinematic style. Films include *King of the Hill* (1993), *Out of Sight* (1998), *Erin Brockovich* (2000), and *Traffic* (2000) for which he won a best director Academy Award.

Spielberg, Steven (1947–) American director, producer, and screenwriter. He made his name with big-budget thrillers, adventures, and science fiction films, such as *Jaws* (1975), *Close Encounters of the Third Kind* (1977), *Raiders of the Lost Ark* (1981), *E.T.: The Extra-Terrestrial* (1982), *Jurassic Park* (1993), and *A.I. Artificial Intelligence* (2001). He has also made serious dramas, such as *The Color Purple* (1985) and *Empire of the Sun* (1987), and has twice won best director Academy Awards: for *Schindler's List* (1993) and *Saving Private Ryan* (1998). Cofounder of the studio DreamWorks SKG, he often coproduces or co–executive produces his films and those of others; he has also written or cowritten some of his films. In 1995, Spielberg received AFI's Life Achievement Award.

Sternberg, Josef von (1894–1969) Austrian-born American director. Von Sternberg scored in Hollywood with *Underworld* (1927), but it was in Germany that he made the classic film that launched Marlene Dietrich: *The Blue Angel* (1930). He and Dietrich worked on six Hollywood films—*Morocco* (1930), *Dishonored* (1931), *Shanghai Express* (1932), *Blonde Venus* (1932), *The Scarlet Empress* (1934), and *The Devil Is a Woman* (1935). After *Shanghai Gesture* (1941), his career went into a permanent tailspin, and he subsequently made few films.

> "Dailies continue to look great. When is something going to go wrong?"
>
> —
>
> *Steven Soderbergh, writing in his diary midway through directing sex, lies, and videotape (1989). The film would win the esteemed Palme d'Or at the Cannes Film Festival.*

John Singleton wrote the screenplay for his 1991 directorial debut, Boyz N the Hood, *which was based on his own experiences.*

"When the last dime is gone, I'll go sit on the curb outside with a pencil and a ten-cent notebook and start the whole thing over again."

Preston Sturges, in the face of impending bankruptcy, circa 1950

Russian filmmaker Andrei Tarkovsky is best known for his works Solaris *(1972) and* Offret/The Sacrifice *(1986), which won three awards at Cannes.*

Stevens, George (1904–1975) American director. Although he made only 25 films, Stevens was one of the most respected directors of his time and winner of a best director Academy Award for *A Place in the Sun* (1951) and *Giant* (1956). He was nominated for *The More the Merrier* (1943), *Shane* (1953), and *The Diary of Anne Frank* (1959). His first film of note was *Alice Adams* (1935). Additional credits include the Fred Astaire–Ginger Rogers vehicle *Swing Time* (1936), the adventure classic *Gunga Din* (1939), *Penny Serenade* (1941), *Woman of the Year* (1942), *The Talk of the Town* (1942), and *The Greatest Story Ever Told* (1965).

Stone, Oliver (1946–) American director, writer, and producer. Stone is a two-time best director Academy Award winner—for *Platoon* (1986), which also won best picture, and for *Born on the Fourth of July* (1989). Stone spent considerable time in Vietnam, first as a teacher and then with the army. His films are often violent and political, and his *JFK* (1991), which posited an assassination conspiracy, generated widespread controversy. Credits include *Salvador* (1986), *Wall Street* (1987), *The Doors* (1991), *Natural Born Killers* (1994), *Nixon* (1995), and *Any Given Sunday* (1999).

Stroheim, Erich von (1885–1957) Austrian-born American director and actor. One of early film's most original, even notorious, directors, von Stroheim remains legendary for his exacting artisanship, the psychological complexity of his films, and the extravagant length and cost of his produtions. The son of a milliner, von Stroheim emigrated to America at the beginning of the 20th century, and began working as the heavy in D.W. Griffith's films. His directorial debut, in which he took total artistic control, was the intriguing and well-received *Blind Husbands* (1919). He directed *The Devil's Passkey* (1920) before the lavish *Foolish Wives* (1922), which barely turned a profit due to its excessive cost. His most famous film was the storied masterpiece *Greed* (1925), which MGM forced him to cut from over nine hours to 140 minutes. The original version has never been completely assembled. Despite conflicts with the studio, von Stroheim directed his dark film

The Merry Widow (1925) and the two-part *The Wedding March/The Honeymoon* (1928), before the profligate *Queen Kelly* (1928), from which he was fired by star Gloria Swanson. He also acted to great effect in Jean Renoir's *Grand Illusion* (1937) and Billy Wilder's *Sunset Boulevard* (1950).

Sturges, Preston (1898–1959) American director, screenwriter, and playwright. Born Edmond P. Biden. A Broadway playwright, he began in Hollywood as a screenwriter whose credits included *The Power and the Glory* (1933) and *Easy Living* (1937). But he gained enduring fame as a director and screenwriter of some of the wittiest comedies ever made, including *The Great McGinty* (1940), *The Lady Eve* (1941), *Sullivan's Travels* (1941), *The Palm Beach Story* (1942), *The Miracle of Morgan's Creek* (1944), and *Hail the Conquering Hero* (1944). After the mid-1940s, he made only a few films; in the 50s, he lived mainly in seclusion.

T

Tarantino, Quentin (1963–) American director, screenwriter, producer, and actor. With criminals as their main characters, his films are marked by graphic violence, offbeat dialogue, and philosophical concerns. He frequently writes and acts in the films he directs, and has also written, produced, and acted in the films of others. He made his feature directorial debut with *Reservoir Dogs* (1992) and followed with *Pulp Fiction* (1994), for which he received an Academy Award for best original screenplay, and *Jackie Brown* (1997). He directed one of the four segments of the omnibus *Four Rooms* (1995).

Tarkovsky, Andrei (1932–1986) Russian director. Tarkovsky's sparse output was acclaimed outside the Soviet Union, winning a number of awards at major film festivals, but his films were mostly ignored or criticized at home. An unorthodox filmmaker, he made his feature debut with *The Roller and the Violin* (1960), followed by the internationally acclaimed *My Name Is Ivan/Ivan's Childhood* (1962). His ensuing films include *Andrei Rublev* (1968), *Solaris* (1972), *The Mirror* (1974), *Nostalghia* (*Nostalgia*) (1983, Italy/USSR), and *Offret* (*Sacrificatio/Le Sacrifice/The Sacrifice*) (1986, Sweden/France).

Tashlin, Frank (1913–1972) American director. A successful screenwriter in the 1940s and 50s, he directed *Son of Paleface* (1952), starring Bob Hope, and a number of Jerry Lewis comedies, including *Artists and Models* (1955), *The Geisha Boy* (1958), *Cinderfella* (1960), *It's Only*

Money (1962), and *The Disorderly Orderly* (1964). His other credits include *Will Success Spoil Rock Hunter?* (1957).

Tati, Jacques (1908–1982) French director and actor. A stage pantomimist before turning to film, he made his directing debut with *L'Ecole des Facteurs* (1947) and followed with *Jour de Fête (Holiday)* (1949). He acted in and wrote the screenplays for most of his films, the comedy of which was built largely on visuals. His work won an international following. Other films include *Les Vacances de Monsieur Hulot (Mr. Hulot's Holiday)* (1953) and *Mon Oncle (My Uncle, Mr. Hulot)* (1956).

Tavernier, Bertrand (1941–) French director, screenwriter, and theorist. A longtime critic and contributor to the film journal *Cahiers du Cinéma*, he was a publicist before directing his first feature, *L'Horloger de Saint-Paul (The Clockmaker of St. Paul)* in 1973. The film was the first of many stylish, intense character studies, including *Le Juge et l'Assassin (The Judge and the Assassin)* (1975), *Des Enfants Gâtes (Spoiled Children)* (1977), *Un Dimanche à la Campagne (A Sunday in the Country)* (1984), *'Round Midnight* (1986), *La Vie et Rien d'Autre (Life and Nothing But)* (1989), *Daddy Nostalgie* (1990), and *Ça Commence Aujourd'hui (It All Starts Today)* (1999).

Taviani, Paolo (1931–) and **Taviani, Vittorio** (1929–) Italian directors and writers. The Taviani brothers codirect and cowrite their movies, which focus mainly on social problems. After two three-director ventures, the brothers began working in tandem. Their fifth joint project, *Padre Padrone (Father Master)* (1977), was the first film to win the Golden Palm and International Critics Prize at the Cannes Film Festival, and *La Notte di San Lorenzo (The Night of the Shooting Stars)* (1982) won the American National Society of Film Critics award for direction. The Tavianis shot *Good Morning, Babilonia (Good Morning, Babylon)* (1987, Italy/France/US) in the US.

Truffaut, François (1932–1984) French director, screenwriter, actor, and critic. As a film critic writing for the magazine *Cahiers du Cinéma*, he helped develop auteur theory and lead the French New Wave. As a director, he established himself with his first feature, *Les Quatre Cents Coups/The 400 Blows* (1959). His films, which he wrote or cowrote and in which he occasionally acted, were tender, atmospheric, and rich in characterization. Films include *Tirez sur le Pianiste (Shoot the Piano Player)* (1960), *Jules et Jim (Jules and Jim)* (1961), and *L'Enfant Sauvage (The Wild Child)* (1970), *La Nuit Américaine (Day for Night)* (1973; best foreign language film Academy Award), and *Le Dernier Métro (The Last Metro)* (1980). Notable books include *Hitchcock/Truffaut* (1983).

U–V

Ulmer, Edgar G. (1904–1972) Austrian-born American director. Ulmer worked with the legendary Max Reinhardt in Berlin and director F.W. Murnau in the United States. Although he directed very low-budget projects, including Yiddish and Ukrainian films, he managed to create a horror classic, *The Black Cat* (1934), with Boris Karloff and Bela Lugosi, and the cult noir classic, *Detour* (1946). His other credits include *Girls in Chains* (1943) and *St. Benny the Dip* (1951).

Vadim, Roger (1928–2000) French director, producer, and actor. Vadim is known for the sensual and visually commanding star vehicles in which his wives and lovers are featured. A journalist and actor, Vadim paved the way for New Wave directors with the daring 1956 film starring his wife Brigitte Bardot, *Et Dieu…Créa la Femme (And God Created Woman)*. He also directed *Les Liaisons Dangereuses* (1960), *La Vice et la Vertu (Vice and Virtue)* (1962), and *La Curée (The Game Is Over)* (1966), and featured his next wife, Jane Fonda, in the erotic cartoon fantasy *Barbarella* (1968). Other films by Vadim include *Pretty Maids All in a Row* (1971), *La Jeune Fille Assassinée (Charlotte)* (1974), *Night Games* (1980), *Surprise Party* (1983), and *Safari* (1991), as well as many television productions.

Van Dyke, W.S. (1889–1943) American director. After working as an assistant on D.W. Griffith's *Intolerance* (1916), Van Dyke directed scores of films, many set in outdoor locations. His direction was so swift and sure that he was known as "One Shot Woody." Films include *White Shadows in the South Seas* (1928), *Trader Horn* (1931), *Tarzan the Ape Man* (1932), *The Thin Man* (1934), *San Francisco* (1936), *The Good Earth* (1937), *The Prisoner of Zenda* (1937), and *Rage in Heaven* (1941).

Van Peebles, Mario (1957–) Mexican-born American director, actor, and screenwriter. The son of director Melvin Van Peebles (1932–), Mario began as an actor in his father's *Sweet Sweetback's Baadasssss Song* (1971). He was an actor and model before getting his directing start in television. His feature debut was *New Jack City* (1991), a well-received crime melodrama. Other films include *Posse* (1993), *Panther* (1995), *Love Kills* (1998), and *Standing Knockdown* (1999).

Verhoeven, Paul (1938–) Dutch-born director of Dutch and American films. He made movies in the Netherlands from the 1970s to the early 80s, in Hollywood thereafter. His films are marked by violence, sex, political satire, and issues of threatened identity. Credits include *Soldier of*

Two slightly different versions of *The Third Man* exist. The British version, released in the UK in 1949, features opening narration by director Carol Reed and runs 104 minutes. The version released in the US by producer David O. Selznick the following year is 11 minutes shorter and replaces Reed's narration with one read by actor Joseph Cotten.

Orange (1979, also sc.), *Spetters* (1980), *De Vierde Man* (*The Fourth Man*) (1983), *Robocop* (1987), *Total Recall* (1990), *Basic Instinct* (1992), *Showgirls* (1995), and *Hollow Man* (2000).

Vidor, King (1894–1982) American director. After a slow start in Hollywood, Vidor moved into the top ranks of silent film directors with *The Big Parade* (1925), starring John Gilbert and Renee Adoree. Subsequently, he earned Academy Award nominations for his work on five films: *The Crowd* (1928), *Hallelujah!* (1929), *The Champ* (1931), *The Citadel* (1938), and *War and Peace* (1956, Italy). Vidor, who was awarded an honorary Academy Award in 1979, also directed some scenes for *The Wizard of Oz* (1939).

Vigo, Jean (1905–1934) French director. Vigo made only four films, but two of them are regarded as classics. He began his career directing a documentary, *A Propos de Nice* (1930), followed by a short. He made his feature debut with *Zéro de Conduite* (*Zero for Conduct*) (1933), a fantasy set in a boys' school. Under pressure, it was withdrawn and not shown again until 1945. His final film was his masterpiece, *L'Atalante* (1934), a poetic attack on the French middle class. The film was drastically censored by its producers. Vigo was only 29 when he died of leukemia.

Silent film director King Vidor (seated, center) successfully made the transition to sound films and received an honorary Academy Award in 1979.

Though shot entirely on video using dozens of meticulously placed digital cameras, Lars von Trier's *Dancer in the Dark* (2000) utilized custom-built anamorphic lenses that allowed the film to be both composed for and projected in a widescreen format.

Visconti, Luchino (1906–1976) Italian director. Visconti, a count but a believer in communism, did not begin working in films until he was 34. His first feature was the neorealistic *Ossessione* (1942). His subsequent credits include the more elaborate *La Terra Trema* (*The Earth Trembled*) (1948), the family epic *Rocco e i Suoi Fratelli* (*Rocco and His Brothers*) (1960), and, with Federico Fellini and Vittorio De Sica, *Boccaccio '70* (1962). His *Il Gattopardo* (*The Leopard*) (1963, Italy/France) and *Stelle dell'Orsa* (*Sandra*) (1965) were internationally honored.

von Trier, Lars (1956–) Danish director, screenwriter, and actor. He debuted as a director of visually dense and imaginative films with *Orchidegartnerer* (1977). After several other films, including *Nocturne* (1980) and *Epidemic* (1988), he had an international smash with *Europa/Zentropa* (1991), an arresting and dynamic thriller. His unusual, heartbreaking love story *Breaking the Waves* (1996) was a popular and critical success and launched the career of actress Emily Watson.

W–X

Wajda, Andrzej (1926–) Polish director. A former Polish Resistance fighter, Wajda established himself as a force in Eastern European filmmaking with his first feature, *A Generation* (1954). He followed with two powerful films, *Kanal* (1957) and *Ashes and Diamonds* (1958). Other films include *Man of Marble* (1977), *Panna Nik* (*Miss Nobody*) (1996), and *Pan Tadeusz* (*Pan Tadeusz: The Last Foray in Lithuania*) (1999, Poland/France).

Walsh, Raoul (1887–1980) American director. An amazingly prolific filmmaker, Walsh began as an actor and assistant director for D.W. Griffith and worked until the 1960s. He lost an eye in 1929 during the shooting of *In Old Arizona*, hence his signature eye patch. His credits include *What Price Glory?* (1927), *They Drive by Night* (1940), *High Sierra* (1941), *White Heat* (1949), *Battle Cry* (1955), and *The Naked and the Dead* (1958). He directed such leading men as Humphrey Bogart, James Cagney, Gary Cooper, and Clark Gable.

Wang, Wayne (1949–) Hong Kong–born director, working in the United States. Wang, who was named after John Wayne, is noted for films with Chinese and Chinese-American themes. He made his feature debut codirecting *A Man, a Woman, and a Killer* (1975). He then directed a low-budget success, *Chan Is Missing* (1981), from his own screenplay. Additional credits include *Dim Sum: A Little Bit of Heart* (1985), *Eat a Bowl of Tea* (1989), *The Joy Luck Club* (1993), and *Anywhere But Here* (1999).

Waters, John (1946–) American director, screenwriter, producer, and cinematographer. Beginning with 8mm shorts and moving into features, he attained national notoriety with his 1972 shocker *Pink Flamingos,* featuring school friend Divine (Harris Glenn Milstead) as the female lead. Later films starring Divine were equally revolting (and amusing) looks at modern life, such as *Female Trouble* (1974) and *Polyester* (1981). Waters entered mainstream movies with the musical comedy *Hairspray* (1988) and *Serial Mom* (1994), both of which display an outrageous brand of humanism.

Weir, Peter (1944–) Australian-born director of Australian and American films. Both before and after moving to Hollywood, where he made his first American film, *Witness* (1985), he made films that are marked by visual poetry and an interest in the clash of cultures. He has written or cowritten some of his films. Directing credits include *Picnic at Hanging Rock* (1975), *Gallipoli* (1981), *The Year of Living Dangerously* (1982), *Dead Poets Society* (1989), and *The Truman Show* (1998).

Welles, Orson (1915–1985) American director, producer, screenwriter, and actor. Born George Orson Welles. His first directorial feature, *Citizen Kane* (1941), which he also produced, coscripted, and starred in, established his reputation as a filmmaker of astonishing talent. Its innovative narrative and cinematographic techniques have influenced generations of directors. His later films, often compromised by studio intervention, never achieved the acclaim of that first film, but many are nevertheless milestones of cinema. He often produced, wrote or cowrote, and acted in his films; he also acted in other people's films. His directorial efforts include *The Magnificent Ambersons* (1942), *The Lady from Shanghai* (1948), *Macbeth* (1948), *Touch of Evil* (1958), *The Trial* (1962), and *Chimes at Midnight* (1966). He received the AFI Life Achievement Award in 1975.

Wellman, William (1896–1975) American director. Wellman was a flying ace during World War I. He directed *Wings* (1929), winner of the first Academy Award for best picture. He was also nominated for Academy Awards for the first film version of *A Star Is Born* (1937), *Battleground* (1949), and *The High and the Mighty* (1954). Among his other notable films are *The Public Enemy* (1931), the classic adventure *Beau Geste* (1939), and *The Ox-Bow Incident* (1943). His final film was *Lafayette Escadrille* (1958), about his World War I unit.

Wenders, Wim (1945–) German director, screenwriter, and producer. His luminous, brooding films have made him one of the most important directors of his generation. He frequently writes and produces his films and sometimes acts in them. He made his debut with *Summer in the City (Dedicated to the Kinks)* (1970) and followed with *Die Angst des Tormanns beim Elfmeter (The Anxiety of the Goalie at the Penalty Kick)* (1972). He directed the quirky *Hammett* (1982, US) and gained international acclaim with *Paris, Texas* (1983, West Germany/France). Additional credits include *Der Himmel über Berlin (Wings of Desire)* (1987) and *Am Ende der Gewalt (The End of Violence)* (1997, France/Germany/US).

Wertmuller, Lina (1928–) Italian director. Wertmuller worked as an assistant director on Federico Fellini's *8 ½*, made her directing debut with *I Basilischi (The Lizards)* (1963), and became an international presence with *Mimi Metallurgico Ferito nell'Onore (The Seduction of Mimi)* (1974). Tough and energetic on the set, she was the first woman nominated for an Academy Award for direction—for *Pasqualino Settebellezze (Seven Beauties)* (1976). Other films include *Travolti da un'Insolito Destino nell'Azzurro Mare d'Agosto (Swept Away by an Unusual Destiny in the Blue Sea of August)* (1974), and *The End of the World in Our Usual Bed in a Night Full of Rain* (1978, Italy/US).

Whale, James (1896–1957) British-born American director who worked exclusively in the United States. Whale made his directing bow with *Journey's End* (1930) but is best known for his classic horror films, including *Frankenstein* (1931), *The Invisible Man* (1933), and *The Bride of Frankenstein* (1935). His credits also include *Show Boat* (1936). After retiring to paint, he drowned in 1957 under mysterious circumstances. His later life was the focus of the 1998 film *Gods and Monsters*, with Ian McKellen as Whale.

Wiene, Robert (1881–1938) German director. Wiene began his career as a screenwriter and began directing in 1914. The highlight of his career is the expressionist classic *Das Kabinett des Dr. Caligari (The Cabinet of Dr. Caligari)* (1919). Although he made many other films, most in Germany, they are generally considered to be of lesser quality. Other works include *Die Rache einer Frau* (1920), *Orlacs Hände (The Hands of Orlac),* and *Der Andere* (1930).

Wilder, Billy (1906–2002) Austrian-born director, screenwriter, and producer. He worked as a screenwriter in Germany until 1933, in the US afterward. He was a screenwriter in Hollywood films until 1942 (credits include *Ninotchka,* 1939, and *Ball of Fire,* 1942), then director and coscreenwriter of his own films. His directorial efforts are marked by witty dialogue, worldly themes, lush cinematography, and riotous comic situations. Films include *Double Indemnity* (1944), *Sunset Boulevard* (1950), *Stalag 17* (1953), *Sabrina* (1954), *The Seven Year Itch* (1955), *Some Like It Hot* (1959), and *The Fortune Cookie* (1966). *The Lost Weekend* (1945) and *The Apartment* (1960) won him best director Academy Awards. He received AFI's Life Achievement Award in 1986.

Director Wim Wenders received international acclaim for Paris, Texas *(1984). He was named best director at Cannes for his 1987 film* Wings of Desire.

Wise, Robert (1914–) American film director, producer, and editor. He started in the cutting department at RKO in 1933 and came to prominence as an editor with *Citizen Kane* (1941) and *The Magnificent Ambersons* (1942). *Citizen Kane*'s success is often attributed to the innovative manipulation of time achieved through the editing process. Later he became a director of horror and science fiction films, such as *The Curse of the Cat People* (1944) and *The Day the Earth Stood Still* (1951). Sometimes producing his films, he achieved his greatest renown for two musicals: *West Side Story* (1961, co-dir.) and *The Sound of Music* (1965); both earned him best director Academy Awards. Other films include *The Andromeda Strain* (1971) and *Star Trek* (1979). In 1998, Wise received the AFI Life Achievement Award.

Woo, John (1946–) Chinese-born director of US and Hong Kong films. Woo made his debut with a martial arts film, *The Young Dragons* (1973). He directed a number of other, often brutally violent action films, frequently starring Chow Yun-Fat; some of these gained cult status. His first US film was *Hard Target* (1993), which he followed with another fast-paced action film, *Broken Arrow* (1997, US) and the John Travolta–Nicolas Cage pairing *Face/Off* (1997, US).

Wood, Edward D., Jr. (1922–1978) American director, producer, and screenwriter. By many accounts, the worst director in history. His films, which he also wrote and produced and in which he sometimes acted, are bad enough to have achieved cult status. Usually centered on the weird and horrific, his films include *Glen or Glenda/I Changed My Sex* (1952), *Bride of the Monster* (1953), and *Plan 9 from Outer Space* (1959). His life and work inspired the Tim Burton film *Ed Wood* (1994).

Y–Z

Yimou, Zhang (1950–) Chinese director. Educated at the Beijing Film Academy, he made his debut with *Red Sorghum* (1988) and followed with such films as *Ju Dou* (1990, China/Japan) and *Raise the Red Lantern* (1991, China/Hong Kong/Taiwan), both nominated for Academy Awards. Additional credits include *To Live* (1994, Hong Kong/China) *Shanghai Triad/Row, Row, Row to Grandma's Bridge* (1995), *Keep Cool* (1997), and *Wo de fu qin muqin (The Red Home)* (1999).

Yorkin, Bud (1926–) American director and producer. Born Alan David Yorkin. A television director and producer during the 1950s, he cofounded Tandem Productions in 1959 and directed (and coproduced) his first film, *Come*

Blow Your Horn, in 1963. Over the next four decades, he has specialized in bright comedies and the occasional drama, with directing-producing credits including *Start the Revolution Without Me* (1970) and *Twice in a Lifetime* (1985).

Zeffirelli, Franco (1923–) Italian director, screenwriter, and production designer of international films. Known for his lavish, operatic design, Zeffirelli's best-loved films are *Romeo and Juliet* (1968) and the television miniseries *Jesus of Nazareth* (1977). After working as an actor and then an assistant director to Luchino Visconti, he directed adaptations of *La Bohème* (1965) and *The Taming of the Shrew* (1967), the latter starring Elizabeth Taylor and Richard Burton. He also directed *Fratello Sole, Sorella Luna/Brother Sun, Sister Moon* (1973), *The Champ* (1979), *Endless Love* (1981), and adaptations of *La Traviata* (1982), *Otello* (1986), *Hamlet* (1990), and *Jane Eyre* (1996), as well as the popular *Un Te con Mussolini/Tea with Mussolini* (1999). His productions, while visually sumptuous, have not always received substantial critical or popular acclaim.

Zinnemann, Fred (1907–1997) Austrian-born American director. Regarded as a master craftsman, he directed two feature films that won Academy Awards for best picture and director, *From Here to Eternity* (1953) and *A Man for All Seasons* (1966, UK) and one film that won for best documentary, short subject, *Benjy* (1951). Other films include *High Noon* (1952), *Oklahoma!* (1955), *The Nun's Story* (1959), *The Sundowners* (1960), and *Julia* (1977).

Zucker, Jerry (1950–) American director, producer, and screenwriter. With brother David Zucker (1947–) and Jim Abrahams (1944–), he shared directing, writing, and producing tasks on such wacky comedies as the genre spoofs *Airplane!* (1980) and *The Naked Gun: From the Files of Police Squad!* (1988, co-sc. and co-exec. prod. only). The partners went on to establish separate careers; Jerry Zucker's other directorial efforts include *Ghost* (1990), *First Knight* (1995), and *Rat Race* (2001).

Zwick, Edward (1952–) American director, producer, and screenwriter. Creator of the television series *thirtysomething* and *Once and Again,* he gained notice as a feature film director for the Civil War drama *Glory* (1989) and later for other expansive dramas, including *Legends of the Fall* (1994) and *Courage Under Fire* (1996). He was a producer of *Shakespeare in Love* (1998).

AT RIGHT: *Director Fred Zinnemann, pictured here with Robert Shaw filming* A Man for All Seasons *(1966), won his third Academy Award for the film.*

> "My films are always concerned with family, friendship, honor and patriotism."
>
> —
>
> *John Woo, 1997*

DIRECTOR
The film's director, Harold Ramis, watches from behind the camera crew. His headphones allow him to clearly hear the sound as it is being recorded. Most contemporary directors also view each take through a video monitor that's connected to the camera. This way, they can immediately see each scene as it will eventually appear onscreen.

STANDS
Lightweight, extendable stands are used by the electrical department to support and position lights. Similar stands are then utilized by the grip department to hold flags, nets, and gel frames that will direct, and diffuse the light to the cinematographer's specifications.

DOLLY
The dolly is a large, wheeled device that the camera can be affixed to and positioned from. Dollies are usually laid on railway-like tracks and are carefully controlled in their movements by a dolly grip, who helps the cinematographer and/or the camera operator achieve a smooth, gliding effect on film. (Grips are the film industry's equivalent to theater's stagehands.)

CINEMATOGRAPHER AND CREW
The film's cinematographer, John Bailey (also known as the director of photography), heads the camera crew. His instructions are relayed to the key grip and the gaffer (or key electrician) who, in turn, filter these directions back to their own crews.

Behind the Scenes

BOOM MIC / BOOM OPERATOR

The boom mic is a microphone attached to a long metal arm, which can then be counterbalanced and positioned just out of camera range when held aloft by a boom operator. In some finished films the boom can seen dipping into the frame.

ANYONE WHO HAS EVER sat through a film's closing credits knows that movies are a collaborative art form. It takes hundreds of people, each performing a specialized task, to guide a motion picture like 1993's *Groundhog Day* from script to screen. But for every self-explanatory make-up artist, costume designer, and editor that scrolls by, there's at least one more—a boom operator, a dolly grip, a focus puller— to baffle even the most ardent filmgoer.

THE ACTOR

Actor Bill Murray is ready for his close-up. After the scene is rehearsed, one of the camera assistants will either use strips of colored tape or a piece of chalk to mark where he will be standing at key points during the take. This is done so the camera can keep Murray in focus as he moved through the scene. An actor's ability to perform this task successfully is referred to in the industry as "hitting the marks."

LOCATION SHOOTING

Groundhog Day was shot on location in towns in Illinois and Pennsylvania, including the film's main setting, Punxsutawney, PA. In such cases, local residents often show up to watch filming, and it's the job of one of the production's many assistant directors (ADs) to "lock up" the crowd to avoid any passers-by inadvertently wandering into a scene or distracting an actor.

CAMERA OPERATOR

The cinematographer may control his own camera, or he may work with a camera operator. The camera operator is assisted by a focus puller, who measures distances from objects to the lens, and camera assistants, who help load and unload film, keep camera reports, and make certain the camera is in working order.

CONTINUITY

The continuity person, or script supervisor, helps preserve the illusion of sequential filming on a motion picture by noting the minute details of each take, including the appearance and exact positioning of performers, props, costumes, and background players in each scene.

SCREENWRITERS

Before a story can be filmed, the screenwriter must tell the story on the page. The screenplay is the blueprint for everything we see on screen.

A

> "What's all this business about being a writer? It's just putting one word after another."
> "Pardon me, Mr. Thalberg; it's putting one right word after another."
>
> —
> *Production executive Irving Thalberg and screenwriter Lenore Coffee, circa 1930*

Anhalt, Edward (1914–2000) American screen and TV writer and cinematographer. Known for his adaptations, he collaborated with his wife Edna on the Academy Award–winning story for *Panic in the Streets* (1950). His screenplays include *The Young Lions* (1958) and *Becket* (1964), for which he won an Academy Award.

Balderston, John L. (1889–1954) American screenwriter, journalist, and playwright. Best known for his work in fantasy and horror, he collaborated on Universal's *Dracula* (1931), *Frankenstein* (1931), and *The Bride of Franken-stein* (1935). His first solo effort was *The Mummy* (1932). Balderston also wrote the screenplay for *Gaslight* (1944).

Bass, Ronald (1943–) American screenwriter, novelist, and producer. Although his work runs from thrillers to romance, it was his collaboration with Barry Morrow on *Rain Man* (1988), about an autistic man, that earned him an Academy Award. Other films include *The Joy Luck Club* (1993) and *My Best Friend's Wedding* (1997).

Bennett, Charles (1899–1995) British-born screenwriter and director of British and American films. Best known for his collaboration on several of Alfred Hitchcock's films, including, in Britain, *Blackmail* (1929), *The Man Who Knew Too Much* (1934), and *The 39 Steps* (1935). His work in the US includes *Foreign Correspondent* (1940) and the remake of *The Man Who Knew Too Much* (1956).

Bolt, Robert (1924–1995) British playwright, screenwriter, and director of British and American films. The theme of man versus society, evident in his play *A Man for All Seasons,* which he turned into an Academy Award–winning screenplay (1966), runs through his work. He also received an Academy Award for *Dr. Zhivago* (1965). Other films include *Lawrence of Arabia* (1962), *Ryan's Daughter* (1970), and *Lady Caroline Lamb* (1972), which he also directed.

Brach, Gérard (1927–) French-born screenwriter of French and international films. Noted for his collaboration with director Roman Polanski on films such as *Repulsion* (1965, UK) and *Cul-de-Sac* (1966, UK). Among his other screenplays are *Jean de Florette* (1986) and *Manon des Sources* (*Manon of the Spring*) (1986).

Brackett, Charles (1892–1969) American screenwriter and producer. Collaborated as a writer and producer with director Billy Wilder on 13 films, from comedies to films noir, including *Ninotchka* (1939) and two that earned Brackett Academy Awards: *The Lost Weekend* (1945) and *Sunset Boulevard* (1950). Without Wilder, Brackett won an Academy Award for *Titanic* (1953).

Brackett, Leigh (1915–1978) American novelist and screenwriter. She created strong men and women in tight spots in the screenplays for five Howard Hawks films, including *The Big Sleep* (1946) and *Rio Bravo* (1959). Brackett also worked on Robert Altman's *The Long Goodbye* (1973) and on *The Empire Strikes Back* (1980).

Buchman, Sidney (1902–1975) American screenwriter and producer. Buchman's metier was comedy, earning him an Academy Award for *The Talk of the Town* (1942). Other films include *Mr. Smith Goes to Washington* (1939) and *Here Comes Mr. Jordan* (1941). Blacklisted in the 1950s, he later contributed to *Cleopatra* (1963).

Burnett, W.R. (William Riley) (1899–1982) American screenwriter and novelist. He left his mark on the American crime movie with films adapted from his novels *Little Caesar* (1931), *High Sierra* (1941), and *The Asphalt Jungle* (1950). His screenwriting includes *High Sierra, This Gun for Hire* (1942), and *The Great Escape* (1963).

Carrière, Jean-Claude (1931–) French screenwriter. He probed the psychological depths of personality, especially in films scripted for director Luis Buñuel, including *Belle de Jour* (1967), *Le Charme Discret de la Bourgeosie (The Discreet Charm of the Bourgeoisie)* (1972), and *Cet Obscur Objet du Désir (That Obscure Object of Desire)* (1977). Carrière also scripted *The Unbearable Lightness of Being* (1988).

Chandler, Raymond (1888–1959) American novelist and screenwriter. The master of hard-boiled detective novels such as *Farewell, My Lovely,* several of which have been adapted for the screen, Chandler also collaborated on screenplays. These include *Double Indemnity* (1944), *The Blue Dahlia* (1946), and *Strangers on a Train* (1951).

Chase, Borden (1900–1971) American screenwriter and novelist. He specialized in westerns, war films, and other adventure genres. Among his films are *Red River* (1948), based on his novel *The Blazing Guns on the Chisholm Trail* (1948), *Winchester '73* (1950), *Bend of the River* (1952), and *Vera Cruz* (1954).

Chayefsky, Paddy (1923–1981) American playwright and screenwriter. He was especially adept at portraying the drama of ordinary people, as in his Academy Award–winning *Marty* (1955). He earned a second Academy Award for *The Hospital* (1971). Other films include *The Bachelor Party* (1957), *The Americanization of Emily* (1964), and *Network* (1976).

Clarke, T.E.B. (Thomas Ernest Bennett) (1907–1989) British screenwriter and novelist. His talent for comedy was most evident in *The Lavender Hill Mob* (1951), which won an Academy Award. Among his other films are *Passport to Pimlico* (1949) and *Sons and Lovers* (1960).

Coffee, Lenore (1897–1984) American screenwriter. From the silent era through the 1950s, she specialized in writing women's melodramas and in fixing ailing scripts. Films include *The Volga Boatman* (1926), *Arsene Lupin* (1932), *Till We Meet Again* (1944), and *The End of the Affair* (1955).

Comden, Betty (1919–) and **Green, Adolph** (1915–) American lyricists and screenwriters. Comden and Green's genius for parody, witty dialogue, and bouncy lyrics have graced some of America's best musical films. These include *On the Town* (1949), *Singin' in the Rain* (1952), *The Band Wagon* (1953), and *Bells Are Ringing* (1960).

Diamond, I.A.L. (1920–1988) Romanian-born American screenwriter and producer. He is best known for succeeding Charles Brackett as director Billy Wilder's coscreenwriter and producer, beginning with *Love in the Afternoon* (1957). His dry and sardonic wit is also found in *Some Like It Hot* (1959) and his Academy Award–winning script for *The Apartment* (1960).

Dunne, Philip (1908–1992) American director and screenwriter. He is known for his adapted screenplays for major films, such as *The Last of the Mohicans* (1936), *How Green Was My Valley* (1941), *Forever Amber* (1947), *Pinky* (1949), *The Robe* (1953), and *Ten North Frederick* (1958). His 1982 book *Take Two* dealt with the blacklist.

Ephron, Nora (1941–) American screenwriter, director, producer, journalist, and novelist. Her work often deals with the twists of modern romance, including the screenplay for *Heartburn* (1985), based on one of her own marriages. She also wrote *Silkwood* (1983) and *When Harry Met Sally…* (1989), for which she acted as an associate producer. She wrote and directed *Sleepless in Seattle* (1993) and *You've Got Mail* (1998). She is the daughter of screenwriters Phoebe and Henry Ephron.

Epstein, Julius J. (1909–2000) and **Epstein, Philip G.** (1909–1952) American screenwriters. Identical twins, they were known for the sophisticated dialogue in their scripts. Their collaborations, mostly on adaptations of stage plays, included *The Man Who Came to Dinner* (1941), *Casablanca* (1942), for which they won an Academy Award, and *Arsenic and Old Lace* (1944).

Eszterhas, Joe (1946–) Hungarian-American screenwriter, producer, and novelist. Known for the large fees he commands and the sex and violence that characterize his scripts, Eszterhas became a bankable name after the commercial success of *Basic Instinct* (1992). Other films include *Jagged Edge* (1985) and *Sliver* (1993), for which he was also a co–executive producer.

Flaino, Ennio (1910–1972) and **Pinelli, Tullio** (1908–) Italian screenwriters. Best known for combining mysticism and irony in their collaborations with Federico Fellini on films such as *Luci del Varietà* (*Variety Lights*) (1951), *La Strada* (1954), *La Dolce Vita* (1960), *Otto e Mezzo* (*8 ½*) (1963), and *Giulietta degli Spiriti* (*Juliet of the Spirits*) (1965). Pinelli also scripted *Il Giardino dei Finzi-Contini* (*The Garden of the Finzi-Continis*) (1971).

Foreman, Carl (1914–1984) American screenwriter, director, and producer. His screenplays are peopled by individuals struggling to maintain their integrity in the face of external pressure. Blacklisted in the 1950s, he only posthumously received his Academy Award for *The Bridge on the River Kwai* (1957), on which he was uncredited. Other films include *Champion* (1949), *High Noon* (1952), and *The Guns of Navarone* (1961).

Frank, Melvin (1913–1988) and **Panama, Norman** (1914–) American screenwriters, producers, and directors. The team's forte was comedy. Films together include *My Favorite Blonde* (1942), *Road to Utopia* (1946), *Mr. Blandings Builds His Dream House* (1948), and *The Court Jester* (1956). Frank scripted several films alone, including *A Touch of Class* (1973).

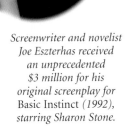

Screenwriter and novelist Joe Eszterhas received an unprecedented $3 million for his original screenplay for Basic Instinct *(1992), starring Sharon Stone.*

Furthman, Jules (1888–1960) American screenwriter. One of Hollywood's most prolific screenwriters, from silent films through *Rio Bravo* (1959), he sometimes collaborated with his brother Charles. His output includes *Morocco* (1930), *Mutiny on the Bounty* (1935), *Only Angels Have Wings* (1939), and *To Have and Have Not* (1944).

Ganz, Lowell (1948–) and **Mandel, Babaloo** (1949–) American screenwriters. This team has specialized in offbeat comedy since the 1980s. Among their scripts are *Night Shift* (1982), *Splash* (1984), *Parenthood* (1989), *City Slickers* (1991), *A League of Their Own* (1992), and *Where the Heart Is* (2000).

Gelbart, Larry (1925–) American screen, stage, and TV writer. One of the screen's most highly paid comedy writers, he has also won Emmy and Tony awards for his writing. Among his films are *The Notorious Landlady* (1960), *Oh God!* (1977), *Tootsie* (1982), and *Blame It on Rio* (1984).

Goldman, Bo (1932–) American screenwriter. A versatile screenwriter and script doctor, Goldman has taken two Academy Awards, for *One Flew over the Cuckoo's Nest* (1975) and *Melvin and Howard* (1980). Other screenplays include *The Rose* (1979), *Shoot the Moon* (1982), *Scent of a Woman* (1992), and *Meet Joe Black* (1998).

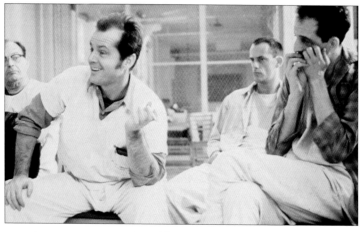

Jack Nicholson (left) starred in One Flew over the Cuckoo's Nest *(1975) with a screenplay adapted from the Ken Kesey novel by Bo Goldman and Lawrence Hauben.*

Goldman, William (1931–) American screenwriter, novelist, playwright, and nonfiction writer. A novelist prior to beginning his screenwriting career in the 1960s, he is known for crafting witty adventures and for his skill as a script doctor. Scripts include two Academy Award winners, *Butch Cassidy and the Sundance Kid* (1969) and *All the President's Men* (1976), along with *Marathon Man* (1976), *The Princess Bride* (1987), and *Hearts in Atlantis* (2001). He dissected the filmmaking process in his nonfiction book *Adventures in the Screen Trade* (1983). His brother James Goldman (1927–1998) was also a screenwriter and playwright.

Goodrich, Frances (1891–1984) and **Hackett, Albert** (1900–1995) American screenwriters and playwrights. The married team worked in several genres and adapted their Tony- and Pulitzer Prize–winning drama *The Diary of Anne Frank* (1959) for the screen. Other films include *The Thin Man* (1934), *It's a Wonderful Life* (1946), *The Pirate* (1948), and *Father of the Bride* (1950).

Gruault, Jean (1924–) French screenwriter. Associated with French New Wave director François Truffaut, Gruault achieved renown with several screenplays for Alain Resnais, including *Mon Oncle d'Amérique* (1980). Among his films are *Jules et Jim* (*Jules and Jim*) (1961), *Les Carabiniers* (1963), *L'Enfant Sauvage* (*The Wild Child*) (1970), and *L'Histoire d'Adèle H.* (*The Story of Adele H.*) (1971).

Guerra, Tonino (1920–) Italian screenwriter, poet, and painter. A creator of fairy-tale worlds, as in his script for Fellini's *Amarcord* (1973), he has worked most closely with director Michelangelo Antonioni. Screenplays for Antonioni include *L'Avventura* (1960), *La Notte* (1961), *L'Eclisse* (*Eclipse*) (1963), *Deserto Rosso* (*The Red Desert*) (1964), *Blow-Up* (1966, UK), and *Zabriskie Point* (1970, US).

Hayes, John Michael (1919–) American screenwriter. He won an Academy Award for Alfred Hitchcock's *Rear Window* (1954) and also scripted the director's *To Catch a Thief* (1955), *The Trouble with Harry* (1955), and *The Man Who Knew Too Much* (1956). Adaptations include *Peyton Place* (1957), *The Matchmaker* (1958), and *The Children's Hour* (1962).

Hecht, Ben (1893–1964) American screenwriter, journalist, novelist, and playwright. His *Underworld* (1927) took the Academy Award the first year it was awarded, and he shared his second, for *The Scoundrel* (1935), with Charles MacArthur, his primary collaborator. A prolific master of sharp and cynical dialogue, working in many genres, he wrote scripts for films such as *Scarface* (1932), *Twentieth Century* (1934), *Nothing Scared* (1937), *Gunga Din* (1939), *Spellbound* (1945), and *Monkey Business* (1952).

Hellman, Lillian (1905–1984) American playwright and dramatist. A major 20th-century dramatist, she adapted some of her plays for the screen, including *These Three* (1936), *The Little Foxes* (1941), and *The Searching Wind* (1946). She also wrote several original screenplays, including *Dead End* (1937) and *The Chase* (1966). Among her plays that have been adapted by others for the screen are *Watch on the Rhine* (1943) and *The Children's Hour* (1962).

Henry, Buck (1930–) American screen and TV writer, actor, and director. Henry's sometimes bizarre sense of humor first brought him cinema fame with his screenplay for *The Graduate* (1967). His other writing for film includes *Catch-22* (1970), *The Owl and the Pussycat* (1970), *What's Up, Doc?* (1972), and *The Day of the Dolphin* (1973).

Howard, Sidney (1891–1939) American screenwriter and playwright. One of the first Broadway playwrights to go to Hollywood with the advent of sound films, Howard became known for using dialogue with economy to support the images on the screen. His scripts, which often convey a social message, include those for *Arrowsmith* (1931) and *Dodsworth* (1936), along with his Academy Award–winning contribution to *Gone with the Wind* (1939).

Jhabvala, Ruth Prawer (1927–) German-born screenwriter and novelist working in India and England. She has portrayed the clash between East and West and, with Ismail Merchant and James Ivory, created literate adaptations of modern novels. Films include *Shakespeare Wallah* (1965, India), her Academy Award–winning *A Room with a View* (1985, UK), *Howards End* (1992, UK), *The Remains of the Day* (1993, UK), and *The Golden Bowl* (2000, UK).

Johnson, Nunnally (1897–1977) Screenwriter, producer, and director. A mainstay of 20th Century–Fox in the studio period who worked in many genres, he is best known for *The Grapes of Wrath* (1940). Films include *The Prisoner of Shark Island* (1936), *Jesse James* (1939), *How to Marry a Millionaire* (1953), and *The Dirty Dozen* (1967).

Kanin, Fay (1917–) American screenwriter and playwright. Born Fay Mitchell. Active in film since the 1950s, she and husband Michael Kanin collaborated on screenplays for *Rhapsody* (1954), *Teacher's Pet* (1958), and *The Right Approach* (1961). Since then, she has written for television. She has been a member of the board of the American Film Institute and has also been president of the Writers Guild of America and the Academy of Motion Picture Arts and Sciences.

Kanin, Garson (1912–1999) and **Gordon, Ruth** (1896–1985) American screenwriters, playwrights, authors, director (Kanin), and actress (Gordon). This husband-and-wife team hit their screenwriting peak with the comedy *Adam's Rib* (1950), starring Spencer Tracy and Katharine Hepburn. Other films written together include *A Double Life* (1947), *Pat and Mike* (1952), and *The Marrying Kind* (1952).

Kanin, Michael (1910–1993) American screenwriter. In film from the 1930s, he is best known for his witty collaboration with Ring Lardner, Jr., on the screenplay for *Woman of the Year* (1942), for which he won an Academy Award. With wife Fay Kanin, he collaborated on screenplays for several films (see above). Among his other screenwriting credits are *Centennial Summer* (1946) and *How to Commit Marriage* (1969). He was the brother of Garson Kanin.

Khouri, Callie (1957–) American screenwriter. With one Academy Award–winning film, *Thelma & Louise* (1991), Khouri made her mark. The feminist road film, in which two women strike a blow for their gender when one kills a rapist and both go on the lam, stirred controversy. Khouri also wrote *Something to Talk About* (1995).

Koch, Howard (1902–1995) American screenwriter. Koch's screenplays were often marked by social concerns, and in the 1950s he was blacklisted. Among his scripts are *Casablanca* (1942), for which he shared an Academy Award, *The Letter* (1940), *Sergeant York* (1941), *Mission to Moscow* (1943), and *The Best Years of Our Lives* (1946).

Koepp, David (1964–) American screenwriter. After writing the psychological thriller *Bad Influence* (1990), Koepp turned to comedy and action films, writing *Death Becomes Her* (1992), *Jurassic Park* (1993), and *Carlito's Way* (1993). He collaborated with his brother Stephen on *The Paper* (1994).

Kräly, Hans (1885–1950) German-born screenwriter of German and American films. He did his most notable work in the silent era, particularly in collaboration with director Ernst Lubitsch. Kräly's screenplays include *Die Austerprinzessin* (*The Oyster Princess*) (1919), *So This Is Paris* (1926), *The Student Prince* (1927), and *100 Men and a Girl* (1937).

Krasna, Norman (1909–1984) American playwright, screenwriter, producer, and director. Light, sophisticated comedy was his specialty, evidenced by *Bachelor Mother* (1939) and his Academy Award–winning *Princess O'Rourke* (1943). Other screenwriting credits include *The Richest Girl in the World* (1934), *The Devil and Miss Jones* (1941), and *Sunday in New York* (1964).

LaGravenese, Richard (1959–) American screenwriter and director. Strong female characters often mark his films. LaGravenese wrote screenplays for *The Fisher King* (1991), *The Bridges of Madison County* (1995), *The Mirror Has Two Faces* (1996), *The Horse Whisperer* (1998), and *Beloved* (1998). He directed and wrote *Living Out Loud* (1998).

Lardner, Ring, Jr. (1915–2000) American screenwriter and journalist. The son of humorist Ring Lardner, he won two Academy Awards, for *Woman of the Year* (1942) and *M*A*S*H* (1970).

"Being in the film industry and living in Hollywood is like being in the car industry and living in Detroit; you hear too much."

—

Richard LaGravenese, on why he resides in New York City

Blacklisted and imprisoned for contempt of Congress as one of the Hollywood Ten, Lardner demonstrated social concern as well as comic and dramatic skills in his scripts. Films also include *Forever Amber* (1947) and *The Cincinnati Kid* (1965).

Lederer, Charles (1910–1975) American screenwriter. He collaborated with Ben Hecht on *Kiss of Death* (1947) and *Ride the Pink Horse* (1947). For Howard Hawks, Lederer skillfully adapted comic material, with his scripts for *His Girl Friday* (1940) and *Gentlemen Prefer Blondes* (1953). He also scripted *The Thing* (1951).

Lehman, Ernest (1920–) American screenwriter and producer. From the 1950s through the 70s, the versatile Lehman was one of Hollywood's most successful writers. His output included two scripts for Alfred Hitchcock, *North by Northwest* (1959) and *Family Plot* (1976), as well as *Sabrina* (1954), *The Sweet Smell of Success* (1957), and *West Side Story* (1961). He produced some of the films he wrote, such as *Hello, Dolly!* (1969). He received and honorary Academy Award in 2001.

Loos, Anita (1893–1981) American screenwriter, playwright, and novelist. She adapted her story collection *Gentlemen Prefer Blondes* twice for the screen (1928 and 1953). A master of cinematic wit and satire, Loos wrote screenplays for more than half a century, often in collaboration with husband John Emerson. Her screenwriting credits include *His Picture in the Papers* (1916), *San Francisco* (1936), and *The Women* (1939).

MacArthur, Charles (1895–1956) American screenwriter, playwright, and director. In collaboration with Ben Hecht, he wrote several plays and screenplays, including two of Broadway and Hollywood's most pungent satires, *The Front Page* (1931) and *Twentieth Century* (1934). MacArthur, separately, wrote *The Senator Was Indiscreet* (1947). He was married to actress Helen Hayes.

Macpherson, Jeannie (1884–1946) American screenwriter and actress. The stage-trained actress entered film in 1908 and appeared regularly on screen in films that included *Enoch Arden* (1911) and *The Merchant of Venice* (1914). From 1915, she turned to screenwriting, working often with Cecil B. De Mille on films such as *Old Wives for New* (1918), *Male and Female* (1919), *The Ten Commandments* (1923), and *Reap the Wild Wind* (1942, co-adaptation only).

Maddow, Ben (1909–1992) American screenwriter, nonfiction writer, and director. Maddow crossed many genres, writing socially conscious documentaries (for which he was blacklisted) as well as feature films. Screenplays include those for *Intruder in the Dust* (1949), *The Asphalt Jungle* (1950), *Johnny Guitar* (1954), *The Savage Eye* (1960), which he also codirected and coproduced, and *The Way West* (1967).

Mahin, John Lee (1902–1984) American screenwriter. Male bonding adventure was his strong point. He worked with Howard Hawks, John Ford, and Victor Fleming. Films include *Scarface* (1932), *Red Dust* (1932), *Captains Courageous* (1937), *Heaven Knows, Mr. Allison* (1957), and *North to Alaska* (1960).

Maltz, Albert (1908–1985) American screenwriter, playwright, and short-story writer. Blacklisted and imprisoned as one of the Hollywood Ten, he wrote socially conscious documentaries as well as some notable war and crime films, including *This Gun for Hire* (1942), *Destination Tokyo* (1944), *Pride of the Marines* (1945), and *The Naked City* (1948).

Mamet, David (1947–) American playwright, screenwriter, and director. Known for his naturalistic dialogue, this playwright has adapted his own and others' work for the screen. Films include *The Verdict* (1982), *The Untouchables* (1987), *Glengarry Glen Ross* (1992), and *Wag the Dog* (1997). He sometimes directs his films, such as *Heist* (2001).

Mankiewicz, Herman J. (1897–1953) American screenwriter and journalist. Brother of Joseph L. Mankiewicz, Herman shared an Academy Award—and an ongoing controversy about who wrote what—with Orson Welles for *Citizen Kane* (1941), in which his trademark witty dialogue is featured. He also worked on *Duck Soup* (1933), *Dinner at Eight* (1933), and *The Pride of the Yankees* (1942).

Marion, Frances (1887–1973) American screenwriter. Known for dramas and melodramas, this major figure in early American cinema won Academy Awards for *The Big House* (1930) and *The Champ* (1931). Films include *Rebecca of Sunnybrook Farm* (1917), *The Son of the Sheik* (1926), *The Wind* (1928), *Anna Christie* (1930), *Dinner at Eight* (1933), and *Camille* (1937). She also wrote the book *How to Write and Sell Film Stories* (1937).

> "Most actors are, unfortunately, not good actors."
>
> —
>
> *David Mamet, 1991*

AT RIGHT:
Frances Marion, one of Hollywood's highest-paid screenwriters, collaborated with Fred De Grasac on the screenplay adaptation of The Son of the Sheik *(1926), which featured Rudolph Valentino (pictured).*

Mathis, June (1892–1927) American screenwriter. Head of Metro's script department, she helped launch the career of actor Rudolph Valentino with adaptations of *The Four Horsemen of the Apocalypse* (1918) and *Blood and Sand* (1922). She also did script editing in condensing Erich von Stroheim's lengthy *Greed* (1925). Other films include *Ben-Hur* (1926) and *Irene* (1926).

Mayer, Edwin Justus (1896–1960) American screenwriter. One of the East Coast writers lured to Hollywood by sound films, Mayer specialized in sophisticated comedy, as in *Desire* (1936) and *To Be or Not to Be* (1942). He also scripted both versions of Cecil B. De Mille's *The Buccaneer* (1938 and 1958).

Miller, Seton I. (1902–1974) American screenwriter and producer. Miller shared an Academy Award for *Here Comes Mr. Jordan* (1941) but usually wrote action films, including seven for Howard Hawks. Films include *The Dawn Patrol* (1930), *Scarface* (1932), *G-Men* (1935), and *The Adventures of Robin Hood* (1938).

Nichols, Dudley (1895–1960) American screenwriter and director. He was arguably the most highly respected screenwriter of the studio period for his literate adaptations, such as John Ford's *The Informer* (1935), for which Nichols won an Academy Award. Nichols wrote 13 other films for Ford. Credits include *Bringing Up Baby* (1938), *Stagecoach* (1939), and *Pinky* (1949).

North, Edmund H. (1911–1990) American screenwriter. Versatile but favoring action genres, North reached a pinnacle when sharing an Academy Award for *Patton* (1970). Among his other films are *One Night of Love* (1934), *The Day the Earth Stood Still* (1951), and *Sink the Bismarck!* (1960, UK).

Nugent, Frank S. (1908–1965) American screenwriter and *New York Times* film critic. He is best known for several John Ford westerns: *Fort Apache* (1948), *She Wore a Yellow Ribbon* (1949), and *Wagonmaster* (1950). He also worked on *The Quiet Man* (1952), *Mister Roberts* (1955), and *The Last Hurrah* (1958).

Peoples, David Webb (date unknown) American screenwriter, director, and editor. Although highly praised for his work on Clint Eastwood's western *Unforgiven* (1992), Peoples has specialized in science fiction since the 1980s. Films include *Blade Runner* (1982), *Leviathan* (1989), and *Soldier* (1998).

Perry, Eleanor (1915–1981) American screenwriter. Known for adaptations and her careful examination of character, Perry wrote mostly for films directed by her husband Frank Perry in the 1960s. Films include *David and Lisa* (1962), *The Swimmer* (1968), *Last Summer* (1969), and *Diary of a Mad Housewife* (1970).

Pierson, Frank (1925–) American screen and TV writer. Academy Award winner for *Dog Day Afternoon* (1975), which played off genre expectations, mixing a sex-change operation with a bank robbery. His *Cat Ballou* (1965) melded comedy with a western. Other films include *Cool Hand Luke* (1967) and *Presumed Innocent* (1990).

Pinter, Harold (1930–) British playwright and screenwriter. A major playwright who has adapted his own works and others', Pinter writes scripts that often evince an air of menace and an undercurrent of personal isolation. Films include *The Servant* (1963), *The Birthday Party* (1968), *The Homecoming* (1973), and *The French Lieutenant's Woman* (1981).

Polonsky, Abraham (1910–1999) American screenwriter and director. Polonsky showed early promise with *Body and Soul* (1947) and *Force of Evil* (1948) but was blacklisted from 1951 to 1967. A poetic sensibility and strong social consciousness often characterize his work. Other films include *Madigan* (1968) and *Tell Them Willie Boy Is Here* (1970).

Prévert, Jacques (1900–1977) French screenwriter and poet. Director Marcel Carné, for whom Prévert wrote *Les Enfants du Paradis (Children of Paradise)* (1945), called him the "poet of the French cinema." Films include *Quai des Brumes (Port of Shadows)* (1938), *Le Jour se Lève (Daybreak)* (1939), and *Les Portes de la Nuit (Gates of the Night)* (1946).

Raphaelson, Samson (1896–1983) American playwright and screenwriter. His forte was sophisticated romantic comedies, especially for Ernst Lubitsch in *One Hour with You* (1932), *Trouble in Paradise* (1932), and *The Shop Around the Corner* (1940). He also worked on Alfred Hitchcock's *Suspicion* (1941). His play *The Jazz Singer* was the basis for the 1927 film.

Ravetch, Irving (1920–) and **Frank, Harriet, Jr.** (date unknown) This husband-and-wife team, whose scripts feature strongly delineated characters, wrote three films for Martin Ritt: *Hud* (1963), *Hombre* (1967), and *Norma Rae* (1979). Other credits include *The Long, Hot Summer* (1958) and *The Sound and the Fury* (1959).

Riskin, Robert (1897–1955) American screenwriter and playwright. An Academy Award winner for *It Happened One Night* (1934), he worked often with that film's director, Frank Capra, on comedies with a social point. Films include *The Whole Town's Talking* (1935), *Mr. Deeds Goes to Town* (1936), *Lost Horizon* (1937), *You Can't Take It with You* (1938), and *Meet John Doe* (1941).

Robinson, Casey (1903–1979) American screenwriter. At Warner Bros. in the 1930s and 40s, working in many genres, Robinson helped

Twelve Monkeys, the 1995 hit science fiction thriller written by David Webb Peoples with his wife Janet, was based on French director Chris Marker's acclaimed short *La Jetée* (1962). Marker's original film is composed almost entirely of black-and-white still photographs.

establish the Errol Flynn screen persona with *Captain Blood* (1935) and scripted six Bette Davis films, including *Dark Victory* (1939) and *Now, Voyager* (1942). *Kings Row* (1942) is another of his prominent scripts.

Rodat, Robert (1953–) American screenwriter. His father, severely wounded in World War II, "has never seen a war film he likes. He thinks they're phony-baloney," Rodat told an interviewer. The result: the iconoclastic war film scripts for *Saving Private Ryan* (1998), for which he won a best original screenplay Academy Award, and *The Patriot* (2000).

Ryskind, Morrie (1895–1985) American playwright and screenwriter. He was a Pulitzer Prize–winning playwright and the recipient of two Academy Awards, for *My Man Godfrey* (1936) and *Stage Door* (1937). Ryskind established his comedy credentials with the Marx Brothers' *The Cocoanuts* (1929), *Animal Crackers* (1930), *A Night at the Opera* (1935), and *Room Service* (1938).

Salt, Waldo (1914–1987) American screenwriter. His Academy Awards for *Midnight Cowboy* (1969) and *Coming Home* (1978) marked Salt's return from the blacklist. Both films manifested the social consciousness underlying much of his work, as did *Serpico* (1973) and *The Day of the Locust* (1975).

Sargent, Alvin (1927–) American screen- and TV writer. Sargent's films show people coping with changes in their lives. In the 1970s, he hit a peak with several adaptations: *The Effect of Gamma Rays* on *Man-in-the-Moon Marigolds* (1972), *Paper Moon* (1973), *Julia* (1977), and *Ordinary People* (1980). The last two earned him Academy Awards.

Saunders, John Monk (1897–1940) American screenwriter. Originally an Army Air Corps officer, he began writing for films in the 1920s, and contributed the stories for several aviation films, including *Wings* (1927), *The Dawn Patrol* (1930), *Devil Dogs of the Air* (1935), and *Dawn Patrol* (1938). He was married to actress Fay Wray (1928–39).

Schiffman, Suzanne (1929–2001) French screenwriter. A script girl for François Truffaut in the 1960s, Schiffman became his collaborator on later films. She shared a César Award for *Le Dernier Métro (The Last Metro)* (1980) and also worked on *La Nuit Américaine (Day for Night)* (1973), *L'Histoire d'Adèle H. (The Story of Adele H.)* (1975), and *L'Homme qui Aimait les Femmes (The Man Who Loved Women)* (1977).

Schnee, Charles (1916–1963) American screenwriter and producer. Although his films include the Howard Hawks western *Red River* (1948), character rather than genre conventions

drove Schnee's scripts. *The Bad and the Beautiful* (1952) earned him an Academy Award. He also wrote *They Live by Night* (1949) and *Butterfield 8* (1960).

Schrader, Paul (1946–) American screenwriter and director. Known for psychologically probing screenplays, Schrader has worked several times with Martin Scorsese, most notably on *Taxi Driver* (1975). Other scripts include *Raging Bull* (1980), *The Last Temptation of Christ* (1988), and *Affliction* (1997), which he also directed. He is the author of *Transcendental Style in Film: Ozu, Bresson, Dreyer*.

Schulberg, Budd (1914–) American novelist and screenwriter. Son of Paramount executive B.P. Schulberg, Budd is best known for his exposé novel of Hollywood, *What Makes Sammy Run?* (1941), and for his Academy Award–winning *On the Waterfront* (1954), as well as *A Face in the Crowd* (1957). A former communist, he publicly identified other radicals during the blacklist era.

Shanley, John Patrick (1950–) American playwright and screenwriter. Coming relatively late to films from the stage, Shanley received an Academy Award for his first screenplay, *Moonstruck* (1987). But comparable success since then has eluded him in screen dramas. Subsequent scripts include *Alive* (1993) and *Congo* (1995).

Silliphant, Sterling (1918–1996) American screen and TV writer. He wrote several popular crime and disaster films and won an Academy Award for *In the Heat of the Night* (1967). Films include *Village of the Damned* (1960, UK), *Charly* (1968), *The New Centurions* (1972), *The Poseidon Adventure* (1972), *The Towering Inferno* (1974), and *The Enforcer* (1976).

Simon, Neil (1927–) American playwright and screenwriter. Broadway's most successful comedy writer has also done well writing screenplays, often adaptations of his own plays. Films include *Barefoot in the Park* (1967), *The Odd Couple* (1968), *Plaza Suite* (1971), *The Sunshine Boys* (1975), *The Goodbye Girl* (1977), and *Biloxi Blues* (1988).

Southern, Terry (1926–1995) American novelist and screenwriter. Author of the best selling novel *Candy* (1964), Southern satirized America's defense establishment in *Dr. Strangelove, or: How I Learned to Stop Worrying and Love the Bomb* (1964, UK), and collaborated on the countercultural road film *Easy Rider* (1969). Other films include *Barbarella* (1968, France/Italy) and *The Telephone* (1988).

Stewart, Donald Ogden (1894–1980) American screenwriter, humorist, and playwright. Specializing in adaptations and working frequently with director George Cukor, Stewart took an Academy Award for *The Philadelphia*

> "No one succeeds in film if he's not hustling. The first thing you think of when you wake up in the morning is, 'Who can I hustle?' And the last thing you think of before you go to bed is, 'Who can I hustle?'"
>
> —
>
> *Paul Schrader, 1998*

Story (1940). Other films include *The Barretts of Wimpole Street* (1934), *Holiday* (1938), and *Kitty Foyle* (1940). The blacklist prematurely ended his career.

Stoppard, Tom (1937–) Czechoslovakian-born British playwright and screen, radio, and TV writer. The acclaimed playwright, known for his experiments with language and structure, has specialized in adapting his writing for the screen. Films include *Brazil* (1985), *Empire of the Sun* (1987), *Rosencrantz and Guildenstern Are Dead* (1990), which he also directed, and *Shakespeare in Love* (1998).

Sullivan, C(harles) Gardner (1879–1965) American screenwriter and producer. Known as the dean of American screenwriters, Sullivan laid the groundwork for the American western with his work on William S. Hart's films, beginning with *The Passing of Two-Gun Hicks* (1914). He worked with both Thomas H. Ince and Cecil B. De Mille. Film credits range from *Civilization* (1916) to *Union Pacific* (1939).

Swerling, Jo (1897–1964) Russian-born American screenwriter, playwright, and journalist. His scripts, especially several for director Frank Capra, stressed a faith in traditional American values and optimism about the future. His work includes *Platinum Blonde* (1931), *The Whole Town's Talking* (1935), *Pride of the Yankees* (1942), and *It's a Wonderful Life* (1946).

Taradash, Daniel (1913–) American screenwriter. Dipping into many genres, Taradash's best screenplays are adaptations of works from other media. They include *Golden Boy* (1939), the Academy Award–winning script for *From Here to Eternity* (1953), *Picnic* (1956), and *Bell, Book, and Candle* (1958).

Tesich, Steve (1942–1996) Yugoslavian-born American screenwriter and playwright. *Breaking Away* (1979), a coming-of-age film in which town-and-gown tensions are worked out in a bike race, made Tesich's screen reputation. Strong characterizations marked other scripts in his brief career, including *Eyewitness* (1981) and *The World According to Garp* (1982).

Towne, Robert (1936–) American screenwriter and director. He is respected for his doctoring of others' scripts—including *Bonnie and Clyde* (1967) and *The Godfather* (1972)—as well as for the high quality of his own. Moral ambiguity underlies his best work: *The Last Detail* (1973), *Chinatown* (1974), his Academy Award winner, and *Shampoo* (1975).

Trotti, Lamar (1900–1952) American screenwriter and producer. In 20 years at Fox and 20th Century–Fox, Trotti dramatized American history with scripts for films such as *In Old Chicago* (1937), *Young Mr. Lincoln* (1939), *The Ox-Bow Incident* (1943), and *Guadalcanal Diary* (1943). He received an Academy Award for *Wilson* (1944).

Trumbo, Dalton (1905–1976) American screenwriter and novelist. Jailed as one of the Hollywood Ten, Trumbo won an Academy Award for *The Brave One* (1956) under a pseudonym. The pursuit of ideals imbues his work. Films include *Kitty Foyle* (1940), *Spartacus* (1960), *Exodus* (1960), *Lonely Are the Brave* (1962), and *Johnny Got His Gun* (1971), adapted from his own antiwar novel.

Vajda, Ernest (1887–1954) Hungarian-born American screenwriter and playwright. He is best known for romantic comedies of the early sound period, particularly for director Ernst Lubitsch, including *The Love Parade* (1929) and *Monte Carlo* (1930). Among his other films are *A Woman Rebels* (1936) and *Marie Antoinette* (1938).

Wilson, Michael (1914–1978) American screenwriter. Blacklisted after his Academy Award for *A Place in the Sun* (1951), Wilson made contributions to *Friendly Persuasion* (1956), *The Bridge on the River Kwai* (1957), and *Lawrence of Arabia* (1962) that went uncredited. He was posthumously awarded an Academy Award for *The Bridge on the River Kwai* (1957) in 1985.

Woods, Frank (1870–1939) American screenwriter and critic. Woods wrote the scenario for D.W. Griffith's first feature film, *Judith of Bethulia* (1914), and collaborated with him on *The Birth of a Nation* (1915) and *Intolerance* (1916). He later helped create story conferences and a supervising producer system at the studio Famous Players–Lasky Corporation.

Zaillian, Steven (1953–) American screenwriter and director. Zaillian worked with Steven Spielberg on two historical films about brutal oppression: *Schindler's List* (1993), for which he received an Academy Award, and *Amistad* (1997). Other films include *Awakenings* (1990), *Searching for Bobby Fischer* (1993), *A Civil Action* (1998), and *Hannibal* (2001).

Zavattini, Cesare (1902–1989) Italian screenwriter, novelist, and film critic. An exponent of neorealism in his screenplays of the 1940s and 50s, he most notably collaborated with Vittorio De Sica. Zavattini's films include *Sciuscia (Shoeshine)* (1946), *Ladri di Bicicletta (The Bicycle Thief)* (1948), *Miracolo a Milano (Miracle in Milan)* (1951), and *Umberto D* (1952).

John Travolta starred in A Civil Action *(1998), which was written and directed by Steven Zaillian.*

PRODUCERS AND BUSINESSPEOPLE

Mavericks. Gamblers. Pragmatists. The men and women who are in the business of getting movies made are all these things and more, and usually all at the same time.

In addition to producing films by such B-movie auteurs as Roger Corman, Mario Bava, Jack Hill, and Larry Cohen, Samuel Z. Arkoff and James Nicholson's American International Pictures provided a testing ground for a number of young, unproven talents. Francis Ford Coppola (*Dementia 13*, 1963), Philip Kaufman (*Fearless Frank*, 1969), Richard Donner (*Lola*, 1972), Martin Scorsese (*Boxcar Bertha*, 1972), Brian De Palma (*Sisters*, 1974), Ivan Reitman (*Cannibal Girls*, 1973), Oliver Stone (*Seizure*, 1974), James Ivory (*The Wild Party*, 1975), and George Miller (*Mad Max*, 1980) all had early pictures released by AIP.

A–C

Arkoff, Samuel Z. (1918–2001) American producer. A cofounder of American International Pictures (AIP) in 1954, Arkoff produced scores of low-budget horror and exploitation movies. With partner James Nicholson, he made *I Was a Teenage Werewolf* (1957), *The Pit and the Pendulum* (1961), *Beach Blanket Bingo* (1965), *Blacula* (1972), and *The Amityville Horror* (1979), among others. AIP launched producers Roger Corman and Bert I. Gordon.

Avnet, Jon (1949–) American producer. Born Jonathan Michael Avnet. After attending the American Film Institute on a directing fellowship, he turned to producing in the 1970s and has since gained note for his lively works. Among them are *Risky Business* (1983), *Fried Green Tomatoes* (1992), and *Up Close and Personal* (1996).

Begelman, David (1921–1995) American executive. The head of Columbia Pictures in the 1970s, Begelman oversaw many hit movies, including *Shampoo* (1974) and *Close Encounters of the Third Kind* (1977), but was fired after a drug and check-forging controversy. He took his own life in 1995.

Berg, Jeff (1948–) American agent. As chairman and CEO of the powerful talent agency International Creative Management (ICM), Berg and his team represent many of Hollywood's top stars. After attending Berkeley in the 1960s, Berg was a script reader and then an agent with Freddie Fields before helping found ICM in 1975 from the union of two former companies, Creative Management Associates and International Famous Agency.

Brillstein, Bernie (1931–) American manager and producer. A dynamic and long-standing Hollywood insider, Brillstein has managed the careers of many film and television personalities, including Jim Henson, John Belushi, and Garry Shandling. With Brad Grey, he formed the production company Brillstein-Grey in 1992, which is now a top producer of talent, film, and television projects. Credits include *The Blues Brothers* (1980), *Ghostbusters* (1984), *Dragnet* (1987), *Ghostbusters II* (1989), and *The Replacement Killers* (1998).

Broccoli, Albert "Cubby" (1919–1996) American producer. He is famous for his long-running string of James Bond films, which spanned three decades and five lead actors, from *Dr. No* (1962) to *Goldeneye* (1996). Broccoli received the Irving Thalberg Award at the 1982 Academy Awards ceremony. He also produced *Chitty Chitty, Bang Bang* (1968).

Bronfman, Edgar, Jr. (1955–) Canadian-born executive. The heir and chairman of the distilling conglomerate Seagram's, Bronfman became a major player in the entertainment world after buying MCA, Inc., parent company of Universal Pictures, in 1995 and becoming its acting chairman. Under his leadership, Universal has had box-office disappointments, such as *Meet Joe Black* (1998), and successes, such as *The Mummy* (1999).

Brown, David (1916–) American producer and executive. A former reporter and studio executive, Brown has produced hit movies across several decades with partner Richard Zanuck. He is married to Helen Gurley Brown, founder of the magazine *Cosmopolitan*. Zanuck-Brown productions include *The Sting* (1973), *Jaws* (1975), *The Verdict* (1982), *Cocoon* (1984), *Driving Miss Daisy* (1989), *The Player* (1992), and *Angela's Ashes* (1999).

Bruckheimer, Jerry (1945–) American producer. Since the 1980s, he has been a creator of high-octane blockbusters. His films were made in collaboration with producing partner Don Simpson until Simpson's death in 1996. Bruckheimer's films include *Flashdance* (1983), *Beverly Hills Cop* (1984), *Top Gun* (1986), *Days of Thunder* (1990), *Bad Boys* (1995), *The Rock* (1996), *Armageddon* (1998), *Coyote Ugly* (2000), and *Pearl Harbor* (2001).

Calley, John (1930–) American communications executive. At NBC from 1951 to 1957, he was director of nighttime programming and director of programming sales. From 1960 to 1969, he was an executive vice president and producer at Filmways Inc. At Warner Bros. from 1970 to 1975, he served as executive vice president in charge of worldwide production, and from 1975 to 1980 he was its president. After being retired for 13 years, he returned to film in 1993 to become president of United Artists and later to become chairman and CEO of Sony Pictures Entertainment.

Canton, Mark (1949–) American film executive. He has been a force at several major studios since the 1970s, when he became vice president for motion picture development at MGM. Among his positions since then have been vice president of production and later vice president for motion picture production at Warner Bros. (1980–91); chairman of Columbia Pictures (1991–94); and chairman of Columbia TriStar Motion Picture Companies (1994–96).

Cohn, Harry (1891–1958) American studio founder. Known for his brash, despotic style, this one-time vaudevillian rose to power as the first head of Columbia Pictures. After working for Carl Laemmle at Universal, Harry and brother Jack left to found what became Columbia Pictures in 1924. Under Cohn, Columbia turned out classic films from directors such as Frank Capra and showcased stars such as Rita Hayworth.

Cooper, Merian C. (1893–1973) American producer and director. With partner Ernest Schoedsack, he produced documentaries and fiction films marked by adventure in exotic places. After making a name with the documentaries *Grass* (1925) and *Chang* (1927), Cooper joined RKO to make the fiction films *The Most Dangerous Game* (1932), *King Kong* (1933), and *Little Women* (1933). In 1952, he received a special Academy Award for his contributions.

D–F

Daly, Robert (1936–) American executive. Daly started out in Hollywood at CBS, rising to become president of its entertainment division in 1977. In 1980, he and Terry Semel (1943–) were hired as cochairmen of Warner Bros. During their regime, they oversaw numerous box-office blockbusters, including the *Lethal Weapon* series and the *Batman* series.

Davis, Martin S. (1927–1999) American executive. The chairman of the parent company of Paramount Pictures in the 1980s and early 90s, Davis began as an assistant at the Samuel Goldwyn Company in the late 1940s before moving, in 1958, to Gulf & Western Industries, which acquired Paramount Pictures in 1966. He became CEO and chairman at Gulf & Western in 1983. He restructured the parent company, focusing on entertainment and publishing and changing its name to Paramount Communications. Viacom purchased Paramount in 1994.

De Laurentiis, Dino (1919–) Italian-born American producer. In Italy, De Laurentiis produced Federico Fellini's *La Strada* (1957) and founded a studio in Rome. When the studio failed, he moved to the US and produced *Death Wish* (1974), *King Kong* (1976), *Conan the Barbarian* (1982), and *Blue Velvet* (1986), among others. Unable to overcome the losses incurred by *Dune* (1985), the company folded in 1988 but was revived by De Laurentiis's daughter Raffaella. Later credits include *Hannibal* (2001).

Diller, Barry (1924–) American executive. Diller began his career at ABC and was head of program development by age 27. In 1974, he took over Paramount Pictures, resigning in 1984 to run 20th Century–Fox, where he developed Fox as a new television network. He left in 1992 to take over the QVC home-shopping network.

Disney, Walt (1901–1966) American producer, director, and studio head. The founder of the Walt Disney Company movie studio, he was a pioneer of animation and one of the most successful and influential filmmakers in history. Following on the success of the first Mickey Mouse sound cartoon, the animated short *Steamboat Willie* (1928), Disney developed his studio into an animation factory, turning out feature-length classics such as *Snow White and the Seven Dwarfs* (1937), *Fantasia* (1940), *Dumbo* (1941), and *Bambi* (1942). He moved into live action with *20,000 Leagues Under the Sea* (1954) and *The Shaggy Dog* (1959), into television with *The Mickey Mouse Club* and finally into theme parks with Disneyland in Anaheim, California, in 1955. After his death, the company continued to grow as an entertainment conglomerate, adding new theme parks and motion picture subsidiaries.

Walt Disney served as a producer or executive producer on more than 80 animated and feature films between 1937 and 1966.

Eisner, Michael (1942–) American studio chief. With colleague Jeffrey Katzenberg, he resurrected the crumbling Disney entertainment empire in the 1980s. After working at ABC and Paramount, Eisner joined Disney in 1984 as chairman and CEO of the Walt Disney Company and began producing adult live-action features while restoring Disney's animation division. The company's box-office successes under his leadership include *The Little Mermaid* (1989), *Pretty Woman* (1990), *Beauty and the Beast* (1991), and *The Lion King* (1994).

Evans, Robert (1930–) American producer and executive. He is known for quality blockbusters produced in the 1970s. At Paramount, he oversaw *Love Story* (1970), *The Godfather* (1972), *The Godfather Part II* (1974), and *Chinatown* (1974). As an independent producer, he made *Urban Cowboy* (1980), *The Cotton Club* (1984), and more recently, *Sliver* (1993) and *The Out-of-Towners* (1999).

Ted Field produced the surprise hit Bill & Ted's Excellent Adventure *(1989), which featured Alex Winter and Keanu Reeves.*

Field, Ted (1952–) American producer and executive. Heir to the Marshall Field's fortune, Field began producing as a young man, founding Interscope Communications, a producer of films and music for Warner Bros. He began with *Revenge of the Nerds* (1984) and continued with such films as *Outrageous Fortune* (1987), *Three Men and a Baby* (1987), *Bill & Ted's Excellent Adventure* (1989), *Arachnophobia* (1990), and *The Hand That Rocks the Cradle* (1992).

Fields, Freddie (1923–) American agent and executive. The founder of Creative Management Associates, Fields sold his company in 1975, when it became part of International Creative Management (ICM). From 1977 to 1983, he produced for Paramount, where he made *Looking for Mr. Goodbar* (1977) and *American Gigolo* (1980), then served as president of MGM from 1983 to 1985. He then became an independent producer of films such as *Glory* (1989).

Fox, William (1879–1952) Hungarian-born American studio founder. Born Wilhelm Fried, he supported his immigrant family while still a child. He built a chain of penny arcades and began producing movies in 1912, forming the Fox Film Corporation in 1915. Fox fell on hard times during the Depression and was forced to sell his shares in the company to a group of bankers in 1930; the company merged with the production company 20th Century to become 20th Century–Fox in 1935. Fox himself later declared bankruptcy and was imprisoned for bribing a judge in his bankruptcy hearing.

Freed, Arthur (1894–1973) American producer. He was instrumental in developing the trademark MGM musical in the 1940s. A songwriter and vaudevillian, Freed was hired by MGM in 1929. Musicals he produced for the studio include *The Wizard of Oz* (1939), *Meet Me in St. Louis* (1944), *An American in Paris* (1951), and *Singin' in the Rain* (1952).

G–J

Geffen, David (1943–) American agent and executive. Geffen began representing musical acts in the early 1970s. He built his agency into a thriving record company, which he sold to MCA in the early 1990s for over $1 billion. He cofounded DreamWorks SKG with Steven Spielberg and Jeffrey Katzenberg in 1994.

Golan, Menachem (1929–) Israeli-born American producer. With partner and cousin Yoram Globus, Golan ran Cannon Pictures, producing formulaic action and horror movies. His films include *The Happy Hooker Goes to Hollywood* (1980), several *Death Wish* sequels, *Bolero* (1984), *Delta Force* (1986), *Night of the Living Dead* (1990), and *Delta Force One: The Last Patrol* (1999).

Goldwyn, Samuel (1882–1974) Polish-born American producer. Born Shmuel Gelbfisz; renamed Samuel Goldfish. From humble beginnings as a penniless immigrant, he moved from glove making to film production, cofounding the Goldwyn Pictures Corporation with Edgar Selwyn in 1916. Goldwyn adopted his name from the company's, which was a blend of Goldfish and Selwyn. The company merged with two others in 1924 to become Metro-Goldwyn-Mayer, but Goldwyn himself was not part of the deal, having been forced out by the stockholders in 1922. Instead, he formed Samuel Goldwyn Productions; as its head, he was a fiercely independent producer of lavish films. His producing credits include *Wuthering Heights* (1939), *The Best Years of Our Lives* (1946), *Hans Christian Andersen* (1952), *Guys* *and Dolls* (1955), and *Porgy and Bess* (1959). His son Samuel Goldwyn, Jr., is also a producer; his grandson Tony Goldwyn is an actor.

Goldwyn, Samuel, Jr. (1926–) American producer and distributor. The son of producer Samuel Goldwyn, he worked as a producer for J. Arthur Rank and Universal. In 1974, he took over the Samuel Goldwyn Company and began producing and distributing medium-budget movies of generally high quality. Films include *The Golden Seal* (1983), *A Prayer for the Dying* (1987), *Mystic Pizza* (1988), and *The Preacher's Wife* (1996).

Gordon, Lawrence (1936–) American producer and executive. Gordon began at ABC as an assistant to Aaron Spelling before moving into film in 1973, where he worked as an executive at Screen Gems and American International Pictures (AIP). He was the president of 20th Century–Fox from 1984 to 1986 before forming Largo Entertainment with his brother Charles. Producing highlights include *Hooper* (1978), *48HRS.* (1982), *Predator* (1987), *Die Hard* (1988), *Field of Dreams* (1989), and *Boogie Nights* (1997).

Grade, Lord Lew (1907–1998) Russian-born British producer and executive. Born Louis Winogradsky. He was a flamboyant media tycoon whose most famous productions were the television miniseries *Jesus of Nazareth* and the series *The Muppet Show*. He became chairman of the European division, Embassy Communications, in 1982, and formed the Grade Company in 1985. Producing credits include *The Cassandra Crossing* (1977) and *Raise the Titanic* (1980).

Grauman, Sid(ney Patrick) (1879–1950) American film exhibitor. He built the legendary Egyptian and Chinese theaters in Hollywood, which are frequently the sites of star-studded premieres. Grauman's Chinese Theatre opened in 1927 and was sold in 1973 to exhibitor Ted Mann, becoming Mann's Chinese Theatre. The theater is famous for the hand- and footprints stars have left in concrete outside its Hollywood Boulevard doors.

Grazer, Brian (1951–) American producer. As partner with director Ron Howard in the production company Imagine Entertainment, he has produced many commercially successful movies. Credits include *Night Shift* (1982), *Splash* (1983), *Parenthood* (1989), *Backdraft* (1991), *The Paper* (1994), *Apollo 13* (1995), *The Nutty Professor* (1996), *Liar Liar* (1997), *Bowfinger* (1999), *Dr. Seuss', How the Grinch Stole Christmas* (2000) and *A Beautiful Mind* (2001).

Guber, Peter (1939–) American producer and executive. Trained as a lawyer, he worked his way up at Columbia Pictures from an entry-level position in 1968 to studio chief by the early 1970s. He left to become an independent producer, cofounding Casablanca Records and Filmworks in 1976. In 1980, he formed Polygram Pictures and established a partnership with Jon Peters. From 1989 to the early 90s, he and Peters jointly headed Columbia Pictures Entertainment, renamed Sony Pictures Entertainment during their tenure. Producing credits include *The Deep* (1977), *An American Werewolf in London* (1981), *The Witches of Eastwick* (1987), *Rain Man* (1988), and *Batman* (1989).

Hearst, William Randolph (1863–1951) American newspaper magnate and occasional film producer. The founder of the media corporation that still bears his name, he began producing films in the late 1910s as star vehicles for his mistress Marion Davies. His production company, Cosmopolitan, was an unsuccessful venture and folded in the 1920s. Hearst's story is famously captured in Orson Welles's *Citizen Kane* (1941).

Hughes, Howard (1905–1976) American industrialist, aviator, and producer. He began producing films as a young man; credits include *The Front Page* (1931) and *Scarface* (1932). He gave the sultry actress Jane Russell her screen debut in *The Outlaw* in 1943, bought and sold the RKO studio and teamed with director and screenwriter Preston Sturges. Despite his many successes, he died a wealthy recluse at the Desert Inn in Las Vegas, Nevada.

Hurd, Gale Ann (1955–) American producer. After attending Stanford, Hurd worked for producer and director Roger Corman at New World Pictures. She teamed with her husband, director James Cameron, to produce *The Terminator* (1984), *Aliens* (1986), *The Abyss* (1989), and *Terminator 2: Judgment Day* (1991). Other producing credits include *The Waterdance* (1992), *The Ghost and the Darkness* (1996), *Dante's Peak* (1997), and *Armageddon* (1998).

Jaffe, Stanley R. (1940–) American producer and executive. He worked as an executive at Paramount and Columbia before going independent in 1979 and producing *Kramer vs. Kramer* (1979). With Sherry Lansing, he formed Jaffe-Lansing Productions in 1984, which produced such hits as *Fatal Attraction* (1987) and *Black Rain* (1989). Jaffe also produced *School Ties* (1992), *Madeline* (1998), and *I Dreamed of Africa* (2000).

Joffe, Charles H. (1929–) American agent and producer. With partner Jack Rollins, he has produced most of director Woody Allen's films from the 1960s to the present. These include *Take the Money and Run* (1969), *Play It Again, Sam* (1972), *Annie Hall* (1977), which won a best picture Academy Award, *Manhattan* (1979), *Hannah and Her Sisters* (1986), *Crimes and Misdemeanors* (1989), *Mighty Aphrodite* (1995), and *Small Time Crooks* (2000).

Gale Ann Hurd certainly likes to keep it in the family. Besides producing *The Terminator* (1984), *Aliens* (1986), and *The Abyss* (1989) while married to director James Cameron, she produced 1992's *Raising Cain* for second husband Brain De Palma, as well as *Armageddon* (1998), which was cowritten by third spouse Jonathan Hensleigh.

K–M

Katzenberg, Jeffrey (1950–) American executive. Katzenberg trained under Barry Diller at Paramount before joining Michael Eisner, chairman of the Walt Disney Company, to whom Katzenberg reported as chairman of Walt Disney Studios from 1984 to 1994. The two recast the ailing movie studio by expanding the live-action offerings and revamping Disney's animated releases. Katzenberg left to form DreamWorks SKG in 1994 with director Steven Spielberg and record and film mogul David Geffen. Katzenberg sued Disney for what he claimed was his share of its success; the two parties reached a settlement in 1999.

Kerkorian, Kirk (1918–) American financier. A billionaire investor whose interests have spanned entertainment, auto manufacturing, and the casino industry, Kerkorian has owned a controlling interest in MGM/UA for decades. He continues to expand his empire of investments and Las Vegas businesses, playing a daily role in the operations of his companies.

Kopelson, Arnold (1935–) American producer. Since the 1980s, he has been known for producing popular films, including *Platoon* (1986), which won a best picture Academy Award. Other credits include *The Fugitive* (1993), *Outbreak* (1995), *The Devil's Advocate* (1997), and *U.S. Marshals* (1998). He often coproduces with his wife Anne Kopelson.

Ladd, Alan, Jr. (1937–) American producer and executive. The son of actor Alan Ladd, he began his career as a talent agent before joining the executive ranks of 20th Century–Fox in 1973. After serving as president of the studio from 1976 to 1979, he formed the Ladd Company production firm. He headed MGM from 1989 to 1993 before returning to producing such films as *The Brady Bunch Movie* (1995), *Braveheart* (1995), and *The Man in the Iron Mask* (1998).

Laemmle, Carl (1867–1939) German-born American founder of Universal Pictures. Laemmle first managed a clothing store but moved into nickelodeons, eventually forming his own production company in 1909. Less than a decade later, he had merged his company into Universal Pictures, where he was president until he sold his interest in 1935. Credited with launching the star system of promoting actors by name as film personalities, Laemmle built Universal City and gave Irving Thalberg and Harry Cohn their starts. His son Carl, Jr., (1908–1979) became the head of production at 21 and in that capacity oversaw Universal's famous monster movies, including *Frankenstein* (1931) and *Dracula* (1931).

Lansing, Sherry (1944–) American producer and executive. After beginning in Hollywood as an actress and model, Lansing worked as an executive at MGM and then at Columbia Pictures. Appointed president of 20th Century–Fox in 1980, she left two years later to form Jaffe-Lansing Productions with coproducer Stanley Jaffe. Her producing credits include *Fatal Attraction* (1987), *The Accused* (1988), and *Indecent Proposal* (1993). She is married to director William Friedkin.

Lasky, Jesse L. (1880–1958) American studio founder. At one time a reporter and a fortune seeker in the Alaska gold rush, Lasky became a talent promoter and cofounded the Jesse L. Lasky Feature Play Company in 1913. The company merged with Adolph Zukor's Famous Players in 1916, forming Famous Players–Lasky Corporation, which became known by the name of its distribution arm, Paramount Pictures Corporation. Under the economic pressures of the Great Depression, Lasky was forced out in 1932, but he remained an independent producer for many years, making, among other films, *Sergeant York* (1941), *The Adventures of Mark Twain* (1944), and *Rhapsody in Blue* (1945).

Lear, Norman (1922–) American television and film producer. Known predominantly as a television producer, Lear created the seminal sitcom *All in the Family* in the early 1970s. Film producing credits include *Come Blow Your Horn* (1963), *The Night They Raided Minsky's* (1968), *The Princess Bride* (1987), and *Fried Green Tomatoes* (1991).

Levine, Joseph E. (1905–1987) American producer and distributor. As a distributor, Levine founded Embassy Pictures in the 1950s to import *Godzilla* movies and other low-budget foreign action pictures. He branched into production and financed films such as Federico Fellini's *8 ½* (1963) and Jean-Luc Godard's *Contempt* (1963). As an independent producer, Levine was responsible for *The Carpetbaggers* (1964), *The Graduate* (1967), *Carnal Knowledge* (1971), and *A Bridge Too Far* (1977).

Lewton, Val (1904–1951) Russian-born American producer, writer, and director. A protégé of David O. Selznick's, then a production executive at the RKO studio in the 1930s, Lewton went on to produce a string of stylish low-budget horror pictures for RKO, including *Cat People* (1942), *The Body Snatcher* (1945), and *Bedlam* (1946).

Lippert, Robert L. (1928–1976) American producer. A B-movie producer during the 1950s and 60s, he is credited with scores of westerns, horror films, and science fiction adventures. Among his most notable films are *The Last of the Wild Horses* (1948), *The Quatermass Experiment* (1956, UK), *The Return of Mr. Moto* (1965), and *The Curse of the Fly* (1965).

"Our formula is simple. A love story, three scenes of suggested horror, and one of actual violence. Fade out. It's all over in less than 70 minutes."

—

Val Lewton, 1940s

Loew, Marcus (1870–1927) American distributor and studio founder. The son of Austrian immigrants and a school dropout at age nine, he began purchasing penny arcades in the early years of the century. In partnership with Adolph Zukor, he expanded to movie theaters and owned about 400 by 1912. His company, Loew's Theatrical Enterprises, bought the studio Metro Pictures in 1920 to produce films for the theaters. In 1924, he acquired a controlling stake in the Goldwyn Pictures Corporation and Louis B. Mayer Pictures and merged the companies to form Metro-Goldwyn-Mayer. He was the father of film executives Arthur M. and David L. Loew.

Mancuso, Frank (1933–) American executive. Mancuso spent nearly 30 years at Paramount Pictures, eventually heading the studio. Having begun his career as a film buyer, he joined Paramount in 1962 as a local film booker. He became chairman in 1984, retiring seven years later in 1991. His son Frank, Jr., is a producer.

Mann, Ted (1916–2001) American film exhibitor and producer. The owner of several theater chains, including National General, Mann moved into production in the late 1960s with *The Illustrated Man* (1969). Other films include *Brubaker* (1980) and *Krull* (1983).

Marshall, Frank (1946–) American producer and director. With wife Kathleen Kennedy, he has produced some of Hollywood's biggest hits, many for Steven Spielberg's production company Amblin Entertainment. Marshall's producing credits include *Raiders of the Lost Ark* (1981), *E.T.: The Extra-Terrestrial* (1982), *The Color Purple* (1985), *Who Framed Roger Rabbit?* (1988), *Cape Fear* (1991), *Congo* (1995), and *The Sixth Sense* (1999).

Mayer, Louis B. (1885–1957) Russian-born American studio founder. Born Eliezer (Lazar) Mayer. He was a scrap dealer, theater owner, film distributor, and producer before helping to found Metro-Goldwyn-Mayer (MGM). In 1924, he merged his production company with two other firms to form MGM and became a vice president and general manager. Though outspoken and brash, Mayer had a keen sense for audience taste and helped shape MGM into a profitable powerhouse. He remained the head of the studio during its golden age, until replaced by former aide Dore Schary in 1951. At one time the highest-paid person in the US (at $1.25 million a year), Mayer received a special Academy Award in 1950 for "distinguished service."

Medavoy, Mike (1941–) Chinese-born American producer and executive. Raised in China and Chile, he began his film career in the Universal mailroom. As an agent, he packaged *The Sting* (1973) and *Jaws* (1975); later, he joined United Artists as a senior vice president, turning out *One Flew over the Cuckoo's Nest* (1975), which won a best picture Academy Award. He left in 1978 to cofound the studio Orion Pictures; he remained there through its release of *The Silence of the Lambs* (1991).

Melnick, Daniel (1934–) American producer and executive. Melnick worked as a TV producer at CBS and ABC before becoming the head of production at MGM. He left MGM to run Columbia in 1978 and then moved into independent production. Films include *That's Entertainment I & II* (1974 and 1976), *All That Jazz* (1979), *Footloose* (1984), *Roxanne* (1987), *L.A. Story* (1991), and *Blue Streak* (1999).

Merchant, Ismail (1936–) Indian-born producer of Indian, British, and American films. With director James Ivory, he has made a series of upscale costume dramas, many of which have won Academy Awards. The Merchant Ivory partnership first gained prominence in 1979 with *The Europeans;* the team's subsequent films include *The Bostonians* (1984), *A Room with a View* (1986), *Howards End* (1992), *The Remains of the Day* (1993), *Surviving Picasso* (1996), and *The Golden Bowl* (2000).

Milchan, Arnon (1949–) Israeli-born American producer. After successfully staging plays in Europe, Milchan moved to Hollywood, where he produced Martin Scorsese's *The King of Comedy* (1983). Other producing credits include *Once Upon a Time in America* (1984), *Brazil* (1985), *The War of the Roses* (1989), *Pretty Woman* (1990), *JFK* (1991), *Under Siege* (1992), *Free Willy* (1993), *Natural Born Killers* (1994), *and L.A. Confidential* (1997).

Morris, William (c. 1860–1932) American agent. He was the founder of the world's oldest talent agency, the William Morris Agency (WMA), formed in 1898. After Morris's death, his son William, Jr., ran the company for more than 30 years. The agency has represented many of the biggest stars of Hollywood, as well as many successful writers and directors. WMA is still one of Hollywood's top agencies, along with International Creative Management (ICM) and Creative Artists Agency (CAA).

Murdoch, Rupert (1931–) Australian-born American media mogul. Murdoch began his empire with several Australian newspapers before expanding to Europe. From there, he purchased media and publishing companies, acquiring 20th Century–Fox in 1985. Under Murdoch's ownership, the studio has turned out such hits as *Home Alone* (1990) and *Independence Day* (1996). Murdoch was instrumental in developing the Fox television network, as well as its myriad cable and satellite channels.

Anthony Hopkins and Diane Venora starred in Surviving Picasso *(1996), a Merchant Ivory film produced by Ismail Merchant.*

N–R

Neufeld, Mace (1928–) American producer. After attending Yale, Neufeld worked at the Dumont TV network. His first big film hit was *The Omen* (1976). With partner Robert Rehme, he produced high-concept techno-thrillers in the 1980s and 90s. Neufeld's producing credits include *No Way Out* (1987), *The Hunt for Red October* (1990), *Patriot Games* (1992), *The Saint* (1997), *Lost in Space* (1998), and *The General's Daughter* (1999).

Obst, Lynda (1950–) American producer. After working as an associate producer on *Flashdance* (1983), Obst produced films for Paramount, Disney, and Columbia. Producing credits include *The Fisher King* (1991), *Sleepless in Seattle* (1993), *One Fine Day* (1996), *Contact* (1997), and *The Siege* (1998).

Ovitz, Michael (1946–) American agent and power broker. The longtime head of Creative Artists Agency (CAA), Ovitz was considered the ultimate deal maker in the 1980s and 90s. He left the William Morris Agency in 1975 to cofound Creative Artists Agency, which he built into one of the most prestigious talent agencies in Hollywood, with a top-drawer client list that allowed him to wield enormous power in negotiations. He was instrumental in putting together movie packages and consulting on studio affairs. He left in 1995 to become president of Walt Disney, a post he left in 1997. After prospecting various fields, Ovitz returned to agenting, cofounding Artists Management Group in 1999.

Peters, Jon (1947–) American producer. A former hairdresser to the stars, Peters rose to become one of Hollywood's top producers with partner Peter Guber. His producing credits include *A Star Is Born* (1976), *Caddyshack* (1980), *Flashdance* (1983), *The Color Purple* (1985), *The Witches of Eastwick* (1987), *Rain Man* (1988), *Batman* (1989), and *Wild Wild West* (1999). From 1989 to 1991, he was cochairman, with Guber, of Columbia Pictures.

Pollock, Thomas (1943–) American film executive. In the film community since the 1960s, he has been business manager for the American Film Institute's marketing division and in 1971 founded the law firm Pollock Bloom and Dekom to serve film clients. From 1973 to 1981, he was chairman of Filmex, and in 1986 he became chairman of MCA's Universal motion picture group. He was later named vicechairman of MCA Inc. In 1996 he was named chairman-designate of AFI's board of trustees.

Puttnam, Sir David (1941–) British producer and executive. Puttnam began as an agent for photographers, then became a producer, collaborating with directors such as Alan Parker and Ridley Scott. He ran Columbia Pictures for 13 months in the 1980s. Producing credits include *Midnight Express* (1978), *Chariots of Fire* (1981), *The Killing Field* (1984), *The Mission* (1986), *Memphis Belle* (1990), *Being Human* (1993), and *My Life So Far* (1999).

Rank, Lord J(oseph) Arthur (1888–1972) British media mogul. Rank's wealthy upbringing allowed him to invest in films at an early age. Soon he was a major player in British film, controlling all aspects of production and owning film processing labs, movie theaters, and studios alike. He remained chairman of the Rank Organization until 1969. He was made a baron in 1957.

Rehme, Robert G. (1935–) American producer and executive. He headed Avco Embassy from 1979 to 1981 and New World Pictures during the 1980s. In 1989, he began teaming with Mace Neufeld to produce a string of action films and techno-thrillers. After *Flight of the Intruder* (1990), Rehme went on to make *Necessary Roughness* (1991), *Patriot Games* (1992), *Beverly Hills Cop III* (1994), *Clear and Present Danger* (1994), *Lost in Space* (1998), and *Bless the Child* (2000). He became president of the Academy of Motion Picture Arts and Sciences in 1997.

Roach, Hal (1892–1992) American producer and director. As head of his own production company, Roach helped shape the careers of such popular comic film stars as Laurel and Hardy and Our Gang, or the Little Rascals. A bit player first, Roach became a director-producer, then focused almost entirely on producing. He developed the *Little Rascals (Our Gang)* in the 1920s, and sold the rights to MGM in 1938. He later turned to television and, in 1984, was honored with a lifetime achievement Academy Award.

Rollins, Jack (1914–) American producer. After cofounding a talent agency with Charles Joffe, he and Joffe became the producers of director Woody Allen's films, including *Take the Money and Run* (1969), *Annie Hall* (1977), *Manhattan* (1979), *Hannah and Her Sisters* (1986), *Crimes and Misdemeanors* (1989), *Mighty Aphrodite* (1995), and *Small Time Crooks* (2000). Other films produced by Rollins include *Arthur* (1981).

Ross, Steven J. (1927–1992) American executive. Born Steven Jay Rechnitz. As head of the conglomerate Kinney National Service, he acquired the floundering studio Warner Bros. in 1969. Renaming the parent company Warner Communications in 1971, he focused on film, television, and publishing. Under his direction, Warner Bros. reemerged as a major studio. Time Inc. acquired Warner Communications in 1989.

Roth, Joe (1948–) American producer, executive, and director. In 1987, he cofounded the independent

---

"The problem is that I've always been a better businessman than artist."

—

Joe Roth, 2001

production company Morgan Creek; in 1989, he took over 20th Century–Fox's film production. He resigned in 1993 to form Caravan Pictures, then moved to Disney in 1994 to head film production there. His producing credits include *Bachelor Party* (1983), *Streets of Gold* (1986), which he also directed, *Young Guns* (1988), *Major League* (1989), *Angels in the Outfield* (1994), and *While You Were Sleeping* (1995).

Rudin, Scott (1958–) American producer. A successful producer of blockbuster films in the 1990s, he began his career as a casting assistant for Broadway, before moving to Los Angeles to work at 20th Century–Fox, where he rose through the ranks to become president in 1986. He resigned a year later to become an independent producer. His producing credits include *The Addams Family* (1991), *The Firm* (1993), *Clueless* (1995), *In and Out* (1997), *The Truman Show* (1998), *Sleepy Hollow* (1999), and *Shaft* (2000).

S–T

Schary, Dore (1905–1980) American producer, executive, screenwriter, director, and playwright. As a screenwriter in the 1930s, he shared an Academy Award for writing *Boys Town* (1938). He was a producer for MGM in the early 1940s, then worked for David O. Selznick. After a year at RKO (1947–48), he returned to MGM, where he became chief of production and, in 1951, replaced Louis B. Mayer as studio head. His films were marked by quality and lavishness. After being fired from MGM in 1956, he wrote and produced the play *Sunrise at Campobello* and became an independent film producer. He directed the film *Act One* (1963).

Schenck, Joseph M. (1876–1961) Russian-born American producer and studio founder. Schenck worked his way up in the drugstore business before branching into amusement parks. He and his brother Nicholas (1880–1969) joined Marcus Loew's film exhibition organization, but Joseph left in 1917 to become an independent producer. He was elected chairman of United Artists in 1924, and in 1935 cofounded 20th Century–Fox, where he was chairman until the early 1940s. Schenck was awarded an honorary Academy Award in 1952 for "long and distinguished service."

Schneer, Charles H. (1920–) American producer. He specialized in producing science fiction and fantasy classics, many of which featured special effects by stop-motion expert Ray Harryhausen. Films include *It Came from Beneath the Sea* (1955), *The Seventh Voyage of Sinbad* (1958), *Mysterious Island* (1961), *Sinbad and the Eye of the Tiger* (1977), and *Clash of the Titans* (1981).

Schulberg, B.P. (Benjamin Percival) (1892–1957) American producer and executive. Formerly a reporter, he began writing screenplays and film publicity in 1911. He went on to work as an executive at the studio Famous Players and launch a career as an independent producer; in the latter capacity, he discovered actress Clara Bow, whom he publicized as the "It" girl. Producing credits include *The Broken Wing* (1923), *Old Ironsides* (1926), *Crime and Punishment* (1935), and *Bedtime Story* (1941). He was the father of Academy Award–winning screenwriter Budd Schulberg (1914–).

Selwyn, Edgar (1875–1944) American producer and studio cofounder. He began his Hollywood career as an actor and writer. In 1912, he cofounded the All-Star Feature Film Company, which merged five years later with the production company of Samuel Goldfish (later Samuel Goldwyn) to form the Goldwyn Pictures Corporation; it in turn merged with two other companies in 1924 to become Metro-Goldwyn-Mayer (MGM). Selwyn worked as a writer and director for MGM in the 1930s and 40s.

Selznick, David O(liver) (1902–1965) American producer and executive. Selznick was one of Hollywood's brightest lights for decades, making his mark with first-rate films. After working for his father Lewis Selznick (1870–1933), a film distributor, he joined MGM in 1926 as an assistant story editor. Moving from MGM to Paramount in 1927, and from there to RKO in 1931, he returned to MGM in 1933 to produce *Dinner at Eight* (1933) and *Anna Karenina* (1935). In 1936, he founded his own company, Selznick International Pictures. There he produced *A Star Is Born* (1937), *The Prizoner of Zenda* (1937), *Gone with the Wind* (1939), which was released by MGM, *Spellbound* (1945), and *The Third Man* (1949), among others. He was married to actress Jennifer Jones from 1949.

Producer David O. Selznick oversaw the signing of contracts by Leslie Howard, Vivien Leigh, and Olivia de Havilland for Gone with the Wind *(1939).*

Selznick, Myron (1898–1944) American producer and agent. The brother of producer David O. Selznick, he worked at the Selznick Company, owned by his father Lewis, running its production arm at age 21. When the company folded in 1923, under competition from Adolph Zukor and Louis B. Mayer, Myron became one of Hollywood's top talent agents.

Shaw, Sir Run Run (1907–) Chinese producer. Famous for his Hong Kong martial-arts films, he had several hits in the US in the 1970s, including *Five Fingers of Death* (1973) and *The Brotherhood* (1976).

Shaye, Robert K. (1939–) American producer and executive. He founded New Line Cinema in 1967. Under his leadership, the independent distribution and production company became famous for low-budget science fiction and horror films, including the *Nightmare on Elm Street* series, beginning in 1984, *Critters* (1986), and *The Hidden* (1987), along with other types of films, such as John Waters's bizarre comedy *Polyester* (1981). In 1991, New Line spun off the subsidiary Fine Line to make more serious films, such as *Glengarry Glen Ross* (1992) and *The Player* (1992). The company was sold to Turner Communications in 1993, with Shaye remaining in charge as New Line's chairman and CEO. Other films include *Frequency* (2000).

Sheinberg, Sidney Jay (1935–) American executive and producer. After graduating from Columbia Law School, Sheinberg joined the entertainment firm MCA Inc., which acquired the Universal movie studio in 1962. Sheinberg rose through the ranks to become MCA's president and COO in 1973. In 1995, after Universal's sale to Seagram's, Sheinberg left that position to become an independent producer of films such as *McHale's Navy* (1997) and *For Richer or Poorer* (1997).

Shutt, Buffy (1950–) American executive. On staff at Paramount from the 1970s, she rose to become president of marketing in the 80s. She later headed marketing at Columbia Pictures and TriStar Pictures and, in 1994, was made president of marketing at Universal Pictures.

George Stevens, Jr., produced the WWII saga The Thin Red Line *(1998), featuring Adrien Brody (pictured) and a star-studded cast.*

Silver, Joel (1952–) American producer. After New York University film school, Silver learned the trade under producer Lawrence Gordon. Since the 1980s, as head of the production company Silver Pictures, he has specialized in blockbuster action films. His credits include *Weird Science* (1985), *Predator* (1987), the *Lethal Weapon* series, the *Die Hard* series, *Demolition Man* (1993), *Conspiracy Theory* (1997), *The Matrix* (1999), and *Romeo Must Die* (2000).

Simpson, Don (1943–1996) American producer. He was president of worldwide production at Paramount in the early 1980s, then partnered with Jerry Bruckheimer to form Simpson-Bruckheimer Productions. The team was responsible for some of the biggest-grossing movies of the decade. Producing credits include *Flashdance* (1983), the *Beverly Hills Cop* series, *Top Gun* (1986), *Days of Thunder* (1990), *Bad Boys* (1995), *Crimson Tide* (1995), and *The Rock* (1996).

Spiegel, Sam (1903–1985) American producer born in Jaroslau, Austria (now Jaroslaw, Poland). A truly independent producer, Spiegel created some of the screen's greatest films. He started as a translator working for Universal in Germany but left when the Nazis rose to power. He became an independent producer in Hollywood in the 1940s. His films include *The African Queen* (1951), *On the Waterfront* (1954; best picture Academy Award), *The Bridge on the River Kwai* (1957; best picture Academy Award), *Suddenly, Last Summer* (1959), *Lawrence of Arabia* (1962; best picture Academy Award), and *The Last Tycoon* (1976). He received the Irving G. Thalberg Award in 1963.

Stark, Ray (1914–) American producer and agent. A onetime talent agent, he has been producing films independently since 1966, including several adaptations of Neil Simon plays. Films include *Funny Girl* (1968), *The Way We Were* (1973), *Funny Lady* (1975), *The Goodbye Girl* (1977), *Brighton Beach Memoirs* (1986), *Peggy Sue Got Married* (1986), *Biloxi Blues* (1988), *Steel Magnolias* (1989), and *Lost in Yonkers* (1993).

Steel, Dawn (1946–1997) American executive and producer. After she dropped out of college, Steel's employment history included jobs as a receptionist and a writer for *Penthouse* magazine. Joining Paramount in the late 1970s, she worked her way up to become president of production in 1985. She left two years later to become president of Columbia Pictures, the first woman to head a major motion picture studio. After Columbia was acquired by Sony in 1989, Steel left to become an independent producer whose credits include *Cool Runnings* (1993) and *City of Angels* (1998).

Stevens, George, Jr. (1932–) American producer and executive. The son of director George Stevens, he assisted his father on a number of films before heading the production unit of the U.S. Information Agency. He went on to become the founding director of the American Film Institute from its inception in 1967 until 1979. As a producer, his films include *America at the Movies* (1976), *George Stevens: A Filmmakers' Journey* (1984), and *The Thin Red Line* (1998).

Stringer, Howard (1942–) Welsh-born American communications executive. With CBS television since the mid-1960s, he has served as an executive producer of documentary broadcasts; a producer-director-writer of *CBS Reports*; and executive producer of the *CBS Evening News* with Dan Rather. He was appointed executive vice president of CBS News Division in 1984; president of CBS News in 1986; president of the CBS/Broadcast Group in 1988; chairman and CEO of Tele-TV in 1995; and later president of the Sony Corporation of America.

Tanen, Ned (1931–) American executive and producer. Tanen joined the entertainment company MCA in 1954, moving up to vice president by 1968. He left to produce independently in 1972 but joined Universal for six years beginning in 1976. As the president of Paramount from 1984 to the 1990s, Tanen oversaw *Sixteen Candles* (1984), *The Breakfast Club* (1985), and *St. Elmo's Fire* (1985). Since resigning from Paramount, he has independently produced such films as *Guarding Tess* (1994) and *Cops and Robbersons* (1994).

Thalberg, Irving G. (1899–1936) American producer. Legendary producer and studio executive known for his meteoric rise, successful track record, and high-quality films. He was working for Carl Laemmle, head of Universal, by the age of 18 and was promoted to head of production by age 20. In 1923, he joined the studio of Louis B. Mayer, which became absorbed into MGM in 1924. There Thalberg presided under studio chief Mayer as a vice president and supervisor of production. He is celebrated for his richly produced films and for inventing the system of testing films through audience sneak previews prior to general release. Producing credits include *Ben-Hur* (1926), *Anna Christie* (1930), *Freaks* (1932), *Mutiny on the Bounty* (1935), *A Night at the Opera* (1935), and *The Good Earth* (1937). He died of pneumonia at the age of 37. The Academy Award for "most consistent high level of production achievement by an individual producer" is named the Irving G. Thalberg Award in his honor.

Turner, Ted (Robert Edward) (1938–) American media mogul. After buying an obscure UHF television station in Atlanta, Georgia, he built a vast media empire. Turner Broadcasting System bought the foundering MGM/UA in 1986, then sold off everything but its library of classic films, which Turner retained to use as programming for his cable stations. Turner became a movie executive when he acquired New Line Cinema and Castle Rock Films in 1993. Turner's company was itself bought by Time-Warner in 1996.

V–Z

Vajna, Andy (1944–) Hungarian-born American producer. With Mario Kassar, he cofounded Carolco in 1976 and went on to produce a number of commercially successful action films. Vajna left Carolco in 1989 to found Cinergi. His producing credits include *First Blood* (1982), *Rambo* (1985), *Angel Heart* (1987), *Total Recall* (1990), *Die Hard with a Vengeance* (1995), *Evita* (1996), and *The Thirteenth Warrior* (1999).

Valenti, Jack (1921–) American executive. A Harvard-trained advertising executive, Valenti served as an adviser to President Lyndon Johnson in the 1960s. Since 1966, he has been president of the Motion Picture Association of America (MPAA), the trade association that represents the Hollywood studios. In that capacity, in 1968 he helped to launch the MPAA system for rating the content of films and has been the public face of the industry for decades. He is also president of two other trade groups, the Motion Picture Export Association (MPEA) and the Alliance of Motion Picture and Television Producers (AMPTP).

Wallis, Hal B. (1899–1986) American producer and executive. A high-school dropout and traveling salesman, he joined the Warner Bros. publicity department in 1923, rising to become executive producer in charge of production by the 1930s. He left Warner Bros. in 1944 to form his own independent production company. Films he oversaw at Warner Bros. include *Jezebel* (1938), *Sergeant York* (1941), *The Maltese Falcon* (1941), and *Casablanca* (1943). His independent productions include *Come Back, Little Sheba* (1952), *King Creole* (1958), *Becket* (1964), *Barefoot in the Park* (1967), *True Grit* (1969), and *Rooster Cogburn* (1975).

Warner, Jack L. (1892–1978) American studio founder. A straight-talking, hard-nosed businessman, Warner is a Hollywood legend. He emigrated from Poland to Ohio with his family, including his brothers Harry (1881–1958), Albert (1884–1967), and Sam (1888–1927). The brothers began with retail stores, then moved into the nickelodeon business in 1903. Expanding from film exhibition to production and distribution, they founded the studio Warner Bros. in 1923. With *The Jazz Singer* (1927), the first talkie, they launched the sound film era and made their studio a major Hollywood player. As chief of production, Jack Warner presided over the studio's golden age in the 1930s and 40s. Harry and Albert sold out in the 1950s, but Jack remained to run the studio until 1967, when he became an independent producer.

Wasserman, Lew (1913–) American agent and executive. A longtime agent and Hollywood deal maker, Wasserman entered the trade under Jules Stein at the talent agency MCA in 1936. He remained involved with MCA for decades, as it grew into an entertainment conglomerate. The gentle but firm Wasserman negotiated deals for stars such as Jimmy Stewart at MCA, before the company acquired Universal in 1962 and moved into film production. Wasserman headed MCA/Universal until 1995, when the company was sold to Seagram's, and remained on the board until 1998.

> "One of my chief functions is to be an observer and sense and feel the moods of the public."
>
> —
>
> *Irving G. Thalberg, 1929*

Weinstein, Bob (1954–) and **Weinstein, Harvey** (1952–) American producers and executives. The Weinstein brothers founded Miramax in 1979 to distribute foreign and low-budget pictures. Their eye for quality and commercial hits proved so sharp that they began producing films in 1989. Productions include *sex, lies and videotape* (1989), *The Crying Game* (1992), the Scream series, *Pulp Fiction* (1994), *The English Patient* (1996), *Good Will Hunting* (1997), *The Cider House Rules* (1999), *Chocolat* (2000), and *The Others* (2001). Miramax was acquired as an autonomous arm of Disney in 1993.

Bob and Harvey Weinstein of Miramax Films produced Good Will Hunting *(1997), which was written by co-stars Ben Affleck (left) and Matt Damon (right).*

> "If you try to superimpose your own taste and feel the public has to like something because you like it, you will fail. I was fortunate."
>
> —
> *Adolph Zukor, 1973*

Winkler, Irwin (1931–) American producer. Winkler has produced films with partner Robert Chartoff since the 1960s. Producing credits include *They Shoot Horses, Don't They?* (1969), *The Gambler* (1974), *Rocky* (1976; best picture Academy Award), *New York, New York* (1977), *Raging Bull* (1980), *The Right Stuff* (1983), *GoodFellas* (1990), and *Life as a House* (2001).

Wolper, David (1928–) American producer and film executive. Founder in the 1960s of Wolper Productions, he produced acclaimed television documentaries before entering film. Among his film credits are *If It's Tuesday, This Must Be Belgium* (1969); *Visions of Eight* (1973), a documentary about the Munich Olympics; *Imagine: John Lennon* (1988); and *L.A. Confidential* (1997). He has also produced numerous television miniseries, movies, series, and specials, including the Emmy Award–winning miniseries *Roots* (1977). In 1985, he received the Jean Hersholt Humanitarian Award.

Zanuck, Darryl F. (1902–1979) American studio founder and producer. He was the head of production at Warner Bros. from 1929 to 1933

but left to cofound 20th Century Pictures, which merged with Fox in 1935 to become 20th Century–Fox. As the firm's chief of production from 1935 to 1956, he helped turn it into a major studio with a reputation for quality. He was later an independent producer of films such as *The Sun Also Rises* (1957) and *The Longest Day* (1962), and returned to head 20th Century–Fox again from the 1960s through 1971.

Zanuck, Richard Darryl (1934–) American producer and executive. The son of legendary studio founder Darryl F. Zanuck, he worked for his father at 20th Century–Fox in various positions, including president from 1969 to 1970. Afterward, he became an independent producer, in partnership with David Brown from the 1970s to 1988, and in partnership with his wife Lili Fini Zanuck thereafter. His producing credits with Brown include *The Sting* (1973), *Jaws* (1975), *The Verdict* (1982), and *Cocoon* (1985). Later credits include *Driving Miss Daisy* (1989), *Mulholland Falls* (1996), *Deep Impact* (1998), *Rules of Engagement* (2000), and *Planet of the Apes* (2001).

Zimbalist, Sam (1904–1958) American producer. A producer at MGM from 1936 to his death, he is best known for overseeing adventure movies and epics. Films include *Tarzan Escapes* (1936), *Tortilla Flats* (1942), *King Solomon's Mines* (1950), *Quo Vadis?* (1951), and *Ben-Hur* (1959).

Zukor, Adolph (1873–1976) Hungarian-born American studio founder. He moved from the fur business to penny arcades in 1903 and from there to film production and distribution. In 1912, he founded the company Famous Players, which specialized in theatrical adaptations. The company merged with the Jesse L. Lasky Feature Play Company in 1916, becoming the Famous Players–Lasky Corporation, with Zukor as president. By the 1920s, it was known as Paramount, taking the name from a distribution company it had absorbed. As president, Zukor helped shape Paramount into one of Hollywood's major studios, with a reputation for high quality. But in 1936, Depression-era economic pressures forced Zukor to step down and become chairman. He received a special Academy Award in 1949 for his "contribution to the industry."

CINEMATOGRAPHERS AND DIRECTORS OF PHOTOGRAPHY

The way we see a film is decided by a cinematograper, who uses an intimate knowledge of photographic science to paint memorable visions of light.

Alcott, John (1931–1986) British cinematographer. He is best known for his work with Stanley Kubrick on *2001: A Space Odyssey* (1968), *A Clockwork Orange* (1971), *Barry Lyndon* (1975; best cinematography Academy Award), and *The Shining* (1980). Other films include *No Way Out* (1987), which was dedicated to him.

Almendros, Nestor (1930–1992) Spanish-born cinematographer of international films. He started his film career as a director of documentaries in Cuba, then worked with Eric Rohmer and François Truffaut on several French New Wave films. In the United States, he filmed *Kramer vs. Kramer* (1979; Academy Award nomination for best cinematography), *Sophie's Choice* (1982), *Places in the Heart* (1984), and *Days of Heaven* (1978; Academy Award for best cinematography). He has also won the French César Prize for *The Last Metro* (1980, France) and was decorated by the Legion of Honor in France (1984).

Alton, John (1901–1996) Hungarian-born American cinematographer. He began his career as a lab technician at MGM, then shot several films in Europe and South America before returning to Hollywood to hone his style on a series of B pictures. His stunning high contrast black-and-white photography helped define the style of 1940s film noir. Films include: *He Walked By Night* (1949), *The Big Combo* (1955), and *Elmer Gantry* (1960). He shared the Academy Award for best color photography on *An American in Paris* (1951). His book, *Painting with Light*, is still considered an invaluable text on cinematography.

August, Joseph (1890–1947) American cinematographer. He began his work in Hollywood on silent films and then shot several John Ford films, including *The Informer* (1935). He helped found the American Society of Cinematographers in 1918.

Bitzer, G.W. (Billy) (1872–1944) American cinematographer. He started work with the Biograph company in the 1910s. He is best known for his groundbreaking camera work on D.W. Griffith's films, including *The Birth of a Nation* (1915) and *Intolerance* (1916). Together they created such technical innovations as the close-up, the iris, the fade, back lighting, and the dolly.

Coutard, Raoul (1924–) French cinematographer. He made his debut with Jean-Luc Godard on *Breathless* (1960). He began his work in the French Military Information Service and also worked for *Time* and *Paris-Match*. His use of a handheld camera and natural light helped create a distinctive look for French New Wave filmmakers in the 1960s. Films include *Jules and Jim* (1961), *Pierrot le Fou* (1965), *Weekend* (1968), and *Wild Innocence* (2001).

Di Palma, Carlo (1925–) Italian cinematographer. He gained experience working with Michelangelo Antonioni on *Deserto Rosso (Red Desert)* (1964) and *Blow-Up* (1966). Beginning in the 1980s, now in the US, he became Woody Allen's cameraman, filming *Hannah and Her Sisters* (1986), *Radio Days* (1987), and *Mighty Aphrodite* (1995).

Edelson, Arthur (1891–1970) American cinematographer. He filmed over 129 features, including *The Maltese Falcon* (1941) and *Casablanca* (1942).

Francis, Freddie (1917–) British cinematographer. He began his work with Michael Powell and Emeric Pressburger in the 1940s and 50s. Twice winning the Academy Award for best cinematography, on *Sons and Lovers* (1960) and *Glory* (1989), he worked on films including *The French Lieutenant's Woman* (1981) and *The Straight Story* (1999). He also directed a number of B horror films in Britain.

"If Mr. Griffith asked for some effect, whether a fadeout or whatever, I tried one way or another to produce what he wanted. When it worked successfully, we were hailed as innovators."

—

Billy Bitzer, in Billy Bitzer, His Story (1973), on D. W. Griffith and the early days of film

351

Polish-born American cinematographer Janusz Kaminski won an Academy Award for his work on Schindler's List *(1993).*

James Wong Howe used several unorthodox methods to achieve his celebrated visual style, including wearing roller skates to photograph the boxing scenes in *Body and Soul* (1947) and pushing his cameraman around in a wheelchair for *He Ran All the Way* (1951).

Freund, Karl (1890–1969) Bohemian-born cinematographer, active in German and American films. He gained experience working for Pathé in France in the early 1900s. He is best known for his work on classic German films, such as *The Last Laugh* (1924), *Variety* (1925), and *Metropolis* (1927), and for his work on American horror films, such as *Dracula* (1931). He won an Academy Award for best cinematography for *The Good Earth* (1937). He also directed a few films, such as *The Mummy* (1932). His artistic use of special lighting effects, camera angles, and camera movement is noteworthy.

Fujimoto, Tak (1939–) Japanese-American cinematographer. He began his career as an apprentice to Haskell Wexler on commercials and is best known as Jonathan Demme's main cameraman. His style is characterized by drenched color and distinctive lighting techniques. Films include *Ferris Bueller's Day Off* (1986), *Married to the Mob* (1988), *The Silence of the Lambs* (1991), *Philadelphia* (1993), and *The Sixth Sense* (1999). He won the National Film Critics award for cinematography for *Devil in a Blue Dress* (1994).

Garmes, Lee (1898–1978) American director of photography. A cameraman from before 1920, he photographed dozens of films, including *The Garden of Allah* (1927), *Shanghai Express* (1932; best cinematography Academy Award), *Scarface* (1932), *Since You Went Away* (1944, co-phot.), *The Desperate Hours* (1955), and *A Big Hand for the Little Lady* (1966). He also filmed a portion of *Gone with the Wind* (1939) but was uncredited. He helped develop lighting techniques and props, including the crab dolly.

Harlan, Russell (1903–1974) American cinematographer. After starting his film career as a stuntman, he worked the camera from the mid-1930s through the 60s. He is known for his work on Howard Hawks's films. Other films include *Witness for the Prosecution* (1957) and *To Kill a Mockingbird* (1963).

Howe, James Wong (1899–1976) Chinese-born American cinematographer. After leaving his career as a professional boxer, he worked for Cecil B. De Mille in the 1920s. In his work for Warner Bros., he used handheld cameras and deep focus, bringing a distinctive look to his films. He won best cinematography Academy Awards for *The Rose Tattoo* (1955) and *Hud* (1963).

Kaminski, Janusz (1959–) Polish-born American cinematographer. He is known for his work with Steven Spielberg on such films as *Schindler's List* (1993; Academy Award for best cinematography), *Amistad* (1997), and *Saving Private Ryan* (1998; Academy Award for best cinematography). He is married to actress Holly Hunter.

Kaufman, Boris (1906–1980) Polish-born cinematographer of French and American films. He worked for the National Film Board of Canada and the US government on propaganda shorts prior to the 1950s, when he became a Hollywood cinematographer. He is known for his work with French director Jean Vigo and American director Sidney Lumet. Kaufman's distinctive style included location shooting and innovative lighting, creating a feeling of spontaneity in his films. Films in France include *Zéro de Conduite* (*Zero for Conduct*) (1933) and *L'Atalante* (1934, co-phot.); films in the US include *On the Waterfront* (1954; Academy Award for best cinematography), *12 Angry Men* (1957), and *Splendor in the Grass* (1961). He is the brother of Soviet directors Dziga Vertov and Mikhail Kaufman.

Kovács, László (1933–) Hungarian-born American cinematographer. He began his career filming B movies such as *Hell's Angels on Wheels* (1967). After shooting the counterculture classic *Easy Rider* (1969), he worked on more mainstream films, including *Ghostbusters* (1984) and *My Best Friend's Wedding* (1997). He is known for his creation of color effects and atmosphere. His name is also familiar as the alias of Jean-Paul Belmondo's character in *Breathless* (1959), Jean-Luc Godard's homage to American film.

Martelli, Otello (1903–) Italian cinematographer. He is known for his work on Italian neorealist films of the 1940s, particularly those of Roberto Rossellini, including *Paisà* (*Paisan*) (1946). In the 1950s, he shot films for Federico Fellini, such as *La Dolce Vita* (1960).

Nykvist, Sven (1922–) Swedish cinematographer. He became famous for his work on Swedish director Ingmar Bergman's films, such as *Cries and Whispers* (1973) and *Fanny and Alexander* (1983; Academy Award for best cinematography). US films include *The Unbearable Lightness of Being* (1988), *Chaplin* (1992, UK/US), and *Sleepless in Seattle* (1993). He received a Lifetime Achievement Award from the American Society of Cinematographers in 1996.

Pratt, Roger (date unknown) Cinematographer. His films include *Batman* (1989), *12 Monkeys* (1995), and *The End of the Affair* (1999; Academy Award for best cinematography).

Rosson, Harold (Hal) (1895–1988) American director of photography. Originally a film actor, he turned to camera work in the mid-1910s, with silent camera credits including *Oliver Twist* (1916) and *Zaza* (1923). Major sound cinematographic works include *The Garden of Allah* (1936; special Academy Award), *Captains Courageous* (1937), *The Wizard of Oz* (1939), and *Singin' in the Rain* (1952). He was married to actress Jean Harlow (1933–35). His brother was silent film director Arthur Rosson (1889–1960).

Ruttenberg, Joseph (1889–1983) Russian-born American cinematographer. He began his career as a newspaper reporter and photographer. He worked on newsreels and silent films prior to the 1930s, when he became a leading cameraman at MGM, shooting such features as *The Great Waltz* (1938), *Mrs. Miniver* (1942), *Somebody Up There Likes Me* (1956), and *Gigi* (1958). These four films won Academy Awards for best cinematography.

Shamroy, Leon (1901–1974) American cinematographer. After photographing experimental films, he moved to features, making a name for himself with his lighting techniques. He used both black-and-white and color well, creating a distinctive look for Fox into the 1960s. He was also one of the pioneers of the CinemaScope process. Four of his films won Academy Awards for best cinematography: *The Black Swan* (1942), *Wilson* (1944), *Leave Her to Heaven* (1945), and *Cleopatra* (1963).

Storaro, Vittorio (1940–) Italian-born cinematographer of international films. He gained international fame for his work with Bernardo Bertolucci. He has won three Academy Awards for best cinematography, for *Apocalypse Now* (1979, US), *Reds* (1981, US), and *The Last Emperor* (1987, Italy/UK/China). Other films include *Last Tango in Paris* (1973, France/Italy), *1900* (1977, Italy/France/Germany), and *Dick Tracy* (1990, US).

Struss, Karl (1891–1981) American cinematographer. He began his career in New York as a commercial photographer. He went to Hollywood in 1919 and worked for Cecil B. De Mille. His innovative use of filters to transform the appearance of actors is evident in *Ben-Hur* (1926) and *Dr. Jekyll and Mr. Hyde* (1931). He also worked for D.W. Griffith and was one of the leading cameramen for Paramount. He shared an Academy Award for best cinematography for *Sunrise* (1927).

Toland, Gregg (1904–1948) American cinematographer. Known for his skills in lighting and optics, he worked primarily for independent producer Samuel Goldwyn. His use of deep focus in *Citizen Kane* (1941) and *The Best Years of Our Lives* (1941) brought him a reputation as one of the most creative cameramen of his day. He won an Academy Award for best cinematography for *Wuthering Heights* (1939).

Totheroh, Roland (1890–1967) American cinematographer. Joined Essanay Studios in 1910. He is best known for his work on comedian Charlie Chaplin's films, including *The Kid* (1921), *The Gold Rush* (1925), *City Lights* (1931), and *Modern Times* (1936).

Unsworth, Geoffrey (1914–1978) British-born cinematographer of British and American films. Known for his color photography, he also helped create several technical improvements for the camera. Films include *2001: A Space Odyssey* (1968, UK), *Cabaret* (1972; best cinematography Academy Award), *Murder on the Orient Express* (1974, UK), and *Superman* (1978; dedicated to his memory).

Wexler, Haskell (1926–) American cinematographer, director, and producer. After beginning his career with documentaries and educational films in the 1940s and 50s, he moved to feature films. Cinematography credits include *The Thomas Crown Affair* (1968), *One Flew over the Cuckoo's Nest* (1975), *Days of Heaven* (1978), and *Mulholland Falls* (1996). He has won two Academy Awards for best cinematography, for *Who's Afraid of Virginia Woolf?* (1966) and *Bound for Glory* (1976).

Willis, Gordon (1931–) American cinematographer. He began his career as a photographer in the US Air Force. He is perhaps best known for his work with Woody Allen, including *Annie Hall* (1977), *Interiors* (1978), *Manhattan* (1979), and *Zelig* (1983), for which he earned an Academy Award nomination for best cinematography. Other films include *The Parallax View* (1975), *All the President's Men* (1976), *Presumed Innocent* (1990), and *The Devil's Own* (1997). He was also nominated for an Academy Award for his work on *The Godfather Part III* (1990).

Zsigmond, Vilmos (1930–) Hungarian-born American cinematographer. He escaped to the United States with friend László Kovács after photographing the Hungarian Revolution of 1956. He has won numerous honors, including an Academy Award for best cinematography for *Close Encounters of the Third Kind* (1977) and nominations for *The Deer Hunter* (1978) and *The River* (1984). Other films include *McCabe and Mrs. Miller* (1971) and *Deliverance* (1972).

Gregg Toland, an American cinematographer, was known for his use of deep focus, shown here in The Best Years of Our Lives *(1941).*

PRODUCTION DESIGNERS AND ART DIRECTORS

The best production designers and art directors work hand-in-hand combining story, setting, and theme to make a film's surroundings seem as vital a character as the on-screen personalities who inhabit it.

"You know, as an artist, you very often instinctively design, and to intellectually justify your creativity is very difficult."

—

Ken Adam, 2001

Adam, Ken (1921–) German-born British art director and production designer. He started his film career as a draftsman for the movie *This Was a Woman* (1947). He did production design for numerous films, including *Dr. Strangelove* (1963), *Chitty Chitty Bang Bang* (1968), and several James Bond films. He won two Academy Awards for art direction, for *Barry Lyndon* (1975) and *The Madness of King George* (1994).

Boyle, Robert (1910–) American art director and production designer. From his first art directing credit, *Saboteur* (1942), he began a long association with director Alfred Hitchcock and was the art director for several of his films, including *Shadow of a Doubt* (1943), *North by Northwest* (1959), and *The Birds* (1964). Among his other art directing credits are *The Thomas Crown Affair* (1968) and *The Shootist* (1976).

Brandenstein, Patrizia von (1948–) American art director and production designer. She began in the 1970s as a costume designer on *Saturday Night Fever* (1977). By the 1980s, she had become a respected production designer for films such as *Silkwood* (1983), *A Chorus Line* (1985), *Working Girl* (1988), and *Shaft* (2000). She won an Academy Award for best art direction for *Amadeus* (1984) and was nominated for *Ragtime* (1981).

Craig, Stuart (1942–) Art director. He worked on both British and American productions during the 1980s and shared Academy Awards for best art direction for *Gandhi* (1982) and *Dangerous Liaisons* (1988). Other films include *The Mission* (1986) and *Notting Hill* (1999).

Day, Richard (1896–1972) Canadian art director. He began his career in 1918 working with Erich von Stroheim and stayed with him through the early 1930s. A well-respected designer, he was known for his creativity and the realism of his sets. He won seven Academy Awards for art direction, for *The Dark Angel* (1935), *Dodsworth* (1936), *How Green Was My Valley* (1941), *This Above All* (1942), *My Gal Sal* (1942), *A Streetcar Named Desire* (1951), and *On the Waterfront* (1954).

Ferretti, Dante (1943–) Italian art director. A leading production designer for European films of the 1970s and 80s, he is best known for his work with Pier Paolo Pasolini and Federico Fellini. Films include *Il Decamerone (The Decameron)* (1971), *E la Nave Va (And the Ship Sails On)* (1983), *The Name of the Rose* (1986, US), and *Bringing Out the Dead* (1999, US).

Furst, Anton (1944–1991) British-born American production designer. He started his career as an architect and designed laser shows for rock concerts. He is best known for his darkly imaginative sets in *Batman* (1989), for which he received an Academy Award for art direction. He also worked on *Full Metal Jacket* (1987) and *Awakenings* (1990).

Garwood, Norman (date unknown) British-born production designer of British and American films. He is known for his imaginative sets that incorporate touches of surrealism and horror. Films include *Time Bandits* (1981), *The Princess Bride* (1987), *Glory* (1989), and *Entrapment* (1999). His work on *Brazil* (1985) earned him an Academy Award nomination for best art direction.

Gibbons, Cedric (1893–1960) Irish-born American art director. Hailed as one of the most influential designers in American cinema history, he also created the Academy Award statuette. As a supervising art director at MGM for 32 years beginning in 1924, he was credited with some 1,500 films and nominated for Academy Awards for best art direction 37 times. He won Academy Awards for 11 of his films, including *Gaslight* (1944), *The Yearling* (1946), *An American in Paris* (1951), and *Julius Caesar* (1956).

Korda, Vincent (1896–1979) Hungarian-born art director of British and American films. Trained in art schools all over Europe, he worked in Britain with his brothers, the directors Alexander and Zoltán Korda, and also worked on Hollywood films. He is best known for his art direction on epic films such as *The Thief of Bagdad* (1940; Academy Award for best art direction), *Jungle Book* (1942; Academy Award nomination for best art direction), and *The Longest Day* (1962; Academy Award nomination for best art direction).

Leven, Boris (1900–1986) Russian-born American art director. After studying painting and architecture, he went to work for Paramount in 1933 as a sketch artist and moved to Fox two years later. As a freelance designer, he earned nine Academy Award nominations for best art direction and won an Academy Award for *West Side Story* (1961). Other films include *Giant* (1956) and *Fletch* (1985).

Menzies, William Cameron (1896–1957) American art director, director, and producer. The first art director to receive a production design credit on a film, he was known for his creativity and artistic vision. He developed a distinctive look for many Hollywood silent films and early talkies. He won the first Academy Award in the "interior design" category, for *The Dove* and *Tempest* (1928). He also earned a special Academy Award for "outstanding achievement in the use of color and the enhancement of dramatic mood" for his work on *Gone with the Wind* (1939). He directed a few films, such as *Things to Come* (1936, UK), for which he served as co–art director, and was an associate producer of *Around the World in 80 Days* (1956).

Platt, Polly (1939–) American production designer, screenwriter, and producer. She began her design work on films by Peter Bogdanovich during the 1960s. She was nominated for an Academy Award for best art direction for *Terms of Endearment* (1983). Other films include *Paper Moon* (1973), *A Star Is Born* (1976), and *The Witches of Eastwick* (1987). She wrote the screenplay for *Pretty Baby* (1978) and produced several films in the 1980s.

Reynolds, Norman (1935–) British-born American production designer and art director. After serving as art director on *Star Wars* (1977; Academy Award for best art direction/set decoration), he worked as the production designer on *The Empire Strikes Back* (1980), *Raiders of the Lost Ark* (1981; Academy Award for best art direction/set decoration), *Return of the Jedi* (1983), *Alien 3* (1992), and *Mission: Impossible* (1996).

Sanders, Thomas (date unknown) Production designer and art director. He worked on *Hook* (1991) as art director and then served as the production designer for *Dracula* (1992), *Braveheart* (1995), and *Saving Private Ryan* (1998). He received Academy Award nominations for best art direction for *Dracula* and *Saving Private Ryan*.

Sylbert, Richard (1928–2002) American art director and production designer. Having trained with William Cameron Menzies, he worked on numerous films from the 1960s to the 90s, including *The Graduate* (1967), *Rosemary's Baby* (1968), *Shampoo* (1975), *Reds* (1981), *The Cotton Club* (1984), *Dick Tracy* (1990), and *My Best Friend's Wedding* (1997). He won an Academy Award for art direction for *Who's Afraid of Virginia Woolf?* (1966).

Tavoularis, Dean (1932–) American production designer. He started his film work doing animation for Disney. His first feature as a production designer was *Bonnie and Clyde* (1967), but he is best known for his work with Francis Ford Coppola. His films include *Little Big Man* (1970), *The Godfather* (1972), *The Godfather Part II* (1974; Academy Award for best art direction), *Apocalypse Now* (1979; Academy Award nomination for best art direction), *The Outsiders* (1983), and *Tucker: The Man and His Dream* (1988; Academy Award nomination for best art direction).

Welch, Bo (date unknown) Production designer. He is known for his creative work on such Tim Burton films as *Beetlejuice* (1988) and *Edward Scissorhands* (1990). He also served as production designer for *The Lost Boys* (1987) and *Men in Black* (1997; Academy Award nomination).

Wheeler, Lyle (1905–1990) American art director. In film from the mid-1930s, he created (or cocreated) memorable sets for an array of films, including *A Star Is Born* (1936), *Laura* (1944), *Twelve O'Clock High* (1949), *Gentlemen Prefer Blondes* (1953), *Peyton Place* (1957), and *Marooned* (1969). He won Academy Awards for art direction for *Gone with the Wind* (1939), *Anna and the King of Siam* (1946), *The Robe* (1953), and *The Diary of Anne Frank* (1957). In 1947, he directed the art department at 20th Century–Fox.

Art director Vincent Korda won an Academy Award for the impressive sets he created for The Thief of Bagdad *(1940).*

355

COSTUME DESIGNERS

The setting may be the distant past or the far-flung future. Costume designers bring research, practicality, and good old-fashioned imagination to the business of dressing actors for their parts.

Adrian (1903–1959) American costume designer. Born Adrian Adolph Greenberg. After early work with Cecil B. De Mille, he became the chief costume designer for MGM through the 1930s, dressing such stars as Greta Garbo, Jean Harlow, and Joan Crawford. Films include *The Forbidden Woman* (1927), *Anna Christie* (1930), *Grand Hotel* (1932), *Anna Karenina* (1935), *Ninotchka* (1939), and *The Wizard of Oz* (1939).

Aldredge, Theoni V. (1932–) Greek-born American costume designer. Born Theoni Vachlioti. She started her career designing for the theater and was a leading designer in Hollywood and on Broadway in the 1960s. Her films include *The Great Gatsby* (1974; Academy Award for best costume design), *The Eyes of Laura Mars* (1978), *The Rose* (1979), *Annie* (1982), and *Moonstruck* (1987). She has also won Tony Awards for her work on Broadway.

Banton, Travis (1894–1958) American costume designer. Educated at Columbia University and the Art Students League, he was a New York fashion designer before coming to Hollywood. Between 1924 and 1939, he designed the diaphanous gowns of Claudette Colbert and Carole Lombard for Paramount, but became best known for creating the signature look of Marlene Dietrich. He was named head stylist at Universal. Films include *The Scarlet Empress* (1934) and *My Man Godfrey* (1936).

Gherardi, Piero (1909–1971) Italian costume designer. He is well known for his work on Federico Fellini's films in the late 1950s and early 60s. He earned Academy Awards for best costume design for *La Dolce Vita* (1961) and *8 ½* (1963). He also worked on set decoration for several films and was nominated for an Academy Award for set decoration/art direction for *La Dolce Vita*.

Head, Edith (1907–1981) American costume designer. She worked for Paramount beginning in the late 1930s and then moved to Universal in 1967. She has won more Academy Awards than any other female personality, with eight Oscars for best costume design to her credit, including awards for *All About Eve* (1950), *Roman Holiday* (1953), *Sabrina* (1954), and *The Sting* (1973). She also worked on *Rear Window* (1953), *Breakfast at Tiffany's* (1961), *Butch Cassidy and the Sundance Kid* (1969), and *The Great Gatsby* (1974).

Jeakins, Dorothy (1914–1995) American costume designer. After working in the theater, she designed gowns and other costumes for many major Hollywood film productions, including *The Ten Commandments* (1956), *The Music Man* (1962), and *The Way We Were* (1973). She won Academy Awards for costume design for *Joan of Arc* (1948), *Samson and Delilah* (1950), and *The Night of the Iguana* (1964).

Louis, Jean (1907–1997) French-born American costume designer. Born Jean Louis Berthault. He worked for Paramount and Universal before establishing his own company. He created glamorous Hollywood designs for Rita Hayworth, Lana Turner, and Kim Novak. His costumes were featured in such films as *The Lady from Shanghai* (1948), *Born Yesterday* (1951), and *A Star Is Born* (1954). Nominated for best costume design more than ten times, he won an Academy Award for *The Solid Gold Cadillac* (1956). Perhaps his most famous design is the strapless gown worn by Hayworth in *Gilda* (1946).

Myers, Ruth (date unknown) British-born costume designer of American films. She began her work in the theater and moved to film in 1969, collaborating with Gene Wilder in the 1970s. Her film credits include *The World's Greatest Lover* (1977), *The Accidental Tourist* (1988), *Emma* (1996), *L.A. Confidential* (1997), and *Proof of Life* (2000).

Orry-Kelly (1897–1964) Australian-born American costume designer. Born John Kelley, he came to America to be an actor, but wound up creating titles for silent films. He went to Hollywood in the early 1930s and became a celebrated designer of gowns for such stars as Bette Davis. He worked for several of the major Hollywood studios, winning three Academy Awards for best costume design for *An American in Paris* (1951, shared), *Les Girls* (1957), and *Some Like It Hot* (1959).

Plunkett, Walter (1902–1982) American costume designer. His most famous creations are the costumes for *Gone with the Wind* (1939). He was nominated for seven Academy Awards for costume design and shared one for *An American in Paris* (1951). Other films include *Stagecoach* (1939), *The Three Musketeers* (1948), and *Singin' in the Rain* (1952).

"Oh, that sweater, I'm so sick of that thing."

—

Costume designer Jean Louis on Lana Turner's sweater, one of his most memorable creations

Costume designer Travis Banton, pictured here with Carole Lombard, designed glamorous gowns for many Hollywood legends, including Marlene Dietrich and Claudette Colbert.

Costume designer Sandy Powell has clothed two very different versions of Queen Elizabeth I: Dame Judi Dench for *Shakespeare in Love* (1998) and flamboyant writer Quentin Crisp in *Orlando* (1992).

Powell, Anthony (date unknown) American costume designer. He won Academy Awards for best costume design for *Travels with My Aunt* (1972), *Death on the Nile* (1978), and *Tess* (1980). Other films include *Hook* (1991), *Indiana Jones and the Temple of Doom* (1984), and *Indiana Jones and the Last Crusade* (1989).

Powell, Sandy (1965–) British costume designer of British and American films. She is best known for her work on period films, including *Orlando* (1992), *Wings of the Dove* (1997), *Shakespeare in Love* (1998), and *The End of the Affair* (1999).

Rose, Helen (1904–1985) American costume designer. She designed costumes in Hollywood from the 1940s though the 60s, primarily with MGM. She won Academy Awards for her costumes for *The Bad and the Beautiful* (1952) and *I'll Cry Tomorrow* (1955) and was nominated for ten other films. She also designed Grace Kelly's wedding dress in 1956.

Runkle, Theodora von (1940–) American costume designer and actress. She started her career as an assistant to Dorothy Jeakins. She is best known for her work on *Bonnie and Clyde* (1967). Her contemporary costumes in the 1960s were trendsetting, but she is also a celebrated designer of period costumes. She has been nominated for three Academy Awards for best costume design. Other films include *The Thomas Crown Affair* (1968), *The Godfather Part II*, (1974), *New York, New York* (1977), and *Peggy Sue Got Married* (1986).

Sharaff, Irene (1910–1993) American costume designer. Trained in both New York and Paris, she is well known for her work on Hollywood musicals. She was nominated for 16 Academy Awards for best costume design, winning or sharing five, including those for the ballet sequence in *An American in Paris* (1951), *The King and I* (1956), and *West Side Story* (1961). She also won solo awards for the costumes in *Cleopatra* (1963) and *Who's Afraid of Virginia Woolf?* (1966).

MAKEUP ARTISTS AND HAIRSTYLISTS

Makeup artists can make the young seem old, the living look dead, and the very beautiful appear even more so. These talented painters and sculptors practice their art on the human form itself.

In addition to designing the video's elaborate and extensive monster makeup, Rick Baker makes a cameo appearance in Michael Jackson's "Thriller." He plays a limping zombie whose arm falls off.

AT RIGHT: *The magic of makeup artist Rick Baker added pounds to Eddie Murphy for his 1996 film* The Nutty Professor.

Archibald, Jan (date unknown) Hairstylist on British and American films. She worked on various films of the 1980s and 90s, including *Orlando* (1992), *Sense and Sensibility* (1995), and *Wings of the Dove* (1997). She was nominated for an Emmy Award for her work on the television miniseries *Joan of Arc* (1999).

Baker, Rick (1950–) American makeup artist. He is best known for his monster makeup and ability to transform actors' faces, such as Eddie Murphy's in *The Nutty Professor* (1996). His creations have appeared in *King Kong* (1976), *Star Wars* (1977), *Men in Black* (1997), and *Planet of the Apes* (2001). He has shared Academy Awards for makeup for *An American Werewolf in London* (1981) and *Ed Wood* (1994), and nominations for *Greystoke: The Legend of Tarzan, Lord of the Apes* (1984; also costume designer) and *Coming to America* (1988). He also worked on Michael Jackson's music video "Thriller" and has appeared in various films in gorilla makeup.

Cannom, Greg (date unknown) American makeup artist. After getting his start working with makeup artist Rick Baker, he became known for his own special effects makeup. He has shared Academy Awards for best makeup for *Mrs. Doubtfire* (1993) and *Bram Stoker's Dracula* (1992). Other films include *Hannibal* (2001).

Chambers, John (1923–2001) Makeup artist. He received an honorary Academy Award in 1968 for his ape makeup for *Planet of the Apes* (1968); he also created the ape makeup in that film's sequels. Other credits include *The List of Adrian Messenger* (1963) and *The Island of Dr. Moreau* (1977).

Dawn, Jack (1892–1961) American makeup artist. He worked on over 150 films from the 1930s through the 50s, including *Dr. Jekyll and Mr. Hyde* (1941), *The Picture of Dorian Gray* (1945), *Easter Parade* (1948), and *Madame Bovary* (1949). He is best known for his work on the character makeup for *The Wizard of Oz* (1939).

Guilaroff, Sydney (1907–1997) American hairstylist. The first hairstylist to be listed in the credits of a film, he worked on over 200 films, including *The Philadelphia Story* (1940), *An American in Paris* (1951), and *The Graduate* (1967). He is credited with creating Lucille Ball's red hair, Claudette Colbert's bangs, and Dorothy's braids in *The Wizard of Oz* (1939).

LaPorte, Steve (date unknown) American makeup artist. Known for his special effects makeup in affiliation with Stan Winston Studio, he worked on *The Golden Child* (1986), *Terminator 2: Judgment Day* (1991), and *Powder* (1995). He shared the Academy Award for best makeup for *Beetlejuice* (1988). He has also done makeup for the televison series *The X Files.*

Manley, Nellie (date unknown) American hairstylist. She worked primarily for Paramount from the late 1930s to the late 60s. She styled hair for such films as *Vertigo* (1958), *The Black Orchid* (1959), *Breakfast at Tiffany's* (1961), *Hud* (1963), and *The Odd Couple* (1968).

Mason, Christine (1950–1999) British-born American hair and makeup artist. She is best known for her work on John Waters's films, including *Polyester* (1981), *Hairspray* (1988), and *Cry Baby* (1990). She also played a bit part in *Hairspray.*

Neill, Ve (date unknown) Makeup artist. She began her career in the 1970s. She has shared best makeup Academy Awards for *Beetlejuice* (1988), *Mrs. Doubtfire* (1993), and *Ed Wood* (1994). She has earned Academy Award nominations for *Edward Scissorhands* (1990), *Batman Returns* (1992), and *Hoffa* (1992). Other credits include *A.I. Artificial Intelligence* (2001).

Pierce, Jack (1889–1968) American makeup artist. He is best known for his monster-movie creations in the 1930s. He acted as the head of the makeup department at Universal from 1936 to the late 1940s. His films include *Frankenstein* (1931), *The Mummy* (1932), *The Bride of Frankenstein* (1936), *Werewolf of London* (1935), *The Wolf Man* (1941), and *Beauty and the Beast* (1962).

Savini, Tom (1946–) American makeup artist. He is known for his gruesome and realistic work in the horror genre, in such films as *Dawn of the Dead* (1979), *Friday the 13th* (1980), and *Creepshow* (1982). He also directed the 1990 remake of *Night of the Living Dead* and has acted in such films as *From Dusk Till Dawn* (1996).

Smit, Howard (date unknown) American makeup artist. He is known for his work on several Hitchcock films, including *The Birds* (1963) and *Marnie* (1964). He also worked on makeup for *The Wizard of Oz* (1939). In the 1970s, he did makeup for various television shows. His local IATSE union, #706, named an award after him to recognize his accomplishments in movie makeup.

Smith, Dick (1922–) American makeup artist. He is best known for his special effects makeup in films such as *The Godfather* (1972), *The Exorcist* (1973), *Altered States* (1980), *The Hunger* (1983), and *Amadeus* (1984; Academy Award for best makeup).

Toussieng, Yolanda (date unknown) American hairstylist. She has shared Academy Awards for best makeup (as a hairstylist on the team) for *Mrs. Doubtfire* (1993) and *Ed Wood* (1994). Her other films include *Beetlejuice* (1988) and *Edward Scissorhands* (1990).

Tuttle, William (date unknown) American makeup artist. He worked for MGM during the 1950s and 60s. He won an honorary Academy Award for transforming Tony Randall into all the characters in *7 Faces of Dr. Lao* (1964). Other films include *Julius Caesar* (1953), *The Time Machine* (1960), *Cat on a Hot Tin Roof* (1958), and *How the West Was Won* (1962).

Westcott, Lisa (date unknown) Makeup artist on British and American films. She is known for her work on large-scale period dramas, including *The Madness of King George* (1994), *Mrs. Brown* (1997), and *Shakespeare in Love* (1998; hair and makeup). She has also done makeup for various television shows.

Westmore family (father **George** [1879–1931], sons **Monte** [1904–1968], **Perc** [1904–1970], **Ernest** [1904–1968], **Wally** [1906–1973], **Bud** [1918–1973], and **Frank** [1923–1985]) American makeup artists. George Westmore, a British-born wigmaker, was a pioneering Hollywood makeup artist from 1917. His six American-born sons continued the dynasty, becoming prestigious Hollywood makeup artists. In 1936, they founded their own cosmetics company, House of Westmore. Descendants of the Westmores, including Michael, Marvin, Kevin, Monty, Jr., and Pamela S., continue the family trade. The family's films include *Dr. Jekyll and Mr. Hyde* (1932; Wally), *Gone with the Wind* (1939; Monte), *The Maltese Falcon* (1941; Perc), *The War of the Worlds* (1953; Wally), *The Ten Commandments* (1956; Frank), *To Kill a Mockingbird* (1962; Bud), *Rocky* (1976) and its sequels (Michael), *Predator 2* (1990; Kevin), and *Practical Magic* (1998; Pamela S.). Michael won the first-ever Academy Award for best makeup, for *Mask* (1985).

As the title character in Beetlejuice *(1988), Michael Keaton wore elaborate makeup by makeup artist Ve Neill.*

Although many films have been adapted from Mary Shelley's *Frankenstein*, Jack Pierce's iconic flat-topped, bolt-necked design for the monster in Universal's 1936 version is the only one exclusively copyrighted by a studio.

SPECIAL EFFECTS/ VISUAL EFFECTS

Special effects artists can make the unreal real and the impossible seem, at the very least, much more than plausible.

> "I really admire what's happening in the digital field, but I still get a lot of letters from fans who say they prefer the old technique because there's more heart in it, and more character."
>
> —
>
> *Retired stop-motion pioneer Ray Harryhausen, commenting on the new technology, 2000*

AT RIGHT: *Special effects master Ray Harryhausen developed a process he called Dynamation, which mixed live actors with animated models and was used in* Jason and the Argonauts *(1963).*

Abbott, L.B. (1908–1985) American special effects artist. He won an Academy Award nomination for special effects for *Journey to the Center of the Earth* (1959) and Academy Awards for special effects for *Dr. Doolittle* (1967) and *Tora! Tora! Tora!* (1970; shared with A.D. Flowers). He was also honored with special achievement awards in 1972 for *The Poseidon Adventure* (shared with A.D. Flowers) and in 1976 for *Logan's Run* (shared with Glen Robinson and Matthew Yuricich).

Dykstra, John (1947–) American special effects artist. Trained in still photography, he headed Industrial Light & Magic before leaving to form his own company, called Apogee. He shared a visual effects Academy Award for *Star Wars* (1977) and a special Academy Award in the scientific/technical category for developing a motion-control system for cameras. He was also nominated for his effects work on *Star Trek—The Motion Picture* (1979).

Edlund, Richard (1940–) American special effects artist. After getting his photography training with the US Navy, he was hired by John Dykstra to work on *Star Wars* (1977) and shared an Academy Award for that film's visual effects. He also won a visual effects Academy Award for *Raiders of the Lost Ark* (1981) and shared special achievement awards for *The Empire Strikes Back* (1980) and *Return of the Jedi* (1983). His scientific awards include one for a device for a composite-picture printer and new camera system (1981), and one for a 65mm optical printer (1986). He worked for Industrial Light & Magic until 1983, when he left to form Boss Film Corporation. Other films include *Bedazzled* (2000).

Edouart, Farciot (1894–1980) American special effects artist. He is known for perfecting the rear-projection technique for creating visual effects. He worked for Paramount in the 1930s and developed a special three-projector system that could intensify the background image. He shared two Academy Awards for special effects, for *I Wanted Wings* (1941) and *Reap the Wild Wind* (1942).

Fulton, John P. (1902–1966) American special effects artist. Trained as an electrical engineer and surveyor, he worked in Hollywood for both Universal and Samuel Goldwyn. He was responsible for the memorable effects in several films, including the invisibility in *The Invisible Man* (1933), the twin effects in *Wonder Man* (1945; Academy Award for special effects), and the parting of the Red Sea in *The Ten Commandments* (1956; Academy Award for special effects). He also worked on such classic horror films as *Frankenstein* (1931), *The Mummy* (1932), and *The Invisible Man* (1933).

Gillespie, A. Arnold (1899–1978) American special effects artist. He worked for MGM in the 1940s and 50s. His 12 Academy Award nominations for best special effects include those for *The Wizard of Oz* (1939), *Flight Command* (1941), *Mrs. Miniver* (1942), *Stand by for Action* (1943), *Forbidden Planet* (1956), and *Mutiny on the Bounty* (1962). He won Academy Awards for *Thirty Seconds over Tokyo* (1944), *Green Dolphin Street* (1947), and *Ben-Hur* (1959).

Harryhausen, Ray (1920–) American special effects artist. Having worked as a stop-motion artist on George Pal's *Puppetoons,* he became an

assistant to legendary effects creator Willis O'Brien in 1946, working with O'Brien on *Mighty Joe Young* (1949). Harryhausen later developed his own method of animating models, called Dynamation. The dueling skeletons in *The Seventh Voyage of Sinbad* (1958) and *Jason and the Argonauts* (1963) are examples of his work. He received a special Academy Award, the Gordon E. Sawyer Award for Special Technical Achievement, in 1992.

Muren, Dennis (1946–) American visual effects creator. Associated with the special effects studio Industrial Light & Magic, he became known for his work on films by producers and directors Stephen Spielberg and George Lucas. His Academy Awards total eight, including best visual effects for *E.T.: The Extra-Terrestrial* (1982), *Indiana Jones and the Temple of Doom* (1984), *Innerspace* (1987), *The Abyss* (1989), *Terminator 2: Judgment Day* (1991), and *Jurassic Park* (1993) and shared special achievement awards for *The Empire Strikes Back* (1980) and *Return of the Jedi* (1983). He received a technical achievement award in 1981 for a device for animation photography. Other films include *Star Wars: Episode I—The Phantom Menace* (1999) and *A.I. Artificial Intelligence* (2001).

O'Brien, Willis (1886–1962) American special effects artist. He started his career as a newspaper cartoonist and sculptor. He began experimenting with special effects in 1914 for short films. He pioneered the technique of stop-motion photography to create lifelike dinosaurs, giant gorillas, and other fantasy creatures on screen. His most celebrated films are *The Lost World* (1925), *King Kong* (1933), and *Mighty Joe Young* (1949).

Pal, George (1908–1980) Hungarian-born American special effects artist, producer, and director. After studying architecture and working in set design in Europe, he came to Hollywood. There he developed a new puppet-animation technique and made film shorts called *Puppetoons*, for which he won a special Academy Award in 1943. He became a producer and special effects artist on several films, including several that won Academy Awards for their special effects: *Destination Moon* (1950), *When Worlds Collide* (1951), *The War of the Worlds* (1953), *Tom Thumb* (1958), and *The Time Machine* (1960). He also directed the latter two films.

Ralston, Ken (date unknown) American special effects artist. Inspired as a child by Ray Harryhausen's work, he began making his own movies at age ten. He has shared a special achievement Academy Award for *Return of the Jedi* (1983) and shared best visual effects

Academy Awards for *Forrest Gump* (1994), *Cocoon* (1985), *Who Framed Roger Rabbit?* (1988), and *Death Becomes Her* (1992). Other films include *Dragonslayer* (1981), *Back to the Future Part II* (1989), and *Cast Away* (2000). He has worked for Sony Pictures Imageworks since 1995.

Robinson, Glen (date unknown) American special effects artist. He has shared special achievement Academy Awards for *Earthquake* (1974), *The Hindenburg* (1975), *King Kong* (1976), and *Logan's Run* (1976).

Whitlock, Albert (1915–) British-born American special effects artist. He is known for his realistic matte paintings, such as those in *The Birds* (1963) and several other Hitchcock films. He shared Academy Awards for his visual effects in *Earthquake* (1974) and *The Hindenburg* (1975). He has also designed effects for television and played a small role in the Mel Brooks film *High Anxiety* (1977).

Winston, Stan (1946–) American special effects and makeup artist. He began his career with Walt Disney before opening his own company, the Stan Winston Studio. He is best known for making animatronic creatures for science fiction and horror films. His work has appeared in *The Thing* (1982), *The Terminator* (1984), *Edward Scissorhands* (1990; Academy Award nomination with Ve Neill), *Interview with the Vampire* (1994), and *A.I. Artificial Intelligence* (2001), among others. He has received Academy Awards for visual effects work on *Aliens* (1986), *Terminator 2: Judgment Day* (1991), and *Jurassic Park* (1993). He also received the best makeup Academy Award for *Terminator 2*.

Hungarian-born effects artist George Pal won five Academy Awards for special effects, including one for When Worlds Collide (1951).

Digital Animation

S INCE THE EARLY DAYS of film, audiences of all ages have delighted in the magic of animated characters that have danced, sang, scampered, flown, hopped, and sometimes bumbled their way across the silver screen. Whether in the brisk, tangy wit of a perfect Chuck Jones short or the fairy-dusted grandeur of a Disney musical, the best animation makes good on the central promise of all film-going, transporting us to a world of total imagination. As the Golden Age of painstakingly hand-drawn cells makes way for the Digital Era's computerized backgrounds, paint programs, and—with 2001's *Monsters, Inc.*— fully-dimensional digitally-rendered characters, what's striking is how the new technology has both preserved and revitalized animation's single best attribute: *humanity*.

BACKGROUND CHARACTERS

These characters were created to move through background scenes of the film, as if they were extras in a live-action film.

CREATING CHARACTERS

Director Pete Docter, with supervising animator Glenn McQueen, oversees the work of the lead animators, who focus on getting consistent performances from each main character. For the multitude of outlandish creatures that crawl through crowd scenes in *Monsters, Inc.*, the artists at Pixar created a "tentacle package" in order to quickly build and animate characters with multiple eyes, arms, and legs. These could then be used to fill out the background of shots.

FREEDOM OF MOVEMENT

In *Toy Story 2* (1999), one character's clothing had to be continually moved by the animators. For this *Monsters, Inc.* (2001), simulation technology was developed that allowed clothing to move independently of body motion. Even still, some visual elements—the little girl Boo's ponytail for example—continued to be animated by hand.

PRE-PRODUCTION

Each Pixar film takes a long time to produce—*Monsters, Inc.* took five years. A great deal of this time is devoted to pre-production, so that the film's story can be fully fleshed out by the writers while new programs are being created. The technology continues to improve at an amazing velocity, however; according to Tom Porter, *Monsters, Inc.'s* supervising technical director, the original *Toy Story* was animated with ⅒th of the computer power now available.

DIGITAL TO FILM

While *Monsters, Inc.* was created entirely with computers, the finished picture still needs to be transferred to 35mm film in order to be exhibited in most theatres. Though Pixar has developed a new laser recording system for transferring digital images to film, only digital projection—still a few years away from becoming the industry standard—offers sound and picture that's closest to the way the filmmakers intended it.

MOTION CONTROL

Every character is built three-dimensionally in the computer and manipulated—marionette-like—through a series of "controls" that allows the animator complete freedom of movement. Each control moves a different part of the body. For example, one control moves the elbow, while three more might be used to impel the wrist. Like the technology itself, these controls have become more sophisticated with each successive film: *Toy Story's* Woody had 300 controls, Sulley in *Monsters, Inc.* possesses close to 500.

VOICE ACTING

Billy Crystal, who vocalizes grinning eyeball Mike Wazowski, was originally approached by Pixar to provide the voice of Buzz Lightyear for the original *Toy Story* (1995). He turned them down on the advice of his agent, a decision he regretted after seeing the finished film. He agreed to do *Monsters, Inc.* after animators showed him test footage of Mike dubbed with Crystal's dialogue from *My Giant* (1998).

SIMULTANEOUS SYNC

The vocal performances for most animated features are recorded separately so that filmmakers can pick and choose the best takes to edit together later. *Monsters, Inc.* has the distinction of being the first Pixar film in which the two leads (Crystal and John Goodman, who plays Sulley) insisted on recording their dialogue at the same time to preserve a sense of energy and spontaneity.

HAIR APPARENT

Each of Sulley's 3.2 million hairs is individually animated. Animators first work with a bald version of the character in order to finalize his movements, while artists model each hair in the computer as if it were a collection of springs and balls. As hair is added, 500 "key" hairs placed throughout Sulley's coat are programmed to influence and coordinate the movements of all the other hairs around them. The result? A stunningly natural covering of shaggy, blue fur.

THE STUDIO

2001 marks the 15th anniversary of Pixar, the computer animation studio behind *Toy Story* (1995), *A Bug's Life* (1998), *Toy Story 2* (1999) and *Monsters, Inc.* Begun as the computer graphics division of George Lucas's Lucasfilm before being purchased by Apple's Steve Jobs in 1986, Pixar is guided by creative vice president John Lasseter. Pioneers in the field of digital animation, the company is responsible for setting the standard for the industry with the creation of Renderman, an Academy Award-winning rendering system responsible for 24 of the 26 films nominated for best visual effects over the last decade.

STUNT PEOPLE

*Whether braving fire, air, earth, or water, stunt people
thrill us by making the most out of dangerous situations.*

Although it is stuntman
Harvey Parry, and not
comedian Harold Lloyd,
who is famously seen
hanging from the clock
tower in several shots from
Safety Last (1923), Parry
had an agreement with the
image-conscious studio to
keep his involvement a
secret. Parry kept his word
until after Lloyd's death.

Canutt, Yakima (1895–1986) American stuntman,
actor, second-unit director, and director. Born
Enos Edward Canutt, he began as a rodeo
performer; from 1917 to 1924, he held the title
World Champion All Round Cowboy. He
started film work in westerns in the 1920s,
eventually doubling for many of the genre's
stars, including John Wayne, Roy Rogers, and
Gene Autry, and developing classic stunts with
moving horses and wagons. In the 1930s, he
took on the role of second-unit director,
overseeing the filming of stunt sequences for
westerns and other films. He also acted in
supporting roles and directed low-budget
westerns. His films as an actor include *The
Riding Comet* (1925), *Westward Ho!* (1935),
Stagecoach (1939; also second-unit director),
Gone with the Wind (1939), and *The Great Train
Robbery* (1941). His films as a second-unit
director include *Dark Command* (1940), *Ben-
Hur* (1959), in which he staged the chariot race,
and *Spartacus* (1960). He was awarded an
honorary Academy Award in 1966 for "creating
the profession of stuntman as it exists today"
and for developing safety devices for stunt people.

Dixon, Shane (1955–1999) American stuntman.
He performed stunts in over 50 films throughout the 1980s and 90s, such as *Lethal Weapon 3*
(1992), *Point of No Return* (1993), and *Lethal
Weapon 4* (1998). He served as stunt coordinator
for *The Mod Squad* (1999). He also performed
stunts for television series such as *Walker, Texas
Ranger* and *Buffy the Vampire Slayer.*

Fetters, Linda (date unknown) American
stuntwoman. She is a specialist in precision and
stunt diving, fights, high falls, and burns. Films
include *The Rocketeer* (1991) and *Batman
Forever* (1995). The president of the Stunt-
women's Association of
Motion Pictures from 1994 to
1996, she is married to actor
Ken Howard.

Finn, Lila (1909–1996)
American stuntwoman.
Known for her diving stunts,
she appeared in such films as
Gone with the Wind (1939)
and *It's a Wonderful Life*
(1946). In 1993, she received a
Lifetime Achievement Award
from Women in Film.

Grace, Dick (1898–1965)
American stuntman. He is best
known as a pioneer of stunt
flying in the 1920s and 30s. He
established crash patterns used
in subsequent films and also
left autobiographical writings
that detail the life of a major
stunt actor. Films include
Wings (1927) and *The Lost
Squadron* (1932).

Hickman, Bill (1920–1986)
American stuntman. He is
best known for his stunt
driving skills as featured in
Bullitt (1968), *The French
Connection* (1971), and *The
Seven-Ups* (1973).

*A former rodeo world champion, legendary stuntman Yakima Canutt also developed and
directed stunt sequences for many films later in his career, including* Ben-Hur *(1959),
starring Charlton Heston.*

SOUND PEOPLE

At its most successful, sound people's work goes unnoticed. Their complex aural tapestries should sound like nothing less than the real world as we see it depicted on screen. Only much louder.

Bender, Lon (date unknown) American sound designer. He founded the sound company, Wallaworks at age 18. He cofounded Soundelux Entertainment Group, where he now works. He has worked with a sound team on *Coal Miner's Daughter* (1980), *Glory* (1989), *Legends of the Fall* (1994), and *Shrek* (2001). He shared an Academy Award for best sound effects editing for *Braveheart* (1996).

Berger, Mark (1943–) American sound mixer. Beginning in the 1970s, he has worked on over 100 films, primarily as a rerecording mixer. He shared Academy Awards for best sound for *The Right Stuff* (1983), *Amadeus* (1984), and *The English Patient* (1996). Other films include *Ghost World* (2001).

Burtt, Ben (1948–) American sound designer and editor. He is best known for his work on Steven Spielberg's, films as a sound effects editor. He won special achievement awards for *Star Wars* (1977) and *Raiders of the Lost Ark* (1981). Films include *Indiana Jones and the Temple of Doom* (1984), *Willow* (1988; Academy Award nomination for best sound effects editing), and *Star Wars: Episode I—The Phantom Menace* (1989).

Jenkins, Chris (date unknown) American sound rerecording mixer. Films include *The Natural* (1984), *Body Heat* (1981), *Heat* (1995), and *Six Days, Seven Nights* (1998). He shared two Academy Awards for best sound, for *Out of Africa* (1985) and *The Last of the Mohicans* (1993). He is the president of Todd-AO Sound Company.

Landaker, Gregg (date unknown) American sound mixer and rerecording mixer. He shared Academy Awards for best sound for *The Empire Strikes Back* (1980), *Raiders of the Lost Ark* (1981), and *Speed* (1994). He also did sound restoration for the 1989 re-release of *Lawrence of Arabia* (1962).

McMillan, David (date unknown) American sound mixer. He has worked on such films as *The Right Stuff* (1983; Academy Award for best sound), *Flatliners* (1990), *Speed* (1994; Academy Award for best sound), and *Apollo 13* (1995; Academy Award for best sound). He often works with Gregg Landaker and Steve Maslow.

Maslow, Steve (date unknown) American sound rerecording mixer. He began as a recording engineer, working with Gregg Landaker and Bill Varney at Warner Bros. With that team, he won Academy Awards for best sound for *The Empire Strikes Back* (1980) and *Raiders of the Lost Ark* (1981). He also shared a best sound Academy Award for *Speed* (1994). He has helped create sound for over 100 films.

Murch, Walter (1943–) American sound designer, editor, and director. He is known for his innovative sound work on *The Conversation* (1974) and *Apocalyspe Now* (1979), both of which earned him Academy Award nominations for best sound; he won for *Apocalypse Now*. He also served as editor and sound editor on *The English Patient* (1996) and *The Talented Mr. Ripley* (1999).

Rydstrom, Gary (1959–) American sound rerecording mixer and sound effects editor. He has shared numerous Academy Awards, often with Gary Summers. He won double Academy Awards (both best sound and best sound effects editing) for *Terminator 2: Judgment Day* (1991), *Jurassic Park* (1993), and *Saving Private Ryan* (1998). Other films include *Mission: Impossible* (1996) and *Titanic* (1997; shared Academy Award for best sound).

Shearer, Douglas (1899–1971) American sound recording technician. A director of the MGM sound department, he refined numerous sound techniques and defined the trademark MGM sound. He won 12 Academy Awards for sound recording, for films including *The Big House* (1930), *Naughty Marietta* (1935), *San Francisco* (1936), *Strike Up the Band* (1940), *Thirty Seconds over Tokyo* (1944), and *The Great Caruso* (1951). In addition, he won a science and technical category Academy Award for helping to develop the Camera 65 system. He was the brother of actress Norma Shearer.

Summers, Gary (date unknown) American sound rerecording mixer. His work with Gary Rydstrom is best known, including *Terminator 2: Judgment Day* (1991), *Jurassic Park* (1993), and *Saving Private Ryan* (1998). He shared Academy Awards for best sound for each of these films.

Varney, Bill (date unknown) American sound rerecording mixer. He shared Academy Awards for best sound for his work on *The Empire Strikes Back* (1980) and *Raiders of the Lost Ark* (1981). He also created sound for *Star Trek—The Motion Picture* (1979), *Poltergeist* (1982), and *Dragonheart* (1996).

Ben Burtt ingeniously blended sounds from the modern world to create the laser blasts, alien languages, and spacecraft heard in *Star Wars* (1977), with one notable exception: The scream of a falling stormtrooper was lifted directly from the 1954 giant-ant film *Them!*

COMPOSERS

A film score can be sweeping, sentimental, or simply terrifying.
A composer sets the tone of a picture, and the best can create
unforgettable marriages of music and imagery.

Bacharach, Burt (1928–) American composer. Known for his popular songwriting, he composed music for such films as *What's New Pussycat?* (1965); *Butch Cassidy and the Sundance Kid* (1969), for which he won two Academy Awards, including one for the song "Raindrops Keep Fallin' on My Head"; and *Arthur* (1981), for which he won two more Academy Awards, for song and score.

Barry, John (1933–) British composer. After starting his career as a rock and roll trumpet player, he composed scores for numerous films, including *Midnight Cowboy* (1969), *King Kong* (1976), *Somewhere in Time* (1980), *Body Heat* (1981), and *Chaplin* (1992). He received Academy Awards for his work on *Born Free* (1966; best score and best song), *The Lion in Winter* (1968; best score), *Out of Africa* (1985; best score), and *Dances with Wolves* (1990; best score). He has also composed music for several James Bond films.

Composer John Barry (right), seen here with Bryan Forbes, scored several James Bond films and won Academy Awards for Born Free *(1966),* The Lion in Winter *(1968), and* Out of Africa *(1985).*

Bernstein, Elmer (1922–) American composer. Served as the first vice president of the Academy of Motion Picture Arts and Sciences. He has also served as president of the Composers and Lyricists Guild of America. He is credited with scoring over 90 major films, including *The Ten Commandments* (1956), *The Magnificent Seven* (1960), *To Kill a Mockingbird* (1963), *The Great Santini* (1979), *Ghostbusters* (1984), *My Left Foot* (1989, Ireland), *The Grifters* (1990), and *The Age of Innocence* (1993). He won an Academy Award for best score in 1967 for *Thoroughly Modern Millie*.

Elfman, Danny (1953–) American composer. Originally part of the rock band Oingo Boingo, he is perhaps best known for his work on Tim Burton's films, such as *Pee-wee's Big Adventure* (1985), *Beetlejuice* (1988), *Batman* (1989), *Edward Scissorhands* (1990), *The Nightmare*

Before Christmas (1993), and *Planet of the Apes* (2001). He has also composed music for television shows such as *Pee-wee's Playhouse, Alfred Hitchcock Presents, Tales from the Crypt,* and the theme of *The Simpsons.*

Glass, Philip (1937–) American composer. Having studied at Juilliard and in France, he became known for his experimental scores and minimalist compositions. Films include *Koyaanisqatsi* (1983), *Mishima* (1985), *Hamburger Hill* (1987), and *Powaqqatsi* (1988).

Goldsmith, Jerry (1929–) American composer. He began his career scoring television shows such as *Playhouse 90* and *Gunsmoke* and also worked with Miklos Rosza at USC. He has composed scores for over 100 films, including *Planet of the Apes* (1968), *Chinatown* (1974), *Star Trek—The Motion Picture* (1979), *Poltergeist* (1982), *Total Recall* (1990), *Basic Instinct* (1992), *L.A. Confidential* (1997), and *The Last Castle* (2001). He received numerous Academy Award nominations and won an Oscar for *The Omen* in 1976.

Hamlisch, Marvin (1944–) American composer. He began as the piano accompanist and straight man for Groucho Marx. He was also a concert pianist and scored several Broadway musicals. He was the first individual to win three Academy Awards in one night, for *The Way We Were* (1973; for original score and title song) and *The Sting* (1973; for adapted score). Other films include *Ordinary People* (1980), *Sophie's Choice* (1982), *A Chorus Line* (1985), and *The Mirror Has Two Faces* (1996).

Hermann, Bernard (1911–1975) American composer. Composing since childhood, he became the conductor of several orchestras, including the New York Philharmonic, the BBC, and CBS radio. He has composed operas, ballets, a cantata, and numerous film scores. His compositions for film are dramatic and often feature strings. He is best known for his work with Alfred Hitchcock and Orson Welles, and his films include *Citizen Kane* (1941), *Vertigo* (1958), *Psycho* (1960), and *Taxi Driver* (1976; dedicated to his memory).

Horner, James (1953–) American composer. He won Grammy Awards for his song "Somewhere Out There" from *An American Tail* (1986) and his instrumental arrangement for *Glory* (1989). Film scores include *Gorky Park* (1983), *Aliens* (1986), *Field of Dreams* (1989), *Apollo 13* (1995), *Braveheart* (1996), *Titanic* (1997), and *Enemy at the Gates* (2001).

Jarre, Maurice (1924–) French-born composer for American and international films. He worked with the French National Theater before scoring films and has also written several ballets. He is known for his use of guitar and other string instruments and his subdued sound. He has composed scores for over 80 films, including *Lawrence of Arabia* (1962; Academy Award for best score), *Doctor Zhivago* (1965; Academy Award for best score), *The Year of Living Dangerously* (1983, Australia), *A Passage to India* (1984, UK; Academy Award for best score), *Witness* (1985), *Gorillas in the Mist* (1988), and *Dead Poets Society* (1989).

Kaper, Bronislaw (or **Bronislau**) (1902–1983) Polish-born international composer. He scored German films until 1933, when he emigrated to the US. In 1935, he wrote his first score, for *Mutiny on the Bounty* (1935), and first songs, for *A Night at the Opera* (1935). Other works for which he wrote songs include *San Francisco* (1936) and *A Day at the Races* (1937). Scored works include *Gaslight* (1944) and *Lili* (1953; Academy Award for scoring of a dramatic or comedy film).

Mancini, Henry (1924–1994) American composer. After beginning his career as a dance-band pianist, he got a job with Universal Pictures in 1951 as a studio composer. He is best known for his suspenseful themes for Blake Edwards's Pink Panther movies. He composed scores for over 100 films, including *Breakfast at Tiffany's* (1961; Academy Awards for best score and best song, "Moon River"), *Days of Wine and Roses* (1962; Academy Award for best song), *The Pink Panther* (1964), and *Victor/Victoria* (1982; Academy Award for best score). He won over 20 Grammy Awards.

Menken, Alan (1949–) American composer. He is best known for his work with lyricist Bill Ashman on *The Little Mermaid* (1989), *Beauty and the Beast* (1991), *Aladdin* (1992), and *Pocahontas* (1995). Each of these collaborations won Academy Awards for both original song and music score. He has also composed music for various theater productions.

Moroder, Giorgio (1940–) Italian-born composer for American films. Specializing in synthesized music, he gained fame with the score to *Midnight Express* (1978; Academy Award for best score). He also won Academy Awards for the title songs to *Flashdance* (1983) and *Top Gun* (1986). Other film scores include *American Gigolo* (1980), *Cat People* (1982), and the revised version of Fritz Lang's *Metropolis* (1983).

Morricone, Ennio (1928–) Italian composer for international films. After beginning his career writing for popular Italian performers and composing chamber music, he gained recognition for his work on Sergio Leone's spaghetti westerns (under the name Dan Davio). He has scored over 120 films, both for Hollywood and for European films, including *Once Upon a Time in America* (1984), *Ginger e Fred (Ginger and Fred)* (1985), *The Mission* (1986, UK), *The Untouchables* (1987), *Hamlet* (1990, UK), and *Malèna* (2000).

Newman, Alfred (1901–1970) American composer. This prolific writer of film scores and music for Broadway began his career as a conductor and went to Hollywood in 1930. He worked primarily for 20th Century–Fox, earning nine Academy Awards for his scores. He was the brother of Robert V. Newman, a studio executive, and Lionel Newman, a composer for Fox. Films include *Stella Dallas* (1937), *Tin Pan Alley* (1940; Academy Award for best score), *The Razor's Edge* (1946), *The Seven Year Itch* (1955), and *How the West Was Won* (1962).

Newman, Randy (1943–) American composer and singer. The nephew of musicians Lionel and Alfred Newman, he is known for his wry, jaunty touch. His best-known popular songs are "Short People" and "I Love L.A." He has scored many films, including *Cold Turkey* (1971), *Ragtime* (1981), *The Natural* (1984), *Avalon* (1990), *Maverick* (1994), and *Meet the Parents* (2000). He was nominated for 16 Academy Awards and finally won for best song for 2001's *Monsters, Inc.*

North, Alex (1910–1991) American composer. Trained with Aaron Copland, he worked on documentary films from 1937 to 1950. He was known for his creative and wide-ranging scores. He was nominated for 15 Academy Awards and won an Honorary Lifetime Achievement Academy Award in 1986 for "brilliant artistry in the creation of memorable music for a host of motion pictures." Films include *A Streetcar Named Desire* (1951), *Spartacus* (1960), *Cleopatra* (1963), *Who's Afraid of Virginia Woolf?* (1966), and *Prizzi's Honor* (1985).

Charles Bronson (left) played the haunting recurring harmonica theme by composer Ennio Morricone in Once Upon a Time in the West *(1968), also starring Jason Robards and Claudia Cardinale.*

367

Although Jesus Christ is never fully shown in the 1959 biblical epic *Ben-Hur*, composer Miklos Rozsa chose to employ an organ to convey His presence.

Previn, Sir André (1929–) French composer for international films. He has served as conductor of the London and Pittsburgh Symphony Orchestras and guest conductor of orchestras throughout the United States and Europe. In film, he is best known for his work on musicals such as *Gigi* (1958; Academy Award for best score), *Porgy and Bess* (1959; Academy Award for best score), *Irma La Douce* (1963; Academy Award for best score), and *Thoroughly Modern Millie* (1967). He was knighted in 1996.

Romberg, Sigmund (1887–1951) Hungarian composer for American films. He wrote comic operas and film scores. Films include *Viennese Nights* (1930), *Broadway Serenade* (1939), and *Central Park* (1948). In his cinematic biography, *Deep in My Heart* (1954), he was portrayed by José Ferrer.

Rota, Nino (1911–1979) Italian composer for Italian and American films. He is best known for scores written for Federico Fellini's and Francis Ford Coppola's films. He also wrote operas, symphonies, concertos, and ballets. His music is simple and melodic, often featuring a solo piano. He won an Academy Award for best score for *The Godfather Part II* (1974, US). Other films include *La Strada* (1954), *La Dolce Vita* (1960), and *The Godfather* (1972, US).

Rozsa, Miklos (1907–1995) Hungarian composer for British and American films. He began his career as a violinist and a composer of ballets and symphonies. He worked with Alexander Korda in the 1930s, moving to Hollywood in the early 40s. Best known for his scores of psychological dramas and historical epics, his films include *Jungle Book* (1942), *Double Indemnity* (1944), *Spellbound* (1945; Academy Award for best score), *A Double Life* (1947; Academy Award for best score), *Ben-Hur* (1959; Academy Award for best score), and *Eye of the Needle* (1981, US/UK).

Shaiman, Marc (1959–) American composer. He began his career as a vocal arranger for Bette Midler. He has worked as music supervisor or arranger on several films, including *Beaches* (1988), *When Harry Met Sally…* (1989), and *Sister Act* (1992). As a composer, he earned three Academy Award nominations for best score, for *The American President* (1995), *Sleepless in Seattle* (1993), and *The First Wives Club* (1996).

Steiner, Max (1888–1971) Viennese-born American composer. A child prodigy who studied under Gustav Mahler, he worked on Broadway musicals for Florenz Ziegfeld after emigrating to the United States in 1914. He went to Hollywood in 1929 to score for films. He has worked on over 200 scores, closely associating the music to the images, but is best known for the score of *Gone with the Wind* (1939), one of the longest scores in film history. He won three Academy Awards for best score, for *The Informer* (1935), *Now, Voyager* (1942), and *Since You Went Away* (1944). Other films include *King Kong* (1933) and *Casablanca* (1943).

Stothart, Herbert (1885–1949) American composer, arranger, and music director. A Broadway composer *(Rose Marie)*, he came to MGM in the late 1920s and was a dominant musical presence there during the 1930s and 40s. In addition to scoring or adapting operettas like *Rose Marie* (1928) and *Naughty Marietta* (1935), he composed an array of scores for comedies such as *A Night at the Opera* (1935), action films such as *Mutiny on the Bounty* (1935), and many of MGM's high-toned productions, including *A Tale of Two Cities* (1935) and *Mrs. Miniver* (1942). He may be best remembered for his original score for *The Wizard of Oz* (1939), for which he won an Academy Award.

Tiomkin, Dmitri (1899–1979) Russian-born American composer. After starting his career as a concert pianist and conductor, he began working in Hollywood in the early 1930s and became a successful composer of film scores. His work is diverse and borrows from various American and European folk traditions. He won Academy Awards for *High Noon* (1952; best score and best song), *The High and Mighty* (1954; best score), and *The Old Man and the Sea* (1958; best score). He is also well known for his work on *Giant* (1956).

Williams, John (1932–) American composer. Best known for his scores accompanying Steven Spielberg films, he won Academy Awards for best score for *Jaws* (1975), *Star Wars* (1977), *E.T: The Extra-Terrestrial* (1982), and *Schindler's List* (1993). He has conducted the Boston Pops Orchestra since 1977. Other films include *The Patriot* (2000) and *A.I. Artificial Intelligence* (2001).

Young, Victor (1900–1956) Polish-born American composer. He studied at the Warsaw conservatory before coming to Hollywood in the early 1920s, where he worked primarily for Paramount. Films include *Anything Goes* (1936), *For Whom the Bell Tolls* (1943), *Samson and Delilah* (1949), *Rio Grande* (1950), and *Shane* (1953).

Zimmer, Hans (1957–) German-born American composer. He began as a musician and producer with the rock band the Buggles. His work using computer technology to combine digital synthesizers and orchestra was revolutionary. He composed scores for such films as *Rain Man* (1988), *Driving Miss Daisy* (1989), *Thelma & Louise* (1991), *Pearl Harbor* (2001), and *Riding in Cars with Boys* (2001). His original score for *The Lion King* (1994) won him an Academy Award, along with a Grammy and a Golden Globe.

Max Steiner received three Academy Awards for his film scores and was nominated for 15 other films.

EDITORS

Editors are responsible for the important final stage of film craftsmanship. They shape the narrative, assembling and honing it in a way that brings out the filmmakers' best intentions.

Allen, Dede (1925–) American editor. Born Dorothea Carothers. After beginning her career at Columbia Pictures as a messenger, she rose to become an accomplished editor. Films include *The Hustler* (1961), *Bonnie and Clyde* (1967), *Little Big Man* (1970), *Serpico* (1973), and *Wonder Boys* (2000). She was nominated for Academy Awards for *Dog Day Afternoon* (1975) and *Reds* (1981). In 1994, she received an Honorary Lifetime Achievement Award from the A.C.E.

Booth, Margaret (1898–) American editor. Credits as editor or supervising editor during her long career include *Strange Interlude* (1932), *Mutiny on the Bounty* (1935), *The Way We Were* (1973), *The Goodbye Girl* (1977), and *Annie* (1985). She received an honorary Academy Award in 1977.

Cattozzo, Leo (date unknown) Italian editor. He is best known for his work with Federico Fellini on such films as *La Strada* (1954), *La Notti di Cabiria (The Nights of Cabiria)* (1957), *La Dolce Vita* (1960), and *Otto e Mezzo (8 ½)* (1963).

Coates, Anne V. (1925–) British editor. A onetime nurse in a plastic surgery hospital, she is best known for her work on *Lawrence of Arabia* (1962), for which she won an Academy Award for best editing. She received Academy Award nominations for her editing of *Becket* (1964) and *The Elephant Man* (1980). Other credits include *Murder on the Orient Express* (1974).

Fields, Verna (1918–1982) American editor. She worked on numerous films throughout the 1960s and 70s, including *American Graffiti* (1973; best editing Academy Award) and *Jaws* (1975). In 1981, she was honored by Women in Film.

Kahn, Michael (1924–) American editor. He is known for his work with Stephen Spielberg, including *Close Encounters of the Third Kind* (1977), *Indiana Jones and the Temple of Doom* (1984), and *Empire of the Sun* (1987). He won an Academy Award for best editing for *Raiders of the Lost Ark* in 1981.

Kern, Hal C. (1894–1985) American editor. A film cutter from 1915, he gained notice in the 1920s and early 30s at United Artists, with works including *The Eagle* (1925) and *Abraham Lincoln* (1930). In 1934, he moved to Selznick International, where he edited many memorable films, including *A Star Is Born* (1937), *Gone with the Wind* (1939; cowinner of an Academy Award for film editing), and *Rebecca* (1940). His brother was film editor Robert J. Kern.

Lovejoy, Ray (date unknown) American editor. Films include *2001: A Space Odyssey* (1968), *The Shining* (1980), *Aliens* (1986; Academy Award nomination for best editing), *Batman* (1989), and *Lost in Space* (1998).

Lyon, William A. (d. 1964) American editor. From 1935 to 1967, he edited over 80 films, including *Rio Grande* (1939), *From Here to Eternity* (1953), and *Barefoot in the Park* (1967). He won an Academy Award for best editing for *Picnic* (1955).

Rosenblum, Ralph (1925–) American editor. After beginning his career in documentaries and television, he gained fame for his editing of Sidney Lumet's and Woody Allen's films of the late 1960s and early 70s. He won the British Film Academy Award for *Annie Hall* (1977). Other films include *The Pawnbroker* (1965), *Sleeper* (1973), and *Love and Death* (1975).

Sewell, Blanche (1899–1949) American editor. She worked on Hollywood films from the 1920s to the 40s. She is best known for her work on *Grand Hotel* (1932) and *The Wizard of Oz* (1939).

Tomasini, George (1909–1964) American editor. He gained recognition as Alfred Hitchcock's editor, working on such films as *Rear Window* (1954), *Vertigo* (1958), *Psycho* (1960), and *The Birds* (1963). He earned an Academy Award nomination for best editing for *North by Northwest* (1959).

Vorkapich, Slavko (1892–1976) Yugoslavian montage expert and special effects artist in American films. He started his career as a commercial artist. He lent his montage skills to both MGM and Columbia on such films as *David Copperfield* (1935), *Boys Town* (1938), and *Mr. Smith Goes to Washington* (1939). He also directed the film *Hanka* (1955) as a demonstration of filmmaking principles.

William A. Lyon edited Picnic *(1955), starring William Holden and Susan Strasberg.*

WRITERS ON FILM

From critics to theorists, they teach us not only what we have to gain from watching a film, but what we can bring to it as well.

As a film critic and scholar, Peter Bogdanovich interviewed director Howard Hawks extensively. As a filmmaker, Bogdanovich freely borrowed from Hawks, particularly in making *What's Up, Doc?* (1972), which was inspired by Hawks's *Bringing Up Baby* (1938). The latter film was a screwball comedy that combined Cary Grant, Katharine Hepburn, a leopard, and a dinosaur skeleton. Bogdanovich nervously showed his script to Hawks, fearing that he had stolen too much. Hawks read the script, then called and indicated he was disappointed about only one thing: Bogdanovich hadn't stolen the leopard or the dinosaur.

Agee, James (1910–1955) American film critic, screenwriter, and novelist. The author of the Pulitzer Prize–winning novel *A Death in the Family* (1957), he reviewed films for publications such as *Time* and *The Nation* throughout the 1940s. Screenplays include *The African Queen* (1951), which he coscripted. His reviews and screenplays are collected in the two volumes of *Agee on Film* (1958, 1960).

Anderson, Lindsay (1923–) Indian-born British director, film critic, and theorist. He was the cofounder and coeditor of the British film journal *Sequence*, which advocated new directions in filmmaking. He later wrote for *Sight and Sound, The London Times, The Observer,* and *The New Statesman.* The topics of his essays include nonfiction films and Alfred Hitchcock's work. Also a filmmaker, he won an Academy Award for best documentary short subject for his film *Thursday's Children* (1954, UK). He also appeared as a schoolmaster in the feature *Chariots of Fire* (1981, UK).

Arnheim, Rudolf (1904–) German-born American film theorist. He was concerned with the properties of film that set it apart from other art forms. *Film as Art* (1957) is a collection of his most influential essays.

Barthes, Roland (1915–1980) French social and literary critic. Interested in language and the way a system of signs creates meaning, he suggested that film is like a visual language in which the various images form meaning only as they become linked together in a certain pattern. Notable works include *Le degré zéro de l'écriture (Writing Degree Zero)* (1953), *Mythologies* (1957), and *A Barthes Reader* (1987), edited by Susan Sontag.

Bazin, André (1918–1958) French film theorist. A cofounder of the French journal *Cahiers du Cinéma* in 1951, he wrote *What Is Cinema?* (1967), a two-volume collection of essays. His work highlights the role of film in capturing reality as it unfolds with no creative interference. According to him, this is best accomplished using deep focus and *mise-en-scène* rather than montage, as in *Citizen Kane* (1941) and Italian neorealist films of the 1940s. He was also a proponent of the auteur theory.

Benjamin, Walter (1892–1940) German philosopher. His work with the Frankfurt School in the 1920s suggested that popular culture was a tool of fascism. According to him, film as an infinitely reproducible work of art is inherently less valuable than a singular art object. He explores this idea in the essay "The Work of Art in the Age of Mechanical Reproduction" (1935). He was mainly concerned with the technological properties of the film medium and how these affect the audience's viewing experience.

Bergman, Andrew (1945–) Film historian, screenwriter, and director. Before turning to screenwriting and directing, he wrote two well-known film histories. *We're in the Money* (1971) examines films made during the Depression, and *James Cagney* (1975) is a biography of the actor. He went on to write or cowrite the screenplays for several successful comedies, including *Blazing Saddles* (1974) and *The In-Laws* (1979). Directing credits include *The Freshman* (1990), for which he also wrote the screenplay.

Bogdanovich, Peter (1939–) American film critic, director, producer, and screenwriter. Before making films himself, he wrote books and articles on other directors for the Museum of Modern Art in New York and *Esquire.* He has written on Howard Hawks, Fritz Lang, Orson Welles, D.W. Griffith, and John Ford and is an outspoken fan of the veteran Hollywood directors he writes about. As a director, his films include *The Last Picture Show* (1971), *Paper Moon* (1973), and *Daisy Miller* (1974).

Bordwell, David (1947–) American film scholar. Pioneer in the study of film formalism, which examines elements of a film that construct the narrative, such as sound, color, lighting, framing of the images, and camera movement. This approach also explores the relationship of the audience to the film's narrative. His books include *Narration in the Fiction Film* (1985), *Film Art* (1993), and *Planet Hong Kong: Popular Cinema and the Art of Entertainment* (2000).

Braudy, Leo (1941–) American film critic and historian. His texts include *Great Film Directors: A Critical Anthology* (1978; editor) and a study of Jean Renoir's films. In his work, he examines components that make up the total experience of the film.

Brownlow, Kevin (1938–) British director, film editor, and film historian. A filmmaker since the 1950s (*It Happened Here,* 1966, UK, co-dir., co-prod., co-sc.), he gained great praise (and honor from the French government) for his nearly lifelong project to restore Abel Gance's 1927 silent film *Napoléon*. Among his well-regarded books are *The Parade's Gone By* (1968) and *Hollywood: The Pioneers* (1979).

Corliss, Richard (1944–) American film and literary critic. He wrote for the *National Review* from 1966 to 1970, and later worked for the Museum of Modern Art in New York. Since 1980, he has been the film reviewer for *Time*. He has written a text on screenwriters, a monograph on *Lolita* (1994), and essays on *Casablanca* and Greta Garbo.

Cowie, Peter (1939–) British film scholar. Best known for his historical texts on various world cinemas, he has written about Swedish, Finnish, and Dutch film, as well as *The Cinema of Orson Welles* (1965, 1973) and *Eighty Years of Cinema* (1978), an overview of world cinema.

Crowther, Bosley (1905–1981) American film critic. He was a longtime film reviewer for *The New York Times*. Books include volumes on MGM and Louis B. Mayer, and *Vintage Films* (1977), a survey of what he considers to be the most important films from 1929 to 1972.

Denby, David (1943–) American film critic. He began his career with the *Boston Phoenix* and then reviewed films for *The Atlantic* from 1970 to 1973. His reviews have appeared in *The New York Times, Harper's, Sight and Sound, Film Quarterly,* and *The New Yorker*. He edited the book *Awake in the Dark: An Anthology of American Film Criticism, 1915–Present* (1977).

Ebert, Roger (1942–) American film critic. He started at the *Chicago Sun-Times* in 1967, and won the Pulitzer Prize for criticism in 1975. He and fellow film critic Gene Siskel (1947–1999) appeared on television in a series of weekly review programs titled *Sneak Previews, At the Movies* and *Siskel & Ebert*. After Siskel's death, Ebert teamed up with Chicago critic Richard Roeper on "Ebert & Roeper." His film reviews are syndicated by Universal Press Syndicate to some 250 newspapers. His books include *A Kiss is Still a Kiss* (1984) annual editions of *Roger Ebert's Movie Yearbook, Roger Ebert's Book of Film,* and *The Great Movies,* essays on 100 classic films. He has been a lecturer on film at the University of Chicago Fine Arts Program since 1969, and is an adjunct professor of cinema studies at the University of Illinois at Urbana, where he holds his annual Overlooked Film Festival.

Eisenstein, Sergei (1898–1948) Russian director and film theorist. Trained as an engineer, he began to sketch caricatures during the advent of the Russian Revolution. While serving in the Red Army, he directed small productions with his fellow servicemen. He also became interested in Japanese culture and the pictographic structure of the language. His ideas about film revolve around the principle of montage—the linking together of disparate images to produce meaning. According to Eisenstein, the images should be in tension with each other and meaning is created from this clash. Films are a means to inform the audience and make social commentary, producing emotions in the viewer. His writings on film are gathered in several texts, including *Film Form* (1949) and *Notes of a Film Director* (1959). He is best known for his films *Strike* (1925), *The Battleship Potemkin* (1925), and *October/Ten Days That Shook the World* (1928), all of which are informed by his theories.

Everson, William K. (1929–) British-born American film historian and collector. Owner of one of the largest independent film collections in the United States, he is also the author of several important film texts, including a history of the silent film era, *American Silent Film* (1978). He has written on westerns, W.C. Fields, and Hal Roach.

Giannetti, Louis D. (1937–) American film scholar. The author of an important introduction to film, *Understanding Movies* (1976), he has also written on the aesthetics of cinema and the films of Jean-Luc Godard.

Greene, Graham (1904–1991) British film critic, novelist, and screenwriter. Born Henry Graham Greene. Best known for his novels, such as *The End of the Affair* (1951), he was a film critic in the late 1930s for *The Spectator*. His reviews are collected in *Graham Greene on Film* (1972) and *The Pleasure-Dome* (1972). Many of his novels were adapted for the screen, some by Greene himself, such as *Brighton Rock/Young Scarface* (1947) and *Our Man in Havana* (1959).

Halliwell, Leslie (1929–1989) British film critic. He authored *The Filmgoer's Companion,* an important reference book that provides information about films, stars, and other aspects of the film industry. He also wrote a guide to films with his personal ratings, *Halliwell's Film Guide,* and a book of film quotes.

Haskell, Molly (1939–) American film critic. She is best known for her examination of the representation of women in film, *From Reverence to Rape* (1974). Other books include *Holding My Own in No Man's Land* (1997). Her film reviews can be heard on National Public Radio and read in *The Village Voice, Vogue,* and *New York* magazine. She is married to film critic Andrew Sarris.

Higham, Charles (1931–) British-born Australian literary and film critic. A prolific and well-respected writer, he compiled reflections by Hollywood's best-known cameramen in *Hollywood Cameramen: Sources of Light* (1970), and wrote *The Art of the American Film, 1900–1971,* a text that combines both the history and aesthetics of American film. Other books include studio and biographies of major film

Sergei Eisenstein's writings on film include: Film Form *(1949) and* Notes of a Film Director *(1959).*

personalities, including Ava Gardner, Marlene Dietrich, Katharine Hepburn, Charles Laughton, and Cecil B. De Mille.

Kael, Pauline (1919–2001) American film critic. She is best known for her reviews for *The New Yorker* beginning in 1968, which often championed popular American films to the dismay of other reviewers. Her writings are collected in several books, including *I Lost It at the Movies* (1965), *Kiss, Kiss, Bang, Bang* (1968), *Hooked* (1989), and *5001 Nights at the Movies* (1991). She has also contributed essays to numerous books on film history, among them "Raising Kane," an essay on *Citizen Kane* that is included in *The Citizen Kane Book* (1971), which she coedited. She also worked briefly in Hollywood as a producer for Warren Beatty. She retired from regular reviewing in 1991.

Kaplan, E. Ann (1936–) British film scholar. Her work highlights the role of women in film, often using theory imported from literary criticism. Texts include *Talking About the Cinema* (1963, 1974), *Women and Film: Both Sides of the Camera* (1983), and *Psychoanalysis and Cinema* (1989). A former lecturer at the British Film Institute, she is on the editorial board of *Cinema Journal* and also writes about other aspects of popular culture, such as music and television.

Katz, Ephraim (d. 1992) American film scholar. He is best known for his comprehensive reference book *The Film Encyclopedia*, a source of information on all aspects of the motion picture industry.

Kauffmann, Stanley (1916–) American film critic, writer, actor, and director. He has reviewed films for *The New York Times,* the *New American Review*, and *The New Republic.* His influential reviews are collected in *Living Images* (1966), *A World on Film* (1971), *Figures of Light* (1970–75), and *Before My Eyes: Film Criticism and Comment* (1980). He is also the editor of *American Film Criticism* (1972), a collection of reviews of important films. His work tends to place films in a broad cultural and historical context.

Kehr, Dave (date unknown) American film critic. He began his career with the *Chicago Reader* in the early 1970s, then wrote for *The Chicago Tribune.* He worked for the *New York Daily News* from 1992 to 1998. His culturally sophisticated reviews have appeared in *Film Comment* and online at CitySearch.com.

Kracauer, Siegfried (1889–1966) German-born American film theorist and historian. He began his career as a newspaper editor in Frankfurt. He worked for the Museum of Modern Art in New York in the early 1940s and wrote a history of German film, *From Caligari to Hitler* (1947). In *Theory of Film* (1960), he highlights the specific properties of the film medium to argue that the

main goal of movies is to reveal elements of our physical reality that we tend not to acknowledge.

Leyda, Jay (1910–) American film critic and filmmaker. Best known for his work on Soviet cinema, he studied with Sergei Eisenstein at the Moscow State Film Institute. He worked for the Museum of Modern Art in New York from 1936 to 1946. Texts include *Kino: A History of the Russian and Soviet Film* (1960) and monographs on Pudovkin, Dovzhenko, and Eisenstein.

McCann, Richard Dyer (date unknown) American film scholar. He is known for his examination of the relationship between movies and society in his texts *Hollywood in Transition* (1962) and *Film and Society* (1964; editor). He also published an overview of film theory, *Film: A Montage of Theories* (1966), and a history of films made by the United States government.

Macdonald, Dwight (1906–1982) American writer and film critic. He was known for his attacks on popular movies and his celebration of more serious films. His reviews appeared in *Fortune, The New Yorker,* and *Esquire.* Many are collected in *Dwight Macdonald on Movies* (1969).

Maltin, Leonard (1950–) American film historian and critic. He is the author of a book on movie shorts from 1930 to 1950; a comprehensive look at Walt Disney's oeuvre, *The Disney Films* (1973); and the popular *Leonard Maltin's Movie & Video Guide* (annual). He is a film reviewer on popular television shows, including *Entertainment Tonight.*

Mast, Gerald (1940–1988) American film scholar. He authored numerous texts on film, including *A Short History of the Movies* (1981), *The Comic Mind: Comedy and the Movies* (1979), *Film/Cinema/Movie: A Theory of Experience* (1977), and *The Movies in Our Midst: Readings in the Cultural History of Film in America* (1982). His successful collection *Film Theory and Criticism,* coedited with Marshall Cohen, has appeared in several editions. His work helped to pioneer the academic study of film.

Metz, Christian (1931–) French film theorist. He is esteemed for his theories applying semiotics, or the study of signs and sign systems, to the cinema. His texts *Language and Cinema* (1974) and *Film Language* (1974) helped establish film as a legitimate field of academic study.

Mitry, Jean (1907–1988) French film theorist, critic, historian, and filmmaker. Mitry made a number of experimental shorts and one feature, *Enigme aux Folies-Bergère* (1959). He was more important as a film theoretician, critic, and historian. He was a founder of France's first film society and of the Cinémathèque Française in 1936. Works include the book *Esthétique et psychologie du cinéma* (1963) and the 30-volume reference work *Filmographie universelle.*

"Very often in cinema, it is the saying that determines absolutely what is said."

—

Christian Metz, 1971

Mulvey, Laura (date unknown) British film theorist and filmmaker. She is best known for her ideas about the role of female spectators in the cinema. Her seminal essay "Visual Pleasure and Narrative Cinema" (1975) encouraged other feminist film scholars to consider the effects of gender on filmmaking and viewing. She coauthored several essays with Peter Wollen and published a critical text on *Citizen Kane.* Her essays are collected in *Visual and Other Pleasures* (1989).

Pudovkin, Vsevolod I. (1893–1953) Russian director and film theorist. Trained at the Moscow State Institute of Cinematography, he worked with Lev Kuleshov beginning in 1922. The notion of montage was central to his theories on film, as it was for Sergei Eisenstein, but unlike that director-theorist, Pudovkin argued that the individual images should be used as building blocks, like words in a sentence. Indebted to D.W. Griffith for his ideas on editing, he believed that the selection of the shot is of utmost importance. Pudovkin's essays are collected in *Film Technique and Film Acting.* His own films, such as *Mother* (1905) and *The End of St. Petersburg* (1927), championed the individual hero rather than the masses, and used narrative and characterization to move the audience.

Sarris, Andrew (1928–) American film critic. A prolific and influential writer, he worked for *The Village Voice* from 1960 to 1989. He is best known for his introduction of the auteur theory to the American public. He also wrote for *Film Culture* in the mid-1950s and 60s. His books include *The Films of Josef von Sternberg,* for the Museum of Modern Art (1966); *Interviews with Film Directors* (1967); *The American Cinema: Directors and Directions* (1968), in which he ranks directors according to the auteur theory; *The Primal Screen* (1973); and *Politics and Cinema* (1978). He has written essays on John Ford, Howard Hawks, and *Citizen Kane.*

Schickel, Richard (1933–) American film critic. He began as a reporter for *Sports Illustrated* and then wrote for *Life* from 1965 to 1972. He has reviewed films for *Time* since 1972. These reviews are collected in *Second Sight* (1972). He is also the author of *The History of an Art and an Institution* (1964), which examines various forces that shape films; *The Disney Version: The Life, Times, Art, and Commerce of Walt Disney* (1968); and *The Making of Star Wars* (1976).

Shalit, Gene (1932–) American film critic who began working for NBC in 1968. Since 1973, he has been a regular film reviewer for that network's *Today* show.

Silverman, Kaja (1947–) American film theorist. Her work examines the female spectator in the cinema, as well as the role of women on screen. *The Subject of Semiotics* (1983) uses a familiar theory from literary criticism to explore the creation of meaning through images. Other books include *The Acoustic Mirror: The Female Voice in Cinema* (1988) and *World Spectators (Cultural Memory in the Present)* (2000).

Siskel, Gene (1946–1999) American film critic. He wrote for *The Chicago Tribune* for more than 30 years as a reviewer and feature columnist and is best known for his 24 year small-screen partnership with Roger Ebert on the weekly review programs *Sneak Previews, At the Movies* and *Siskel & Ebert.* Their television feuding on films attracted millions of viewers each week and created the genre of popular film criticism.

Sitney, P. Adams (date unknown) American film scholar. Since the late 1960s, he has worked for the Anthology Film Archives in New York, an organ-ization that collects and preserves experimental and avant-garde films. He has written on the history of avant-garde film-making. His texts include *Visionary Film: The American Avant-Garde* (1974), *The Essential Cinema* (1975), and a collection of essays from the journal *Film Culture,* which is dedicated to independent films.

Sontag, Susan (1933–) American writer and director. She has written extensively on photography, film, and other media. Her analysis of modern culture calls for a return to emphasis on formal qualities. Her works include *Against Interpretation and Other Essays* (1966) and *On Photography* (1977).

Tyler, Parker (1904–1974) American film critic and writer. He is well known for his examination of sex in the cinema in such texts as *Screening the Sexes: Homosexuality in the Movies* (1972) and *A Pictorial History of Sex in Films* (1974). He also wrote *Magic and Myth of the Movies* (1947), *Underground Film: A Critical History* (1970), and a critical analysis of Charlie Chaplin's films.

Warshow, Robert (1917–1955) American film critic. His writings celebrate gangster and western films as the most important creations of American cinema. Works include *The Immediate Experience: Movies, Comics, Theatre, and Other Aspects of Popular Culture* (1971).

Wollen, Peter (1938–) British-born American filmmaker, film theorist, and critic. He has written on gender in the cinema, Sergei Eisenstein, and semiotics. He discussed the auteur theory in *Signs and Meaning in the Cinema* (1969).

Wood, Robin (Robert) (1931–) British film scholar. He is best known for his seminal studies of great American directors, including Howard Hawks, Alfred Hitchcock, and Arthur Penn. He edited *Working Papers on the Cinema: Sociology and Semiology* (1969) for the British Film Institute and wrote *The American Nightmare: Essays on the Horror Film* (1978).

Saturday Night Fever (1977) fan Gene Siskel bought John Travolta's white suit from the film for $2,000 at a celebrity auction in the early 1980s. At a 1995 auction, it sold for $145,000.

FILMS

Animosity flared between performing brothers when sexy chanteuse Michelle Pfeiffer joined their act in The Fabulous Baker Boys *(1989).*

AFI's Top 100 American Movies of the Last 100 Years

As American filmmaking enters its second century, these motion pictures represent the very best that its finest had to offer.

IN 1998 THE AMERICAN FILM INSTITUTE announced the 100 greatest American movies of the last 100 years, as selected by a blue-ribbon panel of 1,500 leaders from across the film community. The panelists— who included screenwriters, directors, actors, producers, cinematographers, editors, executives, film historians, and critics—chose from a list of 400 nominated films compiled by AFI. The nominated films were all made in the first 100 years of American cinema (1896–1996); movies produced after 1996 were not included.

"This is an exciting moment in American film history," said AFI director and CEO Jean Picker Firstenberg when the results were unveiled. "As the end of this century approaches and we reflect on its defining achievements, among the most powerful and successful is, without question, the motion picture. Through the collective judgment of leaders from across the American film community, from both in front of and behind the camera, AFI has identified 100 movies which set the standard and mark the excellence of the first century of American cinema."

The list of 100 greatest American movies was not intended to close discussion but to open it. Said Firstenberg, "Movies are an intensely personal experience, and it's certain that this list will generate

The Graduate (1967), number seven on AFI's "Top 100 American Movies of the Last 100 Years," starred Anne Bancroft as a middle-aged seductress.

a broad range of opinion and discussion. AFI welcomes this dialogue and hopes to achieve increased regard, respect, and appreciation for this great American art form."

Selection criteria included the following:

FEATURE-LENGTH FICTION FILM: narrative format typically over 60 minutes in length

AMERICAN FILM: English-language film with significant creative and/or financial production elements from the United States

CRITICAL RECOGNITION: formal commendation in print

POPULARITY OVER TIME: including figures for box office adjusted for inflation, television broadcasts and syndication, and home-video sales and rentals

HISTORICAL SIGNIFICANCE: a film's mark on the history of the moving image through technical innovation, visionary narrative devices, or other groundbreaking achievements

CULTURAL IMPACT: a film's mark on American society in matters of style and substance

MAJOR AWARD WINNER: recognition from competitive events, including awards from organizations in the film community and major film festivals

For maximum ease of reference, the films are listed below in three ways: first, in list form in order of preference; second, in alphabetical order; and third, in order of preference with entries that provide the studio, year of release, director, principal cast, and a brief description.

IN ORDER OF PREFERENCE

1. *Citizen Kane* (1941)
2. *Casablanca* (1942)
3. *The Godfather* (1972)
4. *Gone with the Wind* (1939)
5. *Lawrence of Arabia* (1962)
6. *The Wizard of Oz* (1939)
7. *The Graduate* (1967)
8. *On the Waterfront* (1954)
9. *Schindler's List* (1993)
10. *Singin' in the Rain* (1952)
11. *It's a Wonderful Life* (1946)
12. *Sunset Boulevard* (1950)
13. *The Bridge on the River Kwai* (1957)
14. *Some Like It Hot* (1959)
15. *Star Wars* (1977)
16. *All About Eve* (1950)
17. *The African Queen* (1951)
18. *Psycho* (1960)
19. *Chinatown* (1974)
20. *One Flew over the Cuckoo's Nest* (1975)
21. *The Grapes of Wrath* (1940)
22. *2001: A Space Odyssey* (1968)
23. *The Maltese Falcon* (1941)
24. *Raging Bull* (1980)
25. *E.T.: The Extra-Terrestrial* (1982)
26. *Dr. Strangelove or: How I Learned to Stop Worrying and Love the Bomb* (1964)
27. *Bonnie and Clyde* (1967)
28. *Apocalypse Now* (1979)
29. *Mr. Smith Goes to Washington* (1939)
30. *The Treasure of the Sierra Madre* (1948)
31. *Annie Hall* (1977)
32. *The Godfather, Part II* (1974)
33. *High Noon* (1952)
34. *To Kill a Mockingbird* (1962)
35. *It Happened One Night* (1934)
36. *Midnight Cowboy* (1969)
37. *The Best Years of Our Lives* (1946)
38. *Double Indemnity* (1944)

39. *Doctor Zhivago* (1965)
40. *North by Northwest* (1959)
41. *West Side Story* (1961)
42. *Rear Window* (1954)
43. *King Kong* (1933)
44. *The Birth of a Nation* (1915)
45. *A Streetcar Named Desire* (1951)
46. *A Clockwork Orange* (1971)
47. *Taxi Driver* (1976)
48. *Jaws* (1975)
49. *Snow White and the Seven Dwarfs* (1937)
50. *Butch Cassidy and the Sundance Kid* (1969)
51. *The Philadelphia Story* (1940)
52. *From Here to Eternity* (1953)
53. *Amadeus* (1984)
54. *All Quiet on the Western Front* (1930)
55. *The Sound of Music* (1965)
56. *M*A*S*H* (1970)
57. *The Third Man* (1949)
58. *Fantasia* (1941)
59. *Rebel Without a Cause* (1955)
60. *Raiders of the Lost Ark* (1981)
61. *Vertigo* (1958)
62. *Tootsie* (1982)
63. *Stagecoach* (1939)
64. *Close Encounters of the Third Kind* (1977)
65. *The Silence of the Lambs* (1991)
66. *Network* (1976)
67. *The Manchurian Candidate* (1962)
68. *An American in Paris* (1951)
69. *Shane* (1953)
70. *The French Connection* (1971)
71. *Forrest Gump* (1994)
72. *Ben-Hur* (1959)
73. *Wuthering Heights* (1939)
74. *The Gold Rush* (1925)
75. *Dances with Wolves* (1990)
76. *City Lights* (1931)
77. *American Graffiti* (1973)
78. *Rocky* (1976)
79. *The Deer Hunter* (1978)
80. *The Wild Bunch* (1969)
81. *Modern Times* (1936)

Debra Winger provided the alien's voice in E.T.: The Extra-Terrestrial (1982).

continued on next page

82. *Giant* (1956)
83. *Platoon* (1986)
84. *Fargo* (1996)
85. *Duck Soup* (1933)
86. *Mutiny on the Bounty* (1935)
87. *Frankenstein* (1931)
88. *Easy Rider* (1969)
89. *Patton* (1970)
90. *The Jazz Singer* (1927)
91. *My Fair Lady* (1964)
92. *A Place in the Sun* (1951)
93. *The Apartment* (1960)
94. *GoodFellas* (1990)
95. *Pulp Fiction* (1994)
96. *The Searchers* (1956)
97. *Bringing Up Baby* (1938)
98. *Unforgiven* (1992)
99. *Guess Who's Coming to Dinner* (1967)
100. *Yankee Doodle Dandy* (1942)

AFI's Top 100 American Movies of the Last 100 Years

IN ALPHABETICAL ORDER

MOVIE	AFI RANK
The African Queen (1951)	17
All About Eve (1950)	16
All Quiet on the Western Front (1930)	54
Amadeus (1984)	53
American Graffiti (1973)	77
An American in Paris (1951)	68
Annie Hall (1977)	31
The Apartment (1960)	93
Apocalypse Now (1979)	28
Ben-Hur (1959)	72
The Best Years of Our Lives (1946)	37
The Birth of a Nation (1915)	44
Bonnie and Clyde (1967)	27

FACTS ABOUT THE TOP 100 AMERICAN MOVIES

- THE EARLIEST FILM on the roster is *The Birth of a Nation* (1915); the most recent is *Fargo* (1996).
- THE TOP TEN include movies from every decade from the 1930s to the 1990s, with the exception of the 1980s. The 1950s is the most represented decade on the list, with 20 films.
- THE YEAR 1939, widely considered the greatest year in American film history, produced five films on AFI's list: *Gone with the Wind, The Wizard of Oz, Stagecoach, Wuthering Heights,* and *Mr. Smith Goes to Washington.*
- JAMES STEWART and Robert De Niro are the most represented actors in a starring role, each with five films in the top 100. Character actor Ward Bond is the actor who appears in the most films, seven.
- MARLON BRANDO is the only actor to star in two of the top ten films, *The Godfather* (1972) and *On the Waterfront* (1954) .
- KATHARINE HEPBURN is the most represented leading actress, with four films. She is followed by Natalie Wood, Diane Keaton, and Faye Dunaway, with three films each.
- THE GODFATHER, PART II (1974) is the only sequel to make the cut.
- CHARLIE CHAPLIN is the most honored actor-director on the list, with three films in which he performed both tasks: *The Gold Rush* (1925), *City Lights* (1931), and *Modern Times* (1936).
- STEVEN SPIELBERG directed five films on AFI's top 100: *Schindler's List* (1993) at No. 9, *E.T.: The Extra-Terrestrial* (1982) at No. 25, *Jaws* (1975) at No. 48, *Raiders of the Lost Ark* (1981) at No. 60, and *Close Encounters of the Third Kind* (1977) at No. 64.
- ALFRED HITCHCOCK and Billy Wilder each directed four of the films on the list. Hitchcock's include *Psycho* (1960) at No. 18, *North by Northwest* (1959) at No. 40, *Rear Window* (1954) at No. 42, and *Vertigo* (1958) at No. 61. Wilder's include *Sunset Boulevard* (1950) at No. 12, *Some Like It Hot* (1959) at No. 14, *Double Indemnity* (1944) at No. 38, and *The Apartment* (1960) at No. 93.

Steven Spielberg directed five films on AFI's "Top 100 American Movies".

The Bridge on the River Kwai (1957)	13		*Modern Times* (1936)	81
Bringing Up Baby (1938)	97		*Mr. Smith Goes to Washington* (1939)	29
Butch Cassidy and the Sundance Kid (1969)	50		*Mutiny on the Bounty* (1935)	86
Casablanca (1942)	2		*My Fair Lady* (1964)	91
Chinatown (1974)	19		*Network* (1976)	66
Citizen Kane (1941)	1		*North by Northwest* (1959)	40
City Lights (1931)	76		*On the Waterfront* (1954)	8
A Clockwork Orange (1971)	46		*One Flew over the Cuckoo's Nest* (1975)	20
Close Encounters of the Third Kind (1977)	64		*Patton* (1970)	89
Dances with Wolves (1990)	75		*The Philadelphia Story* (1940)	51
The Deer Hunter (1978)	79		*A Place in the Sun* (1951)	92
Doctor Zhivago (1965)	39		*Platoon* (1986)	83
Double Indemnity (1944)	38		*Psycho* (1960)	18
Dr. Strangelove or: How I Learned to Stop Worrying and Love the Bomb (1964)	26		*Pulp Fiction* (1994)	95
Duck Soup (1933)	85		*Raging Bull* (1980)	24
E.T.: The Extra-Terrestrial (1982)	25		*Raiders of the Lost Ark* (1981)	60
Easy Rider (1969)	88		*Rear Window* (1954)	42
Fantasia (1941)	58		*Rebel Without a Cause* (1955)	59
Fargo (1996)	84		*Rocky* (1976)	78
Forrest Gump (1994)	71		*Schindler's List* (1993)	9
Frankenstein (1931)	87		*The Searchers* (1956)	96
The French Connection (1971)	70		*Shane* (1953)	69
From Here to Eternity (1953)	52		*The Silence of the Lambs* (1991)	65
Giant (1956)	82		*Singin' in the Rain* (1952)	10
The Godfather (1972)	3		*Snow White and the Seven Dwarfs* (1937)	49
The Godfather, Part II (1974)	32		*Some Like It Hot* (1959)	14
The Gold Rush (1925)	74		*The Sound of Music* (1965)	55
Gone with the Wind (1939)	4		*Stagecoach* (1939)	63
GoodFellas (1990)	94		*Star Wars* (1977)	15
The Graduate (1967)	7		*A Streetcar Named Desire* (1951)	45
The Grapes of Wrath (1940)	21		*Sunset Boulevard* (1950)	12
Guess Who's Coming to Dinner (1967)	99		*Taxi Driver* (1976)	47
High Noon (1952)	33		*The Third Man* (1949)	57
It Happened One Night (1934)	35		*To Kill a Mockingbird* (1962)	34
It's a Wonderful Life (1946)	11		*Tootsie* (1982)	62
Jaws (1975)	48		*The Treasure of the Sierra Madre* (1948)	30
The Jazz Singer (1927)	90		*2001: A Space Odyssey* (1968)	22
King Kong (1933)	43		*Unforgiven* (1992)	98
Lawrence of Arabia (1962)	5		*Vertigo* (1958)	61
*M*A*S*H* (1970)	56		*West Side Story* (1961)	41
The Maltese Falcon (1941)	23		*The Wild Bunch* (1969)	80
The Manchurian Candidate (1962)	67		*The Wizard of Oz* (1939)	6
Midnight Cowboy (1969)	36		*Wuthering Heights* (1939)	73
			Yankee Doodle Dandy (1942)	100

PREVIOUS PAGE:

Mutiny on the Bounty *(1935)*, *starring Donald Crisp (left) and Charles Laughton (right) was named to AFI's list of "The Top 100 American Movies of the Last 100 Years."*

Renowned as a "woman's director," George Cukor was a natural choice to direct *Gone with the Wind*. After reportedly clashing with star Clark Gable, however, Cukor was replaced partway into shooting by Victor Fleming. But Cukor's famous touch is still apparent in the finished picture: he continued to secretly coach stars Vivien Leigh and Olivia de Havilland throughout the film's production.

AFI's Top 100 American Movies of the Last 100 Years

BRIEF DESCRIPTIONS

1. ***Citizen Kane*** (RKO, 1941) Director: Orson Welles. Orson Welles, Joseph Cotten, Everett Sloane, Agnes Moorehead. Tragic story of newspaper tycoon Charles Foster Kane (Welles), loosely modeled after the life of William Randolph Hearst, founder of the Hearst publishing empire. Acclaimed for its innovations in narrative technique and cinematography, its literate screenplay, and its nuanced portrayal of the central character.

2. ***Casablanca*** (Warner Bros., 1942) Director: Michael Curtiz. Humphrey Bogart, Ingrid Bergman, Paul Henreid, Claude Rains, Dooley Wilson. Romantic drama of wartime sacrifice set in Nazi-occupied French Morocco. Bogart's portrayal of the cynical but heroic saloonkeeper Rick Blaine made him a major star. With a crackling script and the classic song "As Time Goes By" Academy Award for best picture.

3. ***The Godfather*** (Paramount, 1972) Director: Francis Ford Coppola. Marlon Brando, Al Pacino, Robert Duvall, James Caan, Diane Keaton. Tragic, romantic saga of Mob boss Don Corleone (Brando) and the rise of his successor, son Michael (Pacino). The film reimagined the genre of the Mob drama and won Academy Awards for best picture and best actor. Adapted from Mario Puzo's novel, it is marked by taut suspense, rich period detail, and memorable dialogue ("I'll make him an offer he can't refuse").

4. ***Gone with the Wind*** (MGM, 1939) Director: Victor Fleming. Clark Gable, Vivien Leigh, Olivia de Havilland, Leslie Howard, Hattie McDaniel. Inimitable epic of Civil War destruction and the ill-fated romance between Scarlett O'Hara (Leigh) and Rhett Butler (Gable). Endures as a compelling story and an example of studio era greatness. Based on the best-selling novel by Margaret Mitchell, it won four Academy Awards, for best picture, director, actress, and supporting actress.

5. ***Lawrence of Arabia*** (Columbia, 1962) Director: David Lean. Peter O'Toole, Omar Sharif, Alec Guinness, Anthony Quinn, José Ferrer. Majestic adventure and character drama about enigmatic British mapmaker T.E. Lawrence (O'Toole), who transforms himself into the leader of a World War I Arab revolt. Based on T.E. Lawrence's memoir *Seven Pillars*

of Wisdom. Winner of Academy Awards for best picture and best director.

6. ***The Wizard of Oz*** (MGM, 1939) Director: Victor Fleming. Judy Garland, Ray Bolger, Bert Lahr, Jack Haley, Frank Morgan. Magical adaptation of L. Frank Baum's children's fantasy of an enchanted land made Garland a major star and Harold Arlen and E.Y. Harburg's song "Over the Rainbow" a popular standard. Inventive use of color and special effects are still impressive today. A children's movie for all ages.

7. ***The Graduate*** (Embassy, 1967) Director: Mike Nichols. Dustin Hoffman, Anne Bancroft, Katharine Ross. Black comedy of aimless 1960s college graduate (Hoffman) that defined a generation and established Hoffman as a star. Mrs. Robinson's (Bancroft's) seduction of Benjamin (Hoffman) is withering and hilarious. Evocative score by Simon and Garfunkel includes "Mrs. Robinson." Nichols won an Academy Award for best director.

8. ***On the Waterfront*** (Columbia, 1954) Director: Elia Kazan. Marlon Brando, Eva Marie Saint, Karl Malden, Lee J. Cobb. Gritty drama of union corruption memorable for Brando's sensitive performance as a misfit dockworker, epitomized in backseat scene in which he cries "I could've been a contender." Winner of Academy Awards for best picture, actor, and supporting actress.

9. ***Schindler's List*** (Amblin Entertainment/ Universal, 1993) Director: Steven Spielberg. Liam Neeson, Ben Kingsley, Ralph Fiennes. Somber, inspiring adaptation of Thomas Kenneally's fact-based book about a Catholic industrialist able to save several hundred Polish Jews from death during World War II by hiring them to work in his factory. Memorable performances all around, particularly by Fiennes, who plays a brutal Nazi officer. Winner of Academy Awards for best picture and best director.

10. ***Singin' in the Rain*** (MGM, 1952) Directors: Stanley Donen, Gene Kelly. Gene Kelly, Debbie Reynolds, Donald O'Connor, Jean Hagen. Delightful musical send-up of the transition from silent to sound films, with many memorable musical numbers, including "Make 'Em Laugh," "Broadway Rhythm," and the incomparable title song.

11. ***It's a Wonderful Life*** (RKO/Liberty Films, 1946) Director: Frank Capra. James Stewart, Donna Reed, Lionel Barrymore, Thomas Mitchell, Henry Travers. Moving fable of disillusioned family man (Stewart) who is visited by a guardian angel (Travers) and shown what the world would be like if he had never been born. Notable for Stewart's

engrossing Everyman performance as George Bailey. Favorite film of both Capra and Stewart.

12. *Sunset Boulevard* (Paramount, 1950) Director: Billy Wilder. William Holden, Gloria Swanson, Erich von Stroheim, Cecil B. DeMille. The caustic, tragic noir about a screenwriter (Holden) and the deluded silent star (Swanson) who ensnares him won three Academy Awards, including best screenplay. Memorable line: "I am big. It's the pictures that got small."

13. *The Bridge on the River Kwai* (Columbia, 1957) Director: David Lean. Alec Guinness, William Holden, Jack Hawkins, Sessue Hayakawa. Dark World War II drama about stiff-backed British POW colonel (Guinness), his equally unyielding Japanese captor, (Hayakawa), and the bridge that embodies the absurdities of war. Winner of Academy Awards for best picture, director, actor. Memorable use of World War II song and the "Colonel Bogey March."

14. *Some Like It Hot* (Ashton/Mirisch, 1959) Director: Billy Wilder. Jack Lemmon, Tony Curtis, Marilyn Monroe, Joe E. Brown. Hilarious comedy about 1920s musicians (Lemmon and Curtis) who witness the St. Valentine's Day Massacre in Chicago, then join all-female band and evade killers. Memorable throughout, especially for the last line. Adapted screenplay by Wilder and I.A.L. Diamond, for which they won Academy Awards.

15. *Star Wars* (20th Century–Fox, 1977) Director: George Lucas. Mark Hamill, Harrison Ford, Carrie Fisher, Alec Guinness. Spectacular space adventure combined a simple story of good vs. evil with stunning visual effects and endearing robotic characters to revolutionize the science fiction and action genres and make a star of Harrison Ford. Two sequels and a prequel followed.

16. *All About Eve* (20th Century–Fox, 1950) Director: Joseph L. Mankiewicz. Bette Davis, Anne Baxter, George Sanders, Celeste Holm, Thelma Ritter. Classic story of backstage betrayal, with Davis as the aging star Margo Channing and Baxter as the young schemer Eve Harrington. Academy Award winner for best picture, it is memorable for Sanders role as the cynical critic and Marilyn Monroe as his scene-stealing consort.

17. *The African Queen* (United Artists, 1951) Director: John Huston. Humphrey Bogart, Katharine Hepburn, Robert Morley. Rousing romantic adventure yarn of drunken boatman and prim spinster (Bogart and Hepburn) who join forces on the river during World War I. Quintessential Bogart performance won an Academy Award for best actor; the James Agee/John Huston screenplay is based on the C.S. Forester novel.

18. *Psycho* (Paramount, 1960) Director: Alfred Hitchcock. Anthony Perkins, Janet Leigh, John Gavin. Shocking thriller of a woman on the lam (Leigh) and the twisted events at the Bates Motel, under the management of Norman Bates (Perkins). Controversial upon release for its shocking shower scene and sympathetic portrayal of the killer, it has since been influential to horror and thriller filmmakers.

19. *Chinatown* (Paramount, 1974) Director: Roman Polanski. Jack Nicholson, Faye Dunaway, John Huston. Intricate mystery involving an enigmatic woman (Dunaway), her corrupt father (Huston), and LA detective J.J. Gittes (Nicholson), who uncovers their secrets and shady water deals in 1930s LA. Seductive 1930s set design, memorable last line. Won an Academy Award for best original screenplay.

20. *One Flew over the Cuckoo's Nest* (United Artists, 1975) Director: Milos Forman. Jack Nicholson, Louise Fletcher. Earnest adaptation of Ken Kesey's novel about inspired asylum patient Randle McMurphy (Nicholson) and the institution's relentless drive to quash him. Won five Academy Awards—for best picture, actor, actress, director, and screenplay.

21. *The Grapes of Wrath* (20th Century–Fox, 1940) Director: John Ford. Henry Fonda, Jane Darwell, John Carradine, Charley Grapewin. Moving adaptation of John Steinbeck's novel about displaced farmers during the Great Depression, notable for understated performances by Fonda and Jane Darwell, in a supporting role as Ma Joad, which earned her an Academy Award. Ford won an Academy Award for best director.

The 1940 film adaptation of John Steinbeck's classic novel The Grapes of Wrath *starred Dorris Bowden, Jane Darwell, and Henry Fonda.*

22. *2001: A Space Odyssey* (MGM, 1968) Director: Stanley Kubrick. Keir Dullea, Gary Lockwood, William Sylvester, Douglas Rain. Coolly spectacular space drama takes on the history of mankind and a search for alien existence in the galaxy. HAL 9000 the computer, with voice by Rain, is memorable.

23. *The Maltese Falcon* (Warner Bros., 1941) Director: John Huston. Humphrey Bogart, Mary Astor, Peter Lorre, Sydney Greenstreet, Elisha Cook, Jr. Bogart offers the definitive incarnation of Sam Spade in this tight adaptation of Dashiell Hammett's detective story, which is also Huston's first film. Irresistible performance by Astor as the mendacious femme fatale, with equally delectable supporting characterizations provided by Lorre, Cook, and Greenstreet.

24. *Raging Bull* (United Artists, 1980) Director: Martin Scorsese. Robert De Niro, Joe Pesci, Cathy Moriarty. Dark biographical drama of self-destructive boxer Jake La Motta and his path to redemption. Notable for compelling fight scenes and an Academy Award–winning performance by De Niro, who transformed himself physically for the title role.

25. *E.T.: The Extra-Terrestrial* (Universal, 1982) Director: Steven Spielberg. Dee Wallace, Henry Thomas, Drew Barrymore. Touching, exhilarating drama of boy (Thomas) who encounters otherworldly creature who wants only to go home. John Williams's Academy Award–winning score is notable.

26. *Dr. Strangelove or: How I Learned to Stop Worrying and Love the Bomb* (Columbia, 1964) Director: Stanley Kubrick. Peter Sellers, Slim Pickens, George C. Scott, Sterling Hayden. Black comedy of US nuclear bomb launch on Russia, featuring a memorable triad of performances by Sellers (as US president, British officer, and deranged scientist) and Pickens's wild ride on a missile.

Faye Dunaway and Warren Beatty portrayed Depression-era bank robbers Bonnie and Clyde on the big screen in the 1967 film Bonnie and Clyde.

27. *Bonnie and Clyde* (Warner Bros.–Seven Arts, 1967) Director: Arthur Penn. Warren Beatty, Faye Dunaway, Gene Hackman, Estelle Parsons. Influential reimagining of gangster film genre recounts lives and loves of infamous 1930s bank robbers, played by Beatty and Dunaway. Also notable for influence on fashion and its stylized presentation of film violence.

28. *Apocalypse Now* (Zoetrope Studios, 1979) Director: Francis Ford Coppola. Marlon Brando, Martin Sheen, Robert Duvall. Phantasmagoric representation of Vietnam War based on Joseph Conrad's novel *Heart of Darkness*. Features enigmatic performance by Brando (as Kurtz) and dazzling Academy Award–winning cinematography by Vittorio Storaro.

29. *Mr. Smith Goes to Washington* (Columbia, 1939) Director: Frank Capra. James Stewart, Jean Arthur, Claude Rains, Thomas Mitchell. Exhilarating comedy-drama of Washington politics chronicles triumph of idealistic Senator Jefferson Smith (Stewart) over longtime corruption, embodied in mentor Senator Paine (Rains). Stewart's stirring one-man filibuster is especially notable.

30. *The Treasure of the Sierra Madre* (Warner Bros., 1948) Director: John Huston. Humphrey Bogart, Walter Huston, Tim Holt. Morality tale about gold prospectors overcome by greed won Academy Awards for best director, screenplay, and supporting actor (Walter Huston, father of the director and screenwriter).

31. *Annie Hall* (United Artists, 1977) Director: Woody Allen. Woody Allen, Diane Keaton, Tony Roberts. Sophisticated autobiographical comedy of the untenable love affair of two New Yorkers (Allen and Keaton), notable for its witty dialogue and sumptuous rendering of New York City. Won Academy Awards for best picture and actress (Keaton, in title role).

32. *The Godfather—Part II* (Paramount, 1974) Director: Francis Ford Coppola. Al Pacino, Diane Keaton, Robert De Niro, Robert Duvall, Lee Strasberg. Sizzling sequel to *The Godfather* contrasts the rise to power of young Vito Corleone (De Niro) with the maturation and moral decline of his son Don Michael Corleone (Pacino). Outstanding period detail. Winner of Academy Awards for best picture, director, and supporting actor (De Niro).

33. *High Noon* (United Artists, 1952) Director: Fred Zinnemann. Gary Cooper, Grace Kelly, Lloyd Bridges, Thomas Mitchell. Classically drawn western about newlywed marshal (Cooper) deserted by his community in the face of evil. Academy Award winner for best picture, memorable for its tight structure and iconic Academy Award–winning performance by Cooper.

34. *To Kill a Mockingbird* (Universal, 1962) Director: Robert Mulligan. Gregory Peck, Mary Badham, Philip Alford, Brock Peters. Affecting adaptation of Harper Lee's novel about a small-town lawyer's defense of a black man accused of raping a white woman in 1930s South. Remembered for Peck's Academy Award–winning performance as lawyer Atticus Finch and the debut of Robert Duvall as recluse Boo Radley.

35. *It Happened One Night* (Columbia, 1934) Director: Frank Capra. Clark Gable, Claudette Colbert, Roscoe Karns, Walter Connolly. Definitive screwball comedy of runaway heiress bride (Colbert) who learns about life, love, and the Walls of Jericho from a newspaperman (Gable). It was the first film to sweep the four top Academy Awards—winning best picture, actor, actress, and director—and established Capra as the preeminent director of the 1930s. Gable's bare-chested presence onscreen caused a decline in US undershirt sales.

36. *Midnight Cowboy* (United Artists, 1969) Director: John Schlesinger. Dustin Hoffman, Jon Voight, Sylvia Miles, Brenda Vaccaro. Dark, powerful character drama about misfits (Hoffman and Voight) living on the fringes in New York City. Based on the novel by James Lee Herlihy, it was the first and only X-rated film to win an Academy Award for best picture (later edited to gain R rating).

37. *The Best Years of Our Lives* (Goldwyn, RKO, 1946) Director: William Wyler. Fredric March, Myrna Loy, Dana Andrews, Teresa Wright, Harold Russell. Poignant drama of three returning World War II veterans captures their generation's difficulties in readjusting to civilian life. Won Academy Awards for best picture, actor, director, and supporting actor (Harold Russell, as a veteran who lost both hands in the war). Memorable March homecoming scene.

38. *Double Indemnity* (Paramount, 1944) Director: Billy Wilder. Fred MacMurray, Barbara Stanwyck, Edward G. Robinson. Adaptation of James M. Cain novel features a sharp Wilder/Raymond Chandler screenplay and steamy chemistry between an insurance salesman (MacMurray) and schemer (Stanwyck). Robinson provides the moral center as the salesman's dogged boss.

39. *Doctor Zhivago* (MGM, 1965) Director: David Lean. Omar Sharif, Julie Christie, Geraldine Chaplin. Sweeping adaptation of Boris Pasternak's epic novel, with Sharif in title role of a Russian doctor-poet involved with two women amid the turmoil of World War I and the Bolshevik Revolution. Maurice Jarre won an Academy Award for his romantic score.

40. *North by Northwest* (MGM, 1959) Director: Alfred Hitchcock. Cary Grant, Eva Marie Saint, James Mason, Jessie Royce Landis. Witty, baroque mystery that begins with the mistaken identity of Roger Thornhill (Grant) and moves to a cross-country chase that concludes on the carved faces of Mount Rushmore. Other notable scenes include the thrilling crop-dusting airplane sequence.

41. *West Side Story* (United Artists, 1961) Directors: Robert Wise, Jerome Robbins. Natalie Wood, Richard Beymer, Rita Moreno, George Chakiris, Russ Tamblyn. Masterful adaptation of the Leonard Bernstein–Stephen Sondheim musical about gang life and star-crossed love that captures its vigor, color, and tragedy. Earned Academy Awards for best picture, director, and supporting actor and actress. Dramatic songs include "Tonight," "Somewhere," and "America."

42. *Rear Window* (Paramount, 1954) Director: Alfred Hitchcock. James Stewart, Grace Kelly, Thelma Ritter, Raymond Burr. Convalescing Stewart's (and Kelly's and Ritter's) amiable voyeurism uncovers a bona fide murder case in this tight mystery based on a Cornell Woolrich story. Notable for its rendering of 1950s New York City and for Kelly's stylish costumes.

43. *King Kong* (RKO, 1933) Directors: Merian C. Cooper, Ernest B. Schoedsack. Robert Armstrong, Fay Wray, Bruce Cabot. Tragic fantasy-adventure of giant misunderstood ape and the woman (Wray) he adores. Legendary special effects by Willis O'Brien include the closing sequence of the beast and Wray atop the Empire State Building. Pounding score by Max Steiner.

44. *The Birth of a Nation* (Epoch Producing Co., 1915) Director: D.W. Griffith. Lillian Gish, Mae Marsh, Wallace Reid, Henry B. Walthall, Elmo Lincoln. Groundbreaking all-star silent epic of Civil War and Reconstruction strife seen through the eyes of two families, one Union, one Confederate. Notable for intricate narrative that is sustained for over two and a half hours. Controversial since its initial release for its racism and heroic depiction of the Ku Klux Klan.

45. *A Streetcar Named Desire* (Warner Bros., 1951) Director: Elia Kazan. Marlon Brando, Vivien Leigh, Karl Malden, Kim Hunter. Potent adaptation of the Tennessee Williams tragedy about an aging Southern belle (Leigh) that established coarse Brando as a star and gained Academy Awards for Leigh, Malden, and Hunter.

46. *A Clockwork Orange* (Warner Bros., 1971) Director: Stanley Kubrick. Malcolm McDowell, Patrick Magee, Michael Bates. Stunning, stylized adaptation of Anthony Burgess's satiric novel, seen through the eyes of Alex (McDowell), who delights in ultraviolence until he is reprogrammed. The controversial, farsighted work was edited from its original X rating to an R rating.

47. *Taxi Driver* (Columbia, 1976) Director: Martin Scorsese. Robert De Niro, Jodie Foster, Harvey Keitel, Cybill Shepherd. Unsettling urban drama of New York City cabbie Travis Bickle (De Niro), who combats the crime and filth of the city through what he believes to be righteous violence. The sight of Bickle barking

"I went to see Stanley and he said, 'I've got this book for you…' When I read it, I found it very hard going, first time. I thought, what is all this 'malenky' and 'droogies' nonsense?"

—

Malcolm McDowell, on his first being given a copy of Anthony Burgess's novel A Clockwork Orange *by director Stanley Kubrick, 1973*

OVERLEAF:

Stanley Kubrick's classic anti war film Dr. Strangelove *(1964) was based on the Peter George novel* Red Alert.

"You talkin' to me?" to himself in the mirror is still shocking. The moody score by Bernard Herrmann (his last work) captures New York's menacing darkness.

48. *Jaws* (Universal, 1975) Director: Steven Spielberg. Richard Dreyfuss, Robert Shaw, Roy Scheider. Thrilling adventure about a killer shark and the motley crew hunting for it. Notable for lifelike mechanical shark. John Williams's pounding score won an Academy Award.

49. *Snow White and the Seven Dwarfs* (RKO/Walt Disney, 1937) Director: David Hand. Voices of Adrienne Casillotti, Harry Stockwell, Lucille LaVerne. Disney's first full-length animated film is notable for its rich artistic detail, distinctive characterizations, and enduring songs, including "Whistle While You Work" and "Someday My Prince Will Come."

50. *Butch Cassidy and the Sundance Kid* (20th Century–Fox, 1969) Director: George Roy Hill. Paul Newman, Robert Redford, Katharine Ross. Genial character western chronicling the relationship of two bandits (Newman and Redford) and their final attempt to escape the law. Marked by William Goldman's keen Academy Award–winning original screenplay and star turns by the two leads.

51. *The Philadelphia Story* (MGM, 1940) Director: George Cukor. Katharine Hepburn, Cary Grant, James Stewart, Ruth Hussey. Divine adaptation of the Philip Barry marriage comedy features three of the screen's biggest stars at their wittiest and most beautiful. Memorable drunk scenes between Stewart and Hepburn and Stewart and Grant. Stewart won an Academy Award for best actor.

52. *From Here to Eternity* (Columbia, 1953) Director: Fred Zinnemann. Burt Lancaster, Deborah Kerr, Montgomery Clift, Frank Sinatra, Donna Reed. Blistering adaptation of James Jones's novel of army life in Hawaii on the eve of Pearl Harbor captured Academy Awards for best picture and director, as well as a career-rebuilding best supporting actor award for Sinatra. Includes much-imitated waterside love scene between Lancaster and Kerr.

53. *Amadeus* (Orion, 1984) Director: Milos Forman. F. Murray Abraham, Tom Hulce, Elizabeth Berridge. Sweeping drama of the difficult relationship between composers Wolfgang Amadeus Mozart (Hulce) and Antonio Salieri (Abraham) is a study in the excesses of talent and jealousy. Film won an Academy Award for best picture; Abraham was named best actor.

54. *All Quiet on the Western Front* (Universal, 1930) Director: Lewis Milestone. Lew Ayres, Louis Wolheim, John Wray. Powerful adaptation of the Erich Maria Remarque antiwar novel about the experiences of German students who become soldiers during World War I. Winner of Academy Awards for best picture and best director, it was also a box-office success.

55. *The Sound of Music* (20th Century–Fox, 1965) Director: Robert Wise. Julie Andrews, Christopher Plummer, Eleanor Parker, Peggy Wood. Phenomenally popular adaptation of Rodgers and Hammerstein musical about the singing Von Trapp family and their escape from the Nazis. Five Academy Awards, including best picture and director. Memorable opening sequence with Maria (Andrews) and the Alps. Beloved songs include "My Favorite Things," "Edelweiss," "Do Re Mi," and "The Sound of Music."

56. *M*A*S*H* (Aspen/20th Century–Fox, 1970) Director: Robert Altman. Donald Sutherland, Elliot Gould, Sally Kellerman. Black comedy of freewheeling emergency medical unit during the Korean War established Altman as major iconoclastic director and helped usher in a decade of US film experimentation. It also inspired a long-running television series.

57. *The Third Man* (Korda/Selznick Releasing Org., UK, 1949) Director: Carol Reed. Orson Welles, Joseph Cotten, Alida Valli, Trevor Howard. The search for Harry Lime (Welles) is the center of this lithe mystery notable for its Academy Award–winning cinematography and distinctive, zither theme that recurs throughout the film.

58. *Fantasia* (Walt Disney–RKO, 1940) Director (production supervisor): Ben Sharpsteen. Deems Taylor, narrator. Classical music and animation mix in a dazzling eight-part imaginative journey. Musical selections include Dukas's "The Sorcerer's Apprentice" (with Mickey Mouse) and Stravinsky's "Rite of Spring."

59. *Rebel Without a Cause* (Warner Bros., 1955) Director: Nicholas Ray. James Dean, Natalie Wood, Sal Mineo, Jim Backus. Definitive film of 1950s teen disaffection memorable for Dean's iconic turn. Also notable are performances by Mineo as Dean's troubled friend and Backus as Dean's pitiable father.

60. *Raiders of the Lost Ark* (Paramount, 1981) Director: Steven Spielberg. Harrison Ford, Karen Allen, John Rhys-Davies. Rollicking yarn about archeologist Indiana Jones (Ford) and his quest for the Ark of the Covenant. Simultaneously paid homage to the tradition of movie serials and reinvented the adventure film. Followed by two sequels.

61. *Vertigo* (Paramount, 1958) Director: Alfred Hitchcock. James Stewart, Kim Novak, Barbara Bel Geddes. Obsession and suspense combine in this eerie drama about retired police detective John "Scottie" Ferguson's (Stewart's)

"It's like being hit over the head with a Valentine's card every day."

—

Christopher Plummer, on working with Julie Andrews in The Sound of Music

pursuit of a mysterious woman (Novak). Tense score by Bernard Herrmann, memorable credits by Saul Bass. Considered by many film writers and scholars as Hitchcock's most ambitious film.

62. *Tootsie* (Columbia, 1982) Director: Sydney Pollack. Dustin Hoffman, Jessica Lange, Bill Murray (unbilled), Teri Garr. Hilarious comedy about out-of-work actor Michael Dorsey (Hoffman), who becomes a national phenomenon as straight-shooting female soap opera star Dorothy Michaels. Lange won an Academy Award for best supporting actress for her performance as Dorothy's friend and Dorsey's love object.

63. *Stagecoach* (Walter Wanger/United Artists, 1939) Director: John Ford. John Wayne, Claire Trevor, Thomas Mitchell, John Carradine. Absorbing, character study of eventful stagecoach trip elevated the western in dramatic importance and made a star of Wayne, who portrayed the Ringo Kid. Stunning showcase of stunt work by Yakima Canutt. For the role of the drunken doctor, Mitchell won an Academy Award for best supporting actor.

64. *Close Encounters of the Third Kind* (Columbia, 1977) Director: Steven Spielberg. Richard Dreyfuss, François Truffaut, Teri Garr. Spectacular, hopeful mystery of an average man (Dreyfuss) who finds himself called by an otherworldly source, culminating in his rendezvous with alien creatures. Groundbreaking special effects and inviting John Williams score.

65. *The Silence of the Lambs* (Orion, 1991) Director: Jonathan Demme. Jodie Foster, Anthony Hopkins, Scott Glenn. Engrossing adaptation of Thomas Harris's crime novel and character study is notable for the complex relationship between FBI agent Clarice Starling (Foster) and cannibalistic criminal Hannibal Lecter (Hopkins). Won Academy Awards for best picture, actor, actress, and director.

66. *Network* (MGM/United Artists, 1976) Director: Sidney Lumet. William Holden, Faye Dunaway, Peter Finch. Biting satire of a television network's shameless search for ratings. Memorable for its prophetic screenplay by Paddy Chayefsky and the performances of Dunaway and Finch. All three garnered Academy Awards, as did supporting actress Beatrice Straight.

67. *The Manchurian Candidate* (United Artists, 1962) Director: John Frankenheimer. Frank Sinatra, Laurence Harvey, Janet Leigh, Angela Lansbury. Suspense thriller about a Korean War veteran brainwashed by the communists to be an assassin. Notable for its political satire, visual inventiveness, and Lansbury's performance as a scheming mother.

68. *An American in Paris* (MGM, 1951) Director: Vincente Minnelli. Gene Kelly, Leslie Caron, Oscar Levant. Academy Award–winning film about American artist Kelly finding love with Frenchwoman Caron is a showcase for dazzling scenes built around George and Ira Gershwin's lush score. Songs include "I Got Rhythm," "Embraceable You," "'s Wonderful," and "An American in Paris."

69. *Shane* (Paramount, 1953) Director: George Stevens. Alan Ladd, Jean Arthur, Van Heflin, Brandon de Wilde, Jack Palance. Elemental western about lone gunman Shane (Ladd) teaming with settlers to protect land from gunslingers, including Palance. De Wilde's closing call to Shane caps the film.

70. *The French Connection* (20th Century–Fox, 1971) Director: William Friedkin. Gene Hackman, Roy Scheider, Fernando Rey. Gritty action drama about unconventional detective James "Popeye" Doyle (Hackman) tracking international heroin smugglers won five Academy Awards, including best picture and actor. The car chase under the El tracks is among the most spectacular in film.

71. *Forrest Gump* (Paramount, 1994) Director: Robert Zemeckis. Tom Hanks, Sally Field, Gary Sinise, Robin Wright. Poignant drama of a simple, kind man (Hanks) who becomes central to the major events of the late 20th century and finds true love (Wright) along the way. Seamless visual effects place Gump at forefront of historical scenes. This adaptation of Winston Groom's novel won Academy Awards for best picture and best actor.

72. *Ben-Hur* (MGM, 1959) Director: William Wyler. Charlton Heston, Jack Hawkins, Stephen Boyd, Hugh Griffith. Epic character-driven adaptation of Lew Wallace's religious novel set in the time of Christ. The film is notable for impressive action scenes, including its legendary chariot race. Won Academy Awards for best picture, director, and supporting actor (Griffith).

73. *Wuthering Heights* (United Artists, 1939) Director: William Wyler. Laurence Olivier, Merle Oberon, David Niven. Atmospheric adaptation of the Emily Brontë novel features Olivier and Oberon as the doomed romantic couple, framed by stunning Academy Award–winning cinematography by Gregg Toland.

Tom Hanks played the dim-witted but good-hearted Forrest Gump in the award-winning 1994 film of the same name.

74. *The Gold Rush* (United Artists, 1925) Director: Charlie Chaplin. Charlie Chaplin, Georgia Hale, Mack Swain. The Little Tramp finds love and adventure in the Yukon in this poignant comedy that defines Chaplin's silent work. Chaplin also wrote the score and screenplay.

75. *Dances with Wolves* (Orion, 1990) Director: Kevin Costner. Kevin Costner, Mary McDonnell, Graham Greene. Civil War captain Costner finds a new home among the Sioux Indians in this Academy Award–winning movie, Costner's directoral debut. Memorable for its atmospheric location cinematography and feeling portrayal of Native American life.

76. *City Lights* (Chaplin/United Artists, 1931) Director: Charlie Chaplin. Charlie Chaplin, Virginia Cherrill, Florence Lee, Harry Myers. Moving drama about the Little Tramp's (Chaplin's) devotion to a blind girl (Cherrill) and his difficult link to a rich and eccentric lush (Myers). Notable as an exquisite Chaplin-esque blend of drama and pathos.

77. *American Graffiti* (Universal, 1973) Director: George Lucas. Richard Dreyfuss, Ron Howard, Paul LeMat, Harrison Ford. California teenagers on a late-summer night in 1962 mark passage from high school into adulthood. This funny, melancholy film brought the director and Dreyfuss to prominence; use of early rock hits influenced sound tracks for years.

78. *Rocky* (United Artists, 1976) Director: John G. Avildsen. Sylvester Stallone, Talia Shire, Burgess Meredith, Carl Weathers. Crowd-pleasing Cinderella drama of small-time boxer (Stallone) who gets his last chance to prove himself in a championship match against Apollo Creed (Weathers). An Academy Award winner, the film made Stallone a star and sparked four sequels.

79. *The Deer Hunter* (Warner Bros., 1978) Director: Michael Cimino. Robert De Niro, Christopher Walken, Meryl Streep, John Savage, John Cazale. Intense drama about the effects of Vietnam War service on a group of steelworker friends and their western Pennsylvania community. Winner of Academy Awards for best picture and supporting actor (Walken).

80. *The Wild Bunch* (Warner Bros.–Seven Arts, 1969) Director: Sam Peckinpah. William Holden, Robert Ryan, Ernest Borgnine, Ben

Sylvester Stallone wrote the screenplay for Rocky *(1976) in three days, and starred as the title character.*

Johnson. Antiheroic western about a group of aging desperados who plan one last run. Notable for its grittiness and lyrical representation of violence.

81. *Modern Times* (United Artists, 1936) Director: Charlie Chaplin. Charlie Chaplin, Paulette Goddard, Henry Bergman. Poignant comedy-drama about the dehumanization of the machine age. Chaplin's last silent film.

82. *Giant* (Warner Bros., 1956) Director: George Stevens. Elizabeth Taylor, Rock Hudson, James Dean. Generational epic about Texas oil families based on the Edna Ferber novel is notable for its star turns and as Dean's final film.

83. *Platoon* (Orion, 1986) Director: Oliver Stone. Tom Berenger, Willem Dafoe, Charlie Sheen, Forest Whitaker. Intense drama about the Vietnam War depicts harshness and cruelties through the eyes of a soldier played by Sheen. Acclaimed for its realism, the film won Academy Awards for best picture and director.

84. *Fargo* (Gramercy Pictures/Polygram Filmed Entertainment/Working Title Films, 1996) Director: Joel Coen. Frances McDormand, William H. Macy, Steve Buscemi. Dark, jaunty crime drama about Minnesota multiple murder case under the able investigation of pregnant police chief (McDormand). Wood-chipper scene and blinding white exterior shots are notable. Academy Award winner for best actress and best original screenplay.

85. *Duck Soup* (Paramount, 1933) Director: Leo McCarey. Groucho Marx, Harpo Marx, Chico Marx, Zeppo Marx, Margaret Dumont. Quintessential anarchic Marx Brother's comedy about the Prime Minister of Freedonia Rufus T. Firefly (Groucho) and his war on another fictional country, Sylvania. Timeless gags involve a mirror, street vendor, and sidecar. Zeppo's last film.

86. *Mutiny on the Bounty* (MGM, 1935) Director: Frank Lloyd. Clark Gable, Charles Laughton, Franchot Tone. Bracing adaptation of the adventure novel by Charles Nordhoff and James Norman Hall about 18th-century sea justice, with meaty performances by Laughton as cruel Captain Bligh and Gable as noble mutineer Fletcher Christian. Won an Academy Award for best picture.

87. *Frankenstein* (Universal, 1931) Director: James Whale. Colin Clive, Mae Clarke, Boris Karloff. The original sound version of Mary Shelley's classic horror novel is notable for its Gothic atmosphere and haunting makeup and the poignant performance by Karloff as the monster brought to life by the scientist Frankenstein (Clive).

88. *Easy Rider* (Columbia, 1969) Director: Dennis Hopper. Peter Fonda, Dennis Hopper, Jack Nicholson. Definitive countercultural road movie follows motorcycle-riding duo (Hopper and Fonda) across America. Nicholson gained notice for his supporting role as a lawyer, leading to stardom in the 1970s.

89. *Patton* (20th Century–Fox, 1970) Director: Franklin J. Schaffner. George C. Scott, Karl Malden. Intelligent biography of "Blood and Guts" World War II general, notable for its riveting opening sequence and Scott's commanding title performance. Film won an Academy Award for best picture; Scott won (and refused) an award for best actor.

90. *The Jazz Singer* (Warner Bros., 1927) Director: Alan Crosland. Al Jolson, May McAvoy, Warner Oland. Pioneering silent film with sound portions about a cantor's son (Jolson) who enters show business. Helped launch the sound era. Songs include "Blue Skies," "Mammy," and "Toot Toot Tootsie, Goodbye."

91. *My Fair Lady* (Warner Bros., 1964) Director: George Cukor. Rex Harrison, Audrey Hepburn, Stanley Holloway, Wilfrid Hyde-White. Lush adaptation of the Lerner and Loewe musical features Harrison reprising his stage role as Henry Higgins and Hepburn as a spirited Eliza Doolittle. Earned Academy Awards for best picture, actor, and director, but the music is the film's enduring element. Songs include "On the Street Where You Live," "The Rain in Spain," and "I've Grown Accustomed to Her Face."

92. *A Place in the Sun* (Paramount, 1951) Director (and producer): George Stevens. Montgomery Clift, Elizabeth Taylor, Shelley Winters. Atmospheric adaptation of Theodore Dreiser's novel *An American Tragedy* features a smoldering performance from Clift as he pursues the gorgeous, elusive, and rich Taylor.

93. *The Apartment* (United Artists, 1960) Director: Billy Wilder. Jack Lemmon, Shirley MacLaine, Fred MacMurray. In this sparkling office comedy, an insurance clerk (Lemmon) loans his apartment as a love nest for his boss (MacMurray) and falls in love with the building's elevator operator (and the boss's paramour) MacLaine. Winner of Academy Awards for best picture, director, and original screenplay.

94. *GoodFellas* (Warner Bros., 1990) Director: Martin Scorsese. Robert De Niro, Ray Liotta, Joe Pesci, Lorraine Bracco. Violent drama about modern-day New York City Mafia life, as seen through the eyes of former member Henry Hill (Liotta). Based on Nicholas Pileggi's book *Wiseguy*, the film is notable for its unromanticized depiction of underworld life.

95. *Pulp Fiction* (A Band Apart/Jersey Films/Miramax Films, 1994) Director: Quentin Tarantino. John Travolta, Bruce Willis, Samuel L. Jackson, Ving Rhames, Uma Thurman. Multiple stories combine to form a frenetic meditation on underworld honor. The Travolta-Thurman dance scene and metaphysical discussions between Travolta and Jackson are memorable.

96. *The Searchers* (Warner Bros., 1956) Director: John Ford. John Wayne, Natalie Wood, Jeffrey Hunter. Haunting western about Ethan Edwards's (Wayne's) relentless search for niece Debbie (Wood), captured in childhood by Commanche Indians. Indelible closing shot shows the eternal divide between Edwards and his family, and between the frontier and civilization.

97. *Bringing Up Baby* (RKO, 1938) Director: Howard Hawks. Cary Grant, Katharine Hepburn, May Robson. Archetypal screwball comedy about heiress (Hepburn) and her pet leopard Baby who wreak havoc on the life of paleontologist (Grant). Funny and fast, it features song standard "I Can't Give You Anything but Love," sung to the leopard perched on a roof.

98. *Unforgiven* (Malpaso Productions/Warner Bros., 1992) Director: Clint Eastwood. Clint Eastwood, Morgan Freeman, Gene Hackman, Frances Fisher. Meditative western about a reformed killer (Eastwood) called to one last gunfight. Academy Award winner for best picture, director, and supporting actor (Hackman).

99. *Guess Who's Coming to Dinner* (Columbia, 1967) Director (and producer): Stanley Kramer. Katharine Hepburn, Spencer Tracy, Sidney Poitier, Katharine Houghton. Timely drama about parents (Tracy and Hepburn) learning of interracial romance between their daughter (Houghton) and an erudite, well-spoken African-American (Poitier). Tracy's last film, especially poignant for a scene in which he and Hepburn reflect on the power of love. Hepburn won an Academy Award for best actress.

100. *Yankee Doodle Dandy* (Warner Bros., 1942) Director: Michael Curtiz. James Cagney, Joan Leslie, Walter Huston, Irene Manning. Patriotic musical biography of George M. Cohan, with Cagney singing and dancing memorably in the title role, for which he won an Academy Award. Songs include "Give My Regards to Broadway," "Mary's a Grand Old Name," "Yankee Doodle Boy," and "Over There."

Samuel Jackson, John Travolta, and Harvey Keitel shared the screen in Pulp Fiction *(1994).*

The longest movie ever made was the 85-hour *The Cure for Insomnia* (1987). Directed by John Henry Timmis IV, it premiered in its entirety at the School of the Art Institute in Chicago from January 31 to February 3, 1987.

OVERLEAF:

George C. Scott declined the best actor Academy Award for his performance in Patton *(1971) in protest over the nature of the awards.*

Martin Scorsese on Film Preservation

By Martin Scorsese

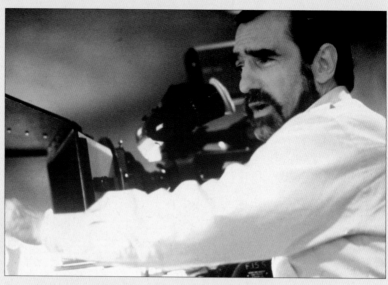

Martin Scorsese's directing credits include Taxi Driver *(1976),* Raging Bull *(1980),* The Color of Money *(1986), and* GoodFellas *(1990).*

CINEMA IS ONLY ONE HUNDRED years old and yet so much of it is gone. The facts about this loss are shocking. Of the more than 21,000 feature-length films produced in the United States before 1951, less than half exist today and 75 percent of all silent films no longer exist. These films are our history. With every foot of film that is lost, we lose a link to our culture, to the world around us, to each other, and to ourselves.

Until the early 1950s, films were printed on nitrate stock, which is highly flammable and deteriorates over time. Nitrate films were also routinely destroyed and recycled for their silver content. The predominant color process used for printing from the early 1930s to the mid-1970s was Technicolor's dye-transfer (a separation process that uses the three secondary colors: yellow, cyan, and magenta). Arguably, no better or more stable color process existed, but shooting film with it was very expensive and required a heavy, cumbersome camera. In the early 1950s, Kodak came out with Eastmancolor stock, which was cheaper and faster (it has multiple emulsion layers on a single strip of film, and the three different color separations are brought out through chemical processing). But Eastmancolor fades: in fact, all films using Eastmancolor during this period have already faded or will fade. Fortuitously, in the early '80s Kodak created a low-fade color printing stock (LPP), which now ensures that film, prints, and negatives can last for sixty to a hundred years if stored properly.

WHY IS IT SO IMPORTANT to save movies? The first and most compelling reason is that films are part of our artistic heritage—some say that film is the art form of the 20th century. Secondly, film is history. Movies made at a certain time, even minor ones, document the way of thinking and speaking, the behavior and the style of living of the people of that of society and the popular music, clothes, and language of that time. It is the most complete record we have of a particular period. And thirdly, older films provide a great source of historical reference for filmmakers, actors, and other creative artists.

When I think of a film, I don't necessarily think of stories or plot lines. I see images, faces, sensations, moods, emotions, the details that surface in textures of light and shadow. The great classical artists of the past knew that narrative—and emotional—power is found in the telling detail.

Think of the Giotti frescoes in the Scrovegni Chapel, the tension captured in the movement of the cloaks, the lances, and torches in his painting "The Betrayal of Christ," which provided visual inspiration for *The Last Temptation of Christ*. In my films, I have tried to develop character through detail. These details reflect the civilization or the society being depicted, so it's important to me to show in detail what people eat, how they dress, the music they listen to.

FOR EXAMPLE, WHILE PREPARING for *The Age of Innocence*, I looked at mutoscopes (paper images viewed through a kind of nickelodeon) from the turn of the century. What fascinated me was the way people moved, the way their clothes fit. In most period films, the actors' costumes fit perfectly. But in these images, the buttons on the vest were a little too heavy, or the vest was pulling. I used some of this everyday awkwardness in creating the look of the film and in directing the actors. It is just such telling details of daily life that vanish when our film heritage disappears.

When Woody Allen, Francis Ford Coppola, Stanley Kubrick, George Lucas, Sydney Pollack, Steven Spielberg, and I created the Film Foundation in 1990, the industry was just beginning to fully understand the value of their film libraries. Over the years we have encouraged efforts to safeguard and restore these libraries, and many classic films have been restored as a result of this partnership including *Sunrise, My Darling Clementine,*

All About Eve, On the Waterfront, and *All Quiet on the Western Front,* to name just a few.

I've repeated some of these facts about film preservation many times before. And I will continue to repeat the message until everyone responsible for our shared cultural patrimony understands how astonishing and heartbreaking those facts really are. Film is history and with every foot lost we lose a vital link to our culture, to the world around us, to each other and to ourselves.

All Quiet on the Western Front *(1930) featured Lew Ayers as a disillusioned German soldier fighting in World War I.*

AFI's 100 Funniest American Movies of All Time

There's an oft-quoted Hollywood deathbed one-liner: Dying is easy, comedy is hard. Here are one hundred films that make it look easy.

IN 2000 THE AMERICAN FILM INSTITUTE announced its 100 Funniest American Movies of All Time, which were selected by a blue-ribbon panel of leaders from across the film community.

"Recognizing the subjective and historical nature of comedy, 'AFI's 100 Years...100 Laughs' salutes the films that have enriched America's film heritage," stated AFI director and CEO Jean Picker Firstenberg. "Often overlooked for major film awards, it was time funny films had the last laugh. AFI hopes this list will continue to spark interest, dialogue, and appreciation for this great American art form."

To create the list, AFI distributed a ballot with 500 nominated films to a jury of 1,800 experts, including film artists (directors, screenwriters, actors, editors, and cinematographers), critics, historians, and film executives. The jurors were asked to select 100 movies with the following criteria in mind:

FEATURE-LENGTH FICTION FILM: The film must be in a narrative format typically more than 60 minutes long

AMERICAN FILM: It must be an English-language film with significant creative and/or financial production elements from the United States

FUNNY: Regardless of genre, the total comedic impact of a film's elements must create an experience greater than the sum of the smile

LEGACY: Laughs that echo across time, enriching America's film heritage and inspiring artists and audiences today

For maximum ease of reference, the films are listed below in three ways: first, in a list by order of preference; second, in alphabetical order; and third, in order of preference with entries that provide the studio, year of release, director, principal cast, and a brief description.

In addition, the alphabetical table includes cross-references for those films included in AFI's Top 100 American Movies of the Last 100 Years.

Christopher Guest played Nigel Tufnel, the dimwitted guitarist of a heavy metal band in Rob Reiner's documentary-style spoof This Is Spinal Tap (1984).

IN ORDER OF PREFERENCE

1. *Some Like It Hot* (1959)
2. *Tootsie* (1982)
3. *Dr. Strangelove or: How I Learned to Stop Worrying and Love the Bomb* (1964)
4. *Annie Hall* (1977)
5. *Duck Soup* (1933)
6. *Blazing Saddles* (1974)
7. *M*A*S*H* (1970)
8. *It Happened One Night* (1934)
9. *The Graduate* (1967)
10. *Airplane!* (1980)
11. *The Producers* (1968)
12. *A Night at the Opera* (1935)
13. *Young Frankenstein* (1974)
14. *Bringing Up Baby* (1938)
15. *The Philadelphia Story* (1940)
16. *Singin' in the Rain* (1952)
17. *The Odd Couple* (1968)
18. *The General* (1927)
19. *His Girl Friday* (1940)
20. *The Apartment* (1960)
21. *A Fish Called Wanda* (1988)
22. *Adam's Rib* (1949)
23. *When Harry Met Sally…* (1989)
24. *Born Yesterday* (1950)
25. *The Gold Rush* (1925)
26. *Being There* (1979)
27. *There's Something About Mary* (1998)
28. *Ghostbusters* (1984)
29. *This Is Spinal Tap* (1984)
30. *Arsenic and Old Lace* (1944)
31. *Raising Arizona* (1987)
32. *The Thin Man* (1934)
33. *Modern Times* (1936)
34. *Groundhog Day* (1993)
35. *Harvey* (1950)
36. *National Lampoon's Animal House* (1978)
37. *The Great Dictator* (1940)
38. *City Lights* (1931)
39. *Sullivan's Travels* (1941)
40. *It's a Mad Mad Mad Mad World* (1963)
41. *Moonstruck* (1987)
42. *Big* (1988)
43. *American Graffiti* (1973)
44. *My Man Godfrey* (1936)
45. *Harold and Maude* (1972)
46. *Manhattan* (1979)
47. *Shampoo* (1975)
48. *A Shot in the Dark* (1964)
49. *To Be or Not to Be* (1942)
50. *Cat Ballou* (1965)
51. *The Seven Year Itch* (1955)
52. *Ninotchka* (1939)
53. *Arthur* (1981)
54. *The Miracle of Morgan's Creek* (1944)
55. *The Lady Eve* (1941)
56. *Abbott and Costello Meet Frankenstein* (1948)
57. *Diner* (1982)
58. *It's a Gift* (1934)
59. *A Day at the Races* (1937)
60. *Topper* (1937)
61. *What's Up, Doc?* (1972)
62. *Sherlock, Jr.* (1924)
63. *Beverly Hills Cop* (1984)
64. *Broadcast News* (1987)
65. *Horse Feathers* (1932)
66. *Take the Money and Run* (1969)
67. *Mrs. Doubtfire* (1993)
68. *The Awful Truth* (1937)
69. *Bananas* (1971)
70. *Mr. Deeds Goes to Town* (1936)
71. *Caddyshack* (1980)
72. *Mr. Blandings Builds His Dream House* (1948)
73. *Monkey Business* (1931)
74. *9 to 5* (1980)
75. *She Done Him Wrong* (1933)
76. *Victor/Victoria* (1982)
77. *The Palm Beach Story* (1942)
78. *Road to Morocco* (1942)
79. *The Freshman* (1925)
80. *Sleeper* (1973)
81. *The Navigator* (1924)
82. *Private Benjamin* (1980)
83. *Father of the Bride* (1950)
84. *Lost in America* (1985)
85. *Dinner at Eight* (1933)

86. *City Slickers* (1991)
87. *Fast Times at Ridgemont High* (1982)
88. *Beetlejuice* (1988)
89. *The Jerk* (1979)
90. *Woman of the Year* (1942)
91. *The Heartbreak Kid* (1972)
92. *Ball of Fire* (1941)
93. *Fargo* (1996)
94. *Auntie Mame* (1958)
95. *Silver Streak* (1976)
96. *Sons of the Desert* (1933)
97. *Bull Durham* (1988)
98. *The Court Jester* (1956)
99. *The Nutty Professor* (1963)
100. *Good Morning, Vietnam* (1987)

Comedian Robin Williams improvised much of his deejay patter in Good Morning, Vietnam *(1987).*

AFI's 100 Funniest American Movies of All Time
IN ALPHABETICAL ORDER

With Cross-References to AFI's Top 100 American Movies of the Last 100 Years

THE 100 FUNNIEST AMERICAN MOVIES of All Time were chosen primarily for their comedic value, but many of them have earned classic status by any standard. It is no surprise, then, that 17 of the 100 Funniest American Movies of All Time have also been honored by inclusion among AFI's Top 100 American Movies of the Last 100 Years. Two of the funniest movies placed in the top ten of the latter list: *The Graduate* (1967) at No. 7 and *Singin' in the Rain* (1952) at No. 10. In the right column of the alphabetical table below, the twice-honored films are noted with their ranking on the list of the Top 100 American Movies in parentheses.

MOVIE	RANK	
Abbott and Costello Meet Frankenstein (1948)	56	
Adam's Rib (1949)	22	
Airplane! (1980)	10	
American Graffiti (1973)	43	(77)
Annie Hall (1977)	4	(31)
The Apartment (1960)	20	(93)
Arsenic and Old Lace (1944)	30	
Arthur (1981)	53	
Auntie Mame (1958)	94	
The Awful Truth (1937)	68	
Ball of Fire (1941)	92	
Bananas (1971)	69	
Beetlejuice (1988)	88	
Being There (1979)	26	
Beverly Hills Cop (1984)	63	
Big (1988)	42	

Blazing Saddles (1974)	6	
Born Yesterday (1950)	24	
Bringing Up Baby (1938)	14	(97)
Broadcast News (1987)	64	
Bull Durham (1988)	97	
Caddyshack (1980)	71	
Cat Ballou (1965)	50	
City Lights (1931)	38	(76)
City Slickers (1991)	86	
The Court Jester (1956)	98	
A Day at the Races (1937)	59	
Diner (1982)	57	
Dinner at Eight (1933)	85	
Dr. Strangelove or: How I Learned to Stop		
Worrying and Love the Bomb (1964)	3	(26)
Duck Soup (1933)	5	(85)
Fargo (1996)	93	(84)
Fast Times at Ridgemont High (1982)	87	
Father of the Bride (1950)	83	
A Fish Called Wanda (1988)	21	
The Freshman (1925)	79	
The General (1927)	18	
Ghostbusters (1984)	28	
The Gold Rush (1925)	25	(74)
Good Morning, Vietnam (1987)	100	
The Graduate (1967)	9	(7)
The Great Dictator (1940)	37	
Groundhog Day (1993)	34	
Harold and Maude (1972)	45	
Harvey (1950)	35	
The Heartbreak Kid (1972)	91	
His Girl Friday (1940)	19	
Horse Feathers (1932)	65	
It Happened One Night (1934)	8	(35)
It's a Gift (1934)	58	
It's a Mad Mad Mad Mad World (1963)	40	
The Jerk (1979)	89	
The Lady Eve (1941)	55	
Lost in America (1985)	84	
M*A*S*H (1970)	7	(56)
Manhattan (1979)	46	
The Miracle of Morgan's Creek (1944)	54	
Modern Times (1936)	33	(81)
Monkey Business (1931)	73	

Moonstruck (1987)	41	
Mr. Blandings Builds		
His Dream House (1948)	72	
Mr. Deeds Goes to Town (1936)	70	
Mrs. Doubtfire (1993)	67	
My Man Godfrey (1936)	44	
National Lampoon's		
Animal House (1978)	36	
The Navigator (1924)	81	
A Night at the Opera (1935)	12	
9 to 5 (1980)	74	
Ninotchka (1939)	52	
The Nutty Professor (1963)	99	
The Odd Couple (1968)	17	
The Palm Beach Story (1942)	77	
The Philadelphia Story (1940)	15	(51)
Private Benjamin (1980)	82	
The Producers (1968)	11	
Raising Arizona (1987)	31	
Road to Morocco (1942)	78	
The Seven Year Itch (1955)	51	
Shampoo (1975)	47	
She Done Him Wrong (1933)	75	
Sherlock, Jr. (1924)	62	
A Shot in the Dark (1964)	48	
Silver Streak (1976)	95	
Singin' in the Rain (1952)	16	(10)
Sleeper (1973)	80	
Some Like It Hot (1959)	1	(14)
Sons of the Desert (1933)	96	
Sullivan's Travels (1941)	39	
Take the Money and Run (1969)	66	
There's Something		
About Mary (1998)	27	
The Thin Man (1934)	32	
This Is Spinal Tap (1984)	29	
To Be or Not to Be (1942)	49	
Tootsie (1982)	2	(62)
Topper (1937)	60	
Victor/Victoria (1982)	76	
What's Up, Doc? (1972)	61	
When Harry Met Sally... (1989)	23	
Woman of the Year (1942)	90	
Young Frankenstein (1974)	13	

PREVIOUS PAGE:

Abbott and Costello Meet Frankenstein (1948) featured the comedy team of Lou Costello (left) and Bud Abbott (not pictured), along with Lon Chaney, Jr. as the Wolf Man (right) and Bela Lugosi as Dracula.

"I didn't like it. They were too irresponsible and also I couldn't get them all together at the same time— one was always missing."

—

Director Leo McCarey, on working with the Marx Brothers on Duck Soup, 1969

AFI's 100 Funniest American Movies of All Time

BRIEF DESCRIPTIONS

MOVIE TITLES MARKED by an asterisk (*) have the distinction of appearing on AFI's Top 100 American Movies list as well as on this list. Descriptions for the asterisked films can be found in the subsection on the Top 100 American Movies. To find their rank on that list, see the chart titled "AFI's 100 Funniest American Movies of All Time, in Alphabetical Order."

1. *Some Like It Hot* (1959)* (see page 383)

2. *Tootsie* (1982)* (see page 389)

3. *Dr. Strangelove or: How I Learned to Stop Worrying and Love the Bomb* (1964)* (see page 384)

4. *Annie Hall* (1977)* (see page 384)

5. *Duck Soup* (1933)* (see page 390)

6. *Blazing Saddles* (Warner Bros., 1974) Director: Mel Brooks. Gene Wilder, Cleavon Little, Harvey Korman, Madeline Kahn. In this send-up of the western, no social convention escapes ridicule, beginning with a heroic sheriff who happens to be a black convict (Little). Gags include a villain (Korman) named Hedley Lamarr and an unforgettable gas-passing binge.

7. *M*A*S*H* (1970)* (see page 388)

8. *It Happened One Night* (1934)* (see page 385)

9. *The Graduate* (1967)* (see page 382)

10. *Airplane!* (Paramount, 1980) Directors: Jim Abrahams, David Zucker, Jerry Zucker. Robert Hays, Leslie Nielsen, Julie Hagerty. Ensemble dramas and disaster films are played for laughs in this zany spoof of *Airport* (1970) and *Grand Hotel* (1932). It was followed by *Airplane II: The Sequel* (1982).

11. *The Producers* (Embassy, 1968) Director: Mel Brooks. Zero Mostel, Gene Wilder, Dick Shawn. Two shysters (Mostel, Wilder) try to fleece investors with a musical about Hitler but are caught when the play becomes a hit. The play's showstopper is the number "Springtime for Hitler."

12. *A Night at the Opera* (MGM, 1935) Director: Sam Wood. Groucho Marx, Chico Marx, Harpo Marx, Kitty Carlisle. The brothers minus Zeppo bring chaos to the opera house, with contractual agreements and staterooms faring no better. This was the Marx Brothers' first movie for MGM.

13. *Young Frankenstein* (20th Century–Fox, 1974) Director: Mel Brooks. Gene Wilder, Teri Garr, Marty Feldman, Cloris Leachman, Madeline Kahn, Peter Boyle. This spoof of Frankenstein films finds relative of the original mad scientist Victor Frankenstein (Wilder) creating a new life in the form of Boyle. Seemingly relentless gags include Feldman's shifting hunchback and the horse neighing whenever Frau Blucher (Leachman) is mentioned.

14. *Bringing Up Baby* (1938)* (see page 391)

15. *The Philadelphia Story* (1940)* (see page 388)

16. *Singin' in the Rain* (1952)* (see page 382)

17. *The Odd Couple* (Paramount, 1968) Directors: Gene Saks, Robert B. Hauser. Jack Lemmon, Walter Matthau, Herb Edelman. In this adaptation of the Neil Simon play, two diametrically opposed divorced men share an apartment and drive each other batty. The roles provided an ideal fit for the two comedic leads. A long-running television series followed.

18. *The General* (United Artists, 1927) Directors: Buster Keaton, Clyde Bruckman. Buster Keaton, Marion Mack, Jim Farley. Beautifully constructed Civil War comedy based on real-life drama of a Union spy's capture of a train in Confederate turf. Remade as *The Great Locomotive Chase* (1956).

19. *His Girl Friday* (Columbia, 1940) Director: Howard Hawks. Cary Grant, Rosalind Russell, Ralph Bellamy, Abner Biberman. The fast-paced remake of *The Front Page* (1931; remade 1974) is a battle between the sexes. Divorced reporter Hildy Johnson (Russell) and editor Walter Burns (Grant) unite one last time to save a wrongly accused man—and, if Grant can manage it, keep Russell from marrying dull Bruce Baldwin (Bellamy). Filled with overlapping dialogue, this is one of the fastest-talking comedies in history. Another remake called *Switching Channels* appeared in 1988.

20. *The Apartment* (1960)* (see page 391)

21. *A Fish Called Wanda* (MGM/UA, 1988) Director: Charles Crichton. John Cleese, Jamie Lee Curtis, Kevin Kline. A barrister (Cleese), a femme fatale (Curtis), and her shady partner

(Kline) mix with a bank robbery scheme to create an off-the-wall farce, with hints of Monty Python and other varieties of offbeat British humor. Kline won an Academy Award for best supporting actor for his flamboyant performance.

22. *Adam's Rib* (MGM, 1949) Director: George Cukor. Spencer Tracy, Katharine Hepburn, Judy Holliday. Tracy and Hepburn are married lawyers who take opposing sides to prosecute (or defend) Holliday in a murder case. The witty screenplay by Ruth Gordon and Garson Kanin plays off Tracy-Hepburn chemistry to detail differences between the sexes.

23. *When Harry Met Sally…* (Columbia, 1989) Director: Rob Reiner. Billy Crystal, Meg Ryan, Carrie Fisher. Two friends (Crystal and Ryan), who vow they will never fall into the trap of love finally do, accompanied by a lot of distress. The scene in the diner is memorable, as is the much-quoted comment by the patron (Reiner's mother).

24. *Born Yesterday* (Columbia, 1950) Director: George Cukor. Judy Holliday, Broderick Crawford, William Holden. Holliday reprises her signature Broadway role as junk dealer's mistress Billie Dawn, who gains culture and courage with the help of a newspaperman (Holden). Her performance earned an Academy Award for best actress. A remake appeared in 1993.

25. *The Gold Rush* (1925)* (see page 390)

26. *Being There* (United Artists, 1979) Director: Hal Ashby. Peter Sellers, Shirley MacLaine, Melvyn Douglas. In this black comedy, a gardener (Sellers) who has absorbed all he knows from television is brought into cultured society, where he is viewed as a sage. Jerzy Kozinski wrote the screenplay, an adaptation of his novel.

27. *There's Something About Mary* (20th Century–Fox, 1998) Directors: Bobby Farrelly, Peter Farrelly. Cameron Diaz, Ben Stiller, Matt Dillon. Lovely, good-hearted Diaz is the object of desire for Stiller and Dillon in this comedy that tests the limits people go to for love. Stiller's bathroom accident is excruciatingly funny.

28. *Ghostbusters* (Columbia, 1984) Director: Ivan Reitman. Bill Murray, Dan Aykroyd, Harold Ramis, Sigourney Weaver, Ernie Hudson. Three underfunded scientists of the paranormal plus an employee (Hudson) get lots of work when ghosts hit New York City. Weaver is memorable as client, love interest, and human vehicle for a ghost. The sequel is *Ghostbusters II* (1989).

29. *This Is Spinal Tap* (Embassy, 1984) Director: Rob Reiner. Michael McKean, Christopher Guest, Harry Shearer. This mock documentary of a legendary British rock band in its twilight years has gained cult status and established the reputation of first-time director Reiner.

30. *Arsenic and Old Lace* (Warner Bros., 1944) Director: Frank Capra. Cary Grant, Priscilla Lane, Peter Lorre, Josephine Hull. Faithful adaptation of the hit Broadway comedy by Joseph Kesselring about two elderly ladies who poison their male visitors with elderberry wine that retains its whimsy and zaniness. It features many of the original stage cast, along with Grant as a shocked nephew.

31. *Raising Arizona* (20th Century–Fox, 1987) Director: Joel Coen. Nicolas Cage, Holly Hunter, John Goodman. Policewoman Hunter and ex-con Cage fulfill their wish for a baby by kidnapping one from a group of quintuplets. Slapstick and chase scenes follow when the quint is discovered missing. Joel and Ethan Coen wrote the zany screenplay.

32. *The Thin Man* (MGM, 1934) Director: W.S. Van Dyke. Myrna Loy, William Powell, Maureen O'Sullivan. The sophisticated sleuth was perfected in stylish married couple Nick and Nora Charles (Powell and Loy), who search for a killer with wit and aplomb. This adaptation of the Dashiell Hammett novel was filmed by master cinematographer James Wong Howe. Five sequels followed (1936–47).

33. *Modern Times* (1936)* (see page 390)

34. *Groundhog Day* (Columbia, 1993) Director: Harold Ramis. Bill Murray, Andie MacDowell, Chris Elliot. Whimsical existentialist comedy about a cynical weatherman (Murray) who discerns the meaning of life after he is forced

Teri Garr, Gene Wilder, Madeline Kahn, and Marty Feldman starred in Mel Brooks's monster movie spoof Young Frankenstein *(1974).*

To shoot the now-legendary close-up of Ben Stiller's ensnared private parts in *There's Something About Mary* (1998), the Farrelly Brothers used a four-foot-tall zipper and mock genitalia that was roughly the size of a soccer ball. The zipper later broke during shooting, and the entire apparatus had to be taken to a flabbergasted tailor for repairs.

A Shot in the Dark (1964) was not originally intended as the sequel to *The Pink Panther* (1964). Based on a hit play by Harry Kurnitz, the film was set to star Peter Sellers when United Artists hired director Blake Edwards, who had just finished a successful collaboration with Sellers on the then still-unreleased *Panther*. Working with William Peter Blatty, Edwards rewrote the script so Sellers could reprise his role as the bumbling Inspector Clouseau. The two films came out within three months of each other, and Edwards would go on to direct six more Panther films, three of which were filmed after Sellers's death in 1980.

AT RIGHT: *The 1936 screwball comedy* My Man Godfrey *featured Carole Lombard and William Powell.*

to relive the same day over and over in Punxsutawney, Pennsylvania. The repetition of the Sonny & Cher song "I Got You Babe" and the "Pennsylvania Polka" are appropriately excruciating.

35. *Harvey* (Universal, 1950) Director: Henry Koster. James Stewart, Josephine Hull, Peggy Dow. This adaptation of the Mary Chase play tells the rambling story of Elwood P. Dowd (Stewart) and his invisible six-foot three-inch rabbit friend Harvey. The pixiled Dowd became one of Stewart's best-known characterizations. Hull reprised her Broadway role as Dowd's sister and won an Academy Award for best supporting actress.

36. *National Lampoon's Animal House* (Universal, 1978) Director: John Landis. John Belushi, Tim Matheson, John Vernon. The definitive frat-house comedy is marked by sight gags and on-screen high jinks led by Belushi as party animal Bluto Blutarsky. Among notorious scenes is the toga party.

37. *The Great Dictator* (United Artists, 1940) Director: Charlie Chaplin. Charlie Chaplin, Paulette Goddard, Jack Oakie. This incisive, broad wartime satire of well-known Nazi and fascist rulers features Chaplin as leader Adenoid Hynkel and Oakie as Benzino Napaloni. Chaplin does double duty as a Jewish barber.

38. *City Lights* (1931)* (see page 390)

39. *Sullivan's Travels* (Paramount, 1941) Director: Preston Sturges. Joel McCrea, Veronica Lake, William Demarest. Disgusted by the mindless entertainment he makes, movie director McCrea tours the country as a pauper (with comrade Lake) and learns what really counts in the cockeyed caravan of life.

40. *It's a Mad Mad Mad Mad World* (United Artists, 1963) Director: Stanley Kramer. Spencer Tracy, Sid Caesar, Edie Adams, Milton Berle, Ethel Merman. The era's great comedians star in this shaggy-dog comedy about a treasure hunt for a trove of cash. Tracy is the detective overseeing the shenanigans.

41. *Moonstruck* (United Artists, 1987) Director: Norman Jewison. Cher, Nicolas Cage, Olympia Dukakis, Vincent Gardenia. This cheery operatic saga depicts an Italian-American family thrown into chaos when one of its members, an engaged widow (Cher), falls in love with her boyfriend's brother (Cage), a one-handed baker. Dukakis won an Academy Award for best supporting actress for her performance as Cher's philosophical mother.

42. *Big* (20th Century–Fox, 1988) Director: Penny Marshall. Tom Hanks, Elizabeth Perkins, Robert Loggia. A boy who wishes to be "big" is transformed into an adult (Hanks), who struggles believably and amusingly with life as a man in the world and a boy at heart.

43. *American Graffiti* (1973)* (see page 390)

44. *My Man Godfrey* (Universal, 1936) Director: Gregory La Cava. William Powell, Carole Lombard, Eugene Pallette, Mischa Auer. Classic screwball comedy about rich socialite (Lombard) who finds what she believes to be a hobo (Powell), then hires him as a butler. Powell's wry diffidence and Lombard's zaniness make for a believable romantic pair that will never quite understand one another. A remake appeared in 1957.

FACTS ABOUT AFI'S 100 FUNNIEST AMERICAN MOVIES OF ALL TIME

CARY GRANT is the most celebrated actor, with eight films in the top 100 funniest films list.

THE MARX BROTHERS and Woody Allen each star in five of the top 100 films.

SPENCER TRACY, Buster Keaton, Charlie Chaplin, and Bill Murray each appear in four of the top 100 funniest films.

KATHARINE HEPBURN and Margaret Dumont share the title of most represented actress; each appears in four films in the top 100.

Bill Murray began a successful film career after leaving TV's Saturday Night Live.

WOODY ALLEN and Billy Wilder each wrote the scripts for five of the top 100 funniest films.

FIVE WOODY ALLEN FILMS are in the top 100 funniest movies, including *Annie Hall,* ranked No. 4, making him the most represented director.

GEORGE CUKOR, Charlie Chaplin, and Preston Sturges each directed four films on the list; Mel Brooks directed three films, all of which placed in the top 15.

FOUR FILMS, including the No. 1 and No. 2 funniest films, involve cross-dressing: *Some Like It Hot* (1959), *Tootsie* (1982), *Mrs. Doubtfire* (1993), and *Victor/Victoria* (1982).

---

45. *Harold and Maude* (Paramount, 1972) Director: Hal Ashby. Ruth Gordon, Bud Cort, Vivian Pickles. Iconoclastic older woman Maude (Gordon) becomes friends with haunted 20-year-old Harold (Cort) in this black comedy that gained cult status in the 1970s.

46. *Manhattan* (United Artists, 1979) Director: Woody Allen. Woody Allen, Diane Keaton, Mariel Hemingway, Meryl Streep. TV writer Allen pointedly observes the mangled relationships around him and looks to young Hemingway for a cleansing innocence. Although its dissection of urban society is on-target, the film is more memorable for its starry depiction of Manhattan, photographed in black-and-white by Gordon Willis.

47. *Shampoo* (Columbia, 1975) Director: Hal Ashby. Warren Beatty, Julie Christie, Goldie Hawn, Lee Grant. The doings of seductive hairdresser Beatty and his well-heeled clientele make for a satire on the liberated Southern California lifestyle. Grant, as a salon client, won an Academy Award for best supporting actress.

48. *A Shot in the Dark* (United Artists, 1964) Director: Blake Edwards. Peter Sellers, Elke Sommer, George Sanders. Sellers's Inspector Clouseau returns in this fast-paced follow-up to *The Pink Panther* (1964) that focuses on the detective's attempted defense of a beautiful murder suspect (Sommer) amid a sea of gags. As in the original, Henry Mancini wrote the smooth score.

49. *To Be or Not to Be* (United Artists, 1942) Director: Ernst Lubitsch. Jack Benny, Carole Lombard, Robert Stack. Benny plays an egotistical actor who, with wife Lombard, finds himself battling Nazis while trying to save his Polish theater group. This black comedy was Lombard's last film. The 1983 remake starred Mel Brooks and Anne Bancroft.

50. *Cat Ballou* (Columbia, 1965) Director: Elliot Silverstein. Lee Marvin, Jane Fonda, Michael Callan. Cat (Fonda) is a schoolmarm gone bad, and Marvin takes a dual role as Tim Shawn/Kid Shelleen—a drunken outlaw with a nasty twin—in this lighthearted western comedy. Marvin was named best actor by the Academy for his two-role performance.

51. *The Seven Year Itch* (20th Century–Fox, 1955) Director: Billy Wilder. Marilyn Monroe, Tom Ewell, Sonny Tufts. Long-married Ewell, flying solo while his family vacations in the country, finds an ideal object of fantasy in upstairs neighbor Monroe. Notable for its witty screenplay adapted by the playwright George Axelrod and Wilder, the film is equally memorable for Monroe's white dress wafting over a street grate.

52. *Ninotchka* (MGM, 1939) Director: Ernst Lubitsch. Greta Garbo, Melvyn Douglas, Ina Claire. As advertised in studio publicity for the film, Garbo laughs in this romantic comedy of love between a tough communist agent (Garbo) and a rakish capitalist playboy (Douglas). Sparkling screenplay by Billy Wilder,

"It had become depressing to go to the movies. I decided it was time to make a movie where people felt better coming out of the theater than when they went in."

—

George Lucas on American Graffiti, *1987*

Charles Brackett, and Walter Reisch. Remade as the musical film *Silk Stockings* in 1957.

53. *Arthur* (Warner Bros., 1981) Director: Steve Gordon. Dudley Moore, Liza Minnelli, John Gielgud. This romantic comedy about a ne'er-do-well millionaire (Moore) who risks his fortune for a waitress (Minnelli) is notable for its oddball cheeriness and Gielgud's Academy Award–winning performance as the valet. The sequel is *Arthur 2: On the Rocks* (1988).

54. *The Miracle of Morgan's Creek* (Paramount, 1944) Director: Preston Sturges. Betty Hutton, Eddie Bracken, William Demarest, Diana Lynn. In the director's most manic, intricate comedy, wartime waif Trudy Kockenlocker (Hutton) gets drunk, pregnant, maybe even married, and can't remember a thing. Here the plot speeds up, the Sturges way. The remake is *Rock-a-Bye Baby* (1958).

55. *The Lady Eve* (Paramount, 1941) Director: Preston Sturges. Henry Fonda, Barbara Stanwyck, Charles Coburn, William Demarest. After being rejected by a snake expert (Fonda) whom she loves, cardsharp Stanwyck disguises herself as the Lady Eve Sidwich and lets him fall in love with her. Elegance, wit, and buffoonery mix. Ocean cruises, train rides, and horses are used to considerable effect.

Eddie Murphy played Axel Foley in Beverly Hills Cop *(1984), and reprised the role in the sequel,* Beverly Hills Cop II *(1987).*

56. *Abbott and Costello Meet Frankenstein* (Universal, 1948) Director: Charles T. Barton. Bud Abbott, Lou Costello, Lon Chaney, Jr., Bela Lugosi. The final sequel in Universal's Frankenstein cycle of the 1930s and 1940s finds deliverymen Abbott and Costello bringing what they think are the dead Dracula and Dr. Frankenstein to a museum. Problems arise when Dracula arises and wants to lend Costello's brain to Frankenstein. Tip-top Abbott and Costello and winning homage to Universal's movie monsters.

57. *Diner* (MGM/UA, 1982) Director: Barry Levinson. Daniel Stern, Mickey Rourke, Steve Gutenberg, Kevin Bacon. The first of Levinson's movies set in Baltimore, this one a wry look at a group of male friends who frequent a local diner in the 1950s. Notable topical scenes include a marriage test about the Baltimore Colts and a debate on the merits of Johnny Mathis vs. Frank Sinatra.

58. *It's a Gift* (Paramount, 1934) Director: Norman Z. McLeod. W.C. Fields, Baby LeRoy, Kathleen Howard. Family man and grocery-store owner Fields takes his brood west, with amusing and exasperating results. Includes memorable encounters with scene-stealing child star LeRoy.

59. *A Day at the Races* (MGM, 1937) Director: Sam Wood. Groucho Marx, Harpo Marx, Chico Marx, Margaret Dumont. Groucho is a horse doctor enlisted to run a sanitarium where Dumont is a patient in this characteristically zany Marx Brothers comedy. Seemingly endless comic bits include Chico selling ice cream and race tips.

60. *Topper* (MGM, 1937) Director: Norman Z. McLeod. Constance Bennett, Cary Grant, Roland Young. This merry adaptation of the Thorne Smith novel offers Bennett and Grant as ghosts who take their quiet friend Cosmo Topper (Young) under their wing. Two sequels followed (1939, 1941).

61. *What's Up, Doc?* (Warner Bros., 1972) Director: Peter Bogdanovich. Barbra Streisand, Ryan O'Neal. This wacky homage to *Bringing Up Baby* (1938) features Streisand as the blithe spirit who disrupts Professor O'Neal's prim life.

62. *Sherlock, Jr.* (Metro, 1924) Director: Buster Keaton. Buster Keaton, Kathryn McGuire, Ward Crane. Projectionist Keaton unwittingly steps into the on-screen antics, with hilarious results. This prototypical Keaton silent film continues to influence filmmakers.

63. *Beverly Hills Cop* (Paramount, 1984) Director: Martin Brest. Eddie Murphy, Judge Reinhold, John Ashton, Bronson Pinchot. Fish-out-of-water crime comedy puts fast-talking Detroit cop Murphy in swank Beverly Hills to solve a friend's death. The humorous support team includes Reinhold as a straight man and Pinchot as a vaguely foreign gallery assistant. Overall, an ideal showcase for Murphy's big, brash talent.

64. *Broadcast News* (20th Century–Fox, 1987) Director: James L. Brooks. William Hurt, Holly Hunter, Albert Brooks. Genial yet pointed send-up of the television news business in which Hunter epitomizes the 1980s career woman who does everything right, except for falling for handsome but empty newsman Hurt. Brooks plays a caustic reporter and would-be paramour to Hunter.

65. *Horse Feathers* (Paramount, 1932) Director: Norman Z. McLeod. Groucho Marx, Chico Marx, Harpo Marx, Zeppo Marx, Thelma Todd. Huxley University head Groucho mobilizes his football team into characteristic Marx Brothers anarchy to defeat rival Darwin U. Notable songs include "Whatever It Is, I'm Against It"; notable dialogue involves the word "swordfish."

66. **Take the Money and Run** (Palomar, 1969) Director: Woody Allen. Woody Allen, Janet Margolin, Marcel Hillaire. In his directorial debut, Allen charts the unsuccessful career of Virgil Starkwell (Allen), inept thief. Hilarious gags include an attempt to escape prison with a gun made of soap that disintegrates in the rain.

67. **Mrs. Doubtfire** (20th Century–Fox, 1993) Director: Chris Columbus. Robin Williams, Sally Field, Pierce Brosnan, Harvey Fierstein. A divorced father (Williams), despondent over not being with his children, transforms himself into British nanny Mrs. Doubtfire and rejoins the household. Classical Williams physical comedy and pathos follow. Based on Anne Fine's novel *Alias Madame Doubtfire*.

68. **The Awful Truth** (Columbia, 1937) Director: Leo McCarey. Irene Dunne, Cary Grant, Ralph Bellamy. In this prototypical screwball comedy, sophisticated couple Dunne and Grant cannot stay divorced, even as they both plan marriages to others. Bellamy creates a romantic comedy archetype as Dunne's other man—a hapless hick poet. Originally filmed in 1925 and 1929, it was remade in 1953 as the musical *Let's Do It Again*.

69. **Bananas** (United Artists, 1971) Director: Woody Allen. Woody Allen, Louise Lasser, Carlos Montalban, Howard Cosell. Absurd romp about Allen leaving his day job to volunteer for a Latin American revolutionary force, which eventually makes him its leader. Marvin Hamlisch wrote the score.

70. **Mr. Deeds Goes to Town** (Columbia, 1936) Director: Frank Capra. Gary Cooper, Jean Arthur, Lionel Stander, George Bancroft. Small-town man Longfellow Deeds (Cooper) inherits $20 million that he doesn't need and plans to donate it to the needy, a situation that captivates hard-boiled reporter Babe Bennett (Arthur). The mix of wisecracking characters and populist sentiment makes it a prototypical Capra comedy. Adapted from the play *Opera Hut* by Clarence Budington Kelland.

71. **Caddyshack** (Warner Bros., 1980) Director: Harold Ramis. Chevy Chase, Rodney Dangerfield, Bill Murray. The exclusive Bushwood Country Club dissolves into chaos with dysfunctional players like Chase and Dangerfield and a staff that includes the gopher-chasing Murray. Sight gags and base jokes abound.

72. **Mr. Blandings Builds His Dream House** (RKO, 1948) Director: H.C. Potter. Cary Grant, Myrna Loy, Melvyn Douglas. The postwar dream of building a house in the country is skewered in this good-natured tale of woe, in which, among other problems, Loy won't get her very specific choices of paint colors.

73. **Monkey Business** (Paramount, 1931) Director: Norman Z. McLeod. Groucho Marx, Harpo Marx, Chico Marx, Zeppo Marx, Thelma Todd. As stowaways on an ocean liner, the four brothers create the usual havoc, notably imitating Maurice Chevalier to qualify for exiting the ship. The film is their first screenplay collaboration with S. J. Perelman. Todd is Groucho's love interest.

74. **9 to 5** (20th Century–Fox, 1980) Director: Colin Higgins. Jane Fonda, Lily Tomlin, Dolly Parton, Dabney Coleman. The ultimate secretarial trio endure and later take revenge on their barbaric boss (Coleman). On-target in its depiction of the male-dominated workplace, the movie was a box-office success. A television series followed.

75. **She Done Him Wrong** (Paramount, 1933) Director: Lowell Sherman. Mae West, Cary Grant, Gilbert Roland. West reprises her Broadway role as Diamond Lil, the Gilded Era siren who cracks wise, sings "Frankie and Johnny," and plies young Grant with the line "Why don't you come up sometime and see me?"

76. **Victor/Victoria** (MGM/UA, 1982) Director: Blake Edwards. Julie Andrews, Robert Preston, James Garner, Alex Karras. Tight sex farce about an out-of-work singer (Andrews) who becomes the toast of Paris cabarets and the object of desire for one audience member (Garner) when she disguises herself as a man. A Broadway musical adaptation followed, also with Andrews in the lead.

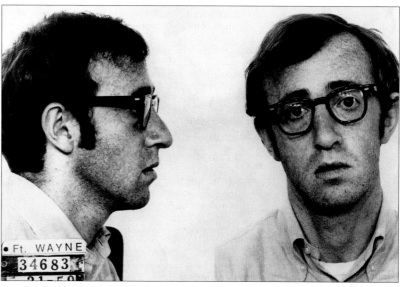

Take the Money and Run *(1969) was Woody Allen's directorial debut.*

Sometimes, even a movie's credits are funny. Mr. Gopher, the golf-course pest that Bill Murray's assistant greens keeper battles in *Caddyshack* (1980), is listed in that film's final cast roll as having been portrayed by one "Chuck Rodent."

OVERLEAF:

Stan Laurel (left) and Oliver Hardy (right) made more than 100 films (including shorts) in their 30 years as a comedy team, including Sons of the Desert *(1933).*

The Jerk (1979) featured comedian Steve Martin in his first starring role. He also cowrote the screenplay.

"I wanted to write what it was like for the kid no one writes about. The high point of his year might be going to a Rod Stewart concert."

—

Cameron Crowe, on his motivation behind going undercover in a contemporary California high school to research Fast Times at Ridgemont High, *1982*

77. **The Palm Beach Story** (Paramount, 1942) Director: Preston Sturges. Claudette Colbert, Joel McCrea, Rudy Vallee, Mary Astor. Sturges-style marital mayhem occurs when happily married Colbert decides to bankroll inventor husband McCrea by marrying multimillionaire Vallee. Also wreaking havoc is the men's group called the Ale and Quail Club, with Colbert as mascot. Top 1920s crooner Vallee sings "Goodnight, Sweetheart."

78. **Road to Morocco** (Paramount, 1942) Director: David Butler. Bob Hope, Bing Crosby, Dorothy Lamour. In the third and most consistently funny of their seven road pictures (the series of comedies that put Hope, Crosby, and Lamour in exotic settings), Hope is sold into slavery by Crosby, which temporarily keeps him from pursuing Lamour.

79. **The Freshman** (Pathé Exchange, 1925) Directors: Sam Taylor, Fred Newmeyer. Harold Lloyd, Jobyna Ralston, Brooks Benedict. Country bumpkin Lloyd wins the girl (Ralston) and the football game in this classic comedy, one of the comedian's most popular films.

80. **Sleeper** (United Artists, 1973) Director: Woody Allen. Woody Allen, Diane Keaton, John Beck. Allen awakens after 200 years of being frozen and finds life vastly different from 1973. The satirical script, written by Allen and Marshall Brickman, features commentary on contemporary mores and obsessions, along with the cloning of a nose.

81. **The Navigator** (MGM, 1924) Directors: Buster Keaton, Donald Crisp. Buster Keaton, Kathryn McGuire, Frederick Vroom. Gag-filled silent movie about an indolent millionaire (Keaton) ending up on a deserted ship with the woman (McGuire) who has just rejected him.

82. **Private Benjamin** (Warner Bros., 1980) Director: Howard Zieff. Goldie Hawn, Eileen Brennan, Armand Assante. Pampered suburban princess (Hawn) is humiliated and later enlightened when she finds herself in the army. A television series followed.

83. **Father of the Bride** (MGM, 1950) Director: Vincente Minnelli. Spencer Tracy, Joan Bennett, Elizabeth Taylor. Daughter Taylor plans her Great American Wedding, to exasperating and poignant effect on her father Tracy. The sequel is *Father's Little Dividend* (1951). The remake, *Father of the Bride*, appeared in 1991.

84. **Lost in America** (Warner Bros., 1985) Director: Albert Brooks. Albert Brooks, Julie Hagerty, Garry Marshall. In this satire of self-fulfillment, yuppies Brooks and Hagerty leave their professional lives to travel the country in a Winnebago.

85. **Dinner at Eight** (MGM, 1933) Director: George Cukor. Jean Harlow, Wallace Beery, Marie Dressler, John Barrymore, Lionel Barrymore. This adaptation of the Edna Ferber and George S. Kaufman play is a comic dissection of the guests at a high-toned New York party, with Dressler delivering the memorable final comment.

86. **City Slickers** (Columbia, 1991) Director: Ron Underwood. Billy Crystal, Bruno Kirby, Daniel Stern, Jack Palance. Amiable, gag-filled comedy about friends in midlife crisis who take a lengthy cattle drive to clear their minds. Palance won an Academy Award for his supporting performance as the crusty drive leader. The sequel is *City Slickers: The Legend of Curly's Gold* (1994).

87. **Fast Times at Ridgemont High** (Universal, 1982) Director: Amy Heckerling. Sean Penn, Jennifer Jason Leigh, Judge Reinhold. Cameron Crowe's book provides the basis for this loopy comedy about Southern California teenage life at high school and in the mall. Penn gained notice for his portrayal of a drugged-out student.

88. **Beetlejuice** (Warner Bros., 1988) Director: Tim Burton. Michael Keaton, Geena Davis, Alec Baldwin, Winona Ryder. The dark spirit Betelgeuse (Keaton) aids a newly dead couple who are upset at the disagreeable family that has taken over their house. Notable for its visual inventiveness and mix of horror and comedy. The clever music is by Danny Elfman.

89. **The Jerk** (Universal, 1979) Director: Carl Reiner. Steve Martin, Bernadette Peters, Bill Macy. The travails of a dim-witted man make for abundant humor and pathos from Martin, in his first lead role.

90. **Woman of the Year** (MGM, 1942) Director: George Stevens. Spencer Tracy, Katharine Hepburn, Fay Bainter. An easygoing sportswriter (Tracy) and a high-strung political reporter (Hepburn) fall in love and learn amusing lessons on their differences along the way. Among these lessons is a well-paced drinking scene. The clever screenplay is by Ring Lardner, Jr., and Michael Kanin. A stage musical followed.

91. **The Heartbreak Kid** (Palomar/20th Century–Fox, 1972) Director: Elaine May. Charles Grodin, Cybill Shepherd, Jeannie Berlin. Based on a story by Bruce Jay Friedman, this is the wry tragicomedy of a newly married Jewish man (Grodin) who becomes obsessed by unobtainable blond beauty Shepherd.

92. **Ball of Fire** (United Artists 1941) Director: Howard Hawks. Gary Cooper, Barbara Stanwyck, Dana Andrews, Oscar Homolka. Seven scholars enlist the help of a nightclub singer (Stanwyck) to compile a slang dictionary but have to think fast when her gangster friends come looking for her. The screenplay for this worldly take-off on *Snow White and the Seven Dwarfs* was written by Billy Wilder and Charles Brackett. The remake is *A Song Is Born* (1948).

93. **Fargo** (1996)* (see page 390)

94. **Auntie Mame** (Warner Bros., 1958) Director: Morton DaCosta. Rosalind Russell, Patric Knowles, Coral Browne. Mame (Russell) towers over New York City with her lush life and eccentricities, all viewed by the young boy she's entrusted to raise. Based on the Broadway play by Jerome Robbins and Robert E. Lee, which was drawn from Patrick Dennis's autobiographical novel *Auntie Mame.* The musical stage and later screen version is *Mame* (film, 1974).

95. **Silver Streak** (20th Century–Fox, 1976) Director: Arthur Hiller. Gene Wilder, Richard Pryor, Jill Clayburgh. The first Wilder-Pryor pairing mixes mystery, fast talk, and physical humor amid a long-distance train trip meant to be a vacation getaway for the hardworking Wilder.

96. **Sons of the Desert** (MGM, 1933) Director: William A. Seiter. Stan Laurel, Oliver Hardy, Mae Busch. Classic Laurel and Hardy high jinks occur when the two men lie to their wives so they can attend a convention in Chicago.

97. **Bull Durham** (Orion, 1988) Director: Ron Shelton. Susan Sarandon, Kevin Costner, Tim Robbins. Picaresque tale about a baseball groupie and counselor (Sarandon) who leads a minor-league greenhorn pitcher (Robbins) to success but falls in love with an aging catcher (Costner) along the way. Location filming and off-the-wall pitcher's mound discussions lend realism and a fanciful sensibility to this celebration of baseball.

98. **The Court Jester** (Paramount, 1956) Directors: Norman Panama, Melvin Frank. Danny Kaye, Glynis Johns, Basil Rathbone. In this melodic swashbuckler, Kaye impersonates a court jester to infiltrate an evil government and finds himself singing, falling in love, and fighting villains along the way.

99. **The Nutty Professor** (Paramount, 1963) Director: Jerry Lewis. Jerry Lewis, Stella Stevens, Del Moore. This Jekyll-and-Hyde story focuses on a milquetoast college professor (Lewis) who, with the aid of his secret potion, becomes arrogant but irresistible Buddy Love. The remake appeared in 1996, starring Eddie Murphy.

100. **Good Morning, Vietnam** (Touchstone/Buena Vista, 1987) Director: Barry Levinson. Robin Williams, Forest Whitaker, Tung Thanh Tran. Williams uses the true story of Vietnam War radio disc jockey Adrian Cronauer as the basis for a highly charged performance in this thoughtful war comedy. Memorable for the star's runaway radio patter.

Tim Robbins portrayed a minor-league ballplayer in the romantic comedy Bull Durham *(1988).*

In 1998, Gene Wilder recalled an encounter he had in the late '70s with legendary actor Cary Grant. Wilder was heading to a function on the 20th Century–Fox lot when a cab pulled up. A moment later, Grant jumped out to tell the astonished young actor that he and his daughter had enjoyed Wilder's *Silver Streak* so much, they'd gone to see it three times in a row. Was the film, Grant wanted to know, based in any way on *North by Northwest*? Wilder confirmed that writer Colin Higgins was indeed a huge fan of the Grant-starring Hitchcock classic. "I knew it!" Wilder remembered the still-suave Grant telling him. "You take an ordinary chap, like you or me, put him in trouble over his head, and watch him try to squirm out of it."

THE BRITISH FILM INSTITUTE'S TOP 100

Favorite British Films of the 20th Century

IN 1999 THE BRITISH FILM INSTITUTE (BFI) announced its 100 Favourite British Films released in the preceding 100 years. The list was determined by 1,000 panelists who worked in all areas of the film and television industries throughout the UK. Among them were producers, directors, writers, actors, technicians, academics, exhibitors, distributors, executives, and critics. Participants were asked to vote for up to 100 "culturally British" feature films released in theaters during the 20th century that they felt had made a strong and lasting impression on the art form and the culture. The final selection in order of preference spans seven decades, from 1935 to 1998.

The Madness of King George *(1994) featured Nigel Hawthorne as the ailing monarch.*

IN ORDER OF PREFERENCE

1. *The Third Man* (1949)
2. *Brief Encounter* (1945)
3. *Lawrence of Arabia* (1962)
4. *The 39 Steps* (1935)
5. *Great Expectations* (1946)
6. *Kind Hearts and Coronets* (1946)
7. *Kes* (1969)
8. *Don't Look Now* (1973)
9. *The Red Shoes* (1948)
10. *Trainspotting* (1996)
11. *The Bridge on the River Kwai* (1957)
12. *If....* (1968)
13. *The Ladykillers* (1955)
14. *Saturday Night and Sunday Morning* (1960)
15. *Brighton Rock* (1947)
16. *Get Carter* (1971)
17. *The Lavender Hill Mob* (1951)
18. *Henry V* (1944)
19. *Chariots of Fire* (1981)
20. *A Matter of Life and Death* (1946)
21. *The Long Good Friday* (1980)
22. *The Servant* (1963)
23. *Four Weddings and a Funeral* (1994)
24. *Whisky Galore!* (1949)
25. *The Full Monty* (1997)
26. *The Crying Game* (1992)
27. *Doctor Zhivago* (1965)
28. *Monty Python's Life of Brian* (1979)
29. *Withnail and I* (1987)
30. *Gregory's Girl* (1980)
31. *Zulu* (1964)
32. *Room at the Top* (1958)
33. *Alfie* (1966)
34. *Gandhi* (1982)
35. *The Lady Vanishes* (1938)
36. *The Italian Job* (1969)
37. *Local Hero* (1983)
38. *The Commitments* (1991)
39. *A Fish Called Wanda* (1988)
40. *Secrets & Lies* (1995)
41. *Dr. No* (1962)
42. *The Madness of King George* (1994)
43. *A Man for All Seasons* (1966)
44. *Black Narcissus* (1947)
45. *The Life and Death of Colonel Blimp* (1943)
46. *Oliver Twist* (1948)

47. *I'm All Right Jack* (1959)

48. *Performance* (1970)

49. *Shakespeare in Love* (1998)

50. *My Beautiful Laundrette* (1985)

51. *Tom Jones* (1963)

52. *This Sporting Life* (1963)

53. *My Left Foot* (1989)

54. *Brazil* (1985)

55. *The English Patient* (1996)

56. *A Taste of Honey* (1961)

57. *The Go-Between* (1971)

58. *The Man in the White Suit* (1951)

59. *The Ipcress File* (1965)

60. *Blow-Up* (1966)

61. *The Loneliness of the Long Distance Runner* (1962)

62. *Sense and Sensibility* (1995)

63. *Passport to Pimlico* (1949)

64. *The Remains of the Day* (1993)

65. *Sunday Bloody Sunday* (1971)

66. *The Railway Children* (1970)

67. *Mona Lisa* (1986)

68. *The Dam Busters* (1955)

69. *Hamlet* (1948)

70. *Goldfinger* (1964)

71. *Elizabeth* (1998)

72. *Goodbye Mr. Chips* (1939)

73. *A Room with a View* (1985)

74. *The Day of the Jackal* (1973)

75. *The Cruel Sea* (1952)

76. *Billy Liar* (1963)

77. *Oliver!* (1968)

78. *Peeping Tom* (1960)

79. *Far from the Madding Crowd* (1967)

80. *The Draughtsman's Contract* (1982)

81. *A Clockwork Orange* (1971)

82. *Distant Voices, Still Lives* (1988)

83. *Darling* (1965)

84. *Educating Rita* (1983)

85. *Brassed Off* (1996)

86. *Genevieve* (1953)

87. *Women in Love* (1969)

88. *A Hard Day's Night* (1964)

89. *Fires Were Started* (1943)

90. *Hope and Glory* (1987)

91. *My Name Is Joe* (1998)

92. *In Which We Serve* (1942)

93. *Caravaggio* (1986)

94. *The Belles of St. Trinian's* (1954)

95. *Life Is Sweet* (1990)

96. *The Wicker Man* (1973)

97. *Nil by Mouth* (1997)

98. *Small Faces* (1995)

99. *Carry On up the Khyber* (1968)

100. *The Killing Fields* (1984)

OVERLEAF:

The Third Man *(1949)*, a thriller directed by Sir Carol Reed, was named the favorite British film of the 20th century by the British Film Institute.

FACTS ABOUT THE BFI'S TOP 100 FILMS OF THE 20TH CENTURY

- BECAUSE OF OVERLAPPING criteria for determining nationality, the No. 1 film on the BFI 100, along with four others, are also listed among AFI's Top 100 American Movies of the Last 100 Years. In alphabetical order, they are as follows:

  The Bridge on the River Kwai (BFI No. 11, AFI No. 13)

  A Clockwork Orange (BFI No. 81, AFI No. 46)

  Doctor Zhivago (BFI No. 27, AFI No. 39)

  Lawrence of Arabia (BFI No. 3, AFI No. 5)

  The Third Man (BFI No. 1, AFI No. 57)

- THE LIST, which spans the years 1935 to 1998, contains no silent films. The earliest film included is the 1935 film *The 39 Steps*.

- OF THE SEVEN DECADES represented (1930s to 1990s), the most represented decade is the 1960s, with 26 films; the least represented is the 1930s, with three films.

- THE ACTOR WITH THE MOST included films to his credit is Sir Alec Guinness, who appears in nine films, three of them in the top ten: *Lawrence of Arabia*, *Great Expectations*, and *Kind Hearts and Coronets*.

- DAVID LEAN DIRECTED six of the 100 films and codirected another, with Noël Coward: *In Which We Serve*.

- MICHAEL CAINE and Julie Christie each star in six films.

Malcolm McDowell was a disturbed English punk in A Clockwork Orange *(1971).*

FILMS SELECTED TO THE NATIONAL FILM REGISTRY, LIBRARY OF CONGRESS

Since 1989, these are the works of cinema that have been chosen for preservation in America's largest and most important library.

WITH THE 1988 NATIONAL FILM Preservation Act, Congress established the National Film Registry, a list of films deemed to have cultural, historic, or aesthetic significance. The law authorizes the Librarian of Congress to select up to 25 films each year for inclusion in the registry. The selection takes place after the Librarian of Congress reviews public suggestions and consults with film experts and the 40 members and alternates of the National Film Preservation Board. The films may include Hollywood productions along with independent, documentary, and avant-garde films. All 300 films chosen from 1989 to 2000 are listed alphabetically below. To nominate films (up to 50 titles per year), forward recommendations to:

National Film Registry
Library of Congress, MBRS Division
Washington, D.C. 20540

Sir Alec Guinness starred in
The Bridge on the River Kwai *(1957).*

IN ALPHABETICAL ORDER

1. *Adam's Rib* (1949)
2. *The Adventures of Robin Hood* (1938)
3. *The African Queen* (1951)
4. *All About Eve* (1950)
5. *All Quiet on the Western Front* (1930)
6. *All That Heaven Allows* (1955)
7. *American Graffiti* (1973)
8. *An American in Paris* (1951)
9. *Annie Hall* (1977)
10. *The Apartment* (1960)
11. *Apocalypse Now* (1979)
12. *The Awful Truth* (1937)
13. *Badlands* (1973)
14. *The Band Wagon* (1953)
15. *The Bank Dick* (1940)
16. *The Battle of San Pietro* (1945)
17. *Ben-Hur* (1926)
18. *The Best Years of Our Lives* (1946)
19. *Big Business* (1929)
20. *The Big Parade* (1925)
21. *The Big Sleep* (1946)
22. *The Birth of a Nation* (1915)
23. *The Black Pirate* (1926)
24. *Blacksmith Scene* (1893)
25. *Blade Runner* (1982)
26. *The Blood of Jesus* (1941)
27. *Bonnie and Clyde* (1967)
28. *Bride of Frankenstein* (1935)
29. *The Bridge on the River Kwai* (1957)
30. *Bringing Up Baby* (1938)
31. *Broken Blossoms* (1919)
32. *Cabaret* (1972)
33. *Carmen Jones* (1954)
34. *Casablanca* (1942)

35. *Castro Street* (1966)

36. *Cat People* (1942)

37. *Chan Is Missing* (1982)

38. *The Cheat* (1915)

39. *Chinatown* (1974)

40. *Chulas Fronteras* (1976)

41. *Citizen Kane* (1941)

42. *The City* (1939)

43. *City Lights* (1931)

44. *Civilization* (1916)

45. *The Conversation* (1974)

46. *The Cool World* (1963)

47. *Cops* (1922)

48. *A Corner in Wheat* (1909)

49. *The Crowd* (1928)

50. *Czechoslovakia 1968* (1968)

51. *David Holzman's Diary* (1968)

52. *The Day the Earth Stood Still* (1951)

53. *Dead Birds* (1964)

54. *The Deer Hunter* (1978)

55. *Destry Rides Again* (1939)

56. *Detour* (1946)

57. *Do the Right Thing* (1989)

58. *The Docks of New York* (1928)

59. *Dr. Strangelove or: How I Learned to Stop
    Worrying and Love the Bomb* (1964)

60. *Dodsworth* (1936)

61. *Dog Star Man* (1964)

62. *Don't Look Back* (1967)

63. *Double Indemnity* (1944)

64. *Dracula* (1931)

65. *Duck Amuck* (1953)

66. *Duck Soup* (1933)

67. *E.T.: The Extra-Terrestrial* (1982)

68. *Easy Rider* (1969)

69. *Eaux d'Artifice* (1953)

70. *El Norte* (1983)

71. *The Emperor Jones* (1933)

72. *The Exploits of Elaine* (1914)

73. *The Fall of the House of Usher* (1928)

74. *Fantasia* (1940)

75. *Fatty's Tintype Tangle* (1915)

76. *Five Easy Pieces* (1970)

77. *Flash Gordon* (serial) (1936)

78. *Footlight Parade* (1933)

79. *Force of Evil* (1948)

80. *The Forgotten Frontier* (1931)

81. *42nd Street* (1933)

82. *The Four Horsemen of the Apocalypse* (1921)

83. *Frank Film* (1973)

84. *Frankenstein* (1931)

85. *Freaks* (1932)

86. *The Freshman* (1925)

87. *From the Manger to the Cross* (1912)

88. *Fury* (1936)

89. *The General* (1927)

90. *Gerald McBoing-Boing* (1951)

91. *Gertie the Dinosaur* (1914)

92. *Gigi* (1958)

93. *The Godfather* (1972)

94. *The Godfather, Part II* (1974)

95. *The Gold Rush* (1925)

96. *Gone with the Wind* (1939)

97. *GoodFellas* (1990)

98. *The Graduate* (1967)

99. *The Grapes of Wrath* (1940)

100. *Grass* (1925)

101. *The Great Dictator* (1940)

102. *The Great Train Robbery* (1903)

103. *Greed* (1924)

104. *Gun Crazy* (1949)

105. *Gunga Din* (1939)

106. *Harlan County, U.S.A.* (1976)

107. *Harold and Maude* (1972)

108. *The Heiress* (1949)

109. *Hell's Hinges* (1916)

110. *High Noon* (1952)

111. *High School* (1968)

112. *Hindenburg Disaster Newsreel Footage* (1937)

113. *His Girl Friday* (1940)

114. *The Hitch-Hiker* (1953)

115. *Hospital* (1970)

116. *The Hospital* (1971)

117. *How Green Was My Valley* (1941)

118. *How the West Was Won* (1962)

119. *The Hustler* (1961)

120. *I Am a Fugitive from a Chain Gang* (1932)

121. *The Immigrant* (1917)

Koyaanisqatsi *(1983), directed by Godfrey Reggio with a score by Philip Glass, took nine years to complete.*

122. *In the Land of the Head Hunters (In the Land of the War Canoes)* (1914)
123. *Intolerance* (1916)
124. *Invasion of the Body Snatchers* (1956)
125. *It Happened One Night* (1934)
126. *It's a Wonderful Life* (1946)
127. *The Italian* (1915)
128. *Jammin' the Blues* (1944)
129. *Jazz on a Summer's Day* (1959)
130. *The Jazz Singer* (1927)
131. *Killer of Sheep* (1977)
132. *King: A Filmed Record...Montgomery to Memphis* (1970)
133. *King Kong* (1933)
134. *The Kiss* (1896)
135. *Kiss Me Deadly* (1955)
136. *Knute Rockne, All American* (1940)
137. *Koyaanisqatsi* (1983)
138. *The Lady Eve* (1941)
139. *Lambchops* (1929)
140. *The Land Beyond the Sunset* (1912)
141. *Lassie Come Home* (1943)
142. *The Last of the Mohicans* (1920)
143. *The Last Picture Show* (1972)
144. *Laura* (1944)
145. *Lawrence of Arabia* (1962)
146. *The Learning Tree* (1969)
147. *Let's All Go to the Lobby* (1957)
148. *Letter from an Unknown Woman* (1948)

149. *The Life and Death of 9413— A Hollywood Extra* (1927)
150. *The Life and Times of Rosie the Riveter* (1980)
151. *The Life of Emile Zola* (1937
152. *Little Caesar* (1930))
153. *The Little Fugitive* (1953)
154. *Little Miss Marker* (1934)
155. *The Living Desert* (1953)
156. *The Lost World* (1925)
157. *Louisiana Story* (1948)
158. *Love Finds Andy Hardy* (1938)
159. *Love Me Tonight* (1932)
160. *Magical Maestro* (1952)
161. *The Magnificent Ambersons* (1942)
162. *The Maltese Falcon* (1941)
163. *The Manchurian Candidate* (1962)
164. *Manhatta* (1921)
165. *March of Time: Inside Nazi Germany—1938* (1938)
166. *Marty* (1955)
167. *M*A*S*H* (1970)
168. *Master Hands* (1936)
169. *Mean Streets* (1973)
170. *Meet Me in St. Louis* (1944)
171. *Meshes of the Afternoon* (1943)
172. *Midnight Cowboy* (1969)
173. *Mildred Pierce* (1945)
174. *Mr. Smith Goes to Washington* (1939)
175. *Modern Times* (1936)
176. *Modesta* (1956)
177. *Morocco* (1930)
178. *Motion Painting No. 1* (1947)
179. *A Movie* (1958)
180. *Multiple Sidosis* (1970)
181. *The Music Box* (1932)
182. *My Darling Clementine* (1946)
183. *My Man Godfrey* (1936)
184. *The Naked Spur* (1953)
185. *Nanook of the North* (1922)
186. *Nashville* (1975)
187. *Network* (1976)
188. *A Night at the Opera* (1935)
189. *The Night of the Hunter* (1955)

190. *Night of the Living Dead* (1968)

191. *Ninotchka* (1939)

192. *North by Northwest* (1959)

193. *Nothing But a Man* (1964)

194. *On the Waterfront* (1954)

195. *One Flew Over the Cuckoo's Nest* (1975)

196. *Out of the Past* (1947)

197. *The Outlaw Josey Wales* (1976)

198. *The Ox-Bow Incident* (1943)

199. *Pass the Gravy* (1928)

200. *Paths of Glory* (1957)

201. *Peter Pan* (1924)

202. *Phantom of the Opera* (1925)

203. *The Philadelphia Story* (1940)

204. *Pinocchio* (1940)

205. *A Place in the Sun* (1951)

206. *The Plow That Broke the Plains* (1936)

207. *Point of Order* (1964)

208. *The Poor Little Rich Girl* (1917)

209. *Porky in Wackyland* (1938)

210. *Powers of Ten* (1978)

211. *President McKinley Inauguration Footage* (1901)

212. *Primary* (1960)

213. *The Prisoner of Zenda* (1937)

214. *The Producers* (1968)

215. *Psycho* (1960)

216. *The Public Enemy* (1931)

217. *Pull My Daisy* (1959)

218. *Raging Bull* (1980)

219. *Raiders of the Lost Ark* (1981)

220. *Rear Window* (1954)

221. *Rebel Without a Cause* (1955)

222. *Red River* (1948)

223. *Regeneration* (1915)

224. *Republic Steel Strike Riot Newsreel Footage* (1937)

225. *Return of the Secaucus 7* (1980)

226. *Ride the High Country* (1962)

227. *Rip Van Winkle* (1896)

228. *The River* (1937)

229. *Road to Morocco* (1942)

230. *Roman Holiday* (1953)

231. *Safety Last* (1923)

232. *Salesman* (1969)

233. *Salomé* (1922)

234. *Salt of the Earth* (1954)

235. *Scarface* (1932)

236. *The Searchers* (1956)

237. *Seventh Heaven* (1927)

238. *Shadow of a Doubt* (1943)

239. *Shadows* (1959)

240. *Shaft* (1971)

241. *Shane* (1953)

242. *She Done Him Wrong* (1933)

243. *Sherlock, Jr.* (1924)

244. *Sherman's March* (1986)

245. *Shock Corridor* (1963)

246. *The Shop Around the Corner* (1940)

247. *Show Boat* (1936)

248. *Singin' in the Rain* (1952)

249. *Sky High* (1922)

250. *Snow White* (1933)

251. *Snow White and the Seven Dwarfs* (1937)

252. *Some Like It Hot* (1959)

253. *Stagecoach* (1939)

254. *A Star Is Born* (1954)

255. *Star Wars* (1977)

256. *Steamboat Willie* (1928)

257. *A Streetcar Named Desire* (1951)

258. *Sullivan's Travels* (1941)

259. *Sunrise* (1927)

Timothy Bottoms and Jeff Bridges played best friends growing up in a small Texas town in The Last Picture Show *(1971).*

260. *Sunset Boulevard* (1950)

261. *Sweet Smell of Success* (1957)

262. *Tabu* (1931)

263. *Tacoma Narrows Bridge Collapse* (1940)

264. *The Tall T* (1957)

265. *Taxi Driver* (1976)

266. *The Ten Commandments* (1956)

267. *Tevye* (1939)

268. *The Thief of Bagdad* (1924)

269. *The Thin Man* (1934)

270. *To Be or Not to Be* (1942)

271. *To Fly* (1976)

272. *To Kill a Mockingbird* (1962)

273. *Tootsie* (1982)

274. *Top Hat* (1935)

275. *Topaz (Home Movie Footage Taken at Japanese American Internment Camp, The Topaz War Relocation Authority Center)* (1943–45)

276. *Touch of Evil* (1958)

277. *Trance and Dance in Bali* (1936–39)

278. *The Treasure of the Sierra Madre* (1948)

279. *Trouble in Paradise* (1932)

280. *Tulips Shall Grow* (1942)

281. *Twelve O'Clock High* (1949)

282. *2001: A Space Odyssey* (1968)

283. *Verbena Tragica* (1939)

284. *Vertigo* (1958)

285. *West Side Story* (1961)

286. *Westinghouse Works, 1904* (1904)

287. *What's Opera, Doc?* (1957)

288. *Where Are My Children?* (1916)

289. *Why We Fight* (Series, 1943–45)

290. *The Wild Bunch* (1969)

291. *Will Success Spoil Rock Hunter?* (1957)

292. *The Wind* (1928)

293. *Wings* (1927)

294. *Within Our Gates* (1920)

295. *The Wizard of Oz* (1939)

296. *Woman of the Year* (1942)

297. *A Woman Under the Influence* (1974)

298. *Woodstock* (1970)

299. *Yankee Doodle Dandy* (1942)

300. *Zapruder Film* (1963)

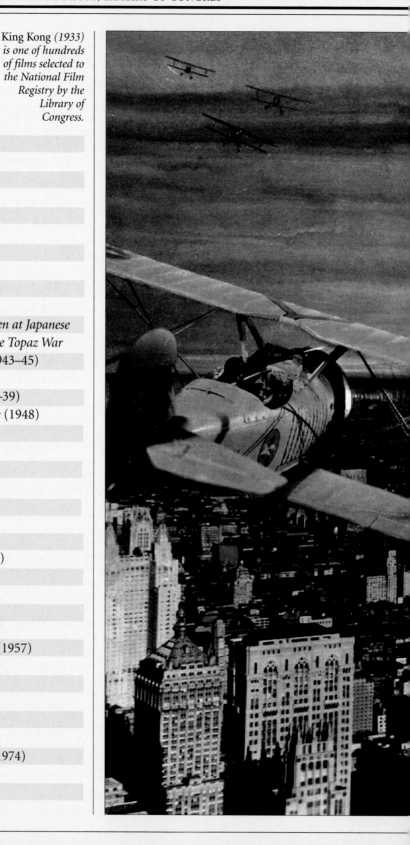

King Kong *(1933) is one of hundreds of films selected to the National Film Registry by the Library of Congress.*

TOP 50 ALL-TIME BOX OFFICE HITS

The following are the top 50 all-time money-making films, as ranked by Variety *in terms of their gross box office receipts in the US as of January 1, 2002.*

MOVIE	GROSS (IN US DOLLARS)
1. *Titanic* (1997)	$600,788,188
2. *Star Wars: Episode IV— A New Hope* (1977)	460,998,007
3. *Star Wars: Episode I— The Phantom Menace* (1999)	431,088,295
4. *E.T.: The Extra-Terrestrial* (1982)	399,804,539
5. *Jurassic Park* (1993)	357,067,947
6. *Forrest Gump* (1994)	329,693,974

Star Wars: Episode I— The Phantom Menace *(1999), starring Natalie Portman, joined the first Star Wars film as one of the biggest US box office hits of all time upon its release.*

HIGHEST-GROSSING FILMS BY GENRE

Film Genre	Movie	Rank
ADVENTURE	*Titanic*	1
WAR	*Saving Private Ryan*	31
HISTORICAL	*Titanic*	1
ROMANTIC	*Titanic*	1
SCIENCE FICTION	*Star Wars*	2
ANIMATED FEATURE	*The Lion King*	7
COMEDY	*Home Alone*	13
HORROR	*The Sixth Sense*	11
BASED ON A COMIC BOOK	*Batman*	17
WESTERN	*Dances With Wolves*	44
MUSICAL	*Grease*	49

7. *The Lion King* (1994)	312,855,561
8. *Return of the Jedi* (1983)	309,205,079
9. *Independence Day* (1996)	306,169,268
10. *Harry Potter and the Sorcerer's Stone* (2001)	294,474,009
11. *The Sixth Sense* (1999)	293,506,292
12. *The Empire Strikes Back* (1980)	290,271,960
13. *Home Alone* (1990)	285,761,243
14. *Shrek* (2001)	267,665,011
15. *Dr. Seuss' The Grinch Who Stole Christmas* (2000)	260,044,825
16. *Jaws* (1975)	260,000,000
17. *Batman* (1989)	251,188,924
18. *Men in Black* (1997)	250,016,330
19. *Toy Story 2* (1999)	245,852,179
20. *Raiders of the Lost Ark* (1981)	242,374,454
21. *Twister* (1996)	241,721,524
22. *Monsters, Inc.* (2001)	240,760,811
23. *Ghostbusters* (1984)	238,600,000
24. *Beverly Hills Cop* (1984)	234,760,478
25. *Cast Away* (2000)	233,632,142
26. *The Lost World: Jurassic Park* (1997)	229,086,123
27. *Rush Hour 2* (2001)	226,164,286
28. *Mrs. Doubtfire* (1993)	219,195,051
29. *Ghost* (1990)	217,631,306
30. *Aladdin* (1992)	217,350,219
31. *Saving Private Ryan* (1998)	216,335,085
32. *Mission: Impossible 2* (2000)	215,409,889
33. *Back to the Future* (1985)	208,242,016
34. *Austin Powers: The Spy Who Shagged Me* (1999)	206,040,086
35. *Terminator 2* (1991)	204,843,345
36. *The Exorcist* (1973)	204,671,011
37. *The Mummy Returns* (2001)	202,019,785

38. *Armageddon* (1998)	201,578,182
39. *Gone with the Wind* (1939)	198,648,910
40. *Pearl Harbor* (2001)	198,542,554
41. *Indiana Jones & The Last Crusade* (1989)	197,171,806
42. *Toy Story* (1995)	191,796,233
43. *Gladiator* (2000)	187,683,805
44. *Dances with Wolves* (1990)	184,208,848
45. *Batman Forever* (1995)	184,031,112
46. *The Fugitive* (1993)	183,875,760
47. *The Perfect Storm* (2000)	182,618,434
48. *The Lord of the Rings: The Fellowship of the Ring* (2001)	182,503,422
49. *Grease* (1978)	181,513,510
50. *Liar Liar* (1997)	181,410,615

SOURCE: VARIETY.COM

VITAL STATISTICS

- THE MOST EXPENSIVE movie ever made was *Titanic* (1997), which cost more than $200 million to make. However, in terms of real costs adjusted for inflation, the most expensive movie ever made was *Cleopatra* (1963). Its budget of $44 million was the equivalent of $306.9 million today.
- THE MOST EXPENSIVE SILENT MOVIE was *Ben-Hur* (1925), which cost $3.9 million, the equivalent of $33 million today.
- THE LEAST EXPENSIVE FEATURE FILM ever made was *The Shattered Illusion* (1927, Australia), a silent movie written and directed by A.G. Harbrow. It cost $1,458 to make.
- THE HIGHEST OPENING-DAY GROSS was that of *Spider-Man* (2002), which took in 39.3 million dollars from 3,615 North American theaters on its first day of exhibition, May 3, 2002. One day later, it also set the record for the best single day in history, with 43.7 million dollars.
- ONLY ONE FILM on the list was released earlier than the 1970s. It is *Gone with the Wind* (1939), at No. 39.
- BECAUSE OF RISING ticket prices, box office grosses are generally higher today than in the past, and that makes recent films appear more popular than older ones. But the appearance is deceptive. If ticket prices are adjusted for inflation, the biggest box office champion in film history is *Gone with the Wind* (1939).

The Top Ten All-Time Foreign Language Film Box Office Hits in North America

AS OF JANUARY 1, 2002.

MOVIE	GROSS (IN MILLIONS OF US DOLLARS)
1. *Crouching Tiger, Hidden Dragon* (2000, China/Taiwan/Hong Kong)	128.1
2. *Life is Beautiful* (1998, Italy)	57.1
3. *Il Postino* (1994, Italy)	21.8
4. *Like Water For Chocolate* (1992, Mexico)	21.7
5. *I am Curious (Yellow)* (1967, Sweden)	20.2
6. *La Dolce Vita* (1960, Italy)	19.5
7. *La Cage aux Folles* (1978, France/Italy)	17.7
8. *Z* (1969, France/Algeria)	15.8
9. *A Man and a Woman* (1966, France)	14.3
10. *Amélie* (2001, France)	14.1

SOURCE: VARIETY.COM

La Cage aux Folles *(1978), featuring Michel Serrault and Ugo Tognazzi, received international acclaim.*

ACADEMY AWARD WINNERS

The Academy Awards have long been the motion picture industry's divining rod, pointing to quality and exposing the roots of the public's ever-shifting taste.

THE ACADEMY AWARDS are the world's best-known film awards. They are granted annually by the Academy of Motion Picture Arts and Sciences, a nonprofit professional organization for the American motion picture industry based in Beverly Hills, California. The first awards, for the films of 1927 to 1928, were presented on May 16, 1929, at a banquet in the Blossom Room of the Hollywood Roosevelt Hotel. The event went on to become an internationally televised spectacle held in Los Angeles in the spring, usually in March.

The first Academy Awards for director and actress were presented to Frank Borzage and Janet Gaynor respectively for Seventh Heaven *(1927).*

The awards are determined by a secret-ballot vote of the Academy's entire 6,000-person membership, following a nomination process in which the Academy's 13 craft branches each select nominees in their categories—actors naming actors, directors naming directors, and so on. The coveted awards take the form of 13½-inch-high gold-plated statuettes known as Oscars. According to Academy lore, the statuette got its nickname when the Academy's librarian and eventual executive director, Margaret Herrick, remarked, "he reminds me of my Uncle Oscar."

Academy Awards honor films made during a 12-month period. From 1927 to 1933, the 12-month period spanned two calendar years; for example, the 1927–28 awards covered films opening in Los Angeles between August 1, 1927, and July 31, 1928. Beginning in 1934, the Academy Awards honored films released during an entire calendar year.

Listed below are all the Academy Award winners from the first ceremony for 1927–28 through the 2001 awards. Our listing of the Academy Awards reflects their evolution and idiosyncrasies. When the nomenclature of an Academy Award presentation changes, we include it. For example, the Academy Awards for screenwriting underwent several permutations, a few of which are highlighted here.

In 1927–28, awards were given in the categories of WRITING—ADAPTATION and WRITING—ORIGINAL STORY. By 1940, categories included WRITING—ORIGINAL STORY and WRITING—SCREENPLAY, and WRITING—ORIGINAL SCREENPLAY had been added. Beginning in 1956, the subcategories changed to WRITING—MOTION PICTURE STORY, WRITING—ADAPTED SCREENPLAY, and WRITING—ORIGINAL SCREENPLAY.

Other rule changes have been instituted across several Academy Award categories, including those for Art Direction, Music Scoring, Sound Recording, and others. A far-reaching change was the elimination of Academy Award subcategory divisions in several categories for black-and-white films and color films. Although the two categories began to be merged during the 1950s, the first year without separate categories for black-and-white and color films was 1967.

Likewise, decades of Academy Awards also saw the creation of categories. For example, the award for Foreign-Language Film was first given regularly in 1956. When an Academy Award category appears for the first time, it marks the first time it was presented.

Among other changes, three named awards were created over the course of Academy Awards history. They are:

—the Irving G. Thalberg Memorial Award, for achievement in production (first presented 1937)

—the Jean Hersholt Humanitarian Award, for charitable activities (1956)

—the Gordon E. Sawyer Award, for technical achievement (1981)

In addition, special or honorary awards have become part of the Academy Awards ceremony. Some, like the special award given to Judy Garland in 1939 for her "outstanding performance as a screen juvenile during the past year," mark discrete achievements. Others, like the 1991 honorary award to director Satyajit Ray, honor lifetime achievement. Explanations for special and honorary awards are given in the text.

——————————— CHRONOLOGY ———————————

1927–28

Best Picture: *Wings*
Artistic Quality of Production: *Sunrise*
Actor: Emil Jannings, *The Last Command*
Actress: Janet Gaynor, *Seventh Heaven*
Director: Frank Borzage, *Seventh Heaven*
Comedy Direction: Lewis Milestone, *Two Arabian Knights*
Writing—Adaptation: Benjamin Glazer, *Seventh Heaven*
Writing—Original Story: Ben Hecht, *Underworld*
Writing—Title Writing: Joseph Farnham, *Telling the World*
Cinematography: Charles Rosher, Karl Struss, *Sunrise*
Interior Decoration: William Cameron Menzies, *The Dove* and *The Tempest*
Engineering Effects: Roy Pomeroy, *Wings*
Special Awards:
—Warner Bros., "for producing *The Jazz Singer*, the outstanding pioneer talking picture, which has revolutionized the industry"
—Charles Chaplin, "for versatility and genius in writing, acting, directing and producing *The Circus*"

1928–29

Best Picture: *Broadway Melody*
Actor: Warner Baxter, *In Old Arizona*
Actress: Mary Pickford, *Coquette*
Director: Frank Lloyd, *The Divine Lady, Weary River,* and *Drag*

Writing: Hans Kraly, *The Patriot*
Cinematography: Clyde DeVinna, *White Shadows in the South Seas*
Interior Decoration: Cedric Gibbons, *The Bridge of San Luis Rey*

1929–30

Best Picture: *All Quiet on the Western Front*
Actor: George Arliss, *Disraeli*
Actress: Norma Shearer, *The Divorcée*
Director: Lewis Milestone, *All Quiet on the Western Front*
Writing: Frances Marion, *The Big House*
Cinematography: Joseph T. Rucker, Willard Van der Veer, *With Byrd at the South Pole*
Interior Decoration: Herman Rosse, *King of Jazz*
Sound Recording: Douglas Shearer, *The Big House*

1930–31

Best Picture: *Cimarron*
Actor: Lionel Barrymore, *A Free Soul*
Actress: Marie Dressler, *Min and Bill*
Director: Norman Taurog, *Skippy*
Writing—Adaptation: Howard Estabrook, *Cimarron*
Writing—Original Story: John Monk Saunders, *The Dawn Patrol*
Cinematography: Floyd Crosby, *Tabu*
Interior Decoration: Max Ree, *Cimarron*
Sound Recording: Paramount Publix Studio Sound Department

"Hollywood was just one big family then, and this was a bouquet — thrown to me, I think, because I was new and because they thought I had a certain freshness. It was nothing then like it is now. My agent didn't call me up the next day with an offer to double my salary. I didn't find a pile of scripts at my door. Photographers weren't camped on my front lawn. I just got up at five a.m. and drove to the studio — as always."

—

Janet Gaynor, recalling her win for the first ever Academy Award for best actress for her performance in Seventh Heaven, *1982*

Frank Capra's classic 1934 screwball comedy It Happened One Night *featured Clark Gable and Claudette Colbert.*

1935 marked the first and, to date, only time in the Academy's history that a write-in candidate has been furnished with a gold statuette, when Hal Mohr won for his cinematography on *A Midsummer Night's Dream.* Mohr heard the news on the radio that night, hurriedly dressed up, and rushed to the ceremony to receive his award.

1931–32

Best Picture: *Grand Hotel*
Actor: Wallace Beery, *The Champ;* Fredric March, *Dr. Jekyll and Mr. Hyde*
Actress: Helen Hayes, *The Sin of Madelon Claudet*
Director: Frank Borzage, *Bad Girl*
Writing—Adaptation: Edwin Burke, *Bad Girl*
Writing—Original Story: Frances Marion, *The Champ*
Cinematography: Lee Garmes, *Shanghai Express*
Interior Decoration: Gordon Wiles, *Transatlantic*
Sound Recording: Paramount Publix Studio Sound Department
Short Subject—Cartoons: *Flowers and Trees*
Short Subject—Comedy: *The Music Box*
Short Subject—Novelty: *Wrestling Swordfish*
Special Award: Walt Disney, "for the creation of Mickey Mouse"

1932–33

Best Picture: *Cavalcade*
Actor: Charles Laughton, *The Private Life of Henry VIII*
Actress: Katharine Hepburn, *Morning Glory*
Director: Frank Lloyd, *Cavalcade*
Writing—Adaptation: Victor Heerman, Sarah Y. Mason, *Little Women*
Writing—Original Story: Robert Lord, *One Way Passage*
Cinematography: Charles Bryant Lang, Jr., *A Farewell to Arms*
Interior Direction: William S. Darling, *Cavalcade*
Sound Recording: Harold C. Lewis, *A Farewell to Arms*
Assistant Director: Charles Barton (Paramount), Scott Beal (Universal), Charles Dorian (MGM), Fred Fox (United Artists), Gordon Hollingshead (Warner Bros.), Dewey Starkey (RKO Radio), William Tummel (Fox)
Short Subject—Cartoons: *The Three Little Pigs*
Short Subject—Comedy: *So This Is Harris*
Short Subject—Novelty: *Krakatoa*

1934

Best Picture: *It Happened One Night*
Actor: Clark Gable, *It Happened One Night*
Actress: Claudette Colbert, *It Happened One Night*
Director: Frank Capra, *It Happened One Night*
Writing—Adaptation: Robert Riskin, *It Happened One Night*
Writing—Original Story: Arthur Caesar, *Manhattan Melodrama*
Cinematography: Victor Milner, *Cleopatra*
Interior Decoration: Cedric Gibbons, Frederic Hope, *The Merry Widow*
Sound Recording: Paul Neal, *One Night of Love*
Assistant Director: John Waters, *Viva Villa*
Song: Con Conrad, "The Continental" for *The Gay Divorcée*
Score: Victor Schertzinger and Gus Kahn, thematic music for *One Night of Love*
Film Editing: Conrad Nervig, *Eskimo*
Short Subject—Cartoons: *The Tortoise and the Hare*
Short Subject—Comedy: *La Cucaracha*
Short Subject—Novelty: *City of Wax*
Special Award: Shirley Temple, "in grateful recognition of her outstanding contribution to screen entertainment during the year of 1934"

1935

Best Picture: *Mutiny on the Bounty*
Actor: Victor McLaglen, *The Informer*
Actress: Bette Davis, *Dangerous*
Director: John Ford, *The Informer*
Writing—Original Story: Ben Hecht, Charles MacArthur, *The Scoundrel*
Writing—Screenplay: Dudley Nichols, *The Informer*
Cinematography: Hal Mohr, *A Midsummer Night's Dream*
Interior Decoration: Richard Day, *The Dark Angel*
Sound Recording: Douglas Shearer, *Naughty Marietta*
Assistant Director: Clem Beauchamp, Paul Wing, *Lives of a Bengal Lancer*
Song: Music by Harry Warren, lyrics by Al Dubin, "Lullaby of Broadway" for *Gold Diggers*
Score: Max Steiner, *The Informer*
Film Editing: Ralph Dawson, *A Midsummer Night's Dream*
Dance Direction: David Gould, "I've Got a Feeling You're Fooling" number in *Broadway Melody of 1936* and "Straw Hat" number in *Folies Bergere*
Short Subject—Cartoons: *Three Orphan Kittens*
Short Subject—Comedy: *How to Sleep*
Short Subject—Novelty: *Wings over Mt. Everest*
Special Award: David Wark Griffith, "for his distinguished creative achievements as director and producer, and his invaluable initiative and contributions to the progress of the motion picture arts"

1936

Best Picture: *The Great Ziegfeld*
Actor: Paul Muni, *The Story of Louis Pasteur*
Actress: Luise Rainer, *The Great Ziegfeld*
Supporting Actor: Walter Brennan, *Come and Get It*
Supporting Actress: Gale Sondergaard, *Anthony Adverse*
Director: Frank Capra, *Mr. Deeds Goes to Town*
Writing—Original Story: Pierre Collings, Sheridan Gibney, *The Story of Louis Pasteur*
Writing—Screenplay: Pierre Collings, Sheridan Gibney, *The Story of Louis Pasteur*
Cinematography: Gaetano Gaudio, *Anthony Adverse*
Interior Decoration: Richard Day, *Dodsworth*
Sound Recording: Douglas Shearer, *San Francisco*
Assistant Director: Jack Sullivan, *The Charge of the Light Brigade*
Song: Music by Jerome Kern, lyrics by Dorothy Fields, "The Way You Look Tonight" for *Swing Time*
Score: Erich Wolfgang Korngold, *Anthony Adverse*
Film Editing: Ralph Dawson, *Anthony Adverse*
Dance Direction: Seymour Felix, "A Pretty Girl Is Like a Melody" number in *The Great Ziegfeld*
Short Subject—Cartoons: *Country Cousin*
Short Subject—One-Reel: *Bored of Education*
Short Subject—Two-Reel: *The Public Pays*
Short Subject—Color: *Give Me Liberty*
Special Awards:
—*March of Time,* "for its significance to motion pictures and for having revolutionized one of the most important branches of the industry—the newsreel"
—W. Howard Greene and Harold Rosson, "for the color cinematography of the Selznick International Production, *The Garden of Allah*"

1937

Best Picture: *The Life of Emile Zola*
Actor: Spencer Tracy, *Captains Courageous*
Actress: Luise Rainer, *The Good Earth*
Supporting Actor: Joseph Schildkraut, *The Life of Emile Zola*
Supporting Actress: Alice Brady, *In Old Chicago*
Director: Leo McCarey, *The Awful Truth*
Writing–Original Story: William A. Wellman, Robert Carson, *A Star Is Born*
Writing—Screenplay: Heinz Herald, Geza Herczeg, Norman Reilly Raine, *The Life of Emile Zola*
Cinematography: Karl Freund, *The Good Earth*
Interior Decoration: Stephen Goosson, *Lost Horizon*
Sound Recording: Thomas Moulton, *The Hurricane*
Assistant Director: Robert Webb, *In Old Chicago*
Song: Harry Owen, "Sweet Leilani" for *Waikiki Wedding*
Score: Universal Studio Music Dept., Charles Previn, head, *One Hundred Men and a Girl*
Film Editing: Gene Havlick and Gene Milford, *Lost Horizon*
Dance Direction: Hermes Pan, "Fun House" number in *Damsel in Distress*
Short Subject—Cartoons: *The Old Mill*
Short Subject—One-Reel: *Private Life of the Gannetts*
Short Subject—Two-Reel: *Torture Money*
Short Subject—Color: *Penny Wisdom*
Irving G. Thalberg Memorial Award: Darryl F. Zanuck
Special Awards:
—Mack Sennett, "for his lasting contributions to the comedy technique of the screen, the basic principles of which are as important today as when they were first put into practice…to the master of fun, discoverer of stars, sympathetic, kindly, understanding comedy genius"
—Edgar Bergen, "for his outstanding comedy creation, Charlie McCarthy"
—The Museum of Modern Art Film Library, "for its significant work in collecting films dating from 1895 to the present and for the first time making available to the public the means of studying the historical and aesthetic development of the motion picture as one of the major arts"
—W. Howard Green, "for the color photography of *A Star Is Born*"

Graham Greene, the esteemed British author of *The Third Man,* was a film critic for the *London Spectator* when he wrote a blistering review of 1936's *The Great Ziegfeld,* calling it a "huge inflated gas-blown object" which "bobs into critical view as irrelevantly as an airship advertising somebody's toothpaste." Despite Greene's qualms, the three-hour musical went on to be both a huge hit and the recipient of that year's best picture Oscar.

Marlene Dietrich starred in The Garden of Allah *(1936), set in the Algerian desert. The film won a special award in 1936 for its color cinematography.*

OVERLEAF:

Frank Capra's Lost Horizon *(1937) received Academy Awards for interior decoration and film editing.*

1938

Best Picture: *You Can't Take It with You*
Actor: Spencer Tracy, *Boys Town*
Actress: Bette Davis, *Jezebel*
Supporting Actor: Walter Brennan, *Kentucky*
Supporting Actress: Fay Bainter, *Jezebel*
Director: Frank Capra, *You Can't Take It with You*
Writing—Original Story: Eleanore Griffin, Dore Schary, *Boys Town*
Writing—Screenplay: George Bernard Shaw; adaptation by Ian Dalrymple, Cecil Lewis, and W.P. Lipscomb, *Pygmalion*
Cinematography: Joseph Ruttenberg, *The Great Waltz*
Interior Decoration: Carl J. Weyl, *The Adventures of Robin Hood*
Sound Recording: Thomas Moulton, *The Cowboy and the Lady*
Song: Music by Ralph Rainger, lyrics by Leo Robin, "Thanks for the Memory" for *The Big Broadcast of 1938*
Score: Alfred Newman, *Alexander's Ragtime Band*
Original Score: Erich Wolfgang Korngold, *The Adventures of Robin Hood*
Film Editing: Ralph Dawson, *The Adventures of Robin Hood*
Short Subject—Cartoons: *Ferdinand the Bull*
Short Subject—One-Reel: *That Mothers Might Live*
Short Subject—Two-Reel: *Declaration of Independence*
Irving G. Thalberg Memorial Award: Hal B. Wallis
Special Awards:
—Deanna Durbin and Mickey Rooney, "for their significant contribution in bringing to the screen the spirit and personification of youth, and as juvenile players setting the standard of ability and achievement"

> "To Father Edward J. Flanagan, whose great human qualities, timely simplicity, and inspiring courage were strong enough to shine through my humble effort."
>
> —
>
> *Spencer Tracy's inscription on his Oscar for* Boys Town *(1938), which he presented to the real-life priest he had won a best actor award for portraying*

—Harry M. Warner, "in recognition of patriotic service in the production of historical short subjects presenting significant episodes in the early struggle of the American people for liberty"
—Walt Disney, "for *Snow White and the Seven Dwarfs,* recognized as a significant screen innovation which has charmed millions and pioneered a great new entertainment field for the motion picture cartoon"
—Oliver Marsh and Allen Davey, "for the color cinematography of the MGM production *Sweethearts*"
—"For outstanding achievement in creating special photographic and sound effects in the Paramount production *Spawn of the North:* special effects by Gordon Jennings, assisted by Jan Domela, Dev Jennings, Irmin Roberts, and Art Smith; transparencies by Farciot Edouart, assisted by Loyal Griggs; sound effects by Loren Ryder, assisted by Harry Mills, Louis H. Mesenkop, and Walter Oberst"
—J. Arthur Ball, "for his outstanding contributions to the advancement of color in motion picture photography"

1939

Best Picture: *Gone with the Wind*
Actor: Robert Donat, *Goodbye, Mr. Chips*
Actress: Vivien Leigh, *Gone with the Wind*
Supporting Actor: Thomas Mitchell, *Stagecoach*
Supporting Actress: Hattie McDaniel, *Gone with the Wind*
Director: Victor Fleming, *Gone with the Wind*
Writing—Original Story: Lewis R. Foster, *Mr. Smith Goes to Washington*
Writing—Screenplay: Sidney Howard, *Gone with the Wind*
Cinematography—Black-and-White: Gregg Toland, *Wuthering Heights*
Cinematography—Color: Ernest Haller, Ray Rennahan, *Gone with the Wind*
Interior Decoration: Lyle Wheeler, *Gone with the Wind*
Sound Recording: Bernard B. Brown, *When Tomorrow Comes*
Song: Music by Harold Arlen; lyrics by E.Y. Harburg, "Over the Rainbow" for *The Wizard of Oz*
Score: Walter Wanger, Richard Hageman, Frank Harling, John Leipold, Leo Shuken, *Stagecoach*
Original Score: Herbert Stothart, *The Wizard of Oz*
Film Editing: Hal C. Kern and James E. Newcom, *Gone with the Wind*
Special Effects: E.H. Hansen (photographic), Fred Sersen (sound), *The Rains Came*
Short Subject—Cartoons: *The Ugly Duckling*
Short Subject—One-Reel: *Busy Little Bears*
Short Subject—Two-Reel: *Sons of Liberty*
Irving G. Thalberg Memorial Award: David O. Selznick

Errol Flynn and Basil Rathbone squared off in The Adventures of Robin Hood *(1938).*

Special Awards:

—Douglas Fairbanks,"recognizing the unique and outstanding contribution of Douglas Fairbanks, first president of the Academy, to the international development of the motion picture"

—The Motion Picture Relief Fund, "acknowledging the outstanding services to the industry during the past year of the Motion Picture Relief Fund and its progressive leadership. Presented to Jean Hersholt, President; Ralph Morgan, Chairman of the Executive Committee; Ralph Block, First Vice President; Conrad Nagel"

—Judy Garland, "for her outstanding performance as a screen juvenile during the past year"

—William Cameron Menzies, "for outstanding achievement in the use of color for the enhancement of dramatic mood in the production *Gone with the Wind*"

—The Technicolor Company, "for its contributions in successfully bringing three-color feature production to the screen"

1940

Best Picture: *Rebecca*
Actor: James Stewart, *The Philadelphia Story*
Actress: Ginger Rogers, *Kitty Foyle*
Supporting Actor: Walter Brennan, *The Westerner*
Supporting Actress: Jane Darwell, *The Grapes of Wrath*
Director: John Ford, *The Grapes of Wrath*
Writing—Original Story: Benjamin Glazer, John S. Toldy, *Arise, My Love*
Writing—Original Screenplay: Preston Sturges, *The Great McGinty*
Writing—Screenplay: Donald Ogden Stewart, *The Philadelphia Story*
Cinematography—Black-and-White: George Barnes, *Rebecca*
Cinematography—Color: George Perinal, *The Thief of Bagdad*
Set Decoration—Black-and-White: Cedric Gibbons, Paul Groesse, *Pride and Prejudice*
Set Decoration—Color: Vincent Korda, *The Thief of Bagdad*
Sound Recording: Douglas Shearer, *Strike Up the Band*
Song: Music by Leigh Harline, lyrics by Ned Washington, "When You Wish upon a Star" for *Pinocchio*
Score: Alfred Newman, *Tin Pan Alley*
Original Score: Leigh Harline, Paul J. Smith, Ned Washington, *Pinocchio*
Film Editing: Anne Bauchens, *North West Mounted Police*
Special Effects: Lawrence Butler (photographic), Jack Whitney (sound), *The Thief of Bagdad*
Short Subject—Cartoons: *Milky Way*
Short Subject—One-Reel: *Quicker 'N a Wink*
Short Subject—Two-Reel: *Teddy, the Rough Rider*
Special Awards:
—Bob Hope, "in recognition of his unselfish services to the motion picture industry"

—Colonel Nathan Levinson, "for his outstanding service to the industry and the Army during the past nine years, which has made possible the present efficient mobilization of the motion picture facilities for the production of Army training films"

1941

Best Picture: *How Green Was My Valley*
Actor: Gary Cooper, *Sergeant York*
Actress: Joan Fontaine, *Suspicion*
Supporting Actor: Donald Crisp, *How Green Was My Valley*
Supporting Actress: Mary Astor, *The Great Lie*
Director: John Ford, *How Green Was My Valley*
Writing—Original Story: Harry Segall, *Here Comes Mr. Jordan*
Writing—Original Screenplay: Herman J. Mankiewicz, Orson Welles, *Citizen Kane*
Writing—Screenplay: Sidney Buchman, Seton I. Miller, *Here Comes Mr. Jordan*
Cinematography—Black-and-White: Arthur Miller, *How Green Was My Valley*
Cinematography—Color: Ernest Palmer, Ray Rennahan, *Blood and Sand*
Interior Decoration—Black-and-White: Richard Day and Nathan Juran (art direction), Thomas Little (set decoration), *How Green Was My Valley*
Interior Decoration—Color: Cedric Gibbons and Urie McCleary (art direction), Edwin B. Willis (set decoration), *Blossoms in the Dust*
Sound Recording: Jack Whitney, General Service, *That Hamilton Woman*
Song: Music by Jerome Kern, lyrics by Oscar Hammerstein II, "The Last Time I Saw Paris" for *Lady Be Good*

Preston Sturges's directorial debut, The Great McGinty *(1940), starred Brian Donlevy, Mariel Angelus, and William Demarest.*

Among the actresses Joan Fontaine beat out for best actress for 1941's *Suspicion* was her older sister, Olivia de Havilland, who was nominated in the same category for *Hold Back the Dawn*. Having also lost the Oscar two years earlier (to her *Gone with the Wind* co-star, Hattie McDaniel, for best supporting actress), the empty-handed de Havilland would go on to win two best actress awards before the decade was over—for *To Each His Own* (1946) and *The Heiress* (1949).

How Green Was My Valley *(1941) followed the lives of a Welsh family over the course of 50 years. The film was nominated for ten Academy Awards and won a total of five.*

Scoring of a Dramatic Picture:
Bernard Herrmann, *All That Money Can Buy*
Scoring of a Musical Picture: Frank Churchill,
Oliver Wallace, *Dumbo*
Film Editing: William Holmes, *Sergeant York*
Special Effects: Farciot Edouart and Gordon
Jennings (photographic), Louis Mesenkop
(sound), *I Wanted Wings*
Short Subject—Cartoons: *Lend a Paw*
Short Subject—One-Reel: *Of Pups and Puzzles*
Short Subject—Two-Reel: *Main Street on the March*
Documentary: *Churchill's Island*
Irving G. Thalberg Memorial Award: Walt Disney
Special Awards:
—Rey Scott, "for his extraordinary achievement
in producing *Kukan,* the film record of China's
struggle, including its photography with a
16mm camera under the most difficult and
dangerous conditions"
—The British Ministry of Information, "for
its vivid and dramatic presentation of the
heroism of the RAF in the documentary film
Target for Tonight"
—Leopold Stokowski and his associates, "for
their unique achievement in the creation of a
new form of visualized music in Walt Disney's
Fantasia, thereby widening the scope of the
motion picture as entertainment and as an
art form"
—Walt Disney, William Garity, John N.A.
Hawkins, and the RCA Manufacturing Company, "for their outstanding contribution to the
advancement of the use of sound in motion
pictures through the production of *Fantasia*"

1942

Best Picture: *Mrs. Miniver*
Actor: James Cagney, *Yankee Doodle Dandy*
Actress: Greer Garson, *Mrs. Miniver*
Supporting Actor: Van Heflin, *Johnny Eager*
Supporting Actress: Teresa Wright,
Mrs. Miniver
Director: William Wyler, *Mrs. Miniver*
Writing—Original Story: Michael Kanin,
Ring Lardner, Jr., *Woman of the Year*
Writing—Screenplay: George Froeschel,
James Hilton, Claudine West, Arthur Wimperis,
Mrs. Miniver
Cinematography—Black-and-White:
Joseph Ruttenberg, *Mrs. Miniver*
Cinematography—Color: Leon Shamroy,
The Black Swan
Interior Decoration—Black-and-White:
Richard Day and Joseph Wright (art direction),
Thomas Little (set decoration), *This Above All*
Interior Decoration—Color: Richard Day and
Joseph Wright (art direction), Thomas Little
(set decoration), *My Gal Sal*
Sound Recording: Nathan Levinson,
Yankee Doodle Dandy
Song: Irving Berlin, "White Christmas" for
Holiday Inn
Scoring of a Dramatic or Comedy Picture:
Max Steiner, *Now, Voyager*
Scoring of a Musical Picture: Ray Heindorf,
Heinz Roemheld, *Yankee Doodle Dandy*
Film Editing: Daniel Mandell,
The Pride of the Yankees
Special Effects: Farciot Edouart, Gordon Jennings,
and William L. Pereira (photographic), Louis
Mesenkop (sound), *Reap the Wild Wind*
Short Subject—Cartoons: *Der Fuehrer's Face*
Short Subject—One-Reel:
Speaking of Animals and Their Families
Short Subject—Two-Reel: *Beyond the Line of Duty*
Documentary: *Battle of Midway*
Irving G. Thalberg Memorial Award:
Sidney Franklin
Special Awards:
—Charles Boyer, "for his progressive cultural
achievement in establishing the French Research
Foundation in Los Angeles as a source of refer-
ence for the Hollywood motion picture industry"
—Noël Coward, "for his outstanding production
achievement in *In Which We Serve*"
—MGM Studio, "for its achievement in
representing the American way of life in the
production of the Andy Hardy series of films"

1943

Best Picture: *Casablanca*
Actor: Paul Lukas, *Watch on the Rhine*
Actress: Jennifer Jones, *The Song of Bernadette*
Supporting Actor: Charles Coburn, *The More
the Merrier*

Supporting Actress: Katina Paxinou, *For Whom the Bell Tolls*
Director: Michael Curtiz, *Casablanca*
Writing—Original Story: William Saroyan, *The Human Comedy*
Writing—Screenplay: Norman Krasna, *Princess O'Rourke*
Cinematography—Black-and-White: Arthur Miller, *The Song of Bernadette*
Cinematography—Color: Hal Mohr, W. Howard Greene, *The Phantom of the Opera*
Interior Decoration—Black-and-White: James Basevi and William Darling (art direction), Thomas Little (set decoration), *The Song of Bernadette*
Interior Decoration—Color: Alexander Golitzen and John B. Goodman (art direction), Russell A. Gausman and Ira S. Webb (set decoration), *The Phantom of the Opera*
Sound Recording: Stephen Dunn, *This Land Is Mine*
Song: Music by Harry Warren, lyrics by Mack Gordon, "You'll Never Know" for *Hello, Frisco, Hello*
Scoring of a Dramatic or Comedy Picture: Alfred Newman, *The Song of Bernadette*
Scoring of a Musical Picture: Ray Heindorf, *This Is the Army*
Film Editing: George Amy, *Air Force*
Special Effects: Fred Sersen (photographic), Roger Heman (sound), *Crash Dive*
Short Subject—Cartoons: *Yankee Doodle Mouse*
Short Subject—One-Reel: *Amphibious Fighters*
Short Subject—Two-Reel: *Heavenly Music*
Documentary—Short Subject: *December 7th*
Documentary—Feature: *Desert Victory*
Irving G. Thalberg Memorial Award: Hal B. Wallis
Special Award: George Pal, "for the development of novel methods and techniques in the production of short subjects known as Puppetoons"

1944

Best Picture: *Going My Way*
Actor: Bing Crosby, *Going My Way*
Actress: Ingrid Bergman, *Gaslight*
Supporting Actor: Barry Fitzgerald, *Going My Way*
Supporting Actress: Ethel Barrymore, *None But the Lonely Heart*
Director: Leo McCarey, *Going My Way*
Writing—Original Story: Leo McCarey, *Going My Way*
Writing—Original Screenplay: Lamar Trotti, *Wilson*
Writing—Screenplay: Frank Butler, Frank Cavett, *Going My Way*
Cinematography—Black-and-White: Joseph LaShelle, *Laura*
Cinematography—Color: Leon Shamroy, *Wilson*
Interior Decoration—Black-and-White: Cedric Gibbons and William Ferrari (art direction), Edwin B. Willis and Paul Huldschinsky (set direction), *Gaslight*
Interior Decoration—Color: Wiard Ihnen (art direction); Thomas Little (set direction), *Wilson*
Sound Recording: E.H. Hansen, *Wilson*
Song: Music by James Van Heusen, lyrics by Johnny Burke, "Swinging on a Star" for *Going My Way*
Scoring of a Dramatic or Comedy Picture: Max Steiner, *Since You Went Away*
Scoring of a Musical Picture: Carmen Dragon, Morris Stoloff, *Cover Girl*
Film Editing: Barbara McLean, *Wilson*
Special Effects: A. Arnold Gillespie, Donald Jahraus, and Warren Newcombe (photographic), Douglas Shearer (sound), *Thirty Seconds over Tokyo*
Short Subject—Cartoons: *Mouse Trouble*

> "I write what I see. This is very difficult for anybody to understand. Especially for anybody with such bad eyesight as I have."
>
> —
>
> *Academy Award-winning composer Max Steiner, on creating the music for the characters he sees onscreen, 1970*

Casablanca (1942), starring Ingrid Bergman and Humphrey Bogart, won Academy Awards for best picture and best director (Michael Curtiz).

In 1946, Harold Russell became the only actor to ever win two Academy Awards for the same performance for his role in *The Best Years of Our Lives.* Wishing to honor the World War Two vet, who had lost both hands in combat, Academy governors gave him an Honorary Oscar. Later that night, Russell beat out Clifton Webb, Claude Rains, William Demarest, and Charles Coburn for the best supporting actor Oscar, for which he was also nominated. He would not appear in another film until 1980's *Inside Moves.*

Ray Milland portrayed an alcoholic in The Lost Weekend *(1945).*

Short Subject—One-Reel:
Who's Who in Animal Land
Short Subject—Two-Reel: *I Won't Play*
Documentary—Short Subject:
With the Marines at Tarawa
Documentary—Feature: *The Fighting Lady*
Irving G. Thalberg Memorial Award:
Darryl F. Zanuck
Special Awards:
—Margaret O'Brien, "outstanding child actress of 1944"
—Bob Hope, "for his many services to the Academy"

1945

Best Picture: *The Lost Weekend*
Actor: Ray Milland, *The Lost Weekend*
Actress: Joan Crawford, *Mildred Pierce*
Supporting Actor: James Dunn, *A Tree Grows in Brooklyn*
Supporting Actress: Anne Revere, *National Velvet*
Director: Billy Wilder, *The Lost Weekend*
Writing—Original Story: Charles G. Booth, *The House on 92nd Street*
Writing—Original Screenplay: Richard Schweizer, *Marie-Louise*
Writing—Screenplay: Charles Brackett, Billy Wilder, *The Lost Weekend*
Cinematography—Black-and-White:
Harry Stradling, *The Picture of Dorian Gray*
Cinematography—Color:
Leon Shamroy, *Leave Her to Heaven*

Interior Decoration—Black-and-White:
Wiard Ihnen (art direction), A. Roland Fields (set decoration), *Blood on the Sun*
Interior Decoration—Color: Hans Dreier and Ernst Fegte (art direction), Sam Comer (set decoration), *Frenchman's Creek*
Sound Recording: Stephen Dunn, *The Bells of St. Mary's*
Song: Music by Richard Rodgers, lyrics by Oscar Hammerstein II, "It Might as Well Be Spring" for *State Fair*
Scoring of a Dramatic or Comedy Picture: Miklos Rozsa, *Spellbound*
Scoring of a Musical Picture: Georgie Stoll, *Anchors Aweigh*
Film Editing: Robert J. Kern, *National Velvet*
Special Effects: John Fulton (photographic), A.W. Johns (sound), *Wonder Man*
Short Subject—Cartoons: *Quiet Please*
Short Subject—One-Reel: *Stairway to Light*
Short Subject—Two-Reel: *Star in the Night*
Documentary—Short Subject: *Hitler Lives?*
Documentary—Feature: *The True Glory*
Special Awards:
—Walter Wanger, "for his six years service as President of the Academy of Motion Picture Arts and Sciences"
—Peggy Ann Garner, "outstanding child actress of 1945"
—*The House I Live In,* tolerance short subject.
—Republic Studio, Daniel J. Bloomberg, and the Republic Sound Department, "for the building of an outstanding musical scoring auditorium which provides optimum recording conditions and combines all elements of acoustic and engineering design"

1946

Best Picture: *The Best Years of Our Lives*
Actor: Fredric March, *The Best Years of Our Lives*
Actress: Olivia de Havilland, *To Each His Own*
Supporting Actor: Harold Russell, *The Best Years of Our Lives*
Supporting Actress: Anne Baxter, *The Razor's Edge*
Director: William Wyler, *The Best Years of Our Lives*
Writing—Original Story: Clemence Dane, *Vacation from Marriage*
Writing—Original Screenplay: Muriel Box, Sydney Box, *The Seventh Veil*
Writing—Screenplay: Robert E. Sherwood, *The Best Years of Our Lives*
Cinematography—Black-and-White: Arthur Miller, *Anna and the King of Siam*
Cinematography—Color: Charles Rosher, Leonard Smith, Arthur Arling, *The Yearling*

Interior Decoration—Black-and-White:
Lyle Wheeler and William Darling
(art direction), Thomas Little and Frank E.
Hughes (set decoration), *Anna and the King of Siam*

Interior Decoration—Color: Cedric Gibbons
and Paul Groesse (art direction), Edwin B.
Willis (set decoration), *The Yearling*

Sound Recording: John Livadary, *The Jolson Story*

Song: Music by Harry Warren, lyrics by
Johnny Mercer, "On the Atchison, Topeka
and Santa Fe" for *The Harvey Girls*

Scoring of a Dramatic or Comedy Picture:
Hugo Friedhofer, *The Best Years of Our Lives*

Scoring of a Musical Picture:
Morris Stoloff, *The Jolson Story*

Film Editing: Daniel Mandell, *The Best Years of Our Lives*

Special Effects: William McGann (visual),
A Stolen Life

Short Subject—Cartoons: *The Cat Concerto*

Short Subject—One-Reel: *Facing Your Danger*

Short Subject—Two-Reel: *A Boy and His Dog*

Documentary—Short Subject: *Seeds of Destiny*

Irving G. Thalberg Memorial Award:
Samuel Goldwyn

Special Awards:
—Laurence Olivier, "for his outstanding
achievement as actor, producer and director
in bringing *Henry V* to the screen"
—Harold Russell, "for bringing hope and courage
to his fellow veterans through his appearance in
The Best Years of Our Lives"
—Ernst Lubitsch, "for his distinguished
contributions to the art of the motion picture"
—Claude Jarman, Jr., "outstanding child actor
of 1946"

1947

Best Picture: *Gentleman's Agreement*

Actor: Ronald Colman, *A Double Life*

Actress: Loretta Young, *The Farmer's Daughter*

Supporting Actor: Edmund Gwenn, *Miracle on 34th Street*

Supporting Actress: Celeste Holm, *Gentleman's Agreement*

Director: Elia Kazan, *Gentleman's Agreement*

Writing—Original Story: Valentine Davies,
Miracle on 34th Street

Writing—Original Screenplay: Sidney Sheldon,
The Bachelor and the Bobby-Soxer

Writing—Screenplay: George Seaton, *Miracle
on 34th Street*

Cinematography—Black-and-White: Guy Green,
Great Expectations

Cinematography—Color: Jack Cardiff, *Black
Narcissus*

Interior Decoration—Black-and-White: John
Bryan (art direction), Wilfred Shingleton (set
decoration), *Great Expectations*

Interior Decoration—Color: Alfred Junge,
Black Narcissus

Sound Recording: Goldwyn Sound Department,
The Bishop's Wife

Song: Music by Allie Wrubel, lyrics by Ray Gilbert,
"Zip-A-Dee-Doo-Dah" for *Song of the South*

Scoring of a Dramatic or Comedy Picture:
Miklos Rozsa, *A Double Life*

Scoring of a Musical Picture: Alfred Newman,
Mother Wore Tights

Film Editing: Francis Lyon, Robert Parrish,
Body and Soul

Special Effects: A. Arnold Gillespie and Warren
Newcombe (visual), Douglas Shearer and
Michael Steinore (audible), *Green Dolphin Street*

Short Subject—Cartoons: *Tweetie Pie*

Short Subject—One-Reel: *Goodbye Miss Turlock*

Short Subject—Two-Reel: *Climbing the Matterhorn*

Documentary—Short Subject: *First Steps*

Documentary—Feature: *Design for Death*

Special Awards:
—James Baskette, "for his able and heartwarming
characterization of Uncle Remus, friend and
storyteller to the children of the world"
—*Bill and Coo*, "in which artistry and patience
blended in a novel and entertaining use of the
medium of motion pictures"
—*Shoeshine*—"the high quality of this motion
picture, brought to eloquent life in a country
scarred by war, is proof to the world that the
creative spirit can triumph over adversity"
—Colonel William N. Selig, Albert E. Smith,
Thomas Armat, and George K. Spoor, "the
small group of pioneers whose belief in a new
medium, and whose contributions to its
development, blazed the trail along which the
motion picture has progressed, in their lifetime,
from obscurity to worldwide acclaim"

*The 1947 film adaptation
of* Great Expectations,
*by Charles Dickens,
starred John Mills.*

Laurence Olivier garnered acclaim for his acting and directing in Hamlet *(1948).*

Sound Recording: 20th Century—Fox Sound Department, *The Snake Pit*

Song: Jay Livingston, Ray Evans, "Buttons and Bows" for *The Paleface*

Scoring of a Dramatic or Comedy Picture: Brian Easdale, *The Red Shoes*

Scoring of a Musical Picture: Johnny Green, Roger Edens, *Easter Parade*

Film Editing: Paul Weatherwax, *The Naked City*

Costume Design—Black-and-White: Roger K. Furse, *Hamlet*

Costume Design—Color: Dorothy Jeakins, Karinska, *Joan of Arc*

Special Effects: Paul Eagler, J. McMillan Johnson, Russell Shearman, Clarence Slifer (visual), Charles Freeman and James G. Stewart (audible), *Portrait of Jennie*

Short Subject—Cartoons: *The Little Orphan*

Short Subject—One-Reel: *Symphony of a City*

Short Subject—Two-Reel: *Seal Island*

Documentary—Short Subject: *Toward Independence*

Documentary—Feature: *The Secret Land*

Irving G. Thalberg Memorial Award: Jerry Wald

Special Awards:

—*Monsieur Vincent* (France), the "most outstanding foreign-language film"

—Ivan Jandl's "outstanding juvenile performance" in *The Search*

—Sid Grauman, "for raising the standard of exhibition of motion pictures"

—Adolph Zukor, "for services to the industry"

—Walter Wanger, "for distinguished service to the industry in adding to its moral stature in the world community by producing *Joan of Arc*"

1948

Best Picture: *Hamlet*

Actor: Laurence Olivier, *Hamlet*

Actress: Jane Wyman, *Johnny Belinda*

Supporting Actor: Walter Huston, *The Treasure of the Sierra Madre*

Supporting Actress: Claire Trevor, *Key Largo*

Director: John Huston, *The Treasure of the Sierra Madre*

Writing—Motion Picture Story: Richard Schweizer, David Wechsler, *The Search*

Writing—Screenplay: John Huston, *The Treasure of the Sierra Madre*

Cinematography—Black-and-White: William Daniels, *The Naked City*

Cinematography—Color: Joseph Valentine, William V. Skall, Winton Hoch, *Joan of Arc*

Art Direction—Black-and-White: Roger K. Furse (art direction), Carmen Dillon (set decoration), *Hamlet*

Art Direction—Color: Hein Heckroth (art direction), Arthur Lawson (set decoration), *The Red Shoes*

1949

Best Picture: *All the King's Men*

Actor: Broderick Crawford, *All the King's Men*

Actress: Olivia de Havilland, *The Heiress*

Supporting Actor: Dean Jagger, *Twelve O'Clock High*

Supporting Actress: Mercedes McCambridge, *All the King's Men*

Director: Joseph L. Mankiewicz, *A Letter to Three Wives*

Writing—Motion Picture Story: Douglas Morrow, *The Stratton Story*

Writing—Screenplay: Joseph L. Mankiewicz, *A Letter to Three Wives*

Cinematography—Black-and-White: Paul C. Vogel, *Battleground*

Cinematography—Color: Winton Hoch, *She Wore a Yellow Ribbon*

Art Direction—Black-and-White: John Meehan and Harry Horner (art direction), Emile Kuri (set decoration), *The Heiress*

Art Direction—Color: Cedric Gibbons and Paul Groesse (art direction), Edwin B. Willis and Jack D. Moore (set decoration), *Little Women*

Sound Recording: 20th Century–Fox Sound Department, *Twelve O'Clock High*

Song: Frank Loesser, "Baby, It's Cold Outside" for *Neptune's Daughter*

Scoring of a Dramatic or Comedy Picture: Aaron Copland, *The Heiress*

Scoring of a Musical Picture: Roger Edens, Lennie Hayton, *On the Town*

Film Editing: Harry Gerstad, *Champion*

Special Effects: RKO Radio, *Mighty Joe Young*

Short Subject—Cartoons: *For Scent-imental Reasons*

Short Subject—One-Reel: *Aquatic House-Party*

Short Subject—Two-Reel: *Van Gogh*

Documentary—Short Subject: *A Chance to Live* and *So Much for So Little*

Documentary—Feature: *Daybreak in Udi*

Special Awards:

—*The Bicycle Thief* (Italy), "voted by the Academy Board of Governors as the most outstanding foreign-language film released in the United States during 1949"

—Bobby Driscoll, "the outstanding juvenile actor of 1949"

—Fred Astaire, "for his unique artistry and his contributions to the technique of musical pictures"

—Cecil B. DeMille, "distinguished motion picture pioneer, for thirty-seven years of brilliant showmanship"

—Jean Hersholt, "for distinguished service to the motion-picture industry"

1950

Best Picture: *All About Eve*

Actor: José Ferrer, *Cyrano de Bergerac*

Actress: Judy Holliday, *Born Yesterday*

Supporting Actor: George Sanders, *All About Eve*

Supporting Actress: Josephine Hull, *Harvey*

Director: Joseph L. Mankiewicz, *All About Eve*

Writing—Motion Picture Story: Edna Anhalt, Edward Anhalt, *Panic in the Streets*

Writing—Screenplay: Joseph L. Mankiewicz, *All About Eve*

Cinematography—Black-and-White: Robert Krasker, *The Third Man*

Cinematography—Color: Robert Surtees, *King Solomon's Mines*

Art Direction—Black-and-White: Hans Dreier and John Meehan (art direction), Sam Comer and Ray Moyer (set decoration), *Sunset Boulevard*

Art Direction—Color: Hans Dreier and Walter Tyler (art direction), Sam Comer and Ray Moyer (set decoration), *Samson and Delilah*

Sound Recording: 20th Century–Fox Sound Department, *All About Eve*

Song: Ray Evans, Jay Livingston, "Mona Lisa" for *Captain Carey*

Scoring of a Dramatic or Comedy Picture: Franz Waxman, *Sunset Boulevard*

Scoring of a Musical Picture: Adolph Deutsch, Roger Edens, *Annie Get Your Gun*

Film Editing: Ralph E. Winters, Conrad A. Nervig, *King Solomon's Mines*

Costume Design—Black-and-White: Edith Head, Charles LeMaire, *All About Eve*

Costume Design—Color: Edith Head, Dorothy Jeakins, Elois Jenssen, Gile Steele, Gwen Wakeling, *Samson and Delilah*

Special Effects: Eagle-Lion, *Destination Man*

Short Subject—Cartoons: *Gerald McBoing-Boing*

Short Subject—One-Reel: *Grandad of Races*

Short Subject—Two-Reel: *In Beaver Valley*

Documentary—Short Subject: *Why Korea?*

Documentary—Feature: *The Titan: Story of Michelangelo*

Irving G. Thalberg Memorial Award: Darryl F. Zanuck

Honorary Awards:

—George Murphy, "for his services in interpreting the film industry to the country at large"

—Louis B. Mayer, "for distinguished service to the motion picture industry"

—*The Walls of Malapaga* (France/Italy)–"voted by the [Academy's] Board of Governors as the most outstanding foreign-language film released in the United States in 1950"

1951

Best Picture: *An American in Paris*

Actor: Humphrey Bogart, *The African Queen*

Actress: Vivien Leigh, *A Streetcar Named Desire*

Supporting Actor: Karl Malden, *A Streetcar Named Desire*

Supporting Actress: Kim Hunter, *A Streetcar Named Desire*

Director: George Stevens, *A Place in the Sun*

Writing—Motion Picture Story: Paul Dehn, James Bernard, *Seven Days to Noon*

Writing—Screenplay: Michael Wilson, Harry Brown, *A Place in the Sun*

Writing—Story and Screenplay: Alan Jay Lerner, *An American in Paris*

Cinematography—Black-and-White: William C. Mellor, *A Place in the Sun*

Cinematography—Color: Alfred Gilks, John Alton, *An American in Paris*

Art Direction—Black-and-White: Richard Day (art direction), George James Hopkins (set decoration), *A Streetcar Named Desire*

Art Direction—Color: Cedric Gibbons and Preston Ames (art direction), Edwin B. Willis and Keogh Gleason (set decoration), *An American in Paris*

Sound Recording: Douglas Shearer, *The Great Caruso*

Song: Music by Hoagy Carmichael, lyrics by Johnny Mercer, "In the Cool, Cool, Cool of the Evening" for *Here Comes the Groom*

Scoring of a Dramatic or Comedy Picture: Franz Waxman, *A Place in the Sun*

Scoring of a Musical Picture: Johnny Green, Saul Chapman, *An American in Paris*

Film Editing: William Hornbeck, *A Place in the Sun*

Costume Design—Black-and-White: Edith Head, *A Place in the Sun*

Before she made the role famous on film, Vivien Leigh played Blanche Dubois in *A Streetcar Named Desire* on the London stage for nine months, in a production directed by Laurence Olivier.

Costume Design—Color: Orry-Kelly, Walter Plunkett, Irene Sharaff, *An American in Paris*
Special Effects: George Pal, Paramount, *When Worlds Collide*
Short Subject—Cartoons: *Two Mouseketeers*
Short Subject—One-Reel: *World of Kids*
Short Subject—Two-Reel: *Nature's Half Acre*
Documentary—Short Subject: *Benjy*
Documentary—Feature: *Kon-Tiki*
Irving G. Thalberg Memorial Award: Arthur Freed
Honorary Awards:
—Gene Kelly, "in appreciation of his versatility as an actor, singer, director and dancer, and specifically for his brilliant achievements in the arts of choreography on film"
—*Rashomon* (Japan), "voted by the [Academy's] Board of Governors as the most outstanding foreign-language film released in the United States during 1951"

Director Vincente Minnelli and actor Kirk Douglas utilized footage from their Oscar–winning collaboration *The Bad and the Beautiful* (1952) to serve as the film-within-a-film when they reunited ten years later for *Two Weeks in Another Town*. Both are movies about moviemaking.

1952

Best Picture: *The Greatest Show on Earth*
Actor: Gary Cooper, *High Noon*
Actress: Shirley Booth, *Come Back, Little Sheba*
Supporting Actor: Anthony Quinn, *Viva Zapata!*
Supporting Actress: Gloria Grahame, *The Bad and the Beautiful*
Director: John Ford, *The Quiet Man*
Writing—Motion Picture Story: Frederic M. Frank, Theodore St. John, Frank Cavett, *The Greatest Show on Earth*
Writing—Screenplay: Charles Schnee, *The Bad and the Beautiful*
Writing—Story and Screenplay: T.E.B. Clarke, *The Lavender Hill Mob*
Cinematography—Black-and-White: Robert Surtees, *The Bad and the Beautiful*
Cinematography—Color: Winton C. Hoch, Archie Stout, *The Quiet Man*
Art Direction—Black-and-White: Cedric Gibbons and Edward Carfagno (art direction), Edwin B. Willis and Keogh Gleason (set decoration), *The Bad and the Beautiful*
Art Direction—Color: Paul Sheriff (art direction), Marcel Vertes (set decoration), *Moulin Rouge*
Sound Recording: London Film Sound Department, *Breaking the Sound Barrier*
Song: Music by Dimitri Tiomkin, lyrics by Ned Washington, "High Noon (Do Not Forsake Me, Oh My Darlin')" for *High Noon*
Scoring of a Dramatic or Comedy Picture: Dimitri Tiomkin, *High Noon*
Scoring of a Musical Picture: Alfred Newman, *With a Song in My Heart*

Film Editing: Elmo Williams, Harry Gerstad, *High Noon*
Costume Design—Black-and-White: Helen Rose, *The Bad and the Beautiful*
Costume Design—Color: Marcel Vertes, *Moulin Rouge*
Special Effects: MGM, *Plymouth Adventures*
Short Subject—Cartoons: *Johann Mouse*
Short Subject—One-Reel: *Light in the Window*
Short Subject—Two-Reel: *Water Birds*
Documentary—Short Subject: *Neighbours*
Documentary—Feature: *The Sea Around Us*
Irving G. Thalberg Memorial Award: Cecil B. DeMille
Honorary Awards:
—George Alfred Mitchell, "for the design and development of the camera which bears his name and for his continued and dominant presence in the field of cinematography"
—Joseph M. Schenk, "for long and distinguished service to the motion picture industry"
—Merian C. Cooper, "for his many innovations and contributions to the art of motion pictures"
—Harold Lloyd, "master comedian and good citizen"
—Bob Hope, "for his contribution to the laughter of the world, his service to the motion-picture industry, and his devotion to the American premise"
—*Forbidden Games* (France), foreign-language film first released in the United States during 1952.

Lee Van Cleef was cast as the villain in numerous westerns following his appearance in High Noon *(1952), which won four Oscars that year.*

1953

Best Picture: *From Here to Eternity*
Actor: William Holden, *Stalag 17*
Actress: Audrey Hepburn, *Roman Holiday*
Supporting Actor: Frank Sinatra, *From Here to Eternity*
Supporting Actress: Donna Reed, *From Here to Eternity*
Director: Fred Zinnemann, *From Here to Eternity*
Writing—Motion Picture Story: Ian McLellan Hunter, *Roman Holiday*
Writing—Screenplay: Daniel Taradash, *From Here to Eternity*
Writing—Story and Screenplay: Charles Brackett, Walter Reisch, Richard Breen, *Titanic*
Cinematography—Black-and-White: Burnett Guffey, *From Here to Eternity*
Cinematography—Color: Loyal Griggs, *Shane*
Art Direction—Black-and-White: Cedric Gibbons and Edward Carfagno (art direction), Edwin B. Willis and Hugh Hunt (set decoration), *Julius Caesar*
Art Direction—Color: Lyle Wheeler, George W. David (art direction), Walter M. Scott, Paul S. Fox (set decoration), *The Robe*
Sound Recording: John P. Livadary, *From Here to Eternity*
Song: Music by Sammy Fain, lyrics by Paul Francis Webster, "Secret Love" for *Calamity Jane*
Scoring of a Dramatic or Comedy Picture: Bronislau Kaper, *Lili*
Scoring of a Musical Picture: Alfred Newman, *Call Me Madam*
Film Editing: William Lyon, *From Here to Eternity*
Costume Design—Black-and-White: Edith Head, *Roman Holiday*
Costume Design—Color: Charles LeMaire, Emile Santiago, *The Robe*
Special Effects: George Pal, Paramount, *War of the Worlds*
Short Subject—Cartoons: *Toot, Whistle, Plunk and Boom*
Short Subject—One-Reel: *The Merry Wives of Windsor Overture*
Short Subject—Two-Reel: *Bear Country*
Documentary—Short Subject: *The Alaskan Eskimo*
Documentary—Feature: *The Living Desert*
Irving G. Thalberg Memorial Award: George Stevens
Honorary Awards:
—Pete Smith, "for his witty and pungent observations on the American scene in his series Pete Smith Specialties"
—20th Century—Fox Film Corporation, "in recognition of their imagination, showmanship and foresight in introducing the revolutionary process known as CinemaScope"
—Joseph I. Breen, "for his conscientious, open-minded and dignified management of the Motion Picture Production Code"
—Bell and Howell Company, "for their pioneering and basic achievements in the advancement of the motion-picture industry"

1954

Best Picture: *On the Waterfront*
Actor: Marlon Brando, *On the Waterfront*
Actress: Grace Kelly, *The Country Girl*
Supporting Actor: Edmond O'Brien, *The Barefoot Contessa*
Supporting Actress: Eva Marie Saint, *On the Waterfront*
Director: Elia Kazan, *On the Waterfront*
Writing—Motion Picture Story: Philip Yordan, *Broken Lance*
Writing—Screenplay: George Seaton, *The Country Girl*
Writing—Story and Screenplay: Budd Schulberg, *On the Waterfront*
Cinematography—Black-and-White: Boris Kaufman, *On the Waterfront*
Cinematography—Color: Milton Krasner, *Three Coins in the Fountain*
Art Direction—Black-and-White: Richard Day, *On the Waterfront*
Art Direction—Color: John Meehan (art direction), Emile Kuri (set decoration), *20,000 Leagues Under the Sea*
Sound Recording: Leslie I. Carey, *The Glenn Miller Story*
Song: Music by Jule Styne, lyrics by Sammy Cahn, "Three Coins in the Fountain" for *Three Coins in the Fountain*
Scoring of a Dramatic or Comedy Picture: Dimitri Tiomkin, *The High and the Mighty*
Scoring of a Musical Picture: Adolph Deutsch, Saul Chaplin, *Seven Brides for Seven Brothers*
Film Editing: Gene Milford, *On the Waterfront*
Costume Design—Black-and-White: Edith Head, *Sabrina*
Costume Design—Color: Sanzo Wada, *Gate of Hell*
Special Effects: Walt Disney Studios, *20,000 Leagues Under the Sea*
Short Subject—Cartoons: *When Magoo Flew*
Short Subject—One-Reel: *The Mechanical Age*
Short Subject—Two-Reel: *A Time Out of War*

The Robe *(1953), starring Richard Burton and Jean Simmons, was the first film shot in CinemaScope.*

"It might be of some interest to know that we rehearsed the entire film *From Here to Eternity* (1953) in detail with props and so on before shooting started. We found that it adds to spontaneity and saves time."

—

From Here to Eternity *director Fred Zinnemann, who received a best director Oscar for his efforts, 1955*

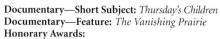

> "The art film must be made, quite frankly, in the hurried, slipshod way that any other low-budget Grade B film is made."
>
> —
>
> *Screenwriter Paddy Chayefsky, who received a best screenplay Oscar for the decidedly low budget, definitely Grade A* Marty *(1955)*

Love Is a Many-Splendored Thing (1955), starring Jennifer Jones and William Holden, received multiple Academy Awards.

Documentary—Short Subject: *Thursday's Children*
Documentary—Feature: *The Vanishing Prairie*
Honorary Awards:
—Bausch & Lomb Optical Company, "for their contributions to the advancement of the motion-picture industry"
—Kemp R. Niver, "for the development of the Renovare Process, which has made possible the restoration of the Library of Congress Paper Film Collection"
—Greta Garbo, "for her unforgettable screen performances"
—Danny Kaye, "for his unique talents, his service to the Academy, the motion picture industry, and the American people"
—Jon Whiteley, "for his outstanding performance in *The Little Kidnappers*"
—Vincent Winter, "for his outstanding performance in *The Little Kidnappers*"
—*Gate of Hell* (Japan), the best foreign-language film first released in the United States during 1954

1955

Best Picture: *Marty*
Actor: Ernest Borgnine, *Marty*
Actress: Anna Magnani, *The Rose Tattoo*
Supporting Actor: Jack Lemmon, *Mister Roberts*
Supporting Actress: Jo Van Fleet, *East of Eden*
Director: Delbert Mann, *Marty*
Writing—Motion Picture Story: Daniel Fuchs, *Love Me or Leave Me*
Writing—Screenplay: Paddy Chayefsky, *Marty*
Writing—Story and Screenplay: William Ludwig, Sonya Levien, *Interrupted Melody*
Cinematography—Black-and-White: James Wong Howe, *The Rose Tattoo*
Cinematography—Color: Robert Burks, *To Catch a Thief*
Art Direction—Black-and-White: Hal Pereira and Tambi Larsen (art direction), Sam Comer and Arthur Krams (set decoration), *The Rose Tattoo*
Art Direction—Color: William Flannery and Jo Mielziner (art direction), Robert Priestley (set decoration), *Picnic*
Sound Recording: Fred Hynes, *Oklahoma!*
Song: Music by Sammy Fain, lyrics by Paul Francis Webster, "Love Is a Many-Splendored Thing" for *Love Is a Many-Splendored Thing*
Scoring of a Dramatic or Comedy Picture: Alfred Newman, *Love Is a Many-Splendored Thing*
Scoring of a Musical Picture: Robert Russell Bennett, Jay Blackton, Adolph Deutsch, *Oklahoma!*
Film Editing: Charles Nelson, William A. Lyon, *Picnic*
Costume Design—Black-and-White: Helen Rose, *I'll Cry Tomorrow*

Costume Design—Color: Charles LeMaire, *Love Is a Many-Splendored Thing*
Special Effects: Paramount, *The Bridges at Toko-Ri*
Short Subject—Cartoons: *Speedy Gonzales*
Short Subject—One-Reel: *Survival City*
Short Subject—Two-Reel: *The Face of Lincoln*
Documentary—Short Subject: *Men Against the Arctic*
Documentary—Feature: *Helen Keller in Her Story*
Honorary Award: *Samurai, The Legend of Musashi* (Japan), a foreign-language film first released in the United States during 1955

1956

Best Picture: *Around the World in 80 Days*
Actor: Yul Brynner, *The King and I*
Actress: Ingrid Bergman, *Anastasia*
Supporting Actor: Anthony Quinn, *Lust for Life*
Supporting Actress: Dorothy Malone, *Written on the Wind*
Director: George Stevens, *Giant*
Foreign-Language Film: *La Strada* (Italy)
Motion Picture Story: Robert Rich (a.k.a. Dalton Trumbo), *The Brave One*
Adapted Screenplay: James Poe, John Farrow, S.J. Perelman, *Around the World in 80 Days*
Original Screenplay: Albert Lamorisse, *The Red Balloon*
Cinematography—Black-and-White: Joseph Ruttenberg, *Somebody Up There Likes Me*
Cinematography—Color: Lionel Linden, *Around the World in 80 Days*
Art Direction—Black-and-White: Cedric Gibbons and Malcolm F. Brown (art direction), Edwin B. Willis and F. Keogh Gleason (set decoration), *Somebody Up There Likes Me*
Art Direction—Color: Lyle R. Wheeler and John DeCuir (art direction), Walter M. Scott and Paul S. Fox (set decoration), *The King and I*
Sound Recording: Carl Faulkner, *The King and I*
Song: Jay Livingston, Ray Evans, "Whatever Will Be, Will Be (Que Sera, Sera)" for *The Man Who Knew Too Much*
Scoring of a Dramatic or Comedy Picture: Victor Young, *Around the World in 80 Days*
Scoring of a Musical Picture: Alfred Newman, Ken Darby, *The King and I*
Film Editing: Gene Ruggiero, Paul Weatherwax, *Around the World in 80 Days*
Costume Design—Black-and-White: Jean Louis, *The Solid Gold Cadillac*
Costume Design—Color: Irene Sharaff, *The King and I*
Special Effects: John Fulton, *The Ten Commandments*
Short Subject—Cartoons: *Mister Magoo's Puddle Jumper*
Short Subject—One-Reel: *Crashing the Water Barrier*
Short Subject—Two-Reel: *The Bespoke Overcoat*
Documentary—Short Subject: *The True Story of the Civil War*

Documentary—Feature: *The Silent World*
1945 Irving G. Thalberg Memorial Award:
Buddy Adler
1946 Jean Hersholt Humanitarian Award:
Y. Frank Freeman
Honorary Award: Eddie Cantor, "for
distinguished service to the film industry"

1957

Best Picture: *The Bridge on the River Kwai*
Actor: Alec Guinness, *The Bridge on the River Kwai*
Actress: Joanne Woodward, *The Three Faces of Eve*
Supporting Actor: Red Buttons, *Sayonara*
Supporting Actress: Miyoshi Umeki, *Sayonara*
Director: David Lean, *The Bridge on the River Kwai*
Foreign Language Film: *The Nights of Cabiria* (Italy)
Adapted Screenplay: Pierre Boulle, *The Bridge on the River Kwai*
Original Screenplay: George Wells, *Designing Woman*
Cinematography: Jack Hildyard, *The Bridge on the River Kwai*
Art Direction: Ted Hayworth (art direction), Robert Priestley (set decoration), *Sayonara*
Sound: George Groves, *Sayonara*
Song: Music by James Van Heusen, lyrics by Sammy Cahn, "All the Way" for *The Joker Is Wild*
Score: Malcolm Arnold, *The Bridge on the River Kwai*
Film Editing: Peter Taylor, *The Bridge on the River Kwai*
Costume Design: Orry-Kelly, *Les Girls*
Special Effects: Walter Rossi, *The Enemy Below*

Short Subject—Cartoons: *Birds Anonymous*
Short Subject—Live Action: *The Wetback Hound*
Documentary—Feature: *Albert Schweitzer*
1947 Jean Hersholt Humanitarian Award: Samuel Goldwyn
Honorary Awards:
—Charles Brackett, "for outstanding service to the Academy"
—B.B. Kahane, "for distinguished service to the motion picture industry"
—Gilbert M. ("Bronco Billy") Anderson, "motion picture pioneer, for his contributions to the development of motion pictures as entertainment"
—The Society of Motion Picture and Television Engineers, "for their contributions to the advancement of the motion picture industry"

1958

Best Picture: *Gigi*
Actor: David Niven, *Separate Tables*
Actress: Susan Hayward, *I Want to Live!*
Supporting Actor: Burl Ives, *The Big Country*
Supporting Actress: Wendy Hiller, *Separate Tables*
Director: Vincente Minnelli, *Gigi*
Foreign Language Film: *My Uncle* (France)
Adapted Screenplay: Alan Jay Lerner, *Gigi*
Original Screenplay: Nathan E. Douglas, Harold Jacob Smith, *The Defiant Ones*
Cinematography—Black-and-White: Sam Leavitt, *The Defiant Ones*
Cinematography—Color: Joseph Ruttenberg, *Gigi*
Art Direction: William A. Horning and Preston Ames (art direction), Henry Grace and Keogh Gleason (set decoration), *Gigi*
Sound: Fred Hynes, *South Pacific*
Song: Music by Frederick Loewe, lyrics by Alan Jay Lerner, "Gigi" for *Gigi*
Scoring of a Dramatic or Comedy Picture: Dimitri Tiomkin, *The Old Man and the Sea*
Scoring of a Musical Picture: André Previn, *Gigi*
Film Editing: Adrienne Fazan, *Gigi*
Costume Design: Cecil Beaton, *Gigi*
Special Effects: Tom Howard, *tom thumb*
Short Subject—Cartoons: *Knighty Knight Bugs*
Short Subject—Live Action: *Grand Canyon*
Documentary—Short Subject: *AMA Girls*
Documentary—Feature: *White Wilderness*
1948 Irving G. Thalberg Memorial Award: Jack L. Warner
Honorary Award: Maurice Chevalier, "for his contributions to the world of entertainment for more than half a century"

AT LEFT: *Robert Loggia, pictured here with Paul Newman, made his screen debut in* Somebody Up There Likes Me *(1956).*

French writer Pierre Boulle, who won the best adapted screenplay Oscar for the film adaptation of his novel, *The Bridge on the River Kwai* (1957), never wrote a word of English in his life, and in fact could barely speak it. Blacklisted screenwriters Carl Foreman and Michael Wilson were the real writers behind *Kwai's* script, a fact that was finally revealed in 1976, well after both writers had returned from exile to Hollywood. It was not until 1985, in a private ceremony, that the widows of Foreman and Wilson received the Oscars that their now late husbands had so long been due.

OVERLEAF:

Gigi, featuring Louis Jordan and Leslie Caron, received nine Academy Awards—including best picture, best director, song, and costume design—in 1958.

Rock Hudson tried to charm Doris Day in Pillow Talk, *which won the 1959 Academy Award for original screenplay.*

1959

Best Picture: *Ben-Hur*
Actor: Charlton Heston, *Ben-Hur*
Actress: Simone Signoret, *Room at the Top*
Supporting Actor: Hugh Griffith, *Ben-Hur*
Supporting Actress: Shelley Winters, *The Diary of Anne Frank*
Director: William Wyler, *Ben-Hur*
Foreign-Language Film: *Black Orpheus*
Adapted Screenplay: Neil Paterson, *Room at the Top*
Original Screenplay: Russell Rouse, Clarence Greene, Stanley Shapiro, Maurice Richlin, *Pillow Talk*
Cinematography—Black-and-White: William C. Mellor, *The Diary of Anne Frank*
Cinematography—Color: Robert L. Surtees, *Ben-Hur*
Art Direction—Black-and-White: Lyle R. Wheeler and George W. Davis (art direction), Walter M. Scott and Stuart A. Reiss (set decoration), *The Diary of Anne Frank*
Art Direction—Color: William A. Horning and Edward Carfagno (art direction), Hugh Hunt (set decoration), *Ben-Hur*
Sound: Franklin E. Milton, *Ben-Hur*
Song: Music by James Van Heusen, lyrics by Sammy Cahn, "High Hopes" for *A Hole in the Head*
Scoring of a Dramatic or Comedy Picture: Miklos Rozsa, *Ben-Hur*
Scoring of a Musical Picture: André Previn, Ken Darby, *Porgy and Bess*
Film Editing: Ralph E. Winters, John D. Dunning, *Ben-Hur*
Costume Design—Black-and-White: Orry-Kelly, *Some Like It Hot*
Costume Design—Color: Elizabeth Haffenden, *Ben-Hur*
Special Effects: A. Arnold Gillespie and Robert MacDonald (visual), Milo Lory (audible), *Ben-Hur*
Short Subject—Cartoons: *Moonbird*
Short Subject—Live Action: *The Golden Fish*
Documentary—Short Subject: *Glass*
Documentary—Feature: *Serengeti Shall Not Die*
Jean Hersholt Humanitarian Award: Bob Hope
Honorary Awards:
—Lee De Forest, "for his pioneering inventions which brought sound to the motion picture"
—Buster Keaton, "for his unique talents which brought immortal comedies to the screen"

Second unit director Yakima Canutt was supervising the filming of *Ben-Hur*'s famed chariot race when his eldest son Joe—doubling for star Charlton Heston—was thrown from his vehicle after it accidentally hit some wreckage on the racecourse. The resulting shot proved so effective that it was left in the finished film, and the screenplay was changed in order to explain it.

1960

Best Picture: *The Apartment*
Actor: Burt Lancaster, *Elmer Gantry*
Actress: Elizabeth Taylor, *Butterfield 8*
Supporting Actor: Peter Ustinov, *Spartacus*
Supporting Actress: Shirley Jones, *Elmer Gantry*
Director: Billy Wilder, *The Apartment*
Foreign-Language Film: *The Virgin Spring* (Sweden)
Adapted Screenplay: Richard Brooks, *Elmer Gantry*
Original Screenplay: Billy Wilder, I.A.L. Diamond, *The Apartment*
Cinematography—Black-and-White: Freddie Francis, *Sons and Lovers*
Cinematography—Color: Russell Metty, *Spartacus*
Art Direction—Black-and-White: Alexander Trauner (art direction), Edward G. Boyle (set decoration), *The Apartment*
Art Direction—Color: Alexander Golitzen and Eric Orbom (art direction), Russell A. Gausman and Julia Heron (set decoration), *Spartacus*
Sound: Gordon E. Sawyer, Fred Hynes, *The Alamo*
Song: Manos Hadjidakis, "Never on Sunday" for *Never on Sunday*
Scoring of a Dramatic or Comedy Picture: Ernest Gold, *Exodus*
Scoring of a Musical Picture: Morris Stoloff, Harry Sukman, *Song Without End*
Film Editing: Daniel Mandell, *The Apartment*
Costume Design—Black-and-White: Edith Head, Edward Stevenson, *The Facts of Life*
Costume Design—Color: Valles, Bill Thomas, *Spartacus*
Special Effects: Gene Warren, Tim Baar, *The Time Machine*
Short Subject—Cartoons: *Munro*
Short Subject—Live Action: *Day of the Painter*
Documentary—Short Subject: *Giuseppina*
Documentary—Feature: *The Horse with the Flying Tail*

Jean Hersholt Humanitarian Award: Sol Lesser
Honorary Awards:
—Gary Cooper, "for his many memorable screen performances and the international recognition he, as an individual, has gained for the motion-picture industry"
—Stan Laurel, "for his creative pioneering in the field of cinema comedy"
—Hayley Mills, for *Pollyanna,* "the most out-standing juvenile performance during 1960"

Honorary Awards:
—William Hendricks, "for his outstanding patriotic service in the conception, writing and production of the Marine Corps film *A Force in Readiness,* which has brought honor to the Academy and the motion-picture industry"
—Fred L. Metzler, "for his dedication and outstanding service to the Academy of Motion Picture Arts and Sciences"
—Jerome Robbins, "for his brilliant achievements in the art of choreography on film"

1961

Best Picture: *West Side Story*
Actor: Maximilian Schell, *Judgment at Nuremberg*
Actress: Sophia Loren, *Two Women*
Supporting Actor: George Chakiris, *West Side Story*
Supporting Actress: Rita Moreno, *West Side Story*
Director: Robert Wise, Jerome Robbins, *West Side Story*
Foreign-Language Film: *Through a Glass Darkly* (Sweden)
Adapted Screenplay: Abby Mann, *Judgment at Nuremberg*
Original Screenplay: William Inge, *Splendor in the Grass*
Cinematography—Black-and-White: Eugen Shuftan, *The Hustler*
Cinematography—Color: Daniel L. Fapp, *West Side Story*
Art Direction—Black-and-White: Harry Horner (art direction), Gene Callahan (set decoration), *The Hustler*
Art Direction—Color: Boris Leven (art direction), Victor A. Gangelin (set decoration), *West Side Story*
Sound: Fred Hynes, Gordon E. Sawyer, *West Side Story*
Song: Music by Henry Mancini, lyrics by Johnny Mercer, "Moon River" for *Breakfast at Tiffany's*
Scoring of a Dramatic or Comedy Picture: Henry Mancini, *Breakfast at Tiffany's*
Scoring of a Musical Picture: Saul Chaplin, Johnny Green, Sid Ramin, Irwin Kostal, *West Side Story*
Film Editing: Thomas Stanford, *West Side Story*
Costume Design—Black-and-White: Piero Gherardi, *La Dolce Vita*
Costume Design—Color: Irene Sharaff, *West Side Story*
Special Effects: Bill Warrington (visual), Vivian C. Greenham (audible), *The Guns of Navarone*
Short Subject—Cartoons: *Ersatz (The Substitute)*
Short Subject—Live Action: *Seawards the Great Ships*
Documentary—Short Subject: *Project Hope*
Documentary—Feature: *Le Ciel et la Boue (Sky Above and Mud Beneath)* (France)
Irving G. Thalberg Memorial Award: Stanley Kramer
Jean Hersholt Humanitarian Award: George Seaton

Jerome Robbins choreographed the groundbreaking musical West Side Story *(1961).*

1962

Best Picture: *Lawrence of Arabia*
Actor: Gregory Peck, *To Kill a Mockingbird*
Actress: Anne Bancroft, *The Miracle Worker*
Supporting Actor: Ed Begley, *Sweet Bird of Youth*
Supporting Actress: Patty Duke, *The Miracle Worker*
Director: David Lean, *Lawrence of Arabia*
Foreign-Language Film: *Sundays and Cybèle* (France)
Adapted Screenplay: Horton Foote, *To Kill a Mockingbird*
Original Screenplay: Ennio de Concini, Alfredo Giannetti, Pietro Germi, *Divorce—Italian Style*
Cinematography—Black-and-White: Jean Bourgoin, Walter Wottitz, *The Longest Day*
Cinematography—Color: Fred A. Young, *Lawrence of Arabia*
Art Direction—Black-and-White: Alexander Golitzen and Henry Bumstead (art direction), Oliver Emert (set decoration), *To Kill a Mockingbird*
Art Direction—Color: John Box, John Stoll (art direction), Dario Simoni (set decoration), *Lawrence of Arabia*

Nominated for best actor seven times between 1962 and 1982, Peter O'Toole holds the record for the most nominated actor never to win an Oscar.

Sound: John Cox, *Lawrence of Arabia*
Song: Music by Henry Mancini, lyrics by Johnny Mercer, "Days of Wine and Roses" for *Days of Wine and Roses*
Music Score—Substantially Original: Maurice Jarre, *Lawrence of Arabia*
Music Score—Adaptation or Treatment: Ray Heindorf, *The Music Man*
Film Editing: Anne Coates, *Lawrence of Arabia*
Costume Design—Black-and-White: Norma Koch, *Whatever Happened to Baby Jane?*
Costume Design—Color: Mary Wills, *The Wonderful World of the Brothers Grimm*
Special Effects: Robert MacDonald (visual), Jacques Maumont (audible), *The Longest Day*
Short Subject—Cartoons: *The Hole*
Short Subject—Live Action: *Heureux Anniversaire* (*Happy Anniversary*), France
Documentary—Short Subject: *Dylan Thomas*
Documentary—Feature: *Black Fox*
Jean Hersholt Humanitarian Award: Steve Broidy

1963

Best Picture: *Tom Jones*
Actor: Sidney Poitier, *Lilies of the Field*
Actress: Patricia Neal, *Hud*
Supporting Actor: Melvyn Douglas, *Tom Jones*
Supporting Actress: Margaret Rutherford, *The V.I.P.s*
Director: Tony Richardson, *Tom Jones*
Foreign-Language Film: *8½* (Italy)
Adapted Screenplay: John Osborne, *Tom Jones*
Original Screenplay: James R. Webb, *How the West Was Won*
Cinematography—Black-and-White: James Wong Howe, *Hud*
Cinematography—Color: Leon Shamroy, *Cleopatra*
Art Direction—Black-and-White: Gene Callahan, *America America*
Art Direction—Color: John DeCuir, Jack Martin Smith, Hilyard Brown, Herman Blumenthal,

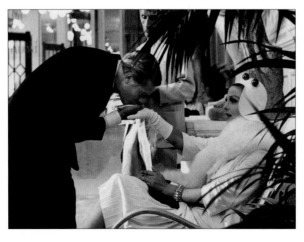

Marcello Mastroianni starred in Federico Fellini's acclaimed film 8½ (1963).

Elven Webb, Maurice Pelling, and Boris Juraga (art direction), Walter M. Scott, Paul S. Fox, and Ray Moyer (set decoration), *Cleopatra*
Sound: Franklin E. Milton, *How the West Was Won*
Song: Music by James Van Heusen, lyrics by Sammy Cahn, "Call Me Irresponsible" for *Papa's Delicate Condition*
Music Score—Substantially Original: John Addison, *Tom Jones*
Scoring of Music—Adaptation or Treatment: André Previn, *Irma La Douce*
Film Editing: Harold F. Kress, *How the West Was Won*
Costume Design—Black-and-White: Piero Gherardi, *8½*
Costume Design—Color: Irene Sharaff, Vittorio Nino Novarese, Renie, *Cleopatra*
Special Visual Effects: Emil Koss, Jr., *Cleopatra*
Sound Effects: Walter G. Elliott, *It's a Mad Mad Mad Mad World*
Short Subject—Cartoons: *The Critic*
Short Subject—Live Action: *An Occurrence at Owl Creek Bridge*
Documentary—Short Subject: *Chagall*
Documentary—Feature: *Robert Frost: A Lover's Quarrel With the World*
Irving G. Thalberg Memorial Award: Sam Spiegel

1964

Best Picture: *My Fair Lady*
Actor: Rex Harrison, *My Fair Lady*
Actress: Julie Andrews, *Mary Poppins*
Supporting Actor: Peter Ustinov, *Topkapi*
Supporting Actress: Lila Kedrova, *Zorba the Greek*
Director: George Cukor, *My Fair Lady*
Foreign-Language Film: *Yesterday, Today, and Tomorrow* (Italy)
Adapted Screenplay: Edward Anhalt, *Becket*
Original Screenplay: S.H. Barnett, Peter Stone, Frank Tarloff, *Father Goose*
Cinematography—Black-and-White: Walter Lassally, *Zorba the Greek*
Cinematography—Color: Harry Stradling, *My Fair Lady*
Art Direction—Black-and-White: Vassilis Fotopoulos, *Zorba the Greek*
Art Direction—Color: Gene Allen and Cecil Beaton (art direction), George James Hopkins (set decoration), *My Fair Lady*
Sound: George R. Groves, *My Fair Lady*
Song: Richard M. Sherman, Robert B. Sherman, "Chim Chim Cher-ee" for *Mary Poppins*
Music Score—Substantially Original: Richard M. Sherman, Robert B. Sherman, *Mary Poppins*
Scoring of Music—Adaptation or Treatment: André Previn, *My Fair Lady*
Film Editing: Cotton Warburton, *Mary Poppins*
Costume Design—Black-and-White: Dorothy Jeakins, *The Night of the Iguana*
Costume Design—Color: Cecil Beaton, *My Fair Lady*

Special Visual Effects: Peter Ellenshaw, Hamilton Luske, Eustace Lycett, *Mary Poppins*
Sound Effects: Norman Wanstall, *Goldfinger*
Short Subject—Cartoons: *The Pink Phink*
Short Subject—Live Action: *Casals Conducts: 1964*
Documentary—Short Subject: *Nine from Little Rock*
Documentary—Feature: *Jacques-Yves Cousteau's World Without Sun*
Honorary Award: William Tuttle, "for his outstanding makeup achievement for *7 Faces of Dr. Lao*"

Julie Andrews portrayed the governess Maria in The Sound of Music *(1965).*

1965

Best Picture: *The Sound of Music*
Actor: Lee Marvin, *Cat Ballou*
Actress: Julie Christie, *Darling*
Supporting Actor: Martin Balsam, *A Thousand Clowns*
Supporting Actress: Shelley Winters, *A Patch of Blue*
Director: Robert Wise, *The Sound of Music*
Foreign-Language Film: *The Shop on Main Street* (Czechoslovakia)
Adapted Screenplay: Robert Bolt, *Doctor Zhivago*
Original Screenplay: Frederic Raphael, *Darling*
Cinematography—Black-and-White: Ernest Laszlo, *Ship of Fools*
Cinematography—Color: Freddie Young, *Doctor Zhivago*
Art Direction—Black-and-White: Robert Clatworthy (art direction), Joseph Kish (set decoration), *Ship of Fools*
Art Direction—Color: John Box and Terry Marsh (art direction), Dario Simoni (set decoration), *Doctor Zhivago*
Sound: James P. Corcoran, Fred Hynes, *The Sound of Music*
Song: Music by Johnny Mandel, lyrics by Paul Francis Webster, "The Shadow of Your Smile" for *The Sandpiper*
Music Score—Substantially Original: Maurice Jarre, *Doctor Zhivago*
Scoring of Music—Adaptation or Treatment: Irwin Kostal, *The Sound of Music*
Film Editing: William Reynolds, *The Sound of Music*
Costume Design—Black-and-White: Julie Harris, *Darling*
Costume Design—Color: Phyllis Dalton, *Doctor Zhivago*
Special Visual Effects: John Stears, *Thunderball*
Sound Effects: Tregoweth Brown, *The Great Race*
Short Subject—Cartoons: *The Dot and the Line*
Short Subject—Live Action: *The Chicken*
Documentary—Short Subject: *To Be Alive!*
Documentary—Feature: *The Eleanor Roosevelt Story*
Irving G. Thalberg Memorial Award: William Wyler
Jean Hersholt Humanitarian Award: Edmond L. DePatie

Honorary Award:
—"Bob Hope, for unique and distinguished service to our industry and the Academy"

1966

Best Picture: *A Man for All Seasons*
Actor: Paul Scofield, *A Man for All Seasons*
Actress: Elizabeth Taylor, *Who's Afraid of Virginia Woolf?*
Supporting Actor: Walter Matthau, *The Fortune Cookie*
Supporting Actress: Sandy Dennis, *Who's Afraid of Virginia Woolf?*
Director: Fred Zinnemann, *A Man for All Seasons*
Foreign-Language Film: *A Man and a Woman* (France)
Adapted Screenplay: Robert Bolt, *A Man for All Seasons*
Original Screenplay: Claude Lelouch, Pierre Uytterhoeven, *A Man and a Woman*
Cinematography—Black-and-White: Haskell Wexler, *Who's Afraid of Virginia Woolf?*
Cinematography—Color: Ted Moore, *A Man for All Seasons*
Art Direction—Black-and-White: Richard Sylbert (art direction), George James Hopkins (set decoration), *Who's Afraid of Virginia Woolf?*
Art Direction—Color: Jack Martin Smith and Dale Hennesy (art direction), Walter M. Scott and Stuart A. Reiss (set decoration), *Fantastic Voyage*
Sound: Franklin E. Milton, *Grand Prix*
Song: Music by Burt Bacharach, lyrics by Hal David, "Alfie" for *Alfie*
Original Music Score: John Barry, *Born Free*
Scoring of Music—Adaptation or Treatment: Ken Thorne, *A Funny Thing Happened on the Way to the Forum*
Film Editing: Frederic Steinkamp, Henry Berman, Stewart Linder, Frank Santillo, *Grand Prix*

"If you took the novel *Doctor Zhivago* as it stands and treated it as a shooting script incident by incident, the resulting film would run at least 60 hours. Therefore, in the film you can have only a twentieth of the book—therefore, you have to turn it into something not only shorter, but quite different."

—

Screenwriter Robert Bolt, who managed to turn his adapted screenplay for Doctor Zhivago (1965) *into Oscar gold*

Costume Design—Black-and-White:
Irene Sharaff, *Who's Afraid of Virginia Woolf?*
Costume Design—Color: Elizabeth Haffenden,
Joan Bridge, *A Man for All Seasons*
Special Visual Effects: Art Cruickshank,
Fantastic Voyage
Sound Effects: Gordon Daniel, *Grand Prix*
Short Subject—Cartoons: *Herb Alpert and the
Tijuana Brass Double Feature*
Short Subject—Live Action: *Wild Wings*
Documentary—Short Subject: *A Year Toward
Tomorrow*
Documentary—Feature: *The War Game*
Irving G. Thalberg Memorial Award:
Robert Wise
Jean Hersholt Humanitarian Award:
George Bagnall
Honorary Awards:
—Y. Frank Freeman, "for unusual and
outstanding service to the Academy during his
thirty years in Hollywood"
—Yakima Canutt, "for achievements as a stunt
man and for developing safety devices to
protect stunt men everywhere"

*Fantastic Voyage
(1966), a journey
inside the human
body, featured award-
winning special effects.*

1967

Best Picture: *In the Heat of the Night*
Actor: Rod Steiger, *In the Heat of the Night*
Actress: Katharine Hepburn, *Guess Who's
Coming to Dinner*
Supporting Actor: George Kennedy,
Cool Hand Luke
Supporting Actress: Estelle Parsons,
Bonnie and Clyde
Director: Mike Nichols, *The Graduate*
Foreign-Language Film: *Closely Watched Trains*
(Czechoslovakia)
Adapted Screenplay: Joseph Strick, Fred Haines,
In the Heat of the Night
Original Screenplay: William Rose, *Guess Who's
Coming to Dinner*
Cinematography: Burnett Guffey, *Bonnie
and Clyde*

Art Direction: John Truscott and Edward Carrere
(art direction), John W. Brown (set decoration),
Camelot
Sound: Samuel Goldwyn Studio Sound
Department, *In the Heat of the Night*
Song: Leslie Bricusse, "Talk to the Animals" for
Doctor Dolittle
Original Music Score: Elmer Bernstein,
Thoroughly Modern Millie
Scoring of Music—Adaptation or Treatment:
Alfred Newman, Ken Darby, *Camelot*
Film Editing: Hal Ashby, *In the Heat of the Night*
Costume Design: John Truscott, *Camelot*
Special Visual Effects: L.B. Abbott, *Doctor Dolittle*
Sound Effects: John Poyner, *The Dirty Dozen*
Short Subject—Cartoons: *The Box*
Short Subject—Live Action: *A Place to Stand*
Documentary—Short Subject: *The Redwoods*
Documentary—Feature: *The Anderson Platoon*
Irving G. Thalberg Memorial Award:
Alfred Hitchcock
Jean Hersholt Humanitarian Award:
Gregory Peck
Honorary Award: Arthur Freed, "for
distinguished service to the Academy and the
production of six top-rated awards telecasts"

1968

Best Picture: *Oliver!*
Actor: Cliff Robertson, *Charly*
Actress: Katharine Hepburn, *The Lion in Winter,*
Barbra Streisand, *Funny Girl*
Supporting Actor: Jack Albertson,
The Subject Was Roses
Supporting Actress: Ruth Gordon,
Rosemary's Baby
Director: Carol Reed, *Oliver!*
Foreign-Language Film: *War and Peace* (Russia)
Adapted Screenplay: James Goldman,
The Lion in Winter
Original Screenplay: Mel Brooks, *The Producers*
Cinematography: Pasqualino De Santis,
Romeo and Juliet
Art Direction: John Box and Terrence Marsh
(art direction), Vernon Dixon and Ken
Muggleston (set decoration), *Oliver!*
Sound: Shepperton Studio Sound Deptartment,
Oliver!
Song: Music by Michel Legrand, lyrics by Alan
and Marilyn Bergman, "The Windmills of Your
Mind" for *The Thomas Crown Affair*
Original Score for a Motion Picture:
John Barry, *The Lion in Winter*
Scoring of a Musical Picture: John Green, *Oliver!*
Film Editing: Frank P. Keller, *Bullitt*
Costume Design: Danilo Donati, *Romeo and Juliet*
Special Visual Effects: Stanley Kubrick,
2001: A Space Odyssey
Short Subject—Cartoons: *Winnie the Pooh and
the Blustery Day*
Short Subject—Live Action: *Robert Kennedy
Remembered*

Mark Lester played the title role in Oliver! *(1968), a musical adaptation of the Charles Dickens tale.*

Documentary—Short Subject: *Why Man Creates*
Documentary—Feature: *Journey into Self*
Jean Hersholt Humanitarian Award:
Martha Raye
Honorary Awards:
—John Chambers, "for his outstanding makeup achievement for *Planet of the Apes*"
—Onna White, "for her outstanding choreography achievement for *Oliver!*"

1969

Best Picture: *Midnight Cowboy*
Actor: John Wayne, *True Grit*
Actress: Maggie Smith, *The Prime of Miss Jean Brodie*
Supporting Actor: Gig Young, *They Shoot Horses, Don't They?*
Supporting Actress: Goldie Hawn, *Cactus Flower*
Director: John Schlesinger, *Midnight Cowboy*
Foreign-Language Film: *Z* (France/Algeria)
Adapted Screenplay: Waldo Salt, *Midnight Cowboy*
Original Screenplay: William Goldman, *Butch Cassidy and the Sundance Kid*
Cinematography: Conrad Hall, *Butch Cassidy and the Sundance Kid*
Art Direction: John DeCuir, Jack Martin Smith, and Herman Blumenthal (art direction), Walter M. Scott, George Hopkins, and Raphael Bretton (set direction), *Hello, Dolly!*
Sound: Jack Solomon, Murray Spivack, *Hello, Dolly!*
Song: Music by Burt Bacharach, lyrics by Hal David, "Raindrops Keep Fallin' on My Head" for *Butch Cassidy and the Sundance Kid*
Original Score for a Motion Picture: Burt Bacharach, *Butch Cassidy and the Sundance Kid*
Score of a Musical Picture: Lennie Hayton, Lionel Newman, *Hello, Dolly!*
Film Editing: Françoise Bonnot, *Z*

Costume Design: Margaret Furse, *Anne of the Thousand Days*
Special Visual Effects: Robbie Robertson, *Marooned*
Short Subject—Cartoons: *It's Tough to Be a Bird*
Short Subject—Live Action: *The Magic Machines*
Documentary—Short Subject: *Czechoslovakia 1968*
Documentary—Feature: *Arthur Rubinstein*
Jean Hersholt Humanitarian Award: George Jessel
Honorary Award: Cary Grant, "for his unique mastery of the art of screen acting with the respect and affection of his colleagues"

1970

Best Picture: *Patton*
Actor: George C. Scott, *Patton*
Actress: Glenda Jackson, *Women in Love*
Supporting Actor: John Mills, *Ryan's Daughter*
Supporting Actress: Helen Hayes, *Airport*
Director: Franklin J. Schaffner, *Patton*
Foreign-Language Film: *Investigation of a Citizen Above Suspicion* (Italy)
Adapted Screenplay: Ring Lardner, Jr., *M*A*S*H*
Original Screenplay: Francis Ford Coppola, Edmund H. North, *Patton*
Cinematography: Freddie Young, *Ryan's Daughter*
Art Direction: Urie McCleary, Gil Parrondo (art direction), Antonio Mateos, Pierre-Louis Thevenet (set decoration), *Patton*
Sound: Douglas Williams, Don Bassman, *Patton*
Song: Music by Fred Karlin, lyrics by Robb Royer and James Griffin (a.k.a. Robb Wilson and Arthur James), "For All We Know" for *Lovers and Other Strangers*
Original Score: Francis Lai, *Love Story*
Original Song Score: The Beatles, *Let It Be*
Film Editing: Hugh S. Fowler, *Patton*
Costume Design: Nino Novarese, *Cromwell*
Special Visual Effects: A.D. Flowers, L.B. Abbott, *Tora! Tora! Tora!*
Short Subject—Cartoons: *Is It Always Right to Be Right?*
Short Subject—Live Action: *The Resurrection of Bronco Billy*
Documentary—Short Subject: *Interviews with My Lai Veterans*
Documentary—Feature: *Woodstock*
Irving G. Thalberg Memorial Award: Ingmar Bergman
Jean Hersholt Humanitarian Award: Frank Sinatra
Honorary Awards:
—Lillian Gish, "for superlative artistry and for distinguished contribution to the progress of motion pictures"
—Orson Welles, "for superlative artistry and versatility in the creation of motion pictures"

"Although I have received no official notification, elements of the international press have informed me that I have recently been nominated for an Academy Award. Once again I respectfully request that you withdraw my name from the list of nominees."
—
The award-shy George C. Scott, in a cable sent to the Motion Picture Academy from Spain, after learning that he had just received his third Oscar nomination, this time for Patton *(1970). Although Scott won the award, he refused to attend the ceremony, and his statuette was later returned to the Academy, where it rests in a vault to this day.*

OVERLEAF:

Ryan's Daughter (1970), starring Sarah Miles and Robert Mitchum, was recognized by the Academy for its cinematography.

The hip action film Shaft *(1971) featured Richard Roundtree in the title role. Isaac Hayes's memorable theme won the Oscar for best song.*

For the elevated subway train crash that climaxes the famous chase scene in *The French Connection* (1971), the producers didn't have the money to destroy a real train, so director William Friedkin mounted a camera inside the subway car and shot the scene in reverse, then under cranked the film to give the impression that the train was moving at high speed. In the finished picture, Friedkin cuts away just before the moment of impact, using crashing sound effects to effectively complete the illusion.

1971

Best Picture: *The French Connection*
Actor: Gene Hackman, *The French Connection*
Actress: Jane Fonda, *Klute*
Supporting Actor: Ben Johnson, *The Last Picture Show*
Supporting Actress: Cloris Leachman, *The Last Picture Show*
Director: William Friedkin, *The French Connection*
Foreign-Language Film: *Il Giardino de Finzi-Contini/The Garden of the Finzi-Continis* (Italy)
Adapted Screenplay: Ernest Tidyman, *The French Connection*
Original Screenplay: Paddy Chayefsky, *The Hospital*
Cinematography: Oswald Morris, *Fiddler on the Roof*
Art Direction: John Box, Ernest Archer, Jack Maxsted, and Gil Parrondo (art direction), Vernon Dixon (set decoration), *Nicholas and Alexandra*
Sound: Gordon K. McCallum, David Hildyard, *Fiddler on the Roof*
Song: Isaac Hayes, "Theme from Shaft" for *Shaft*
Original Dramatic Score: Michel Legrand, *Summer of '42*
Scoring–Adaptation and Original Song Score: John Williams, *Fiddler on the Roof*
Film Editing: Jerry Greenberg, *The French Connection*
Costume Design: Yvonne Blake, Antonio Castillo, *Nicholas and Alexandra*
Special Visual Effects: Alan Maley, Eustace Lycett, Danny Lee, *Bedknobs and Broomsticks*
Short Subject—Animated: *The Crunch Bird*
Short Subject—Live Action: *Sentinels of Silence*
Documentary—Short Subject: *Sentinels of Silence*
Documentary—Feature: *The Hellstrom Chronicle*
Honorary Award: Charlie Chaplin, "for the incalculable effect he has had in making motion pictures the art form of this century"

1972

Best Picture: *The Godfather*
Actor: Marlon Brando, *The Godfather*
Actress: Liza Minnelli, *Cabaret*
Supporting Actor: Joel Grey, *Cabaret*
Supporting Actress: Eileen Heckart, *Butterflies Are Free*
Director: Bob Fosse, *Cabaret*
Foreign-Language Film: *The Discreet Charm of the Bourgeoisie* (France)
Adapted Screenplay: Mario Puzo, Francis Ford Coppola, *The Godfather*
Original Screenplay: Jeremy Larner, *The Candidate*
Cinematography: Geoffrey Unsworth, *Cabaret*
Art Direction: Rolf Zehetbauer and Jürgen Kiebach (art direction), Herbert Strabel (set decoration), *Cabaret*
Sound: Robert Knudson, David Hildyard, *Cabaret*
Song: Al Kasha, Joel Hirschhorn, "The Morning After" for *The Poseidon Adventure*
Original Dramatic Score: Charles Chaplin, Raymond Rasch, Larry Russell, *Limelight*
Scoring—Adaptation and Original Song Score: Ralph Burns, *Cabaret*
Film Editing: David Bretherton, *Cabaret*
Costume Design: Anthony Powell, *Travels with My Aunt*
Short Subject—Animated: *A Christmas Carol*
Short Subject—Live Action: *Norman Rockwell's World… An American Dream*
Documentary—Short Subject: *This Tiny World*
Documentary—Feature: *Marjoe*
Jean Hersholt Humanitarian Award: Rosalind Russell
Honorary Awards:
—Charles S. Boren, "leader for 38 years of the industry's enlightened labor relations and architect of its policy of nondiscrimination. With the respect and affection of all who work in films"
—Edward G. Robinson, "who achieved greatness as a player, a patron of the arts and a dedicated citizen…in sum, a Renaissance man. From his friends in the industry he loves"
Special Achievement Award—For Visual Effects: L.B. Abbott and A.D. Flowers, for *The Poseidon Adventure*

1973

Best Picture: *The Sting*
Actor: Jack Lemmon, *Save the Tiger*
Actress: Glenda Jackson, *A Touch of Class*
Supporting Actor: John Houseman, *The Paper Chase*
Supporting Actress: Tatum O'Neal, *Paper Moon*
Director: George Roy Hill, *The Sting*
Foreign-Language Film: *La Nuit américaine/Day for Night* (France)
Adapted Screenplay: William Peter Blatty, *The Exorcist*

Original Screenplay: David S. Ward, *The Sting*
Cinematography: Sven Nykvist,
  Cries and Whispers
Art Direction/Set Decoration: Henry Bumstead
  (art direction), James Payne (set decoration),
  The Sting
Sound: Robert Knudson, Chris Newman,
  The Exorcist
Song: Music by Marvin Hamlisch, lyrics by
  Alan and Marilyn Bergman, "The Way We
  Were" for *The Way We Were*
Original Dramatic Score: Marvin Hamlisch,
  The Way We Were
**Scoring—Original Song Score and/or
  Adaptation:** Marvin Hamlisch, *The Sting*
Film Editing: William Reynolds, *The Sting*
Costume Design: Edith Head, *The Sting*
Short Subject—Animated: *Frank Film*
Short Subject—Live Action: *The Bolero*
Documentary—Short Subject: *Princeton: A Search
  for Answers*
Documentary—Feature: *The Great American
  Cowboy*
Irving G. Thalberg Memorial Award:
  Lawrence Weingarten
Jean Hersholt Humanitarian Award:
  Lew Wasserman
Honorary Awards:
—Henri Langlois, "for his devotion to the art of
  film, his massive contributions in preserving its
  past and his unswerving faith in its future"
—Groucho Marx, "in recognition of his brilliant
  creativity and for the unequaled achievements
  of the Marx Brothers in the art of motion-
  picture comedy"

1974

Best Picture: *The Godfather, Part II*
Actor: Art Carney, *Harry and Tonto*
Actress: Ellen Burstyn, *Alice Doesn't Live Here
  Anymore*
Supporting Actor: Robert De Niro,
  The Godfather, Part II
Supporting Actress: Ingrid Bergman,
  Murder on the Orient Express
Director: Francis Ford Coppola,
  The Godfather, Part II
Foreign-Language Film: *Amarcord* (Italy)
Original Screenplay: Robert Towne, *Chinatown*
Adapted Screenplay: Francis Ford Coppola,
  Mario Puzo, *The Godfather, Part II*
Cinematography: Fred Koenekamp, Joseph
  Biroc, *The Towering Inferno*
Art Direction/Set Decoration: Dean Tavoularis,
  Angelo Graham (art direction), George R.
  Nelson (set decoration), *The Godfather, Part II*
Sound: Ronald Pierce, Melvin Metcalfe, Sr.,
  Earthquake
Song: Al Kasha, Joel Hirschhorn, "We May Never
  Love Like This Again" for *The Towering Inferno*
Original Dramatic Score: Nino Rota, Carmine
  Coppola, *The Godfather, Part II*

**Scoring—Original Song Score and/or
  Adaptation:** Nelson Riddle, *The Great Gatsby*
Film Editing: Harold F. Kress, Carl Kress,
  The Towering Inferno
Costume Design: Theoni V. Aldredge,
  The Great Gatsby
Short Subject—Animated: *Closed Mondays*
Short Subject—Live Action: *One-Eyed Men
  Are Kings*
Documentary—Short Subject: *Don't*
Documentary—Feature: *Hearts and Minds*
Jean Hersholt Humanitarian Award:
  Arthur B. Krim
Honorary Awards:
—Howard Hawks, "a master American filmmaker
  whose creative efforts hold a distinguished
  place in world cinema"
—Jean Renoir, "a genius who, with grace, respon-
  sibility, and enviable devotion through silent
  film, sound film, feature, documentary and
  television, has won the world's admiration"
Special Achievement Award—For Visual Effects:
  Frank Brendel, Glen Robinson, and Albert
  Whitlock for *Earthquake*

1975

Best Picture: *One Flew over the Cuckoo's Nest*
Actor: Jack Nicholson, *One Flew over the
  Cuckoo's Nest*
Actress: Louise Fletcher,
  One Flew over the Cuckoo's Nest
Supporting Actor: George Burns,
  The Sunshine Boys
Supporting Actress: Lee Grant, *Shampoo*
Director: Milos Forman,
  One Flew over the Cuckoo's Nest
Foreign-Language Film:
  Dersu Uzala
  (USSR/Japan)
Original Screenplay:
  Frank Pierson,
  Dog Day Afternoon
Adapted Screenplay:
  Lawrence Hauben,
  Gladys Hill, *One Flew
  over the Cuckoo's Nest*
Cinematography:
  John Alcott,
  Barry Lyndon
**Art Direction/Set
  Decoration:** Ken Adam
  and Roy Walker (art
  direction), Vernon Dixon
  (set decoration), *Barry Lyndon*
Sound: Robert L. Hoyt, Roger Herman,
  Earl Madery, John Carter, *Jaws*
Original Song: Keith Carradine, "I'm Easy"
  for *Nashville*
Original Score: John Williams, *Jaws*
Scoring—Original Score and/or Adaptation:
  Leonard Rosenman, *Barry Lyndon*
Film Editing: Verna Fields, *Jaws*

Legendary producer
Roger Corman has
appeared as a bureaucrat
in several Oscar-worthy
films, first as a senator in
Francis Coppola's *The
Godfather, Part II* (1974),
and followed by turns as
the director of the F.B.I.
in Jonathan Demme's
The Silence of the Lambs
(1991), and then as a
penny-pinching
congressman in Ron
Howard's *Apollo 13*
(1995). There is a
connection, of course:
All three directors had
early films produced
by Corman.

The Sunshine Boys
*(1975) featured Walter
Matthau (left) and
George Burns (right)
as old vaudevillian
partners sharing a
love-hate relationship.*

"I'm astounded by people who take 18 years to write something. That's how long it took that guy to write *Madame Bovary*. And was that ever on the bestseller list? No. It was a lousy book and it made a lousy movie."

—

Sylvester Stallone, who allegedly wrote his award-winning script for Rocky *in three days, 1976*

Costume Design: Ulla-Britt Soderlund, Milena Canonero, *Barry Lyndon*
Short Subject—Animated: *Great*
Short Subject—Live Action: *Angel and Big Joe*
Documentary—Short Subject: *The End of the Game*
Documentary—Feature: *The Man Who Skied Down Everest*
Irving G. Thalberg Memorial Award: Mervyn LeRoy
Jean Hersholt Humanitarian Award: Jules C. Stein
Honorary Award: Mary Pickford, "in recognition of her unique contributions to the film industry and the development of film as an artistic medium"
Special Achievement Awards:
—For Sound Effects: Peter Berkos, for *The Hindenburg*
—For Visual Effects: Albert Whitlock and Glen Robinson, for *The Hindenburg*

1976

Best Picture: *Rocky*
Actor: Peter Finch, *Network*
Actress: Faye Dunaway, *Network*
Supporting Actor: Jason Robards, *All the President's Men*
Supporting Actress: Beatrice Straight, *Network*
Director: John G. Avildsen, *Rocky*
Foreign-Language Film: *Black and White in Color* (France/Ivory Coast)
Original Screenplay: Paddy Chayefsky, *Network*
Adapted Screenplay: William Goldman, *All the President's Men*
Cinematography: Haskell Wexler, *Bound for Glory*
Art Direction/Set Decoration: George Jenkins (art direction), George Gaines (set decoration), *All the President's Men*

Peter Finch won the best actor Oscar for his portrayal of a television newscaster in Network *(1976).*

Sound: Arthur Piantadosi, Les Fresholtz, Dick Alexander, Jim Webb, *All the President's Men*
Original Song: Music by Barbra Streisand, lyrics by Paul Williams, "Evergreen (Love Theme from *A Star Is Born*)" for *A Star Is Born*
Original Score: Jerry Goldsmith, *The Omen*
Original Song Score and Its Adaptation or Adaptation Score: Leonard Rosenman, *Bound for Glory*
Film Editing: Richard Halsey, Scott Conrad, *Rocky*
Costume Design: Danilo Donati, *Fellini's Casanova*
Short Subject—Animated: *Leisure*
Short Subject—Live Action: *In the Region of Ice*
Documentary—Short Subject: *Number Our Days*
Documentary—Feature: *Harlan County, U.S.A.*
Irving G. Thalberg Memorial Award: Pandro S. Berman
Special Achievement Awards:
—For Visual Effects: Carlo Rambaldi, Glen Robinson, Frank Van Der Veer, for *King Kong*
—For Visual Effects: L.B. Abbott, Glen Robinson, Matthew Yuricich, for *Logan's Run*

1977

Best Picture: *Annie Hall*
Actor: Richard Dreyfuss, *The Goodbye Girl*
Actress: Diane Keaton, *Annie Hall*
Supporting Actor: Jason Robards, *Julia*
Supporting Actress: Vanessa Redgrave, *Julia*
Director: Woody Allen, *Annie Hall*
Foreign-Language Film: *Madame Rosa* (France)
Original Screenplay: Woody Allen, Marshall Brickman, *Annie Hall*
Adapted Screenplay: Alvin Sargent, *Julia*
Cinematography: Vilmos Zsigmond, *Close Encounters of the Third Kind*
Art Direction/Set Decoration: John Barry, Norman Reynolds and Leslie Dilley (art direction), Roger Christian (set decoration), *Star Wars*
Sound: Don MacDougall, Ray West, Bob Minkler, Derek Ball, *Star Wars*
Original Song: Joseph Brooks, "You Light Up My Life" for *You Light Up My Life*
Original Score: John Williams, *Star Wars*
Original Song Score and Its Adaptation or Adaptation Score: Jonathan Tunick, *A Little Night Music*
Film Editing: Paul Hirsch, Marcia Lucas, Richard Chew, *Star Wars*
Costume Design: John Mollo, *Star Wars*
Visual Effects: John Stears, John Dykstra, Richard Edlund, Grant McCune, Robert Blalack, *Star Wars*
Short Subject—Animated: *Sand Castle*
Short Subject—Live Action: *I'll Find a Way*
Documentary—Short Subject: *Gravity Is My Enemy*
Documentary—Feature: *Who Are the DeBolts? And Where Did They Get Nineteen Kids?*
Irving G. Thalberg Memorial Award: Walter Mirisch

Jean Hersholt Humanitarian Award:
Charlton Heston
Honorary Awards:
—Margaret Booth, "for her exceptional contributions to the art of film editing in the motion picture industry"
—Gordon E. Sawyer and Sidney P. Solow, "in appreciation for outstanding service and dedication in upholding the high standards of the Academy of Motion Picture Arts and Sciences"
Special Achievement Awards:
—For Sound Effects Editing: Frank Warner, for *Close Encounters of the Third Kind*
—For Sound Effects: Benjamin Burtt, Jr., for the creation of the alien creature, and robot voices in *Star Wars*

—King Vidor, "for his incomparable achievements as a cinematic creator and innovator"
—The Museum of Modern Art Department of Film, "for the contribution it has made to the public's perception of movies as an art form"
—Linwood G. Dunn, Loren L. Ryder, and Walden O. Watson, "in appreciation for outstanding service and dedication in upholding the high standards of the Academy of Motion Picture Arts and Sciences"
Special Achievement Award—For Visual Effects:
Les Bowie, Colin Chilvers, Denys Coop, Roy Field, Derek Meddings, Zoran Perisic, for *Superman*

1978

Best Picture: *The Deer Hunter*
Actor: Jon Voight, *Coming Home*
Actress: Jane Fonda, *Coming Home*
Supporting Actor: Christopher Walken, *The Deer Hunter*
Supporting Actress: Maggie Smith, *California Suite*
Director: Michael Cimino, *The Deer Hunter*
Foreign-Language Film: *Get Out Your Handkerchiefs* (France)
Original Screenplay: Story by Nancy Dowd, screenplay by Waldo Salt and Robert C. Jones, *Coming Home*
Adapted Screenplay: Oliver Stone, *Midnight Express*
Cinematography: Nestor Almendros, *Days of Heaven*
Art Direction: Paul Sylbert and Edwin O'Donovan (art direction), George Gaines (set decoration), *Heaven Can Wait*
Sound: Richard Portman, William McCaughey, Aaron Rochin, Darrin Knight, *The Deer Hunter*
Original Song: Paul Jabara, "Last Dance" for *Thank God It's Friday*
Original Score: Giorgio Moroder, *Midnight Express*
Original Song Score and Its Adaptation or Adaptation Score: Joe Renzetti, *The Buddy Holly Story*
Film Editing: Peter Zinner, *The Deer Hunter*
Costume Design: Anthony Powell, *Death on the Nile*
Short Subject—Animated: *Special Delivery*
Short Subject—Live Action: *Teenage Father*
Documentary—Short Subject: *The Flight of the Gossamer Condor*
Documentary—Feature: *Scared Straight!*
Jean Hersholt Humanitarian Award: Leo Jaffe
Honorary Awards:
—Walter Lantz, "for bringing joy and laughter to every part of the world through his unique animated motion pictures"
—Laurence Olivier, "for the full body of his work, for the unique achievements of his entire career and his lifetime contribution to the art of film"

1979

Best Picture: *Kramer vs. Kramer*
Actor: Dustin Hoffman, *Kramer vs. Kramer*
Actress: Sally Field, *Norma Rae*
Supporting Actor: Melvyn Douglas, *Being There*
Supporting Actress: Meryl Streep, *Kramer vs. Kramer*
Director: Robert Benton, *Kramer vs. Kramer*
Foreign-Language Film: *The Tin Drum* (West Germany)
Original Screenplay: Steve Tesich, *Breaking Away*
Adapted Screenplay: Robert Benton, *Kramer vs. Kramer*
Cinematography: Vittorio Storaro, *Apocalypse Now*
Art Direction: Philip Rosenberg and Tony Walton (art direction), Edward Stewart and Gary Brink (set decoration), *All That Jazz*
Sound: Walter Murch, Mark Berger, Richard Beggs, Nat Boxer, *Apocalypse Now*
Original Song: Music by David Shire, lyrics by Norman Gimbel, "It Goes Like It Goes" for *Norma Rae*

Cycling fanatic Dennis Christopher received help from his friends—played by Jackie Earle Haley, Daniel Stern, and Dennis Quaid—in an important race in Breaking Away *(1979).*

The famous scene of Harrison Ford, as globetrotting archaeologist Indiana Jones, gunning down the marketplace swordsman in *Raiders of the Lost Ark* (1981) almost didn't come to pass. A lengthy fight had been scripted between the two, but on the day it was scheduled to be shot, Ford was sick with the flu and wanted to go home early, so he asked director Steven Spielberg if it would be all right if he just shot him instead.

Original Score: Georges Delerue, *A Little Romance*

Original Song Score and Its Adaptation or Adaptation Score: Ralph Burns, *All That Jazz*

Film Editing: Alan Heim, *All That Jazz*

Costume Design: Albert Wolsky, *All That Jazz*

Visual Effects: H.R. Giger, Carlo Rambaldi, Brian Johnson, Nick Allder, Denys Ayling, *Alien*

Short Subject—Animated: *Every Child*

Short Subject—Live Action: *Board and Care*

Documentary—Short Subject: *Paul Robeson*

Documentary—Feature: *Best Boy*

Irving G. Thalberg Memorial Award: Ray Stark

Jean Hersholt Humanitarian Award: Robert Benjamin

Honorary Awards:

—Hal Elias, "for his dedication and distinguished service to the Academy of Motion Picture Arts and Sciences"

—Alec Guinness, "for advancing the art of screen acting through a host of memorable and distinguished performances"

—John O. Aalberg, Charles G. Clarke, and John G. Frayne, "in appreciation for outstanding service and dedication in upholding the high standards of the Academy of Motion Picture Arts and Sciences"

Special Achievement Award—For Sound Editing: Alan Splet, for *Black Stallion*

1980

Best Picture: *Ordinary People*

Actor: Robert De Niro, *Raging Bull*

Actress: Sissy Spacek, *Coal Miner's Daughter*

Supporting Actor: Timothy Hutton, *Ordinary People*

Supporting Actress: Mary Steenburgen, *Melvin and Howard*

Director: Robert Redford, *Ordinary People*

Foreign-Language Film: *Moscow Does Not Believe in Tears* (USSR)

Original Screenplay: Bo Goldman, *Melvin and Howard*

Adapted Screenplay: Alvin Sargent, *Ordinary People*

Cinematography: Geoffrey Unsworth, Ghislain Cloquet, *Tess*

Art Direction: Pierre Guffroy, Jack Stevens, *Tess*

Sound: Bill Varney, Steve Maslow, Gregg Landaker, Peter Sutton, *The Empire Strikes Back*

Original Song: Music by Michael Gore, lyrics by Dean Pitchford, "Fame" for *Fame*

Original Score: Michael Gore, *Fame*

Award-winning Ordinary People *(1980), Robert Redford's directorial debut, featured Timothy Hutton and Donald Sutherland as son and father.*

Film Editing: Thelma Schoonmaker, *Raging Bull*

Costume Design: Anthony Powell, *Tess*

Short Subject—Animated: *The Fly*

Short Subject—Live Action: *The Dollar Bottom*

Documentary—Short Subject: *Karl Hess: Toward Liberty*

Documentary—Feature: *From Mao to Mozart: Isaac Stern in China*

Special Achievement Award—For Visual Effects: Brian Johnson, Richard Edlund, Dennis Muren, Bruce Nicholson, for *The Empire Strikes Back*

Honorary Awards:

—Henry Fonda, "the consummate actor, in recognition of his brilliant accomplishments and enduring contribution to the art of motion pictures"

—Fred Hynes, "in appreciation for outstanding service and dedication in upholding the high standards of the Academy of Motion Picture Arts and Sciences"

1981

Best Picture: *Chariots of Fire*

Actor: Henry Fonda, *On Golden Pond*

Actress: Katharine Hepburn, *On Golden Pond*

Supporting Actor: John Gielgud, *Arthur*

Supporting Actress: Maureen Stapleton, *Reds*

Director: Warren Beatty, *Reds*

Foreign-Language Film: *Mephisto* (Hungary)

Original Screenplay: Colin Welland, *Chariots of Fire*

Adapted Screenplay: Ernest Thompson, *On Golden Pond*

Cinematography: Vittorio Storaro, *Reds*

Art Direction: Norman Reynolds and Leslie Dilley (art direction), Michael Ford (set decoration), *Raiders of the Lost Ark*

Sound: Bill Varney, Steve Maslow, Gregg Landaker, Roy Charman, *Raiders of the Lost Ark*

Original Song: Burt Bacharach, Carole Bayer Sager, Christopher Cross, Peter Allen, "Arthur's Theme (Best That You Can Do)" for *Arthur*
Original Score: Vangelis, *Chariots of Fire*
Film Editing: Michael Kahn, *Raiders of the Lost Ark*
Costume Design: Milena Canonero, *Chariots of Fire*
Makeup: Rick Baker, *An American Werewolf in London*
Visual Effects: Richard Edlund, Kit West, Bruce Nicholson, Joe Johnston, *Raiders of the Lost Ark*
Short Subject—Animated: *Crac*
Short Subject—Live Action: *Violet*
Documentary—Short Subject: *Close Harmony*
Documentary—Feature: *Genocide*
Irving G. Thalberg Memorial Award: Albert R. "Cubby" Broccoli
Jean Hersholt Humanitarian Award: Danny Kaye
Gordon E. Sawyer Award: Joseph B. Walker
Honorary Award: Barbara Stanwyck, "for superlative creativity and unique contribution to the art of screen acting"
Special Achievement Award—For Sound Effects Editing: Benjamin P. Burtt, Jr., and Richard L. Anderson, for *Raiders of the Lost Ark*

1982

Best Picture: *Gandhi*
Actor: Ben Kingsley, *Gandhi*
Actress: Meryl Streep, *Sophie's Choice*
Supporting Actor: Louis Gossett, Jr., *An Officer and a Gentleman*
Supporting Actress: Jessica Lange, *Tootsie*
Director: Richard Attenborough, *Tootsie*
Foreign-Language Film: *Volver a Empezar (To Begin Again)* (Spain)
Original Screenplay: John Briley, *Gandhi*
Adapted Screenplay: Costa-Gavras, Donald Stewart, *Missing*
Cinematography: Billy Williams, Ronnie Taylor, *Gandhi*
Art Direction: Stuart Craig, Bob Laing (art direction), Michael Seirton (set decoration), *Gandhi*
Sound: Gerry Humphreys, Robin O'Donoghue, Jonathan Bates, Simon Kaye, *Gandhi*
Original Song: Music by Jack Nitzsche and Buffy Sainte-Marie, lyrics by Will Jennings, "Up Where We Belong" for *An Officer and a Gentleman*
Original Score: John Williams, *E.T.: The Extra-Terrestrial*
Film Editing: John Bloom, *Gandhi*
Costume Design: John Mollo, Bhanu Athaiya, *Gandhi*
Makeup: (credits in controversy), *Quest for Fire*
Visual Effects: Carlo Rambaldi, Dennis Muren, Kenneth F. Smith, *E.T.: The Extra-Terrestrial*
Sound Effects Editing: Charles L. Campbell, Ben Burtt, *E.T.: The Extra-Terrestrial*
Short Subject—Animated: *Tango*

Short Subject—Live Action: *A Shocking Accident*
Documentary—Short Subject: *If You Love This Planet*
Documentary—Feature: *Just Another Missing Kid*
Jean Hersholt Humanitarian Award: Walter Mirisch
Gordon E. Sawyer Award: John O. Aalberg, "for his technological contributions to the motion picture industry"
Honorary Award: Mickey Rooney, "for fifty years of versatility in a variety of memorable film performances"

1983

Best Picture: *Terms of Endearment*
Actor: Robert Duvall, *Tender Mercies*
Actress: Shirley MacLaine, *Terms of Endearment*
Supporting Actor: Jack Nicholson, *Terms of Endearment*
Supporting Actress: Linda Hunt, *The Year of Living Dangerously*
Director: James L. Brooks, *Terms of Endearment*
Foreign-Language Film: *Fanny and Alexander* (Sweden)
Original Screenplay: Horton Foote, *Tender Mercies*
Adapted Screenplay: James L. Brooks, *Terms of Endearment*
Cinematography: Sven Nykvist, *Fanny and Alexander*
Art Direction: Susanne Lingheim, *Fanny and Alexander*
Sound: Mark Berger, Tom Scott, Randy Thom, David MacMillan, *The Right Stuff*
Song: Music by Giorgio Moroder, lyrics by Keith Forsey, Irene Cara, "Flashdance…What a Feeling" for *Flashdance*
Original Score: Bill Conti, *The Right Stuff*
Original Song Score or Adaptation Score: Michel Legrand, Alan and Marilyn Bergman, *Yentl*
Film Editing: Glenn Farr, Lisa Fruchtman, Stephan A. Rotter, Douglas Steward, Tom Rolf, *The Right Stuff*
Costume Design: Marik Vos, *Fanny and Alexander*
Sound Effects Editing: Jay Boekelheide, *The Right Stuff*

Dennis Quaid played a US Mercury 7 astronaut in The Right Stuff *(1983).*

"I think you've got to have nutty goals in life. I'd like to win more Oscars than Walt Disney, and I'd like to win them in every category."

—

Jack Nicholson, accepting his best supporting actor award for 1983's Terms of Endearment, *1984*

> "This was my first time working with a movie star. A movie star is a person I saw when I was ten or eleven on a big screen."
>
> —
>
> *Martin Scorsese, on directing Paul Newman in* The Color of Money *(1987), who reprised his role as pool shark Fast Eddie Felson from Robert Rossen's* The Hustler *(1961). Scorsese directed Newman to a best actor Oscar.*

Short Subject—Animated: *Sundae in New York*
Short Subject—Live Action: *Boys and Girls*
Documentary—Short Subject: *Flamenco at 5:15*
Documentary—Feature:
   He Makes Me Feel Like Dancin'
Jean Hersholt Humanitarian Award:
   M.J. "Mike" Frankovich
Gordon E. Sawyer Award: Dr. John G. Frayne
Honorary Award: Hal Roach, "in recognition of his unparalleled record of distinguished contributions to the motion picture art form"
Special Achievement Award—For Visual Effects: Richard Edlund, Dennis Muren, Ken Ralston, Phil Tippett, for *Return of the Jedi*

1984

Best Picture: *Amadeus*
Actor: F. Murray Abraham, *Amadeus*
Actress: Sally Field, *Places in the Heart*
Supporting Actor: Haing S. Ngor,
   The Killing Fields
Supporting Actress: Peggy Ashcroft,
   A Passage to India
Director: Milos Forman, *Amadeus*
Foreign-Language Film: *Dangerous Moves*
   (Switzerland)
Original Screenplay: Robert Benton,
   Places in the Heart
Adapted Screenplay: Peter Shaffer, *Amadeus*
Cinematography: Chris Menges, *The Killing Fields*
Art Direction: Patrizia Von Brandenstein
   (art direction), Karel Cerny (set decoration),
   Amadeus
Sound: Mark Berger, Tom Scott, Todd
   Boekelheide, Chris Newman, *Amadeus*
Song: Stevie Wonder, "I Just Called to Say I Love
   You," for *The Woman in Red*
Original Score: Maurice Jarre,
   A Passage to India

Sally Field delivered an award-winning performance in Places in the Heart *(1984).*

Original Song Score: Prince, *Purple Rain*
Film Editing: Jim Clark, *The Killing Fields*
Costume Design: Theodor Pistek, *Amadeus*
Makeup: Paul LeBlanc, Dick Smith, *Amadeus*
Visual Effects: Dennis Muren, Michael McAlister,
   Lorne Peterson, George Gibbs, *Indiana Jones
   and the Temple of Doom*
Short Subject—Animated: *Charade*
Short Subject—Live Action: *Up*
Documentary—Short Subject: *The Stone Carvers*
Documentary—Feature:
   The Times of Harvey Milk
Jean Hersholt Humanitarian Award:
   David L. Wolper
Gordon E. Sawyer Award: Linwood G. Dunn
Honorary Awards:
—National Endowment for the Arts, "for
   supporting filmmakers"
—James Stewart, "for 50 years of meaningful
   performances, for his high ideals, both on and
   off the screen, with the respect and affection of
   his colleagues"
**Special Achievement Award—Sound Effects
   Editing:** Kay Rose, for *The River*

1985

Best Picture: *Out of Africa*
Actor: William Hurt, *Kiss of the Spider Woman*
Actress: Geraldine Page, *The Trip to Bountiful*
Supporting Actor: Don Ameche, *Cocoon*
Supporting Actress: Anjelica Huston,
   Prizzi's Honor
Director: Sydney Pollack, *Out of Africa*
Foreign-Language Film: *The Official Story*
   (Argentina)
Original Screenplay: Earl W. Wallace and
   William Kelley (screenplay), William Kelley,
   Pamela Wallace, and Earl W. Wallace (story),
   Witness
Adapted Screenplay: Kurt Luedtke, *Out of Africa*
Cinematography: David Watkin, *Out of Africa*
Art Direction: Stephen Grimes (art direction),
   Josie MacAvin (set decoration), *Out of Africa*
Sound: Chris Jenkins, Gary Alexander, Larry
   Stensvold, Peter Handford, *Out of Africa*
Song: Lionel Richie, "Say You, Say Me" for
   White Knights
Original Score: John Barry, *Out of Africa*
Film Editing: Thom Noble, *Witness*
Costume Design: Emi Wada, *Ran*
Makeup: Michael Westmore, Zoltan Elek, *Mask*
Visual Effects: Ken Ralston, Ralph McQuarrie,
   Scott Farrar, David Berry, *Cocoon*
Sound Effects Editing: Charles L. Campbell,
   Robert Rutledge, *Back to the Future*
Short Subject—Animated: *Anna & Bella*
Short Subject—Live Action: *Molly's Pilgrim*
Documentary—Short Subject: *Witness to War:
   Dr. Charlie Clements*
Documentary—Feature: *Broken Rainbow*
Jean Hersholt Humanitarian Award:
   Charles "Buddy" Rogers

Honorary Awards:
—Paul Newman, "in recognition of his many memorable and compelling screen performances and for his personal integrity and dedication to his craft"
—Alex North, "in recognition of his brilliant artistry in the creation of memorable music for a host of distinguished motion pictures"
—John H. Whitney, "for cinematic pioneering"

A Room with a View charmed critics and audiences alike in 1986.

1986

Best Picture: *Platoon*
Actor: Paul Newman, *The Color of Money*
Actress: Marlee Matlin, *Children of a Lesser God*
Supporting Actor: Michael Caine, *Hannah and Her Sisters*
Supporting Actress: Dianne Wiest, *Hannah and Her Sisters*
Director: Oliver Stone, *Platoon*
Foreign-Language Film: *The Assault* (The Netherlands)
Original Screenplay: Woody Allen, *Hannah and Her Sisters*
Adapted Screenplay: Ruth Prawer Jhabvala, *A Room With a View*
Cinematography: Chris Menges, *The Mission*
Art Direction: Gianni Quaranta and Brian Ackland-Snow (art direction), Brian Savegar and Elio Altramura (set decoration), *A Room with a View*
Sound: John "Doc" Wilkinson, Richard Rogers, Charles "Bud" Grenzbach, Simon Kaye, *Platoon*
Song: Music by Giorgio Moroder, lyrics by Tom Whitlock, "Take My Breath Away" for *Top Gun*
Original Score: Herbie Hancock, *'Round Midnight*
Film Editing: Claire Simpson, *Platoon*
Costume Design: Jenny Beaven, John Bright, *A Room with a View*
Makeup: Chris Walas, Stephen Dupuis, *The Fly*
Visual Effects: Robert Skotak, Stan Winston, John Richardson, Suzanne Benson, *Aliens*
Sound Effects Editing: Don Sharpe, *Aliens*

Short Subject—Animated: *A Greek Tragedy*
Short Subject—Live Action: *Precious Images*
Documentary—Short Subject: *Women—For America, for the World*
Documentary—Feature: *Artie Shaw: Time Is All You've Got* and *Down and Out in America*
Irving G. Thalberg Memorial Award: Steven Spielberg
Honorary Awards:
—Ralph Bellamy, "for his unique artistry and his distinguished service to the profession of acting"
—E.M. "Al" Lewis, "in appreciation for outstanding service in upholding the Academy standards"

1987

Best Picture: *The Last Emperor*
Actor: Michael Douglas, *Wall Street*
Actress: Cher, *Moonstruck*
Supporting Actor: Sean Connery, *The Untouchables*
Supporting Actress: Olympia Dukakis, *Moonstruck*
Director: Bernardo Bertolucci, *The Last Emperor*
Foreign-Language Film: *Babette's Feast* (Denmark)
Original Screenplay: John Patrick Shanley, *Moonstruck*
Adapted Screenplay: Mark Peploe, Bernardo Bertolucci, *The Last Emperor*
Cinematography: Vittorio Storaro, *The Last Emperor*
Art Direction: Ferdinando Scarfiotti (art direction), Bruno Cesari (set decoration), *The Last Emperor*
Sound: Bill Rowe, Ivan Sharrock, *The Last Emperor*
Song: Music by Franke Previte, John DeNicola, and Donald Markowitz, lyrics by Franke Previte, "(I've Had) The Time of My Life" for *Dirty Dancing*
Original Score: Ryuichi Sakamoto, David Byrne, Cong Su, *The Last Emperor*
Film Editing: Gabriella Cristiani, *The Last Emperor*
Costume Design: James Acheson, *The Last Emperor*
Makeup: Rick Baker, *Harry and the Hendersons*
Visual Effects: Dennis Muren, William George, Harley Jessup, Kenneth Smith, *Innerspace*
Short Subject—Animated: *The Man Who Planted Trees*
Short Subject—Live Action: *Ray's Male Heterosexual Dance Hall*
Documentary—Short Subject: *Young at Heart*
Documentary—Feature: *The Ten-Year Lunch: The Wit and Legend of the Algonquin Round Table*
Irving G. Thalberg Memorial Award: Billy Wilder
Gordon E. Sawyer Award: Fred Hynes
Special Achievement Award—For Sound Effects Editing: Stephen Flick, John Pospisil, for *Robocop*

Dr. Haing S. Ngor had no acting experience when he was chosen to play photographer Dith Pran in the searing Cambodian-set drama *The Killing Fields* (1984), but he did have experience of another kind. A gynecologist in his native Cambodia, he was captured and tortured by Khmer Rouge guerillas before escaping to Thailand and, later, to California. After winning the best supporting actor Oscar for his heartfelt portrayal, Ngor worked with international human rights organizations to improve conditions in Cambodia. He was found shot to death in the garage of his Los Angeles apartment building in 1996, and some have speculated that the killing was an act of revenge for his outspoken opposition to the Khmer Rouge.

Tom Cruise discovered he had an autistic brother, played by Dustin Hoffman, in Rain Man *(1988).*

"Genres are not dead as long as they are treated with sophistication."

—

Kevin Costner, who breathed life into the long-dormant western (and carried off two Oscars, as director and producer) with Dances With Wolves *(1990)*

1988

Best Picture: *Rain Man*
Actor: Dustin Hoffman, *Rain Man*
Actress: Jodie Foster, *The Accused*
Supporting Actor: Kevin Kline,
    A Fish Called Wanda
Supporting Actress: Geena Davis,
    The Accidental Tourist
Director: Barry Levinson, *Rain Man*
Foreign-Language Film: *Pelle the Conqueror*
    (Denmark/Sweden)
Original Screenplay: Barry Morrow, *Rain Man*
Adapted Screenplay: Christopher Hampton,
    Dangerous Liaisons
Cinematographer: Peter Biziou,
    Mississippi Burning
Art Direction: Stuart Craig (art direction), Gerard
    James (set direction), *Dangerous Liaisons*
Sound: Les Fresholtz, Dick Alexander, Vern Poore,
    Willie D. Burton, *Bird*
Original Song: Carly Simon, "Let the River Run"
    for *Working Girl*
Original Score: Dave Grusin,
    The Milagro Beanfield War
Film Editing: Arthur Schmidt,
    Who Framed Roger Rabbit
Costume Design: James Acheson,
    Dangerous Liaisons
Makeup: Ve Neill, Steve LaPorte, Robert Short,
    Beetlejuice
Sound Effects Editing: Charles L. Campbell,
    Louis L. Edemann, *Who Framed Roger Rabbit*
Visual Effects: Ken Ralston, Richard Williams,
    Edward Jones, George Gibbs, *Who Framed
    Roger Rabbit*
Short Subject—Animated: *Tin Toy*
Short Subject—Live Action:
    The Appointments of Dennis Jennings
Documentary—Short Subject: *You Don't Have
    to Die*
Documentary—Feature: *Hotel Terminus: The Life
    and Times of Klaus Barbie*
Gordon E. Sawyer Award: Gordon Henry Cook
Honorary Awards:
—Eastman Kodak, "in recognition of the
    company's fundamental contributions to the art

of motion pictures during the first century of
film history"
—The National Film Board of Canada, "in
    recognition of its 50th anniversary and its
    dedicated commitment to original artistic,
    creative, and technological activity and
    excellence in every area of filmmaking"
**Special Achievement Award—For Animation
    Direction:** Richard Williams

1989

Best Picture: *Driving Miss Daisy*
Actor: Daniel Day-Lewis, *My Left Foot*
Actress: Jessica Tandy, *Driving Miss Daisy*
Supporting Actor: Denzel Washington, *Glory*
Supporting Actress: Brenda Fricker, *My Left Foot*
Director: Oliver Stone, *Born on the Fourth of July*
Foreign-Language Film: *Cinema Paradiso* (Italy)
Original Screenplay: Tom Schulman,
    Dead Poets Society
Adapted Screenplay: Alfred Uhry,
    Driving Miss Daisy
Cinematographer: Freddie Francis, *Glory*
Art Direction: Anton Furst (art direction),
    Peter Young (set direction), *Batman*
Sound: Donald O. Mitchell, Gregg C. Rudloff,
    Elliott Tyson, Russell Williams II, *Glory*
Original Song: Music by Alan Menken, lyrics
    by Howard Ashman, "Under the Sea" for *The
    Little Mermaid*
Original Score: Alan Menken, *The Little Mermaid*
Film Editing: David Brenner, Joe Hutshing,
    Born on the Fourth of July
Costume Design: Phyllis Dalton, *Henry V*
Makeup: Manlio Rochetti, Lynn Barber, Kevin
    Haney, *Driving Miss Daisy*
Sound Effects Editing: Ben Burtt, Richard
    Hymns, *Indiana Jones and the Last Crusade*
Visual Effects: John Bruno, Dennis Muren, Hoyt
    Yeatman, Dennis Skotak, *The Abyss*
Short Subject—Animated: *Balance*
Short Subject—Live Action: *Work Experience*
Documentary—Short Subject:
    The Johnstown Flood
Documentary—Feature: *Common Threads:
    Stories from the Quilt*
Jean Hersholt Humanitarian Award:
    Howard W. Koch
Gordon E. Sawyer Award: Pierre Angenieux
Honorary Award: Akira Kurosawa, "for
    accomplishments that have inspired, delighted,
    enriched, and entertained audiences and
    influenced filmmakers throughout the world"

1990

Best Picture: *Dances with Wolves*
Actor: Jeremy Irons, *Reversal of Fortune*
Actress: Kathy Bates, *Misery*
Supporting Actor: Joe Pesci, *GoodFellas*

Supporting Actress: Whoopi Goldberg, *Ghost*
Director: Kevin Costner, *Dances with Wolves*
Foreign-Language Film: *Journey of Hope* (Switzerland)
Original Screenplay: Bruce Joel Rubin, *Ghost*
Adapted Screenplay: Michael Blake, *Dances with Wolves*
Cinematographer: Dean Semier, *Dances with Wolves*
Art Direction: Richard Sylbert (art direction), Rick Simpson (set decoration), *Dick Tracy*
Sound: Russell Williams II, Jeffrey Perkins, Bill W. Benton, Greg Watkins, *Dances with Wolves*
Original Song: Stephen Sondheim, "Sooner or Later (I Always Get My Man)" for *Dick Tracy*
Original Score: John Barry, *Dances with Wolves*
Film Editing: Neil Travis, *Dances with Wolves*
Costume Design: Franca Squaricapino, *Cyrano de Bergerac*
Makeup: John Caglione, Jr., Doug Drexler, *Dick Tracy*
Sound Effects Editing: Cecelia Hall, George Watters II, *The Hunt for Red October*
Short Subject—Animated: *Creature Comforts*
Short Subject—Live Action: *The Lunch Date*
Visual Effects: Eric Brevig, Rob Bottin, Tim McGovern, Alex Funke, *Total Recall*
Documentary—Short Subject: *Days of Waiting*
Documentary—Feature: *American Dream*
Gordon E. Sawyer Award: Stefan Kudelski
Honorary Awards: Sophia Loren and Myrna Loy, "for lifetime achievement in acting"

1991

Best Picture: *The Silence of the Lambs*
Actor: Anthony Hopkins, *The Silence of the Lambs*
Actress: Jodie Foster, *The Silence of the Lambs*
Supporting Actor: Jack Palance, *City Slickers*
Supporting Actress: Mercedes Ruehl, *The Fisher King*
Director: Jonathan Demme, *The Silence of the Lambs*
Foreign-Language Film: *Mediterraneo* (Italy)
Original Screenplay: Callie Khouri, *Thelma & Louise*
Adapted Screenplay: Ted Tally, *The Silence of the Lambs*
Cinematographer: Robert Richardson, *JFK*
Art Direction: Dennis Gassner (art direction), Nancy Haigh (set decoration), *Bugsy*
Sound: Tom Johnson, Gary Rydstrom, Gary Summers, Lee Orloff, *Terminator 2: Judgment Day*
Original Song: Alan Menken, "Beauty and the Beast," for *Beauty and the Beast*
Original Score: Alan Menken, *Beauty and the Beast*
Film Editing: Joe Hutshing, Pietro Scalia, *JFK*
Costume Design: Albert Wolsky, *Bugsy*
Makeup: Stan Sinston, Jeff Dawn, *Terminator 2: Judgment Day*
Sound Effects Editing: Gary Rydstrom, Gloria S.

Borders, *Terminator 2: Judgment Day*
Visual Effects: Dennis Muren, Stan Winston, Gene Warren, Jr., Robert Skotak, *Terminator 2: Judgment Day*
Short Subject—Animated: *Manipulation*
Short Subject—Live Action: *Session Man*
Documentary—Short Subject: *Deadly Deception: General Electric, Nuclear Weapons, and Our Environment*
Documentary—Feature: *In the Shadow of the Stars*
Gordon E. Sawyer Award: Ray Harryhausen
Honorary Award: Satyajit Ray, "for lifetime achievement in directing"

1992

Best Picture: *Unforgiven*
Actor: Al Pacino, *Scent of a Woman*
Actress: Emma Thompson, *Howards End*
Supporting Actor: Gene Hackman, *Unforgiven*
Supporting Actress: Marisa Tomei, *My Cousin Vinny*
Director: Clint Eastwood, *Unforgiven*
Foreign-Language Film: *Indochine* (France)
Original Screenplay: Neil Jordan, *The Crying Game*
Adapted Screenplay: Ruth Prawer Jhabvala, *Howards End*
Cinematographer: Philippe Rousselot, *A River Runs Through It*
Art Direction: Luciana Arrighi (art direction), Ian Whittaker (set decoration), *Howards End*
Sound: Chris Jenkins, Doug Hemphill, Mark Smith, Simon Kaye, *The Last of the Mohicans*

The Crying Game (1992), starring Jaye Davidson and Stephen Rea, shocked viewers with a surprise plot twist.

Original Song: Alan Menken, "Whole New World" for *Aladdin*
Original Score: Alan Menken, *Aladdin*
Film Editing: Joel Cox, *Unforgiven*
Costume Design: Elko Ishioka, *Bram Stoker's Dracula*
Makeup: Greg Cannon, Michele Burke, Matthew W. Mungle, *Bram Stoker's Dracula*
Sound Effects Editing: Tom C. McCarthy, David E. Stone, *Bram Stoker's Dracula*
Visual Effects: Ken Ralston, Doug Chiang, Doug Smythe, Tom Woodruff, *Death Becomes Her*
Short Subject—Animated: *Mona Lisa Descending a Staircase*
Short Subject—Live Action: *Omnibus*
Documentary—Short Subject: *Educating Peter*
Documentary—Feature: *The Panama Deception*
Jean Hersholt Humanitarian Award:
—Audrey Hepburn, for her UNICEF work
—Elizabeth Taylor, for her support of AIDS research
Gordon E. Sawyer Award: Erich Kaestner, "whose technical contributions have brought credit to the motion-picture industry"
Honorary Award: Federico Fellini, "in recognition of his cinematic accomplishments that have thrilled and entertained worldwide audiences"

Writer John O'Brien committed suicide two weeks before production began on the film adaptation of his novel *Leaving Las Vegas* (1995). Both the book and the film are about a self-destructive writer who decides to drink himself to death.

1993

Best Picture: *Schindler's List*
Actor: Tom Hanks, *Philadelphia*
Actress: Holly Hunter, *The Piano*
Supporting Actor: Tommy Lee Jones, *The Fugitive*
Supporting Actress: Anna Paquin, *The Piano*
Director: Steven Spielberg, *Schindler's List*
Foreign-Language Film: *Belle Époque* (Spain)
Original Screenplay: Jane Campion, *The Piano*
Adapted Screenplay: Steven Zaillian, *Schindler's List*
Cinematographer: Janusz Kaminski, *Schindler's List*
Art Direction: Allan Starski (art direction), Ewa Braun (set direction), *Schindler's List*
Sound: Gary Summers, Gary Rydstrom, Shawn Murphy, Ron Judkins, *Jurassic Park*
Original Song: Bruce Springsteen, "Streets of Philadelphia" for *Philadelphia*
Original Score: John Williams, *Schindler's List*
Film Editing: Michael Kahn, *Schindler's List*

Holly Hunter and Anna Paquin played mother and daughter in The Piano *(1993).*

Costume Design: Gabriella Pescucci, *The Age of Innocence*
Makeup: Greg Cannom, Ve Neill, Yolanda Toussieng, *Mrs. Doubtfire*
Sound Effects Editing: Gary Rydstrom, Richard Hymns, *Jurassic Park*
Visual Effects: Dennis Muren, Stan Winston, Phil Tippett, Michael Lantieri, *Jurassic Park*
Short Subject—Animated: *The Wrong Trousers*
Short Subject—Live Action: *Black Rider (Schwarzfahrer)*
Documentary—Short Subject: *Defending Our Lives*
Documentary—Feature: *I Am a Promise: The Children of Stanton Elementary School*
Jean Hersholt Humanitarian Award: Paul Newman, "for his humanitarian efforts"
Gordon E. Sawyer Award: Petro Vlahos, "whose technical contributions have brought credit to the motion picture industry"
Honorary Award: Deborah Kerr, for career achievement

1994

Best Picture: *Forrest Gump*
Actor: Tom Hanks, *Forrest Gump*
Actress: Jessica Lange, *Blue Sky*
Supporting Actor: Martin Landau, *Ed Wood*
Supporting Actress: Dianne Wiest, *Bullets Over Broadway*
Director: Robert Zemeckis, *Forrest Gump*
Foreign-Language Film: *Burnt by the Sun* (Russia)
Original Screenplay: Quentin Tarantino, *Pulp Fiction*
Adapted Screenplay: Eric Roth, *Forrest Gump*
Cinematographer: John Toll, *Legends of the Fall*
Art Direction: Ken Adam (art direction), Carolyn Scott (set direction), *The Madness of King George*
Sound: Gregg Landaker, Steve Maslow, Bob Reemer, David R.B. MacMillan, *Speed*
Original Song: Music by Elton John, lyrics by Tim Rice, "Can You Feel the Love Tonight" for *The Lion King*
Original Score: Hans Zimmer, *The Lion King*
Film Editing: Arthur Schmidt, *Forrest Gump*
Costume Design: Lizzy Gardiner, Tim Chappel, *The Adventures of Priscilla, Queen of the Desert*
Makeup: Rick Baker, Ve Neill, Yolanda Toussieng, *Ed Wood*
Sound Effects Editing: Stephen Hunter Flick, *Speed*
Visual Effects: Ken Ralston, George Murphy, Stephen Rosenbaum, Allen Hall, *Forrest Gump*
Short Subject—Animated: *Bob's Birthday*
Short Subject—Live Action: *Franz Kafka's It's a Wonderful Life*
Documentary—Short Subject: *A Time for Justice*
Documentary—Feature: *Maya Lin: A Strong Clear Vision*
Irving R. Thalberg Memorial Award: Clint Eastwood

Jean Hersholt Humanitarian Award:
   Quincy Jones
Gordon E. Sawyer Award:
—Petro Vlahos, Paul Vlahos, "for concept and development of the Ultimate Electronic Blue Screen Compositing Process"
—Eastman Kodak, "for development of the EXR Color Intermediate Film 5244"
Honorary Award: Michelangelo Antonioni, for lifetime achievement

Dead Man Walking (1995) featured Sean Penn and Susan Sarandon.

1995

Best Picture: *Braveheart*
Actor: Nicolas Cage, *Leaving Las Vegas*
Actress: Susan Sarandon, *Dead Man Walking*
Supporting Actor: Kevin Spacey, *The Usual Suspects*
Supporting Actress: Mira Sorvino, *Mighty Aphrodite*
Director: Mel Gibson, *Braveheart*
Foreign-Language Film: *Antonia's Line* (The Netherlands/Belgium/UK)
Original Screenplay: Christopher McQuarrie, *The Usual Suspects*
Adapted Screenplay: Emma Thompson, *Sense and Sensibility*
Cinematographer: John Toll, *Braveheart*
Art Direction: Eugenio Zanetti, *Restoration*
Sound: Rick Dior, Steve Pederson, Scott Millan, David MacMillan, *Apollo 13*
Original Song: Music by Alan Menken, lyrics by Steven Schwartz, "Colors of the Wind" for *Pocahontas*
Original Score: Luis Bacalov, *Il Postino (The Postman)*
Film Editing: Mike Hill, Dan Hanley, *Apollo 13*
Costume Design: James Acheson, *Restoration*
Makeup: Peter Frampton, Paul Pattison, Lois Burwell, *Braveheart*
Visual Effects: Scott E. Anderson, Charles Gibson, Neal Scanlan, John Cox, *Babe*
Sound Effects Editing: Lon Bender, Per Hallberg, *Braveheart*

Short Subject—Animated: *A Close Shave*
Short Subject—Live Action: *Lieberman in Love*
Documentary—Short Subject: *One Survivor Remembers*
Documentary—Feature: *Anne Frank Remembered*
Gordon E. Sawyer Award: Donald C. Rogers
Honorary Awards:
—Kirk Douglas, "for 50 years as a creative and moral force in the motion picture community"
—Chuck Jones, "for the creation of classic cartoons and cartoon characters whose animated lives have brought joy to our real ones for more than half a century"
—John Lasseter, "for the development and inspired application of techniques that have made possible the first feature-length computer animated film"

1996

Best Picture: *The English Patient*
Actor: Geoffrey Rush, *Shine*
Actress: Frances McDormand, *Fargo*
Supporting Actor: Cuba Gooding, Jr., *Jerry Maguire*
Supporting Actress: Juliette Binoche, *The English Patient*
Director: Anthony Minghella, *The English Patient*
Foreign-Language Film: *Kolya* (Czech Republic)
Original Screenplay: Ethan Coen, Joel Coen, *Fargo*
Adapted Screenplay: Billy Bob Thornton, *Sling Blade*
Cinematographer: John Seale, *The English Patient*
Art Direction: Stuart Craig (art direction), Stephanie McMillan (set decoration), *The English Patient*
Sound: Walter Murch, Mark Berger, David Parker, Chris Newman, *The English Patient*
Original Song: Music by Andrew Lloyd Webber, lyrics by Tim Rice, "You Must Love Me" for *Evita*
Original Dramatic Score: Gabriel Yared, *The English Patient*
Original Musical or Comedy Score: Rachel Portman, *Emma*
Film Editing: Walter Murch, *The English Patient*
Costume Design: Ann Roth, *The English Patient*
Makeup: Rick Baker, David LeRoy Anderson, *The Nutty Professor*
Sound Effects Editing: Bruce Stambler, *The Ghost and the Darkness*
Visual Effects: Volker Engel, Douglas Smith, Clay Pinney, Joseph Viskocil, *Independence Day*
Short Subject—Animated: *Quest*
Short Subject—Live Action: *Dear Diary*
Documentary—Short Subject: *Breathing Lessons: The Life and Work of Mark O'Brien*
Documentary—Feature: *When We Were Kings*
Irving G. Thalberg Memorial Award: Saul Zaentz
Career Achievement Award: Michael Kidd

There's a rather overt nod to 1969's best picture winner *Midnight Cowboy* in 1994's best picture, *Forrest Gump.* It comes when crippled Vietnam War vet Gary Sinise is crossing a busy New York street with Tom Hanks's title character; as a cab pulls into the intersection and nearly hits Sinise, he screams "Hey, I'm walkin' here!" —exactly the line that Dustin Hoffman has in *Cowboy* when he's nearly hit by a cab while crossing the street with Jon Voight. However, it's not the first time Gump director Robert Zemeckis has paid tribute to John Schlesinger's classic: Zemeckis used the same gag, and had a character quote the same line of dialogue, in his time travel comedy *Back to the Future Part II* (1989).

1997

Best Picture: *Titanic*
Actor: Jack Nicholson, *As Good as It Gets*
Actress: Helen Hunt, *As Good as It Gets*
Supporting Actor: Robin Williams, *Good Will Hunting*
Supporting Actress: Kim Basinger, *L.A. Confidential*
Director: James Cameron, *Titanic*
Foreign-Language Film: *Character* (Netherlands)
Original Screenplay: Ben Affleck, Matt Damon, *Good Will Hunting*
Adapted Screenplay: Brian Helgeland, Curtis Hanson, *L.A. Confidential*
Cinematographer: Russell Carpenter, *Titanic*
Art Direction: Peter Lamont (art direction), Michael Ford (set decoration), *Titanic*
Sound: Gary Rydstrom, Tom Johnson, Gary Summers, Mark Ulano, *Titanic*
Original Song: Music by James Horner, lyrics by Will Jennings, "My Heart Will Go On" for *Titanic*
Original Dramatic Score: James Horner, *Titanic*
Original Musical or Comedy Score: Anne Dudley, *The Full Monty*
Film Editing: Conrad Buff, James Cameron, Richard A. Harris, *Titanic*
Costume Design: Deborah L. Scott, *Titanic*
Makeup: Rick Baker, David LeRoy Anderson, *Men in Black*
Sound Effects Editing: Tom Bellfort, Christopher Boyes, *Titanic*
Visual Effects: Robert Legato, Mark Lasoff, Thomas L. Fisher, Michael Kanfer, *Titanic*
Short Subject—Animated: *Geri's Game*
Short Subject—Live Action: *Visas and Virtue*
Documentary—Short Subject: *A Story of Healing*
Documentary—Feature: *The Long Way Home*
Honorary Award:
—Stanley Donen, "in appreciation of a body of work marked by grace, elegance, wit and visual innovation"
—John A. Bonner Medal of Commendation: Pete Clark, "for outstanding service and dedication in upholding the high standards of the Academy"
Academy Award of Merit: Gunnar P. Michelson, "for the engineering and development of an improved, electronic, high-speed, precision light valve for use in motion-picture printing machines"

After co-executive producing *Good Will Hunting* (1997), writer-director Kevin Smith convinced Ben Affleck and Matt Damon to spoof their Oscar-winning creations in his comic caper *Jay and Silent Bob Strike Back* (2001). Affleck and Damon, along with *Hunting* co-star Scott William Winters and director Gus Van Sant, appear as themselves on the set of a mock sequel entitled *Good Will Hunting II: Hunting Season.*

1998

Best Picture: *Shakespeare in Love*
Actor: Roberto Benigni, *Life Is Beautiful*
Actress: Gwyneth Paltrow, *Shakespeare in Love*
Supporting Actor: James Coburn, *Affliction*
Supporting Actress: Judi Dench, *Shakespeare in Love*
Director: Steven Spielberg, *Saving Private Ryan*
Foreign-Language Film: *Life Is Beautiful* (Italy)
Original Screenplay: Marc Norman, Tom Stoppard, *Shakespeare in Love*
Adapted Screenplay: Bill Condon, *Gods and Monsters*
Cinematography: Janusz Kaminski, *Saving Private Ryan*
Art Direction: Martin Childs (art direction), Jill Quertier (set decoration), *Shakespeare in Love*
Sound: Gary Rydstrom, Gary Summers, Andy Nelson, Ronald Judkins, *Saving Private Ryan*
Original Song: Stephen Schwartz, "When You Believe" for *The Prince of Egypt*
Original Dramatic Score: Nicola Piovani, *Life Is Beautiful*
Original Musical or Comedy Score: Stephen Warbeck, *Shakespeare in Love*
Film Editing: Michael Kahn, *Saving Private Ryan*
Costume Design: Sandy Powell, *Shakespeare in Love*
Makeup: Jenny Shircore, *Elizabeth*
Visual Effects: Joel Hynk, Nicholas Brooks, Stuart Robertson, Kevin Mack, *What Dreams May Come*
Sound Effects Editing: Gary Rydstrom, Richard Hymns, *Saving Private Ryan*
Short Subject—Animated: *Bunny*
Short Subject—Live Action: *Election Night*
Documentary—Short Subject: *The Personals: Improvisations on Romance in the Golden Years*
Documentary—Feature: *The Last Days*
Irving G. Thalberg Memorial Award: Norman Jewison
Honorary Award: Elia Kazan, "for lifetime achievement in directing"

1999

Best Picture: *American Beauty*
Actor: Kevin Spacey, *American Beauty*
Actress: Hilary Swank, *Boys Don't Cry*
Supporting Actor: Michael Caine, *The Cider House Rules*
Supporting Actress: Angelina Jolie, *Girl, Interrupted*
Director: Sam Mendes, *American Beauty*
Foreign-Language Film: *All About My Mother* (Spain)
Original Screenplay: Alan Ball, *American Beauty*
Adapted Screenplay: John Irving, *The Cider House Rules*
Cinematographer: Conrad L. Hall, *American Beauty*
Art Direction: Rick Heinrichs (art direction), Peter Young (set direction), *Sleepy Hollow*

Gwyneth Paltrow and Joseph Fiennes starred in the surprise Academy Award–winning hit Shakespeare in Love *(1998).*

Sound: John Reitz, Gregg Rudloff, David Campbell, David Lee, *The Matrix*
Original Song: Phil Collins, "You'll Be in My Heart" for *Tarzan*
Original Score: John Corigliano, *The Red Violin*
Film Editing: Zach Staenberg, *The Matrix*
Costume Design: Lindy Hemming, *Topsy-Turvy*
Makeup: Christine Blundell, Trefor Proud, *Topsy-Turvy*
Sound Effects Editing: Dane A. Davis, *The Matrix*
Visual Effects: John Gaeta, Janek Sirrs, Steve Courtley, Jon Thum, *The Matrix*
Short Subject—Animated: *The Old Man and the Sea*
Short Subject—Live Action: *My Mother Dreams the Satan's Disciples in New York*
Documentary—Short Subject: *King Gimp*
Documentary—Feature: *One Day in September*
Irving G. Thalberg Memorial Award: Warren Beatty
Honorary Award: Andrzej Wajda, "one of the most respected filmmakers of our time, a man whose films have given audiences around the world an artist's view of history, democracy and freedom, and who in so doing has himself become a symbol of courage and hope for millions of people in postwar Europe"

2000

Best Picture: *Gladiator*
Actor: Russell Crowe, *Gladiator*
Actress: Julia Roberts, *Erin Brockovich*
Supporting Actor: Benicio Del Toro, *Traffic*
Supporting Actress: Marcia Gay Harden, *Pollock*
Director: Steven Soderbergh, *Traffic*
Foreign-Language Film: *Crouching Tiger, Hidden Dragon* (China/Taiwan/Hong Kong/US)
Original Screenplay: Cameron Crowe, *Almost Famous*
Adapted Screenplay: Stephen Gaghan, *Traffic*
Cinematographer: Peter Pau, *Crouching Tiger, Hidden Dragon*
Art Direction: Tim Yip, *Crouching Tiger, Hidden Dragon*
Sound: Scott Millan, Bob Beemer, Ken Weston, *Gladiator*
Original Song: Bob Dylan, "Things Have Changed" for *Wonder Boys*
Original Score: Tan Dun, *Crouching Tiger, Hidden Dragon*
Film Editing: Stephen Mirrione, *Traffic*
Costume Design: Janty Yates, *Gladiator*
Makeup: Rick Baker, Gail Ryan, *Dr. Seuss' How the Grinch Stole Christmas*
Sound Editing: Jon Johnson, *U-571*
Visual Effects: John Nelson, Neil Corbould, Tim Burke, Rob Harvey, *Gladiator*
Short Subject—Animated: *Father and Daughter*
Short Subject—Live Action: *Quiero Ser (I want to be…)*
Documentary–Short Subject: *Big Mama*
Documentary–Feature: *Into the Arms of Strangers: Stories of the Kindertransport*
Gordon E. Sawyer Award: Irwin W. Young

Irving G. Thalberg Memorial Award: Dino De Laurentiis
Honorary Award:
—Ernest Lehman, "for achievement in screenwriting"
—Jack Cardiff, "for achievement in cinematography"

2001

Best Picture: *A Beautiful Mind*
Actor: Denzel Washington, *Training Day*
Actress: Halle Berry, *Monster's Ball*
Supporting Actor: Jim Broadbent, *Iris*
Supporting Actress: Jennifer Connelly, *A Beautiful Mind*
Director: Ron Howard, *A Beautiful Mind*
Foreign-Language Film: *No Man's Land* (Bosnia and Herzegovina)
Animated Feature: *Shrek*
Original Screenplay: Julian Fellowes, *Gosford Park*
Adapted Screenplay: Akiva Goldsman, *A Beautiful Mind*
Cinematographer: Andrew Lesnie, *The Lord of the Rings: The Fellowship of the Ring*
Art Direction: Catherine Martin, Brigitte Broch *Moulin Rouge*
Sound: Michael Minkler, Myron Nettinga, Chris Munro, *Black Hawk Down*
Original Song: Randy Newman, "If I Didn't Have You" from *Monsters, Inc.*
Original Score: Howard Shore, *The Lord of the Rings: The Fellowship of the Ring*
Film Editing: Pietro Scalia, *Black Hawk Down*
Costume Design: Catherine Martin and Angus Strathie, *Moulin Rouge*
Makeup: Peter Owen, Richard Taylor, *Lord of the Rings: The Fellowship of the Ring*
Sound Editing: George Watters II, Christopher Boyes, *Pearl Harbor*
Visual Effects: Jim Rygiel, Randall William Cook, Richard Taylor, Mark Stetson, *Lord of the Rings: The Fellowship of the Ring*
Short Subject—Animated: *For the Birds*
Short Subject—Live Action: *The Accountant*
Documentary—Short Subject: *Thoth*
Documentary—Feature: *Murder on a Sunday Morning*
Gordon E. Sawyer Award: Edmund M. Di Giulio
Jean Hersholt Humanitarian Award: Arthur Hiller, "by the wide diversity of his charitable and educational interests"
Honorary Award:
—Sidney Poitier, "for his extraordinary performances and unique presence on the screen, and for representing the motion picture industry with dignity, style and intelligence"
—Robert Redford, "Actor, Director, Producer, Creator of Sundance, inspiration to independent and innovative filmmakers everywhere"
—John A. Bonner Medal of Commendation: Ray Feeney, "for his pioneering efforts to improve visual effects in the motion picture industry"

Patrick Fugit (second from left) played a teenage journalist touring with a rock-and-roll band in Cameron Crowe's semi-autobiographical Almost Famous *(2000).*

Although the picture was shot entirely in Mandarin, neither Chow Yun-Fat nor Michelle Yeoh, the stars of *Crouching Tiger, Hidden Dragon* (2000), speak the language. Mandarin is the language of Mainland China; Yun-Fat and Yeoh both hail from Hong Kong, where the predominant tongue is Cantonese. To overcome this discrepancy, the two actors were forced to learn their dialogue phonetically.

THE COST
At $200 million, the movie cost more than the actual *Titanic* did. The cost to construct the ship at the time (1909 to 1912) was £1.5 million, or $7.5 million US. Accounting for inflation, this brings the total to about $120-$150 million in 1997 dollars.

THE DETAILS
To keep costs down, the number of some repeated components on the full-scale model (such as windows) was reduced, while other parts (such as the funnels and lifeboats) were built at the same ninety-percent scale as the rest of the ship to maintain a consistent visual appearance.

THE SHIP
In total, seven *Titanic* replicas were built for the film, including a 45-foot, $\frac{1}{20}$-scale model that took five months to construct. This model was used for long shots showing the whole ship's exterior, which were later augmented with computer-generated images of strolling passengers, rolling waves, and billowing smoke courtesy of Cameron's visual effects company, Digital Domain.

Historical Accuracy in Movies

"WE CAN'T CATER TO A HANDFUL of people who know Paris," MGM's Irving Thalberg, calling for an ocean in the French capital, told one of his directors back in 1925. "Whatever you put there, they'll believe that's how it is." Just as then, such is it still whenever Hollywood decides to tackle historical subject matter. While some recent films, such as *Schindler's List* (1993) and *Thirteen Days* (2000), have been applauded by scholars for their faithfulness to recorded texts, there are many more that either distort the facts for dramatic effect, or else are forced, by the constraints of time and storytelling, to simply bend the truth a little. (Vietnam vets, for example, derided the Russian roulette scenes in 1978's *The Deer Hunter*.) Eschewing Thalberg's decades-old advice, writer-director James Cameron, with his 1997 blockbuster *Titanic*, went to great— and sometimes extreme—lengths to get almost everything right.

THE DAVITS

The davits in the film were built by the same company that built them for the real *RMS Titanic*. When the original ship was constructed, there was some concern that they might not be able to support the weight of the fully-loaded lifeboats. In the finished film, they can clearly be seen flexing under the strain as the boats are being lowered.

THE LENGTH

Does size matter? The real *Titanic* was 882 feet, nine inches long, and took three years to complete. The architects of Cameron's *Titanic* used the original ship's blueprints to create a ninety-percent (775-foot) scale replica of its predecessor. Construction of both the ship and the Fox Studios-Baja facility— which included a six-acre, 17-million gallon open air water tank and four indoor soundstages—took place at Rosarito Beach, Baja California, Mexico and lasted 100 days. After filming wrapped, the remains of the full-size set were torn down and sold as scrap metal.

PORT AND STARBOARD

Because only the starboard side of the exterior set was completed, all the shots of the *Titanic* at the Southampton Docks were reversed to give the appearance that the ship was docked on its *port* side, exactly as it had been in 1912. Specially reversed costumes and signs had to be made, and the illusion was completed in post-production by simply reversing the image.

THE EXTRAS

Instead of having to constantly find new extras that would then have had to be fit for costumes and coached in 1912 mannerisms, time was saved by hiring a group of 150 "core extras" for use throughout the entire production. Proper 1912 behavior was taught in a 3-hour course led by Lynne Hockney, the film's choreographer. Hockney also produced a video, *Titanic Etiquette: A Time Traveler's Guide,* that played continuously in the film's wardrobe department.

THE LOVE SCENE

Rose (played by Kate Winslet, pictured above) and Jack's famously steamy love scene in the Renault touring car has some basis in fact. There actually was a Renault onboard the *Titanic,* owned by William E. Carter and stored on the ship's G-deck. Working from pictures from the wreckage, as well as insurance records, Cameron had an exact replica of the car built for the film.

BEYOND THE ACADEMY: OTHER NOTABLE FILM AWARDS

The Academy Awards are not the whole story. The following are several organizations that grant film awards annually.

THIS SECTION SURVEYS seven organizations that grant film awards annually. For each, there is a brief description of the institution that presents the awards, then a list of the films honored as best picture of the year or the equivalent. The honored films are shown chronologically, from the first year the given award was conferred to the present. For balance, the Golden Raspberry Awards, which dishonor what they claim are the worst films of the year, are included.

Cannes Film Festival Awards

THE FESTIVAL HAS RECOGNIZED excellence in world cinema since its founding in 1946. The grand prize for best picture is the *Palme d'Or* (Golden Palm), first awarded in 1955. Awards are presented at the festival held in Cannes, a small city in southeastern France, each May. The jury is composed of film professionals worldwide. Current categories include the Grand Prix for the film that shows the "most

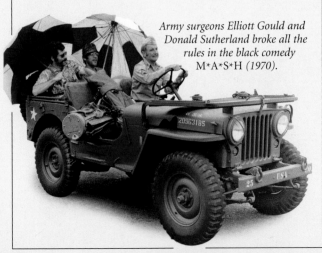

Army surgeons Elliott Gould and Donald Sutherland broke all the rules in the black comedy M*A*S*H (1970).

originality," best actress, best actor, best director, the Jury Prize (the nature of which is "determined each year"), best screenwriter, and best cinematography. Films made within the twelve months before the submission date may be entered.

PALME D'OR

1955 *Marty* (US)

1956 *Le Monde du silence (The Silent World)* (France)

1957 *Friendly Persuasion* (US)

1958 *Letjat zhuravli (The Cranes Are Flying)* (USSR)

1959 *Orfeu Negro (Black Orpheus)* (France)

1960 *La Dolce Vita* (Italy)

1961 *Viridiana* (Spain/Mexico); *Une Aussi Longue Absence (A Long Absence)* (France/Italy)

1962 *O Pagador de Promessas (The Given Word)* (Brazil)

1963 *Il Gattopardo (The Leopard)* (France/Italy)

1964 *Les Parapluies de Cherbourg (The Umbrellas of Cherbourg)* (France/West Germany)

1965 *The Knack* (UK)

1966 *Un Homme et une Femme (A Man and a Woman)* (France); *Signore and Signori (The Birds, the Bees, and the Italians)* (France/Italy)

1967 *Blow-Up* (UK/Italy)

1968 Festival canceled

1969 *If…* (UK)

1970 *M*A*S*H* (US)

1971 *The Go-Between* (UK)

1972 *Il Caso Mattei (The Mattei Affair)* (Italy); *La Classe operaia va in paradiso (The Working Class Go to Heaven)* (Italy)

1973 *Scarecrow* (US); *The Hireling* (UK)

1974 *The Conversation* (US)

1975 *Chronique des Années de Braise*
   (Chronicle of the Burning Years)
   (Algeria)

1976 *Taxi Driver* (US)

1977 *Padre padrone* (Italy)

1978 *L'Albero degli Zoccoli*
   (The Tree of Wooden Clogs) (Italy)

1979 *Die Blechtrommel (The Tin Drum)*
   (West Germany); Apocalypse Now (US)

1980 *Kagemusha* (Japan); *All That Jazz* (US)

1981 *Czloweik z Zelaza (Man of Iron)*
   (Poland)

1982 *Missing* (US); *Yol (The Way)* (Turkey)

1983 *Narayama Bushiko (The Ballad*
   of Narayama) (Japan)

1984 *Paris, Texas* (West Germany)

1985 *Otac na Sluzbenom Putu (When Father Was*
   Away on Business) (Yugoslavia)

1986 *The Mission* (UK)

1987 *Sous le Soleil de Satan (Under Satan's Sun)*
   (France)

1988 *Pelle Erobreren (Pelle the Conqueror)* (Sweden)

1989 *sex, lies, and videotape* (US)

1990 *Wild at Heart* (US)

1991 *Barton Fink* (US)

1992 *Den Goda Viljan (The Best Intentions)*
   (Sweden)

1993 *The Piano* (Australia/France); *Ba Wang Bie Ji*
   (Farewell My Concubine) (China/Hong Kong)

1994 *Pulp Fiction* (US)

1995 *Bila Jednom Jedna Zemlja (Underground)*
   (Yugoslavia/France/Germany/Hungary)

1996 *Secrets & Lies* (UK)

1997 *Ta'm e Guilass (The Taste of Cherry)* (Iran);
   Unagi (The Eel) (Japan)

1998 *Mia Aiwniothta kai Mia Mera (Eternity and*
   a Day) (Greece)

1999 *Rosetta* (Belgium)

2000 *Dancer in the Dark*
   (Denmark/Sweden/France)

2001 *La Stanza del figlio (The Son's Room)*
   (Italy/France)

Marianne Jean-Baptiste (standing, right) discovered that Brenda Blethyn (left) was her biological mother in Secrets and Lies *(1996), also starring Phyllis Logan.*

Directors Guild of America Awards

AWARDED ANNUALLY BY the Directors Guild of America (DGA) to honor the achievement of its members. The DGA is a trade organization representing directors in film and television; established in 1960, it is based in Los Angeles. The prizes are given each March and have been awarded since 1948, although originally by the Screen Directors Guild, which was founded in 1937. Current categories include Directing Excellence in film, television, movie of the week, commercial, documentary, and student Film, and a Lifetime Achievement Award.

FILM DIRECTOR'S AWARD

 1948 Joseph Mankiewicz—*A Letter to Three Wives*

 1949 Robert Rossen—*All the King's Men*

 1950 Joseph Mankiewicz—*All About Eve*

 1951 George Stevens—*A Place in the Sun*

 1952 John Ford—*The Quiet Man*

 1953 Fred Zinnemann—*From Here to Eternity*

 1954 Elia Kazan—*On the Waterfront*

 1955 Delbert Mann—*Marty*

 1956 George Stevens—*Giant*

 1957 David Lean—*Bridge on the River Kwai*

 1958 Vincente Minnelli—*Gigi*

 1959 William Wyler—*Ben-Hur*

The star-studded cast of Apollo 13 *(1995), which revisited the problematic 1970 space mission of the same name, included Kevin Bacon.*

1960 Billy Wilder—*The Apartment*
1961 Robert Wise and Jerome Robbins—
  West Side Story
1962 David Lean—*Lawrence of Arabia*
1963 Tony Richardson—*Tom Jones*
1964 George Cukor—*My Fair Lady*
1965 Robert Wise—*The Sound of Music*
1966 Fred Zinnemann—*A Man for All Seasons*
1967 Mike Nichols—*The Graduate*
1968 Anthony Harvey—*The Lion in Winter*
1969 John Schlesinger—*Midnight Cowboy*
1970 Franklin J. Schaffner—*Patton*
1971 William Friedkin—*The French Connection*
1972 Francis Ford Coppola—*The Godfather*
1973 George Roy Hill—*The Sting*
1974 Francis Ford Coppola—*The Godfather, Part II*
1975 Milos Forman—*One Flew over the Cuckoo's Nest*
1976 John G. Avildsen—*Rocky*
1977 Woody Allen—*Annie Hall*
1978 Michael Cimino—*The Deer Hunter*
1979 Robert Benton—*Kramer vs. Kramer*
1980 Robert Redford—*Ordinary People*
1981 Warren Beatty—*Reds*
1982 Richard Attenborough—*Gandhi*
1983 James Brooks—*Terms of Endearment*
1984 Milos Forman—*Amadeus*
1985 Steven Spielberg—*The Color Purple*
1986 Oliver Stone—*Platoon*
1987 Bernardo Bertolucci—*The Last Emperor*

1988 Barry Levinson—*Rain Man*
1989 Oliver Stone—*Born on the Fourth of July*
1990 Kevin Costner—*Dances with Wolves*
1991 Jonathan Demme—*The Silence of the Lambs*
1992 Clint Eastwood—*Unforgiven*
1993 Steven Spielberg—*Schindler's List*
1994 Robert Zemeckis—*Forrest Gump*
1995 Ron Howard—*Apollo 13*
1996 Anthony Minghella—*The English Patient*
1997 James Cameron—*Titanic*
1998 Steven Spielberg—*Saving Private Ryan*
1999 Sam Mendes—*American Beauty*
2000 Ang Lee—*Crouching Tiger, Hidden Dragon*
2001 Ron Howard—*A Beautiful Mind*

Golden Globe Awards

THE HOLLYWOOD FOREIGN PRESS Association has awarded the Golden Globes every January since 1944. The association is composed of film critics and journalists who cover Hollywood for foreign press organizations, newspapers, and magazines. Golden Globes represent a number of categories that span television and film. The major awards include best motion picture–drama, best motion picture–comedy or musical, and best director, actress, actor, cinematography, and documentary, as well as best television series–drama, best television series–comedy, and best television actress and actor. The Lifetime Achievement Award is named after film director Cecil B. DeMille.

BEST MOTION PICTURE—DRAMA

1944 *The Song of Bernadette*
1945 *Going My Way*
1946 *The Lost Weekend*
1947 *The Best Years of Our Lives*
1948 *Gentleman's Agreement*
1949 *Treasure of the Sierra Madre; Johnny Belinda*
1950 *All the King's Men*
1951 *Sunset Boulevard*
1952 *A Place in the Sun*
1953 *The Greatest Show on Earth*
1954 *The Robe*

1955 *On the Waterfront*
1956 *East of Eden*
1957 *Around the World in 80 Days*
1958 *The Bridge on the River Kwai* (UK)
1959 *The Defiant Ones*
1960 *Ben-Hur*
1961 *Spartacus*
1962 *The Guns of Navarone*
1963 *Lawrence of Arabia* (UK)
1964 *The Cardinal*
1965 *Becket* (UK)
1966 *Doctor Zhivago*
1967 *A Man for All Seasons* (UK)
1968 *In the Heat of the Night*
1969 *The Lion in Winter* (UK)
1970 *Anne of a Thousand Days* (UK)
1971 *Love Story*
1972 *The French Connection*
1973 *The Godfather*
1974 *The Exorcist*
1975 *Chinatown*
1976 *One Flew over the Cuckoo's Nest*
1977 *Rocky*
1978 *The Turning Point*
1979 *Midnight Express*
1980 *Kramer vs. Kramer*
1981 *Ordinary People*
1982 *On Golden Pond*
1983 *E.T.: The Extra-Terrestrial*
1984 *Terms of Endearment*
1985 *Amadeus*
1986 *Out of Africa*
1987 *Platoon*
1988 *The Last Emperor*
        (Italy/UK/China)
1989 *Rain Man*
1990 *Born on the Fourth of July*
1991 *Dances with Wolves*
1992 *Bugsy*
1993 *Scent of a Woman*
1994 *Schindler's List*
1995 *Forrest Gump*
1996 *Sense and Sensibility* (US/UK)
1997 *The English Patient*

1998 *Titanic*
1999 *Saving Private Ryan*
2000 *American Beauty*
2001 *Gladiator*

BEST MOTION PICTURE—COMEDY OR MUSICAL

1952 *An American in Paris*
1953 *With a Song in My Heart*
1955 *Carmen Jones*
1956 *Guys and Dolls*
1957 *The King and I*
1958 *Les Girls*
1959 *Gigi* (Musical)
        Auntie Mame (Comedy)
1960 *Porgy and Bess* (Musical)
        Some Like It Hot (Comedy)
1961 *Song Without End* (Musical)
        The Apartment (Comedy)

Gene Kelly choreographed and starred in An American in Paris *(1951).*

1962	*West Side Story* (Musical)
	A Majority of One (Comedy)
1963	*The Music Man* (Musical)
	That Touch of Mink (Comedy)
1964	*Tom Jones* (UK)
1965	*My Fair Lady*
1966	*The Sound of Music*
1967	*The Russians Are Coming!*
	The Russians Are Coming!
1968	*The Graduate*
1969	*Funny Girl*
1970	*The Secret of Santa Vittoria*
1971	*M*A*S*H*
1972	*Fiddler on the Roof*
1973	*Cabaret*
1974	*American Graffiti*
1975	*The Longest Yard*
1976	*The Sunshine Boys*
1977	*A Star Is Born*
1978	*The Goodbye Girl*
1979	*Heaven Can Wait*
1980	*Breaking Away*
1981	*Coal Miner's Daughter*
1982	*Arthur*
1983	*Tootsie*
1984	*Yentl*
1985	*Romancing the Stone*
1986	*Prizzi's Honor*
1987	*Hannah and Her Sisters*
1988	*Hope and Glory* (UK)
1989	*Working Girl*
1990	*Driving Miss Daisy*
1991	*Green Card*
1992	*Beauty and the Beast*
1993	*The Player*
1994	*Mrs. Doubtfire*
1995	*The Lion King*
1996	*Babe* (Australia)
1997	*Evita*
1998	*As Good as It Gets*
1999	*Shakespeare in Love* (US/UK)
2000	*Toy Story 2*
2001	*Almost Famous*

Golden Raspberry Awards

FOUNDED BY AUTHOR JOHN WILSON in 1980, the Golden Raspberry Awards, or "Razzies," are probably the best-publicized bad-movie awards. According to the awarding body, the Golden Raspberry Award Foundation, the awards target "Hollywood's High-Profile Humiliations" rather than "the easier target of low-budget/drive-in fare." They are presented in the Los Angeles area every spring. Categories include worst picture, worst actor, worst actress, worst screen couple, worst director, worst remake or sequel, and the Joe Eszterhas Dis-Honorarial Worst Screenplay Award.

WORST PICTURE AWARDS

1980	*Can't Stop the Music*
1981	*Mommie Dearest*
1982	*Inchon*
1983	*The Lonely Lady*
1984	*Bolero*
1985	*Rambo: First Blood Part II*
1986	*Howard the Duck; Under the Cherry Moon*
1987	*Leonard Part 6*
1988	*Cocktail*
1989	*Star Trek V*
1990	*Adventures of Ford Fairlane; Ghosts Can't Do It*
1991	*Hudson Hawk*
1992	*Shining Through*
1993	*Indecent Proposal*
1994	*Color of Night*
1995	*Showgirls*
1996	*Striptease*
1997	*The Postman*
1998	*An Alan Smithee Film: Burn, Hollywood, Burn!*
1999	*Wild Wild West*
2000	*Battlefield Earth*
2001	*Freddy Got Fingered*

The Postman (1997) was directed by Kevin Costner, who also starred in the film.

Terry Gilliam of Monty Python fame wrote and directed Brazil *(1985), starring Jonathan Pryce.*

Los Angeles Film Critics Awards

AWARDED EACH DECEMBER since 1975 by members of the Los Angeles Film Critics Association, which is composed of film critics and journalists working in Los Angeles. Categories include best picture, best foreign film, best director, best actress, best actor, best cinematography, and a career achievement award.

BEST PICTURE

1975	*Dog Day Afternoon;*
	One Flew over the Cuckoo's Nest
1976	*Rocky*
1977	*Star Wars*
1978	*Coming Home*
1979	*Kramer vs. Kramer*
1980	*Raging Bull*
1981	*Atlantic City*
1982	*E.T.: The Extra-Terrestrial*
1983	*Terms of Endearment*
1984	*Amadeus*
1985	*Brazil*
1986	*Hannah and Her Sisters*
1987	*Hope and Glory* (UK)
1988	*Little Dorrit* (UK)
1989	*Do the Right Thing*
1990	*GoodFellas*
1991	*Bugsy*
1992	*Unforgiven*
1993	*Schindler's List*
1994	*Pulp Fiction*
1995	*Leaving Las Vegas*
1996	*Secrets & Lies* (UK)
1997	*L.A. Confidential*
1998	*Saving Private Ryan*
1999	*The Tiger*
2000	*Crouching Tiger, Hidden Dragon*
2001	*In The Bedroom*

OVERLEAF:

The British film Hope and Glory *(1987), starring Geraldine Muir and Sebastian Rice-Edwards, was honored as best picture at the Los Angeles Film Critics Awards.*

473

National Society of Film Critics Awards

AWARDED IN DECEMBER OR JANUARY since 1966 and selected by the National Society of Film Critics, an association of critics and journalists writing for national newspapers and magazines, most in Los Angeles or New York City. Categories include best picture, best foreign film, best director, best actress, best actor, and best screenplay.

BEST PICTURE

1966 *Blow-Up* (UK/Italy)
1967 *Persona* (Sweden)
1968 *Skammen (The Shame)* (Sweden)
1969 *Z* (France/Algeria)
1970 *M*A*S*H* (US)
1971 *Genou de Claire (Claire's Knee)* (France)
1972 *Le Charme Discret de la Bourgeoisie
        (The Discreet Charm of the Bourgeoisie)*
        (France/Spain/Italy)
1973 *La Nuit américaine (Day for Night)* (France)
1974 *Scener ur ett Äktenskap (Scenes from a
        Marriage)* (Sweden)
1975 *Nashville* (US)
1976 *All the President's Men* (US)
1977 *Annie Hall* (US)
1978 *Days of Heaven* (US); *Préparez vous Mouchoirs
        (Get Out Your Handkerchiefs)* (France)
1979 *Breaking Away* (US)
1980 *Melvin and Howard* (US)
1981 *Atlantic City* (US)

Burt Lancaster played an aging gangster in Atlantic City *(1981).*

1982 *Tootsie* (US)
1983 *La Notte di San Lorenzo
        (The Night of the Shooting Stars)* (Italy)
1984 *Stranger Than Paradise* (US)
1985 *Ran* (Japan)
1986 *Blue Velvet* (US)
1987 *The Dead* (UK); *Hope and Glory* (UK)
1988 *The Unbearable Lightness of Being* (US)
1989 *Drugstore Cowboy* (US)
1990 *GoodFellas* (US)
1991 *Life Is Sweet* (UK)
1992 *Unforgiven* (US)
1993 *Schindler's List* (US)
1994 *Pulp Fiction* (US)
1995 *Babe* (Australia)
1996 *Breaking the Waves*
        (Denmark/Sweden/
        France/Netherlands)
1997 *L.A. Confidential* (US)
1998 *Out of Sight* (US)
1999 *Being John Malkovich* (US); *Topsy Turvy* (UK)
2000 *Yi Yi (Taiwan/ Japan)*
2001 *Mulholland Dr.* (US)

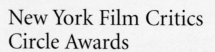

Babe (1995) used live animals, puppets, and animatronics.

New York Film Critics Circle Awards

AWARDED EVERY DECEMBER by the New York Film Critics Circle, an association of film critics and writers working in New York City. The awards began in 1935 as a response to the Hollywood politics that influenced the selection of the Academy Awards. Categories include best picture, best foreign film, best director, best actress, best actor, and best cinematography.

BEST PICTURE

1935 *The Informer*
1936 *Mr. Deeds Goes to Town*
1937 *The Life of Emile Zola*
1938 *The Citadel*
1939 *Wuthering Heights*
1940 *The Grapes of Wrath*
1941 *Citizen Kane*

1942 *In Which We Serve*

1943 *Watch on the Rhine*

1944 *Going My Way*

1945 *The Lost Weekend*

1946 *The Best Years of Our Lives*

1947 *Gentleman's Agreement*

1948 *The Treasure of the Sierra Madre*

1949 *All the King's Men*

1950 *All About Eve*

1951 *A Streetcar Named Desire*

1952 *High Noon*

1953 *From Here to Eternity*

1954 *On the Waterfront*

1955 *Marty*

1956 *Around the World in 80 Days*

1957 *Bridge on the River Kwai* (UK)

1958 *The Defiant Ones*

1959 *Ben-Hur*

1960 *The Apartment*

1961 *West Side Story*

1962 No award given (newspaper strike)

1963 *Tom Jones* (UK)

1964 *My Fair Lady*

1965 *Darling*

1966 *A Man for All Seasons* (UK)

1967 *In the Heat of the Night*

1968 *The Lion in Winter* (UK)

1969 *Z* (France/Algeria)

1970 *Five Easy Pieces*

1971 *A Clockwork Orange*

1972 *Viskninger och Rop (Cries and Whispers)*
(Sweden)

1973 *La Nuit américaine (Day for Night)* (France)

1974 *Amarcord* (Italy)

1975 *Nashville*

1976 *All the President's Men*

1977 *Annie Hall*

1978 *The Deer Hunter*

1979 *Kramer vs. Kramer*

1980 *Ordinary People*

1981 *Reds*

1982 *Gandhi* (US/UK/India)

1983 *Terms of Endearment*

1984 *A Passage to India* (UK)

Kathleen Turner starred in Prizzi's Honor *(1985), a black comedy about the Mob.*

1985 *Prizzi's Honor*

1986 *Hannah and Her Sisters*

1987 *Broadcast News*

1988 *The Accidental Tourist*

1989 *My Left Foot* (Ireland/UK)

1990 *GoodFellas*

1991 *The Silence of the Lambs*

1992 *The Player*

1993 *Schindler's List*

1994 *Quiz Show*

1995 *Leaving Las Vegas*

1996 *Fargo*

1997 *L.A. Confidential*

1998 *Saving Private Ryan*

1999 *Topsy-Turvy*

2000 *Traffic*

2001 *Mulholland Dr.*

MOVIE QUOTATIONS

Movies have given us some of the most memorable phrases in history. Here is a compendium of more than 300 quotations from the earliest talkies to the present.

Quotes are presented chronologically by year of release. To include the greatest possible number of films, no film has been represented by more than one quotation. With each quotation, the actor speaking the line is named, with his or her character's name in parentheses.

"Wait a minute, wait a minute, you ain't heard nothin' yet!"

—*Al Jolson (Jakie Rabinowitz/Jack Robin),* The Jazz Singer *(1927), first line in a sound feature*

"I'll meet you tonight under the moon. Oh, I can see you now, you and the moon. You wear a necktie so I'll know you."

—*Groucho Marx (Mr. Hammer) to Margaret Dumont (Mrs. Potter),* The Cocoanuts *(1929)*

"Would you be shocked if I put on something more comfortable?"

—*Jean Harlow (Helen) to Ben Lyon (Monte Rutledge),* Hell's Angels *(1930)*

"Mother of Mercy! Is this the end of Rico?"

—*Edward G. Robinson (Caesar Enrico Bandelli), as he dies in the movie's finale,* Little Caesar *(1930), last line*

"Listen to them. Children of the night. What music they make."

—*Bela Lugosi (Count Dracula) on wolves,* Dracula *(1931)*

"It's alive! It's alive!"

—*Colin Clive (Henry Frankenstein) on creating his monster,* Frankenstein *(1931)*

"I'd love to kiss you, but I just washed my hair."

—*Bette Davis (Madge),* Cabin in the Cotton *(1932)*

"Grand Hotel. Always the same. People come. People go. Nothing ever happens."

—*Lewis Stone (Dr. Otternschlag),* Grand Hotel *(1932)*

"I'd horsewhip you, if I had a horse."

—*Groucho Marx (Professor Quincy Adams Wagstaff) to Zeppo Marx (Frank Wagstaff),* Horse Feathers *(1932)*

Cloakroom Girl: "Goodness, what beautiful diamonds!" *Mae West (Mandie Triplett):* "Goodness had nothing to do with it, dearie."

—Night After Night *(1932)*

Jean Harlow (Kitty Packard): "I was reading a book the other day....Do you know that the guy said that machinery is going to take the place of every profession." *Marie Dressler (Carlotta Vance):* "Oh, my dear, that's something you need never worry about."

—Dinner at Eight *(1933)*

Margaret Dumont (Mrs. Teasdale): "Oh, Your Excellency!" *Groucho Marx (Rufus T. Firefly):* "You're not so bad yourself."

—Duck Soup *(1933)*

"And, Sawyer, you're going out a youngster, but you've got to come back a star!"

—*Warner Baxter (Julian Marsh) to Ruby Keeler (Peggy Sawyer),* 42ND Street *(1933)*

"Chance is the fool's name for fate."

—*Fred Astaire (Guy Holden) to Edward Everett Horton (Egbert Fitzgerald),* The Gay Divorcée *(1934)*

"We'll begin with a reign of terror—a few murders here and there. Murders of great men, murders of little men. Just to show we make no distinction."

—*Claude Rains (Jack Griffin) to William Harrigan (Kemp),* The Invisible Man *(1933)*

"Beulah, peel me a grape."

—*Mae West (Tira) to Gertrude Howard (Beulah),* I'm No Angel *(1933)*

Charles Laughton (Dr. Moreau): "What is the law?" *Bela Lugosi (Sayer of the Law):* "Not to run on all fours. That is the law. Are we not men?"

—Island of Lost Souls *(1933)*

"Oh no. It wasn't the airplanes. It was Beauty killed the Beast."

—*Robert Armstrong (Carl Denham) to a police officer, concerning King Kong's death in the finale,* King Kong *(1933)*

"Why don't you come up sometime and see me?"

—*Mae West (Lady Lou) to Cary Grant (Captain Cummings),* She Done Him Wrong *(1933)*

Mae West played a floozy with a penchant for extortion in I'm No Angel *(1933)*

"Well, here's another nice mess you've gotten me into!"

—*Oliver Hardy (Himself) to Stan Laurel (Himself),* Sons of the Desert *(1933)*

"My soul, woman, I give you three murders and you're still not satisfied."

—*William Powell (Nick Charles) to Myrna Loy (Nora Charles),* The Thin Man *(1934)*

"Well, I proved once and for all that the limb is mightier than the thumb."

—*Claudette Colbert (Ellie Andrews) to Clark Gable (Peter Warne), on raising her skirt to hitch a ride,* It Happened One Night *(1934)*

"The only fun I get is feeding the goldfish, and they only eat once a day."

—*Bette Davis (Marie Roark),* Bordertown *(1935)*

"'Twas I informed on your son, Mrs. McPhillip. Forgive me."

—*Victor McLaglen (Gypo Nolan) to Una O'Connor (Mrs. McPhillip),* The Informer *(1935)*

"I'll take my chance against the law. You'll take yours against the sea."

—*Clark Gable (Fletcher Christian) to Charles Laughton (Captain Bligh),* Mutiny on the Bounty *(1935)*

Groucho Marx (Otis B. Driftwood): "Have you got any milk-fed chickens?" *Waiter:* "Yes, sir." *Marx:* "Well, squeeze the milk out of one and bring me a glass."

—A Night at the Opera *(1935)*

"It's a far, far better thing I do than I have ever done. It's a far, far better rest I go to than I have ever known."

—*Ronald Colman (Sidney Carton), A Tale of Two Cities (1935), last line*

"Allow us to introduce ourselves. We are Bates."

—*Eric Blore (Bates) to Fred Astaire (Jerry Travers), Top Hat (1935)*

"I've got to have more steps. I need more steps. I've got to get higher, higher!"

—*William Powell (Florenz Ziegfeld), The Great Ziegfeld (1936), last line*

William Powell and Luise Rainer starred in The Great Ziegfeld *(1936), a biography of showman Florenz Ziegfeld*

"Why, everybody in Mandrake Falls is pixilated—except us."

—*Margaret Seddon (Jane Faulkner), Mr. Deeds Goes to Town (1936)*

"Never give a sucker an even break."

—*W.C. Fields (Professor Eustace McGargle) to Rochelle Hudson (Poppy), Poppy (1936)*

"Is it this or that—all the universe or nothing? Which shall it be, Passworthy? Which shall it be?"

—*Raymond Massey (John/Oswald Cabal) to Edward Chapman (Pippa/Raymond Passworthy), Things to Come (1936, UK), last line*

"To you, my little prairie flower: I'm thinkin' of you every hour. Though now you're just a friend to me, I wonder what the end will be. Oh, you would make my life divine If you would change your name to mine."

—*Ralph Bellamy (Daniel Leeson) to Irene Dunne (Lucy Warriner), The Awful Truth (1937)*

"O-Lan, you are the earth."

—*Paul Muni (Wang Lung) to Luise Rainer (O-Lan), The Good Earth (1937), last line*

"The calla lilies are in bloom again."

—*Katharine Hepburn (Terry Randall), Stage Door (1937)*

"Hello, everybody. This is Mrs. Norman Maine."

—*Janet Gaynor (Esther Blodgett/Vicki Lester), A Star Is Born (1937), last line; reprised by Judy Garland in the same role in A Star Is Born (1954), last line*

"Welcome to Sherwood, my lady!"

—*Errol Flynn (Robin Hood) to Olivia de Havilland (Maid Marian), The Adventures of Robin Hood (1938)*

Joseph Calleia (Slimane): "I'm sorry, Pepe. He thought you were going to escape." *Charles Boyer (Pepe Le Moko, dying):* "And so I have, my friend."

—Algiers *(1938), last lines*

ROCKY DIES YELLOW KILLER COWARD AT END

—*Newspaper headline describing how James Cagney (Rocky Sullivan) acted at his execution,* Angels with Dirty Faces *(1938)*

"In a pinch I can be tougher than you are, and I guess maybe this is the pinch."

—*Spencer Tracy (Father Flanagan) to Mickey Rooney (Whitey Marsh),* Boys Town *(1938)*

"Because I just went gay all of a sudden!"

—*Cary Grant (David Huxley) to May Robson (Aunt Elizabeth), explaining why he is wearing a woman's negligee,* Bringing Up Baby *(1938)*

"Frankly, my dear, I don't give a damn."

—*Clark Gable (Rhett Butler), to Vivian Leigh (Scarlett O'Hara), on her question about her future,* Gone with the Wind *(1939)*

"Very regimental, Din."

—*Cary Grant (Cutter) to Sam Jaffe (Gunga Din),* Gunga Din *(1939)*

"Dad always used to say the only causes worth fighting for were the lost causes."

—*James Stewart (Jefferson Smith) to Claude Rains (Senator Joseph Paine),* Mr. Smith Goes to Washington *(1939)*

"Ninotchka, it's midnight. One half of Paris is making love to the other half."

—*Melvyn Douglas (Count Leon Dalga) to Greta Garbo (Lena "Ninotchka" Yakushova),* Ninotchka *(1939)*

"I'm hard to get, Geoff. All you have to do is ask me."

—*Jean Arthur (Bonnie Lee) to Cary Grant (Geoff Carter),* Only Angels Have Wings *(1939)*

"Well, they're saved from the blessings of civilization."

—*George Bancroft (Sheriff Curly Wilcox) to Thomas Mitchell (Dr. Josiah Boone), on the escape of John Wayne (the Ringo Kid) and Claire Trevor (Dallas),* Stagecoach *(1939), last line*

"Toto, I've a feeling we're not in Kansas anymore."

—*Judy Garland (Dorothy) to her dog Toto on arriving in Oz,* The Wizard of Oz *(1939)*

"There's a name for you ladies, but it isn't used in high society— outside of a kennel."

—*Joan Crawford (Crystal Allen),* The Women *(1939)*

"If you can't sleep at night, it isn't the coffee— it's the bunk."

—*Dick Powell (Jimmy MacDonald), coining an advertising slogan,* Christmas in July *(1940)*

"Wherever there's a fight so hungry people can eat, I'll be there. Wherever there's a cop beatin' up a guy, I'll be there. I'll be in the way guys yell when they're mad. I'll be in the way kids laugh when they're hungry an' they know supper's ready. An' when the people are eatin' the stuff they raise, livin' in the homes they build—I'll be there, too."

—*Henry Fonda (Tom Joad) to Jane Darwell (Ma Joad),* The Grapes of Wrath *(1940)*

"Well, who's gonna read the second paragraph?"

—*Cary Grant (Walter Burns) offering editorial advice to reporter Rosalind Russell (Hildy Johnson),* His Girl Friday *(1940)*

"My, she was yare."

—*Katharine Hepburn (Tracy Lord) on her favorite boat,* The Philadelphia Story *(1940)*

"I'm going to show you what yum-yum is. Here's yum. Here's the other yum. And here's yum-yum."

—*Barbara Stanwyck (Sugarpuss O'Shea) kissing Gary Cooper (Professor Bertram Potts),* Ball of Fire *(1941)*

"Rosebud."

—*Orson Welles (Charles Foster Kane), dying,* Citizen Kane *(1941), first line*

"My business is anything that comes between man and the spirit of God."

—*Walter Pidgeon (Mr. Gruffydd), a minister, to Arthur Shields (Mr. Parry),* How Green Was My Valley *(1941)*

"See, Hopsy, you don't know very much about girls. The best ones aren't as good as you probably think, and the worst aren't as bad. Not nearly as bad."

—*Barbara Stanwyck (Jean Harrington) to Henry Fonda (Charles Pike),* The Lady Eve *(1941)*

"Yes, angel, I'm gonna send you over."

—*Humphrey Bogart (Sam Spade), preparing to deliver Mary Astor (Brigid O'Shaughnessy) to the police,* The Maltese Falcon *(1941)*

"All those nice, sweet, lovable people become heelots. A lotta heels!"

—*Walter Brennan (The Colonel),* Meet John Doe *(1941)*

"I was in love with a beautiful blond once. She drove me to drink, 'Tis the one thing I'm indebted to her for."

—*W.C. Fields (The Great Man),* Never Give a Sucker an Even Break *(1941)*

"There's a lot to be said for making people laugh. Did you know that's all some people have? It isn't much, but it's better than nothing in this cockeyed caravan. Boy."

—*Joel McCrea (John L. Sullivan),* Sullivan's Travels *(1941), last line*

"Even a man who is pure in heart, And says his prayers by night, May become a wolf when the wolfbane blooms, And the autumn moon is bright."

—*Poem recited by Evelyn Ankers (Gwen Conliffe), Claude Rains (Sir John Talbot), and Fay Helm (Jenny Williams),* The Wolf Man *(1941)*

Bobby Stewart (Bambi, a deer): "What happened, Mother? Why did we all run?" *Bambi's mother:* "Man was in the forest."

—Bambi *(1942)*

"We'll always have Paris."

—*Humphrey Bogart (Rick Blaine) to Ingrid Bergman (Ilsa Lund),* Casablanca *(1942)*

"This is the people's war. It is our war. We are the fighters. Fight it, then. Fight it with all that is in us, and may God defend the right."

—*Henry Wilcoxon (Vicar),* Mrs. Miniver *(1942), last line*

"Oh, Jerry, don't let's ask for the moon. We have the stars."

—*Bette Davis (Charlotte Vale) to Paul Henreid (Jerry Durrance),* Now, Voyager *(1942), last line*

"There are a lot of inconveniences to yachting that most people don't know anything about."

—*Rudy Vallee (John D. Hackensacker III) to Claudette Colbert (Gerry Jeffers),* The Palm Beach Story *(1942)*

"People all say that I've had a bad break, but today—today I consider myself the luckiest man on the face of the earth."

—*Gary Cooper (Lou Gehrig) to his fans,* The Pride of the Yankees *(1942)*

"My mother thanks you. My father thanks you. My sister thanks you. And I thank you."

—*James Cagney (George M. Cohan) to audience,* Yankee Doodle Dandy *(1942)*

"To the gallant officers and men of the silent service, to our submarines now on war patrol in hostile waters, good luck and good hunting."

—*Lou Marcelle (Narrator),* Destination Tokyo *(1943), last line*

"There comes a time in every woman's life when the only thing that helps is a glass of champagne."

—*Bette Davis (Kitty Marlowe),* Old Acquaintance *(1943)*

"Insanity runs in my family. It practically gallops."

—*Cary Grant (Mortimer Brewster) to Priscilla Lane (Elaine Harper),* Arsenic and Old Lace *(1944)*

"I killed him for money and for a woman. And I didn't get the money and I didn't get the woman. Pretty, isn't it?"

—*Fred MacMurray (Walter Neff) recording a confession of his murder of the husband of Barbara Stanwyck (Phyllis Dietrichson) for insurance investigator Edward G. Robinson (Barton Keyes),* Double Indemnity *(1944)*

"Y'know, at one time I had quite a decision to make: whether to write the nation's songs or go my way."

—*Bing Crosby (Father Chuck O'Malley),* Going My Way *(1944)*

"A doll in Washington Heights once got a fox fur out of me."

—*Dana Andrews (Mark McPherson) to Clifton Webb (Waldo Lydecker), on whether he has ever been in love,* Laura *(1944)*

"Nobody believes good unless they have to, if they've got a chance to believe something bad."

—*Diana Lynn (Emmy) to Betty Hutton (Trudy Kockenlocker),* The Miracle of Morgan's Creek *(1944)*

"The Thirty-Nine Steps is an organization of spies, collecting information on behalf of the foreign office of—"

—*Wylie Watson (Mr. Memory),* Thirty Seconds Over Tokyo *(1944)*

Bing Crosby (Father Chuck O'Malley): "If you ever need anything, no matter what it is or wherever you happen to be—" *Ingrid Bergman (Sister Benedict):* "Yes, I know. I just dial O for O'Malley."

—The Bells of St. Mary's *(1945)*

"Personally, Veda's convinced me that alligators have the right idea. They eat their young."

—*Eve Arden (Ida) to Joan Crawford (Mildred Pierce),* Mildred Pierce *(1945)*

Joan Crawford, pictured here with Jack Carson, won an Academy Award for Mildred Pierce *(1945).*

Bud Abbott (Dexter): "Now on the St. Louis team we have Who's on first, What's on second, I Don't Know is on third—" *Lou Costello (Sebastian):* "That's what I want to find out. I want you to tell me the names of the fellows on the St. Louis team." *Abbott:* "I'm telling you: Who's on first, What's on Second, I Don't Know is on third…"

—The Naughty Nineties *(1945)*

Humphrey Bogart (Philip Marlowe): "What's wrong with you?" *Lauren Bacall (Vivian):* "Nothing you can't fix."

—The Big Sleep *(1946), last lines*

"If I'd been a ranch, they would've named me the Bar Nothing."

—Rita Hayworth (Gilda) to a male escort, Gilda *(1946)*

"Dear George, remember no man is a failure who has friends. Thanks for the wings! Love Clarence."

—Written message left by Henry Travers (Clarence Odbody, Angel Second Class) for James Stewart (George Bailey), It's a Wonderful Life *(1946)*

"Ma'am, I sure like that name—Clementine."

—Henry Fonda (Wyatt Earp) to Cathy Downs (Clementine Carter), My Darling Clementine *(1946), last line*

Ingrid Bergman (Alicia Huberman): "This is a very strange love affair." *Cary Grant (Bruce Devlin):* "Why?" *Bergman:* "Maybe the fact that you don't love me."

—Notorious *(1946)*

"One thing I can't stand, it's a dame that's drunk."

—Edward G. Robinson (Johnny Rocco), Key Largo *(1948)*

"If you ain't eating Wham, you ain't eating ham."

—Louise Beavers (Gussie), Mr. Blandings Builds His Dream House *(1948)*

Gilda *(1946) helped seal Rita Hayworth's reputation as a Hollywood bombshell.*

"There are eight million stories in the naked city. This has been one of them."

—Mark Hellinger (Narrator), The Naked City *(1948)*

"When we get back to the ranch, I want you to change the brand. It'll be like this, the Red River D, and we'll add a name to it. You don't mind that, do you?… You've earned it."

—John Wayne (Tom Dunson) to Montgomery Clift (Matthew Garth), revising his brand for the steer to add Clift's name, Red River *(1948), last line*

"Badges? We ain't got no badges! We don't need no badges! I don't have to show you any stinking badges!"

—Alfonso Bedoya (Gold Hat) to Humphrey Bogart (Fred C. Dobbs), The Treasure of the Sierra Madre *(1948)*

"I'm old-fashioned. I like two sexes."

—Spencer Tracy (Adam Bonner) to Katharine Hepburn (Amanda Bonner), Adam's Rib *(1949)*

"What can I do, old man? I'm dead, aren't I?"

—Orson Welles (Harry Lime) to Joseph Cotton (Holly Martins), The Third Man *(1949, UK)*

"What a dump."

—*Bette Davis (Rosa Moline),*
Beyond the Forest *(1949)*

"Don't apologize. It's
a sign of weakness."

—*John Wayne
(Capt. Nathan Brittles),*
She Wore a Yellow Ribbon *(1949)*

"Fasten your seat belts, it's
going to be a bumpy night."

—*Bette Davis (Margo Channing) to
party group,* All About Eve *(1950)*

"In this world, Elwood, you
must be, oh so smart, or oh
so pleasant. For years, I was
smart. I recommend
pleasant. And you
may quote me."

—*James Stewart (Elwood P. Dowd)
repeating his mother's advice to
Cecil Kellaway (Dr. Chumley),*
Harvey *(1950)*

"I am big. It's the pictures
that got small."

—*Gloria Swanson (Norma
Desmond), faded silent-screen star,
to William Holden (Joe Gillis),*
Sunset Boulevard *(1950)*

"Nature, Mr. Allnut,
is what we are put in this
world to rise above."

—*Katharine Hepburn (Rose Sayer)
to Humphrey Bogart
(Charlie Allnut),*
The African Queen *(1951)*

"Gort. Klaatu baraada nikto."

—*Patricia Neal (Helen Benson)
giving an alien message to robot Lock
Martin (Gort),* The Day the Earth
Stood Still *(1951)*

"Hey, Stella! Hey, Stella!"

—*Marlon Brando (Stanley
Kowalski) to Kim Hunter (Stella),* A
Streetcar Named Desire *(1951),
last line*

"Every one of you listening
to my voice, tell the world.
Tell this to everybody,
wherever they are. Watch the
skies, everywhere, keep
looking. Keep watching
the skies."

—*Douglas Spencer (Ned "Scotty"
Scott),* The Thing from Another
World *(1951), last line*

"You wanna bite
somebody?…
Well, pick your spot."

—*Gloria Grahame (Angel) to
Charlton Heston (Brad),* The
Greatest Show on Earth *(1952)*

"The judge has left town,
Harvey's quit, and I'm havin'
trouble gettin' deputies."

—*Gary Cooper (Marshal Will Kane)
to Lon Chaney, Jr. (Martin Howe),*
High Noon *(1952)*

"And I can't stan' 'im."

—*Jean Hagen (Lina Lamont)
practicing her diction,*
Singin' in the Rain *(1952)*

"Not much meat on her, but
what's there is cherce."

—*Spencer Tracy (Mike Conovan)
on Katharine Hepburn (Pat
Pemberton),* Pat and Mike *(1952)*

"No pattyfingers, if you
please. The proprieties at
all times. Hold on
to your hats."

—*Barry Fitzgerald (Michaeleen
Flynn) to Victor McLaglen (Red Will
Danaher) and Mildred Natwick
(Mrs. Sarah Tillane),*
The Quiet Man *(1952), last line*

"I can stand anything
but pain."

—*Oscar Levant (Lester Marton),*
The Band Wagon *(1953)*

"I never knew it could
be like this."

—*Deborah Kerr (Karen
Holmes) to Burt Lancaster
(Sgt. Milton Warden),*
From Here to Eternity *(1953)*

"I always say a kiss on the
hand might feel very good
but a diamond tiara
lasts forever."

—*Marilyn Monroe (Lorelei) to
Charles Coburn (Sir Francis
Beekman),* Gentlemen Prefer
Blondes *(1953)*

OVERLEAF:

The beach love scene in From
Here to Eternity *(1953), starring
Deborah Kerr and Burt Lancaster,
became one of Hollywood's most
recognizable screen moments.*

"There it is, Wendy. Second star to the right and straight on till morning."

—*Bobby Driscoll (Peter Pan) to Kathryn Beaumont (Wendy),* Peter Pan *(1953)*

"He forgave you from the cross. Can I do less?"

—*Michael Rennie (St. Peter) to Richard Burton (Marcellus Gallio),* The Robe *(1953)*

"The Mouth of Truth. Legend is that if you're given to lying, you put your hand in there, it'll be bitten off."

—*Gregory Peck (Joe Bradley) to Audrey Hepburn (Princess Anne),* Roman Holiday *(1953)*

"Pa's got things for you to do, and Mother wants you. I know she does. Shane. Shane. Come back. 'Bye, Shane."

—*Brandon de Wilde (Joey Starrett) to Alan Ladd (Shane),* Shane *(1953), last line*

"Nobody has ever escaped from Stalag 17. Not alive, anyway."

—*Otto Preminger (Oberst Von Scherbach) to prisoners,* Stalag 17 *(1953)*

"Ah, but the strawberries! That's…that's where I had them."

—*Humphrey Bogart (Captain Queeg),* The Caine Mutiny *(1954)*

Woman in Bar:
"Hey, Johnny, what are you rebelling against?"
Marlon Brando (Johnny):
"What've you got?"

—The Wild One *(1953)*

"You don't understand! I could've had class. I could've been a contender. I could've been somebody, instead of a bum, which is what I am."

—*Marlon Brando (Terry Malloy),* On the Waterfront *(1954)*

"Nobody ever invented a polite word for a killing yet."

—*Thelma Ritter (Stella) to Grace Kelly (Lisa Fremont),* Rear Window *(1954)*

"Democracy can be a wickedly unfair thing. Nobody poor was ever called democratic for marrying somebody rich."

—*John Williams (Thomas Fairchild) to Audrey Hepburn (Sabrina Fairchild),* Sabrina *(1954)*

"Let's just say we're doing it for a pal in the army."

—*Bing Crosby (Bob Wallace) to Danny Kaye (Phil Davis),* White Christmas *(1954)*

"If you're impatient, you have no business growing trees."

—*Rock Hudson (Ron Kirby) to Jane Wyman (Cary Scott),* All That Heaven Allows *(1955)*

"We have not missed, you and I—we have not missed that many-splendored thing."

—*William Holden (Mark Elliott) to Jennifer Jones (Han Suyin),* Love Is a Many-Splendored Thing *(1955), last line*

"Captain, it is I, Ensign Pulver, and I just threw your stinking palm tree overboard. Now, what's all this crud about no movie tonight?"

—*Jack Lemmon (Ensign Pulver) to James Cagney (Captain Morton),* Mister Roberts *(1955), last line*

"Would you like me to tell you the little story of right hand, left hand? The story of good and evil? H-A-T-E. It was with this left hand that old brother Cain struck the blow that laid his brother low. L-O-V-E. You see these fingers, dear hearts? These fingers has veins that run straight to the soul of man— the right hand, friends, the hand of love."

—*Robert Mitchum (Preacher Harry Powell),* The Night of the Hunter *(1955)*

"You want a leg or a breast?"

—*Grace Kelly (Frances Stevens) to Cary Grant (John Robie, "The Cat"), To Catch a Thief (1955)*

"Monsters, John. Monsters from the Id."

—*Warren Stevens (Lieutenant Doc Ostrow), Forbidden Planet (1956)*

"Desire, ambition, faith— without them life is so simple."

—*Larry Gates (Dan Kaufman), Invasion of the Body Snatchers (1956)*

"Et cetera, et cetera, et cetera."

—*Yul Brynner (King of Siam), The King and I (1956)*

"Let's go home, Debbie."

—*John Wayne (Ethan Edwards) to Natalie Wood (Debbie Edwards), The Searchers (1956)*

"Oh, Moses, Moses, you stubborn, splendid, adorable fool!"

—*Anne Baxter (Nefretiri) to Charlton Heston (Moses), The Ten Commandments (1956)*

"Madness. Madness."

—*James Donald (Major Clipton) surveying the wreckage of the bridge, The Bridge on the River Kwai (1957, UK), last line*

"I don't want to stop. I like it. Take the picture, take the picture."

—*Audrey Hepburn (Jo Stockton) to Fred Astaire (Dick Avery), Funny Face (1957)*

"That's silly, honey. People just don't get smaller."

—*Randy Stuart (Louise Carey) to Grant Williams (Scott Carey), The Incredible Shrinking Man (1957)*

Yul Brynner starred as the King of Siam in the 1956 film The King and I.

"Killed him? She executed him."

—*Charles Laughton (Sir Wilfrid Robarts), Witness for the Prosecution (1957)*

"Life is a banquet, and most poor suckers are starving to death!"

—*Rosalind Russell (Mame Dennis) to Peggy Cass (Agnes Gooch), Auntie Mame (1958)*

"He was some kind of a man. What does it matter what you say about people?"

—*Marlene Dietrich (Tanya) about Orson Welles (Hunic Quinlan), Touch of Evil (1958)*

"We keep you alive to serve this ship. Row well and live."

—*Charlton Heston (Judah Ben-Hur) to the galley slaves, Ben-Hur (1959)*

"Mama, Mama, I didn't mean it. I didn't mean it. Mama, do you hear me, I'm sorry, I'm sorry, Mama. Mama, I did love you."

—*Susan Kohner (Sara Jane at 18), at coffin of Juanita Moore (Annie Johnson), Imitation of Life (1959)*

"If there's anything worse than a woman living alone, it's a woman saying she likes it."

—*Thelma Ritter (Alma) to Doris Day (Jan Morrow), Pillow Talk (1959)*

"It's going to be a long night…
and I don't particularly
like the book I started."

—*Eva Marie Saint (Eve Kendall) to
Cary Grant (Roger Thornhill),
North by Northwest (1959)*

"I guess they'll let you in the
front door from now on."

—*John Wayne (John T. Chance) to
Dean Martin (Dude),
Rio Bravo (1959)*

"Well, nobody's perfect."

—*Joe E. Brown
(Osgood Fielding III) on discovering
his fiancée, Jack Lemmon
(Jerry/Daphne), is a man, Some
Like It Hot (1959), last line*

"A boy's best friend
is his mother."

—*Anthony Perkins
(Norman Bates),
Psycho (1960)*

*Jack Lemmon and
Shirley MacLaine
starred in The
Apartment
(1960).*

"I am more interested
in the 'Rock of Ages'
than I am in the age
of rocks."

—*Fredric March (Matthew Brady)
to Spencer Tracy
(Henry Drummond),
Inherit the Wind (1960)*

"Mama, face it.
I was the slut of all time."

—*Elizabeth Taylor (Gloria
Wandrous) to Mildred Dunnock
(Mrs. Wandrous),
Butterfield 8 (1960)*

"The old man was right, only
the farmers won. We lost.
We'll always lose."

—*Yul Brynner (Chris),
The Magnificent Seven (1960),
last line*

"Shut up and deal."

—*Shirley MacLaine
(Fran Kubelik) to Jack Lemmon
(C.C. Baxter),
The Apartment (1960),
last line*

"I'm Spartacus! I'm
Spartacus! I'm Spartacus!"

—*Rebel slaves, beginning with
Tony Curtis (Antoninus),
Spartacus (1960)*

"Are you a good girl,
Tuggle?"

—*Jim Hutton (TV Thompson) to
Paula Prentiss (Tuggle Carpenter),
Where the Boys Are (1960)*

"I mean, any gentleman with
the slightest chic will give a
girl a fifty-dollar bill for the
powder room."

—*Audrey Hepburn (Holly Golightly)
to George Peppard (Paul Varjak),
Breakfast at Tiffany's (1961)*

Paul Newman (Eddie Felson): "Fat man, you shoot a great game of pool."
Jackie Gleason (Minnesota Fats): "So do you, Fast Eddie."

—The Hustler *(1961), last lines*

Marilyn Monroe (Roslyn Taber): "How do you find your way back in the dark?"
Clark Gable (Gay Langland): "Just head for that big star straight on. The highway's under it, and it'll take us right home."

—The Misfits *(1961)*

"*Te adoro*, Anton."

—*Natalie Wood (Maria) to her deceased love Richard Beymer (Tony),* West Side Story *(1961), last line*

"Bond. James Bond."

—*Sean Connery (James Bond), introducing himself to Eunice Gayson (Sylvia Trench),* Dr. No *(1962, UK)*

"Sherif Ali, so long as the Arabs fight tribe against tribe, so long will they be a little people, a silly people, greedy, barbarous, and cruel as you are."

—*Peter O'Toole (T.E. Lawrence) to Omar Sharif (Sherif Ali),* Lawrence of Arabia *(1962, UK)*

"Sing out, Louise. Sing out."

—*Rosalind Russell (Rose) to Diane Pace (Baby Louise),* Gypsy *(1962)*

"No, sir. This is the West, sir. When the legend becomes fact, print the legend."

—*Carleton Young (Maxwell Scott) to James Stewart (Ransom Stoddard),* The Man Who Shot Liberty Valance *(1962)*

"Made to commit acts too unspeakable to be cited here by an enemy who had captured his mind and soul, he freed himself at last and in the end heroically and unhesitatingly gave his life to save his country. Raymond Shaw....Hell....Hell."

—*Frank Sinatra (Bennett Marco) on Laurence Harvey (Raymond Shaw),* The Manchurian Candidate *(1962)*

Audrey Hepburn (Regina Lambert): "Do you know what's wrong with you?"
Cary Grant (Peter Joshua): "No, what?"
Hepburn: "Nothing."

—Charade *(1963)*

Sean Connery (James Bond): "Do you expect me to talk?"
Gert Frobe (Goldfinger): "No, Mr. Bond. I expect you to die."

—Goldfinger *(1964, UK)*

"Gentlemen, you can't fight in here, this is the war room!"

—*Peter Sellers (President Merkin Muffley) to George C. Scott (General Buck Turgidson) and Peter Bull (Russian Ambassador de Sadesky),* Dr. Strangelove or: How I Learned to Stop Worrying and Love the Bomb *(1964)*

"Eliza? Where the devil are my slippers?"

—*Rex Harrison (Professor Henry Higgins) to Audrey Hepburn (Eliza Doolittle),* My Fair Lady *(1964), last line*

"The Von Trapp children don't play. They march."

—*Norma Varden (Frau Schmidt) to Julie Andrews (Maria),* The Sound of Music *(1965)*

"It's the first time I've tasted women. They're rather good."

—*Sean Connery (James Bond) to Claudine Auger (Domino),* Thunderball *(1965, UK)*

"Listen, Meg, when a man takes an oath, he's holding his own self in his own hands like water. And if he opens his fingers then, he needn't hope to find himself again."

—*Paul Scofield (Sir Thomas More) to Susannah York (Margaret More),* A Man for All Seasons *(1966, UK)*

"We rob banks."

—*Warren Beatty (Clyde Barrow),*
Bonnie and Clyde *(1967)*

"What we've got here is a failure to communicate."

—*Strother Martin (Captain) to
Paul Newman (Luke),*
Cool Hand Luke *(1967)*

"I just want to say one word to you—just one word....Plastics."

—*Walter Brooke (Mr. Maguire) to
Dustin Hoffman (Benjamin
Braddock),* The Graduate *(1967)*

"They call me Mr. Tibbs."

—*Sidney Poitier (Virgil Tibbs),*
In the Heat of the Night *(1967)*

"Hello, gorgeous."

—*Barbra Streisand (Fanny Brice) to
mirror,* Funny Girl *(1968), first line*

"How dear of you to let me out of jail."

—*Katharine Hepburn (Eleanor of
Aquitane) to Peter O'Toole (Henry
II),* The Lion in Winter *(1968)*

"Kill the brain and you kill the ghoul."

—*TV announcer,*
Night of the Living Dead *(1968)*

"It took me three hours to figure out 'F.U.' was Felix Unger. It's not your fault, Felix; it's a rotten combination, that's all."

—*Walter Matthau (Oscar Madison)
to Jack Lemmon (Felix Unger),*
The Odd Couple *(1968)*

"Please, sir. I want some more."

—*Mark Lester (Oliver Twist),*
Oliver! *(1968, UK), first line*

"Get your stinking paws off me, you damn dirty ape."

—*Charlton Heston (George Taylor)
to gorilla,* Planet of the Apes *(1968)*

"I'm wet! I'm wet! I'm hysterical and I'm wet!"

—*Gene Wilder (Leo Bloom) to Zero
Mostel (Max Bialystock),*
The Producers *(1968)*

"Dave, stop.
Stop, will you? Stop, Dave.
Will you stop, Dave?
Stop, Dave. I'm afraid.
I'm afraid, Dave. Dave, my mind is going. I can feel it.
I can feel it. My mind is going. There is no question about it."

—*Douglas Rain (voice of HAL 9000
computer) to Keir Dullea
(David Bowman),*
2001: A Space Odyssey *(1968, UK)*

"I'm walking here! I'm walking here!"

—*Dustin Hoffman (Ratso Rizzo) to
cabdriver,* Midnight Cowboy *(1969)*

"Little girls, I am in the business of putting old heads on young shoulders, and all my pupils are the crème de la crème. Give me a girl at an impressionable age and she is mine for life."

—*Maggie Smith (Jean Brodie) to her
pupils,* The Prime of Miss Jean
Brodie *(1969, UK), last line*

"Please put fifty thousand dollars into this bag and abt natural as I am pointing a gub at you."

—*Woody Allen's (Virgil Starkwell's)
illegible holdup note,* Take the
Money and Run *(1969)*

"Well, come see a fat old man sometime!"

—*John Wayne (Reuben J. "Rooster"
Cogburn) to Kim Darby (Mattie
Ross),* True Grit *(1969), last line*

"Grab him! He's got a bomb!"

—*Airplane passenger, talking about
Van Heflin (D.O. Guerrero),*
Airport *(1970)*

"Love means never having to say you're sorry."

—*Ryan O'Neal (Oliver Barrett IV)
to Ray Milland (Oliver Barrett III),*
Love Story *(1970), last line*

"Now all you have to do is hold the chicken, bring me the toast, give me a check for the chicken salad sandwich, and you haven't broken any rules."

—*Jack Nicholson (Robert Dupeau) to waitress,* Five Easy Pieces *(1970)*

"This isn't a hospital! It's an insane asylum!"

—*Sally Kellerman (Major "Hot Lips" Houlihan) to Roger Bowen (Colonel Henry Blake),* M*A*S*H *(1970)*

"I love it. God help me, I do love it so. I love it more than my life."

—*George C. Scott (General George S. Patton, Jr.) on war,* Patton *(1970)*

"I know what you're thinking. Did he fire six shots or only five? Well, to tell you the truth, in all this excitement, I've kind of lost track myself. But being as this is a .44 magnum, the most powerful handgun in the world, and would blow your head clean off, you've got to ask yourself one question: 'Do I feel lucky?' Well, do ya, punk?"

—*Clint Eastwood (Harry Callahan) to bank robber,* Dirty Harry *(1971)*

"You ever been to Poughkeepsie? Huh? Have you ever been to Poughkeepsie?"

—*Gene Hackman (Popeye Doyle),* The French Connection *(1971)*

Gene Hackman portrayed a narcotics detective in the thriller The French Connection *(1971), which was based on a true story.*

Timothy Bottoms (Sonny Crawford): "Could have been worse." *Ben Johnson (Sam the Lion):* "Yeah, you can say that about nearly everything, I guess."

—The Last Picture Show *(1971)*

"In the summer of '42 we raided the Coast Guard station four times, we saw five movies, we had nine days of rain. Benjie broke his watch. Oscy gave up the harmonica, and in a very special way, I lost Hermie forever."

—*Gary Grimes (Hermie),* Summer of '42 *(1971), last line*

"I was cured, all right."

—*Malcolm McDowell (Alex),* A Clockwork Orange *(1972, UK), last line*

"I'm gonna make him an offer he can't refuse."

—*Marlon Brando (Don Vito Corleone) to Al Martino (Johnny Fontane); repeated by Al Pacino (Michael Corleone) to John Cazale (Fredo),* The Godfather *(1972)*

"Greet the dawn with a breath of fire."

—*Ruth Gordon (Maude) to Bud Cort (Harold),* Harold and Maude *(1972)*

"When I pray to him, I find I'm talking to myself."

—*Peter O'Toole (Jack), a mad aristocrat who is convinced he is God,* The Ruling Class *(1972, UK)*

"Okay, Toad, we'll take 'em all."

—*Paul LeMat (John Milner) to Charles Martin Smith (Terry Fields),* American Graffiti *(1973)*

"From here on in, I rag nobody."

—*Michael Moriarty (Henry Wiggen),* Bang the Drum Slowly *(1973), last line*

"What an excellent day for an exorcism."

—*Mercedes McCambridge (voice of demon) to Jason Miller (Father Karras),* The Exorcist *(1973)*

"Yes, according to history, over one hundred years ago a man named Albert Shanker got ahold of a nuclear warhead."

—*Bartlett Robinson (Dr. Orva),* Sleeper *(1973)*

"Best year, 1945. No, '45, '46…"

—*Robert Redford (Hubbell Gardiner) to Bradford Dillman (J.J.),* The Way We Were *(1973)*

"Ooh, a wed wose. How womantic."

—*Madeline Kahn (Lili Von Shtupp) to Cleavon Little (Bart),* Blazing Saddles *(1974)*

"Forget it, Jake, it's Chinatown."

—*Bruce Glover (Duffy) to Jack Nicholson (J.J. Gittes),* Chinatown *(1974)*

Jack Nicholson and Faye Dunaway starred in Roman Polanski's suspenseful Chinatown *(1974).*

"Tom, you know, you surprise me. If anything in this life is certain, if history has taught us anything, it's that you can kill anyone."

—*Al Pacino (Michael Corleone) to Robert Duvall (Tom Hagen),* The Godfather, Part II *(1974)*

"That's Frahnk-en-steen."

—*Gene Wilder (Dr. Frederick Frankenstein) to student,* Young Frankenstein *(1974)*

"Attica! Attica!"

—*Al Pacino (Sonny) to crowd,* Dog Day Afternoon *(1975)*

"You're gonna need a bigger boat."

—*Roy Scheider (Martin Brody) to Robert Shaw (Quint),* Jaws *(1975)*

"I'm French. Why do think I have this outrageous accent, you silly king?"

—*John Cleese (French sentry) to Graham Chapman (King Arthur),* Monty Python and the Holy Grail *(1975, UK)*

"Follow the money."

—*Hal Holbrook (Deep Throat) to Robert Redford (Bob Woodward),* All the President's Men *(1976)*

"Is it safe?"

—*Laurence Olivier (Szell) to Dustin Hoffman (Babe Levy),* Marathon Man *(1976)*

"I want you to get up now. I want all of you to get up out of your chairs. I want you to get up right now and go the window. Open it, and stick your head out, and yell, 'I'm as mad as hell, and I'm not going to take this anymore!'"

—*Peter Finch (Howard Beale),* Network *(1976)*

"I love you more than God."

—*Audrey Hepburn (Maid Marian) to Sean Connery (Robin Hood),* Robin and Marian *(1976, UK)*

"Yo, Adrienne!"

—*Sylvester Stallone (Rocky Balboa)
to Talia Shire (Adrienne),*
Rocky *(1976)*

"You talking to me?
You talking to me?
You talking to me?
Well, who the hell else
are you talking to?
You talking to me?
Well, I'm the only one here.
Who the f__k do you think
you're talking to?"

—*Robert De Niro (Travis Bickle) to
his image in the mirror,*
Taxi Driver *(1976)*

"Well, I guess that's pretty
much now how I feel about
relationships. You know,
they're totally irrational and
crazy and absurd—but, uh,
I guess we keep goin'
through it because most
of us need the eggs."

—*Woody Allen (adult Alvy Singer),*
Annie Hall *(1977), last line*

"This means something. This
is important."

—*Richard Dreyfuss (Roy Neary) to
his family,* Close Encounters of the
Third Kind *(1977)*

"That kid gets no tip."

—*Mel Brooks (Richard Thorndyke)
after being attacked by a bellhop,*
High Anxiety *(1977)*

"The last miracle I did was
the 1969 Mets. Before that,
I think you have to go back
to the Red Sea."

—*George Burns (God),*
Oh God! *(1977)*

"May the Force be with you."

—*Harrison Ford (Han Solo) to
Mark Hamill (Luke Skywalker),*
Star Wars *(1977)*

"You have to think
about one shot. One shot
is what it's all about.
The deer has to be taken
with one shot."

—*Robert De Niro (Michael) to
Christopher Walken (Nick),*
The Deer Hunter *(1978)*

"I never drink when I fly."

—*Christopher Reeve (Clark
Kent/Superman) to Margot Kidder
(Lois Lane),* Superman *(1978, UK)*

"I love the smell of
napalm in the morning....
Smells like—victory."

—*Robert Duvall (Lieutenant Colonel
Kilgore),* Apocalypse Now *(1979)*

"I like to watch TV."

—*Peter Sellers (Chauncey Gardener)
to Laurie Jefferson (a TV reporter),*
Being There *(1979)*

"Blessed are the
cheesemakers."

—*Ken Colley (Jesus) as
misunderstood by listeners,*
Monty Python's Life of Brian
(1979, UK)

Robert Hayes (Ted Striker):
"Surely you can't be serious."
Leslie Nielsen (Dr. Rumack):
"I am serious, and don't call
me Shirley."

—Airplane! *(1980)*

"They're not gonna catch us.
We're on a mission
from God."

—*Dan Aykroyd (Elwood)
to John Belushi (Jake),*
The Blues Brothers *(1980)*

"Never tell me the odds."

—*Harrison Ford (Han Solo) to
Anthony Daniels (C3PO),*
The Empire Strikes Back *(1980)*

"Go get 'em, champ....
I'm the boss, I'm the boss,
I'm the boss, I'm the boss,
I'm the boss...boss boss boss
boss boss boss."

—*Robert De Niro (Jake La Motta) to
the mirror,* Raging Bull *(1980),
last line*

"He-e-e-e-re's Johnnie!"

—*Jack Nicholson (Jack Torrance) to
Shelley Duvall (Wendy Torrance),*
The Shining *(1980, UK)*

"The Atlantic Ocean was something then. Yes, you should have seen the Atlantic Ocean in those days."

—*Burt Lancaster (Lou) to Robert Joy (Dave),* Atlantic City *(1981)*

"You're not too smart, are you? I like that in a man."

—*Kathleen Turner (Matty Walker) to William Hurt (Ned Racine),* Body Heat *(1981)*

"Norman. Come here. Come here, Norman. Hurry up. The loons! The loons! They're welcoming us back."

—*Katharine Hepburn (Ethel Thayer) to Henry Fonda (Norman Thayer, Jr.),* On Golden Pond *(1981), first line*

"Snakes. Why did it have to be snakes?"

—*Harrison Ford (Indiana Jones),* Raiders of the Lost Ark *(1981)*

"Don't rewrite what I write."

—*Warren Beatty (John Reed) to Gene Hackman (Pete Van Wherry),* Reds *(1981)*

"E.T. phone home."

—*E.T.,* E.T.: The Extra-Terrestrial *(1982)*

"If you are a minority of one, the truth is the truth."

—*Ben Kingsley (Mohandas Gandhi) to Martin Sheen (Walker),* Gandhi *(1982, UK)*

"Ah, Kirk, my old friend, do you know the Klingon proverb that tells us revenge is a dish that is best served cold? It is very cold in space."

—*Ricardo Montalban (Khan), talking to himself about his projected revenge on William Shatner (Admiral James T. Kirk),* Star Trek II: The Wrath of Khan *(1982)*

"God, I begged you to get some therapy."

—*Sydney Pollack (George Fields) to transvestite Dustin Hoffman (Michael Dorsey),* Tootsie *(1982)*

"There is no other music, not in my house."

—*Kevin Kline (Harold) to friends,* The Big Chill *(1983)*

"Go ahead, make my day."

—*Clint Eastwood (Harry Callahan) to thug,* Sudden Impact *(1983)*

"A strange game. The only winning move is not to play. How about a nice game of chess?"

—*James Ackerman (voice of Joshua the Computer),* WarGames *(1983)*

"This is the cleanest and nicest police car I've ever been in in my life. This thing's nicer than my apartment."

—*Eddie Murphy (Axel Foley) to policemen,* Beverly Hills Cop *(1984)*

"Back off, man. I'm a scientist."

—*Bill Murray (Dr. Peter Venkman),* Ghostbusters *(1984)*

"Is this the big secret that you've been keeping from me? Is it that you're a mermaid, or is there something else?"

—*Tom Hanks (Allen Bauer) to Daryl Hannah (Madison),* Splash *(1984)*

"I'll be back."

—*Arnold Schwarzenegger (the Terminator),* The Terminator *(1984)*

"I think that the problem may have been that there was a Stonehenge monument on the stage that was in danger of being crushed by a dwarf. That tended to understate the hugeness of the object."

—*Michael McKean (David St. Hubbins),* This Is Spinal Tap *(1984)*

"Roads? Where we're going we don't need—roads."

—Chistopher Lloyd (Dr. Emmett Brown) to Michael J. Fox (Marty McFly) and Claudia Wells (Jennifer), Back to the Future (1985), last line

Michael J. Fox found himself in the past in Back to the Future (1985), also starring Christopher Lloyd.

"I'm poor, black. I may even be ugly, but, dear God, I'm here. I'm here!"

—Whoopi Goldberg (Celie) to Danny Glover (Albert Johnson), The Color Purple (1985)

"I had a farm in Africa."

—Meryl Streep (Karen Blixen-Finecke), Out of Africa (1985)

"Yeah, right here on the Oriental, with all the lights on."

—Anjelica Huston (Maerose Prizzi), seducing Jack Nicholson (Charley Partanna), Prizzi's Honor (1985)

"To survive a war, you've got to become war."

—Sylvester Stallone (John Rambo), Rambo: First Blood Part II (1985)

"You be careful out among them English."

—Jan Rubes (Eli Lapp) to Harrison Ford (John Book), Witness (1985), last line

"Get away from her, you bitch."

—Sigourney Weaver (Ripley) to alien queen, Aliens (1986)

"That's not a knife. That's a knife."

—Paul Hogan (Michael J. "Crocodile" Dundee) to mugger as Hogan pulls out a big knife, Crocodile Dundee (1986, Australia)

"No. Be afraid. Be very afraid."

—Geena Davis (Veronica Quaife) to Joy Boushel (Tawny), The Fly (1986)

"They're ba-a-ck!"

—Heather O'Rourke (Carol Anne Freeling), Poltergeist II (1986)

"I'm not gonna be ignored, Dan."

—Glenn Close (Alex Forrest) to Michael Douglas (Dan Gallagher), Fatal Attraction (1987)

"I am Gunnery Sergeant Hartman, your senior drill instructor. From now on, you will speak only when spoken to, and the first and last words out of your filthy sewers will be 'Sir!' Do you maggots understand this?"

—Lee Ermey (Gunnery Sergeant Hartman) to new Marine recruits, Full Metal Jacket (1987), first line

"But love don't make things nice. It ruins everything. It breaks your heart. It makes things a mess. We aren't here to make things perfect. The snowflake is perfect. The stars are perfect. Not us. Not us. We are here to ruin ourselves and to break our hearts and love the wrong people and die."

—Nicolas Cage (Ronny Cammareri) to Cher (Loretta Castorini), Moonstruck (1987)

"Hello. My name is Inigo Montoya. You killed my father. Prepare to die!"

—Mandy Patinkin (Inigo Montoya) to Chris Sarandon (Prince Humperdinck), The Princess Bride (1987)

"I'll be taking these Huggies and, uh, whatever cash you got."

—Nicolas Cage (H.I. McDonnough) to convenience-store clerk, Raising Arizona (1987)

"Thank you for your cooperation."

—Peter Weller (Robocop) to thief, Robocop (1987)

"What do I wanna pay? I wanna pay nothing."

—Richard Dreyfuss (Bill "B.B." Babowsky) to car salesman, Tin Men (1987)

Reporter: "They say they're going to repeal Prohibition. What will you do then?" Kevin Costner (Eliot Ness): "I think I'll have a drink."

—The Untouchables (1987), last lines

"Greed, for lack of a better word, is good. Greed is right. Greed works. Greed clarifies, cuts through, and captures the essence of the evolutionary spirit. Greed, in all of its forms."

—Michael Douglas (Gordon Gekko), Wall Street (1987)

"Okay, well, this is the damnedest season I've ever seen. I mean, the Durham Bulls can't lose and I can't get laid."

—Susan Sarandon (Annie Savoy) to Kevin Costner (Crash Davis), Bull Durham (1988)

"It's beyond my control."

—John Malkovich (Vicomte de Valmont) to Michelle Pfeiffer (Madame de Tourvel), Dangerous Liaisons (1988)

"Wilbur…it's the times, they're a-changin'. Something's blowin' in the wind. Fetch me my diet pill, would you, hon?"

—Divine (Edna Turnblad) to Jerry Stiller (Wilbur), Hairspray (1988)

"I want a divawce."

—Michelle Pfeiffer (Angela DeMarco) to Alec Baldwin (Frank DeMarco), Married to the Mob (1988)

"Down here they say rattlesnakes don't commit suicide."

—Gene Hackman (Rupert Anderson), Mississippi Burning (1988)

"I'll let you in on a little secret, Ray. Kmart sucks."

—Tom Cruise (Charlie Babbitt) to Dustin Hoffman (Raymond Babbitt), Rain Man (1988)

"I'm not bad, I'm just drawn that way."

—Kathleen Turner (voice of Jessica Rabbit), Who Framed Roger Rabbit (1988)

"I have a head for business and a bod for sin."

—Melanie Griffith (Tess McGill) to Harrison Ford (Jack Trainer), Working Girl (1988)

"I'll have what she's having."

—Estelle Reiner (Customer) to waitress, When Harry Met Sally… (1989)

Meg Ryan tried to prove to Billy Crystal that men and women can be "just friends" in When Harry Met Sally…(1989).

"Can somebody tell me what kind of a world we live in where a man dressed up as a bat gets all of my press?"

—*Jack Nicholson (Joker/Jack Napier)*, Batman *(1989)*

Ossie Davis (Da Mayor): "Always do the right thing."
Spike Lee (Mookie): "That's it?"
Davis: "That's it."
Lee: "I got it, I'm gone."

—Do the Right Thing *(1989)*

"You're my best friend."

—*Jessica Tandy (Daisy Werthan) to Morgan Freeman (Hoke Colburn),* Driving Miss Daisy *(1989)*

"If you build it, he will come."

—*Ray Liotta ("Shoeless" Joe Jackson) to Kevin Costner (Ray Kinsella),* Field of Dreams *(1989)*

"Just when I thought I was out, they pull me back in."

—*Al Pacino (Michael Corleone),* The Godfather, Part III *(1990)*

"Listen, I…I appreciate this whole seduction scene you got going, but let me give you a tip: I'm a sure thing."

—*Julia Roberts (Vivian Ward), a prostitute, to Richard Gere (Edward Lewis),* Pretty Woman *(1990)*

Billy Crystal (Mitch Robbins): "Hi, Curly, kill anyone today?"
Jack Palance (Curly): "Day ain't over yet."

—City Slickers *(1991)*

"Face it girls, I'm older and I have more insurance."

—*Kathy Bates (Evelyn Couch) to two obnoxious young women,* Fried Green Tomatoes *(1991)*

"A census taker once tried to test me. I ate his liver with some fava beans and a nice Chianti."

—*Anthony Hopkins (Hannibal Lecter),* The Silence of the Lambs *(1991)*

"*Hasta la vista*, baby."

—*Arnold Schwarzenegger (the Terminator) to Robert Patrick (T-1000),* Terminator 2: Judgment Day *(1991)*

"Brains will only get you so far, and luck always runs out."

—*Harvey Keitel (Hal) to Steven Tobolowsky (Max),* Thelma & Louise *(1991)*

"You can't handle the truth!"

—*Jack Nicholson (Colonel Nathan Jessep) to Tom Cruise (Lieutenant Daniel Kaffee),* A Few Good Men *(1992)*

"First prize is a Cadillac Eldorado. Second prize is a set of steak knives. Third prize is you're fired."

—*Alec Baldwin (Blake),* Glengarry Glen Ross *(1992)*

"I didn't do wrong. Did I?"

—*Anthony Hopkins (Henry Wilcox) to Emma Thompson (Margaret Schlegel),* Howards End *(1992)*

"We didn't land on Plymouth Rock, Plymouth Rock landed on us."

—*Denzel Washington (Malcolm X) to an assembly of African-Americans,* Malcolm X *(1992)*

Joe Pesci (Vincent La Guardia Gambino): "Your Honor, may I have permission to treat Miss Vito as a hostile witness?"
Marisa Tomei (Mona Lisa Vito): "You think I'm hostile now, wait 'til you see me tonight."

—My Cousin Vinny *(1992)*

"It's amusing to me to torture a cop."

—*Michael Madsen (Mr. Blonde/Vic) to Kirk Baltz (Marvin Nash),* Reservoir Dogs *(1992)*

"I'm just gettin' warmed up."

—*Al Pacino (Lieutenant Colonel Frank),* Scent of a Woman *(1992)*

"It's better than sex!
No, no, I've heard."

—*Whoopi Goldberg (Deloris) to
fellow nuns,* Sister Act *(1992)*

*Jaimz Woolvett
(The Schofield Kid):* "Well, I
guess they had it comin'."
*Clint Eastwood (William
Munny):* "We all have it
comin', kid."

—Unforgiven *(1992)*

"My, my, my, my, my.
What a mess."

—*Tommy Lee Jones (Deputy Samuel
Gerard),* The Fugitive *(1993)*

"I'm a god. I'm not
the God—
I don't think."

—*Bill Murray (Phil),*
Groundhog Day *(1993)*

"All right, look, I want you
to explain this to me like
I'm a six-year-old, okay?"

—*Denzel Washington (Joe Miller) to
potential client,* Philadelphia *(1993)*

"I could have got one more
person, but I didn't."

—*Liam Neeson (Oskar Schindler)
to workers he saved from Nazi
concentration camps,*
Schindler's List *(1993)*

"I'm not even supposed to
be here today!"

—*Brian O'Halloran (Dante Hicks),*
Clerks *(1994)*

"My mama always said, life
was like a box of chocolates.
You never know what you're
gonna get."

—*Tom Hanks (Forrest Gump)
to a listener at a bus stop,*
Forrest Gump *(1994)*

Samuel L. Jackson (Jules):
"First, I'm gonna deliver this
case to Marcellus. Then,
basically, I'm just gonna
walk the earth."
John Travolta (Vincent):
"What you mean,
walk the earth?"
Jackson: "You know, like
Caine in *Kung Fu.*"

—Pulp Fiction *(1994)*

"Houston, we have a
problem."

—*Tom Hanks (Jim Lovell),*
Apollo 13 *(1995)*

"Every man dies, not every
man really lives."

—*Mel Gibson (William Wallace),*
Braveheart *(1995)*

"This kind of certainty comes
but once in a lifetime."

—*Clint Eastwood (Robert Kincaid),*
The Bridges of
Madison County *(1995)*

"The greatest trick the devil
ever pulled was convincing
the world he didn't exist."

—*Kevin Spacey (Verbal Kint),*
The Usual Suspects *(1995)*

"Swoon. I'll catch you."

—*Ralph Fiennes (Count László
Almásy) to Kristin Scott Thomas
(Katharine Clifton),*
The English Patient *(1996)*

"And I guess that was your
accomplice in the
woodchipper."

—*Frances McDormand (Marge
Gunderson),* Fargo *(1996)*

"Show me the money!"

—*Cuba Gooding, Jr. (Rod Tidwell),*
Jerry Maguire *(1996)*

"Some people call it a sling
blade. I call it a kaiser blade."

—*Billy Bob Thornton (Karl
Childers),* Sling Blade *(1996)*

"You make me want to
be a better man."

—*Jack Nicholson (Melvin Udall)
to Helen Hunt (Carol Connelly),*
As Good as It Gets *(1997)*

"Shall we shag now, or
shall we shag later?"

—*Mike Myers (Austin Powers),*
Austin Powers: International
Man of Mystery *(1997)*

"Look, you're my best friend, so don't take this the wrong way. In 20 years, if you're still livin' here, comin' over to my house to watch the Patriots games, still workin' construction, I'll f___in' kill you. That's not a threat. Now, that's a fact. I'll f___in' kill you."

—Ben Affleck (Chuckie) to Matt Damon (Will Hunting), Good Will Hunting (1997)

"Off the record, on the QT, and very hush-hush."

—Danny DeVito (Sid Hudgens), L.A. Confidential (1997)

Geoffrey Rush (Philip Henslowe): "Mr. Fennyman, allow me to explain about the theater business. The natural condition is one of insurmountable obstacles on the road to imminent disaster."
Tom Wilkinson (Hugh Fennyman): "So what do we do?"
Rush: "Nothing. Strangely enough, it all turns out well."
Wilkinson: "How?"
Rush: "I don't know. It's a mystery."

—Shakespeare in Love (1998)

"Earn this."

—Tom Hanks (Captain John Miller), dying, to Matt Damon (Private James Francis Ryan), Saving Private Ryan (1998)

"Maybe I'm spending too much of my time starting up clubs and putting on plays. I should probably be trying harder to score chicks."

—Jason Schwartzmann (Max Fischer), Rushmore (1998)

"Sometimes there's so much beauty in the world I feel like I can't take it, like my heart's going to cave in."

—Wes Bentley (Ricky Fitts), American Beauty (1999)

"You see the world through John Malkovich's eyes. Then, after about 15 minutes, you're spit out into a ditch on the side of the New Jersey Turnpike!"

—John Cusack (Craig Schwartz), Being John Malkovich (1999)

"The way it works is, you do the thing you're scared s___less of, and you get the courage after you do it, not before you do it."

—George Clooney (Archie Gates), Three Kings (1999)

"If you think that Mick Jagger will still be doing the whole rock star thing at age 50, well, then, you are sorely, sorely mistaken."

—Jimmy Fallon (Dennis Hopper), Almost Famous (2000)

"I see dead people."

—Haley Joel Osment (Cole Sear), The Sixth Sense (1999)

"At my signal, unleash hell."

—Russell Crowe (Maximus), Gladiator (2000)

Russell Crowe cemented his box-office status with Gladiator (2000).

501

WORLD CINEMA

Films from around the globe have much to teach us about other cultures and foreign lands. But while they may display our differences, the best serve to show us what we all have in common.

FILM IS AN INTERNATIONAL medium. In a recent issue of *Variety International Film Guide*, the present-day film industries of no fewer than 70 nations are profiled, from Algeria to Venezuela, from Armenia to Zimbabwe; others have been active in the past, from those of the now defunct Soviet Union to the now divided Czechoslovakia. (The Czech Republic, Slovakia, and the former Soviet republics all continue to release films.) This section pays homage to 22 of the leading nations of world cinema, nations that together represent every continent except Antarctica. For each of these countries, a brief alphabetical list of notable films is provided, including directors and years of release. In addition, one of the films is spotlighted by a brief description.

The nationality of films mentioned in the text of a spotlight entry is the same as that of the country under discussion, unless otherwise indicated. Because of its long-lived and distinctive

Zdenek Sverak and Andrej Chalimon starred in the Czech film Kolya *(1996).*

film industry, Hong Kong is treated as a country, although it was a British colony until 1997 when it was ceded to China. For the convenience of readers who might not be familiar with foreign-language articles such as "El" and "Les," these are treated like any other words in the alphabetization of titles, even when they appear at the beginning of a phrase. However, films are not alphabetized by the English-language articles "A," "An," and "The" when they occur at the beginning of a title. Variant English-language titles are also included.

Regarding titles: In many cases, both English-language and foreign-language titles are listed. However, some foreign films, often ones with universally understood titles (e.g., *Kolya, Viridiana*), do not have English titles, and many foreign films are best known worldwide by their English-language titles. Finally, some films are known under several different titles, like *Zêmlya/Earth/Soil* (1930), and we have tried to include them.

Argentina

SPOTLIGHT ON ARGENTINIAN FILMS:
La Casa del Ángel (The House of the Angel/End of Innocence) (1957).
Director: Leopoldo Torre Nilsson. Elsa Daniel, Lautaro Murúa, Guillermo Battaglia, Yordana Fain. Set in the 1920s, this drama concerns a sheltered Catholic girl's first love affair and her subsequent shame. A critique of bourgeois morality, the film was a departure from more conventional Argentinian melodramas and comedies. It won acclaim at the Cannes Film Festival, bringing international notice to its director and his country.

NOTABLE FILMS

Boda Secreta (Secret Wedding) (1989), Director: Alejandro Agresti

Camila (1984, Argentina/Spain), Director: María Luisa Bemberg

El Amor es una Mujer Gorda (Love Is a Fat Woman) (1987), Director: Alejandro Agresti

El Grito de este pueblo (The Cry of the People) (1972), Director: Humberto Ríos

La Caída (The Fall) (1958), Director: Leopoldo Torre Nilsson

La Casa del Ángel (The House of the Angel/ End of Innocence) (1957), Director: Leopoldo Torre Nilsson

La Historia Oficial (The Official Version/The Official Story) (1985), Director: Luis Puenzo

La Hora de los Hornos (The Hour of the Furnaces) (1968), Director: Fernando E. Solanas

La Mano en la Trampa (The Hand in the Trap) (1961), Director: Leopoldo Torre Nilsson

Las Aguas Bajan Turbias (Dark River/The River of Blood) (1952), Director: Hugo del Carril

Muñequitas Porteñas (1931), Director: José A. Ferreyra

No Habrá más Penas ni Olvido (A Funny Dirty Little War) (1983), Director: Héctor Olivera

Señora de Nadie (Nobody's Wife) (1982), Director: María Luisa Bemberg

Sur (The South) (1988), Director: Fernando E. Solanas

Tango Bar (1988), Director: Marcos Zurinaga

Tangos, l'Exil de Gardel (Tangos, the Exile of Gardel) (1985, Argentina/France), Director: Fernando E. Solanas

Tiempo de Revancha (A Time for Revenge) (1981), Director: Adolfo Aristarain

Últimas Imágenes del Naufragio (Last Images of the Shipwreck) (1989), Director: Elisea Subielo

Veronico Cruz (La Deuda Interna) (1987), Director: Miguel Pereira

Australia

SPOTLIGHT ON AUSTRALIAN FILMS:
Mad Max 2/The Road Warrior (1981). Director: George Miller. Mel Gibson, Bruce Spence, Vernon Wells, Mike Preston. This postapocalyptic action film recounts the efforts of loner Max to survive in a lawless wasteland populated by various warring gangs. Miller's film draws on conventions used in other genres, such as the western and the horror film and is said by many to reflect themes in Australian culture. A sequel to *Mad Max* (1979), which also starred Gibson, it helped make the actor an international star and spawned another sequel, *Mad Max Beyond Thunderdome* (1985).

Mad Max Beyond Thunderdome *(1985) was the third film in a series starring Mel Gibson.*

NOTABLE FILMS

The Adventures of Priscilla, Queen of the Desert (1994), Director: Stephan Elliott

Babe (1995, US/Australia), Director: Chris Noonan

Breaker Morant (1979), Director: Bruce Beresford

The Chant of Jimmie Blacksmith (1978), Director: Fred Schepisi

Mad Max (1979), Director: George Miller

Mad Max 2/The Road Warrior (1981), Director: George Miller

Muriel's Wedding (1994), Director: P.J. Hogan

My Brilliant Career (1979), Director: Gillian Armstrong

Newsfront (1978), Director: Phil Noyce

Nice Coloured Girls (1987), Director: Tracey Moffat

Picnic at Hanging Rock (1975), Director: Peter Weir

Proof (1991), Director: Jocelyn Moorhouse

Queensland (1976), Director: John Ruane

The Sentimental Bloke (1919), Director: Raymond Longford

Sirens (1994), Director: John Duigan

Strictly Ballroom (1992), Director: Baz Luhrmann

Sunday Too Far Away (1975), Director: Ken Hannan

Brazil

SPOTLIGHT ON BRAZILIAN FILMS:
Central do Brasil (Central Station)
(1998, Brazil/France). Director: Walter
Salles. Fernanda Montenegro, Soia
Lira, Vinícius de Oliveira, Marília
Pêra. This internationally acclaimed
film is set in Rio de Janeiro's main
train station, where Dora supports
herself by writing and mailing
letters for the uneducated.
She becomes entangled
in people's lives as she
reads the letters aloud
to her neighbor and
then decides whether
or not to send them.
After one of her clients
is killed, she is forced to
take a more active role as
caretaker of the woman's
young son. Salles beautifully captures
Dora's emotional transformation
from a greedy businesswoman to a
surrogate mother. The film was
nominated for an Academy Award for
best foreign-language film and earned
actress Montenegro awards from the
Berlin International Film Festival and
the Los Angeles Film Critics Circle.

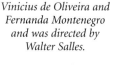

*The critically acclaimed
Brazilian film* Central
Station *(1998) starred
Vinicius de Oliveira and
Fernanda Montenegro
and was directed by
Walter Salles.*

NOTABLE FILMS
Alma Corsária (Buccaneer Soul) (1993), Director:
  Carlos Reichenbach
Antonio das Mortes (1969), Director: Glauber
  Rocha
Central do Brasil (Central Station) (1998, Brazil/
  France), Director: Walter Salles
Dona Flor and Her Two Husbands (1978),
  Director: Bruno Barreto
Ele, o Boto (The Dolphin) (1987), Director:
  Walter Lima, Jr.
Filho sem Mãe (Motherless Son) (1925), Director:
  Tancredo Seabra
A Lei do Mais Fraco/Pixote (1981), Director:
  Hector Babenco
Vidas Secas (Barren Lives) (1963), Director:
  Nelson Pereira dos Santos
Xica da Silva/Xica (1976), Director: Carlos
  Diegues

Canada

SPOTLIGHT ON CANADIAN FILMS:
The Sweet Hereafter (1997). Director:
Atom Egoyan. Ian Holm, Sarah Polley,
Arsinée Khanjian, Maury Chaykin. This
film is a moving account of a town
trying to recover after a tragic school bus
accident that left numerous children
dead. As a lawyer probes the pain of the
community to encourage a lawsuit, its
members' hidden deceptions slowly
come to light. One of the best-known
Canadian directors, Egoyan has a subtle
filmmaking style that beautifully reveals
the deviance of his seemingly normal
characters. The film captured the grand
prize at the Cannes Film Festival and
Egoyan was nominated for an Academy
Award for best director.

NOTABLE FILMS
The Apprenticeship of Duddy Kravitz (1974),
  Director: Ted Kotcheff
Decline of the American Empire (1985), Director:
  Denys Arcand
Emporte-Moi (Set Me Free) (1998), Director:
  Léa Pool
Goin' Down the Road (1970), Director: Don
  Shebib
The Hanging Garden (1997), Director: Thom
  Fitzgerald
Hen Hop (1942), Director: Norman McLaren
I've Heard the Mermaids Singing (1988), Director:
  Patricia Rozema
*La Vie Heureuse de Léopold Z. (The Merry World
  of Leopold Z)* (1965), Director: Gilles Carle
Le Confessional (1995), Director: Robert LePage
Léolo (1992), Director: Jean-Claude Lauzon
Les Bons Débarras (1978), Director: Francis
  Mankiewicz
Les Ordres (The Orders) (1974), Director:
  Michel Brault
Mon Oncle Antoine (My Uncle Antoine) (1971),
  Director: Claude Jutra
My American Cousin (1985), Director: Sandy
  Wilson
Nobody Waved Goodbye (1965), Director:
  Don Owen
Not a Love Story: A Film About Pornography
  (1981), Director: Bonnie Sherr Klein
The Red Violin (1998), Director: François Girard
Roadkill (1989), Director: Bruce McDonald
The Sweet Hereafter (1997), Director: Atom
  Egoyan
Videodrome (1982), Director: David Cronenberg
Wavelength (1967), Director: Michael Snow

China

SPOTLIGHT ON CHINESE FILMS: *Hong Gao Liang (Red Sorghum)* (1987). Director: Zhang Yimou. Gong Li, Jiang Wen, Liu Ji, Teng Rijun. An epic romance with fairy-tale overtones, this film concerns a pair of rural lovers who face the Japanese invasion of the 1930s. It is famous for its CinemaScope cinematography, vivid storytelling, and rich portrayal of Chinese rural life. Female lead Gong Li starred in subsequent Zhang features, including *Raise the Red Lantern* (1991, China/Taiwan/ Hong Kong).

NOTABLE FILMS

Ba Wang Bie Ji (Farewell My Concubine) (1993, China/Hong Kong), Director: Chen Kaige

Da hong deng long gao gao gua/Raise the Red Lantern (1991, China/Taiwan/Hong Kong), Director: Zhang Yimou

Da Yue Bing (The Big Parade) (1986), Director: Chen Kaige

Dao Ma Zei (The Horse Thief) (1986), Director: Tian Zhuangzhuang

Fu Rong Zhen (Hibiscus Town) (1986), Director: Xie Jin

Hai Zi Wang (King of the Children) (1988), Director: Chen Kaige

Hei Pao Shi Jian (The Black Cannon Incident) (1985), Director: Huang Jianxin

Hong Gao Liang (Red Sorghum) (1987), Director: Zhang Yimou

Ju Dou (1990), Directors: Zhang Yimou, Yang Fengliang

Juexiang (Swan Song) (1985), Director: Zhang Zeming

Lao Jing (The Old Well) (1987), Director: Wu Tianming

The Last Emperor (1987, Italy/UK/China), Director: Bernardo Bertolucci

Pai Mao Nu (The White-Haired Girl) (1970), Director: Sang Hu

Qing Chun Ji (Sacrificed Youth) (1985), Director: Zhang Nuanxing

The Song of the Fishermen (1934), Director: Tsai Chu-sheng

The Story of Qiuju (1992), Director: Zhang Yimou

Wan Zhong (Evening Bell) (1987), Director: Wu Ziniu

Wild Torrent (1933), Director: Cheng Bu-kao

Wo Hu Cang Long (Crouching Tiger, Hidden Dragon) (2000, China/Taiwan/Hong Kong/US), Director: Ang Lee

Wutai Jiemei (Two Stage Sisters) (1964), Director: Xie Jin

Wuya Yu Maque (Crows and Sparrows) (1949), Director: Zheng Junli

Yi Jiang Chun Shui Xiang Dong Liu (Spring River Flows East/Tears of the Yangtse) (1947), Director: Cai Chusheng, Zheng Junli

Yuanli Zhanzhengde Niandai (Far from War) (1988), Director: Hu Mei

Zuihou Yige Dongri (The Last Day of Winter) (1986), Director: Wu Ziniu

Czech Republic

SPOTLIGHT ON CZECH FILMS: *Ostre Sledované Vlaky (Closely Watched Trains)* (1966). Director: Jiří Menzel. Václav Neckár, Jitka Bendova, Vladimir Valenta. Menzel's sex comedy follows the coming of age of a young man during the German occupation in World War II. After repeated failures to perform sexually and an attempted suicide, Miloš succeeds in his quest, only to be gunned down in a mission. Punctuated by tragic moments, the film captures the Czech spirit of perseverance and humor in the face of horrible circumstances. Based on the novel of the same name by Bohumil Hrabal, the film won a 1967 Academy Award for best foreign-language film.

NOTABLE FILMS

The Coward (1961), Director: Jiří Weiss

Démanty noci/Diamonds of the Night (1964), Director: Ján Nemec

Intimi osvetleni/Intimate Lighting (1966), Director: Ivan Passer

Kolya (1996), Director: Jan Sverák

Loves of a Blonde/A Blonde in Love (1965), Director: Milos Forman

Musíme si Pomáhat (Divided We Fall) (2000), Director: Jan Hřebejk

Not Angels, But Angels (1994), Director: Wiktor Grodecki

Obchod na Korze (The Shop on Main Street/Shop on the High Street) (1965), Director: Ján Kadár and Elmar Klos

Ostre Sledované Vlaky (Closely Watched Trains) (1966), Director: Jiří Menzel

Řeka (The River) (1933), Director: Josef Rovenskř

Ruka (The Hand) (1965), Director: Jiří Trnka

Gong Li played a young woman who becomes the fourth wife of a rich, elderly man when she is sold by her mother in Raise the Red Lantern *(1991).*

Denmark

SPOTLIGHT ON DANISH FILMS: *Babettes gæstebud (Babette's Feast)* (1987). Director: Gabriel Axel. Stephane Audran, Jean-Philippe Lafont, Bibi Andersson. Full of beautiful visual and aural details, this film tells the story of two unmarried sisters who live with their father in a strict Protestant community. Reluctantly, they take in a French Catholic refugee, Babette, who becomes their cook and maid. When the father dies, she is entrusted with preparing a feast to mark what would have been his 100TH birthday. The film vividly captures the splendor of the feast, which is a glorious success for the whole village. Adapted from a novel by Isak Dinesen, the film won an Academy Award for best foreign-language film.

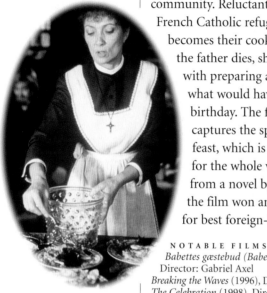

Stephane Audran portrayed a housekeeper who is also a world-class chef in Babette's Feast (Babettes Gæstebud) *(1987).*

NOTABLE FILMS

Babettes gæstebud (Babette's Feast) (1987), Director: Gabriel Axel
Breaking the Waves (1996), Director: Lars von Trier
The Celebration (1998), Director: Thomas Vinterberg
Dancer in the Dark (2000, Denmark/Sweden/France), Director: Lars von Trier
Det hemmelighedsfulde X (Sealed Orders) (1913), Director: Benjamin Christensen
La Passion de Jeanne d'Arc (The Passion of Joan of Arc) (1928), Director: Carl Theodor Dreyer
Mifune (1999), Director: Søren Kragh-Jacobsen
Pelle Erobreren/Pelle the Conqueror (1988), Director: Bille August

Egypt

SPOTLIGHT ON EGYPTIAN FILMS: *Iskandiriya—Leh? (Alexandria—Why?)* (1978, Egypt/Algeria). Director: Youssef Chahine. Mohsen Mohiedin, Naglaa Fathi, Farid Shawki, Ezzat el-Alayli. Directed by Egypt's best-known filmmaker, this is an autobiographical account of a film-crazed schoolboy growing up in Alexandria during World War II and yearning to become a star. The film won the Special Jury Prize at the 1979 Berlin Festival and generated a sequel, *Hadduta Misriya (An Egyptian Story)* (1982).

NOTABLE FILMS

Al-Asfour (The Sparrow) (1973), Director: Youssef Chahine
Al-Wedaa Ya Bonaparte (Adieu Bonaparte) (1984, Egypt/France), Director: Youssef Chahine
Bab el-Hadid (Cairo Station/Cairo: Central Station) (1958), Director: Youssef Chahine
The Civil Servant (1923), Director: Mohamed Bayoumi
Determination (1940), Director: Kamal Selim
El-Ard (The Land/The Earth) (1968), Director: Youssef Chahine
Hadduta Misrija (An Egyptian Story) (1982), Director: Youssef Chahine
Iskandiriya—Leh? (Alexandria—Why?) (1978, Egypt/Algeria), Director: Youssef Chahine
Kit Kat (1991), Director: Daoud Abdel Sayed
Shahateen wa-Nubalaa (Beggars and Noblemen) (1992), Director: Asma el-Bakri
The Vagabonds (1985), Director: Daoud Abdel Sayed

France

SPOTLIGHT ON FRENCH FILMS: *Les Quatre Cent Coups (The 400 Blows)* (1959). Director: François Truffaut. Jean-Pierre Léaud, Claire Maurier, Albert Rémy. This film about a young loner, Antoine Doinel, who tests the boundaries of society launched the French New Wave movement; among its hallmarks is its realist camera work. The title refers to a French expression, faire les 400 coups, which means "to make mischief." Truffaut returns to the character of Antoine in several later films, including *Stolen Kisses* (1968) and *Bed and Board* (1970). Antoine is said by some critics and scholars to represent the director's alter ego.

NOTABLE FILMS

A Bout de souffle (Breathless) (1959), Director: Jean-Luc Godard
A Nous la liberté (1931), Director: René Clair
Au Revoir, les Enfants (1987), Director: Louis Malle

Baise-Moi (Rape Me) (2000), Director: Coralie/ Virginie Despentes

Café au Lait (1994), Director: Mathieu Kassovitz

Hiroshima, Mon Amour (1959), Director: Alain Resnais

J'Accuse! (I Accuse) (1919), Director: Abel Gance

Jean de Florette (1986), Director: Claude Berri

L'Atalante (1934), Director: Jean Vigo

La Belle et la Bête (Beauty and the Beast) (1946), Director: Jean Cocteau

La Grande Illusion (Grand Illusion) (1937), Director: Jean Renoir

La Jetée (1962), Director: Chris Marker (Christian François Bouche-Villeneuve)

La Règle du Jeu (Rules of the Game) (1939), Director: Jean Renoir

La Voyage dans la Lune/A Trip to the Moon (1902), George Méliès

Le Bonheur/Happiness (1965), Director: Agnès Varda

Le Fabuleux Destin D'Amélie Poulain (Amélie) (2001, France/Germany), Director: Jean-Pierre Jeunet

Le Jour se lève/Daybreak (1939), Director: Marcel Carné

Le Salaire de la Peur (The Wages of Fear) (1952, France/Italy), Director: Henri-Georges Clouzot

Les Diaboliques/Diabolique (1955), Director: Henri-Georges Cluzot

Les Quatre Cent Coups (The 400 Blows) (1959), Director: François Truffaut

Les Parapluies de Cherbourg/The Umbrellas of Cherbourg (1963), Director: Jacques Demy

Les Vacances de M. Hulot (Mr. Hulot's Holiday) (1953), Director: Jacques Tati

Ma Nuit Chez Maud (My Night at Maud's) (1969), Director: Eric Rohmer

Madame de…(The Earrings of Madame de…) (1953), Director: Max Ophuls

Nikita (La Femme Nikita) (1990, France/Italy), Director: Luc Besson

The Seashell and the Clergyman (1928), Director: Germaine Dulac

37.2 au Matin (Betty Blue) (1985), Director: Jean-Jacques Beineix

Germany

SPOTLIGHT ON GERMAN FILMS: *Die Ehe der Maria Braun (The Marriage of Maria Braun)* (1978). Director: Rainer Werner Fassbinder. Hanna Schygulla, Klaus Löwitsch, Ivan Desny, Gisela Uhlen. The most prolific German director of the New German cinema, Fassbinder tackles the issue of power in his films, including this one, which follows Maria (Schygulla) as she climbs the social ladder in the bedroom while

her husband is thought to be dead in World War II. After his return provokes a row, she accidentally kills her lover and is left to deal with a pregnancy.

A mixture of dark comedy, soap opera, political satire, and history, the film represents the postwar German national spirit. Schygulla won the best actress award at the Berlin International Film Festival, and the production team was also honored for its work on the film.

Die Ehe Der Maria Braun (The Marriage of Maria Braun) *(1978), starring Hanna Schygulla, exemplified New German cinema.*

NOTABLE FILMS

Abschied von Gestern (Yesterday Girl) (1965–66), Director: Alexander Kluge

Aguirre, der Zorn Gottes (Aguirre: The Wrath of God) (1972), Director: Werner Herzog

Bekenntnisse des Hochstaplers Felix Krull (The Confessions of Felix Krull) (1957), Director: Kurt Hoffmann

Das Boot (The Boat) (1981), Director: Wolfgang Peterson

Das Cabinet des Dr. Caligari (The Cabinet of Dr. Caligari) (1919), Director: Robert Wiene

Der Amerikanische Freund (The American Friend) (1976–77), Director: Wim Wenders

Der Blaue Engel (The Blue Angel) (1930), Director: Josef von Sternberg

Deutschland, Bleiche Mutter (Germany, Pale Mother) (1979–80), Director: Helma Sanders-Brahms

Die Büchse der Pandora (Pandora's Box) (1928), Director: G.W. Pabst

Die Ehe der Maria Braun (The Marriage of Maria Braun) (1978), Director: Rainer Werner Fassbinder

Die Legende von Paul und Paula (The Legend of Paul and Paula) (1972), Director: Heiner Carow

Die Verlorene Ehre der Katharina Blum (The Lost Honor of Katharina Blum) (1975), Director: Margarethe von Trotta, Volker Schlöndorff

Heimat (1984), Director: Edgar Reitz

Ich War Neunzehn (I Was Nineteen) (1967), Director: Konrad Wolf

M (1931), Director: Fritz Lang

Nobody Loves Me (1994), Director: Doris Dörrie

Nosferatu—Eine Symphonie des Grauens/ Nosferatu the Vampire/Nosferatu (1921), Director: F.W. Murnau

Parsifal (1982), Director: Hans-Jürgen Syberberg

Triumph of the Will (1935), Director: Leni Riefenstahl

DONNIE YEN

Donnie Yen is a Boston native who went to China and Hong Kong to perform in martial arts competitions, where he began his acting career after being discovered by Yuen Woo-ping—a legendary HK action director, and the renowned stunt coordinator behind both *The Matrix* (1999) and *Crouching Tiger, Hidden Dragon*. Yen fought Jet Li's Wong Fei-hong in 1991's *Once Upon a Time in China II*, then went on to star as the father of the young Fei-hong in Woo-ping's *Iron Monkey* (1993). Of the three actors in this scene, he's the only one with a proper martial arts background.

BRIGITTE LIN

Brigitte Lin Chin-hsia made a name for herself in Taiwanese melodramas in the 1970s before becoming the star of such swordplay and kung fu flicks as *Zu: Warriors from the Magic Mountain* (1983), *Swordsman II* (1992), *The East is Red* and *The Bride with White Hair* (both 1993). She retired from the entertainment industry in 1994.

WIRE WORK

The high-flying, gravity-defying fight scenes featured in director Ching Siu-tung's *Dragon Inn* have long been a staple, not only of his films (such as the *Chinese Ghost Story* trilogy, produced between 1987-91), but of HK cinema in general. To achieve this effect, the actors are attached to wires and physically lifted into the air, allowing for a thrilling, supernatural onscreen grace. While the wires are still readily visible in some older films, digital technology now allows for them to be completely erased. Though wire work has been criticized by some martial arts fans as a form of cheating, the style caught on Stateside with *The Matrix*, and has since been incorporated into such hit films as *X-Men* (2000), *Charlie's Angels* (2000), and *Crouching Tiger, Hidden Dragon*.

HISTORY AND MYTH

This thrilling desert duel is taken from *Dragon Inn* (1992), a film set during the Ming Dynasty and based on 1966's *Dragon Gate Inn*. Many Hong Kong films draw on China's rich history and mythology, and their abundance throughout the '90s is thanks in no small part to prolific producer/director Tsui Hark, whose hit *Once Upon a Time in China* (1991)—along with star Jet Li and a seemingly endless string of sequels— re-popularized the real-life exploits of a turn-of-the-century Chinese folk hero named Wong Fei-hong and whetted a national appetite for sweeping period action pictures.

Hong Kong Cinema

*Danny Lee
in John Woo's
The Killer
(1989).*

MAN OF ACTION

Hong Kong action
pictures such as *A
Better Tomorrow* (1986),
The Killer (left, 1989),
and *Hard-Boiled* (1992)
helped establish director
John Woo's signature visual motifs: poetic slow-motion
shoot-outs, tense stand-offs, and a hero brandishing twin
automatic pistols, a style that has since been referenced in
American films as varied as *Reservoir Dogs* (1992),
Desperado (1995), and *The Matrix*. Woo, who began his
career directing comedies, uses *The Killer*'s DVD
commentary track to pay tribute to his own influences,
which encompass everything from Martin Scorsese and
Sam Peckinpah to *Singin' in the Rain* (1952), *The Shining*
(1980), Jean-Pierre Melville's French New Wave gangster
classic *Le Samourai* (1967), and, bizarrely enough, *MAD*
magazine's comic espionage series "Spy vs. Spy."

Bᴇᴛᴡᴇᴇɴ ᴛʜᴇ ᴇᴀʀʟʏ '80s ᴅᴇᴄʟɪɴᴇ of the mass-
produced "chop socky" pictures that all but
defined the Western perception of Asian cinema, and the
imminence of mainland China's takeover in 1997, Hong
Kong filmmakers and actors produced an astonishing
output of internationally successful films that were as
singular as they were diverse. By the mid-1990s, the Hong
Kong film industry was the world's third largest, tailing only
Hollywood and Bombay. Even now, with some of its top
talent emigrating to the US, Hong Kong's worldwide
reputation still endures.

The influence of this recent wave of Hong Kong cinema
has permeated these shores for more than a decade. It is
visible in the work of such prominent American filmmakers
as Quentin Tarantino and the Wachowski brothers, in
the hiring of HK stars to add creative juice to Hollywood
blockbusters, in the Oscar-winning crossover hit *Crouching
Tiger, Hidden Dragon* (2000), and even evident in a 2001
BMW ad directed by HK iconoclast Wong Kar-wai.

Hong Kong movies cover all the bases—from *film
noir* and gangster pictures to lush romances, supernatural
thrillers, wild erotica, way-out comedies, period swordfight
flicks, and every conceivable combination and sub-genre in
between. Actors, too, are able to effortlessly shift genres in a
way that recalls the versatility of Hollywood's
Golden Age of contract players. It's this
eclecticism that makes Hong Kong one of
the most exciting—and readily accessible—
film centers in the world.

BOX OFFICE

The weekend of February 23, 1996, marked
something of a landmark for Hong Kong cinema,
as the top two films in North America both had
strong HK connections: the English-dubbed kung
fu adventure, *Rumble in the Bronx* ($9.6M),
starring Jackie Chan, and the military action
picture *Broken Arrow* ($8.4M), directed by John
Woo. (*Arrow* had spent the previous two weeks at
number one.) Woo is currently the only Asian
director to have a film (*Mission: Impossible 2*,
2000) among *Variety*'s top fifty domestic hits of all
time, and Chan, the only Asian star (*Rush Hour 2*,
2001). Other HK directors who have made films in
the US include Ringo Lam (*Maximum Risk*, 1996),
Tsui Hark (*Double Team*, 1997), Stanley Tong (*Mr.
Magoo*, 1997), and Ronny Yu (*Bride of Chucky*,
1998). Among the HK actors to have made the
leap are Michelle Yeoh (*Tomorrow Never Dies*,
1997), Woo favorite, Chow Yun-Fat (*Anna and the
King*, 1999), and Jet Li (*Kiss of the Dragon*, 2001).

MAGGIE CHEUNG

Born in Hong Kong but raised in England, Maggie Cheung Man-yuk has
starred in over 74 films in 15 years, receiving international acclaim for
her roles in the art-house pictures of director Wong Kar-wai, including
In The Mood For Love (2000). In 1992, she became the first Chinese
actress to win an international acting award when she was given the
Silver Bear in Berlin for her portrayal of the silent film star Ruan Ling-
yu, China's Greta Garbo, in Stanley Kwan's *Yuen Ling-yuk* (*The Actress*).
Cheung also co-starred with Jackie Chan in his *Police Story* series
(1985–1992), which resulted in a severe head injury during a stunt for
1988's *Police Story 2* that saw her hospitalized with several stitches.

Greece

SPOTLIGHT ON GREEK FILMS: *Stella* (1955). Director: Michael Cacoyannis. Melina Mercouri, Yiorgo Fountas (George Foundas), Alekos Alexandrikis, Sophia Vembo. This melodrama about a freespirited but doomed singer (Mercouri) received praise at the 1956 Cannes Film Festival and put Greek cinema on the international map. A second feature for Cacoyannis, who became Greece's leading director of his day, and screen debut for Mercouri, who developed into an international star.

NOTABLE FILMS
Alexis Zorbas (Zorba the Greek) (1964), Director: Michael Cacoyannis
Antigoni (Antigone) (1961), Director: Yorgos Javellas (George Tzavellas)
Astero (1929), Director: Dimitris Gaziadis
Elektra (Electra) (1962), Director: Michael Cacoyannis
Haroumeni Imera (Happy Day) (1976), Director: Pantelis Voulgaris
To Homa vaftike kokkino (Blood on the Land) (1964), Director: Vassilis Georgiadis
Magos tis Athinas (1931), Director: Ahilleas Madras
Maria Pentagiotissa (1929), Director: Ahilleas Madras
Mavri gi, I (1952), Director: Stelios Tatasopoulos
Mikres Aphrodites (Young Aphrodites) (1963), Director: Nikos Koundouros
O Thiassos (The Traveling Players) (1975), Director: Theo Angelopoulos
Pote tin Kyriaki (Never on Sunday) (1960), Director: Jules Dassin
Stella (1955), Director: Michael Cacoyannis

Hong Kong

SPOTLIGHT ON HONG KONG FILMS: *Diexue Shuang Xiong (The Killer)* (1989). Director: John Woo. Chow Yun-Fat, Danny Lee, Sally Yeh, Chu Kong, Shing Fui-On. This action-packed, tightly built thriller concerns a hit man who accidentally blinds a singer, then accepts a final assignment to pay for her needed eye operation. A top example of Hong Kong action filmmaking, the movie is influenced by Italian spaghetti westerns, Chinese martial chivalry films, and other sources. Director Woo and male lead Chow went on to work in Hollywood as well as in other Hong Kong films.

NOTABLE FILMS
A Better Tomorrow (1986), Director: John Woo
Bullet in the Head (1990), Director: John Woo
Come Drink with Me (1965), Director: King Hu
Die Xue Shuang Xiong (The Killer) (1989), Director: John Woo
Fu Zi Qing (Father and Son) (1981), Director: Allen Fong (Fong Yuk-Ping)
Project A (1983), Director: Jackie Chan
Tang shan da xiong/Fists of Fury/The Big Boss (1971), Director: Lo Wei
A Touch of Zen (1969), Director: King Hu
Yan Zhi Kou (Rouge) (1987), Director: Stanley Kwan (Guan Jinpang)
The Young Master (1980), Director: Jackie Chan

India

SPOTLIGHT ON INDIAN FILMS: *Pather Panchali (Song of the Little Road)* (1955). Director: Satyajit Ray. Kanu Banerji, Karuna Banerji, Uma Das Gupta, Chunibala Devi. Perhaps the best known Indian filmmaker outside of India, Ray turned his back on Indian cinematic conventions in this film, using no star, songs, or dances, and shooting on location to tell the tragic story of a young Bengali boy and his family. Won the Jury Prize at the 1956 Cannes Film Festival. Based on a novel by B.B. Bandapaddhay, this is the first film in Ray's Apu trilogy.

NOTABLE FILMS
Anjali (1990), Director: Mani Rathnam
Asoaka (2001), Director: Santosh Sivan
Awara (The Vagabond) (1951), Director: Raj Kapoor
Bandit Queen (1994), Director: Shekhar Kapur
Chandralekha (1948), Director: S.S. Vasan
Devdas (1935), Director: P.C. Barua
Dilwale Dulhania Le Jayenge (Lovers Will Walk Off with the Bridge) (1995), Director: Aditya Chopra
Dr. Kotnis Ki Amar Kahani (The Immortal Story of Dr. Kotnis) (1946), Director: Vankudre Shantaram
Ekdin Pratidin (And Quiet Rolls the Dawn) (1979), Director: Mrinal Sen
Kismet (1943), Director: Gyan Mukherjee

Satyajit Ray made his directorial debut with Pather Panchali (1955).

Mother India (1957), Director: Mehboob Khan

Nagarik (The Citizen) (1952), Director: Ritwik Ghatak

Pather Panchali (Song of the Little Road) (1955), Director: Satyajit Ray

Pyaasa (1957), Director: Guru Dutt

Sant Tukaram (1936), Directors: Sheikh Fatellal, V.G. Damle

Seeta (1934), Director: Debaki Bose

Sholay (Flames of the Sun) (1975), Director: Ramesh Sippy

Tarang (The Wave) (1984), Director: Kumar Shahani

Iran

SPOTLIGHT ON IRANIAN FILMS: *Gaav (The Cow)*(1970). Director: Daryush Mehrjui. Ezat Entezami, Ali Nassirian, Jamshid Mashayekhi. This symbolic drama of a villager's obsessive attachment to his cow was initially banned by the government of Iran for its portrayal of rural poverty. After its release in 1970, a year after its completion, it attracted worldwide attention to Iranian cinema and established the director's reputation. The film vividly depicts both the details of rural life and the growing madness of the protagonist following his cow's death.

NOTABLE FILMS

And Life Goes On.../Life, and Nothing More (1992), Director: Abbas Kiarostami

Ansuyeh Atash (Beyond the Fire) (1988), Director: Kianoush Ayari

Bad ma ra khahad bord (The Wind Will Carry Us) (1999), Director: Abbas Kiarostami

Baghé Sangui (Garden of Stones) (1976), Director: Parviz Kimiavi

Come Stranger! (1969), Director: Massoud Kimiai

The Crow (1977), Director: Bahram Beyzai

Dastforoush (The Peddler) (1987), Director: Mohsen Makhmalbaf

Davandeh (The Runner) (1984), Director: Amir Naderi

Dayereh Mina (The Cycle) (1977), Director: Daryush Mehrjui

Gaav (The Cow) (1970), Director: Daryush Mehrjui

Goodbye, My Friend (1971), Director: Amir Naderi

Gharibeh Va Meh (The Stranger and the Fog) (1974), Director: Bahram Beyzai

Hamoun (The Desert) (1990), Director: Daryush Mehrjui

Lost Time (1990), Director: Pouran Derakhshandeh

Ragbar (Downpour) (1971), Director: Bahram Beyzai

Saiehaien Bolan De Bad (Tall Shadows of the Wind) (1978), Director: Bahman Farmanara

Ta'm e Guilass (The Taste of Cherry) (1997), Director: Abbas Kiarostami

Where Is the Friend's Home? (1987), Director: Abbas Kiarostami

Italy

SPOTLIGHT ON ITALIAN FILMS: *Roma, Città Aperta (Rome, Open City)* (1945). Director: Roberto Rossellini. Aldo Fabrizi, Anna Magnani. A quintessential example of Italian Neorealism, this film depicts the struggle of the Italian people in postwar Rome. Although Rossellini faced a scarcity of film stock, actors, and money, he turned these hardships into the characteristic elements of a new film style, utilizing untrained actors and shooting on location with a handheld camera. The natural, unpolished look of the film echoed the harsh reality of life at the time and helped portray Rossellini's sympathy for the people of Rome.

NOTABLE FILMS

C'eravamo tanto/We All Loved Each Other So Much (1974), Director: Ettore Scola

Caro Diario (1994), Director: Nanni Moretti

Cinema Paradiso (1988), Director: Giuseppe Tornatore

Dillinger è Morto (Dillinger Is Dead) (1969), Director: Marco Ferreri

8 ½ (1963), Director: Federico Fellini

Il Decamerone (The Decameron) (1970), Director: Pier Paolo Pasolini

L'Avventura (1960), Director: Michelangelo Antonioni

La Notte di San Lorenzo/Night of the Shooting Stars (1982), Directors: Paolo and Vittorio Taviani

La Stanza del Figlio (The Son's Room) (2001, Italy/ France), Director: Nanni Moretti

La Strada (1954), Director: Federico Fellini

La Terra Trema (1947), Director: Luchino Visconti

La Vita e Bella (Life Is Beautiful) (1997), Director: Roberto Benigni

Ladri di Biciclette (The Bicycle Thief) (1947), Director: Vittorio De Sica

Mediterraneo (1991), Director: Gabriele Salvatores

FACTS ABOUT WORLD CINEMA

- INDIA PRODUCES MORE feature films than any other country. In its peak year, 1990, India produced 948 films.

- THE RECORD FOR GREATEST annual movie theater attendance is held by China. In 1988, there were 21.8 billion movie theater visits in that country.

- HONG KONG HOLDS the record for the world's longest movie series. More than 100 movies have been made in Hong Kong about the 19th-century martial arts hero Huang Fei-Hong. The first in the series was *The True Story of Huang Fei-Hong* (1949). A more recent example is *Once upon a Time in China 5* (1995).

- THE HIGHEST-GROSSING African movie is *Sankofa* (1993, Ethiopia), directed by Haile Gerima. It grossed $2.69 million in the US alone.

Pane e Cioccolata/Bread and Chocolate (1978), Director: Franco Brusati

Per un Pugno di Dollari/A Fistful of Dollars (1964), Director: Sergio Leone

Prima della Rivoluzione (Before the Revolution) (1964), Director: Bernardo Bertolucci

Roma, Città Aperta (Rome, Open City) (1945), Director: Roberto Rossellini

Seven Beauties (1976), Director: Lina Wertmuller

Travolti da un Insolito Destino nell'Azzurro Mare d'Agosto/Swept Away...by an unusual destiny in the blue sea of August (1975), Director: Lina Wertmuller

Tre Fratelli (Three Brothers) (1981), Director: Francesco Rosi

Japan

SPOTLIGHT ON JAPANESE FILMS: *Shichinin no samurai (Seven Samurai)* (1954). Director: Akira Kurosawa. Takashi Shimura, Toshiro Mifune. Generally considered Kurosawa's best film, it centers on a small farming village that plans to defend itself against gangs of bandits by enlisting the help of the samurai, whom they traditionally fear. Set in the 16th century, the film reworks a typical western theme of the gunfighter coming to town and is characterized by Kurosawa's fast editing cuts. It won awards at the Venice Film Festival and the Academy Awards. Kurosawa's narrative and filmmaking style influenced directors all over the world, most notably George Lucas.

NOTABLE FILMS

Bukushu (Early Summer) (1951), Director: Yasujiro Ozu

The Burmese Harp (1956), Director: Kon Ichikawa

Chuji tabi nikki (A Diary of Chuji's Travels) (1927), Director: Daisuke Ito

Furyo shonen (Bad Boys) (1961), Director: Susumu Hani

Jigokumon (Gate of Hell) (1953), Director: Teinosuke Kinugasa

Kyoya erimise (Kyoya, the Collar Shop) (1922), Director: Eizo Tanaka

My Neighbor Totoro (1988), Director: Hayao Miyazaki

Musashi Miyamoto/The Samurai Trilogy (1956), Director: Hiroshi Inagaki

Nihon no yoru to kiri (Night and Fog in Japan) (1960), Director: Nagisa Oshima

Rashomon (1950), Director: Akira Kurosawa

Shichinin no samurai (Seven Samurai; The Magnificent Seven) (1954), Director: Akira Kurosawa

Susa no onna (Woman in the Dunes) (1964), Director: Hiroshi Teshigahara

Ugetsu monogatari/Ugetsu (Tales of the Pale and Silvery Moon After the Rain) (1953), Director: Kenji Mizoguchi

Akira Kurosawa wrote and directed Shichinin no Samurai (The Seven Samurai) *(1954), considered by many to be his masterpiece.*

Mexico

SPOTLIGHT ON MEXICAN FILMS: *Como Agua para Chocolate (Like Water for Chocolate)*. (1992) Director: Alfonso Arau. Lumi Cavazos, Regina Torné, Yareli Arizmendi. Vivid colors and striking visual details highlight this epicurean fantasy, which follows a pair of doomed lovers who are forced apart by tradition. The title suggests the water temperature that will melt chocolate, but it is also a metaphor for sexual excitement. The film, adapted from the novel by Laura Esquivel, was also nominated for a Golden Globe Award in the best foreign language-film category.

NOTABLE FILMS
Amores Perros (Love's a Bitch) (2000), Director: Alejandro Gonzales Iñarita
Así es la Vida (Such is Life) (2000) Director: Arturo Ripstein
Como Agua para Chocolate (Like Water for Chocolate) (1992), Director: Alfonso Arau
Cronos (1992), Director: Guillermo del Toro
Danzón (1991), Director: María Novaro
El Compadre Mendoza (1933), Director: Fernando de Fuentes
El Topo (The Mole) (1969), Director: Alejandro Jodorowsky
En el Balcón Vacío (On the Empty Balcony) (1961), Director: Jomí García Ascot
Espaldas Mojadas (Wetbacks) (1953), Director: Alejandro Galindo
La Banda del Automovil gris (The Gray Car Gang) (1919), Directors: Joaqín Coss, Juan de Homs, Enrique Rosas
La Perla (The Pearl) (1946), Director: Emilio Fernández
Mecánica Nacional (1971), Director: Luis Alcoriza
Nosotros los Pobres (We the Poor) (1947), Director: Ismael Rodríguez
Santa (1931), Director: Antonio Moreno
Yanco (1961), Director: Servando González

Russia

SPOTLIGHT ON RUSSIAN FILMS: *The Battleship Potemkin (Potemkin)* (1925). Director: Sergei Eisenstein. The best example of Soviet montage and a chronicle of an actual massacre by Russian soldiers in Odessa. The film is composed of five parts, a structure that mirrors the unity of classical drama and serves as a celebration of the Russian people. Eisenstein's masterful editing creates meaning from the contrast of individual shots, and his powerful images incite emotion and pathos for the masses. The well-known "Odessa Steps" sequence has been echoed in several subsequent films, most notably Brian DePalma's *The Untouchables* (1987).

NOTABLE FILMS
Andrei Roublev (1966), Director: Andrei Tarkovsky
The Battleship Potemkin (Potemkin) (1925), Director: Sergei Eisenstein
Burnt by the Sun (1994), Director: Nikita Mikhalkov
The Extraordinary Adventures of Mr. West in the Land of the Bolsheviks (1924), Director: Lev Kuleshov
Giorgobistve (Falling Leaves) (1966), Director: Otar Yoseliani
Letjat zhuravli (The Cranes Are Flying) (1957), Director: Mikhail Kalatozov
Malenkaya Vera (Little Vera) (1988), Director: Vasily Pichul
Man with the Movie Camera/Moscow Today (Living Russia, or The Man with the Camera) (1929), Director: Dziga Vertov
Mat (Mother) (1926), Director: Vsevolod Pudovkin
Monanieba (Repentance) (1987), Director: Tengiz Abuladze
Moskva slezam ne verit (Moscow Does Not Believe in Tears) (1979), Director: Vladimir Menshov
Moj Drug, Ivan Lapshin (My Friend, Ivan Lapshin) (1983), Director: Alexei German
Pervy Uchitel (The First Teacher) (1965), Director: Andrei Konchalovsky
Seasons (1972), Director: Artavazd Pelechian
Sorok pervy (The Forty-First) (1956), Director: Grigori Chukhrai
Tini zabutykh predkiv (Shadows of Forgotten Ancestors) (1964), Director: Sergei Paradzhanov
Voskhozhdeniye (The Ascent) (1977), Director: Larisa Shepitko
Zêmlya/Earth/Soil (1930), Director: Alexander Dovzhenko

The Mexican fairytale Como Agua para Chocolate (Like Water for Chocolate) *(1992) starred Marco Leonardi and Lumi Cavazos.*

Senegal

SPOTLIGHT ON SENEGALESE FILMS: *Ceddo (The People)* (1976) Director: Ousmane Sembène. Ismaila Diagne, Tabara N'Diaye, Moustapha Yade, Ousmane Camara. This drama concerns the clash between an Imam (Muslim religious leader) who is trying to force the population to convert to Islam and a princess who rises against him. As directed by Sembène, who is widely regarded as the leading filmmaker of Sub-Saharan Africa, the film is an allegory of Senegalese history and was banned in Senegal for its critique of Islam.

NOTABLE FILMS

Camp Thiaroye (Camp de Thiaroye) (1988, Senegal/Algeria/Tunisia), Directors: Ousmane Sembène, Thierno Faty Sow
Ceddo (The People) (1976), Director: Ousmane Sembène
Emitai (1972), Director: Ousmane Sembène
Hyènes/Hyenas (1992), Director: Djibril Diop Mambéty
Jom (1982), Director: Ababacar Samb Makharam
Kaddu Beykat (Letter from My Village) (1975), Director: Safi Faye
La Noire de... (Black Girl) (1966), Director: Ousmane Sembène
Le Mandat (Mandabi/The Money Order) (1968), Director: Ousmane Sembène
Man Say Yay (I Your Mother) (1980), Director: Safi Faye
Mossane (1996), Director: Safi Faye
Touki-Bouki (1973), Director: Djibril Diop Mambéty
Xala (The Curse) (1974), Director: Ousmane Sembène

Julieta Serrano, Antonio Banderas, and Maria Barranco starred in Pedro Almodovar's 1988 film Mujerres al Borde do un Ataque de Nervios (Women on the Edge of a Nervous Breakdown) (1988).

Spain

SPOTLIGHT ON SPANISH FILMS: *Mujerres al Borde de un Ataque de Nervios (Women on the Verge of a Nervous Breakdown)* (1988). Director: Pedro Almodóvar. Carmen Maura, Antonio Banderas, Julieta Serrano, Rossy de Palma. This comedy of errors features an array of wacky characters fighting over lovers and drinking spiked gazpacho. Almodóvar has emerged as one of the most prolific directors of the new Spanish cinema. The film won a New York Film Critics Circle Award for best foreign-language film.

NOTABLE FILMS

Amantes (Lovers) (1990), Director: Vicente Aranda
Asignatura Pendiente (Unfinished Business) (1977), Director: José Luis Garci
Belle Époque (1992), Director: Fernando Trueba
Beltenebros (Prince of Shadows) (1991), Director: Pilar Miró
El Desencanto (Disenchantment) (1976), Director: Jaime Chávarri
El Sur (The South) (1983), Director: Víctor Erice
Furtivos (Poachers) (1975), Director: José Luis Borau
Jamón, Jamón (Salami, Salami) (1992), Director: Bigas Luna
Juana la Loca (Madness in Love) (2001), Director: Vicente Aranda
La Aldea Maldita (The Cursed Village) (1929), Director: Florián Rey
La Caza (The Hunt) (1965), Director: Carlos Saura
La Escopeta Nacional (The National Shotgun) (1977), Director: Luis García Berlanga
Las Hurdes/Tierra sin Pan (Land Without Bread/Unpromised Land) (1932), Director: Luis Buñuel
Muerte de un Ciclista (Death of a Cyclist) (1955), Director: Juan Antonio Bardem
Mujerres al Borde de un Ataque de Nervios (Women on the Verge of a Nervous Breakdown) (1988), Director: Pedro Almodóvar
Vacas (Cows) (1992), Director: Julio Medem
Viridiana (1961, Spain/Mexico), Director: Luis Buñuel

Sweden

SPOTLIGHT ON SWEDISH FILMS: *Det Sjunde Inseglet (The Seventh Seal)* (1956). Director: Ingmar Bergman. Max von Sydow, Bengt Ekerot, Bibi Andersson, Nils Poppe. First internationally recognized film by Bergman, the master of Swedish cinema. Allegorical story of a medieval knight who must play a game of chess against Death in order to gain time to contemplate the meaning of his life. The knight loses the game and must die, but the film is ultimately hopeful as the delay has caused a family to escape the hands of Death. Bergman's love of the theater is demonstrated by the inclusion of a band of players whose brightly lit scenes help to balance the grim chess game.

NOTABLE FILMS
Adalen '31 (1969), Director: Bo Widerberg
Det Sjunde Inseglet (The Seventh Seal) (1956), Director: Ingmar Bergman
Fanny and Alexander (1983), Director: Ingmar Bergman
Hets (Torment) (1944), Director: Alf Sjöberg
Käre John (Dear John) (1966), Director: Lars-Magnus Lindgren
The Legend of Gösta Berling/The Gosta Berling Saga (1924), Director: Victor Sjöström
My Life as a Dog (1985), Director: Lasse Hallström
The Outlaw and His Wife (1918), Director: Victor Sjöström
Utvandrarna (The Emigrants) (1971), Director: Jan Troell

United Kingdom

SPOTLIGHT ON BRITISH FILMS:
Trainspotting (1996). Director: Danny Boyle. Ewan McGregor, Ewen Bremner, Jonny Lee Miller, Robert Carlyle, Kelly MacDonald. This film reveals the underbelly of dole society in Edinburgh, Scotland as it follows the exploits of a group of heroin-addled friends. Boyle's use of handheld cameras and sometimes graphic scenes of drug use lend this film a gritty reality. Well-received by critics internationally, it earned writer John Hodge an Academy Award for best adaptation. The film helped to launch the careers of Ewan McGregor, Robert Carlyle, and Jonny Lee Miller. It is based on the novel of the same name by Irvine Welsh.

NOTABLE FILMS
Billy Elliot (2000, UK/France), Director: Stephen Daldry
Black Narcissus (1947), Director: Michael Powell
Caravaggio (1986), Director: Derek Jarman
Carry on Sergeant (1959), Director: Gerald Thomas
Chariots of Fire (1981), Director: Hugh Hudson
Chocolat (2000, UK/US), Director: Lasse Hallström
The Crying Game (1992), Director: Neil Jordan
Don't Look Now (1973), Director: Nicholas Roeg
The Draughtsman's Contract (1982), Director: Peter Greenaway
Four Weddings and a Funeral (1994), Director: Mike Newell
The Full Monty (1997), Director: Peter Cattaneo
The Gamekeeper (1980), Director: Kenneth Loach
Gandhi (1982), Director: Richard Attenborough
Gregory's Girl (1981), Director: Bill Forsyth
A Hard Day's Night (1964), Director: Richard Lester
Howards End (1992), Director: James Ivory
The Killing Fields (1984), Director: Roland Joffe
Kind Hearts and Coronets (1949), Director: Robert Hamer
Lair of the White Worm (1988), Director: Ken Russell
The Lavender Hill Mob (1951), Director: Charles Crichton
Lawrence of Arabia (1962), Director: David Lean
The Man in the White Suit (1951), Director: Alexander MacKendrick
My Beautiful Laundrette (1985), Director: Stephen Frears
Orlando (1992), Director: Sally Potter
Rescued by Rover (1905), Director: Cecil Hepworth
Secrets & Lies (1996), Director: Mike Leigh
Spare Time (1939), Director: Humphrey Jennings
The Third Man (1949), Director: Carol Reed
Tom Jones (1963), Director: Tony Richardson
Trainspotting (1996), Director: Danny Boyle
2001: A Space Odyssey (1968), Director: Stanley Kubrick

Ewan McGregor portrayed a Scottish junkie who goes to London to get clean and finds himself involved with a drug deal in Trainspotting *(1996).*

NOTABLE FILMS BY GENRE

Genres define the kinds of films we choose to watch. The best genre pictures not only define our expectations, but also redefine the genre.

A GENRE IS A GROUP OF FILMS that share similar plots, character types, techniques, and themes. Genre is an inexact category many films straddling several. Therefore, some films can be found on more than one list in this section. It should also be noted that some films have been remade often or have acquired many sequels. Generally, only the original or best-known version is listed here, although remakes and sequels may be noted when they are of exceptional quality. The following film genres are surveyed in this section, each with a brief history and a chronological list of representative films.

Action-Adventure, Animation, Avant-Garde, Biopic, Children's, Comedy, Crime, Cult Movies, Documentary, Drama, Historical, Horror, Melodrama, Musical, Mystery, Romance, Science Fiction and Fantasy, Serials, War, and Western.

Action-Adventure

THE ACTION-ADVENTURE FILM has been a staple of filmmaking since at least 1903, when American filmmaker Edwin S. Porter made the classic 12-minute western *The Great Train Robbery*. Action-adventure films focus primarily on physical activity rather than characterization: they depict a protagonist's struggle against life-threatening obstacles in pursuit of some goal. Though close in

meaning, "action" and "adventure" have slightly different connotations: the former emphasizes fighting and violence, the latter the twists and turns of the heroic journey. Some adventure films have little

Thomas Mitchell and Richard Barthelmess starred in Only Angels Have Wings (1939).

or no violence between humans, depicting instead struggle against technology or the elements; examples include the aerial-adventure film *Only Angels Have Wings* (1939), the man-versus-shark story *Jaws* (1975), and the space disaster film *Apollo 13* (1995). Action-adventure films that are high in thrills may be called thrillers, although that term is also used for horror films; those high in suspense, such as the films of director Alfred Hitchcock, may be called suspense films.

Heroes and villains in action-adventure films are often two-dimensional, although some adventure films are more morally nuanced, such as *The Treasure of the Sierra Madre* (1948). Men dominate most action-adventure stories, with women playing love interests and accomplices, although in some examples—such as *La Femme Nikita* (1990)—women are the heroes. Other hallmarks of the genre are amazing stunts—chases by car, plane, foot, or horseback; and spectacular forms of destruction, such as fires, floods, and explosions.

The action-adventure film has many subgenres, including westerns, war movies, and crime films. Horror, science fiction, and fantasy films often have action-adventure elements. In addition, action-adventure readily blends with other elements to form hybrids, such as the comedy-action film *Beverly Hills Cop* (1984) and the romance-adventure *The African Queen* (1951).

Besides the subgenres noted above, the action film has taken several distinct forms. The swashbuckler, which involves swordplay in the medieval or early modern periods, reached a high point in the silent era with *Robin Hood* (1922) and other films starring Douglas Fairbanks. Errol Flynn inherited Fairbanks's mantle in the sound era in films such as *The Adventures of Robin Hood* (1938). The disaster film, which pits characters against a natural or human-made cataclysm, has been a perennial favorite from *The Hurricane* in 1937 to *The Perfect Storm* in 2000. Treasure hunts often figure in adventure films, such as the search for the temple of gold in *Gunga Din* (1939) and Indiana Jones's quest for archaeological treasures in *Raiders of the Lost Ark* (1981). The series of films about superspy James Bond that began with *Dr. No* (1962), themselves influenced by Hitchcock films such as *North by Northwest* (1959), launched a subgenre of spectacular spy thrillers.

The 1970s saw the entrance of African-American action heroes, in so-called blaxploitation films such as *Shaft.* In the 1980s and 1990s, action films became ever more fast-paced, violent, and laden with special effects, as in *Die Hard* (1988). Another subgenre of the action film is the Asian martial arts film, of which Hong Kong is a principal exporter. Bruce Lee and Jackie Chan are among this subgenre's best-known stars.

George Clooney battled against nature for his life in The Perfect Storm *(2000).*

REPRESENTATIVE FILMS

The Great Train Robbery (1903)
The Mark of Zorro (1920; remade 1940)
The Three Musketeers (1921; remade 1948)
Robin Hood (1922)
The Thief of Bagdad (1924; remade 1940, UK)
The Hurricane (1937)
The Adventures of Robin Hood (1938)
The Four Feathers (1939, UK)
Gunga Din (1939)
Only Angels Have Wings (1939)
The Sea Hawk (1940)
Saboteur (1942)
To Have and Have Not (1944)
The Treasure of the Sierra Madre (1948)
The African Queen (1951)
The Crimson Pirate (1952)
Le Salaire de la Peur (The Wages of Fear) (1952, France/Italy)
The High and the Mighty (1954)
Shichinin no samurai (Seven Samurai; The Magnificent Seven) (1954, Japan)
North by Northwest (1959)
Dr. No (1962, UK)
Goldfinger (1964, UK)
Airport (1970)
Dirty Harry (1971)
Shaft (1971; remade 2000)
Tang shan da xiong/Fists of Fury/The Big Boss (1971, Hong Kong)
The Poseidon Adventure (1972)

Jaws (1975)
The Man Who Would Be King (1975)
Black Sunday (1977)
Star Wars (1977)
Superman (1978)
Raiders of the Lost Ark (1981)
Project A (1983, Hong Kong)
Beverly Hills Cop (1984)
The Terminator (1984)
Rambo: First Blood Part II (1985)
Lethal Weapon (1987)
The Untouchables (1987)
Die Hard (1988)
Batman (1989)
La Femme Nikita (1990, France/Italy)
Thelma & Louise (1991)
The Last of the Mohicans (1992)
The Fugitive (1993)
True Lies (1994)
Apollo 13 (1995)
Braveheart (1995)
Mission Impossible (1996)
Air Force One (1997)
Face/Off (1997)
Titanic (1997)
Rush Hour (1998)
The Matrix (1999)
Three Kings (1999)
Charlie's Angels (2000)
The Perfect Storm (2000)
Spy Kids (2001)

The most profitable series of films in history is the James Bond series, which began with *Dr. No* (1962, UK). Together, the spy thrillers have grossed a total of more than $3.2 billion worldwide.

OVERLEAF:

Lauren Bacall and Humphrey Bogart (far right) met on the set of To Have and Have Not *(1944)—also starring Marcel Dalio (center)—and later married.*

Bob Hoskins and Christopher Lloyd shared the screen with animated bombshell Jessica Rabbit and other "toons" in Who Framed Roger Rabbit *(1988).*

Animation

AN ANIMATED FILM conveys its story through drawn and colored characters and scenes or, in some cases, through three-dimensional puppets or computer generation. Human actors often provide voices for the animated characters and occasionally—such as in *Anchors Aweigh* (1945) and *Who Framed Roger Rabbit* (1988)—live humans and drawn characters share the film frame. Silent animated cartoons featuring Krazy Kat and others gained popularity during the 1910s, and Walt Disney's first sound cartoons in the late 1920s revolutionized the medium. Beginning in the 1930s, cartoons became a standard part of the movie show repertoire, and many major studios formed animation units to create cartoons. Among them were MGM, which created Tom and Jerry; Universal, with Oswald the Rabbit; and,

besides Disney, the most enduring, Warner Bros., with its *Looney Tunes* and *Merrie Melodies.*

The animated film reached another milestone in 1937, when the first animated feature film was released: Walt Disney's *Snow White and the Seven Dwarfs* (1937). While Disney films came to dominate the market with features such as *Bambi* (1942), *Fantasia* (1940), and *Sleeping Beauty* (1959), other notable animated films have been released, among them Max Fleischer's *Gulliver's Travels* (1939) and Ralph Bakshi's *Fritz the Cat* (1972). Since the 1980s, computer-animation techniques have defined animated movies, with titles that include *The Little Mermaid* (1989), *Beauty and the Beast* (1991), and *Toy Story* (1995). Like the best of their predecessors, they combine complex technologies and universal stories to appeal to children and adults alike.

REPRESENTATIVE FILMS
Snow White and the Seven Dwarfs (1937)
Gulliver's Travels (1939)
Fantasia (1940)
Pinocchio (1940)
Dumbo (1941)
Hoppity Goes to Town (1941)
Bambi (1942)
Anchors Aweigh (1945)
Alice in Wonderland (1951)
Peter Pan (1953)
Lady and the Tramp (1955)
Sleeping Beauty (1959)
101 Dalmatians (1961)
The Sword in the Stone (1963)
A Boy Named Charlie Brown (1969)
Bedknobs and Broomsticks (1971)
Fritz the Cat (1972)
Snoopy, Come Home (1972)
Charlotte's Web (1973)
The Land Before Time (1988)
Who Framed Roger Rabbit (1988)
The Little Mermaid (1989)
Beauty and the Beast (1991)
The Lion King (1994)
Toy Story (1995)
The Rugrats Movie (1998)
Toy Story 2 (1999)
Shrek (2001)

Avant-Garde

AN AVANT-GARDE FILM uses experimental moviemaking techniques or film grammar to push the limits of narrative convention and achieve a purer, more direct form of cinema. The concept of the avant-garde was introduced in France with the founding of the Seventh Art Club, a group aimed at promoting the liberation of the art of film, and by 1920, several varieties of experimental film arose in Europe. These works have often embodied the precepts of broader artistic movements of that era, such as dadaism, expressionism, and surrealism, nearly all of which aimed to create a purer poetic form free of traditional narrative constraints. Notable directors of the 1910s, 1920s, and 1930s include Marcel Duchamp, Luis Buñuel, and Viking Eggeling, with works such as *Anemic Cinema* (1925), *Un Chien Andalou (An Andalusian Dog)* (1929), and *Vertikal-Horizontale Symphonie* (1919), respectively.

By midcentury, the US underground-film movement was creating its own avant-garde works, which countered the polished studio look with a shaky, hand-shot authenticity. Examples encompass the experimental *Mothlight* (1963) and the political *Walden* (1970). In the 1980s and 1990s, the video camera influenced avant-garde filmmaking by making the craft more accessible, and music videos widened the boundaries of film grammar. The result is broader acceptance of avant-garde filmmaking and more experimental films, from directors such as Todd Haynes, whose works include *Poison* (1991). Since the personal-computer revolution in the 1990s, experimental films have been made and distributed online, to growing popularity and critical acceptance.

REPRESENTATIVE FILMS
Vertikal-Horizontale Symphonie (1919, Germany)
Fièvre (1921, France)
Manhattan (1921)
Eldorado (1922, France)
The Extraordinary Adventures of Mr. West in the Land of the Bolsheviks (1924, Russia)
Anemic Cinema (1925, France)
Berlin: Symphony of a City (1927, Germany)
H_2O (1929)
The Life and Death of 9413—A Hollywood Extra (1929)
The Man with the Movie Camera (1929, Russia)
Un Chien Andalou (An Andalusian Dog) (1929, France)
L'Age d'Or/The Golden Age (1930, France)
Le Sang d'un Poète/The Blood of a Poet (France, 1930)
A Propos de Nice (1930, France)
Komposition in Blau (1933, German)
Song of Ceylon (1934, UK)
Synchronization (1934)
Colour Box (1935, UK)
Meshes in the Afternoon (1943)
Dreams That Money Can Buy (1946)
Inauguration of the Pleasure Dome (1954)
Pull My Daisy (1959)
Mothlight (1963)
Blow Job (1964)
Hag in a Black Leather Jacket (1964)
The War Game (1966)
Walden (1970)
Pink Flamingos (1972)
Liquid Sky (1983)
Journeys from Berlin/1971 (1984)
Video Americana (1985)
Poison (1991)
Safe (1995)
Asylum (2000)

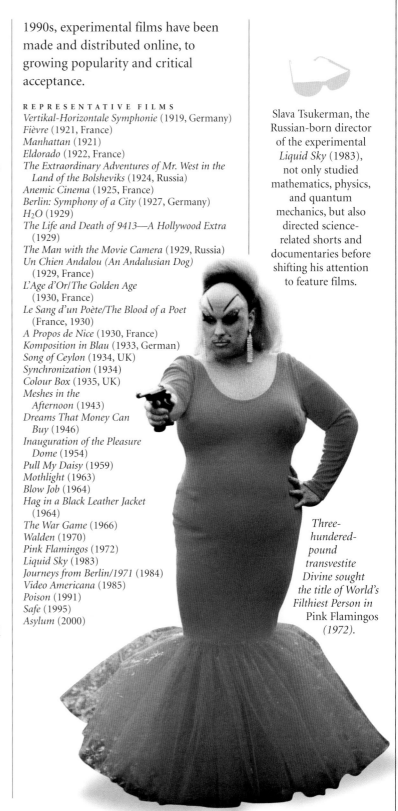

Slava Tsukerman, the Russian-born director of the experimental *Liquid Sky* (1983), not only studied mathematics, physics, and quantum mechanics, but also directed science-related shorts and documentaries before shifting his attention to feature films.

Three-hundred-pound transvestite Divine sought the title of World's Filthiest Person in *Pink Flamingos* (1972).

Biopic

A BIOPIC IS A DRAMATIZED BIOGRAPHY of a notable individual or group that leads to greater understanding of the subject or the era in which they lived. The biopic has been a screen staple since the silent era, when saints, biblical subjects, and western figures dominated subject matter in films such as *Joan of Arc* (1895), *Judith of Bethulia* (1914), and *Jesse James* (1927). During the 1930s, famous public figures became popular subjects for edifying biographical dramas, such as *The Life of Emile Zola* (1937) and *The Story of Alexander Graham Bell* (1939). Presidents have been regular subjects for biopics, with Abraham Lincoln a particularly rich subject. By the 1940s, several biographies had been made in his name. Military figures have also been popular, in films ranging from *Lawrence of Arabia* (1962) to *Patton* (1970). Once the film community had established its own history, entertainers became quarry for biopics; *The Jolson Story* (1946) was an early critical and popular success. In the postwar era, psychological concerns became important, and in films ranging from *Lust for Life* (1956), about Vincent van Gogh, to *Lenny* (1974), about comedian Lenny Bruce, the subject's inner demons became as much a focus of the film as his or her accomplishments. Strong characters worthy of films often elicited award-winning performances from actors. James Cagney, George C. Scott, and Sissy Spacek are a few of the actors winning Academy Awards for their biographical performances in films about George M. Cohan, General George Patton, and Loretta Lynn, respectively.

> "Muhammad Ali is Coca-Cola, he is IBM, he is the Ferrari logo. I wasn't interested in making a biopic or a documentary. I wanted to show the more extreme experience of being Ali, to experience what Ali experienced."
>
> —
>
> *Michael Mann, director of Ali, 2001*

Sissy Spacek portrayed country singer Loretta Lynn in the biographical tale Coal Miner's Daughter *(1980)*, also starring Robert Duvall.

REPRESENTATIVE FILMS
Judith of Bethulia (1914)
Jesse James (1927; remade 1939)
La Passion de Jeanne d'Arc (1928, France)
Abraham Lincoln (1930)
The Great Ziegfeld (1934)
The Life of Emile Zola (1937)
Juarez (1939)
The Story of Alexander Graham Bell (1939)
Young Mr. Lincoln (1939)
Abe Lincoln in Illinois (1940)
Edison, the Man (1940)
Gentleman Jim (1942)
Yankee Doodle Dandy (1942)
Wilson (1944)
The Jolson Story (1946)
The Magnificent Yankee (1950)
The Glenn Miller Story (1954)
Lust for Life (1956)
Spirit of St. Louis (1957)
Sunrise at Campobello (1960)
Lawrence of Arabia (1962)
Funny Girl (1968)
Patton (1970)
Lenny (1974)
Julia (1977)
Coal Miner's Daughter (1980)
Gandhi (1982, UK/India)
Silkwood (1983)
Gorillas in the Mist (1988)
My Left Foot (1989, Ireland)
Chaplin (1992)
Malcolm X (1992)
Ed Wood (1994)
Elizabeth (1998, UK)
Pollock (2000)

Children's

CHILDREN'S FILMS ARE works whose plot, characterizations, and cinematography are tailored to appeal to juvenile audiences. Animation composes a large part of children's works, but because that genre is discussed separately on page 520, only live-action children's works are discussed here. In the 1920s, Rin Tin Tin films introduced the animal as film star and demonstrated its appeal for young audiences. Since then, juvenile films (or adult films with juvenile appeal) have starred animals, children, or both. Other animals that became central to children's films include the dogs Toto, Lassie, Benji, and Beethoven, Francis the talking mule, Trigger the horse, and Babe the pig. Beginning in the sound era, child actors also featured prominently in juvenile films made by many of the major studios. Shirley Temple, Our Gang (reissued for television as the Little Rascals), the Dead End Kids, and young Judy Garland and Mickey Rooney were among the major children's movie stars of the 1930s and early 1940s.

Beginning in the 1950s, television reduced the audience for children's live-action movies, although Walt Disney Studios continued to produce juvenile fare, including *Old Yeller* (1957), *Pollyanna* (1960), and *Mary Poppins* (1964), which combined live action and animation. However, children's film production increased again during the last two decades of the 20th century to meet the desires of the children of baby-boomer parents. A few films in this era, such as *E.T.: The Extra-Terrestrial* (1982) and *Babe* (1995), showed the appeal to both adults and children exhibited by crossover movies of the past, such as the enduring classic *The Wizard of Oz* (1939).

REPRESENTATIVE FILMS
Pollyanna (1920; remade 1960)
Where the North Begins (1923)
Find Your Man (1924)
Rinty of the Desert (1928)
Skippy (1931)
Spanky (1932, short film)
Forgotten Babies (1933, short film)
Kentucky Kernels (1934)
The Little Colonel (1935)
The Littlest Rebel (1935)
Three Smart Girls (1936)
Heidi (1937)
Rebecca of Sunnybrook Farm (1938)
Angels Wash Their Faces (1939)
Babes in Arms (1939)
The Little Princess (1939; remade as *A Little Princess*, 1995)
The Wizard of Oz (1939)
Pride of the Bowery (1940)
Strike Up the Band (1940)
The Swiss Family Robinson (1940; remade 1960, 1975)
National Velvet (1944)
Song of the South (1946)
The Yearling (1946)
Francis (1950)
Francis Goes to the Races (1951)
Hans Christian Anderson (1952)
The 5,000 Fingers of Dr. T (1953)
Old Yeller (1957)
The Absent-Minded Professor (1961)
Mary Poppins (1964)
Born Free (1966, UK)
Doctor Doolittle (1967)
Chitty Chitty Bang Bang (1968)
Willy Wonka and the Chocolate Factory (1971)
Benji (1974)
E.T.: The Extra-Terrestrial (1982)
A Christmas Story (1983)
Honey, I Shrunk the Kids (1989)
Home Alone (1990)
Beethoven (1992)
Free Willy (1993)
The Santa Clause (1994)
Babe (1995, US/Australia)
Madeline (1998)
Dr. Seuss' How the Grinch Stole Christmas (2000)
Harry Potter and the Sorcerer's Stone (2001)

INSET: Free Willy *(1993) featured Jason James Richter as Willy the whale's human friend.*

In addition to penning the surreal children's film *The 5,000 Fingers of Dr. T* (1953), famed children's author Dr. Seuss also wrote the 1945 documentary *Your Job in Germany* for director Frank Capra.

OVERLEAF:

Roy Rowland directed the first nonanimated Dr. Seuss film, The 5,000 Fingers of Dr. T *(1953).*

Comedy

A FILM COMEDY PRESENTS the events of life as a source of humor and amusement. One of the earliest film staples, the silent comedy adapted well to the absence of sound through physical and slapstick humor. Many critics still consider silent comedians such as Charlie Chaplin, Fatty Arbuckle, Harold Lloyd, Mack Sennett, and Buster Keaton among the cinema's most important comedic contributors. Silent comedies were particularly popular in the US, where they were well suited to audiences composed in part of non-English-speaking immigrants. Early sound comedy stars include the Marx Brothers, who combined physical comedy and polished dialogue to create social chaos, as well as masters of the wisecrack such as Mae West and W.C. Fields. During the 1930s, two lasting subgenres took shape: the romantic comedy and its frothy yet tightly structured relative, the screwball comedy. Combining romance, challenges to society, and Shakespearean reversals, the screwball comedy became a hallmark of the sound era. Definitive examples include *Bringing Up Baby* (1938), *The Awful Truth* (1937), and *The Lady Eve* (1941).

> "*Monty Python* touched a communal nerve. *Monty* had connotations of people with seedy little mustaches trying to pretend that they'd had something to do with the war in the desert. And *Python* was all the treachery of a musical agent type."
>
> —
>
> *Monty Python founding member John Cleese, on the origins of his comedy troupe's name, circa 1970s.*

In postwar Europe, offbeat comedies became popular, notably the anti-authoritarian British Ealing comedies, such as *Kind Hearts and Coronets* (1949) and *The Lavender Hill Mob* (1951), and the zany comedies of Jacques Tati, such as *Mr. Hulot's Holiday* (1953) and others. In the United States, postwar comedies ranged from star vehicles such as *The Paleface* (1948), with Bob Hope, to works that hedged on the subversive, such as *Some Like It Hot* (1959).

By the 1960s and 1970s, comedy became darker and more absurdist, featuring black comedies and satires like *Dr. Strangelove* (1964, UK) and *M*A*S*H* (1970), and off-the-wall works like *Young Frankenstein* (1974). The last two decades of the century saw the reliable romantic comedy reimagined as a satire on gender (*Tootsie*, 1982) and a slapstick comedy of humiliation (*There's Something About Mary,* 1998) filled with gags worthy of the silent era. There was also the traditional romantic comedy, *Pretty Woman* (1990), which follows the convention of a rich, idiosyncratic woman disrupting the life of a settled man—except that instead of being a runaway heiress, the main character is a prostitute.

Never Give a Sucker an Even Break (1941) marked the last appearance in a feature film by comedian W.C. Fields.

REPRESENTATIVE FILMS

Jack Fat and Slim Jim at Coney Island (1910)
Max dans sa Famille (1911, France)
Cohen Collects a Debt (1912)
Tillie's Punctured Romance (1914)
Fatty and Mabel Adrift/Mabel, Fatty, and the Law (1916)
Why Worry? (1923)
The Freshman (1925)
The General (1927)
The Cocoanuts (1929)
Duck Soup (1932)
She Done Him Wrong (1933)
It Happened One Night (1934)
A Night at the Opera (1935)
My Man Godfrey (1936)
The Awful Truth (1937)
Bringing Up Baby (1938; remade as *What's Up, Doc?*, 1972)

His Girl Friday (1940)
The Philadelphia Story (1940)
The Lady Eve (1941)
Never Give a Sucker an Even Break (1941)
Road to Morocco (1942)
The Paleface (1948)
Adam's Rib (1949)
Kind Hearts and Coronets (1949, UK)
Born Yesterday (1950)
Harvey (1950)
The Lavender Hill Mob (1951, UK)
Mr. Hulot's Holiday (1953)
The Seven Year Itch (1955)
Pillow Talk (1959)
Some Like It Hot (1959)
The Apartment (1960)
Dr. Strangelove or: How I Learned to Stop Worrying and Love the Bomb (1964, UK)
The Pink Panther (1964)
Play-Time/Playtime (1967, France)
The Producers (1967)
M*A*S*H (1970)
Sleeper (1973)
Blazing Saddles (1974)
Young Frankenstein (1974)
Annie Hall (1977)
Life of Brian (1979, UK)
National Lampoon's Animal House (1979)
Caddyshack (1980)
Tootsie (1982)
Splash (1984)
Moonstruck (1987)
A Fish Called Wanda (1988)
When Harry Met Sally... (1989)
Pretty Woman (1990)
Clerks (1994)
The Full Monty (1997, UK/US)
There's Something About Mary (1998)
Bridget Jones's Diary (2001, US/UK/France)

Crime

A CRIME MOVIE dramatically renders the effects of a crime or life of crime on the victims, perpetrators, or both. In the early sound era, crime films became screen staples, branching into subgenres that have endured for decades. One of these is the prison crime film. Although not all films set in prisons are crime movies, those that are, like *The Big House* (1930) and *Each Dawn I Die* (1939), center on the drama of life behind bars. Gangster films also emerged during the 1930s, with films such as *Little Caesar* (1930) and *Scarface* (1932), which simultaneously glorified and castigated criminals. Countering these sympathetic views of criminals were tough glorifications of crime fighters on either side of the law, such as *"G" Men* (1935), starring James Cagney, the quintessential tough guy.

Postwar crime movies often fell into the category of film noir, which is French for "dark" or "black" film. This style of filmmaking was characterized visually by gloomy lighting, stark shadows, and unsettling camera angles and thematically by pessimism, fatalism, and cynicism. Because the subject matter of film noir was often small-time crime, as in *The Killers* (1946) and *The Asphalt Jungle* (1950), many darkly drawn crime films of the 1940s and 1950s could also be classified as film noir.

In the 1960s, the crime genre was reinvigorated with the character drama *Bonnie and Clyde* (1967), which portrayed the title characters as misfit heroes. Similarly, the gangster drama gained gravitas in the 1970s with *The Godfather* (1972) and *The Godfather Part II* (1974), and realistic urban edginess in films from *Mean Streets* in the 1970s to *GoodFellas* in the 1990s.

REPRESENTATIVE FILMS
The Big House (1930)
Little Caesar (1930)
I Am a Fugitive from a Chain Gang (1932)
Scarface (1932; remade 1983)
"G" Men (1935)
The Petrified Forest (1936)
Dead End (1937)
Angels with Dirty Faces (1938)
Each Dawn I Die (1939)
The Roaring Twenties (1939)
Double Indemnity (1944)
Detour (1945)
The Killers (1946)
The Postman Always Rings Twice (1946)
The Asphalt Jungle (1950)
The Killing (1956)
Bonnie and Clyde (1967)
The Thomas Crown Affair (1968; remade 1999)
The French Connection (1971)

Al Pacino starred as a frustrated bank robber in Dog Day Afternoon *(1975), a thriller based on a true story.*

Actor Tom Neal, who portrayed one of *film noir's* most notorious losers in Edgar G. Ulmer's *Detour* (1945), led a life that imitated his art. He was sent to prison for the murder of his wife.

It's fairly well known among film aficionados that the science fiction cult classic *Forbidden Planet* (1956) is loosely based on Shakespeare's *The Tempest.* What's less well known is that many of *Forbidden Planet's* costumes were recycled two years later for the campy Zsa Zsa Gabor vehicle, *Queen of Outer Space* (1958).

The Godfather (1972)
Mean Streets (1973)
Serpico (1973)
The Godfather, Part II (1974)
Dog Day Afternoon (1975)
Escape from Alcatraz (1979)
The Untouchables (1987)
The Godfather Part, III (1990)
GoodFellas (1990)
Thelma & Louise (1991)
The Shawshank Redemption (1994)
The Usual Suspects (1995)
Out of Sight (1998)
Training Day (2001)

Cult Movies

CULT MOVIES ARE works that, because of their subject matter or timeliness (or both), capture a devoted following. Usually a film develops into a cult film over time, as it builds word-of-mouth interest and an audience of repeat viewers, who, through audience participation and fan-club membership, among other activities, become involved in the film. The crown jewel of the transgender comedy cult films is *The Rocky Horror Picture Show* (1975), now in its third decade of audience involvement. Sometimes a film becomes a cult item years after its initial release, as new generations encounter it fresh. A case in point is *It's a Wonderful Life,* which was overshadowed upon its 1946 release by *The Best Years of Our Lives,* but in the 1970s became a cult (and later mainstream) yuletide favorite, helped along by repeated television airings. Past films about present

The Rocky Horror Picture Show *(1975), starring Tim Curry as a transsexual alien, became a cult camp phenomenon.*

concerns are also prime candidates for cult followings. The 1936 antimarijuana film *Reefer Madness* has been seen by some as a humorous anachronism since the popularization of the drug in the 1960s, and *Glen or Glenda* (1952) is appreciated for both its cinematic ineptness and its compassion for transvestism.

Some of the more stylized genres, notably science fiction and soap opera, have their cult representatives, such as *Forbidden Planet* (1956) and *An Affair to Remember* (1957), respectively. There is also the cult following arising from pornographic movies that gain special notoriety, such as *Behind the Green Door* (1972), which starred Ivory Snow model Marilyn Chambers. While most films edge from obscurity to cult-film success, a few move from wide popularity to cult adoration when new viewers appreciate it differently or the original audience encounters it differently over time. A recent example of this phenomenon is the 1965 musical *The Sound of Music,* which was rereleased in 1999 and 2000 to become a Rocky Horror–type participatory event.

REPRESENTATIVE FILMS
Reefer Madness (1936)
The Wizard of Oz (1939)
It's a Wonderful Life (1946)
Glen or Glenda (1952)
Forbidden Planet (1956)
An Affair to Remember (1957)
Plan 9 from Outer Space (1959)
Little Shop of Horrors (1960; remade 1986)
The Sound of Music (1965)
Behind the Green Door (1972)
Harold and Maude (1972)
Pink Flamingos (1972)
The Rocky Horror Picture Show (1975)
Attack of the Killer Tomatoes (1980)
Pink Floyd—The Wall (1982, UK)
Repo Man (1984)
This Is Spinal Tap (1984)
Evil Dead II (1987)
Henry Fool (1998)

Documentary

A DOCUMENTARY IS A nonfiction film that depicts some element of the human condition. Throughout its existence, this genre's aims have varied from persuading audiences to offering an objective view of an event. The form began in the United States and France during the early 20th century with the newsreel, which recorded contemporary events or reconstructed them for the screen. Multireel documentaries appeared widely during the 1910s in Britain and the US, with propagandistic films dominating the genre during World War I. During the 1920s, several international filmmakers developed the genre artistically. In the US, there was Robert Flaherty with *Nanook of the North* (1922); Marc Allégret in France with *Finnis Terrae* (1929); and Sergei Eisenstein in the USSR with *October/ Ten Days That Shook the World* (1928). The term "documentary" was coined in a 1926 review of Flaherty's *Moana*. During the 1930s and 1940s, the documentary developed into an efficient propaganda tool, in films such as Leni Riefenstahl's *Triumph des Willens (Triumph of the Will)* (1935, Germany) and *In Which We Serve* (1942, UK), directed by David Lean and Noël Coward. The form opened up in subject and technique after World War II, reflecting the influences of television and more streamlined film equipment. Notable postwar titles include *The Endless Summer* (1966) and *Harlan County, USA* (1976). The documentary has continued to flourish as a medium hospitable to independent filmmakers across dozens of countries and to explorations of controversial subjects.

REPRESENTATIVE FILMS

The Durbar at Delhi (The Delhi Durbar) (1911, UK)
The Life of Villa (1914)
Thirty Leagues Under the Sea (1914)
How Life Begins (1916)
Nanook of the North (1922)
Cinema Eye (1924, USSR)
Grass (1925)
Moana (1926)
Berlin—Symphony of a Big City (1927, Germany)
Voyage au Congo (1927, France)
October/Ten Days That Shook the World (1928, USSR)
Drifters (1929, UK)
Finnis Terrae (1929, France)
Man With a Movie Camera (1929, USSR)
Las Hurdes (Land Without Bread) (1932)
Coal Face (1935)
Triumph des Willens (Triumph of the Will) (1935, Germany)
The Plow That Broke the Plains (1936)
The Spanish Earth (1937)
The City (1939)
The 400 Million (1939)
Valley Town (1940)
In Which We Serve (1942, UK)
Desert Victory (1943, UK)
Prelude to War (1943)
The Memphis Belle (1944)
Victory in the Ukraine (1945, USSR)
Louisiana Story (1948)
The Living Desert (1953)
Nuit et Brouillard (Night and Fog) (1955, France)
The Silent World (1956)
Four Days in November (1964)
The Eleanor Roosevelt Story (1965)
The Endless Summer (1966)
Why Man Creates (1968)
Le Chagrin et la Pitié/The Sorrow and the Pity (1971, Switzerland)
The Hellstrom Chronicle (1971)
Hearts and Minds (1974)
Brother Can You Spare a Dime? (1975)
Harlan County, USA (1976)
The Children of Theatre Street (1977)
Let's Get Lost (1988)
Roger and Me (1989)
The Thin Blue Line (1989)
Paris Is Burning (1990)
Hoop Dreams (1994)
When We Were Kings (1996)
Endurance: Shackleton's Legendary Antarctic Expedition (2000, UK/US)

INSET: *The award-winning documentary* Hoop Dreams *(1994) focused on two inner-city high school basketball stars.*

For his 1997 film *Fast, Cheap & Out of Control*, documentarian Errol Morris created a groundbreaking device called the Interrotron. With a two-way camera and video monitor system assembled around a traditional film camera, it allows—for the first time—both interviewer and interviewee to make something resembling direct eye contact through the lens.

OVERLEAF:

Sergei Eisenstein's commemoration of the tenth anniversary of the 1917 Revolution, the documentary October *(1928), underwent extensive last minute editing before its release due to changes in the political climate.*

Gregory Peck played a Southern lawyer defending a black man in the film adaptation of the novel To Kill a Mockingbird *(1962).*

"If I could make that movie from now on, even if it never came out…if I could just keep making *that,* I would do it."

—

Actor/screenwriter Billy Bob Thornton on his 1996 directorial debut, Sling Blade, *2001.*

Drama

A DRAMATIC FILM depicts characters in serious conflict with other people, nature, or themselves. The form dominates the cinema, with the bulk of films falling into its broad borders. In fact, the category is so large that several dramatic subgenres have developed over the years, including the crime drama (pages 527–528), historical drama (pages 533-534), and most westerns (pages 546–547) and mysteries (page 540), among others. Because these subgenres are discussed in separate listings, this section concentrates on nonperiod dramas that focus on character rather than physical action.

Within this definition, there has been great variety over the decades, which in part reflects the fact that social and cultural concerns drive the drama. For example, dramas of the 1930s like *Street Scene* (1931) focused on class divisions. In the 1950s, dramas such as

Rebel Without a Cause (1955) showcased generational conflict. Civil rights were central to several dramas in the 1960s, including *To Kill a Mockingbird* (1962) and *Guess Who's Coming to Dinner* (1967). Studies of human character perennially make for strong dramas; a good example is *Citizen Kane* (1941). But the most enduring concern of film drama remains family conflict. Whether the conflict comes from within or without, the subject has resulted in many of the most lauded films in history, of which *The Grapes of Wrath* (1940), *A Streetcar Named Desire* (1951), and *American Beauty* (1999) are just a few.

REPRESENTATIVE FILMS
The Squaw Man (1914; remade 1918, 1931)
Broken Blossoms (1919)
Way Down East (1920)
The Jazz Singer (1927; remade 1953, 1980)
Seventh Heaven (1927)
Sunrise (1927)
Min and Bill (1930)
Street Scene (1931)
Grand Hotel (1932)
The Informer (1935)
Dead End (1937)
Boys Town (1938)
Goodbye, Mr. Chips (1939, US/UK)
The Grapes of Wrath (1940)
Rebecca (1940)
Citizen Kane (1941)
How Green Was My Valley (1941)
Casablanca (1942)
The Lost Weekend (1945)
The Best Years of Our Lives (1946)
Gentlemen's Agreement (1947)
All About Eve (1950)
Sunset Boulevard (1950)
A Place in the Sun (1951)
A Streetcar Named Desire (1951)
Come Back, Little Sheba (1952)
The Country Girl (1954)
On the Waterfront (1954)
Marty (1955)
Rebel Without a Cause (1955)
Giant (1956)
To Kill a Mockingbird (1962)
Doctor Zhivago (1965)
Guess Who's Coming to Dinner (1967)
Midnight Cowboy (1969)
The Prime of Miss Jean Brodie (1969)
One Flew Over the Cuckoo's Nest (1975)
Network (1976)

Kramer vs. Kramer (1979)
Ordinary People (1980)
Raging Bull (1980)
Sophie's Choice (1982)
Rain Man (1988)
Driving Miss Daisy (1989)
Philadelphia (1993)
Forrest Gump (1994)
Quiz Show (1994)
The English Patient (1996)
Sling Blade (1996)
As Good as It Gets (1997)
Good Will Hunting (1997)
La Vita e Bella/Life Is Beautiful (1998, Italy)
American Beauty (1999)
Traffic (2000)

Historical

A HISTORICAL FILM aims to recreate an important past event or era to preserve it for future generations or cast it in a modern light. There is some overlap between this genre and the biopic, although historical films focus more on the force of events rather than the intricacies of the human psyche. Also called costume dramas because they depict the wardrobe of vanished times, historical films usually blend fictional characters with historical fact. They have been a screen staple since the silent era, when an account of the Civil War and Reconstruction called *The Birth of a Nation* (1915) revealed how cinematically complex the historical film could be. The film employed multiple human dramas to convey the scope of events, which would become a standard practice in like dramas from *Gone with the Wind* (1939) to *Schindler's List* (1993). Because it undercut its historical reliability through its heroic representation of the Ku Klux Klan, *The Birth of a Nation* also pointed to how ideologically fraught the genre could be.

This conflict between truth and dramatic license has created controversies throughout film history, arising from movies as diverse as *The Battleship Potemkin* (1925, USSR) and *JFK* (1991). Still, although audiences appreciate veracity, it does not ensure a historical film's popularity. The 1944 film *Wilson* may have been historically accurate, but it was also a flop. Audiences that year preferred the social history rendered by the period musical *Meet Me in St. Louis,* starring Judy Garland.

Historical film blends easily with other genres. The adventure film *The Adventures of Robin Hood* (1938) is also a historical depiction of England's King Richard I and Prince John. *Titanic* (1997) mixes elements of the historical, adventure, and romance genres. Within the historical genre, there are also distinct subgenres. Westerns, described separately on pages 546–547, are historical films about America's western frontier in the late 19th century. War films, discussed separately on pages 544–545, are historical films when they feature real wars from the past. Swashbucklers, described separately under the heading "Action-Adventure" (pages 516–517), are historical films about the late medieval and early Renaissance periods. Another subgenre is the biblical epic, which usually has a strong religious viewpoint, as in *The Ten Commandments* (1923). This subgenre

The greatest number of costumes ever used in one movie was 32,000; these were worn in the Roman costume drama *Quo Vadis?* (1951).

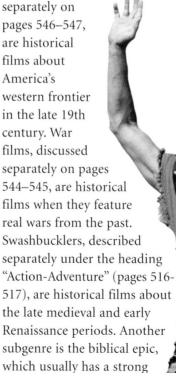

Kirk Douglas starred in Spartacus *(1960), the true story of a gladiator who led a slave a rebellion in ancient Rome.*

To accomplish the parting of the Red Sea in the 1923 version of *The Ten Commandments,* two blocks of Jell-O, carved with waves, were held together on a huge table with water rushing over them. On cue, winches separated the blocks, creating the parting effect. Double exposures then provided the illusion that horses, riders, and chariots had tumbled into the parting "sea." The final images were so realistic for their time that the Society for the Prevention of Cruelty to Animals was convinced that horses had actually been mistreated in the making the film.

includes "swords-and-sandals" films, which may depict biblical history or secular events from antiquity, such as the slave revolt depicted in *Spartacus* (1960). When swords-and-sandals films include mythological material, they intersect with the fantasy genre.

REPRESENTATIVE FILMS
The Birth of a Nation (1915)
The Ten Commandments (1923; remade 1956)
The Battleship Potemkin (1925, USSR)
Ben-Hur (1926; remade 1959)
King of Kings (1927; remade 1961)
The Sign of the Cross (1932)
Cavalcade (1933)
The Last Days of Pompeii (1935; remade 1960, Italy)
The Adventures of Robin Hood (1938)
Drums Along the Mohawk (1939)
Gone with the Wind (1939)
Northwest Passage (1940)
Meet Me in St. Louis (1944)
Wilson (1944)
Samson and Delilah (1949)
Quo Vadis? (1951; remade 1985, Italy)
The Robe (1953)
Spartacus (1960)
The Longest Day (1962)
The Fall of the Roman Empire (1964)
Hawaii (1966)
A Man for All Seasons (1966, UK)
Barry Lyndon (1975)
Julia (1977)
Reds (1981)
The Last Emperor (1987, Italy/UK/China)
JFK (1991)
Gettysburg (1993)
Schindler's List (1993)
Braveheart (1995)
Titanic (1997)
Gladiator (2000)
The Patriot (2000)

Horror

A HORROR FILM is one whose principal end is the production of fear and revulsion. Often the horrifying element is supernatural in origin (vampires, werewolves, demons, ghosts); in other cases, it is a product of science (the Frankenstein monster; Dr. Jekyll's alter ego, Mr. Hyde) or dementia (the serial killer Norman Bates in *Psycho*). The possibility of death and dismemberment is usually close at hand. Synonyms that have been used for the horror film include chiller, spookfest, scary movie, and thriller, although thriller can also refer to other kinds of film with frightening content. A film about the FBI tracking a serial killer might be called a thriller, but it would not be a horror film unless the focus wasthe fear and revulsion caused by the killer's acts, rather than the excitement and intricacies of the chase. *The Silence of the Lambs* (1991) straddles these two genres, generating both horror and police-procedural suspense.

In the silent era and the early days of sound, typical horror movies were Gothic in style: these films features decaying castles, spooky old houses, creepy monsters, fog, shadows, a Gothic or Victorian air, and violence that was more often suggested than shown. German Expressionism gave Gothic horror films much of their cinematic vocabulary and generated one of the earliest examples of the genre, *The Cabinet of Dr. Caligari* (1919). Universal Studios was famed for its Gothic horror productions of the 1930s and 1940s, which included *Frankenstein* and *Dracula* (both 1931).

Director Oliver Stone's controversial film JFK *(1991) proposed that the assassination of President John F. Kennedy was part of a conspiracy.*

In the 1950s, horror went atomic, with often gigantic monsters (e.g., *Godzilla,* 1956, Japan) supplied by radioactive spills, space invasions, or other scientific mishaps.

Beginning with Alfred Hitchcock's *Psycho* (1960), horror filmmakers came to focus on deranged murderers plying their trade with ever increasing explicitness (the "slasher" subgenre). Special effects and makeup artists became increasingly important—notably in *The Exorcist* (1973)—as they labored to make the gore ever more realistic. Two popular films of 1999, *The Blair Witch Project* and *The Sixth Sense,* marked a return to the psychological suggestiveness of early horror cinema.

Max Schreck starred in *Nosferatu* (1922), a vampire film based on Bram Stoker's Dracula.

REPRESENTATIVE FILMS

The Cabinet of Dr. Caligari (1919, Germany)
Nosferatu, the Vampire (1922, Germany)
The Hunchback of Notre Dame (1923)
The Phantom of the Opera (1925)
Dracula (1931)
Frankenstein (1931)
Dr. Jekyll and Mr. Hyde (1932)
Freaks (1932)
The Mummy (1932)
The Invisible Man (1933)
Island of Lost Souls (1933)
King Kong (1933)
The Bride of Frankenstein (1935)
The Wolf Man (1941)
Cat People (1942)
The Uninvited (1944)
Dead of Night (1946, UK)
Godzilla, King of the Monsters (1956, Japan)

The Fly (1958; remade 1986)
The Horror of Dracula (1958)
Les Yeux sans Visage (Eyes Without a Face/ The Horror Chamber of Dr. Faustus) (1959, France/Italy)
Psycho (1960)
What Ever Happened to Baby Jane? (1962)
The Haunting (1963)
The Tomb of Ligeia (1964, UK)
Night of the Living Dead (1968)
Rosemary's Baby (1968)
The Exorcist (1973)
The Texas Chainsaw Massacre (1974)
Carrie (1976)
The Omen (1976)
Halloween (1978)
The Shining (1980)
The Evil Dead (1983)
A Nightmare on Elm Street (1984)
Re-Animator (1985)
The Silence of the Lambs (1991)
From Dusk till Dawn (1996)
Scream (1996)
I Know What You Did Last Summer (1997)
The Blair Witch Project (1999)
The Sixth Sense (1999)
The Others (2001)

In *Halloween* (1978), the knife-wielding Michael Myers hides his face behind a customized William Shatner mask.

OVERLEAF:

Universal produced numerous horror films in the early 1930s, including Frankenstein *(1931), starring Colin Clive as Henry Frankenstein and Boris Karloff as the Monster.*

Melodrama

A MELODRAMA PORTRAYS in heightened terms the human dramas of everyday life and conveys their meaning (with rare exceptions) through one or more central female characters. Endurance and resolve, rather than physical strength and bravery, characterize melodrama heroines. They will suffer, sacrifice, and surmount great fears to secure true love, sustain friendships, and protect their families. Films of this sort are also called soapers, soap operas, women's pictures, chick flicks, and weepies.

When *Ghost* (1990) was screened for audiences in Monterrey, Mexico, female audience members were distributed envelopes marked "solo para mujeres"; translated, "for women only." Inside the envelope? Tissues.

In this genre, threats to love and family come from both society and the families themselves and reflect the concerns of the prevailing culture. Some early silent and sound melodrama such as *Stella Dallas* (1925, 1937) focused on the stigma of poverty by championing poor female characters who sacrifice to help their children rise in society. But excessive maternal devotion can backfire and destroy family happiness, as in *Mildred Pierce* (1945), in which Pierce (Joan Crawford) pampers her only child, Veda (Ann Blyth), and produces a murderous ingrate. Other inequities of society break up soap opera families, as in *Imitation of Life* (1959), in which the effects of racism drive apart mother (Juanita Moore) and daughter (Susan Kohner), until the final scene, in which Kohner races to embrace her dead mother's hearse. Personal temptations also

Ryan O'Neal and Ali McGraw were young lovers from different worlds in Love Story *(1970).*

create familial conflict—with one of the most common vehicles being the lure of show business. Perhaps the most durable of show business weepies is *A Star Is Born,* which has seen three incarnations over five decades (1937, 1954, 1976).

In melodrama since the 1970s, the families that must be preserved have been redefined. For example, in *An Unmarried Woman* (1978), it is a newly single woman seeking self-realization. *Waiting to Exhale* (1995) features traditional soap opera concerns, using an African-American cast. However, despite social changes over the century, the grandest, most enduring problem driving an effective melodrama is death. It has been the center of the weepie throughout film history, in films ranging from *Dark Victory* (1939) to *Love Story* (1970) to *Dying Young* (1991). In melodrama, nothing succeeds like a pretty, long death.

REPRESENTATIVE FILMS

Way Down East (1920; remade 1935)
Stella Dallas (1925; remade 1937 and in 1990 as *Stella*)
Street Angel (1928)
Back Street (1931; remade 1941, 1961)
Imitation of Life (1934; remade 1959)
Magnificent Obsession (1935; remade 1954)
A Star Is Born (1937; remade 1954, 1976)
Dark Victory (1939; remade as *The Stolen Hours*, 1963)
Love Affair (1939; remade as *An Affair to Remember*, 1957)
Now, Voyager (1942)
Old Acquaintance (1943; remade as *Rich and Famous*, 1981)
Mildred Pierce (1945)
All That Heaven Allows (1955; remade as *Ali—Fear Eats the Soul*, 1974, Germany)
A Summer Place (1959)
Love Story (1970)
An Unmarried Woman (1978)
Kramer vs. Kramer (1979)
Terms of Endearment (1983)
Beaches (1988)
Ghost (1990)
Dying Young (1991)
Waiting to Exhale (1995)

Musical

A MUSICAL FILM is a work created to showcase music, often developing characters and propelling the plot through dramatic song and orchestration. Early musicals, in the late 1920s, were marked by spectacle and the novelty of capturing music on film. Notable examples include *The Broadway Melody* (1929), which became the first musical to win an Academy Award for best picture. Musicals gained greater variety during the 1930s, with studios offering varied fare, including sleek Fred Astaire–Ginger Rogers vehicles, sumptuous Busby Berkeley spectacles, and high-toned Nelson Eddy–Jeanette MacDonald operatic musicals.

One of the most enduring of 1930s musicals fits into none of these categories: that is *The Wizard of Oz* (1939). Its stunning use of color ushered in two decades of lavish color musicals, many of which were produced at MGM by Arthur Freed, who worked with musical directors such as Vincente Minnelli and Stanley Donen and stars such as Judy Garland and Gene Kelly. The Freed Unit created definitive musicals such as *Meet Me in St. Louis* (1944), *Singin' in the Rain* (1952), *An American in Paris* (1951), and *Gigi* (1958), the last two winning Academy Awards for best picture.

Screen adaptations of stage musicals marked the 1960s, when four musicals won the Academy Awards for best picture, among them *West Side Story* (1961) and *The Sound of Music* (1965). By the 1970s, however, the screen musical diminished in popularity, and over the next three decades, relatively few were produced. Representative titles include *Saturday Night Fever* (1977), *Grease* (1978), and the musical biography *Selena* (1997).

REPRESENTATIVE FILMS
The Broadway Melody (1929)
Show Boat (1929; remade 1936, 1951)
Footlight Parade (1933)
42nd Street (1933)
Gold Diggers of 1933 (1933)
The Gay Divorcée (1934)
The Great Ziegfeld (1934)
Broadway Melody of 1936 (1935)
The Little Colonel (1935)
Top Hat (1935)
Rose Marie (1936)
Swing Time (1936)
The Wizard of Oz (1939)
Strike Up the Band (1940)
Holiday Inn (1942)
Stage Door Canteen (1943)
Meet Me in St. Louis (1944)
Anchors Aweigh (1945)
Easter Parade (1948)
The Red Shoes (1948)
On the Town (1949)
An American in Paris (1951)
Singin' in the Rain (1952)
The Band Wagon (1953)
Seven Brides for Seven Brothers (1954)
A Star Is Born (1954)
White Christmas (1954)
Funny Face (1957)
Gigi (1958)
West Side Story (1961)
A Hard Day's Night (1964, UK)
Mary Poppins (1964)
My Fair Lady (1964)
The Sound of Music (1965)
Funny Girl (1968)
Saturday Night Fever (1977)
Grease (1978)
Pennies from Heaven (1981)
Footloose (1984)
Shall We Dance? (1996, Japan)
Selena (1997)
Dancer in the Dark (2000)

"I have no desire to prove anything by it. I have never used it as an outlet or as a means of expressing myself. I just dance."

—

Fred Astaire, 1959

INSET: *Barbra Streisand starred as comedian Fanny Brice in* Funny Girl *(1968).*

Mystery

MYSTERY FILMS focus on solving a crime. Many films, such as *Notorious* (1946) (and most of Alfred Hitchcock's films) and *The Silence of the Lambs* (1991), contain elements of a mystery, but if detection is subordinated to other concerns, such as suspense or horror, they may be more properly categorized as suspense films or horror films or some other genre.

Mysteries have been a movie genre since the silent era and staples since the 1930s, when detective series based on established literary detectives were very popular. Notable among them were Sherlock Holmes, Charlie Chan, Philo Vance, and Bulldog Drummond, who together starred in dozens of movies before and after World War II. The books of mystery maven Agatha Christie have provided solid sources for film mysteries over the decades, ranging from *And Then There Were None* (1945) to *Murder on the Orient Express* (1974).

Frances McDormand played a pregnant police chief investigating a kidnapping in the unconventional mystery Fargo *(1996).*

Highly influential to the mystery film is the hard-boiled detective novel, particularly those by Raymond Chandler and Dashiell Hammett. These tough mysteries often meshed well with the cinematic elements of film noir, a style of filmmaking characterized by gloomy lighting and cynical or pessimistic content. (See also "Crime" [page 527] for further discussion of film noir.) Notable film noir mysteries include *The Maltese Falcon* (1941) and *Murder, My Sweet* (1944), with tough-guy leads such as Humphrey Bogart and Dick Powell.

Some film mysteries combine comedy and crime-solving, notably the *Thin Man* series, starring William Powell and Myrna Loy, and *The Pink Panther* and its sequels, featuring Peter Sellers. In part because television has eroded the market for straight mystery, recent film mysteries have been unconventional, such as *Fargo* (1996) and *The Talented Mr. Ripley* (1999).

REPRESENTATIVE FILMS
Sherlock Holmes (1922)
Behind That Curtain (1929)
The Canary Murder Case (1929)
The Kennel Murder Case (1933)
The Thin Man (1934)
Charlie Chan in Paris (1936)
The Adventures of Sherlock Holmes (1939)
The Hound of the Baskervilles (1939)
The Maltese Falcon (1941)
Laura (1944)
Murder, My Sweet (1944; remade as *Farewell, My Lovely*, 1975)
And Then There Were None (1945; remade as *Ten Little* Indians, 1966, 1975, 1989)
The Big Sleep (1946)
Notorious (1946)
Witness for the Prosecution (1957)
The Pink Panther (1964)
A Shot in the Dark (1964)
Chinatown (1974)
Murder on the Orient Express (1974, UK)
The Big Easy (1987)
The Usual Suspects (1995)
Fargo (1996)
L.A. Confidential (1997)
A Simple Plan (1998)
The Talented Mr. Ripley (1999)

Romance

A ROMANCE OR ROMANTIC DRAMA centers on the search for and declaration of love. Although many films, such as romantic comedies and soap operas, contain a love interest, it is often subordinate to the primary aim; be it humor or family drama. In a romance, love is the aim and the obstacles to attaining love, while fueling the plot, are secondary.

That allows seemingly different films like *Wuthering Heights* (1939) and *Jerry Maguire* (1996), or films that overlap with other genres, like *An Affair to Remember* (1957) and *The Way We Were* (1973), to be considered romances.

One element of the romance that has changed markedly over the decades is the nature of the romantic lead. The 1920s were marked by the exotic lover, epitomized in men such as Rudolph Valentino and Ramon Novarro, and in women by Theda Bara (whose name was said to be an anagram of "Arab Death"). Continental European romantic leads were prominent in the 1930s and part of the 1940s, represented by Maurice Chevalier, Charles Boyer, Robert Taylor, Greta Garbo, and others. But even in that era, uncontrived and openly sexual romantic leads such as Clark Gable were gaining prominence in films.

Within a decade, they would dominate, encompassing over a half-century of heartthrobs of both sexes, including Cary Grant, Ingrid Bergman, Paul Newman, Marilyn Monroe, Robert Redford, Michelle Pfeiffer, Tom Cruise, Julia Roberts, and Ben Affleck.

REPRESENTATIVE FILMS
Camille (1915; remade 1917, 1921, 1937)
The Sheik (1921)
Son of the Sheik (1926)
History Is Made at Night (1937)
Love Affair (1939; remade as *An Affair to Remember*, 1957)
Wuthering Heights (1939)
Now, Voyager (1942)
Three Coins in the Fountain (1954)
Love is a Many Splendored Thing (1955)
Summertime (1955)
Jules and Jim (1961, France)
The Umbrellas of Cherbourg (1964, France)
A Man and a Woman (1966, France)
The Way We Were (1973)
Witness (1980)
Say Anything (1989)
When Harry Met Sally... (1989)
Before Sunrise (1994)
Jerry Maguire (1996)
Shakespeare in Love (1998)
Kate and Leopold (2001)

Ethan Hawke and Julia Delpy starred as young twentysomethings who meet while traveling on a European train and spend 14 hours together in Vienna, Austria discussing life and love in Richard Linklater's Before Sunrise *(1994).*

Before director Ridley Scott completed his "director's cut" in 1992, aerial shots at the end of the original theatrical and video release prints of *Blade Runner* (1982), with stars Harrison Ford and Sean Young escaping to the countryside, was actually comprised of unused footage from *The Shining* (1980).

Maurice Evans appeared as the ape Dr. Zaius in the 1968 classic *Planet of the Apes (1968)*.

Science Fiction and Fantasy

SCIENCE FICTION AND FANTASY FILMS work their magic by depicting phenomena that are not yet possible and may never be. Often set in the future, science fiction films base their wonders on known science, or at least the trappings of science, such as spaceships and robots. In contrast, fantasy films dispense with the need for scientific explanation, presenting fairy-tale or mythological events often in a legendary past. Science fiction and fantasy frequently overlap: the space fantasy *Star Wars* (1977), for example, is set "a long time ago in a galaxy far, far away." Both science fiction and fantasy often blend with action-adventure and horror (see pages 516–517 and 534–535 for separate discussions of these genres). In fact, most science fiction and fantasy films are adventure stories, and those that focus primarily on frightening creatures, such as *The Thing from Another World* (1951) and *Alien* (1979), can also be categorized as horror films. Special effects and imaginative production design are essential to making most science fiction and fantasy films plausible, although some, such as *Gattaca* (1997), rely primarily on characterization and performances for impact. French filmmaker Georges Méliès pioneered the science fiction and fantasy genre, producing a panoply of special effects in such silent films as *A Trip to the Moon* (1902). Fritz Lang's silent classic

Metropolis (1926, Germany), a nightmare vision of the future plight of urban workers, established the tradition of using science fiction to comment on contemporary society, a tradition taken up by films from *Things to Come* in the 1930s to *The Truman Show* in the 1990s. Alongside such serious aspirations, comic book–style escapism has been part of the genre since the *Flash Gordon* and *Buck Rogers* serials of the 1930s. The two kinds of content coexisted particularly well in the 1950s; *The Day the Earth Stood Still* (1951) brought a sober message about world peace, while *The War of the Worlds* (1953) and various other alien-invasion films went for thrills. *2001: A Space Odyssey* (1968, UK) set a new standard for futuristic realism and serious thematic content, but the success of *Star Wars* (1977) and its sequels led to a plethora of action-packed, eye-popping films that were the cinematic equivalent of roller-coaster rides. Some of these, such as *Batman* (1989), were directly based on comic book superheroes. Occasionally, spectacular action and philosophical concerns blend, as in *The Matrix* (1999).

Pure fantasy film is even more likely than science fiction to be sheerly escapist. *The Thief of Bagdad* (1940, UK) and *The 7th Voyage of Sinbad* (1958), with their genies and magical creatures, are examples of this type of fanciful film. But the fairy-tale format has also been used for more meditative purposes, as Jean Cocteau's *Beauty and the Beast* (1946, France) and Wim Wenders's tale of modern-day angels, *Wings of Desire* (1988, West Germany/ France).

REPRESENTATIVE FILMS

Voyage dans la Lune (A Trip to the Moon)
   (1902, France)
The Thief of Bagdad (1924; remade 1940, UK)
Metropolis (1926, Germany)
Things to Come (1936, UK)
La Belle et la Bête (Beauty and the Beast)
   (1946, France)
Destination Moon (1950)
The Day the Earth Stood Still (1951)
The Thing from Another World (1951)
The War of the Worlds (1953)
This Island Earth (1955)
Forbidden Planet (1956)
Invasion of the Body Snatchers (1956)
The 7th Voyage of Sinbad (1958)
The Time Machine (1960)
The Day of the Triffids (1963, UK)
Jason and the Argonauts (1963, UK)
Fantastic Voyage (1966)
Planet of the Apes (1968)
2001: A Space Odyssey (1968, UK)
The Andromeda Strain (1971)
A Clockwork Orange (1971)
Logan's Run (1976)
Close Encounters of the Third Kind (1977)

Star Wars (1977; sequels in 1980, 1983, 1999)
Superman (1978)
Alien (1979)
Star Trek—The Motion Picture (1979)
Raiders of the Lost Ark (1981)
Blade Runner (1982)
E.T.: The Extra-Terrestrial (1982)
The Terminator (1984)
Back to the Future (1985)
Brazil (1985)
Aliens (1986)
Der Himmel über Berlin/Wings of Desire
   (1988, West Germany/France)
Batman (1989)
Twelve Monkeys (1995)
Independence Day (1996)
Le Cinquième element/The Fifth Element
   (1997, France)
The Devil's Advocate (1997)
Gattaca (1997)
Starship Troopers (1997)
Armageddon (1998)
The Truman Show (1998)
The Matrix (1999)
The Cell (2000)
A.I. Artificial Intelligence (2000)

*Uma Thurman
portrayed a "perfect"
human in the genetically
engineered world of*
Gattaca *(1997).*

Serials

A SERIAL CONSISTS of a lengthy sequence of melodramatic, action-filled episodes that are shown in installments to entice audiences to return to the theater. Serials gained popularity before 1910 in France and became US staples during the 1910s, largely with serials that featured plucky heroines such as *The Perils of Pauline* (1914), starring Pearl White.

Buster Crabble played the title role in the adventure serial favorite Flash Gordon *(1936).*

Other notable female heroines of the time included Grace Cunard and Ruth Roland. Usually running for several weeks, a serial could extend up to three years, as did *The Hazards of Helen,* which ran from 1914 to 1917.

Beginning in the 1920s, US serials turned to male heroes who usually fought nefarious villains or the impending destruction of the universe. The heroes might be detectives like Ace Drummond, western figures like Jesse James, or comic strip principals like the Green Hornet or Buck Rogers. Popular serial actors include Buster Crabbe, the lead in the *Flash Gordon* adventures (1936). As a genre, the serial ended in 1956 with *Blazing the Overland Trail,* but it would be reincarnated in a different form decades later by George Lucas's *Star Wars* (1977) and Steven Spielberg's *Raiders of the Lost Ark* (1981), and their sequels.

REPRESENTATIVE FILMS
The Perils of Pauline (1914)
The Hazards of Helen (1914–17)
The Exploits of Elaine (1915)
The Fatal Ring (1917)
Judex (1917, France)
I Topi Grigi (1917–18, Italy)
Tih Minh (1918, France)
Barabbas (1920, France)
Homunculus (1920, Germany)
The Ace of Scotland Yard (1929)
The Galloping Ghost (1931)
Flash Gordon (1936)
Dick Tracy: The Original Serial, Vol. 1 (1937)
The Green Hornet (1939)
Drums of Fu Manchu (1940)
Flash Gordon Conquers the Universe (1940)
The Adventures of Captain Marvel (1941)
The Adventures of Smilin' Jack (1943)
The Adventures of Frank and Jesse James (1947)
Superman: The Serial, Vol. 1 (1948)
Blazing the Overland Trail (1956)

War

A WAR MOVIE centers on the action taking place in a military conflict and its effects on the characters involved. Homefront and historical dramas set during wartime often overlap with the war film but usually focus on war's effects on society, rather than on the conflict itself. Screen staples since the silent era, war movies often fall into one of two camps: tales of personal

heroism and sacrifice like *Objective, Burma!* (1945) and *Saving Private Ryan* (1998), or indictments against war like *All Quiet on the Western Front* (1930). Generally, the need to maintain a country's morale during wartime has meant that films made during a war's duration support national interests. This accounts for the many dozens of supportive, even propagandistic, World War II war films that range from *Action in the North Atlantic* (1943) to *...One of Our Aircraft Is Missing* (1941, UK). The passage of time allows for films with a more critical perspective, like *Paths of Glory* (1957) and *The Bridge on the River Kwai* (1957), both of which depict the madness and moral ambiguity of war. An unpopular war, however, may generate critical films during its duration (or just after it). For example, the Vietnam War generated a spate of antiwar films, most notably *The Deer Hunter* (1975) and *Apocalypse Now* (1979).

REPRESENTATIVE FILMS
The Birth of a Nation (1915)
The Four Horsemen of the Apocalypse (1921)
The Big Parade (1927)
Wings (1927)
All Quiet on the Western Front (1930)
La Grande Illusion/Grand Illusion (1937, France)
Alexander Nevsky (1938, USSR)
The Four Feathers (1939, UK)
...One of Our Aircraft Is Missing (1941, UK)
Action in the North Atlantic (1943)
Thirty Seconds Over Tokyo (1944)
Wing and a Prayer (1944)
Back to Bataan (1945)
Objective, Burma! (1945)
They Were Expendable (1945)
Battleground (1949)
Twelve O'Clock High (1950)
From Here to Eternity (1953)
Stalag 17 (1953)
Battle Cry (1955)
The Bridges at Toko-Ri (1955)
To Hell and Back (1955)
The Bridge on the River Kwai (1957)
Paths of Glory (1957)
The Alamo (1960)
The Longest Day (1962)
The Great Escape (1963)
The Dirty Dozen (1967)
M*A*S*H (1970)
The Deer Hunter (1975)
Apocalypse Now (1979)
Platoon (1986)
Full Metal Jacket (1987)
Saving Private Ryan (1998)
Three Kings (1999)
Pearl Harbor (2001)

The D-day invasion of Normandy was seen through the eyes of the Americans, French, British, and Germans in The Longest Day *(1962).*

"My film is not about Vietnam. It *is* Vietnam. It's what it was really like."

—

Francis Ford Coppola on Apocalypse Now *(1979)*

Western

THE WESTERN DEPICTS a struggle between good and evil in a setting where civilization and wilderness are in transition. Early silent westerns included Edwin S. Porter's pioneering narrative film *The Great Train Robbery* (1903). As movies became increasingly character—and star—driven, the western adapted and created its own stars. During the 1910s, the dominant western star was the serious reformed bad man William S. Hart, while the more boisterous 1920s featured flamboyant cowboy star Tom Mix. Definitive western director John Ford directed his first westerns, including the influential movie *The Iron Horse* (1924), in this decade.

During the early sound era, westerns remained popular. Some were big-budget productions such as *The Big Trail* (1930) and *Cimarron* (1931); the latter won an Academy Award for best picture.

More numerous were low-budget westerns and musical westerns with singing "King of the Cowboys" Gene Autry (who would be succeeded in the 1940s by Roy Rogers).

In 1939, westerns gained stature as a film genre with John Ford's character-based film *Stagecoach.* The movie also established John Wayne as the definitive laconic western hero. Through the 1940s, westerns were a dominant genre, with notable productions including *The Westerner* (1940), *Western Union* (1941), and *My Darling Clementine* (1946). Like films in other genres, postwar westerns embodied darker themes and more complex reflections on the nature of violence. Significant films included *Red River* (1948), *High Noon* (1952), *Shane* (1953), *The Tall T* (1957), and *The Searchers* (1956).

Beginning in the 1960s, the traditional western was replaced by comedic, satiric, and violent variations on the genre. Influential films include *Butch Cassidy and the Sundance Kid* (1969), *The Wild Bunch* (1969), and the spaghetti westerns of Italian director Sergio Leone. His films, including *A Fistful of Dollars* (1964) and *The Good, the Bad, and the Ugly* (1966), introduced a new, detached hero, portrayed by Clint Eastwood. A few revisionist westerns, reflecting the critical spirit of the 1960s and 1970s, rewrote the

The 1938 western *The Terror of Tiny Town* is notable for one reason, and one reason only: It's the only film in the history of Hollywood to feature a cast made up entirely of midgets.

Graham Greene received an Academy Award nomination for best supporting actor for his portrayal of Kicking Bird in Dances With Wolves *(1990).*

Director Sam Peckinpah's highly acclaimed 1969 western The Wild Bunch *starred Ernest Borgnine.*

history of frontier expansionism from a Native American perspective, for instance, *Little Big Man* (1970). In the latter part of the 20th century, the western declined precipitously in popularity. The only notable films were elegies such as *The Shootist* (1976) or revisionist meditations such as *Dances with Wolves* (1990) and *Unforgiven* (1992).

REPRESENTATIVE FILMS
The Great Train Robbery (1903)
The Passing of Two-Gun Hicks (1914)
Truthful Tulliver (1916)
The Heart of Texas Ryan (1917)
The Covered Wagon (1923)
The Iron Horse (1924)
Riders of the Purple Sage (1925)
Tumbleweeds (1925)
The Big Trail (1930)
Cimarron (1931)
Tumblin' Tumbleweeds (1935)
Rhythm of the Saddle (1938)

Stagecoach (1939)
The Westerner (1940)
Western Union (1941)
King of the Cowboys (1943)
My Darling Clementine (1946)
Red River (1948)
She Wore a Yellow Ribbon (1949)
Winchester '73 (1950)
High Noon (1952)
The Naked Spur (1953)
Shane (1953)
The Searchers (1956)
Seven Men from Now (1956)
Gunfight at the O.K. Corral (1957)
The Tall T (1957)
Rio Bravo (1959)
Guns of Navarone (1961)
The Man Who Shot Liberty Valance (1962)
A Fistful of Dollars (1964)
The Good, the Bad, and the Ugly (1966)
Butch Cassidy and the Sundance Kid (1969)
The Wild Bunch (1969)
Little Big Man (1970)
Buffalo Bill & the Indians (1976)
The Shootist (1976)
Silverado (1985)
Young Guns (1988)
Dances with Wolves (1990)
Unforgiven (1992)
Wyatt Earp (1994)

Having recently lived in the desert with the Navajo Indians for three months gave director Delmer Daves an interesting perspective when he came to direct his western *3:10 to Yuma* (1957). In all the previous westerns he'd either seen or made (1950's *Broken Arrow,* among others), Daves noticed that the desert shadows were far too light, because the filmmakers had used reflector boards to brighten the outdoor scenes for the camera. But in the desert, Daves knew, the intense sunlight makes all shadows vividly black. By eliminating reflectors during *Yuma's* exterior photography, Daves was better able to suggest the feeling of a bleached, drought-worn landscape, and the effect was so successful that the director used it a year later on *Cowboy* (1958).

SOURCES

Washington Irving's tale of the headless horseman was brought to life in Tim Burton's 1999 film Sleepy Hollow, *starring Christina Ricci.*

SOURCES OF INFORMATION

Addresses, phone numbers, web sites, and recommended reading for every facet of the film world can be found in this section.

Producers and Distributors

WHEN USING THE INFORMATION provided in this chapter, note that companies often change locations and phone numbers. Double-check addresses with a phone call or Web site check before writing or visiting the featured places. Note that Los Angeles has several area codes and companies there are sometimes assigned new ones. Directory assistance can supply the updated data if there has been a change. Web sites change even more rapidly than physical locations, but unless a site becomes defunct, you will usually be directed to the new Web address by clicking on the old one.

THE MAJOR HOLLYWOOD STUDIOS

DreamWorks SKG
100 Universal City Plaza, Building 477
Universal City, CA 91608
(818) 733-7000
www.dreamworks.com

DreamWorks SKG was founded in 1994 by film director Steven Spielberg, former Walt Disney Company executive Jeffrey Katzenberg, and talent agent turned music mogul David Geffen. The "SKG" in the title refers to the founders' surnames. The company produces feature films, television programming, and music. Feature films include *Amistad* (1997), *Saving Private Ryan* (1998), the best picture Academy Award–winning *American Beauty* (1999), and *Almost Famous* (2000).

"Ah don't believe Ah know which pictures are yours. Do you make the Mickey Mouse brand?"

—

William Faulkner to Irving Thalberg of MGM, circa 1930s

Metro-Goldwyn-Mayer/United Artists, Inc. (MGM)
2500 Broadway Street
Santa Monica, CA 90404
(310) 449-3000
(310) 449-3100 (fax)
www.mgmua.com

MGM was formed in 1924 as a merger between Metro Picture Corporation (founded 1915), Goldwyn Picture Corporation, and Louis B. Mayer Pictures. In the 1930s and 1940s, its golden age, it was the most prestigious Hollywood studio, with talent that included directors George Cukor and Victor Fleming and stars Greta Garbo, Clark Gable, Mickey Rooney, and Judy Garland. Classic films include *Greed* (1925), *Grand Hotel* (1932), *Boys Town* (1938), *The Wizard of Oz* (1939), and *Gone with the Wind* (1939). Dore Schary replaced the founding studio chief Louis B. Mayer after a power struggle in 1951. In 1952 following an antitrust suit, the studio divested from Loews Theatres, to which it was formerly connected. Notable MGM films of the 1950s and 1960s include *Singin' in the Rain* (1952), *Ben-Hur* (1959), *Doctor Zhivago* (1966), and *2001: A Space Odyssey* (1968).

MGM stopped distributing films in 1973 and transferred licensing to United Artists. MGM acquired United Artists in 1981 and changed its name to MGM/UA in 1983. The studio passed through many owners in the 1980s and 1990s. In 1996 financier Kirk Kerkorian purchased it. Since the 1983 formation of MGM/UA, the studio's films have included *Thelma and Louise* (1991), *Leaving Las Vegas* (1995), *The World Is Not Enough* (1999), and *Tea with Mussolini* (1999).

Paramount Pictures
5555 Melrose Avenue
Los Angeles, CA 90038
(323) 956-5000
www.paramount.com

This film and television studio originated in a 1916 merger between Adolf Zukor's Famous Players Film Company and the Jesse L. Lasky Feature Play Company. The new company, Famous Players–Lasky Corporation, grew steadily, producing films with Gary Cooper, Claudette Colbert, and Marlene Dietrich, and became known as Paramount, initially the name

of its distribution arm. Following more mergers and theater acquisitions, the Paramount Publix Corporation was founded in 1930. Soon after, the company went bankrupt from a rough transition to sound films and the effects of the Great Depression. In 1935 the company was able to re-form as Paramount Pictures and began producing films with stars that included Mae West and Bing Crosby and featured directors such as Cecil B. DeMille, Preston Sturges, and Billy Wilder. The studio sold its theater chain in 1949 following antitrust litigation. Notable films in the 1950s included *Shane* (1953) and DeMille's remake of his own *The Ten Commandments* (1956).

Paramount Pictures was sold to the Gulf & Western Corporation in 1966 and had a number of hits in the turbulent 1970s including the Academy Award–winning movie *The Godfather* (1972) and its sequel *The Godfather, Part II* (1974), plus three lucrative movies in the late 1970s, *Saturday Night Fever* (1977), *Grease* (1978), and *Heaven Can Wait* (1978). In 1984 Gulf & Western became Paramount Communications and expanded into television production. The company was sold to Viacom in 1993. Paramount films include *Beverly Hills Cop* (1984) and its sequels, the *Star Trek* franchise, *Ghost* (1990), *The Firm* (1993), *Forrest Gump* (1994), *Mission: Impossible* (1996), *The Truman Show* (1998), and *Mission: Impossible II* (2000).

Sony Pictures Entertainment (Columbia Pictures/TriStar Pictures/Sony Classics)
10202 West Washington Boulevard
Culver City, CA 90232
(310) 244-4000
(310) 244-2696 (fax)
www.spe.sony.com
The parent organization of Columbia Pictures, TriStar Pictures, and Sony Classics, Columbia was founded in 1920 as CBC Film Sales Company by partners Harry Cohn, Jack Cohn, and Joe Brandt. It found success in the 1930s with films such as *It Happened One Night* (1934) and others by star director Frank Capra. Successful through the 1940s, Columbia was unaffected by the government antitrust suit that forced other studios to sell off theaters. It produced a string of hits in the 1950s, including *From Here to Eternity* (1953) and *Bridge on the River Kwai* (1957), and founded its television

production arm, Screen Gems. Fiscal problems in the 1960s caused Columbia to merge with Screen Gems and become Columbia Pictures Industries in 1968. The new company was led by David Begelman until he was forced out after a 1978 embezzlement scandal.

Columbia created TriStar Pictures with partners HBO and CBS television in 1982. Five years later, Columbia merged with TriStar and was bought by the Coca-Cola Company. Columbia and TriStar were sold to Sony Corporation in 1989. Notable movies of the late 1980s and 1990s include the *Batman* series, *A Few Good Men* (1992), *Jerry Maguire* (1996), and *Erin Brockovich* (2000).

Today Sony Pictures Entertainment produces films under its Columbia TriStar Motion Picture Group. Other divisions include the Family Entertainment Group and Sony Pictures Classics. Sony Pictures Entertainment also produces television, music, and new-media entertainment.

20th Century–Fox Film Corp.
10201 West Pico Boulevard
Los Angeles, CA 90035
(310) 369-1000
www.foxworld.com
Founded in 1915 by Hungarian immigrant William Fox, who began producing films after running a successful penny arcade business in New York City. Fox was a major studio by the

Alan Ladd (far left) played a mysterious drifter named Shane in the 1953 Paramount Pictures film of the same name, also starring Van Heflin, and Jean Arthur.

Titanic, *a 20th Century–Fox film featuring Leonardo DiCaprio and Kate Winslet, broke box-office records upon its release in 1997.*

The world's largest movie studio complex is Universal City, the Los Angeles home of Universal Studios. It comprises 420 acres with 561 buildings and 34 sound stages and is informally known as the Back Lot.

end of the 1920s, employing stars like Tom Mix and esteemed directors such as John Ford. In 1927 the studio created the Movietone sound system that soon became the industry standard. In 1935 Fox merged with Twentieth Century Film Corporation, a studio founded by Joseph Schenk and Darryl Zanuck in 1933, to create 20th Century–Fox. To compete with the allure of a new form of entertainment—television—Fox developed the wide-screen CinemaScope system in the 1950s. After 20 years as the head of production, Zanuck resigned in 1955 only to return to run Fox in 1962 and bring son Richard on as chief of production. The son and father were forced out in 1970 and 1971, respectively, and Dennis Stanfill became the chairman and CEO. He oversaw the company through the 1970s, profitable mostly due to the science fiction hit *Star Wars* (1977). 20th Century–Fox was bought by financier Marvin Davis in 1981 and sold to Australian newspaper magnate Rupert Murdoch in 1985. Under Murdoch, the studio became part of Fox Filmed Entertainment, a division of Fox Inc. Related film units include Fox 2000, Fox Family Films, and the art house distributor Fox Searchlight. Recent notable films include *Home Alone* (1990), *Speed* (1994), *Titanic* (1997), *There's Something About Mary* (1998), *Star Wars Episode 1—The Phantom Menace* (1999), and *X-Men* (2000).

Universal Studios, Inc.

100 Universal City Plaza
Universal City, CA 91608
(818) 777-1000
(818) 733-1506 (fax)
www.mca.com/studio
Founded by Carl Laemmle in 1912, the studio today not only produces film and television entertainment—it owns theme parks in California and Florida as well. Laemmle established company headquarters at Universal City in 1915, a 230-acre lot in Los Angeles for producing films. Universal employed stars such as Rudolph Valentino and Lon Chaney, Jr., and in the 1930s and 1940s produced a string of successful horror classics, including *Dracula* (1931) and *Frankenstein* (1931), but it still nearly went bankrupt during the Great Depression. It eventually bounced back through a series of lucrative musicals, adventure films, and Abbott and Costello pictures.

Universal merged with International Films in 1946 and was, until 1950, Universal International. After being bought by Decca Records in the 1950s, both companies were purchased by MCA, Inc., originally a talent agency founded by Jules Stein in 1924.

The 1970s brought financial success to the company, the result of several box-office hits, including *The Sting* (1973), *Jaws* (1975), and *Animal House* (1978), and the opening of the Universal City Studio Tour in the early 1970s. The Universal Studios Florida theme park opened in 1990. MCA was sold in 1990 to the Japanese electronics firm Matsushita, which retained studio head Lew Wasserman, who had been with MCA since 1936. Wasserman remained in charge until the firm's 1995 sale to the beverage giant Seagram's. Recent films include *Jurassic Park* (1993), *Apollo 13* (1995), *Men in Black* (1997), and *How the Grinch Stole Christmas* (2000).

The Walt Disney Company

500 South Buena Vista Street
Burbank, CA 91521
(818) 560-1000
(818) 840-5737 (fax)
www. disney.go.com/StudioOperations
Profitable and long-standing studio empire specializing in live-action films, animated films, television and radio programming, merchandising, and theme parks. Founded by animator Walt Disney and brother Roy Disney in 1923. The introduction of Mickey Mouse in the 1928 animated short *Steamboat Willie* launched the company's reputation for quality and profitability. Disney produced its first full-length animated feature, *Snow White and the Seven Dwarfs*, in 1937, beginning a long tradition of successful animated films that has continued through *Tarzan* (1999). The company expanded in the 1950s to include television programming and live-action nature films, such as *The Living Desert* (1953). Production of live-action features began in 1954, with Jules Verne's *20,000 Leagues Under the Sea*.

The company moved into live entertainment when it founded the Disneyland theme park in Anaheim, California, in 1955. After Walt Disney's death in 1966, the company built the profitable Walt Disney World in Orlando, Florida, in 1971, and later Disney Tokyo in 1983 and Disneyland Paris (Euro Disney) in 1992. All the parks exploit the popularity of Disney's animated characters. But film production in the 1970s proved less lucrative. Revitalization began in 1983 when Walt Disney's son-in-law Ron Miller founded Touchstone Pictures to produce live-action films for adults, and Disney moved into cable television with the Disney Channel. Michael Eisner replaced Miller as chairman and CEO in 1984. With Eisner at the helm, aided by Jeffrey Katzenberg as head of production, Disney turned out a string of live-action hits, including *Down and Out in Beverly Hills* (1986), *Three Men and a Baby* (1988), and *Pretty Woman* (1990). The animated films division was brought back to life with successes such as *The Little Mermaid* (1989), *Beauty and the Beast* (1991), and *The Lion King* (1994).

In 1994, Katzenberg was ousted in a power struggle with Eisner, who took over production. Disney merged with Capital Cities/ABC that same year. Superagent Michael Ovitz was brought in to run the studio in 1995, until Eisner fired him a year later and took control once again. The company continues to be financially successful in both entertainment and merchandising. Studio divisions include Touchstone Pictures, Hollywood Pictures, Caravan Pictures, and Miramax. Recent hits include *Pulp Fiction* (1994), *Toy Story* (1995), *Shine* (1996), *The English Patient* (1996), *Good Will Hunting* (1997), and *The Sixth Sense* (1999).

Warner Bros., Inc.

4000 Warner Boulevard
Burbank, CA 91522
(818) 954-6000
www.wb.com

This studio began in 1905 when the Warner brothers, Jack, Harry, Sam, and Albert, went into the nickelodeon business. They eventually moved from distributing films to producing them and, in 1923, incorporated their film company as Warner Bros. and absorbed Vitagraph and First National Pictures by 1925. Warner produced the first sound feature, in 1927, *The Jazz Singer*, starring Al Jolson. It went on to produce popular gangster pictures and adventure movies in the 1930s and 1940s.

Warner was purchased by Seven Arts Productions in 1967 and subsequently by Kinney National Service, which was run by Stephen J. Ross. Ross broadened the scope of Warner Bros. into publishing, television, and music with the creation of Warner Communications in 1971. Warner Bros. box-office hits of the 1970s included *The Exorcist* (1973) and *Superman* (1978). In the 1980s and 1990s, studio chairman Robert Daly and president Terry Semel continued Warner Bros.' financial success with the *Lethal Weapon* series, the *Batman* series, *GoodFellas* (1990), *The Fugitive* (1993), and *The Matrix* (1999). Warner Communications, the studio's parent company, merged with Time Inc. in 1989, forming Time-Warner, a publishing, news, cable, film, and television giant. Time-Warner and AOL merged in 2000, forming AOL Time Warner.

The first Walt Disney-produced motion picture to receive an R-rating was the 1986 hit *Down and Out in Beverly Hills.* The film was released by Touchstone, an adult-oriented division of Disney.

The first "talkie" feature motion picture was the Warner Bros. film The Jazz Singer *(1927), starring Al Jolson.*

African-American director Spike Lee's production company, Forty Acres & a Mule, is named for General William T. Sherman's Civil War order that a 30-mile inland tract of land along the southern coast of Charleston be set aside for the exclusive settlement of blacks. Each family, it was decreed, would receive forty acres of land and an army mule. Later that year, the order was repealed and the land returned to the ex-Confederates.

SMALLER PRODUCERS AND DISTRIBUTORS

IN ADDITION TO THE MAJOR motion picture studios, there are dozens of smaller companies producing and distributing feature films. (See *The International Motion Picture Almanac* for more listings.) These companies sometimes work in collaboration with the large Hollywood studios, sometimes independently. Below are some of the best-known producers and distributors outside the major studios.

American Zoetrope
916 Kearny Street
San Francisco, CA 94133
(415) 788-7500
(415) 989-7910 (fax)
www.zoetrope.com
The Godfather (1972), *Peggy Sue Got Married* (1986), *The Virgin Suicides* (2000)

Imagine Entertainment brought Dr. Seuss's classic tale How the Grinch Stole Christmas *(2000), starring Taylor Momsen and Jim Carrey, to the theaters.*

Artisan Entertainment
2700 Colorado Avenue, 2nd Floor
Los Angeles, CA 90404
(310) 449-9200
www.artisanent.com
The Blair Witch Project (1999), *Dr. T. and the Women* (2000), *Requiem for a Dream* (2000)

Jerry Bruckheimer Films
1631 10th Street
Santa Monica, CA 90403
(310) 664-6260
(310) 664-6261 (fax)
Armageddon (1998), *Coyote Ugly* (2000)

Castle Rock Entertainment
335 North Maple Drive, Suite 135
Beverly Hills, CA 90210
(310) 285-2300
(310) 285-2345 (fax)
www.castle-rock.warnerbros.com
When Harry Met Sally. . . (1989), *The Shawshank Redemption* (1994), *Miss Congeniality* (2000)

Forty Acres & a Mule Filmworks
124 Dekalb Avenue
Brooklyn, NY 11217
(718) 624-3703
(718) 624-2008 (fax)
She's Gotta Have It (1986), *Do the Right Thing* (1989), *Bamboozled* (2000)

Imagine Entertainment
9465 Wilshire Boulevard, 7th Floor
Beverly Hills, CA 90212
(310) 858-2000
(310) 858-2020 (fax)
www.imagine-entertainment.com
Kindergarten Cop (1990), *Apollo 13* (1995), *How the Grinch Stole Christmas* (2000)

Kennedy-Marshall Company
1351 4th Street, 4th Floor
Santa Monica, CA 90401
(310) 656-8400
(310) 656-8430 (fax)
The Indian in the Cupboard (1995), *Congo* (1995), *Snow Falling on Cedars* (1999)

Kopelson Entertainment
2121 Avenue of the Stars, Suite 1400
Los Angeles, CA 90067
(310) 369-7500
(310) 369-7501 (fax)
The Devil's Advocate (1997), *U.S. Marshals* (1998)

Lightstorm Entertainment, Inc.
919 Santa Monica Boulevard
Santa Monica, CA 90401
(310) 656-6100
(310) 656-6102 (fax)
Terminator 2: Judgment Day (1991), *True Lies* (1994), *Titanic* (1997)

Lions Gate Films
561 Broadway, Suite 12B
New York, NY 10012
(212) 966-4670
(212) 966-2544 (fax)
www.lionsgatefilms.com
A Wedding (1978), *Gods and Monsters* (1998), *American Psycho* (2000)

Lucasfilm, Ltd.
P.O. Box 2009
San Rafael, CA 94912
(415) 662-1800
(415) 662-2437 (fax)
www.lucasfilm.com
Star Wars (1977), *Raiders of the Lost
Ark* (1981), *Star Wars Episode I—
The Phantom Menace* (1999)

Merchant Ivory Productions
250 West 57th Street
New York, NY 10107
(212) 582-8049
ww.westmerchantivory.com
A Room with a View (1986),
Howards End (1992), *A Soldier's
Daughter Never Cries* (1998)

Miramax Films Corp.
375 Greenwich Street
New York, NY 10013
(212) 941-3800
(212) 941-3949 (fax)
www.miramax.com
Pulp Fiction (1994), *Shakespeare in
Love* (1998), *Chocolat* (2000)

Morgan Creek Productions
4000 Warner Boulevard,
Building #76
Burbank, CA 91522
(818) 954-4800
(818) 954-4811 (fax)
www.morgancreek.com
The Last of the Mohicans (1992), *Ace Ventura: Pet
Detective* (1994), *The Whole Nine Yards (2000)*

New Line Cinema Corp.
888 Seventh Avenue, 20th Floor
New York, NY 10106
(212) 649-4900
(212) 649-4966 (fax)
www.newline.com
A Nightmare on Elm Street (1984), *Austin Powers:
International Man of Mystery* (1997),
15 Minutes (2001)

Polygram Filmed Entertainment
9333 Wilshire Boulevard
Beverly Hills, CA 90210
(310) 777-7700
Trainspotting (1996), *Lock, Stock and Two
Smoking Barrels* (1998)

RKO Pictures
1875 Century Park East, Suite 2140
Los Angeles, CA 90067
(310) 277-0707
(310) 226-2490 (fax)
info@rko.com (e-mail)
www.rko.com
King Kong (1933), *Top Hat* (1935), *The Best Years
of Our Lives* (1946), *Hamburger Hill* (1987),
Mighty Joe Young (1998)

Silver Productions
c/o Warner Bros. Pictures
4000 Warner Boulevard, Building 90
Burbank, CA 91522-0001
(818) 954-4490
(818) 954-3237 (fax)
Lethal Weapon (1987), *Die Hard* (1988), *The
Matrix* (1999), *Exit Wounds* (2001)

Troma Entertainment, Inc.
733 Ninth Avenue
New York, NY 10019
(212) 757-4555
(212) 399-9885 (fax)
www.troma.com/home
The Toxic Avenger (1985), *Class of Nuke 'Em High*
(1986), *Terror Firmer* (1999)

USA Films
(formerly Gramercy Pictures)
9333 Wilshire Boulevard
Beverly Hills, CA 90210
(310) 385-4400
(310) 385-4408 (fax)
www.usafilms.net
Fargo (1996), *Being John Malkovich* (1999),
Traffic (2000)

The Zanuck Company
202 North Canon Drive
Beverly Hills, CA 90210
(310) 274-0261
(310) 273-9217 (fax)
Driving Miss Daisy (1989), *True Crime* (1999),
Planet of the Apes (2001)

*John Malkovich played
himself in the quirky
Spike Jonze film* Being
John Malkovich *(1999)
released by USA films.*

"This whole
company is
run according
to Taoism."

—

*Lloyd Kaufman, former
Yale Chinese studies major,
producer/director of the
Toxic Avenger series, and
co-founder of Troma
Entertainment, 2001*

Film Festivals and Markets

FILM FESTIVALS ARE EXHIBITION programs organized to showcase new films. They often occur annually in the same city or town and can last days or weeks. Although the marketing of films to potential distributors and exhibitors is an important component of many film festivals, these events usually have an artistic orientation, and may offer prizes in various categories. Film markets, by contrast, are strictly trade events organized to bring films to market.

Hundreds of film festivals and markets are held worldwide every year, including festivals in most major US cities. The following are some of the most important events in film. For more festival listings, see *The International Motion Picture Almanac, Variety International Film Guide,* or www.marklitwak.com.

Kenneth Lonergan wrote, directed, and starred in You Can Count On Me *(2000), also starring Laura Linney, which received AFI's New Directions Prize and Best New Writer Award.*

AFI Los Angeles International Film Festival (AFI Fest)
c/o American Film Institute
2021 North Western Avenue
Los Angeles, CA 90027
(323) 856-7707
(323) 462-4049 (fax)
www.afi.com
 Los Angeles's most prestigious film festival, AFI Fest has been held annually since 1986, usually in October. It has three juried contests: International Competition; New Directions from American Independents; and Documentary Competition. Awards include the Grand Jury Prize for the best feature film in International Competition; the New Directions Prize for the best film in the New Directions from American Independents section; the Discovery Documentary Competition Prize; Best New Writer; and Producer to Watch.

American Film Market (AFM)
10850 Wilshire Boulevard, 9th Floor
Los Angeles, CA 90024
(310) 446-1000
info@afma.com (e-mail)
www.afma.com
 Billed as the world's largest film trade event, the AFM has brought representatives from more than 70 countries to Santa Monica, California, each February since 1981. Sponsored by the American Film Marketing Association (AFMA), a trade organization of American producers and distributors with films for sale on the international market, the marketplace provides a forum for international sales of domestic film and television productions.

Aspen Filmfest
110 East Hallam Street, Suite 102
Aspen, CO 81611
(303) 925-6882
(303) 925-1967 (fax)
www.aspenfilm.org
 Nonprofit film festival that promotes independent cinema. Held each year in September or October since 1979, it screens features, documentaries, and short films. The Filmfest offers seminars, discussions, and other forums to promote the understanding and enjoyment of film. In addition, the organization sponsors Oscar screenings during winter and puts on the Shortsfest festival of short films in April.

Berlin International Film Festival (Internationale Filmfestspiele Berlin)
Budapesterstrasse 50
Berlin 10787 Germany
(49-30) 254-890
(49-30) 254-892 (fax)
www.berlinale.de
 Annual international film festival founded in 1951 and held in February. Known for its efficient organization, the festival includes screenings and panel discussions and has presented juried awards since its inception. Winners are awarded the Silver Bear for best film in several categories and the Golden Bear for the best film overall.

Cannes Film Festival (Festival International du Film de Cannes)
99 Boulevard Malesherbes
Paris 75008 France
(33-01) 45-61-66-00
(33-01) 45-61-97-60 (fax)
festival@festival-cannes.fr (e-mail)
www.festival-cannes.org
 Major international film festival sponsored by the Association Française du Festival

International du Film. The festival was launched in 1946 to provide an international cultural exchange and marketplace for film. Since 1951, it has been held each May in Cannes, France, and serves as a showcase for motion pictures, an environment for deal making, and a closely watched entertainment event in itself. The festival screens films, presents retrospectives, and hosts panel discussions. The prestigious Palme d'Or Award, presented first in 1955, is bestowed upon the film judged best overall by a distinguished international jury. The jury awards a variety of other prizes including best director, best actress, and best actor.

Chicago International Film Festival
32 West Randolph Street, Suite 600
Chicago, IL 60601
(312) 425-9400
(312) 425-0944 (fax)
info@chicagofilmfestival.com (e-mail)
www.chicagofilmfestival.com
Annual international film festival held in October. Organized since 1964 by Cinema/Chicago, the festival is the oldest competitive film festival in North America. Prizes are awarded for feature films, first- and second-time directors, documentaries, animation, and student productions. The Gold Hugo prize is awarded for best all-around film.

Independent Feature Film Market (IFFM)
104 West 29th Street, 12th Floor
New York, NY 10011
(212) 465-8200
(212) 465-8525 (fax)
ifpny@ifp.org (e-mail)
www.ifp.org
Film festival and market featuring productions by independent producers and companies working outside the Hollywood studio system. Sponsored by the Independent Feature Project, IFFM has been held in New York City each September since 1978. It includes exhibitions, conferences, and workshops promoting independent filmmaking.

London Film Festival (LFF)
South Bank
Waterloo
London SE1 8XT UK
(44-171) 815-1322
(44-171) 633- 0786 (fax)
sarah.lutton@bfi.org.uk (e-mail)
www.lff.org.uk
Held annually in November or December since 1956, LFF exhibits international feature films, documentaries, and shorts and provides educational forums, panels, and other informational exhibits. Festival awards include best picture, chosen by the international film critics association FIPRESCI (La Federation International de la Presse Cinematographique), and the Satyajit Ray Award presented to a

filmmaker's first film that expresses "compassion and humanism." The festival is organized by the nonprofit British Film Institute, which provides funding resources, preservation services, and cultural and educational outreach for the art of film.

MIFED
Fiera Internazionale di Milano
Largo Dommodossola 1
Milano 20145 Italy
(39 2) 48012 912 x. 2920
(39 2) 49977 020 (fax)
mifed@fmd.it (e-mail)
www.fmd.it/mifed
International entertainment trade show and exhibition organized by the business association Fiera Internazionale di Milano. MIFED promotes business exchange among its participants, members of the film and television industries from more than 70 countries. Originally held twice a year, in April and October, the convention consolidated in the 1980s into a single fall event.

Montreal World Film Festival
1432 De Bleury Street
Montreal, Quebec H3A 2J1 Canada
(514) 848-3883
(514) 848-3886 (fax)
ffm@qc.aira.com (e-mail)
www.ffm-montreal.org
The Montreal World Film Festival, which screens more then 400 films, bills itself as the "largest publicly attended film festival in the western world." Held annually in late August–early September, the festival was founded in 1977 and features a wide range of international films. A jury awards prizes, including the Grand Prix of the Americas Award for best film.

Helen Mirren starred in The Cook, the Thief, His Wife, and Her Lover *(1989) with Alan Howard, Richard Bohringer, and Michael Gambon.*

Of Thee I Sting, Giant Spider Invasion, and *Termites from Mars* are just some of the films and shorts that have been shown over the years at The Insect Fear Film Festival at the University of Illinois. Entomology graduate students organize this weekend-long event, which aims to educate people about the world of insects and the misconceptions surrounding them.

New York Film Festival
Film Society of Lincoln Center
70 Lincoln Center Plaza
New York, NY 10023
(212) 875-5638
(212) 875-5636 (fax)
  filmlinc@dti.net (e-mail)
    www.filmlinc.com/nyff/nyff.htm
      Held in late September–early October
in New York City at Lincoln Center since
1962. Organized by the Film Society of
Lincoln Center, the festival features a
small, highly selective group of films
geared toward a discerning public and
a film industry crowd—those deemed
the best films from other festivals. The
festival does not award prizes.

Nortel Networks Palm Springs
International Film Festival
  1700 East Tahquitz Canyon Way, Suite 3
  Palm Springs, CA 92262
  (800) 898-7256
    (760) 322-4087 (fax)
    info@psfilmfest.org (e-mail)
    www.psfilmfest.org
      Nonprofit international film festival
sponsored by Nortel Networks and
held in Palm Springs, California.
Organized each January since 1989,
the festival offers exhibitions, business forums, press conferences, panel
discussions, and educational and professional
resources and awards prizes for films in competition. Over 150 films are screened at the festival.

San Francisco International Film Festival
1521 Eddy Street
San Francisco, CA 94115
(415) 929-5000
(415) 921-5032 (fax)
sfiff@sfiff.org (e-mail)
www.sfiff.org
  Nonprofit film festival founded by the San
Francisco Film Society in 1957 and held in late
April–early May. The festival features an
international film exhibition, educational
forums, and other programs to foster film
appreciation.

Santa Barbara International Film Festival
1216 State Street, Suite 710
Santa Barbara, CA 93101
(805) 963-0023
(805) 962-2524 (fax)
info@sbfilmfestival.org (e-mail)
www.sbfilmfestival.org
  Nonprofit festival showcasing independent
American and international films. Held each
March since 1985, the event exhibits full-length
features, short films, documentaries, video,
and animation. It also promotes independent
filmmaking, honors excellence in filmmaking,
and provides educational seminars and
workshops.

Pop star and politician Sonny Bono appeared with singer Debbie Harry in the John Waters's film Hairspray *(1988).*

ShoWest
116 North Robertson, Suite 708
Los Angeles, CA 90048
(212) 246-5897
(212) 541-9327 (fax)
ShoWest@aol.com (e-mail)
www.showest.com
  Annual trade show for motion picture
exhibitors held each March in Las Vegas,
Nevada. ShoWest and the ShoEast convention
held each October in New York City are
presented by Sunshine Worldwide, a company
that produces international film conventions.
Industry professionals from more than 40
countries attend ShoWest. It features
mainstream motion pictures from the major
studios and also gives awards to film professionals, popular actors, and future stars.

Sundance Film Festival
P.O. Box 16450
Salt Lake City, UT 84116
(801) 328-FILM
(801) 394-4662 (fax)
sundance@xmission.com (e-mail)
www.sundancefilm.com
  Independent film festival and market. Founded
in Salt Lake City, Utah, in 1978 as the United
States Film Festival, the festival moved to Park
City, Utah, in 1981 and joined the Sundance
Institute, a nonprofit organization dedicated
to promoting independent films, in 1985.
Renamed in 1991, the festival is held in January
and is probably the best-known US
independent-film festival.

Telluride Film Festival
c/o National Film Preserve, Ltd.
P.O. Box B1156
Hanover, NH 03755
(603) 643-1255
(603) 643-5938 (fax)
tellufilm@aol.com (e-mail)
www.telluridefilmfestival.com
  Held each Labor Day weekend since its founding in 1974 in the town of Telluride, Colorado.
Fewer than 40 films are selected for screening.
The list of films to be exhibited is kept secret
until the schedule is announced on opening day.

Toronto International Film Festival
2 Carlton
Toronto, Ontario M5B 1J3 Canada
(416) 968-FILM
(416) 967-9477 (fax)
tiffg@torfilmfest.ca (e-mail)
www.e.bell.ca/filmfest
  Nonprofit film festival and market held each
September. Founded in 1976 to showcase the
best films from film festivals worldwide, the
Toronto International Film Festival has grown
into one of the largest exhibitions and film
conventions in North America. It exhibits more
than 400 films ranging from obscure to
anticipated titles.

Valladolid International Film Festival
Teatro Calderón
c/Leopoldo Cano
s/n 4ᵃ planta
Apartado de Correos 646
P.O. Box 646
Valladolid 47003 Spain
(34-83) 305-700
(34-83) 309-835 (fax)
festvalladolid@seminci.com
www.seminci.com

Founded in 1956 to bring international films to Spain and to celebrate the state of the art. The festival was often the only place to see certain films from outside Spain during Franco's dictatorship (1939–1975). The range of the festival continues to grow, today including feature films, documentaries, animation, shorts, and television programming.

Venice Film Festival (Biennale)
Mostra Internazionale d'Arte Cinematografica,
    La Biennale
San Marco
Cà Giustinian
Venice 30124 Italy
(39-41) 521-8711
(39-41) 423-6374 (fax)
segregen@labiennale.com (e-mail)
www.labiennaledivenezia.net

The oldest film festival still in existence, it is organized by the Biennale de Venezia, which was founded as a quasi-governmental organization in 1895 to promote the arts in Venice. Although the first Venice Film Festival was held in 1932, the gathering has been sporadic throughout the years. Since 1979, however, the festival has been held regularly in late August–early September. The festival features an international competition; awards include the Golden Lion for best film, as well as prizes for performances, directing and career achievement.

WorldFest—Houston
P.O. Box 56566
Houston, TX 77256
(713) 965-9955
(713) 965-9960 (fax)
worldfest@aol.com (e-mail)
www.worldfest.com

Founded in 1968, WorldFest was one of the first North American film festivals. Then and now, it showcases independent films, and does not allow films with distribution deals to be exhibited or submitted for awards. WorldFest screens no more than 50 films including features, short films, documentaries, and titles in its newest category, "Family/Children's Film." It is held each November in Houston, Texas.

Associations

**Academy of Motion Picture Arts and Sciences
    (AMPAS)**
8949 Wilshire Boulevard
Beverly Hills, CA 90211-1972
(310) 247-3000
(310) 859-9351 or (310) 859-9619 (fax)
ampas@oscars.org (e-mail)
oscars.org; academy.org
Membership: 6,000 members

Nonprofit honorary professional organization for the motion picture industry. Founded in May 1927, with Douglas Fairbanks, Sr., as its first president. Membership is by invitation of the organization's Board of Governors and is limited to people who have achieved distinction in the field. The Academy's 13 branches represent different filmmaking professions including actors, directors, and studio executives. Best known for its annual Academy Awards celebration where the Oscars are awarded, the Academy also supports cultural and educational activities through its subsidiary, the Academy Foundation; sponsors technical research; publishes reference works; and maintains the Center for Motion Picture Study.

Alliance of Motion Picture and Television Producers (AMPTP)
15503 Ventura Boulevard
Encino, CA 91436
(818) 995-3600
(818) 382-1793 (fax)
www.mpaa.org
Membership: 25 members

Originally the Association of Motion Picture Producers, the organization was founded in 1924 by the major film studios to jointly negotiate contracts with film industry workers, navigate public and government relations, and help the studios work together. In 1964 the name was changed to the Association of Motion

"I've been to Paris, France, and I've been to Paris, Paramount. I think I prefer Paris, Paramount."

—

Ernst Lubitsch, circa 1930s, referring to Paramount's famous studio lot

Douglas Fairbanks, Sr., seen here in The Mark of Zorro *(1920), was the first president of the Academy of Motion Picture Arts and Sciences, founded in 1927.*

Picture and Television Producers following a merger with the Alliance of Television Film Producers. In 1975, Paramount Pictures and Universal Pictures broke away from the association, but the rejoined in 1982. The new organization was called the Alliance of Motion Picture and Television Producers. Today, it includes the major studios, independent production companies, and film processing laboratories.

American Film Institute (AFI)

2021 North Western Avenue
Los Angeles, CA 90027
(323) 856-7600
(323) 467-4578 (fax)
info@afi.com (e-mail)
www.afi.com

AFI National Film Theater
John F. Kennedy Center for
the Performing Arts

Washington, DC 20566
(202) 833-AFIT (2348)
(202) 659-1970 (fax)
A private, nonprofit organization founded in 1967, AFI has become the preeminent national organization dedicated to advancing and preserving the art of film, television, video, and the digital arts. Its mission includes educating and training moving image artists; coordinating and assisting moving image preservation activities; gathering and databasing documentation on America's moving image heritage; and offering recognition to artists through the annual AFI Life Achievement Award, the AFI Los Angeles International Film Festival (AFI Fest), and other competitions and honors. AFI publishes the newsletter *American Film*, which honors the American movie heritage and tells the story of AFI with rare movie memorabilia and exhibits on film production, film preservation, and recipients of the AFI Life Achievement Award. AFI programs described within this chapter include AFI Fest (see "Film Festivals and Markets," page 556–559), the National Center for Film and Video Preservation at AFI and the Louis B. Mayer Library (see "Libraries and Research Centers," page 566–567); the AFI Catalog project (see "Books," page 582–583), the National Moving Image Database (NAMID) (see "Online Resources," page 587–589), and the AFI Conservatory (see "Educational Programs," pages 571–574). Additional information about

AFI Fest 2000 featured the US premiere of Joel and Ethan Cohen's O Brother, Where Art Thou?, starring John Turturro, Tim Blake Nelson, and George Clooney.

AFI and its activities is available on its Web site and at the AFI Showcase at the Disney-MGM Studios in Orlando, Florida.

American Film Marketing Association (AFMA)

10850 Wilshire Boulevard, 9th Floor
Los Angeles, CA 90024
(310) 446-1000
(310) 446-1600 (fax)
info@afma.com (e-mail)
www.afma.com
Membership: 164 members
Trade association of feature film producers and distributors. Founded in 1980, AFMA serves to promote the international purchase and distribution of its members' films. Services include contract negotiation, legal assistance, standardization of distribution, and international arbitration. AFMA also produces the American Film Market, the world's largest film trade event, held each February in Santa Monica, California, since 1981 (see "Film Festivals and Markets," pages 556–559).

American Society of Composers, Authors and
Publishers (ASCAP)

One Lincoln Plaza
New York, NY 10023
(212) 621-6000
(212) 724-9064 (fax)
info@ascap.com (e-mail)
www.ascap.com
Membership: 39,000 members
Trade organization of musical composers, lyricists, and publishers, founded in 1914. ASCAP works to support the rights of performers by negotiating contracts, managing royalties, enforcing copyrights, and supervising the remuneration process. It also offers annual awards for excellence in the field and creates several publications, including a membership directory and the bimonthly magazine *Playback*.

Association of Film Commissioners
International (AFCI)

7060 Hollywood Boulevard, Suite 614
Los Angeles, CA 90028
(323) 462-6092
(323) 462-6091 (fax)
afci@afci.org (e-mail)
www.afci.org
Membership: 228 members
International association of local, state, regional, and national film commissions founded in 1981. AFCI helps its members promote the film and television production industry within their regions by facilitating the exchange of information and resources among its members, providing educational resources, and producing the annual AFCI Locations trade show in Los Angeles. AFCI recognizes outstanding members with its annual Crystal Vision Award and publishes the annual journal *AFCI Locations*.

Association of Independent Video and Filmmakers (AIVF)

304 Hudson Street, 6th Floor
New York, NY 10013
(212) 807-1400
(212) 463-8519 (fax)
info@aivf.org (e-mail)
www.aivf.org
Membership: 5,000 members

Nonprofit organization promoting independent film production as cultural expression. Founded in 1974, AIVF provides financing, education, and business support. It also publishes *The Independent Film and Video Monthly* and a variety of guides, including *The Film and Video Self-Distribution Toolkit*, *The AIVF Guide to Film and Video Exhibitors*, and *The Guide to International Film and Video Festivals*. The AIVF organizes symposia, seminars, and exhibitions of members' works and maintains a library and database about funding, legal matters, and business promotion for members.

Association of Moving Image Archivists

8949 Wilshire Boulevard
Beverly Hills, CA 90211
(310) 550-1300
(310) 550-1363 (fax)
amia@amianet.org (e-mail)
www.amianet.org
Membership: 650 members

Professional association that brings together people concerned with the collection, preservation, exhibition, and use of moving image materials. It was founded in 1990, although its history dates from meetings of archivists in the 1960s.

Broadcast Music, Inc. (BMI)

320 West 57th Street
New York, NY 10019
(212) 586-2000
(212) 956-2059 (fax)
newyork@bmi.com (e-mail)
www.bmi.com
Membership: more than 250,000 members

Nonprofit licensing association for musicians, music publishers, and writers. Founded in 1940 to provide musicians and songwriters copyright protections and royalties distribution, today BMI boasts 12 regional branches and 41 affiliated licensing organizations worldwide. Services include assistance with licensing, payment schedules, and payment allocation for its member performers and companies. BMI also sponsors educational workshops, competitions, and annual grants to student musicians and publishes *BMI Music World* quarterly.

The Film Society of Lincoln Center

70 Lincoln Center Plaza
New York, NY 10023
(212) 875-5610
(212) 875-5636 (fax)
mgoglio@filmlinc.com (e-mail)

www.filmlinc.com
Membership: more than 2,000 members

Organized in 1962 to exhibit special interest and international films and quality independent productions. Holds screenings year-round at the Walter Reade Theatre in Lincoln Center and hosts the New York Film Festival (see "Film Festivals and Markets," page 556–559), the New Directors/New Films exhibition, and the New York Video Festival and publishes *Film Comment* magazine. The association honors the filmmakers and film actors at the Film Society Gala Tribute held each May.

The Independent Feature Project (IFP)

104 West 29th Street, 12th Floor
New York, NY 10001
(212) 465-8200
(212) 465-5825 (fax)
ifpny@ifp.org (e-mail)
www.ifp.org
Membership: 3,000 members

Nonprofit association providing support to independent filmmakers. Founded in 1979, the IFP consists of five regional groups, in Chicago, Los Angeles, Miami, Minneapolis, and New York. It promotes the business of independent film with information services, seminars, screenings, conferences, workshops, and an annual presence at the Berlin Film Festival. It also organizes the Independent Feature Film Market, an annual event held in September in New York (see "Film Festivals and Markets," page 556–559).

International Federation of Film Archives (FIAF)

1 Rue Defacqz B-1000
Brussels, Belgium
(32-2) 538 3065
(32-2) 534 4774 (fax)
info@fiafnet.org (e-mail)

The International Federation of Film Archives (FIAF) unites institutions around the world

The Film Society of Lincoln Center showed Before Night Falls *(2000), starring Javier Bardem and Olivier Martinez, at the 2000 New York Film Festival.*

Producer's rep John Pierson has been involved in the backing and selling of some of the most successful indie pictures of the '80s and '90s, including *She's Gotta Have It* (1986), *Roger & Me* (1989), *Slacker* (1991), and *Clerks* (1994). Variety has called him the "guru of independent film."

La Belle et La Bête
(Beauty and the Beast,
1946), a Jean Cocteau
film, is one of many films
that has been restored and
preserved through the use
of modern technology.

Why is the work of film
preservationists urgent?
Consider this statistic: of
the more than 21,000
feature-length films
produced in the United
States before 1951, only
half still exist. The rest
have been lost or
destroyed or have decayed
beyond repair. For
newsreels, documentaries,
and television programs,
the survival rate is less
than half.

dedicated to preserving films. Founded in Paris in 1938, FIAF is a collaborative association of the world's leading film archives. Its affiliated organizations today include more than 100 archives around the world. In addition to film preservation, its goals include the promotion of film culture and historical research through the collection of documents about films and other cinema-related materials.

Motion Picture Association of America (MPAA)
15503 Ventura Boulevard
Encino, CA 91436
(818) 995-6600
(818) 382-1799 (fax)
www.mpaa.org

Trade organization representing the major Hollywood studios. It was founded in 1922 as the Motion Picture Producers and Distributors of America to improve the public image of the film industry. Renamed in 1945, MPAA monitors censorship and copyright infringement and leads an antipiracy program in the United States and abroad. It also provides voluntary ratings for films released in the United States. MPAA is affiliated with the Motion Picture Export Association (MPEA), a trade organization founded in 1945 to promote American films around the world.

National Association of Theatre Owners (NATO)
4605 Lankershim Boulevard, Suite 340
North Hollywood, CA 91602
(818) 506-1778
(818) 506-0269 (fax)
nato@chq.com (e-mail)

www.hollywood.com/nato
Membership: 18,000 members

Trade association for owners, operators, and executives of motion picture exhibition theaters. Founded in 1966 to assist with the exhibition of theatrical films, today NATO also promotes technological and legal advances in the industry. It merged with the Allied States Association of Motion Picture Exhibitors and Theatre Owners of America in 1993. The organization publishes an annual *Encyclopedia of Exhibition* that includes industry economic statistics, a member directory, and production information. It also sponsors the ShoWest trade show in Las Vegas each March, and the NATO/ShowEast in Atlantic City each October. The ShoWest convention honors popular entertainers with the annual NATO Stars of the Year award.

National Board of Review of Motion Pictures (NBRMP)
245 East 72nd Street
New York, NY 10021
(212) 628-1594
Membership: 8,500 members

Cultural association of industry professionals and enthusiasts interested in promoting and celebrating the art of film. The organization was formed in 1909 to fight the censorship of motion pictures and promote creative expression in the new medium. Members include teachers, artists, film craftspeople, actors, and writers. NBRMP maintains libraries and biographies and has published the bimonthly *Films in Review* magazine since 1920. It honors industry professionals with annual awards that include best film, director, actress, actor, and career achievement awards.

National Film Preservation Foundation (NFPF)
870 Market Street, Suite 1113
San Francisco, CA 94102
(415) 392-7291
(415) 392-7293 (fax)
info@filmpreservation.org (e-mail)
www.filmpreservation.org

An arm of the Library of Congress, this nonprofit organization was created by the US Congress to ensure the preservation of America's film heritage. Chartered in 1997, it is funded in part by the Academy of Motion Picture Arts and Sciences and the Film Foundation. NFPF promotes the protection of historical film stock, supports educational outreach and study, provides preservation grants, and organizes film cooperatives.

National Music Publisher's Association (NMPA)
711 Third Avenue
New York, NY 10017
(212) 370-5330
(212) 953-2384 (fax)
clientservice@harryfox.com (e-mail)
www.nmpa.org

Membership: more than 700 members
   Trade organization for music publishers.
   Founded in 1917 as the Music Publishers
   Protective Association, the NMPA works to
   provide copyright safeguards for its members
   through public relations, legislative support,
   and public education. The organization also
   monitors technological advances and promotes
   international expansion of music markets.
   It publishes the quarterly newsletter *News
   and Views*.

Society of Composers and Lyricists (SCL)
400 South Beverly Drive, Suite 214
Beverly Hills, CA 90212
(310) 281-2812
(818) 990-0601 (fax)
scladmin@filmscore.org (e-mail)
www.filmscore.org
   Professional society of composers and lyricists
   working in the film industry. Formed in 1983
   to promote the rights and fair employment
   practices of film composers, SCL continues a
   tradition begun by the Composers and
   Lyricists Guild of America (CLGA) in 1955.
   Although CLGA was disbanded after a
   crippling 1979 legal judgment in the studios'
   favor, composers regrouped under SCL with
   the aid of the Writers Guild of America.

Society of Motion Picture and Television Engineers (SMPTE)
595 Hartsdale Avenue
White Plains, NY 10607
(914) 761-1100
(914) 761-3115 (fax)
smpte@smpte.org (e-mail)
www.smpte.org
Membership: 10,000 members
   Professional organization of entertainment and
   communications engineers that promotes the
   advancement of the science and technology of
   film, television and imaging. C.F. Jenkins, the
   inventor of the first motion picture projector,
   was president of the society when it was
   founded in 1916. Today SMPTE provides
   members with cutting-edge information about
   the art of engineering and maintains standards
   for audio and visual production and measure-
   ments. It also publishes the monthly *SMPTE
   Journal*, which features the latest news about
   the industry.

Theatre Authority (TA)
729 Seventh Avenue, 11th Floor
New York, NY 10019
(212) 764-0156
(212) 764-0158 (fax)
taeinc@juno.com (e-mail)
   Nonprofit organization that coordinates with
   entertainment unions to arrange for entertainers to perform at charity events and on
   telethons. The organization also supports actor-
   oriented charities. It was founded in 1934. It
   publishes the journal *The Source*.

Guilds and Unions

Actors' Equity Association (AEA)
165 West 46th Street
New York, NY 10036
(212) 869-8530
(212) 719-9815 (fax)
www.actorsequity.org
Membership: 40,000 members
   Trade organization representing the actors and
   stage managers in the United States. Actors'
   Equity was founded in 1913 to secure minimum
   wages, negotiate agreements with employers,
   and establish fair working conditions for its
   members. The union is a member of the umbrella organization Associated Actors and Artists
   of America (AAAA). Actors' Equity publishes the
   monthly newsletter *Equity News*.

American Cinema Editors (ACE)
1041 North Formosa Avenue
West Hollywood, CA 90046
(323) 850-2900
(323) 850-2922 (fax)
amercinema@earthlink.net (e-mail)
www.ace-filmeditors.org
Membership: 450 members
   Nonprofit honorary professional organization to
   promote the advancement of film editing.
   Founded in 1950, ACE is composed of distinguished film editors who are invited to become
   members. ACE has granted the film editing
   award since 1951, known since 1965 as the Eddie.
   ACE also sponsors educational activities, hosts
   student competitions, and has published
   Cinemeditor magazine since 1951.

American Federation of Musicians (AFM)
1501 Broadway
New York, NY 10036
(212) 869-1330
(212) 764-6134 (fax)
info@afm.org (e-mail)
www.afm.org
Membership: 250 guilds/112,000 members
   Trade organization representing musicians in
   the United States and Canada. Founded in
   October 1896, when delegates from several
   musicians' organizations chartered a single,
   unified trade union under the guidance of the
   American Federation of Labor. The organization establishes minimum wages and working
   conditions on a local-by-local basis and
   provides negotiated agreements and benefits
   protection for more than 250 local guilds in
   North America. AFM also publishes the
   monthly magazine *International Musician*.

American Guild of Musical Artists (AGMA)
1727 Broadway
New York, NY 10019
(212) 265-3687
(212) 262-9088 (fax)
agma@musicalartists.org (e-mail)
www.musicalartists.com

The Coen Brothers have
edited most of their films
themselves, but don't look
for their names in the
credits — it's a well-known
secret that they choose to
work under the joint
pseudonym "Roderick
Jaynes." However, that fact
didn't stop the Motion
Picture Academy from
nominating Jaynes for best
editing for *Fargo* (1996).

Membership: 5,500 members

Trade organization representing classical singers, ballet and modern dancers, stage directors, stage managers, and choreographers. AGMA was founded in 1936 and is a member of the AFL-CIO. The guild provides protection and support for its members, offers educational activities, and publishes *AGMAzine*.

American Guild of Variety Artists (AGVA)

184 Fifth Avenue
New York, NY 10010
(212) 675-1003
agvany@aol.com (e-mail)
home.earthlink.net/~agvala/agva1.html
Membership: 5,000 members

Trade organization representing entertainers performing on Broadway, and Off-Broadway and in cabaret productions, nightclubs, and theme parks. Founded in 1939 under the guidance of the American Federation of Labor, the guild works for wage minimums and improved employment conditions and assists with contractual negotiation. It has long-standing agreements with New York City's Radio City Music Hall and with Disneyland.

American Society of Cinematographers (ASC)

1782 North Orange Drive
Hollywood, CA 90028
(323) 882-5080
(323) 882-6391 (fax)
office@theasc.com (e-mail)
www.cinematographer.com
Membership: 225 members

Nonprofit honorary professional organization for cinematographers. Chartered in January 1919 by members of the Camera Club of New York and the Static Camera Club of America based in Los Angeles. Today, ASC includes film and television cinematographers, and visual effects experts.

Award-winning Chinese-American cinematographer James Wong Howe was honored in 2001 with a retrospective at the University of California at Los Angeles.

Associated Actors and Artists of America (AAAA)

165 West 46th Street
New York, NY 10036
(212) 869-0358
(212) 869-1746 (fax)
Membership: 7 unions/93,000 members

An umbrella trade organization of actors and related artists that is directly affiliated with the AFL-CIO. Founded in 1919, the 4 A's, as it is called is now comprised of the Actors' Equity Association (AEA), the American Federation of Television and Radio Artists (AFTRA), the American Guild of Musical Artists (AGMA), the American Guild of Variety Artists (AGVA), the Screen Actors Guild (SAG), the Italian Actors Union (IAU), and the Hebrew Actors Union (HAU).

Association of Talent Agents (ATA)

9255 Sunset Boulevard, Suite 930
Los Angeles, CA 90069
(310) 274-0628
(310) 274-5063 (fax)
agentassoc@aol.com (e-mail)
Membership: 120 members

Trade organization for talent agents who represent actors, directors, and writers. Founded in 1937, when it was known as the Artists Managers Guild, the ATA provides members with contractual and arbitration support and liaison services with California labor commissions. It also conducts seminars and symposia, compiles statistics on the industry, and publishes a monthly bulletin.

The Authors Guild, Inc. (AG)

330 West 42nd Street, 29th Floor
New York, NY 10036-6902
(212) 563-5904
(212) 564-8363 (fax)
staff@authorsguild.org (e-mail)
www.authorsguild.org
Membership: 7,000 members

Professional trade organization representing authors of books, short stories, poetry, articles, and other literary works that may be used in film development. Founded in 1921, the guild serves to provide members support and information about the craft and protection for members' works. AG offers educational symposia on subjects such as copyright, taxation, editing, criticism, and reviewing. The guild is affiliated with the Authors League of America and publishes a quarterly bulletin for professional authors.

The Authors League of America

330 West 42nd Street, 29th Floor
New York, NY 10036
(212) 564-8350
(212) 564-8363 (fax)
staff@authorsguild.org (e-mail)
Membership: more than 14,000 members

An umbrella organization composed of the Authors Guild and the Dramatists Guild that represents authors, playwrights, composers, and lyricists. The league was founded in 1912 and provides member support regarding copyright, freedom of expression, taxation, and legal issues.

Directors Guild of America (DGA)

7920 Sunset Boulevard
Los Angeles, CA 90046
(310) 289-2000
(310) 289-2029 (fax)
darrellh@dga.org (e-mail)
www.dga.org
Membership: more than 10,000 members

Professional trade organization representing directors and assistant directors of theatrical, industrial, and educational films, as well as directors of documentaries, television, commercial, radio and video, and unit production managers. DGA was formed in 1960 through a merger of the Screen Directors Guild and the Radio and Television Directors Guild. Today it provides its international membership wage negotiation, work regulations, and benefits. It also offers many educational programs, including the Assistant Directors Training Program. DGA publishes an annual membership directory and a monthly newsletter and each March presents awards for outstanding direction.

The Dramatists Guild of America
1501 Broadway, Suite 701
New York, NY 10036
(212) 398-9366
(212) 944-0420 (fax)
www.dramaguild.com
Membership: more than 7,000 members
Professional organization of playwrights, composers, and lyricists, open to all dramatists. It provides legal, business, and educational resources for its members. It also publishes a bimonthly magazine, *The Dramatists*, and a biennial resource directory. The Dramatists Guild, which was founded in 1920, and the Authors Guild together form the Authors League of America (see page 564).

Hollywood Film and Broadcasting Labor Council
11365 Ventura Boulevard, Suite 315
Studio City, CA 91604
(818) 762-9995
(818) 762-9997 (fax)
Trade organization founded in 1947 to mediate between Hollywood unions and motion picture producers. The Hollywood Film and Broadcasting Labor Council is undergoing reorganization.

International Alliance of Theatrical Stage Employees and Moving Picture Machine Operators, Artists and Allied Crafts of the U.S. and Canada (IATSE)
1515 Broadway, Suite 601
New York, NY 10036
(212) 730-1770
(212) 730-7809 (fax)
www.iatse.lm.com
Membership: more than 800 local unions with more than 100,000 members
Trade organization representing hundreds of unions working in every facet of entertainment production. Founded in 1893 by a group of 17 stage employees in New York City, the union was chartered as the National Alliance of Theatrical Stage Employees by the American Federation of Labor in 1894. IATSE, also called IA, works on behalf of its membership to secure minimum wages, negotiate agreements with employers, and establish fair working conditions. IA includes over 800 local unions across the US and Canada. These locals represent accountants, art directors, cameramen, cartoonists, costume designers, costumers, crafts

services, distribution employees, editors, first aid employees, grips, illustrators and matte artists, lighting technicians, mechanics, model makers, office coordinators, painters, property craftsmen, publicists, scenic artists, script supervisors, set designers, set painters, sound effects, story analysts, studio teachers and welfare workers, title artists, and wardrobe assistants. The union also provides training programs and scholarships through its foundation. Its *Official Bulletin* is published quarterly.

International Brotherhood of Electrical Workers (IBEW)
1125 15th Street, NW
Washington, DC 20005
(202) 833-7000
(202) 728-6056 (fax)
www.ibew.org
Membership: 750,000 members
Trade organization of electrical workers in the United States and Canada. Founded in 1891, IBEW is a member of the AFL-CIO and provides its members with collective bargaining agreements, minimum wage rates, negotiations, and contracts and fights for fair working conditions. The IBEW also provides education and training to its members and publishes the monthly *IBEW Journal*.

Producers Guild of America (PGA)
6363 Sunset Boulevard, 9th Floor
Los Angeles, CA 90028
(310) 557-0807
(310) 557-0436 (fax)
info@producersguild.com (e-mail)
www.producersguildonline.com
Membership: more than 1,500 members
Nonprofit professional organization representing individual producers working in television and film. Founded in 1950 as the Screen Producers Guild, the guild serves its international membership through business and legal support, negotiations, and information. The PGA hosts the annual Golden Laurel Awards, which honor the best theatrical film and best television show of the year. It also publishes *P.O.V.* magazine.

Screen Actors Guild (SAG)
5757 Wilshire Boulevard
Los Angeles, CA 90036
(213) 954-1600
(213) 549-6484 (fax)
www.sag.com
Membership: more than 90,000 members
Trade organization representing motion picture and television performers. It was founded in July 1933 by a group of 18 character actors who elected actor Ralph Morgan as their first president. A member of the AFL-CIO and a constituent member of the Associated Actors and Artists of America (see page 564), SAG

> "I have learned that *nothing matters but the final picture.*"
> —
> *David O. Selznick, 1957*

Prior to his 1980 election as president of the United States, Ronald Reagan—seen here with Diana Lynn in Bedtime for Bonzo *(1951)—was president of the Screen Actors Guild from 1947–52 and 1959–60.*

provides negotiations on contracts, workplaces and member welfare in the film, television, and multimedia industries. SAG also provides archives, lobbying services, and educational services. The guild publishes the *Hollywood Call Sheet* and *Screen Actor* magazine, both bimonthly.

The Songwriters Guild of America (SGA)
1500 Harbor Boulevard
Weehauken, NJ 07087
(201) 867-7603
(201) 867-7535 (fax)
songnews@aol.com (e-mail)
www.songwriters.org
Membership: 4,000 members
  Volunteer professional association advancing, promoting, and benefiting songwriters. Founded in 1931 as the Songwriters Protective Association, the group changed its name in 1982 to the American Guild of Authors and Composers before becoming the Songwriters Guild of America in 1986. SGA promotes the rights of songwriters, including the fair payment of royalties, and provides support and services to its members. It also offers scholarships and publishes the *Songwriters Guild of America News* three times yearly.

Stuntmen's Association of Motion Pictures
10660 Riverside Drive, 2nd Floor, Suite E
Toluca Lake, CA 91602
(818) 766-4334
(818) 766-5943 (fax)
samp@stuntmen.com (e-mail)
www.stuntmen.com
Membership: 150 members
  Nonprofit honorary professional organization for stunt performers who work in the motion picture and television industries. Founded in 1961 with 50 charter members and Dale van Sickle as the first president, the association promotes safety and excellence in physical stunts.

Writers Guild of America, West (WGAw)
7000 West Third Street
Los Angeles, CA 90048
(213) 951-4000
(213) 782-4800 (fax)
www.wga.org
Membership: 7,000 members

Writers Guild of America, East (WGAe)
555 West 57th Street
New York, NY 10019
(212) 767-7800
(212) 582-1909 (fax)
www.wgae.org
Membership: 4,000 members
  Trade organization representing writers

in the motion picture, broadcast, cable, interactive, and new media industries. The Writers Guild of America, West, and its counterpart, the Writers Guild of America, East, are two semiautonomous parts of the same organization, whose territories are separated by the Mississippi River. Although governed by a national board, the two separate guilds have their own officers. All members share pension and contractual benefits. The Writers Guild was established in 1954, unifying members of the Authors Guild, Dramatists Guild, Radio Writers Guild, Television Writers Group, and Screen Writers Guild.

Libraries and Research Centers

THE RESEARCHER WHO WANTS to view rare films or study film-related books and documents depends on the hard work of film curators, archivists, librarians, and booksellers. This section lists addresses and phone numbers of some of the principal film museums, archives, and libraries in the US and around the world. A selection of the best-known film and entertainment bookstores in the US is also included. Brief descriptions are provided for those research institutions associated with AFI.

UNITED STATES
Academy of Motion Picture Arts and Sciences
Center for Motion Picture Study
  Academy Film Archive
  Margaret Herrick Library
  333 South La Cienega Boulevard
  Beverly Hills, CA 90211
  (310) 247-3027
  (310) 657-5431(fax)
  www.oscars.org/cmps

American Film Institute
Louis B. Mayer Library
2021 North Western Avenue
  Los Angeles, CA 90027
  (323) 856-7654
  www.afi.com
    Resource library specializing in film and television open to AFI Fellows, scholars, and the general public. Holdings include more than 14,000

Members of the Stuntmen's Association of Motion Pictures work in television as well as movies. Member Hugh Aodh O'Brien, a veteran of films such as *The Replacement Killers* (1998), has done stunts in TV commercials for Levi's and Taco Bell.

AT RIGHT: *Bette Davis portrayed a teaching governess in* All This and Heaven Too *(1940).*

books, approximately 100 industry journals, more than 5,000 unpublished scripts, oral-history transcripts, filmmakers' papers, and other special collections.

American Film Institute
National Center for Film and Video Preservation
2021 North Western Avenue
Los Angeles, CA 90027
(323) 856-7708
www.afi.com

Established in 1984, the National Center for Film and Video Preservation coordinates and supports national film and television preservation activities. The center's activities include gathering, databasing, and making accessible comprehensive documentation on America's moving image heritage. The Center implements the National Moving Image Database (NAMID) (see "Online Resources," pages 587–589) and researches and publishes *The AFI Catalog* (see "Books," pages 582–584). It also locates and acquires films for the American Film Institute Collection housed at the Library of Congress, which includes more than 27,500 titles, primarily theatrical features and short films produced from 1894 to the present. Some AFI Collection films are housed in other archives nationwide. For more information about the contents of the AFI Collection, contact the center directly; for information about access to the AFI Collection, contact the Library of Congress, Motion Picture, Broadcasting and Recorded Sound Division (see below).

American Museum of the Moving Image
3601 35th Avenue
Astoria, NY 11106
(718) 784-4520
www.ammi.org

Association of Moving Image Archivists
See "Associations," pages 559–563.

George Eastman House
900 East Avenue
Rochester, NY 14607
(716) 271-3361
(716) 271-3970 (fax)
www.eastman.org

Harvard Film Archive
Carpenter Center for the Visual Arts
Harvard University
24 Quincy Street
Cambridge, MA 02138
(617) 495-4700
www.harvardfilmarchive.org

Library of Congress
Motion Picture, Broadcasting and Recorded Sound Division
Washington, DC 20540-4690
(202) 707-5840
www.loc.gov/film

The New York Public Library for the Performing Arts
40 Lincoln Center Plaza
New York, NY 10023-7498
(212) 870-1630
performingarts@nypl.org (e-mail)
www.nypl.org/research/lpa

Museum of Modern Art
Department of Film and Video
11 West 53rd Street
New York, NY 10019
(212) 708-9602
education@moma.org (e-mail)
www.moma.org

National Archives and Records Administration
Motion Picture, Sound and Video Branch
8601 Adelphi Road
College Park, MD 20740
(703) 713-7050
inquire@nara.gov (e-mail)
www.nara.gov

National Film Preservation Foundation (NFPF)
See "Associations," pages 559–563.

National Museum of Natural History
National Anthropological Archives
Smithsonian Institution
10th Street and Constitution Avenue NW
Washington, DC 20560-0152
(202) 357-3349; (202) 357-3356
haa@nmnh.si.edu (e-mail)
www.nmnh.si.edu

Pacific Film Archive
University Art Museum
2625 Durant Avenue
Berkeley, CA 94720
(510) 642-1412
www.bampfa.berkeley.edu/pfa

UCLA Film and Television Archive
UCLA Theatre Arts Library
302 East Melnitz Hall
University of California
405 Hilgard Avenue
Los Angeles, CA 90024
(310) 206-8013
(310) 206-3129 (fax)
arsc@ucla.edu (e-mail)
www.cinema.ucla.edu

Wisconsin Center for Film and Theater Research
Film and Photo Archive
816 State Street
Madison, WI 53706
(608) 264-6466
(608) 262-5554 (fax)
www.shsw.wisc.edu/wcftr

Many museums show critically acclaimed films that are otherwise rarely seen in public, such as Andrei Tarkovsky's Solaris *(1972).*

The American Museum of the Moving Image, located in the borough of Queens, New York City, houses the largest and most comprehensive collection of moving image artifacts in the United States—including turn-of-the-century photographic studies and antique televisions, as well as props, costumes, and scripts from countless films—for a total of over 83,000 items.

Museums, Archives, and Libraries: Foreign Institutions

ARGENTINA
Fundacion Cinemateca Argentina
Salta 1915 piso 2
Buenos Aires 1137
Argentina
(54-11) 43-06-05-61 ; 43- 06-05-62 ; 43-06-05-48
(54-11) 43-06-05-92 (fax)
cinematecaargentina@yahoo.com.ar (e-mail)
www.cinemateca.org.ar

AUSTRALIA
Screensound Australia
National Film and Sound Archive
GPO Box 2002
Canberra ACT 2601
Australia
Street address:
McCoy Circuit
Acton ACT 2601
Australia
(61-2) 6248-22-22
(61-2) 6248-21-65 (fax)
www.screensound.gov.au

CANADA
**Archives Visuelles et Sonores
(Visual and Sound Archives)
Archives Nationales du Canada
(National Archives of Canada)**
395 Wellington Street
Ottawa K1A ON3
Canada
(613) 995-7504
(613) 995-6575 (fax)
www.archives.ca

CHINA
China Film Archive
N°3, Wen Hui Yuan Road
Xiao Xi Tian,
Haidian District
Beijing 100088
China
(86-10) 6225-09-16;6225-04-38
(86-10) 6225-93-15 (fax)
cfafad@263.net (e-mail)

EGYPT
Al-Archive Al-Kawmy Lil-Film
(National Film Archive)
c/o Egyptian Film Center
City of Arts
Pyramids Avenue
Guiza
Egypt
(20-2) 585-47-81; 585-03-46; 585-48-01; 585-08-97
(20-2) 585-47-01 (fax)

FRANCE
Cinémathèque Française
Musée du cinéma
4 Rue de Longchamp
Paris 75116
France
(33-1) 53-65-74-74
(33-1) 53-65-74-97 (fax)
cinematec-fr@magic.fr (e-mail)
www.cinematheque.tm.fr

GERMANY
Deutsche Kinemathek (Film Museum Berlin)
Postdamer Strasse 2
Berlin 10785
Germany
(49-30) 300-90-30
(49-30) 300-903-13
info@filmmuseum-berlin.de (e-mail)
www.kinemathek.de

HONG KONG
Hong Kong Film Archive
50 Lei King Road
Sai Wan Ho
Hong Kong
China

A TALE OF TWO CINEMATHEQUES

THE CINÉMATHÈQUE FRANÇAISE in Paris is one of the world's most famous film archives. Founded in the 1930s by archivist Henri Langlois and director Georges Franju, it grew into a vast collection of films and film-related materials. Musée du Cinéma, an associated film museum, was founded in 1972. Given the mission of its French namesake, one might think the American Cinematheque is also an archive. But it isn't. It is an unrelated nonprofit cultural arts organization in Hollywood dedicated to public exhibition of films and videos, including classics and new and innovative works. It was founded in 1981, and organizes year-round weekly film series at the historic 1922 Egyptian Theatre, which it helped to renovate. To see what's playing this week, visit the Egyptian Theatre at 6712 Hollywood Boulevard, Hollywood, CA 90028. Or contact American Cinematheque:

American Cinematheque
1800 North Highland Avenue,
Suite 717
Hollywood, CA 90028
(323) 466-FILM
(recorded information)
(323) 461-2020 (office)
(323) 461-9737 (fax)
amcin@msn.com (e-mail)
www.egyptiantheatre.com

The Adventures of Priscilla, Queen of the Desert *(1994) starred Hugo Weaving, Terence Stamp, and Guy Pearce as two drag queens and one transsexual traveling through the Australian Outback.*

"There is a kind of acting in the United States, especially in the movies, where the personality remains the same in every part. I like changing as much as possible. The Swedish idea of acting is that you change; you play another person each time. To me, doing that is natural."

—

Ingrid Bergman, 1962

(852) 2739-2139
(852) 2311-5229 (fax)
ccfliu@lcsd.gov.hk (e-mail)
www.lcsd.gov.hk/hk/CE/CulturalService/HKFA/
    index.html

INDIA
National Film Archive of India
Law College Road
Pune 411 004
India
(91-20) 565-22-59
(91-20) 567-00-27 (fax)

ITALY
Fondazione Scuola Nazionale Di Cinema
Cineteca Nazionale
Via Tuscolana 1524
Rome 00173
Italy
(39-06) 72-29-41
(39-06) 721-16-19 (fax)
scn@snc.it (e-mail)
www.snc.it

JAPAN
National Film Center
The National Museum of Modern Art, Tokyo
3-7-6, Kyobashi
Chuo-ku, Tokyo104-0031
Japan
(81-3) 3561-0823
(81-3) 3561-0830 (fax)
okajima@momat.go.jp (e-mail)
www.momat.go.jp/

MEXICO
Cineteca Nacional
Ave. México-Coyoacán 389
Col. Xoco
C.P. 03330
Mexico, D.F.
Mexico
(52-5) 688-88-14 ; 604-14-49
(52-5) 688-42-11 ; 688-12-08 (fax)
acvcntk@conaculta.gob.mx (e-mail)
cineteca.conaculta.gob.mx

SWEDEN
Cinemateket
Svenska Filminstitutet
PB 27126
S-102 52 Stockholm
Sweden
Street address:
Filmhuset
Borgvägen 1-5
Stockholm
Sweden
(46-8) 665-11-00
(46-8) 661-18-20 (fax)
www.sfi.se

UK
**British Film Institute (BFI) Collections
    Department**
National Film and Television Archive
21 Stephen Street
London W1P 2LN UK
(44-171) 255-14-44
(44-171) 580-75-03 (fax)
www.bfi.org.uk

Film and Entertainment Bookstores

> "Let me tell you about writing for films. You finish your book. Now, you know where the California state line is? Well, you drive right up to that line, take your manuscript, and pitch it across —No, on second thought, don't pitch it across. First, let them toss the money over. *Then* you throw it over, pick up the money, and get the hell out of there."
>
> *Ernest Hemingway during preproduction for* The Old Man and the Sea, *circa 1957*

Applause
211 West 71st Street
New York, NY 10021
(800) 496-7511
www.applause.com

Cinema Books
4753 Roosevelt Way NE
Seattle, WA 98105
(206) 547-7667
www.isomedia.com

Elliot M. Katt: Books on the Performing Arts
8568 Melrose Avenue
Los Angeles, CA 90069
(310) 652-5178; (800) 445-4561 outside California
filmbok@leonardo.net (e-mail)
www.abebooks.com/home/filmbook

Gotham Book Mart
41 West 47th Street
New York, NY 10036
(212) 719-4448

Jerry Ohlinger's Movie Material Store, Inc.
242 West 14th Street
New York, NY 10011
(212) 989-0869
(212) 989-1660 (fax)
JOMMS@aol.com (e-mail)
www.moviematerials.com

Larry Edmunds Bookshop
6644 Hollywood Boulevard
Hollywood, CA 90028
(323) 463-3273
(323) 463-4275 (fax)
www.larryedmunds.com

Limelight Film and Theatre Bookstore
1803 Market Street
San Francisco, CA 94103
(415) 864-2265

Samuel French Theatre and Film Bookshop
(two locations)
7623 Sunset Boulevard
Hollywood, CA 90046
(323) 876-0570
(323) 876-6822 (fax)
11963 Ventura Boulevard
Studio City, CA 91604
(818) 762-0535
samuelfrench@earthlink.net (e-mail)
www.samuelfrench.com

Script City
8033 Sunset Boulevard, Suite 1500
Hollywood, CA 90046
(800) 676-2522 in the US, (818) 764-4120 worldwide
(818) 764-4132 (fax)
ww.scriptcity.net

The Writers Store
2040 Westwood Boulevard
Los Angeles, CA 90025
(800) 272-8927
(800) 486-4006 (fax)
sales@writersstore.com (e-mail)
www.writersstore.com

In Batman *(1989), starring Michael Keaton in the title role, the superhero used high-tech gadgets to fend off the Joker, played by Jack Nicholson.*

Educational Programs

GIVEN WIDESPREAD PUBLIC INTEREST, many colleges and universities offer undergraduate majors in film. Some offer graduate degrees: master of arts (MA), master of fine arts (MFA), and doctor of philosophy (PhD). Many aspiring filmmakers regard an MFA. as an indispensable part of learning the trade and making contacts, especially if the degree comes from a top film school in Los Angeles or New York City. Others prefer to acquire their training on the job or through nondegree classes, workshops, and seminars. Screenwriting workshops, in particular, have become a mainstay in many communities where people long to make movies. It should be noted that some nondegree programs, such as the labs offered by the Sundance Institute, are as prestigious as the degree program of any film school.

Graduate programs, plus some of the better-known nondegree film studies programs and screenwriting classes, workshops, and seminars, are listed below.

GRADUATE PROGRAMS IN FILM

ALABAMA
University of Alabama
Telecommunication and Film Department
Box 870152
Tuscaloosa, AL 35487-0152
(205) 348-6350
(205) 348-5162 (fax)
www.tcf.ua.edu

ARIZONA
University of Arizona
Media Arts Department
Tuscon, AZ 85723
(520) 621-7352
gradmar@e-mail.arizona.edu (e-mail)
www.arts.arizona.edu

CALIFORNIA
American Film Institute
AFI Conservatory
2021 North Western Avenue
Los Angeles, CA 90027
(323) 856-7600
(323) 467-4578 (fax)
info@afi.com (e-mail)
www.afi.com

Brooks Institute of Photography
Media Center
801 Alston Road
Santa Barbara, CA 93108
(888) 304-FILM (3456)
admissions@brooks.edu (e-mail)
www.brooks.edu

California Institute of the Arts
School of Film and Video
24700 McBean Parkway
Valencia, CA 91355-2397
(800) 545-2787; in California (800) 292-ARTS
   (2787)
admissions@calarts.edu (e-mail)
www.calarts.edu

Chapman University
School of Film and Television
Cecil B. DeMille Hall
333 North Glassell Street
Orange, CA 92866
(714) 997-6815
(714) 997-6700 (fax)
ftvinfo@chapman.edu (e-mail)
www.chapman.edu

The students in Dead Poets Society *(1989) were inspired by an unconventional English teacher played by Robin Williams.*

John Belushi and the cast of National Lampoon's Animal House *(1978) wreaked havoc on a college campus.*

Humboldt State University
Theater Arts Department
Arcata, CA 95521-8299
(707) 826-3011
(707) 826-6194 (fax)
hsuinfo@humboldt.edu (e-mail)
www.humboldt.edu

Loyola Marymount University
School of Film and Television
7900 Loyola Boulevard
Los Angeles, CA 90045
(310) 338-2750
www.lmu.edu

San Francisco State University
Cinema Department
1600 Holloway Avenue
San Francisco, CA 94132-1722
(415) 338-1629
sfuin@sfsu.edu (e-mail)
www.sfsu.edu

Stanford University
Communication Department
Stanford, CA 94305-2050
(415) 723-2300
www.stanford.edu

University of California, Los Angeles
School of Theater, Film, and Television
102 East Melnitz Hall
405 Hilgard Avenue
Box 951622
Los Angeles, CA 90025-1622
(310) 825-5761
(310) 825-3383 (fax)
www.tft.ucla.edu

University of Southern California
Student Affairs
School of Cinema-Television
Los Angeles, CA 90089-0911
(213) 740-2311
www.usc.edu

DISTRICT OF COLUMBIA
The American University
School of Communications
4400 Massachusetts Avenue NW
Washington, DC 20016-8001
(202) 885-2061
einfo@american.edu (e-mail)
www.american.edu

Howard University
Radio, Television and Film Department
525 Bryant Street NW
Washington, DC 20059
(202) 806-6100
www.howard.edu

FLORIDA
Florida State University
School of Motion Picture, Television and
    Recording Arts
1346 University Center
Tallahassee, FL 32306-2084
(850) 644-2525
www.fsu.edu

University of Miami
School of Communication
P.O. Box 248127
Coral Gables, FL 33124
(305) 284-2265
(305) 284-3648 (fax)
communication@miami.edu (e-mail)
www.miami.edu

ILLINOIS
Columbia College
Department of Film and Video
600 South Michigan Avenue
Chicago, IL 60605
(312) 663-1600, ext. 300
www.colum.edu

Northern Illinois University
Department of Communication Studies
DeKalb, IL 60115-2854
(815) 753-1000
www.niu.edu

Northwestern University
Department of Radio, Television and Film
1905 Sheridan Road
Evanston, IL 60201
(847) 491-7315
(847) 491-2389 (fax)
www.northwestern.edu

University of Chicago
Committee on Cinema and Media Studies
Gates-Blake 405
5845 South Ellis Avenue
Chicago, IL 60637
(773) 834-1077
(773) 702-9042 (fax)
cine-media@uchicago.edu (e-mail)
www.uchicago.com

INDIANA
Indiana University
Film Studies Program
Bloomington, IN 47405
(815) 855-4848
www.iub.edu

IOWA
University of Iowa
College of Liberal Arts
Department of Cinema and
    Comparative Literature
425 English-Philosophy Building
Iowa City, IA 52242
(319) 335-0330
cinema-comlit@uiowa.edu (e-mail)
www.uiowa.edu

KANSAS
University of Kansas
Department of Theater and Film
356 Murphy Hall
Lawrence, KS 66045
(913) 864-3511
www.ukans.edu

MASSACHUSETTS
Boston University
College of Communications
640 Commonwealth Avenue
Boston, MA 02215
(617) 353-3483
comgrad@bu.edu (e-mail)
www.bu.edu

NEW YORK
Bard College
Milton Avery Graduate School of the Arts Dept.
P.O. Box 5000

Annandale-on-Hudson, NY 12504-5000
(845) 758-7481
www.bard.edu

**City University of New York,
    College of Staten Island**
Department of Performing and Creative Arts
2800 Victory Boulevard
Staten Island, NY 10314
(718) 982-2000
www.csi.cuny.edu

City University of New York, Queens College
Department of Media Studies
65-30 Kissena Boulevard
Flushing, NY 11367-1597
(718) 997-2950
www.qc.edu

Columbia University School of the Arts
Film Division
305 Dodge Hall
2960 Broadway
New York, NY 10027
(212) 854-2815
film@columbia.edu (e-mail)
www.columbia.edu

New York University
Tisch School of the Arts
721 Broadway, 6th Floor
New York, NY 10003
(212) 998-1600
(212) 995-4061 (fax)
www.nyu.com

Syracuse University
Department of Art Media Studies
102 Shaffer Art
Syracuse, NY 13244-1210
(315) 443-1033
(315) 443-1303 (fax)
grad@gwmail.syr.edu (e-mail)
www.syr.edu

**University of
    Rochester**
Department of Film
Rush Rhees, Room 427
Rochester, NY 14627
(716) 275-5757
www.rochester.edu

Director Alexander Mackendrick (*The Sweet Smell of Success*, 1957) was appointed dean of the film department at the California Institute of the Arts in the late 1960s, where his students included director James Mangold (*Girl, Interrupted*, 1999).

Honor student Buster Keaton tried out for every sport in college in order to keep the interest of a girl infatuated with an athlete in College *(1927).*

NORTH CAROLINA
University of North Carolina, Chapel Hill
Radio, Television and Motion Pictures Department
Chapel Hill, NC 27599-6235
(919) 962-2211
www.unc.edu

University of North Carolina, Greensboro
Division of Broadcasting and Cinema
241 Mossman Building
P.O. Box 26176
Greensboro, NC 27402
(336) 334-5596
(336) 334-4424 (fax)
inquiries@uncg.edu (e-mail)
www.uncg.edu

OHIO
Ohio University
School of Film
378 Lindley Hall
Athens, OH 45701
(740) 593-1323
(740) 593-1328 (fax)
filmdept@www.ohiou.edu (e-mail)
www.ohiou.edu

OKLAHOMA
University of Oklahoma
Department of Film
Dale Hall Tower, Room 806
College of Arts and Sciences
Norman, OK 73019
(405) 325-3020
www.ou.edu

PENNSYLVANIA
Temple University
School of Communications and Theater
Department of Radio, Television and Film
2020 North 13th Street
Philadelphia, PA 19122
(215) 204-8422
(215) 204-6641 (fax)
www.temple.edu

TEXAS
University of North Texas
Department of Radio, Television & Film
Box 13108
Denton, TX 76203
(940) 565-2537
(940) 369-7838 (fax)
rtuf.unt.edu (e-mail)
www.unt.edu

University of Texas, Austin
Department of Radio, Television and Film
CMA 6.114
Austin, TX 78712-1091
(512) 471-3532
(512) 471-4077 (fax)
www.utexas.edu/coc/rtf

UTAH
University of Utah
Department of Film
206 Pab Building
Salt Lake City, UT 84112
(801)581-6448
www.utah.edu

VIRGINIA
Virginia Commonwealth University
School of the Arts
Department of Photography and Film
P.O. Box 842519
325 Harviman Street
Richmond, VA 23284
(804) 828-0100
gradschool@vcu.edu (e-mail)
www.vcu.edu

WISCONSIN
University of Wisconsin, Milwaukee
School of the Arts
Department of Film
Mitchell Hall
3203 North Downer Avenue, MIT B-69
Milwaukee, WI 53211
(414) 229-6015
(414) 229-5901 (fax)
www.uwm.edu/soa/film

Nondegree Programs

THERE ARE MANY WAYS to get training in the film arts besides completing graduate degree programs. Classes open to the general public are offered by the American Film Institute (see below) and, through UCLA Extension, by the University of California, Los Angeles (see preceding section). Many of the film craft guilds also offer training resources (see "Guilds and Unions," pages 563–566). The following nondegree programs are particularly well known.

Actors Studio
432 West 44th Street
New York, New York 10036
(212) 757-0870

The Actors Studio, Inc.
8341 DeLongpre Avenue
West Hollywood, CA 90060-2601
(323) 654-7125
(323) 654-8266 (fax)

> "I decided to become an actor because I was failing in school and needed the credits."
>
> —
>
> *Dustin Hoffman, 1979*

Prestigious workshop for actors. Actors must be professionals with previous training who audition to participate. Not a school but a place for actors to hone their skills in company with other actors.

American Film Institute
2021 North Western Avenue
Los Angeles, CA 90027
(323) 856-7600
(323) 467-4578 (fax)
info@afi.com (e-mail)
www.afi.com
Directing Workshop for Women
(323) 856-7691
Intensive training workshop for women in narrative filmmaking. Since its inception in 1974, more than 150 women have participated in this highly competitive program. Workshop participants are women with a minimum of five years experience in television, film, video, or dramatic arts but no professional credits as a narrative film director. Online application is available.

Hollywood Film Institute
1223 Olympic Boulevard
Santa Monica, CA 90404
(310) 399-6699
(310) 581-0919 (fax)
dov@webfilmschool.com (e-mail)
www.WebFilmSchool.com
Independent film school for adults founded by film producer and educator Dov S-S Simens. It offers weekend-long intensive crash courses for adults who want to learn how to produce, write, direct, shoot, or edit independent and digital feature films.

Sundance Institute
225 Santa Monica Boulevard, 8th Floor
Santa Monica, CA 90401
(310) 394-4662
P.O. Box 16450
Salt Lake City, UT 84116
(801) 328-3456
(801) 575-5175 (fax)
www.sundance.org
Founded by actor-director Robert Redford in 1980 to encourage independent filmmaking by developing and training filmmakers and showcasing their work. The Sundance Film Festival has become one of cinema's most prestigious annual events (see "Film Festivals and Markets," see pages 556–559). The Santa Monica office conducts screenwriting and filmmakers labs, while the Utah location holds labs for playwrights, producers, composers, and choreographers. Admission is highly selective.

* * *

SCREENWRITING CLASSES, WORKSHOPS, AND SEMINARS

Robert McKee Two Arts, Inc.
P.O. Box 452930
Los Angeles, CA 90045
(888) 676-2533
(310) 645-6928 (fax)
contact@mckeestory.com (e-mail)
www.mckeystory.com
Acclaimed screenwriting educator Robert McKee offers a three-day "Story Seminar" that teaches the principles of screenwriting, focusing on the relationship between story structure and character. He regularly brings the seminar to other locations in tours of the United States, Europe, and Australia.

Truby Writer's Studio (TWS)
751 Hartzell Street
Pacific Palisades, CA 90272
(800) 338-7829; outside US (310) 573-9630
www.truby.com
Story structure teacher John Truby offers courses on audio tape, along with software aimed at helping writers develop their screenplays.

Wisconsin Screenwriters Forum
University of Wisconsin
Madison Communication Programs
610 Langdon Street
Madison, WI 53703
(888) 282-6776
www.wiscreenwritersforum.org
Established in 1982, this Wisconsin-based organization is run by screenwriters for screenwriters. It offers seminars, a script critique service, an annual screenplay contest, meetings for members in Wisconsin and California, and networking with industry professionals.

Writer's Boot Camp
2525 Michigan Avenue Building I
Santa Monica, CA 90404
(310) 998-1199
(310) 998-1140 (fax)
www.writersbootcamp.com
Offers twelve-week sessions aimed at getting writers to complete scripts, with peer group support for the writing of new scripts after the course is over. A six-week course is available for alumni. Requires participants to commit ten hours weekly to their creative work.

AFI's Conservatory offers MFA degrees in cinematography, directing, editing, producing, production design, and screenwriting. Many acclaimed film and television artists have been educated at the Conservatory; some have gone on to participate in the Conservatory's direction, including film directors Jon Avnet, Carl Franklin, and Ed Zwick.

Robert Redford (right) founded the Sundance Institute and highly esteemed Sundance Film Festival, naming them after his character in Butch Cassidy and The Sundance Kid *(1969), also starring Paul Newman (left).*

Services for Filmmakers

FILM IS A COLLABORATIVE art that could not exist without the services of many different professionals. This section spotlights three kinds of services: talent agencies, government agencies, and production services, a catchall category that includes everything from special effects to stock footage and classic-car rentals.

TALENT AGENCIES

Artists Management Group (AMG)
9465 Wilshire Boulevard
Beverly Hills, CA 90212-2604
(310) 860-8000
(310) 860-8100 (fax)

Creative Artists Agency (CAA)
9830 Wilshire Boulevard
Beverly Hills, CA 90212
(310) 288-4545
(310) 288-4800 (fax)
www.caa.com

International Creative Management (ICM)
8942 Wilshire Boulevard
Beverly Hills, CA 90211
(310) 550-4000
(310) 550-4100 (fax)

William Morris Agency, Inc.
151 El Camino Drive
Beverly Hills, CA 90212
(310) 859-4000
(310) 859-4462 (fax)
www.wma.com

United Talent Agency
9560 Wilshire Boulevard, 5th Floor
Beverly Hills, CA 90212
(213) 273-6700
(213) 247-1111 (fax)

The William Morris Agency is the world's oldest and largest talent and literary agency. Founded in 1898, it made its reputation representing vaudeville stars such as Will Rogers and Al Jolson.

Nicole Kidman (seen here with Ewan McGregor in Moulin Rouge, 2001) *is represented by Creative Artists Agency.*

FINDING AN AGENT

IF YOU ARE NEW TO THE FILM industry, finding an agent to represent you is no guarantee of success, but it is a mark of professionalism. It is not hard to locate the agents: guilds such as the Screen Actors Guild (SAG) and Writers Guild of America (WGA) supply complete lists of reputable agents, which are accessible on the Web to both members and nonmembers (see "Guilds and Unions," pages 563-566). The Hollywood Creative Directory (www. hcdonline.com) sells online and print versions of its directory of agents and managers. The hard part is to convince an agent to take you on as a client and to make sure your agent works hard for you and has the clout to make a difference. Here are a few tips from experts on how to find an agent. For more in-depth advice, see the titles under "Career Help and Professional Resources" in the "Books" section (pages 582-584).

NETWORK. Meet as many people as you can in the industry. Ask them for recommendations of reputable agents.

WHEN READING LISTS of agents, look for agents who list themselves as willing to consider clients new to the business.

BE PROFESSIONAL. If you're an actor, submit headshots, résumés, and tapes of your professional work (if any). If you're a writer, send a query letter describing your script and asking if the agent is interested before sending the script.

IT IS EASIER TO GET an agent with a personal referral than with an unsolicited letter. If you have a contact who already works in the industry and knows an agent, ask him or her to call the agent on your behalf.

LOOK OUT FOR SCAMS. Agents should not charge money up-front or in excess of their 10- to 15-percent commission or demand sexual favors in return for representation.

BE PERSISTENT.

Government Agencies

FILM OFFICES AND COMMISSIONS

CALIFORNIA
California Film Commission
7080 Hollywood Boulevard, Suite 900
Hollywood, CA 90028
(800) 858-4PIX
(323) 860-2972 (fax)
filmca@commerce.ca.gov (e-mail)

County of Los Angeles
Entertainment Industry Development Corporation
Los Angeles Film Office
7083 Hollywood Boulevard, Suite 500
Hollywood, CA 90028
(323) 957-1000
(323) 962-4966 (fax)
www.commerce.ca.gov

FLORIDA
Orlando/Central Florida Film and TV Office
200 East Robinson Street, Suite 600
Orlando, FL 32801-1950
(407) 422-7159
(407) 841-9069 (fax)
filminfo@film-orlando.org (e-mail)
www.film-orlando.org

ILLINOIS
City of Chicago Film Office
One North LaSalle Street, Suite 2165
Chicago, IL 60602
(312) 744-6415
(312) 744-1378 (fax)
filmoffice@ci.chi.il.us (e-mail)
www.ci.chi.il.us

Illinois Film Office
100 West Randolph Street, Suite 3-400
Chicago, IL 60601
(312) 814-3600
(312) 814-8874 (fax)
www.commerce.state.il.us/film

NEW YORK
**City of New York Mayor's Office of Film,
  Theatre and Broadcasting**
1697 Broadway, 6th Floor
New York, NY 10019
(212) 489-6710
(212) 307-6237 (fax)
www.ci.nyc.ny.us/html/film.com/

**New York State Governor's Office for Motion
  Picture and Television Development**
633 Third Avenue, 33rd Floor
New York, NY 10017
(212) 803-2330
(212) 803-2339 (fax)
NYFILM@empire.state.ny.us (e-mail)

FEDERAL GOVERNMENT AGENCIES

Library of Congress Copyright Office
Madison Building
101 Independence Avenue, SE
Washington, DC 20559-6000
(202) 707-3000
(202) 707-2600 (fax)
www.loc.gov/copyright

**National Endowment for the Arts
Creation and Presentation, Media Arts Program**
1100 Pennsylvania Avenue NW, Room 726
Washington, DC 20506
(202) 682-5452
(202) 682-5721 (fax)
webmgr@artsendow.gov (e-mail)
www.arts.endow.gov

**National Endowment for the Humanities
Humanities Projects in Media,
  Division of Public Programs**
1100 Pennsylvania Avenue NW, Room 426
Washington, DC 20506
(202) 606-8278
(202) 606-8557 (fax)
info@neh.gov (e-mail)
www.neh.fed.us

MILITARY LIAISONS FOR FILMMAKERS
Army Chief of Public Affairs
10880 Wilshire Boulevard,
  Room 10104
Los Angeles, CA 90024-3688
(310) 235-7621
(310) 235-6075 (fax)

Marine Corps Public Affairs
10880 Wilshire Boulevard, Suite 1230
Los Angeles, CA 90024
(310) 235-7272
(310) 235-7274 (fax)

**U.S. Air Force Motion Picture
  and Television Liaison
  Office**
10880 Wilshire Boulevard,
  Room 10114
Los Angeles, CA 90024
(310) 235-7522
(310) 235-7500 (fax)

**U.S. Coast Guard
  Motion Picture and
  Television Office**
10880 Wilshire
  Boulevard, Suite 1210
Los Angeles, CA 90024
(310) 235-7817
(310) 235-7851 (fax)
www.uscg.mil

The US Military has had a close relationship with Hollywood since their heavy involvement throughout the production of 1927's best picture winner, *Wings*. Sometimes, script changes are required before the army decides to cooperate, as was the case with *From Here to Eternity* (1953), which was not allowed to film at Hawaii's Schofield Barracks until its depictions of Army brig atrocities were toned down. The makers of *Top Gun* (1986) was given free access to an aircraft carrier, planes, and technical advice as long as the Navy was allowed to censor anything in the script it found to be less than flattering.

Goldie Hawn starred in and produced Private Benjamin *(1980), in which she played a young woman who impulsively joins the Army.*

Production Services

HERE IS A SAMPLING of companies that provide assorted services to filmmakers, from animation to prop rentals. Additional listings can be found in *The International Motion Picture Almanac.*

ANIMATION

Fleischer Studios, Inc.
10160 Cielo Drive
Beverly Hills, CA 90210
(310) 276-7503
(310) 276-1559 (fax)
stanhandmans@man.com (e-mail)

Jim Henson Productions
c/o Raleigh Studios
5358 Melrose Avenue
West Building, 3rd Floor
Hollywood, CA 90038
(213) 960-4096
(213) 960-4935 (fax)

Pixar Animation Studios
1200 Park Avenue
Emeryville, CA 94608
(510) 752-3000
(510) 752-3151 (fax)
www.pixar.com

Period costumes are among the multitude of items that can be rented from a prop-rental establishment.

CASTING ORGANIZATIONS

Casting Society of America
606 N. Larchmont Boulevard, #4B
Los Angeles, CA 90004
(213) 463-1925
(213) 463-5753 (fax)
castsoc@earthlink.net (e-mail)
www.castingsociety.com

Communications Corporation of America
(specializing in preteen, teen, and young adult actors)
2501 North Sheffield Avenue
Chicago, IL 60614
(773) 348-0001
(773) 472-7398 (fax)

Hollywood Screen Parents Association
P.O. Box 1612
Burbank, CA 91507-1612
(818) 955-6510

Ron Smith's Celebrity Look-Alikes
(celebrity impersonators)
7060 Hollywood Boulevard, #1215
Hollywood, CA 90028
(323) 467-3030
(323) 467-6720 (fax)

Lynn Stalmaster & Associates
500 South Sepulveda Boulevard,
Suite 600
Los Angeles, CA 90049
(310) 552-0983

CONSULTANTS AND TECHNICAL ADVISERS

Blackstone Magik Enterprises, Inc.
(magic technical advisers, consultants)
12800 Puesta Del Sol
Redlands, CA 92373
(909) 792-1227
(909) 794-2737 (fax)
magik@blackstonemagik.com (e-mail)
www.blackstonemagik.com

Call the Cops
(police tactics, homicide procedures)
P.O. Box 911
Agoura Hills, CA 91376
(818) 595-5125
(661) 245-2677 (fax)
www.call-the-cops.com

Mademoiselle Irene UJDA
(period reenactment and historical consultants)
2546 ½ Corralitas Drive
Los Angeles, CA 90039
(213) 664-0227; (310) 244-8028

U.S. Film Force
(military and government coordination, technical advice)
8306 Wilshire Boulevard, Suite 2659
Beverly Hills, CA 90211
(213) 468-0282
(213) 651-0380 (fax)
filmforce@aol.com (e-mail)

COSTUME AND PROP RENTALS

Classic Car Suppliers
1905 Sunset Plaza Drive
West Hollywood, CA 90069
(310) 657-7823
www.hollywoodmoviecars.com

House of Props
(fine-arts prop rentals)
1117 Gower Street
Hollywood, CA 90038-1801
(323) 463-3166
(323) 463-8302 (fax)
houseprops@aol.com (e-mail)

Western Costume Company
11041 Van Owen Street
North Hollywood, CA 91605
(818) 760-0902
(818) 508-2190 (fax)
mailroom@westerncostume.com (e-mail)

FILM PRESERVATION AND SERVICES

Deluxe Laboratories, Inc.
(full-service film lab)
1377 North Serrano Avenue
Hollywood, CA 90027
(323) 462-6171
(323) 467-9787 (fax)
www.bydeluxe.com

Foto-Kem Foto-Tronics, Film-Video Lab
(preservation, processing, repair, storage, transfer)
2880 West Clive Avenue
Burbank, CA 91505
(818) 846-3101
(818) 841-2130 (fax)

Hollywood Vaults, Inc.
(film preservation and off-site storage)
1780 Prospect Avenue (office)
Santa Barbara, CA 93103
(805) 569-5336
(805) 569-1657 (fax)
vault@hollywoodvaults.com (e-mail)
www.hollywoodvaults.com

MARKET RESEARCH AND ANALYSIS

Paul Kagan Associates
126 Clock Tower Place
Carmel, CA 93923
(408) 624-1536
(408) 625-3225 (fax)
info@kagan.com
www.pkbaseline.com

SOUND STUDIOS

Dolby Laboratories, Inc.
3375 Barham Boulevard
Los Angeles, CA 90068
(213) 845-1880
(415) 863-1373 (fax)
www.dolby.com

SPECIAL EFFECTS

Industrial Light and Magic (ILM)
P.O. Box 2459
San Rafael, CA 94912
(415) 258-2000
www.ilm.com

Stan Winston Studio
7032 Valjean Avenue
Van Nuys, CA 91406
(818) 782-0870
info@swfx.com (e-mail)
www.swfx.com

STOCK SHOTS

Archive Films/Archive Photos
75 Varick Street
New York, NY 10013
(646) 613-4100; (800) 447-0733
(646) 613-4140 (fax)
sales@archivefilms.com (e-mail)
www.archivefilms.com

Film Bank
425 South Victory Boulevard
Burbank, CA 91502
(818) 841-9176
(818) 567-4235 (fax)
filmbank@primenet.com (e-mail)
www.filmbank.com

Hollywood Newsreel Syndicate, Inc.
1622 North Gower Street
Hollywood, CA 90028
(323) 469-7307
(323) 469-8251 (fax)

STUDIO AND EDITING EQUIPMENT RENTALS

Walt Disney/MGM Studios
3300 North Bonnett Creek Road
Lake Buena Vista, FL 32830
(407) 560-5353; (407) 560-6188

Kaufman Astoria Studios
34-12 36th Street
Astoria, NY 11106
(718) 392-5600
(718) 706-7733 (fax)
www.kaufmanastoria.com

Warner Bros. Studios Facilities
4000 Warner Boulevard
Burbank, CA 91522
(818) 954-3000
(818) 954-2577 (fax)
wbsf@warnerbros.com (e-mail)
www.wbsf.com

SUBTITLING AND CAPTIONING

National Captioning Institute
(closed-captioning, subtitling)
303 North Glenoaks Boulevard,
  Suite 200
Burbank, CA 91502
(818) 238-0068
(818) 238-4266 (fax)
dougroberts@earthlink.net
  (e-mail)
www.ncicap.org/nci

P.F.M. Dubbing International
(produces and dubs
  English-language versions of foreign-
  language films)
1007 Montana Avenue, Suite 306
Santa Monica, CA 90403
(310) 451-6068
(310) 451-6058 (fax)

* * *

Studio equipment rental facilities carry cameras, lights, and sound equipment.

AT RIGHT: *Sex symbol Kim Novak, seen here with her name in lights on a movie marquee, epitomized glamour in the 1950s.*

Film Exhibition

THE DESIRED ENDPOINT for every film is exhibition: its presentation to an audience in a multiplex, at a campus film society, or at home on video. This section provides information on the major theater circuits, places to obtain 16-millimeter or 35-millimeter release prints, and sources for rare videos that can be borrowed or purchased for home viewing.

According to *The International Motion Picture Almanac 2000,* there are 34,186 screens for public exhibition of films in the US. Of them, 33,440 are indoor screens; and 776 are screens at drive-in movie theaters. The top ten theater circuits control more than 50 percent (54.9 percent) of all US screens.

TOP TEN THEATER CIRCUITS

AMC Entertainment, Inc.
208 theaters, 2,559 screens in US
106 West 14th Street, Suite 1700
Kansas City, MO 64141
(816) 221-4000
(816) 480-4617 (fax)
www.amctheaters.com

Carmike Cinemas, Inc.
484 theaters, 2,467 screens in US
1301 First Avenue
P.O. Box 391
Columbus, GA 31902-0391
(706) 576-3400
(706) 576-3441 (fax)
www.carmike.com

Cinemark USA, Inc.
180 theaters, 1,967 screens in US
3900 Dallas Parkway, Suite 500
Plano, TX 75093
(972) 665-1000
(972) 665-1004 (fax)
www.cinemark.com

Edwards Theatres
87 theaters, 752 screens in US
300 Newport Center Drive
Newport Beach, CA 92660
(949) 640-4600
(949) 721-7170 (fax)
www.edwardscinemas.com

General Cinema Theatres
A subsidiary of GC Companies, Inc.
140 theaters, 1,100 screens in US
1280 Boylston Street
Chestnut Hill, MA 02467
(617) 277-4320
(617) 277-8875 (fax)
www.generalcinema.com

Hoyts Cinemas Corporation
119 theaters, 970 screens in the US
One Exeter Plaza
Boston, MA 02116-2836
(617) 646-5700
(617) 262-0707 (fax)
www.hoyts.com

Loews Cineplex Entertainment Corporation
(includes Loews Theatres, Sony Theatres, Cineplex Odeon, Magic Johnson Theatres, Star Theatres)
451 theaters, 2,787 screens in US, including two IMAX
711 Fifth Avenue
New York, NY 10022-3109
(212) 833-6275
www.loewscineplex.com

National Amusements
97 theaters, 890 screens in US
P.O. Box 9126
Dedham, MA 02026
(781) 461-1600
(781) 326-1306 (fax)
www.nationalamusements.com

Regal Cinemas, Inc.
386 theaters, 3,237 screens, 8 entertainment centers in the US
7132 Commercial Park Drive
Knoxville, TN 37918
(865) 922-1123
(865) 922-3188 (fax)
www.regalcinemas.com

United Artists Theatre Circuit, Inc.
307 theaters, 2,102 screens in the US
9110 East Nichols Avenue, Suite 200
Englewood, CO 80112
(303) 792-3600
www.natc.com

Sources for Release Prints

Crown International Pictures, Inc.
8701 Wilshire Boulevard
Beverly Hills, CA 90211
(310) 657-6700
(310) 657-4489 (fax)
www.crownintlpictures.com

Em Gee Film Library
6924 Canby Avenue, Suite 103
Reseda, CA 91335
(818) 881-8110
(818) 981-5506 (fax)
mglass@worldnet.att.net (e-mail)

Kino International
333 West 39th Street, Suite 503
New York, NY 10018
(212) 629-6880
(212) 714-0871 (fax)
www.kino.com

Kit Parker Films
P.O. Box 16022
Monterey, CA 93942
(831) 393-0303
(831) 393-0304 (fax)
info@kitparker.com (e-mail)
www.kitparker.com

New Yorker Films
16 West 61st Street
New York, NY 10023
(212) 247-6110
info@newyorkerfilms.com (e-mail)
www.newyorkerfilms.com

Swank Motion Pictures
201 South Jefferson Avenue
St. Louis, MO 63103
(800) 876-5577
(314) 289-2192 (fax)
www.swank.com

Toho International
1501 Broadway
New York, NY 10036
(212) 391-9058

Sources for Videos

WHEN TRYING TO FIND MOVIES to watch on your VCR, your local video store is a good place to look first. But when the store's new release section is unappetizing and you have long since exhausted its older titles, try these

ABOUT RELEASE PRINTS

TO RENT A 16-MILLIMETER or 35-millimeter film to show in a theater or other setting, you need to consult a film distributor. You may need to go straight to the studio's distribution department if it has retained the rights: the studios' main numbers are listed in "Producers and Distributors" (see pages 550–555) and they may have local distribution affiliates. But there are also general film distribution companies that market films from a variety of studios, and it may be more convenient to work with them.

Films have theatrical and nontheatrical distribution rights, and there is considerable variety in how the rights are apportioned. Frequently, nontheatrical rights are granted to general distributors, with theatrical rights to films, particularly recent or popular releases, kept with the studio. But a general distributor may have further limitations on its rights, such as renting the film only in 16-millimeter or for nontheatrical purposes.

Despite these kinds of restrictions, many films are available through several sources. In choosing a distributor, geography generally is not a factor, because films can be sent by overnight services. To ensure a high-quality print, ask about the distributor's maintenance procedures.

Many distributors rent both 16- and 35-millimeter films, although not every film is available in both formats.

mail-order sources, known for stocking videos that are hard to find elsewhere. Videos may be available for sale and/or rental; contact the company for details.

A Million and One World-Wide Videos
P.O. Box 349
Orchard Hill, GA 30266
(800) 849-7309 in US; (770) 227-7309 worldwide
(800) 849-0873 in US; (770) 227-0873 (fax)
information@wwvideos.com (e-mail)
www.wwvideos.com

Eddie Brandt's Saturday Matinee Video
5006 Vineland Avenue
North Hollywood, CA 91601
(818) 506-4242

Facets
1517 West Fullerton Avenue
Chicago, IL 60614
(800) 331-6197
(773) 929-5437 (fax)
sales@facets.org (e-mail)
www.facets.org

For a brief time in the late 1990s, the burgeoning DVD format had a competitor in a system called Divx. Designed to do away with rental returns and late fees, Divx, like DVD, came in a digital disc format, and could be watched on most DVD players. Unlike DVD, however, Divx was only viewable for a 48-hour-period. Available for a one-time purchase price of $4.49, consumers could then watch the movie again by paying $3.25 for another 48 hours. The disposable discs, lacking both consumer and major studio support, never caught on, and were discontinued in 1999.

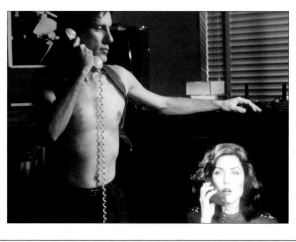

James Woods portrayed a cable-TV programmer who becomes engrossed in a sexual, violent pirated TV show in Videodrome (1983).

Kim's Video
6 St. Mark's Place
New York, NY 10003
(800) 617-5467
(212) 995-5586 (fax)
info@kimsvideo.com (e-mail)
www.kimsvideo.com

Movies Unlimited
3015 Darnell Road
Philadelphia, PA 19154
(800) 466-8437, (215) 637-4444
(215) 637-2350 (fax)
movies@moviesunlimited.com (e-mail)
www.moviesunlimited.com

Reel.com
(*See* "Online Resources," page 587–589)

TLA Video
234 Market Street
Philadelphia, PA 19106
(800) 333-8521; (215) 733-0608
(215) 733-0668 (fax)
sales@tlavideo.com (e-mail)
www.tlavideo.com

Video Yesteryear
Box C
Sandy Hook, CT 06482
(800) 243-0987
(203) 797-0819 (fax)
video@yesteryear.com (e-mail)
www.yesteryear.com

Videofinders
4401 Sunset Boulevard
Los Angeles, CA 90027
(800) 343-4727
(323) 953-5645 (fax)
www.videofinders.com

Vidiots
302 Pico Boulevard
Santa Monica, CA 90405
(310) 392-8508

Sources of Additional Information

THIS SECTION LISTS PUBLICATIONS, both print and electronic, useful to the film professional or researcher. Publications are listed under the following categories: Books, Periodicals, Online Resources, and Software.

BOOKS
GENERAL REFERENCE

American Film Institute Catalog of Motion Pictures Produced in the United States (also known as *The AFI Catalog*).
Film Beginnings, 1893–1910–A Work in Progress. 2 vols. Lanham, MD: Scarecrow Press, 1995.
Feature Films, 1911–1920. 2 vols. Berkeley, CA: University of California Press, 1989.
Feature Films, 1921–1930. 2 vols. Berkeley, CA: University of California Press, 1997.
Feature Films, 1931–1940. 3 vols. Berkeley, CA: University of California Press, 1993.
Feature Films, 1941–1950. 3 vols. Berkeley, CA: University of California Press, 1999.
Feature Films, 1951–1970. 2 vols. Berkeley, CA: University of California Press, 1997.
Within Our Gates: Ethnicity in American Feature Films, 1911–1960. Berkeley, CA: University of California Press, 1997.
Bergan, Ronald, and Robyn Karney. *The Faber Companion to Foreign Films.* Boston: Faber and Faber, 1992.
Bogle, Donald. *Blacks in American Films and Television: An Encyclopedia.* New York: Fireside, 1989.
Boller, Jr., Paul F., and Ronald L. Davis. *Hollywood Anecdotes.* New York: Ballantine Books, 1987.
Brown, Gene. *Movie Time: A Chronology of Hollywood and the Movie Industry from Its Beginnings to the Present.* New York: Macmillan, 1995.
_____. *The New York Times Encyclopedia of Film.* 14 vols. New York: Times Books, 1984.
Corey, Melinda, and George Ochoa. *A Cast of Thousands: A Compendium of Who Played What in Film.* 3 vols. New York: Facts on File, 1992.
_____. *The Dictionary of Film Quotations.* New York: Crown, 1995.
_____. *The Man in Lincoln's Nose: Funny, Profound, and Quotable Quotes of Screenwriters, Movie Stars, and Moguls.* New York: Fireside, 1990.
_____. *Movies and TV: The New York Public Library Book of Answers.* New York: Fireside, 1992.
Cowie, Peter, ed. *Variety International Film Guide 2000.* London: Faber and Faber, 1999.

Gifford, Denis. *The British Film Catalogue 1895–1985*. New York: Facts on File, 1986.

Jarvis, Everett G. *Final Curtain: Deaths of Noted Movie and T.V. Personalities 1915–1992*. New York: Citadel Press, 1992.

Halliwell, Leslie and John Walker. *Halliwell's Film and Video Guide 2001*. New York: Harper & Row, 2000.

Halliwell, Leslie and John Walker. *Halliwell's Who's Who in the Movies*, 13th ed. New York: HarperCollins, 1999.

Katz, Ephraim. *The Film Encyclopedia*, 4th ed. Revised by Fred Klein and Ronald Dean Nolen. New York: Harper Resource, 2001.

Konigsberg, Ira. *The Complete Film Dictionary*. New York: Meridian, 1989.

Maltin, Leonard, ed. *Leonard Maltin's Movie & Video Guide*. New York: Plume, published annually.

Monaco, James, et al. *The Encyclopedia of Film*. New York: Perigee, 1991.

Nash, Jay Robert and Stanley Ralph Ross. *The Motion Picture Guide*. Chicago: Cinebooks, 1985.

_____. *The Motion Picture Guide Annual*. Chicago: Cinebooks, published annually.

Peary, Danny. *Cult Movies: The Classics, the Sleepers, the Weird, and the Wonderful*. New York: Delta/Dell Publishing, 1981.

Pickard, Roy. *Who Played Who in the Movies*. New York: Schocken, 1979.

Reves, Luis and Peter Rubie. *Hispanics in Hollywood*. Los Angeles: Lone Eagle, 2000.

Sackett, Susan. *The Hollywood Reporter Book of Box Office Hits*. New York: Billboard Books, 1990.

Slide, Anthony. *The American Film Industry: A Historical Dictionary*. New York: Limelight Editions, 1990.

The Variety Insider. New York: Perigee, 1999.

Videohound's Golden Movie Retriever. Detroit: Visible Ink Press, published annually.

Weldon, Michael. *The Psychotronic Encyclopedia of Film*. New York: Ballantine Books, 1983.

Wiley, Mason, and Damien Bona. *Inside Oscar: The Unofficial History of the Academy Awards*, 10th anniversary ed. New York: Ballantine Books, 1996.

Wlaschin, Ken. *The Illustrated Encyclopedia of the World's Great Movie Stars and Their Films*. London: Salamander, 1979.

FILM THEORY AND CRITICISM

Agee, James. *Agee on Film*. New York: Grosset & Dunlap, 1969.

Arnheim, Rudolf. *Film as Art*. Berkeley, CA: University of California Press, 1957.

Balázs, Béla. *Theory of the Film: The Character and Growth of a New Art*. London: Dennis Dobson, 1952.

Basinger, Jeanine. *A Woman's View: How Hollywood Spoke to Women 1930–1960*. New York: Knopf/Random House, 1993.

Bazin, André. *What Is Cinema?* 2 vols. Berkeley, CA: University of California Press, 1967, 1971.

Bogdanovich, Peter. *Pieces of Time: Peter Bogdanovich on the Movies*. New York: Arbor House/Esquire, 1973.

Bordwell, David, et al. *The Classical Hollywood Cinema: Film Style & Mode of Production to 1960*. New York: Columbia University Press, 1985.

Braudy, Leo. *The World in a Frame: What We See in Films*. Chicago: University of Chicago Press, 1984.

Braudy, Leo and Marshall Cohen, eds. *Film Theory and Criticism: Introductory Readings*, 5th ed. Oxford, UK: Oxford University Press, 1998.

Cavell, Stanley. *Pursuits of Happiness: The Hollywood Comedy of Remarriage*. Cambridge, MA: Harvard University Press, 1984.

Cawelti, John. *The Six-Gun Mystique*. Bowling Green, OH: Bowling Green University Popular Press, 1970.

Eisenstein, Sergei. *Towards a Theory of Montage*. Richard Taylor and Michael Glenny, eds. Michael Glenny, trans. London: BFI, 1992.

Harvey, James. *Romantic Comedy in Hollywood from Lubitsch to Sturges*. New York: Da Capo Press, 1998.

Haskell, Molly. *From Reverence to Rape: The Treatment of Women in the Movies*. Chicago: University of Chicago Press, 1987.

Hill, John, and Pamela Church Gibson, eds. *The Oxford Guide to Film Studies*. Oxford, UK: Oxford University Press, 1998.

Kael, Pauline. *5001 Nights at the Movies*. New York: Henry Holt, 1991.

Kracauer, Siegfried. *From Caligari to Hitler*. Princeton, NJ: Princeton University Press, 1947.

Books were burned in a world where reading material is banned in François Truffaut's adaptation of the Ray Bradbury novel Fahrenheit 451 (1966).

> "I never cover
> myself when I
> shoot. I take it
> only from one
> angle…
> I believe that
> every shot has
> only ONE
> angle,
> ONE lens."
>
> —
>
> *François Truffaut, 1973*

AT RIGHT: *Abel Gance's
silent masterpiece*
Napoleon *(1927),
starring Albert Dieudonne,
featured technical
innovations in tinting,
superimposed images,
editing, and camerawork
and helped establish high
standards for the genre of
historical films.*

Metz, Christian. *Film Language: A Semiotics of the Cinema.* Michael Taylor, trans. Chicago: University of Chicago Press, 1991.

Mulvey, Laura. *Visual and Other Pleasures (Theories of Representation and Difference).* Bloomington, IN: Indiana University Press, 1989.

Munsterberg, Hugo. *The Photoplay: A Psychological Study.* New York: Appleton, 1916.

Sarris, Andrew, ed. *The American Cinema: Directors and Directions, 1929–1968.* New York: E.P. Dutton, 1968.

Sklar, Robert. *Movie-Made America.* New York: Vintage, 1976.

Warshow, Robert. *The Immediate Experience.* New York: Doubleday, 1962.

Wollen, Peter. *Signs and Meaning in the Cinema,* rev. ed. London: Secker & Warburg,1972.

Wood, Robin. *Hollywood from Vietnam to Reagan.* New York: Columbia University Press, 1986

FILM HISTORY AND MEMOIR

Behlmer, Rudy. *Behind the Scenes: The Making of... Hollywood;* Samuel French, 1989.

Bogdanovich, Peter. *Who the Devil Made It.* New York: Knopf, 1997.

Brownlow, Kevin. *The Parade's Gone By.* London: Secker & Warburg, 1968.

Everson, William K. *American Silent Film.* New York: Da Capo Press, 1998.

Gabler, Neal. *An Empire of Their Own: How the Jews Invented Hollywood.* New York: St. Martin's Press, 1988.

Goldman, William. *Adventures in the Screen Trade: A Personal View of Hollywood and Screenwriting.* New York: Warner Books, 1988.

_____. *Which Lie Did I Tell? or, More Adventures in the Screen Trade.* New York: Pantheon Books, 2000.

Gomery, Douglas. *The Hollywood Studio System.* New York: St. Martin's Press, 1986.

McGilligan, Pat. *Backstory: Interviews with Screenwriters of Hollywood's Golden Age.* Berkeley, CA: University of California Press, 1986.

Mast, Gerald. *A Short History of the Movies.* New York: Macmillan, 1986.

Nowell-Smith, Geoffrey. *The Oxford History of World Cinema.* Oxford, UK: Oxford University Press, 1996.

Schatz, Thomas. *The Genius of the System: Hollywood Filmmaking in the Studio Era.* New York: Pantheon, 1988.

Truffaut, François and Helen G. Scott. *Hitchcock,* rev. ed. New York: Simon & Schuster, 1985.

CAREER HELP AND PROFESSIONAL RESOURCES

Agents & Managers. Hollywood, CA: Hollywood Creative Directory, published semiannually.

Buzzell, Linda. *How to Make It in Hollywood,* 2nd ed. New York: HarperPerennial, 1996.

Field, Syd. *The Foundations of Screenwriting,* rev. ed. New York: Dell, 1994.

Hollywood Reporter Blu-Book Directory. Los Angeles: Hollywood Reporter, published annually.

International Motion Picture Almanac. La Jolla, CA: Quigley, published annually.

LA 411. Los Angeles: LA 411 Published annually. Directory of Los Angeles film and tape production industries.

Laskin, Emily, ed. *Getting Started in Film: The Official AFI Guide to Exciting Film Careers.* New York: Prentice Hall, 1992.

_____, ed. dir. *The American Film Institute Guide to College Courses in Film and Television,* 8th ed. New York: Prentice Hall, 1990.

Lone Eagle Directories. Los Angeles: Lone Eagle Publishing. Directories of film professionals, including *Film Directors: A Complete Guide* by Michael Singer and *Film Actors Guide* by Steve LuKanic.

Producer's Masterguide. New York: Producer's Masterguide, published annually.

Resnik, Gail, and Scott Trost. *All You Need to Know About the Movie and TV Business.* New York: Fireside, 1996.

Seger, Linda. *Making a Good Script Great: A Guide to Writing and Rewriting by a Hollywood Script Consultant.* Hollywood, CA: Samuel French Trade, 1987.

Squire, Jason E., ed. *The Movie Business Book,* 2nd ed. New York: Fireside, 1992.

Stolberg, Shael. *International Film Festival Guide.* Toronto: Toronto Festival Products, 1998.

Taylor, Hugh. *The Hollywood Job-Hunter's Survival Guide: An Insider's Winning Strategies for Getting That (All-Important) First Job...And Keeping It.* Los Angeles: Lone Eagle, 1993.

U.S. Directory of Entertainment Employers. Van Nuys, CA: Monumental Communications, published annually.

PERIODICALS

American Cinematographer
A.S.C. Holding Corporation
1782 North Orange Drive
Hollywood, CA 90028
(213) 876-5080
www.cinematographer.com

**American Movie
    Classics Magazine**
Working Media, Inc.
18 Shawmut Street
Boston, MA 02116
(800) 669-1002
www.amctv.com

Black Film Review
Sojourner Productions, Inc.
2025 Eye Street NW
Washington, DC 20006
(202) 466-2753

Boxoffice
155 South El Molino Avenue,
    Suite 100
Pasadena, CA 91101
(626) 396-0250
(626) 396-0248
www.boxoff.com

Cahiers du Cinéma
Editions de l'Etoile
9 Passage de la Boule Blanche
Paris 75012
France
www.cahiersducinema.com

Cineaste
P.O. Box 2242
New York, NY 10009
(212) 982-1241
www.cineaste.com

Cinefantastique
P.O. Box 270
Oak Park, IL 60303
(708) 366-5566
mail@cfq.com (e-mail)
www.cfq.com

Cinefex
Box 20027
Riverside, CA 92516
(909) 781-1917
(909) 788-1793 (fax)
editorial@cinefax.com (e-mail)
www.cinefax.com

Cinema Journal
University of Texas Press
Journals Division
2100 Comal
Austin, TX 78722-2550
www.cinemastudies.org/cj.htm

Creative Screenwriting
6404 Hollywood Boulevard, Suite 415
Los Angeles, CA 90028
(323) 957-1405
www.creativescreenwriting.com

DGA Magazine
Directors Guild of America
7920 Sunset Boulevard
Hollywood, CA 90046-3388
(310) 289-5333
www.dga.org

Entertainment Employment Journal
5632 Van Nuys Boulevard, Suite 320
Van Nuys, CA 91401
(818) 920-0060; (800) 335-4335 outside California
www.eej.com

Entertainment Weekly
1675 Broadway
New York, NY 10019
(212) 522-5600
www.ew.com

Fangoria
Starlog Group
475 Park Avenue South
New York, NY 10016-6989
(212) 689-2830
www.fangoria2000.com

Film and Video: The Production Magazine
8455 Beverly Boulevard, Suite 508
Los Angeles, CA 90048
(213) 653-8053
(213) 653-8190 (fax)
www.filmandvideomagazine.com

Magazines such as Photoplay, Motion Picture, *and* Cinema *were precursors to modern entertainment magazines such as* Premiere *and* Entertainment Weekly.

Comedian Mike Myers spoofed spy films in Austin Powers: International Man of Mystery *(1997).*

Film Comment
Film Society of Lincoln Center
70 Lincoln Center Plaza
New York, NY 10023
(212) 875-5614
filmcomment@filmline.com (e-mail)
www.filmline.com/fcm/fcm.htm

Filmfax
Box 1900
Evanston, IL 60204-1900
(708) 866-7155
www.filmfax.com

Filmmaker—The Magazine of Independent Film
501 Fifth Avenue, Suite 1714
New York, NY 10017
(212) 581-8080
(212) 973-0318 (fax)
publisher@filmmakermagazine.com (e-mail)
www.filmmakermagazine.com

Film Quarterly
University of California Press
2120 Berkeley Way
Berkeley, CA 94702
(510) 601-9070
www.ucpress.edu/journals/fq

Films in Review
P.O. Box 589
New York, NY 10021
(212) 628-1594
www.filmsinreview.com

Hollywood Reporter
5055 Wilshire Boulevard
Los Angeles, CA 90036-4396
(323) 525-2000
(323) 525-2377 (fax)
www.hollywoodreporter.com

The Independent Film and Video Monitor
Association for Independent Video and
   Filmmakers
304 Hudson Street, 6th Floor
New York, NY 10013
(212) 807-1400
(212) 463-8519 (fax)
info@aivf.org (e-mail)
www.aivf.org/the_independent/

Jump Cut: A Review of Contemporary Media
P.O. Box 865
Berkeley, CA 94701
(510) 658-7721
(510) 658-7769 (fax)
www.tcf.ua.edu/jumpcut

Millennium Film Journal
Millennium Film Workshop
66 East Fourth Street
New York, NY 10003
(212) 673-0090
www.mfj-online.org

Millimeter
5 Penn Plaza, 13th Floor
New York, NY 10001
(212) 613-9700
(212) 563-3028 (fax)
www.millimete.com

Movieline
1141 South Beverly Drive
Los Angeles, CA 90035-1155
(619) 745-2809
www.movielinemag.com

Movie Maker Magazine
2265 Westwood Boulevard #479
Los Angeles, CA 90064
(888) MAKE-MOVIES (625-3668)
(316) 234-9293 (fax)
staff@moviemaker.com (e-mail)
www.moviemaker.com

Premiere
1633 Broadway, 41st Floor
New York, NY 10016
(212) 767-6000
premiere@hfnm.com (e-mail)
www.premiere.com

Scenario: The Magazine of
    Screenwriting Art
3200 Tower Oaks Boulevard
Rockville, MD 20852
(800) 222-2654
(301) 984-3203 (fax)
www.scenariomag.com

Sight and Sound
British Film Institute
21 Stephen Street
London W1T 1LN UK
(44-020) 7957-8971
www.bfi.org.uk/sightandsound

Spectator—USC Journal of Film and
    Television Criticism
USC School of Cinema-Television
Division of Critical Studies
University of Southern California
Los Angeles, CA 90089-2211
(213) 740-3334

Total Film
Future Publishing
99 Baker Street
London W1M 1FE UK
(44-145) 827-1130
www.totalfilm.co.uk

Variety and Daily Variety
5700 Wilshire Boulevard
Suite 120
Los Angeles, CA 90036
(323) 857-6600
(323) 857-0494 (fax)
comments@variety.cahners.com (e-mail)
www.variety.com

Velvet Light Trap
University of Texas Press
Box 7819
Austin, TX 78713-7819
(512) 471-7233
(512) 232-7178 (fax)
journals@uts.cc.utexas.edu (e-mail)
www.utexas.edu/utpress/
    journals/jvlt.html

Written By
Writers Guild of America, West
7000 West Third Street
Los Angeles, CA 90048
(323) 782-4522
www.wga.org

* * *

ONLINE RESOURCES

For the Web sites of Hollywood studios, see
"The Major Hollywood Studios," (pages 550–553).

About Movies
www.about.com/movies/index.htm
    Offers a search engine, links, news articles, and
    forums about films. Site is subdivided into
    categories such as Classic Movies, Film Making,
    Hollywood Movies/Reviews, and World Film.

American Film Institute Online Resources
www.afi.com
    Official Web site of the American Film Institute,
    provides information on AFI's programs and
    the films and stars honored by the organization.

American Film Institute Catalog
www.afi.chadwyck.com
    Online version of *The American Film Institute
    Catalog of Motion Pictures Produced in the
    United States*, which provides definitive
    filmographies on all feature-length motion
    pictures produced in the United States on a
    decade-by-decade basis. Purchase on a CD-
    ROM or on the Web for an annual maintenance
    fee. For print editions, see "Books," pages
    582–584.

National Moving Image Database (NAMID)
    By permission only. Stores comprehensive data
    on the film, television, and video holdings of
    American archives and producers consisting of
    more than 200,000 records. Because of the
    proprietary nature of some of the material,
    access to the database is limited. For more
    information, phone (323) 856-7702.

Ain't It Cool News
www.aint-it-cool-news.com
    "Outlaw" site featuring unauthorized reviews of
    films shown in previews, rumors and news
    about productions in progress, and forums to
    discuss the latest industry gossip.

Baseline
See HollywoodPro, page 588.

Coming Attractions by Corona
www.corona.bc.ca/films/
    News and rumors about film projects in
    development.

Cyber Film School
www.cyberfilmschool.com
    Home of the Movie School Encyclopedia, which
    features video demonstrations and tips from
    Hollywood filmmakers. Also offers articles,
    columns, forums, and links to other movie sites.

Dark Horizons
www.darkhorizons.com
    News about film projects in development.
    Includes prerelease reviews, clips, and images.

The first teaser trailer for
*Lord of the Rings: The
Fellowship of the Ring* was
released to the Web in the
spring of 2000 and
downloaded 1.7 million
times in the first twenty-
four hours alone.

The success of the Web campaign that preceded the release of *The Blair Witch Project* (1999) has inspired other films, such as *Fight Club* (1999) and *Requiem for a Dream* (2000), to build eye-catching, interactive Web sites as part of a movie's promotional process. But one of the most elaborate —and puzzled over— was the complex Web presence structured around Steven Spielberg's 2001 science fiction film *A.I.*; an elaborate cyber murder-mystery that featured an interconnected series of characters, interlocking Web pages, real phone numbers to call, and cryptic hints that were strewn throughout the film's ad campaign. Although entire newsgroups devoted to solving the online enigma quickly sprang up in the site's wake, the hype had little to do with *A.I.*'s actual storyline, and the film was met with disappointing box office.

E!Online
www.eonline.com
> Movie news, reviews, features, games, and shopping.

Film.com
www.film.com
> Movie reviews, news, interviews, information about home videos, and video order service through Reel.com.

Filmmaker.com
www.filmmaker.com
> Online resource for filmmakers on a budget. Filmmakers exchange information helpful to getting films made and distributed. Site includes articles, FAQs, links, downloadable files, forums, and LOAFS—the Library of Annotated Film Schools.

The Greatest Films
www.filmsite.org
> Descriptions, reviews, reproductions of posters, and historical and reference information about classic films.

Hollywood.com
www.hollywood.com
> Presents movie industry news, reviews, features, games, shopping, and movie trailers.

Hollywood Creative Directory Online
www.hcdonline.com
> Offers access for paid subscribers to online directories of agents, producers, distributors, and other film professionals. Also sells print copies of its directories and hosts a free entertainment industry job board.

HollywoodPro (a.k.a. Baseline)
www.hollywoodpro.com
www.pkbaseline.com
> Preeminent entertainment industry resource for film and television information. Database contains more than 1.5 million records, updated daily, about projects in production, cast and crew credits, box-office grosses, celebrity biographies, talent contact information, company directories, and industry news. Available by subscription or on an à la carte basis. Some features are free, such as movie news, reviews, and box-office rankings.

indieWIRE.com
www.indiewire.com
> Online trade newspaper for independent filmmakers. Includes news, reviews, interviews, and forums about movies. Specializes in coverage of film festivals.

The Internet Movie Database
www.imdb.com
> Widely regarded as the Web's most useful, and usually accurate, free resource about film. Includes information on virtually every movie ever released, including cast, credits, distribution information, reviews, quotes, trivia, and show times (if the film is currently in release). Offers video purchasing through Amazon.com.

Mark Litwak's Entertainment Law Resources for Film, TV, and Multimedia Producers
www.marklitwak.com
> Useful information on deal making and legal aspects of filmmaking from veteran entertainment lawyer. Includes many links, especially links to film festival Web sites.

Sandra Bullock played a reclusive systems analyst whose Net-surfing habit puts her life in jeopardy in The Net *(1995).*

Mr. Showbiz
www.mrshowbiz.go.com
Reviews, movie times, news, and interviews.

The Motion Picture Industry:
    Behind-the-Scenes
The ThinkQuest Library of Entries
www.library.thinkquest.org/10015/
    Educational Web site about the film industry
    designed by students participating in a
    ThinkQuest contest. Features ScriptBuddy, a
    free screenwriting utility.

Moviefone
www.moviefone.com
    Offers movie-time information and ticket
    buying service.

The Movie Review Query Engine
www.mrqe.com
    Exhaustive searchable index of the movie reviews
    available on the Web from both commercial
    sources and Usenet movie review groups.

Oscar.com
www.oscar.com
    The official Academy Awards site includes a
    database of past award winners.

Reel.com
www.reel.com
    Offers video and DVD ordering, movie news,
    and reviews.

Roger Ebert on Movies
www.suntimes.com/ebert/index.html
    Current and archived reviews written by the
    esteemed critic, plus his "Movie Answer Man"
    column, interviews, essays, and other features.

Screenit.com
www.screenit.com
    Entertainment reviews for parents. Site covers
    movies, music, videos, and DVDs, scrutinizing
    entertainment for the child friendliness of its
    content, rating films according to categories
    such as "blood/gore," "nudity," and "profanity."

Toby's Film Stills
www.filmstills.freeservers.com
    Film still archive.

24 Frames Per Second: Projections on Film
www.24framespersecond.com
    Online film journal that offers local information
    on theaters, festivals, education, and filmmaking
    opportunities in cities around the world.

Variety.com
www.variety.com
    Official Web site of the show business trade
    magazine *Variety*. Offers industry news,
    columns, movie reviews, box-office charts, and
    other useful tools, including the "Slanguage
    Dictionary" of *Variety* jargon.

WebMovie.com
www.webmovie.com
    Web guide for motion
    picture producers.
    Search thousands of
    sites selling film and
    video production
    services, facilities, and
    technologies.

SOFTWARE
Screenwriting Assistance
    Maintaining proper
    screenplay format, with
    its profusion of centered text and abbreviations,
    may distract the screenwriter from telling a story
    and creating characters. Screenwriting programs
    such as those listed below format your script
    correctly as you type and simplify script plan-
    ning and revision. Some, such as *Dramatica Pro
    4.0*, also serve as a "writing coach," helping you
    brainstorm ideas and build your narrative.

Dramatica Pro 4.0. Screenplay Systems.
    Macintosh, Windows 95/98/Me. CD-ROM.

Final Draft 5.0. Final Draft. Macintosh, Windows
    95/98/NT/2000/Me. CD-ROM.
Hollywood Screenwriter. Screenplay Systems.
    Windows 95/98/Me. CD-ROM.

Movie Magic Screenwriter 2000. Screenplay
    Systems. Windows 95/98/NT/2000/Me.
    CD-ROM.

Film Production Assistance
    Despite the perceived glamour of movie-
    making, the process is full of pesky details that
    may be easier when computerized. Software
    programs such as those listed below can help
    film producers and production staff manage
    such mundane elements as scheduling,
    budgeting, script breakdowns, production
    boards, and call sheets.

Boardmaster Storyboard and Timing Software.
    Windows 95/98/NT. CD-ROM.

Cinergy 2000 Scheduling and *Cinergy 2000
    Budgeting*. Mindstar. Windows 95/98/NT.
    CD-ROM.

Easy Budget. Macintosh or Windows.

*How to Make Your Movie: An Interactive Film
    School*. Ohio University/Electronic Vision.
    Windows 95/98/NT. CD-ROM.

Industry Labor Rates for Movie Magic Budgeting.
    Macintosh, Windows 95/NT.

Movie Magic Scheduling and *Movie Magic
    Budgeting*. Screenplay Systems. Macintosh,
    Windows 95/98/2000/NT. CD-ROM.

*Boston police officer
Anthony Franklin, played
by Forest Whitaker,
conducts an investigation
on the computer in
Blown Away (1994).*

INDEX

PHOTO CREDITS

Page location of images is denoted as follows: top (T), bottom (B), left (L), right (R), center (C).

The Kobal Collection/20th Century Fox/Aspen: p. 468

The Kobal Collection/20th Century Fox: pp. 89, 115, 122, 128, 193, 197, 239, 269, 301 TR, 302, 383, 392-393, 403, 432, 439-440, 447-448, 455, 473, 477, 489, 493, 528, 542, 545, 575-576

The Kobal Collection/20th Century Fox/Paramount: p. 467

The Kobal Collection/ABC/Allied Artists: p. 261

The Kobal Collection/Alexander, Kenneth/United Artists: p. 427

The Kobal Collection/Allarts/Erato: p. 557

The Kobal Collection/Amblin/Universal: p. 497

The Kobal Collection/Anglo Enterprise/Vineyard: p. 583

The Kobal Collection/Appleby, David/Mandalay Ent: p. 8 CL Row 1

The Kobal Collection/Arau/Cinevista/Aviacsa: p. 513

The Kobal Collection/Artisan Pics: pp. 131, 319

The Kobal Collection/Bachrach, Ernest: p. 35

The Kobal Collection/Bailey, Alex/Working Title: p. 135

The Kobal Collection/Barius, Claudette/Warner Bros: p. 517

The Kobal Collection/Batzdorff, Ron/Imagine Ent: p. 554

The Kobal Collection/Batzdorff, Ron/Universal: p. 470

The Kobal Collection/Betzer-Panorama Film/Danish Film Inst: p. 506

The Kobal Collection/Biever, John/Columbia: p. 317

The Kobal Collection/Biograf, Jan: p. 502

The Kobal Collection/BIP: p. 47

The Kobal Collection/Brandenstein, Gabrielle/Castle Rock/Detour: p. 541

The Kobal Collection/Bray, Phil/Tiger Moth/Miramax: pp. 226-227

The Kobal Collection/Bryna/Universal: p. 533

The Kobal Collection/Buitendijk, Jaap/Dreamworks/Universal: p. 501

The Kobal Collection/Bull, Clarence Sinclair/MGM: p. 253

The Kobal Collection/Bunuel-Dali: p. 45

The Kobal Collection/Carolco: pp. 114, 201 T, 333

The Kobal Collection/Caruso, Phillip/Columbia: p. 168

The Kobal Collection/Castle Rock/Nelson/Columbia: p. 498

The Kobal Collection/Castle Rock Entertainment: p. 231

The Kobal Collection/Chaplin/United Artists: p. 56

The Kobal Collection/Chen, Linda R./Miramax/Buena Vista: p. 391

The Kobal Collection/Chuen, Chan Kam/Columbia/Sony: p. 134

The Kobal Collection/Ciby 2000: p. 469

The Kobal Collection/Cinerama: p. 407

The Kobal Collection/Circle Films: p. 176

The Kobal Collection/Coburn, Robert/Columbia: p. 484

The Kobal Collection/Columbia: pp. 57, 86, 93, 143, 183, 265, 272, 295, 313, 329, 360, 369, 416, 419, 426, 428-429, 449, 474-475, 486-487, 539, 588

The Kobal Collection/Columbia/Goldman, Louis: pp. 330-331

The Kobal Collection/Coote, Clive: pp. 548-549

The Kobal Collection/Cristaldifilm/Films Ariane: p. 218

The Kobal Collection/Cronenweth, Frank: p. 580

The Kobal Collection/Daza, Daniel/El Mar/Grandview: p. 561

The Kobal Collection/Decla/Bioscop: p. 38

The Kobal Collection/Di Novi/Columbia: p. 298

The Kobal Collection/Digital Domain/20th Century Fox/Paramount: p. 200 TL

The Kobal Collection/Dreamland Productions: p. 521

The Kobal Collection/Edison: p. 23

The Kobal Collection/El Desea-Lauren: p. 514

The Kobal Collection/Embassy: p. 376, 396

The Kobal Collection/EMI/Columbia/Warner Bros: p. 106

The Kobal Collection/Epic: p. 32

The Kobal Collection/ERA International: p. 505

The Kobal Collection/Essenay: pp. 14-15

The Kobal Collection/Fefer, Stephane: pp. 312, 327

The Kobal Collection/Ferorelli, Enrico: p. 152

The Kobal Collection/Figment/Noel Gay/Channel 4: p. 515

The Kobal Collection/Film Workshop: p. 509

The Kobal Collection/Films Andre Paulve: p. 562

The Kobal Collection/Fine Line/Kartemquin: p. 529

The Kobal Collection/Flaherty: p. 39

The Kobal Collection/Fox Films: p. 192

The Kobal Collection/Freulich, Roman: p. 30

The Kobal Collection/Geffen/Warner Bros: p. 359

The Kobal Collection/Gladden: pp. 374-375

The Kobal Collection/Golden Harvest: p. 235

The Kobal Collection/Goldwyn/RKO: p. 353

The Kobal Collection/Gordon Melinda Sue/Touchstone/Universal: p. 560

The Kobal Collection/Goskino: p. 225

The Kobal Collection/Govt of W. Bengal: p. 510

The Kobal Collection/Hal Roach/MGM: pp. 408-409

The Kobal Collection/Halsband, Michael/20th Century Fox: p. 289

The Kobal Collection/Hamshere, Keith/ Lucasfilm: p. 422

The Kobal Collection/Handmade Films: p. 7 BL

The Kobal Collection/Harvey, Shane/ Gramercy Pictures: p. 8 R Row 5

The Kobal Collection/Hawk Films Productions/Columbia: pp. 386-387

The Kobal Collection/Histrionic Film: p. 20

The Kobal Collection/Hurrell, George: p. 241

The Kobal Collection/Image Ten: p. 220

The Kobal Collection/Indo-British/INT Film Investors: p. 113

The Kobal Collection/James, David/ Dreamworks, LLC: p. 158

The Kobal Collection/James, David/ Touchstone: p. 339

The Kobal Collection/Jan Chapman Prods/Ciby 2000: p. 462

The Kobal Collection/Keystone: p. 31

The Kobal Collection/Konow, Rolf/ Castle Rock/Dakota Films: p. 243

The Kobal Collection/Korda: p. 355

The Kobal Collection/Kraychyk, George/Miramax: p. 350

The Kobal Collection/Ladd Company/ Warner Bros: pp. 198, 457

The Kobal Collection/Lee, David/40 Acres & A Mule: p. 155

The Kobal Collection/Lee, David/ Warner Bros: p. 124

The Kobal Collection/Lion's Gate/ Buillard, Jeanne Louise: p. 8 L Row 5

The Kobal Collection/Lippman, Irving/Columbia: pp. 292, 516

The Kobal Collection/Lockwood, Elise/ Polygram/Australian Film Finance: p. 569

The Kobal Collection/London Films/ United Artists: p. 194

The Kobal Collection/London Films: pp. 53, 414-415

The Kobal Collection/Lucasfilm/20th Century Fox: p. 96

The Kobal Collection/Lucasfilm Ltd./ Paramount: pp. 108, 378

The Kobal Collection/Lumiere Bros: p. 16

The Kobal Collection/Marshak, Bob/ Universal: p. 142

The Kobal Collection/Melies: p. 22

The Kobal Collection/Merchant Ivory/ Goldcrest: p. 459

The Kobal Collection/MGM /Pathe: p. 271

The Kobal Collection/MGM: pp. 50, 52, 54, 59-60, 64, 67, 83, 91, 195, 260, 300, 311, 364, 380-381, 441-443, 450-453, 471, 480

The Kobal Collection/Michaels, Darren/ Columbia: pp. 8 R Row 4, 543

The Kobal Collection/Miramax/ Dimension Films/Tursi, Mario: p. 136

The Kobal Collection/Mirisch/United Artists: p. 259

The Kobal Collection/Mirisch-7 Arts/ United Artists: p. 445

The Kobal Collection/Moad, Phil: 280, 301 BC

The Kobal Collection/Montain, Peter/ Warner Bros: p. 132

The Kobal Collection/Morton, Merrick/ Warner Bros: p. 8 CR Row 1

The Kobal Collection/Mos Film: p. 567

The Kobal Collection/Moseley, Melissa/ Touchstone Pictures: p. 238

The Kobal Collection/New Line/Saul Zanetz/Wing Nut: p. 137

The Kobal Collection/New Line Cinema: p. 558

The Kobal Collection/New Line Production: p. 586

The Kobal Collection/NSDAP: p. 55

The Kobal Collection/Orion: 342, 546

The Kobal Collection/Palace Pictures: p. 461

The Kobal Collection/Paramount/ Rafran: p. 367

The Kobal Collection/Paramount: pp. 8 L Row 1, 8 R Row 2, 40, 46, 66, 84, 99, 107, 116, 167, 190, 229, 249, 293, 336, 361, 373, 389, 406, 434, 456, 476 BL, 479, 494, 538, 551, 556

The Kobal Collection/Polygram/ Channel 4/Working Title: p. 126

The Kobal Collection/Ponti – DeLaurentis: p. 309

The Kobal Collection/Prana-Film: p. 535

The Kobal Collection/Prandini, Paula/ Sony Pictures Classics: p. 504

The Kobal Collection/Preston, Neal/ DreamWorks LLC: p. 465

The Kobal Collection/Prods Artistes Associes/Da Ma: p. 423

The Kobal Collection/Produzione de Sica: p. 70

The Kobal Collection/Python Pictures/ EMI: p. 262

The Kobal Collection/Rank: pp. 246, 435

The Kobal Collection/Regan, Ken/ Orion: p. 123

The Kobal Collection/Regency/ Monarchy: p. 138

The Kobal Collection/Renaissance Films/ABC/Curzon Films: p. 233

The Kobal Collection/Reteitalia/Scena Film: p. 181

The Kobal Collection/Richee, E.R.: p. 77

The Kobal Collection/Richee, E.R./ Paramount: pp. 2, 36

The Kobal Collection/RKO: pp. 6 LC, 63, 65, 420-421

The Kobal Collection/Road Movies/ Argos Films/WDR: p. 7 TR

The Kobal Collection/Rubin, Seth/ Warner Bros./Merchant Ivory: p. 345

The Kobal Collection/Saul Zaentz Company: p. 287

The Kobal Collection/Schiffman, Bonnie: p. 398

The Kobal Collection/Schwartz, Andrew/ MGM: p. 291

The Kobal Collection/Sebastian, Lorey/ DreamWorks, LLC: p. 120

The Kobal Collection/Selznick/MGM: pp. 8 R Row 1, 48, 347

The Kobal Collection/Selznick/ United Artists: p. 62

The Kobal Collection/SGF/Gaumont: p. 584

The Kobal Collection/Sorel, Peter/ 20th Century Fox: p. 306

The Kobal Collection/Sovkino: pp. 530-531

The Kobal Collection/Sparham, Laurie/ Miramax Films/Universal Pictures: p. 464

The Kobal Collection/Stanley Kramer/ United Artists: p. 438

The Kobal Collection/Tackett, Michael/ Working Title/Polygram: p. 540

The Kobal Collection/Talamon, Bruce/ Lucasfilm Ltd./Paramount: p. 297

The Kobal Collection/Todd, Demmie/ Working Title/Havoc: p. 463

The Kobal Collection/TOHO/Kurosawa: p. 169

The Kobal Collection/TOHO: p. 512

The Kobal Collection/Touchstone/ Amblin: p. 520

The Kobal Collection/Touchstone: pp. 240, 571

The Kobal Collection/Tri Star: pp. 310, 458

The Kobal Collection/Trilogy Entertainment: p. 589

The Kobal Collection/Trio/Albatros/ WDR: p. 507

The Kobal Collection/Two Cities/Rank: p. 436

The Kobal Collection/UFA: p. 44

The Kobal Collection/UGC/Studio Canal+: p. 6 TR

The Kobal Collection/United Artists/ Fantasy Films: p. 334

The Kobal Collection/United Artists: pp. 71, 95, 111, 157, 221, 277, 320, 390, 454, 460, 490, 559, 573

The Kobal Collection/Universal: pp. 68, 103, 117, 171, 255, 267, 352, 358, 377, 395, 400-401, 404, 410, 444, 476 TR, 522, 526, 532, 536-537, 544, 555, 565, 572, 582

The Kobal Collection/View Askew: p. 145

The Kobal Collection/Wallace, Merie W./ 20th Century Fox/Paramount: pp. 466-467, 552

The Kobal Collection/Wallace, Merie W./ 20th Century Fox: p. 348

The Kobal Collection/Walt Disney: p. 341

The Kobal Collection/Wark Producing Company: p. 24

The Kobal Collection/Warner Bros./ DC Comics: p. 570

The Kobal Collection/Warner Bros: pp. 10-11, 43, 79, 101, 119, 178, 244, 274, 279, 282, 384, 413, 430, 433, 472, 483, 503, 518-519, 527, 534, 547, 553, 577

The Kobal Collection/Warner Brothers/First National: pp. 51, 566

The Kobal Collection/Wolper/Warner Bros: 8 L Row 2

The Kobal Collection/XI'AN Film Studio: p. 118

The Kobal Collection/Yanco/Tao/ Recorded Picture: p. 184

The Kobal Collection/Zahedi, Firooz/ Sam Goldwyn/Channel Four/Close Call: p. 412

The Kobal Collection/Zoetrope/United Artists: p. 104

The Kobal Collection: pp. 8 C Row 2, 25, 26, 28-29, 31, 33-34, 42, 58, 69, 72, 75, 80, 140, 144, 160, 162, 164, 179-180, 208, 237, 250, 257-258, 268, 270, 281, 284, 290, 304-305, 307, 314, 321, 323-324, 326, 357, 366, 368, 371, 394, 405, 418, 424, 431, 446, 564, 585

Alexander, Max: p. 212

American Film Institute: p. 9

Disney: pp. 8 L Row 4, 127, 151

Disney Enterprises, Inc./Pixar Animation: pp. 362-363

King, Dave: pp. 8 L Row 3, 8 R Row 3, 8 C Row 5, 19, 76, 150-151, 161, 172, 186-187, 201-202, 206, 210, 217

O'Neill, Terry: p. 146

Salem, Lee: p. 216

Setchfield, Neil: p. 5

Shone, Karl: p. 18

Ward, Richard: p. 188

Dragon Inn courtesy of Colin Geddes, Toronto, Ontario: pp. 508-509

. . .

ACKNOWLEDGMENTS

THE STONESONG PRESS would also like to acknowledge the contributions of the following individuals to this book: Margie Steinmann, Bob Cosenza and Jamie Vuignier of The Kobal Collection. Ann Abel, Ariane Barbanell, Gillian Belnap, Celia Bland, Tom Burke, Jean Cotterell, Denny Downs, Justine Gardner, Colin Geddes, Phil Mariani, and Sarah Scheffel. Index prepared by Cohen & Carruth.

"Last night I was in the
Kingdom of Shadows."

———

*Maxim Gorky, on his first encounter with the cinema,
1896. The great Russian writer had just seen a
program of Lumière films.*